PONS
Fachwörterbuch Wirtschaft

Vorwort

Das PONS Fachwörterbuch Wirtschaft enthält einen etwa 8000 Stichwörter und Wendungen umfassenden Basiswortschatz aus allen Bereichen der britischen und amerikanischen Wirtschaftssprache. Dabei werden die verschiedensten Situationen, vom Büro über die Börse bis hin zu internationalen Messen berücksichtigt.

Die Stichwörter und Wendungen werden in leicht verständlichem Englisch erklärt, um den Bedürfnissen des Fremdsprachenlerners Rechnung zu tragen. Der Definitionswortschatz beschränkt sich im wesentlichen auf die als Stichwörter aufgenommenen Termini — nur etwa 470 zusätzliche Wörter werden verwendet.

Den Bedeutungserklärungen folgen jeweils die deutschen Entsprechungen. In den Fällen, wo Termini oder Institutionen von der Bedeutung oder Funktion her vom Deutschen abweichen, lassen sich nicht immer direkte Übersetzungsäquivalente finden. Solche Ausdrücke bleiben entweder unübersetzt, oder aber es wird eine ungefähre Entsprechung im Deutschen angegeben, die durch den Zusatz "entspricht" gekennzeichnet ist.

Anhand zahlreicher englischer Beispiele wird die Verwendung der Stichwörter und Wendungen im Kontext aufgezeigt.

Bei jedem Stichwort ist die Wortklasse vermerkt. Wörtern, die bestimmte grammatikalische Probleme aufwerfen, sind kurze Erklärungen ("Notes"), beispielsweise mit Angaben zu unregelmäßigen Verb- oder Pluralformen, Konstruktionen oder sonstigen nützlichen Hinweisen beigefügt. Unterschiede zwischen britischem und amerikanischem Sprachgebrauch werden ebenfalls berücksichtigt.

Englisch ist die Sprache der internationalen Geschäftswelt. Daher enthält das Wörterbuch kurze Zitate aus englischsprachigen Zeitschriften und Magazinen vieler Länder der Welt, darunter England, USA, Kanada, Australien, Hongkong and Nigeria. Sie zeigen dem Wörterbuchbenutzer typische, authentische Verwendungszusammenhänge auf.

Im zweiten Teil des Wörterbuchs sind die übersetzten deutschen Wirtschaftstermini noch einmal mit ihren englischen Entsprechungen in einem alphabetischen Register aufgelistet. Das bietet den Vorteil, daß das Nachschlagen von Wörtern und Wendungen sowohl ausgehend vom Englischen als auch vom Deutschen erfolgen kann. Damit vereinigt das PONS Fachwörterbuch Wirtschaft die Vorzüge eines einsprachigen Erklärungswörterbuchs mit denen eines zweisprachigen Nachschlagewerks.

Der Anhang enthält verschiedene Bank- und Geschäftsdokumente, Anleitungen zum Verfassen von Geschäftsbriefen und Führen von Telefonaten, eine Liste der wichtigsten Weltwährungen sowie Zahlen, Maße und geläufige Abkürzungen.

Durch seine Kenntnis der Wirtschaftssprache leistete Dr. Rainer Merkel einen wertvollen Beitrag bei der Übersetzung ins Deutsche.

Englisch-Deutsches
Wörterbuch

Aa

AAA letters indicating that a share *or* bond *or* bank is very reliable **AAA (Bewertung);** *these bonds have an AAA rating*
NOTE: you say 'triple A'

"A" shares *plural noun* ordinary shares with limited voting rights **dividendenberechtigte Aktien mit beschränktem Stimmrecht**

A1 *adjective*
(a) best **1A, erstklassig;** *we sell only goods in A1 condition*
(b) ship which is A1 at Lloyd's = ship which is in best condition according to Lloyd's Register **Schiff, das bei Lloyd's als in erstklassigem Zustand beschrieben wird**
◇ **A1, A2, A3, A4, A5** *noun* standard international sizes of paper **DIN A1, A2, A3, A4, A5;** *you must photocopy the spreadsheet on A3 paper; we must order some more A4 headed notepaper*

abandon *verb*
(a) to give up *or* not to continue **aufgeben;** *we abandoned the idea of setting up a New York office; the development programme had to be abandoned when the company ran out of cash;* **to abandon an action** = to give up a court case **eine Klage zurückziehen**
(b) to leave (something) **verlassen, aufgeben;** *the crew abandoned the sinking ship*
◇ **abandonment** *noun* act of giving something up **Verlassen, Aufgabe; abandonment of a ship** = giving up a ship and cargo to the underwriters against payment for total loss **Aufgabe eines Schiffes, Abandon**

abatement *noun* act of reducing **Senkung, Kürzung; tax abatement** = reduction of tax **Steuernachlaß**

abroad *adverb* to or in another country **ins od im Ausland;** *the consignment of cars was shipped abroad last week; the chairman is abroad on business; half of our profit comes from sales abroad*

absence *noun* not being at work *or* at a meeting **Abwesenheit, Fernbleiben, Nichterscheinen; in the absence of** = when someone is not there **in Abwesenheit von;** *in the absence of the chairman, his deputy took the chair;* **leave of absence** = being allowed to be absent from work **Beurlaubung;** *he asked for leave of absence to visit his mother in hospital*
NOTE: no plural
◇ **absent** *adjective* not at work *or* not at a meeting **abwesend;** *ten of the workers are absent with flu; the chairman is absent in Holland on business*
◇ **absentee** *noun* worker who stays away from work for no good reason **Abwesender, Nichterschienener**
◇ **absenteeism** *noun* staying away from work for no good reason **Nichterscheinen (am Arbeitsplatz), Abwesenheit;** *absenteeism is high in the week before Christmas; the rate of absenteeism or the absenteeism rate always increases in fine weather*
NOTE: no plural

absolute *adjective* complete *or* total **absolut, unbeschränkt; absolute monopoly** = situation where only one producer or supplier produces or supplies something **unumschränktes Monopol;** *the company has an absolute monopoly of imports of French wine*
◇ **absolutely** *adverb* completely **absolut, voll und ganz;** *we are absolutely tied to our suppliers' schedules*

absorb *verb*
(a) to take in a small item so as to form part of a larger one **absorbieren, aufnehmen; to absorb a surplus** = to take back surplus stock so that it does not affect a business **Warenbestände zurücknehmen; overheads have absorbed all our profits** = all our profits have gone in paying overhead expenses **die laufenden Kosten haben unsere ganzen Gewinne geschluckt; to absorb a loss by a subsidiary** = to write a subsidiary company's loss into the main accounts **den Verlust einer Tochtergesellschaft auffangen**
(b) business which has been absorbed by a competitor = a small business which has been made part of a larger one **Unternehmen, das von der Konkurrenz übernommen wurde**
◇ **absorption** *noun* making a smaller business part of a larger one **Übernahme**
NOTE: no plural

abstract *noun* short form of a report *or* document **Zusammenfassung, Übersicht;** *to make an abstract of the company accounts*

a/c *or* **acc** = ACCOUNT

accelerated *adjective* made faster **beschleunigt; accelerated depreciation** = system of depreciation which reduces the value of assets at a high rate in the early years to encourage companies, because of tax advantages, to invest in new equipment **(steuerbegünstigte) vorzeitige Abschreibung, Sonderabschreibung**

accept *verb*
(a) to take something which is being offered **annehmen; to accept a bill** = to sign a bill of exchange to indicate that you promise to pay it **einen Wechsel akzeptieren; to accept delivery of a shipment** = to take goods into the warehouse officially when they are delivered **eine Warensendung annehmen**
(b) to say "yes" *or* to agree to something **akzeptieren, annehmen;** *she accepted the offer of a job in Australia; he accepted £200 for the car*

◇ **acceptable** *adjective* which can be accepted **akzeptabel, annehmbar;** *the offer is not acceptable to both parties*

◇ **acceptance** *noun*
(a) signing a bill of exchange to show that you agree to pay it **Akzept, Annahme; to present a bill for acceptance** = for payment by the person who has accepted it **einen Wechsel zum Akzept vorlegen; acceptance house** *or* *US* **acceptance bank** = = ACCEPTING HOUSE
(b) acceptance of an offer = agreeing to an offer **Annahme eines Angebotes; to give an offer a conditional acceptance** = to accept provided that certain things happen *or* that certain terms apply **ein Angebot unter Vorbehalt annehmen; we have his letter of acceptance** = we have received a letter from him accepting the offer **wir haben seine Annahmeerklärung erhalten; acceptance sampling** = testing a small part of a batch to see if the whole batch is good enough **Qualitätskontrolle mittels Stichprobe**

◇ **accepting house** *noun* firm which accepts bills of exchange (i.e. promises to pay them) and is paid a commission for this **Akzepthaus**

access
1 *noun* **to have access to something** = to be able to obtain *or* reach something **zu etwas Zugang haben;** *he has access to large amounts of venture capital;* **access time** = time taken by a computer to find data stored in it **Zugriffszeit;** NOTE: no plural
2 *verb* to call up (data) which is stored in a computer **aufrufen, zugreifen auf;** *she accessed the address file on the computer*

accident *noun* something unpleasant which happens by chance (such as the crash of a plane) **Unfall, Unglück; industrial accident** = accident which takes place at work **Betriebs-, Arbeitsunfall; accident insurance** = insurance which will pay when an accident takes place **Unfallversicherung**

accommodation *noun*
(a) money lent for a short time **Überbrückungskredit**
(b) to reach an accommodation with creditors = to agree terms for settlement **mit Gläubigern zu einer Übereinkunft kommen**
(c) accommodation bill = bill of exchange where the person signing is helping someone to raise a loan **Gefälligkeitswechsel**
(d) place to live **Unterkunft;** *visitors have difficulty in finding hotel accommodation during the summer; they are living in furnished accommodation;* **accommodation address** = address used for receiving messages but which is not the real address of the company **Briefkastenadresse**
NOTE: no plural in GB English, but US English can have **accommodations** for meaning (d)

> QUOTE an airline ruling requires airlines to provide a free night's hotel accommodation for full fare passengers in transit
> *Business Traveller*
>
> QUOTE any non-resident private landlord can let furnished or unfurnished accommodation to a tenant
> *Times*
>
> QUOTE the airline providing roomy accommodations at below-average fares
> *Dun's Business Month*

accompany *verb* to go with **begleiten;** *the chairman came to the meeting accompanied by the finance director; they sent a formal letter of complaint, accompanied by an invoice for damage*
NOTE: accompanied **by** something

accordance *noun* **in accordance with** = in agreement with *or* according to **in Übereinstimmung mit;** *in accordance with your instructions we have deposited the money in your current account; I am submitting the claim for damages in accordance with the advice of our legal advisers*

◇ **according to** *preposition* as someone says or writes **nach, laut, gemäß;** *the computer was installed according to the manufacturer's instructions*

◇ **accordingly** *adverb* in agreement with what has been decided **(dem)entsprechend;** *we have received your letter and have altered the contract accordingly*

> QUOTE the budget targets for employment and growth are within reach according to the latest figures
>
> *Australian Financial Review*

account

1 *noun*

(a) record of money paid *or* owed **Abrechnung; Konto;** *please send me your account or a detailed or an itemized account;* **expense account** = money which a businessman is allowed by his company to spend on travelling and entertaining clients in connection with his business **Spesenkonto;** *he charged his hotel bill to his expense account*

(b) *(in a shop)* arrangement which a customer has to buy goods and pay for them at a later date (usually the end of the month) **Kunden(kredit)konto;** *to have an account or a charge account or a credit account with Harrods; put it on my account or charge it to my account; (of a customer)* **to open an account** = to ask a shop to supply goods which you will pay for at a later date **ein Kundenkonto eröffnen, einrichten; to open an account** *or* **to close an account** = to start *or* to stop supplying a customer on credit **ein Kundenkonto eröffnen/einrichten; ein Kundenkonto sperren; to settle an account** = to pay all the money owed on an account **ein Konto be-, ausgleichen; to stop an account** = to stop supplying a customer until he has paid what he owes **ein Kundenkonto sperren; on account** = as part of a total bill **als Teilzahlung; to pay money on account** = to pay to settle part of a bill **eine Anzahlung leisten, Geld anzahlen; advance on account** = money paid as a part payment **eine Teilzahlung leisten**

(c) customer who does a large amount of business with a firm and has an account **Kreditkunde;** *he is one of our largest accounts; our salesmen call on their best accounts twice a month;* **account executive** = employee who looks after certain customers *or* who is the link between certain customers and his company **Kundenbetreuer**

(d) the accounts of a business *or* **a company's accounts** = detailed record of a company's financial affairs **Geschäftsbücher, Bücher; to keep the accounts** = to write each sum of money in the account book **die Bücher führen;** *the accountant's job is to enter all the money received in the accounts;* **annual accounts** = accounts prepared at the end of a financial year **Jahresabschluß, Jahresbilanz; management accounts** = financial information (sales, expenditure, credit, and profitability) prepared for a manager so that he can take decisions **Rechnungsbericht für die besonderen Zwecke der Unternehmensleitung; Geschäftsbilanz; profit and loss account** = accounts for a company with expenditure and income balanced to show a final profit or loss **Gewinn- und Verlustrechnung; accounts department** = department in a company which deals with money paid, received, borrowed or owed **Buchhaltung; accounts manager** = manager of an accounts department **Leiter/-in der Buchhaltung; accounts payable** = money owed by a company **Verbindlichkeiten; accounts receivable** = money owed to a company **Außenstände**

(e) bank account *or US* **banking account** = arrangement to keep money in a bank **Bankkonto;** *building society account; savings bank account; Girobank account; Lloyds account; he has an account with Lloyds; I have an account with the Halifax Building Society; to put money in(to) your account; to take money out of your account or to withdraw money from your account;* **budget account** = bank account where you plan income and expenditure to allow for periods when expenditure is high **Budget-Konto; current account** *or* **cheque account** *or US* **checking account** = account which pays some or no interest but from which the customer can withdraw money when he wants by writing cheques **laufendes Konto, Girokonto; deposit account** = account which pays interest but on which notice usually has to be given to withdraw money **Sparkonto (ohne gesetzliche Kündigungsfrist); external account** = account in a British bank of someone who is living in another country **Auslandskonto; frozen account** = account where the money cannot by used or moved because of a court order **gesperrtes Konto; joint account** = account for two people **gemeinsames Konto, Gemeinschaftskonto;** *most married people have joint accounts so that they can each take money out when they want it;* **overdrawn account** = account where you have taken out more money than you have put in (i.e. where the bank is lending you money) **überzogenes Konto; savings account** = account where you put money in regularly and which pays interest, often at a higher rate than a deposit account **Sparkonto; to open an account** = to start an account by putting money in **ein Konto eröffnen/einrichten;** *she opened an account with the Halifax Building Society;* **to close an account** = to take all money out of a bank account and stop the account **ein Konto auflösen;** *he closed his account with Lloyds*

(f) *(Stock Exchange)* period of credit (usually fourteen days) at the end of which you must pay for shares bought **(14-tägige) Abrechnung; account day** = day on which shares which have been bought must be paid for **Abrechnungstag;** *share prices rose at the end of the account or the account end*

(g) notice **Berücksichtigung; to take account of inflation** *or* **to take inflation into account** = to assume that there will be a certain percentage inflation when making calculations **die Inflation in Betracht ziehen**

2 *verb* **to account for** = to explain and record a money deal **Rechenschaft ablegen, sich verantworten;** *to account for a loss or a discrepancy; the reps have to account for all their expenses to the sales manager*

◇ **accountancy** *noun* work of an accountant **Buchhaltung, Rechnungswesen;** *he is studying accountancy or he is an accountancy student*

NOTE: no plural

◇ **accountant** *noun* person who keeps a company's accounts *or* person who advises a company on its finances *or* person who examines accounts **Buchhalter/-in; Steuerberater/-in; Rechnungs-, Wirtschaftsprüfer/-in;** *the chief accountant of a manufacturing group; I send all my income tax queries to my accountant;* **certified accountant** = accountant who has passed the professional examinations and is a member of the Association of Certified Accountants; *entspricht* **amtlich zugelassener Wirtschaftsprüfer;** *US* **certified public accountant** = accountant who has passed professional examinations; *entspricht* **Wirtschaftsprüfer; chartered accountant** = accountant who has passed the professional examinations and is a member of the Institute of Chartered Accountants; *entspricht* **beeidigter Wirtschaftsprüfer; cost accountant** = accountant who gives managers information about their business costs **Kostenrechner/-in; management accountant** = accountant who prepares financial information for managers so that they can take decisions **Finanzbuchhalter**

◇ **accounting** *noun* work of recording money paid, received, borrowed or owed **Buchhaltung, Rechnungswesen;** *accounting machine; accounting methods or accounting procedures; accounting system;* **accounting period** = period usually covered by a firm's accounts **Abrechnungszeitraum; cost accounting** = preparing special accounts of manufacturing and sales costs **Kostenrechnung; current cost accounting** = method of accounting which notes the cost of replacing assets at current prices, rather than valuing assets at their original cost **Rechnungslegung zum Wiederbeschaffungswert**

NOTE: no plural

> QUOTE applicants will be professionally qualified and have a degree in Commerce or Accounting
>
> *Australian Financial Review*

accredited *adjective* (agent) who is appointed by a company to act on its behalf **akkreditiert, autorisiert, bevollmächtigt**

accrual *noun* gradual increase by addition **Auflaufen, Zuwachs; accrual of interest** = automatic addition of interest to capital **Auflaufen von Zinsen, Zinsthesaurierung**

◇ **accrue** *verb* to increase and be due for payment at a later date **auflaufen, anwachsen;** *interest accrues from the beginning of the month; accrued interest is added quarterly;* **accrued dividend** = dividend earned since the last dividend was paid **aufgelaufene Dividenden**

acct = ACCOUNT

accumulate *verb* to grow larger by adding **akkumulieren, anhäufen;** *to allow dividends to accumulate;* **accumulated profit** = profit which is not paid as dividend but is taken over into the accounts of the following year **Gewinnvortrag**

accurate *adjective* correct **genau, exakt, fehlerfrei;** *the sales department made an accurate forecast of sales; the designers produced an accurate copy of the plan*

◇ **accurately** *adverb* correctly **genau, exakt, fehlerfrei;** *the second quarter's drop in sales was accurately forecast by the computer*

accuse *verb* to say that someone has committed a crime **beschuldigen, anklagen;** *she was accused of stealing from the petty cash box; he was accused of industrial espionage*

NOTE: you accuse someone **of** a crime or **of** doing something

achieve *verb* to succeed in doing something *or* to do something successfully **erreichen, schaffen, erlangen;** *the company has achieved great success in the Far East; we achieved all our objectives in 1985*

> QUOTE the company expects to move to profits of FFr 2m for 1985 and achieve equally rapid growth in following years
>
> *Financial Times*

acknowledge *verb* to tell a sender that a letter *or* package *or* shipment has arrived **bestätigen;** *he has still not acknowledged my letter of the 24th; we acknowledge receipt of your letter of June 14th*

◇ **acknowledgement** *noun* act of acknowledging **Bestätigung;** *she sent an acknowledgement of receipt; they sent a letter of acknowledgement*

acquire *verb* to buy **erwerben;** *to acquire a company*

◇ **acquirer** *noun* person *or* company which buys something **Erwerber, Ankäufer**

◇ **acquisition** *noun* thing bought; act of getting *or* buying something **Anschaffung, Erwerb;** *the chocolate factory is his latest acquisition;* **data acquisition** *or* **acquisition of data** = obtaining and classifying data **Datenerfassung**

acre *noun* measure of the area of land (= 0.45 hectares) **Morgen**

NOTE: the plural is used with figures, except before a noun: **he has bought a farm of 250 acres** *or* **he has bought a 250 acre farm**

across-the-board *adjective* applying to everything *or* everyone **allgemein, global;** *an across-the-board price increase*

act

1 *noun*

(a) law passed by a parliament which must be obeyed by the people **Gesetz, Erlaß;** *GB* **Companies Act** = Act which rules how companies should do their business; *entspricht* **Unternehmensrecht; Health and Safety at Work Act** = Act which rules how the health of workers should be protected by the companies they work for; *entspricht* **Gesetz zum Schutz der Gesundheit und Unfallverhütung am Arbeitsplatz; Finance Act** = annual Act of Parliament which gives the government power to raise taxes as proposed in the budget **Finanzgesetz**

(b) act of God = something you do not expect to happen, and which cannot be avoided (such as storms *or* floods) **höhere Gewalt**

2 *verb*

(a) to work **fungieren, handeln, agieren;** *to act as an agent for an American company; to act for someone or to act on someone's behalf*

(b) to do something **handeln;** *the board will have to act quickly if the company's losses are going to be reduced; the lawyers are acting on our instructions;* **to act on a letter** = to do what a letter asks to be done **etwas auf einen Brief hin unternehmen**

◇ **acting** *adjective* working in place of someone for a short time **stellvertretend;** *acting manager; the Acting Chairman*

◇ **action** *noun*

(a) thing which has been done **Handlung, Vorgehen; to take action** = to do something **etwas/Schritte unternehmen;** *you must take action if you want to stop people cheating you*

(b) direct action = strike or go-slow by the workforce **Direktaktion; to take industrial action** = to do something (usually to go on strike) to show that you are not happy with conditions at work **in den Arbeitskampf treten**

(c) case in a law court where a person or company sues another person or company **Klage, Prozeß, Rechtsstreit; to take legal action** = to sue someone **Klage erheben, klagen, verklagen;** *action for damages; action for libel or libel action; to bring an action for damages against someone;* **civil action** = case brought by a person *or* company against someone who has done them wrong **Zivilprozeß, zivilrechtliche Klage; criminal action** = case brought by the state against someone who is charged with a crime **Strafprozeß; strafrechtliche Verfolgung**

◇ **active** *adjective* busy **aktiv, tätig; active partner** = partner who works in the company **tätiger Teilhaber, Geschäftspartner;** *an active demand for oil shares; oil shares are very active; an active day on the Stock Exchange; business is active*

◇ **actively** *adverb* in a busy way **aktiv, tätig;** *the company is actively recruiting new personnel*

◇ **activity** *noun* being active *or* busy **Aktivität, Betriebsamkeit;** *a low level of business activity; there was a lot of activity on the Stock Exchange;* **activity chart** = plan showing work which has been done so that it can be compared to the plan of work to be done **Terminplan; monthly activity report** = report by a department on what has been done during the past month **monatlicher Tätigkeitsbericht**

NOTE: no plural

> QUOTE preliminary indications of the level of business investment and activity during the March quarter will provide a good picture of economic activity in 1985
>
> *Australian Financial Review*

actual

1 *adjective* real *or* correct **tatsächlich, effektiv;** *what is the actual cost of one unit? the actual figures for directors' expenses are not shown to the shareholders*

2 *plural noun* real figures; *these figures are the actuals for 1984* **Effektiveinnahmen**

actuary *noun* person employed by an insurance company to calculate premiums **Versicherungsmathematiker**

◇ **actuarial** *adjective* calculated by an actuary **versicherungsmathematisch;** *the premiums are worked out according to actuarial calculations;* **actuarial tables** =

lists showing how long people of certain ages are likely to live, used to calculate life assurance premiums **Sterbetabellen**

ad *noun* = ADVERTISEMENT

add *verb*
(a) to put figures together to make a total **addieren, hinzurechnen;** *to add interest to the capital; interest is added monthly*
(b) to put things together to make a large group **hinzufügen;** *we are adding to the sales force; they have added two new products to their range;* **this all adds to the company's costs** = this makes the company's costs higher **all dies erhöht die Unkosten der Firma**

◇ **add up** *verb* to put several figures together to make a total **zusammenzählen, addieren;** *to add up a column of figures;* **the figures do not add up** = the total given is not correct **die Zahlen stimmen nicht**

◇ **add up to** *verb* to make a total **ergeben, sich belaufen auf;** *the total expenditure adds up to more than £1,000*

◇ **adding machine** *noun* machine which adds numbers **Addiermaschine**

◇ **addition** *noun*
(a) thing or person added **Ergänzung; Zugang;** *the management has stopped all additions to the staff; we are exhibiting several additions to our product line; the marketing director is the latest addition to the board*
(b) in addition to = added to *or* as well as **zusätzlich, dazu, extra;** *there are twelve registered letters to be sent in addition to this packet*
(c) putting numbers together **Addition;** *you don't need a calculator to do simple addition*

◇ **additional** *adjective* **zusätzlich, zuzüglich** extra which is added; *additional costs; additional charges; additional clauses to a contract; additional duty will have to be paid*

address
1 *noun* details of number, street and town where an office is or a person lives **Adresse;** *my business address and phone number are printed on the card;* **accommodation address** = address used for receiving messages but which is not the real address of the company **Briefkastenadresse; cable address** = short address for sending cables **Telegrammanschrift; forwarding address** = address to which a person's mail can be sent on **Nachsendeadresse; home address** = address of a house or flat where someone lives **Privatadresse;** *please send the documents to my home address;* **address list** = list of addresses **Adressenliste;** *we keep an address list of two thousand addresses in Europe*
2 *verb*
(a) to write the details of an address on an envelope, etc. **adressieren, richten an;** *to address a letter or a parcel; a letter addressed to the managing director; incorrectly addressed package*
(b) to speak **sprechen zu;** *to address a meeting*

◇ **addressee** *noun* person to whom a letter *or* package is addressed **Adressat/-in; Empfänger/-in**

◇ **addressing machine** *noun* machine which puts addresses on envelopes automatically **Adressiermaschine**

adequate *adjective*
(a) large enough **adäquat, angemessen, hinlänglich; to operate without adequate cover** = to act without being completely protected by insurance **ohne hinreichenden Versicherungsschutz handeln**
(b) more or less satisfactory **zufriedenstellend;** *the results of the tests on the product were adequate*

adjourn *verb* to stop a meeting for a period **vertagen;** *to adjourn a meeting; the chairman adjourned the meeting until three o'clock; the meeting adjourned at midday*

◇ **adjournment** *noun* act of adjourning **Vertagung;** *he proposed the adjournment of the meeting*

adjudicate *verb* to give a judgement between two parties in law; to decide a legal problem **entscheiden, Urteil fällen;** *to adjudicate a claim; to adjudicate in a dispute;* **he was adjudicated bankrupt** = he was declared legally bankrupt **über ihn wurde der Konkurs verhängt**

◇ **adjudication** *noun* act of giving a judgement *or* of deciding a legal problem **Entscheidung; Gerichtsentscheidung; adjudication order** *or* **adjudication of bankruptcy** = order by a court making someone bankrupt **Konkurseröffnungsbeschluß; adjudication tribunal** = group which adjudicates in industrial disputes **Schlichtungskommission**

◇ **adjudicator** *noun* person who gives a decision on a problem **Schlichter;** *an adjudicator in an industrial dispute*

adjust *verb* to change something to fit new conditions **anpassen, angleichen;** *to adjust prices to take account of inflation; prices are adjusted for inflation*

◇ **adjuster** *noun* person who calculates losses for an insurance company **Schadenssachverständiger; average adjuster**

= person who calculates how much of an insurance is to be paid **Schadenregulierer**

◊ **adjustment** *noun* act of adjusting; slight change **Anpassung, Angleichung;** *tax adjustment; wage adjustment; to make an adjustment to salaries; adjustment of prices to take account of rising costs;* **average adjustment** = calculation of the share of cost of damage or loss of a ship **Dispache**

◊ **adjustor** *noun* = ADJUSTER

> QUOTE inflation-adjusted GNP moved up at a 1.3% annual rate
> *Fortune*
>
> QUOTE Saudi Arabia will no longer adjust its production to match short-term supply with demand
> *Economist*

adman *noun informal* man who works in advertising **Werbefachmann;** *the admen are using balloons as promotional material*

admin *noun informal*

(a) work of administration, especially paperwork **Verwaltung;** *all this admin work takes a lot of my time; there is too much admin in this job; admin costs seem to be rising each quarter; the admin people have sent the report back*

(b) administration staff **Verwaltungsangestellte;** *admin say they need the report immediately*

NOTE: no plural; as a group of people it can have a plural verb

◊ **administer** *verb* to organize *or* to manage **verwalten;** *he administers a large pension fund; US* **administered price** = price fixed by a manufacturer which cannot be varied by a retailer **Richtpreis**

◊ **administration** *noun* organization *or* control *or* management of a company **Verwaltung, Führung; the expenses of the administration** *or* **administration expenses** = costs of management, not including production, marketing or distribution costs **Verwaltungskosten; letters of administration** = letter given by a court to allow someone to deal with the estate of a person who has died **Bestallungsurkunde zum Nachlaßverwalter**

◊ **administrative** *adjective* referring to administration **administrativ, verwaltungstechnisch;** *administrative details; administrative expenses*

◊ **administrator** *noun*

(a) person who directs the work of other employees in a business **Verwalter; Bürovorsteher**

(b) person appointed by a court to manage the affairs of someone who dies without leaving a will **Nachlaßverwalter**

admission *noun*

(a) allowing someone to go in **Eintritt, Zutritt;** *there is a £1 admission charge; admission is free on presentation of this card; free admission on Sundays*

(b) saying that something really happened **Eingeständnis; Geständnis;** *he had to resign after his admission that he had passed information to the rival company*

admit *verb*

(a) to allow someone to go in **Zutritt gewähren;** *children are not admitted to the bank; old age pensioners are admitted at half price*

(b) to say that something is correct *or* to say that something really happened **zugeben, eingestehen;** *the chairman admitted he had taken the cash from the company's safe*

NOTE: **admitting - admitted**

◊ **admittance** *noun* allowing someone to go in **Zutritt;** *no admittance except on business*

NOTE: no plural

adopt *verb* to agree to (something) *or* to accept (something) **annehmen;** *to adopt a resolution; the proposals were adopted unanimously*

ad valorem duty *or* **tax** *noun* tax calculated according to the value of the goods taxed **Wertsteuer**

advance

1 *noun*

(a) money paid as a loan or as a part of a payment to be made later **Vorschuß; Anzahlung; Darlehen;** *bank advance; a cash advance; to receive an advance from the bank; an advance on account; to make an advance of £100 to someone; to pay someone an advance against a security; can I have an advance of £50 against next month's salary?*

(b) in advance = early *or* before something happens **im voraus, vorab;** *to pay in advance; freight payable in advance; price fixed in advance*

(c) increase **Fortschritt, Verbesserung; Erhöhung;** *advance in trade; advance in prices*

2 *adjective* early **im voraus, vorab;** *advance booking; advance payment; you must give seven days' advance notice of withdrawals from the account*

3 *verb*

(a) to lend **leihen; vorschießen;** *the bank advanced him £10,000 against the security of his house*

(b) to increase **steigen, anziehen;** *prices generally advanced on the stock market*

(c) to make something happen earlier **vorverlegen;** *the date of the AGM has been* *advanced to May 10th; the meeting with the German distributors has been advanced from 11.00 to 09.30*

advantage *noun* something useful which may help you to be successful **Vorteil;** *fast typing is an advantage in a secretary; knowledge of two foreign languages is an advantage; there is no advantage in arriving at the exhibition before it opens;* **to take advantage of something** = to use something which helps you **sich etwas zunutze machen**

adverse *adjective* bad *or* not helpful **ungünstig, nachteilig, defizitär; adverse balance of trade** = situation when a country imports more than it exports **passive Handelsbilanz; adverse trading conditions** = bad conditions for trade **ungünstige/widrige Handelsbedingungen**

advertise *verb* to announce that something is for sale *or* that a job is vacant *or* that a service is offered **eine Anzeige schalten, annoncieren; per Anzeige suchen; Reklame machen für;** *to advertise a vacancy; to advertise for a secretary; to advertise a new product*

◊ **ad** *noun informal* = ADVERTISEMENT *we put an ad in the paper; she answered an ad in the paper; he found his job through an ad in the paper;* **classified ads** *or* **small ads** *or* **want ads** = advertisements listed in a newspaper under special headings (like "property for sale","jobs wanted") **Kleinanzeigen;** *look in the small ads to see if anyone has a computer for sale;* **coupon ad** = advertisement with a form attached, which is to be cut out and returned to the advertiser with your name and address for further information **Couponanzeige; display ad** = advertisement which is well designed to attract attention **Großanzeige**

◊ **advert** *noun GB informal* = ADVERTISEMENT *to put an advert in the paper; to answer an advert in the paper; classified adverts; display advert*

◊ **advertisement** *noun* notice which shows that something is for sale *or* that a service is offered *or* that someone wants something *or* that a job is vacant, etc. **Anzeige, Annonce; Reklame, Werbung;** *to put an advertisement in the paper; to answer an advertisement in the paper;* **classified advertisements** = advertisements listed in a newspaper under special headings (such as "property for sale" or "jobs wanted") **Kleinanzeigen; display advertisement** = advertisement which is well designed to attract attention **Großanzeige; advertisement manager** = manager in charge of the advertisement section of a newspaper **Anzeigenleiter**

◊ **advertiser** *noun* person *or* company which advertises **Inserent, Anzeigenkunde;** *the catalogue gives a list of advertisers*

◊ **advertising** *noun* business of announcing that something is for sale *or* of trying to persuade customers to buy a product or service **Werbung(sbranche), Reklame;** *she works in advertising; he has a job in advertising; advertising agent; advertising budget; advertising campaign;* **advertising agency** = office which plans, designs and manages advertising for other companies **Werbeagentur; advertising manager** = manager in charge of advertising a company's products **Werbeleiter; advertising rates** = amount of money charged for advertising space in a newspaper *or* advertising time on TV **Anzeigenkosten; Werbetarif; advertising space** = space in a newspaper set aside for advertisements **Anzeigenraum; to take advertising space in a paper** = to put an advertisement in a newspaper **in einer Zeitung inserieren**
NOTE: no plural

advice *noun*
(a) advice note = written notice to a customer giving details of goods ordered and shipped but not yet delivered **Versandanzeige, Avis; as per advice** = according to what is written on the advice note **laut Benachrichtigung/Avis**
(b) opinion as to what action to take **Rat, Empfehlung; to take legal advice** = to ask a lawyer to say what should be done **sich juristisch beraten lassen;** *the accountant's advice was to send the documents to the police; we sent the documents to the police on the advice of the accountant or we took the accountant's advice and sent the documents to the police*
NOTE: no plural

advise *verb*
(a) to tell someone what has happened **in Kenntnis setzen, informieren, unterrichten;** *we are advised that the shipment will arrive next week*
(b) to suggest to someone what should be done **raten, empfehlen;** *we are advised to take the shipping company to court; the accountant advised us to send the documents to the police*

◊ **advise against** *verb* to suggest that something should not be done **abraten;** *the bank manager advised against closing the account; my stockbroker has advised against buying those shares*

◊ **adviser** *or* **advisor** *noun* person who suggests what should be done **Berater/-in; Ratgeber/-in;** *he is consulting the company's legal adviser;* **financial adviser** = person *or* company which gives advice on financial problems for a fee **Finanzberater/-in**

◇ **advisory** *adjective* as an adviser **beratend;** *he is acting in an advisory capacity;* **an advisory board** = a group of advisers **Beratungsgremium, Beirat**

affair *noun* business *or* dealings **Geschäft, Handel; Sache, Angelegenheit;** *are you involved in the copyright affair? his affairs were so difficult to understand that the lawyers had to ask accountants for advice*

affect *verb* to change *or* to have a bad effect on (something) **betreffen, sich auswirken auf, angehen;** *the new government regulations do not affect us; the company's sales in the Far East were seriously affected by the embargo*

QUOTE the dollar depreciation has yet to affect the underlying inflation rate
Australian Financial Review

affiliated *adjective* connected with *or* owned by another company **angeschlossen, Zweig-, Tochter-;** *one of our affiliated companies*

affirmative *adjective* meaning "yes" **affirmativ, bejahend, zustimmend; the answer was in the affirmative** = the answer was yes **die Antwort war positiv/zustimmend;** *US* **affirmative action program** = programme to avoid discrimination in employment **aktives Förderungsprogramm zugunsten von Minderheiten**

NOTE: the GB equivalent is "equal opportunities"

affluent *adjective* very rich **wohlhabend, reich;** *we live in an affluent society*

afford *verb* to be able to pay *or* buy **sich leisten (können); aufbringen;** *we could not afford the cost of two telephones; the company cannot afford the time to train new staff*

NOTE: only used after **can, cannot, could, could not, able to**

AFL-CIO = AMERICAN FEDERATION OF LABOR - CONGRESS OF INDUSTRIAL ORGANIZATIONS an organization linking US trade unions **Dachverband der amerikanischen Gewerkschaften - Industriegewerkschaftsbund**

after-hours *adjective* **after-hours buying** *or* **selling** *or* **dealing** = buying *or* selling *or* dealing in shares after the Stock Exchange has officially closed for the day **Nachbörse**

◇ **after-sales service** *noun* service of a machine carried out by the seller for some time after the machine has been bought **Kundendienst**

◇ **after-tax profit** *noun* profit after tax has been deducted **Gewinn nach Abzug der Steuern**

against *preposition* relating to *or* part of **gegen;** *to pay an advance against a security; can I have an advance against next month's salary? the bank advanced him £10,000 against the security of his house*

QUOTE investment can be written off against the marginal rate of tax
Investors Chronicle

QUOTE the index for the first half of 1985 shows that the rate of inflation went down by about 12.9 per cent against the rate as at December last year
Business Times (Lagos)

agency *noun*

(a) office *or* job of representing another company in an area **Agentur, Vertretung;** *they signed an agency agreement or an agency contract;* **sole agency** = agreement to be the only person to represent a company *or* to sell a product in a certain area **Alleinvertretung; Alleinvertrieb;** *he has the sole agency for Ford cars*

(b) office *or* business which arranges things for other companies **Agentur; advertising agency** = office which plans *or* designs and manages advertising for companies **Werbeagentur; employment agency** = office which finds jobs for staff **Stellenvermittlung; estate agency** = office which arranges for the sale of properties **Grundstücks- und Immobilienmakler(büro); news agency** = office which distributes news to newspapers and television stations **Nachrichtenagentur, Nachrichtendienst; travel agency** = office which arranges travel for customers **Reisebüro**

NOTE: plural is **agencies**

agenda *noun* list of things to be discussed at a meeting **Tagesordnung;** *the conference agenda or the agenda of the conference; after two hours we were still discussing the first item on the agenda; the secretary put finance at the top of the agenda; the chairman wants two items removed from or taken off the agenda*

agent *noun*

(a) person who represents a company *or* another person in an area **Vertreter/-in;** *to be the agent for IBM;* **sole agent** = person who has the sole agency for a company in an area **Alleinvertreter;** *he is the sole agent for Ford cars;* **agent's commission** = money

(often a percentage of sales) paid to an agent **Vertreterprovision**
(b) person in charge of an agency **Makler/-in, Agent/-in;** *advertising agent; estate agent; travel agent;* **commission agent** = agent who is paid by commission, not by fee **Provisionsagent; forwarding agent** = person *or* company which arranges shipping and customs documents **Spediteur; insurance agent** = person who arranges insurance for clients **Versicherungsvertreter; land agent** = person who runs a farm *or* a large area of land for the owner **Gutsverwalter**
(c) *US* **(business) agent** = chief local official of a trade union **Gewerkschaftsfunktionär**

aggregate *adjective* total *or* with everything added together **Gesamt-, gesamt, angesammelt;** *aggregate output*

agio *noun* charge made for changing money of one currency into another **Agio, Aufgeld**

AGM *noun* = ANNUAL GENERAL MEETING

agree *verb*
(a) to approve **genehmigen, sich einverstanden erklären;** *the auditors have agreed the accounts; the figures were agreed between the two parties; we have agreed the budgets for next year; terms of the contract are still to be agreed; he has agreed your prices*
(b) to say yes *or* to accept **vereinbaren; zustimmen;** *it has been agreed that the lease will run for 25 years; after some discussion he agreed to our plan; the bank will never agree to lend the company £250,000; we all agreed on the plan* (NOTE: to agree **to** *or* **on** a plan)
(c) to agree to do something = to say that you will do something **sich einverstanden od bereit erklären, etwas zu tun;** *she agreed to be chairman; will the finance director agree to resign?*
(d) to be the same as **übereinstimmen;** *the two sets of calculations do not agree*

◇ **agree with** *verb*
(a) to say that your opinions are the same as someone else's **übereinstimmen mit;** *I agree with the chairman that the figures are lower than normal*
(b) to be the same as **übereinstimmen mit;** *the auditors' figures do not agree with those of the accounts department*

◇ **agreed** *adjective* which has been accepted by everyone **vereinbart, abgemacht;** *an agreed amount; on agreed terms*

◇ **agreement** *noun* contract between two parties which explains how they will act **Vereinbarung, Abkommen, Abmachung;** *written agreement; unwritten or verbal agreement; to draw up or to draft an agreement; to break an agreement; to sign an agreement; to witness an agreement; an agreement has been reached or concluded or come to; to reach an agreement or to come to an agreement on prices or salaries; an international agreement on trade; collective wage agreement; an agency agreement; a marketing agreement;* **blanket agreement** = agreement which covers many different items **Gesamtvereinbarung; exclusive agreement** = agreement where a company is appointed sole agent for a product in a market **Alleinvertretungsvereinbarung; gentleman's agreement** = verbal agreement between two parties who trust each other **Vereinbarung auf Treu und Glauben, Gentleman's Agreement**

> QUOTE after three days of tough negotiations the company has reached agreement with its 1,200 unionized workers
> *Toronto Star*

agribusiness *noun* farming, and making products used by farmers **Agrarindustrie**
NOTE: no plural

agriculture *noun* use of land for growing crops *or* raising animals **Landwirtschaft**
NOTE: no plural

◇ **agricultural** *adjective* referring to agriculture *or* referring to farms **landwirtschaftlich, Landwirtschafts-, agrar-, Agrar-; agricultural co-operative** = farm run by groups of workers who are the owners and share the profits **landwirtschaftliche Genossenschaft; agricultural economist** = person who specializes in the study of finance and investment in agriculture **Agrarökonom; Common Agricultural Policy** = agreement between members of the EC to protect farmers by paying subsidies to fix prices of farm produce **Agrarpolitik der Europäischen Gemeinschaft**

ahead *adverb* in front of **vor, voraus** better than **voraus, an der Spitze;** *we are already ahead of our sales forecast; the company has a lot of work ahead of it if it wants to increase its market share*

aim
1 *noun* something which you try to do **Ziel, Bestrebung;** *one of our aims is to increase the quality of our products;* **the company has achieved all its aims** = the company has done all the things it had hoped to do **das Unternehmen hat seine Ziele erreicht**

2 *verb* to try to do something **streben nach;** *we aim to be No. 1 in the market in two years' time; each salesman must aim to double his previous year's sales*

air

1 *noun* **by air** method of travelling *or* sending goods using aircraft **auf dem Luftwege, per Luftpost;** *to send a letter or a shipment by air;* **air carrier** = company which sends cargo *or* passengers by air **Flug-, Luftfahrtgesellschaft Luftverkehrsgesellschaft siehe airline unten; air forwarding** = arranging for goods to be shipped by air **Luftfrachtspedition; air letter** = special sheet of thin blue paper which when folded can be sent by air mail without an envelope **Luftpostbrief(papier)**
2 *verb* **to air a grievance** = to talk about *or* to discuss a grievance **eine Beschwerde vorbringen;** *the management committee is useful because it allows the workers' representatives to air their grievances*

◇ **air cargo** *noun* goods sent by air **Luftfracht**

◇ **aircraft** *noun* machine which flies in the air, carrying passengers or cargo **Flugzeug;** *the airline has a fleet of ten commercial aircraft; the company is one of the most important American aircraft manufacturers;* **to charter an aircraft** = to hire an aircraft for a special purpose **ein Flugzeug chartern**
NOTE: no plural: **one aircraft, two aircraft**

◇ **air freight** *noun* method of shipping goods in an aircraft **Luftfracht;** *to send a shipment by air freight; air freight charges or rates*

◇ **airfreight** *verb* to send goods by air **per Luftfracht senden;** *to airfreight a consignment to Mexico; we airfreighted the shipment because our agent ran out of stock*

◇ **airline** *noun* company which carries passengers or cargo by air **Fluggesellschaft, Airline**

◇ **airmail**
1 *noun* way of sending letters *or* parcels by air **Luftpost;** *to send a package by airmail; airmail charges have risen by 15%;* **airmail envelope** = very light envelope for sending airmail letters **Luftpostumschlag; airmail sticker** = blue sticker with the words "by air mail" which can be stuck to an envelope or packet to show it is being sent by air **Luftpostaufkleber**
NOTE: no plural
2 *verb* to send letters *or* parcels by air **per Luftpost schicken;** *to airmail a document to New York*

◇ **airport** *noun* place where planes land and take off **Flughafen;** *we leave from London Airport at 10.00; O'Hare Airport is the main airport for Chicago;* **airport bus** = bus which takes passengers to and from an airport **Flughafenbus; airport tax** = tax added to the price of the air ticket to cover the cost of running an airport **Flughafengebühr; airport terminal** = main building at an airport where passengers arrive and depart **Terminal, Abfertigungshalle**

◇ **air terminal** *noun* building in a town where passengers meet to be taken by bus to an airport outside the town **Terminal/Abfertigungsgebäude in der Innenstadt**

◇ **airtight** *adjective* which does not allow air to get in **luftdicht;** *the goods are packed in airtight containers*

◇ **airworthiness** *noun* being able and safe to fly **Flugtauglichkeit; certificate of airworthiness** = certificate to show that an aircraft is safe to fly **Lufttüchtigkeitszeugnis**
NOTE: no plural

all

adjective & pronoun everything *or* everyone **alle, gesamt;** *all (of) the managers attended the meeting; the salesman should know the prices of all the products he is selling*

◇ **all-in** *adjective* including everything **Inklusiv-, alles inbegriffen; all-in price** *or* **rate** = price which covers all items in a purchase (goods, delivery, tax, insurance) **Inklusivpreis**

allocate

verb to divide (a sum of money) in various ways and share it out **zuweisen, zuteilen;** *we allocate 10% of revenue to publicity; $2,500 was allocated to office furniture*

◇ **allocation** *noun*
(a) dividing a sum of money in various ways **Zuteilung, Zuweisung;** *allocation of capital; allocation of funds to a project*
(b) share allocation *or* **allocation of shares** = spreading a small number of shares among a large number of people who have applied for them **Aktienzuteilung**

allot

verb to share out **zuteilen, zuweisen; to allot shares** = to give a certain number of shares to people who have applied for them **Aktien zuteilen**
NOTE: **allotting - allotted**

◇ **allotment** *noun*
(a) sharing out funds by giving money to various departments **Zuteilung;** *allotment of funds to a project*
(b) giving some shares in a new company to people who have applied for them **(Aktien)zuteilung;** *share allotment; payment in full on allotment;* **letter of allotment** *or* **allotment letter** = letter which tells someone who has applied for shares in a

new company how many shares he has been allotted **Zuteilungsanzeige**

all-out *adjective* complete *or* very serious **total;** *(campaign)* **massiv;** *the union called for an all-out strike; the personnel manager has launched an all-out campaign to get the staff to work on Friday afternoons*

allow *verb*
(a) to say that someone can do something **bewilligen, gestatten;** *junior members of staff are not allowed to use the chairman's lift; the company allows all members of staff to take six days' holiday at Christmas*
(b) to give **gewähren;** *to allow someone a discount; to allow 5% discount to members of staff; to allow 10% interest on large sums of money*
(c) to agree *or* to accept legally **anerkennen; stattgeben;** *to allow a claim or an appeal*

◇ **allow for** *verb* to give a discount for *or* to add an extra sum to cover something **einrechnen, vergüten;** *to allow for money paid in advance; to allow 10% for packing;* **delivery is not allowed for** = delivery charges are not included **Liefergebühren sind nicht eingerechnet; allow 28 days for delivery** = calculate that delivery will take at least 28 days **Lieferzeit bis zu 28 Tagen**

◇ **allowable** *adjective* legally accepted **zulässig, erlaubt; allowable expenses** = expenses which can be claimed against tax **abzugsfähige Ausgaben**

◇ **allowance** *noun*
(a) money which is given for a special reason **Zuschuß; Beihilfe; Spesen;** *travel allowance or travelling allowance; foreign currency allowance;* **cost-of-living allowance** = addition to normal salary to cover increases in the cost of living **Teuerungszulage; entertainment allowance** = money which a manager is allowed to spend each month on meals with visitors **Aufwands-, Bewirtungsentschädigung**
(b) part of an income which is not taxed; *allowances against tax or tax allowances; personal allowances* **Steuerfreibetrag; wife's earned income allowance** = tax allowance to be set against money earned by the wife of the main taxpayer **zusätzlicher Steuerfreibetrag für Erwerbseinkünfte der Ehefrau**
(c) money removed in the form of a discount **Nachlaß, Rabatt;** *allowance for depreciation; allowance for exchange loss*
(d)

◇ **allowed time** *noun* paid time which the management agrees a worker can spend on rest *or* cleaning *or* meals, not working **Erholungspause**

◇ **baggage allowance** amount of baggage which a passenger can take with him free on a plane **Freigepäck**

> QUOTE most airlines give business class the same baggage allowance as first class
> *Business Traveller*
>
> QUOTE the compensation plan includes base, incentive and car allowance totalling $50,000+
> *Globe and Mail (Toronto)*

all-risks policy *noun* insurance policy which covers risks of any kind, with no exclusions **Kombination verschiedener Versicherungsarten**

all-time *adjective* **all-time high** *or* **all-time low** = highest or lowest point ever reached **absoluter Höchststand; absoluter Tiefstand;** *sales have fallen from their all-time high of last year*

alphabet *noun* the 26 letters used to make words **Alphabet**
◇ **alphabetical order** *noun* arrangement of records (such as files, index cards) in the order of the letters of the alphabet (A,B,C,D, etc.) **alphabetische Reihenfolge**

alter *verb* to change **ab-, verändern;** *to alter the terms of a contract*
◇ **alteration** *noun* change which has been made **Änderung, Abänderung;** *he made some alterations to the terms of a contract; the agreement was signed without any alterations*

alternative
1 *noun* thing which can be done instead of another **Alternative;** *what is the alternative to firing half the staff?;* **we have no alternative** = there is nothing else we can do **wir haben keine Alternative / andere Wahl**
2 *adjective* other *or* which can take the place of something **Alternativ-; to find someone alternative employment** = to find someone another job **für jdn eine andere Arbeitsstelle finden**

altogether *adverb* putting everything together **insgesamt;** *the staff of the three companies in the group come to 2,500 altogether; the company lost £2m last year and £4m this year, making £6m altogether for the two years*

a.m. *adverb* in the morning *or* before 12 midday **vormittags, ante meridiem;** *the flight leaves at 9.20 a.m.; telephone calls before 6 a.m. are charged at the cheap rate*

amend *verb* to change and make more correct *or* acceptable **(ab)ändern, berichtigen;**

please amend your copy of the contract accordingly

◇ **amendment** *noun* change to a document **Änderung, Abänderung;** *to propose an amendment to the constitution; to make amendments to a contract*

Amex *noun informal* = AMERICAN STOCK EXCHANGE; AMERICAN EXPRESS

amortize *verb* to pay off (a debt) by putting money aside regularly over a period of time **amortisieren;** *the capital cost is amortized over five years*

◇ **amortizable** *adjective* which can be amortized **amortisierbar;** *the capital cost is amortizable over a period of ten years*

◇ **amortization** *noun* act of amortizing **Amortisation;** *amortization of a debt*

amount
1 *noun* quantity of money **Betrag, Summe;** *amount paid; amount deducted; amount owing; amount written off; what is the amount outstanding? a small amount invested in gilt-edged stock*
2 *verb* **to amount to** = to make a total of **sich belaufen auf, betragen;** *their debts amount to over £1m*

analog computer *noun* computer which works on the basis of electrical impulses representing numbers **Analogrechner**

analyse *or* **analyze** *verb* to examine in detail **analysieren, auswerten;** *to analyse a statement of account; to analyse the market potential*

◇ **analysis** *noun* detailed examination and report **Analyse, Auswertung;** *job analysis; market analysis; sales analysis; to carry out an analysis of the market potential; to write an analysis of the sales position;* **cost analysis** = examination in advance of the costs of a new product **Kostenanalyse; systems analysis** = using a computer to suggest how a company can work more efficiently by analysing the way in which it works at present **Systemanalyse**
NOTE: plural is **analyses**

◇ **analyst** *noun* person who analyses **Analytiker/-in;** *market analyst; systems analyst*

announce *verb* to tell something to the public **ankündigen, bekanntgeben;** *to announce the results for 1984; to announce a programme of investment*

◇ **announcement** *noun* telling something in public **Ankündigung, Bekanntmachung;** *announcement of a cutback in expenditure; announcement of the appointment of a new managing director; the managing director made an announcement to the staff*

annual *adjective* for one year **jährlich;** *annual statement of income; he has six weeks' annual leave; the annual accounts; annual growth of 5%;* **annual report** = report of a company's financial situation at the end of a year, sent to all the shareholders **Geschäftsbericht; on an annual basis** = each year **einmal pro Jahr;** *the figures are revised on an annual basis*

◇ **annual general meeting** *noun* meeting of all the shareholders, when the company's financial situation is discussed with the directors **ordentliche Jahreshauptversammlung**

◇ **annualized** *adjective* shown on an annual basis **jährlich; annualized percentage rate** = rate of interest (such as on a hire-purchase agreement) shown on an annual compound basis **Jahreszinssatz**

◇ **annually** *adverb* each year **jährlich;** *the figures are updated annually*

QUOTE real wages have risen at an annual rate of only 1% in the last two years
Sunday Times

QUOTE the remuneration package will include an attractive salary, profit sharing and a company car together with four weeks annual holiday
Times

annuity *noun* money paid each year to a retired person, usually in return for a lump-sum payment **Jahresrente;** *he has a government annuity or an annuity from the government; to buy or to take out an annuity ;* **annuity for life** *or* **life annuity** = annual payments made to someone as long as he is alive **Leibrente; reversionary annuity** = annuity paid to someone on the death of another person **einseitige Überlebensrente**
NOTE: plural is **annuities**

◇ **annuitant** *noun* person who receives an annuity **Empfänger einer Jahresrente**

annul *verb* to cancel *or* to stop something being legal **annullieren; rückgängig machen; für ungültig erklären;** *the contract was annulled by the court*
NOTE: **annulling - annulled**

◇ **annullable** *adjective* which can be cancelled **annullierbar, aufhebbar**

◇ **annulling**
1 *adjective* which cancels **Annulierungs-; Nichtigkeits-; Ungültigkeits-;** *annulling clause*
2 *noun* act of cancelling **Annullierung;** *the annulling of a contract*

◇ **annulment** *noun* act of cancelling **Annullierung, Aufhebung;** *annulment of a contract*

answer
1 *noun* reply *or* letter or conversation coming after someone has written or spoken **Antwort, Bescheid;** *I am writing in answer to your letter of October 6th; my letter got no answer or there was no answer to my letter; I tried to phone his office but there was no answer*
2 *verb* to speak or write after someone has spoken or written to you **(be)antworten; to answer a letter** = to write a letter in reply to a letter which you have received **einen Brief beantworten; to answer the telephone** = to lift the telephone when it rings and listen to what the caller is saying **das Telefon abnehmen**
◇ **answering** *noun* **answering machine** = machine which answers the telephone automatically when someone is not in the office **Anrufbeantworter; answering service** = office which answers the telephone and takes messages for someone *or* for a company **Fernsprechauftragsdienst**

antedate *verb* to put an earlier date on a document **zurückdatieren;** *the invoice was antedated to January 1st*

anti- *prefix* against **Anti-**
◇ **anti-dumping** *adjective* which protects a country against dumping **Anti-Dumping-;** *anti-dumping legislation*
◇ **anti-inflationary** *adjective* which tries to restrict inflation **anti-, gegeninflationär;** *anti-inflationary measures*
◇ **anti-trust** *adjective* which attacks monopolies and encourages competition **Antitrust-;** *anti-trust laws or legislation*

AOB = ANY OTHER BUSINESS item at the end of an agenda, where any matter can be raised **Verschiedenes**

aperture *noun* hole **Öffnung; aperture envelope** = envelope with a hole in it so that the address on the letter inside can be seen **Fenster(brief)umschlag**

apologize *verb* to say you are sorry **sich entschuldigen;** *to apologize for the delay in answering; she apologized for being late*
◇ **apology** *noun* saying you are sorry **Entschuldigung;** *to write a letter of apology; I enclose a cheque for £10 with apologies for the delay in answering your letter*

appeal
1 *noun*
(a) being attractive **Reiz, Anziehungskraft; customer appeal** = being attractive to customers **Kundenattraktivität; sales appeal** = quality which makes customers want to buy **Kaufanreiz**
(b) asking a court *or* a government department to change its decision **Berufung(santrag), Revision(santrag);** *the appeal against the planning decision will be heard next month; he lost his appeal for damages against the company;* **she won her case on appeal** = her case was lost in the first court, but the appeal court said that she was right **sie gewann den Prozeß in der Berufung/Revision/Rechtsmittelinstanz**
NOTE: no plural for (a)
2 *verb*
(a) to attract **ansprechen, reizen;** *this record appeals to the under-25 market; the idea of working in Australia for six months appealed to her*
(b) to ask a government department *or* a law court to alter its decision **Berufung/Revision einlegen;** *the company appealed against the decision of the planning officers*
NOTE: you appeal **to** a court or a person **against** a decision

appear *verb* to seem **scheinen;** *the company appeared to be doing well; the managing director appears to be in control*

apply *verb*
(a) to ask for something, usually in writing **beantragen, nachsuchen;** *(um eine Stelle)* **sich bewerben;** *(für Aktien)* **zeichnen;** *to apply for a job; to apply for shares; to apply in writing; to apply in person*
(b) to affect *or* to touch **gelten, Anwendung finden;** *this clause applies only to deals outside the EC*

◇ **applicant** *noun* person who applies for something **Antragsteller/-in;** *(für eine Stelle)* **Bewerber/-in;** *(für Aktien)* **Zeichner;** *applicant for a job or job applicant; there were thousands of applicants for shares in the new company*

◇ **application** *noun* asking for something, usually in writing **Antrag, Gesuch, Ersuchen;** *(für eine Stelle)* **Bewerbung;** *(für Aktien)* **Zeichnung;** *application for shares; shares payable on application; attach the cheque to the share application form; application for a job or job application;* **application form** = form to be filled in when applying **Bewerbungsformular; Antragsformular;** *to fill in an application (form) for a job or a job application (form)* ; **letter of application** = letter in which someone applies for a job **Bewerbungsschreiben**

appoint *verb* to choose someone for a job **ernennen, berufen;** *to appoint James Smith (to the post of) manager; we have appointed a new distribution manager*
NOTE: you appoint a person **to** a job

◇ **appointee** *noun* person who is appointed to a job **Ernannter, Kandidat/-in**

◇ **appointment** *noun*
(a) arrangement to meet **Termin;** *to make or to fix an appointment for two o'clock; to make an appointment with someone for two o'clock; he was late for his appointment; she had to cancel her appointment;* **appointments book** = desk diary in which appointments are noted **Terminkalender**
(b) being appointed to a job **Ernennung; Einsetzung; Berufung; on his appointment as manager** = when he was made manager **bei seiner Ernennung zum Manager; letter of appointment** = letter in which someone is appointed to a job **Einstellungsschreiben; Ernennungsschreiben**
(c) job **Stelle, Amt; staff appointment** = job on the staff **feste Anstellung; appointments vacant** = list (in a newspaper) of jobs which are available **Stellenangebote**

apportion *verb* to share out (costs) **zu-, verteilen; umlegen;** *costs are apportioned according to projected revenue*

◇ **apportionment** *noun* sharing out of (costs) **Zu-, Verteilung; Umlegung**

appraise *verb* to assess *or* to calculate the value of something **ab-, einschätzen, bewerten**

◇ **appraisal** *noun* calculation of the value of someone *or* something **Ab-, Einschätzung, Bewertung; staff appraisal** = reports on how well each member of staff is working **Personalbeurteilung**

appreciate *verb*
(a) to notice how good something is **zu schätzen wissen, schätzen;** *the customer always appreciates efficient service; tourists do not appreciate long delays at banks*
(b) to increase in value **(im Wert) steigen;** *the dollar has appreciated in terms of the yen; these shares have appreciated by 5%*

◇ **appreciation** *noun*
(a) increase in value **Wertsteigerung, Wertzuwachs;** *these shares show an appreciation of 10%; the appreciation of the dollar against the peseta*
(b) valuing something highly **Anerkennung, Würdigung, Wertschätzung;** *he was given a rise in appreciation of his excellent work*
NOTE: no plural

apprentice
1 *noun* young person who works under contract with a skilled workman to learn from him **Auszubildender, Lehrling**
2 *verb* **to be apprenticed to someone** = to work with a skilled workman to learn from him **jdm als Lehrling unterstellt sein**

◇ **apprenticeship** *noun* time spent learning a skilled trade **Ausbildung, Lehre;** *he served a six-year apprenticeship in the steel works*

appro *noun* = APPROVAL; **to buy something on appro** = to buy something which you will only pay for if it is satisfactory **etwas zur Probe/zur Ansicht kaufen**

approach
1 *noun* getting in touch with someone with a proposal **Herantreten, Herangehen(sweise);** *the company made an approach to the supermarket chain; the board turned down all approaches on the subject of mergers; we have had an approach from a Japanese company to buy our car division*
2 *verb* to get in touch with someone with a proposal **herantreten an, sich wenden an;** *he approached the bank with a request for a loan; the company was approached by an American publisher with the suggestion of a merger; we have been approached several times but have turned down all offers*

appropriate *verb* to put a sum of money aside for a special purpose **zuweisen, bereitstellen;** *to appropriate a sum of money for a capital project*

◇ **appropriation** *noun* act of putting money aside for a special purpose **Zuweisung, Bereitstellung;** *appropriation of funds to the reserve;* **appropriation account** = part of a profit and loss account which shows how the profit has been dealt with (i.e. how much has been given to the shareholders as dividends, how much is being put into the reserves, etc.) **Gewinnverteilungsrechnung**
NOTE: no plural

approve *verb*
(a) to approve of = to think something is good **billigen, gutheißen;** *the chairman approves of the new company letter heading; the sales staff do not approve of interference from the accounts division*
(b) to agree to something officially **genehmigen; ratifizieren;** *to approve the terms of a contract; the proposal was approved by the board*

◇ **approval** *noun*
(a) agreement **Genehmigung;** *to submit a budget for approval;* **certificate of approval** =

document showing that an item has been approved officially **Genehmigungszertifikat**
(b) on approval = sale where the buyer only pays for goods if they are satisfactory **zur Probe; versuchsweise;** *to buy a photocopier on approval*
NOTE: no plural

approximate *adjective* not exact, but almost correct **ungefähr, annähernd;** *the sales division has made an approximate forecast of expenditure*

◊ **approximately** *adverb* almost correctly **circa, etwa, annähernd;** *expenditure is approximately 10% down on the previous quarter*

◊ **approximation** *noun* rough calculation **annähernde Berechnung;** *(Zahl)* **Näherungswert;** *approximation of expenditure; the final figure is only an approximation*

APR = ANNUAL(IZED) PERCENTAGE RATE

arbitrage *noun* selling on one market and buying on another at almost the same time to profit from different exchange rates; buying shares in companies which are likely to be taken over and so rise in price **Arbitrage; arbitrage syndicate** = group of people formed to raise the capital to invest in arbitrage deals **Arbitrage-Konsortium**

◊ **arbitrager** *or* **arbitrageur** *noun* person whose business is arbitrage **Arbitrageur, Arbitragehändler**

arbitrate *verb (of an outside party)* to be chosen by both sides to try to settle an industrial dispute **schlichten;** *to arbitrate in a dispute*

◊ **arbitration** *noun* settling of a dispute by an outside person, chosen by both sides **Schlichtung(sverfahren);** *to submit a dispute to arbitration; to refer a question to arbitration; to take a dispute to arbitration; to go to arbitration;* **arbitration board** *or* **arbitration tribunal** = group which arbitrates **Schlichtungskommission; industrial arbitration tribunal** = court which decides in industrial disputes **Schiedsgericht für wirtschaftliche Streitigkeiten;** *to accept the ruling of the arbitration board*
NOTE: no plural

◊ **arbitrator** *noun* person not concerned with a dispute who is chosen by both sides to try to settle it **Schlichter/-in; Schiedsrichter/-in;** *industrial arbitrator; to accept or to reject the arbitrator's ruling*

area *noun*
(a) measurement of the space taken up by something (calculated by multiplying the length by the width) **Fläche, Raum;** *the area of this office is 3,400 square feet; we are looking for a shop with a sales area of about 100 square metres*
(b) region of the world **Gebiet, Zone; free trade area** = group of countries practising free trade **freie Handelszone; dollar area** *or* **sterling area** = areas of the world where the dollar *or* the pound is the main trading currency **Dollarzone; Sterlingzone**
(c) subject **Bereich;** *a problem area or an area for concern*
(d) district *or* part of a town **Viertel, Teil;** *the office is in the commercial area of the town; their factory is in a very good area for getting to the motorways and airports*
(e) part of a country, a division for commercial purposes **Gebiet;** *his sales area is the North-West; he finds it difficult to cover all his area in a week*

◊ **area code** *noun* special telephone number which is given to a particular area **Vorwahl, Ortsnetzkennzahl;** *the area code for London is 071*

◊ **area manager** *noun* manager who is responsible for a part of the country **Bezirks-, Gebietsleiter**

argue *verb* to discuss something about which you do not agree **streiten, sich auseinandersetzen;** *they argued over or about the price; we spent hours arguing with the managing director about the site for the new factory; the union officials argued among themselves over the best way to deal with the ultimatum from the management*
NOTE: you argue **with** someone **about** *or* **over** something

◊ **argument** *noun* discussing something without agreeing **Auseinandersetzung, Streit;** *they got into an argument with the customs officials over the documents; he was sacked after an argument with the managing director*

around *preposition* approximately **um, circa;** *the office costs around £2,000 a year to heat; his salary is around $85,000*

arrange *verb*
(a) to put in order **(an)ordnen, gruppieren;** *the office is arranged as an open-plan area with small separate rooms for meetings; the files are arranged in alphabetical order; arrange the invoices in order of their dates*
(b) to organize **arrangieren, einrichten;** *we arranged to have the meeting in their offices; she arranged for a car to meet him at the airport*

NOTE: you arrange **for** someone to do something; you arrange **for** something to be done; or you arrange **to** do something

◇ **arrangement** *noun*

(a) way in which something is organized **Arrangement, Plan;** *the company secretary is making all the arrangements for the AGM*

(b) settling of a financial dispute **Vergleich; Übereinkunft;** *to come to an arrangement with the creditors*

arrears *plural noun* money which is owed, but which has not been paid at the right time **Rückstände;** *arrears of interest; to allow the payments to fall into arrears; salary with arrears effective from January 1st;* **in arrears** = owing money which should have been paid earlier **im Rückstand;** *the payments are six months in arrears; he is six weeks in arrears with his rent*

arrive *noun*

(a) to reach a place **ankommen, eingehen, eintreffen;** *the consignment has still not arrived; the shipment arrived without any documentation; the plane arrives in Sydney at 04.00; the train leaves Paris at 09.20 and arrives at Bordeaux two hours later*

NOTE: you arrive **at** *or* **in** a place or town, but only **in** a country

(b) to arrive at = **gelangen/kommen zu** to calculate and agree; *to arrive at a price; after some discussion we arrived at a compromise*

◇ **arrival** *noun* reaching a place **Ankunft; Eingang; Eintreffen;** *we are waiting for the arrival of a consignment of spare parts;* **"to await arrival"** = note written on an envelope to ask for it to be kept safe until the person it is addressed to arrives **nicht nachsenden; arrivals** = part of an airport dealing with passengers who are arriving **Ankunft**

article *noun*

(a) product *or* thing for sale **Artikel;** *to launch a new article on the market; a black market in luxury articles*

(b) section of a legal agreement **Artikel, Paragraph, Absatz, Klausel;** *see article 8 of the contract*

(c) articles of association *or US* **articles of incorporation** = document which sets up a company and says what work it will do **Gesellschaftsvertrag, Satzung;** *director appointed under the articles of the company; this procedure is not allowed under the articles of association of the company*

◇ **articled** *adjective* **articled clerk** = clerk who is bound by contract to work in a lawyer's office for some years to learn the law **Anwaltsreferendar**

articulated lorry *or* **articulated vehicle** *noun* large lorry formed of two parts, the second pulled by the first **Sattelschlepper, Sattelkraftfahrzeug**

asap = AS SOON AS POSSIBLE

aside *adverb* to one side *or* out of the way **zur Seite, beiseite; to put aside** *or* **to set aside** = to save (money) **auf die Seite legen;** *he is putting £50 aside each week to pay for his car*

ask *verb*

(a) to put a question to someone **fragen;** *he asked the information office for details of companies exhibiting at the motor show; ask the salesgirl if the bill includes VAT*

(b) to tell someone to do something **bitten;** *he asked the switchboard operator to get him a number in Germany; she asked her secretary to fetch a file from the managing director's office; the customs officials asked him to open his case*

◇ **ask for** *verb*

(a) to say that you want *or* need something **verlangen; fragen nach; bitten;** *he asked for the file on 1984 debtors; they asked for more time to repay the loan; there is a man in reception asking for Mr Smith*

(b) to put a price on something for sale **verlangen, fordern;** *they are asking £24,000 for the car*

◇ **asking price** *noun* price which the seller asks for the goods being sold **geforderter Preis; Verhandlungsbasis;** *the asking price is £24,000*

assay mark *noun* mark put on gold or silver items to show that the metal is of the correct quality **Feingehaltsstempel**

assemble *verb* to put a product together from various parts **montieren, zusammenbauen;** *the engines are made in Japan and the bodies in Scotland, and the cars are assembled in France*

◇ **assembly** *noun*

(a) putting an item together from various parts **Montage, Zusammenbau;** *there are no assembly instructions to show you how to put the computer together;* **car assembly plant** = factory where cars are put together from parts made in other factories **Auto-Montagewerk**

(b) meeting **Versammlung;** (NOTE: no plural for (a); plural for (b) is **assemblies)**

◇ **assembly line** *noun* production system where the product (such as a car) moves slowly through the factory with new sections added to it as it goes along **Montageband, Fließband, Fertigungsstraße;** *he* *works on an assembly line or he is an assembly line worker*

assess *verb* to calculate the value of something **schätzen;** *to assess damages at £1,000; to assess a property for the purposes of insurance*

◇ **assessment** *noun* calculation of value **Schätzung;** *assessment of damages; assessment of property; tax assessment;* **staff assessment** = report on how well members of staff are working **Personalbeurteilung**

asset *noun* thing which belongs to company or person, and which has a value **Aktiva, Vermögenswert;** *he has an excess of assets over liabilities; her assets are only £640 as against liabilities of £24,000;* **capital assets** *or* **fixed assets** = property *or* machinery which a company owns and uses **Anlagevermögen; current assets** = assets used by a company in its ordinary work (such as materials, finished goods, cash) **Umlaufvermögen; frozen assets** = assets of a company which cannot be sold because someone has a claim against them **eingefrorene/blockierte Vermögenswerte; intangible assets** = assets which have a value, but which cannot be seen (such as goodwill, or a patent, or a trademark) **immaterielle Vermögenswerte; liquid assets** = cash, or bills which can be quickly converted into cash **flüssige Mittel; personal assets** = moveable assets which belong to a person **bewegliches Privatvermögen; tangible assets** = assets which are solid (such as furniture or jewels or cash) **materielle Vermögenswerte; bilanzirbare Sachwerte; asset value** = value of a company calculated by adding together all its assets **Vermögenswert; asset stripper** = person who buys a company to sell its assets **Aufkäufer (un)rentabler Unternehmen, der anschließend deren Vermögenswerte verkauft; asset stripping** = buying a company to sell its assets **Aufkauf (un)rentabler Unternehmen, deren Vermögenswerte anschließend verkauft werden**

> QUOTE many companies are discovering that a well-recognised brand name can be a priceless asset that lessens the risk of introducing a new product
>
> *Duns Business Month*

assign *verb*
(a) to give legally **übertragen, abtreten;** *to assign a right to someone; to assign shares to someone*
(b) to give someone a job of work **beauftragen, betrauen;** *he was assigned the job of checking the sales figures*

◇ **assignation** *noun* legal transfer **Übertragung, Abtretung;** *assignation of shares to someone; assignation of a patent*

◇ **assignee** *noun* person who receives something which has been assigned **Abtretungsempfänger**

◇ **assignment** *noun*
(a) legal transfer of a property *or* of a right **Abtretung; Übertragung;** *assignment of a patent or of a copyright; to sign a deed of assignment*
(b) particular job of work **Aufgabe, Auftrag;** *he was appointed managing director with the assignment to improve the company's profits; the oil team is on an assignment in the North Sea*

◇ **assignor** *noun* person who assigns something to someone **Abtretender**

assist *verb* to help **helfen, unterstützen;** *can you assist the stock controller in counting the stock? he assists me with my income tax returns*
NOTE: you assist someone **in** doing something or **with** something

◇ **assistance** *noun* help **Hilfe, Unterstützung; financial assistance** = help in the form of money **Finanzhilfe**
NOTE: no plural

◇ **assistant** *noun* person who helps **Assistent, Gehilfe, Mitarbeiter; personal assistant** = secretary who also helps the boss in various ways **persönlicher Assistent; shop assistant** = person who serves the customers in a shop **Verkäufer/-in; assistant manager** = person who helps a manager **stellvertretender Manager**

associate
1 *adjective* linked **assoziiert; associate company** = company which is partly owned by another **Beteiligungsgesellschaft; associate director** = director who attends board meetings, but has not been elected by the shareholders; *entspricht* **außerordentliches Verwaltungsratsmitglied**
2 *noun* person who works in the same business as someone **Geschäftspartner;** *she is a business associate of mine*

◇ **associated** *adjective* linked **assoziiert; Beteiligungs-;** *Smith Ltd and its associated company, Jones Brothers*

◇ **association** *noun*
(a) group of people *or* of companies with the same interest **Gesellschaft, Verband, Bund;** *trade association; employers' association; manufacturers' association*
(b) articles of association = document which sets up a company and says what work it will do **Gesellschaftsvertrag, Satzung**

assume *verb* to take **übernehmen;** *to assume all risks; he has assumed responsibility for marketing*

◊ **assumption** *noun* taking **Übernahme;** *assumption of risks*

assure *verb* to insure *or* to have a contract with a company where if regular payments are made, the company will pay compensation if you die **versichern, eine Versicherung abschließen für;** *to assure someone's life; he has paid the premiums to have his wife's life assured;* **the life assured** = the person whose life has been covered by the life assurance **der Versicherte (in einer Lebensversicherung)**

◊ **assurance** *noun* insurance *or* agreement that in return for regular payments, a company will pay compensation for loss of life **Versicherung;** *assurance company; assurance policy;* **life assurance** = insurance which pays a sum of money when someone dies **Lebensversicherung**

◊ **assurer** *or* **assuror** *noun* insurer *or* company which insures **Versicherungsträger**

NOTE: **assure** and **assurance** are used in Britain for insurance policies relating to something which will certainly happen (such as death); for other types of policy use **insure** and **insurance**

at best *phrase* **sell at best** = instruction to stockbroker to sell shares at the best price possible **bestens verkaufen**

at par *phrase* **share at par** = share whose value on the stock market is the same as its face value **Aktie zum Nennwert/al pari**

ATM *noun* = AUTOMATIC TELLING MACHINE

attach *verb* to fasten *or* to link **befestigen, anhängen;** *(document to a letter)* **beiheften;** *(Bedeutung)* **beimessen;** *I am attaching a copy of my previous letter; please find attached a copy of my letter of June 24th; the machine is attached to the floor so it cannot be moved; the bank attaches great importance to the deal*

◊ **attache** *noun* junior diplomat who does special work **Attaché; commercial attaché** = diplomat whose job is to promote the commercial interests of his country **Handelsattaché; attaché case** = small case for carrying papers and documents **Aktenkoffer**

◊ **attachment** *noun* holding a debtor's property to prevent it being sold until debts are paid **dinglicher Arrest**

attempt

1 *noun* trying to do something **Versuch, Bemühung;** *the company made an attempt to break into the American market; the takeover attempt was turned down by the board; all his attempts to get a job have failed*

2 *verb* to try **versuchen, sich bemühen;** *the company is attempting to get into the tourist market; we are attempting the takeover of a manufacturing company; he attempted to have the sales director sacked*

attend *verb* to be present at **anwesend sein, beiwohnen;** *the chairman has asked all managers to attend the meeting; none of the shareholders attended the AGM*

◊ **attend to** *verb* to give careful thought to (something) and deal with it **sich kümmern um;** *the managing director will attend to your complaint personally; we have brought in experts to attend to the problem of installing the new computer*

◊ **attention** *noun* giving careful thought **Aufmerksamkeit, Beachtung;** *for the attention of the Managing Director; your orders will have our best attention*

attorney *noun*

(a) person who is legally allowed to act on behalf of someone else **Bevollmächtigter, rechtlicher Vertreter; power of attorney** = legal document giving someone the right to act on someone's behalf in legal matters **Handlungsvollmacht;** *his solicitor was granted power of attorney*

(b) *US* lawyer **Rechtsanwalt**

attract *verb* to make something or someone join *or* come in **anziehen, gewinnen;** *the company is offering free holidays in Spain to attract buyers; we have difficulty in attracting skilled staff to this part of the country*

◊ **attractive** *adjective* which attracts **attraktiv, zugkräftig; attractive prices** = prices which are cheap enough to make buyers want to buy **verlockende Preise; attractive salary** = good salary to make high-quality applicants apply for the job **verlockendes/ansprechendes Gehalt**

> QUOTE airlines offer special stopover rates and hotel packages to attract customers and to encourage customer loyalty
>
> *Business Traveller*

attributable *adjective* **attributable profits** = profits which can be shown to come from a particular area **zurechenbare Gewinne**

auction

1 *noun* selling of goods where people offer bids, and the item is sold to the person who makes the highest offer **Auktion, Versteigerung;** *sale by auction; auction*

rooms; to sell goods by auction or ; US at auction; **to put something up for auction** = to offer an item for sale at an auction **etwas zur Versteigerung anbieten; Dutch auction** = auction where the auctioneer offers an item for sale at a high price and gradually reduces the price until someone makes a bid **holländische Versteigerung**
2 *verb* to sell at an auction **versteigern;** *the factory was closed and the machinery was auctioned off*

◇ **auctioneer** *noun* person who conducts an auction **Auktionator/-in**

audio-typing *noun* typing to dictation from a recording **Tippen nach Phonodiktat**
NOTE: no plural

◇ **audio-typist** *noun* typist who types to dictation from a recording on a dictating machine **Phonotypist/-in**

audit
1 *noun* examination of the books and accounts of a company **Buch-, Rechnungsprüfung, Revision;** *to carry out the annual audit;* **external audit** *or* **independent audit** = audit carried out by an independent auditor **außerbetriebliche/unabhängige Rechnungsprüfung/Revision; internal audit** = audit carried out by a department inside the company **innerbetriebliche Rechnungsprüfung/Revision;** *he is the manager of the internal audit department*
2 *verb* to examine the books and accounts of a company **Rechnungsprüfungen vornehmen;** *to audit the accounts; the books have not yet been audited*

◇ **auditing** *noun* action of examining the books and accounts **Rechnungsprüfung, Revision**

◇ **auditor** *noun* person who audits **Rechnungsprüfer, Revisor;** *the AGM appoints the company's auditors;* **external auditor** = independent person who audits the company's accounts **unabhängiger Rechnungsprüfer/Revisor; internal auditor** = member of staff who audits a company's accounts **betriebsinterner Rechnungsprüfer/Revisor**

authenticate *verb* to say that something is true **beglaubigen, beurkunden**

authority *noun*
(a) power to do something **Befugnis, Ermächtigung;** *he has no authority to act on our behalf*
(b) local authority = elected section of government which runs a small area of a country **örtliche Behörde; the authorities** = the government *or* the people in control **die Behörden**
NOTE: no plural for (a)

authorize *verb*
(a) to give permission for something to be done **genehmigen, bewilligen;** *to authorize payment of £10,000*
(b) to give someone the authority to do something **ermächtigen, autorisieren, bevollmächtigen;** *to authorize someone to act on the company's behalf*

◇ **authorization** *noun* permission *or* power to do something **Genehmigung, Bevollmächtigung, Ermächtigung;** *do you have authorization for this expenditure?; he has no authorization to act on our behalf*
NOTE: no plural

◇ **authorized** *adjective* permitted **befugt, autorisiert, bevollmächtigt; authorized capital** = amount of capital which a company is allowed to have, as stated in the articles of association **genehmigtes Grundkapital; authorized dealer** = person *or* company (such as a bank) which is allowed to buy and sell foreign currency **Geldhändler**

> QUOTE in 1934 Congress authorized President Franklin D. Roosevelt to seek lower tariffs with any country willing to reciprocate
> *Duns Business Month*

automated *adjective* worked automatically by machines **automatisiert;** *fully automated car assembly plant; US* **automated teller machine** = = AUTOMATIC TELLING MACHINE

◇ **automation** *noun* use of machines to do work with very little supervision by people **Automatisierung**
NOTE: no plural

automatic *adjective* which works *or* takes place without any person making it happen **(voll)automatisch;** *there is an automatic increase in salaries on January 1st;* **automatic data processing** = data processing done by a computer **elektronische Datenverarbeitung; automatic telling machine** *or* machine which gives out money when a special card is inserted and special instructions given **Geldautomat; automatic vending machine** = machine which provides drinks, cigarettes, etc. when a coin is put in **Automat**

◇ **automatically** *adverb* working without a person giving instructions **automatisch;** *the invoices are sent out automatically; addresses are typed in automatically; a demand note is sent automatically when the invoice is overdue*

available *adjective* which can be obtained *or* bought **erhältlich, verfügbar;** *available in all branches; item no longer* *available; items available to order only; funds which are made available for investment in small businesses;* **available capital** = capital which is ready to be used **verfügbares Kapital, flüssige Gelder**

◇ **availability** *noun* being easily obtained **Verfügbarkeit, Disponibilität; offer subject to availability** = the offer is valid only if the goods are available **solange Vorrat reicht**

NOTE: no plural

average

1 *noun*

(a) number calculated by adding together several figures and dividing by the number of figures added **Durchschnitt, Mittelwert;** *the average for the last three months or the last three months' average; sales average or average of sales;* **weighted average** = average which is calculated taking several factors into account, giving some more value than others **Bewertungsdurchschnitt; on an average** = in general **im Durchschnitt, durchschnittlich;** *on an average, £15 worth of goods are stolen every day*

(b) sharing of the cost of damage or loss of a ship between the insurers and the owners **Havarie, Havarei; average adjuster** = person who calculates how much of an insurance is to be paid **Schadenregulierer; general average** = sharing of the cost of the lost goods of a ship by all parties to an insurance **große Havarie; particular average** = situation where part of a shipment is lost or damaged and the insurance costs are borne by the owner of the lost goods and not shared among all the owners of the shipment **besondere Havarie**

2 *adjective*

(a) middle (figure) **durchschnittlich;** *average cost per unit; average price; average sales per representative; the average figures for the last three months; the average increase in prices*

(b) not very good **durchschnittlich, Durchschnitts-;** *the company's performance has been only average; he is an average worker*

3 *verb* to produce as an average figure **sich durchschnittlich belaufen auf, durchschnittlich betragen;** *price increases have averaged 10% per annum; days lost through sickness have averaged twenty-two over the last four years*

◇ **average due date** *noun* date when several payments (due at different dates) are settled in one payment **mittlerer Zahlungstermin**

◇ **average out** *verb* to come to a figure as an average **durchschnittlich betragen;** *it averages out at 10% per annum; sales increases have averaged out at 15%*

◇ **averager** *noun* person who buys the same share at various times and at various prices to give an average price **Person, die zu verschiedenen Kursen und Zeitpunkten Aktien kauft, um so einen besseren Durschnittskurs zu erzielen**

◇ **average-sized** *adjective* not large or small **mittelgroß;** *they are an average-sized company; he has an average-sized office*

◇ **averaging** *noun* buying shares at different times and at different prices to give an average price **Kauf von Aktien zu verschiedenen Kursen und Zeitpunkten, um so einen besseren Durschschnittskurs zu erzielen**

NOTE: no plural

> QUOTE a share with an average rating might yield 5 per cent and have a PER of about 10
> *Investors Chronicle*
>
> QUOTE the average price per kilogram for this season to the end of April has been 300 cents
> *Australian Financial Review*

avoid

avoid *verb* to try not to do something **vermeiden, umgehen;** *the company is trying to avoid bankruptcy; my aim is to avoid paying too much tax; we want to avoid direct competition with Smith Ltd*

NOTE: you avoid something or avoid **doing** something

◇ **avoidance** *noun* trying not to do something **Vermeidung, Umgehung;** *avoidance of an agreement or of a contract;* **tax avoidance** = trying (legally) to pay as little tax as possible **Steuerverkürzung**

NOTE: no plural

avoirdupois

avoirdupois *noun* old system of weights used in Britain, shown in pounds, ounces, etc. **britisches Handelsgewicht;** *one ounce avoirdupois*

await

await *verb* to wait for **warten auf, erwarten;** *we are awaiting the decision of the planning department; they are awaiting a decision of the court; the agent is awaiting our instructions*

award

1 *noun* decision which settles a dispute **Schiedsspruch;** *an award by an industrial tribunal; the arbitrator's award was set aside on appeal*

2 *verb* to decide the amount of money to be given to someone **zuerkennen, zusprechen;** *to award someone a salary increase; to award damages; the judge awarded costs to the defendant;* **to award a contract to someone** = to decide that someone will have the contract to do work **einen Auftrag/Vertrag an jdn vergeben**

away

away *adverb* not here or somewhere else **abwesend;** *the managing director is away on business; my secretary is away sick; the* *company is moving away from its downmarket image*

awkward *adjective* difficult to deal with **schwierig;** *(Fragen)* **unangenehm, peinlich;** *the board is trying to solve the awkward problem of the managing director's son; when he asked for the loan the bank started to ask some very awkward questions; he is being very awkward about giving us further credit*

axe
1 *noun* **the project got the axe** = the project was stopped **das Projekt wurde gestrichen**
2 *verb* to cut *or* to stop **radikal kürzen;** *(Stellen)* **streichen, abbauen;** *to axe expenditure; several thousand jobs are to be axed*

Bb

"B" shares *plural noun* ordinary shares with special voting rights (often owned by the founder of a company and his family) **Aktien mit besonderem Stimmrecht**

baby bonds *plural noun US* bonds in small denominations (i.e. $100) which the small investor can afford to buy **Baby Bonds**

back
1 *noun* opposite side to the front **Rückseite;** *write your address on the back of the envelope; the conditions of sale are printed on the back of the invoice; please endorse the cheque on the back*
2 *adjective* referring to the past **zurück, Rück-; back interest** = interest not yet paid **Zinsrückstand; back orders** = orders received in the past and not fulfilled (usually because the item is out of stock) **unerledigte Aufträge;** *after the strike it took the factory six weeks to clear all the accumulated back orders;* **back pay** = salary which has not been paid **Lohnrückstand;** *I am owed £500 in back pay;* **back payment** = paying money which is owed **Nach-, Rückzahlung;** *the salesmen are claiming for back payment of unpaid commission;* **back payments** = payments which are due **Rückstände; back rent** = rent owed **Mietrückstand;** *the company owes £100,000 in back rent*
3 *adverb* as things were before **zurück;** *he will pay back the money in monthly instalments; the store sent back the cheque because the date was wrong; the company went back on its agreement to supply at £1.50 a unit*
4 *verb*
(a) to back someone = to help someone financially **jdn (finanziell) unterstützen;** *the bank is backing him to the tune of £10,000; he is looking for someone to back his project*
(b) to back a bill = to sign a bill promising to pay it if the person it is addressed to is not able to do so **(als Dritter) einen Wechsel unterzeichnen**

◇ **backdate** *verb* to put an earlier date on a cheque *or* an invoice **zurückdatieren;** *backdate your invoice to April 1st; the pay increase is backdated to January 1st*

◇ **backer** *noun*
(a) person who backs someone **Geldgeber; Sponsor; Hintermann;** *he has an Australian backer; one of the company's backers has withdrawn*
(b) backer of a bill = person who backs a bill **Wechselgarant**

◇ **background** *noun*
(a) past work *or* experience **Werdegang; Vorbildung; Ausbildung;** *his background is in the steel industry; the company is looking for someone with a background of success in the electronics industry; she has a publishing background; what is his background or do you know anything about his background?*
(b) past details **Hintergründe, Zusammenhänge;** *he explained the background of the claim; I know the contractual situation as it stands now, but can you fill in the background details?*

◇ **backhander** *noun informal* bribe *or* money given to someone to get him to help you **Schmiergeld**

◇ **backing** *noun*
(a) financial support **finanzielle Unterstützung;** *he has the backing of an Australian bank; the company will succeed only if it has sufficient backing; who is providing the backing for the project or where does the backing for the project come from?*
(b) currency backing = gold or government securities which maintain the strength of a currency **Währungsgarantie**
NOTE: no plural

◇ **backlog** *noun* work (such as orders *or* letters) which has piled up waiting to be done **Rückstand;** *the warehouse is trying to cope with a backlog of orders; my secretary can't cope with the backlog of paperwork*
NOTE: no plural

◇ **back out** *verb* to stop being part of a deal *or* an agreement **aussteigen, zurücktreten von;** *the bank backed out of the contract; we had to cancel the project when our German partners backed out*

◇ **back up** *verb* to support *or* to help **unterstützen;** *he brought along a file of documents to back up his claim; the finance director said the managing director had refused to back him up in his argument with the VAT office*

◇ **backup** *adjective* supporting *or* helping **zusätzlich, Unterstützungs-;** *we offer a free backup service to customers; after a series of sales tours by representatives, the sales director sends backup letters to all the contacts;* **backup copy** = copy of a computer disk to be kept in case the original disk is damaged **Sicherungskopie**

◇ **backwardation** *noun* penalty paid by the seller when postponing delivery of shares to the buyer **Deport**

> QUOTE the businesses we back range from start-up ventures to established companies in need of further capital for expansion
> *Times*
>
> QUOTE the company has received the backing of a number of oil companies who are willing to pay for the results of the survey
> *Lloyd's List*

bad *adjective* not good **schlecht; bad bargain** = item which is not worth the price asked **schlechtes Geschäft; bad buy** = thing bought which was not worth the money paid for it **schlechter Kauf; bad debt** = debt which will not be paid **uneinbringliche Forderung, nicht einziehbare Außenstände;** *the company has written off £30,000 in bad debts*

bag *noun* thing made of paper, cloth, or plastic for carrying items **Tüte, Beutel, Tasche;** *he brought his files in a Harrods bag; we gave away 5,000 plastic bags at the exhibition;* **shopping bag** = bag used for carrying shopping **Einkaufstasche**

baggage *noun* suitcases *or* bags for carrying clothes when travelling **Gepäck; free baggage allowance** = amount of baggage which a passenger can take with him free on a plane **Freigepäck;** *US* **baggage room** = room where cases can be left while passengers are waiting for a plane or train **Gepäckaufbewahrung**

NOTE: no plural; to show one suitcase, etc., you can say **a piece of baggage**

bail *noun* payment made to a court as guarantee that a prisoner will return after being released **Kaution;** *to stand bail of £3,000 for someone; he was released on bail of $3,000 or he was released on payment of $3,000 bail;* **to jump bail** = not to appear in court after having been released on bail **die Kaution (durch Nichterscheinen) verfallen lassen**

NOTE: no plural

◇ **bail out** *verb*

(a) to rescue a company which is in financial difficulties **aus (finanziellen) Schwierigkeiten helfen**

(b) to bail someone out = to pay money to a court as a guarantee that someone will return to face charges **für jdn Kaution stellen;** *she paid $3,000 to bail him out*

◇ **bail-out** *noun* rescue of a company in financial difficulties **Hilfe aus (finanziellen) Schwierigkeiten**

> QUOTE the government has decided to bail out the bank which has suffered losses to the extent that its capital has been wiped out
> *South China Morning Post*

balance

1 *noun*

(a) amount in an account which makes the total debits and credits equal **Saldo; credit balance** = balance in an account showing that more money has been received than is owed **Kredit-, Aktivsaldo; debit balance** = balance in an account showing that more money is owed than has been received **Sollsaldo;** *the account has a credit balance of £100; because of large payments to suppliers, the account has a debit balance of £1,000;* **balance in hand** = cash held to pay small debts **Kassenbestand; balance brought down** = amount entered in an account at the end of a period to balance income and expenditure **Saldo; balance brought forward** *or* **balance carried forward** = amount entered in an account at the end of a period to balance the expenditure and income which is then taken forward to start the new period **Saldovortrag**

(b) rest of an amount owed **Restbetrag, Differenz;** *you can pay £100 deposit and the balance within 60 days;* **balance due to us** = amount owed to us which is due to be paid **fälliger Rechnungsbetrag**

(c) balance of payments = the international financial position of a country, including invisible as well as visible trade **Zahlungsbilanz; balance of trade** *or* **trade balance** = international trading position of a country, excluding invisible trade **Handelsbilanz; adverse** *or* **unfavourable balance of trade** = situation where a country imports more than it exports **passive Handelsbilanz; favourable trade balance** = situation where a country exports more than it imports **aktive Handelsbilanz;** *the country has had an adverse balance of trade for the second month running*

(d) bank balance = state of an account at a bank at a particular time **Kontostand**

NOTE: no plural

2 *verb*
(a) to calculate the amount needed to make the two sides of an account equal **saldieren;** *I have finished balancing the accounts for March;* **the February accounts do not balance** = the two sides are not equal **der Februar-Abschluß ist nicht ausgeglichen**
(b) to plan a budget so that expenditure and income are equal **ausgleichen;** *the president is planning for a balanced budget*

◊ **balance sheet** *noun* statement of the financial position of a company at a particular time, such as the end of the financial year or the end of a quarter **Bilanz;** *the company balance sheet for 1984 shows a substantial loss; the accountant has prepared the balance sheet for the first half-year*

bale

1 *noun* large pack of wool *or* paper *or* cotton,etc. **Ballen;** *a bale of cotton; 2,520 bales of wool were destroyed in the fire*
2 *verb* to tie wool *or* paper *or* cotton to make a bale **in Ballen packen, bündeln**

ballot

1 *noun*
(a) election where people vote for someone by marking a cross on a paper with a list of names **(geheime) Wahl; ballot paper** = paper on which the voter marks a cross to show who he wants to vote for **Wahl-, Stimmzettel; ballot box** = sealed box into which ballot papers are put **Wahlurne; postal ballot** = election where the voters send their ballot papers by post **Briefwahl; secret ballot** = election where the voters vote in secret **geheime Wahl**
(b) selecting by taking papers at random out of a box **Losverfahren;** *the share issue was oversubscribed, so there was a ballot for the shares*
2 *verb* to take a vote by ballot **abstimmen, eine (geheime) Wahl abhalten;** *the union is balloting for the post of president*

◊ **ballot-rigging** *noun* illegal arranging of the votes in a ballot, so that a particular candidate or party wins **Manipulation der Wahlresultate**
NOTE: no plural

ban

1 *noun* order which forbids someone from doing something **Verbot;** *a government ban on the import of weapons; a ban on the export of computer software;* **overtime ban** = order by a trade union which forbids overtime work by its members **Überstundenverbot; to impose a ban on smoking** = to make an order which forbids smoking **Rauchverbot erlassen; to lift the ban on smoking** = to allow people to smoke **das Rauchverbot aufheben; to beat the ban on something** = to do something which is forbidden - usually by doing it rapidly before a ban is imposed, or by finding a legal way to avoid a ban **ein Verbot umgehen**
2 *verb* to forbid something *or* to make something illegal **verbieten, mit einem Verbot belegen;** *the government has banned the sale of alcohol*
NOTE: **banning - banned**

band

noun **rubber band** = thin ring of rubber for attaching things together **Gummiband;** *put a band round the filing cards to stop them falling on the floor*

bank

1 *noun*
(a) business which holds money for its clients, which lends money at interest, and trades generally in money **Bank;** *Lloyds Bank; The First National Bank; The Royal Bank of Scotland; he put all his earnings into his bank; I have had a letter from my bank telling me my account is overdrawn;* **bank loan** *or* **bank advance** = loan from a bank **Bankkredit, Bankdarlehen;** *he asked for a bank loan to start his business;* **bank borrowing** = money borrowed from a bank **Bankdarlehen;** *the new factory was financed by bank borrowing;* **bank borrowings have increased** = loans given by banks have increased **die Kreditvergaben haben zugenommen; bank deposits** = all money placed in banks **Bankeinlagen**
(b) central bank = main government-controlled bank in a country, which controls the financial affairs of the country by fixing main interest rates, issuing currency and controlling the foreign exchange rate **Zentral-, Notenbank; the Bank of England** = central British bank, owned by the state, which, together with the Treasury, regulates the nation's finances **die Bank von England; the Federal Reserve Banks** = central banks in the USA which are owned by the state, and directed by the Federal Reserve Board **die 12 Banken des Federal Reserve Systems; the World Bank** = central bank, controlled by the United Nations, whose funds come from the member states of the UN and which lends money to member states **die Weltbank**
(c) savings bank = bank where you can deposit money and receive interest on it **Sparkasse; merchant bank** = bank which lends money to companies and deals in international finance; *entspricht* **Investmentbank; the High Street banks** = main British banks which accept deposits from and allow withdrawals by individuals **die größten Bankinstitute in Großbritanien**
(d) data bank = store of information in a computer **Datenbank**

2 *verb* to deposit money into a bank or to have an account with a bank **bei einer Bank einzahlen; ein Konto bei einer Bank haben;** *he banked the cheque as soon as he received it;* **where do you bank?** = where do you have a bank account? **bei welcher Bank haben Sie Ihr Konto?;** *I bank at or with Barclays*

◇ **bankable** *adjective* which a bank will accept as security for a loan **bankfähig;** *a bankable paper*

◇ **bank account** *noun* account which a customer has with a bank, where the customer can deposit and withdraw money **Bankkonto;** *to open a bank account; to close a bank account; how much money do you have in your bank account? she has £100 in her savings bank account; if you let the balance in your bank account fall below £100, you have to pay bank charges*

◇ **bank balance** *noun* state of a bank account at any particular time **Kontostand;** *our bank balance went into the red last month*

◇ **bank bill** *noun*
(a) *GB* order by one bank telling another bank to pay money to someone **Bankwechsel**
(b) *US* piece of printed paper money **Banknote, Schein**

◇ **bank book** *noun* book, given by a bank, which shows money which you deposit or withdraw from your savings account **Sparbuch**

◇ **bank charges** *plural noun* charges which a bank makes for carrying out work for a customer **Bankgebühren**

◇ **bank clerk** *noun* person who works in a bank, but not a manager **Bankangestellter**

◇ **bank draft** *noun* order by one bank telling another bank to pay money to someone **Banktratte; Bankwechsel**

◇ **banker** *noun*
(a) person who is in an important position in a bank **Bankier, Banker; merchant banker** = person who has a high position in a merchant bank; *entspricht* **Bankier in einer Investmentbank**
(b) generally, a bank **Bank; banker's bill** = order by one bank telling another bank to pay money to someone **Bankwechsel; banker's order** = order written by a customer asking a bank to make a regular payment **Dauerauftrag;** *he pays his subscription by banker's order*

◇ **bank giro** *noun GB* method used by clearing banks to transfer money rapidly from one account to another **Bankgiro**

◇ **bank holiday** *noun* a weekday which is a public holiday when the banks are closed **öffentlicher Feiertag;** *New Year's Day is a bank holiday*

◇ **banking** *noun* the business of banks **Bankgeschäft, Bankgewerbe;** *he is studying banking; she has gone into banking; US* **banking account** = account which a customer has with a bank **Bankkonto; a banking crisis** = crisis affecting the banks **Bankenkrise; banking hours** = hours when a bank is open for its customers **Banköffnungszeiten, Schalterstunden;** *you cannot get money out of the bank after banking hours*
NOTE: no plural

◇ **bank manager** *noun* person in charge of a branch of a bank **Bankdirektor;** *he asked his bank manager for a loan*

◇ **bank note** *or* **banknote** *noun* piece of printed paper money **Banknote, Schein;** *he pulled out a pile of used bank notes*

◇ **bank on** *verb* to do something because you are sure something will happen **sich verlassen auf;** *he is banking on getting a loan from his father to set up in business; do not bank on the sale of your house*

◇ **bankroll** *verb informal* to pay for *or* to finance (a project) **finanzieren**

◇ **bank statement** *noun* written statement from a bank showing the balance of an account **Kontoauszug**

bankrupt

1 *noun* (person *or* company) which has been declared by a court not to be capable of paying its debts and whose affairs are put into the hands of a receiver **Konkursschuldner**
2 *adjective* not capable of paying debts **bankrott, zahlungsunfähig, insolvent;** *he was adjudicated or declared bankrupt; a bankrupt property developer; he went bankrupt after two years in business;* **certificated bankrupt** = bankrupt who has been discharged from bankruptcy with a certificate to show he was not at fault .OJ OFF **rehabilitierter Konkursschuldner; discharged bankrupt** = person who has been released from being bankrupt because he has paid his debts **entlasteter Konkursschuldner; undischarged bankrupt** = person who has been declared bankrupt and has not been released from that state **nicht entlasteter Konkursschuldner**
3 *verb* to make someone become bankrupt **ruinieren, in den Konkurs treiben;** *the recession bankrupted my father*

◇ **bankruptcy** *noun* state of being bankrupt **Bankrott, Konkurs;** *the recession has caused thousands of bankruptcies;* **adjudication of bankruptcy** *or* **declaration of bankruptcy** = legal order making someone bankrupt **Konkurseröffnungsbeschluß; discharge in bankruptcy** = being released from bankruptcy after paying debts **Entlastung des Konkursschuldners; to file a**

petition in bankruptcy = to apply officially to be made bankrupt *or* to ask officially for someone else to be made bankrupt **den Konkurs anmelden, Antrag auf Konkurseröffnung stellen**

bar *noun*
(a) place where you can buy and drink alcohol **Bar, Lokal;** *the sales reps met in the bar of the hotel*
(b) sandwich bar = small shop where you can buy sandwiches to take away **Sandwich Bar; snack bar** = small restaurant where you can get simple meals **Imbißstube**
(c) thing which stops you doing something **Hindernis, Hemmnis;** *government legislation is a bar to foreign trade*
(d) *GB* the profession of barrister **Anwalt (vor Gericht); to be called to the bar** = to become a barrister **als Anwalt (vor Gericht) zugelassen sein**

◇ **bar chart** *noun* chart where values *or* quantities are shown as thick columns of different heights **Balken-, Stab-, Säulendiagramm**

◇ **bar code** *noun* system of lines printed on a product which when read by a computer give a reference number or price **Strichkodierung, Bar-Code**

bareboat charter *noun* system of chartering a ship where the owner provides only the ship, but not the crew, fuel or insurance **Chartern eines Schiffes ohne Besatzung etc., Bareboat Charter**

barely *adverb* almost not **kaum;** *there is barely enough money left to pay the staff; she barely had time to call her lawyer*

bargain
1 *noun*
(a) agreement on the price of something **Handel, Geschäft;** *to make a bargain;* **to drive a hard bargain** = to be a difficult negotiator **hart verhandeln, harte Bedingungen stellen; to strike a hard bargain** = to agree a deal which is favourable to you **ein Geschäft zufriedenstellend abschließen; it is a bad bargain** = it is not worth the price **das ist ein schlechtes Geschäft**
(b) thing which is cheaper than usual **Schnäppchen, Gelegenheitskauf;** *that car is a (real) bargain at £500;* **bargain hunter** = person who looks for cheap deals **jd, der auf Sonderangebote aus ist**
(c) sale of one lot of shares on the Stock Exchange **Börsengeschäft, Abschluß; bargains done** = number of deals made on the Stock Exchange during a day **Anzahl der Abschlüsse/Börsengeschäfte**
2 *verb* to discuss a price for something **(aus)handeln;** *you will have to bargain with the dealer if you want a discount; they spent two hours bargaining about or over the price*
NOTE: you bargain **with** someone **over** *or* **about** *or* **for** something

◇ **bargain basement** *noun* basement floor in a shop where goods are sold cheaply **Abteilung für Sonderangebote im Untergeschoß eines Kaufhauses; I'm selling this at a bargain basement price** = I'm selling this very cheaply **ich verkaufe dies zu einem Sonderpreis**

◇ **bargain counter** *noun* counter in a shop where goods are sold cheaply **Sonderangebotsstand, Sondertisch**

◇ **bargain offer** *noun* sale of a particular type of goods at a cheap price **Sonderangebot, günstiges Angebot;** *this week's bargain offer - 30% off all carpet prices*

◇ **bargain price** *noun* cheap price **Sonderpreis, Spottpreis;** *these carpets are for sale at a bargain price*

◇ **bargain sale** *noun* sale of all goods in a store at cheap prices **Ausverkauf**

◇ **bargaining** *noun* act of discussing a price, usually wage increases for workers **Handeln, Aushandeln; (free) collective bargaining** = negotiations between employers and workers' representatives over wage increases and conditions **(autonome) Tarifverhandlungen; bargaining power** = strength of one person or group when discussing prices *or* wage settlements **Verhandlungsstärke; bargaining position** = statement of position by one group during negotiations **Verhandlungsposition**

barrel *noun*
(a) large round container for liquids **Faß;** *he bought twenty-five barrels of wine; to sell wine by the barrel*
(b) amount of liquid contained in a barrel **Barrel;** *the price of oil has reached $30 a barrel*

> QUOTE if signed, the deals would give effective discounts of up to $3 a barrel on Saudi oil
> *Economist*
>
> QUOTE US crude oil stocks fell last week by nearly 2.6m barrels
> *Financial Times*
>
> QUOTE the average spot price of Nigerian light crude oil for the month of July was 27.21 dollars a barrel
> *Business Times (Lagos)*

barrier *noun* thing which stops someone doing something, especially sending goods from one place to another **Schranke; customs barriers** *or* **tariff barriers** = customs duty intended to make trade more difficult **Zollschranken; to impose trade barriers on**

certain goods = to restrict the import of certain goods by charging high duty **bestimmte Güter mit Handelsschranken belegen;** *the unions have asked the government to impose trade barriers on foreign cars;* **to lift trade barriers from imports** = to remove restrictions on imports **Handelsschranken für Importe aufheben;** *the government has lifted trade barriers on foreign cars*

barrister *noun GB* lawyer (especially in England) who can speak *or* argue a case in one of the higher courts **Rechtsanwalt, Rechtsanwältin, Barrister**

barter
1 *noun* system where goods are exchanged for other goods and not sold for money **Tauschhandel; barter agreement** *or* **barter arrangement** *or* **barter deal** = agreement to exchange goods by barter **Tauschabkommen;** *the company has agreed a barter deal with Bulgaria*
NOTE: no plural
2 *verb* to exchange goods for other goods, but not buy them for money **Tauschhandel treiben;** *they agreed a deal to barter tractors for barrels of wine*

◇ **bartering** *noun* act of exchanging goods for other goods and not for money **Tauschhandel**
NOTE: no plural

> QUOTE under the barter agreements, Nigeria will export 175,000 barrels a day of crude oil in exchange for trucks, food, planes and chemicals
> *Wall Street Journal*

base
1 *noun*
(a) lowest or first position **Basis, Ausgangspunkt, Grundlage;** *turnover increased by 200%, but starting from a low base;* **base year** = first year of an index, against which later years' changes are measured **Basis-, Vergleichsjahr; bank base rate** = basic rate of interest which a bank charges on loans to its customers **Eckzins;** *see* DATABASE
(b) place where a company has its main office or factory *or* place where a businessman has his office **Sitz, Standort;** *the company has its base in London and branches in all European countries; he has an office in Madrid which he uses as a base while he is travelling in Southern Europe*
2 *verb*
(a) to start to calculate *or* to negotiate from a position **basieren, gründen;** *we based our calculations on the forecast turnover;* **based on** = calculating from **basieren auf, auf der Grundlage von;** *based on last year's figures; based on population forecasts*
(b) to set up a company *or* a person in a place **stationieren;** *the European manager is based in our London office; our overseas branch is based in the Bahamas; a London-based sales executive*

◇ **basement** *noun* section of a shop which is underground **Untergeschoß; bargain basement** = basement floor in a shop where goods are sold cheaply **Abteilung für Sonderangebote im Untergeschoß eines Kaufhauses;** *I am selling this at a bargain basement price*

> QUOTE the base lending rate, or prime rate, is the rate at which banks lend to their top corporate borrowers
> *Wall Street Journal*
> QUOTE other investments include a large stake in the Chicago-based insurance company
> *Lloyd's List*

basic
1 *adjective*
(a) normal **Grund-, Basis-; eigentlich; basic pay** *or* **basic salary** *or* **basic wage** = normal salary without extra payments **Ecklohn; Grundgehalt; basic discount** = normal discount without extra percentages **Grundrabatt;** *our basic discount is 20%, but we offer 5% extra for rapid settlement*
(b) most important **wesentlich, hauptsächlich, Haupt-; basic commodities** = ordinary farm produce, produced in large quantities (such as corn, rice, sugar, etc.) **Grundstoffe**
(c) simple *or* from which everything starts **Grund-, elementar;** *he has a basic knowledge of the market; to work at the cash desk, you need a basic qualification in maths*

◇ **basics** *plural noun* simple and important facts **Grundlagen, Grundsachverhalt;** *he has studied the basics of foreign exchange dealing;* **to get back to basics** = to consider the basic facts again **zum Kern der Sache/zu den Grundlagen zurückkommen**

◇ **basically** *adverb* seen from the point from which everything starts **im Grunde, eigentlich**

◇ **BASIC** *noun* = BEGINNER'S ALL-PURPOSE SYMBOLIC INSTRUCTION CODE simple language for computer programming **BASIC**

basis *noun*
(a) point *or* number from which calculations are made **Grundlage, Basis;** *we forecast the turnover on the basis of a 6% price increase*
(b) general terms of agreement **Basis, Grundlage; on a short-term** *or* **long-term basis** = for a short *or* long period **kurzfristig; langfristig; on a freelance basis als freier Mitarbeiter;** *he has been appointed on a*

short-term basis; we have three people working on a freelance basis
NOTE: the plural is **bases**

basket *noun*
(a) container made of thin pieces of wood *or* metal *or* plastic **Korb;** *a basket of apples;* **filing basket** = container kept on a desk for documents which have to be filed **Ablage; shopping basket** = basket used for carrying shopping **Einkaufskorb; waste paper basket** = container into which paper or pieces of rubbish can be thrown **Papierkorb**
(b) group of prices *or* currencies taken as a standard **Warenkorb; Währungskorb;** *the pound has fallen against a basket of European currencies; the price of the average shopping basket or; US the market basket has risen by 6%*

> QUOTE as a basket of European currencies, the ecu is protected from exchange-rate swings
> *Economist*

batch
1 *noun*
(a) group of items which are made at one time **Serie; Auflage;** *this batch of shoes has the serial number 25-02*
(b) group of documents which are processed at the same time **Stapel, Stoß;** *a batch of invoices; today's batch of orders; the accountant signed a batch of cheques; we deal with the orders in batches of fifty;* **batch processing** = system of data processing where information is collected into batches before being loaded into the computer **Stapelverarbeitung, Batch-Betrieb**
2 *verb* to put items together in groups **stapeln;** *to batch invoices or cheques*

◇ **batch number** *noun* number attached to a batch **Seriennummer; Auflagennummer;** *when making a complaint always quote the batch number on the packet*

battery *noun* small object for storing electric power **Batterie;** *the calculator needs a new battery; a battery-powered calculator*

battle *noun* fight **Kampf; boardroom battles** = arguments between directors **Auseinandersetzungen in der Vorstandsetage; circulation battle** = fight between two newspapers to sell more copies in the same section of the market **Kampf um die Auflagenhöhe (einer Zeitung)**

bay *noun* **loading bay** = section of road in a warehouse, where lorries can drive in to load or unload **Ladeplatz**

b/d = BARRELS PER DAY

bear
1 *noun*
(a) large wild animal covered in fur **Bär;** *their advertising symbol is a bear*
(b) *(Stock Exchange)* dealer who sells shares because he thinks the price will fall and he will be able to buy them again more cheaply later **Baissier; bear market** = period when Stock Exchange prices fall because shareholders are selling **Baissemarkt;** *see* BULL
2 *verb*
(a) to give interest **tragen, bringen;** *government bonds which bear 5% interest*
(b) to have (a name) *or* to have something written on it **tragen, aufweisen;** *the cheque bears the signature of the company secretary; envelope which bears a London postmark; a letter bearing yesterday's date; the share certificate bears his name*
(c) to pay costs **tragen, übernehmen;** *the costs of the exhibition will be borne by the company; the company bore the legal costs of both parties*
NOTE: **bearing - bore - has borne**

◇ **bearer** *noun* person who holds a cheque *or* certificate **Überbringer/-in, Inhaber/-in; the cheque is payable to bearer** = is paid to the person who holds it, not to any particular name written on it **zahlen Sie diesen Scheck an den Überbringer**

◇ **bearer bond** *noun* bond which is payable to the bearer and does not have a name written on it **Inhaberschuldverschreibung**

◇ **bearing** *adjective* which bears *or* which produces **tragend, bringend;** *certificate bearing interest at 5%; interest-bearing deposits*

beat *verb*
(a) to win in a fight against someone **schlagen, drücken;** *they have beaten their rivals into second place in the computer market*
(b) to beat a ban = to do something which is forbidden by doing it rapidly before the ban is enforced **ein Verbot umgehen**
NOTE: **beating - beat - has beaten**

become *verb* to change into something different **werden;** *the export market has become very difficult since the rise in the dollar; the company became very profitable in a short time*
NOTE: **becoming - became - has become**

bed-and-breakfast deal *noun* arrangement where shares are sold one day and bought back the following day, in order to establish a profit or loss for tax declaration **kurzfristiger Verkauf und Rückkauf von Aktien zu Steuerzwecken**

begin *verb* to start **anfangen, beginnen;** *the company began to lose its market share; he began the report which the shareholders had asked for; the auditors' report began with a description of the general principles adopted*
NOTE: you begin something *or* begin **to do** something *or* begin **with** something. Note also: **beginning - began - has begun**

◇ **beginning** *noun* first part **Anfang, Beginn;** *the beginning of the report is a list of the directors and their shareholdings*

behalf *noun* **on behalf of** = acting for (someone *or* a company) **im Interesse von; im Namen von; im Auftrag von;** *I am writing on behalf of the minority shareholders; she is acting on my behalf; solicitors acting on behalf of the American company*

behind
1 *preposition* at the back *or* after **hinter;** *the company is No. 2 in the market, about £4m behind their rivals*
2 *adverb* after; **we have fallen behind our rivals** = we have fewer sales *or* make less profit than our rivals **wir sind hinter unsere Konkurrenz zurückgefallen; the company has fallen behind with its deliveries** = it is late with its deliveries **die Firma ist mit ihren Lieferungen in Verzug gekommen**

believe *verb* to think that something is true **glauben;** *we believe he has offered to buy 25% of the shares; the chairman is believed to be in South America on business*

belong *verb*
(a) to belong to = to be the property of **gehören zu;** *the company belongs to an old American banking family; the patent belongs to the inventor's son*
(b) to belong with = to be in the correct place with **gehören (zu);** *those documents belong with the sales reports*

below *preposition* lower down than *or* less than **unter;** *we sold the property at below the market price; you can get a ticket for New York at below £150 from a bucket shop*

◇ **below-the-line** *adjective* **below-the-line expenditure** = exceptional payments which are separated from a company's normal accounts **außerordentliche Aufwendungen**

benchmark *noun* point in an index which is important, and can be used to compare with other figures **Eckwert**

> QUOTE the US bank announced a cut in its prime, the benchmark corporate lending rate, from 10+% to 10%
>
> *Financial Times*
>
> QUOTE the dollar dropped below three German marks - a benchmark with more psychological than economic significance - for the first time since October
>
> *Fortune*

beneficial *adjective* **beneficial occupier** = person who occupies a property but does not own it fully **Nießbrauchberechtigter; beneficial interest** = interest which allows someone to occupy or receive rent from a property, but not to own it **Nießbrauch**

◇ **beneficiary** *noun* person who gains money from something **Begünstigter; Nutznießer;** *the beneficiaries of a will*

> QUOTE the pound sterling was the main beneficiary of the dollar's weakness
>
> *Business Times (Lagos)*

benefit
1 *noun*
(a) payments which are made to someone under a national or private insurance scheme **Leistung; Zuschuß, Beihilfe;** *she receives £20 a week as unemployment benefit; the sickness benefit is paid monthly; the insurance office sends out benefit cheques each week;* **death benefit** = money paid to the family of someone who dies in an accident at work **Sterbegeld**
(b) fringe benefits = extra items given by a company to workers in addition to their salaries (such as company cars, private health insurance) **Leistungsanreize für Arbeitnehmer**
2 *verb*
(a) to make better *or* to improve **nützen, zugute kommen;** *a fall in inflation benefits the exchange rate*
(b) to benefit from *or* **by something** = to be improved by something *or* to gain more money because of something **profitieren von, den Nutzen ziehen aus;** *exports have benefited from the fall in the exchange rate; the employees have benefited from the profit-sharing scheme*

> QUOTE the retail sector will also benefit from the expected influx of tourists
> *Australian Financial Review*
> QUOTE what benefits does the executive derive from his directorship? Compensation has increased sharply in recent years and fringe benefits for directors have proliferated
> *Duns Business Month*
> QUOTE salary is negotiable to £30,000, plus car and a benefits package appropriate to this senior post
> *Financial Times*
> QUOTE California is the latest state to enact a program forcing welfare recipients to work for their benefits
> *Fortune*

bequest *noun* property, money, etc., given to someone in a will **Vermächtnis;** *he made several bequests to his staff*

berth
1 *noun* place in a harbour where a ship can tie up **Liegeplatz**
2 *verb* to tie up at a berth **anlegen;** *the ship will berth at Rotterdam on Wednesday*

BES = BUSINESS EXPANSION SCHEME

best
1 *adjective* very good *or* better than all others **bester;** *his best price is still higher than all the other suppliers; 1985 was the company's best year ever*
2 *noun* very good effort **der/die/das beste;** *the salesmen are doing their best, but the stock simply will not sell at that price*
◊ **best-seller** *noun* item (especially a book) which sells very well **Verkaufsschlager;** *(book)* **Bestseller**
◊ **best-selling** *adjective* which sells very well **absatzstark, am meisten verkauft;** *these computer disks are our best-selling line*

bet
1 *noun* amount deposited when you risk money on the result of a race *or* of a game **Wetteinsatz, Wette**
2 *verb* to risk money on the result of something **wetten;** *he bet £100 on the result of the election; I bet you £25 the dollar will rise against the pound;* **betting tax** = tax levied on betting on horses *or* dogs, etc. **Wettsteuer**
NOTE: **betting - bet - has bet**

better *adjective* very good compared with something else **besser;** *this year's results are better than last year's; we will shop around to see if we can get a better price*

beware *verb* to be careful **sich vorsehen, sich in acht nehmen; beware of imitations** = be careful not to buy cheap low-quality items which are made to look like more expensive items **vor Imitationen wird gewarnt**

bi- *prefix* twice **Bi-, bi-; bi-monthly** = (i) twice a month; (ii) every two months **(i) zweimal monatlich; (ii) jeden zweiten Monat; bi-annually** = twice a year **zweimal jährlich, halbjährlich**

bid
1 *noun*
(a) offer to buy something at a certain price **Gebot, Angebot; to make a bid for something** = to offer to buy something **ein Angebot/Gebot für etwas machen;** *he made a bid for the house; the company made a bid for its rival;* **to make a cash bid** = to offer to pay cash for something **ein Bargebot machen; to put in a bid for something** *or* **to enter a bid for something** = to offer (usually in writing) to buy something **ein Angebot abgeben; opening bid** = first bid **Eröffnungsgebot; closing bid** = last bid at an auction *or* the bid which is successful **Höchstgebot**
(b) offer to do some work at a certain price **Kosten(vor)anschlag, Angebot;** *he made the lowest bid for the job; US* offer to sell something at a certain price **Angebot;** *they asked for bids for the supply of spare parts*
(c) takeover bid = offer to buy all or a majority of shares in a company so as to control it **Übernahmeangebot;** *to make a takeover bid for a company; to withdraw a takeover bid;* **the company rejected the takeover bid** = the directors recommended that the shareholders should not accept it **das Unternehmen hat das Übernahmeangebot zurückgewiesen**
2 *verb* **to bid for something** = to offer to buy something **für/auf etwas bieten; he bid £1,000 for the jewels** = he offered to pay £1,000 for the jewels **er bot £1.000 für den Schmuck**
NOTE: **bidding - bid - has bid**
◊ **bidder** *noun* person who makes a bid (usually at an auction) **Bieter/-in;** *several bidders made offers for the house;* **the property was sold to the highest bidder** = to the person who had made the highest bid *or* who offered the most money **der Besitz wurde an den Meistbietenden verkauft; the tender will go to the lowest bidder** = to the person who offers the best terms *or* the lowest price for services **der Auftrag wird an den Mindestbietenden vergeben**
◊ **bidding** *noun* action of making offers to buy (usually at an auction) **Bieten, Gebot; Abgabe von Angeboten; the bidding started at £1,000** = the first and lowest bid was £1,000 **£1.000 war das Mindestgebot; the bidding stopped at £250,000** = the last bid (and the successful bid) was for £250,000 **£250.000 war das Höchstgebot; the auctioneer**

started the bidding at £100 = he suggested that the first bid should be £100 **der Auktionator setzte das Erstgebot mit £100 an**
NOTE: no plural

Big Board *noun US informal* = NEW YORK STOCK EXCHANGE

bilateral *adjective* between two parties *or* countries **bilateral, zweiseitig;** *the minister signed a bilateral trade agreement*

bill
1 *noun*
(a) written list of charges to be paid **Rechnung;** *the salesman wrote out the bill; does the bill include VAT? the bill is made out to Smith Ltd; the builder sent in his bill; he left the country without paying his bills;* **to foot the bill** = to pay the costs **die Rechnung begleichen/bezahlen**
(b) list of charges in a restaurant **Rechnung;** *can I have the bill please? the bill comes to £20 including service; does the bill include service? the waiter has added 10% to the bill for service*
(c) written paper promising to pay money **Wechsel; Tratte; bill of exchange** = document which tells a bank to pay a person (usually used in payments in foreign currency) **Wechsel; Tratte; accommodation bill** = bill of exchange where the person signing is helping someone else to raise a loan **Gefälligkeitswechsel; bank bill** = bill of exchange endorsed by a bank **Bankwechsel, Bankakzept; demand bill** = bill of exchange which must be paid when payment is asked for **Sichtwechsel; to accept a bill** = to sign a bill of exchange to show that you promise to pay it **einen Wechsel akzeptieren; to discount a bill** = to buy a bill of exchange at a lower price than that written on it in order to cash it later **einen Wechsel diskontieren; bills payable** = bills which a debtor will have to pay **Wechselverbindlichkeiten; bills receivable** = bills which a creditor will receive in the end **Wechselforderungen**
(d) bill of lading = list of goods being shipped, which the transporter gives to the person sending the goods to show that the goods have been loaded **Konnossement**
(e) *US* piece of paper money **Banknote, Schein;** *a $5 bill*
(f) bill of sale = document which the seller gives to the buyer to show that the sale has taken place **Kaufvertrag**
(g) draft of a new law which will be discussed in Parliament **Gesetzesvorlage, Gesetzentwurf**
2 *verb* to present a bill to someone so that it can be paid **berechnen, in Rechnung stellen;** *the builders billed him for the repairs to his neighbour's house*

◊ **billing** *noun US* writing of invoices or bills **Ausstellen von Rechnungen**
NOTE: no plural

billion number one thousand million *or* one million million; *Brit* **Billion;** *US* **Milliarde**
NOTE: in the US it means 1,000 million, but in GB it usually means one million million. With figures it is usually written **bn: $5bn** say 'five billion dollars'

> QUOTE gross wool receipts for the selling season to end June 30 appear likely to top $2 billion
> *Australian Financial Review*
>
> QUOTE at its last traded price the bank was capitalized at around $1.05 billion
> *South China Morning Post*

bin *noun* large container **Behälter, Kiste; dump bin** = display container like a large box, filled with goods for sale **Wühltisch**

bind *verb* to tie *or* to attach **binden;** *the company is bound by its articles of association; he does not consider himself bound by the agreement which was signed by his predecessor*
NOTE: **binding - bound**

◊ **binder** *noun*
(a) stiff cardboard cover for papers **Hefter; ring binder** = cover with rings in it which fit into special holes made in sheets of paper **Ringbuch**
(b) *US* temporary agreement for insurance sent before the insurance policy is issued **vorläufiger Versicherungsschein, Deckungszusage**
NOTE: the GB English for this is **cover note**

◊ **binding** *adjective* which legally forces someone to do something **verbindlich, bindend;** *a binding contract; this document is not legally binding;* **the agreement is binding on all parties** = all parties signing it must do what is agreed **die Vereinbarung ist für alle Beteiligten verbindlich/bindend**

black
1 *adjective*
(a) black market = buying and selling goods in a way which is not allowed by law (as in a time of rationing) **Schwarzmarkt;** *there is a flourishing black market in spare parts for cars; you can buy gold coins on the black market;* **to pay black market prices** = to pay high prices to get items which are not easily available **Schwarzmarktpreise bezahlen**
(b) black economy = work which is paid for in cash, and therefore not declared for tax **Schattenwirtschaft**
(c) in the black = in credit **in den schwarzen Zahlen;** *the company has moved into the black; my bank account is still in the black*

2 *verb* to forbid trading in certain goods or with certain suppliers **boykottieren;** *three firms were blacked by the government; the union has blacked a trucking firm*

◊ **blackleg** *noun* worker who goes on working when there is a strike **Streikbrecher**

◊ **black list** *noun* list of goods *or* people *or* companies which have been blacked **schwarze Liste**

◊ **blacklist** *verb* to put goods *or* people *or* a company on a black list **auf die schwarze Liste setzen;** *his firm was blacklisted by the government*

blame

1 *noun* saying that someone has done something wrong *or* that someone is responsible **Schuld;** *the sales staff got the blame for the poor sales figures*
2 *verb* to say that someone has done something wrong *or* is responsible for a mistake **beschuldigen, Vorwürfe machen;** *the managing director blamed the chief accountant for not warning him of the loss; the union is blaming the management for poor industrial relations*

blank

1 *adjective* with nothing written **leer, unausgefüllt; a blank cheque** = a cheque with no amount of money or name written on it, but signed by the drawer **ein Blankoscheck**
2 *noun* space on a form which has to be completed **leere Stelle, Lücke;** *fill in the blanks and return the form to your local office*

blanket *noun* thick woollen cover for a bed **Decke; blanket agreement** = agreement which covers many items **Gesamtvereinbarung; blanket insurance** = insurance which covers various items (such as a house and its contents) **Kombination mehrerer Versicherungsarten; blanket refusal** = refusal to accept many different items **allgemeine Ablehnung**

blister pack *noun* type of packing where the item for sale is covered with a stiff plastic sheet sealed to a card backing **Schrumpffolienverpackung**

block

1 *noun*
(a) series of items grouped together **Paket, Partie;** *he bought a block of 6,000 shares;* **block booking** = booking of several seats *or* rooms at the same time **Gruppenbuchung;** *the company has a block booking for twenty seats on the plane or for ten rooms at the hotel;* **block vote** = voting of a large number of votes at the same time (such as those of a trade union delegation) **Blockabstimmung, geschlossene Stimmabgabe**
(b) series of buildings forming a square with streets on all sides **Häuserblock;** *they want to redevelop a block in the centre of the town;* **a block of offices** *or* **an office block** = a large building which only contains offices **Bürohaus**
(c) block capitals *or* **block letters** = capital letters (as A,B,C) **Druck-, Blockschrift;** *write your name and address in block letters*
2 *verb* to stop something taking place **blockieren, stoppen, sperren;** *he used his casting vote to block the motion; the planning committee blocked the redevelopment plan;* **blocked currency** = currency which cannot be taken out of a country because of exchange controls **nicht frei konvertierbare und nicht frei transferierbare Währung;** *the company has a large account in blocked roubles*

blue *adjective* **blue-chip investments** *or* **blue-chip shares** *or* **blue chips** = risk-free shares in good companies **erstklassige, sichere Wertpapieranlage, Blue-chips; blue-collar worker** = manual worker in a factory **Fabrikarbeiter; blue-collar union** = trade union formed mainly of blue-collar workers **Arbeitergewerkschaft**

blurb *noun* piece of advertising, especially an advertisement written by a publisher for a book **Werbung**

bn = BILLION

board

1 *noun*
(a) *GB* **board of directors** = group of directors elected by the shareholders to run a company **Board of Directors;** *entspricht* **(Firmen)vorstand, Aufsichtsrat (nach britischem Recht);** *the bank has two representatives on the board; he sits on the board as a representative of the bank; two directors were removed from the board at the AGM;* **she was asked to join the board** = she was asked to become a director; *entspricht* **sie wurde in den Vorstand od Aufsichtsrat berufen; board meeting** = meeting of the directors of a company; *entspricht* **Vorstands-, Aufsichtsratssitzung**
(b) *US* **board of directors** = group of people elected by the shareholders to draw up company policy and to appoint the president and other executive officers who are responsible for managing the company **Board of Directors (nach amerikanischem Recht)**

NOTE: the board of an American company may be made up of a large number of non-executive

directors and only one or two executive officers; a British board has more executive directors
(c) group of people who run a trust *or* a society **Ausschuß; advisory board** = group of advisors **Beratungsgremium, Beirat; editorial board** = group of editors **Redaktion, Redaktionskomitee**
(d) on board = on a ship *or* plane **an Bord** on a train **im Zug; free on board (f.o.b.)** = price includes all the seller's costs until the goods are on the ship for transportation **frei an Bord, f.o.b**
2 *verb* to go on to a ship *or* plane **an Bord gehen;** *(Zug)* **einsteigen;** *customs officials boarded the ship in the harbour*

◇ **boarding card** *or* **boarding pass** *noun* card given to passengers who have checked in for a flight to allow them to board the plane **Bordkarte**

◇ **boardroom** *noun* room where the directors of a company meet **Sitzungssaal; boardroom battles** = arguments between directors **Auseinandersetzungen in der Vorstandsetage**

> QUOTE a proxy is the written authorization an investor sends to a stockholder meeting conveying his vote on a corporate resolution or the election of a company's board of directors
> *Barrons*
>
> QUOTE CEOs, with their wealth of practical experience, are in great demand and can pick and choose the boards they want to serve on
> *Duns Business Month*

boat *noun* ship **Boot, Schiff;** *cargo boat; passenger boat; we took the night boat to Belgium; boats for Greece leave every morning*

bona fide *adjective* trustworthy *or* which can be trusted **in gutem Glauben; a bona fide offer** = an offer which is made honestly **ein Bona-Fide-Angebot**

bonanza *noun* great wealth; very profitable business **Goldgrube; Blütezeit;** *the oil well was a bonanza for the company; 1984 was a bonanza year for the computer industry*

bond *noun*
(a) contract document promising to repay money borrowed by a company *or* by the government **Schuldverschreibung, Obligation; government bonds Staatsanleihen; Schatzanweisung;** *government bonds or treasury bonds;* **municipal bond** *or* **local authority bond** = bond issued by a town or district **Kommunalobligation**
(b) contract document promising to repay money borrowed by a person **Schuldschein; bearer bond** = bond which is payable to the bearer and does not have a name written on it **Inhaberschuldverschreibung; debenture bond** = certificate showing that a debenture has been issued **Schuldverschreibung, Obligation; mortgage bond** = certificate showing that a mortgage exists and that property is security for it **Hypothekenpfandbrief;** *GB* **premium bond** = government bond, part of the National Savings scheme, which pays no interest, but gives the owner the chance to win a weekly or monthly prize **Sparprämienanleihe**
(c) goods (held) in bond = goods held by the customs until duty has been paid **Waren unter Zollverschluß; entry of goods under bond** = bringing goods into a country in bond **Einfuhr von Waren unter Zollverschluß; to take goods out of bond** = to pay duty on goods so that they can be released by the customs **Waren aus dem Zollverschluß nehmen**

◇ **bonded** *adjective* held in bond **unter Zollverschluß; bonded warehouse** = warehouse where goods are stored in bond until duty is paid **Zollager**

◇ **bondholder** *noun* person who holds government bonds **Pfandbrief-, Obligationsinhaber**

◇ **bond-washing** *noun* selling American Treasury bonds with the interest coupon, and buying them back ex coupon, so as to reduce tax **Ankauf und Verkauf von US-Schatzanleihen zur Einkommenssteuerausweichung**

bonus *noun* extra payment **Prämie, Zulage, Bonus; capital bonus** = extra payment by an insurance company which is produced by capital gain **Bonus aus Kapitalerträgen; cost-of-living bonus** = money paid to meet the increase in the cost of living **Teuerungszuschlag; Christmas bonus** = extra payment made to staff at Christmas **Weihnachtsgeld; incentive bonus** = extra pay offered to a worker to encourage him to work harder **Leistungsprämie; productivity bonus** = extra payment made because of increased productivity **Produktivitätsprämie; bonus share** = extra share given to an existing shareholder **Gratisaktie; no-claims bonus** = reduction of premiums on an insurance because no claims have been made **Schadenfreiheitsrabatt**
NOTE: plural is **bonuses**

book
1 *noun*
(a) set of sheets of paper attached together **Buch; a company's books** = the financial records of a company **Geschäftsbücher; account book** = book which records sales and purchases **Rechnungsbuch; cash book** = record of cash **Kassenbuch; order book** = record of orders **Auftragsbuch, Bestellbuch;**

the company has a full order book = it has sufficient orders to keep the workforce occupied **das Unternehmen hat volle Auftragsbücher; purchase book** = records of purchases **Wareneingangsbuch; sales book** = records of sales **Warenverkaufsbuch; book sales** = sales as recorded in the sales book **Absatz laut Verkaufsbuch; book value** = value as recorded in the company's books **Buch-, Bilanzwert**

(b) bank book = book which shows money which you have deposited or withdrawn from a bank account **Sparbuch; cheque book** = book of new cheques **Scheckheft; phone book** *or* **telephone book** = book which lists names of people or companies with their addresses and telephone numbers **Telefonbuch**

2 *verb* to order **bestellen** to reserve something **buchen, reservieren;** *to book a room in a hotel or a table at a restaurant or a ticket on a plane; I booked a table for 7.45; he booked a ticket through to Cairo;* **to book someone into a hotel** *or* **onto a flight** = to order a room *or* a plane ticket for someone **für jdn ein Zimmer od ein Flugticket buchen;** *he was booked on the 09.00 flight to Zurich;* **the hotel** *or* **the flight is fully booked** *or* **is booked up** = all the rooms *or* seats are reserved **das Hotel od der Flug ist ausgebucht;** *the restaurant is booked up over the Christmas period*

◇ **booking** *noun* act of ordering a room *or* a seat **Buchung;** *hotel bookings have fallen since the end of the tourist season;* **booking clerk** = person who sells tickets in a booking office **Kartenverkäufer; Schalterbeamter; booking office** = office where you can book seats at a theatre *or* tickets for the railway **Vorverkaufsstelle/Vorverkaufskasse; Fahrkartenschalter; block booking** = booking of several seats *or* rooms at the same time **Gruppenbuchung; to confirm a booking** = to say that a booking is certain **eine Buchung bestätigen; double booking** = booking by mistake of two people into the same hotel room *or* the same seat on a plane **Doppelbuchung; Doppelbelegung**

◇ **bookkeeper** *noun* person who keeps the financial records of a company **Buchhalter/-in**

◇ **bookkeeping** *noun* keeping of the financial records of a company *or* an organization **Buchführung; single-entry bookkeeping** = noting a deal with only one entry **einfache Buchführung; double-entry bookkeeping** = noting of both credit and debit sides of an account **doppelte Buchführung**

NOTE: no plural

◇ **booklet** *noun* small book with a paper cover **Broschüre**

◇ **bookseller** *noun* person who sells books **Buchhändler**

◇ **bookshop** *noun* shop which sells books **Buchhandlung**

◇ **bookstall** *noun* small open bookshop (as in a railway station) **Bücherstand**

◇ **bookstore** *noun US* bookshop **Buchhandlung**

◇ **bookwork** *noun* keeping of financial records **Buchführungsarbeit**

NOTE: no plural

boom

1 *noun* time when sales *or* production *or* business activity are increasing **Aufschwung, Boom, Hochkonjunktur, Hausse;** *a period of economic boom; the boom of the 1970s;* **boom industry** = industry which is expanding rapidly **Konjunkturindustrie; a boom share** = share in a company which is expanding **steigende Aktie; the boom years** = **Jahre des Aufschwungs** years when there is an economic boom

2 *verb* to expand *or* to become prosperous **einen Aufschwung haben;** *business is booming; sales are booming*

◇ **booming** *adjective* which is expanding *or* becoming prosperous **florierend, blühend;** *a booming industry or company; technology is a booming sector of the economy*

boost

1 *noun* help to increase **Auftrieb, Aufschwung, Förderung;** *this publicity will give sales a boost; the government hopes to give a boost to industrial development*

2 *verb* to make something increase **ankurbeln, fördern, in die Höhe treiben;** *we expect our publicity campaign to boost sales by 25%; the company hopes to boost its market share; incentive schemes are boosting production*

> QUOTE the company expects to boost turnover this year to FFr 16bn from FFr 13.6bn in 1984
> *Financial Times*

booth *noun*

(a) small place for one person to stand or sit **Kabine; telephone booth** = public box with a telephone **Telefonzelle; ticket booth** = place outdoors where a person sells tickets **Kartenverkaufsstand**

(b) *US* section of a commercial fair where a company exhibits its products or services **Stand, Messestand**

NOTE: the GB English for this is **stand**

borrow *verb* to take money from someone for a time, possibly paying interest for it, and repaying it at the end of the period **leihen, borgen;** *he borrowed £1,000 from the bank; the company had to borrow heavily to* *repay its debts; they borrowed £25,000 against the security of the factory;* **to borrow short** *or* **long** = to borrow for a short *or* long period **kurzfristig od langfristig aufnehmen**

◇ **borrower** *noun* person who borrows **Kredit-, Darlehensnehmer; Entleiher;** *borrowers from the bank pay 12% interest*

◇ **borrowing** *noun*
(a) action of borrowing money **Kreditaufnahme;** *the new factory was financed by bank borrowing;* **borrowing power** = amount of money which a company can borrow **Kreditfähigkeit**
(b) borrowings = money borrowed **aufgenommene Schulden; Fremdkapital;** *the company's borrowings have doubled;* **bank borrowings** = loans made by banks **Kreditvergaben**

boss *noun informal* employer *or* person in charge of a company *or* an office **Chef, Boss;** *if you want a pay rise, go and talk to your boss; he became a director when he married the boss's daughter*

bottleneck *noun* position when business activity is slowed down because one section of the operation cannot cope with the amount of work **Engpaß;** *a bottleneck in the supply system; there are serious bottlenecks in the production line*

bottom
1 *noun* lowest part *or* point **Tiefpunkt; Tiefststand; sales have reached rock bottom** = the very lowest point of all **die Verkaufszahlen haben einen Tiefpunkt erreicht; the bottom has fallen out of the market** = sales have fallen below what previously seemed to be the lowest point **die Marktpreise haben einen Tiefststand erreicht; bottom price** = lowest price **niedrigster Preis; rock-bottom price** = lowest price of all **Tiefst-, Schleuderpreis; bottom line** = last line on a balance sheet indicating profit or loss **Saldo; the boss is interested only in the bottom line** = he is only interested in the final profit **der Chef ist nur am Saldo interessiert**
2 *verb* **to bottom (out)** = to reach the lowest point **den tiefsten Stand erreichen; the market has bottomed out** = has reached the lowest point and does not seem likely to fall further **der Markt hat seinen tiefsten Stand erreicht**

bottomry *noun* mortgage of a ship to pay for repairs **Schiffshypothek, Bodmerei**

bought *see* BUY; **bought ledger** = book in which expenditure is noted **Einkaufsbuch**

bounce *verb (einen Scheck)* to be returned to the person who has tried to cash it, because there is not enough money in the payer's account to pay it **platzen;** *he paid for the car with a cheque that bounced*

bounty *noun* government subsidy made to help an industry **Subvention**

boutique *noun* small specialized shop, especially for up-to-date clothes; section of a department store selling up-to-date clothes **Boutique;** *a jeans boutique; a ski boutique*

box *noun*
(a) cardboard *or* wood *or* plastic container **Schachtel, Kasten;** *the goods were sent in thin cardboard boxes; the watches are prepacked in plastic display boxes;* **paperclips come in boxes of two hundred** = packed two hundred to a box **Büroklammern sind in Schachteln zu zweihundert erhältlich; box file** = file (for papers) made like a box **kastenförmiger Aktenordner**
(b) box number = reference number used in a post office or an advertisement to avoid giving an address **Chiffre;** *(Postamt)* **Postfach;** *please reply to Box No. 209; our address is: P.O. Box 74209, Edinburgh*
(c) cash box = metal box for keeping cash **Geldkassette; letter box** *or* **mail box** = place where incoming mail is put **Briefkasten; call box** = outdoor telephone kiosk **Telefonzelle**

◇ **boxed** *adjective* put in a box *or* sold in a box **in Kisten od Schachteln verpackt; boxed set** = set of items sold together in a box **in einer Schachtel verpacktes Set**

boycott
1 *noun* refusal to buy *or* to deal in certain products **Boykott;** *the union organized a boycott against or of imported cars*
2 *verb* to refuse to buy *or* to deal in a certain product **boykottieren;** *we are boycotting all imports from that country;* **the management has boycotted the meeting** = has refused to attend the meeting **die Leitung hat das Treffen boykottiert**

bracket
1 *noun* group of items *or* people taken together **Gruppe, Klasse, Stufe; people in the middle-income bracket** = people with average incomes, not high or low **Personen der mittleren Einkommensstufe; he is in the top tax bracket** = he pays the highest level of tax **er ist in der höchsten Steuerklasse**
2 *verb* **to bracket together** = to treat several items together in the same way **zusammenfassen;** *in the sales reports, all the European countries are bracketed together*

branch
1 *noun* local office of a bank or large business; local shop of a large chain of shops **Filiale, Geschäfts-, Zweigstelle, Niederlassung;** *the bank or the store has branches in most towns in the south of the country; the insurance company has closed its branches in South America; he is the manager of our local branch of Lloyds bank; we have decided to open a branch office in Chicago; the manager of our branch in Lagos or of our Lagos branch;* **branch manager** = manager of a branch **Filialleiter**
2 *verb* **to branch out** = to start a new (but usually related) type of business **in fremde/andere Branchen einsteigen;** *from car retailing, the company branched out into car leasing*

> QUOTE a leading manufacturer of business, industrial and commercial products requires a branch manager to head up its mid-western Canada operations based in Winnipeg
> *Globe and Mail (Toronto)*

brand *noun* make of product, which can be recognized by a name or by a design **Marke;** *the top-selling brands of toothpaste; the company is launching a new brand of soap;* **brand name** = name of a brand **Markenname; brand image** = idea of a product which is associated with the brand name **Markenprofil, Produkt-Image; brand loyalty** = loyalty by the customer who always buys the same brand **Markentreue; own brand** = name of a store which is used on products which are specially packed for that store **Hausmarke**

◇ **branded** *adjective* **branded goods** = goods sold under brand names **Markenartikel**

◇ **brand new** *adjective* quite new or very new **völlig neu**

breach *noun* failure to carry out the terms of an agreement **Verletzung, Verstoß; breach of contract** = failing to do something which is in a contract **Vertragsbruch; the company is in breach of contract** = it has failed to carry out the duties of the contract **das Unternehmen ist vertragsbrüchig geworden; breach of warranty** = supplying goods which do not meet the standards of the warranty applied to them **Garantieverletzung; Verletzung der Gewährleistungspflicht**

break
1 *noun* short space of time, when you can rest **Pause;** *she typed for two hours without a break;* **coffee break** or **tea break** = rest time during work when the workers can drink coffee or tea **Kaffeepause; Teepause**
2 *verb*
(a) to fail to carry out the duties of a contract **nicht einhalten, verletzen;** *the company has broken the contract or the agreement;* **to break an engagement to do something** = not to do what has been agreed **eine Verpflichtung nicht einhalten**
(b) to cancel (a contract) **lösen;** *the company is hoping to be able to break the contract*
NOTE: **breaking - broke - has broken**

◇ **breakages** *plural noun* breaking of items **Bruch; Bruchschaden;** *customers are expected to pay for breakages*

◇ **break down** *verb*
(a) to stop working because of mechanical failure **ausfallen;** *the telex machine has broken down; what do you do when your photocopier breaks down?*
(b) to stop **scheitern;** *negotiations broke down after six hours*
(c) to show all the items in a total list of costs or expenditure **aufschlüsseln, spezifizieren;** *we broke the expenditure down into fixed and variable costs; can you break down this invoice into spare parts and labour?*

◇ **breakdown** *noun*
(a) stopping work because of mechanical failure **Betriebsstörung, Ausfall;** *we cannot communicate with our Nigerian office because of the breakdown of the telex lines*
(b) stopping talking **Scheitern;** *a breakdown in wage negotiations*
(c) showing details item by item **Aufschlüsselung, Spezifizierung;** *give me a breakdown of investment costs*

◇ **break even** *verb* to balance costs and receipts, but not make a profit **kostendeckend arbeiten;** *last year the company only just broke even; we broke even in our first two months of trading*

◇ **breakeven point** *noun* point at which sales cover costs, but do not show a profit **Kostendeckungspunkt, Break-even-Point**

◇ **break off** *verb* to stop **abbrechen;** *we broke off the discussion at midnight; management broke off negotiations with the union*

◇ **break up** *verb*
(a) to split something large into small sections **aufteilen;** *the company was broken up and separate divisions sold off*
(b) to come to an end **(sich) auflösen;** *the meeting broke up at 12.30*

bribe
1 *noun* money given to someone in authority to get him to help **Bestechungs-, Schmiergeld;** *the minister was dismissed for taking bribes*
2 *verb* to pay someone money to get him to do something for you **bestechen, schmieren;** *we had to bribe the minister's secretary before she would let us see her boss*

bridging loan *noun* short-term loan to help someone buy a new house when he has not yet sold his old one **Überbrückungskredit**

brief *verb* to explain to someone in detail **instruieren, informieren;** *the salesmen were briefed on the new product; the managing director briefed the board on the progress of the negotiations*

◇ **briefcase** *noun* case with a handle for carrying papers and documents **Aktenkoffer;** *he put all the files into his briefcase*

◇ **briefing** *noun* telling someone details **Besprechung;** *all salesmen have to attend a sales briefing on the new product*

bring *verb* to come to a place with someone or something **bringen;** *he brought his documents with him; the finance director brought his secretary to take notes of the meeting;* **to bring a lawsuit against someone** = to tell someone to appear in court to settle an argument **jdn verklagen**
NOTE: **bringing - brought**

◇ **bring down** *verb*
(a) to reduce **senken;** *petrol companies have brought down the price of oil*
(b) to add a figure to an account at the end of a period to balance expenditure and income **eine Bilanz saldieren;** *balance brought down: £365.15*

◇ **bring forward** *verb*
(a) to make earlier **vorverlegen;** *to bring forward the date of repayment; the date of the next meeting has been brought forward to March*
(b) to take a balance brought down as the starting point for the next period in a balance sheet **vor-, übertragen;** *balance brought forward: £365.15*

◇ **bring in** *verb* to earn (an interest) **bringen, einbringen;** *the shares bring in a small amount*

◇ **bring out** *verb* to produce something new **herausbringen;** *they are bringing out a new model of the car for the Motor Show*

◇ **bring up** *verb* to refer to something for the first time **zur Sprache bringen;** *the chairman brought up the question of redundancy payments*

brisk *adjective* selling actively **lebhaft, rege;** *sales are brisk; the market in oil shares is particularly brisk; a brisk market in oil shares*

broadside *noun US* publicity leaflet **Prospekt**

brochure *noun* publicity booklet **Prospekt, Broschüre;** *we sent off for a brochure about holidays in Greece or about postal services*

broke *adjective informal* having no money **pleite;** *the company is broke; he cannot pay for the new car because he is broke;* **to go broke** = to become bankrupt **pleite machen/bankrott gehen;** *the company went broke last month*

broker *noun*
(a) dealer **Makler, Händler; foreign exchange broker** = **Devisenhändler, Devisenmakler** person who buys and sells foreign currency on behalf of other people; **insurance broker** = person who sells insurance to clients **Versicherungsvertreter; ship broker** = person who sells shipping *or* transport of goods to clients **Schiffsmakler**
(b) (stock)broker = person who buys or sells shares for clients **Börsenmakler**

◇ **brokerage** *or* **broker's commission** *noun* payment to a broker for a deal carried out **Maklergebühr; Courtage**

◇ **broking** *noun* dealing in stocks and shares **Maklergeschäft**

bubble pack *noun* = BLISTER PACK

buck
1 *noun US informal* dollar **Dollar**
2 *verb* **to buck the trend** = to go against the trend **gegen den Strom schwimmen**

bucket shop *noun informal* travel agent selling airline tickets at a discount **unseriöses Reisebüro**

budget
1 *noun*
(a) plan of expected spending and income (usually for one year) **Budget; Haushalt; Etat;** *to draw up a budget; we have agreed the budgets for next year;* **advertising budget** = money planned for spending on advertising **Werbeetat; cash budget** = plan of cash income and expenditure **Einnahmen- und Ausgabenplanung; overhead budget** = plan of probable overhead costs **Festkostenvoranschlag; publicity budget** = money allowed for expected expenditure on publicity **Werbeetat; sales budget** = plan of probable sales **Absatzplanung**
(b) the Budget = the annual plan of taxes and government spending proposed by a finance minister **der Staatshaushalt;** *the minister put forward a budget aimed at boosting the economy;* **to balance the budget** = to plan income and expenditure so that they balance **den Etat ausgleichen;** *the president is planning for a balanced budget*

(c) *(Bank)* **budget account** = bank account where you plan income and expenditure to allow for periods when expenditure is high, by paying a set amount each month **Budget-Konto**
(d) *(Geschäft)* cheap **Billig-; budget department** = cheaper department **Sonderangebotsabteilung; budget prices** = low prices **Sparpreise**
2 *verb* to plan probable income and expenditure **das Budget planen, budgetieren;** *we are budgeting for £10,000 of sales next year*

◇ **budgetary** *adjective* referring to a budget **Finanz-, Budget-, Etat-, Haushalts-; budgetary policy** = policy of planning income and expenditure **Budgetpolitik; budgetary control** = keeping check on spending **Budgetkontrolle; budgetary requirements** = spending or income required to meet the budget forecasts **Budgetbedarf**

◇ **budgeting** *noun* preparing of budgets to help plan expenditure and income **Budgetierung, Finanzplanung; Kalkulation**
NOTE: no plural

> QUOTE he budgeted for further growth of 150,000 jobs (or 2.5 per cent) in the current financial year
> *Sydney Morning Herald*
> QUOTE the minister is persuading the oil, gas, electricity and coal industries to target their advertising budgets towards energy efficiency
> *Times*
> QUOTE the Federal government's budget targets for employment and growth are within reach according to the latest figures
> *Australian Financial Review*

build *verb* to make by putting pieces together **bauen, aufbauen;** *to build a sales structure;* **to build on past experience** = to use experience as a base on which to act in the future **sich auf gemachte Erfahrungen stützen**
NOTE: **building - built**

◇ **building** *noun* house *or* factory *or* office block, etc. **Gebäude;** *they have redeveloped the site of the old office building;* **the Shell Building** = the office block where the head office of Shell is **das Shell-Gebäude**

◇ **building and loan association** *noun US* = SAVINGS AND LOAN ASSOCIATION

◇ **building society** *noun GB* financial institution which accepts and pays interest on deposits and lends money to people who are buying property **Bausparkasse**
NOTE: the US English for this is **savings and loan association** *he put his savings into a building society or into a building society account; I have an account with the Halifax Building Society; I saw the building society manager to ask for a mortgage*

◇ **build into** *verb* to add something to something being set up **einbeziehen;** *you must build all the forecasts into the budget;* **we have built 10% for contingencies into our cost forecast** = we have added 10% to our basic forecast to allow for items which may appear suddenly **wir haben 10% für unvorhergesehene Ausgaben in unsere Prognosen einbezogen**

◇ **build up** *verb*
(a) to create something by adding pieces together **aufbauen;** *he bought several shoe shops and gradually built up a chain*
(b) to expand something gradually **aufbauen;** *to build up a profitable business; to build up a team of salesmen*

◇ **buildup** *noun* gradual increase **Steigerung;** *a buildup in sales or a sales buildup; there will be a big publicity buildup before the launch of the new model*

◇ **built-in** *adjective* forming part of the system *or* of a machine **eingebaut;** *the micro has a built-in clock; the accounting system has a series of built-in checks*

bulk *noun* large quantity of goods **Masse, Menge; in bulk** = in large quantities **en gros, in Massen, in Mengen;** *to buy rice in bulk;* **bulk buying** *or* **bulk purchase** = buying large quantities of goods at a lower price **Mengen-, Posteneinkauf; bulk carrier** = ship which carries large quantities of loose goods (such as coal) **Massengutfrachter; bulk shipments** = shipments of large quantities of goods **Massengütertransport**
NOTE: no plural

◇ **bulky** *adjective* large and awkward **sperrig;** *the Post Office does not accept bulky packages*

bull *noun Stock Exchange* dealer who believes the market will rise, and therefore buys shares to sell at a higher price later **Haussier; bull market** = period when share prices rise because people are optimistic and buy shares **Haussemarkt;** *see* BEAR

> QUOTE lower interest rates are always a bull factor for the stock market
> *Financial Times*

bullion *noun* gold or silver bars **Barren;** *gold bullion; the price of bullion is fixed daily; to fix the bullion price for silver*
NOTE: no plural

bumper *noun* very large crop **Rekordernte;** *a bumper crop of corn;* **1984 was a bumper year for computer sales** = 1984 was an excellent year for sales **1984 war ein Rekordjahr für den Verkauf von Computern**

bumping *noun US* situation where a senior employee takes the place of a junior (in a restaurant *or* in a job) **Verdrängung eines untergeordneten Angestellten vom Tisch im (Betriebs-)Restaurant; Personalpolitik nach dem LIFO-Prinzip**

bureau *noun* office which specializes **Büro; computer bureau** = office which offers to do work on its computers for companies which do not own their own computers **Rechenzentrum; EDV-Servicebüro; employment bureau** = office which finds jobs for people **Stellenvermittlung; information bureau** = office which gives information **Information, Auskunft; trade bureau** = office which specializes in commercial enquiries **Handels-, Wirtschaftsbüro; visitors' bureau** = office which deals with visitors' questions **Besucherinformation; word-processing bureau** = office which specializes in word-processing **(Computer-)Schreibbüro;** *we farm out the office typing to a local bureau*
NOTE: the plural is **bureaux**

◊ **bureau de change** *noun* office where you can change foreign currency **Wechselstube**

burn *verb* to destroy by fire **verbrennen;** *the chief accountant burnt the documents before the police arrived*
NOTE: **burning - burnt**

◊ **burn down** *verb* to destroy completely in a fire **abbrennen;** *the warehouse burnt down and all the stock was destroyed; the company records were all lost when the offices were burnt down*

bus *noun* motor vehicle for carrying passengers **Bus;** *he goes to work by bus; she took the bus to go to her office;* **bus company** = company which runs the buses in a town **Busunternehmer; Verkehrsgesellschaft**

bushel *noun* measure of dry goods, such as corn (= 56 pounds) **Scheffel**

business *noun*
(a) work in buying or selling **Geschäft; Gewerbe;** *business is expanding; business is slow; he does a thriving business in repairing cars; what's your line of business?;* **business call** = visit to talk to someone on business **Geschäftsbesuch; business centre** = part of a town where the main banks, shops and offices are located **Geschäftsviertel; business class** = type of airline travel which is less expensive than first class and more comfortable than tourist class **Business Class; business college** *or* **business school** = place where commercial studies are taught **Wirtschaftsinstitut; business correspondent** = journalist who writes articles on business news for newspapers **Wirtschaftskorrespondent; business efficiency exhibition** = exhibition which shows products (computers, word-processors) which help a business to be efficient **Ausstellung von arbeitssparenden Büroeinrichtungen; business letter** = letter about commercial matters **Geschäftsbrief; business lunch** = lunch to discuss business matters **Geschäftsessen; business trip** = trip to discuss business matters with clients **Geschäftsreise, Dienstreise; to be in business** = to be in a commercial firm **im Geschäft sein; to go into business** = to start a commercial firm **ein Geschäft gründen;** *he went into business as a car dealer;* **to go out of business** = to stop trading **das Geschäft aufgeben;** *the firm went out of business during the recession;* **on business** = on commercial work **geschäftlich, dienstlich;** *he had to go abroad on business; the chairman is in Holland on business*
(b) commercial company **Unternehmen, Geschäft, Betrieb;** *he owns a small car repair business; she runs a business from her home; he set up in business as an insurance broker;* **business address** = details of number, street and town where a company is located **Geschäftsadresse; business card** = card showing a businessman's name and the name and address of the company he works for **Visitenkarte; business correspondence** = letters concerned with a business **Geschäftskorrespondenz; business equipment** = machines used in an office **Büroeinrichtung, Büroausstattung; business expansion scheme** = system in Britain where money invested for some years in a new company is free from tax **Steuerbefreiung bei Investitionen in Betriebsneugründung; business expenses** = money spent on running a business, not on stock or assets **Betriebskosten; business hours** = time (usually 9 a.m. to 5 p.m.) when a business is open **Geschäftsstunden, Geschäftszeit; big business** = very large commercial firms **Großunternehmertum, Großindustrie**
(c) affairs discussed **Angelegenheit, Sache;** *the main business of the meeting was finished by 3 p.m.;* **any other business** = item at the end of an agenda, where any matter can be raised **Verschiedenes**
NOTE: no plural for meanings (a) and (c); (b) has the plural **businesses**

◊ **business agent** *noun US* chief local official of a trade union **Gewerkschaftsvertreter**

◊ **businessman** *or* **businesswoman** *noun* man *or* woman engaged in business **Geschäftsmann; Geschäftsfrau; she's a good businesswoman** = she is good at commercial deals **sie ist eine gute Geschäftsfrau; a small businessman** = man who owns a small business **Kleinunternehmer**

bust *adjective informal* **to go bust** = to become bankrupt **pleite machen/bankrott gehen**

busy *adjective* occupied in doing something/in working **beschäftigt;** *he is busy preparing the annual accounts; the manager is busy at the moment, but he will be free in about fifteen minutes; the busiest time of year for stores is the week before Christmas; summer is the busy season for hotels;* **the line is busy** = the telephone line is being used **die Leitung ist besetzt**

buy
1 *verb* to get something by paying money **(ein)kaufen;** *he bought 10,000 shares; the company has been bought by its leading supplier; to buy wholesale and sell retail; to buy for cash;* **to buy forward** = to buy foreign currency before you need it, in order to be sure of the exchange rate **auf Termin kaufen**
NOTE: **buying - bought**
2 *noun* **good buy** *or* **bad buy** = thing bought which is *or* is not worth the money paid for it **guter Kauf; schlechter Kauf;** *that watch was a good buy; this car was a bad buy*

◊ **buy back** *verb* to buy something which you have sold **zurückkaufen;** *he sold the shop last year and is now trying to buy it back*

◊ **buyer** *noun*
(a) person who buys **Käufer/-in; there were no buyers** = no one wanted to buy **es gab keine Käufer; a buyers' market** = market where products are sold cheaply because there are few buyers **Käufermarkt; impulse buyer** = person who buys something when he sees it, not because he was planning to buy it **Spontankäufer**
(b) person who buys a certain type of goods wholesale, which are then stocked by a large store **Einkäufer; head buyer** = most important buyer in a store **Einkaufsleiter;** *she is the shoe buyer for a London department store*

◊ **buy in** *verb (Auktion)* to buy the thing which you are trying to sell because no one will pay the price you want **rückkaufen**

◊ **buying** *noun* getting something for money **Kaufen, Einkaufen; bulk buying** = getting large quantities of goods at low prices **Mengen-, Posteneinkauf; forward buying** *or* **buying forward** = buying shares *or* commodities *or* currency for delivery at a later date **Terminkauf; impulse buying** = buying items which you have just seen, not because you had planned to buy them **Impuls-, Spontankäufe; panic buying** = rush to buy something at any price because stocks may run out **Panikkäufe; buying department** = department in a company which buys raw materials or goods for use in the company **Einkaufsabteilung; buying power** = ability to buy **Kaufkraft;** *the buying power of the pound has fallen over the last years*
NOTE: no plural

◊ **buyout** *noun* **management buyout** = takeover of a company by a group of employees (usually managers and directors) **Übernahme eines Unternehmens durch das Management; leveraged buyout** = buying all the shares in a company by borrowing money against the security of the shares to be bought **Leveraged Buyout: Unternehmenserwerb unter Ausnutzung des Leverage-Effekts**

> QUOTE we also invest in companies whose growth and profitability could be improved by a management buyout
> *Times*
>
> QUOTE in a normal leveraged buyout, the acquirer raises money by borrowing against the assets or cash flow of the target company
> *Fortune*

by-product *noun* product made as a result of manufacturing a main product **Neben-, Abfallprodukt;** *soap is a useful by-product of oil*

byte *noun* storage unit in a computer, equal to one character **Byte 1**

Cc

cabinet *noun* piece of furniture for storing records or display **Schrank;** *last year's correspondence is in the bottom drawer of the filing cabinet;* **display cabinet** = piece of furniture with a glass top or glass doors for showing goods for sale **Vitrine**

cable
1 *noun* telegram *or* message sent by telegraph **Telegramm;** *he sent a cable to his office asking for more money;* **cable address** = specially short address for sending cables **Telegrammanschrift**
2 *verb* to send a message *or* money by telegraph **telegrafieren;** *he cabled his office to ask them to send more money; the office cabled him £1,000 to cover his expenses*

◊ **cablegram** *noun* telegram *or* message sent by telegraph **Telegramm**

calculate *verb*
(a) to find the answer to a problem using numbers **(be)rechnen, ermitteln;** *the bank clerk calculated the rate of exchange for the dollar*
(b) to estimate **kalkulieren, schätzen;** *I calculate that we have six months' stock left*

◇ **calculating machine** *noun* machine which calculates **Rechenmaschine**

◇ **calculation** *noun* answer to a problem in mathematics **Berechnung, Ermittlung; rough calculation** = approximate answer **grobe Kalkulation;** *I made some rough calculations on the back of an envelope; according to my calculations, we have six months' stock left;* **we are £20,000 out in our calculations** = we have £20,000 too much or too little **wir haben uns um £20.000 verrechnet**

◇ **calculator** *noun* electronic machine which works out the answers to problems in mathematics **Taschenrechner;** *my pocket calculator needs a new battery; he worked out the discount on his calculator*

calendar *noun* book *or* set of sheets of paper showing the days and months in a year, often attached to pictures **Kalender;** *for the New Year the garage sent me a calendar with photographs of old cars ;* **calendar month** = a whole month as on a calendar, from the 1st to the 30th or 31st **Kalendermonat; calendar year** = year from the 1st January to 31st December **Kalenderjahr**

call
1 *noun*
(a) conversation on the telephone **Anruf, Gespräch; local call** = call to a number on the same exchange **Ortsgespräch; trunk call** *or* **long-distance call** = call to a number in a different zone *or* area **Ferngespräch; overseas call** *or* **international call** = call to another country **Auslandsgespräch; person-to-person call** = call where you ask the operator to connect you with a named person **Gespräch mit namentlicher Voranmeldung; transferred charge call** *or US* **collect call** = call where the person receiving the call agrees to pay for it **R-Gespräch; to make a call** = to dial and speak to someone on the telephone **telefonieren, anrufen; to take a call** = to answer the telephone **ein Gespräch annehmen; to log calls** = to note all details of telephone calls made **Gespräche registrieren**
(b) demand for repayment of a loan by a lender **Zahlungsaufforderung; money at call** *or* **money on call** *or* **call money** = money loaned for which repayment can be demanded without notice **Tagesgeld**
(c) *Stock Exchange* demand to pay for new shares **Aufruf; call option** = option to buy shares at a certain price **Kaufoption**
(d) visit **Besuch;** *the salesmen make six calls a day;* **business call** = visit to talk to someone on business **Geschäftsbesuch; cold call** = sales visit where the salesman has no appointment and the client is not an established customer **unangemeldeter Besuch; call rate** = number of calls (per day or per week) made by a salesman **Besuchshäufigkeit**
2 *verb*
(a) to telephone to someone **anrufen;** *I'll call you at your office tomorrow*
(b) to call on someone = to visit **jdn besuchen;** *our salesmen call on their best accounts twice a month*
(c) to ask someone to do something **aufrufen; the union called a strike** = the union told its members to go on strike **die Gewerkschaft hat zum Streik ausgerufen**

◇ **callable bond** *noun* bond which must be repaid at notice **kündbare Schuldverschreibung**

◇ **call-back pay** *noun* pay given to a worker who has been called back to work after his normal working hours **Überstundenlohn**

◇ **call box** *noun* outdoor telephone kiosk **Telefonzelle**

◇ **called up capital** *noun* share capital in a company which has been paid for **eingezahltes Kapital**

◇ **caller** *noun*
(a) person who telephones **Anrufer/-in**
(b) person who visits **Besucher/-in**

◇ **call in** *verb*
(a) to visit **vorbeikommen;** *the sales representative called in twice last week*
(b) to telephone to make contact **anrufen;** *we ask the reps to call in every Friday to report the weeks' sales*
(c) to ask for a debt to be paid **zurückfordern**

◇ **call off** *verb* to ask for something not to take place **absagen; rückgängig machen; abbrechen;** *the union has called off the strike; the deal was called off at the last moment*

◇ **call up** *verb* to ask for share capital to be paid **aufrufen**

calm *adjective* quiet *or* not excited **ruhig;** *the markets were calmer after the government statement on the exchange rate*

campaign *noun* planned method of working **Kampagne, Aktion; sales campaign** = planned work to achieve higher sales **Verkaufsaktion; publicity campaign** *or* **advertising campaign** = planned period when publicity takes place **Werbekampagne,**

Werbeaktion; *they are working on a campaign to launch a new brand of soap*

cancel *verb*
(a) to stop something which has been agreed *or* planned **absagen; annullieren; stornieren; aufheben;** *to cancel an appointment or a meeting; to cancel a contract; the government has cancelled the order for a fleet of buses*
(b) to cancel a cheque = to stop payment of a cheque which you have signed **einen Scheck stornieren**
NOTE: GB English: **cancelling - cancelled** but US English: **canceling - canceled**
◇ **cancellation** *noun* stopping something which has been agreed *or* planned **Absage; Annullieren; Stornierung; Aufhebung;** *cancellation of an appointment; cancellation of an agreement;* **cancellation clause** = clause in a contract which states the terms on which the contract may be cancelled **Rücktrittsklausel**
◇ **cancel out** *verb* to balance and so make invalid *or* even **aufheben;** *the two clauses cancel each other out; costs have cancelled out the sales revenue*

candidate *noun* person who applies for a job **Kandidat/-in, Bewerber/-in;** *there are six candidates for the post of assistant manager*

canvass *verb* to visit people to ask them to buy goods *or* to vote *or* to say what they think **werben; Wahlwerbung betreiben; befragen;** *he's canvassing for customers for his hairdresser's shop; we have canvassed the staff about raising the prices in the staff restaurant*
◇ **canvasser** *noun* person who canvasses **Vertreter; Wahlhelfer; Meinungsforscher**
◇ **canvassing** *noun* action of asking people to buy *or* to vote *or* to say what they think **Vertreterbesuche; Wahlwerbung; Meinungsumfrage;** *canvassing techniques; door-to-door canvassing*
NOTE: no plural

CAP = COMMON AGRICULTURAL POLICY

capable *adjective*
(a) capable of = able *or* clever enough to do something **können, fähig sein zu;** *she is capable of very fast typing speeds; the sales force must be capable of selling all the stock in the warehouse*
(b) efficient **fähig, leistungsfähig;** *she is a very capable departmental manager*
NOTE: you are capable **of** something or **of doing** something

capacity *noun*
(a) amount which can be produced *or* amount of work which can be done **Kapazität;** *industrial or manufacturing or production capacity;* **to work at full capacity** = to do as much work as possible **voll ausgelastet sein; to use up spare** *or* **excess capacity** = to make use of time *or* space which is not fully used **überschüssige Kapazitäten ausnutzen**
(b) amount of space **Fassungsvermögen; Kapazität; storage capacity** = space available for storage **Lagerkapazität; warehouse capacity** = space available in a warehouse **Lagerhauskapazität**
(c) ability **Befähigung, Eignung;** *he has a particular capacity for business;* **earning capacity** = amount of money someone is able to earn **Verdienstmöglichkeiten**
(d) in a capacity = acting as **in einer Funktion/Eigenschaft;** *in his capacity as chairman;* **the manager, speaking in his official capacity, said** = speaking officially **in seiner Eigenschaft als Manager sagte er**
NOTE: no plural for (a), (b) and (c)

> QUOTE analysts are increasingly convinced that the industry simply has too much capacity
> *Fortune*

capita *see* PER CAPITA

capital *noun*
(a) money, property and assets used in a business **Kapital;** *company with £10,000 capital or with a capital of £10,000;* **authorized capital** = maximum capital which is permitted by a company's articles of association **genehmigtes Grundkapital; capital account** = account of dealings (money invested in the company, or taken out of the company) by the owners of a company **Kapitalkonto; capital assets** = property *or* machines, etc. which a company owns and uses **Anlagevermögen; capital bonus** = bonus payment by an insurance company which is produced by capital gain **Bonus aus Kapitalerträgen; capital equipment** = equipment which a factory or office uses to work **Produktionsmittel; capital expenditure** *or* **investment** *or* **outlay** = money spent on fixed assets (property, machines, furniture) **Investitionen; capital gains** = money made by selling a fixed asset *or* by selling shares **Veräußerungsgewinn; capital gains tax** = tax paid on capital gains **Veräußerungsgewinnsteuer; capital goods** = goods used to manufacture other goods (i.e. machinery) **Anlagegüter; capital levy**= tax on the value of a person's property and possessions **Vermögenssteuer; capital loss** = loss made by selling assets **Kapitalverlust; capital reserves** = part of share capital which can be used only when a company is

wound up **Kapitalreserven; capital structure of a company** = way in which a company's capital is set up **Kapitalstruktur eines Unternehmens; capital transfer tax** = tax on gifts or bequests of money or property **Kapitaltransfersteuer; circulating capital** = capital required in the form of raw materials, finished products and work in progress for a company to carry on its business **Umlaufvermögen; equity capital** = amount of a company's capital which is owned by the shareholders **Eigenkapital; fixed capital** = capital in the form of buildings and machinery **Anlagevermögen; issued capital** = amount of capital issued as shares to the shareholders **ausgegebenes Kapital; paid-up capital** = amount of money paid for the issued capital shares **einbezahltes Kapital; risk capital** *or* **venture capital** = capital for investment which may easily be lost in risky projects **Risiko-, Wagniskapital; share capital** = value of the assets of a company held as shares, less its debts **Aktienkapital; working capital** = capital in cash and stocks needed for a company to be able to work **Working Capital**
(b) money for investment **Kapital; movements of capital** = changes of investments from one country to another **Kapitalverkehr; flight of capital** = rapid movement of capital out of one country because of lack of confidence in that country's economic future **Kapitalflucht; capital market** = places where companies can look for investment capital **Kapitalmarkt**
(c) capital letters *or* **block capitals**= letters written as A, B, C, D, etc., and not a, b, c, d **Großbuchstaben, Versalien;** *write your name in block capitals at the top of the form*
NOTE: no plural for (a) and (b)

◇ **capitalism** *noun* economic system where each person has the right to invest money, to work in business, to buy and sell, with no restriction from the state **Kapitalismus**

◇ **capitalist**
1 *noun* person who invests money in a business **Kapitalist/-in**
2 *adjective* working according to the principles of capitalism **kapitalistisch;** *a capitalist economy; the capitalist system; the capitalist countries or world*

◇ **capitalize** *verb* to have money as capital in a company **kapitalisieren; company capitalized at £10,000** = company with a working capital of £10,000 **Unternehmen mit einem Kapital von £10.000**

◇ **capitalize on** *verb* to make a profit from **Kapital schlagen aus;** *to capitalize on one's market position*

◇ **capitalization** *noun* **market capitalization** = value of a company calculated by multiplying the price of its shares on the stock exchange by the number of shares issued **Börsenwert;** *company with a £1m capitalization;* **capitalization of reserves** = issuing free bonus shares to shareholders **Kapitalisierung von Rücklagen**

QUOTE to prevent capital from crossing the Atlantic in search of high US interest rates and exchange-rate capital gains
Duns Business Month

QUOTE Canadians' principal residences have always been exempt from capital gains tax
Toronto Star

QUOTE issued and fully paid capital is $100 million, comprising 2340 shares of $100 each and 997,660 ordinary shares of $100 each
Hongkong Standard

QUOTE at its last traded price the bank was capitalized at around $1.05 billion with 60 per cent in the hands of the family
South China Morning Post

captive market *noun* market where one supplier has a monopoly and the buyer has no choice over the product which he must purchase **monopolistischer Absatzmarkt**

capture *verb* to take *or* to get control of something **erobern, einnehmen; to capture 10% of the market** = to sell hard, and so take a 10% market share **10% des Marktes erobern; to capture 20% of a company's shares** = to buy shares in a company rapidly and so own 20% of it **Firmenanteile von 10% erwerben**

car *noun* small motor vehicle for carrying people **Auto, Wagen; company car**= car owned by a company and lent to a member of staff to use as if it were his own **Firmenwagen**

◇ **car-hire** *noun* business of lending cars to people for money **Autovermietung, Autoverleih;** *he runs a car-hire business*

carat *noun*
(a) measure of the quality of gold (pure gold being 24 carat) **Karat;** *a 22-carat gold ring*
(b) measure of the weight of precious stones **Karat;** *a 5-carat diamond*
NOTE: no plural

carbon *noun*
(a) carbon paper **Durchschlag-, Kohlepapier;** *you forgot to put a carbon in the typewriter*
(b) carbon copy **Durchschlag;** *make a top copy and two carbons*

◇ **carbon copy** *noun* copy made with carbon paper **Durchschlag;** *give me the original, and file the carbon copy*

◇ **carbonless** *adjective* which makes a copy without using carbon paper

selbstdurchschreibend; *our reps use carbonless order pads*

◇ **carbon paper** *noun* sheet of paper with a black material on one side, used in a typewriter to make a copy **Durchschlagpapier, Kohlepapier;** *you put the carbon paper in the wrong way round*

card *noun*
(a) stiff paper **Pappe, Karton;** *we have printed the instructions on thick white card* NOTE: no plural
(b) small piece of stiff paper or plastic **Karte; business card** = card showing a businessman's name and the address of the company he works for **Visitenkarte; cash card** = plastic card used to obtain money from a cash dispenser **Geldautomatenkarte; charge card**= plastic card which allows you to buy goods and pay for them later **Kundenkreditkarte; cheque (guarantee) card** = plastic card from a bank which guarantees payment of a cheque **Scheckkarte; credit card** = plastic card which allows you to borrow money or to buy goods without paying for them immediately **Kreditkarte; filing card** = card with information written on it, used to classify information in correct order **Karteikarte; index card** = card used to make a card index **Karteikarte; punched card** = card with holes punched in it which a computer can read **Lochkarte**
(c) postcard **Karte, Postkarte, Ansichtskarte; reply paid card** = card to be sent back to the sender with a reply on it, the sender having already paid the postage **freigemachte/frankierte Antwortkarte**
(d) to get one's cards = to be dismissed **entlassen werden**

◇ **cardboard** *noun* thick stiff brown paper **Karton, Pappe; cardboard box** = box made of cardboard **Pappkarton, Pappschachtel**
NOTE: no plural

◇ **card index** *noun* series of cards with information written on them, kept in special order so that the information can be found easily **Kartei; card-index file** = information kept on filing cards **Kartei**

◇ **card-index** *verb* to put information onto a card index **Karteikarten anlegen**

◇ **card-indexing** *noun* putting information onto a card index **Anlegen von Karteikarten;** *no one can understand her card-indexing system*

care of *phrase (in an address)* words to show that the person lives at the address, but only as a visitor **bei;** *Herr Schmidt, care of Mr W. Brown*

career *noun* job which you are trained for, and which you expect to do all your life **Beruf, Karriere, Laufbahn;** *he made his career in electronics;* **career woman** *or* **girl** = woman who is working in business and does not plan to stop working to look after the house or children **Karrierefrau**

cargo *noun* load of goods which are sent in a ship *or* plane, etc. **Fracht, Ladung, Kargo; the ship was taking on cargo** = was being loaded with goods **das Schiff nahm Fracht auf; to load cargo** = to put cargo on a ship **Fracht verladen; air cargo** = goods sent by air **Luftfracht; cargo ship** = ship which carries only cargo and not passengers **Frachter, Fracht-, Transportschiff; cargo plane** plane which carries only cargo and not passengers **Transportflugzeug**
NOTE: plural is **cargoes**

carnet *noun* international document which allows dutiable goods to cross several European countries by road without paying duty until the goods reach their final destination **Carnet**

carriage *noun* transporting goods from one place to another; cost of transport of goods **Transport; Transportkosten;** *to pay for carriage; to allow 10% for carriage; carriage is 15% of the total cost;* **carriage free** = deal where the customer does not pay for the shipping **frachtfrei; carriage paid** = deal where the seller has paid for the shipping **frachtfrei; carriage forward** = deal where the customer will pay for the shipping when the goods arrive **Frachtnachnahme**
NOTE: no plural

carrier *noun*
(a) company which transports goods **Spedition, Transportunternehmen;** *we only use reputable carriers;* **air carrier**= company which sends cargo *or* passengers by air **Flug-, Luftfahrtsgesellschaft**
(b) vehicle *or* ship which transports goods **Transporter; bulk carrier** = ship which carries large quantities of loose goods (such as corn) **Massengutfrachter**

carry *verb*
(a) to take from one place to another **befördern;** *to carry goods; a tanker carrying oil from the Gulf; the train was carrying a consignment of cars for export*
(b) to vote to approve **annehmen; the motion was carried** = the motion was accepted after a vote **der Antrag wurde angenommen**
(c) to produce **bringen, tragen;** *the bonds carry interest at 10%*

(d) to keep in stock **führen, auf Lager haben;** *to carry a line of goods; we do not carry pens*

◇ **carry forward** *verb* to take a balance brought down as the starting point for the next period or page **vortragen; balance carried forward** = amount entered in an account at the end of a period to balance the income and expenditure which is then taken forward to start the next period **Saldovortrag**

◇ **carrying** *noun* transporting from one place to another **Beförderung, Transport;** *carrying charges; carrying cost*
NOTE: no plural

◇ **carry on** *verb* to continue *or* to go on doing something **weitermachen, weiter-;** *the staff carried on working in spite of the fire;* **to carry on a business** = to be active in running a business **ein Geschäft betreiben**

◇ **carry over** *verb*
(a) to carry over a balance = to take a balance from the end of one page or period to the beginning of the next **einen Saldo vortragen**
(b) to carry over stock = to hold stock from the end of one stocktaking period to the beginning of the next **Waren übertragen (in das neue Finanzjahr)**

cartage *noun* carrying goods by road **Transport**
NOTE: no plural

cartel *noun* group of companies which try to fix the price *or* to regulate the supply of a product because they can then profit from this situation **Kartell**

carter *noun* person who transports goods by road **Fuhrunternehmer**

carton *noun*
(a) thick cardboard **Karton, Pappe;** *a folder made of carton*
(b) box made of cardboard **Pappkarton, Karton;** *(Zigaretten)* **Stange;** *(Milch)* **Tüte;** *a carton of cigarettes*
NOTE: no plural for (a)

case
1 *noun*
(a) suitcase *or* box with a handle for carrying clothes and personal belongings when travelling **Koffer;** *the customs made him open his case; she had a small case which she carried onto the plane*
(b) cardboard or wooden box for packing and carrying goods **Kiste; six cases of wine** = six boxes, each containing twelve bottles **sechs Kisten Wein; a packing case** = large wooden box for carrying items which can be easily broken **Kiste**
(c) display case = table or counter with a glass top, used for displaying items for sale **Schau-, Glaskasten, Vitrine**
(d) court case = legal action or trial **Gerichtsverfahren; Prozeß; Rechtsstreit; the case is being heard next week** = the case is coming to court **der Fall wird nächste Woche vor Gericht verhandelt**
2 *verb* to pack in a case **in Kisten verpacken**

cash
1 *noun*
(a) money in coins or notes **Bargeld; cash in hand** = money and notes in the till, kept to pay small debts **Barbestand, Bargeld; hard cash=** money in notes and coins, as opposed to cheques or credit cards **Bargeld; petty cash** = small amounts of money **Porto-, Barkasse; ready cash** = money which is immediately available for payment **Bargeld; cash account** = account which records the money which is received and spent **Kassen-, Kassakonto; cash advance=** loan in cash against a future payment **Barvorschuß; cash balance** = balance in cash, as opposed to amounts owed **Bar-, Kassenbestand; cash book** = book in which cash transactions are entered **Kassenbuch; cash box** = metal box for keeping cash **Geldkassette; cash budget=** plan of cash income and expenditure **Einnahmen- und Ausgabenplanung; cash card** = card used to obtain money from a cash dispenser **Geldautomatenkarte; cash desk** = place in a store where you pay for the goods bought **Kasse; cash dispenser** = machine which gives out money when a special card is inserted and instructions given **Geldautomat; cash float** = cash put into the cash box at the beginning of the day or week to allow business to start **Wechselgeld; cash offer** = offer to pay in cash **Barzahlungsangebot; cash payment** = payment in cash **Barzahlung; cash purchases** = purchases made in cash **Barkäufe; cash register** *or* **cash till** = machine which shows and adds the prices of items bought, with a drawer for keeping the cash received **Registrierkasse; cash reserves** = a company's reserves in cash, deposits or bills, kept in case of urgent need **Bar-, Liquiditätsreserven**
(b) using money in coins or notes **Barzahlung; to pay cash down** = to pay in cash immediately **(in) bar zahlen; cash price** *or* **cash terms** = lower price *or* terms which apply if the customer pays cash **Bar(zahlungs)preis; Barzahlungsbedingungen; settlement in cash** *or* **cash settlement** = paying a bill in cash **Barzahlung; cash sale** *or* **cash transaction** = transaction paid for in cash **Bar-, Kassegeschäft; terms: cash with order** = terms of sale showing the payment has to be made in cash when the order is placed **Bedingungen: Barzahlung bei Bestellung; cash on delivery** = payment in

cash when goods are delivered **per Nachnahme; cash discount** *or* **discount for cash** = discount given for payment in cash **Barzahlungsrabatt, Diskont**
NOTE: no plural
2 *verb* **to cash a cheque** = to exchange a cheque for cash **einen Scheck einlösen**

◊ **cashable** *adjective* which can be cashed **einlösbar;** *a crossed cheque is not cashable at any bank*

◊ **cash and carry** *noun* large store, selling goods at low prices, where the customer pays cash and has to take the goods away himself **(Verbraucher-)Abholmarkt;** *cash and carry warehouse*

◊ **cash flow** *noun* cash which comes into a company from sales less the money which goes out in purchases or overhead expenditure **Cashflow; cash flow forecast** = forecast of when cash will be received or paid out **Cashflow-Prognose; cash flow statement** = report which shows cash sales and purchases **Cashflow-Bericht; net cash flow** = difference between the money coming in and the money going out **Netto-Cashflow; negative cash flow** = situation where more money is going out of a company than is coming in **negativer Cashflow; positive cash flow** = situation where more money is coming into a company than is going out **positiver Cashflow; the company is suffering from cash flow problems** = cash income is not coming in fast enough to pay the expenditure going out **das Unternehmen hat Cashflow-Probleme**

◊ **cashier** *noun* person who takes money from customers in a shop; person who deals with customers' money in a bank **Kassierer/-in**

◊ **cash in** *verb* to sell (shares) for cash **gegen bar verkaufen**

◊ **cash in on sth** *verb* to profit from **sich etwas zunutze machen, aus etwas Kapital schlagen;** *the company is cashing in on the interest in computer games*

◊ **cash up** *verb* to add up the cash in a shop at the end of the day **Kasse machen**

cassette *noun* small plastic box with a magnetic tape on which words or information can be recorded **Kassette;** *copy the information from the computer onto a cassette*

casting vote *noun* vote used by the chairman in the case where the votes for and against a proposal are equal **ausschlaggebende Stimme;** *the chairman has the casting vote; he used his casting vote to block the motion*

casual *adjective* not permanent *or* not regular **Aushilfs-; flüchtig; casual labour** = workers who are hired for a short period **Aushilfsarbeiter; casual work** = work where the workers are hired for a short period **Aushilfsarbeit; casual labourer** *or* **casual worker** = worker who can be hired for a short period **Aushilfsarbeiter**

catalogue *or* *US* **catalog**
1 *noun* list of items for sale, usually with prices **Katalog, Prospekt, Liste;** *an office equipment catalogue; they sent us a catalogue of their new range of desks;* **mail order catalogue** = catalogue from which a customer orders items to be sent by mail **Versandhauskatalog; catalogue price** = price as marked in a catalogue **Katalog-, Listenpreis**
2 *verb* to put an item into a catalogue **katalogisieren**

category *noun* type *or* sort of item **Klasse, Kategorie;** *we deal only in the most expensive categories of watches*

cater for *verb* to deal with *or* to provide for **ausgerichtet sein auf;** *the store caters mainly for overseas customers*

◊ **caterer** *noun* person who supplies food and drink, especially for parties **Lebensmittellieferant**

◊ **catering** *noun*
(a) supply of food and drink for a party, etc. **gastronomische Betreuung; the catering trade** = food trade, especially supplying food ready to eat **Gaststättengewerbe**
(b) catering for = which provides for **ausgerichtet auf;** *store catering for overseas visitors*
NOTE: no plural

cause
1 *noun* thing which makes something happen **Ursache, Grund;** *what was the cause of the bank's collapse? the police tried to find the cause of the fire*
2 *verb* to make something happen **verursachen, der Grund sein für;** *the recession caused hundreds of bankruptcies*

caveat *noun* warning **Warnung; to enter a caveat** = to warn legally that you have an interest in a case, and that no steps can be taken without your permission **Einspruch einlegen**

◊ **caveat emptor** = LET THE BUYER BEWARE phrase meaning that the buyer is himself responsible for checking that what he buys is in good order **Ausschluß der Gewährleistung**

cc = COPIES
NOTE: **cc** is put on a letter to show who has received a copy of it

ceiling *noun*
(a) top part which covers a room **Decke; ceiling light** = electric light attached to the ceiling **Deckenleuchte**
(b) highest point **Höchstgrenze;** *output has reached a ceiling; to fix a ceiling to a budget;* **ceiling price** *or* **price ceiling** = highest price that can be reached **oberste Preisgrenze**

cent
(a) *noun* small coin, one hundredth of a dollar **Cent;** *the stores are only a 25-cent bus ride away; they sell oranges at 99 cents each*
NOTE: **cent** is usually written c in prices: 25c, but not when a dollar price is mentioned: $1.25
(b) *see* PER CENT

centimetre *noun* measurement of length (one hundredth of a metre) **Zentimeter;** *the paper is fifteen centimetres wide*
NOTE: **centimetre** is usually written cm after figures: 260cm

central *adjective* organized by one main point **zentral; central bank** = main government-controlled bank in a country, which controls the financial affairs of the country by fixing main interest rates, issuing currency and controlling the foreign exchange rate **Zentral-, Notenbank; central office** = main office which controls all smaller offices **Hauptbüro, Zentrale; central purchasing** = purchasing organized by a central office for all branches of a company **Zentraleinkauf**
◇ **centralization** *noun* organization of everything from a central point **Zentralisierung**
NOTE: no plural
◇ **centralize** *verb* to organize from a central point **zentralisieren;** *all purchasing has been centralized in our main office; the group benefits from a highly centralized organizational structure*

QUOTE the official use of the ecu remains limited, since most interventions by central banks on the market are conducted in dollars
Economist
QUOTE central bankers in Europe and Japan are reassessing their intervention policy
Duns Business Month

centre *or* *US* **center** *noun*
(a) business centre = part of a town where the main banks, shops and offices are **Geschäftsviertel**
(b) important town **Zentrum;** *industrial centre; manufacturing centre; the centre for the shoe industry*
(c) *GB* **job centre** = government office which lists jobs which are vacant; *entspricht* **Arbeitsamt; Stellenvermittlung; shopping centre** = group of shops linked together with car parks and restaurants **Einkaufszentrum; cost centre** = person or group whose costs can be itemized **Kostenstelle; profit centre** = person or department which is considered separately for the purposes of calculating a profit **Profit Center**

CEO *US* = CHIEF EXECUTIVE OFFICER

certain *adjective*
(a) sure **sicher, gewiß;** *the chairman is certain we will pass last year's total sales*
(b) a certain = one particular **ein bestimmter, ein gewisser; a certain number** *or* **a certain quantity** = some **eine bestimmte Anzahl/Menge**

certificate *noun* official document which shows that something is true **Bescheinigung, Beglaubigung, Bestätigung; clearance certificate** = document showing that goods have been passed by customs **Zollabfertigungs-, Ausklarierungsschein; savings certificate** = document showing you have invested money in a government savings scheme **Sparbrief; share certificate** = document proving that you own shares **Aktienzertifikat; certificate of airworthiness** = document to show that an aircraft is safe to fly **Lufttüchtigkeitszeugnis; certificate of approval** = document showing that an item has been officially approved **Genehmigungszertifikat; certificate of deposit** = document from a bank showing that money has been deposited **Einzahlungsschein; certificate of origin** = document showing where goods were made **Herkunftszertifikat; certificate of registration** = document showing that an item has been registered **Eintragungsbescheinigung, Meldeschein**
◇ **certificated** *adjective* **certificated bankrupt** = bankrupt who has been discharged from bankruptcy with a certificate to show that he was not at fault **rehabilitierter Konkursschuldner**

certify *verb* to make an official declaration in writing **bescheinigen, bestätigen, beglaubigen;** *I certify that this is a true copy; the document is certified as a true copy;* **certified accountant** = accountant who has passed the professional examinations and is a member of the Association of Certified Accountants; *entspricht* **amtlich zugelassener Wirtschaftsprüfer; certified cheque** *or* *US* **certified check** = cheque which a bank says is good and will be paid out of money put aside from the bank account **bestätigter Scheck**

cession *noun* giving up property to someone (especially a creditor) **Abtretung, Zession**

chain *noun* series of stores belonging to the same company **Kette;** *a chain of hotels or a hotel chain; the chairman of a large do-it-yourself chain; he runs a chain of shoe shops; she bought several shoe shops and gradually built up a chain*
◇ **chain store** *noun* one store in a chain **Filiale, Kettenladen**

> QUOTE the giant US group is better known for its chain of cinemas and hotels rather than its involvement in shipping
> *Lloyd's List*

chair
1 *noun* position of the chairman, presiding over a meeting **Vorsitz;** *to be in the chair; she was voted into the chair;* **Mr Jones took the chair** = Mr Jones presided over the meeting **Mr Jones führte den Vorsitz; to address the chair** = in a meeting, to speak to the chairman and not to the rest of the people at the meeting **sich an den Vorsitzenden wenden;** *please address your remarks to the chair*
2 *verb* to preside over a meeting **den Vorsitz führen bei;** *the meeting was chaired by Mrs Smith*
◇ **chairman** *noun*
(a) person who is in charge of a meeting **Vorsitzender;** *Mr Howard was chairman or acted as chairman;* **Mr Chairman** *or* **Madam Chairman** = way of speaking to the chairman **Herr Vorsitzender; Frau Vorsitzende**
(b) person who presides over the board meetings of a company **Vorsitzender des Aufsichtsrates;** *the chairman of the board or the company chairman;* **the chairman's report** = annual report from the chairman of a company to the shareholders **Jahresbericht des Aufsichtsratsvorsitzenden**
◇ **chairmanship** *noun* being a chairman **Vorsitz, Leitung;** *the committee met under the chairmanship of Mr Jones*
◇ **chairperson** *noun* person who is in charge of a meeting **Vorsitzender**
◇ **chairwoman** *noun* woman who is in charge of a meeting **Vorsitzende**
NOTE: the plurals are **chairmen, chairpersons, chairwomen.** Note also that in a US company the president is less important than the chairman of the board

> QUOTE the corporation's entrepreneurial chairman seeks a dedicated but part-time president. The new president will work a three-day week
> *Globe and Mail (Toronto)*

Chamber of Commerce *noun* group of local businessmen who meet to discuss problems which they have in common and to promote commerce in their town **Handelskammer**

chambers *plural noun* office of a judge **Richterzimmer; the judge heard the case in chambers** = in his private office, and not in court **der Richter verhandelte den Fall ohne Öffentlichkeit im Richterzimmer**

chance *noun*
(a) being possible **Möglichkeit, Chance;** *the company has a good chance of winning the contract; his promotion chances are small*
(b) opportunity to do something **Chance;** *she is waiting for a chance to see the managing director; he had his chance of promotion when the finance director's assistant resigned*
NOTE: you have a chance **of doing** something or **to do** something

Chancellor of the Exchequer *noun GB* chief finance minister in the government **Finanzminister, Schatzkanzler**

chandler *noun* person who deals in goods, especially supplies to ships **Schiffslieferant;** *ship chandler*

◇ **chandlery** *noun* chandler's shop **Schiffsausrüster**

change
1 *noun*
(a) money in coins or small notes **Wechselgeld; small change** = coins **Kleingeld; to give someone change for £10** = to give someone coins or notes in exchange for a ten pound note **jdm £10 wechseln; change machine** = machine which gives small change for a larger coin **Wechselautomat, Geldwechsler**
(b) money given back by the seller, when the buyer can pay only with a larger note *or* coin than the amount asked **Wechselgeld;** *he gave me the wrong change; you paid the £5.75 bill with a £10 note, so you should have £4.25 change;* **keep the change** = keep it as a tip (said to waiters, etc.) **der Rest ist für Sie**
2 *verb*
(a) to change a £10 note = to give change in smaller notes or coins for a £10 note **einen £10 Schein wechseln**
(b) to give one type of currency for another **wechseln, tauschen;** *to change £1,000 into dollars; we want to change some traveller's cheques*

(c) to change hands = to be sold to a new owner **den Besitzer wechseln;** *the shop changed hands for £100,000*

◇ **changer** *noun* person who changes money **Geldwechsler**

channel *noun* way in which information or goods are passed from one place to another **Kanal, Weg; to go through the official channels** = to deal with government officials (especially when making a request) **den Amtsweg/Dienstweg beschreiten; to open up new channels of communication** = to find new ways of communicating with someone **neue Kommunikationswege erschließen; distribution channels** *or* **channels of distribution** = ways of sending goods from the manufacturer for sale by retailers **Vertriebswege**

charge

1 *noun*

(a) money which must be paid *or* price of a service **Gebühr, Kosten;** *to make no charge for delivery; to make a small charge for rental; there is no charge for service or no charge is made for service;* **admission charge** *or* **entry charge** = price to be paid before going into an exhibition, etc. **Eintritt(sgebühr); bank charges** = charges made by a bank for carrying out work for a customer **Bankgebühren; handling charge** = money to be paid for packing *or* invoicing *or* dealing with goods which are being shipped **Bearbeitungsgebühr; inclusive charge** = charge which includes all items **Gesamtgebühr, Pauschale; interest charges** = money paid as interest on a loan **Zinsbelastung, Sollzinsen; scale of charges** = list showing various prices **Gebührenordnung; service charge** = charge added to a bill in a restaurant to pay for service **Bedienung;** *a 10% service charge is added; does the bill include a service charge?;* **charge account** = arrangement which a customer has with a store to buy goods and to pay for them at a later date, usually when the invoice is sent at the end of the month **Kundenkreditkonto; charges forward** = charges which will be paid by the customer **Nachnahme; a token charge is made for heating** = a small charge is made which does not cover the real costs at all **nominelle Heizkostenpauschale; free of charge** = free *or* with no payment to be made **kostenlos, gebührenfrei**

(b) debit on an account **Belastung;** *it appears as a charge on the accounts*

(c) being formally accused in a court **Anklage;** *he appeared in court on a charge of embezzling or on an embezzlement charge*

2 *verb*

(a) to ask someone to pay for services later **in Rechnung stellen, berechnen; to charge the packing to the customer** *or* **to charge the customer with the packing** = the customer has to pay for packing **dem Kunden Verpackungskosten in Rechnung stellen**

(b) to ask for money to be paid **erheben, berechnen, in Rechnung stellen;** *to charge £5 for delivery; how much does he charge?;* **he charges £6 an hour** = he asks to be paid £6 for an hour's work **er nimmt £6 pro Stunde**

(c) *(in a court)* to accuse someone formally of having committed a crime **anklagen;** *he was charged with embezzling his clients' money*

◇ **chargeable** *adjective* which can be charged **anrechenbar, zu berechnen;** *repairs chargeable to the occupier;* **sums chargeable to the reserve** = sums which can be debited to a company's reserves **Beträge, die von den Rücklagen getragen werden**

◇ **chargee** *noun* person who has the right to force a debtor to pay **Gläubiger**

◇ **chargehand** *noun* chief of a group of workers under a foreman **Vorarbeiter**

> QUOTE traveller's cheques cost 1% of their face value - some banks charge more for small amounts
>
> *Sunday Times*

chart *noun* diagram showing information as a series of lines *or* blocks, etc. **Diagramm; bar chart** = diagram where quantities and values are shown as thick columns of different heights *or* lengths **Balken-, Stabdiagramm; flow chart** = diagram showing the arrangement of various work processes in a series **Arbeitsablauf-, Flußdiagramm; organization chart** = diagram showing how a company *or* an office is organized **Stellenbesetzungsplan; Diagramm der Unternehmensstruktur; pie chart** = diagram where information is shown as a circle cut up into sections of different sizes **Kreisdiagramm; sales chart** = diagram showing how sales vary from month to month **Umsatz-, Absatzdiagramm**

charter

1 *noun*

(a) bank charter = official government document allowing the establishment of a bank **Bankkonzession**

(b) hiring transport for a special purpose **Chartern; Charterung; charter flight** = flight in an aircraft which has been hired for that purpose **Charterflug; charter plane** = plane which has been chartered **Charterflugzeug; boat on charter to Mr Smith** = boat which Mr Smith has hired for a voyage **Boot, das von Mr Smith gechartert wurde**

2 *verb* to hire for a special purpose **chartern; mieten;** *to charter a plane or a boat or a bus*

◊ **chartered** *adjective*
(a) chartered accountant = accountant who has passed the professional examinations and is a member of the Institute of Chartered Accountants; *entspricht* **beeidigter Wirtschaftsprüfer**
(b) (company) which has been set up by charter, and not registered as a company **durch Hoheitsakt geschaffene Gesellschaft;** *a chartered bank*
(c) chartered ship *or* **plane** *or* **bus** = ship *or* bus *or* plane which has been hired for a special purpose **gechartertes Schiff od Flugzeug; gemieteter Bus**

◊ **charterer** *noun* person who hires a ship, etc., for a special purpose **Charterer; Mieter/-in**

◊ **chartering** *noun* act of hiring for a special purpose **Chartern; Mieten**

chartist *noun* person who studies stock market trends and forecasts future rises or falls **Chartist**

chase *verb*
(a) to run after someone *or* something to try to catch them **verfolgen, jagen**
(b) to try to speed up work by asking how it is progressing **antreiben, vorantreiben;** *we are trying to chase up the accounts department for the cheque; we will chase your order with the production department*

◊ **chaser** *noun*
(a) progress chaser = person whose job is to check that work is being carried out on schedule *or* that orders are fulfilled on time **Terminprüfer**
(b) letter to remind someone of something (especially to remind a customer that an invoice has not been paid) **Mahnung**

chattels *plural noun* goods *or* moveable property **bewegliches Eigentum, Mobiliar**

cheap *adjective & adverb* not costing a lot of money *or* not expensive **billig, preiswert; cheap labour** = workforce which does not earn much money **billige Arbeitskräfte;** *we have opened a factory in the Far East because of the cheap labour or because labour is cheap;* **cheap money** = money which can be borrowed at low interest **billiges Geld; cheap rate** = rate which is not expensive **niedriger Tarif;** *cheap rate phone calls;* **to buy something cheap** = at a low price **etwas billig/preiswert kaufen;** *he bought two companies cheap and sold them again at a profit;* **they work out cheaper by the box** = these items are cheaper per unit if you buy a box of them **sie kommen billiger pro Kiste**

◊ **cheaply** *adverb* without paying much money **billig;** *the salesman was living cheaply at home and claiming a high hotel bill on his expenses*

◊ **cheapness** *noun* being cheap **niedriger Preis; Schwäche;** *the cheapness of the pound means that many more tourists will come to London*
NOTE: no plural

cheat *verb* to trick someone so that he loses money **betrügen, übervorteilen;** *he cheated the Income Tax out of thousands of pounds; she was accused of cheating clients who came to ask her for advice*

check
1 *noun*
(a) sudden stop **Sperre, Hemmnis, Hindernis; Einhalt; to put a check on imports** = to stop some imports **Importe beschränken**
(b) check sample = sample to be used to see if a consignment is acceptable **Stichprobe**
(c) investigation *or* examination **Überprüfung, Kontrolle;** *the auditors carried out checks on the petty cash book; a routine check of the fire equipment;* **baggage check** = examination of passengers' baggage to see if it contains bombs **Gepäckkontrolle**
(d) *US (Restaurant)* bill **Rechnung**
(e) *US* = CHEQUE
(f) *US* mark on paper to show that something is correct **Haken;** *make a check in the box marked "R"*
2 *verb*
(a) to stop *or* to delay **hemmen, bremsen, lahmlegen;** *to check the entry of contraband into the country*
(b) to examine *or* to investigate **überprüfen, kontrollieren;** *to check that an invoice is correct; to check and sign for goods;* **he checked the computer printout against the invoices** = he examined the printout and the invoices to see if the figures were the same **er verglich den Computerausdruck mit den Rechnungen**
(c) *US* to mark with a sign to show that something is correct **abhaken;** *check the box marked "R"*

◊ **check in** *verb*
(a) *(Hotel)* to arrive at a hotel and sign for a room **sich anmelden;** *he checked in at 12.15*
(b) *(Flughafen)* to give in your ticket to show you are ready to take the flight **einchecken**
(c) to check baggage in = to pass your baggage to the airline to put it on the plane for you **Gepäck aufgeben**

◊ **check-in** *noun* place where passengers give in their tickets for a flight **Flugabfertigung;** *the check-in is on the first floor;* **check-in counter** = counter where passengers check in **Abfertigung(sschalter);**

check-in time = time at which passengers should check in **Eincheckzeit**

◇ **checking** *noun*

(a) examination *or* investigation **Überprüfung;** *the inspectors found some defects during their checking of the building*

(b) *US* **checking account** = bank account on which you can write cheques **laufendes Konto, Girokonto**

NOTE: no plural

◇ **checkoff** *noun US* system where union dues are automatically deducted by the employer from a worker's paycheck **Abzug der Gewerkschaftsbeiträge durch den Betrieb**

◇ **check out** *verb (Hotel)* to leave and pay for a room **abreisen;** *we will check out before breakfast*

◇ **checkout** *noun*

(a) *(Supermarkt)* place where you pay for the goods you have bought **Kasse**

(b) *(Hotel)* **checkout time is 12.00** = time by which you have to leave your room **um 12 Uhr müssen die Zimmer geräumt sein**

◇ **checkroom** *noun US* place where you leave your coat *or* luggage, etc. **Garderobe; Gepäckaufbewahrung**

cheque *noun* note to a bank asking them to pay money from your account to the account of the person whose name is written on the note **Scheck;** *a cheque for £10 or a £10 cheque;* **cheque account** = bank account which allows the customer to write cheques **laufendes Konto, Girokonto; cheque to bearer** = cheque with no name written on it, so that the person who holds it can cash it **Überbringer-, Inhaberscheck; crossed cheque** = cheque with two lines across it showing that it can only be deposited at a bank and not exchanged for cash **Verrechnungsscheck; open** *or* **uncrossed cheque** = cheque which can be cashed anywhere **Barscheck; blank cheque** = cheque with the amount of money and the payee left blank, but signed by the drawer **Blankoscheck; pay cheque** *or* **salary cheque** = monthly cheque by which an employee is paid **Lohn-, Gehaltsscheck; traveller's cheques** = cheques taken by a traveller, which can be cashed in a foreign country **Reiseschecks; dud cheque** *or* **bouncing cheque** *or* **cheque which bounces** *or US* **rubber check** = cheque which cannot be cashed because the person writing it has not enough money in the account to pay it **ungedeckter Scheck**

(b) to cash a cheque = to exchange a cheque for cash **einen Scheck einlösen; to endorse a cheque** = to sign a cheque on the back to show that you accept it **einen Scheck girieren; to make out a cheque to someone** = to write someone's name on a cheque **jdm einen Scheck ausstellen;** *who shall I make the cheque out to?;* **to pay by cheque** = to pay by writing a cheque, and not using cash or a credit card **mit (einem) Scheck bezahlen; to pay a cheque into your account** = to deposit a cheque **einen Scheck auf das Konto einzahlen; the bank referred the cheque to drawer** = returned the cheque to the person who wrote it because there was not enough money in the account to pay it **die Bank gab den Scheck zurück an den Aussteller; to sign a cheque** = to sign on the front of a cheque to show that you authorize the bank to pay the money from your account **einen Scheck unterschreiben; to stop a cheque** = to ask a bank not to pay a cheque which you have written **einen Scheck sperren lassen**

◇ **cheque book** *noun* booklet with new cheques **Scheckheft**

◇ **cheque guarantee card** *noun* plastic card from a bank which guarantees payment of a cheque up to a certain amount, even if there is no money in the account **Scheckkarte**

chief *adjective* most important **erster, höchster, Haupt-,;** *he is the chief accountant of an industrial group;* **chief executive** *or US* **chief executive officer** = executive in charge of a company; *entspricht* **geschäftsführender Direktor**

chip *noun*

(a) a computer chip = a small piece of silicon able to store data, used in computers **ein Computerchip**

(b) blue chip = very safe investment *or* risk-free share in a good company **Blue-chip**

chit *noun* bill (for food or drink in a club) **Bon, Gutschein**

choice

1 *noun*

(a) thing which is chosen **Wahl;** *you must give the customer time to make his choice*

(b) range of items to choose from **Auswahl, Sortiment;** *we have only a limited choice of suppliers;* **the shop carries a good choice of paper** = the shop carries many types of paper to choose from **das Geschäft hat eine gute Auswahl an Papieren**

2 *adjective* specially selected (food) **Qualitäts-;** *choice meat; choice wines; choice foodstuffs*

choose *verb* to decide to do a particular thing *or* to buy a particular item (as opposed to something else) **wählen, auswählen;** *there were several good candidates to choose from; they chose the only woman applicant as sales director; you*

must give the customers plenty of time to choose
NOTE: **choosing - chose - chosen**

chronic *adjective* permanently bad **chronisch;** *the company has chronic cash flow problems; we have a chronic shortage of skilled staff;* **chronic unemployment** = being unemployed for more than six months **Dauerarbeitslosigkeit**

chronological order *noun* arrangement of records (files, invoices, etc.) in order of their dates **chronologische Reihenfolge**

c.i.f. = COST, INSURANCE AND FREIGHT

circular
1 *adjective* sent to many people **Rund-; circular letter of credit** = letter of credit sent to all branches of the bank which issues it **Akkreditiv**
2 *noun* leaflet *or* letter sent to many people **Rundschreiben, Umlauf;** *they sent out a circular offering a 10% discount*

◇ **circularize** *verb* to send a circular to **Rundschreiben verschicken;** *the committee has agreed to circularize the members; they circularized all their customers with a new list of prices*

◇ **circulate** *verb*
(a) *(Geld)* **to circulate freely** = to move about without restriction by the government **in freiem Umlauf sein**
(b) to send *or* to give out without restrictions **in Umlauf bringen, zirkulieren lassen, verbreiten; to circulate money** = to issue money *or* to make money available to the public and industry **Geld in Umlauf bringen**
(c) to send information to **in Umlauf bringen;** *they circulated a new list of prices to all their customers*

◇ **circulating** *adjective* which is moving about freely **umlaufend, zirkulierend, im Umlauf befindlich; circulating capital** = capital required in cash, raw materials, finished products and work in progress for a company to carry on its business **Umlaufvermögen**

◇ **circulation** *noun*
(a) movement **Verbreitung;** *the company is trying to improve the circulation of information between departments;* **circulation of capital** = movement of capital from one investment to another **Kapitalverkehr**
(b) to put money into circulation = to issue new notes to business and the public **Geld in Umlauf/in den Verkehr bringen;** *the amount of money in circulation increased more than was expected*
(c) *(von Zeitungen)* number of copies sold **Auflage, Auflagenhöhe;** *the audited circulation of a newspaper; the new editor hopes to improve the circulation;* **a circulation battle** = competition between two papers to try to sell more copies in the same market **Kampf um die Auflagenhöhe verschiedener Zeitung**
NOTE: no plural for (a) and (b)

> QUOTE the level of currency in circulation increased to N4.9 billion in the month of August
> *Business Times (Lagos)*

city *noun*
(a) large town **Stadt, Großstadt;** *the largest cities in Europe are linked by hourly flights;* **capital city** = main town in a country, where the government is located **Hauptstadt; inter-city** = between cities **Intercity-;** *inter-city train services are often quicker than going by air*
(b) the City = old centre of London, where banks and large companies have their main offices; the British financial centre **die City, das Banken- und Börsenviertel in London;** *he works in the City or he is in the City;* **City desk** = section of a newspaper office which deals with business news **Finanz- und Wirtschaftsredaktion; City editor** = business *or* finance editor of a British paper **Finanz- und Wirtschaftsredakteur; they say in the City that the company has been sold** = the business world is saying that the company has been sold **in der City wird gesagt, daß das Unternehmen verkauft wurde**

civil *adjective* referring to ordinary people **bürgerlich, zivil-, Zivil-; civil action** = court case brought by a person *or* a company against someone who has done them wrong **Zivilprozeß, zivilrechtliche Klage; civil law** = laws relating to people's rights and agreements between individuals **Zivilrecht, bürgerliches Recht**

◇ **civil service** *noun* organization and personnel which administer a country **öffentlicher Dienst; Beamtenschaft;** *you have to pass an examination to get a job in the civil service or to get a civil service job*

◇ **civil servant** *noun* person who works in the civil service **Beamter im öffentlichen Dienst**

claim
1 *noun*
(a) asking for money **Forderung, Anspruch; wage claim** = asking for an increase in wages **Lohnforderung; the union put in a 6% wage claim** = the union asked for a 6%

increase in wages for its members **die Gewerkschaft forderte 6% mehr Lohn**
(b) legal claim = statement that you think you own something legally **Rechtsanspruch, rechtmäßiger Anspruch;** *he has no legal claim to the property*
(c) insurance claim = asking an insurance company to pay for damages *or* for loss **Versicherungsanspruch; claims department** = department of an insurance company which deals with claims **Schadenabteilung; claim form** = form to be filled in when making an insurance claim **Schadensformular, Antragsformular auf Schadensersatz; claims manager** = manager of a claims department **Leiter der Schadenabteilung; no claims bonus** = lower premium paid because no claims have been made against the insurance policy **Schadenfreiheitsrabatt; to put in a claim** = to ask the insurance company officially to pay damages **einen Anspruch geltend machen, Schadensansprüche stellen;** *to put in a claim for repairs to the car; she put in a claim for £250,000 damages against the driver of the other car;* **to settle a claim** = to agree to pay what is asked for **eine Forderung od einen Schadensersatz-, Versicherungsanspruch regulieren;** *the insurance company refused to settle his claim for storm damage*
(d) small claims court = court which deals with claims for small amounts of money **Gericht, das für Geldansprüche bis zu einer gewissen Höhe zuständig ist** *entspricht* **Amtsgericht**
2 *verb*
(a) to ask for money **fordern, einfordern;** *he claimed £100,000 damages against the cleaning firm; she claimed for repairs to the car against her insurance*
(b) to say that something is your property **Anspruch erheben auf;** *he is claiming possession of the house; no one claimed the umbrella found in my office*
(c) to state that something is a fact **behaupten;** *he claims he never received the goods; she claims that the shares are her property*

◊ **claimant** *noun* person who claims **Kläger/-in; Antrag-, Anspruchsteller/-in; rightful claimant** = person who has a legal claim to something **Anspruchsberechtigter**

◊ **claim back** *verb* to ask for money to be paid back **zurückfordern**

◊ **claimer** *noun* = CLAIMANT

◊ **claiming** *noun* act of making a claim **Anspruchstellung, Forderung**

class *noun* category *or* group into which things are classified according to quality or price **Kategorie, Klasse, Güteklasse; first-class** = top quality *or* most expensive **erstklassig;** *he is a first-class accountant;* **economy class** *or* **tourist class** = lower quality *or* less expensive way of travelling **Touristenklasse;** *I travel economy class because it is cheaper; tourist class travel is less comfortable than first class; he always travels first class because tourist class is too uncomfortable; GB* **first-class mail** = more expensive mail service, designed to be faster **Briefpost erster Klasse;** *a first-class letter should get to Scotland in a day;* **second-class mail** = less expensive, slower mail service **Briefpost zweiter Klasse;** *the letter took three days to arrive because he sent it second class*

classify *verb* to put into classes *or* categories **klassifizieren, einstufen; classified advertisements** = advertisements listed in a newspaper under special headings (such as "property for sale" or "jobs wanted") **Kleinanzeigen; classified directory** = book which lists businesses grouped under various headings (such as computer shops *or* newsagents) **Branchenverzeichnis**

◊ **classification** *noun* way of putting into classes **Klassifizierung, Einstufung; job classification** = describing jobs listed in various groups **Berufsklassifikation**

clause *noun* section of a contract **Klausel, Paragraph, Absatz;** *there are ten clauses in the contract; according to clause six, payments will not be due until next year;* **exclusion clause** = clause in an insurance policy *or* warranty which says which items are not covered by the policy **Ausschlußklausel, Freizeichnungsklausel; penalty clause** = clause which lists the penalties which will happen if the contract is not fulfilled **Strafklausel; termination clause** = clause which explains how and when a contract can be terminated **Kündigungsklausel**

claw back *verb* to take back money which has been allocated **sich zurückholen; zurückfordern;** *income tax claws back 25% of pensions paid out by the government; of the £1m allocated to the project, the government clawed back £100,000 in taxes*

◊ **clawback** *noun* money taken back **Zurückholung; Rückforderung**

clear
1 *adjective*
(a) easily understood **klar, deutlich, verständlich;** *he made it clear that he wanted the manager to resign; you will have to make it clear to the staff that productivity is falling*

(b) clear profit = profit after all expenses have been paid **Reingewinn;** *we made $6,000 clear profit on the sale*
(c) free *or* total period of time **frei; ganz; three clear days** = three whole working days **drei ganze/volle Tage;** *allow three clear days for the cheque to be paid into the bank*
2 *verb*
(a) to sell cheaply in order to get rid of stock **räumen, ausverkaufen;** *"demonstration models to clear"*
(b) to clear goods through the customs = to have all documentation passed by the customs so that goods can leave the country **Güter zollamtlich abfertigen**
(c) to clear 10% *or* **$5,000 on a deal** = to make 10% *or* $5,000 clear profit **bei einem Geschäft 10% od $5.000 Gewinn machen; we cleared only our expenses** = the sales revenue only paid for the costs and expenses without making any profit **wir konnten nur unsere Unkosten decken**
(d) to clear a cheque = to pass a cheque through the banking system, so that the money is transferred from the payer's account to another **einen Scheck einlösen;** *the cheque took ten days to clear or the bank took ten days to clear the cheque*

◇ **clearance** *noun*
(a) customs clearance = passing goods through the customs so that they can enter or leave the country **Zollabfertigung; to effect customs clearance** = to clear goods through the customs **die Zollabfertigung vornehmen; clearance certificate** = certificate showing that goods have been passed by the customs **Zollabfertigungs-, Ausklarierungsschein**
(b) clearance sale = sale of items at low prices to get rid of stock **Räumungsverkauf**
(c) clearance of a cheque = passing of a cheque through the banking system, transferring money from one account to another **Einlösen eines Schecks;** *you should allow six days for cheque clearance*

◇ **clearing** *noun*
(a) clearing of goods through the customs = passing of goods through the customs **Verzollung von Waren**
(b) clearing of a debt = paying all of a debt **Schuldenbegleichung, Schuldentilgung**
(c) clearing bank = bank which clears cheques, one of the major British High Street banks **Giro-, Abrechnungsbank, Clearingbank; clearing house** = central office where clearing banks exchange cheques **Abrechnungs-, Clearing-, Girokasse**

◇ **clear off** *verb* **to clear off a debt** = to pay all of a debt **Schulden begleichen/tilgen**

clerical *adjective* (work) done in an office *or* done by a clerk **Büro-, Schreib-; clerical error** = mistake made in an office **Schreibfehler; clerical staff** = staff of an office **Büropersonal, Schreibkräfte; clerical work** = paperwork done in an office **Schreib-, Büroarbeit; clerical worker** = person who works in an office **Büroangestellter**

clerk
1 *noun*
(a) person who works in an office **Büroangestellter, Sachbearbeiter; articled clerk** = clerk who is bound by a contract to work in a lawyer's office for some years to learn the trade **Anwaltsreferendar; chief clerk** *or* **head clerk** = most important clerk **Bürochef; filing clerk** = clerk who files documents **Angestellter in der Registratur; invoice clerk** = clerk who deals with invoices **Fakturist/-in; shipping clerk** = clerk who deals with shipping documents **Reedereiangestellter;** *US* **Spediteur**
(b) bank clerk = person who works in a bank **Bankangestellter; booking clerk** = person who works in a booking office **Kartenverkäufer;** *US* **sales clerk** = person who sells in a store **Verkäufer/-in**
2 *verb US* to work as a clerk **Verkäufer/-in sein**

◇ **clerkess** *noun (in Scotland)* woman clerk **Büroangestellte, Sachbearbeiterin**

clever *adjective* intelligent *or* able to learn quickly **klug, geschickt, schlau;** *he is very clever at spotting a bargain; clever investors have made a lot of money on the share deal*

client *noun* person with whom business is done *or* person who pays for a service **Kunde/Kundin, Auftraggeber/-in**

◇ **clientele** *noun* all the clients of a business; all the customers of a shop **Kundschaft, Kundenkreis, Klientel**
NOTE: no plural

climb *verb* to go up **steigen, klettern;** *the company has climbed to No. 1 position in the market; profits climbed rapidly as the new management cut costs*

clinch *verb* to settle (a business deal) *or* to come to an agreement **abschließen;** *he offered an extra 5% to clinch the deal; they need approval from the board before they can clinch the deal*

clipping service *noun* service of cutting out references to a client in newspapers or magazines and sending them to him **Presseausschnittdienst**

clock *noun* machine which shows the time **Uhr;** *the office clock is fast; the micro has a built-in clock;* **digital clock** = clock which shows the time using numbers (as 12:05) **Digitaluhr**

◇ **clock card** *noun* special card which a worker puts into the time clock when clocking on or off **Stechkarte**

◇ **clock in** *or* **clock on** *verb (Arbeiter)* to record the time of arriving for work by putting a card into a special timing machine **Arbeitsbeginn registrieren, stempeln**

◇ **clock out** *or* **clock off** *verb (Arbeiter)* to record the time of leaving work by putting a card into a special timing machine **Arbeitsschluß registrieren, stempeln**

◇ **clocking in** *or* **clocking on** *noun* arriving for work and recording the time on a time-card **Registrieren des Arbeitsbeginns, Stempeln**

◇ **clocking out** *or* **clocking off** *noun* leaving work and recording the time on a time-card **Registrieren des Arbeitsschlusses, Stempeln**

close

1 *noun* end **Schluß;** *at the close of the day's trading the shares had fallen 20%*
NOTE: no plural
2 *adjective* **close to** = very near *or* almost **nahe daran, fast;** *the company was close to bankruptcy; we are close to meeting our sales targets*
3 *verb* to end **beenden, schließen, abschließen**
(a) to stop doing business for the day **schließen, zumachen;** *the office closes at 5.30; we close early on Saturdays*
(b) to close the accounts = to come to the end of an accounting period and make up the profit and loss account **die Bücher abschließen**
(c) to close an account = (i) to stop supplying a customer on credit; (ii) to take all the money out of a bank account and stop the account **(i) ein Kundenkreditkonto sperren; (ii) ein Konto auflösen; he closed his building society account** = he took all the money out and stopped using the account **er löste sein Konto bei der Bausparkasse auf**
(d) the shares closed at $15 = at the end of the day's trading the price of the shares was $15 **die Aktien erreichten eine Schlußnotierung von $15**

◇ **close company** *or US* **close(d) corporation** *noun* privately owned company where the public may own a small number of shares **Personengesellschaft**

◇ **closed** *adjective*
(a) shut *or* not open *or* not doing business **geschlossen;** *the office is closed on Mondays; all the banks are closed on the National Day*
(b) closed shop = system where a company agrees to employ only union members in certain jobs **gewerkschaftspflichtiger Betrieb;** *a closed shop agreement; the union is asking the management to agree to a closed shop;* **closed market** = market where a supplier deals only with one agent *or* distributor and does not supply any others direct **geschlossener Markt;** *they signed a closed market agreement with an Egyptian company*

◇ **close down** *verb* to shut a shop *or* factory for a long period or for ever **schließen; stillegen;** *the company is closing down its London office; the strike closed down the railway system*

◇ **close-out sale** *noun US* selling goods cheaply to try to get rid of them **Räumungs-, Ausverkauf**

◇ **closing**
1 *adjective*
(a) final *or* coming at the end **Abschluß-, Schluß-, abschließend; closing bid** = last bid at an auction *or* the bid which is successful **Höchstgebot; closing date** = last date **Schließungstag;** *(für Inserate)* **Anzeigenschluß;** *(für Ausschreibungsangebot)* **Ausschreibungsschluß;** *the closing date for tenders to be received is May 1st;* **closing price** = price of a share at the end of a day's trading **Schlußkurs, Schlußnotierung**
(b) at the end of an accounting period **Abschluß-;** *closing balance; closing stock*
2 *noun*
(a) shutting of a shop *or* being shut **Schließung; Sunday closing** = not opening a shop on Sundays **geschäftsfreier Sonntag; closing time** = time when a shop or office stops work **Geschäftsschluß; Ladenschluß; early closing day** = weekday (usually Wednesday or Thursday) when many shops close in the afternoon **Tag mit frühem Ladenschluß**
(b) closing of an account = act of stopping supply to a customer on credit **Sperrung eines Kundenkreditkontos**
NOTE: no plural

◇ **closing down** *noun* **closing-down sale** = sale of goods when a shop is closing for ever **Totalaus-, Räumungsverkauf**

◇ **closure** *noun* act of closing **Schließung; Stillegung**

> QUOTE Toronto stocks closed at an all-time high, posting their fifth straight day of advances in heavy trading
> *Financial Times*
>
> QUOTE the best thing would be to have a few more plants close down and bring supply more in line with current demand
> *Fortune*

club *noun* group of people who have the same interest; place where these people meet **Klub, Verein;** *if you want the managing director, you can phone him at his club; he has applied to join the sports club;* **club**

membership = all the members of a club **Klub-, Vereinsmitgliedschaft; club subscription** = money paid to belong to a club **Klub-, Vereins-, Mitgliedsbeitrag; staff club** = club for the staff of a company, which organizes staff parties, sports and meetings **Betriebsverein**

cm = CENTIMETRE

c/o = CARE OF

Co. = COMPANY *J. Smith & Co. Ltd*

co- *prefix* working *or* acting together **Mit-, mit-**
◇ **co-creditor** *noun* person who is a creditor of the same company as you are **Solidargläubiger**
◇ **co-director** *noun* person who is a director of the same company as you **Mitdirektor**
◇ **co-insurance** *noun* insurance policy where the risk is shared among several insurers **Mitversicherung**

COD *or* **c.o.d.** = CASH ON DELIVERY

code *noun*
(a) system of signs *or* numbers *or* letters which mean something **Code, Chiffre; area code** = numbers which indicate an area for telephoning **Vorwahl, Ortsnetzkennzahl;** *what is the code for Edinburgh?;* **bar code** = system of lines printed on a product which can be read by a computer to give a reference number or price **Strichkodierung, Bar-Code; international dialling code** = numbers used for dialling to another country **Auslandsvorwahl; machine-readable codes** = sets of signs or letters (such as bar codes *or* post codes) which can be read by computers **maschinenlesbare Codes; post code** *or US* **zip code** = letters and numbers used to indicate a town or street in an address on an envelope **Postleitzahl; stock code** = numbers and letters which refer to an item of stock **Warencode**
(b) set of rules **Kodex; code of practice** = rules drawn up by an association which the members must follow when doing business **Richtlinien**
◇ **coding** *noun* act of putting a code on something **Kodierung; Verschlüsselung, Chiffrierung;** *the coding of invoices*

coin *noun* piece of metal money **Münze, Geldstück;** *he gave me two 10-franc coins in my change; I need some 10p coins for the telephone*
◇ **coinage** *noun* system of metal money used in a country **Hartgeldwährung**
NOTE: no plural

cold *adjective*
(a) not hot **kalt;** *the machines work badly in cold weather; the office was so cold that the staff started complaining; the coffee machine also sells cold drinks*
(b) without being prepared **unvorbereitet; cold call** = sales call where the salesman has no appointment and the client is not an established customer **unangemeldeter Vertreterbesuch; cold start** = starting a new business *or* opening a new shop where there was none before **ein völliger Neubeginn**

collaborate *verb* to work together **zusammenarbeiten;** *to collaborate with a French firm on a building project; they collaborated on the new aircraft*
NOTE: you collaborate **with** someone **on** something
◇ **collaboration** *noun* working together **Zusammenarbeit;** *their collaboration on the project was very profitable*
NOTE: no plural

collapse
1 *noun*
(a) sudden fall in price **Sturz, Zusammenbruch;** *the collapse of the market in silver; the collapse of the dollar on the foreign exchange markets*
(b) sudden failure of a company **Zusammenbruch;** *investors lost thousands of pounds in the collapse of the company*
2 *verb*
(a) to fall suddenly **zusammenbrechen;** *the market collapsed; the yen collapsed on the foreign exchange markets*
(b) to fail suddenly **zusammenbrechen;** *the company collapsed with £25,000 in debts*

collar *noun* part of a coat *or* shirt which goes round the neck **Kragen; blue-collar worker** = manual worker in a factory **Arbeiter/-in; white-collar worker** = office worker **Büroangestellter; he has a white-collar job** = he works in an office **er hat eine Stelle im Büro**

collateral
1 *noun* (security) used to provide a guarantee for a loan **Sicherheit, Deckung**
2 *adjective* in addition **zusätzlich, Zusatz-, Neben-**

> QUOTE examiners have come to inspect the collateral that thrifts may use in borrowing from the Fed
> *Wall Street Journal*

collect
1 *verb*

(a) to make someone pay money which is owed **einziehen, eintreiben; to collect a debt** = to go and make someone pay a debt **Schulden einziehen/eintreiben**
(b) to take things away from a place **abholen;** *we have to collect the stock from the warehouse; can you collect my letters from the typing pool?;* **letters are collected twice a day** = the post office workers take them from the letter box to the post office for dispatch **die Briefkästen werden zweimal täglich geleert**
2 *adverb & adjective US* **collect call** phone call where the person receiving the call agrees to pay for it **R-Gespräch;** *to make a collect call; he called his office collect*

◊ **collecting agency** *noun* agency which collects money owed to other companies for a commission **Inkassobüro**

◊ **collection** *noun*
(a) getting money together *or* making someone pay money which is owed **Einziehung, Eintreibung;** *tax collection or collection of tax;* **debt collection** = collecting money which is owed **Schuldeneintreibung, Forderungseinziehung; debt collection agency** = company which collects debts for other companies for a commission **Inkassobüro; bills for collection** = bills where payment is due **fällige Rechnungen; fälliger Inkassowechsel**
(b) fetching of goods **Abholung;** *the stock is in the warehouse awaiting collection;* **collection charges** *or* **collection rates** = charge for collecting something **Abholgebühren; to hand something in for collection** = to leave something for someone to come and collect **etwas für jdn hinterlegen**
(c) collections = money which has been collected **Sammlung**
(d) taking of letters from a letter box or mail room to the post office for dispatch **Leerung;** *there are six collections a day from the letter box*

◊ **collective** *adjective* working together **gemeinsam, Gemeinschafts-; free collective bargaining** = negotiations about wage increases and working conditions between management and trade unions **autonome Tarifverhandlungen; collective farm** = state-owned farm which is run by the workers **landwirtschaftliche Produktionsgenossenschaft; collective ownership** = ownership of a business by the workers who work in it **Kollektivinhaberschaft; they signed a collective wage agreement** = an agreement was signed between management and the trade union about wages **sie haben einen Lohntarifvertrag unterzeichnet**

◊ **collector** *noun* person who makes people pay money which is owed **Inkassobeauftragter; Schuldeneintreiber; Einziehungsbeamter;** *collector of taxes or tax collector; debt collector*

college *noun* place where people can study after they have left full-time school **College, Institut; business college** = college which teaches general business methods **Wirtschaftsinstitut; commercial college** college which teaches general business methods **Handelsinstitut; secretarial college** = college which teaches shorthand, typing and word-processing **Sekretärinnenschule**

column *noun*
(a) series of numbers, one under the other **Kolonne, Spalte;** *to add up a column of figures; put the total at the bottom of the column;* **credit column** = right-hand side in accounts showing money received **Kreditspalte; debit column** = left-hand side in accounts showing money paid or owed **Debetspalte**
(b) section of printed words in a newspaper *or* magazine **Kolumne, Spalte; column-centimetre** = space in centimetres in a newspaper column, used for calculating charges for advertising **Zentimeterpreis**

combine
1 *noun* large financial or commercial group **Verband, Kartell;** *a German industrial combine*
2 *verb* to join together **sich zusammenschließen;** *the workforce and management combined to fight the takeover bid*

◊ **combination** *noun*
(a) several things which are joined together **Kombination, Verbindung;** *a combination of cash flow problems and difficult trading conditions caused the company's collapse*
(b) series of numbers which open a special lock **Kombination;** *I have forgotten the combination of the lock on my briefcase; the office safe has a combination lock*

comfort *noun* **letter of comfort** *or* **comfort letter** = letter supporting someone who is trying to get a loan **Bonitätsbestätigung**

commerce *noun* business *or* buying and selling of goods and services **Handel, Handelsverkehr; Chamber of Commerce** = group of local businessmen who meet to discuss problems which they have in common and to promote business in their town **Handelskammer**

◊ **commercial**
1 *adjective*
(a) referring to business **Handels-,**

Geschäfts-, kommerziell; commercial aircraft = aircraft used to carry cargo *or* passengers for payment **Verkehrsflugzeug; commercial artist** = artist who designs advertisements *or* posters, etc. for payment **Werbegrafiker; commercial attaché** = diplomat who represents and tries to promote his country's business interests **Handelsattaché; commercial college** = college which teaches business studies **Handelsinstitut; commercial course** = course where business skills are studied **kaufmännischer Lehrgang;** *he took a commercial course by correspondence;* **commercial directory** = book which lists all the businesses and business people in a town **Branchenadreßbuch; commercial district** = part of a town where offices and shops are **Gewerbegebiet; commercial law** = laws regarding business **Handelsrecht (Teil des Wirtschaftsrechts); commercial port** = port which has only goods traffic **Handelshafen; commercial traveller** = salesman who travels round an area visiting customers on behalf of his company **Handelsvertreter; commercial vehicle** = van *or* truck, etc. used for business purposes **Nutzfahrzeug; sample only - of no commercial value** = not worth anything if sold **unverkäufliche Warenprobe**
(b) profitable **wirtschaftlich, gewinnbringend; not a commercial proposition** = not likely to make a profit **kein gewinnbringendes Geschäft; commercial load** = amount of goods *or* number of passengers which a bus *or* train *or* plane has to carry to make a profit **wirtschaftliche Auslastung**
2 *noun* advertisement on television **Werbespot, Werbung**

◇ **commercialization** *noun* making something into a business proposition **Kommerzialisierung;** *the commercialization of museums*
NOTE: no plural

◇ **commercialize** *verb* to make something into a business **kommerzialisieren;** *the holiday town has become so commercialized that it is unpleasant*

◇ **commercially** *adverb* in a business way **geschäftlich, gewerblich, kommerziell; not commercially viable** = not likely to make a profit **unrentabel**

commission *noun*
(a) money paid to a salesman *or* an agent, usually a percentage of the sales made **Provision, Kommission(sgebühr), Maklergebühr;** *she gets 10% commission on everything she sells;* **he charges 10% commission** = he asks for 10% of sales as his payment **er erhebt 10% Provision; commission agent** = agent who is paid a percentage of sales **Provisionsagent; commission rep** = representative who is not paid a salary, but receives a commission on sales **Provisionsvertreter; commission sale** *or* **sale on commission** = sale where the salesman is paid a commission **Verkauf auf Kommissionsbasis**
(b) group of people officially appointed to examine some problem **Kommission, Ausschuß;** *the government has appointed a commission of inquiry to look into the problems of small exporters; he is the chairman of the government commission on export subsidies*

commit *verb* to carry out (a crime) **begehen**
NOTE: **committing - committed**

committee *noun* official group of people who organize or plan for a larger group **Ausschuß, Gremium, Komitee;** *to be a member of a committee or to sit on a committee; he was elected to the committee of the staff club; the new plans have to be approved by the committee members;* **to chair a committee** = to be the chairman of a committee **einem Ausschuß/Gremium/Komitee vorsitzen;** *he is the chairman of the planning committee; she is the secretary of the finance committee;* **management committee** = committee which manages a club *or* a pension fund,etc. **geschäftsführender Ausschuß; Vorstandsgremium**

commodity *noun* thing sold in very large quantities, especially raw materials and food such as metals or corn **Ware; primary** *or* **basic commodities** = farm produce grown in large quantities, such as corn, rice, cotton **Grundstoffe; staple commodity** = basic food or raw material which is most important in a country's economy **Haupterzeugnis; commodity market** *or* **commodity exchange** = place where people buy and sell commodities **Warenbörse; commodity futures** = trading in commodities for delivery at a later date **Warentermingeschäft;** *silver rose 5% on the commodity futures market yesterday;* **commodity trader** = person whose business is buying and selling commodities **Warenterminhändler**

common *adjective*
(a) which happens very often **häufig, weitverbreitet, allgemein, normal;** *putting the carbon paper in the wrong way round is a common mistake; being caught by the customs is very common these days*
(b) belonging to several different people or to everyone **gemeinsam, Gemeinschafts-, Gemein-; common carrier** = firm which carries goods or passengers, and which anyone can use **Spedition,**

Transportunternehmen; Verkehrsunternehmen; common ownership = ownership of a company *or* a property by a group of people **Miteigentum; common pricing** = illegal fixing of prices by several businesses so that they all charge the same price **Preisabsprache;** *US* **common stock** = ordinary shares in a company, giving shareholders a right to vote at meetings and to receive dividends **Stammaktien;** *(EG)* **Common Agricultural Policy** = agreement between members of the EEC to protect farmers by paying subsidies to fix prices of farm produce **Agrarpolitik der Europäischen Gemeinschaft**

◇ **Common Market** *noun* **the Common Market** = the European Community *or* organization which links several European countries for the purposes of trade **der Gemeinsame Markt; the Common Market finance ministers** = the finance ministers of all the Common Market countries meeting as a group **die Finanzminister der Europäischen Gemeinschaft**

communicate *verb* to pass information to someone **sich verständigen, kommunizieren;** *he finds it impossible to communicate with his staff; communicating with head office has been quicker since we installed the telex*

◇ **communication** *noun*
(a) passing of information **Verständigung, Kommunikation;** *communication with the head office has been made easier by the telex;* **to enter into communication with someone** = to start discussing something with someone, usually in writing **mit jdm in Verbindung treten;** *we have entered into communication with the relevant government department*
(b) official message **Mitteilung;** *we have had a communication from the local tax inspector*
(c) communications = being able to contact people *or* to pass messages **Verbindungen, Verkehrsverbindung;** *after the flood all communications with the outside world were broken*

community *noun*
(a) group of people living or working in the same place **Gemeinschaft; Gemeinde; the local business community** = the business people living and working in the area **die örtliche Geschäftswelt**
(b) the European Community = the Common Market **die Europäische Gemeinschaft; the Community ministers** = the ministers of member states of the Common Market **die Minister der Europäischen Gemeinschaft**

commute *verb*
(a) to travel to work from home each day **pendeln;** *he commutes from the country to his office in the centre of town*
(b) to change a right into cash **umwandeln;** *he decided to commute part of his pension rights into a lump sum payment*

◇ **commuter** *noun* person who commutes to work **Pendler/-in; he lives in the commuter belt** = area of country where the commuters live round a town **er wohnt im städtischen Einzugsbereich/Einzugsgebiet; commuter train** = train which commuters take in the morning and evening **Pendler-, Nahverkehrszug**

company *noun* business *or* group of people organized to buy, sell or provide a service **Firma, Unternehmen; Gesellschaft**
(a) to put a company into liquidation = to close a company by selling its assets for cash **ein Unternehmen liquidieren; to set up a company** = to start a company legally **eine Firma gründen; associate company** = company which is partly owned by another company **Beteiligungsgesellschaft; family company** = company where most of the shares are owned by members of a family **Familienunternehmen; holding company** = company which exists only to own shares in subsidiary companies **Dach-, Holdinggesellschaft; joint-stock company** = company whose shares are held by many people **Aktiengesellschaft (die nicht an der Börse notiert ist); limited (liability) company** = company where a shareholder is responsible for repaying the company's debts only to the face value of the shares he owns; *entspricht* **Gesellschaft mit beschränkter Haftung; listed company** = company whose shares can be bought or sold on the Stock Exchange **börsenfähiges/an der Börse notiertes Unternehmen; parent company** = company which owns more than half of another company's shares **Muttergesellschaft; private (limited) company** = company with a small number of shareholders, whose shares are not traded on the Stock Exchange; *entspricht* **Gesellschaft mit beschränkter Haftung; public limited company (plc)** = company whose shares can be bought on the Stock Exchange; *entspricht* **Aktiengesellschaft; subsidiary company** = company which is owned by a parent company **Tochtergesellschaft**
(b) finance company = company which provides money for hire-purchase **Finanzierungsgesellschaft; insurance company** = company whose business is insurance **Versicherungsgesellschaft; shipping company** = company whose business is in transporting goods **Reederei; a tractor** *or* **chocolate company** = company

which makes tractors *or* chocolate **Traktorenhersteller; Schokoladenhersteller**
(c) company car = car which belongs to a company and is lent to an employee to use personally **Firmenwagen; company doctor** = (i) doctor who works for a company and looks after sick workers; (ii) specialist businessman who rescues companies which are in difficulties **(i) Betriebsarzt; (ii) Krisenmanager; company director** = person appointed by the shareholders to help run a company **geschäftsführender Direktor/Manager;** *(AG)* **Vorstandsvorsitzender; company law** = laws which refer to the way companies may work **Unternehmensrecht;** *GB* **company secretary** = person responsible for the company's legal and financial affairs **Manager mit Aufgabenbereich Finanzen und Verwaltung;** *GB* **the Companies Act** = Act of Parliament which states the legal limits within which companies may do their business; *entspricht* **Unternehmensrecht**

compare *verb* to look at several things to see how they differ **vergleichen;** *the finance director compared the figures for the first and second quarters*

◇ **compare with** *verb* to put two things together to see how they differ **vergleichen mit;** *how do the sales this year compare with last year's? compared with 1982, last year was a boom year*

◇ **comparable** *adjective* which can be compared **vergleichbar, Vergleichs-;** *the two sets of figures are not comparable;* **which is the nearest company comparable to this one in size?** = which company is of a similar size and can be compared with this one? **welches Unternehmen ist von vergleichbarer Größe?**

◇ **comparability** *noun* being able to be compared **Vergleichbarkeit; pay comparability** = similar pay system in two different companies **Vergleichslohn**
NOTE: no plural

◇ **comparison** *noun* way of comparing **Vergleich;** *sales are down in comparison with last year;* **there is no comparison between overseas and home sales** = overseas and home sales are so different they cannot be compared **die Verkaufzahlen des Inlandes lassen sich nicht mit den Exportziffern vergleichen**

compensate *verb* to pay for damage done **entschädigen;** *to compensate a manager for loss of commission*
NOTE: you compensate someone **for** something

◇ **compensation** *noun*
(a) compensation for damage = payment for damage done **Schadensersatz; compensation for loss of earnings** = payment to someone who has stopped earning money *or* who is not able to earn money **Verdienstausfallentschädigung; compensation for loss of office** = payment to a director who is asked to leave a company before his contract ends **Entlassungsabfindung**
(b) *US* salary **Lohn, Gehalt; Vergütung; compensation package** = salary, pension and other benefits offered with a job **Gesamtvergütung**

> QUOTE it was rumoured that the government was prepared to compensate small depositors
> ***South China Morning Post***
> QUOTE golden parachutes are liberal compensation packages given to executives leaving a company
> ***Publishers Weekly***

compete *verb* **to compete with someone** *or* **with a company** = to try to do better than another person *or* another company **mit jdm od mit einem Unternehmen konkurrieren;** *we have to compete with cheap imports from the Far East; they were competing unsuccessfully with local companies on their home territory;* **the two companies are competing for a market share** *or* **for a contract** = each company is trying to win a larger part of the market *or* to win the contract **die beiden Unternehmen stehen in Konkurrenz um einen Marktanteil od einen Vertrag**

◇ **competing** *adjective* which competes **konkurrierend; competing firms** = firms which compete with each other **konkurrierende Unternehmen; competing products** = products from different companies which have the same use and are sold in the same markets at similar prices **Konkurrenzprodukte**

◇ **competition** *noun*
(a) trying to do better than another supplier **Wettbewerb, Konkurrenz; free competition** = being free to compete without government interference **freier Wettbewerb; keen competition** = strong competition **scharfer Wettbewerb;** *we are facing keen competition from European manufacturers*
(b) the competition = companies which are trying to compete with your product **die Konkurrenz;** *we have lowered our prices to beat the competition; the competition have brought out a new range of products*
NOTE: singular, but can take a plural verb

◇ **competitive** *adjective* which competes fairly **wettbewerbs-, konkurrenzfähig; competitive price** = low price aimed to compete with a rival product **wettbewerbs-, konkurrenzfähiger Preis; competitive pricing** = putting low prices on goods so as to compete with other products **wettbewerbs-, konkurrenzfähige Auspreisung; competitive**

products = products made to compete with existing products **Konkurrenzartikel, Konkurrenzprodukte; konkurrenzfähige Produkte**

◇ **competitively** *adverb* **competitively priced** = sold at a low price which competes with the price of similar products from other companies **mit wettbewerbsfähigen Preisen**

◇ **competitiveness** *noun* being competitive **Wettbewerbs-, Konkurrenzfähigkeit**

NOTE: no plural

◇ **competitor** *noun* person *or* company which competes **Konkurrent/-in;** *two German firms are our main competitors*

> QUOTE profit margins in the industries most exposed to foreign competition are worse than usual
>
> *Sunday Times*
>
> QUOTE competition is steadily increasing and could affect profit margins as the company tries to retain its market share
>
> *Citizen (Ottawa)*
>
> QUOTE the company blamed fiercely competitive market conditions in Europe for a £14m operating loss last year
>
> *Financial Times*
>
> QUOTE farmers are increasingly worried by the growing lack of competitiveness for their products on world markets
>
> *Australian Financial Review*
>
> QUOTE sterling labour costs continue to rise between 3% and 5% a year faster than in most of our competitor countries
>
> *Sunday Times*

competence *or* competency *noun*

the case falls within the competence of the court = the court is legally able to deal with the case **der Rechtsfall fällt in die Zuständigkeit des Gerichts**

◇ **competent** *adjective*

(a) able to do something *or* efficient **fähig, kompetent;** *she is a competent secretary or a competent manager*

(b) the court is not competent to deal with this case = the court is not legally able to deal with the case **das Gericht ist nicht zuständig für diesen Rechtsfall**

complain *verb*

to say that something is no good *or* does not work properly **sich beschweren, sich beklagen;** *the office is so cold the staff have started complaining; she complained about the service; they are complaining that our prices are too high; if you want to complain, write to the manager*

◇ **complaint** *noun* statement that you feel something is wrong **Beschwerde;** *when making a complaint, always quote the reference number; she sent her letter of complaint to the managing director;* **to make** *or* **lodge a complaint against someone** = to write and send an official complaint to someone's superior **gegen jdn Beschwerde einlegen; complaints department** = department which deals with complaints from customers **Beschwerde-, Reklamationsabteilung; complaints procedure** = agreed way for workers to make complaints to the management about working conditions **Beschwerdeweg**

complete

1 *adjective* whole *or* with nothing missing **komplett, vollständig;** *the order is complete and ready for sending; the order should be delivered only if it is complete*

2 *verb* to finish **beenden, fertigstellen;** *the factory completed the order in two weeks; how long will it take you to complete the job?*

◇ **completely** *adverb* all *or* totally **völlig, vollkommen;** *the cargo was completely ruined by water; the warehouse was completely destroyed by fire*

◇ **completion** *noun* act of finishing something **Beendigung, Abschluß, Fertigstellung; completion date** = date when something will be finished **Abschlußtermin; completion of a contract** = signing of a contract for the sale of a property when the buyer pays and the seller passes ownership to the buyer **Vertragsabschluß**

complex

1 *noun* series of large buildings **Komplex;** *a large industrial complex*

NOTE: plural is **complexes**

2 *adjective* with many different parts **komplex, differenziert;** *a complex system of import controls; the specifications for the machine are very complex*

complimentary *adjective*

complimentary ticket = free ticket, given as a present **Freikarte**

◇ **compliments slip** *noun* piece of paper with the name of the company printed on it, sent with documents *or* gifts, etc. instead of a letter **Kurzmitteilung**

comply *verb*

to comply with a court order = to obey an order given by a court **sich an einen Gerichtsbeschluß halten**

◇ **compliance** *noun* agreement to do what is ordered **Befolgung, Einhaltung**

NOTE: no plural

component *noun*

piece of machinery *or* section which will be put into a final product **Bestandteil;** *the assembly line stopped because supply of a component was delayed;* **components factory** = factory which makes parts which are used in other factories to make finished products **Zulieferant**

composition *noun* agreement between a debtor and creditors to settle a debt by repaying only part of it **Vergleich**

compound
1 *adjective* **compound interest** = interest which is added to the capital and then earns interest itself **Zinseszins(en)**
2 *verb* to agree with creditors to settle a debt by paying part of what is owed **einen Vergleich schließen**

comprehensive *adjective* which includes everything **umfassend; comprehensive insurance** = insurance policy which covers you against all risks which are likely to happen **kombinierte Haftpflicht- und Vollkaskoversicherung**

compromise
1 *noun* agreement between two sides, where each side gives way a little **Kompromiß;** *management offered £5 an hour, the union asked for £9, and a compromise of £7.50 was reached*
2 *verb* to reach an agreement by giving way a little **einen Kompromiß schließen;** *he asked £15 for it, I offered £7 and we compromised on £10*

comptometer *noun* machine which counts automatically **Zählmaschine**

comptroller *noun* financial controller **Rechnungsprüfer**

compulsory *adjective* which is forced *or* ordered **obligatorisch, verbindlich, Pflicht-, Zwangs-; compulsory liquidation** = liquidation which is ordered by a court **Zwangsliquidation**

compute *verb* to calculate *or* to do calculations **aus-, be-, errechnen, kalkulieren, überschlagen**

◇ **computable** *adjective* which can be calculated **be-, errechen-, kalkulier-, überschlagbar**

◇ **computation** *noun* calculation **Be-, Errechnung, Kalkulation, Überschlag**

◇ **computational** *adjective* **computational error** = mistake made in calculating **Rechen-, Berechnungsfehler**

◇ **computer** *noun* electronic machine which calculates *or* stores information and processes it automatically **Computer, Rechner; computer bureau** = office which offers to do work on its computers for companies which do not have their own computers **Rechenzentrum; EDV-Servicebüro; computer department** = department in a company which manages the company's computers **EDV-Abteilung; computer error** = mistake made by a computer **Computerfehler; computer file** = section of information on a computer (such as the payroll, list of addresses, customer accounts) **Computerdatei; computer language** = system of signs, letters and words used to instruct a computer **Computersprache; computer listing** = printout of a list of items taken from data stored in a computer **Computerausdruck; computer manager** = person in charge of a computer department **Leiter der EDV-Abteilung; computer program** = instructions to a computer, telling it to do a particular piece of work **Computerprogramm; computer programmer** = person who writes computer programs **Computerprogrammierer, Programmierer; computer services** = work using a computer, done by a computer bureau **EDV-Service; computer time** = time when a computer is being used (paid for at an hourly rate) **Betriebszeit;** *running all those sales reports costs a lot in computer time;* **business computer** = powerful small computer which is programmed for special business uses **kommerzieller Rechner; personal computer** *or* **home computer** = small computer which can be used in the home **Personalcomputer, PC**

◇ **computerize** *verb* to change from a manual system to one using computers **computerisieren, auf Computer/Datenverarbeitung/EDV umstellen;** *our stock control has been completely computerized*

◇ **computerized** *adjective* worked by computers **computerisiert, EDV-;** *a computerized invoicing system*

◇ **computer-readable** *adjective* which can be read and understood by a computer **maschinell lesbar;** *computer-readable codes*

◇ **computing** *noun* referring to computers **Computer-, Rechen-, Datenverarbeitungs-, EDV-; computing speed** = speed at which a computer calculates **Rechengeschwindigkeit**

con
1 *noun informal* trick done to try to get money from someone **Schwindel, Trick;** *trying to get us to pay him for ten hours' overtime was just a con*
2 *verb informal* to trick someone to try to get money **jdn durch einen Trick dazu bringen, etwas zu tun;** *they conned the bank into lending them £25,000 with no security; he conned the finance company out of £100,000*
NOTE: **con - conning - conned**

concealment *noun* hiding for criminal purposes **Unterschlagung, Verschleierung; concealment of assets** = hiding assets so that creditors do not know they exist **Vermögensverschleierung**

concern
1 *noun*
(a) business *or* company **Konzern; his business is a going concern** = the company is working (and making a profit) **er hat ein dynamisches Unternehmen; sold as a going concern** = sold as an actively trading company **als rentables Unternehmen verkauft**
(b) being worried about a problem **Besorgnis, Sorge, Anteil, Interesse;** *the management showed no concern at all for the workers' safety*
2 *verb* to deal with *or* to be connected with **betreffen, angehen, zu tun haben mit;** *the sales staff are not concerned with the cleaning of the store; he filled in a questionnaire concerning computer utilization*

concession *noun*
(a) right to use someone else's property for business purposes **Konzession; mining concession** = right to dig a mine on a piece of land **Abbaurecht, Bergbaukonzession**
(b) right to be the only seller of a product in a place **Alleinvertrieb;** *she runs a jewellery concession in a department store*
(c) allowance **Vergünstigung; tax concession** = allowing less tax to be paid **Steuervergünstigung**
◇ **concessionnaire** *noun* person who has the right to be the only seller of a product in a place **Konzessionär**
◇ **concessionary** *adjective* **concessionary fare** = reduced fare for certain types of passenger (such as employees of the transport company) **Vorzugsfahrpreis**

conciliation *noun* bringing together the parties in a dispute so that the dispute can be settled **Schlichtung**

conclude *verb*
(a) to complete successfully **abschließen;** *to conclude an agreement with someone*
(b) to believe from evidence **schlußfolgern, zu dem Schluß kommen;** *the police concluded that the thief had got into the building through the main entrance*

condition *noun*
(a) term of a contract *or* duties which have to be carried out as part of a contract *or* something which has to be agreed before a contract becomes valid **Bedingung, Kondition, Auflage; conditions of employment** *or* **conditions of service** = terms of a contract of employment **Arbeitsvertragsbedingungen; conditions of sale** = agreed ways in which a sale takes place (such as discounts *or* credit terms) **Verkaufsbedingungen; on condition that** = provided that **unter der Bedingung, daß ...;** *they were granted the lease on condition that they paid the legal costs*
(b) general state **Zustand, Bedingungen;** *the union has complained of the bad working conditions in the factory; item sold in good condition; what was the condition of the car when it was sold? adverse trading conditions*
◇ **conditional** *adjective* provided that certain things take place **mit Auflagen, unter Vorbehalt, bedingt; to give a conditional acceptance** = to accept, provided that certain things happen *or* certain terms apply **unter Vorbehalt annehmen; the offer is conditional on the board's acceptance** = provided the board accepts **das Angebot ist abhängig von der Zustimmung des Vorstands; he made a conditional offer** = he offered to buy, provided that certain terms applied **er machte ein bedingtes Angebot**

condominium *noun US* system of ownership, where a person owns an apartment in a building, together with a share of the land, stairs, roof, etc. **Eigentumswohnung**

conduct *verb* to carry on **leiten, führen;** *to conduct negotiations; the chairman conducted the negotiations very efficiently*

conference *noun*
(a) meeting of people to discuss problems **Konferenz, Besprechung, Tagung; to be in conference** = to be in a meeting **sich in einer Konferenz/Besprechung befinden; conference phone** = telephone so arranged that several people can speak into it from around a table **Konferenztelefon: Lautfernsprecher mit Freisprecheinrichtung; conference room** = room where small meetings can take place **Besprechungszimmer; press conference** = meeting where newspaper and TV reporters are invited to hear news of a new product *or* a takeover bid, etc. **Pressekonferenz; sales conference** = meeting of sales managers, representatives, publicity staff, etc., to discuss future sales plans **Konferenz zur Absatzförderung**
(b) meeting of an association *or* a society *or* a union **Konferenz, Tagung;** *the annual conference of the Electricians' Union; the conference of the Booksellers' Association; the conference agenda or the agenda of the conference was drawn up by the secretary;* **Trades Union Congress** = annual meeting of TUC **jährliche Tagung des TUC**

confidence *noun*

(a) feeling sure *or* being certain **Vertrauen;** *the sales teams do not have much confidence in their manager; the board has total confidence in the managing director*
(b) in confidence = in secret **vertraulich;** *I will show you the report in confidence*

◇ **confidence trick** *noun* business deal where someone gains another person's confidence and then tricks him **Schwindel, Bauernfängerei, Betrug**

◇ **confidence trickster** *noun* person who carries out a confidence trick on someone **Schwindler, Bauernfänger, Betrüger**

◇ **confident** *adjective* certain *or* sure **zuversichtlich;** *I am confident the turnover will increase rapidly; are you confident the sales team is capable of handling this product?*

◇ **confidential** *adjective* secret *or* not to be told or shown to other people **vertraulich;** *he sent a confidential report to the chairman; please mark the letter "Private and Confidential"*

◇ **confidentiality** *noun* being secret **Vertraulichkeit; he broke the confidentiality of the discussions** = he told someone about the secret discussions **er brach die Vertraulichkeit der Unterredungen**

confirm *verb* to say that something is certain **bestätigen, bekräftigen;** *to confirm a hotel reservation or a ticket or an agreement or a booking;* **to confirm someone in a job** = to say that someone is now permanently in the job **jdn nach einer Probezeit fest anstellen**

◇ **confirmation** *noun*
(a) being certain **Bestätigung, Bekräftigung; confirmation of a booking** = checking that a booking is certain **Buchungsbestätigung**
(b) document which confirms something **Bestätigungsschreiben;** *he received confirmation from the bank that the deeds had been deposited*

conflict *noun* **conflict of interest** = situation where a person may profit personally from decisions which he takes in his official capacity **Interessenkonflikt**

confuse *verb* to make it difficult for someone to understand something *or* to make something difficult **verwirren, verwechseln;** *the chairman was confused by all the journalists' questions; to introduce the problem of VAT will only confuse the issue*

conglomerate *noun* group of subsidiary companies linked together and forming a group making very different types of products **Mischkonzern**

congratulate *verb* to give someone your good wishes for having done something well **beglückwünschen, gratulieren;** *the sales director congratulated the salesmen on doubling sales; I want to congratulate you on your promotion*

◇ **congratulations** *plural noun* good wishes **Glückwünsche, Gratulationen;** *the staff sent him their congratulations on his promotion*

conman *noun informal* = CONFIDENCE TRICKSTER
NOTE: plural is **conmen**

connect *verb*
(a) to link *or* to join **verbinden;** *the company is connected to the government because the chairman's father is a minister*
(b) the flight from New York connects with a flight to Athens = the plane from New York arrives in time for passengers to catch the plane to Athens **der Flug von New York hat Anschluß an den Flug nach Athen**

◇ **connecting flight** *noun* plane which a passenger will be on time to catch and which will take him to his final destination **Anschlußflug;** *check at the helicopter desk for connecting flights to the city centre*

◇ **connection** *noun*
(a) link *or* something which joins **Verbindung, Beziehung;** *is there a connection between his argument with the director and his sudden move to become warehouse manager?;* **in connection with** = referring to **in Zusammenhang mit;** *I want to speak to the managing director in connection with the sales forecasts*
(b) connections = people you know *or* customers *or* contacts **Beziehungen, Verbindungen;** *he has useful connections in industry*

conservative *adjective* careful *or* not overestimating **vorsichtig;** *a conservative estimate of sales; his forecast of expenditure is very conservative;* **at a conservative estimate** = calculation which probably underestimates the final figure **bei vorsichtiger Schätzung;** *their turnover has risen by at least 20% in the last year, and that is probably a conservative estimate*

◇ **conservatively** *adverb* not overestimating **vorsichtig;** *the total sales are conservatively estimated at £2.3m*

consider *verb* to think seriously about something **bedenken, überlegen; to consider the terms of a contract** = to examine and discuss if the terms are acceptable **die Vertragsbedingungen prüfen**

◇ **consideration** *noun*

(a) serious thought **Überlegung, Erwägung;** *we are giving consideration to moving the head office to Scotland*
(b) something valuable exchanged as part of a contract **Gegenleistung; for a small consideration** = for a small fee *or* payment **für ein geringes Entgelt**
NOTE: no plural for (a)

considerable *adjective* quite large **beträchtlich, erheblich;** *we sell considerable quantities of our products to Africa; they lost a considerable amount of money on the commodity market*

◊ **considerably** *adverb* quite a lot **beträchtlich, erheblich;** *sales are considerably higher than they were last year*

consign *verb* **to consign goods to someone** = to send goods to someone for him to use or to sell for you **Waren in Kommission geben**

◊ **consignation** *noun* act of consigning **Versand, Versenden**

◊ **consignee** *noun* person who receives goods from someone for his own use or to sell for the sender **Empfänger**

◊ **consignment** *noun*
(a) sending of goods to someone who will sell them for you **Versand, Versenden; consignment note** = note saying that goods have been sent **Versandanzeige, Frachtbrief; goods on consignment** = goods kept for another company to be sold on their behalf for a commission **Kommissionsware**
(b) group of goods sent for sale **Warensendung, Lieferung;** *a consignment of goods has arrived; we are expecting a consignment of cars from Japan*

◊ **consignor** *noun* person who consigns goods to someone **Ab-, Versender**

consist of *verb* to be formed of **bestehen aus, sich zusammensetzen aus;** *the trade mission consists of the sales directors of ten major companies; the package tour consists of air travel, six nights in a luxury hotel, all meals and visits to places of interest*

consolidate *verb*
(a) to put the accounts of several subsidiary companies into the accounts of the main group **konsolidieren**
(b) to group goods together for shipping **zusammenlegen**

◊ **consolidation** *noun* grouping together of goods for shipping **Zusammenlegung**

◊ **consolidated** *adjective*
(a) consolidated accounts = accounts of subsidiary companies grouped together into the accounts of the parent company **konsolidierte Bilanz**
(b) consolidated shipment = goods from different companies grouped together into a single shipment **Sammelladung**

consols *plural noun GB* government bonds which pay an interest but do not have a maturity date **Konsols, konsolidierte Staatsanleihen**

consortium *noun* group of companies which work together **Konsortium;** *a consortium of Canadian companies or a Canadian consortium; a consortium of French and British companies is planning to construct the new aircraft*

constitution *noun* written rules *or* regulations of a society *or* association *or* club *or* state **Satzung, Verfassung;** *under the society's constitution, the chairman is elected for a two-year period; payments to officers of the association are not allowed by the constitution*

◊ **constitutional** *adjective* according to a constitution **verfassungsmäßig; satzungsgemäß;** *the reelection of the chairman is not constitutional*

construct *verb* to build **bauen; konstruieren;** *the company has tendered for the contract to construct the new airport*

◊ **construction** *noun* building **Bau; Konstruktion; construction company** = company which specializes in building **Bauunternehmen; under construction** = being built **in/im Bau (befindlich);** *the airport is under construction*

◊ **constructive** *adjective* which helps in the making of something **konstruktiv;** *she made some constructive suggestions for improving management-worker relations; we had a constructive proposal from a distribution company in Italy;* **constructive dismissal** = situation when a worker leaves his job voluntarily but because of pressure from the management **erzwungene Kündigung**

◊ **constructor** *noun* person *or* company which constructs **Erbauer/-in, Konstrukteur/-in**

consult *verb* to ask an expert for advice **konsultieren, zu Rate ziehen;** *he consulted his accountant about his tax*

◊ **consultancy** *noun* act of giving specialist advice **Beratung;** *a consultancy firm; he offers a consultancy service*

◊ **consultant** *noun* specialist who gives advice **Berater/-in, Gutachter/-in;** *engineering consultant; management consultant; tax consultant*

◇ **consulting** *adjective* person who gives specialist advice **beratend;** *consulting engineer*

consumable *adjective* **consumable goods** = goods which are bought by members of the public and not by companies **Verbrauchs-, Konsumgüter**

◇ **consumables** *plural noun* = CONSUMABLE GOODS

◇ **consumer** *noun* person *or* company which buys and uses goods and services **Verbraucher/-in, Konsument/-in;** *gas consumers are protesting at the increase in prices; the factory is a heavy consumer of water;* **consumer council** = group representing the interests of consumers **Verbraucherberatung; consumer credit** = credit given by shops, banks and other financial institutions to consumers so that they can buy goods **Kundenkredit; Abzahlungskredit; consumer durables** = items such as washing machines *or* refrigerators *or* cookers which are bought and used by the public **langlebige Gebrauchs-, Konsumgüter; consumer goods** = goods bought by consumers *or* by members of the public **Verbrauchs-, Konsumgüter; consumer panel** = group of consumers who report on products they have used so that the manufacturers can improve them or use what the panel says about them in advertising **Verbrauchertestgruppe;** *US* **consumer price index** = index showing how prices of consumer goods have risen over a period of time, used as a way of measuring inflation and the cost of living **Verbraucherpreisindex; consumer protection** = protecting consumers against unfair *or* illegal traders **Verbraucherschutz; consumer research** = research into why consumers buy goods and what goods they really want to buy **Konsumforschung; consumer resistance** = lack of interest by consumers in buying a product **Kaufunlust;** *the latest price increases have produced considerable consumer resistance;* **consumer society** = type of society where consumers are encouraged to buy goods **Kosumgesellschaft; consumer spending** = spending by consumers **Ausgaben der Privathaushalte**

> QUOTE analysis of the consumer price index for the first half of 1985 shows that the rate of inflation went down by about 12.9 per cent
> *Business Times (Lagos)*

consumption *noun* buying or using goods or services **Konsum, Verbrauch;** *a car with low petrol consumption; the factory has a heavy consumption of coal;* **home consumption** *or* **domestic consumption** = use of something in one's own country **Inlandsverbrauch**
NOTE: no plural

contact
1 *noun*
(a) person you know *or* person you can ask for help or advice **Verbindung, Kontakt(person);** *he has many contacts in the city; who is your contact in the ministry?*
(b) act of getting in touch with someone **Kontakt, Verbindung; I have lost contact with them** = I do not communicate with them any longer **ich habe den Kontakt zu ihnen verloren; he put me in contact with a good lawyer** = he told me how to get in touch with a good lawyer **er hat mir einen guten Anwalt vermittelt**
NOTE: no plural for (b)
2 *verb* to get in touch with someone *or* to communicate with someone **sich in Verbindung setzen mit, Kontakt aufnehmen mit;** *he tried to contact his office by phone; can you contact the managing director at his club?*

contain *verb* to hold something inside **enthalten;** *each crate contains two computers and their peripherals; a barrel contains 250 litres; we have lost a file containing important documents*

◇ **container** *noun*
(a) box *or* bottle *or* can, etc. which can hold goods **Behälter;** *the gas is shipped in strong metal containers; the container burst during shipping*
(b) very large metal case of a standard size for loading and transporting goods on trucks, trains and ships **Container;** *container ship; container berth; container port; container terminal; to ship goods in containers;* **a container-load of spare parts** = a shipment of spare parts sent in a container **eine Containerladung mit Ersatzteilen**

◇ **containerization** *noun* to start shipping in containers **Umstellung auf Containertransport**

◇ **containerize** *verb* to start using containers; to start shipping goods in containers **auf Container umstellen**

contango *noun* payment of interest by a stockbroker for carrying payment for shares from one account day to the next **Reportgeschäft; contango day** = day when the rate of contango payments is fixed **Reporttag**

content *noun* the ideas inside a letter, etc. **Gehalt; the content of the letter** = the real meaning of the letter **der Gehalt des Briefes**

◊ **contents** *plural noun* things contained *or* what is inside something **Inhalt;** *the contents of the bottle poured out onto the floor; the customs officials inspected the contents of the crate;* **the contents of the letter** = the words written in the letter **der Inhalt des Briefes**

contested takeover *noun* takeover where the board of the company do not recommend it to the shareholders and try to fight it **angefochtene Übernahme**

contingency *noun* possible state of emergency when decisions will have to be taken quickly **unvorhergesehenes Ereignis; contingency fund** *or* **contingency reserve** = money set aside in case it is needed urgently **Fonds für außerordentliche Rückstellungen; contingency plans** = plans which will be put into action if something happens which no one expects **Krisenplan; to add on 10% to provide for contingencies** = to provide for further expenditure which may be incurred **10% für Sonderausgaben aufschlagen;** *we have built 10% for contingencies into our cost forecast*

◊ **contingent** *adjective*

(a) contingent expenses = expenses which will be incurred only if something happens **unvorhergesehene Sonderausgaben**

(b) contingent policy = policy which pays out only if something happens (as if the person named in the policy dies before the person due to benefit) **Eventualversicherung; Risikoversicherung**

continue *verb* to go on doing something *or* to do something which you were doing earlier **andauern; fortsetzen, fortfahren mit;** *the chairman continued speaking in spite of the noise from the shareholders; the meeting started at 10 a.m. and continued until six p.m.; negotiations will continue next Monday*

◊ **continual** *adjective* which happens again and again **ständig, ununterbrochen;** *production was slow because of continual breakdowns*

◊ **continually** *adverb* again and again **ständig, ununterbrochen;** *the photocopier is continually breaking down*

◊ **continuation** *noun* act of continuing **Fortsetzung, Fortführung**

◊ **continuous** *adjective* with no end *or* with no breaks **kontinuierlich, stetig, gleichmäßig;** *continuous production line;* **continuous feed** = device which feeds continuous stationery into a printer **Endlospapiereinzug; continuous stationery** = paper made as one long sheet, used in the computer printers **Endlospapier**

contra

1 *noun* **contra account** = account which offsets another account **Gegenkonto; Gegenrechnung; contra entry** = entry made in the opposite side of an account to make an earlier entry worthless (i.e. a debit against a credit) **Gegenbuchung; per contra** *or* **as per contra** = words showing that a contra entry has been made **als Gegenbuchung**

2 *verb* **to contra an entry** = to enter a similar amount in the opposite side of an account **einen Eintrag zurückbuchen**

contraband *noun* **contraband (goods)** = goods brought into a country illegally, without paying customs duty **Schmuggelware**

contract

1 *noun*

(a) legal agreement between two parties **Vertrag, Vereinbarung;** *to draw up a contract; to draft a contract; to sign a contract;* **the contract is binding on both parties** = both parties signing the contract must do what is agreed **beide Vertragspartner sind an den Vertrag gebunden; to be under contract** = bound by the terms of a contract **unter Vertrag stehen;** *the firm is under contract to deliver the goods by November;* **to void a contract** = to make a contract invalid **einen Vertrag aufheben/für nichtig erklären; contract of employment** = contract between management and employee showing all conditions of work **Arbeitsvertrag; service contract** = contract between a company and a director showing all conditions of work **Dienstvertrag; exchange of contracts** = point in the sale of a property when the buyer and seller both sign the contract of sale which then becomes binding **Vertragsunterzeichnung**

(b) contract law *or* **law of contract** = laws relating to agreements **Vertragsrecht; Schuldrecht; by private contract** = by private legal agreement **durch Privatabkommen; contract note** = note showing that shares have been bought or sold but not yet paid for **Ausführungsanzeige**

(c) agreement for supply of a service or goods **Liefervertrag;** *contract for the supply of spare parts; to enter into a contract to supply spare parts; to sign a contract for £10,000 worth of spare parts;* **to put work out to contract** = to decide that work should be done by another company on a contract, rather than employing members of staff to do it **Unteraufträge vergeben; to award a contract to a company** *or* **to place a contract with a company** = to decide that a company shall have the contract to do work for you **einen Auftrag an eine Firma vergeben; to**

tender for a contract = to put forward an estimate of cost for work under contract **sich (im Ausschreibungsweg) um einen Auftrag bewerben;** *conditions of contract or contract conditions;* **breach of contract** = breaking the terms of a contract **Vertragsbruch; the company is in breach of contract** = the company has failed to do what was agreed in the contract **die Firma ist vertragsbrüchig geworden; contract work** = work done according to a written agreement **Auftragsarbeit**

2 *verb* to agree to do some work by contract **sich vertraglich verpflichten;** *to contract to supply spare parts or to contract for the supply of spare parts;* **the supply of spare parts was contracted out to Smith Ltd** = Smith Ltd was given the contract for supplying spare parts **der Vertrag für den Ersatzteilevertrieb wurde an Smith Ltd vergeben; to contract out of an agreement** = to withdraw from an agreement with written permission of the other party **sich von einer vertraglichen Verpflichtung befreien**

◇ **contracting** *adjective* **contracting party** = person or company which signs a contract **Vertragspartner**

◇ **contractor** *noun* person or company which does work according to a written agreement **Auftragnehmer; haulage contractor** = company which transports goods by contract **Transport-, Fuhrunternehmer; Spediteur; government contractor** = company which supplies the government with goods by contract **Unternehmen mit Staatsaufträgen**

◇ **contractual** *adjective* according to a contract **vertraglich, vertragsmäßig; contractual liability** = legal responsibility for something as stated in a contract **Vertragshaftung; to fulfill your contractual obligations** = to do what you have agreed to do in a contract **seine vertraglichen Verpflichtungen erfüllen; he is under no contractual obligation to buy** = he has signed no agreement to buy **er ist vertraglich nicht verpflichtet zu kaufen**

◇ **contractually** *adverb* according to a contract **vertraglich, durch Vertrag;** *the company is contractually bound to pay his expenses*

contrary *noun* opposite **Gegenteil; failing instructions to the contrary** = unless different instructions are given **sofern Sie nichts Gegenteiliges hören; on the contrary** = quite the opposite **im Gegenteil;** *the chairman was not annoyed with his assistant - on the contrary, he promoted him*

contribute *verb* to give money *or* to add to money **beisteuern, einen Beitrag leisten;** *to contribute 10% of the profits; he contributed to the pension fund for 10 years*

◇ **contribution** *noun* money paid to add to a sum **Beitrag; contribution of capital** = money paid to a company as additional capital **Investition; employer's contribution** = money paid by an employer towards a worker's pension **Arbeitgeberanteil; National Insurance contributions** = money paid each month by a worker and the company to the National Insurance **Sozialversicherungsbeiträge; pension contributions** = money paid by a company or worker into a pension fund **Rentenversicherungsbeiträge**

◇ **contributor** *noun* **contributor of capital** = person who contributes capital **Investor**

◇ **contributory** *adjective*

(a) contributory pension plan *or* **scheme** = pension plan where the employee has to contribute a percentage of salary **beitragspflichtige Rentenversicherung**

(b) which helps to cause **beitragend, mitverursachend;** *falling exchange rates have been a contributory factor in or to the company's loss of profits*

con trick *noun informal* = CONFIDENCE TRICK

control

1 *noun*

(a) power *or* being able to direct something **Leitung, Kontrolle, Macht, Aufsicht;** *the company is under the control of three shareholders; the family lost control of its business;* **to gain control of a business** = to buy more than 50% of the shares so that you can direct the business **die Aktienmehrheit an einem Unternehmen erwerben; to lose control of a business** = to find that you have less than 50% of the shares in a company, and so are not longer able to direct it **die Aktienmehrheit an einem Unternehmen verlieren**

(b) restricting *or* checking something *or* making sure that something is kept in check **Kontrolle, Überwachung; under control** = kept in check **unter Kontrolle;** *expenses are kept under tight control; the company is trying to bring its overheads back under control;* **out of control** = not kept in check **außer Kontrolle;** *costs have got out of control;* **budgetary control** = keeping check on spending **Budgetkontrolle; credit control** = checking that customers pay on time and do not exceed their credit limits **Kreditkontrolle; quality control** = making sure that the quality of a product is good **Qualitätskontrolle; stock control** = making sure that movements of stock are noted **Lagersteuerung**

(c) exchange controls = government restrictions on changing the local currency into foreign currency **Devisenkontrolle;** *the government has imposed exchange controls; they say the government is going to lift exchange controls;* **price controls** = legal measures to prevent prices rising too fast **Preiskontrollen; Preisüberwachung**
(d) control group = small group which is used to check a sample group **Kontrollgruppe; control systems** = systems used to check that a computer system is working correctly **Steuerungssysteme**
2 *verb*
(a) to control a business = to direct a business **die Mehrheit an einem Unternehmen haben;** *the business is controlled by a company based in Luxemburg; the company is controlled by the majority shareholder*
(b) to make sure that something is kept in check *or* is not allowed to develop **kontrollieren, steuern;** *the government is fighting to control inflation or to control the rise in the cost of living*
NOTE: **controlling - controlled**

◇ **controlled** *adjective* ruled *or* kept in check **kontrolliert, gesteuert; government-controlled** = ruled by a government **unter staatlicher Aufsicht; controlled economy** = economy where the most business activity is directed by orders from the government **staatlich gelenkte Wirtschaft**

◇ **controller** *noun*
(a) person who controls (especially the finances of a company) **Controller; stock controller** = person who notes movements of stock **Lagerverwalter**
(b) *US* chief accountant in a company **Leiter der Buchhaltung**

◇ **controlling** *adjective* **to have a controlling interest in a company** = to own more than 50% of the shares so that you can direct how the company is run **die Mehrheitsbeteiligung an einem Unternehmen haben**

convene *verb* to ask people to come together **einberufen; zusammenrufen;** *to convene a meeting of shareholders*

convenience *noun* **at your earliest convenience** = as soon as you find it possible **baldmöglichst; convenience foods** = food which is prepared by the shop before it is sold, so that it needs only heating to be made ready to eat **Fertiggerichte; ship sailing under a flag of convenience** = flying the flag of a country which may have no ships of its own but allows ships of other countries to be registered in its ports **ein Schiff, das unter Billigflagge fährt**

◇ **convenient** *adjective* suitable *or* handy **passend; praktisch;** *a bank draft is a convenient way of sending money abroad; is 9.30 a convenient time for the meeting?*

convenor *noun* trade unionist who organizes union meetings **Gewerkschaft(l)er**

conversion *noun* change **Umwandlung, Konvertierung**
(a) conversion of funds = using money which does not belong to you for a purpose for which it is not supposed to be used **Veruntreuung von Geldmitteln, Umleitung von Geldmitteln für eigene Zwecke**
(b) conversion price *or* **conversion rate** = rate at which a currency is changed into a foreign currency; price at which preference shares are converted into ordinary shares **Umrechnungskurs**

◇ **convert** *verb* to change money of one country for money of another **(um)tauschen;** *we converted our pounds into Swiss francs;* **to convert funds to one's own use** = to use someone else's money for yourself **Gelder veruntreuen/umleiten**

◇ **convertibility** *noun* ability to exchange one currency for another easily **Konvertierbarkeit**

◇ **convertible** *adjective* **convertible currency** = currency which can be exchanged for another easily **frei konvertierbare Währung; convertible loan stock** = stock which can be exchanged for shares at a later date **Wandelanleihe**

conveyance *noun* legal document which transfers a property from the seller to the buyer **Übertragungsurkunde**

◇ **conveyancer** *noun* person who draws up a conveyance **Notar**

◇ **conveyancing** *noun* legally transferring a property from a seller to a buyer **Eigentumsübertragung; do-it-yourself conveyancing** = drawing up a legal conveyance without the help of a lawyer **Aufsetzen einer Übertragungsurkunde ohne notarielle Hilfe**

cooling off *noun* **cooling off period** = during an industrial dispute, a period when negotiations have to be carried on and no action can be taken by either side; period when a person is allowed to think about something which he has agreed to buy on hire-purchase and possibly change his mind; *(Arbeitskampf)* **Friedenspflicht;** *(vor Vertragsabschluß)* **Überlegungsfrist**

co-op *noun* = CO-OPERATIVE 2

◇ **co-operate** *verb* to work together **kooperieren, zusammenarbeiten;** *the* *governments are co-operating in the fight against piracy; the two firms have co-operated on the computer project*

◇ **co-operation** *noun* working together **Kooperation, Zusammenarbeit, Mitarbeit;** *the project was completed ahead of schedule with the co-operation of the workforce*

◇ **co-operative**

1 *adjective* willing to work together **kooperativ;** *the workforce has not been co-operative over the management's productivity plan;* **co-operative society** = society where the customers and workers are partners and share the profits **Genossenschaft**

2 *noun* business run by a group of workers who are the owners and who share the profits **Kooperative;** *agricultural co-operative; to set up a workers' co-operative*

co-opt *verb* **to co-opt someone onto a committee** = to ask someone to join a committee without being elected **jdn in ein Komitee kooptieren**

co-owner *noun* person who owns something with another person **Mitinhaber; Miteigentümer (zur gesamten Hand od nach Bruchteilen);** *the two sisters are co-owners of the property*

◇ **co-ownership** *noun* arrangement where partners *or* workers have shares in a company **Miteigentum**

copartner *noun* person who is a partner in a business with another person **Teilhaber/-in**

◇ **copartnership** *noun* arrangement where partners *or* workers have shares in the company **Teilhaberschaft**

cope *verb* to manage to do something **zurechtkommen, fertigwerden;** *the new assistant manager coped very well when the manager was on holiday; the warehouse is trying to cope with the backlog of orders*

copier *noun* = COPYING MACHINE, PHOTOCOPIER

coproperty *noun* ownership of property by two or more people together **Miteigentum**

◇ **coproprietor** *noun* person who owns a property with another person or several other people **Miteigentümer**

copy

1 *noun*

(a) document which is made to look the same as another **Kopie, Durchschlag; carbon copy** = copy made with carbon paper **Durchschlag; certified copy** = document which is certified as being the same as another **beglaubigte Kopie; file copy** = copy of a document which is filed in an office for reference **Aktenkopie**

(b) document **Ausfertigung; fair copy** *or* **final copy** = document which is written or typed with no changes or mistakes **Reinschrift; hard copy** = printout of a text which is on a computer *or* printed copy of something which is on microfilm **Ausdruck; Kopie; Abzug; rough copy** = draft of a document which, it is expected, will have changes made to it **Konzept, Entwurf; top copy** = first or top sheet of a document which is typed with carbon copies **Original**

(c) publicity copy = text of a proposed advertisement before it is printed **Werbetextentwurf;** *she writes copy for a travel firm;* **knocking copy** = advertising material which criticizes competing products **aggressive, herabsetzende Werbung**

(d) a book *or* a newspaper **Ausgabe, Exemplar;** *have you kept yesterday's copy of the "Times"? I read it in the office copy of "Fortune"; where is my copy of the telephone directory?*

NOTE: no plural for (c)

2 *verb* to make a second document which is like the first **kopieren; einen Durchschlag/eine Abschrift machen;** *he copied the company report at night and took it home*

◇ **copier** *or* **copying machine** *noun* machine which makes copies of documents **Kopierer**

◇ **copyright**

1 *noun* legal right (lasting for fifty years after the death of a writer) which a writer has to publish his own work and not to have it copied **Copyright, Urheberrecht; copyright act** = Act of Parliament making copyright legal, and controlling the copying of copyright material **Urheberrechtsgesetz; copyright law** = laws concerning copyright **Urheberrechtschutzgesetz; work which is out of copyright** = work by a writer who has been dead for fifty years **Werk, das nicht mehr urheberrechtlich geschützt ist; work still in copyright** = work by a living writer, or by a writer who has not been dead for fifty years **urheberrechtlich geschütztes Werk; infringement of copyright** *or* **copyright infringement** = act of illegally copying a work which is in copyright **Verletzung des Urheberrechts; copyright notice** = note in a book showing who owns the copyright and the date of ownership **Urheberrechtsvermerk**

NOTE: no plural

2 *verb* to confirm the copyright of a written work by inserting a copyright notice and publishing the work **urheberrechtlich schützen**

3 *adjective* covered by the laws of copyright **urheberrechtlich geschützt;** *it is illegal to photocopy a copyright work*

◇ **copyrighted** *adjective* in copyright **verlagsrechtlich geschützt**

copy typing *noun* typing documents from originals, not from dictation **Abtippen von Dokumenten**

◇ **copy typist** *noun* person who types documents from originals, not from dictation **Schreibkraft (ohne Diktat)**

copywriter *noun* person who writes advertisements **Werbetexter/-in**

corner
1 *noun*
(a) place where two streets *or* two walls join **Ecke, Straßenecke;** *the Post Office is on the corner of the High Street and London Road;* **corner shop** = small general store in a town on a street corner **Eckladen**
(b) place where two sides join **Ecke;** *the box has to have specially strong corners; the corner of the crate was damaged*
(c) situation where one person or a group controls the supply of a certain commodity **Monopol**
2 *verb* **to corner the market** = to own most or all of the supply of a certain commodity and so control the price **den Markt beherrschen;** *the syndicate tried to corner the market in silver*

corp *US* = CORPORATION

corporate *adjective* referring to a whole company **Firmen-, Unternehmens-; corporate image** = idea which a company would like the public to have of it **Firmenimage; corporate plan** = plan for the future work of a whole company **langfristiger Unternehmensplan; corporate planning** = planning the future work of a whole company **langfristige Unternehmensplanung; corporate profits** = profits of a corporation **Unternehmensgewinne**

◇ **corporation** *noun*
(a) large company **Unternehmen; Kapitalgesellschaft; finance corporation** = company which provides money for hire purchase **Finanzierungsgesellschaft; corporation tax** = tax on profits made by companies **Körperschaftssteuer**
(b) *US* company which is incorporated in the United States **Kapital-, Aktiengesellschaft; corporation income tax** = tax on profits made by incorporated companies **Körperschaftssteuer**

> QUOTE the prime rate is the rate at which banks lend to their top corporate borrowers
> *Wall Street Journal*
> QUOTE corporate profits for the first quarter showed a 4 per cent drop from last year
> *Financial Times*
> QUOTE if corporate forecasts are met, sales will exceed $50 million in 1985
> *Citizen (Ottawa)*

correct
1 *adjective* accurate *or* right **richtig, korrekt;** *the published accounts do not give a correct picture of the company's financial position*
2 *verb* to remove mistakes from something **korrigieren, verbessern;** *the accounts department have corrected the invoice; you will have to correct all these typing errors before you send the letter*

◇ **correction** *noun* making something correct; change which makes something correct **Korrektur, Verbesserung;** *he made some corrections to the text of the speech*

correspond *verb*
(a) to correspond with someone = to write letters to someone **mit jdm korrespondieren/in Briefwechsel stehen**
(b) to correspond with something = to fit *or* to match something **(sich) entsprechen, übereinstimmen**

◇ **correspondence** *noun* letters which are exchanged **Korrespondenz, Schriftwechsel; business correspondence** = letters concerned with a business **Geschäftskorrespondenz, Geschäftsbriefe; to be in correspondence with someone** = to write letters to someone and receive letters back **mit jdm korrespondieren/in Briefwechsel stehen; correspondence clerk** = clerk whose responsibility it is to answer correspondence **Korrespondent/-in**
NOTE: no plural

◇ **correspondent** *noun*
(a) person who writes letters **Briefeschreiber, Korrespondent/-in**
(b) journalist who writes articles for a newspaper on specialist subjects **Korrespondent/-in;** *a financial correspondent; the "Times" business correspondent; he is the Paris correspondent of the "Telegraph"*

cost
1 *noun*
(a) amount of money which has to be paid for something **Kosten; Preis;** *what is the cost of a first class ticket to New York? computer costs are falling each year; we cannot afford the cost of two telephones;* **to cover costs** = to produce enough money in sales to pay for the costs of production **die Kosten decken;** *the sales revenue barely covers the costs of advertising or the manufacturing costs;* **to**

sell at cost = to sell at a price which is the same as the cost of manufacture or the wholesale cost **zum Selbstkostenpreis verkaufen; fixed costs** = business costs which do not rise with the quantity of the product made **Fixkosten; Gemeinkosten; labour costs** = cost of hourly-paid workers employed to make a product **Lohnkosten; manufacturing costs** *or* **production costs** = costs of making a product **Herstellungs-, Produktionskosten; operating costs** *or* **running costs** = cost of the day-to-day organization of a company **Betriebskosten; variable costs** = production costs which increase with the quantity of the product made (such as wages, raw materials) **variable Kosten; cost accountant** = accountant who gives managers information about their business costs **Kostenrechner/-in; cost accounting** = specially prepared accounts of manufacturing and sales costs **Kostenrechnung; cost analysis** = calculating in advance what a new product will cost **Kostenanalyse; cost centre** = group *or* machine whose costs can be itemized and to which fixed costs can be allocated **Kostenstelle; cost, insurance and freight** = estimate of a price, which includes the cost of the goods, the insurance and the transport charges **Kosten, Versicherung und Fracht, cif; cost price** = selling price which is the same as the price which the seller paid for the item (i.e. either the manufacturing cost or the wholesale price) **Selbstkostenpreis; cost of sales** = all the costs of a product sold, including manufacturing costs and the staff costs of the production department **Absatz-, Vertriebskosten**

(b) costs = expenses involved in a court case **Gerichtskosten; to pay costs** = to pay the expenses of a court case **Gerichtskosten tragen;** *the judge awarded costs to the defendant; costs of the case will be borne by the prosecution*

2 *verb*

(a) to have a price **kosten;** *how much does the machine cost? this cloth costs £10 a metre*

(b) to cost a product = to calculate how much money will be needed to make a product, and so work out its selling price **den Preis eines Produktes kalkulieren**

◇ **cost-benefit** *noun* **cost-benefit analysis** = examining the ratio between costs and benefits, especially in comparing different production processes **Kosten-Nutzen-Analyse**

◇ **cost-cutting** *noun* reducing costs **Kostensenkung;** *we have taken out the telex as a cost-cutting exercise*

◇ **cost-effective** *adjective* which gives value, especially when compared with something else **kostenwirksam;** *we find advertising in the Sunday newspapers very cost-effective*

◇ **cost-effectiveness** *noun* being cost-effective **Kostenrentabilität;** *can we calculate the cost-effectiveness of air freight against shipping by sea?*

◇ **costing** *noun* calculation of the manufacturing costs, and so the selling price of a product **Kostenberechnung;** *the costings give us a retail price of $2.95; we cannot do the costing until we have details of all the production expenditure*

◇ **costly** *adjective* expensive *or* costing a lot of money **teuer, kostspielig**

◇ **cost of living** *noun* money which has to be paid for food, heating, rent etc. **Lebenshaltungskosten;** *to allow for the cost of living in the salaries;* **cost-of-living allowance** = addition to normal salary to cover increases in the cost of living **Teuerungszulage; cost-of-living bonus** = extra money paid to meet the increase in the cost of living **Teuerungszulage; cost-of-living increase** = increase in salary to allow it to keep up with the increased cost of living **Gehaltszulage zur Anpassung an gestiegene Lebenshaltungskosten; cost-of-living index** = way of measuring the cost of living which is shown as a percentage increase on the figure for the previous year **Lebenshaltungskostenindex**

◇ **cost plus** *noun* system of charging, where the buyer pays the costs plus a percentage commission to the seller **Kosten plus prozentualer Aufschlag;** *we are charging for the work on a cost plus basis*

◇ **cost-push inflation** *noun* inflation caused by increased wage demands which lead to higher prices and in turn lead to further wage demands **kostentreibende Inflation**

council *noun* official group chosen to run something *or* to advise on a problem **Rat; Behörde; consumer council** = group representing the interests of consumers **Verbraucherberatung; town council** = representatives elected to run a town **Stadtrat**

counsel *noun* lawyer acting for one of the parties in a legal action **Anwalt/Anwältin;** *defence counsel; prosecution counsel; GB* **Queen's Counsel** = senior lawyer **Kronanwalt**
NOTE: no plural

count *verb*

(a) to add figures together to make a total **(zusammen)zählen;** *he counted up the sales for the six months to December*

(b) to include **(mit)rechnen, (mit)zählen;** *did you count my trip to New York as part of my sales expenses?*

◇ **counting house** *noun* department dealing with cash **Buchhaltung(sabteilung)**

◇ **count on** *verb* to expect something to happen **rechnen mit, sich verlassen auf;** *they are counting on getting a good response from the TV advertising; do not count on a bank loan to start your business*

counter *noun* long flat surface in a shop for displaying and selling goods **Ladentisch, Tresen; over the counter** = legally **legal (verkaufen); goods sold over the counter** = retail sales of goods in shops **im Einzelhandel gegen bar verkaufte Waren;** *some drugs are sold over the counter, but others need to be recommended by a doctor;* **over-the-counter sales** = legal selling of shares which are not listed in the official Stock Exchange list **Verkauf im Freiverkehr; under the counter** = illegally **(illegal) unter dem Ladentisch; under-the-counter sales** = black market sales **ungesetzliche Verkäufe; bargain counter** = counter where things are sold cheaply **Sonderangebotsstand, Sondertisch; check-in counter** = place where plane passengers have to check in **Abfertigung(sschalter); ticket counter** = place where tickets are sold **Kartenschalter; trade counter** = shop in a factory *or* warehouse where goods are sold to retailers **Warenausgabe für den Einzelhandel, Großhandelsverkauf; glove counter** = section of a shop where gloves are sold **Handschuhabteilung; counter staff** = sales staff who serve behind counters **Verkaufspersonal hinter dem Ladentisch**

counter- *prefix* against **Gegen-**

◇ **counterbid** *noun* higher bid in reply to a previous bid **Gegengebot;** *when I bid £20 he put in a counterbid of £25*

◇ **counter-claim**
1 *noun* claim for damages made in reply to a previous claim **Gegenforderung; Widerklage;** *Jones claimed £25,000 in damages against Smith, and Smith entered a counter-claim of £50,000 for loss of office*
2 *verb* to put in a counter-claim **eine Gegenforderung stellen; Widerklage erheben;** *Jones claimed £25,000 in damages and Smith counter-claimed £50,000 for loss of office*

◇ **counterfeit**
1 *adjective* false *or* imitation (money) **gefälscht, Falsch-**
2 *verb* to make imitation money **fälschen**

◇ **counterfoil** *noun* slip of paper kept after writing a cheque *or* an invoice *or* a receipt, as a record of the deal which has taken place **Kontrollabschnitt**

◇ **countermand** *verb* **to countermand an order** = to say that an order must not be carried out **einen Auftrag stornieren**

◇ **counter-offer** *noun* higher offer made in reply to another offer **Gegengebot;** *Smith Ltd made an offer of £1m for the property, and Blacks replied with a counter-offer of £1.4m*

◇ **counterpart** *noun* person who has a similar job in another company **Kollege; Gegenstück, Pendant; John is my counterpart in Smith's** = he has the same post as I have here **John hat bei Smith den gleichen Posten wie ich**

◇ **countersign** *verb* to sign a document which has already been signed by someone else **gegenzeichnen;** *all cheques have to be countersigned by the finance director; the sales director countersigns all my orders*

country *noun*
(a) land which is separate and governs itself **Land, Staat;** *the contract covers distribution in the countries of the Common Market; some African countries export oil; the Organization of Petroleum Exporting Countries;* **the managing director is out of the country** = he is on a business trip abroad **der Generaldirektor ist außer Landes/im Ausland**
(b) land which is not near a town **Land;** *distribution is difficult in country areas; his territory is mainly the country, but he is based in the town*

couple *noun* two things or people taken together **zwei;** *we only have enough stock for a couple of weeks; a couple of the directors were ill, so the board meeting was cancelled;* **the negotiations lasted a couple of hours** = the negotiations went on for about two hours **die Verhandlungen dauerten über zwei Stunden**

coupon *noun*
(a) piece of paper used in place of money **Gutschein; gift coupon** = coupon from a store which is given as a gift and which must be exchanged in that store **Geschenkgutschein**
(b) piece of paper which replaces an order form **Coupon; coupon ad** = advertisement with a form attached, which is to be cut out and returned to the advertiser with your name and address if you want further information about the product advertised **Couponanzeige; reply coupon** = form attached to a coupon ad, which must be filled in and returned to the advertiser **Antwortcoupon**
(c) interest coupon = slip of paper attached to a government bond certificate which can be cashed to provide the annual interest

Zinsschein; cum coupon = with a coupon attached **cum/mit Kupon; ex coupon** = without the interest coupons **ex/ohne Kupon**

courier *noun*
(a) motorcyclist who takes messages from one place another in a town **Kurier, Eilbote**
(b) person who goes with a party of tourists to guide them on a package tour **Reiseleiter**

course *noun*
(a) in the course of = during *or* while something is happening **während, im Verlauf/Lauf;** *in the course of the discussion, the managing director explained the company's expansion plans; sales have risen sharply in the course of the last few months*
(b) series of lessons **Kurs(us), Lehrgang;** *she has finished her secretarial course; the company has paid for her to attend a course for trainee sales managers*
(c) of course = naturally **selbstverständlich, natürlich;** *of course the company is interested in profits; are you willing to go on a sales trip to Australia? - of course!*

court *noun* place where a judge listens to a case and decides legally which of the parties in the argument is right **Gericht, Gerichtssaal; court case** = legal action *or* trial **Gerichtsverfahren; Prozeß; Rechtsstreit; to take someone to court** = to tell someone to appear in court to settle an argument **gerichtlich gegen jdn vorgehen; a settlement was reached out of court** *or* **the two parties reached an out-of-court settlement** = the dispute was settled between the two parties privately without continuing the court case **es kam zu einem außergerichtlichen Vergleich**

covenant
1 *noun* legal contract **Vertrag, Abkommen; deed of covenant** = official signed agreement to pay someone a sum of money each year **Vertragsurkunde (über die jährliche Zahlung eines bestimmten Betrages)**
2 *verb* to agree to pay a sum of money each year by contract **vertraglich vereinbaren (jährlich einen bestimmten Betrag zu zahlen);** *to covenant to pay £10 per annum*

cover
1 *noun*
(a) thing put over a machine, etc. to keep it clean **Schutz, Hülle;** *put the cover over your micro when you leave the office; always keep a cover over the typewriter*
(b) insurance cover = protection guaranteed by an insurance policy **Versicherungsschutz;** *do you have cover against theft?;* **to operate without adequate cover** = without being protected by insurance **ohne ausreichenden Versicherungsschutz sein; to ask for additional cover** = to ask the insurance company to increase the amount for which you are insured **Erhöhung der Versicherungssumme beantragen; full cover** = insurance against all risks **voller Versicherungsschutz; cover note** = letter from an insurance company giving details of an insurance policy and confirming that the policy exists **vorläufiger Versicherungsschein, Deckungszusage**
NOTE: the US English for this is **binder**
(c) security to guarantee a loan **Deckung, Sicherheit;** *do you have sufficient cover for this loan?*
(d) *(Restaurant)* **cover charge** = charge in addition to the charge for food **Gedeck, Couvert**
(e) dividend cover = ratio of profits to dividend **Dividendendeckung, Verhältnis Gewinn-Dividende**
(f) to send something under separate cover = in a separate envelope **mit getrennter Post schicken; to send a magazine under plain cover** = in an ordinary envelope with no company name printed on it **eine Zeitschrift in neutralem Umschlag verschicken**
2 *verb*
(a) to put something over a machine, etc. to keep it clean **abdecken, zudecken;** *don't forget to cover your micro before you go home*
(b) to cover a risk = to be protected by insurance against a risk **ein Risiko decken; to be fully covered** = to have insurance against all risks **vollen Versicherungsschutz haben;** *the insurance covers fire, theft and loss of work*
(c) to have enough money to pay; to ask for security against a loan which you are making **(ab)decken; the damage was covered by the insurance** = the insurance company paid for the damage **der Schaden wurde von der Versicherung bezahlt; to cover a position** = to have enough money to be able to pay for a forward purchase **eine Position abdecken**
(d) to earn enough money to pay for costs, expenses etc. **decken;** *we do not make enough sales to cover the expense of running the shop; breakeven point is reached when sales cover all costs;* **the dividend is covered four times** = profits are four times the dividend paid out **das Verhältnis Gewinn-Dividende ist 4:1**

◇ **coverage** *noun*
(a) press coverage *or* **media coverage** = reports about something in the newspapers *or* on TV, etc. **Berichterstattung durch die Presse od die Medien;** *the company had good media coverage for the launch of its new model*
(b) *US* protection guaranteed by insurance **Versicherungsschutz;** *do you have coverage against fire damage?*

NOTE: no plural

◇ **covering letter** *or* **covering note** *noun* letter or note sent with documents to say why you are sending them **Begleitschreiben**

> QUOTE three export credit agencies have agreed to provide cover for large projects in Nigeria
> *Business Times (Lagos)*

crane *noun* machine for lifting heavy objects **Kran;** *the container slipped as the crane was lifting it onto the ship; they had to hire a crane to get the machine into the factory*

crash
1 *noun*
(a) accident to a car *or* plane *or* train **Kollision; Absturz;** *the car was damaged in the crash; the plane crash killed all the passengers or all the passengers were killed in the plane crash*
(b) financial collapse **Börsenkrach, Crash; finanzieller Zusammenbruch;** *financial crash; he lost all his money in the crash of 1929*
2 *verb*
(a) to hit something and be damaged **kollidieren; abstürzen;** *the plane crashed into the mountain; the lorry crashed into the post office*
(b) to collapse financially **bankrott gehen, zusammenbrechen;** *the company crashed with debts of over £1 million*

crate
1 *noun* large wooden box **Kiste;** *a crate of oranges*
2 *verb* to put goods into crates **in Kisten verpacken**

create *verb* to make something new **schaffen;** *by acquiring small unprofitable companies he soon created a large manufacturing group; the government scheme aims at creating new jobs for young people*

◇ **creation** *noun* making **Schaffung; job creation scheme** = government-backed scheme to make work for the unemployed **Arbeitsbeschaffungs-, Beschäftigungsprogramm,**

> QUOTE he insisted that the tax advantages he directed towards small businesses will help create jobs and reduce the unemployment rate
> *Toronto Star*

credere *see* DEL CREDERE

credit
1 *noun*
(a) time given to a customer before he has to pay **Kredit, Darlehen;** *to give someone six months' credit; to sell on good credit terms;* **extended credit** = credit on very long repayment terms **verlängerter/prolongierter Kredit; interest-free credit** = arrangement to borrow money without paying interest on the loan **zinsloses Darlehen; long credit** = terms allowing the borrower a long time to pay **Kredit mit langer Laufzeit; open credit** = bank credit given to good customers without security **offener (ungedeckter) Kredit, Blankokredit; short credit** = terms allowing the customer only a short time to pay **kurzfristiger Kredit; credit account** = account which a customer has with a shop which allows him to buy goods and pay for them later **Kundenkreditkonto;** *to open a credit account;* **credit agency** *or US* **credit bureau** = company which reports on the creditworthiness of customers to show whether they should be allowed credit **Kreditauskunftei; credit bank** = bank which lends money **Kreditbank; credit control** = check that customers pay on time and do not owe more than their credit limit **Kreditkontrolle; credit facilities** = arrangement with a bank or supplier to have credit so as to buy goods **Kreditmodalitäten; credit freeze** *or* **credit squeeze** = period when lending by banks is restricted by the government **Einfrieren von Krediten; letter of credit** = letter from a bank, allowing someone credit and promising to repay at a later date **Akkreditiv; irrevocable letter of credit** = letter of credit which cannot be cancelled **unwiderrufliches Akkreditiv; credit limit** = fixed amount which is the most a customer can owe on credit **Kreditlinie, Kreditlimit; he has exceeded his credit limit** = he has borrowed more money than he is allowed **er hat seinen Kredit überzogen; to open a line of credit** *or* **a credit line** = to make credit available to someone **eine Kreditlinie einräumen; credit rating** = amount which a credit agency feels a customer should be allowed to borrow **Bonitätsbeurteilung; on credit** = without paying immediately **auf Kredit;** *to live on credit; we buy everything on sixty days credit; the company exists on credit from its suppliers* (NOTE: no plural)
(b) money received by a person *or* company and recorded in the accounts **Haben, Kredit;** *to enter £100 to someone's credit; to pay in £100 to the credit of Mr Smith;* **debit and credit** = money which a company owes and which it receives **Soll und Haben; credit balance** = balance in an account showing that more money has been received than is owed by the company **Kredit-, Aktivsaldo;** *the account has a credit balance of £1,000;* **credit column** = right-hand column in accounts showing money received **Kredit-, Habenspalte; credit entry** = entry on the credit side of an account **Habenbuchung,**

Gutschrift; credit note = note showing that money is owed to a customer **Gutschriftsanzeige;** *the company sent the wrong order and so had to issue a credit note;* **credit side** = right-hand side of accounts showing money received **Habenseite; account in credit** = account where the credits are higher than the debits **Konto, das nicht überzogen ist, Konto mit Habensaldo; bank credit** = loans or overdrafts from a bank to a customer **Bankkredit; tax credit** = part of a dividend on which the company has already paid tax, so that the shareholder is not taxed on it **Steuergutschrift**
2 *verb* to put money into someone's account; to note money received in an account **gutschreiben;** *to credit an account with £100 or to credit £100 to an account*

◇ **credit card** *noun* plastic card which allows you to borrow money and to buy goods without paying for them immediately **Kreditkarte**

◇ **creditor** *noun* person who is owed money **Gläubiger; creditors' meeting** = meeting of all persons to whom a bankrupt company owes money, to decide how to obtain the money owed **Gläubigerversammlung**

◇ **credit union** *noun US* group of people who pay regular subscriptions which are used to help members of the group who are ill or in financial difficulties **Kreditgenossenschaft**

◇ **creditworthy** *adjective* able to buy goods on credit **kreditwürdig**

◇ **creditworthiness** *noun* ability of a customer to pay for goods bought on credit **Kreditwürdigkeit, Bonität**

crew *noun* group of people who work on a plane *or* ship, etc. **Besatzung, Crew, Mannschaft;** *the ship carries a crew of 250*

crime *noun* act which is against the law **Straftat, Verbrechen, Delikt;** *crimes in supermarkets have risen by 25%*

◇ **criminal** *adjective* illegal **kriminell, verbrecherisch, strafbar;** *misappropriation of funds is a criminal act;* **criminal action** = court case brought by the state against someone who is charged with a crime **Strafprozeß; strafrechtliche Verfolgung**

crisis *noun* serious economic situation where decisions have to be taken rapidly **Krise;** *international crisis; banking crisis; financial crisis;* **to take crisis measures** = to take severe measures rapidly to stop a crisis developing **Krisenmaßnahmen ergreifen**
NOTE: plural is **crises**

criticize *verb* to say that something *or* someone is wrong *or* is working badly, etc. **kritisieren;** *the MD criticized the sales manager for not improving the volume of sales; the design of the new catalogue has been criticized*

cross *verb*
(a) to go across **überqueren;** *Concorde only takes three hours to cross the Atlantic; to get to the bank, you turn left and cross the street at the post office*
(b) to cross a cheque = to write two lines across a cheque to show that it has to be paid into a bank **einen Scheck zur Verrechnung ausstellen; crossed cheque** = cheque which has to be paid into a bank **Verrechnungsscheck**

◇ **cross holding** *noun* situation where two companies hold shares in each other **wechselseitiger Aktienbesitz**

◇ **cross off** *verb* to remove something from a list **streichen;** *he crossed my name off his list; you can cross him off our mailing list*

◇ **cross out** *verb* to put a line through something which has been written **durchstreichen;** *she crossed out £250 and put in £500*

◇ **cross rate** *noun* exchange rate between two currencies expressed in a third currency **Kreuzkurs**

crude (oil) *noun* raw petroleum, taken from the ground **Roh(öl);** *the price for Arabian crude has slipped*
NOTE: no plural

cubic *adjective* measured in volume by multiplying length, depth and width **Kubik-, Raum-;** *the crate holds six cubic metres;* **cubic measure** = volume measured in cubic feet or metres **Kubik-, Raummaß** six cubic metres;
ten cubic feet

cum *preposition* with **mit, cum; cum dividend** = price of a share including the next dividend still to be paid **mit Dividende; cum coupon** = with a coupon attached **mit/cum Coupon**

cumulative *adjective* which is added automatically each year **kumulativ, anhäufend; cumulative interest** = interest which is added to the capital each year **Zins und Zinseszins; cumulative preference share** *or US* **cumulative preferred stock** = preference share which will have the dividend paid at a later date even if the company is not able to pay a dividend in the current year **kumulative Vorzugsaktien**

currency *noun* money in coins and notes which is used in a particular country **Währung; convertible currency** = currency which can easily be exchanged for another **frei konvertierbare Währung; foreign currency** = currency of another country **Devisen, Fremdwährung; foreign currency account** = bank account in the currency of another country (e.g. a dollar account) **Devisen-, Fremdwährungskonto; foreign currency reserves** = a country's reserves in currencies of other countries **Devisenreserven; hard currency** = currency of a country which has a strong economy and which can be changed into other currencies easily **harte Währung;** *to pay for imports in hard currency; to sell raw materials to earn hard currency;* **legal currency** = money which is legally used in a country **gesetzliches Zahlungsmittel; soft currency** = currency of a country with a weak economy, which is cheap to buy and difficult to exchange for other currencies **weiche Währung; currency backing** = gold *or* securities which maintain the international strength of a currency **Währungsgarantie; currency note** = bank note **Banknote, Schein**

NOTE: currency has no plural when it refers to the money of one country: **he was arrested trying to take currency out of the country**

QUOTE the strong dollar's inflationary impact on European economies, as national governments struggle to support their sinking currencies and push up interest rates

Duns Business Month

QUOTE today's wide daily variations in exchange rates show the instability of a system based on a single currency, namely the dollar

Economist

QUOTE the level of currency in circulation increased to N4.9 billion in the month of August

Business Times (Lagos)

current *adjective* referring to the present time **derzeitig, gegenwärtig; current account** = account in an bank from which the customer can withdraw money when he wants **laufendes Konto, Girokonto;** *to pay money into a current account;* **current assets** = assets used by a company in its ordinary work (such as materials, finished products, cash) **Umlaufvermögen; current cost accounting** = method of accounting which notes the cost of replacing assets at current prices, rather than valuing assets at their original cost **Rechnungslegung zum Wiederbeschaffungswert; current liabilities** = debts which a company has to pay within the next accounting period **kurzfristige Verbindlichkeiten; current price** = today's price **Tagespreis; current rate of exchange** = today's rate of exchange **Tageskurs; current yield** = dividend calculated as a percentage of the price paid per share **laufende Ertrag**

◇ **currently** *adverb* at the present time **gegenwärtig, zur Zeit;** *we are currently negotiating with the bank for a loan*

QUOTE crude oil output plunged during the past month and is likely to remain at its current level for the near future

Wall Street Journal

QUOTE customers' current deposit and current accounts also rose to $655.31 million at the end of December

Hongkong Standard

curriculum vitae *noun* summary of a person's life story showing details of education and work experience **Lebenslauf;** *candidates should send a letter of application with a curriculum vitae to the personnel officer*

NOTE: the plural is **curriculums** *or* **curricula vitae.** Note also that the US English is **résumé**

curve *noun* line which bends round **Kurve;** *the graph shows an upward curve;* **sales curve** = graph showing how sales increase or decrease **Absatzkurve**

cushion *noun*

(a) soft bag for sitting on **Kissen, Polster;** *she put a cushion on her chair as it was too hard*

(b) money which allows you to make a loss **Polster, Puffer;** *we have sums on deposit which are a useful cushion when cash flow is tight*

custom *noun*

(a) use of a shop by regular shoppers **Kundschaft, Klientel; to lose someone's custom** = to do something which makes a regular customer go to another shop **jdn als Kunden verlieren; custom-built** *or* **custom-made** = made specially for one customer **spezialangefertigt;** *he drives a custom-built Rolls Royce*

(b) the customs of the trade = general way of working in a trade **Handelsbrauch, Usance**

NOTE: no plural for (a)

◇ **customer** *noun* person *or* company which buys goods **Kunde/Kundin;** *the shop was full of customers; can you serve this customer first please? he is a regular customer of ours;* **customer appeal** = what attracts customers to a product **Kundenattraktivität; customer service department** = department which deals with customers and their complaints and orders **Kundendienst**

◇ **customize** *verb* to change something to fit the special needs of a customer **individuell anpassen, auf Bestellung anfertigen;** *we used customized computer terminals*

◇ **customs** *plural noun* the government department which organizes the collection of taxes on imports; office of this department at a port *or* airport **Behörde für Zölle und Verbrauchssteuern; Zoll(behörden); to go through the customs** = to pass through the area of a port or airport where customs officials examine goods **den Zoll passieren; to get something through the customs** = to carry something illegal through the customs area without declaring it **etwas durch den Zoll schmuggeln;** *he was stopped by the customs; her car was searched by the customs;* **customs barrier** = customs duty intended to prevent imports **Zollschranke; customs broker** = person *or* company which takes goods through the customs for a shipping company **Zollagent; customs clearance** = document given by customs to a shipper to show that customs duty has been paid and the goods can be shipped **Zollabfertigung;** *to wait for customs clearance;* **customs declaration** = statement showing goods being imported on which duty will have to be paid **Zollerklärung;** *to fill in a customs (declaration) form;* **customs duty** = tax paid on goods brought into or taken out of a country **Zoll(abgabe); the crates had to go through a customs examination** = the crates had to be examined by customs officials **die Kisten wurden vom Zoll untersucht; customs formalities** = declaration of goods by the shipper and examination of them by the customs **Zollformalitäten; customs officer** *or* **customs official** = person working for the customs **Zollbeamter; customs tariff** = list of duties to be paid on imported goods **Zollgebühren; customs union** = agreement between several countries that goods can travel between them, without paying duty, while goods from other countries have to pay special duties **Zollunion**

cut

1 *noun*

(a) sudden lowering of a price *or* salary *or* numbers of jobs **Senkung; Kürzung;** *price cuts or cuts in prices; salary cuts or cuts in salaries;* **job cuts** = reductions in the number of jobs **Arbeitsplatzkürzungen; he took a cut in salary** = he accepted a lower salary **er nahm eine Gehaltskürzung hin**

(b) share in a payment **Anteil, Teil;** *he introduces new customers and gets a cut of the salesman's commission*

2 *verb*

(a) to lower suddenly **senken; kürzen;** *we are cutting prices on all our models;* **to cut (back) production** = to reduce the quantity of products made **die Produktion zurückschrauben;** *the company has cut back its sales force; we have taken out the telex in order to try to cut costs*

(b) to stop *or* to reduce the number of something **streichen; abbauen; reduzieren; to cut jobs** = to reduce the number of jobs by making people redundant **Arbeitsplätze streichen; he cut his losses** = he stopped doing something which was creating a loss **er hat seine Verluste reduziert**

NOTE: **cutting - cut - has cut**

◇ **cutback** *noun* reduction **Kürzung;** *cutbacks in government spending*

◇ **cut down (on)** *verb* to reduce suddenly the amount of something used **kürzen;** *the government is cutting down on welfare expenditure; the office is trying to cut down on electricity consumption; we have installed a word-processor to cut down on paperwork*

◇ **cut in** *verb informal* **to cut someone in on a deal** = to give someone a share in the profits of a deal **jdn an einem Geschäft beteiligen**

◇ **cut-price** *adjective* sold at a cheaper price than usual **zu herabgesetzten Preisen;** *cut-price goods; cut-price petrol;* **cut-price store** = store selling cut-price goods **Niedrigpreisgeschäft, Billigladen**

◇ **cut-throat** *adjective* **cut-throat competition** = sharp competition by cutting prices and offering high discounts **mörderischer Wettbewerb**

◇ **cutting** *noun*

(a) cost cutting = reducing costs **Kostensenkung;** *we have made three secretaries redundant as part of our cost-cutting programme;* **price cutting** = sudden lowering of prices **Preissenkung; price-cutting war** = competition between companies to get a larger market share by cutting prices **Preiskrieg**

(b) press cutting agency = company which cuts out references to a client from newspapers and magazines and sends them on to him **Presseausschnittdienst; press cuttings** = references to a client *or* person *or* product cut out of newspapers or magazines **Zeitungsausschnitte;** *we have a file of press cuttings on our rivals' products*

NOTE: no plural for (a)

> QUOTE state-owned banks cut their prime rates a percentage point to 11%
> *Wall Street Journal*
>
> QUOTE the US bank announced a cut in its prime from 10+ per cent to 10 per cent
> *Financial Times*
>
> QUOTE Opec has on average cut production by one third since 1979
> *Economist*

cwt = HUNDREDWEIGHT

CV *noun* = CURRICULUM VITAE *please apply in writing, enclosing a current CV*

cycle *noun* period of time when something leaves its original position and then returns to it **Zyklus, Kreislauf; economic**

cycle *or* **trade cycle** *or* **business cycle** = period during which trade expands, then slows down and then expands again **Konjunkturzyklus**

◇ **cyclical** *adjective* which happens in cycles **zyklisch; cyclical factors** = way in which a trade cycle affects businesses **zyklische Faktoren**

Dd

daily *adjective* done every day **täglich; daily consumption** = amount used each day **täglicher Verbrauch, Tagesverbrauch; daily production of cars** = number of cars produced each day **Tagesproduktion an Autos; daily sales returns** = reports of sales made each day **Tagesumsatz; a daily newspaper** *or* **a daily** = newspaper which is produced every day **Tageszeitung**

damage
1 *noun*
(a) harm done to things **Schaden, Beschädigung; fire damage** = damage caused by a fire **Brandschaden; storm damage** = damage caused by a storm **Sturmschaden; to suffer damage** = to be harmed **Schaden erleiden/nehmen;** *we are trying to assess the damage which the shipment suffered in transit;* **to cause damage** = to harm something **beschädigen, Schaden verursachen/anrichten;** *the fire caused damage estimated at £100,000;* **damage survey** = survey of damage done **Schadensprüfung**
NOTE: no plural
(b) damages = money claimed as compensation for harm done **Schadensersatz, Entschädigung;** *to claim £1000 in damages; to be liable for damages; to pay £25,000 in damages;* **to bring an action for damages against someone** = to take someone to court and claim damages **jdn auf Schadensersatz verklagen**
2 *verb* to harm **beschädigen;** *the storm damaged the cargo; stock which has been damaged by water*

◇ **damaged** *adjective* which has suffered damage *or* which has been harmed **beschädigt, schadhaft;** *goods damaged in transit;* **fire-damaged goods** = goods harmed in a fire **brandgeschädigte Waren**

damp down *verb* to reduce **dämpfen, abschwächen;** *to damp down demand for domestic consumption of oil*

danger *noun* possibility of being harmed or killed **Gefahr, Risiko;** *there is danger to the workforce in the old machinery;* **there is no danger of the sales force leaving** = it is not likely that the sales force will leave **es besteht keine Gefahr, daß das Verkaufspersonal geht; to be in danger of** = which may easily happen **Gefahr laufen;** *the company is in danger of being taken over; she is in danger of being made redundant*

◇ **danger money** *noun* extra money paid to workers in dangerous jobs **Gefahrenzulage;** *the workforce has stopped work and asked for danger money*

◇ **dangerous** *adjective* which can be harmful **gefährlich, riskant; dangerous job** = job where the workers may be killed or hurt **gefährlicher Beruf**

data *noun* information (letters or figures) available on computer **Daten; data acquisition** = getting information **Datenerfassung; data bank** *or* **bank of data** = store of information in a computer **Datenbank; data processing** = selecting and examining data in a computer to produce special information **Datenverarbeitung**
NOTE: **data** is usually singular: **the data is easily available**

◇ **database** *noun* store of information in a large computer **Datenbank;** *we can extract the lists of potential customers from our database*

date
1 *noun*
(a) number of day, month and year **Datum;** *I have received your letter of yesterday's date;* **date stamp** = rubber stamp for marking the date on letters received **Datumsstempel; date of receipt** = date when something is received **Eingangs-, Empfangsdatum**
(b) up to date = current *or* recent *or* modern **aktuell, auf dem neuesten Stand;** *an up-to-date computer system;* **to bring something up to date** = to add the latest information to something **etwas auf den neuesten Stand bringen; to keep something up to date** = to keep adding information to something so that it is always up to date **etwas auf dem laufenden halten/aktualisieren;** *we spend a lot of time keeping our mailing list up to date*
(c) to date = up to now **bis jetzt/heute; interest to date** = interest up to the present time **Zinsen bis auf den heutigen Tag**
(d) out of date = old-fashioned **veraltet, altmodisch, unzeitgemäß;** *their computer system is years out of date; they are still using out-of-date machinery*
(e) maturity date = date when a government stock will mature **Fälligkeitstermin; date of bill** = date when a bill will mature **Fälligkeitstermin eines Wechsels**

2 *verb* to put a date on a document **datieren;** *the cheque was dated March 24th; you forgot to date the cheque;* **to date a cheque forward** = to put a later date than the present one on a cheque **einen Scheck vordatieren**

◇ **dated** *adjective* with a date written on it **datiert;** *thank you for your letter dated June 15th;* **long-dated bill** = bill which is payable more than three months from now **langfristiger Wechsel; short-dated bill** = bill which is payable within a few days **kurzfristiger Wechsel**

day *noun*

(a) period of 24 hours **Tag;** *there are thirty days in June; the first day of the month is a public holiday;* **settlement day** = day when accounts have to be settled **Abrechnungstag; three clear days** = three whole working days **drei (volle) Werk-/Arbeitstage;** *to give ten clear days' notice; allow four clear days for the cheque to be paid into the bank*
(b) period of work from morning to night **Tag; she took two days off** = she did not come to work for two days **sie hat zwei Tage freigenommen; he works three days on, two days off** = he works for three days, then has two days' holiday **er arbeitet drei Tage und hat dann zwei Tage frei; to work an eight-hour day** = to spend eight hours at work each day **einen achtstündigen Arbeitstag haben; day shift** = shift which works during the daylight hours such as from 8 a.m. to 5.30 p.m. **Tagschicht;** *there are 150 men on the day shift; he works the day shift;* **day release** = arrangement where a company allows a worker to go to college to study for one or two days each week **Freistellung zur beruflichen Fortbildung;** *the junior sales manager is attending a day release course*

◇ **daybook** *noun* book with an account of sales and purchases made each day **Journal**

◇ **day-to-day** *adjective* ordinary *or* which goes on all the time **täglich, Tages-;** *he organizes the day-to-day running of the company; sales only just cover the day-to-day expenses*

◇ **day worker** *noun* person who works the day shift **Tagarbeiter**

DCF = DISCOUNTED CASH FLOW

dead *adjective*

(a) not alive **tot, verstorben;** *six people were dead as a result of the accident; the founders of the company are all dead*
(b) not working **unproduktiv, ertraglos; dead account** = account which is no longer used **umsatzloses Konto; the line went dead** = the telephone line suddenly stopped working **die Verbindung wurde unterbrochen; dead loss** = total loss **Totalverlust;** *the car was written off as a dead loss;* **dead money** = money which is not invested to make a profit **totes Kapital; dead season** = time of year when there are few tourists about **Nebensaison**

◇ **deadline** *noun* date by which something has to be done **(letzter) Termin, Stichtag; to meet a deadline** = to finish something in time **eine Frist einhalten;** *we've missed our October 1st deadline*

◇ **deadlock**
1 *noun* point where two sides in a dispute cannot agree **Stillstand;** *the negotiations have reached a deadlock;* **to break a deadlock** = to find a way to start discussions again **aus einer Sackgasse herausfinden**
2 *verb* to be unable to agree to continue discussing **zum Stillstand bringen; talks have been deadlocked for ten days** = after ten days the talks have not produced any agreement **nach zehn Tagen sind die Gespräche an einem toten Punkt angekommen**

◇ **deadweight** *noun* heavy goods like coal, iron or sand **schwere Güter; deadweight cargo** = heavy cargo which is charged by weight, not by volume **Schwergut; deadweight capacity** *or* **deadweight tonnage** = largest amount of cargo which a ship can carry safely **Gesamtnutzlast**

deal

1 *noun*
(a) business agreement *or* affair *or* contract **Abkommen, Abschluß, Geschäft, Handel;** *to arrange a deal or to set up a deal or to do a deal; to sign a deal; the sales director set up a deal with a Russian bank; the deal will be signed tomorrow; they did a deal with an American airline;* **to call off a deal** = to stop an agreement **ein Abkommen rückgängig machen;** *when the chairman heard about the deal he called it off;* **cash deal** = sale done for cash **Barverkauf; package deal** = agreement where several different items are agreed at the same time **Pauschalarrangement, Verhandlungspaket;** *they agreed a package deal, which involves the construction of the factory, training of staff and purchase of the product*
(b) a great deal *or* **a good deal of something** = a large quantity of something **viel, eine Menge;** *he has made a good deal of money on the stock market; the company lost a great deal of time asking for expert advice*
2 *verb*
(a) to deal with = to organize **sich befassen mit;** *leave it to the filing clerk - he'll deal with it;* **to deal with an order** = to supply an order **eine Bestellung ausführen**
(b) to trade *or* to buy and sell **handeln, Handel treiben; to deal with someone** = to do business with someone **mit jdm Geschäfte**

machen, mit jdm in Geschäftsverbindung stehen; to deal in leather *or* **to deal in options** = to buy and sell leather *or* options **in der Lederbranche tätig sein; Optionsgeschäfte machen; he deals on the Stock Exchange** = his work involves buying and selling shares on the Stock Exchange for clients **er ist als Börsenhändler tätig**

◊ **dealer** *noun* person who buys and sells **Händler/-in, Kaufmann/Kauffrau;** *dealer in tobacco or tobacco dealer;* **foreign exchange dealer** = person who buys and sells foreign currencies **Devisenhändler, Devisenmakler; retail dealer** = person who sells to the general public **Einzelhändler; wholesale dealer** = person who sells in bulk to retailers **Großhändler**

◊ **dealing** *noun*
(a) buying and selling on the Stock Exchange **Effektenhandel; fair dealing** = legal trade *or* legal buying and selling of shares **legaler Handel; geordneter Effektenhandel; foreign exchange dealing** = buying and selling foreign currencies **Devisenhandel; forward dealings** = buying or selling commodities forward **Termingeschäfte; insider dealing** = illegal buying or selling of shares by staff of a company who have secret information about the company's plans **Insiderhandel; option dealing** = buying and selling share options **Optionsgeschäft**
(b) buying and selling goods **Handel; to have dealings with someone** = to do business with someone **mit jdm Geschäfte machen, mit jdm in Geschäftsbeziehungen stehen**

dear *adjective*

(a) expensive *or* costing a lot of money **teuer, kostspielig;** *property is very dear in this area;* **dear money** = money which has to be borrowed at a high interest rate **teures Geld**
(b) way of starting a letter **Liebe(r); Sehr geehrte(r); Dear Sir** *or* **Dear Madam** = addressing a man or woman whom you do not know **Sehr geehrte Damen und Herren; Dear Sirs** = addressing a firm **Sehr geehrte Damen und Herren; Dear Mr Smith** *or* **Dear Mrs Smith** *or* **Dear Miss Smith** = addressing a man or woman whom you know **Lieber/Sehr geehrter Herr Smith; Liebe/Sehr geehrte Frau Smith; Dear James** *or* **Dear Julia** = addressing a friend *or* a person you do business with **Lieber James; Liebe Julia**

death *noun*

act of dying **Tod, Sterben; death benefit** = insurance benefit paid to the family of someone who dies in an accident at work **Sterbegeld; death in service** = insurance benefit or pension paid when someone dies while employed by a company **Versicherungszahlung im Todesfall eines Betriebsangehörigen;** *US* **death duty** *or* **death tax** = tax paid on the property left by a dead person **Erbschaftssteuer**

debenture *noun*

agreement to repay a debt with fixed interest using the company's assets as security **gesicherte Schuldverschreibung;** *the bank holds a debenture on the company;* **mortgage debenture** = debenture where the lender can be repaid by selling the company's property **Hypothekenpfandbrief; debenture issue** *or* **issue of debentures** = borrowing money against the security of the company's assets **Ausgabe von Schuldverschreibungen; debenture bond** = certificate showing that a debenture has been issued **Schuldverschreibung, Obligation; debenture capital** *or* **debenture stock** = capital borrowed by a company, using its fixed assets as security **Anleihekapital; debenture holder** = person who holds a debenture for money lent **Obligationär; debenture register** *or* **register of debentures** = list of debenture holders of a company **Verzeichnis der Obligationäre**

debit

1 *noun* money which a company owes **Schuldposten, Soll, Debet; debits and credits** = money which a company owes and money it receives **Soll und Haben; debit balance** = balance in an account, showing that the company owes more money than it has received **Sollsaldo; debit column** = left-hand column in accounts showing the money paid or owed to others **Debetspalte; debit entry** = entry on the debit side of an account **Sollbuchung, Lastschrift; debit side** = left-hand side of an account showing the money paid or owed to others **Debetseite; debit note** = note showing that a customer owes money **Lastschriftanzeige;** *we undercharged Mr Smith and had to send him a debit note for the extra amount;* **direct debit** = system where a customer allows a company to charge costs to his bank account automatically and where the amount charged can be increased or decreased with the agreement of the customer **Direktabbuchung;** *I pay my electricity bill by direct debit*
2 *verb* **to debit an account** = to charge an account with a cost **ein Konto belasten;** *his account was debited with the sum of £25*

◊ **debitable** *adjective* which can be debited **belastbar**

debt *noun*

(a) money owed for goods or services **Schulden;** *the company stopped trading with debts of over £1 million;* **to be in debt** = to owe money **Schulden haben; he is in debt to**

the tune of £250 = he owes £250 **er hat Schulden in Höhe von £250; to get into debt** = to start to borrow more money than you can pay back **sich verschulden, Schulden machen; the company is out of debt** = the company does not owe money any more **das Unternehmen ist aus den Schulden heraus; to pay back a debt** = to pay all the money owed **Schulden zurückzahlen; to pay off a debt** = to finish paying money owed **Schulden begleichen/tilgen; to service a debt** = to pay interest on a debt **für Schulden Zinsen bezahlen;** *the company is having problems in servicing its debts;* **bad debt** = money owed which will never be paid back **uneinbringliche Forderung, nicht einziehbare Außenstände;** *the company has written off £30,000 in bad debts;* **secured debts** *or* **unsecured debts** = debts which are guaranteed or not guaranteed by assets **gesicherte Verbindlichkeiten; ungesicherte Verbindlichkeiten; debt collection** = collecting money which is owed **Forderungseinziehung, Schuldeneintreibung; debt collection agency** = company which collects debts for a commission **Inkassofirma; debt collector** = person who collects debts **Inkassobeauftragter;** *umg* **Schuldeneintreiber; debts due** = money owed which is due for repayment **fällige Schulden (b) funded debt** = part of the National Debt which pays interest, but where there is no date for repayment of the principal **fundierte Schuld; the National Debt** = money borrowed by a government **Staatsverschuldung**

◊ **debtor** *noun* person who owes money **Schuldner/-in; Kreditnehmer; debtor side** = debit side of an account **Soll-, Debetspalte; debtor nation** = country whose foreign debts are larger than money owed to it by other countries **Schuldnerland**

> QUOTE the United States is now a debtor nation for the first time since 1914, owing more to foreigners than it is owed itself
> *Economist*

deceit *or* **deception** *noun* making a wrong statement to someone in order to trick him into paying money **Täuschung, Betrug, Betrügerei;** *he obtained £10,000 by deception*

decentralize *verb* to organize from various points, away from the centre **dezentralisieren;** *the group has a policy of decentralized purchasing where each division is responsible for its own purchasing*

◊ **decentralization** *noun* organization from various points, away from the centre **Dezentralisierung;** *the decentralization of the buying departments*

decide *verb* to make up your mind to do something **entscheiden, beschließen, sich entschließen;** *to decide on a course of action; to decide to appoint a new managing director*

◊ **deciding** *adjective* **deciding factor** = most important factor which influences a decision **entscheidender Faktor**

decile *noun* one of a series of nine figures below which one tenth or several tenths of the total fall **Zehntelstelle, Ezil**

decimal *noun* **decimal system** = system based on the number 10 **Dezimalsystem; correct to three places of decimals** = correct to three figures after the decimal point (e.g. 3.485) **korrekt bis zu drei Stellen nach dem Komma/bis auf drei Dezimalstellen; decimal point** = dot which indicates the division between the whole unit and its smaller parts (such as 4.75) **Dezimalstelle**

◊ **decimalization** *noun* changing to a decimal system **Dezimalisierung**

◊ **decimalize** *verb* to change to a decimal system **auf das Dezimalsystem umstellen**

decision *noun* making up one's mind to do something **Entscheidung, Beschluß, Entschluß;** *to come to a decision or to reach a decision;* **decision making** = act of coming to a decision **Entscheidungsfindung, Beschlußfassung; the decision-making processes** = ways in which decisions are reached **Entscheidungsprozeß; decision maker** = person who has to decide **Person, die Entscheidungen trifft**

deck *noun* flat floor in a ship **Deck; deck cargo** = cargo carried on the open top deck of a ship **Deckladung; deck hand** = ordinary sailor on a cargo ship **unausgebildeter Seemann**

declaration *noun* official statement **Erklärung, Deklaration; declaration of bankruptcy** = official statement that someone is bankrupt **Konkurseröffnungsbeschluß; declaration of income** = statement declaring income to the tax office **Einkommenssteuererklärung; customs declaration** = statement declaring goods brought into a country on which customs duty should be paid **Zolldeklaration; VAT declaration** = statement declaring VAT income to the VAT office **Mehrwertsteuererklärung**

◊ **declare** *verb* to make an official statement *or* to announce to the public **Erklärung abgeben, erklären, bekanntgeben;** *to declare someone bankrupt; to declare a dividend of 10%;* **to declare goods to the**

customs = to state that you are importing goods which are liable to duty **Waren deklarieren, Waren zur Verzollung anmelden;** *the customs officials asked him if he had anything to declare;* **to declare an interest** = to state in public that you own shares in a company being investigated **seine Beteiligungen offenlegen**

◇ **declared** *adjective* which has been made public or officially stated **erklärt; declared value** = value of goods entered on a customs declaration **angemeldeter/angegebener Wert**

decline

1 *noun* gradual fall **Rückgang, Abnahme, Abschwächung, Sinken;** *the decline in the value of the franc; a decline in buying power; the last year has seen a decline in real wages*
2 *verb* to fall slowly **zurückgehen, abnehmen, sinken, geringer/weniger werden;** *shares declined in a weak market; imports have declined over the last year; the economy declined during the last government*

> QUOTE in 1984 the profits again declined to L185bn from the 1983 figure of L229.7bn
> *Financial Times*
> QUOTE Saudi oil production has declined by three quarters to around 2.5m barrels a day
> *Economist*
> QUOTE this gives an average monthly decline of 2.15 per cent during the period
> *Business Times (Lagos)*

decontrol *verb* to stop controls **freigeben, liberalisieren; to decontrol the price of petrol** = to stop controlling the price of petrol so that it can be reached freely by the market **den Benzinpreis freigeben; to decontrol wages** = to allow wage increases to be given freely **Lohnkontrollen aufheben**
NOTE: **decontrolling - decontrolled**

decrease

1 *noun* fall *or* reduction **Rückgang, Abnahme, Verminderung, Fall, Reduzierung;** *decrease in price; decrease in value; decrease in imports; exports have registered a decrease; sales show a 10% decrease on last year*
2 *verb* to fall *or* to become less **zurückgehen, abnehmen, nachlassen, fallen, sich vermindern/reduzieren;** *imports are decreasing; the value of the pound has decreased by 5%*

deduct *verb* to remove money from a total **abziehen;** *to deduct £3 from the price; to deduct a sum for expenses; after deducting costs the gross margin is only 23%; expenses are still to be deducted;* **tax deducted at source** = tax which is removed from a salary, interest payment *or* dividend payment on shares before the money is paid **Quellensteuer**

◇ **deductible** *adjective* which can be deducted **abziehbar; tax-deductible** = which can be deducted from an income before tax is paid **steuerlich absetzbar/abzugsfähig; these expenses are not tax-deductible** = tax has to be paid on these expenses **diese Ausgaben sind nicht (von der Steuer) absetzbar**

◇ **deduction** *noun* removing of money from a total *or* money removed from a total **Abzug, Abziehen;** *net salary is salary after deduction of tax and social security;* **deductions from salary** *or* **salary deductions** *or* **deductions at source** = money which a company removes from salaries to give to the government as tax, national insurance contributions, etc. **Lohnabzüge; tax deductions** = (i) money removed from a salary to pay tax; (ii); *US* business expenses which can be claimed against tax **(i) Steuerabzüge; (ii) (von der Steuer) absetzbare Ausgaben**

deed *noun* legal document *or* written agreement **Dokument, Urkunde; deed of assignment** = document which legally transfers a property from a debtor to a creditor **Übereignungsurkunde; deed of covenant** = signed legal agreement **Vertragsurkunde; deed of partnership** = agreement which sets up a partnership **Gesellschaftsvertrag; deed of transfer** = document which transfers the ownership of shares **Zessionsurkunde; title deeds** = document showing who owns a property **Grundeigentumsurkunde;** *entspricht* **Grundbucheintrag;** *we have deposited the deeds of the house in the bank*

defalcation *noun* illegal use of money by someone who is not the owner but who has been trusted to look after it **Veruntreuung, Unterschlagung**

default

1 *noun* failure to carry out the terms of a contract, especially failure to pay back a debt **Nichterfüllung, Versäumnis, Unterlassung, Vertragsverletzung; in default of payment** = with no payment made **bei Zahlungsverzug; the company is in default** = the company has failed to carry out the terms of the contract **die Firma befindet sich in Verzug; by default** = because no one else will act **im Unterlassungsfall; he was elected by default** = he was elected because all the other candidates withdrew **er wurde in Ermangelung anderer Kandidaten gewählt**
NOTE: no plural
2 *verb* to fail to carry out the terms of a contract, especially to fail to pay back a debt **nicht erfüllen, nicht bezahlen, in (Zahlungs)verzug geraten, unterlassen; to default on payments** = not to make

payments which are due under the terms of a contract **mit Zahlungen in Verzug geraten**

◇ **defaulter** *noun* person who defaults **säumiger Schuldner**

defeat

1 *noun* loss of a vote **Niederlage;** *the chairman offered to resign after the defeat of the proposal at the AGM*

2 *verb* to beat someone **schlagen** to beat something in a vote **ablehnen;** *the proposal was defeated by 10 votes to 23; he was heavily defeated in the ballot for union president*

defect *noun* something which is wrong *or* which stops a machine from working properly **Defekt, Fehler, Mangel;** *a computer defect or a defect in the computer*

◇ **defective** *adjective*

(a) faulty *or* not working properly **defekt, fehlerhaft, schadhaft;** *the machine broke down because of a defective cooling system*

(b) not legally valid **unzulänglich, ungültig;** *his title to the property is defective*

defence *or US* **defense** *noun*

(a) protecting someone *or* something against attack **Verteidigung, Abwehr;** *the merchant bank is organizing the company's defence against the takeover bid*

(b) fighting a lawsuit on behalf of a defendant **Verteidigung; defence counsel** = lawyer who represents the defendant in a lawsuit **Verteidiger**

◇ **defend** *verb* to fight to protect someone *or* something which is being attacked **verteidigen;** *the company is defending itself against the takeover bid; he hired the best lawyers to defend him against the tax authorities;* **to defend a lawsuit** = to appear in court to state your case when accused of something **einen Prozeß als Beklagter führen**

◇ **defendant** *noun* person who is sued *or* who is accused of doing something to harm someone **Beklagter**

defer *verb* to put back to a later date *or* to postpone **ver-, aufschieben, zurückstellen, vertagen;** *to defer payment; the decision has been deferred until the next meeting*

NOTE: **deferring - deferred**

◇ **deferment** *noun* postponement *or* putting back to a later date **Aufschub, Zurückstellung, Vertagung;** *deferment of payment; deferment of a decision*

◇ **deferred** *adjective* put back to a later date **aufgeschoben, vertagt; deferred creditor** = person who is owed money by a bankrupt but who is paid only after all other creditors **nachrangiger (Konkurs)gläubiger; deferred payment** = payment for goods by instalments over a long period **Ratenzahlung; deferred stock** = shares which receive a dividend after all other dividends have been paid **Nachzugsaktien**

deficiency *noun* lack; money lacking **Mangel; Defizit, Fehlbetrag;** *there is a £10 deficiency in the petty cash;* **to make up a deficiency** = to put money into an account to balance it **einen Fehlbetrag ausgleichen**

deficit *noun* amount by which spending is higher than income **Defizit, Minusbetrag, Verlust; the accounts show a deficit** = the accounts show a loss **die Bilanz weist einen Verlust auf; to make good a deficit** = to put money into an account to balance it **ein Defizit ausgleichen; balance of payments deficit** = situation when a country imports more than it exports **Zahlungsbilanzdefizit; deficit financing** = planning by a government to borrow money to cover the shortfall between tax income and expenditure **Defizitwirtschaft**

deflate *verb* **to deflate the economy** = to reduce activity in the economy by cutting the supply of money **eine restriktive Wirtschaftspolitik betreiben**

◇ **deflation** *noun* reduction in economic activity **Deflation**

◇ **deflationary** *adjective* which can cause deflation **deflationär;** *the government has introduced some deflationary measures in the budget*

QUOTE the strong dollar's deflationary impact on European economies as national governments push up interest rates

Duns Business Month

defray *verb* to provide money to pay (costs) **aufkommen für, tragen, übernehmen;** *the company agreed to defray the costs of the exhibition*

degearing *noun* reduction in gearing *or* reducing a company's loan capital in relation to the value of its ordinary shares **den Verschuldungsgrad reduzieren**

NOTE: no plural

delay

1 *noun* time when someone *or* something is later than planned **Verspätung, Verzögerung, Verzug;** *there was a delay of thirty minutes before the AGM started or the AGM started after a thirty minute delay; we are sorry for the delay in supplying your order or in replying to your letter*

2 *verb* to be late; to make someone late **sich verspäten/verzögern; aufhalten;** *he was delayed because his taxi had an accident;*

the company has delayed payment of all invoices

del credere

noun **del credere agent** = agent who receives a high commission because he guarantees payment by customers **Delkredereagent**

delegate

1 *noun* person who represents others at a meeting **Delegierter, Bevollmächtigter;** *the management refused to meet the trade union delegates*
2 *verb* to pass authority or responsibility to someone else **delegieren, bevollmächtigen, Vollmacht erteilen;** *to delegate authority;* **he cannot delegate** = he wants to control everything himself and refuses to give up any of his responsibilities to his subordinates **er kann nicht delegieren**

◇ **delegation** *noun*
(a) group of delegates **Delegation, Abordnung;** *a Chinese trade delegation; the management met a union delegation*
(b) act of passing authority or responsibility to someone else **Bevollmächtigung, Übertragung**

delete

verb to cut out words in a document **streichen;** *they want to delete all references to credit terms from the contract; the lawyers have deleted clause two*

deliver

verb to transport goods to a customer **liefern, zustellen; goods delivered free** *or* **free delivered goods** = goods transported to the customer's address at a price which includes transport costs **frei Haus gelieferte Waren; goods delivered on board** = goods transported free to the ship *or* plane but not to the customer's warehouse **frei Bord; delivered price** = price which includes packing and transport **Lieferpreis**

◇ **delivery** *noun*
(a) delivery of goods = transport of goods to a customer's address **Warenlieferung, Warenzustellung;** *parcels awaiting delivery; free delivery or delivery free; delivery date; delivery within 28 days; allow 28 days for delivery; delivery is not allowed for or is not included;* **delivery note** = list of goods being delivered, given to the customer with the goods **Lieferschein; delivery order** = instructions given by the customer to the person holding his goods, to tell him to deliver them **Lieferauftrag; the store has a delivery service to all parts of the town** = the store will deliver goods to all parts of the town **das Geschäft liefert in alle Stadtteile; delivery time** = number of days before something will be delivered **Lieferzeit; delivery van** = goods van for delivering goods to retail customers **Lieferwagen; express delivery** = very fast delivery **Eilzustellung; recorded delivery** = mail service where the letters are signed for by the person receiving them **Einschreiben;** *we sent the documents (by) recorded delivery;* **cash on delivery** = payment in cash when the goods are delivered **gegen Nachnahme; to take delivery of goods** = to accept goods when they are delivered **eine Lieferung abnehmen/übernehmen;** *we took delivery of the stock into our warehouse on the 25th*
(b) goods being delivered **Lieferung;** *we take in three deliveries a day; there were four items missing in the last delivery*
(c) transfer of a bill of exchange **Übertragung**

demand

1 *noun*
(a) asking for payment **Forderung, Aufforderung; payable on demand** = which must be paid when payment is asked for **zahlbar bei Sicht/auf Verlangen; demand bill** = bill of exchange which must be paid when payment is asked for **Sichtwechsel;** *US* **demand deposit** = money in a bank account which can be taken out when you want it by writing a cheque **Kontokorrentkonto, laufendes Konto, Sichteinlage; final demand** = last reminder from a supplier, after which he will sue for payment **letzte Mahnung**
(b) need for goods at a certain price **Nachfrage, Bedarf;** *there was an active demand for oil shares on the stock market;* **to meet a demand** *or* **to fill a demand** = to supply what is needed **den Bedarf decken;** *the factory had to increase production to meet the extra demand; the factory had to cut production when demand slackened; the office cleaning company cannot keep up with the demand for its services;* **there is not much demand for this item** = not many people want to buy it **dieser Artikel ist nicht sehr gefragt; this book is in great demand** *or* **there is a great demand for this book** = many people want to buy it **dieses Buch ist sehr gefragt; effective demand** = actual demand for a product which can be paid for **effektive Nachfrage; demand price** = price at which a certain quantity of goods will be bought **Nachfragepreis; supply and demand** = amount of a product which is available and the amount which is wanted by customers **Angebot und Nachfrage; law of supply and demand** = general rule that the amount of a product which is available is related to the needs of potential customers **Gesetz von Angebot und Nachfrage**
2 *verb* to ask for something and expect to get it **fordern, verlangen;** *she demanded a refund; the suppliers are demanding immediate payment of their outstanding invoices*

◇ **demand-led inflation** *noun* inflation caused by rising demand which cannot be met **Nachfrageinflation**

> QUOTE spot prices are now relatively stable in the run-up to the winter's peak demand
> *Economist*
> QUOTE the demand for the company's products remained strong throughout the first six months of the year with production and sales showing significant increases
> *Business Times (Lagos)*
> QUOTE growth in demand is still coming from the private rather than the public sector
> *Lloyd's List*

demarcation dispute *noun* argument between different trade unions over who shall do different parts of a job **Kontroverse um den Zuständigkeitsbereich, Kompetenzstreit;** *production of the new car was held up by demarcation disputes*

demise *noun*
(a) death **Tod, Ableben;** *on his demise the estate passed to his daughter*
(b) granting of a property on a lease **Verpachtung**
NOTE: no plural for (a)

demonetize *verb* to stop a coin or note being used as money **entwerten, einziehen**

◇ **demonetization** *noun* stopping a coin or note being used as money **Entwertung, Außerkurssetzung**

demonstrate *verb* to show how something works **vorführen;** *he was demonstrating a new tractor when he was killed; the managers saw the new stock control system being demonstrated*

◇ **demonstration** *noun* showing how something works **Vorführung;** *we went to a demonstration of new telex equipment;* **demonstration model** = piece of equipment used in demonstrations and later sold off cheaply **Vorführmodell**

◇ **demonstrator** *noun* person who demonstrates pieces of equipment **Vorführer/-in**

demote *verb* to give someone a less important job **niedriger einstufen, zurückstufen;** *he was demoted from manager to salesman; she lost a lot of salary when she was demoted*

◇ **demotion** *noun* giving someone a less important job **niedrigere Einstufung, Zurückstufung;** *he was very angry at his demotion*

demurrage *noun* money paid to a customer when a shipment is delayed at a port *or* by the customs **Liegegeld**

denationalize *verb* to put a nationalized industry back into private ownership **(re)privatisieren;** *the government has plans to denationalize the steel industry*

◇ **denationalization** *noun* act of denationalizing **(Re)privatisierung;** *the denationalization of the aircraft industry*

denomination *noun* unit of money (on a coin, banknote or stamp) **Nennwert, Stückelung;** *coins of all denominations; small denomination notes*

depart *verb*
(a) to leave **abreisen, abfahren; abfliegen;** *the plane departs from Paris at 11.15*
(b) to depart from normal practice = to act in a different way from the normal practice **von der üblichen Verfahrensweise abweichen**

◇ **department** *noun*
(a) specialized section of a large company **Abteilung;** *complaints department; design department; dispatch department; export department; legal department;* **accounts department** = section which deals with money paid or received **Buchhaltung; new issues department** = section of a bank which deals with issues of new shares **Emissionsabteilung; personnel department** = section of a company dealing with the staff **Personalabteilung; head of department** *or* **department head** *or* **department manager** = person in charge of a department **Abteilungsleiter**
(b) section of a large store selling one type of product **Abteilung;** *you will find beds in the furniture department;* **budget department** = department in a large store which sells cheaper goods **Sonderangebotsabteilung**
(c) section of the British government containing several ministries **Ministerium;** *the Department of Trade and Industry; the Department of Education and Science*

◇ **department store** *noun* large store with sections for different types of goods **Kaufhaus**

◇ **departmental** *adjective* referring to a department **Abteilungs-; departmental manager** = manager of a department **Abteilungsleiter**

departure *noun*
(a) going away **Abreise, Abfahrt; Abflug;** *the plane's departure was delayed by two hours;* **departures** = part of an airport terminal which deals with passengers who are leaving **Abflug(halle); departure lounge** =

room in an airport where passengers wait to get on their planes **Warteraum**
(b) new venture *or* a new type of business **Neubeginn, Start, Neuerung;** *selling records will be a departure for the local bookshop*

depend *verb*
(a) to depend on = to need someone *or* something to exist **angewiesen sein auf;** *the company depends on efficient service from its suppliers; we depend on government grants to pay the salary bill*
(b) to happen because of something **abhängig sein von;** *the success of the launch will depend on the publicity;* **depending on** = which varies according to something **abhängig von, je nach;** *depending on the advertising budget, the new product will be launched on radio or on TV*

deposit
1 *noun*
(a) money placed in a bank for safe keeping or to earn interest **Einzahlung, Einlage; certificate of deposit** = certificate from a bank to show that money has been deposited **Einzahlungsbeleg; bank deposits** = all the money placed in banks **Bankeinlagen;** *bank deposits are at an all-time high;* **fixed deposit** = deposit which pays a fixed interest over a fixed period **Festgeld; deposit account** = bank account which pays interest but on which notice has to be given to withdraw money **Sparkonto; deposit at 7 days' notice** = money deposited which you can withdraw by giving seven days' notice **Sparkonto mit 7tägiger Kündigungsfrist; deposit slip** = piece of paper stamped by the cashier to prove that you have paid money into your account **Einzahlungsbeleg**
(b) safe deposit = bank safe where you can leave jewellery or documents **Tresor; safe deposit box** = small box which you can rent, in which you can keep jewellery or documents in a bank's safe **Bankschließfach**
(c) money given in advance so that the thing which you want to buy will not be sold to someone else **Anzahlung;** *to pay a deposit on a watch; to leave £10 as deposit*
2 *verb*
(a) to put documents somewhere for safe keeping **in Verwahrung geben, deponieren;** *to deposit shares with a bank; we have deposited the deeds of the house with the bank; he deposited his will with his solicitor*
(b) to put money into a bank account **einzahlen;** *to deposit £100 in a current account*

◇ **depositary** *noun US* person *or* company with whom money or documents can be deposited **Depot, Hinterlegungsstelle; Verwahrer**

◇ **depositor** *noun* person who deposits money in a bank **Einzahler, Einleger**

◇ **depository** *noun*
(a) furniture depository = warehouse where you can store household furniture **Möbellager**
(b) person or company with whom money or documents can be deposited **Depot, Hinterlegungsstelle; Verwahrer**

depot *noun* central warehouse for goods; centre for transport **Depot, Lagerhaus; Depot;** *bus depot; freight depot; goods depot; oil storage depot*

depreciate *verb*
(a) to reduce the value of assets in accounts **abschreiben;** *we depreciate our company cars over three years*
(b) to lose value **fallen, sinken, an Wert verlieren;** *share which has depreciated by 10% over the year; the pound has depreciated by 5% against the dollar*

◇ **depreciation** *noun*
(a) reduction in value of an asset **Abschreibung; depreciation rate** = rate at which an asset is depreciated each year in the accounts **Abschreibungssatz; accelerated depreciation** = system of depreciation which reduces the value of assets at a high rate in the early years to encourage companies, as a result of tax advantages, to invest in new equipment **vorzeitige Abschreibung, Sonderabschreibung; annual depreciation** = reduction in the book value of an asset at a certain rate per year **jährliche Abschreibung; straight line depreciation** = depreciation calculated by dividing the cost of an asset by the number of years it is likely to be used **lineare Abschreibung**
(b) loss of value **Fall, Wertminderung, Wertverlust;** *a share which has shown a depreciation of 10% over the year; the depreciation of the pound against the dollar*
NOTE: no plural

> QUOTE this involved reinvesting funds on items which could be depreciated against income for three years
> ***Australian Financial Review***
> QUOTE buildings are depreciated at two per cent per annum on the estimated cost of construction
> ***Hongkong Standard***

depress *verb* to reduce **herabsetzen, drücken, senken, vermindern, verringern;** *reducing the money supply has the effect of depressing demand for consumer goods*

◇ **depressed** *adjective* **depressed area** = part of a country suffering from depression **von einer Wirtschaftskrise betroffenes Gebiet; depressed market** = market where there are more goods than customers **flauer Markt**

◇ **depression** *noun* period of economic crisis with high unemployment and loss of trade **Depression, Flaute, Tiefstand;** *an economic depression;* **the Great Depression** = the world economic crisis of 1929-1933 **die Weltwirtschaftskrise (von 1929)**

dept = DEPARTMENT

deputy *noun* person who takes the place of another **Stellvertreter;** *to act as deputy for someone or to act as someone's deputy; deputy chairman; deputy manager; deputy managing director*

◇ **deputize** *verb* **to deputize for someone** = to take the place of someone who is absent **jdn vertreten, als Stellvertreter für jdn fungieren;** *he deputized for the chairman who had a cold*

deregulation *noun US* reducing government control over an industry **Deregulation, Abbau einschränkender Bestimmungen;** *the deregulation of the airlines*

describe *verb* to say what someone *or* something is like **beschreiben, ausführen, schildern;** *the leaflet describes the services the company can offer; the managing director described the company's difficulties with cash flow*

◇ **description** *noun* words which show what something is like **Beschreibung, Schilderung; false description of contents** = wrongly stating the contents of a packet to trick customers into buying it **unkorrekte Inhaltsbeschreibung; job description** = official document from the management which says what a job involves **Tätigkeitsbeschreibung; trade description** = description of a product to attract customers **Warenkennzeichnung**

design

1 *noun* planning *or* drawing of a product before it is built or manufactured **Design, Entwurf; industrial design** = design of products made by machines (such as cars and refrigerators) **Industriedesign; product design** = design of consumer products **Produktgestaltung; design department** = department in a large company which designs the company's products or its advertising **Design-Abteilung; Werbeabteilung; design studio** = independent firm which specializes in creating designs **Design-Studio**

2 *verb* to plan *or* to draw something before it is built or manufactured **entwerfen;** *he designed a new car factory; she designs garden furniture*

◇ **designer** *noun* person who designs **Designer/-in;** *she is the designer of the new computer*

designate *adjective* person who has been appointed to a job but who has not yet started work **designiert;** *the chairman designate*

NOTE: always follows a noun

desk *noun*

(a) writing table in an office, usually with drawers for stationery **Schreibtisch;** *desk diary; desk drawer; desk light;* **a three-drawer desk** = desk with three drawers **ein Schreibtisch mit drei Schubladen; desk pad** = pad of paper kept on a desk for writing notes **Schreibblock**

(b) cash desk *or* **pay desk** = place in a store where you pay for goods bought **Kasse;** *please pay at the desk*

(c) section of a newspaper **Redaktion, Ressort; the city desk** = the department which deals with business news **die Wirtschaftsredaktion**

despatch = DISPATCH

destination *noun* place to which something is sent *or* to which something is going **Bestimmungsort;** *the ship will take ten weeks to reach its destination;* **final destination** *or* **ultimate destination** = place reached at the end of a journey after stopping at several places en route **Zielort**

detail

1 *noun* small part of a description **Detail, Einzelheit;** *the catalogue gives all the details of our product range; we are worried by some of the details in the contract;* **in detail** = giving many particulars **detailliert;** *the catalogue lists all the products in detail*

2 *verb* to list in detail **detailliert beschreiben;** *the catalogue details the payment arrangements for overseas buyers; the terms of the licence are detailed in the contract*

◇ **detailed** *adjective* in detail **detailliert, ausführlich; detailed account** = account which lists every item **detaillierte Rechnung**

determine *verb* to fix *or* to arrange *or* to decide **bestimmen, festlegen, festsetzen;** *to determine prices or quantities; conditions still to be determined*

Deutschmark *noun* unit of money used in Germany **(Deutsche) Mark**

NOTE: also called a **mark;** when used with a figure, usually written **DM** before the figure: **DM250** (say "two hundred and fifty Deutschmarks")

devalue *verb* to reduce the value of a currency against other currencies **abwerten;** *the pound has been devalued by 7%; the government has devalued the pound by 7%*

◇ **devaluation** *noun* reduction in value of a currency against other currencies **Abwertung;** *the devaluation of the franc*

develop *verb*
(a) to plan and produce **entwickeln;** *to develop a new product*
(b) to plan and build an area **erschließen;** *to develop an industrial estate*

◇ **developer** *noun* **a property developer** = person who plans and builds a group of new houses *or* new factories **Bauunternehmer**

◇ **developing country** *or* **developing nation** *noun* country which is not fully industrialized **Entwicklungsland**

◇ **development** *noun*
(a) planning the production of a new product **Entwicklung;** *research and development*
(b) industrial development = planning and building of new industries in special areas **industrielle Erschließung; development area** *or* **development zone** = area which has been given special help from a government to encourage businesses and factories to be set up there **Förderungsgebiet**

device *noun* small useful machine **Gerät, Vorrichtung;** *he invented a device for screwing tops on bottles*

diagram *noun* drawing which shows something as a plan or a map **Diagramm, grafische Darstellung, Schaubild;** *diagram showing sales locations; he drew a diagram to show how the decision-making processes work; the paper gives a diagram of the company's organizational structure;* **flow diagram** = diagram showing the arrangement of work processes in a series **Arbeitsablauf-, Flußdiagramm**

◇ **diagrammatic** *adjective* **in diagrammatic form** = in the form of a diagram **grafisch dargestellt, in einem Diagramm dargestellt;** *the chart showed the sales pattern in diagrammatic form*

◇ **diagrammatically** *adverb* using a diagram **in einem Diagramm/Schaubild;** *the chart shows the sales pattern diagrammatically*

dial *verb* to call a telephone number on a telephone **wählen;** *to dial a number; to dial the operator;* **to dial direct** = to contact a phone number without asking the operator to do it for you **durchwählen;** *you can dial New York direct from London*

NOTE: GB English is **dialling - dialled,** but US spelling is **dialing - dialed**

◇ **dialling** *noun* act of calling a telephone number **Wählen; dialling code** = special series of numbers which you use to make a call to another town or country **Vorwahl, Kennzahlen;** *in BRD* **Ortsnetzkennzahlen; dialling tone** = noise made by a telephone to show that it is ready for you to dial a number **Freizeichen; international direct dialling** = calling telephone numbers in other countries direct **internationaler Selbstwählferndienst**
NOTE: no plural

diary *noun* book in which you can write notes or appointments for each day of the week **Terminkalender, Tagebuch;** *desk diary*

Dictaphone *noun* trademark for a brand of dictating machine; *entspricht* **Diktaphon**

dictate *verb* to say something to someone who then writes down your words **diktieren;** *to dictate a letter to a secretary; he was dictating orders into his pocket dictating machine;* **dictating machine** = machine which records what someone dictates, which a secretary can play back and type out the text **Diktiergerät**

◇ **dictation** *noun* act of dictating **Diktat; to take dictation** = to write down what someone is saying **ein Diktat aufnehmen;** *the secretary was taking dictation from the managing director;* **dictation speed** = number of words per minute which a secretary can write down in shorthand **Silbenzahl pro Minute**

differ *verb* not to be the same as something else **sich unterscheiden;** *the two products differ considerably - one has an electric motor, the other runs on oil*

◇ **difference** *noun* way in which two things are not the same **Unterschied;** *what is the difference between these two products? differences in price or price differences*

◇ **different** *adjective* not the same **unterschiedlich, verschieden;** *our product range is quite different in design from that of our rivals; we offer ten models each in six different colours*

◇ **differential**
1 *adjective* which shows a difference **unterschiedlich, verschieden; differential tariffs** = different tariffs for different classes of goods **Differentialtarif, Staffeltarif**
2 *noun* **price differential** = difference in price between products in a range **Preisunterschied, Preisgefälle; wage differentials** = differences in salary between workers in similar types of jobs **Lohngefälle;**

to erode wage differentials = to reduce differences in salary gradually **Lohngefälle abbauen**

difficult *adjective* not easy **schwierig, schwer;** *the company found it difficult to sell into the European market; the market for secondhand computers is very difficult at present*
◇ **difficulty** *noun* problem *or* thing which is not easy **Schwierigkeit, Problem;** *they had a lot of difficulty selling into the European market; we have had some difficulties with the customs over the export of computers*

digit *noun* single number **Ziffer;** *a seven-digit phone number*
◇ **digital** *adjective* **digital clock** = clock which shows the time as a series of figures (such as 12:05:23) **Digitaluhr; digital computer** = computer which calculates on the basis of numbers **Digitalcomputer**

dilution *noun* **dilution of equity** *or* **of shareholding** = situation where the ordinary share capital of a company has been increased but without an increase in the assets, so that each share is worth less than before **Wertminderung von Aktien**
NOTE: no plural

dime *noun US informal* ten cent coin **Zehncentstück, Dime**

diminish *verb* to become smaller **abnehmen, sich verringern/vermindern;** *our share of the market has diminished over the last few years;* **law of diminishing returns** = general rule that as more factors of production (land, labour and capital) are added to the existing factors, so the amount they produce is proportionately smaller **Gesetzmäßigkeit vom abnehmenden Ertragszuwachs**

dip
1 *noun* sudden small fall **kurzfristiger Rückgang;** *last year saw a dip in the company's performance*
2 *verb* to fall in price **fallen, sinken;** *shares dipped sharply in yesterday's trading*
NOTE: **dipping - dipped**

diplomat *or* **diplomatist** *noun* person (such as an ambassador) who is the official representative of his country in another country **Diplomat/-in**
◇ **diplomatic** *adjective* referring to diplomats **diplomatisch; diplomatic immunity** = being outside the control of the laws of the country you are living in because of being a diplomat **diplomatische Immunität;** *he claimed diplomatic immunity to avoid being arrested;* **to grant someone diplomatic status** = to give someone the rights of a diplomat **jdn in den Diplomatenstand erheben**

direct
1 *verb* to manage *or* to organize **leiten, führen;** *he directs our South-East Asian operations; she was directing the development unit until last year*
2 *adjective* straight *or* with no interference **direkt, unmittelbar; direct action** = strike *or* go-slow, etc. **Arbeitskampfmaßnahmen; direct cost** = production cost of a product **Selbstkosten; direct debit** = system where a customer allows a company to charge costs to his bank account automatically and where the amount charged can be increased or decreased with the agreement of the customer **Direktabbuchung;** *I pay my electricity bill by direct debit;* **direct mail** = selling a product by sending publicity material to possible buyers through the post **Direktversand; Direktwerbung;** *these calculators are only sold by direct mail; the company runs a successful direct-mail operation;* **direct-mail advertising** = advertising by sending leaflets to people through the post **Briefwerbung; direct selling** = selling a product direct to the customer without going through a shop **Direktverkauf; direct taxation** = tax, such as income tax, which is paid direct to the government **direkte Besteuerung;** *the government raises more money by direct taxation than by indirect*
3 *adverb* straight *or* with no third party involved **direkt, unmittelbar;** *we pay income tax direct to the government;* **to dial direct** = to contact a phone number yourself without asking the operator to do it for you **durchwählen;** *you can dial New York direct from London if you want*
◇ **direction** *noun*
(a) organizing *or* managing **Leitung, Führung;** *he took over the direction of a multinational group*
(b) directions for use = instructions showing how to use something **Gebrauchsanweisung**
NOTE: no plural for (a)
◇ **directly** *adverb*
(a) immediately **sofort, gleich;** *he left for the airport directly after receiving the telephone message*
(b) straight *or* with no third party involved **direkt, unmittelbar;** *we deal directly with the manufacturer, without using a wholesaler*
◇ **director** *noun*
(a) person appointed by the shareholders to help run a company **Direktor/-in, Aufsichtsratsmitglied; managing director** = director who is in charge of the whole

company **geschäftsführender Direktor, Geschäftsführer; chairman and managing director** = managing director who is also chairman of the board of directors **Vorsitzender und Geschäftsführer; board of directors** = all the directors of a company **Board of Directors;** *entspricht* **(Firmen)vorstand; Aufsichtsrat (nach britischem Recht); directors' report** = annual report from the board of directors to the shareholders **Jahresbericht; associate director** = director who attends board meetings but has not been elected by the shareholders; *entspricht* **außerordentliches Verwaltungsratsmitglied; executive director** = director who actually works full-time in the company **geschäftsführender Direktor; non-executive director** = director who attends board meetings only to give advice; *entspricht* **Aufsichtsratsmitglied; outside director** = director who is not employed by the company **unternehmensfremder Direktor**
(b) person who is in charge of a project, an official institute, etc. **Leiter/-in, Direktor/-in;** *the director of the government research institute; she was appointed director of the organization*

◇ **directorate** *noun* group of directors **Direktion, Direktorium, Geschäftsleitung; Aufsichtsrat**

◇ **directorship** *noun* post of director **Direktorenstelle;** *he was offered a directorship with Smith Ltd*

> QUOTE the research director will manage and direct a team of business analysts reporting on the latest developments in retail distribution throughout the UK
>
> *Times*
>
> QUOTE what benefits does the executive derive from his directorship? In the first place compensation has increased sharply in recent years
>
> *Duns Business Month*

directory *noun* list of people *or* businesses with information about their addresses and telephone numbers **Adreßbuch; Telefonbuch; classified directory** = list of businesses grouped under various headings, such as computer shops *or* newsagents **Branchenverzeichnis; commercial directory** *or* **trade directory** = book which lists all the businesses and business people in a town **Branchenadreßbuch; street directory** = list of people living in a street **Adreßbuch** map of a town which lists all the streets in alphabetical order in an index **Stadtplan; telephone directory** = book which lists all people and businesses in alphabetical order with their phone numbers **Telefonbuch;** *to look up a number in the telephone directory; his number is in the London directory*

disallow *verb* not to accept a claim for insurance **nicht anerkennen;** *he claimed £2,000 for fire damage, but the claim was disallowed*

disaster *noun*
(a) very bad accident **Unglück, Unglücksfall;** *ten people died in the air disaster*
(b) financial collapse **finanzielle Katastrophe; the company is heading for disaster** *or* **is on a disaster course** = the company is going to collapse **die Firma geht einem finanziellem Fiasko entgegen; the advertising campaign was a disaster** = the advertising campaign was very bad *or* did not have the required effect **die Werbekampagne erwies sich als Desaster**
(c) accident in nature **Katastrophe;** *a storm disaster on the south coast; flood disaster damage*

◇ **disastrous** *adjective* very bad **katastrophal, verheerend;** *the company suffered a disastrous drop in sales*

disburse *verb* to pay money **aus(be)zahlen, ausgeben**

◇ **disbursement** *noun* payment of money **Auszahlung, Ausgabe, Auslage**

discharge
1 *noun*
(a) discharge in bankruptcy = being released from bankruptcy after paying one's debts **Entlastung eines Konkursschuldners, Konkursaufhebung**
(b) payment of debt **Tilgung, Begleichung, Bezahlung; in full discharge of a debt** = paying a debt completely **Schuldentilgung in voller Höhe; final discharge** = final payment of what is left of a debt **letzte Tilgungsrate**
(c) in discharge of his duties as director = carrying out his duties as director **bei der Erfüllung seiner Pflichten als Direktor**
2 *verb*
(a) to discharge a bankrupt = to release someone from bankruptcy because he has paid his debts **einen Konkursschuldner entlasten**
(b) to discharge a debt *or* **to discharge one's liabilities** = to pay a debt *or* one's liabilities in full **eine Schuld begleichen, eine Verbindlichkeit erfüllen**
(c) to dismiss *or* to sack **entlassen;** *to discharge an employee*

disciplinary *adjective* **disciplinary procedure** = way of warning a worker officially that he is breaking rules *or* that he is working badly **Disziplinarverfahren**

disclaimer *noun* legal refusal to accept responsibility **Haftungsablehnungserklärung**

disclose *verb* to tell details **preisgeben, aufdecken, enthüllen;** *the bank has no right to disclose details of my account to the tax office*

◇ **disclosure** *noun* act of telling details **Preisgabe, Aufdeckung, Enthüllung;** *the disclosure of the takeover bid raised the price of the shares*

discontinue *verb* to stop stocking *or* selling *or* making (a product) **auslaufen lassen, die Produktion einstellen;** *these carpets are a discontinued line*

discount
1 *noun*
(a) percentage by which a full price is reduced to a buyer by the seller **Rabatt, Preisnachlaß;** *to give a discount on bulk purchases;* **to sell goods at a discount** *or* **at a discount price** = to sell goods below the normal price **Waren mit Rabatt verkaufen; basic discount** = normal discount without extra percentages **Normal-, Grundrabatt;** *we give 25% as a basic discount, but can add 5% for cash payment;* **quantity discount** = discount given to people who buy large quantities **Mengenrabatt; 10% discount for quantity purchases** = you pay 10% less if you buy a large quantity **10% Mengenrabatt; 10% discount for cash** *or* **10% cash discount** = you pay 10% less if you pay in cash **10% Skonto bei Barzahlung; trade discount** = discount given to a customer in the same trade **Händler-, Wiederverkäuferrabatt**
(b) discount house = (i) financial company which specializes in discounting bills; (ii) shop which specializes in selling cheap goods bought at a high discount **(i) Diskontbank; (ii) Diskontladen, Diskonter, Billigladen; discount rate** = percentage taken when a bank buys bills **Diskontsatz; discount store** = shop which specializes in cheap goods bought at a high discount **Diskontladen, Billigladen**
(c) shares which stand at a discount = shares which are lower in price than their face value **Aktien, die unter pari sind**
2 *verb* to reduce prices to increase sales **Rabatt gewähren; to discount bills of exchange** = to buy bills of exchange for less than the value written on them in order to cash them later **Wechsel diskontieren; shares are discounting a rise in the dollar** = shares have risen in advance of a rise in the dollar price **die Aktien nehmen eine Aufwertung des Dollar vorweg; discounted cash flow** = calculating the forecast return on capital investment in current terms, with reductions for current interest rates **diskontierter Cashflow; discounted value** = difference between the face value of a share and its lower market price **Diskontwert**

◇ **discountable** *adjective* which can be discounted **diskontfähig;** *these bills are not discountable*

◇ **discounter** *noun* (i) company which discounts bills; (ii) Company which sells goods at a discount **(i) Diskonthaus; (ii) Diskontladen, Diskonter**

> QUOTE pressure on the Federal Reserve Board to ease monetary policy and possibly cut its discount rate mounted yesterday
> *Financial Times*
>
> QUOTE banks refrained from quoting forward US/Hongkong dollar exchange rates as premiums of 100 points replaced the previous day's discounts of up to 50 points
> *South China Morning Post*
>
> QUOTE a 100,000 square-foot warehouse generates ten times the volume of a discount retailer; it can turn its inventory over 18 times a year, more than triple a big discounter's turnover
> *Duns Business Month*

discover *verb* to find something new **entdecken, ausfindig machen, herausfinden;** *we discovered that our agent was selling our rival's products at the same price as ours; the auditors discovered some errors in the accounts*

discrepancy *noun* situation where totals do not add up correctly in accounts **Diskrepanz; there is a discrepancy in the accounts** = there is an error **in den Büchern ist eine Unstimmigkeit; statistical discrepancy** = amount by which sets of figures differ **statistische Abweichung**

discretion *noun* being able to decide correctly what should be done **Ermessen, Entscheidungsfreiheit; I leave it to your discretion** = I leave it for you to decide what to do **ich stelle es in Ihr Ermessen, ich lasse Ihnen freie Hand; at the discretion of someone** = if someone decides **nach jds Ermessen;** *membership is at the discretion of the committee*
NOTE: no plural

◇ **discretionary** *adjective* which can be done if someone wants **beliebig; the minister's discretionary powers** = powers which the minister could use if he thought he should do so **die Ermessensbefugnis des Ministers**

discrimination *noun* treating people in different ways because of class, religion, race, language, colour or sex **Diskriminierung; sexual discrimination** *or* **sex discrimination** *or* **discrimination on grounds of sex** = treating men and women in different ways **Diskriminierung aufgrund des Geschlechts**
NOTE: no plural

discuss *verb* to talk about a problem **diskutieren, besprechen, erörtern;** *they spent two hours discussing the details of the contract; the committee discussed the question of import duties on cars; the board will discuss wage rises at its next meeting; we discussed delivery schedules with our suppliers*

◊ **discussion** *noun* talking about a problem **Diskussion, Besprechung, Erörterung, Debatte;** *after ten minutes' discussion the board agreed the salary increases; we spent the whole day in discussions with our suppliers*

disenfranchise *verb* to take away someone's right to vote **das Wahlrecht nehmen;** *the company has tried to disenfranchise the ordinary shareholders*

dishonour *verb* **to dishonour a bill** = not to pay a bill **einen Wechsel nicht bezahlen; dishonoured cheque** = cheque which the bank will not pay because there is not enough money in the account to pay it **nichteingelöster Scheck**

disinflation *noun* reducing inflation in the economy by increasing tax, reducing the level of money supply, etc. **Inflationsbekämpfung**

disinvest *verb* to reduce investment by not replacing capital assets when they wear out **desinvestieren**

◊ **disinvestment** *noun* reduction in capital assets by not replacing them when they wear out **Desinvestition**

NOTE: no plural

disk *noun* round flat object, used to store information in computers **Diskette; floppy disk** = small disk for storing information through a computer **Floppy Disk; hard disk** = solid disk which will store a large amount of computer information in a sealed case **Festplatte; disk drive** = part of a computer which makes a disk spin round in order to read it or store information on it **Diskettenlaufwerk**

◊ **diskette** *noun* very small floppy disk **Diskette**

dismiss *verb* **to dismiss an employee** = to remove an employee from a job **einen Angestellten entlassen;** *he was dismissed for being late*

◊ **dismissal** *noun* removal of an employee from a job **Entlassung; constructive dismissal** = situation where an employee leaves his job voluntarily, but because of pressure from the management **erzwungene Kündigung; unfair dismissal** = removing someone from a job for reasons which are not fair **ungerechtfertigte Entlassung; wrongful dismissal** = removing someone from a job for reasons which are wrong **unrechtmäßige Entlassung; dismissal procedures** = correct way of dismissing someone according to the contract of employment **Entlassungsverfahren**

dispatch

1 *noun*

(a) sending of goods to a customer **Versand;** *the strike held up dispatch for several weeks;* **dispatch department** = department which deals with the packing and sending of goods to customers **Versandabteilung; dispatch note** = note saying that goods have been sent **Versandschein; dispatch rider** = motorcyclist who delivers messages or parcels in a town **Motorrad-Bote**

(b) goods which have been sent **Sendung;** *the weekly dispatch went off yesterday*

2 *verb* to send goods to customers **(ver)senden, schicken**

◊ **dispatcher** *noun* person who sends goods to customers **Expedient; Absender**

dispenser *noun* machine which automatically provides something (an object *or* a drink *or* some food), often when money is put in **Automat;** *automatic dispenser; towel dispenser;* **cash dispenser** = machine which gives out money when a special card is inserted and instructions given **Geldautomat**

display

1 *noun* showing of goods for sale **Auslage;** *the shop has several car models on display; an attractive display of kitchen equipment;* **display advertisement** = advertisement which is well designed to attract attention **Großanzeige; display cabinet** *or* **display case** = piece of furniture with a glass top or glass doors for showing goods for sale **Vitrine, Schaukasten; display material** = posters, photographs, etc., to be used to attract attention to goods which are for sale **Dekorationsmaterial; display pack** *or* **display box** = special box for showing goods for sale **Schaupackung, Präsentationspackung;** *the watches are prepacked in plastic display boxes;* **display stand** *or* **display unit** = special stand for showing goods for sale **Auslagenstand, Vollsichtregal; visual display unit** *or* **visual display terminal** = screen attached to a computer which shows the information stored in the computer **Monitor, Bildschirm**

2 *verb* to show **ausstellen, zeigen;** *the company was displaying three new car models at the show*

dispose *verb* **to dispose of** = to get rid of *or* to sell cheaply **veräußern, losschlagen;** *umg* **verramschen;** *to dispose of excess stock; to dispose of one's business*

◇ **disposable** *adjective*

(a) which can be used and then thrown away **Wegwerf-, Einweg-;** *disposable cups*

(b) disposable personal income = income left after tax and national insurance have been deducted **(frei) verfügbares Einkommen nach Steuerabzug**

◇ **disposal** *noun* sale **Verkauf, Veräußerung, Absatz;** *disposal of securities or of property;* **lease** *or* **business for disposal** = lease *or* business for sale **langfristiger Pachtvertrag od Unternehmen zu verkaufen**

dispute *noun* **industrial disputes** *or* **labour disputes** = arguments between management and workers **Arbeitskampf; to adjudicate** *or* **to mediate in a dispute** = to try to settle a dispute between other parties **einen Disput schlichten**

dissolve *verb* to bring to an end **auflösen, aufheben;** *to dissolve a partnership or a company*

◇ **dissolution** *noun* ending (of a partnership) **Auflösung, Aufhebung**

distress merchandise *noun US* goods sold cheaply to pay a company's debts **stark herabgesetzte Ware**

distribute *verb*

(a) to share out dividends **ausschütten;** *profits were distributed among the shareholders*

(b) to send out goods from a manufacturer's warehouse to retail shops **vertreiben;** *Smith Ltd distributes for several smaller companies*

◇ **distribution** *noun*

(a) act of sending goods from the manufacturer to the wholesaler and then to retailers **Vertrieb;** *distribution costs; distribution manager;* **channels of distribution** *or* **distribution channels** = ways of sending goods from the manufacturer to the retailer **Vertriebswege; distribution network** = series of points *or* small warehouses from which goods are sent all over a country **Verteiler-, Vertriebsnetz**

(b) distribution slip = paper attached to a document *or* a magazine showing all the people in an office who should read it **Verteilerzettel**

NOTE: no plural

◇ **distributor** *noun* company which sells goods for another company which makes them **Verteiler, Wiederverkäufer, Händler; sole distributor** = retailer who is the only one in an area who is allowed by the manufacturer to sell a certain product **Alleinvertrieb; a network of distributors** = a series of distributors spread all over a country **Verteilernetz**

◇ **distributorship** *noun* position of being a distributor for a company **Vertrieb**

district *noun* section of a country *or* of a town **Gebiet; Stadtteil, Viertel;** *district manager;* **the commercial district** *or* **the business district** = part of a town where offices and shops are located **Geschäftsviertel**

diversification *noun* adding another quite different type of business to a firm's existing trade **Diversifikation; product diversification** *or* **diversification into new products** = adding new types of products to the range already made **Erweiterung des Produktangebots, Sortimentserweiterung**

◇ **diversify** *verb*

(a) to add new types of business to existing ones **diversifizieren, erweitern;** *to diversify into new products*

(b) to invest in different types of shares or savings so as to spread the risk of loss **verteilt/gestreut anlegen**

divest *verb* **to divest oneself of something** = to get rid of something **sich einer Sache entledigen;** *the company had divested itself of its US interests*

divide *verb* to cut into separate sections **aufteilen, teilen;** *the country is divided into six representative's areas; the two companies agreed to divide the market between them*

dividend *noun* percentage of profits paid to shareholders **Dividende; to raise** *or* **to increase the dividend** = to pay out a higher dividend than in the previous year **Dividende erhöhen; to maintain the dividend** = to keep the same dividend as in the previous year **Dividenden in gleicher Höhe ausschütten; to pass the dividend** = to pay no dividend **keine Dividende ausschütten, die Dividende ausfallen lassen; final dividend** = dividend paid at the end of a year **Schlußdividende, Restdividende; interim dividend** = dividend paid at the end of a half-year **Abschlags-, Zwischendividende; dividend cover** = the ratio of profits to dividend **Dividendendeckung (im Verhältnis zum Gewinn); the dividend is covered four**

times = the profits are four times the dividend **die Dividenden sind vierfach gedeckt; dividend warrant** = cheque which makes payment of a dividend **Dividendenzahlungsanweisung, Kupon; dividend yield** = dividend expressed as a percentage of the price of a share **Dividendenertrag; cum dividend** = share sold with the dividend still to be paid **mit/cum Dividende; ex dividend** = share sold after the dividend has been paid **ohne/ex Dividende; the shares are quoted ex dividend** = the share price does not include the right to the dividend **die Aktien werden ex Dividende notiert**

division *noun*
(a) main section of a large company **Abteilung;** *marketing division; production division; retail division; the paints division of ICI; the hotel division of THF; he is in charge of one of the major divisions of the company*
(b) company which is part of a large group **Unternehmensbereich;** *Smith's is now a division of the Brown group of companies*
◇ **divisional** *adjective* referring to a division **Abteilungs-;** *a divisional director; the divisional headquarters*

DIY = DO-IT-YOURSELF

DM *or* **D-mark** = DEUTSCHMARK, MARK

dock
1 *noun* harbour *or* place where ships can load or unload **Hafen, Kai;** *loading dock; a dock worker; the dock manager;* **the docks** = part of a town where the harbour is **Hafen; dock dues** = money paid by a ship going into or out of a dock, used to keep the dock in good repair **Dockgebühren**
2 *verb*
(a) to go into dock **ins Dock gehen, am Kai festmachen;** *the ship docked at 17.00*
(b) to remove money from someone's wages **einbehalten, kürzen;** *we will have to dock his pay if he is late for work again; he had £20 docked from his pay for being late*
◇ **docker** *noun* person who works in a dock **Hafenarbeiter**
◇ **dockyard** *noun* place where ships are built **Werft**

docket *noun* list of contents of a package which is being sent **Inhaltsverzeichnis, Warenbegleitschein**

doctor *noun* specialist who examines people when they are sick to see how they can be made well **Arzt/Ärztin;** *the staff are all sent to see the company doctor once a year;* **doctor's certificate** = document written by a doctor to say that a worker is ill and cannot work **Attest, ärztliche Bescheinigung;** *he has been off sick for ten days and still has not sent in a doctor's certificate;* **company doctor** = (i) doctor who works for a company and looks after sick workers; (ii) specialist businessman who rescues businesses which are in difficulties **(i) Betriebsarzt; (ii) Krisenmanager**

document *noun* paper with writing on it **Dokument, Urkunde, Akte;** *legal document*
◇ **documentary** *adjective* in the form of documents **dokumentarisch, urkundlich;** *documentary evidence; documentary proof*
◇ **documentation** *noun* all documents referring to something **Dokumentation;** *please send me the complete documentation concerning the sale*
NOTE: no plural

dogsbody *noun informal* person who does all types of work in an office for very low wages **Mädchen für alles; Kalfaktor**

do-it-yourself *adjective* done by an ordinary person, not by a skilled worker **Do-it-yourself; do-it-yourself conveyancing** = drawing up a legal conveyance by the person selling a property, without the help of a lawyer **Übertragungsurkunde ohne notarielle Hilfe; do-it-yourself magazine** = magazine with articles on work which the average person can do to repair or paint his house **Do-it-yourself Magazin, Heimwerkermagazin**

dole *noun* money given by the government to unemployed people **Arbeitslosengeld; Arbeitslosenhilfe; he is receiving dole payments** *or* **he is on the dole** = he is receiving unemployment benefits **Arbeitslosenunterstützung beziehen;** *umg* **stempeln gehen; dole queues** = lines of people waiting to collect the dole **Arbeitslosenschlange**

dollar *noun*
(a) money used in the USA and other countries **Dollar;** *the US dollar rose 2%; fifty Canadian dollars; it costs six Australian dollars;* **five dollar bill** = banknote for five dollars **Fünfdollarschein**
(b) the currency used in the USA **(US) Dollar; dollar area** = area of the world where the dollar is the main trading currency **Dollarzone; dollar balance** = a country's trade balances expressed in US dollars **Handelsbilanz in Dollar; dollar crisis** = fall in the exchange rate for the US dollar **Dollarkrise; dollar gap** *or* **dollar shortage** =

situation where the supply of dollars is not enough to satisfy the demand for them from overseas buyers **Dollarlücke; dollar stocks** = shares in US companies **US Aktien**
NOTE: usually written $ before a figure: **$250.** The currencies used in different countries can be shown by the initial letter of the country: **C$** (Canadian dollar) **A$** (Australian dollar), etc.

domestic *adjective* referring to the home market *or* the market of the country where the business is situated **Innen-, Binnen-, einheimisch, im Inland;** *domestic sales; domestic turnover;* **domestic consumption** = consumption on the home market **Inlandsverbrauch;** *domestic consumption of oil has fallen sharply;* **domestic market** = market in the country where a company is based **Binnen-, Inlandmarkt;** *they produce goods for the domestic market;* **domestic production** = production of goods for domestic consumption **Inlandsproduktion**

domicile
1 *noun* place where someone lives *or* where a company's office is registered **Wohnsitz; Sitz, Niederlassung**
2 *verb* **he is domiciled in Denmark** = he lives in Denmark officially **er hat seinen Wohnsitz in Dänemark, er ist in Dänemark ansässig; bills domiciled in France** = bills of exchange which have to be paid in France **in Frankreich zahlbare Wechsel**

door *noun* piece of wood *or* metal, etc. which closes the entrance to a building *or* room **Tür;** *the finance director knocked on the chairman's door and walked in; the sales manager's name is on his door;* **the store opened its doors on June 1st** = the store started in business on June 1st **das Geschäft öffnete am 1. Juni (erstmals) seine Türen; door-to-door canvassing** to sell goods at the door **Hausieren; door-to-door salesman** rep calling on house **Vertreter/-in; door-to-door selling** selling directly through rep **Verkauf durch Vertreter**

dot *noun* small round spot **Tupfen, Punkt, Pünktchen;** *the order form should be cut off along the line shown by the row of dots*
◇ **dot-matrix printer** *noun* printer which makes letters by printing many small dots **Matrixdrucker**
◇ **dotted line** *noun* line made of a series of dots **punktierte Linie;** *please sign on the dotted line; do not write anything below the dotted line*

double
1 *adjective*
(a) twice as large *or* two times the size **doppelt;** *their turnover is double ours;* **to be on double time** = to earn twice the usual wages for working on Sundays or other holidays **das Doppelte verdienen; double-entry bookkeeping** = system of bookkeeping where both credit and debit sides of an account are noted **doppelte Buchführung; double taxation** = taxing the same income twice **Doppelbesteuerung; double taxation agreement** = agreement between two countries that a person living in one country shall not be taxed in both countries on the income earned in the other country **Doppelbesteuerungsabkommen**
(b) in double figures = with two figures *or* 10 to 99 **zweistellig;** *inflation is in double figures; we have had double-figure inflation for some years*
2 *verb* to become twice as big; to make something twice as big **verdoppeln;** *we have doubled our profits this year or our profits have doubled this year; the company's borrowings have doubled*
◇ **double-book** *verb* to let the same hotel room *or* plane seat, etc., to more than one person at a time **doppelt belegen, doppelt buchen;** *we had to change our flight as we were double-booked*
◇ **double-booking** *noun* letting by a travel agent of the same hotel room *or* the same plane seat to more than one person at a time **Doppelbelegung, Doppelbuchung**

Dow Jones Average *noun* index of share prices on the New York Stock Exchange, based on a group of major companies **Dow-Jones Aktienindex;** *the Dow Jones Average rose ten points; general optimism showed in the rise on the Dow Jones Average*

down
1 *adverb & preposition* in a lower position *or* to a lower position **unten, herunter, hinunter, niedrig, gefallen;** *the inflation rate is gradually coming down; shares are slightly down on the day; the price of petrol has gone down;* **to pay money down** = to make a deposit **Geld anzahlen;** *he paid £50 down and the rest in monthly instalments*
2 *verb* **to down tools** = to stop working **die Arbeit niederlegen**
◇ **downgrade** *verb* to reduce the importance of someone *or* of a job **herunterstufen, niedriger einstufen;** *his job was downgraded in the company reorganization*
◇ **down market** *adjective & adverb* cheaper *or* appealing to a less wealthy section of the population **Billig-, Massen-; billig, massen;** *the company has adopted a down-market image;* **the company has decided to go down market** = the company has decided to make products which appeal to a wider section of

the public **die Firma hat beschlossen, sich dem Massenmarkt zuzuwenden**

◇ **down payment** *noun* part of a total payment made in advance **Anzahlung;** *he made a down payment of $100*

◇ **downside** *noun* **downside factor** = possibility of making a loss (in an investment) **Verlustfaktor; the sales force have been asked to give downside forecasts** = they have been asked for pessimistic forecasts **das Verkaufspersonal wurde aufgefordert, in der Prognose eine Abwärtsbewegung aufzuzeigen**

◇ **down time** *noun* time when a machine is not working because it is broken *or* being mended, etc.; time when a worker cannot work because machines have broken down, because components are not available, etc. **Stillstand-, Ausfall-, Verlustzeit**

◇ **downtown** *noun* in the central business district of a town **Stadtzentrum, Geschäftsviertel, Innenstadt** *adverb* in the central district of a town **in der Innenstadt gelegen;** *his office is in downtown New York; a downtown store; they established a business downtown*

◇ **downturn** *noun* movement towards lower prices *or* sales *or* profits **Rückgang, Abflauen, Flaute;** *a downturn in the market price; the last quarter saw a downturn in the economy*

◇ **downward** *adjective* towards a lower position **nach unten, abwärts, rückgängig, rückläufig**

◇ **downwards** *adverb* towards a lower position **nach unten, abwärts;** *the company's profits have moved downwards over the last few years*

dozen *noun* twelve **Dutzend;** *to sell in sets of one dozen;* **cheaper by the dozen** = the product is cheaper if you buy twelve at a time **im Dutzend billiger**

draft

1 *noun*

(a) order for money to be paid by a bank **Bankwechsel; Banktratte;** *banker's draft;* **to make a draft on a bank** = to ask a bank to pay money for you **einen Wechsel auf eine Bank ziehen; sight draft** = bill of exchange which is payable when it is presented **Sichtwechsel, Sichttratte**

(b) first rough plan *or* document which has not been finished **Entwurf, Fassung, Konzept;** *draft of a contract or draft contract; he drew up the draft agreement on the back of an envelope; the first draft of the contract was corrected by the managing director; the finance department has passed the final draft of the accounts;* **rough draft** = plan of a document which may have changes made to it before it is complete **Rohentwurf, Konzept**

2 *verb* to make a first rough plan of a document **entwerfen, konzipieren;** *to draft a letter; to draft a contract; the contract is still being drafted or is still in the drafting stage*

◇ **drafter** *noun* person who makes a draft **Verfasser/-in;** *the drafter of the agreement*

◇ **drafting** *noun* act of preparing the draft of a document **Verfassen, Formulieren;** *the drafting of the contract took six weeks*

drain

1 *noun*

(a) pipe for taking dirty water from a house **Abflußrohr**

(b) gradual loss of money flowing away **Belastung;** *the costs of the London office are a continual drain on our resources*

2 *verb* to remove something gradually **aufbrauchen, aufzehren;** *the expansion plan has drained all our profits; the company's capital resources have drained away*

draw *verb*

(a) to take money away **abheben;** *to draw money out of an account;* **to draw a salary** = to have a salary paid by the company **ein Gehalt beziehen;** *the chairman does not draw a salary*

(b) to write a cheque **ausstellen;** *he paid the invoice with a cheque drawn on an Egyptian bank*

NOTE: **drawing - drew - has drawn**

◇ **drawback** *noun*

(a) thing which is not convenient *or* likely to cause problems **Nachteil;** *one of the main drawbacks of the scheme is that it will take six years to complete*

(b) paying back customs duty when imported goods are then re-exported **Zollrückvergütung, Rückzoll**

◇ **drawee** *noun* person or bank asked to make a payment by a drawer **Bezogener, Trassat**

◇ **drawer** *noun* person who writes a cheque *or* a bill asking a drawee to pay money to a payee **Aussteller, Trassant; the bank returned the cheque to drawer** = the bank would not pay the cheque because the person who wrote it did not have enough money in the account to pay it **die Bank schickte den Scheck an den Aussteller zurück**

◇ **drawing** *noun* **drawing account** = current account *or* account from which the customer may take money when he wants **Kontokorrentkonto, laufendes Konto, Girokonto**

◇ **draw up** *verb* to write a legal document **aufsetzen, konzipieren, aufstellen;** *to draw up a contract or an agreement; to draw up a company's articles of association*

drift *verb* to move slowly **treiben, sich langsam bewegen;** *shares drifted lower in a dull market; strikers are drifting back to work*

drive

1 *noun*

(a) energy *or* energetic way of working **Elan, Schwung; economy drive** = vigorous effort to save money or materials **Sparkampagne; sales drive** = vigorous effort to increase sales **Verkaufskampagne; he has a lot of drive** = he is very energetic in business **er hat viel Elan**

(b) part of a machine which makes other parts work **Antrieb; disk drive** = part of a computer which makes the disk spin round in order to store information on it **Diskettenlaufwerk**

2 *verb*

(a) to make a car *or* lorry, etc. go in a certain direction **fahren;** *he was driving to work when he heard the news on the car radio; she drives a company car*

(b) he drives a hard bargain = he is a difficult negotiator **er schließt bei Verhandlungen keine Kompromisse**

NOTE: **driving - drove - has driven**

drop

1 *noun*

(a) fall **Rückgang, Sturz;** *drop in sales; sales show a drop of 10%; a drop in prices*

(b) drop shipment = delivery of a large order from the manufacturer direct to a customer's shop or warehouse without going through an agent or wholesaler **Direktlieferung**

2 *verb* to fall **zurückgehen, stürzen, fallen;** *sales have dropped by 10% or have dropped 10%; the pound dropped three points against the dollar*

NOTE: **dropping - dropped**

◇ **drop ship** *verb* to deliver a large order direct to a customer **direkt an den Kunden liefern**

> QUOTE while unemployment dropped by 1.6 per cent in the rural areas, it rose by 1.9 per cent in urban areas during the period under review
> *Business Times (Lagos)*
>
> QUOTE corporate profits for the first quarter showed a 4 per cent drop from last year's final three months
> *Financial Times*
>
> QUOTE since last summer American interest rates have dropped by between three and four percentage points
> *Sunday Times*

drug *noun* medicine **Arzneimittel, Medikament; a drug on the market** = product which is difficult to sell because it has already been sold in large quantities and the market is satisfied **Ladenhüter, schwer verkäufliche Ware**

dry *adjective* not wet **trocken; dry goods** = cloth, clothes **Textilwaren und Trockenwaren; dry measure** = way of calculating loose dry produce (such as corn) **Trockenmaß**

duck *see* LAME DUCK

dud

1 *noun informal* false *or* not good coin or banknote **Blüte;** *the £50 note was a dud*

2 *adjective* false *or* not good **falsch, gefälscht, wertlos; dud cheque** = cheque which the bank refuses to pay because the person writing it has not enough money in his account to pay it **ungedeckter Scheck**

due *adjective*

(a) owed **fällig;** *sum due from a debtor; bond due for repayment;* **to fall due** *or* **to become due** = to be ready for payment **fällig sein/werden; bill due on May 1st** = bill which has to be paid on May 1st **eine am 1. Mai fällige Rechnung; balance due to us** = amount owed to us which should be paid **fälliger Rechnungsbetrag**

(b) the plane is due at 10.30 = the plane is expected to arrive at 10.30 **das Flugzeug soll um 10.30 Uhr ankommen**

(c) in due form = written in the correct legal form **vorschriftsmäßig, rechtsgültig;** *receipt in due form; contract drawn up in due form;* **after due consideration** = after thinking seriously **nach reiflicher Überlegung**

(d) caused by **aufgrund, wegen;** *supplies have been delayed due to a strike at the manufacturers; the company pays the wages of staff who are absent due to illness*

◇ **dues** *plural noun*

(a) dock dues *or* **port dues** *or* **harbour dues** = payment which a ship makes to the harbour authorities for the right to use the harbour **Hafengebühren**

(b) orders taken but not supplied until new stock arrives **Vorbestellungen**

> QUOTE many expect the US economic indicators for April, due out this Thursday, to show faster economic growth
> *Australian Financial Review*

dull *adjective* not exciting *or* not full of life **langweilig, lahm, schleppend; dull market** = market where little business is done **flauer Markt**

◇ **dullness** *noun* being dull **Flaute, Stagnation;** *the dullness of the market*

duly *adverb*

(a) properly **vorschriftsmäßig, ordnungsgemäß;** *duly authorized representative*
(b) as was expected **erwartungsgemäß;** *we duly received his letter of 21st October*

dummy *noun* imitation product to test the reaction of potential customers to its design **Aufmachungsmuster;** *von Buch* **Blindband; dummy pack** = empty pack for display **Attrappe, Schau-, Leerpackung; dummy run** = test run **Probelauf**

dump *verb* **to dump goods on a market** = to get rid of large quantities of excess goods cheaply in an overseas market **Waren billig auf einen ausländischen Markt bringen**

◇ **dump bin** *noun* display container like a large box which is filled with goods for sale **Wühltisch**

◇ **dumping** *noun* act of getting rid of excess goods cheaply in an overseas market **Dumping;** *the government has passed anti-dumping legislation; dumping of goods on the European market;* **panic dumping of sterling** = rush to sell sterling at any price because of possible devaluation **Panik-Dumping von Sterling**
NOTE: no plural

> QUOTE a serious threat lies in the 400,000 tonnes of subsidized beef in EEC cold stores. If dumped, this meat will have disastrous effects in Pacific Basin markets
> *Australian Financial Review*

duplicate
1 *noun* copy **Duplikat, Zweitschrift, Kopie;** *he sent me the duplicate of the contract ;* **duplicate receipt** *or* **duplicate of a receipt** = copy of a receipt **Quittungsduplikat; in duplicate** = with a copy **in doppelter/zweifacher Ausfertigung; receipt in duplicate** = two copies of a receipt **Quittung in doppelter Ausfertigung;** *to print an invoice in duplicate*
2 *verb*
(a) *(of a bookkeeping entry)* **to duplicate with another** = to repeat another entry *or* to be the same as another entry **miteinander übereinstimmen**
(b) to duplicate a letter = to make a copy of a letter **einen Brief kopieren, von einem Brief ein Duplikat anfertigen**

◇ **duplicating** *noun* copying **Kopieren; duplicating machine** = machine which makes copies of documents **Vervielfältigungsgerät; Kopiergerät; duplicating paper** = special paper to be used in a duplicating machine **Saugpostpapier, Matrizenpapier**

◇ **duplication** *noun* copying of documents **Vervielfältigung; duplication of work** = work which is done twice without being necessary **doppelte Arbeit**

◇ **duplicator** *noun* machine which makes copies of documents **Vervielfältigungsgerät, Kopiergerät**

durable
1 *adjective* **durable goods** = goods which will be used for a long time (such as washing machines or refrigerators) **langlebige Güter; durable effects** = effects which will be felt for a long time **langanhaltende Auswirkungen;** *the strike will have durable effects on the economy*
2 *noun* **consumer durables** = goods bought by the public which will be used for a long time (such as washing machines or refrigerators) **langlebige Gebrauchsgüter**

Dutch *adjective* **Dutch auction** = auction where the auctioneer offers an item for sale at a high price and then gradually reduces the price until someone makes a bid **holländische Versteigerung; to go Dutch** = to share the bill in a restaurant **getrennt bezahlen, getrennte Kasse machen**

dutiable *adjective* **dutiable goods** *or* **dutiable items** = goods on which a customs duty has to be paid **zollpflichtig**

◇ **duty** *noun* tax which has to be paid **Steuer;** *to take the duty off alcohol; to put a duty on cigarettes;* **ad valorem duty** = duty calculated on the sales value of the goods **Wertsteuer; customs duty** *or* **import duty** = tax on goods imported into a country **Zoll, Einfuhrzoll; excise duty** = tax on goods (such as alcohol and petrol) which are produced in the country **Verbrauchssteuer; goods which are liable to duty** = goods on which customs duty has to be paid **zu verzollende Güter; duty-paid goods** = goods where the duty has been paid **verzollte Waren; stamp duty** = tax on legal documents (such as the conveyance of a property to a new owner) **Stempelgebühr; estate duty** *or US* **death duty** = tax paid on the property left by a dead person **Erbschaftssteuer**

◇ **duty-free** *adjective & adverb* sold with no duty to be paid **zollfrei;** *he bought a duty-free watch at the airport or he bought the watch duty-free;* **duty-free shop** = shop at an airport *or* on a ship where goods can be bought without paying duty **Duty-free-Shop**

> QUOTE Canadian and European negotiators agreed to a deal under which Canada could lower its import duties on $150 million worth of European goods
> *Globe and Mail (Toronto)*
> QUOTE the Department of Customs and Excise collected a total of N79m under the new advance duty payment scheme
> *Business Times (Lagos)*

Ee

e.& o.e. = ERRORS AND OMISSIONS EXCEPTED

eager *adjective* wanting to do something **sehr interessiert, erpicht;** *the management is eager to get into the Far Eastern markets; our salesmen are eager to see the new product range*

early *adjective & adverb*
(a) before the usual time **frühzeitig, früher, vorzeitig;** *the mail left early;* **early closing day** = weekday when most shops in a town close in the afternoon **Tag, an dem die Geschäfte nachmittags geschlossen sind; at your earliest convenience** = as soon as possible **so bald wie möglich; at an early date** = very soon **bald**
(b) at the beginning of a period of time **früh;** *he took an early flight to Paris;* **we hope for an early resumption of negotiations** = we hope negotiations will start again soon **wir hoffen, daß die Verhandlungen schon bald wieder aufgenommen werden**

earmark *verb* to reserve for a special purpose **vorsehen;** *to earmark funds for a project; the grant is earmarked for computer systems development*

earn *verb*
(a) to be paid money for working **verdienen;** *to earn £50 a week; our agent in Paris certainly does not earn his commission; GB* **wife's earned income allowance** = tax allowance to be set against money earned by the wife of the taxpayer **Freibetrag für Erwerbseinkommen der Ehefrau**
(b) to produce interest *or* dividends **(ein)bringen;** *what level of dividend do these shares earn? account which earns interest at 10%*
◊ **earning** *noun* **earning capacity** *or* **earning power** = amount of money someone should be able to earn **Verdienstmöglichkeit;** *he is such a fine dress designer that his earning power is very large;* **earning potential** = amount of money a person should be able to earn; amount of dividend a share should produce **Erwerbsfähigkeit, Ertragsfähigkeit**
◊ **earnings** *plural noun*
(a) salary *or* wages, profits and dividends *or* interest received **Einkommen, Einkünfte; compensation for loss of earnings** = payment to someone who has stopped earning money *or* who is not able to earn money **Verdienstausfallentschädigung; invisible earnings** = foreign currency earned by a country in providing services (such as banking, tourism), not in selling goods **unsichtbare Einkünfte, Einkünfte aus unsichtbaren Leistungen**
(b) money which is earned in interest *or* dividend **Gewinn, Profit, Ertrag; earnings per share** *or* **earnings yield** = money earned in dividends per share, shown as a percentage of the market price of one share **Gewinnrendite; gross earnings** = earnings before tax and other deductions **Bruttoeinkommen, Bruttoeinnahmen; price/earnings ratio (P/E ratio)** = ratio between the market price of a share and the current dividend it produces **Kurs-Gewinn-Verhältnis;** *these shares sell at a P/E ratio of 7;* **retained earnings** = profits which are not paid out to shareholders as dividend **einbehaltene Gewinne**

> QUOTE if corporate forecasts are met, sales will exceed $50 million in 1985 and net earnings could exceed $7 million
> *Citizen (Ottawa)*
>
> QUOTE the US now accounts for more than half of our world-wide sales. It has made a huge contribution to our earnings turnaround
> *Duns Business Month*
>
> QUOTE last fiscal year the chain reported a 116% jump in earnings, to $6.4 million or $1.10 a share
> *Barrons*

earnest *noun* money paid as a down payment **Hand-, Draufgeld,**

ease *verb* to fall a little **nachlassen, nachgeben;** *the share index eased slightly today*

easement *noun* right which someone has to use land belonging to someone else (such as for a path to a garage) **Grunddienstbarkeit**

easy *adjective*
(a) not difficult **einfach, leicht; easy terms** = terms which are not difficult to accept *or* price which is easy to pay **günstige Bedingungen, Zahlungserleichterungen;** *the shop is let on very easy terms;* **the loan is repayable in easy payments** = with very small sums paid back regularly **das Darlehen ist unter erleichterten Bedingungen zurückzuzahlen; easy money** = (i) money which can be earned with no difficulty; (ii) money available on easy repayment terms **(i) leicht verdientes Geld; (ii) billiges Geld; easy money policy** = government policy of expanding the economy by making money more easily available **Politik des billigen Geldes**
(b) easy market = market where few people are buying, so prices are low **ruhiger Markt;**

the Stock Exchange was easy yesterday; **share prices are easier** = prices have fallen slightly **die Aktienpreise sind günstiger**

◇ **easily** *adverb*
(a) without any difficulty **einfach, leicht;** *we passed through the customs easily*
(b) much *or* a lot (compared to something else) **bei weitem;** *he is easily our best salesman; the firm is easily the biggest in the market*

EC = EUROPEAN COMMUNITY

ECGD = EXPORT CREDIT GUARANTEE DEPARTMENT

echelon *noun* group of people of a certain grade in an organization **Ebene, Schicht;** *the upper echelons of industry*

econometrics *plural noun* study of the statistics of economics, using computers **Ökonometrie**
NOTE: takes a singular verb

economic *adjective*
(a) which provides enough money **rentabel;** *the flat is let at an economic rent; it is hardly economic for the company to run its own warehouse*
(b) referring to the financial state of a country **Wirtschafts-;** *economic planner; economic planning; the government's economic policy; the economic situation; the country's economic system; economic trends;* **economic crisis** *or* **economic depression** = state where a country is in financial collapse **Wirtschaftskrise;** *the government has introduced import controls to solve the current economic crisis;* **economic cycle** = period during which trade expands, then slows down, then expands again **Konjunkturzyklus; economic development** = expansion of the commercial and financial situation **wirtschaftliche Enwicklung;** *the economic development of the region has totally changed since oil was discovered there;* **economic growth** = increase in the national income **Wirtschaftswachstum;** *the country enjoyed a period of economic growth in the 1960s;* **economic indicators** = statistics which show how the economy is going to perform in the short or long term **Schlüsselwerte für die Wirtschaft, Konjunkturindikatoren; economic sanctions** = restrictions on trade with a country in order to make its government change policy **Wirtschaftssanktionen;** *the western nations imposed economic sanctions on the country;* **the European Community** = the Common Market **die Europäische Gemeinschaft**

◇ **economical** *adjective* which saves money or materials *or* which is cheap **sparsam, rationell; economical car** = car which does not use much petrol; **im Benzinverbrauch sparsames Auto economical use of resources** = using resources as carefully as possible **sparsamer Umgang mit Ressourcen**

◇ **economics** *plural noun*
(a) study of production, distribution, selling and use of goods and services **Volkswirtschaft, Wirtschaftswissenschaft**
(b) study of financial structures to show how a product or service is costed and what returns it produces **ökonomischer Aspekt, Ökonomie;** *the economics of town planning; I do not understand the economics of the coal industry*
NOTE: takes a singular verb

◇ **economist** *noun* person who specializes in the study of economics **Volkswirt, Wirtschaftswissenschaftler;** *agricultural economist*

◇ **economize** *verb* **to economize on petrol** = to save petrol **mit Benzin sparsam umgehen/haushalten**

◇ **economy** *noun*
(a) being careful not to waste money or materials **Sparsamkeit, Wirtschaftlichkeit; an economy measure** = an action to save money or materials **Sparmaßnahme; to introduce economies** *or* **economy measures** = to start using methods to save money or materials **Sparmaßnahmen einführen; economies of scale** = making a product more profitable by manufacturing it in larger quantities **Größendegression; economy car** = car which does not use much petrol **im Benzinverbrauch sparsames Auto; economy class** = cheapest class on a plane **Touristenklasse;** *to travel economy class;* **economy drive** = campaign to save money or materials **Sparkampagne; economy size** = large size *or* large packet which is a bargain **Sparpackung**
(b) financial state of a country *or* way in which a country makes and uses its money **Wirtschaft;** *the country's economy is in ruins;* **black economy** = work which is paid for in cash or goods, but not declared to the tax authorities **Schattenwirtschaft; capitalist economy** = system where each person has the right to invest money, to work in business, to buy and sell with no restrictions from the state **kapitalistisches Wirtschaftssystem; controlled economy** = system where business activity is controlled by orders from the government **staatlich gelenkte Wirtschaft; free market economy** = system where the government does not interfere in business activity in

any way **freie Marktwirtschaft; mixed economy** = system which contains both nationalized industries and private enterprise **Mischwirtschaft; planned economy** = system where the government plans all business activity **Planwirtschaft**

> QUOTE each of the major issues on the agenda at this week's meeting is important to the government's success in overall economic management
> *Australian Financial Review*
>
> QUOTE believers in free-market economics often find it hard to sort out their views on the issue
> *Economist*
>
> QUOTE the European economies are being held back by rigid labor markets and wage structures, huge expenditures on social welfare programs and restrictions on the free movement of goods within the Common Market
> *Duns Business Month*

ecu *or* **ECU** *noun* = EUROPEAN CURRENCY UNIT

> QUOTE the official use of the ecu remains limited. Since its creation in 1981 the ecu has grown popular because of its stability
> *Economist*

edge

1 *noun*

(a) side of a flat thing **Kante, Rand;** *he sat on the edge of the managing director's desk; the printer has printed the figures right to the edge of the printout*

(b) advantage **Vorteil;** *having a local office gives us a competitive edge over Smith Ltd;* **to have the edge on a rival company** = to be slightly more profitable *or* to have a slightly larger share of the market than a rival **einer Konkurrenzfirma gegenüber im Vorteil sein**

2 *verb* to move a little **sich langsam bewegen, sich verschieben;** *prices on the stock market edged upwards today; sales figures edged downwards in January*

editor *noun* person in charge of a newspaper or a section of a newspaper **Herausgeber/-in, Redakteur/-in;** *the editor of the "Times";* **the City editor** = business *or* finance editor of a British newspaper **Wirtschaftsredakteur**

◊ **editorial**

1 *adjective* referring to an editor **redaktionell, Redaktions-; editorial board** = group of editors (on a newspaper, etc.) **Redaktion, Redaktionskomitee**

2 *noun* main article in a newspaper, written by the editor **Leitartikel**

EDP = ELECTRONIC DATA PROCESSING

EEC = EUROPEAN ECONOMIC COMMUNITY *EEC ministers met today in Brussels; the USA is increasing its trade with the EEC*

effect

1 *noun*

(a) result **Auswirkung, Effekt;** *the effect of the pay increase was to raise productivity levels;* **terms of a contract which take effect** *or* **come into effect from January 1st** = terms which start to operate on January 1st **Vertragsbedingungen, die am 1. Januar in Kraft treten; prices are increased 10% with effect from January 1st** = new prices will apply from January 1st **mit Wirkung vom 1. Januar werden die Preise um 10% erhöht; to remain in effect** = to continue to be applied **wirksam/gültig bleiben**

(b) meaning **Sinn; clause to the effect that** = clause which means that **Klausel, die zum Inhalt hat/Klausel, die ... beinhaltet; we have made provision to this effect** = we have put into the contract terms which will make this work **wir haben für diesen Fall Klauseln eingebaut**

(c) personal effects = personal belongings **Gegenstände des persönlichen Gebrauchs**

2 *verb* to carry out **aus-, durchführen; to effect a payment** = to make a payment **eine Zahlung leisten; to effect customs clearance** = to clear something through customs **zollamtlich abfertigen lassen; to effect a settlement between two parties** = to bring two parties together and make them agree to a settlement **einen Vergleich zustande bringen**

◊ **effective** *adjective*

(a) effective demand = actual demand for a product which can be paid for **effektive Nachfrage; effective yield** = actual yield shown as a percentage **Effektivertrag, Effektivrendite**

(b) effective date = date on which a rule *or* a contract starts to be applied **Stichtag, Tag des Inkrafttretens; clause effective as from January 1st** = clause which starts to be applied on January 1st **Klausel mit Wirkung vom 1. Januar**

(c) which works *or* which produces results **effektiv, wirksam;** *advertising in the Sunday papers is the most effective way of selling; see* COST-EFFECTIVE

◊ **effectiveness** *noun* working *or* producing results **Wirksamkeit;** *I doubt the effectiveness of television advertising; see* COST-EFFECTIVENESS

◊ **effectual** *adjective* which produces a correct result **wirksam**

efficiency *noun* ability to work well *or* to produce the right result or the right work quickly **Fähigkeit, Leistungsfähigkeit, Effizienz;** *with a high degree of efficiency; a*

business efficiency exhibition; an efficiency expert
NOTE: no plural

◇ **efficient** *adjective* able to work well *or* to produce the right result quickly **fähig, leistungsfähig, effizient, tüchtig;** *the efficient working of a system; he needs an efficient secretary to look after him; efficient machine*

◇ **efficiently** *adverb* in an efficient way **gut, effizient;** *she organized the sales conference very efficiently*

> QUOTE increased control means improved efficiency in purchasing, shipping, sales and delivery
> *Duns Business Month*

efflux *noun* flowing out **Abfluß;** *efflux of capital to North America*

effort *noun* using the mind or body to do something **Anstrengung, Mühe;** *the salesmen made great efforts to increase sales; thanks to the efforts of the finance department, overheads have been reduced; if we make one more effort, we should clear the backlog of orders*

e.g. for example *or* such as **z.B.;** *the contract is valid in some countries (e.g. France and Belgium) but not in others*

EGM = EXTRAORDINARY GENERAL MEETING

elastic *adjective* which can expand or contract easily because of small changes in price **elastisch**

◇ **elasticity** *noun* ability to change easily **Elastizität; elasticity of supply and demand** = changes in supply and demand of an item depending on its market price **Elastizität von Angebot und Nachfrage**
NOTE: no plural

elect *verb* to choose someone by a vote **wählen;** *to elect the officers of an association; she was elected president*

◇ **-elect** *suffix* person who has been elected but has not yet started the term of office **designiert;** *she is the president-elect*
NOTE: the plural is **presidents-elect**

◇ **election** *noun* act of electing **Wahl;** *the election of officers of an association; the election of directors by the shareholders;* **general election** = choosing of representatives by all the voters in a country; *GB* **Parlamentswahl**

electricity *noun* current used to make light *or* heat *or* power **Elektrizität, Strom;** *the electricity was cut off this morning, so the computers could not work; our electricity bill has increased considerably this quarter; electricity costs are an important factor in our overheads*

◇ **electric** *adjective* worked by electricity **elektrisch;** *an electric typewriter*

◇ **electrical** *adjective* referring to electricity **elektrisch, Elektrizitäts-;** *the engineers are trying to repair an electrical fault*

electronic *adjective* **electronic data processing** = selecting and examining data stored in a computer to produce information **elektronische Datenverarbeitung; electronic engineer** = engineer who specializes in electronic machines **Elektroniker/-in; electronic mail** = system of sending messages from one computer terminal to another, via telephone lines **elektronische Post, E-Mail; electronic point of sale** = system where sales are charged automatically to a customer's credit card and stock is controlled by the shop's computer **(elektronischer) Kassenterminal, Datenkasse**

◇ **electronics** *plural noun* applying the scientific study of electrons to produce manufactured products, such as computers, calculators or telephones **Elektronik;** *the electronics industry; an electronics specialist or expert; electronics engineer*
NOTE: takes a singular verb

element *noun* basic part **Grundlage, Grundbestandteil;** *the elements of a settlement*

elevator *noun US* lift *or* machine which carries passengers or goods from one floor to another in a building **Fahrstuhl, Lift, Aufzug;** *take the elevator to the 26th floor*

eligible *adjective* person who can be chosen **wählbar;** *she is eligible for re-election*

◇ **eligibility** *noun* being eligible **Wählbarkeit;** *the chairman questioned her eligibility to stand for re-election*

eliminate *verb* to remove **eliminieren, ausschalten, ausschließen, beseitigen;** *to eliminate defects in the system; using a computer should eliminate all possibility of error*

embargo
1 *noun* government order which stops a type of trade **Embargo, Handelsverbot; to lay** *or* **put an embargo on trade with a country** = to say that trade with a country must not

take place **ein Handelsembargo über ein Land verhängen;** *the government has put an embargo on the export of computer equipment;* **to lift an embargo** = to allow trade to start again **ein Embargo aufheben;** *the government has lifted the embargo on the export of computers;* **to be under an embargo** = to be forbidden **einem Embargo unterliegen**
NOTE: plural is **embargoes**
2 *verb* to stop trade *or* not to allow trade **ein Embargo verhängen;** *the government has embargoed trade with the Eastern countries*

> QUOTE the Commerce Department is planning to loosen export controls for products that have been embargoed but are readily available elsewhere in the West
> *Duns Business Month*

embark *verb*
(a) to go on a ship **einschiffen;** *the passengers embarked at Southampton*
(b) to embark on = to start **mit etwas beginnen;** *the company has embarked on an expansion programme*

◇ **embarkation** *noun* going on to a ship **Einschiffung; port of embarkation** = port at which you get on to a ship **Einschiffungshafen; embarkation card** = card given to passengers getting on to a plane or ship **Bordkarte**

embezzle *verb* to use money which is not yours, or which you are looking after for someone **unterschlagen, veruntreuen;** *he was sent to prison for six months for embezzling his clients' money*

◇ **embezzlement** *noun* act of embezzling **Unterschlagung, Veruntreuung;** *he was sent to prison for six months for embezzlement*

◇ **embezzler** *noun* person who embezzles **jd, der Geld unterschlagen hat**

emergency *noun* dangerous situation where decisions have to be taken quickly **Notlage, Notfall, Notstand; the government declared a state of emergency** = the government decided that the situation was so dangerous that the police or army had to run the country **die Regierung hat den Notstand ausgerufen; to take emergency measures** = to take action rapidly to stop a crisis developing **Krisenmaßnahmen ergreifen;** *the company had to take emergency measures to stop losing money;* **emergency reserves** = ready cash held in case it is needed suddenly **Notfonds**

emoluments *plural noun* pay, salary or fees, or the earnings of directors who are not employees **Einkommen, Honorar, Bezüge**

employ *verb* to give someone regular paid work **beschäftigen, an-, einstellen; to employ twenty staff** = to have twenty people working for you **zwanzig Angestellte haben; to employ twenty new staff** = to give work to twenty new people **zwanzig neue Mitarbeiter einstellen**

◇ **employed**
1 *adjective*
(a) in regular paid work **beschäftigt, angestellt; he is not gainfully employed** = he has no regular paid work **er ist nicht erwerbstätig; self-employed** = working for yourself **selbständig;** *he worked in a bank for ten years but now is self-employed*
(b) (money) used profitably **arbeitend, gewinnbringend angelegt;** *return against capital employed*
2 *plural noun* people who are working **Arbeitnehmer;** *the employers and the employed;* **the self-employed** = people who work for themselves **die Selbständigen**

◇ **employee** *noun* worker *or* person employed by a company **Arbeitnehmer/-in, Angestellter;** *employees of the firm are eligible to join a profit-sharing scheme; relations between management and employees have improved; the company has decided to take on new employees*

◇ **employer** *noun* person *or* company which has regular workers and pays them **Arbeitgeber; employers' organization** *or* **association** = group of employers with similar interests **Arbeitgeberverband; employer's contribution** = money paid by an employer towards a worker's pension **Arbeitgeberanteil**

◇ **employment** *noun* regular paid work **Beschäftigung, Anstellung, Arbeit, Stelle; full employment** = situation where everyone in a country who can work has a job **Vollbeschäftigung; full-time employment** = work for all of a working day **Ganztagsbeschäftigung;** *to be in full-time employment;* **part-time employment** = work for part of a working day *or* part of a week **Halbtagsbeschäftigung; Teilzeitbeschäftigung; temporary employment** = work which does not last for more than a few months **Zeitarbeit; to be without employment** = to have no work **ohne Arbeit/erwerbslos sein; to find someone alternative employment** = to find another job for someone **für jdn eine andere Stelle finden; conditions of employment** = terms of a contract where someone is employed **Arbeitsvertragsbedingungen; contract of employment** *or* **employment contract** = contract between management and an employee showing all the conditions of work **Arbeitsvertrag; security of employment** = feeling by a worker that he has the right to keep his job until he retires

Arbeitsplatzsicherheit; employment office *or* **bureau** *or* **agency** = office which finds jobs for people **Stellenvermittlung**
NOTE: no plural

> QUOTE 70 per cent of Australia's labour force was employed in service activity
> *Australian Financial Review*
> QUOTE the blue-collar unions are the people who stand to lose most in terms of employment growth
> *Sydney Morning Herald*
> QUOTE companies introducing robotics think it important to involve individual employees in planning their introduction
> *Economist*

emporium *noun* large shop **Warenhaus**
NOTE: plural is **emporia**

empower *verb* to give someone the power to do something **ermächtigen, Vollmacht erteilen;** *she was empowered by the company to sign the contract*

emptor *see* CAVEAT

empty
1 *adjective* with nothing inside **leer;** *the envelope is empty; you can take that filing cabinet back to the storeroom as it is empty; start the computer file with an empty workspace*
2 *verb* to take the contents out of something **leeren, leer-, ausräumen;** *she emptied the filing cabinet and put the files in boxes; he emptied the petty cash box into his briefcase*
◇ **empties** *plural noun* empty bottles *or* cases **Leergut; returned empties** = empty bottles which are taken back to a shop to get back a deposit paid on them **Pfandflaschen**

EMS = EUROPEAN MONETARY SYSTEM

encash *verb* to cash a cheque *or* to exchange a cheque for cash **einlösen**
◇ **encashable** *adjective* which can be cashed **einlösbar**
◇ **encashment** *noun* act of exchanging for cash **Einlösung, Inkasso**

enc *or* **encl** = ENCLOSURE note put on a letter to show that a document is enclosed with it **Anlage**

enclose *verb* to put something inside an envelope with a letter **beilegen, beifügen;** *to enclose an invoice with a letter; I am enclosing a copy of the contract; letter enclosing a cheque; please find the cheque enclosed herewith*
◇ **enclosure** *noun* document enclosed with a letter **An-, Beilage;** *letter with enclosures*

encourage *verb*
(a) to make it easier for something to happen **fördern, anregen, begünstigen;** *the general rise in wages encourages consumer spending; leaving your credit cards on your desk encourages people to steal* *or* *encourages stealing; the company is trying to encourage sales by giving large discounts*
(b) to help someone to do something by giving advice **ermutigen;** *he encouraged me to apply for the job*
◇ **encouragement** *noun* giving advice to someone to help him to succeed **Anregung, Ermutigung;** *the designers produced a very marketable product, thanks to the encouragement of the sales director*

end
1 *noun* final point *or* last part **Ende, Beendigung;** *at the end of the contract period;* **at the end of six months** = after six months have passed **nach Ablauf von sechs Monaten; account end** = the end of an accounting period **Ende des Buchungszeitraumes; month end** = the end of the month, when accounts have to be drawn up **Monatsende; end product** = manufactured product, made at the end of a production process **Endprodukt;** *after six months' trial production, the end product is still not acceptable;* **end user** = person who actually uses a product **Endverbraucher;** *the company is creating a computer with the end user in mind;* **in the end** = at last *or* after a lot of problems **schließlich;** *in the end the company had to pull out of the US market; in the end they signed the contract at the airport; in the end the company had to call in the police;* **on end** = for a long time *or* with no breaks **ununterbrochen;** *the discussions continued for hours on end; the workforce worked at top speed for weeks on end to finish the order on time;* **to come to an end** = to finish **zu Ende gehen, auslaufen;** *our distribution agreement comes to an end next month*
2 *verb* to finish **beenden;** *the distribution agreement ends in July; the chairman ended the discussion by getting up and walking out of the meeting*
◇ **end in** *verb* to have as a result **enden mit, ausgehen;** *the AGM ended in the shareholders fighting on the floor*
◇ **end up** *verb* to finish **enden;** *we ended up with a bill for £10,000*

endorse *verb* **to endorse a bill** *or* **a cheque** = to sign a bill *or* a cheque on the back to show that you accept it **einen Wechsel indossieren; einen Scheck girieren**

◇ **endorsee** *noun* person whose name is written on a bill *or* a cheque as having the right to cash it **Indossat**

◇ **endorsement** *noun*
(a) act of endorsing; signature on a document which endorses it **Indossament**
(b) note on an insurance policy which adds conditions to the policy **Zusatzklausel**

◇ **endorser** *noun* person who endorses a bill which is then paid to him **Indossant**

endowment *noun* giving money to provide a regular income **Stiftung; endowment insurance** *or* **endowment policy** = insurance policy where a sum of money is paid to the insured person on a certain date, or to his heirs if he dies earlier **Versicherung auf den Erlebens- und Todesfall; endowment mortgage** = mortgage backed by an endowment policy **mit einer gemischten Lebensversicherung gekoppelte Hypothek**

energy *noun*
(a) force *or* strength **Energie, Kraft;** *he hasn't the energy to be a good salesman; they wasted their energies on trying to sell cars in the German market*
(b) power from electricity *or* petrol, etc. **Energie;** *we try to save energy by switching off the lights when the rooms are empty; if you reduce the room temperature to eighteen degrees, you will save energy*
NOTE: no plural for (b)

◇ **energetic** *adjective* with a lot of energy **aktiv;** *the salesmen have made energetic attempts to sell the product*

◇ **energy-saving** *adjective* which saves energy **energiesparend;** *the company is introducing energy-saving measures*

enforce *verb* to make sure something is done *or* is obeyed **erzwingen, Geltung verschaffen, durchsetzen;** *to enforce the terms of a contract*

◇ **enforcement** *noun* making sure that something is obeyed **Erzwingung, Durchsetzung;** *enforcement of the terms of a contract*
NOTE: no plural

engage *verb*
(a) to engage someone to do something = to make someone do something legally **jdn zu etwas verpflichten;** *the contract engages us to a minimum annual purchase*
(b) to employ **jdn an-, einstellen, engagieren;** *we have engaged the best commercial lawyer to represent us; the company has engaged twenty new salesmen*
(c) to be engaged in = to be busy with **sich befassen mit, tätig sein;** *he is engaged in work on computers; the company is engaged in trade with Africa*

◇ **engaged** *adjective* busy (telephone) **besetzt;** *you cannot speak to the manager - his line is engaged;* **engaged tone** = sound made by a telephone when the line dialled is busy **Besetztzeichen;** *I tried to phone the complaints department but got only the engaged tone*

◇ **engagement** *noun*
(a) agreement to do something **Verpflichtung, Vereinbarung; to break an engagement to do something** = not to do what you have legally agreed **eine Verbindlichkeit nicht erfüllen, eine Abmachung nicht einhalten;** *the company broke their engagement not to sell our rivals' products*
(b) engagements = arrangements to meet people **Termine;** *I have no engagements for the rest of the day; she noted the appointment in her engagements diary*

engine *noun* machine which drives something **Motor;** *a car with a small engine is more economic than one with a large one; the lift engine has broken down again - we shall just have to walk up to the 4th floor*

◇ **engineer** *noun* person who looks after technical equipment **Ingenieur, Techniker; civil engineer** = person who specializes in the construction of roads, bridges, railways, etc. **Bauingenieur; consulting engineer** = engineer who gives specialist advice **beratender Ingenieur; product engineer** = engineer in charge of the equipment for making a product **Fertigungsingenieur; project engineer** = engineer in charge of a project **Projektingenieur; programming engineer** = engineer in charge of programming a computer system **Systemprogrammierer, Systemanalytiker**

◇ **engineering** *noun* science of technical equipment **Tiefbau, Grundbau; civil engineering** = construction of roads, bridges, railways, etc. **Bauingenieurwesen; the engineering department** = section of a company dealing with equipment **technische Abteilung; an engineering consultant** = an engineer who gives specialist advice **ein technischer Berater**
NOTE: no plural

enquire = INQUIRE

◇ **enquiry** = INQUIRY

en route *adverb* on the way **unterwegs;** *the tanker sank when she was en route to the Gulf*

entail

1 *noun* legal condition which passes ownership of a property only to certain persons **festgelegte Erbfolge für Grundbesitz, Fideikommiß**
2 *verb* to involve **erforderlich machen, zur Folge haben;** *itemizing the sales figures will entail about ten days' work*

enter *verb*

(a) to go in **hereinkommen, hineingehen, einsteigen;** *they all stood up when the chairman entered the room; the company has spent millions trying to enter the do-it-yourself market*
(b) to write **eintragen;** *to enter a name on a list; the clerk entered the interest in my bank book; to enter up an item in a ledger;* **to enter a bid for something** = to offer (usually in writing) to buy something **für etwas ein Angebot machen; to enter a caveat** = to warn legally that you have an interest in a case, and that no steps can be taken without your permission **Einspruch einlegen**
(c) to enter into = to begin **aufnehmen, eingehen;** *to enter into relations with someone; to enter into negotiations with a foreign government; to enter into a partnership with a legal friend; to enter into an agreement* or *a contract*
◇ **entering** *noun* act of writing items in a record **Eintragung**
NOTE: no plural

enterprise *noun*

(a) system of carrying on a business **Unternehmertum; free enterprise** = system of business free from government interference **freies Unternehmertum; private enterprise** = businesses which are owned privately, not nationalized **Privatwirtschaft;** *the project is completely funded by private enterprise*
(b) business **Unternehmen; a small-scale enterprise** = a small business **ein Kleinbetrieb; a state enterprise** = a state-controlled company **staatliches Unternehmen, Staatsbetrieb;** *bosses of state enterprises are appointed by the government*
NOTE: no plural for (a)

entertain *verb*

(a) to offer meals *or* hotel accommodation *or* theatre tickets, etc. to (business) visitors **unterhalten, bewirten**
(b) to be ready to consider (a proposal) **in Erwägung/Betracht ziehen, erwägen;** *the management will not entertain any suggestions from the union representatives*
◇ **entertainment** *noun* offering meals, etc. to business visitors **Unterhaltung, Bewirtung; entertainment allowance** = money which a manager is allowed by his company to spend on meals with visitors **Aufwands-, Bewirtungsentschädigung; entertainment expenses** = money spent on giving meals to business visitors **Bewirtungsspesen**

entitle *verb* to give the right to something **berechtigen; he is entitled to a discount** = he has the right to be given a discount **er hat Anspruch auf Rabatt**

◇ **entitlement** *noun* right **Anspruch, Berechtigung; holiday entitlement** = number of days' paid holiday which a worker has the right to take **Urlaubsanspruch;** *she has not used up all her holiday entitlement;* **pension entitlement** = amount of pension which someone has the right to receive when he retires **Rentenanspruch**

entrance *noun* way in **Eingang;** *the taxi will drop you at the main entrance; deliveries should be made to the London Road entrance;* **entrance (charge)** = money which you have to pay to go in **Eintritt;** *entrance is £1.50 for adults and £1 for children*

entrepot *noun* **entrepot port** = town with a large international commercial port dealing in re-exports **Wiederausfuhrhafen**

entrepreneur *noun* person who directs a company and takes commercial risks **Unternehmer**

◇ **entrepreneurial** *adjective* taking commercial risks **unternehmerisch;** *an entrepreneurial decision*

entrust *verb* **to entrust someone with something** *or* **to entrust something to someone** = to give someone the responsibility for looking after something **jdm etwas anvertrauen;** *he was entrusted with the keys to the office safe*

entry *noun*

(a) written information put in an accounts ledger **Eintrag; credit entry** *or* **debit entry** = entry on the credit *or* debit side of an account **Gutschrift, Habenbuchung; Lastschrift, Sollbuchung; single-entry bookkeeping** = noting a deal with only one entry **einfache Buchführung; double-entry bookkeeping** = noting of both debit and credit sides of an account **doppelte Buchführung; to make an entry in a ledger** = to write in details of a deal **einen Eintrag in das Hauptbuch machen; contra entry** = entry made in the opposite side of an account to make an earlier entry worthless (such as a debit entry against a credit) **Gegenbuchung; to contra an entry** = to enter a similar

amount on the opposite side of the account **einen Eintrag zurückbuchen**
(b) act of going in; place where you can go in **Eintritt, Eingang;** *to pass a customs entry point; entry of goods under bond;* **entry charge** = money which you have to pay before you go in **Eintritt; entry visa** = visa allowing someone to go into a country **Einreisevisum; multiple entry visa** = entry visa which allows someone to enter a country as often as he likes **Visum zur mehrmaligen Einreise**

envelope *noun* flat paper cover for sending letters **Briefumschlag; airmail envelope** = very light envelope for airmail letters **Luftpostumschlag; aperture envelope** = envelope with a hole in it so that the address on the letter inside can be seen **Fensterumschlag; window envelope** = envelope with a hole covered with film so that the address on the letter inside can be seen **Fensterumschlag; sealed** *or* **unsealed envelope** = envelope where the flap has been stuck down to close it *or* envelope where the flap has been pushed into the back of the envelope **verschlossener Briefumschlag; offener Briefumschlag;** *to send the information in a sealed envelope;* **a stamped addressed envelope** = an envelope with your own address written on it and a stamp stuck on it to pay for return postage **freigemachter/frankierter Rückumschlag;** *please send a stamped addressed envelope for further details and our latest catalogue*

epos *or* **EPOS** = ELECTRONIC POINT OF SALE

equal
1 *adjective* exactly the same **gleich;** *male and female workers have equal pay;* **equal opportunities programme** = programme to avoid discrimination in employment **Chancengleichheitsplan**
NOTE: the US equivalent is **affirmative action**
2 *verb* to be the same as **gleichkommen;** *production this month has equalled our best month ever*
NOTE: **equalling - equalled** but US: **equaling - equaled**

◇ **equalize** *verb* to make equal **aus-, angleichen;** *to equalize dividends*

◇ **equalization** *noun* process of making equal **Ausgleich, Angleichung**

◇ **equally** *adverb* in the same way **gleichmäßig, gleichermaßen;** *costs will be shared equally between the two parties; they were both equally responsible for the disastrous launch*

equip *verb* to provide with machinery **ausrüsten, ausstatten;** *to equip a factory with new machinery; the office is fully equipped with word-processors*

◇ **equipment** *noun* machinery and furniture required to make a factory or office work **Ausrüstung, Ausstattung, Einrichtung;** *office equipment or business equipment; office equipment supplier; office equipment catalogue;* **capital equipment** = equipment which a factory *or* office uses to work **Investitionsgüter; heavy equipment** = large machines, such as for making cars or for printing **Industriegüter, Schwermaschinen**
NOTE: no plural

equity *noun*
(a) right to receive dividends as part of the profit of a company in which you own shares **Dividendenanspruch**
(b) shareholders' equity *or* **equity capital** = amount of a company's capital which is owned by shareholders **Eigenkapital**

◇ **equities** *plural noun* ordinary shares **Stammaktien**

> QUOTE in the past three years commercial property has seriously underperformed equities and dropped out of favour as a result
> *Investors Chronicle*
> QUOTE investment trusts can raise more capital but this has to be done as a company does it, by a rights issue of equity
> *Investors Chronicle*

equivalence *noun* being equivalent **Gleichwertigkeit, Äquivalenz**

◇ **equivalent** *adjective* **to be equivalent to** = to have the same value as *or* to be the same as **gleichkommen, gleich/gleichwertig sein;** *the total dividend paid is equivalent to one quarter of the pretax profits*

ergonomics *plural noun* study of people at work and their working conditions **Ergonomie, Ergonomik**
NOTE: takes a singular verb

◇ **ergonomist** *noun* scientist who studies people at work and tries to improve their working conditions **Ergonomiker/-in**

erode *verb* to wear away gradually **aushöhlen, auswaschen; to erode wage differentials** = to reduce gradually differences in salary between different grades **Lohnunterschiede abbauen**

error *noun* mistake **Fehler;** *he made an error in calculating the total; the secretary must have made a typing error;* **clerical error** = mistake made in an office **Schreibfehler; computer error** = mistake made by a computer **Computerfehler; margin**

of error = number of mistakes which are accepted in a document *or* in a calculation **Fehlerspielraum; errors and omissions excepted** = words written on an invoice to show that the company has no responsibility for mistakes in the invoice **Irrtümer und Auslassungen vorbehalten; error rate** = number of mistakes per thousand entries *or* per page **Fehlerquote; in error** *or* **by error** = by mistake **versehentlich, irrtümlich;** *the letter was sent to the London office in error*

escalate *verb* to increase steadily **eskalieren, ansteigen**

◇ **escalation** *noun* **escalation of prices** = steady increase in prices **Preiseskalation, Preisanstieg; escalation clause** = ESCALATOR CLAUSE

◇ **escalator clause** *noun* clause in a contract allowing for regular price increases because of increased costs **Preisgleitklausel**

escape *noun* getting away from a difficult situation **Ausbruch, Entkommen; escape clause** = clause in a contract which allows one of the parties to avoid carrying out the terms of the contract under certain conditions **Befreiungs-, Rücktrittsklausel**

escrow *noun* **in escrow** = held in safe keeping by a third party **treuhänderisch hinterlegt; document held in escrow** = document given to a third party to keep and to pass on to someone when money has been paid **bei einem Treuhänder verwahrtes Dokument;** *US* **escrow account** = account where money is held in escrow until a contract is signed *or* until goods are delivered, etc. **Treuhandkonto**

NOTE: no plural

espionage *noun* **industrial espionage** = trying to find out the secrets of a competitor's work or products, usually by illegal means **Werks-, Wirtschaftsspionage**

NOTE: no plural

essential *adjective* very important **wesentlich, unerläßlich, unbedingt notwendig;** *it is essential that an agreement be reached before the end of the month; the factory is lacking essential spare parts*

◇ **essentials** *plural noun* goods *or* products which are very important **Güter des täglichen Bedarfs**

establish *verb* to set up *or* to make *or* to open **gründen, schaffen, bilden, einrichten;** *the company has established a branch in Australia; the business was established in Scotland in 1823; it is a young company - it has been established for only four years;* **to establish oneself in business** = to become successful in a new business **sich geschäftlich durchsetzen/etablieren**

◇ **establishment** *noun*

(a) commercial business **Firma, Geschäft, Betrieb, Unternehmen;** *he runs an important printing establishment*

(b) establishment charges = cost of people and property in a company's accounts **Unternehmens-Fixkosten**

(c) number of people working in a company **Personalbestand; to be on the establishment** = to be a full-time employee **zum Personal gehören, fest angestellt sein; office with an establishment of fifteen** = office with a budgeted staff of fifteen **Büro mit fünfzehn Mitarbeitern**

estate *noun*

(a) real estate = property (land or buildings) **Grundbesitz, Immobilien; estate agency** = office which arranges for the sale of property **Grundstücks- und Immobilienfirma; estate agent** = person in charge of an estate agency **Grundstücks- und Immobilienmakler**

(b) industrial estate *or* **trading estate** = area of land near a town specially for factories and warehouses **Gewerbe-, Industriegebiet**

(c) property left by a dead person **Nachlaß; estate duty** = tax on property left by a dead person **Erbschaftssteuer**

estimate

1 *noun*

(a) calculation of probable cost *or* size *or* time of something **Schätzung; rough estimate** = very approximate calculation **grobe Schätzung/Berechnung; at a conservative estimate** = calculation which probably underestimates the final figure **bei vorsichtiger Schätzung;** *their turnover has risen by at least 20% in the last year, and that is a conservative estimate;* **these figures are only an estimate** = these are not the final accurate figures **diese Beträge sind nur Schätzwerte;** *can you give me an estimate of how much time was spent on the job?*

(b) calculation of how much something is likely to cost in the future, given to a client so as to get him to make an order **Kostenvoranschlag;** *estimate of costs or of expenditure; before we can give the grant we must have an estimate of the total costs involved; to ask a builder for an estimate for building the warehouse;* **to put in an estimate** = to give someone a written calculation of the probable costs of carrying out a job **einen Kostenvoranschlag machen;** *three firms put in estimates for the job*

2 *verb*
(a) to calculate the probable cost *or* size *or* time of something **schätzen;** *to estimate that it will cost £1m or to estimate costs at £1m; we estimate current sales at only 60% of last year*
(b) to estimate for a job = to state in writing the future costs of carrying out a piece of work so that a client can make an order **einen Kostenvoranschlag für einen Auftrag einreichen;** *three firms estimated for the fitting of the offices*

◇ **estimated** *adjective* calculated approximately **geschätzt, veranschlagt;** *estimated sales; estimated figure*

◇ **estimation** *noun* approximate calculation **Schätzung**

◇ **estimator** *noun* person whose job is to calculate estimates for carrying out work **Schätzer/-in**

etc. and so on **usw., etc.;** *the import duty is to be paid on luxury items including cars, watches, etc.*

Euro- *prefix* referring to Europe or the European Community **Euro-**

◇ **Eurobond** *noun* bond issued by an international corporation or government outside its country of origin and sold to Europeans who pay in Eurodollars **Eurobond, Euroanleihe;** *the Eurobond market*

◇ **Eurocheque** *noun* cheque which can be cashed in a European bank **Euroscheck**

◇ **Eurocurrency** *noun* European currencies used for trade within Europe but outside their countries of origin **Eurowährung;** *a Eurocurrency loan; the Eurocurrency market*

◇ **Eurodollar** *noun* US dollar in a European bank, used for trade within Europe **Eurodollar;** *a Eurodollar loan; the Eurodollar market*

◇ **Euromarket** *noun* the European Community seen as a potential market for sales **Euromarkt**

◇ **Europe** *noun* group of countries to the West of Asia and the North of Africa **Europa;** *most of the countries of Western Europe are members of the Common Market; Canadian exports to Europe have risen by 25%*

◇ **European** *adjective* referring to Europe **europäisch; the European Community** = the Common Market **die Europäische Gemeinschaft; the European Monetary System** = system of controlled exchange rates between some member countries of the Common Market **das Europäische Währungssystem**

evade *verb* to try to avoid something **ausweichen, umgehen, sich entziehen; to evade tax** = to try illegally to avoid paying tax **Steuer hinterziehen**

evaluate *verb* to calculate a value **ab-, einschätzen, festsetzen, berechnen;** *to evaluate costs*

◇ **evaluation** *noun* calculation of value **Ein-, Abschätzung, Festsetzung; job evaluation** = examining different jobs within a company to see what skills and qualifications are needed to carry them out **Arbeitsplatzbewertung**

evasion *noun* avoiding **Umgehung, Ausweichen; tax evasion** = illegally trying not to pay tax **Steuerhinterziehung**

evidence *noun* written or spoken report at a trial **Aussage; documentary evidence** = evidence in the form of documents **Urkundenbeweis; the secretary gave evidence against her former employer** = the secretary was a witness, and her report suggested that her former employer was guilty **die Sekretärin sagte gegen ihren ehemaligen Vorgesetzten aus**
NOTE: no plural

ex- *preposition*
(a) out of *or* from **ab; price ex warehouse** = price for a product which is to be collected from the manufacturer's or agent's warehouse and so does not include delivery **Preis ab Lager; price ex works** *or* **ex factory** = price not including transport from the maker's factory **Preis ab Werk**
(b) ex coupon = bond without the interest coupon **ohne/ex Kupon; share quoted ex dividend** = share price not including the right to receive the next dividend **ex Dividende notierte Aktie;** *the shares went ex dividend yesterday*
(c) formerly **ehemalig, Ex-;** *Mr Smith, the ex-chairman of the company*
(d) to be ex-directory = telephone number which is not printed in the telephone book **nicht im Telefonbuch aufgeführt sein;** *he has an ex-directory number*

exact *adjective* very correct **genau, exakt;** *the exact time is 10.27; the salesgirl asked me if I had the exact sum, since the shop had no change*

◇ **exactly** *adverb* very correctly **genau;** *the total cost was exactly £6,500*

examine *verb* to look at someone *or* something very carefully to see if it can be accepted **untersuchen, (über)prüfen;** *the customs officials asked to examine the* *inside of the car; the police are examining the papers from the managing director's safe*

◇ **examination** *noun*
(a) looking at something very carefully to see if it is acceptable **Untersuchung, Prüfung, Überprüfung; customs examination** = looking at goods *or* baggage by customs officials **Zollkontrolle**
(b) test to see if someone has passed a course **Prüfung, Examen;** *he passed his accountancy examinations; she came first in the final examination for the course; he failed his proficiency examination and so had to leave his job*

example *noun* something chosen to show **Modell, Muster, Probe;** *the motor show has many examples of energy-saving cars on display;* **for example** = to show one thing out of many **zum Beispiel;** *the government wants to encourage exports, and, for example, it gives free credit to exporters*

exceed *verb* to be more than **übersteigen, überschreiten, hinausgehen über;** *discount not exceeding 15%; last year costs exceeded 20% of income for the first time;* **he has exceeded his credit limit** = he has borrowed more money than he is allowed **er hat seinen Kredit überzogen**

excellent *adjective* very good **ausgezeichnet, erstklassig, hervorragend;** *the quality of the firm's products is excellent, but its sales force is not large enough*

except *preposition & conjunction* not including **außer;** *VAT is levied on all goods and services except books, newspapers and children's clothes; sales are rising in all markets except the Far East*

◇ **excepted** *adverb* not including **ausgenommen; errors and omissions excepted** = note on an invoice to show that the company has no responsibility for mistakes in the invoice **Irrtümer und Auslassungen vorbehalten**

◇ **exceptional** *adjective* not usual *or* different **außergewöhnlich; exceptional items** = items in a balance sheet which do not appear there each year **Sonderposten**

excess *noun* amount which is more than what is allowed **Überschuß, Mehrbetrag;** *an excess of expenditure over revenue;* **excess baggage** = extra payment at an airport for taking baggage which is heavier than the normal passenger's allowance **Übergewicht; excess capacity** = spare capacity which is not being used **Überkapazität; excess fare** = extra fare to be paid (such as for travelling first class with a second class ticket) **Nachlösegebühr; in excess of** = above *or* more than **über, mehr als;** *quantities in excess of twenty-five kilos;* **excess profits** = profit which is more than what is thought to be normal **Mehrgewinn; excess profits tax** = tax on excess profits **Steuer zur Abschöpfung von Höchstgewinnen**

◇ **excessive** *adjective* too large **übermäßig;** *excessive costs*

> QUOTE most airlines give business class the same baggage allowance as first class, which can save large sums in excess baggage
> *Business Traveller*
>
> QUOTE control of materials provides manufacturers with an opportunity to reduce the amount of money tied up in excess materials
> *Duns Business Month*

exchange
1 *noun*
(a) giving of one thing for another **Tausch, Austausch; to offer** *or* **take something in part exchange** giving *or* taking an old product as part of the payment for a new one **etwas in Zahlung geben od nehmen;** *to take a car in part exchange;* **exchange of contracts** = point in the sale of property when the buyer and the seller both sign the contract of sale which then becomes binding **Unterzeichnung des Kaufvertrags von Grundbesitz**
(b) foreign exchange = money of another country **Devisen;** *the company has more than £1m in foreign exchange;* **foreign exchange broker** = person who buys and sells foreign currency on behalf of other people **Devisenhändler, Devisenmakler; foreign exchange market** = dealings in foreign currencies **Devisenmarkt;** *he trades on the foreign exchange market; foreign exchange markets were very active after the dollar devalued;* **rate of exchange** *or* **exchange rate** = price at which one currency is exchanged for another **Wechselkurs;** *the current rate of exchange is 10.95 francs to the pound;* **exchange control** = control by a government of the way in which its currency may be exchanged for foreign currencies **Devisenkontrolle;** *the government had to impose exchange controls to stop the rush to buy dollars;* **exchange dealer** = person who buys and sells foreign currency **Devisenhändler; exchange dealings** = buying and selling foreign currency **Devisenhandel;** *GB* **Exchange Equalization Account** = account with the Bank of England used by the government when buying or selling foreign currency to influence the sterling exchange rate **Währungsausgleichsfonds; exchange premium** = extra cost above the normal rate for buying a foreign currency **Agio, Aufgeld**

(c) bill of exchange = document which tells a bank to pay a person (usually used in foreign currency payments) **Wechsel, Tratte**
(d) Stock Exchange = place where stocks and shares are bought and sold **Börse;** *the company's shares are traded on the New York Stock Exchange; he works on the Stock Exchange;* **commodity exchange** = place where commodities are bought and sold **Warenbörse**
NOTE: no plural for (b)
2 *verb*
(a) to exchange one article for another = to give one thing in place of something else **einen Artikel gegen einen anderen umtauschen;** *he exchanged his motorcycle for a car; if the trousers are too small you can take them back and exchange them for a larger pair; goods can be exchanged only on production of the sales slip*
(b) to exchange contracts = to sign a contract when buying a property (done by both buyer and seller at the same time) **beim Kauf von Grundbesitz den Vertrag unterschreiben**
(c) to change money of one country for money of another **wechseln, tauschen;** *to exchange francs for pounds*

◇ **exchangeable** *adjective* which can be exchanged **austauschbar, umtauschbar**

◇ **exchanger** *noun* person who buys and sells foreign currency **Devisenhändler**

> QUOTE under the barter agreements, Nigeria will export crude oil in exchange for trucks, food, planes and chemicals
> *Wall Street Journal*
>
> QUOTE can free trade be reconciled with a strong dollar resulting from floating exchange rates
> *Duns Business Month*
>
> QUOTE a draft report on changes in the international monetary system casts doubt on any return to fixed exchange-rate parities
> *Wall Street Journal*

Exchequer

Exchequer *noun GB* **the Exchequer** = government department dealing with public revenue **Finanzministerium, Schatzamt; the Chancellor of the Exchequer** = the chief British finance minister **Finanzminister, Schatzkanzler**

excise

1 *noun*
(a) excise duty = tax on certain goods produced in a country (such as alcohol) **Verbrauchssteuer;** *to pay excise duty on wine*
(b) Customs and Excise *or* **Excise Department** = government department which deals with taxes on imports and on products such as alcohol produced in the country **Behörde für Zölle und Verbrauchssteuern;** *Excise officer*
2 *verb* to cut out **herausschneiden;** *please excise all references to the strike in the minutes*

◇ **exciseman** *noun* person who works in the Excise Department **Steuereinnehmer**

exclude

exclude *verb* to keep out *or* not to include **ausschließen;** *the interest charges have been excluded from the document; damage by fire is excluded from the policy*

◇ **excluding** *preposition* not including **außer, ausgenommen;** *all salesmen, excluding those living in London, can claim expenses for attending the sales conference*

◇ **exclusion** *noun* act of not including **Ausschluß; exclusion clause** = clause in an insurance policy *or* warranty which says which items are not covered **Ausschlußklausel, Freizeichnungsklausel**

◇ **exclusive** *adjective*
(a) exclusive agreement = agreement where a person is made sole agent for a product in a market **Alleinvertretungsvereinbarung; exclusive right to market a product** = right to be the only person to market the product **Rechte zum Alleinvertrieb eines Produktes**
(b) exclusive of = not including **exklusive, ausschließlich;** *all payments are exclusive of tax; the invoice is exclusive of VAT*

◇ **exclusivity** *noun* exclusive right to market a product **Alleinvertrieb**

excuse

1 *noun* reason for doing something wrong **Entschuldigung; Ausrede;** *his excuse for not coming to the meeting was that he had been told about it only the day before;* **the managing director refused to accept the sales manager's excuses for the poor sales** = he refused to believe that there was a good reason for the poor sales **der leitende Direktor weigerte sich, die Ausreden des Verkaufsleiters für den schlechten Umsatz zu akzeptieren**
2 *verb* to forgive a small mistake **entschuldigen;** *she can be excused for not knowing the French for "photocopier"*

execute

execute *verb* to carry out (an order) **ausführen**

◇ **execution** *noun* carrying out of an order **Aus-, Durchführung; stay of execution** = temporary stopping of a legal order **Vollstreckungsaufschub;** *the court granted the company a two-week stay of execution*
NOTE: no plural

◇ **executive**
1 *adjective* which puts decisions into action **exekutiv, Exekutiv-; executive committee** = committee which runs a society *or* a club **Vorstand; executive director** = director who actually works full-time in the company

geschäftsführender Direktor; executive powers = right to put decisions into actions **ausübende Gewalt, Exekutivgewalt;** *he was made managing director with full executive powers over the European operation*
2 *noun* person in a business who takes decisions *or* manager *or* director **Führungskraft, leitender Angestellter;** *sales executive; senior or junior executive;* **account executive** = employee who is the link between his company and certain customers **Kundenbetreuer; chief executive** = executive director in charge of a company; *entspricht* **geschäftsführender Direktor**

executor *noun* person who sees that the terms of a will are carried out **Testamentsvollstrecker;** *he was named executor of his brother's will*

exempt
1 *adjective* not covered by a law; not forced to obey a law **ausgenommen, befreit; exempt from tax** *or* **tax-exempt** = not required to pay tax **von der Steuer befreit, steuerfrei;** *as a non-profit-making organization we are exempt from tax*
2 *verb* to free something from having tax paid on it or from having to pay tax **befreien;** *non-profit-making organizations are exempted from tax; food is exempted from sales tax; the government exempted trusts from tax*
◇ **exemption** *noun* act of exempting something from a contract *or* from a tax **Befreiung; exemption from tax** *or* **tax exemption** = being free from having to pay tax **Steuerbefreiung;** *as a non-profit-making organization you can claim tax exemption*

exercise
1 *noun* use of something **Anwendung, Ausübung; exercise of an option** = using an option *or* putting an option into action **Ausübung einer Option**
2 *verb* to use **anwenden, ausüben; to exercise an option** = to put an option into action **eine Option ausüben;** *he exercised his option to acquire sole marketing rights for the product; the chairwoman exercised her veto to block the motion*

ex gratia *adjective* **an ex gratia payment** = payment made as a gift, with no other obligations **Zahlung ohne Anerkennung einer Rechtspflicht**

exhibit
1 *noun*
(a) thing which is shown **Ausstellungsstück;** *the buyers admired the exhibits on our stand*
(b) single section of an exhibition **Ausstellungsstand;** *the British Trade Exhibit at the International Computer Fair*
2 *verb* **to exhibit at the Motor Show** = to display new models of cars **auf der Fahrzeugausstellung ausstellen**
◇ **exhibition** *noun* showing goods so that buyers can look at them and decide what to buy **Ausstellung;** *the government has sponsored an exhibition of good design; we have a stand at the Ideal Home Exhibition; the agricultural exhibition grounds;* **exhibition room** *or* **hall** = place where goods are shown so that buyers can look at them and decide what to buy **Ausstellungsraum, Messehalle; exhibition stand** = separate section of an exhibition where a company exhibits its products or services **Messestand**
◇ **exhibitor** *noun* person *or* company which shows products at an exhibition **Aussteller**

exist *verb* to be **existieren;** *I do not believe the document exists - I think it has been burnt*

exit *noun* way out of a building **Ausgang;** *the customers all rushed towards the exits;* **fire exit** = door which leads to a way out of a building if there is a fire **Notausgang**

ex officio *adjective & adverb* because of an office held **ex officio, von Amts wegen;** *the treasurer is ex officio a member or an ex officio member of the finance committee*

expand *verb* to increase *or* to get bigger *or* to make something bigger **erweitern, (sich) ausweiten/vergrößern, expandieren, ausbauen;** *an expanding economy; the company is expanding fast; we have had to expand our sales force*
◇ **expansion** *noun* increase in size **Erweiterung, Ausweitung, Vergrößerung, Expansion, Ausbau;** *the expansion of the domestic market; the company had difficulty in financing its current expansion programme; GB* **business expansion scheme** = system where money invested in a new company for some years is free from tax **Steuerbefreiung bei Investition in Betriebsneugründung**

QUOTE inflation-adjusted GNP moved up at a 1.3% annual rate, its worst performance since the economic expansion began
Fortune

QUOTE the businesses we back range from start-up ventures to established businesses in need of further capital for expansion
Times

QUOTE the group is undergoing a period of rapid expansion and this has created an exciting opportunity for a qualified accountant
Financial Times

expect *verb* to hope that something is going to happen **erwarten;** *we are expecting him to arrive at 10.45; they are expecting a cheque from their agent next week; the house was sold for more than the expected price*

◊ **expectancy** *noun* **life expectancy** = number of years a person is likely to live **Lebenserwartung**

> QUOTE he observed that he expected exports to grow faster than imports in 1985-86
> *Sydney Morning Herald*
>
> QUOTE American business as a whole has seen profits well above the levels normally expected at this stage of the cycle
> *Sunday Times*

expenditure *noun* amounts of money spent **Ausgaben, Aufwendungen; below-the-line expenditure** = exceptional payments which are separated from a company's normal accounts **außerordentliche Aufwendungen; capital expenditure** = money spent on fixed assets (such as property or machinery) **Investitionen; the company's current expenditure programme** = the company's spending according to the current plan **der Plan für laufende Aufwendungen des Unternehmens; heavy expenditure on equipment** = spending large sums of money on equipment **beträchtliche Ausgaben für die Ausstattung**

NOTE: no plural

◊ **expense** *noun*

(a) money spent **Ausgabe, Kosten;** *it is not worth the expense; the expense is too much for my bank balance;* **at great expense** = having spent a lot of money **mit hohen Kosten, kostenintensiv; he furnished the office regardless of expense** = without thinking how much it cost **er möblierte das Büro, ohne auf die Kosten zu achten**

(b) expense account = money which a businessman is allowed by his company to spend on travelling and entertaining clients in connection with his business **Spesenkonto;** *I'll put this lunch on my expense account; expense account lunches form a large part of our current expenditure*

NOTE: no plural

◊ **expenses** *plural noun* money paid for doing something **Unkosten, Spesen;** *the salary offered is £10,000 plus expenses;* **all expenses paid** = with all costs paid by the company **mit Vergütung aller Unkosten;** *the company sent him to San Francisco all expenses paid;* **to cut down on expenses** = to try to reduce spending **die Unkosten einschränken; allowable expenses** = business expenses which are allowed against tax **abzugsfähige Ausgaben; business expenses** = money spent on running a business, not on stock or assets **Betriebskosten; entertainment expenses** = money spent on giving meals to business visitors **Bewirtungsspesen; fixed expenses** = money which is spent regularly (such as rent, electricity, telephone) **Fixkosten; incidental expenses** = small amounts of money spent at various times, in addition to larger amounts **Nebenkosten; legal expenses** = money spent on fees paid to lawyers **Anwaltskosten; overhead expenses** *or* **general expenses** *or* **running expenses** = money spent on the day-to-day cost of a business **Betriebskosten, allgemeine Unkosten, Festkosten; travelling expenses** = money spent on travelling and hotels for business purposes **Reisespesen**

◊ **expensive** *adjective* which costs a lot of money **teuer, kostspielig;** *first-class air travel is becoming more and more expensive*

experience

1 *noun* having lived through various situations and therefore knowing how to make decisions **Erfahrung;** *he is a man of considerable experience; she has a lot of experience of dealing with German companies; he gained most of his experience in the Far East; some experience is required for this job*

2 *verb* to live through a situation **durchmachen, erleben, erfahren;** *the company experienced a period of falling sales*

◊ **experienced** *adjective* person who has lived through many situations and has learnt from them **erfahren, sachkundig;** *he is the most experienced negotiator I know; we have appointed a very experienced woman as sales director*

expert *noun* person who knows a lot about something **Experte/Expertin, Fachmann, Sachverständiger;** *an expert in the field of electronics or an electronics expert; the company asked a financial expert for advice or asked for expert financial advice;* **expert's report** = report written by an expert **Sachverständigengutachten, Expertise**

◊ **expertise** *noun* specialist knowledge **Fachwissen, Sachkenntnis;** *we hired Mr Smith because of his financial expertise or because of his expertise in the African market*

NOTE: no plural

expiration *noun* coming to an end **Ablauf, Fälligwerden, Erlöschen;** *expiration of an insurance policy; to repay before the expiration of the stated period;* **on expiration of the lease** = when the lease comes to an end **nach Ablauf des Mietvertrages**

NOTE: no plural

◊ **expire** *verb* to come to an end **fällig werden, ablaufen, erlöschen;** *the lease expires in 1987;* **his passport has expired** = his passport is no longer valid **sein Paß ist abgelaufen**

◊ **expiry** *noun* coming to an end **Ablauf, Verfall, Erlöschen;** *expiry of an insurance policy;* **expiry date** = date when something will end **Ablauf-, Verfallsdatum, Fälligkeitstag**

explain *verb* to give reasons for something **erklären;** *he explained to the customs officials that the two computers were presents from friends; can you explain why the sales in the first quarter are so high? the sales director tried to explain the sudden drop in unit sales*

◊ **explanation** *noun* reason for something **Erklärung;** *the VAT inspector asked for an explanation of the invoices; at the AGM, the chairman gave an explanation for the high level of interest payments*

exploit *verb* to use something to make a profit **(aus)nutzen; ausbeuten;** *the company is exploiting its contacts in the Ministry of Trade; we hope to exploit the oil resources in the China Sea*

explore *verb* to examine carefully **untersuchen, sondieren;** *we are exploring the possibility of opening an office in London*

export

1 *noun*

(a) exports = goods sent to a foreign country to be sold **Exporte;** *exports to Africa have increased by 25%*

(b) action of sending goods to a foreign country to be sold **Export, Ausfuhr;** *the export trade or the export market;* **export department** = section of a company which deals in sales to foreign countries **Exportabteilung; export duty** = tax paid on goods sent out of a country for sale **Export-, Ausfuhrzoll; export house** = company which specializes in the export of goods made by other manufacturers **Exportfirma; export licence** = government permit allowing something to be exported **Exportlizenz;** *the government has refused an export licence for computer parts;* **export manager** = person in charge of an export department in a company **Exportleiter; Export Credit Guarantee Department** = British government department which insures exports sold on credit; *entspricht* **Hermes Kreditversicherung; staatliche Exportkreditversicherung**

NOTE: usually used in the plural, but the singular form is used before a noun

2 *verb* to send goods to foreign countries for sale **exportieren, ausführen;** *50% of our production is exported; the company imports raw materials and exports the finished products*

◊ **exportation** *noun* act of sending goods to foreign countries for sale **Ausfuhr, Export**

NOTE: no plural

◊ **exporter** *noun* person *or* company *or* country which sells goods in foreign countries **Exporteur, Exportfirma;** *a major furniture exporter; Canada is an important exporter of oil or an important oil exporter*

◊ **exporting** *adjective* which exports **Ausfuhr-, Export-; oil exporting countries** = countries which produce oil and sell it to other countries **erdölexportierende Länder**

exposition *noun US* = EXHIBITION

exposure *noun* amount of risk which a lender runs **Risiko;** *he is trying to cover his exposure in the property market*

NOTE: no plural

express

1 *adjective*

(a) rapid *or* very fast **Expreß-, Eil-, per Expreß;** *express letter; express delivery*

(b) clearly shown in words **ausdrücklich;** *the contract has an express condition forbidding sale in Africa*

2 *verb*

(a) to put into words or diagrams **ausdrücken;** *this chart shows home sales expressed as a percentage of total turnover*

(b) to send very fast **per Expreß/ als Eilsendung schicken;** *we expressed the order to the customer's warehouse*

◊ **expressly** *adverb* clearly in words **ausdrücklich;** *the contract expressly forbids sales to the United States*

ext = EXTENSION

extend *verb*

(a) to make available *or* to give **gewähren;** *to extend credit to a customer*

(b) to make longer **verlängern, prolongieren;** *to extend a contract for two years*

◊ **extended credit** *noun* credit allowing the borrower a very long time to pay **langfristiger Kredit;** *we sell to Australia on extended credit*

◊ **extension** *noun*

(a) allowing longer time **Verlängerung, Prolongation; to get an extension of credit** = to get more time to pay back **eine Kreditverlängerung gewährt bekommen; extension of a contract** = continuing the contract for a further period **Vertragsverlängerung**

(b) *(in an office)* individual telephone linked to the main switchboard **Anschluß,**

Nebenstelle, Apparat; *can you get me extension 21? extension 21 is engaged; the sales manager is on extension 53*

◇ **extensive** *adjective* very large *or* covering a wide area **umfangreich, ausgedehnt, weit, breit, umfassend;** *an extensive network of sales outlets*

> QUOTE the White House refusal to ask for an extension of the auto import quotas
> *Duns Business Month*

external *adjective*
(a) outside a country **ausländisch; external account** = account in a British bank of someone who is living in another country **Auslandskonto; external trade** = trade with foreign countries **Außenhandel**
(b) outside a company **außerbetrieblich, extern; external audit** = audit carried out by an independent auditor **außerbetriebliche/unabhängige Rechnungsprüfung/Revision**

extra
1 *adjective* which is added *or* which is more than usual **extra, zusätzlich;** *there is no extra charge for heating; to charge 10% extra for postage; he had £25 extra pay for working on Sunday; service is extra*
2 *plural noun* **extras** = items which are not included in a price **Nebenkosten, Neben-, Sonderausgaben;** *packing and postage are extras*

extract *noun* printed document which is part of a larger document **Auszug;** *he sent me an extract of the accounts*

extraordinary *adjective* different from normal **außerordentlich, außergewöhnlich; Extraordinary General Meeting** = special meeting of shareholders *or* members of a club, etc., to discuss an important matter which cannot wait until the next AGM **außerordentliche Hauptversammlung;** *to call an Extraordinary General Meeting;* **extraordinary items** = items in accounts which do not appear each year **Sonderposten;** *the auditors noted several extraordinary items in the accounts*

extremely *adverb* very much **äußerst, höchst;** *it is extremely difficult to break into the US market; their management team is extremely efficient*

Ff

face value *noun* value written on a coin *or* banknote *or* share **Nominal-, Nennwert**

> QUOTE travellers cheques cost 1% of their face value - some banks charge more for small amounts
> *Sunday Times*

facility *noun*
(a) being able to do something easily **Erleichterung, Fazilität;** *we offer facilities for payment*
(b) total amount of credit which a lender will allow a borrower **Kredit; credit facilities** = arrangement with a bank *or* supplier to have credit so as to buy goods **Kreditmodalitäten; overdraft facility** = arrangement with a bank to have an overdraft **Überziehungskredit**
(c) facilities = equipment *or* buildings which make it easy to do something **Einrichtungen;** *storage facilities; harbour facilities; transport facilities; there are no facilities for passengers; there are no facilities for unloading or there are no unloading facilities*
(d) *US* single large building **Anlage, Betriebsanlage;** *we have opened our new warehouse facility*

facsimile *noun* = fax, FAX

fact *noun* something which is true and real **Tatsache, Faktum;** *the chairman asked to see all the facts on the income tax claim; the sales director can give you the facts and figures about the African operation;* **the fact of the matter is** = what is true is that **Tatsache ist, ...;** *the fact of the matter is that the product does not fit the market;* **in fact** = really **eigentlich, tatsächlich;** *the chairman blamed the finance director for the loss when in fact he was responsible for it himself*

◇ **fact-finding** *adjective* looking for information **Erkundungs-, Untersuchungs-; a fact-finding mission** = visit, usually by a group of people, to search for information about a problem **Untersuchungsausschuß;** *the minister went on a fact-finding tour of the region*

factor
1 *noun*
(a) thing which is important *or* which influences **Faktor;** *the drop in sales is an important factor in the company's lower profits;* **cost factor** = problem of cost **Kostenfaktor; cyclical factors** = way in which a trade cycle affects businesses **zyklische Faktoren; deciding factor** = most important factor which influences a decision **entscheidender/ausschlaggebender Faktor; load factor** = number of seats in a bus *or*

plane *or* train which are occupied by passengers who have paid the full fare **Auslastung, Kapazitätsfaktor; factors of production** = things needed to produce a product (land, labour and capital) **Produktionsfaktoren**
(b) a factor of ten = ten times **ein Faktor von zehn**
(c) person or company which is responsible for collecting debts for companies, by buying debts at a discount on their face value **Factor**
2 *verb* to buy debts from a company at a discount **Forderungen ankaufen**

◇ **factoring** *noun* business of buying debts at a discount **Factoring; factoring charges** = cost of selling debts to a factor for a commission **Factoring-Gebühren**

factory

factory *noun* building where products are manufactured **Fabrik, Werk;** *car factory; shoe factory;* **factory hand** *or* **factory worker** = person who works in a factory **Fabrikarbeiter; factory inspector** *or* **inspector of factories** = government official who inspects factories to see if they are well run **Gewerbeaufsichtsbeamter; the factory inspectorate** = all factory inspectors **Gewerbeaufsichtsamt; factory price** *or* **price ex factory** = price not including transport from the maker's factory **Fabrikpreis, Preis ab Werk; factory unit** = single building on an industrial estate **Fabrikgebäude**

fail

fail *verb*
(a) not to do something which you were trying to do **keinen Erfolg haben, unterlassen, scheitern;** *the company failed to notify the tax office of its change of address; the prototype failed its first test*
(b) to be unsuccessful commercially **bankrott gehen; the company failed** = the company went bankrupt **das Unternehmen ging bankrott;** *he lost all his money when the bank failed*

◇ **failing**
1 *noun* weakness **Fehler, Schwäche;** *the chairman has one failing - he goes to sleep at board meetings*
2 *preposition* if something does not happen **mangels; ansonsten, widrigenfalls; failing instructions to the contrary** = unless someone gives opposite instructions **falls keine gegenteiligen Instruktionen erfolgen; failing prompt payment** = if the payment is not made on time **bei nicht termingerechter Zahlung; failing that** = if that does not work **sonst, widrigenfalls;** *try the company secretary, and failing that the chairman*

◇ **failure** *noun*
(a) breaking down *or* stopping **Scheitern, Versagen;** *the failure of the negotiations*
(b) failure to pay a bill = not having paid the bill **Nichtbezahlen einer Rechnung**
(c) commercial failure = financial collapse *or* bankruptcy **kommerzieller Mißerfolg/kommerzielle Pleite;** *he lost all his money in the bank failure*

fair

1 *noun* **trade fair** = large exhibition and meeting for advertising and selling a certain type of product **Handels-, Fachmesse;** *to organize or to run a trade fair; the fair is open from 9 a.m. to 5 p.m.; the computer fair runs from April 1st to 6th; there are two trade fairs running in London at the same time - the carpet manufacturers' and the computer dealers'*
2 *adjective*
(a) honest *or* correct **gerecht, fair; fair deal** = arrangement where both parties are treated equally **faire Abmachung;** *the workers feel they did not get a fair deal from the management;* **fair dealing** = legal buying and selling of shares **geordneter Effektenhandel; fair price** = good price for both buyer and seller **angemessener Preis; fair trade** = (i) international business system where countries agree not to charge import duties on certain items imported from their trading partners; (ii); *US* = RESALE PRICE MAINTENANCE **(i) Nichtdiskriminierung im Außenhandel; fair trading** *or* **fair dealing** = way of doing business which is reasonable and does not harm the consumer **lauterer Wettbewerb;** *GB* **Office of Fair Trading** = government department which protects consumers against unfair or illegal business **Amt für Verbraucherschutz; fair wear and tear** = acceptable damage caused by normal use **normale Abnutzungs- und Verschleißerscheinungen;** *the insurance policy covers most damage, but not fair wear and tear to the machine*
(b) fair copy = document which is written or typed with no changes or mistakes **Reinschrift**

◇ **fairly** *adverb* quite **ziemlich, recht;** *the company is fairly close to financial collapse; she is a fairly fast keyboarder*

faith

faith *noun* **to have faith in something** *or* **someone** = to believe that something *or* a person is good or will work well **Vertrauen in etwas/jdn setzen;** *the salesmen have great faith in the product; the sales teams do not have much faith in their manager; the board has faith in the managing director's judgement;* **to buy something in good faith** = to buy something thinking that is of good quality *or* that it has not been stolen *or* that it is not an imitation **etwas in gutem Glauben kaufen**

NOTE: no plural

◇ **faithfully** *adverb* **yours faithfully** = used as an ending to a formal business letter not addressed to a named person **Mit freundlichen Grüßen, Hochachtungsvoll**
NOTE: not used in US English

fake

1 *noun* imitation *or* copy made for criminal purposes **Fälschung, Imitation, Falsifikat;** *the shipment came with fake documentation*
2 *verb* to make an imitation for criminal purposes **fälschen, fingieren, imitieren;** *faked documents; he faked the results of the test*

fall

1 *noun* sudden drop *or* suddenly becoming smaller *or* loss of value **Sinken, Fallen;** *a fall in the exchange rate; fall in the price of gold; a fall on the Stock Exchange; profits showed a 10% fall*
2 *verb*
(a) to drop suddenly to a lower price **sinken, fallen;** *shares fell on the market today; gold shares fell 10% or fell 45 cents on the Stock Exchange; the price of gold fell for the second day running; the pound fell against other European currencies*
(b) to happen *or* to take place **fallen, liegen;** *the public holiday falls on a Tuesday;* **payments which fall due** = payments which are now due to be made **fällige Zahlungen**
NOTE: **falling - fell - has fallen**

◇ **fall away** *verb* to become less **zurückgehen, abnehmen, sinken;** *hotel bookings have fallen away since the tourist season ended*

◇ **fall back** *verb* to become lower or cheaper after rising in price **erneut sinken;** *shares fell back in light trading*

◇ **fall back on** *verb* to have to use money kept for emergencies **zurückgreifen auf;** *to fall back on cash reserves*

◇ **fall behind** *verb* to be late in doing something **in Rückstand/Verzug geraten;** *he fell behind with his mortgage repayments*

◇ **falling** *adjective* which is growing smaller *or* dropping in price **fallend, sinkend, abnehmend; a falling market** = market where prices are coming down **Baissemarkt; the falling pound** = the pound which is losing its value against other currencies **das an Wert verlierende Pfund**

◇ **fall off** *verb* to become lower *or* cheaper *or* less **zurückgehen, abnehmen, fallen;** *sales have fallen off since the tourist season ended*

◇ **fall out** *verb* **the bottom has fallen out of the market** = sales have fallen below what previously seemed to be their lowest point **die Preise sind ins Bodenlose gesunken**

◇ **fall through** *verb* not to happen *or* not to take place **fehlschlagen, mißlingen, scheitern;** *the plan fell through at the last moment*

> QUOTE market analysts described the falls in the second half of last week as a technical correction to the market
> ***Australian Financial Review***
>
> QUOTE for the first time since mortgage rates began falling in March a financial institution has raised charges on homeowner loans
> ***Globe and Mail (Toronto)***
>
> QUOTE falling profitability means falling share prices
> ***Investors Chronicle***

false *adjective* not true *or* not correct **falsch, unrichtig;** *to make a false entry in the balance sheet;* **under false pretences** = doing or saying something to cheat someone **unter Vorspiegelung falscher Tatsachen;** *he was sent to prison for obtaining money by false pretences;* **false weight** = weight on shop scales which is wrong and so cheats customers **falsches Gewicht**

◇ **falsify** *verb* to change something to make it wrong **fälschen;** *to falsify the accounts*

◇ **falsification** *noun* action of making false entries in accounts **Verfälschung, Fälschung**

famous *adjective* very well known **berühmt;** *the company owns a famous department store in the centre of London*

fancy *adjective*
(a) fancy goods = small attractive items **Modeartikel**
(b) fancy prices = high prices **Phantasiepreise;** *I don't want to pay the fancy prices they ask in London shops*

fare *noun* price to be paid for a ticket to travel **Fahrpreis; Flugpreis;** *train fares have gone up by 5%; the government is asking the airlines to keep air fares down;* **concessionary fare** = reduced fare for certain types of passenger (such as employees of the transport company) **Vorzugsfahrpreis; full fare** = ticket for a journey by an adult paying the full price **voller Fahrpreis; half fare** = half-price ticket for a child **halber Fahrpreis; single fare** *or US* **one-way fare** = fare for a journey from one place to another **einfacher Fahrpreis; return fare** *or US* **round-trip fare** = fare for a journey from one place to another and back again **Hin- und Rückfahrpreis**

farm

1 *noun* property in the country where crops are grown *or* where animals are raised for sale **Bauernhof; collective farm** = state-owned farm which is run by the workers **landwirtschaftliche**

Produktionsgenossenschaft; fish farm = place where fish are grown for food **Fischzucht; mixed farming** = farm which has both animals and crops **gemischte Landwirtschaft**
2 *verb* to own a farm **Landwirtschaft betreiben;** *(Land)* **bewirtschaften;** *he farms 150 acres*

◇ **farming** *noun* job of working on a farm *or* of raising animals for sale *or* of growing crops for food **Landwirtschaft;** *chicken farming; fish farming; mixed farming*

◇ **farm out** *verb* **to farm out work** = to hand over work for another person *or* company to do it for you **Arbeit/Aufträge weitervergeben;** *she farms out the office typing to various local bureaux*

fast *adjective & adverb* quick *or* quickly **schnell;** *the train is the fastest way of getting to our supplier's factory; home computers sell fast in the pre-Christmas period*

◇ **fast-moving** *or* **fast-selling** *adjective* **fast-selling items** = items which sell fast **schnellverkäufliche Artikel, Selbstläufer;** *dictionaries are not fast-moving stock*

fault *noun*
(a) being to blame for something which is wrong **Verschulden; Schuld;** *it is the stock controller's fault if the warehouse runs out of stock; the chairman said the lower sales figures were the fault of a badly motivated sales force*
(b) wrong working **Defekt, Fehler;** *the technicians are trying to correct a programming fault; we think there is a basic fault in the product design*

◇ **faulty** *adjective* which does not work properly **defekt, fehlerhaft;** *faulty equipment; they installed faulty computer programs*

favour *or US* **favor**
1 *noun*
(a) as a favour = to help *or* to be kind to someone **aus Gefälligkeit;** *he asked the secretary for a loan as a favour*
(b) in favour of = in agreement with *or* feeling that something is right **für; zugunsten;** *six members of the board are in favour of the proposal, and three are against it*
2 *verb* to agree that something is right *or* to vote for something **bevorzugen; begünstigen;** *the board members all favour Smith Ltd as partners in the project*

◇ **favourable** *adjective* which gives an advantage **vorteilhaft, günstig; favourable balance of trade** = situation where a country's exports are more than the imports **aktive Handelsbilanz; on favourable terms** = on specially good terms **zu sehr günstigen Bedingungen;** *the shop is let on very favourable terms*

◇ **favourite** *adjective* which is liked best **bevorzugt, Lieblings-, Spitzen-;** *this brand of chocolate is a favourite with the children's market*

fax *or* **FAX**
1 *noun informal* exact copy of a document **Fax, Telefax**
2 *verb* to send a fax **faxen, telefaxen;** *we will send a fax of the design plan; I've faxed the documents to our New York office*

feasibility *noun* ability to be done **Durchführbarkeit, Realisierbarkeit;** *to report on the feasibility of a project;* **feasibility report** = report saying if something can be done **Durchführbarkeitsstudie; to carry out a feasibility study on a project** = to carry out an examination of costs and profits to see if the project should be started **eine Durchführbarkeitsstudie zu einem Projekt anfertigen**
NOTE: no plural

federal *adjective* referring to a system of government where a group of states are linked together in a federation **Bundes-;** *most federal offices are in Washington*

◇ **the Fed** *noun US informal* = FEDERAL RESERVE BOARD

◇ **Federal Reserve Bank** *noun US* one of the twelve central banks in the USA which are owned by the state and directed by the Federal Reserve Board **eine der 12 Banken des "Federal Reserve System";** *entspricht* **Zentralbank**

◇ **Federal Reserve Board** *noun US* government organization which runs the central banks in the USA; *entspricht* **Zentralbankrat**

◇ **federation** *noun* group of societies *or* companies *or* organizations which have a central organization which represents them and looks after their common interests **Verband, Syndikat;** *federation of trades unions; employers' federation*

> QUOTE indications of weakness in the US economy were contained in figures from the Fed on industrial production for April
> **Financial Times**
>
> QUOTE federal examiners will determine which of the privately-insured savings and loans qualify for federal insurance
> **Wall Street Journal**
>
> QUOTE pressure on the Federal Reserve Board to ease monetary policy mounted yesterday with the release of a set of pessimistic economic statistics
> **Financial Times**
>
> QUOTE since 1978 America has freed many of its industries from federal rules that set prices and controlled the entry of new companies
> **Economist**

fee *noun*
(a) money paid for work carried out by a professional person (such as an accountant *or* a doctor *or* a lawyer) **Honorar;** *we charge a small fee for our services; director's fees; consultant's fee*
(b) money paid for something **Gebühr;** *entrance fee or admission fee; registration fee*

feed
1 *noun* device which puts paper into a printer *or* into a photocopier **Einzug, Vorschub;** *the paper feed has jammed;* **continuous feed** = device which feeds in continuous computer stationery into a printer **Endlospapiereinzug; sheet feed** = device which puts in one sheet at a time into a printer **Einzelblatteinzug**
2 *verb* to put information into a computer **speisen, eingeben**
NOTE: **feeding - fed**

◊ **feedback** *noun* information, especially about people's reactions **Reaktion, Resonanz, Feedback;** *have you any feedback from the sales force about the customers' reaction to the new model?*
NOTE: no plural

feint *noun* very light lines on writing paper **feine Linien**

ferry *noun* boat which takes passengers or goods across water **Fähre;** *we are going to take the night ferry to Belgium;* **car ferry** = ferry which carries cars **Autofähre; passenger ferry** = ferry which only carries passengers **Passagierfähre**

fetch *verb*
(a) to go to bring something **holen, abholen;** *we have to fetch the goods from the docks; it is cheaper to buy at a cash and carry warehouse, provided you have a car to fetch the goods yourself*
(b) to be sold for a certain price **erzielen, einbringen;** *to fetch a high price; it will not fetch more than £200; these computers fetch very high prices on the black market*

few *adjective & noun*
(a) not many **wenige;** *we sold so few of this item that we have discontinued the line; few of the staff stay with us more than six months*
(b) a few = some **ein paar, einige;** *a few of our salesmen drive Rolls-Royces; we get only a few orders in the period from Christmas to the New Year*

fiat *noun* **fiat money** = notes which are not worth much as paper or metal, but are said by the government to have a value **ungedecktes Geld**

fictitious *adjective* false *or* which do not exist **falsch, fiktiv, Schein-; fictitious assets** = assets which do not really exist, but are entered as assets to balance the accounts **Scheinaktiva**

fiddle
1 *noun informal* cheating **Schiebung, Trickserei, Manipulation;** *it's all a fiddle;* **he's on the fiddle** = he is trying to cheat **er macht faule Geschäfte/dreht krumme Dinger**
2 *verb informal* to cheat **frisieren, tricksen;** *he tried to fiddle his tax returns; the salesman was caught fiddling his expense account*

fide *see* BONA FIDE

fiduciary *noun* person acting as trustee for someone else **Treuhänder** *adjective* relating to a trust and trustee **treuhänderisch**

field *noun*
(a) piece of ground on a farm **Feld, Acker, Weide;** *the cows are in the field*
(b) in the field = outside the office *or* among the customers **im Außendienst;** *we have sixteen reps in the field;* **to be first in the field** = first company to bring out a product *or* to start a service **etwas als Erster auf den Markt bringen, führend sein;** *Smith Ltd has a great advantage in being first in the field with a reliable electric car;* **field sales manager** = manager in charge of a group of salesmen **Außendienstleiter; field work** = examination of the situation among possible customers **Felduntersuchung;** *he had to do a lot of field work to find the right market for the product*

FIFO = FIRST IN FIRST OUT

fifty-fifty *adjective & adverb* half **halbe-halbe, fifty-fifty; to go fifty-fifty** = to share the costs equally **halbe-halbe/fifty-fifty machen; he has a fifty-fifty chance of making a profit** = he has an equal chance of making a profit or a loss **seine Chancen, Gewinne zu machen, stehen fifty-fifty**

figure *noun*
(a) number *or* cost written in numbers **Zahl, Ziffer; Summe;** *the figure in the accounts for heating is very high;* **he put a very low figure on the value of the lease** = he calculated the value of the lease as very low **er setzte im Pachtvertrag eine sehr niedrige Summe an**
(b) figures = written numbers **Zahlen, Ziffern; sales figures** = total sales **Verkaufs-, Absatzzahlen; to work out the figures** = to calculate **Kalkulationen vornehmen; his income runs into five figures** *or* **he has a five-figure income** = his income is more than £10,000 **er hat ein fünfstelliges Einkommmen; in round figures** = not totally accurate, but correct to the nearest 10 or 100 **aufgerundet; abgerundet;** *they have a workforce of 2,500 in round figures*
(c) figures = results for a company **Zahlen;** *the figures for last year or last year's figures*

file
1 *noun*
(a) cardboard holder for documents, which can fit in the drawer of a filing cabinet **Aktenordner;** *put these letters in the customer file; look in the file marked "Scottish sales";* **box file** = cardboard box for holding documents **kastenförmiger Aktenordner**
(b) documents kept for reference **Akte; to place something on file** = to keep a record of something **etwas zu den Akten nehmen; to keep someone's name on file** = to keep someone's name on a list for reference **jdn in den Akten führen; file copy** = copy of a document which is kept for reference in an office **Aktenkopie; card-index file** = information kept on filing cards **Kartei**
(c) section of data on a computer (such as payroll, address list, customer accounts) **Datei;** *how can we protect our computer files?*
2 *verb*
(a) to file documents = to put documents in order so that they can be found easily **Dokumente in Akten ablegen;** *the correspondence is filed under "complaints"*
(b) to make an official request **einreichen, vorlegen, erheben; to file a petition in bankruptcy** = to ask officially to be made bankrupt *or* to ask officially for someone else to be made bankrupt **Antrag auf Konkurseröffnung stellen**
(c) to register something officially **einreichen, vorlegen;** *to file an application for a patent; to file a return to the tax office*

◊ **filing** *noun* documents which have to be put in order **Ablage;** *there is a lot of filing to do at the end of the week; the manager looked through the week's filing to see what letters had been sent;* **filing basket** *or* **filing tray** = container kept on a desk for documents which have to be filed **Ablage; filing cabinet** = metal box with several drawers for keeping files **Aktenschrank; filing card** = card with information written on it, used to classify information into the correct order **Karteikarte; filing clerk** = clerk who files documents **Angestellter in der Registratur; filing system** = way of putting documents in order for reference **Ablagesystem**
NOTE: no plural

fill
1 *verb*
(a) to make something full **füllen, ausfüllen;** *we have filled our order book with orders for Africa; the production department has filled the warehouse with unsellable products*
(b) to fill a gap = to provide a product *or* service which is needed, but which no one has provided before **eine Lücke schließen;** *the new range of small cars fills a gap in the market*
(c) to fill a post *or* **a vacancy** = to find someone to do a job **eine Stelle besetzen;** *your application arrived too late - the post has already been filled*

◊ **filler** *noun* something which fills a space **Füller, Lückenfüller; stocking filler** = small item which can be used to put into a Christmas stocking **kleines Geschenk für den Weihnachtsstrumpf;** *see* SHELF FILLER

◊ **fill in** *verb* to write in the blank spaces in a form **ausfüllen, eintragen;** *fill in your name and address in block capitals*

◊ **filling station** *noun* place where you can buy petrol **Tankstelle;** *he stopped at the filling station to get some petrol before going on to the motorway*

◊ **fill out** *verb* to write the required information in the blank spaces in a form **ausfüllen;** *to get customs clearance you must fill out three forms*

◊ **fill up** *verb*
(a) to make something completely full **voll machen, ausfüllen;** *he filled up the car with petrol; my appointments book is completely filled up*
(b) to finish writing on a form **ausfüllen;** *he filled up the form and sent it to the bank*

final *adjective* last *or* coming at the end of a period **letzter, Schluß-, End-, Abschluß-;** *to pay the final instalment; to make the final payment; to put the final details on a document;* **final date for payment** = last date by which payment should be made **letzter**

Zahlungstermin; final demand = last reminder from a supplier, after which he will sue for payment **letzte Mahnung/Zahlungsaufforderung; final discharge** = last payment of what is left of a debt **letzte Tilgungsrate; final dividend** = dividend paid at the end of the year **Schlußdividende; final product** = manufactured product, made at the end of a production process **Endprodukt**

◇ **finalize** *verb* to agree final details **endgültig festlegen, abschließen, zum Abschluß bringen;** *we hope to finalize the agreement tomorrow; after six weeks of negotiations the loan was finalized yesterday*

◇ **finally** *adverb* in the end **schließlich, zum Schluß;** *the contract was finally signed yesterday; after weeks of trials the company finally accepted the computer system*

finance

1 *noun*

(a) money used by a company, provided by the shareholders or by loans **finanzielle Mittel, Kapital;** *where will they get the necessary finance for the project?;* **finance company** *or* **finance corporation** *or* **finance house** = company which provides money for hire-purchase **Finanzierungsgesellschaft; finance market** = place where large sums of money can be lent or borrowed **Finanzmarkt; high finance** = lending, investing and borrowing of very large sums of money, organized by financiers **Hochfinanz**

(b) money (of a club, local authority, etc.) **finanzielle Mittel;** *she is the secretary of the local authority finance committee*

(c) finances = money *or* cash which is available **Finanzenmittel;** *the bad state of the company's finances*

2 *verb* to provide money to pay for something **finanzieren;** *to finance an operation*

◇ **Finance Act** *noun GB* annual act of parliament which gives the government the power to obtain money from taxes as proposed in the Budget **Finanzgesetz**

◇ **financial** *adjective* concerning money **finanziell, Finanz-; financial adviser** = person *or* company which gives advice on financial matters for a fee **Finanzberater; financial assistance** = help in the form of money **Finanzhilfe; financial correspondent** = journalist who writes articles on money matters for a newspaper **Wirtschaftskorrespondent; financial position** = state of a company's bank balance (assets and debts) **Finanzlage;** *he must think of his financial position;* **financial resources** = money which is available for investment **finanzielle Mittel;** *a company with strong financial resources;* **financial risk** = possibility of losing money **finanzielles Risiko;** *there is no financial risk in selling to East European countries on credit;* **financial statement** = document which shows the financial situation of a company **Finanzbericht;** *the accounts department has prepared a financial statement for the shareholders;* **Financial Times (Ordinary) index** = index published by the "Financial Times", giving share prices on the London Stock Exchange based on a group of major companies **Aktienindex der Financial Times; financial year** = the twelve months' period for a firm's accounts **Rechnungs-, Geschäftsjahr**

◇ **financially** *adverb* regarding money **finanziell, finanz-; company which is financially sound** = company which is profitable and has strong assets **die Firma ist finanziell gesund/finanzkräftig**

◇ **financier** *noun* person who lends large amounts of money to companies **Financier, Geldgeber**

◇ **financing** *noun* providing money **Finanzierung;** *the financing of the project was done by two international banks;* **deficit financing** = planning by a government to borrow money to cover the shortfall between expenditure and income from taxation **Defizitwirtschaft**

find *verb*

(a) to get something which was not there before **finden;** *to find backing for a project*

(b) to make a legal decision in court **befinden; urteilen; entscheiden;** *the tribunal found that both parties were at fault;* **the judge found for the defendant** = the judge decided that the defendant was right **der Richter entschied für den Angeklagten**

NOTE: **finding - found**

◇ **findings** *plural noun* **the findings of a commission of enquiry** = the recommendations of the commission **Ergebnisse einer Untersuchungskommission**

◇ **find time** *verb* to make enough time to do something **Zeit finden;** *we must find time to visit the new staff sports club; the chairman never finds enough time to play golf*

fine

1 *noun* money paid because of something wrong which has been done **Geldstrafe; gebührenpflichtige Verwarnung;** *he was asked to pay a $25,000 fine; we had to pay a $10 parking fine*

2 *verb* to punish someone by making him pay money **zu einer Geldstrafe verurteilen; mit einer Geldstrafe belegen; eine gebührenpflichtige Verwarnung erteilen;** *to fine someone £2,500 for obtaining money by false pretences*

3 *adverb* very thin *or* very small **dünn, fein; we are cutting our margins very fine** = we are reducing our margins to the smallest possible **unsere Gewinnspannen sind sehr knapp bemessen**

finish

1 *noun*

(a) final appearance **Finish, Oberflächenfinish, Oberfläche, Verarbeitung;** *the product has an attractive finish*

(b) end of a day's trading on the Stock Exchange **Börsenschluß;** *oil shares rallied at the finish*

2 *verb*

(a) to do something *or* to make something completely **abschließen, erledigen, fertig machen;** *the order was finished in time; she finished the test before all the other candidates*

(b) to come to an end **(be)enden, auslaufen;** *the contract is due to finish next month*

◇ **finished** *adjective* **finished goods** = manufactured goods which are ready to be sold **Fertigwaren**

fink *noun US informal* worker hired to replace a striking worker **Streikbrecher**

fire

1 *noun* thing which burns **Feuer;** *the shipment was damaged in the fire on board the cargo boat; half the stock was destroyed in the warehouse fire;* **to catch fire** = to start to burn **Feuer fangen, in Brand geraten;** *the papers in the waste paper basket caught fire;* **fire damage** = damage caused by fire **Brandschaden, Feuerschaden;** *he claimed £250 for fire damage;* **fire-damaged goods** = goods which have been damaged in a fire **brandgeschädigte Waren; fire door** = special door to prevent fire going from one part of a building to another **Feuertür; fire escape** = door *or* stairs which allow staff to get out of a building which is on fire **Feuertreppe, Feuerleiter; to be a fire hazard** *or* **fire risk** = situation *or* goods which could start a fire **eine Feuergefahr darstellen;** *that warehouse full of paper is a fire hazard;* **fire insurance** = insurance against damage by fire **Feuerversicherung**

2 *verb* **to fire someone** = to dismiss someone from a job **jdn entlassen/feuern;** *the new managing director fired half the sales force;* **to hire and fire** = to employ new staff and dismiss existing staff very frequently **oft einstellen und entlassen**

◇ **fireproof** *adjective* which cannot be damaged by fire **feuerfest, feuersicher;** *we packed the papers in a fireproof safe; it is impossible to make the office completely fireproof*

firm

1 *noun* business *or* partnership **Firma; Unternehmen;** *he is a partner in a law firm; a manufacturing firm; an important publishing firm*

2 *adjective*

(a) which cannot be changed **stabil, fest, beständig, verbindlich;** *to make a firm offer for something; to place a firm offer for two aircraft; they are quoting a firm price of £1.22 per unit*

(b) not dropping in price, and possibly going to rise **stabil, fest, beständig;** *sterling was firmer on the foreign exchange markets; shares remained firm*

3 *verb* to remain at a price and seem likely to go up **sich festigen;** *the shares firmed at £1.50*

◇ **firmness** *noun* being steady at a price *or* being likely to rise **Stabilität, Festigkeit, Beständigkeit;** *the firmness of the pound*

◇ **firm up** *verb* to finalize *or* to agree final details **abschließen, unter Dach und Fach bringen;** *we expect to firm up the deal at the next trade fair*

> QUOTE some profit-taking was noted, but underlying sentiment remained firm
> *Financial Times*

first *noun* person *or* thing which is there at the beginning *or* earlier than others **der/die/das erste;** *our company was one of the first to sell into the European market;* **first quarter** = three months' period from January to the end of March **erstes Quartal; first half** *or* **first half-year** = six months' period from January to the end of June **erstes Halbjahr; first in first out (FIFO)** = (i) redundancy policy, where the people who have been working longest are the first to be made redundant; (ii) accounting policy where stock is valued at the price of the oldest purchases **(i) Personalpolitik nach der FIFO-Methode; (ii) FIFO-Abschreibungsmethode**

◇ **first-class** *adjective*

(a) top quality *or* most expensive **erstklassig, Spitzen-;** *he is a first-class accountant*

(b) most expensive and comfortable type of travel *or* type of hotel **Erster Klasse; erstklassig;** *to travel first-class; first-class travel provides the best service; a first-class ticket; to stay in first-class hotels;* **first-class mail** = *GB* most expensive mail service, designed to be faster;; *US* mail service for letters and postcards **Briefpost erster Klasse;** *a first-class letter should get to Scotland in a day*

◇ **first-line** *adjective* **first-line management** = the managers who have immediate contact with the workers **unterste Leitungsebene**

fiscal *adjective* referring to tax *or* to government revenues **Finanz-, Steuer-, steuerlich;** *the government's fiscal policies;* **fiscal measures** = tax changes made by a government to improve the working of the economy **steuerpolitische Maßnahmen; fiscal year** = twelve-month period on which taxes are calculated (in the UK, April 6th to April 5th) **Steuerjahr**

> QUOTE the standard measure of fiscal policy - the public sector borrowing requirement - is kept misleadingly low
> *Economist*

fit *verb* to be the right size for something **passen;** *the paper doesn't fit the typewriter*
NOTE: **fitting - fitted**

◇ **fit in** *verb* to make something go into a space **(hinein)passen;** *will the computer fit into that little room? the chairman tries to fit in a game of golf every afternoon; my appointments diary is full, but I shall try to fit you in tomorrow afternoon*

◇ **fit out** *verb* to provide equipment *or* furniture for a business **ausrüsten, ausstatten;** *they fitted out the factory with computers; the shop was fitted out at a cost of £10,000;* **fitting out of a shop** = putting shelves *or* counters in for a new shop **ein Geschäft ausstatten/einrichten**

◇ **fittings** *plural noun* items in a property which are sold with it but are not permanently fixed (such as carpets or shelves) **Einbauten; fixtures and fittings** = objects in a property which are sold with the property, both those which cannot be removed and those which can **Installationen und Einbauten**

fix *verb*
(a) to arrange *or* to agree **beschließen; festlegen, festsetzen;** *to fix a budget; to fix a meeting for 3 p.m.; the date has still to be fixed; the price of gold was fixed at $300; the mortgage rate has been fixed at 11%*
(b) to mend **in Ordnung bringen, reparieren;** *the technicians are coming to fix the telephone switchboard; can you fix the photocopier?*

◇ **fixed** *adjective* permanent *or* which cannot be removed **fest, Fest-, gebunden; fixed assets** = property *or* machinery which a company owns and uses **Anlagevermögen; fixed capital** = capital in the form of buildings and machinery **Anlagekapital; fixed costs** = costs paid to produce a product which do not increase with the amount of product made (such as rent) **Fixkosten; Gemeinkosten; fixed deposit** = deposit which pays a stated interest over a set period **Festgeld; fixed expenses** = money which is spent regularly (such as rent, electricity, telephone) **Fixkosten; fixed income** = income which does not change (as from an annuity) **festes Einkommen, feste Einkünfte; fixed-interest investments** = investments producing an interest which does not change **festverzinsliche Kapitalanlagen; fixed-price agreement** = agreement where a company provides a service *or* a product at a price which stays the same for the whole period of the agreement **Festpreisvereinbarung; fixed scale of charges** = rate of charging which cannot be altered **verbindliche Gebührenordnung**

◇ **fixer** *noun informal* person who has a reputation for arranging business deals (often illegally) **Fixer/-in**

◇ **fixing** *noun*
(a) arranging **Festsetzung, Festlegung;** *fixing of charges; fixing of a mortgage rate*
(b) price fixing = illegal agreement between companies to charge the same price for competing products **Preisabsprache**
(c) the London gold fixing = system where the world price for gold is set each day in London **London Gold Fixing**
NOTE: no plural

> QUOTE coupons are fixed by reference to interest rates at the time a gilt is first issued
> *Investors Chronicle*
>
> QUOTE you must offer shippers and importers fixed rates over a reasonable period of time
> *Lloyd's List*

◇ **fixtures** *plural noun* items in a property which are permanently attached to it (such as sinks and lavatories) **Installationen; fixtures and fittings** = objects in a property which are sold with the property, both those which cannot be removed and those which can **Installationen und Einbauten**

◇ **fix up with** *verb* to arrange **besorgen, beschaffen;** *my secretary fixed me up with a car at the airport; can you fix me up with a room for tomorrow night?*

flag
1 *noun*
(a) piece of cloth with a design on it which shows which country it belongs to **Flagge, Fahne;** *a ship flying a British flag;* **ship sailing under a flag of convenience** = ship flying the flag of a country which may have no ships of its own, but allows ships of other countries to be registered in its ports **ein Schiff, das unter Billigflagge fährt**
(b) mark which is attached to information in a computer so that the information can be found easily **Kennzeichen, Markierung**
2 *verb* to insert marks on information in a computer so that the information can be found easily **Kennzeichen/Markierungen setzen**
NOTE: **flagging - flagged**

flat
1 *adjective*
(a) falling because of low demand **lustlos;** *the market was flat today*
(b) fixed *or* not changing; **flat rate** = charge which always stays the same **Einheitssatz;** *we pay a flat rate for electricity each quarter; he is paid a flat rate of £2 per thousand*
2 *noun* set of rooms for one family in a building with other sets of similar rooms **Wohnung;** *he has a flat in the centre of town; she is buying a flat close to her office;* **company flat** = flat owned by a company and used by members of staff from time to time **Firmenwohnung**
NOTE: US English is **apartment**
◇ **flat out** *adverb* working hard *or* at full speed **auf Hochtouren;** *the factory worked flat out to complete the order on time*

flea market *noun* market, usually in the open air, for selling cheap secondhand goods **Flohmarkt**

fleet *noun* group of cars belonging to a company and used by its staff **Wagen-, Fuhrpark;** *a company's fleet of representatives' cars;* **a fleet car** = car which is one of a fleet of cars **ein Wagen des Fuhrparks; fleet discount** = specially cheap price for purchase or rental of a company's cars **Preisnachlaß bei Anmietung od Kauf aller Wagen einer Firma; fleet rental** = renting all a company's cars at a special price **Anmietung des gesamten Fuhrparks**

flexible *adjective* which can be altered *or* changed **flexibel;** *flexible budget; flexible prices; flexible pricing policy;* **flexible working hours** = system where workers can start or stop work at different hours of the morning or evening provided that they work a certain number of hours per day or week **flexible Arbeitszeit, Gleitzeit;** *we work flexible hours*
◇ **flexibility** *noun* being easily changed **Flexibilität;** *there is no flexibility in the company's pricing policy*
NOTE: no plural
◇ **flexitime** *noun* system where workers can start or stop work at different hours of the morning or evening, provided that they work a certain number of hours per day or week **Gleitzeit;** *we work flexitime; the company introduced flexitime working two years ago*
NOTE: no plural

flier *or* **flyer** *noun*
(a) high flier = (i) person who is very successful *or* who is likely to rise to a very important position; (ii) share whose market price is rising rapidly **(i) Senkrechtstarter; (ii) schnell steigende Aktien**
(b) small advertising leaflet designed to encourage customers to ask for more information about the product for sale **Handzettel**

flight *noun*
(a) journey by an aircraft, leaving at a regular time **Flug;** *flight AC 267 is leaving from Gate 46; he missed his flight; I always take the afternoon flight to Rome; if you hurry you will catch the six o'clock flight to Paris*
(b) rapid movement of money out of a country because of a lack of confidence in the country's economic future **Flucht;** *the flight of capital from Europe into the USA; the flight from the franc into the dollar*
(c) series of steps **Treppe; top-flight** = in the most important position *or* very efficient **Spitzen-;** *top-flight managers can earn very high salaries*

flip chart *noun* way of showing information to a group of people by writing on large sheets of paper which can then be turned over to show the next sheet **Flip-Chart**

float
1 *noun*
(a) cash taken from a central supply and used for running expenses **Kleingeld;** *the sales reps have a float of £100 each;* **cash float** = cash put into the cash box at the beginning of the day to allow business to start **Wechselgeld;** *we start the day with a £20 float in the cash desk*
(b) starting a new company by selling shares in it on the Stock Exchange **Gesellschaftsgründung durch Emission von Aktien an der Börse;** *the float of the new company was a complete failure*
2 *verb*
(a) to float a company = to start a new company by selling shares in it on the Stock Exchange **eine Gesellschaft gründen durch Aktienemission an der Börse; to float a loan** = to raise a loan on the financial market by asking banks and companies to subscribe to it **eine Anleihe auflegen**
(b) to let a currency find its own exchange rate on the international markets and not be fixed **floaten, freigeben;** *the government has let sterling float; the government has decided to float the pound*
◇ **floating**
1 *noun*
(a) floating of a company = starting a new company by selling shares in it on the Stock Exchange **Gesellschaftsgründung durch Aktienemission**

(b) the floating of the pound = letting the pound find its own exchange rate on the international market **das Floaten/die Wechselkursfreigabe des Pfundes**
NOTE: no plural
2 *adjective* which is not fixed **frei, frei schwankend, variabel;** *floating exchange rates; the floating pound*

> QUOTE in a world of floating exchange rates the dollar is strong because of capital inflows rather than weak because of the nation's trade deficit
> *Duns Business Month*

flood
1 *noun* large quantity **Flut, Strom;** *we received a flood of orders; floods of tourists filled the hotels*
2 *verb* to fill with a large quantity of something **überschwemmen;** *the market was flooded with cheap imitations; the sales department is flooded with orders or with complaints*

floor *noun*
(a) part of the room which you walk on **Fußboden, Boden; floor space** = area of floor in an office *or* warehouse **Grund-, Bodenfläche;** *we have 3,500 square metres of floor space to let;* **the factory floor** = main works of a factory **Fabrikhalle; on the shop floor** = in the works *or* in the factory *or* among the ordinary workers **im Betrieb;** *the feeling on the shop floor is that the manager does not know his job*
(b) all rooms on one level in a building **Stockwerk, Etage;** *the shoe department is on the first floor; her office is on the 26th floor;* *US* **floor manager** = person in charge of the sales staff in a department store **Abteilungsleiter**
NOTE: the numbering of floors is different in GB and the USA. The floor at street level is the **ground floor** in GB, but the **first floor** in the USA. Each floor in the USA is one number higher than the same floor in GB.
◇ **floorwalker** *noun* employee of a department store who advises the customers, and supervises the shop assistants in a department **Ladenaufsicht**

flop
1 *noun* failure *or* not being a success **Reinfall, Flop, Pleite;** *the new model was a flop*
2 *verb* to fail *or* not to be a success **ein Reinfall/Flop/eine Pleite sein;** *the flotation of the new company flopped badly*
NOTE: **flopping - flopped** *noun* **floppy disk** = small disk for storing information in a computer **Floppy Disk;** *the data is on 5 inch floppies*

flotation *noun* **the flotation of a new company** = starting a new company by selling shares in it **Gesellschaftsgründung durch Emission von Aktien**

flotsam *noun* **flotsam and jetsam** = rubbish floating in the water after a ship has been wrecked and rubbish washed on to the land **Treib-, Strandgut**
NOTE: no plural

flourish *verb* to be prosperous *or* to do well in business **florieren, blühen;** *the company is flourishing; trade with Nigeria flourished*
◇ **flourishing** *adjective* profitable **florierend, blühend, gutgehend; flourishing trade** = trade which is expanding profitably **reger/florierender Handel;** *he runs a flourishing shoe business*

flow
1 *noun*
(a) movement **Fluß;** *the flow of capital into a country; the flow of investments into Japan*
(b) cash flow = cash which comes into a company from sales and goes out in purchases or overhead expenditure **Cashflow; discounted cash flow** = calculation of forecast sales of a product in current terms with reductions for current interest rates **diskontierter Cashflow; the company is suffering from cash flow problems** = cash income is not coming in fast enough to pay for the expenditure going out **das Unternehmen hat Cashflow Probleme/Liquiditätsprobleme**
(c) flow chart *or* **flow diagram** = chart which shows the arrangement of work processes in a series **Arbeitsablauf-, Flußdiagramm**
2 *verb* to move smoothly **ruhig laufen;** *production is now flowing normally after the strike*

fluctuate *verb* to move up and down **fluktuieren, schwanken;** *prices fluctuate between £1.10 and £1.25; the pound fluctuated all day on the foreign exchange markets*
◇ **fluctuating** *adjective* moving up and down **fluktuierend, schwankend;** *fluctuating dollar prices*
◇ **fluctuation** *noun* up and down movement **Fluktuation, Schwankung;** *the fluctuations of the franc; the fluctuations of the exchange rate*

fly *verb* to move through the air in an aircraft **fliegen;** *the chairman is flying to Germany on business; the overseas sales manager flies about 100,000 miles a year visiting the agents*
◇ **fly-by-night** *adjective* company which is not reliable *or* which might disappear to

avoid paying debts **unseriöses Unternehmen; flüchtiger Schuldner;** *I want a reputable builder, not one of these fly-by-night outfits*

FOB *or* **f.o.b.** = FREE ON BOARD

fold *verb*
(a) to bend a flat thing, so that part of it is on top of the rest **falten, zusammenlegen;** *she folded the letter so that the address was clearly visible*
(b) *informal* **to fold (up)** = to stop trading **eingehen;** *the business folded up last December; the company folded with debts of over £1m*
◇ **-fold** *suffix* times **-fach; four-fold** = four times **um das Vierfache**

> QUOTE the company's sales have nearly tripled and its profits have risen seven-fold since 1982
> *Barrons*

◇ **folder** *noun* cardboard envelope for carrying papers **Aktenmappe, -deckel;** *put all the documents in a folder for the chairman*

folio
1 *noun* page with a number, especially two facing pages in an account book which have the same number **Folio**
2 *verb* to put a number on a page **paginieren, mit Seitenzahlen versehen**

follow *verb* to come behind *or* to come afterwards **folgen;** *the samples will follow by surface mail; we will pay £10,000 down, with the balance to follow in six months' time*
◇ **follow up** *verb* to examine something further **nachgehen; nachfassen;** *I'll follow up your idea of putting our address list on to the computer;* **to follow up an initiative** = to take action once someone else has decided to do something **eine Initiative aufgreifen**
◇ **follow-up letter** *noun* letter sent to someone who has not acted on the instructions in a previous letter, or to discuss in more detail points which were raised earlier **Nachfaß-, Folgeschreiben**

food *noun* things which are eaten **Essen, Nahrung, Lebensmittel;** *he is very fond of Indian food; the food in the staff restaurant is excellent*
◇ **foodstuffs** *plural noun* **essential foodstuffs** = very important food, such as bread or rice **Grundnahrungsmittel**

foolscap *noun* large size of writing paper 13 1/4 x 16 1/2 inches; *the letter was on six sheets of foolscap;* **a foolscap envelope** = large envelope which takes foolscap paper
NOTE: no plural

foot
1 *noun*
(a) part of the body at the end of the leg **Fuß; on foot** = walking **zu Fuß;** *the reps make most of their central London calls on foot; the rush hour traffic is so bad that it is quicker to go to the office on foot*
(b) bottom part **Fuß, Seitenende;** *he signed his name at the foot of the invoice*
(c) measurement of length (= 30cm) **Fuß;** *the table is six feet long; my office is ten feet by twelve*
NOTE: the plural is **feet** for (a) and (c); there is no plural for (b). In measurements, **foot** is usually written **ft** or **'** after figures: **10ft; 10'**
2 *verb*
(a) to foot the bill = to pay the bill **die Rechnung begleichen/bezahlen;** *the director footed the bill for the department's Christmas party*
(b) *US* **to foot up an account** = to add up a column of numbers **die Spalten eines Kontos addieren**

forbid *verb* to tell someone not to do something *or* to say that something must not be done **verbieten, nicht erlauben;** *the contract forbids resale of the goods to the USA; the staff are forbidden to use the front entrance*
NOTE: **forbidding - forbade - forbidden**

force
1 *noun*
(a) strength **Kraft; to be in force** = to be operating *or* working **in Kraft sein;** *the rules have been in force since 1946;* **to come into force** = to start to operate *or* work **in Kraft treten;** *the new regulations will come into force on January 1st*
(b) labour force *or* **workforce** = all the workers in a company *or* in an area **Belegschaft; Arbeitskräfte, Arbeiterschaft;** *the management has made an increased offer to the labour force; we are opening a new factory in the Far East because of the cheap local labour force;* **sales force** = group of salesmen **Verkaufspersonal, Verkäuferstab**
(c) force majeure = something which happens which is out of the control of the parties who have signed a contract (such as strike, war, storm) **höhere Gewalt**
NOTE: no plural for (a) and (c)
2 *verb* to make someone do something **zwingen;** *competition has forced the company to lower its prices*
◇ **forced** *adjective* **forced sale** = sale which takes place because a court orders it *or* because it is the only way to avoid a financial crisis **Zwangs-, Notverkauf**
◇ **force down** *verb* to make something become lower **drücken; to force prices down**

= to make prices come down **die Preise drücken;** *competition has forced prices down*

◊ **force up** *verb* to make something become higher **hochtreiben; to force prices up** = to make prices go up **die Preise hochtreiben;** *the war forced up the price of oil*

forecast

1 *noun* description *or* calculation of what will probably happen in the future **Prognose, Voraussage, Vorausberechnung;** *the chairman did not believe the sales director's forecast of higher turnover; we based our calculations on the forecast turnover;* **cash flow forecast** = forecast of when cash will be received or paid out **Cashflow-Prognose; population forecast** = calculation of how many people will be living in a country *or* in a town at some point in the future **Prognose über die Bevölkerungszahlen; sales forecast** = calculation of future sales **Absatzprognose**

2 *verb* to calculate *or* to say what will probably happen in the future **voraussagen, prognostizieren;** *he is forecasting sales of £2m; economists have forecast a fall in the exchange rate*

NOTE: **forecasting - forecast**

◊ **forecasting** *noun* calculating what will probably happen in the future **Voraussage, Prognose,; manpower forecasting** = calculating how many workers will be needed in the future, and how many will actually be available **Personalbesetzungsplan**

NOTE: no plural

foreclose *verb* to sell a property because the owner cannot repay money which he has borrowed (using the property as security) **(aus einer Hypothek) zwangsvollstrecken lassen;** *to foreclose on a mortgaged property*

◊ **foreclosure** *noun* act of foreclosing **Zwangsvollstreckung**

foreign *adjective* not belonging to one's own country **ausländisch, Auslands-;** *foreign cars have flooded our market; we are increasing our trade with foreign countries;* **foreign currency** = money of another country **Devisen, Fremdwährung; foreign goods** = goods manufactured in other countries **Auslandswaren; foreign investments** = money invested in other countries **Auslandsinvestitionen; foreign money order** = money order in a foreign currency which is payable to someone living in a foreign country **Auslandszahlungsanweisung; foreign trade** = trade with other countries **Außenhandel**

◊ **foreign exchange** *noun* **(a)** money of another country **Devisen; foreign exchange broker** *or* **dealer** = person who deals on the foreign exchange market **Devisenhändler, Devisenmakler; foreign exchange dealing** = buying and selling foreign currencies **Devisenhandel; the foreign exchange market** = market where people buy and sell foreign currencies **Devisenmarkt; foreign exchange reserves** = foreign money held by a government to support its own currency and pay its debts **Devisenreserven; foreign exchange transfer** = sending of money from one country to another **Devisentransfer**

◊ **foreigner** *noun* person from another country **Ausländer/-in**

QUOTE the dollar recovered a little lost ground on the foreign exchanges yesterday
Financial Times

QUOTE a sharp setback in foreign trade accounted for most of the winter slowdown
Fortune

QUOTE the treasury says it needs the cash to rebuild its foreign reserves which have fallen from $19 billion when the government took office to $7 billion in August
Economist

foreman *or* **forewoman** *noun* skilled worker in charge of several other workers **Vorarbeiter/-in**

NOTE: plural is **foremen** *or* **forewomen**

forex *or* **Forex** = FOREIGN EXCHANGE

QUOTE the amount of reserves sold by the authorities were not sufficient to move the $200 billion Forex market permanently
Duns Business Month

forfeit

1 *noun* taking something away as a punishment **Verfall; Verwirkung; forfeit clause** = clause in a contract which says that goods *or* deposit will be taken away if the contract is not obeyed **Verfallsklausel; the goods were declared forfeit** = the court said that the goods had to be taken away from their owner **die Waren wurden für verwirkt erklärt**

2 *verb* to have something taken away as a punishment **verwirken; konfiszieren; to forfeit a patent** = to lose a patent because payments have not been made **ein Patent verfallen lassen; to forfeit a deposit** = to lose a deposit which was left for an item because you have decided not to buy that item **eine Anzahlung verlieren/verwirken**

◊ **forfeiture** *noun* act of forfeiting a property **Konfiskation; Verwirkung**

NOTE: no plural

forge *verb* to copy money or a signature illegally *or* to make a document which looks like a real one **fälschen, nachmachen;** *he tried to enter the country with forged documents*

◇ **forgery** *noun*
(a) making an illegal copy **Fälschen;** *he was sent to prison for forgery*
NOTE: no plural
(b) illegal copy **Fälschung;** *the signature was proved to be a forgery*

forget *verb* not to remember **vergessen;** *she forgot to put a stamp on the envelope; don't forget we're having lunch together tomorrow*
NOTE: **forgetting - forgot - forgotten**

fork-lift truck *noun* type of small tractor with two metal arms in front, used for lifting and moving pallets **Gabelstapler**

form
1 *noun*
(a) form of words = words correctly laid out for a legal document **Form; Formulierung; receipt in due form** = correctly written receipt **ordnungsgemäße Quittung**
(b) official printed paper with blank spaces which have to be filled in with information **Formular, Vordruck;** *you have to fill in form A20; customs declaration form; a pad of order forms;* **application form** = form which has to be filled in to apply for something **Antragsformular; Bewerbungsformular; claim form** = form which has to be filled in when making an insurance claim **Schadensformular**
2 *verb* to start *or* to organize **gründen;** *the brothers have formed a new company*

◇ **formation** *or* **forming** *noun* act of organizing **Gründung;** *the formation of a new company*
NOTE: no plural

forma *see* PRO FORMA

formal *adjective* clearly and legally written **offiziell; formell; förmlich;** *to make a formal application; to send a formal order*

◇ **formality** *noun* something which has to be done to obey the law **Formalität; customs formalities** = declaration of goods by the shipper and examination of them by the customs **Zollformalitäten**

◇ **formally** *adverb* in a formal way **offiziell, formell;** *we have formally applied for planning permission for the new shopping precinct*

former *adjective* before *or* at an earlier time **ehemalig, vormalig;** *the former chairman has taken a job with the rival company*

◇ **formerly** *adverb* at an earlier time **vorher, früher;** *he is currently managing director of Smith Ltd, but formerly he worked for Jones*

fortnight *noun* two weeks **zwei Wochen;** *I saw him a fortnight ago; we will be on holiday during the last fortnight of July*

fortune *noun* large amount of money **Vermögen, Besitz;** *he made a fortune from investing in oil shares; she left her fortune to her three children*

forward
1 *adjective* in advance *or* to be paid at a later date **im voraus, Voraus-; forward buying** *or* **buying forward** = buying shares *or* currency *or* commodities at today's price for delivery at a later date **Terminkauf; forward contract** = agreement to buy foreign currency *or* shares *or* commodities for delivery at a later date at a certain price **Abschluß auf Termin; forward market** = market for purchasing foreign currency *or* oil *or* commodities for delivery at a later date **Terminmarkt; forward (exchange) rate** = rate for purchase of foreign currency at a fixed price for delivery at a later date **Devisenterminkurs;** *what are the forward rates for the pound?;* **forward sales** = sales for delivery at a later date **Terminverkäufe**
2 *adverb*
(a) to date a cheque forward = to put a later date than the present one on a cheque **einen Scheck vordatieren; carriage forward** *or* **freight forward** = deal where the customer pays for transporting the goods **Frachtnachnahme; charges forward** = charges which will be paid by the customer **Gebühr bezahlt Empfänger**
(b) to buy forward = to buy foreign currency before you need it, in order to be certain of the exchange rate **auf Termin kaufen; to sell forward** = to sell foreign currency for delivery at a later date **auf Termin verkaufen**
(c) balance brought forward *or* **carried forward** = balance which is entered in an account at the end of a period and is then taken to be the starting point of the next period **Saldovortrag**
3 *verb* **to forward something to someone** = to send something to someone **jdm etwas nachsenden;** *to forward a consignment to Nigeria;* **please forward** *or* **to be forwarded** = words written on an envelope, asking the person receiving it to send it on to the person whose name is written on it **bitte nachsenden**

◇ **(freight) forwarder** *noun* person *or* company which arranges shipping and customs documents for several shipments from different companies, putting them together to form one large shipment **Spediteur; Spedition**

◇ **forwarding** *noun*
(a) arranging shipping and customs documents **Spedition; Abfertigung; air forwarding** = arranging for goods to be shipped by air **Luftfrachtspedition; forwarding agent** = FORWARDER; **forwarding instructions** *or* **instructions for forwarding** = instructions showing how the goods are to be shipped and delivered **Versandanweisungen**
(b) forwarding address = address to which a person's mail can be sent on **Nachsendeadresse**
NOTE: no plural

foul *adjective* **foul bill of lading** = bill of lading which says that the goods were in bad condition when received by the shipper **unreines Konnossement**

founder *noun* person who starts a company **Gründer/-in; founder's shares** = special shares issued to the person who starts a company **Gründeraktien**

fourth *adjective* coming after third **vierter; fourth quarter** = period of three months from October to the end of the year **viertes Quartal**

Fr = FRANC

fraction *noun* very small amount **Bruchteil;** *only a fraction of the new share issue was subscribed*

◇ **fractional** *adjective* very small **geringfügig; fractional certificate** = certificate for part of a share **Bruchteilsaktie**

fragile *adjective* which can be easily broken **zerbrechlich;** *there is an extra premium for insuring fragile goods in shipment*

franc *noun* money used in France, Belgium, Switzerland and many other countries **Franc;** *French francs or Belgian francs or Swiss francs; it costs twenty-five Swiss francs;* **franc account** = bank account in francs **Franc-Konto**
NOTE: in English usually written **Fr** before the figure: **Fr2,500** (say: "two thousand, five hundred francs"). Currencies of different countries can be shown by the initial letters of the countries: **FFr** (French francs); **SwFr** (Swiss francs); **BFr** (Belgian francs)

franchise
1 *noun* licence to trade using a brand name and paying a royalty for it **Franchise;** *he has bought a printing franchise or a hot dog franchise*
2 *verb* to sell licences for people to trade using a brand name and paying a royalty **auf Franchise-Basis vergeben;** *his sandwich bar was so successful that he decided to franchise it*

◇ **franchisee** *noun* person who runs a franchise **Franchisenehmer**

◇ **franchiser** *noun* person who licenses a franchise **Franchisegeber**

◇ **franchising** *noun* act of selling a licence to trade as a franchise **Franchising;** *he runs his sandwich chain as a franchising operation*
NOTE: no plural

◇ **franchisor** *noun* = FRANCHISER

franco *adverb* free **frei**

frank *verb* to stamp the date and postage on a letter **frankieren, freimachen; franking machine** = machine which marks the date and postage on letters so that the sender does not need to use stamps **Frankiermaschine**

fraud *noun* making money by making people believe something which is not true **Betrug;** *he got possession of the property by fraud; he was accused of frauds relating to foreign currency;* **to obtain money by fraud** = to obtain money by saying or doing something to cheat someone **auf betrügerische Weise Geld erlangen; fraud squad** = special police department which investigates frauds **Betrugsdezernat**

◇ **fraudulent** *adjective* not honest *or* aiming to cheat people **betrügerisch;** *a fraudulent transaction*

◇ **fraudulently** *adverb* not honestly **auf betrügerische Weise;** *goods imported fraudulently*

free
1 *adjective & adverb*
(a) not costing any money **kostenlos, gratis, Frei-;** *to be given a free ticket to the exhibition; the price includes free delivery; goods are delivered free; catalogue sent free on request;* **carriage free** = the customer does not pay for the shipping **frachtfrei; free gift** = present given by a shop to a customer who buys a certain amount of goods **Werbegeschenk;** *there is a free gift worth £25 to any customer buying a washing machine;* **free sample** = sample given free to advertise a product **Gratisprobe; free trial** = testing of a machine with no payment involved **kostenlos zur Probe;** *to send a piece of equipment for two weeks' free trial;* **free of charge** = with no payment to be made

kostenlos; free on board = (i) price including all the seller's costs until the goods are on the ship for transportation; (ii); *US* price includes all the seller's costs until the goods are delivered to a certain place **(i) f.o.b., frei an Bord; (ii) f.o.b. einschließlich Fracht; free on rail** = price including all the seller's costs until the goods are delivered to the railway for shipment **frei Bahn**

(b) with no restrictions **frei, unabhängig; free collective bargaining** = negotiations over wage increases and working conditions between the management and the trade unions **autonome Tarifverhandlungen; free competition** = being free to compete without government interference **freier Wettbewerb, Wettbewerbsfreiheit; free currency** = currency which is allowed by the government to be bought and sold without restriction **frei konvertierbare Währung; free enterprise** = system of business with no interference from the government **freies Unternehmertum; free market economy** = system where the government does not interfere in business activity in any way **freie Marktwirtschaft; free port** *or* **free trade zone** = port *or* area where there are no customs duties **Freihafen; Freihandelszone; free of tax** *or* **tax-free** = with no tax having to be paid **steuerfrei;** *he was given a tax-free sum of £25,000 when he was made redundant; interest free of tax or tax-free interest;* **interest-free credit** *or* **loan** = credit *or* loan where no interest is paid by the borrower **zinsloses Darlehen; free of duty** *or* **duty-free** = with no duty to be paid **zollfrei;** *to import wine free of duty or duty-free;* **free trade** = system where goods can go from one country to another without any restrictions **Freihandel;** *the government adopted a free trade policy;* **free trade area** = group of countries practising free trade **Freihandelszone; free trader** = person who is in favour of free trade **Befürworter des Freihandels**

(c) not busy *or* not occupied **frei; unbesetzt;** *are there any free tables in the restaurant? I shall be free in a few minutes; the chairman always keeps Friday afternoon free for a game of bridge*

2 *verb* to make something available *or* easy **flüssigmachen;** *the government's decision has freed millions of pounds for investment*

> QUOTE American business as a whole is increasingly free from heavy dependence on manufacturing
>
> *Sunday Times*
>
> QUOTE can free trade be reconciled with a strong dollar resulting from floating exchange rates?
>
> *Duns Business Month*
>
> QUOTE free traders hold that the strong dollar is the primary cause of the nation's trade problems
>
> *Duns Business Month*

◊ **freehold** *noun* **freehold property** = property which the owner holds for ever and on which no rent is paid **unbeschränkter Grundbesitz**

◊ **freeholder** *noun* person who owns a freehold property **freier Grundeigentümer**

◊ **freelance**
1 *noun* independent worker who works for several different companies but is not employed by any of them **freier Mitarbeiter;** *we have about twenty freeelances working for us*
2 *adjective* independent **freiberuflich (tätig);** *she is a freelance journalist*
3 *adverb* selling one's work to various firms, but not being employed by any of them **freiberuflich;** *he works freelance as a designer*
4 *verb*
(a) to do work for several firms but not be employed by any of them **freiberuflich tätig sein, als freier Mitarbeiter tätig sein;** *she freelances for the local newspapers*
(b) to send work out to be done by a freelancer **Arbeit an freie Mitarbeiter vergeben;** *we freelance work out to several specialists*

◊ **freelancer** *noun* freelance worker **freier Mitarbeiter**

◊ **freely** *adverb* with no restrictions **frei, unbeschränkt;** *money should circulate freely within the Common Market*

◊ **freephone** *noun GB* system where one can telephone to reply to an advertisement *or* to place an order *or* to ask for information and the seller pays for the call; *entspricht* **SERVICE 130**

◊ **freepost** *noun GB* system where one can write to an advertiser *or* to place an order *or* to ask for information to be sent, and the seller pays the postage **Gebühr bezahlt Empfänger**

freeze

1 *noun* **credit freeze** = period when lending by banks is restricted by the government **Einfrieren von Krediten; wages and prices freeze** *or* **a freeze on wages and prices** = period when wages and prices are not allowed to be increased **Lohn- und Preisstopp**
2 *verb* to keep money *or* costs, etc., at their present level and not allow them to rise **einfrieren;** *we have frozen expenditure at last year's level; to freeze wages and prices; to freeze credits; to freeze company dividends*
NOTE: **freezing - froze - has frozen**

◊ **freeze out** *verb* **to freeze out competition** = to trade successfully and cheaply and so prevent competitors from operating **Konkurrenz verdrängen**

freight

1 *noun*

(a) cost of transporting goods by air, sea or land **Frachtgebühren;** *at an auction, the buyer pays the freight;* **freight charges** *or* **freight rates** = money charged for transporting goods **Frachtgebühren;** *freight charges have gone up sharply this year;* **freight costs** = money paid to transport goods **Transport-, Frachtkosten; freight forward** = deal where the customer pays for transporting the goods **Frachtnachnahme**

(b) air freight = shipping of goods in an aircraft **Luftfracht;** *to send a shipment by air freight;* **air freight charges** *or* **rates** = money charged for sending goods by air **Luftfrachtgebühren**

(c) goods which are transported; **to take on freight** = to load goods onto a ship, train or truck **Fracht aufnehmen/aufladen;** *US* **freight car** = railway wagon for carrying goods **Güterwagen, Waggon; freight depot** = central point where goods are collected before being shipped **Güterdepot; freight elevator** = strong lift for carrying goods **Warenaufzug; freight plane** = aircraft which carries goods, not passengers **Transportflugzeug; freight train** = train used for carrying goods **Güterzug**

2 *verb* **to freight goods** = to send goods **verfrachten;** *we freight goods to all parts of the USA*

◊ **freightage** *noun* cost of transporting goods **Frachtkosten**

◊ **freighter** *noun*

(a) aircraft or ship which carries goods **Transportflugzeug; Frachter**

(b) person *or* company which organizes the transport of goods **Befrachter**

◊ **freightliner** *noun* train which carries goods in containers **Containerzug;** *the shipment has to be delivered to the freightliner depot*

frequent *adjective* which comes *or* goes *or* takes place often **häufig;** *there is a frequent ferry service to France; we send frequent telexes to New York; how frequent are the planes to Birmingham?*

◊ **frequently** *adverb* often **oft, häufig;** *the photocopier is frequently out of use; we telex our New York office very frequently - at least four times a day*

friendly society *noun* group of people who pay regular subscriptions which are used to help members of the group when they are ill or in financial difficulties; *entspricht* **Versicherungsverein auf Gegenseitigkeit**

fringe benefits *plural noun* extra items given by a company to workers in addition to a salary (such as company cars, private health insurance) **Leistungsanreize für Arbeitnehmer**

front *noun*

(a) part of something which faces away from the back **Fassade, Vorderseite;** *the front of the office building is on the High Street; the front page of the company report has a photograph of the managing director; our ad appeared on the front page of the newspaper*

(b) in front of = before *or* on the front side of something **vor;** *they put up a "for sale" sign in front of the factory; the chairman's name is in front of all the others on the staff list*

(c) business or person used to hide an illegal trade **Tarnung; Strohmann;** *his restaurant is a front for a drugs organization*

(d) money up front = payment in advance **Vorauszahlung;** *they are asking for £10,000 up front before they will consider the deal; he had to put money up front before he could clinch the deal*

◊ **front-line** *adjective* **front-line management** = managers who have immediate contact with the workers **Management, das direkten Kontakt zu den Arbeitern hat; unterste Leitungsebene**

◊ **front man** *noun* person who seems honest but is hiding an illegal trade **Strohmann**

frozen *adjective* not allowed to be changed or used **gesperrt, blockiert, eingefroren; frozen account** = bank account where the money cannot be changed or used because of a court order **gesperrtes Konto; frozen assets** = a company's assets which by law cannot be sold because someone has a claim against them **eingefrorene/blockierte Vermögenswerte; frozen credits** = credit in an account which cannot be moved **eingefrorene Kredite; his assets have been frozen by the court** = the court does not allow him to sell his assets **seine Vermögenswerte wurden vom Gericht blockiert;** *see also* FREEZE

ft = FOOT

fuel

1 *noun* material (like oil, coal, gas) used to give power **Brenn-, Kraftstoff;** *the annual fuel bill for the plant has doubled over the last years; he has bought a car with low fuel consumption*

2 *verb* to add to **anheizen;** *market worries were fuelled by news of an increase in electricity charges; the rise in the share price was fuelled by rumours of a takeover bid*

fulfil *or US* **fulfill** *verb* to complete something in a satisfactory way **erfüllen, ausführen;** *the clause regarding payments has not been fulfilled;* **to fulfil an order** = to supply the items which have been ordered **eine Bestellung ausführen;** *we are so understaffed that we cannot fulfil any more orders before Christmas*

◇ **fulfilment** *noun* carrying something out in a satisfactory way **Erfüllung, Ausführung; order fulfilment** = supplying items which have been ordered **Auftragserfüllung**

full *adjective*
(a) with as much inside it as possible **voll;** *the train was full of commuters; is the container full yet? we sent a lorry full of spare parts to our warehouse; when the disk is full, don't forget to make a backup copy*
(b) complete *or* including everything **völlig, vollständig; we are working at full capacity** = we are doing as much work as possible **wir sind voll ausgelastet; full costs** = all the costs of manufacturing a product, including both fixed and variable costs **Vollkosten; full cover** = insurance cover against all risks **voller Versicherungsschutz; in full discharge of a debt** = paying a debt completely **Schuldentilgung in voller Höhe; full employment** = situation where all the people who can work have jobs **Vollbeschäftigung; full fare** = ticket for a journey by an adult at full price **voller Fahrpreis; full price** = price with no discount **voller Preis;** *he bought a full-price ticket*
(c) in full = completely **voll, ganz, vollständig;** *give your full name and address or your name and address in full; he accepted all our conditions in full; full refund or refund paid in full; he got a full refund when he complained about the service;* **full payment** *or* **payment in full** = paying all money owed **Zahlung in voller Höhe**

◇ **full-scale** *adjective* complete *or* very thorough **total, umfassend;** *the MD ordered a full-scale review of credit terms*

◇ **full-time** *adjective & adverb* working all the normal working time (i.e. about eight hours a day, five days a week) **ganztägig, Ganztags-, hauptberuflich;** *she is in full-time work or she works full-time or she is in full-time employment; he is one of our full-time staff*

◇ **full-timer** *noun* person who works full-time **ganztätig Beschäftigter**

◇ **fully** *adverb* completely **voll, ganz, vollständig; fully-paid shares** = shares where the full face value has been paid **voll bezahlte Aktien; fully paid-up capital** = all money paid for the issued capital shares **voll einbezahltes Kapital**

QUOTE a tax-free lump sum can be taken partly in lieu of a full pension
Investors Chronicle

QUOTE issued and fully paid capital is $100 million
Hongkong Standard

QUOTE the administration launched a full-scale investigation into maintenance procedures
Fortune

function
1 *noun* duty *or* job **Funktion, Aufgabe; management function** *or* **function of management** = the duties of being a manager **Aufgaben der Betriebsleitung, Führungsfunktion**
2 *verb* to work **funktionieren;** *the advertising campaign is functioning smoothly; the new management structure does not seem to be functioning very well*

fund
1 *noun* money set aside for a special purpose **Fonds, zweckgebundene Mittel; contingency fund** = money set aside in case it is needed urgently **Fonds für außerordentliche Rückstellungen; pension fund** = money which provides pensions for retired members of staff **Rentenfonds; the International Monetary Fund** = (part of the United Nations) a type of bank which helps member states in financial difficulties, gives financial advice to members and encourages world trade **Weltwährungsfonds**
2 *plural noun*
(a) money which is available for spending **verfügbares Kapital;** *the company has no funds to pay for the research programme;* **the company called for extra funds** = the company asked for more money **das Unternehmen bat um zusätzliche Geldmittel; somebody is running out of funds** = to come to the end of the money available **jdm geht das Geld aus; public funds** = government money available for expenditure **öffentliche Mittel;** *the cost was paid for out of public funds;* **conversion of funds** = using money which does not belong to you for a purpose for which it is not supposed to be used **Veruntreuung von Geldmitteln, Umleitung von Geldmitteln für eigene Zwecke; to convert funds to another purpose** = to use money for a wrong purpose **Gelder veruntreuen; to convert funds to one's own use** = to use someone else's money for yourself **Gelder veruntreuen/umleiten**
(b) *GB* **the Funds** = government stocks and securities **Staatspapiere**
3 *verb* to provide money for a purpose **finanzieren; to fund a company** = to provide money for a company to operate **ein Unternehmen finanzieren;** *the company does not have enough resources to fund its expansion programme*

◇ **funded** *adjective* backed by long-term loans **fundiert;** *long-term funded capital; GB* **funded debt** = part of the National Debt which pays interest, but where there is no date for repayment of the principal **fundierte Schuld**

◇ **funding** *noun*
(a) providing money for spending **Finanzierung;** *the bank is providing the funding for the new product launch*
(b) changing a short-term debt into a long-term loan **Fundieren, Konsolidieren;** *the capital expenditure programme requires long-term funding*
NOTE: no plural

> QUOTE the S&L funded all borrowers' development costs, including accrued interest
> *Barrons*
> QUOTE small innovative companies have been hampered for lack of funds
> *Sunday Times*
> QUOTE the company was set up with funds totalling NorKr 145m
> *Lloyd's List*

furnish *verb*
(a) to supply *or* to provide **beliefern, versorgen**
(b) to put furniture into an office *or* room **einrichten, möblieren, ausstatten;** *he furnished his office with secondhand chairs and desks; the company spent £10,000 on furnishing the chairman's office;* **furnished accommodation** = flat *or* house, etc. which is let with furniture in it **möblierte Unterkunft**

furniture *noun* chairs, tables, beds, etc. **Mobiliar, Möbel; office furniture** = chairs, desks, filing cabinets used in an office **Büromöbel;** *he deals in secondhand office furniture; an office furniture store;* **furniture depository** = warehouse where you can store the furniture from a house **Möbellager**

further
1 *adjective*
(a) at a larger distance away **weiter;** *the office is further down the High Street; the flight from Paris terminates in New York - for further destinations you must change to internal flights*
(b) additional *or* extra **weiter, zusätzlich;** *further orders will be dealt with by our London office; nothing can be done while we are awaiting further instructions; to ask for further details or particulars; he had borrowed £100,000 and then tried to borrow a further £25,000; the company is askin*
(c) further to = referring to something in addition **im Nachtrag, über ... hinaus; further to our letter of the 21st** = in addition to what we said in our letter **bezugnehmend auf unser Schreiben vom 21.; further to your letter of the 21st** = here is information which you asked for in your letter **bezugnehmend auf Ihr Schreiben vom 21.; further to our telephone conversation** = here is some information which we discussed **bezugnehmend auf unser Telefongespräch**
2 *verb* to help *or* to promote **fördern, unterstützen;** *he was accused of using his membership of the council to further his own interests*

future
1 *adjective* referring to time to come *or* to something which has not yet happened **zukünftig, Zukunfts-; future delivery** = delivery at a later date **Terminlieferung**
2 *noun* time which has not yet happened **Zukunft;** *try to be more careful in future; in future all reports must be sent to Australia by air*

◇ **futures** *plural noun* trading in shares or commodities for delivery at a later date **Termingeschäfte, Futures;** *gold rose 5% on the commodity futures market yesterday*

Gg

g = GRAM

gain
1 *noun*
(a) increase *or* becoming larger **Zuwachs, Zunahme; gain in experience** = getting more experience **Gewinn an Erfahrung; gain in profitability** = becoming more profitable **Rentabilitätssteigerung**
(b) increase in profit *or* price *or* value **Gewinn;** *oil shares showed gains on the Stock Exchange; property shares put on gains of 10%-15%;* **capital gains** = money made by selling a fixed asset **Veräußerungsgewinne; capital gains tax** = tax paid on capital gains **Veräußerungsgewinnsteuer; short-term gains** = increase in price made over a short period **kurfristige Gewinne**
2 *verb*
(a) to get *or* to obtain **erwerben, erlangen;** *he gained some useful experience working in a bank;* **to gain control of a business** = to buy more than 50% of the shares so that you can direct the business **die Aktienmehrheit an einem Unternehmen erlangen**
(b) to rise in value **steigen, an Wert gewinnen;** *the dollar gained six points on the foreign exchange markets*

◇ **gainful** *adjective* **gainful employment** = employment which pays money **einträgliche Beschäftigung, Erwerbstätigkeit**

◇ **gainfully** *adverb* **gainfully employed** = working and earning money **erwerbstätig sein**

gallon *noun* measure of liquids (= 4.5 litres) **Gallone; the car does twenty-five miles per gallon** *or* **the car does twenty-five miles to the gallon** = the car uses one gallon of petrol in travelling twenty-five miles **das Auto verbraucht eine Gallone auf fünfundzwanzig Kilometer**
NOTE: usually written **gal** after figures: **25gal**

galloping inflation *noun* very rapid inflation which is almost impossible to reduce **galoppierende Inflation**

gap *noun* empty space **Lücke; gap in the market** = opportunity to make a product which is needed but which no one has sold before **Marktlücke;** *to look for or to find a gap in the market; this computer has filled a real gap in the market;* **dollar gap** = situation where the supply of dollars is not enough to satisfy the demand for them from overseas buyers **Dollarlücke; trade gap** = difference in value between a country's imports and exports **Außenhandelsdefizit**

> QUOTE these savings are still not great enough to overcome the price gap between American products and those of other nations
> *Duns Business Month*

gate *noun*
(a) door leading into a field **Tor**
(b) door leading to an aircraft at an airport **Flugsteig, Gate;** *flight AZ270 is now boarding at Gate 23*
(c) number of people attending a sports match **Zuschauerzahl;** *there was a gate of 50,000 at the football final*

gather *verb*
(a) to collect together *or* to put together **zusammenpacken, sammeln;** *he gathered his papers together before the meeting started; she has been gathering information on import controls from various sources*
(b) to understand *or* to find out **schließen, folgen; entnehmen;** *I gather he has left the office; did you gather who will be at the meeting?*

GATT = GENERAL AGREEMENT ON TARIFFS AND TRADE

gazump *verb* **he was gazumped** = his agreement to buy the house was cancelled because someone offered more money **entgegen mündlicher Zusage wurde das Haus, das er kaufen wollte, an einen Höherbietenden verkauft**

◇ **gazumping** *noun* offering more money for a house than another buyer has done, so as to be sure of buying it **das akzeptierte Angebot eines Käufers für ein Haus überbieten**

GDP = GROSS DOMESTIC PRODUCT

gear *verb*
(a) to link to *or* to connect with **abstellen, ausrichten auf, anpassen an;** *bank interest rates are geared to American interest rates;* **salary geared to the cost of living** = salary which rises as the cost of living increases **Gehalt, das den Lebenshaltungskosten angepaßt ist**
(b) a company which is highly geared *or* **a highly-geared company** = company which has a high proportion of its funds from fixed-interest borrowings **Unternehmen mit hohem Anteil an Fremdkapital**
◇ **gear up** *verb* to get ready **sich bereit machen; to gear up for a sales drive** = to make all the plans and get ready for a sales drive **sich für eine Verkaufskampagne rüsten;** *the company is gearing itself up for expansion into the African market*
◇ **gearing** *noun*
(a) ratio between a company's capital borrowed at fixed interest and the value of its ordinary shares **Verhältnis Fremdkapital/Eigenkapital, Verschuldungsgrad**
(b) borrowing money at fixed interest which is then used to produce more money than the interest paid **festverzinsliche Fremdkapitalaufnahme**
NOTE: no plural

general *adjective*
(a) ordinary *or* not special **allgemein, generell; general expenses** = all kinds of minor expenses *or* money spent on the day-to-day costs of running a business **allgemeine Unkosten; general manager** = manager in charge of the administration of a company **geschäftsführender Direktor; general office** = main administrative office of a company **Zentrale**
(b) dealing with everything *or* with everybody **allgemein; general audit** = examining all the books and accounts of a company **ordentliche Buchprüfung; general average** = sharing of the cost of lost goods between all parties to an insurance **große Havarie; general election** = election of a government by all the voters in a country **Bundestagswahl;** *GB* **Parlamentswahl; general meeting** = meeting of all the shareholders of a company **Hauptversammlung; general strike** = strike of all the workers in a country **Generalstreik; Annual General Meeting** = meeting of all the shareholders, when the company's financial situation is discussed with the directors **ordentliche**

Jahreshauptversammlung; Extraordinary General Meeting = special meeting of shareholders to discuss an important matter **außerordentliche Hauptversammlung**
(c) the General Agreement on Tariffs and Trade = international organization which aims to try to reduce restrictions in trade between countries **Allgemeines Zoll- und Handelsabkommen**
(d) general trading = dealing in all types of goods **allgemeiner Handel; general store(s)** = small country shop which sells a large range of goods **Gemischtwarenhandlung**

◇ **generally** *adverb* normally *or* usually **im allgemeinen;** *the office is generally closed between Christmas and the New Year; we generally give a 25% discount for bulk purchases*

generous *adjective* (person) who is glad to give money **großzügig;** *the staff contributed a generous sum for the retirement present for the manager*

gentleman *noun*
(a) "gentlemen" = way of starting to talk to a group of men **"meine Herren";** *"good morning, gentlemen; if everyone is here, the meeting can start"; "well, gentlemen, we have all read the report from our Australian office";* **"ladies and gentlemen"** = way of starting to talk to a group of women and men **"meine Damen und Herren"**
(b) man **Herr, Gentleman; gentleman's agreement** *or US* **gentlemen's agreement** = verbal agreement between two parties who respect each other **Vereinbarung auf Treu und Glauben, Gentleman's Agreement;** *they have a gentleman's agreement not to trade in each other's area*

genuine *adjective* true *or* real **echt;** *this old table is genuine; a genuine leather purse;* **the genuine article** = real article, not an imitation **Markenartikel; genuine purchaser** = someone who is really interested in buying **ernsthafter Käufer**

◇ **genuineness** *noun* being real *or* not being an imitation **Echtheit**

get *verb*
(a) to receive **bekommen, erhalten;** *we got a letter from the solicitor this morning; when do you expect to get more stock? he gets £250 a week for doing nothing; she got £5,000 for her car*
(b) to arrive at a place **ankommen;** *the shipment got to Canada six weeks late; she finally got to the office at 10.30*
NOTE: **getting - got - has got** *or US*

◇ **get across** *verb* to make someone understand something **verständlich machen;** *the manager tried to get across to the workforce why some people were being made redundant*

◇ **get along** *verb* to manage **zurechtkommen;** *we are getting along quite well with only half the staff*

◇ **get back** *verb* to receive something which you had before **zurückbekommen;** *I got my money back after I had complained to the manager; he got his initial investment back in two months*

◇ **get on** *verb*
(a) to work *or* to manage **zurechtkommen;** *how is the new secretary getting on?*
(b) to succeed **Fortschritte machen, sich machen;** *my son is getting on well - he has just been promoted*

◇ **get on with** *verb*
(a) to be friendly *or* to work well with someone **auskommen mit, sich verstehen mit;** *she does not get on with her new boss*
(b) to go on doing work **vorankommen; weitermachen mit;** *the staff got on with the work and finished the order on time*

◇ **get out** *verb*
(a) to produce something (on time) **herausbringen; vorlegen;** *the accounts department got out the draft accounts in time for the meeting*
(b) to sell an investment **aussteigen;** *he didn't like the annual report, so he got out before the company collapsed*

◇ **get out of** *verb* to stop trading in (a product *or* an area) **aufgeben; herausgehen;** *the company is getting out of computers; we got out of the South American market*

◇ **get round** *verb* to avoid **umgehen;** *we tried to get round the embargo by shipping from Canada*

◇ **get through** *verb*
(a) to speak to someone on the phone **durchkommen;** *I tried to get through to the complaints department*
(b) to be successful **durchkommen;** *he got through his exams, so he is now a qualified engineer*
(c) to try to make someone understand **verständlich machen;** *I could not get through to her that I had to be at the airport by 2.15*

gift *noun* thing given to someone **Geschenk; gift coupon** *or* **gift token** *or* **gift voucher** = card, bought in a store, which is given as a present and which must be exchanged in that store for goods **Geschenkgutschein;** *we gave her a gift token for her birthday;* **gift shop** = shop selling small items which are given as presents **Geschenkboutique; gift inter vivos** = present given to another living person **Schenkung zu Lebzeiten; free gift** = present given by a shop to a customer who buys a certain amount of goods **Werbegeschenk**

◊ **gift-wrap** *verb* to wrap a present in attractive paper **als Geschenk einpacken;** *do you want this book gift-wrapped?*

◊ **gift-wrapping** *noun*
(a) service in a store for wrapping presents for customers **Geschenkverpackungsdienst**
(b) attractive paper for wrapping presents **Geschenkpapier**

gilts *plural noun GB* government securities **Staatspapiere**

◊ **gilt-edged** *adjective* investment which is very safe **solide; gilt-edged stock** *or* **securities** = government securities **Staatspapiere**

gimmick *noun* clever idea *or* trick **Gag;** *a publicity gimmick; the PR men thought up this new advertising gimmick*

giro *noun* **the giro system** = banking system in which money can be transferred from one account to another without writing a cheque **das Girosystem;** *GB* **National Giro** = banking system, run by the Post Office, which allows account holders to move money from one account to another free of cost; *entspricht* **Postgirodienst;** *a giro cheque; giro account; giro account number; she put £25 into her giro account; to pay by bank giro transfer*

◊ **Girobank** *noun* bank in a giro system; *entspricht* **Girobank;** *a National Girobank account*

give *verb*
(a) to pass something to someone as a present **schenken; überreichen;** *the office gave him a clock when he retired*
(b) to pass something to someone **geben;** *she gave the documents to the accountant; can you give me some information about the new computer system? do not give any details to the police*
(c) to organize **geben; veranstalten;** *the company gave a party on a boat to publicize its new discount system*
NOTE: **giving - gave - has given**

◊ **give away** *verb* to give something as a free present **verschenken, vergeben;** *we are giving away a pocket calculator with each £10 of purchases*

◊ **giveaway**
1 *adjective* **to sell at giveaway prices** = to sell at very cheap prices **zu Schleuderpreisen verkaufen**
2 *noun* thing which is given as a free gift when another item is bought **Werbegeschenk**

glue
1 *noun* material which sticks items together **Klebstoff, Leim;** *she put some glue on the back of the poster to fix it to the wall; the glue on the envelope does not stick very well*
2 *verb* to stick things together with glue **kleben, leimen;** *he glued the label to the box*

glut
1 *noun* **a glut of produce** = too much produce, which is then difficult to sell **Produktüberangebot;** *a coffee glut or a glut of coffee;* **glut of money** = situation where there is too much money available to borrowers **Geldschwemme**
2 *verb* to fill the market with something which is then difficult to sell **überschwemmen;** *the market is glutted with cheap cameras*
NOTE: **glutting - glutted**

gm = GRAM

gnome *noun informal* **the gnomes of Zurich** = important Swiss international bankers **die Gnome von Zürich**

GNP = GROSS NATIONAL PRODUCT

go *verb*
(a) to move from one place to another **gehen;** *the cheque went to your bank yesterday; the plane goes to Frankfurt, then to Rome; he is going to our Lagos office*
(b) to be placed **hingehören;** *the date goes at the top of the letter*
NOTE: **going - went - has gone**

◊ **go-ahead**
1 *noun* **to give something the go-ahead** = to approve something *or* to say that something can be done **etwas grünes Licht geben;** *his project got a government go-ahead; the board refused to give the go-ahead to the expansion plan*
2 *adjective* energetic *or* keen to do well **dynamisch, progressiv;** *he is a very go-ahead type; she works for a go-ahead clothing company*

◊ **go back on** *verb* not to do what has been promised **zurücknehmen;** *two months later they went back on the agreement*

◊ **going** *adjective*
(a) active *or* busy **gutgehend; in Betrieb; to sell a business as a going concern** = to sell a business as an actively trading company **ein rentables Unternehmen verkaufen; it is a going concern** = the company is working (and making a profit) **es ist dynamisches Unternehmen**
(b) the going price = the usual *or* current price *or* the price which is being charged now **üblicher Preis;** *what is the going price for*

secondhand 1975 Volkswagens?; **the going rate** = the usual *or* current rate of payment **üblicher Satz;** *we pay the going rate for typists; the going rate for offices is £10 per square metre*

◇ **going to** *verb* **to be going to do something** = to be just about to start doing something **beabsichtigen, etwas zu tun;** *the firm is going to open an office in New York next year; when are you going to answer my letter?*

◇ **go into** *verb*
(a) to go into business = to start in business **in das Geschäftsleben einsteigen;** *he went into business as a car dealer; she went into business in partnership with her son*
(b) to examine carefully **untersuchen; überprüfen;** *the bank wants to go into the details of the inter-company loans*

◇ **go on** *verb*
(a) to continue **weiter-, etwas weiter tun;** *the staff went on working in spite of the fire; the chairman went on speaking for two hours*
(b) to work with **sich stützen auf;** *the figures for 1982 are all he has to go on; we have to go on the assumption that sales will not double next year*
NOTE: you go on **doing** something

◇ **go out** *verb* **to go out of business** = to stop trading **das Geschäft/den Betrieb schließen/aufgeben;** *the firm went out of business last week*

goal *noun* aim *or* something which you try to do **Ziel;** *our goal is to break even within twelve months; the company achieved all its goals*

godown *noun* warehouse (in the Far East) **Lagerhaus**

gofer *noun US* person who does all types of work in an office for low wages **Mädchen für alles, Kalfaktor**

gold *noun*
(a) very valuable yellow metal **Gold;** *to buy gold; to deal in gold; gold coins;* **gold bullion** = bars of gold **Barrengold**
(b) the country's gold reserves = the country's store of gold kept to pay international debts **die Goldreserven des Landes; the gold standard** = linking of the value of a currency to the value of a quantity of gold **die Goldwährung; the pound came off the gold standard** = the pound stopped being linked to the value of gold **das Pfund wurde von der Goldwährung gelöst**
(c) gold point = amount by which a currency which is linked to gold can vary in price **Goldpunkt**
(d) gold shares *or* **golds** = shares in gold mines **Goldminenaktien**
NOTE: no plural, except for (d)

◇ **golden handshake** *or US* **golden parachute** *noun* large, usually tax-free, sum of money given to a director who retires from a company before the end of his service contract **großzügige Entlassungsabfindung;** *when the company was taken over, the sales director received a golden handshake of £25,000*

◇ **goldmine** *noun* mine which produces gold **Goldmine; that shop is a little goldmine** = that shop is a very profitable business **das Geschäft ist eine kleine Goldgrube**

good *adjective*
(a) not bad **gut; a good buy** = excellent item which has been bought cheaply **ein guter Kauf; to buy something in good faith** = to buy something thinking it is of good quality *or* that it has not been stolen *or* that it is not an imitation **etwas in gutem Glauben kaufen**
(b) a good deal of = a large quantity of **viel, eine Menge;** *we wasted a good deal of time discussing the arrangements for the AGM; the company had to pay a good deal for the building site;* **a good many** = very many **ziemlich viele;** *a good many staff members have joined the union*

◇ **goods** *plural noun*
(a) goods and chattels = moveable personal possessions **Hab und Gut, beweglicher Besitz**
(b) items which can be moved and are for sale **Waren; goods in bond** = imported goods held by the customs until duty is paid **Waren unter Zollverschluß; capital goods** = machinery, buildings and raw materials which are used to make other goods **Anlagegüter; consumer goods** *or* **consumable goods** = goods bought by the general public and not by businesses **Konsum-, Verbrauchsgüter; dry goods** = cloth and clothes **Textilwaren; finished goods** = manufactured goods which are ready to be sold **Fertigwaren; household goods** = items which are used in the home **Haushaltswaren; luxury goods** = expensive items which are not basic necessities **Luxusartikel; manufactured goods** = items which are made by machine **Industriegüter**
(c) goods depot = central warehouse where goods can be stored until they are moved **Güterdepot; goods train** = train for carrying freight **Güterzug**

◇ **goodwill** *noun* good reputation of a business **Firmenansehen; Goodwill;** *he paid £10,000 for the goodwill of the shop and £4,000 for the stock*
NOTE: no plural

> QUOTE profit margins in the industries most exposed to foreign competition - machinery, transportation equipment and electrical goods
> *Sunday Times*
> QUOTE the minister wants people buying goods ranging from washing machines to houses to demand facts on energy costs
> *Times*

go-slow *noun* slowing down of production by workers as a protest against the management **Bummelstreik;** *a series of go-slows reduced production*

govern *verb* to rule a country **regieren;** *the country is governed by a group of military leaders*

◇ **government** *noun*
(a) organization which administers a country **Regierung; central government** = main organization dealing with the affairs of the whole country **Zentralregierung; local government** = organizations dealing with the affairs of a small area of the country **Kommunal-, Gemeindeverwaltung; provincial government** *or* **state government** = organization dealing with the affairs of a province *or* of a state **Provinzialregierung; Landesregierung**
(b) coming from the government *or* referring to the government **staatlich, der Regierung, Regierungs-, Staats-;** *government employees; local government staff; government intervention or intervention by the government; a government ban on the import of arms; a government investigation into organized crime; government officials prevented him leaving the country; government policy is outlined in the booklet; government regulations state that import duty has to be paid on luxury items; he invested all his savings in government securities;* **government support** = financial help given by the government **staatliche Unterstützung;** *the computer industry relies on government support;* **government annuity** = money paid each year by the government **staatliche Rente; government contractor** = company which supplies goods or services to the government on contract **Betrieb mit Staatsaufträgen**

◇ **governmental** *adjective* referring to a government **staatlich, Staats-, Regierungs-**

◇ **government-backed** *adjective* backed by the government **mit staatlicher Unterstützung**

◇ **government-controlled** *adjective* under the direct control of the government **unter staatlicher Aufsicht;** *advertisements cannot be placed in the government-controlled newspapers*

◇ **government-regulated** *adjective* regulated by the government **staatlich vorgeschrieben/gelenkt**

◇ **government-sponsored** *adjective* encouraged by the government and backed by government money **staatlich gefördert;** *he is working in a government-sponsored scheme to help small businesses*

grace *noun* favour shown by granting a delay **Nachfrist; Aufschub;** *to give a creditor a period of grace or two weeks' grace*
NOTE: no plural

grade
1 *noun* level *or* rank **Rang, Stufe;** *top grade of civil servant; to reach the top grade in the civil service;* **high-grade** = of very good quality **hochwertig, Qualitäs-;** *high-grade petrol;* **a high-grade trade delegation** = a delegation made up of important people **eine hochrangige Handelsdelegation; low-grade** = not very important *or* not of very good quality **untergeordnet; minderwertig;** *a low-grade official from the Ministry of Commerce; the car runs well on low-grade petrol;* **top-grade** = most important *or* of the best quality **Spitzen, hoher;;** *top-grade petrol*
2 *verb*
(a) to sort something into different levels of quality **in Güteklassen einteilen, klassifizieren, einstufen;** *to grade coal*
(b) to make something rise in steps according to quantity **abstufen, staffeln; graded advertising rates** = rates which become cheaper as you take more advertising space **degressive Werbesätze; graded tax** = tax which rises according to income **Steuern, die der Progression unterliegen**
(c) graded hotel = good quality hotel **Sterne-Hotel**

gradual *adjective* slow *or* step by step **allmählich;** *1984 saw a gradual return to profits; his CV describes his gradual rise to the position of company chairman*

◇ **gradually** *adverb* slowly *or* step by step **allmählich;** *the company has gradually become more profitable; she gradually learnt the details of the import-export business*

graduate *noun* person who has a degree from a university or polytechnic **Graduierter/Graduierte, Akademiker/-in; graduate entry** = entry of graduates into employment with a company **Einstellung von Hochschulabgängern;** *the graduate entry into the civil service;* **graduate training scheme** = training scheme for graduates **Ausbildungsprogramm für Hochschulabgänger;**

graduate trainee = person in a graduate training scheme **Hochschulabgänger in der Berufsausbildung**

◊ **graduated** *adjective* rising in steps according to quantity **gestaffelt, der Progression unterliegend;** *graduated income tax;* **graduated pension scheme** = pension scheme which is calculated on the salary of each person in the scheme **gestaffeltes Rentensystem; graduated taxation** = tax system where the percentage of tax paid rises as the income rises **Steuersystem mit Progression**

gram *or* **gramme** *noun* measure of weight (one thousandth of a kilo) **Gramm**
NOTE: usually written **g** or **gm** with figures: **25g**

grand
1 *adjective* important **großartig, bedeutend; grand plan** = major plan **großer/großartiger Plan;** *he explained his grand plan for redeveloping the factory site;* **grand total** = final total made by adding several subtotals **Gesamtsumme, Endbetrag**
2 *noun informal* one thousand pounds *or* dollars **tausend Pfund; tausend Dollar;** *they offered him fifty grand for the information*
NOTE: no plural

grant
1 *noun* money given by the government to help pay for something **Stipendium; Beihilfe, Zuschuß; Subvention;** *the laboratory has a government grant to cover the cost of the development programme; the government has allocated grants towards the costs of the scheme;* **grant-aided scheme** = scheme which is funded by a government grant **subventioniertes Programm**
2 *verb* to agree to give someone something **gewähren, bewilligen;** *to grant someone a loan or a subsidy; the local authority granted the company an interest-free loan to start up the new factory*

> QUOTE the budget grants a tax exemption for $500,000 in capital gains
> *Toronto Star*

graph *noun* diagram which shows statistics as a drawing **Schaubild, Diagramm;** *to set out the results in a graph; to draw a graph showing the rising profitability; the sales graph shows a steady rise;* **graph paper** = special paper with many little squares, used for drawing graphs **Millimeterpapier**

gratia *see* EX GRATIA

gratis *adverb* free *or* not costing anything **gratis, umsonst;** *we got into the exhibition gratis*

gratuity *noun* money given to someone who has helped you **Geldgeschenk; Gratifikation;** *the staff are instructed not to accept gratuities*

great *adjective* large **groß; a great deal of** = very much **sehr viel;** *he made a great deal of money on the Stock Exchange; there is a great deal of work to be done before the company can be made really profitable*

greenback *noun US informal* dollar bill **Dollarschein**

◊ **green card** *noun*
(a) special British insurance certificate to prove that a car is insured for travel abroad **grüne Versicherungskarte, Grüne Karte**
(b) work permit for a person going to live in the USA **Arbeitserlaubnis**

◊ **greenmail** *noun* making a profit by buying a large number of shares in a company, threatening to take the company over, and then selling the shares back to the company at a higher price **(spekulativer) Kauf eines Aktienpakets**
NOTE: no plural

> QUOTE proposes that there should be a limit on greenmail, perhaps permitting payment of a 20% premium on a maximum of 8% of the stock
> *Duns Business Month*

◊ **Green Paper** *noun* report from the British government on proposals for a new law to be discussed in Parliament; *entspricht* **Enquettekommissionsbericht**

◊ **green pound** *noun* value of the British pound as used in calculating agricultural prices and subsidies in the EC **grünes Pfund**

grid *noun* system of numbered squares **Planquadrat; grid structure** = structure based on a grid **Gitterstruktur**

grievance *noun* complaint made by a trade union or a worker to the management **Beschwerde; grievance procedure** = way of presenting complaints from a trade union to the management **Beschwerdeweg**

gross
1 *noun* twelve dozen (144) **Gros;** *he ordered four gross of pens*
NOTE: no plural
2 *adjective*
(a) total *or* with no deductions **brutto, Brutto-; gross earnings** = total earnings before tax and other deductions **Bruttoeinkommen; gross income** *or* **gross salary** = salary before tax is deducted **Bruttoverdienst; gross margin** = percentage difference between sales income and the cost of sales **Bruttomarge; gross profit** = profit calculated as sales income less the cost of sales

Bruttogewinn; gross receipts = total amount of money received before expenses are deducted **Bruttoeinnahmen; gross yield** = profit from investments before the deduction of tax **Bruttoertrag**

(b) gross domestic product = annual value of goods sold and services paid for inside a country **Bruttoinlandsprodukt; gross national product** = annual value of goods and services in a country including income from other countries **Bruttosozialprodukt**

(c) gross tonnage = total amount of space in a ship **Bruttotonnage; gross weight** = weight of both the container and its contents **Brutto-, Rohgewicht**

3 *adverb* with no deductions **brutto;** *his salary is paid gross*

4 *verb* to make a gross profit **brutto verdienen; brutto einnehmen;** *the group grossed £25m in 1985*

> QUOTE news that gross national product increased only 1.3% in the first quarter of the year sent the dollar down on foreign exchange markets
>
> *Fortune*
>
> QUOTE gross wool receipts for the selling season to end June appear likely to top $2 billion
>
> *Australian Financial Review*

ground *noun*

(a) soil *or* earth **Boden, Erdboden; the factory was burnt to the ground** = the factory was completely destroyed in a fire **die Fabrik brannte bis auf die Grundmauern nieder; ground hostesses** = women who look after passengers at the airport before they board the plane; *entspricht* **weibliches Bodenpersonal; ground landlord** = person *or* company which owns the freehold of a property which is then leased and subleased **Grundeigentümer; ground lease** = first lease on a freehold building; *entspricht* **Grundstückspacht; ground rent** = rent paid by a lessee to the ground landlord; *entspricht* **Grundzins**

(b) grounds = basic reasons **Grund;** *does he have good grounds for complaint? there are no grounds on which we can be sued; what are the grounds for the demand for a pay rise?*

◊ **ground floor** *noun* floor (in a shop *or* office) which is level with the ground **Erdgeschoß;** *the men's department is on the ground floor; he has a ground-floor office*
NOTE: in the USA this is the **first floor**

group

1 *noun*

(a) several things or people together **Gruppe;** *a group of the staff has sent a memo to the chairman complaining about noise in the office*

(b) several companies linked together in the same organization **Konzern, Firmengruppe;** *the group chairman or the chairman of the group; group turnover or turnover for the group; the BPCC Group;* **group results** = results of a group of companies taken together **Konzernergebnisse**

2 *verb* **to group together** = to put several items together **zusammenfassen;** *sales from six different agencies are grouped together under the heading "European sales"*

grow *verb*

to become larger **wachsen, zunehmen;** *the company has grown from a small repair shop to a multinational electronics business; turnover is growing at a rate of 15% per annum; the computer industry grew fast in the 1980s*
NOTE: **growing - grew - has grown**

◊ **growth** *noun* increase in size **Wachstum, Zunahme; the company is aiming for growth** = is aiming to expand rapidly **das Unternehmen strebt Expansion an; economic growth** = rate at which a country's national income grows **Wirtschaftswachstum; a growth area** *or* **a growth market** = an area where sales are increasing rapidly **wachsender Absatzmarkt; a growth industry** = industry which is expanding rapidly **expandierender Industriezweig; growth rate** = speed at which something grows **Wachstumsrate; growth share** *or* **growth stock** = share which people think is likely to rise in value **Wachstumsaktie**
NOTE: no plural

> QUOTE a general price freeze succeeded in slowing the growth in consumer prices
>
> *Financial Times*
>
> QUOTE the thrift had grown from $4.7 million in assets in 1980 to $1.5 billion
>
> *Barrons*
>
> QUOTE growth in demand is still coming from the private rather than the public sector
>
> *Lloyd's List*
>
> QUOTE population growth in the south-west is again reflected by the level of rental values
>
> *Lloyd's List*

guarantee

1 *noun*

(a) legal document which promises that a machine will work properly *or* that an item is of good quality **Garantie;** *certificate of guarantee or guarantee certificate; the guarantee lasts for two years; it is sold with a twelve-month guarantee;* **the car is still under guarantee** = is still covered by the maker's guarantee **das Auto hat noch Garantie**

(b) promise that someone will pay another person's debts **Bürgschaft; to go guarantee for someone** = to act as security for someone's debts **für jdn bürgen/haften**

(c) thing given as a security **Sicherheit;** *to leave share certificates as a guarantee*

2 *verb* to give a promise that something will happen **garantieren; sich verbürgen; to guarantee a debt** = to promise that you will pay a debt made by someone else **sich für eine Schuld verbürgen; to guarantee an associate company** = to promise that an associate company will pay its debts **sich für ein Konzernunternehmen verbürgen; to guarantee a bill of exchange** = to promise that the bill will be paid **eine Wechselbürgschaft leisten; the product is guaranteed for twelve months** = the manufacturer says that the product will work well for twelve months, and will mend it free of charge if it breaks down **die Ware hat zwölf Monate Garantie; guaranteed wage** = wage which a company promises will not fall below a certain figure **garantierter Mindestlohn**

◇ **guarantor** *noun* person who promises to pay someone's debts **Bürge/-in;** *he stood guarantor for his brother*

guess

1 *noun* calculation made without any real information **Schätzung;** *the forecast of sales is only a guess;* **he made a guess at the pretax profits** = he tried to calculate roughly what the pretax profits would be **er gab eine Schätzung der Gewinne vor Abzug der Steuern ab; it is anyone's guess** = no one really knows what is the right answer **das weiß keiner**

2 *verb* **to guess (at) something** = to try to calculate something without any information **etwas schätzen; etwas raten;** *they could only guess at the total loss; the sales director tried to guess the turnover of the Far East division*

◇ **guesstimate** *noun informal* rough calculation **grobe Schätzung**

guidelines *noun* unofficial suggestions from the government as to how something should be done **Richtlinien;** *the government has issued guidelines on increases in incomes and prices; the increase in retail price breaks or goes against the government guidelines*

guild *noun* association of merchants *or* of shopkeepers **Gilde, Innung, Zunft;** *trade guild; the guild of master bakers*

guillotine *noun* machine for cutting paper **Papierschneider**

guilty *adjective* (person) who has done something wrong **schuldig;** *he was found guilty of libel; the company was guilty of not reporting the sales to the auditors*

gum *noun* glue **Klebstoff;** *he stuck the label to the box with gum*

◇ **gummed** *adjective* with glue on it **gummiert; gummed label** = label with dry glue on it, which has to be made wet to make it stick **Klebeetikett, Aufkleber**

Hh

ha = HECTARE

haggle *verb* to discuss prices and terms and try to reduce them **feilschen, handeln;** *to haggle about or over the details of a contract; after two days' haggling the contract was signed*

half

1 *noun* one of two parts into which something is divided **Hälfte;** *the first half of the agreement is acceptable;* **the first half** *or* **the second half of the year** = the periods from January 1st to June 30th *or* from June 30th to December 31st **die erste Jahreshälfte; die zweite Jahreshälfte; we share the profits half and half** = we share the profits equally **wir teilen uns die Gewinne halb und halb**

NOTE: plural is **halves**

2 *adjective* divided into two parts **halb; half a per cent** *or* **a half per cent** = 0.5% **ein halbes Prozent; his commission on the deal is twelve and a half per cent** = 12.5% **seine Kommission bei diesem Abschluß beträgt zwölfeinhalb Prozent; half a dozen** *or* **a half-dozen** = six **ein halbes Dutzend; to sell goods off at half price** = at 50% of the price for which they were sold before **Waren zum halben Preis verkaufen; a half-price sale** = sale of all goods at half the price **Ausverkauf zum halben Preis**

◇ **half-dollar** *noun US* fifty cents **halber Dollar**

◇ **half-year** *noun* six months of an accounting period **Halbjahr; first half-year** *or* **second half-year** = first six months *or* second six months of a company's accounting year **erstes Halbjahr; zweites Halbjahr; to announce the results for the half-year to June 30th** *or* **the first half-year's results** = results for the period January 1st to June 30th **die Ergebnisse des ersten Halbjahres/die Halbjahresergebnisse bis zum 30. Juni bekanntgeben;** *we look forward to improvements in the second half-year*

◇ **half-yearly**

1 *adjective* happening every six months *or* referring to a period of six months

halbjährlich, Halbjahres-; *half-yearly accounts; half-yearly payment; half-yearly statement; a half-yearly meeting*
2 *adverb* every six months **halbjährlich;** *we pay the account half-yearly*

> QUOTE economists believe the economy is picking up this quarter and will do better in the second half of the year
> *Sunday Times*

hallmark
1 *noun* mark put on gold or silver items to show that the metal is of the correct quality **Feingehaltsstempel**
2 *verb* to put a hallmark on a piece of gold or silver **mit einem Feingehaltsstempel versehen;** *a hallmarked spoon*

hammer
1 *noun* **auctioneer's hammer** = wooden hammer used by an auctioneer to hit his desk, showing that an item has been sold **Auktionshammer; to go under the hammer** = to be sold by auction **versteigert werden, unter den Hammer kommen; all the stock went under the hammer** = all the stock was sold by auction **der ganze Warenbestand kam unter den Hammer**
2 *verb* to hit hard **hämmern; to hammer the competition** = to attack and defeat the competition **die Konkurrenz aus dem Feld schlagen; to hammer prices** = to reduce prices sharply **Preise drastisch senken**

◇ **hammered** *adjective (on the Stock Exchange)* **he was hammered** = he was removed from the Stock Exchange because he could not pay his debts **er wurde für zahlungsunfähig/insolvent erklärt**

◇ **hammering** *noun*
(a) beating **Schlappe; the company took a hammering in Europe** = the company had large losses in Europe *or* lost parts of its European markets **die Firma hat in Europa eine Schlappe erlitten; we gave them a hammering** = we beat them commercially **wir haben ihnen eine Schlappe beigebracht**
(b) *(on the Stock Exchange)* removal of a member because he cannot pay his debts **Insolvenzfeststellung**

◇ **hammer out** *verb* **to hammer out an agreement** = to agree something after long and difficult negotiations **eine Vereinbarung aushandeln/ausarbeiten;** *the contract was finally hammered out*

hand *noun*
(a) part of the body at the end of each arm **Hand; to shake hands** = to hold someone's hand when meeting to show you are pleased to meet him or to show that an agreement has been reached **sich die Hand geben;** *the two negotiating teams shook hands and sat down at the conference table;* **to shake hands on a deal** = to shake hands to show that a deal has been agreed **einen Abschluß mit Handschlag besiegeln**
(b) by hand = using the hands, not a machine **von Hand, hand-;** *these shoes are made by hand;* **to send a letter by hand** = to ask someone to carry and deliver a letter personally, not sending it through the post **einen Brief durch Boten überbringen lassen**
(c) in hand = kept in reserve **vorrätig, zur Verfügung; balance in hand** *or* **cash in hand** = cash held to pay small debts and running costs **Kassen-, Barbestand; Bargeld;** *we have £10,000 in hand;* **work in hand** = work which is in progress but not finished **noch nicht fertiggestellte Arbeit**
(d) goods left on hand = unsold goods left with the retailer or manufacturer **unverkaufte Ware;** *they were left with half the stock on their hands*
(e) to hand = here *or* present **zur Hand; I have the invoice to hand** = I have the invoice in front of me **ich habe die Rechnung zur Hand**
(f) show of hands = vote where people show how they vote by raising their hands **Abstimmung durch Handheben;** *the motion was carried on a show of hands*
(g) to change hands = to be sold to a new owner **in andere Hände übergehen, den Besitzer wechseln;** *the shop changed hands for £100,000*
(h) note of hand = document where someone promises to pay money at a stated time without conditions **Schuldschein; in witness whereof, I set my hand** = I sign as a witness **ich bestätige die Richtigkeit durch meine Unterschrift**
(i) worker **Arbeiter, Arbeitskraft;** *to take on ten more hands;* **deck hand** = ordinary sailor on a ship **unausgebildeter Seemann; factory hand** = worker in a factory **Fabrikarbeiter**

◇ **handbill** *noun* sheet of printed paper handed out to members of the public as an advertisement **Reklame-, Handzettel**

◇ **handbook** *noun* book which gives instructions on how something is to be used **Handbuch, Bedienungsanleitung;** *the handbook does not say how you open the photocopier; look in the handbook to see if it tells you how to clean the typewriter;* **service handbook** = book which shows how to service a machine **Wartungsbuch**

◇ **hand in** *verb* to deliver (a letter) by hand **abgeben; he handed in his notice** *or* **he handed in his resignation** = he resigned **er reichte seine Kündigung ein**

◇ **hand luggage** *noun* small cases which passengers can carry themselves (and so can take with them into a plane) **Handgepäck**

◇ **handmade** *adjective* made by hand, not by machine **handgearbeitet, handgemacht;** *he writes all his letters on handmade paper*

◇ **hand-operated** *adjective* worked by hand, not automatically **handbetrieben, von Hand bedient;** *a hand-operated machine*

◇ **handout** *noun*
(a) publicity handout = information sheet which is given to members of the public **Werbeprospekt, Reklamezettel; Flugblatt**
(b) free gift **Zuwendung;** *the company exists on handouts from the government*

◇ **hand over** *verb* to pass something to someone **übergeben, überreichen;** *she handed over the documents to the lawyer;* **he handed over to his deputy** = he passed his responsibilities to his deputy **er übergab (die Verantwortung) an seinen Stellvertreter**

◇ **handover** *noun* passing of responsibilities to someone else **Übergabe;** *the handover from the old chairman to the new went very smoothly; when the ownership of a company changes, the handover period is always difficult*

◇ **handshake** *noun* **golden handshake** = large, usually tax-free, sum of money given to a director who retires from a company before the end of his service contract **großzügige Entlassungsabfindung;** *the retiring director received a golden handshake of £25,000*

◇ **handwriting** *noun* writing done by hand **Handschrift; to send a letter of application in your own handwriting** = written by you with a pen, and not typed **einen handgeschriebenen Bewerbungsbrief schicken**
NOTE: no plural

◇ **handwritten** *adjective* written by hand, not typed **von Hand geschrieben, handgeschrieben;** *it is more professional to send in a typed rather than a handwritten letter of application*

handle *verb*
(a) to deal with something *or* to organize something **bearbeiten, sich befassen mit, erledigen;** *the accounts department handles all the cash; we can handle orders for up to 15,000 units; they handle all our overseas orders*
(b) to sell *or* to trade in (a sort of product) **führen, handeln mit;** *we do not handle foreign cars; they will not handle goods produced by other firms*

◇ **handling** *noun* moving something *or* dealing with something **Beförderung, Umschlag; Bearbeitung, Erledigung, Handhabung; handling charges** = money to be paid for packing and invoicing *or* for dealing with something in general *or* for moving goods from one place to another **Bearbeitungsgebühr; Umschlagspesen;** *the bank adds on a 5% handling charge for changing travellers' cheques;* **materials handling** = moving materials from one part of a factory to another in an efficient way **innerbetriebliches Transportwesen, Materialfluß**

> QUOTE shipping companies continue to bear the extra financial burden of cargo handling operations at the ports
> *Business Times (Lagos)*

handy *adjective* useful *or* convenient **praktisch, handlich;** *they are sold in handy-sized packs; this small case is handy for use when travelling*

hang *verb* to attach something to a hook, nail, etc. **(auf)hängen;** *hang your coat on the hook behind the door; he hung his umbrella over the back of his chair*
NOTE: **hanging - hung**

◇ **hang on** *verb* to wait (while phoning) **dranbleiben, warten;** *if you hang on a moment, the chairman will be off the other line soon*

◇ **hang up** *verb* to stop a telephone conversation by putting the telephone back on its hook **aufhängen, auflegen;** *when I asked him about the invoice, he hung up*

happen *verb* to take place by chance **sich ereignen, geschehen, passieren;** *the accident happened when the managing director was away on holiday;* **what has happened to** = what went wrong with *or* what is the matter with *or* where is **was ist mit ... passiert?;** *what has happened to that order for Japan?*

happy *adjective* very pleased **zufrieden, erfreut;** *we will be happy to supply you at 25% discount; the MD was not at all happy when the sales figures came in*

harbour *noun* port *or* place where ships come to load or unload **Hafen; harbour dues** = payment which a ship makes to the harbour authorities for the right to use the harbour **Hafengebühren; harbour installations** *or* **harbour facilities** = buildings *or* equipment in a harbour **Hafenanlagen**

hard
1 *adjective*
(a) strong *or* not weak **hart; to take a hard line in trade union negotiations** = to refuse to accept any proposal from the other side **in Verhandlungen mit der Gewerkschaft hart sein/eine harte Linie verfolgen**
(b) difficult **schwierig, schwer;** *these typewriters are hard to sell; it is hard to get good people to work on low salaries*

(c) solid **hart; hard cash** = money in notes and coins which is ready at hand **Bargeld;** *he paid out £100 in hard cash for the chair;* **hard copy** = printout of a text which is on a computer *or* printed copy of a document which is on microfilm **Ausdruck; Kopie; Abzug;** *he made the presentation with diagrams and ten pages of hard copy;* **hard disk** = computer disk which has a sealed case and can store large quantities of information **Festplatte**
(d) hard bargain = bargain with difficult terms **ein Abkommen mit harten Bedingungen; to drive a hard bargain** = to be a difficult negotiator **hart verhandeln, harte Bedingungen stellen; to strike a hard bargain** = to agree a deal where the terms are favourable to you **ein gutes Geschäft machen; after weeks of hard bargaining** = after weeks of difficult discussions **nach Wochen schwierigen/harten Verhandelns**
(e) hard currency = currency of a country which has a strong economy and which can be changed into other currencies easily **harte Währung;** *exports which can earn hard currency for the Soviet Union; these goods must be paid for in hard currency; a hard currency deal*
2 *adverb* with a lot of effort **hart, kräftig, mit aller Kraft;** *the sales team sold the new product range hard into the supermarkets; if all the workforce works hard, the order should be completed on time*

◊ **harden** *verb* **prices are hardening** = are settling at a higher price **die Preise ziehen an**

◊ **hardening** *noun* **a hardening of prices** = becoming settled at a higher level **das Anziehen der Preise**

◊ **hardness** *noun* **hardness of the market** = being strong *or* not being likely to fall **Festigung des Marktes**

◊ **hard sell** *noun* **to give a product the hard sell** = to make great efforts to persuade people to buy it **für ein Produkt aggressive Verkaufsmethoden anwenden; he tried to give me the hard sell** = he put a lot of effort into trying to make me buy **er versuchte mit allen Mitteln, mich zum Kauf zu überreden**

◊ **hard selling** *noun* act of selling by using great efforts **aggressive Verkaufspolitik;** *a lot of hard selling went into that deal*

◊ **hardware** *noun*
(a) computer hardware = machines used in data processing, including the computers and printers, but not the programs **Computer Hardware;** *hardware maintenance contract*
(b) military hardware = guns *or* rockets *or* tanks, etc. **Wehrmaterial**
(c) solid goods for use in the house (such as frying pans or hammers) **Haushaltswaren, Eisenwaren;** *a hardware shop*
NOTE: no plural

> QUOTE hard disks help computers function more speedily and allow them to store more information
> ***Australian Financial Review***
> QUOTE few of the paper millionaires sold out and transformed themselves into hard cash millionaires
> ***Investors Chronicle***

harm
1 *noun* damage done **Schaden;** *the recession has done a lot of harm to export sales*
NOTE: no plural
2 *verb* to damage **schaden;** *the bad publicity has harmed the company's reputation*

hatchet man *noun* recently appointed manager, whose job is to make staff redundant and reduce expenditure **(Krisen-)Manager mit kostenreduzierendem Mandat**

haul *noun* distance travelled with a load of cargo **Transportweg;** *it is a long haul from Birmingham to Athens;* **short-haul flight** = flight over a short distance (up to 1000 km) **Kurzstreckenflug; long-haul flight** = long-distance flight, especially between continents **Langstrecken-, Fernflug**

◊ **haulage** *noun*
(a) road haulage = moving of goods by road **Güterkraftverkehr; road haulage depot** = centre for goods which are being moved by road, and the lorries which carry them **Güterkraftverkehrdepot; haulage contractor** = company which arranges for goods to be moved by road or rail under contract **Transport-, Fuhrunternehmer; Spediteur; haulage costs** *or* **haulage rates** = cost *or* rates of transporting goods by road **Transportkosten; haulage firm** *or* **company** = company which transports goods by road **Spedition**
(b) cost of transporting goods by road **Transport-, Beförderungskosten;** *haulage is increasing by 5% per annum*
NOTE: no plural

◊ **haulier** *noun* **road haulier** = company which transports goods by road **Spediteur, Fernspediteur**

haven *noun* safe place **Zufluchtsort; tax haven** = country where taxes are low which encourages companies to set up their main offices there **Steueroase**

hawk *verb* to sell goods from door to door or in the street **hausieren; to hawk something round** = to take a product *or* an idea *or* a project to various companies to see if one will accept it **mit etwas hausieren;** *he hawked his idea for a plastic car body round all the major car constructors*

◊ **hawker** *noun* person who sells goods from door to door or in the street **Hausierer/-in**

hazard *noun* **fire hazard** = situation *or* goods which could start a fire **Feuerrisiko;** *that warehouse full of wood and paper is a fire hazard*

head
1 *noun*
(a) most important person **Leiter, Chef, Vorstand; head of department** *or* **department head** = person in charge of a department **Abteilungsleiter**
(b) most important *or* main **Haupt-, Ober-;** *head clerk; head porter; head salesman; head waiter;* **head buyer** = most important buyer in a department store **Einkaufsleiter; head office** = main office, where the board of directors works and meets **Hauptgeschäftsstelle, Zentrale, Direktion**
(c) top part *or* first part **Spitze, oberes Ende;** *write the name of the company at the head of the list*
(d) person **Kopf;** *representatives cost on average £25,000 per head per annum*
(e) heads of agreement = draft agreement with not all the details complete **Hauptaspekte eines Abkommens**
2 *verb*
(a) to be the manager *or* to be the most important person **leiten, vorstehen;** *to head a department; he is heading a buying mission to China*
(b) to be first **anführen, an der Spitze stehen;** *the two largest oil companies head the list of stock market results*

◊ **headed** *adjective* **headed paper** = notepaper with the name of the company and its address printed on it **Papier mit Briefkopf**

◊ **head for** *verb* to go towards **zugehen/zusteuern auf, auf dem Weg sein zu/nach; the company is heading for disaster** = the company is going to collapse **die Firma steuert auf eine Katastrophe zu**

◊ **headhunt** *verb* to look for managers and offer them jobs in other companies **nach Führungskräften suchen; he was headhunted** = he was approached by a headhunter and offered a new job **er wurde abgeworben**

◊ **headhunter** *noun* person *or* company which looks for top managers and offers them jobs in other companies **Headhunter, Talentsucher**

◊ **heading** *noun*
(a) words at the top of a piece of text **Überschrift;** *items are listed under several headings; look at the figure under the heading "Costs 85-86"*
(b) letter heading *or* **heading on notepaper** = name and address of a company printed at the top of a piece of notepaper **Briefkopf**

◊ **headlease** *noun* lease from a freehold owner to a lessee **Hauptmietvertrag; Hauptpachtvertrag; Vermietung; Verpachtung**

◊ **headquarters** *plural noun* main office, where the board of directors meets and works **Hauptsitz, Hauptgeschäftsstelle, Zentrale, Direktion;** *the company's headquarters are in New York;* **divisional headquarters** = main office of a division of a company **Zentrale eines Firmenbereiches; to reduce headquarters staff** = to have fewer people working in the main office **das Personal in der Zentrale reduzieren**

◊ **head up** *verb* to be in charge of **führen, leiten;** *he has been appointed to head up our European organization*

> QUOTE reporting to the deputy managing director, the successful candidate will be responsible for heading up a team which provides a full personnel service
> *Times*

health *noun*
(a) being fit and well, not ill **Gesundheit;** *GB* **Health and Safety at Work Act** = Act of Parliament which rules how the health of workers should be protected by the companies they work for; *entspricht* **Gesetz zum Schutz der Gesundheit und Unfallverhütung am Arbeitsplatz; health insurance** = insurance which pays the cost of treatment for illness, especially when travelling abroad **Krankenversicherung; a private health scheme** = insurance which will pay for the cost of treatment in a private hospital, not a state one **private Krankenversicherung**
(b) to give a company a clean bill of health = to report that a company is trading profitably **bescheinigen, daß eine Firma mit Profit arbeitet**
NOTE: no plural

◊ **healthy** *adjective* **a healthy balance sheet** = balance sheet which shows a good profit **eine gesunde Bilanz; the company made some very healthy profits** *or* **a very healthy profit** = made a large profit **die Firma machte beachtliche Gewinne**

hear *verb*
(a) to sense a sound with the ears **hören;** *you can hear the printer in the next office; the traffic makes so much noise that I cannot hear my phone ringing*
(b) to have a letter *or* a phone call from someone **hören;** *we have not heard from them for some time; we hope to hear from the lawyers within a few days*
NOTE: **hearing - heard**

heavy *adjective*
(a) large *or* in large quantities **hoch, groß, bedeutend, umfangreich;** *a programme of heavy investment overseas; he had heavy losses on the Stock Exchange; the company is a heavy user of steel or a heavy consumer of electricity; the government imposed a heavy tax on luxury goods;* **heavy costs** *or* **heavy expenditure** = spending large sums of money **hohe Ausgaben**
(b) which weighs a lot **schwer;** *the Post Office refused to handle the package because it was too heavy;* **heavy industry** = industry which makes large products (such as steel bars, ships or railway lines) **Schwerindustrie; heavy machinery** = large machines **Schwermaschinen**

◇ **heavily** *adverb* **he is heavily in debt** = he has many debts **er ist stark verschuldet; they are heavily into property** = they have large investments in property **sie haben viel Grundbesitz; the company has had to borrow heavily to repay its debts** = the company has had to borrow large sums of money **die Firma hat viel Geld aufnehmen müssen, um ihre Schulden zu bezahlen**

QUOTE the steel company had spent heavily on new equipment
Fortune

QUOTE heavy selling sent many blue chips tumbling in Tokyo yesterday
Financial Times

hectare *noun* measurement of area of land (= 2.47 acres) **Hektar**
NOTE: usually written **ha** after figures: **16ha**

hectic *adjective* wild *or* very active **hektisch;** *a hectic day on the Stock Exchange; after last week's hectic trading, this week has been very calm*

hedge
1 *noun* protection **Schutz, Absicherung; a hedge against inflation** = investment which should increase in value more than the increase in the rate of inflation **Inflationssicherung;** *he bought gold as a hedge against exchange losses*
2 *verb* **to hedge one's bets** = to make investments in several areas so as to be protected against loss in one of them **sich absichern; to hedge against inflation** = to buy investments which will rise in value faster than the increase in the rate of inflation **sich gegen Inflationsverluste absichern**

◇ **hedging** *noun* buying investments at a fixed price for delivery later, so as to protect oneself against possible loss **Kurssicherungsgeschäft, Hedging**

QUOTE during the 1970s commercial property was regarded by investors as an alternative to equities, with many of the same inflation-hedge qualities
Investors Chronicle

height *noun*
(a) measurement of how tall *or* high something is **Höhe;** *what is the height of the desk from the floor? he measured the height of the room from floor to ceiling*
(b) highest point **Höhepunkt, Gipfel;** *it is difficult to find hotel rooms at the height of the tourist season*
NOTE: no plural

heir *noun* person who will receive property when someone dies **Erbe/Erbin;** *his heirs split the estate between them*

helicopter *noun* aircraft with a large propeller on top which allows it to lift straight off the ground **Hubschrauber;** *he took the helicopter from the airport to the centre of town; it is only a short helicopter flight from the centre of town to the factory site*

help
1 *noun* thing which makes it easy to do something **Hilfe, Unterstützung;** *she finds the word-processor a great help in writing letters; the company was set up with financial help from the government; her assistant is not much help in the office - he cannot type or drive* NOTE: no plural
2 *verb* to make it easy for something to be done **helfen, unterstützen;** *he helped the salesman carry his case of samples; the computer helps in the rapid processing of orders or helps us to process orders rapidly; the government helps exporting companies with easy credit*
NOTE: you help someone *or* something **to do** something

hereafter *adverb* from this time on **künftig, in Zukunft, im folgenden, nachstehend**

◇ **hereby** *adverb* in this way *or* by this letter **hiermit;** *we hereby revoke the agreement of January 1st 1982*

◇ **herewith** *adverb* together with this letter **beiliegend, in der Anlage;** *please find the cheque enclosed herewith*

hereditament *noun* property, including land and buildings **Grundbesitz**

hesitate *verb* not to be sure what to do next **zögern, unschlüssig sein;** *the company is hesitating about starting up a new computer* *factory; she hesitated for some time before accepting the job*

hidden *adjective* which cannot be seen **versteckt, verdeckt, verborgen; hidden assets** = assets which are valued much less in the company's accounts than its true market value **stille Reserven; hidden reserves** = illegal reserves which are not declared in the company's balance sheet **stille Reserven; hidden defect in the program** = defect which was not noticed when the program was tested **versteckter/verdeckter Mangel im Programm**

high
1 *adjective*
(a) tall **hoch, hoher;** *the shelves are 30 cm high; the door is not high enough to let us get the machines into the building; they are planning a 30-storey high office block*
(b) large *or* not low **hoher;** *high overhead costs increase the unit price; high prices put customers off; they are budgeting for a high level of expenditure; investments which bring in a high rate of return; high interest rates are killing small businesses;* **high finance** = lending, investing and borrowing of very large sums of money organized by financiers **Hochfinanz; high flier** = (i) person who is very successful *or* who is likely to get a very important job; (ii) share whose market price is rising rapidly **(i) Senkrechtstarter; (ii) schnell steigende Aktie; high sales** = large amount of revenue produced by sales **hoher Absatz; high taxation** = taxation which imposes large taxes on incomes *or* profits **hohe Besteuerung; highest tax bracket** = the group which pays the most tax **höchste Steuerklasse; high volume (of sales)** = large number of items sold **hoher Absatz**
(c) highest bidder = person who offers the most money at an auction **Meistbietender;** *the property was sold to the highest bidder;* **a decision taken at the highest level** = decision taken by the most important person or group **eine auf höchster Ebene getroffene Entscheidung**
2 *adverb* **prices are running high** = prices are above their usual level **die Preise sind gestiegen**
3 *noun* point where prices *or* sales are very large **Höchststand;** *share prices have dropped by 10% since the high of January 2nd; the highs and lows on the Stock Exchange;* **sales volume has reached an all-time high** = has reached the highest point it has ever been at **das Umsatzvolumen hat einen absoluten Höchststand erreicht**

◊ **high-grade** *adjective* of very good quality **hochwertig, erstklassig;** *high-grade petrol;* **a high-grade trade delegation** = a delegation made up of very important people **eine hochrangige/hochgestellte Handelsdelegation**

◊ **high-income** *adjective* which gives a large income **mit hohem Einkommen;** *high-income shares; a high-income portfolio*

◊ **high-level** *adjective*
(a) very important **auf höchster Ebene, Spitzen-; a high-level meeting** *or* **delegation** = meeting *or* delegation of the most important people (such as ministers, managing directors) **ein Treffen auf höchster Ebene, eine Spitzendelegation; a high-level decision** = decision taken by the most important person or group **eine auf höchster Ebene getroffene Entscheidung**
(b) high-level computer language = programming language which uses normal words and figures **höhere Programmiersprache**

◊ **highly** *adverb* very **hoch, höchst; highly-geared company** = company which has a high proportion of its funds from fixed-interest borrowings **Untenehmen mit hohem Fremdkapitalanteil; highly-paid** = earning a large salary **hochbezahlt; highly-placed** = occupying an important post **hochgestellt;** *the delegation met a highly-placed official in the Trade Ministry;* **highly-priced** = with a large price **teuer; she is highly thought of by the managing director** = the managing director thinks she is very competent **der Generaldirektor hält große Stücke auf sie/hat eine hohe Meinung von ihr**

◊ **high pressure** *noun* strong force by other people to do something **großer Druck; working under high pressure** = working with a manager telling you what to do and to do it quickly *or* with customers asking for supplies urgently **unter großem Druck arbeiten; high-pressure salesman** = salesman who forces the customer to buy something he does not really need **aggressiver Verkäufer; high-pressure sales techniques** *or* **high-pressure selling** = forcing a customer to buy something he does not really want **aggressive Verkaufsmethoden**

◊ **high-quality** *adjective* of very good quality **Qualitäts-, hochwertig;** *high-quality goods; high-quality steel*

◊ **High Street** *noun* main shopping street in a British town **Hauptgeschäftsstraße;** *the High Street shops; a High Street bookshop;* **the High Street banks** = main British banks which accept deposits from individual customers **die größten Bankinstituten in Großbritanien**

QUOTE American interest rates remain exceptionally high in relation to likely inflation rates

Sunday Times

QUOTE faster economic growth would tend to push US interest rates, and therefore the dollar, higher

Australian Financial Review

QUOTE in a leveraged buyout the acquirer raises money by selling high-yielding debentures to private investors

Fortune

hike
1 *noun US* increase **Anstieg, Erhöhung; pay hike** = increase in salary **Lohnerhöhung**
2 *verb US* to increase **erhöhen;** *the union hiked its demand to $3 an hour*

hire
1 *noun*
(a) paying money to rent a car *or* boat *or* piece of equipment for a time **Mieten, Leihen;** *car hire; truck hire;* **car hire firm** *or* **equipment hire firm** = company which owns cars *or* equipment and lends them to customers for a payment **Autoverleih(firma); Geräteverleih; hire car** = car which has been rented **Leih-, Mietwagen;** *he was driving a hire car when the accident happened*
(b) "for hire" = sign on a taxi showing it is empty **"frei"**
(c) *US* **for hire contract** = freelance contract **Vertrag als freier Mitarbeiter; to work for hire** = to work freelance **freiberuflich arbeiten**
2 *verb*
(a) to hire staff = to engage new staff to work for you **Personal einstellen; to hire and fire** = to employ new staff and dismiss existing staff frequently **(oft) einstellen und entlassen;** *they hired a small company to paint the offices*
(b) to hire a car *or* **a crane** = to pay money to use a car *or* a crane for a time **einen Wagen mieten; einen Kran mieten;** *he hired a truck to move his furniture*
(c) to hire out cars *or* **equipment** = to lend cars *or* equipment to customers who pay for their use **Wagen vermieten; Geräte vermieten**

◊ **hired** *adjective* **a hired car** = car which has been rented **ein Mietwagen**

◊ **hire purchase** *noun* system of buying something by paying a sum regularly each month **Raten-, Teilzahlungskauf;** *to buy a refrigerator on hire purchase;* **to sign a hire-purchase agreement** = to sign a contract to pay for something by instalments **einen Teilzahlungskaufvertrag unterschreiben; hire-purchase company** = company which provides money for hire purchase **Teilzahlungsfinanzierungsgesellschaft**

◊ **hiring** *noun* employing **Einstellung;** *hiring of new personnel has been stopped*

historic *or* **historical** *adjective* which goes back over a period of time **historisch; historic(al) cost** = actual cost of something which was made some time ago **ursprüngliche Anschaffungskosten; ursprüngliche Herstellungskosten; historical figures** = figures which were current in the past **historische Beträge**

QUOTE the Federal Reserve Board has eased interest rates in the past year, but they are still at historically high levels

Sunday Times

hit *verb*
(a) to knock against something **anstoßen, schlagen, treffen;** *he hit his head against the table;* **we have hit our export targets** = we have reached our targets **wir haben unsere Exportziele erreicht**
(b) to hurt *or* to damage **(be)treffen;** *the company was badly hit by the falling exchange rate; our sales of summer clothes have been hit by the bad weather; the new legislation has hit the small companies hardest*
NOTE: **hitting - hit**

hive off *verb* to split off part of a large company to form a smaller subsidiary **abspalten, ausgliedern;** *the new managing director hived off the retail sections of the company*

hoard *verb* to buy and store food in case of need *or* to keep cash instead of investing it **horten, ansammeln;** *umg* **hamstern**

◊ **hoarder** *noun* person who buys and stores food in case of need **Hamsterer**

◊ **hoarding** *noun*
(a) hoarding of supplies = buying large quantities of money *or* food to keep in case of need **Horten von Vorräten**
(b) advertisement hoarding = large board for posters **Reklame-, Plakatwand**
NOTE: no plural for (a)

QUOTE as a result of hoarding, rice has become scarce with prices shooting up

Business Times (Lagos)

hold *verb*
(a) to own *or* to keep **(be)halten, besitzen;** *he holds 10% of the company's shares;* **you should hold these shares - they look likely to rise** = you should keep these shares and not sell them **du solltest diese Aktien behalten - sie werden wahrscheinlich steigen**
(b) to contain **enthalten, fassen;** *the carton holds twenty packets; each box holds 250 sheets of paper; a bag can hold twenty kilos of sugar*
(c) to make something happen **(ab)halten, stattfinden;** *to hold a meeting or a discussion;*

the computer show will be held in London next month; board meetings are held in the boardroom; the AGM will be held on March 24th; the receiver will hold an auction of the company's assets; the accountants held a revi

(d) *(on telephone)* **hold the line please** = please wait **bleiben Sie bitte am Apparat, bitte warten;** *the chairman is on the other line - will you hold?*

NOTE: **holding - held**

◇ **hold back** *verb* to wait *or* not to go forward **(sich) zurückhalten, zögern; investors are holding back until after the Budget** = investors are waiting until they hear the details of the Budget before they decide whether to buy or sell **Kapitalanleger halten sich zurück bis zur Verkündigung des Haushaltplans; he held back from signing the lease until he had checked the details** = he delayed signing the lease until he had checked the details **er wartete mit der Unterzeichnung des Pachtvertrages, bis er einzelne Punkte überprüft hatte; payment will be held back until the contract has been signed** = payment will not be made until the contract has been signed **die Zahlungen werden zurückgehalten, bis der Vertrag unterzeichnet ist**

◇ **hold down** *verb*

(a) to keep at a low level **niedrig halten;** *we are cutting margins to hold our prices down*

(b) to hold down a job = to manage to do a difficult job **sich in einer Stellung halten**

◇ **holder** *noun*

(a) person who owns *or* keeps something **Besitzer/-in, Inhaber/-in;** *holders of government bonds or bondholders; holder of stock or of shares in a company; holder of an insurance policy or policy holder;* **credit card holder** = person who has a credit card **Kreditkarteninhaber; debenture holder** = person who holds a debenture for money lent **Obligationär**

(b) thing which keeps something *or* which protects something **Halter, Hülle; card holder** = frame which protects a card **Kartenhülle; credit card holder** = plastic wallet for keeping credit cards **Kreditkartenhülle**

◇ **holding** *noun*

(a) group of shares owned **Anteil, Beteiligung, Aktienbesitz;** *he has sold all his holdings in the Far East; the company has holdings in German manufacturing companies*

(b) cross holdings = situation where two companies own shares in each other in order to stop each from being taken over **wechselseitiger Aktienbesitz, gegenseitige Beteiligung;** *the two companies have protected themselves from takeover by a system of cross holdings*

◇ **holding company** *noun* company which exists only to own shares in subsidiary companies **Holding-, Dachgesellschaft**

◇ **hold on** *verb* to wait *or* not to change **(ab)warten, festhalten an; the company's shareholders should hold on and wait for a better offer** = they should keep their shares and not sell them **die Aktionäre der Gesellschaft sollten die Aktien behalten und ein besseres Angebot abwarten**

◇ **hold out for** *verb* to wait and ask for **auf etwas bestehen; you should hold out for a 10% pay rise** = do not agree to a pay rise of less than 10% **Sie sollten auf einer Lohnerhöhung von 10% bestehen**

◇ **hold over** *verb* to postpone *or* to put back to a later date **vertagen, verschieben;** *discussion of item 4 was held over until the next meeting*

◇ **hold to** *verb* not to allow something to change **festhalten an, einhalten; we will try to hold him to the contract** = we will try to stop him going against the contract **wir werden versuchen, ihn zur Einhaltung des Vertrages zu zwingen; the government hopes to hold wage increases to 5%** = the government hopes that wage increases will not be more than 5% **die Regierung hofft, an Lohnerhöhungen unter 5% festhalten zu können**

◇ **hold up** *verb*

(a) to stay at a high level **hochbleiben;** *share prices have held up well; sales held up during the tourist season*

(b) to delay **verzögern, aufhalten;** *the shipment has been held up at the customs; payment will be held up until the contract has been signed; the strike will hold up dispatch for some weeks*

◇ **hold-up** *noun* delay **Verzögerung;** *the strike caused hold-ups in the dispatch of goods*

> QUOTE real wages have been held down; they have risen at an annual rate of only 1% in the last two years
>
> *Sunday Times*
>
> QUOTE as of last night, the bank's shareholders no longer hold any rights to the bank's shares
>
> *South China Morning Post*

holiday *noun*

(a) bank holiday = weekday which is a public holiday when the banks are closed **Feiertag;** *New Year's Day is a bank holiday;* **public holiday** = day when all workers rest and enjoy themselves instead of working **Feiertag; statutory holiday** = holiday which is fixed by law **gesetzlicher Feiertag;** *the office is closed for the Christmas holiday*

(b) period when a worker does not work, but rests, goes away and enjoys himself **Urlaub;** *to take a holiday or to go on holiday; when is the manager taking his holidays? my secretary is off on holiday tomorrow; he*

is away on holiday for two weeks; **the job carries five weeks' holiday** = one of the conditions of the job is that you have five weeks' holiday **in dieser Stellung bekommt man fünf Wochen Urlaub; the summer holidays** = holidays taken by the workers in the summer when the weather is good and children are not at school **Sommerferien, Sommerurlaub; holiday entitlement** = number of days' paid holiday which a worker has the right to take **Urlaubsanspruch; holiday pay** = salary which is still paid during the holiday **Urlaubsgeld**
(c) tax holiday = period when a new business is exempted from paying tax **Steuerbefreiung**

home *noun*
(a) place where a person lives **Wohnung, Zuhause;** *please send the letter to my home address, not my office*
(b) home country = country where a company is based **Heimatland; home sales** *or* **sales in the home market** = sales in the country where a company is based **Inlandsabsatz; home-produced products** = products manufactured in the country where the company is based **einheimische Erzeugnisse**
(c) house **Haus; new home sales** = sales of new houses **Verkauf von neuen Häusern; home loan** = loan by a bank *or* a building society to a person buying a house **Kredit zum Hauskauf**

◊ **homegrown** *adjective* which has been developed in a local area *or* in a country where the company is based **einheimisch;** *a homegrown computer industry; India's homegrown car industry*

◊ **homemade** *adjective* made in a home **hausgemacht;** *homemade jam*

◊ **homeowner** *noun* person who owns a private house **Hausbesitzer; homeowner's insurance policy** = insurance policy covering a house and its contents and the personal liability of the people living in it **kombinierte Haus- und Hausratversicherung**

◊ **homeward** *adjective* going towards the home country **Heim-;** *homeward freight; homeward journey*

◊ **homewards** *adverb* towards the home country **heim, nach Hause;** *cargo homewards*

hon = HONORARY; **hon sec** = honorary secretary **ehrenamtlicher Sekretär**

honest *adjective* respected *or* saying what is right **ehrlich, redlich; to play the honest broker** = to act for the parties in a negotiation to try to make them agree to a solution **die Rolle des Vermittlers spielen**

◊ **honestly** *adverb* saying what is right *or* not cheating **ehrlich**

honorarium *noun* money paid to a professional person, such as an accountant *or* a lawyer, when he does not ask for a fee **Honorar**
NOTE: plural is **honoraria**

◊ **honorary** *adjective* person who is not paid a salary **ehrenamtlich, Ehren-;** *honorary secretary; honorary president;* **honorary member** = member who does not have to pay a subscription **Ehrenmitglied**

honour *verb* to pay something because it is owed and is correct **begleichen;** *to honour a bill;* **to honour a signature** = to pay something because the signature is correct **seine Unterschrift einlösen**

hope *verb* to expect *or* to want something to happen **hoffen;** *we hope to be able to dispatch the order next week; he is hoping to break into the US market; they had hoped the TV commercials would help sales*

horizontal *adjective* flat *or* going from side to side, not up and down **horizontal, waagerecht; horizontal integration** = joining similar companies *or* taking over a company in the same line of business **horizontale Integration; horizontal communication** = communication between workers at the same level **horizontale Kommunikation**

horse trading *noun* hard bargaining which ends with someone giving something in return for a concession from the other side **Kuhhandel**

hostess *noun* woman who looks after passengers *or* clients **Hosteß; air hostess** = woman who looks after passengers in a plane **Stewardeß; ground hostess** = woman who looks after passengers before they get into the plane **weibliches Bodenpersonal**

hot *adjective*
(a) very warm **heiß;** *the staff complain that the office is too hot in the summer and too cold in the winter; the drinks machine sells coffee, tea and hot soup; switch off the machine if it gets too hot*
(b) not safe *or* very bad **unsicher, schwierig; illegal; to make things hot for someone** = to make it difficult for someone to work *or* to trade **jdm einheizen;** *customs officials are making things hot for the drug smugglers;* **hot money** = money which is moved from country to country to get the best interest rates **heißes Geld; he is in the hot seat** = his

job involves making many difficult decisions **er sitzt auf dem Schleudersitz**

hotel *noun* building where you can rent a room for a night, or eat in a restaurant **Hotel;** *hotel bill; hotel expenses; hotel manager; hotel staff;* **hotel accommodation** = rooms available in hotels **Hotelunterbringung;** *all hotel accommodation has been booked up for the exhibition;* **hotel chain** *or* **chain of hotels** = group of hotels owned by the same company **Hotelkette; the hotel trade** = business of running hotels **Hotelgewerbe**

◇ **hotelier** *noun* person who owns a hotel **Hotelier**

hour *noun*

(a) period of time lasting sixty minutes **Stunde; to work a thirty-five hour week** = to work seven hours a day each weekday **eine 35-Stunden-Woche arbeiten; we work an eight-hour day** = we work for eight hours a day, e.g. from 8.30 to 5.30 with one hour for lunch **wir haben einen Achtstundentag**

(b) sixty minutes of work **Stunde;** *he earns £4 an hour; we pay £6 an hour;* **to pay by the hour** = to pay people a fixed amount of money for each hour worked **pro Stunde bezahlen**

(c) banking hours = time when a bank is open for its customers **Schalterstunden, Banköffnungszeiten;** *you cannot get money out of a bank outside banking hours;* **office hours** = time when an office is open **Bürozeit, Dienststunden;** *do not telephone during office hours;* **outside hours** *or* **out of hours** = when the office is not open **außerhalb der Bürozeit;** *he worked on the accounts out of hours;* **the shares rose in after-hours trading** = in trading after the Stock Exchange had closed **die Aktien stiegen an der Nachbörse**

◇ **hourly** *adverb* per hour **stündlich, stundenweise; hourly-paid workers** = workers paid at a fixed rate for each hour worked **stundenweise bezahlter Arbeiter; hourly rate** = amount of money paid for an hour worked **Stundenlohn**

house *noun*

(a) building in which someone lives **Haus; house property** = private houses, not shops, offices or factories **Hausbesitz; house agent** = estate agent who deals in buying or selling houses **Häuser-, Immobilienmakler**

(b) company **Haus, Firma;** *a French business house; the largest London finance house; he works for a broking house or a publishing house;* **clearing house** = central office where clearing banks exchange cheques **Abrechnungs-, Clearing-, Girokasse; discount house** = financial company which specializes in discounting bills **Diskontbank; export house** = company which specializes in the export of goods manufactured by other companies **Exportfirma; house journal** *or* **house magazine** *or US* **house organ** = magazine produced for the workers or shareholders in a company to give them news about the company **Betriebszeitung, Hausnachrichten; house telephone** = internal telephone for calling from one office to another **Haustelefon**

(c) the House = (i) the London Stock Exchange; (ii) the House of Commons **(i) die Londoner Börse; (ii) das Unterhaus**

◇ **household** *noun* people living in a house **Haushalt; household expenses** = money spent on running a private house **Haushaltungskosten, Wirtschaftsgeld; household goods** = goods which are used in a house **Haushaltswaren**

◇ **householder** *noun* person who owns a private house **Hausbesitzer**

◇ **house starts** *or US* **housing starts** *plural noun* number of new private houses or flats of which the construction has begun during a year **Neubauten**

◇ **house-to-house** *adjective* **house-to-house selling** going from one house to the next, asking people to buy something **Direktverkauf, Verkauf an der Haustür;** *house-to-house canvassing; house-to-house salesman; house-to-house selling*

HP = HIRE PURCHASE

hundredweight *noun* weight of 112 pounds (about fifty kilos) **Zentner**
NOTE: usually written **cwt** after figures: **20cwt**

hurry

1 *noun* doing things fast **Eile;** *there is no hurry for the figures, we do not need them until next week;* **in a hurry** = very fast **schnell;** *the sales manager wants the report in a hurry*

2 *verb* to do something *or* to make something *or* to go very fast **sich beeilen; eilen; antreiben, beschleunigen;** *the production team tried to hurry the order through the factory; the chairman does not want to be hurried into making a decision; the directors hurried into the meeting*

◇ **hurry up** *verb* to make something go faster **vorantreiben;** *can you hurry up that order - the customer wants it immediately?*

hurt *verb* to harm *or* to damage **schaden, Schaden zufügen;** *the bad publicity did not hurt our sales; sales of summer clothes were hurt by the bad weather; the company has not been hurt by the recession*
NOTE: **hurting - hurt**

hype
1 *noun* excessive claims made in advertising **übertriebene/reißerische Werbung;** *all the hype surrounding the launch of the new soap*
2 *verb* to make excessive claims in advertising **übertriebene Werbung machen**

hyper- *prefix meaning* very large **Super-, Hyper-**

◇ **hyperinflation** *noun* inflation which is so rapid that it is almost impossible to reduce **Hyperinflation**
NOTE: no plural

◇ **hypermarket** *noun* very large supermarket, usually on the outside of a large town **Verbrauchergroßmarkt**

Ii

idea *noun* thing which you think of **Gedanke, Idee;** *one of the salesman had the idea of changing the product colour; the chairman thinks it would be a good idea to ask all directors to itemize their expenses*

ideal *adjective* perfect *or* very good for something **ideal;** *this is the ideal site for a new hypermarket*

◇ **Ideal Home Exhibition** *noun* annual exhibition in London showing new houses, new kitchens, etc.

idle *adjective*
(a) not working **unbeschäftigt, erwerbslos;** *2,000 employees were made idle by the recession*
(b) idle machinery *or* **machines lying idle** = machinery not being used **stillstehende Maschinen**
(c) idle capital = capital not being used productively **totes Kapital; money lying idle** *or* **idle money** = money which is not being used to produce interest *or* which is not invested in business **stilliegendes Geld, nicht arbeitendes Kapital**

i.e. that is **d.h.;** *the largest companies, i.e. Smith's and Brown's, had a very good first quarter; the import restrictions apply to expensive items, i.e. items costing more than $2,500*

illegal *adjective* not legal *or* against the law **illegal, ungesetzlich, rechtswidrig, unrechtmäßig**

◇ **illegality** *noun* being illegal **Illegalität, Ungesetzlichkeit, Rechtswidrigkeit, Unrechtmäßigkeit**

◇ **illegally** *adverb* against the law **illegal;** *he was accused of illegally importing arms into the country*

illicit *adjective* not legal *or* not permitted **unerlaubt, verboten;** *illicit sale of alcohol; trade in illicit alcohol*

ILO = INTERNATIONAL LABOUR ORGANIZATION

image *noun* general idea which the public has of a product *or* a company **Image;** *they are spending a lot of advertising money to improve the company's image; the company has adopted a down-market image;* **brand image** = picture which people have in their minds of a product associated with the brand name **Markenprofil, Produkt-Image; corporate image** = idea which a company would like the public to have of it **Firmenimage; to promote a corporate image** = to publicize a company so that its reputation is improved **das Firmenimage pflegen**

IMF = INTERNATIONAL MONETARY FUND

imitate *verb* to do what someone else does **nachmachen, kopieren, imitieren;** *they imitate all our sales gimmicks*

◇ **imitation** *noun* thing which copies another **Nachahmung, Kopie, Imitation; beware of imitations** = be careful not to buy low quality goods which are made to look like other more expensive items **vor Imitationen wird gewarnt**

immediate *adjective* happening at once **umgehend, prompt, sofort;** *he wrote an immediate letter of complaint; your order will receive immediate attention*

◇ **immediately** *adverb* at once **umgehend, gleich, sofort;** *he immediately placed an order for 2,000 boxes; as soon as he heard the news he immediately telexed his office; can you phone immediately you get the information?*

immovable *adjective* which cannot be moved **unbeweglich; immovable property** = houses and other buildings on land **unbewegliches Vermögen**

immunity *noun* protection against arrest **Immunität; diplomatic immunity** = being outside a country's laws because of being a diplomat **diplomatische Immunität; he was**

granted immunity from prosecution = he was told he would not be prosecuted **ihm wurde Freiheit von Strafverfolgung gewährt, ihm wurde strafrechtliche Immunität gewährt**
NOTE: no plural

impact *noun* shock *or* strong effect **Wirkung, Auswirkung, Druck;** *the impact of new technology on the cotton trade; the new design has made little impact on the buying public*
NOTE: no plural

> QUOTE the strong dollar's deflationary impact on European economies as governments push up interest rates to support their sinking currencies
> *Duns Business Month*

imperfect *adjective* not perfect **fehlerhaft;** *sale of imperfect items; to check a batch for imperfect products*
◇ **imperfection** *noun* part of an item which is not perfect **Mangel, Fehler;** *to check a batch for imperfections*

impersonal *adjective* without any personal touch *or* as if done by machines **unpersönlich;** *an impersonal style of management*

implement
1 *noun* tool *or* instrument used to do some work **Gerät, Arbeitsgerät, Werkzeug**
2 *verb* to put into action **aus-, durchführen, vollziehen;** *to implement an agreement*
◇ **implementation** *noun* putting into action **Aus-, Durchführung, Vollzug;** *the implementation of new rules*
NOTE: no plural

import
1 *noun*
(a) imports = goods brought into a country from abroad for sale **Importe, Einfuhren;** *imports from Poland have risen to $1m a year;* **invisible imports** = services (such as banking, tourism) which are paid for in foreign currency **unsichtbare Importe; visible imports** = real goods which are imported **sichtbare Importe**
(b) import ban = forbidding imports **Einfuhrverbot, Einfuhrstopp;** *the government has imposed an import ban on arms;* **import duty** = tax on goods imported into a country **Einfuhrzoll; import levy** = tax on imports, especially in the EC a tax on imports of farm produce from outside the EC **Einfuhrzoll;** *EG* **Abschöpfung; import licence** *or* **import permit** = government licence *or* permit which allows goods to be imported **Importlizenz, Importgenehmigung; import quota** = fixed quantity of a particular type of goods which the government allows to be imported **Einfuhrkontingent, Importquote;** *the government has imposed an import quota on cars;* **import surcharge** = extra duty charged on imported goods, to try to prevent them from being imported and to encourage local manufacture **Importabgabe**
NOTE: usually used in the plural, but the singular form is used before a noun
2 *verb* to bring goods from abroad into a country for sale **importieren, einführen;** *the company imports television sets from Japan; this car was imported from France; the union organized a boycott of imported cars*

> QUOTE European manufacturers rely heavily on imported raw materials which are mostly priced in dollars
> *Duns Business Month*

◇ **importation** *noun* act of importing **Import, Einfuhr;** *the importation of arms is forbidden*
NOTE: no plural
◇ **importer** *noun* person *or* company which imports goods **Importeur, Importfirma;** *a cigar importer; the company is a big importer of foreign cars*
◇ **import-export** *adjective* dealing with both bringing foreign goods into a country and sending locally made goods abroad **Import/Export-;** *import-export trade; he is in import-export*
◇ **importing**
1 *adjective* which imports **Import-, Einfuhr-;** *oil-importing countries; an importing company*
2 *noun* act of bringing foreign goods into a country for sale **Import, Einfuhr;** *the importing of arms into the country is illegal*
NOTE: no plural

importance *noun* having a value *or* mattering a lot **Wichtigkeit, Bedeutung;** *the bank attaches great importance to the deal*
NOTE: no plural
◇ **important** *adjective* which matters a lot **wichtig, bedeutend;** *he left a pile of important papers in the taxi; she has an important meeting at 10.30; he was promoted to a more important job*

> QUOTE each of the major issues on the agenda at this week's meeting is important to the government's success in overall economic management
> *Australian Financial Review*

impose *verb* to put a tax *or* a duty on goods **erheben, belegen mit; verhängen;** *to impose a tax on bicycles; they tried to impose a ban on smoking; the government imposed a special duty on oil; the customs have imposed a 10% tax increase on luxury items; the unions have asked the* *government to impose trade barriers on foreign cars*

◇ **imposition** *noun* putting a tax on goods or services **Verhängung**
NOTE: no plural

impossible *adjective* which cannot be done **unmöglich;** *getting skilled staff is becoming impossible; government regulations make it impossible for us to export*

impound *verb* to take something away and keep it until a tax is paid **beschlagnahmen;** *the customs impounded the whole cargo*

◇ **impounding** *noun* act of taking something and keeping it until a tax is paid **gerichtliche Verwahrung, Sicherstellung**
NOTE: no plural

imprest *noun* **the imprest system** = system of controlling petty cash, where cash is paid out against a written receipt and the receipt is used to get more cash to bring the float to the original level **System der Wiederauffüllung nach Abrechnung**

improve *verb* to make something better *or* to become better **verbessern;** *we are trying to improve our image with a series of TV commercials; they hope to improve the company's cash flow position; we hope the cash flow position will improve or we will have difficulty in paying our bills;* **export trade has improved sharply during the first quarter** = export trade has increased **der Exporthandel hat während des ersten Quartals einen deutlichen Aufschwung genommen**

◇ **improved** *adjective* better **höher;** *the union rejected the management's improved offer*

◇ **improvement** *noun*
(a) getting better **Verbesserung, Besserung;** *there is no improvement in the cash flow situation; sales are showing a sharp improvement over last year*
(b) thing which is better **Verbesserung; improvement on an offer** = making a better offer **Erhöhung eines Angebotes**

◇ **improve on** *verb* to do better than **übertreffen, überbieten; he refused to improve on his previous offer** = he refused to make a better offer **er weigerte sich, über sein ursprüngliches Angebot hinauszugehen**

> QUOTE the management says the rate of loss-making has come down and it expects further improvement in the next few years
> *Financial Times*
> QUOTE we also invest in companies whose growth and profitability could be improved by a management buyout
> *Times*

impulse *noun* sudden decision **Impuls; impulse buying** = buying things which you have just seen, not because you had planned to buy them **Impuls-, Spontankäufe;** *the store puts racks of chocolates by the checkout to attract the impulse buyer;* **impulse purchase** = thing bought as soon as it is seen **Impulskauf; to do something on impulse** = to do something because you have just thought of it, not because it was planned **etwas spontan/impulsiv tun**

in = INCH

inactive *adjective* not active *or* not busy **untätig, flau, unbelebt; inactive market** = stock market with few buyers or sellers **lustloser/umsatzschwacher Markt**

Inc *US* = INCORPORATED

incentive *noun* thing which encourages staff to work better **Anreiz, Incentive; staff incentives** = pay and better conditions offered to workers to make them work better **Leistungsanreize für das Personal; incentive bonus** *or* **incentive payment** = extra pay offered to a worker to make him work better **Leistungszulage, Prämie; incentive scheme** = plan to encourage better work by paying higher commission or bonuses **leistungsabhängiges System, Anreizsystem;** *incentive schemes are boosting production*

> QUOTE some further profit-taking was seen yesterday as investors continued to lack fresh incentives to renew buying activity
> *Financial Times*

inch *noun* measurement of length (= 2.54cm) **Inch;** *entspricht* **Zoll**
NOTE: usually written **in** or " after figures: **2in** or **2"**

incidental
1 *adjective* which is not important, but connected with something else **nebensächlich, Neben-; incidental expenses** = small amounts of money spent at various times in addition to larger amounts **Nebenausgaben**
2 *noun* **incidentals** = incidental expenses **Nebenkosten**

include *verb* to count something along with other things **einschließen, einbeziehen, enthalten;** *the charge includes VAT; the total comes to £1,000 including freight; the total is £140 not including insurance and freight; the account covers services up to and including the month of June*

◇ **inclusive** *adjective* which counts something in with other things **inklusive, einschließlich;** *inclusive of tax; not inclusive of VAT;* **inclusive sum** *or* **inclusive charge** = charge which includes all costs **Pauschale, Gesamtgebühr; the conference runs from the 12th to the 16th inclusive** = it starts on the morning of the 12th and ends on the evening of the 16th **die Konferenz geht vom 12. bis einschließlich 16.**

income *noun*
(a) money which a person receives as salary or dividends **Einkommen, Einkünfte; annual income** = money received during a calendar year **Jahreseinkommen; disposable income** = income left after tax and national insurance have been deducted **verfügbares Einkommen (nach Steuerabzug), Nettoeinkommen; earned income** = money received as a salary or wages **Erwerbseinkünfte, Arbeitseinkommen; earned income allowance** = tax allowance to be set against money earned by the wife or children of the main taxpayer **Freibetrag für Erwerbseinkünfte; fixed income** = income which does not change from year to year **festes Einkommen; gross income** = income before tax has been deducted **Bruttoeinkommen; net income** = income left after tax has been deducted **Nettoeinkommen; private income** = income from dividends *or* interest *or* rent which is not part of a salary **Privateinkommen; personal income** = income received by an individual person **persönliches Einkommen; retained income** = profits which are not paid out to shareholders as dividends **nicht ausgeschüttete Gewinne; unearned income** = money received from interest or dividends **Kapitaleinkommen, Vermögenseinkünfte; lower** *or* **upper income bracket** = groups of people who earn low or high salaries considered for tax purposes **niedrige Einkommensstufe; hohe Einkommensstufe; he comes into the higher income bracket** = he is in a group of people earning high incomes and therefore paying more tax **er gehört einer hohen Einkommensstufe an**
(b) the government's incomes policy = the government's ideas on how incomes should be controlled **die Lohn-/Einkommenspolitik der Regierung**
(c) income tax = tax on a person's income **Einkommenssteuer; income tax form** = form to be completed which declares all income to the tax office **Einkommenssteuerformular; declaration of income** *or* **income tax return** = statement declaring income to the tax office **Einkommenssteuererklärung**
(d) money which an organization receives as gifts or from investments **Einkünfte;** *the hospital has a large income from gifts*
(e) *US* **income statement** = accounts for a company which show expenditure and sales balanced to give a final profit or loss **Gewinn- und Verlustrechnung, Aufwands- und Ertragsrechnung**

QUOTE there is no risk-free way of taking regular income from your money much higher than the rate of inflation

Guardian

QUOTE the company will be paying income tax at the higher rate in 1985

Citizen (Ottawa)

incoming *adjective*
(a) incoming call = phone call coming into the office from someone outside **eingehendes Telefongespräch; incoming mail** = mail which comes into an office **Posteingang**
(b) which have recently been elected *or* appointed **neu, nachfolgend; the incoming board of directors** = the new board which is about to start working **der neuernannte Board of Directors;** *the incoming chairman or president*

incompetent *adjective* who cannot work well **inkompetent, unfähig, unzulänglich;** *the sales manager is quite incompetent; the company has an incompetent sales director*

inconvertible *adjective* (currency) which cannot be easily converted into other currencies **nicht konvertierbar/einlösbar**

incorporate *verb*
(a) to bring something in to form part of a main group **integrieren, eingliedern, verbinden;** *income from the 1984 acquisition is incorporated into the accounts*
(b) to form a registered company **eine Kapitalgesellschaft gründen, amtlich eintragen;** *a company incorporated in the USA; an incorporated company; J. Doe Incorporated*

◇ **incorporation** *noun* act of incorporating a company **Gesellschaftsgründung, amtliche Eintragung**

incorrect *adjective* wrong *or* not correct **ungenau, fehlerhaft;** *the minutes of the meeting were incorrect and had to be changed*

◇ **incorrectly** *adverb* wrongly *or* not correctly **falsch, ungenau;** *the package was incorrectly addressed*

increase
1 *noun*
(a) growth *or* becoming larger **Erhöhung, Steigerung, Zunahme, Zuwachs;** *increase in tax or tax increase; increase in price or price increase; profits showed a 10% increase or an increase of 10% on last year;* **increase in the cost of living** = rise in the annual cost of living **Steigerung der Lebenshaltungskosten**
(b) higher salary **Lohnzulage, Gehaltserhöhung, Gehaltsaufbesserung;** *increase in pay or pay increase; increase in salary or salary increase; the government hopes to hold salary increases to 3%;* **he had two increases last year** = his salary went up twice **er bekam letztes Jahr zwei Lohnerhöhungen; cost-of-living increase** = increase in salary to allow it to keep up with higher cost of living **Gehaltszulage zur Anpassung an gestiegene Lebenshaltungskosten; merit increase** = increase in pay given to a worker whose work is good **Leistungszulage**
(c) on the increase = growing larger *or* becoming more frequent **(ständig) zunehmen, im Wachsen begriffen sein;** *stealing in shops is on the increase*
2 *verb*
(a) to grow bigger *or* higher **(sich) erhöhen/steigern, zunehmen, wachsen, (an)steigen;** *profits have increased faster than the increase in the rate of inflation; exports to Africa have increased by more than 25%; the price of oil has increased twice in the past week;* **to increase in price** = to cost more **teurer werden; to increase in size** *or* **in value** = to become larger *or* more valuable **größer werden; im Wert steigen**
(b) the company increased his salary to £20,000 = the company gave him a rise in salary to £20,000 **die Firma erhöhte sein Gehalt auf £20.000**

◇ **increasing** *adjective* which is growing bigger **wachsend, steigend, zunehmend;** *increasing profits; the company has an increasing share of the market*

◇ **increasingly** *adverb* more and more **immer mehr, zunehmend;** *the company has to depend increasingly on the export market*

> QUOTE competition is steadily increasing and could affect profit margins as the company tries to retain its market share
> *Citizen (Ottawa)*
>
> QUOTE turnover has potential to be increased to over 1 million dollars with energetic management and very little capital
> *Australian Financial Review*

increment *noun* regular automatic increase in salary **Gehaltserhöhung;** *annual increment;* **salary which rises in annual increments of £500** = each year the salary is increased by £500 **Gehalt, das jährlich um £500 steigt**

◇ **incremental** *adjective* which rises automatically in stages **Zuwachs-, zunehmend; incremental cost** = cost of making a single extra unit above the number already planned **Grenzkosten; incremental increase** = increase in salary according to an agreed annual increment **jährliche Gehaltszulage; incremental scale** = salary scale with regular annual salary increases **Gehaltssteigerungstabelle**

incur *verb* to make yourself liable to **übernehmen, auf sich nehmen, eingehen; to incur the risk of a penalty** = to make it possible that you risk paying a penalty **das Risiko einer Geldstrafe eingehen; to incur debts** *or* **costs** = to do something which means that you owe money *or* that you will have to pay costs **Schulden machen; sich Unkosten aufladen;** *the company has incurred heavy costs to implement the expansion programme*
NOTE: **incurring - incurred**

> QUOTE the company blames fiercely competitive market conditions in Europe for a £14m operating loss last year, incurred despite a record turnover
> *Financial Times*

indebted *adjective* owing money to someone **verschuldet;** *to be indebted to a property company*
◇ **indebtedness** *noun* **state of indebtedness** = being in debt *or* owing money **Verschuldung**

indemnification *noun* payment for damage **Entschädigung, Schadensersatz**
◇ **indemnify** *verb* to pay for damage **entschädigen, Schadensersatz leisten;** *to indemnify someone for a loss*
◇ **indemnity** *noun* guarantee of payment after a loss **Entschädigung, Vergütung;** *he had to pay an indemnity of £100;* **letter of indemnity** = letter promising payment as compensation for a loss **(schriftliche) Schadloshaltungs-, Ausfallbürgschaftserklärung**

indent
1 *noun*
(a) order placed by an importer for goods from overseas **Auslandsauftrag, Warenbestellung (aus dem Ausland), Indentgeschäft;** *he put in an indent for a new stock of soap*
(b) line of typing which starts several spaces from the left-hand margin **Einrückung, Einzug**
2 *verb*

(a) to indent for something = to put in an order for something **einen Auslandsauftrag erteilen, etwas aus dem Ausland bestellen;** *the department has indented for a new computer*
(b) to start a line of typing several spaces from the left-hand margin **einrücken, einziehen;** *indent the first line three spaces*

indenture

1 *noun* **indentures** *or* **articles of indenture** = contract by which an apprentice works for a master for some years to learn a trade **Ausbildungsvertrag, Lehrvertrag**
2 *verb* to contract with an apprentice who will work for some years to learn a trade **in die Lehre nehmen;** *he was indentured to a builder*

independent

adjective free *or* not controlled by anyone **unabhängig, ungebunden; independent company** = company which is not controlled by another company **unabhängiges Unternehmen; independent trader** *or* **independent shop** = shop which is owned by an individual proprietor, not by a chain **selbständiger Händler; unabhängiges Geschäft; the independents** = shops or companies which are owned by private individuals **unabhängige Unternehmen**

index

noun
(a) list of items classified into groups or put in alphabetical order **Index, Register; index card** = small card used for filing **Karteikarte; card index** = series of cards with information written on them, kept in a special order so that the information car be found easily **Kartei; index letter** *or* **number** = letter or number of an item in an index **Karteibuchstabe; Karteinummer**
(b) regular statistical report which shows rises and falls in prices, etc. **Index; growth index** = index showing how something has grown **Wachstumsindex; cost-of-living index** = way of measuring the cost of living, shown as a percentage increase on the figure for the previous year **Lebenshaltungskostenindex; retail price index** *or US* **consumer price index** = index showing how prices of consumer goods have risen over a period of time, used as a way of measuring inflation and the cost of living **Verbraucherpreisindex; wholesale price index** = index showing rises and falls of prices of manufactured goods as they leave the factory **Großhandelspreisindex; the Financial Times Index** = index which shows percentage rises or falls in shares prices on the London Stock Exchange based on a small group of major companies **Aktienindex der Financial Times; index number** = number which shows the percentage rise of something over a period of time **Indexzahl, Indexziffer**
NOTE: plural is **indexes** or **indices**

◊ **indexation** *noun* linking of something to an index **Indexbindung, Indexierung; indexation of wage increases** = linking of wage increases to the percentage rise in the cost of living **Indexierung von Gehaltserhöhungen**
NOTE: no plural

◊ **index-linked** *adjective* which rises automatically by the percentage increase in the cost of living **indexgebunden, der Inflationsrate angeglichen;** *index-linked pensions; his pension is index-linked; index-linked government bonds*

> QUOTE the index of industrial production sank 0.2 per cent for the latest month after rising 0.3 per cent in March
> *Financial Times*
>
> QUOTE an analysis of the consumer price index for the first half of 1985 shows that the rate of inflation went down by 12.9 per cent
> *Business Times (Lagos)*

indicate

verb to show **(an)zeigen, hinweisen auf;** *the latest figures indicate a fall in the inflation rate; our sales for 1985 indicate a move from the home market to exports*

◊ **indicator** *noun* thing which indicates **Indikator; government economic indicators** = statistics which show how the country's economy is going to perform in the short or long term **staatliche Konjunkturindikatoren**

> QUOTE it reduces this month's growth in the key M3 indicator from about 19% to 12%
> *Sunday Times*
>
> QUOTE we may expect the US leading economic indicators for April to show faster economic growth
> *Australian Financial Review*
>
> QUOTE other indicators, such as high real interest rates, suggest that monetary conditions are extremely tight
> *Economist*

indirect

adjective not direct **indirekt, mittelbar; indirect expenses** *or* **costs** = costs which are not directly attached to the making of a product (such as cleaning, rent, administration) **Fertigungsgemeinkosten; indirect labour costs** = costs of paying workers who are not directly involved in making a product (such as secretaries, cleaners) **Lohngemeinkosten; indirect taxation** = taxes (such as sales tax) which are not paid direct to the government **indirekte Besteuerung;** *the government raises more money by indirect taxation than by direct*

individual

1 *noun* one single person **Einzelperson, Individuum;** *savings plan made to suit the requirements of the private individual*

2 *adjective* single *or* belonging to one person **einzeln, individuell;** *a pension plan designed to meet each person's individual requirements; we sell individual portions of ice cream; US* **Individual Retirement Account** = private pension plan, where persons can make contributions separate from a company pension plan; *entspricht* **Privataltersversorgung, steuerfreies Sparkonto**

inducement *noun* thing which helps to persuade someone to do something **Anreiz, Ansporn;** *they offered him a company car as an inducement to stay*

induction *noun* starting a new person in a new job **Einführung, Einweisung; induction courses** *or* **induction training** = courses to train people starting new jobs **Einführungskurse**

NOTE: no plural

industry *noun*

(a) all factories *or* companies *or* processes involved in the manufacturing of products **Industrie;** *all sectors of industry have shown rises in output;* **basic industry** = most important industry of a country (such as coal, steel, agriculture) **Schlüssel-, Grundstoffindustrie; a boom industry** *or* **a growth industry** = industry which is expanding rapidly **Wachstumsbranche; heavy industry** = industry which deals in heavy raw materials (such as coal) or makes large products (such as ships or engines) **Schwerindustrie; light industry** = industry making small products (such as clothes, books, calculators) **Leichtindustrie; primary industry** = industry dealing with basic raw materials (such as coal, wood, farm produce) **Rohstoffindustrie; secondary industry** = industry which uses basic raw materials to produce manufactured goods **verarbeitende Industrie; service industry** *or* **tertiary industry** = industry which does not produce raw materials or manufacture products but offers a service (such as banking, retailing, accountancy) **Dienstleistungsbranche**

(b) group of companies making the same type of product **Branche, Wirtschaftszweig;** *the aircraft industry; the building industry; the car industry; the food processing industry; the mining industry; the petroleum industry*

◇ **industrial**

1 *adjective* referring to manufacturing work **Industrie-, industriell; industrial accident** = accident which takes place at work **Betriebs-, Arbeitsunfall; to take industrial action** = to go on strike or go-slow **Arbeitskampfmaßnahmen ergreifen, in den Ausstand treten; industrial capacity** = amount of work which can be done in a factory or several factories **Fertigungskapazität; industrial centre** = large town with many industries **Industriezentrum;** *GB* **industrial court** = court which can decide in industrial disputes if both parties agree to ask it to judge between them **Schiedsgericht; industrial tribunal** = court which can decide in disputes over employment **Arbeitsgericht; industrial design** = design of products made by machines (such as cars, refrigerators) **Industriedesign; industrial disputes** = arguments between management and workers **Arbeitskampf; industrial espionage** = trying to find out the secrets of a competitor's work or products, usually by illegal means **Werks-, Wirtschaftsspionage; industrial estate** *or* **industrial park** = area of land near a town specially for factories and warehouses **Industriegebiet, Industriegelände; industrial expansion** = growth of industries in a country *or* a region **industrielle Expansion; industrial injuries** = injuries which happen to workers at work **Berufsschäden; industrial process** = process involved in manufacturing products in factories **Herstellungsprozeß; industrial relations** = relations between management and workers **Arbeitgeber-Arbeitnehmer-Beziehungen; good industrial relations** = situation where management and workers understand each others' problems and work together for the good of the company **gute Beziehungen zwischen Arbeitgebern und Arbeitnehmern; industrial training** = training of new workers to work in an industry **betriebliche Ausbildung; land zoned for light industrial use** = land where planning permission has been given to build small factories for light industry **für Leichtindustrie vorgesehenes Land**

2 *noun* **industrials** = shares in manufacturing companies **Industriepapiere, Industriewerte**

◇ **industrialist** *noun* owner *or* director of a factory **Industrieller**

◇ **industrialization** *noun* changing of an economy from being based on agriculture to industry **Industrialisierung**

NOTE: no plural

◇ **industrialize** *verb* to set up industries in a country which had none before **industrialisieren; industrialized societies** = countries which have many industries **Industriegesellschaft**

> QUOTE indications of renewed weakness in the US economy were contained in figures on industrial production for April
> *Financial Times*
>
> QUOTE central bank and finance ministry officials of the industrialized countries will continue work on the report
> *Wall Street Journal*
>
> QUOTE with the present overcapacity in the airline industry, discounting of tickets is widespread
> *Business Traveller*

inefficiency *noun* lack of efficiency **Ineffizienz, Inkompetenz, Unfähigkeit;** *the report criticized the inefficiency of the sales staff*

◇ **inefficient** *adjective* not efficient *or* not doing a job well **ineffizient, inkompetent, unfähig;** *an inefficient sales director*

inertia *noun* being lazy **Trägheit; inertia selling** = method of selling items by sending them when they have not been ordered and assuming that if the items are not returned, the person who has received them is willing to buy them **negative Option, Trägheitsverkauf**
NOTE: no plural

inexpensive *adjective* cheap *or* not expensive **preiswert, preisgünstig**

◇ **inexpensively** *adverb* without spending much money **preiswert, preisgünstig**

inferior *adjective* not as good as others **minderwertig, zweitklassig;** *inferior products or products of inferior quality*

inflate *verb*
(a) to inflate prices = to increase prices without any reason **Preise in die Höhe treiben;** *tourists don't want to pay inflated London prices*
(b) to inflate the economy = to make the economy more active by increasing the money supply **die Wirtschaft anheizen**

◇ **inflated** *adjective*
(a) inflated prices = prices which are increased without any reason **überhöhte Preise**
(b) inflated currency = currency which is too high in relation to other currencies **Inflationswährung**

◇ **inflation** *noun* situation where prices rise to keep up with increased production costs **Inflation; we have 15% inflation** *or* **inflation is running at 15%** = prices are 15% higher than at the same time last year **die Inflation beträgt 15%;** *to take measures to reduce inflation; high interest rates tend to increase inflation;* **rate of inflation** *or* **inflation rate** = percentage increase in prices over a twelve-month period **Inflationsrate; galloping inflation** *or* **runaway inflation** = very rapid inflation which it is almost impossible to reduce **galoppierende Inflation; spiralling inflation** = inflation where price rises make workers ask for higher wages which then increase prices again **eine sich spiralartig entwickelnde Inflation**
NOTE: no plural

◇ **inflationary** *adjective* which tends to increase inflation **Inflations-, inflatorisch, inflationsbedingt;** *inflationary trends in the economy;* **the economy is in an inflationary spiral** = in a situation where price rises encourage higher wage demands which in turn make prices rise **die Wirtschaft befindet sich in einer Inflationsspirale; anti-inflationary measures** = measures to reduce inflation **Maßnahmen zur Inflationsbekämpfung**

> QUOTE the decision by the government to tighten monetary policy will push the annual inflation rate above the year's previous high
> *Financial Times*
>
> QUOTE when you invest to get a return, you want a "real" return -above the inflation rate
> *Investors Chronicle*

inflow *noun* flowing in **Zustrom; inflow of capital into the country** = capital which is coming into a country in order to be invested **Kapitalzufluß in das Land**

> QUOTE the dollar is strong because of capital inflows rather than weak because of the trade deficit
> *Duns Business Month*

influence
1 *noun* effect which is had on someone *or* something **Einfluß, Auswirkung;** *the price of oil has a marked influence on the price of manufactured goods; we are suffering from the influence of a high exchange rate*
2 *verb* to have an effect on someone *or* something **beeinflussen;** *the board was influenced in its decision by the memo from the managers; the price of oil has influenced the price of manufactured goods; high inflation is influencing our profitability*
NOTE: you influence someone **to do** something

influx *noun* rushing in **Zufluß, Zufuhr, Zustrom;** *an influx of foreign currency into the country; an influx of cheap labour into the cities*
NOTE: plural is **influxes**

> QUOTE the retail sector will also benefit from the expected influx of tourists
> *Australian Financial Review*

inform *verb* to tell someone officially **informieren, mitteilen, benachrichtigen,**

unterrichten, in Kenntnis setzen; *I regret to inform you that your tender was not acceptable; we are pleased to inform you that your offer has been accepted; we have been informed by the Department of Trade that new tariffs are coming into force*

◊ **information** *noun*

(a) details which explain something **Information, Informationsmaterial, Unterlagen;** *please send me information on or about holidays in the USA; have you any information on or about deposit accounts? I enclose this leaflet for your information; to disclose a piece of information; to answer a request for information; for further information, please write to Department 27;* **disclosure of confidential information** = telling someone information which should be secret **Enthüllung/Offenlegung vertraulicher Informationen; flight information** = information about flight times **Fluginformation; tourist information** = information for tourists **Fremdenverkehrsbüro**

(b) information technology = working with computer data **Informationstechnologie; information retrieval** = storing and then finding data in a computer **Datenabruf, Wiederauffinden von Information**

(c) information bureau *or* **information office** = office which gives information to tourists *or* visitors **Fremdenverkehrsamt; Auskunft, Information; information officer** = person whose job is to give information about a company *or* an organization *or* a government department to the public **Pressereferent**

NOTE: no plural; for one item say **a piece of information**

infrastructure *noun*

(a) basic structure **Infra-, Grundstruktur; the company's infrastructure** = how the company is organized **die Grundstruktur des Unternehmens**

(b) basic services **Infrastruktur; a country's infrastructure** = the road and rail systems, education and legal systems, etc. **die Infrastruktur eines Landes**

infringe *verb* to break a law *or* a right **verletzen, übertreten; to infringe a copyright** = to copy a copyright text illegally **das Urheberrecht verletzen; to infringe a patent** = to make a product which works in the same way as a patented product and not pay a royalty to the patent holder **das Patentrecht verletzen**

◊ **infringement** *noun* breaking a law *or* a right **Verletzung, Übertretung; infringement of copyright** *or* **copyright infringement** = act of illegally copying a work which is in copyright **Verstoß gegen das Urheberrecht;** *infringement of patent or patent infringement*

ingot *noun* bar of gold or silver **Barren**

inherit *verb* to get something from a person who has died **erben;** *when her father died she inherited the shop; he inherited £10,000 from his grandfather*

◊ **inheritance** *noun* property which is received from a dead person **Erbe, Erbschaft**

NOTE: no plural

in-house *adverb & adjective* working inside a company's building **betriebsintern, innerbetrieblich;** *the in-house staff; we do all our data processing in-house;* **in-house training** = training given to staff at their place of work **innerbetriebliche Ausbildung**

initial

1 *adjective* first *or* starting **anfänglich, Anfangs-; initial capital** = capital which is used to start a business **Start-, Gründungskapital;** *he started the business with an initial expenditure or initial investment of £500;* **initial sales** = first sales of a new product **Anfangsverkauf;** *the initial response to the TV advertising has been very good*

2 *noun* **initials** = first letters of the words in a name **Initialien, Anfangsbuchstaben;** *what do the initials IMF stand for? the chairman wrote his initials by each alteration in the contract he was signing*

3 *verb* to write your initials on a document to show you have read it and approved **abzeichnen, paraphieren;** *to initial an amendment to a contract; please initial the agreement at the place marked with an X*

> QUOTE the founding group has subscribed NKr 14.5m of the initial NKr 30m share capital
> *Financial Times*
>
> QUOTE career prospects are excellent for someone with potential, and initial salary is negotiable around $45,000 per annum
> *Australian Financial Review*

initiate *verb* to start **einleiten, in Gang setzen;** *to initiate discussions*

◊ **initiative** *noun* decision to start something **Initiative; to take the initiative** = to decide to do something **die Initiative ergreifen; to follow up an initiative** = to take action once someone else has decided to do something **eine Initiative aufgreifen**

inject *verb* **to inject capital into a business** = to put money into a business **Kapital in ein Unternehmen pumpen**

◊ **injection** *noun* **a capital injection of £100,000** *or* **an injection of £100,000 capital**

= putting £100,000 into an existing business **eine Kapitalzuführung von £100.000**

injunction *noun* court order telling someone not to do something **einstweilige Verfügung;** *he got an injunction preventing the company from selling his car; the company applied for an injunction to stop their rival from marketing a similar product*

injure *verb* to hurt (someone) **verletzen;** *two workers were injured in the fire*

◇ **injured party** *noun* party in a court case which has been harmed by another party **der/die Geschädigte, geschädigte Partei**

◇ **injury** *noun* hurt caused to a person **Verletzung; injury benefit** = money paid to a worker who has been hurt at work **Unfallgeld; Versehrtenrente; industrial injuries** = injuries caused to workers at work **Berufsschäden; Betriebsunfälle**

inking pad *noun* small pad with ink on it, used for putting ink on a rubber stamp **Stempelkissen**

inland *adjective*
(a) inside a country **Binnen-, Inlands-; inland postage** = postage for a letter to another part of the country **Inlandsporto; inland freight charges** = charges for carrying goods from one part of the country to another **Inlandsfrachtkosten**
(b) *GB* **the Inland Revenue** = government department dealing with tax **Finanzamt, Finanzverwaltung;** *he received a letter from the Inland Revenue*

innovate *verb* to bring in new ideas *or* new methods **Neuerungen einführen**

◇ **innovation** *noun* new idea *or* new method *or* new product **Neueinführung, Neuheit**

◇ **innovative** *adjective* (person or thing) which is new and makes changes **innovatorisch, progressiv**

◇ **innovator** *noun* person who brings in new ideas and methods **Neuerer**

> QUOTE small innovative companies in IT have been hampered for lack of funds
> *Sunday Times*

input
1 *noun* **input of information** *or* **computer input** = data fed into a computer **Dateneingabe; input lead** = lead for connecting the electric current to the machine **Stromzufuhrkabel; input tax** = VAT paid on goods or services which a company buys **Vorsteuer**
2 *verb* **to input information** = to put data into a computer **Daten eingeben**
NOTE: **inputting - inputted**

inquire *verb* to ask questions about something **sich erkundigen, Erkundigungen einziehen;** *he inquired if anything was wrong; she inquired about the mortgage rate;* **"inquire within"** = ask for more details inside the office *or* shop **"Näheres im Geschäft"**

◇ **inquire into** *verb* to investigate *or* to try to find out about something **Nachforschungen anstellen;** *we are inquiring into the background of the new supplier*

◇ **inquiry** *noun* official question **An-, Nachfrage;** *I refer to your inquiry of May 25th; all inquiries should be addressed to this department*

insert
1 *noun* thing which is put inside something **Beilage; an insert in a magazine mailing** *or* **a magazine insert** = advertising sheet put into a magazine when it is mailed **Werbebeilage**
2 *verb* to put something in **beilegen, hineinstecken; einfügen;** *to insert a clause into a contract; to insert a publicity piece into a magazine mailing*

inside
1 *adjective & adverb* in, especially in a company's office or building **Innen-, betriebsintern; innen;** *we do all our design work inside;* **inside worker** = worker who works in the office or factory (not in the open air, not a salesman) **Angestellter im Innendienst**
2 *preposition* in **in, innerhalb;** *there was nothing inside the container; we have a contact inside our rival's production department who gives us very useful information*

◇ **insider** *noun* person who works in an organization and therefore knows its secrets **Insider; insider dealings** *or* **insider trading** = illegal buying or selling of shares by staff of a company who have secret information about the company's plans **Insiderhandel**

insolvent *adjective* not able to pay debts **zahlungsunfähig, insolvent; he was declared insolvent** = he was officially stated to be insolvent **er wurde zahlungsunfähig erklärt**

◇ **insolvency** *noun* not being able to pay debts **Zahlungsunfähigkeit, Insolvenz; he was in a state of insolvency** = he could not pay his debts **er war zahlungsunfähig**
NOTE: no plural

inspect *verb* to examine in detail **prüfen, kontrollieren, untersuchen;** *to inspect a machine or an installation; to inspect the accounts;* **to inspect products for defects** = to look at products in detail to see if they have any defects **Produkte auf Mängel prüfen**

◇ **inspection** *noun* close examination of something **Prüfung, Kontrolle, Untersuchung, Überprüfung;** *to make an inspection or to carry out an inspection of a machine or an installation; inspection of a product for defects;* **to carry out a tour of inspection** = to visit various places *or* offices *or* factories to inspect them **eine Inspektionstour machen; to issue an inspection order** = to order an official inspection **eine Kontrolle anordnen; inspection stamp** = stamp placed on something to show it has been inspected **Kontrollsiegel**

◇ **inspector** *noun* official who inspects **Kontrolleur/-in, Prüfer/-in; inspector of factories** *or* **factory inspector** = government official who inspects factories to see if they are safely run **Gewerbeaufsichtsbeamter; inspector of taxes** *or* **tax inspector** = official of the Inland Revenue who examines tax returns and decides how much tax people should pay **Leiter des Finanzamtes; Steuerprüfer; inspector of weights and measures** = government official who inspects weighing machines and goods sold in shops to see if the quantities and weights are correct **Eichmeister**

◇ **inspectorate** *noun* all inspectors; **the factory inspectorate = Aufsichtsbehörde** all inspectors of factories **Gewerbeaufsichtsamt**

inst = INSTANT; **your letter of the 6th inst** = your letter of the 6th of this month **Ihr Brief vom 6.d.M.**

instability *noun* being unstable *or* moving up and down **Unbeständigkeit, Veränderlichkeit, Instabilität; period of instability in the money markets** = period when currencies fluctuate rapidly **Zeit der Unsicherheit auf dem Geldmarkt**
NOTE: no plural

install *verb* to put (a machine) into an office *or* into a factory **installieren, aufstellen;** *to install new machinery; to install a new data processing system*

◇ **installation** *noun*
(a) machines, equipment and buildings **Anlage;** *harbour installations; the fire seriously damaged the oil installations*
(b) putting new machines into an office *or* a factory **Installation, Aufstellen, Einbau;** *to supervise the installation of new equipment*

◇ **instalment** *or US* **installment** *noun* part of a payment which is paid regularly until the total amount is paid **Rate;** *the first instalment is payable on signature of the agreement;* **the final instalment is now due** = the last of a series of payments should be paid now **die letzte Rate ist fällig; to pay £25 down and monthly instalments of £20** = to pay a first payment of £25 and the rest in payments of £20 each month **£25 anbezahlen und den Rest in Monatsraten von £20 bezahlen; to miss an instalment** = not to pay an instalment at the right time **mit einer Rate in Rückstand geraten**

◇ **installment plan** *noun US* system of buying something by paying a sum regularly each month **Ratenzahlung, Teilzahlungssystem;** *to buy a car on the installment plan*
NOTE: GB English is **hire purchase**

instance *noun* particular example *or* case **Fall;** *in this instance we will overlook the delay*

instant *adjective*
(a) this month **dieses Monats; our letter of the 6th instant** = our letter of the 6th of this current month **unser Brief vom 6. dieses Monats**
(b) immediately available **sofort, unverzüglich;** *instant credit*

institute
1 *noun* official organization **Institut; research institute** = organization set up to do research **Forschungsinstitut**
2 *verb* to start **einleiten, einrichten, gründen;** *to institute proceedings against someone*

◇ **institution** *noun* organization *or* society set up for a particular purpose **Institut, Gesellschaft; financial institution** = bank *or* investment trust *or* insurance company whose work involves lending or investing large sums of money **Finanz-, Kreditinstitut**

◇ **institutional** *adjective* referring to an institution **institutionell, Instituts-; institutional buying** *or* **selling** = buying or selling shares by financial institutions **Effektenkauf od Effektenverkauf von Finanzinstituten; institutional investors** = financial institutions who invest money in securities **Kapitalsammelstellen**

> QUOTE during the 1970s commercial property was regarded by big institutional investors as an alternative to equities
> *Investors Chronicle*

instruct *verb*
(a) to give an order to someone **anweisen, beauftragen; to instruct someone to do something** = to tell someone officially to do something **jdm Anweisung geben, etwas zu**

tun; *he instructed the credit controller to take action*
(b) to instruct a solicitor = to give orders to a solicitor to start legal proceedings on your behalf **einen Anwalt beauftragen**

◇ **instruction** *noun* order which tells what should be done *or* how something is to be used **Anweisung, Auftrag;** *he gave instructions to his stockbroker to sell the shares immediately;* **to await instructions** = to wait for someone to tell you what to do **auf Anweisungen warten; to issue instructions** = to tell everyone what to do **Anweisungen geben; in accordance with** *or* **according to instructions** = as the instructions show **in Übereinstimmung mit, vorschriftsmäßig, auftragsgemäß; failing instructions to the contrary** = unless someone tells you to do the opposite **falls nichts Gegenteiliges angewiesen; forwarding instructions** *or* **shipping instructions** = details of how goods are to be shipped and delivered **Versandvorschriften, Versandanweisungen**

◇ **instructor** *noun* person who shows how something is to be done **Ausbilder/-in, Lehrer/-in**

instrument *noun*

(a) tool *or* piece of equipment **Gerät, Apparat, Instrument;** *the technician brought instruments to measure the output of electricity*
(b) legal document **Urkunde, Dokument; negotiable instrument** = document (such as a bill of exchange *or* a cheque) which can be exchanged for cash **übertragbares/begebbares Wertpapier**

insure *verb*

insure *verb* to have a contract with a company where, if regular small payments are made, the company will pay compensation for loss, damage, injury or death **versichern, Versicherung abschließen;** *to insure a house against fire; to insure someone's life; he was insured for £100,000; to insure baggage against loss; to insure against bad weather; to insure against loss of earnings;* **the life insured** = the person whose life is covered by a life assurance **der/die Versicherte (in einer Lebensversicherung); the sum insured** = the largest amount of money that an insurer will pay under an insurance **die Versicherungssumme**

◇ **insurable** *adjective* which can be insured **versicherungsfähig, versicherbar**

◇ **insurance** *noun*
(a) agreement that in return for regular small payments, a company will pay compensation for loss, damage, injury or death **Versicherung; to take out an insurance against fire** = to pay a premium, so that if a fire happens, compensation will be paid **eine Feuerversicherung abschließen; to take out an insurance on the house** = to pay a premium, so that if the house is damaged compensation will be paid **eine Gebäudeversicherung abschließen; the damage is covered by the insurance** = the insurance company will pay for the damage **der Schaden ist durch die Versicherung abgedeckt;** *repairs will be paid for by the insurance;* **to pay the insurance on a car** = to pay premiums to insure a car **die Versicherung(sprämie) für ein Auto bezahlen**
(b) accident insurance = insurance which will pay if an accident takes place **Unfallversicherung; car insurance** *or* **motor insurance** = insuring a car, the driver and passengers in case of accident **Kraftfahrzeugversicherung; comprehensive insurance** = insurance which covers against all risks which are likely to happen **kombinierte Haftpflicht- und Vollkaskoversicherung; endowment insurance** = situation where a sum of money is paid to the insured person on a certain date or to his heir if he dies before that date **Versicherung auf den Erlebens- und Todesfall; fire insurance** = insurance against damage by fire **Feuerversicherung; house insurance** = insuring a house and its contents against damage **Haus- und Hausratsversicherung; life insurance** = situation which pays a sum of money when someone dies **Lebensversicherung; medical insurance** = insurance which pays the cost of medical treatment, especially when travelling abroad **Krankenversicherung; term insurance** = life insurance which covers a person's life for a fixed period of time **zeitlich begrenzte Lebensversicherung; third-party insurance** = insurance which pays compensation if someone who is not the insured person incurs loss or injury **Haftpflichtversicherung; whole-life insurance** = insurance where the insured person pays premiums for all his life and the insurance company pays a sum when he dies **Lebensversicherung auf den Todesfall, Risikoversicherung**
(c) insurance agent *or* **insurance broker** = person who arranges insurance for clients **Versicherungsvertreter, Versicherungsagent; insurance claim** = asking an insurance company to pay for damage **Versicherungs-, Schadensanspruch; insurance company** = company whose business is to receive payments and pay compensation for loss or damage **Versicherungsgesellschaft; insurance contract** = agreement by an insurance company to insure **Versicherungsvertrag; insurance cover** = protection guaranteed by an insurance policy **Versicherungsschutz; insurance policy** = document which shows the conditions of an insurance **Versicherungspolice; insurance premium** = payment made by the insured

person to the insurer **Versicherungsbeitrag, Versicherungsprämie**
(d) *GB* **National Insurance** = state insurance, organized by the government, which pays for medical care, hospitals, unemployment benefits, etc. **Sozialversicherung; National Insurance contributions** = money paid by a worker and the company each month to the National Insurance **Sozialversicherungsbeiträge**
◊ **insurer** *noun* company which insures **Versicherer, Versicherungsträger**
NOTE: no plural for (b), (c) and (d). Note also that for life insurance, GB English prefers to use **assurance, assure, assurer**

intangible *adjective* which cannot be touched **immateriell, nicht greifbar; intangible assets** = assets which have a value, but which cannot be seen (such as goodwill, patent or a trademark) **immaterielle Vermögenswerte**

integrate *verb* to link things together to form one whole group **zusammenfassen, zusammenschließen, integrieren**
◊ **integration** *noun* bringing several businesses together under a central control **Zusammenfassung, Zusammenschluß, Integration; horizontal integration** = joining similar companies *or* taking over a company in the same line of business as yourself **horizontale Integration; vertical integration** = joining business together which deal with different stages in the production or sale of a product **vertikale Integration**

intend *verb* to plan *or* to expect to do something **beabsichtigen, vorhaben;** *the company intends to open an office in New York next year; we intend to offer jobs to 250 unemployed young people*

intensive *adjective* **intensive farming** = farming small areas of expensive land, using machines and fertilizers to obtain high crops **intensive Landwirtschaft; capital-intensive industry** = industry which needs a large amount of capital investment in plant to make it work **kapitalintensiver Industriezweig; labour-intensive industry** = industry which needs large numbers of workers *or* where labour costs are high in relation to turnover **arbeitsintensiver Industriezweig**

intent *noun* what is planned **Absicht; letter of intent** = letter which states what a company intends to do if something happens **Absichtserklärung**

inter- *prefix* between **Zwischen-, zwischen-; inter-bank loan** = loan from one bank to another **Bank-an-Bank-Kredit; the inter-city rail services are good** = train services between cities are good **die Intercity-Verbindungen sind gut; inter-company dealings** = dealings between two companies in the same group **konzerninterne/zwischenbetriebliche Abmachungen; inter-company comparisons** = comparing the results of one company with those of another in the same product area **Vergleiche zwischen Unternehmen aus dem gleichen Bereich**

interest
1 *noun*
(a) special attention **Interesse;** *the MD takes no interest in the staff club; the buyers showed a lot of interest in our new product range*
(b) payment made by a borrower for the use of money, calculated as a percentage of the capital borrowed **Zinsen; simple interest** = interest calculated on the capital only, and not added to it **einfache Zinsen; compound interest** = interest which is added to the capital and then earns interest itself **Zinseszins; accrual of interest** = automatic addition of interest to capital **Auflaufen von Zinsen, Zinsthesaurierung; accrued interest** = interest which is accumulating and is due for payment at a later date **aufgelaufene Zinsen; back interest** = interest which has not yet been paid **Zinsrückstand; fixed interest** = interest which is paid at a set rate **feste Zinsen; high** *or* **low interest** = interest at a high or low percentage **hohe Zinsen; niedrige Zinsen; interest charges** = cost of paying interest **Zinsbelastung, Sollzinsen; interest rate** *or* **rate of interest** = percentage charge for borrowing money **Zinssatz; interest-free credit** *or* **loan** = credit or loan where no interest is paid by the borrower **zinsfreies Darlehen;** *the company gives its staff interest-free loans*
(c) money paid as income on investments or loans **Zinsen, Kapitalertrag;** *the bank pays 10% interest on deposits; to receive interest at 5%; the loan pays 5% interest; deposit which yields or gives or produces or bears 5% interest; account which earns interest at 10% or which earns 10% interest;* **interest-bearing deposits** = deposits which produce interest **zinstragende Spareinlagen**
(d) money invested in a company *or* financial share in a company **Beteiligung, Anteil; beneficial interest** = situation where someone is allowed to occupy or receive rent from a house without owning it **Nießbrauch; he has a controlling interest in the company** = he owns more than 50% of the shares and so can direct how the

company is run **er hat eine Mehrheitsbeteiligung an dem Unternehmen; life interest** = situation where someone benefits from a property as long as he is alive **Nutzungsrecht auf Lebensdauer; majority interest** *or* **minority interest** = situation where someone owns a majority *or* a minority of shares in a company **Mehrheitsbeteiligung; Minderheitsbeteiligung;** *he has a majority interest in a supermarket chain;* **to acquire a substantial interest in the company** = to buy a large number of shares in a company **einen beträchtlichen Anteil an einem Unternehmen erwerben; to declare an interest** = to state in public that you own shares in a company **seine Beteiligungen offenlegen**

NOTE: no plural for (a), (b) and (c)

2 *verb* to attract someone's attention **interessieren, Interesse hervorrufen;** *he tried to interest several companies in his new invention;* **interested in** = paying attention to **sich interessieren für, Interesse haben an;** *the managing director is interested only in increasing profitability;* **interested party** = person *or* company with a financial interest in a company **Beteiligter**

◇ **interesting** *adjective* which attracts attention **interessant;** *they made us a very interesting offer for the factory*

> QUOTE since last summer American interest rates have dropped by between three and four percentage points
> *Sunday Times*
>
> QUOTE a lot of money is said to be tied up in sterling because of the interest-rate differential between US and British rates
> *Australian Financial Review*

interface

1 *noun* link between two different computer systems or pieces of hardware **Schnittstelle, Interface, Anschlußstelle**

2 *verb* to meet and act with **anschließen, verbinden;** *the office micros interface with the mainframe computer at head office*

interfere *verb* to get involved *or* to try to change something which is not your concern **sich einmischen, eingreifen, intervenieren**

◇ **interference** *noun* the act of interfering **Einmischung, Eingreifen, Intervention;** *the sales department complained of continual interference from the accounts department*

interim *noun* **interim dividend** = dividend paid at the end of a half-year **Abschlags-, Zwischendividende; interim payment** = payment of part of a dividend **Abschlags-, Interimszahlung; interim report** = report given at the end of a half-year **Halbjahres-, Zwischenbericht; in the interim** = meanwhile *or* for the time being **einstweilig, in der Zwischenzeit**

> QUOTE the company plans to keep its annual dividend unchanged at Y7.5 per share, which includes a Y3.75 interim payout
> *Financial Times*

intermediary *noun* person who is the link between parties who do not agree or who are negotiating **Vermittler/-in;** *he refused to act as an intermediary between the two directors*

internal *adjective*

(a) inside a company **intern, innerbetrieblich; we decided to make an internal appointment** = we decided to appoint an existing member of staff to the post, and not bring someone in from outside the company **wir beschlossen, die Stelle intern zu besetzen; internal audit** = audit carried out by a department within the company **interne Revision; internal audit department** *or* **internal auditor** = department *or* member of staff who audits the accounts of the company he works for **betriebsinterne Revision; betriebsinterner Revisor; internal telephone** = telephone which is linked to other phones in an office **Haustelefon**

(b) inside a country **Inlands-, Binnen-, Innen-; an internal flight** = flight to a town inside the same country **Inlandsflug;** *US* **Internal Revenue Service** = government department which deals with tax **Finanzamt, Finanzverwaltung; internal trade** = trade between various parts of a country **Binnenhandel**

◇ **internally** *adverb* inside a company **intern, innerbetrieblich;** *the job was advertised internally*

international *adjective* working between countries **international; international call** = telephone call to another country **Auslandsgespräch; international dialling code** = number used to make a telephone call to another country **Vorwahl, internationale Kennzahl; International Labour Organization** = section of the United Nations, an organization which tries to improve working conditions and workers' pay in member countries **Internationale Arbeitsorganisation; international law** = laws governing relations between countries **internationales Recht, Völkerrecht; the International Monetary Fund** = (part of the United Nations) a type of bank which helps member states in financial difficulties, gives financial advice to members and encourages world trade **internationaler Währungsfonds, Weltwährungsfonds; international trade** = trade between different countries **Welthandel**

interpret *verb* to translate what someone has said into another language **dolmetschen;** *my assistant knows Greek, so he will interpret for us*

◇ **interpreter** *noun* person who translates what someone has said into another language **Dolmetscher/-in;** *my secretary will act as interpreter*

intervene *verb* to try to make a change in a system **intervenieren, sich einmischen; to intervene in a dispute** = to try to settle a dispute **bei einem Streit vermitteln**

◇ **intervention** *noun* acting to make a change in a system **Intervention, Einmischung, Eingriff;** *the government's intervention in the foreign exchange markets; the central bank's intervention in the banking crisis; the government's intervention in the labour dispute;* **intervention price** = price at which the EEC will buy farm produce which farmers cannot sell, in order to store it **Interventionspreis, garantierter Mindestpreis**

interview
1 *noun*
(a) talking to a person who is applying for a job **Vorstellungsgespräch;** *we called six people for interview; I have an interview next week* or *I am going for an interview next week*
(b) asking a person questions as part of an opinion poll **Befragung, Interview**
2 *verb* to talk to a person applying for a job to see if he is suitable **ein Vorstellungsgespräch führen;** *we interviewed ten candidates, but did not find anyone suitable*

◇ **interviewee** *noun* person who is being interviewed **Kandidat/-in, Befragter, Interviewter**

◇ **interviewer** *noun* person who is conducting the interview **Gesprächsleiter; Interviewer**

inter vivos *phrase* **gift inter vivos** = gift given to another living person **Schenkung zu Lebzeiten**

intestate *adjective* **to die intestate** = to die without having made a will **ohne Hinterlassung eines Testaments sterben**

in transit *adverb* **goods in transit** = goods being transported **Transitgüter**

in tray *noun* basket on a desk for letters or memos which have been received and are waiting to be dealt with **Eingänge**

introduce *verb* to make someone get to know a new person or thing **vorstellen, einführen; to introduce a client** = to bring in a new client and make him known to someone **einen Kunden/Klienten einführen; to introduce a new product on the market** = to produce a new product and launch it on the market **ein neues Produkt auf den Markt bringen**

◇ **introduction** *noun*
(a) letter making someone get to know another person **Einführungsbrief;** *I'll give you an introduction to the MD - he is an old friend of mine*
(b) bringing into use **Einführung; the introduction of new technology** = putting new machines (usually computers) into a business or industry **die Einführung neuer Technologien**

◇ **introductory** *adjective* **introductory offer** = special price offered on a new product to attract customers **Einführungspreis**

invalid *adjective* not valid or not legal **ungültig, nichtig, rechtsunwirksam;** *permit that is invalid; claim which has been declared invalid*

◇ **invalidate** *verb* to make something invalid **für ungültig erklären;** *because the company has been taken over, the contract has been invalidated*

◇ **invalidation** *noun* making invalid **Aufhebung, Ungültigkeitserklärung, Annullierung**

◇ **invalidity** *noun* being invalid **Ungültigkeit, Nichtigkeit, Rechtsungültigkeit;** *the invalidity of the contract*

invent *verb* to make something which has never been made before **erfinden;** *she invented a new type of computer terminal; who invented shorthand? the chief accountant has invented a new system of customer filing*

◇ **invention** *noun* thing which has been invented **Erfindung;** *he tried to sell his latest invention to a US car manufacturer*

◇ **inventor** *noun* person who invents something **Erfinder/-in;** *he is the inventor of the all-plastic car*

inventory
1 *noun*
(a) stock or goods in a warehouse or shop **Lagerbestände, Warenbestände;** *to carry a high inventory; to aim to reduce inventory;* **inventory control** = system of checking that there is not too much stock in a warehouse, but just enough to meet requirements **Bestandskontrolle**
(b) list of the contents of a house for sale, of an office for rent, etc. **Inventarverzeichnis,**

Inventarliste; *to draw up an inventory of fixtures;* **to agree the inventory** = to agree that the inventory is correct **die Inventarliste bestätigen**
2 *verb* to make a list of stock or contents **inventarisieren, Inventar/Bestände aufnehmen**

> QUOTE a warehouse needs to tie up less capital in inventory and with its huge volume spreads out costs over bigger sales
> *Duns Business Month*

invest *verb*

(a) to put money into shares, bonds, a building society, hoping that it will produce interest and increase in value **investieren, (Geld) anlegen;** *he invested all his money in an engineering business; she was advised to invest in real estate or in government bonds;* **to invest abroad** = to put money into shares *or* bonds in overseas countries **Kapital/Geld im Ausland anlegen**
(b) to spend money on something which you believe will be useful **investieren;** *to invest money in new machinery; to invest capital in a new factory*

◊ **investment** *noun*
(a) placing of money so that it will increase in value and produce interest **Investition, Kapital-, Vermögensanlage;** *they called for more government investment in new industries; investment in real estate; to make investments in oil companies;* **return on investment** = interest or dividends shown as a percentage of the money invested **Kapitalrendite, Ertrag aus investiertem Kapital**
(b) shares, bonds, deposits bought with invested money **Wertpapiere; long-term investment** *or* **short-term investment** = shares, etc., which are likely to increase in value over a long or short period **langfristige Anlage; kurzfristige Anlage; safe investment** = shares, etc. which are not likely to fall in value **sichere Kapitalanlage; blue-chip investments** = risk-free shares of good companies **erstklassige Effekten, Spitzenanlagen; he is trying to protect his investments** = he is trying to make sure that the money he has invested is not lost **er versucht, seine Investitionen vor Verlusten zu bewahren**
(c) investment adviser = person who advises people on what investments to make **Anlageberater; investment company** *or* **investment trust** = company whose shares can be bought on the Stock Exchange, and whose business is to make money by buying and selling stocks and shares **Kapitalanlagegesellschaft; Investmenttrust; investment grant** = government grant to a company to help it to invest in new machinery **Investitionszuschuß, Investitionsbeihilfe; investment income** = income (such as interest and dividends) from investments **Kapitaleinkünfte, Kapitalerträge**

◊ **investor** *noun* person who invests money **Investor, Kapitalanleger; the small investor** *or* **the private investor** = person with a small sum of money to invest **Kleinanleger; the institutional investor** = organization (like a pension fund or insurance company) with large sums of money to invest **Kapitalsammelstelle**

> QUOTE we have substantial venture capital to invest in good projects
> *Times*
>
> QUOTE investment trusts, like unit trusts, consist of portfolios of shares and therefore provide a spread of investments
> *Investors Chronicle*
>
> QUOTE investment companies took the view that prices had reached rock bottom and could only go up
> *Lloyd's List*

investigate *verb* to examine something which may be wrong **untersuchen, überprüfen, ermitteln, einer Sache nachgehen**

◊ **investigation** *noun* examination to find out what is wrong **Untersuchung, Überprüfung;** *to conduct an investigation into irregularities in share dealings*

◊ **investigator** *noun* person who investigates **Untersuchungs-, Ermittlungsbeamter, Rechercheur;** *government investigator*

invisible

1 *adjective* **invisible assets** = assets which have a value but which cannot be seen (such as goodwill or patents) **unsichtbare Vermögenswerte; invisible earnings** = foreign currency earned by a country by providing services, not selling goods **unsichtbare Einkünfte, Einkünfte aus unsichtbaren Leistungen; invisible imports** *or* **exports** = services which are paid for in foreign currency or earn foreign currency without actually selling a product (such as banking or tourism) **unsichtbare Einfuhren; unsichtbare Ausfuhren**
2 *plural noun* **invisibles** = invisible imports and exports **unsichtbare Ein- und Ausfuhren**

invite *verb* to ask someone to do something *or* to ask for something **auffordern;** *to invite someone to an interview; to invite someone to join the board; to invite shareholders to subscribe a new issue; to invite tenders for a contract*

◊ **invitation** *noun* asking someone to do something **Aufforderung;** *to issue an invitation to someone to join the board; invitation to tender for a contract; invitation to subscribe a new issue*

invoice
1 *noun*
(a) note asking for payment for goods or services supplied **Rechnung;** *your invoice dated November 10th; they sent in their invoice six weeks late; to make out an invoice for £250; to settle or to pay an invoice;* **the total is payable within thirty days of invoice** = the total sum has to be paid within thirty days of the date on the invoice **der volle Betrag ist innerhalb von dreißig Tagen nach Rechnungsdatum zahlbar; VAT invoice** = invoice which includes VAT **Mehrwertsteuerrechnung**
(b) invoice clerk = office worker who deals with invoices **Fakturist/-in; invoice price** = price as given on an invoice (including discount and VAT) **Rechnungspreis; total invoice value** = total amount on an invoice, including transport, VAT, etc. **voller Rechnungsbetrag**
2 *verb* to send an invoice to someone **Rechnung ausstellen, fakturieren;** *to invoice a customer;* **we invoiced you on November 10th** = we sent you the invoice on November 10th **wir stellten Ihre Rechnung zum 10. November aus**

◇ **invoicing** *noun* sending of an invoice **Abrechnung, Rechnungsausstellung;** *our invoicing is done by the computer;* **invoicing department** = department in a company which deals with preparing and sending invoices **Rechnungsabteilung; invoicing in triplicate** = preparing three copies of invoices **Rechnungsausstellung in dreifacher Ausfertigung; VAT invoicing** = sending of an invoice including VAT **Rechnungsausstellung inklusive Mehrwertsteuer**
NOTE: no plural

inward *adjective* towards the home country **Binnen-, Inlands-; inward bill** = bill of lading for goods arriving in a country **Importkonnossement; inward mission** = visit to your home country by a group of foreign businessmen **Auslandsdelegation**

IOU *noun* = I OWE YOU signed document promising that you will pay back money borrowed **Schuldschein;** *to pay a pile of IOUs*

IRA *US* = INDIVIDUAL RETIREMENT ACCOUNT

irrecoverable *adjective* which cannot be recovered **nicht einziehbar; irrecoverable debt** = debt which will never be paid **uneinbringliche Forderung**

irredeemable *adjective* which cannot be redeemed **nicht einlösbar; irredeemable bond** = bond which has no date of maturity and which therefore provides interest but can never be redeemed at full value **unkündbare/untilgbare Anleihe**

irregular *adjective* not correct *or* not done in the correct way **vorschriftswidrig, nicht ordnungsgemäß, unstatthaft;** *irregular documentation; this procedure is highly irregular*
◇ **irregularity** *noun*
(a) not being regular *or* not being on time **Unregelmäßigkeit;** *the irregularity of the postal deliveries*
(b) irregularities = things which are not done in the correct way and which are possibly illegal **Verstöße, Vorschriftswidrigkeiten, Vergehen;** *to investigate irregularities in the share dealings*

irrevocable *adjective* which cannot be changed **unwiderruflich; irrevocable acceptance** = acceptance which cannot be withdrawn **unwiderrufliche Annahme; irrevocable letter of credit** = letter of credit which cannot be cancelled or changed **unwiderrufliches Akkreditiv**

IRS *US* = INTERNAL REVENUE SERVICE

issue
1 *noun* giving out new shares **Emission, Ausgabe; bonus issue** *or* **scrip issue** = new shares given free to shareholders **Ausgabe von Gratisaktien; issue of debentures** *or* **debenture issue** = borrowing money by giving lenders debentures **Ausgabe von Schuldverschreibungen; issue of new shares** *or* **share issue** = selling new shares in a company to the public **Aktienausgabe, Emission neuer Aktien; rights issue** = giving shareholders the right to buy more shares at a lower price **Bezugsrechtsemission; new issues department** = section of a bank which deals with issues of new shares in companies **Emissionsabteilung; issue price** = price of shares when they are offered for sale for the first time **Emissions-, Ausgabekurs**
2 *verb* to put out *or* to give out **ausstellen, herausgeben, veröffentlichen, ausgeben, emittieren;** *to issue a letter of credit; to issue shares in a new company; to issue a writ against someone; the government issued a report on London's traffic*
◇ **issued** *adjective* **issued capital** = amount of capital which is given out as shares to shareholders **ausgegebenes Kapital; issued price** = price of shares in a new company

when they are offered for sale for the first time **Emissions-, Ausgabekurs**

◇ **issuing** *adjective* which organizes an issue of shares **Emissions-, Ausgabe-; issuing bank** *or* **issuing house** = bank which organizes the selling of shares in a new company **Emissionsbank**

> QUOTE the rights issue should overcome the cash flow problems
> *Investors Chronicle*
>
> QUOTE the company said that its recent issue of 10.5 per cent convertible preference shares at A$8.50 a share has been oversubscribed
> *Financial Times*
>
> QUOTE issued and fully paid capital is $100 million
> *Hongkong Standard*

IT = INFORMATION TECHNOLOGY

item *noun*
(a) thing for sale **Artikel, Gegenstand; cash items** = goods sold for cash **Barposten; we are holding orders for out of stock items** = for goods which are not in stock **wir haben Bestellungen für Artikel, die nicht am Lager sind;** *please find enclosed an order for the following items from your catalogue*
(b) piece of information **Posten;** *items on a balance sheet;* **extraordinary items** = items in accounts which do not appear each year and need to be noted **Sonderposten; item of expenditure** = goods or services which have been paid for and appear in the accounts **Ausgabeposten**
(c) point on a list **Punkt; we will now take item four on the agenda** = we will now discuss the fourth point on the agenda **wir gehen jetzt zu Punkt vier der Tagesordnung über**

◇ **itemize** *verb* to make a detailed list of things **einzeln aufführen, spezifizieren;** *itemizing the sales figures will take about two days;* **itemized account** = detailed record of money paid or owed **spezifizierte Abrechnung; itemized invoice** = invoice which lists each item separately **aufgegliederte Rechnung**

itinerary *noun* list of places to be visited on one journey **Reiseroute;** *a salesman's itinerary*

Jj

jam
1 *noun*
(a) sweet food made with fruit and sugar **Marmelade**
(b) blocking **Stockung; Stau; Verstopfung; traffic jam** = situation where there is so much traffic on the road that it moves only very slowly **Verkehrsstau**
2 *verb* to stop working *or* to be blocked **verklemmen, blockieren;** *the paper feed has jammed; the switchboard was jammed with calls*
NOTE: **jamming - jammed**

jetsam *noun* **flotsam and jetsam** = rubbish floating in the water after a ship has been wrecked and rubbish washed on to the land **Treib-, Strandgut**
NOTE: no plural

jettison *verb* to throw cargo from a ship into the sea to make the ship lighter **über Bord werfen**

jingle *noun* **advertising jingle** *or* **publicity jingle** = short and easily remembered tune to advertise a product on television, etc. **Werbung begleitende Melodie, Jingle**

job *noun*
(a) piece of work **Arbeit, Aufgabe; to do a job of work** = to be given a job of work to do **eine Arbeit/Aufgabe erledigen; to do odd jobs** = to do various pieces of work **Gelegenheitsarbeiten verrichten;** *he does odd jobs for us around the house;* **odd-job-man** = person who does various pieces of work **Gelegenheitsarbeiter; to be paid by the job** = to be paid for each piece of work done **im Stücklohn bezahlt werden**
(b) order being worked on **Auftrag;** *we are working on six jobs at the moment; the shipyard has a big job starting in August*
(c) regular paid work **Arbeitsplatz, Stellung;** *he is looking for a job in the computer industry; he lost his job when the factory closed; she got a job in a factory; to apply for a job in an office;* **office job** *or* **white-collar job** = job in an office **Angestelltenstelle, Schreibtischjob; to give up one's job** = to resign from one's work **seine Stelle aufgeben; to look for a job** = to try to find work **auf Stellungssuche sein, Arbeit suchen; to retire from one's job** = to leave work and take a pension **in den Ruhestand treten; to be out of a job** = to have no work **arbeitslos sein**
(d) job analysis = detailed examination and report on the duties of a job **Arbeitsplatzanalyse; job application** *or* **application for a job** = asking for a job in writing **Bewerbung, Stellengesuch;** *you have to fill in a job application form;* **job centre** = government office which lists jobs which are vacant; *entspricht* **Arbeitsamt; Arbeitsvermittlung; job classification** =

describing jobs listed under various classes **Berufszugehörigkeit; job creation scheme** = government-backed plan to make work for the unemployed **Arbeitsplatzbeschaffungs-, Beschäftigungsprogramm; job description** = official document from the management which says what a job involves **Stellen-, Tätigkeitsbeschreibung; job evaluation** = examining different jobs within an organization to see what skills and qualifications are needed to carry them out **Arbeitsplatzbewertung; job satisfaction** = a worker's feeling that he is happy in his place of work and pleased with the work he does **Zufriedenheit am Arbeitsplatz; job security** = feeling which a worker has that he has a right to keep his job, or that his job will never end **Sicherheit des Arbeitsplatzes; job specification** = very detailed description of what is involved in a job **Stellen-, Arbeitsplatzbeschreibung; job title** = name given to a person in a certain job **Berufsbezeichnung;** *her job title is "Chief Buyer";* **on-the-job training** = training given to workers at their place of work **betriebliche Ausbildung; off-the-job training** = training given to workers away from their place of work (i.e. at a college) **außerbetriebliche Ausbildung**

(e) job lot = group of miscellaneous items sold together **Warenposten;** *he sold the household furniture as a job lot*

(f) difficulty **Schwierigkeiten;** *they will have a job to borrow the money they need for the expansion programme; we had a job to find a qualified secretary*

◇ **jobber** *noun*

(a) (stock) jobber = person who buys and sells shares from other traders on the Stock Exchange **Börsenhändler**

(b) *US* wholesaler **Großhändler**

◇ **jobbing** *noun*

(a) (stock) jobbing = buying and selling shares from other traders on the Stock Exchange **Handel an der Börse**

(b) doing small pieces of work **Jobben, Gelegenheitsarbeiten verrichten; jobbing gardener** *or* **jobbing printer** = person who does odd jobs in the garden *or* who does small printing jobs **Lohngärtner; Akzidenzdrucker**

◇ **jobless** *noun* **the jobless** = people with no jobs *or* the unemployed **die Arbeitslosen**
NOTE: takes a plural verb

QUOTE he insisted that the tax advantages he directed toward small businesses will help create jobs
Toronto Star

QUOTE the contradiction between the jobless figures and latest economic review
Sunday Times

QUOTE warehouse clubs buy directly from manufacturers, eliminating jobbers and wholesale middlemen
Duns Business Month

join *verb*

(a) to put things together **verbinden, anfügen;** *the offices were joined together by making a door in the wall; if the paper is too short to take all the accounts, you can join an extra piece on the bottom*

(b) to join a firm = to start work with a company **eine Stelle in einer Firma antreten; he joined on January 1st** = he started work on the January 1st **er trat seine Stelle am 1. Januar an**

(c) to join an association *or* **a group** = to become a member of an association *or* a group **einem Verband/einer Gruppe beitreten;** *all the staff have joined the company pension plan; he was asked to join the board; Smith Ltd has applied to join the trade association*

joint *adjective*

(a) combined *or* with two or more organizations linked together **gemeinschaftlich-, gemeinsam, Gemeinschafts-, Mit-, Joint-; joint commission of inquiry** *or* **joint committee** = commission *or* committee with representatives of various organizations on it **gemeinsamer Untersuchungsausschuß; gemeinsamer Ausschuß; joint discussions** = discussions between management and workers before something is done; *entspricht* **Betriebsratsgespräch; joint management** = management done by two or more people **gemeinsame Geschäftsführung; joint venture** = very large business project where two or more companies join together **Joint-venture, Gemeinschaftsunternehmen**

(b) joint account = bank account for two people **Gemeinschaftskonto, gemeinsames Konto; joint-stock bank** = bank which is a public company quoted on the Stock Exchange **Aktienbank; joint-stock company** = public company whose shares are owned by very many people **Aktiengesellschaft (die nicht an der Börse notiert ist)**

(c) one of two or more people who work together *or* who are linked **Gemeinschafts-, Mit-, Partner-;** *joint beneficiary; joint managing director; joint owner; joint signatory;* **joint ownership** = owning of a property by several owners **Miteigentum**

◇ **jointly** *adverb* together with one or more other people **gemeinsam;** *to own a property jointly; to manage a company jointly; they are jointly liable for damages*

journal *noun*
(a) book with the account of sales and purchases made each day **Journal**
(b) magazine **Zeitschrift; house journal** = magazine produced for the workers in a company to give them news about the company **Werkszeitung; trade journal** = magazine produced for people or companies in a certain trade **Branchen-, Fachblatt**

◇ **journalist** *noun* person who writes for a newspaper **Journalist/-in**

journey *noun* long trip, especially a trip done by a salesman **Reise;** *he planned his journey to visit all his accounts in two days;* **journey order** = order given by the shopkeeper to a salesman when he calls **Auftrag an Vertreter**

◇ **journeyman** *noun US* skilled craftsman who has completed an apprenticeship **Geselle**

judge
1 *noun* person who decides in a legal case **Richter/-in;** *the judge sent him to prison for embezzlement*
2 *verb* to decide **beurteilen, entscheiden;** *he judged it was time to call an end to the discussions*

◇ **judgement** *or* **judgment** *noun* legal decision *or* official decision **Gerichtsurteil; Urteil; to pronounce judgement** *or* **to give one's judgement on something** = to give an official or legal decision about something **ein Urteil verkünden; judgment debtor** = debtor who has been ordered by a court to pay a debt **Urteilsschuldner**
NOTE: the spelling **judgment** is used by lawyers

judicial *adjective* referring to the law **Justiz-, Rechts-; judicial processes** = the ways in which the law works **Rechtsweg, Verfahrensformen**

jumble sale *noun* sale of odd secondhand items organized by a club or organization to raise money; *entspricht* **Wohltätigkeitsbasar**

jump
1 *noun* sudden rise **sprunghafter Anstieg, Sprung;** *jump in prices; jump in unemployment figures*
2 *verb*
(a) to go up suddenly **emporschnellen, plötzlich steigen;** *oil prices have jumped since the war started; share values jumped on the Stock Exchange*
(b) to move suddenly **springen; to jump bail** = not to appear in court after having been released on bail **die Kaution (durch Nichterscheinen) verfallen lassen; to jump the gun** = to start to do something too early *or* before you should **voreilig sein/handeln; to jump the queue** = to go in front of someone who has been waiting longer **sich vordrängeln;** *they jumped the queue and got their export licence before we did;* **to jump ship** = to leave a ship where you work as a sailor and not to go back **ohne Erlaubnis abheuern**

◇ **jumpy** *adjective* nervous *or* excited **nervös, schreckhaft; the market is jumpy** = the stock market is nervous and share prices are likely to fluctuate **die Börse ist unsicher**

junior
1 *adjective* younger *or* lower in rank **junior; untergeordnet; junior clerk** = clerk, usually young, who has lower status than a senior clerk **untere Angestellter; junior executive** *or* **junior manager** = young manager in a company **Nachwuchsmanager; junior partner** = person who has been made a partner more recently than others **Juniorpartner; John Smith, Junior** = the younger John Smith (i.e. the son of John Smith, Senior) **John Smith, junior**
2 *noun*
(a) barrister who is not a Queen's counsel **Rechtsanwaltsassessor**
(b) office junior = young man or woman who does all types of work in an office **Bürohilfe**

junk *noun* rubbish *or* useless items **Plunder, Trödel;** *you should throw away all that junk;* **junk bonds** = bonds raised as debentures on the security of a company which is the subject of a takeover bid **Junk Bonds; Risikoanleihen; junk mail** = advertising material sent through the post **Reklamesendungen**
NOTE: no plural

jurisdiction *noun* **within the jurisdiction of the court** = in the legal power of a court **in der Zuständigkeit des Gerichts**

Kk

K *abbreviation* one thousand **eintausend; "salary: £15K+ "** = salary more than £15,000 per annum **"Gehalt über £15.000"**

keen *adjective*
(a) eager *or* active **eifrig, aktiv; keen competition** = strong competition **scharfer Wettbewerb;** *we are facing some keen competition from European manufacturers;* **keen demand** = wide demand **große Nachfrage;** *there is a keen demand for home computers*
(b) keen prices = prices which are kept low so as to be competitive **günstige Preise;** *our prices are the keenest on the market*

keep *verb*
(a) to go on doing something **etwas weiter tun;** *they kept working, even when the boss told them to stop; the other secretaries complain that she keeps singing when she is typing*
(b) to do what is necessary **(ein)halten, befolgen; to keep an appointment** = to be there when you said you would be **eine Verabredung einhalten; to keep the books of a company** *or* **to keep a company's books** = to note the accounts of a company accurately **die Bücher einer Firma führen**
(c) to hold items for sale *or* for information **auf Lager halten, führen; we always keep this item in stock** = we always have this item in our warehouse *or* shop **wir haben dieses Produkt immer auf Lager; to keep someone's name on file** = to have someone's name on a list for reference **jds Namen in den Akten führen**
(d) to hold things at a certain level **halten;** *we must keep our mailing list up to date; to keep spending to a minimum; the price of oil has kept the pound at a high level; the government is encouraging firms to keep prices low; lack of demand for typewriters has kept prices down*
NOTE: **keeping - kept**
◇ **keep back** *verb* to hold on to something which you could give to someone **zurück-, einbehalten;** *to keep back information or to keep something back from someone; to keep £10 back from someone's salary*
◇ **keeping** *noun* **safe keeping** = being looked after carefully **Verwahrung;** *we put the documents into the bank for safe keeping*
NOTE: no plural
◇ **keep on** *verb* to continue to do something **weitermachen, etwas weiter tun;** *the factory kept on working in spite of the fire; we keep on receiving orders for this item although it was discontinued two years ago*
◇ **keep up** *verb* to hold at a certain high level **beibehalten, aufrechterhalten;** *we must keep up the turnover in spite of the recession; she kept up a rate of sixty words per minute for several hours*

Keogh plan *noun US* private pension plan for self-employed businessmen

key *noun*
(a) piece of metal used to open a lock **Schlüssel;** *we have lost the keys to the computer room;* **key money** = premium paid when taking over the keys of a flat or office which you are renting **Abstand, Mietvorauszahlung**
(b) part of a computer *or* typewriter which you press with your fingers **Drucktaste;** *there are sixty-four keys on the keyboard;* **control key** = key on a computer which works part of a program **Kontrolltaste; shift key** = key which makes a typewriter *or* computer move to capital letters **Umschalt-, Shifttaste**
(c) important **Schlüssel-;** *key factor; key industry; key personnel; key post; key staff*
◇ **keyboard**
1 *noun* part of a typewriter or computer with keys which are pressed to make a letter or figure **Tastatur; qwerty keyboard** = English language keyboard, where the first letters are Q-W-E-R-T-Y **englische Tastatur;** *the computer has a normal qwerty keyboard*
2 *verb* to press the keys on a keyboard to type something **eingeben;** *he is keyboarding our address list*
◇ **keyboarder** *noun* person who types information into a computer **Datentypist/-in**
◇ **keyboarding** *noun* act of typing on a keyboard **Dateneingabe;** *keyboarding costs have risen sharply*
NOTE: no plural
◇ **keypad** *noun* small keyboard **Kleintastatur; numeric keypad** = part of a computer keyboard which is a programmable set of numbered keys **Zehnertastatur, numerische Tastatur**

kickback *noun* illegal commission paid to someone (especially a government official) who helps in a business deal **Schmiergeld**

killing *noun informal* huge profit **Riesengewinn, Reibach;** *he made a killing on the stock market*

kilo *or* **kilogram** *noun* measure of weight (= one thousand grams) **Kilo, Kilogramm**
◇ **kilobyte** *noun* unit of storage in a computer (= 1,024 bytes) **Kilobyte**

◇ **kilometre** *or US* **kilometer** *noun* measure of length (= one thousand metres) **Kilometer; the car does fifteen kilometres to the litre** = the car uses a litre of petrol to travel fifteen kilometres **der Wagen verbraucht einen Liter auf fünfzehn Kilometer**

kind *noun* sort *or* type **Art, Gattung, Sorte;** *the printer produces two kinds of printout; our drinks machine has three kinds of soups;* **payment in kind** = payment made by giving goods or food, but not money **Bezahlung in Naturalien, Sachleistung**

kiosk *noun* small wooden shelter, for selling goods out of doors **Kiosk;** *a newspaper kiosk;* **telephone kiosk** = shelter with a public telephone in it **Telefonzelle**

kite
1 *noun*
(a) to fly a kite = to put forward a proposal to try to interest people **ein lockendes Angebot machen; kite flier** = person who tries to impress by putting forward a proposal **jd, der hochtrabende Pläne macht, Angeber/-in; kite-flying** = trying to impress by putting forward grand plans **angeben**
(b) *GB* **kite mark** = mark on goods to show they meet official standards **Gütezeichen**
2 *verb US informal* to get money by using bad cheques **Schecks fälschen**

kitty *noun* money which has been collected by a group of people to be used later (such as for an office party) **gemeinsame Kasse**

km = KILOMETRE

knock *verb*
(a) to hit something **stoßen, anschlagen;** *she knocked her head on the filing cabinet*
(b) to knock the competition = to hit competing firms hard by vigorous selling **die Konkurrenz schlagen; knocking copy** = advertising material which criticizes competing products **herabsetzender Werbetext**
◇ **knock down** *verb* **to knock something down to a bidder** = to sell something at an auction **jdm etwas zuschlagen, jdm den Zuschlag erteilen;** *the stock was knocked down to him for £10,000*
◇ **knockdown** *noun* **knockdown prices** = very low prices **Spottpreise;** *he sold me the car at a knockdown price*
◇ **knock off** *verb*
(a) to stop work **Feierabend machen**
(b) to reduce a price by an amount **nachlassen;** *he knocked £10 off the price for cash*
◇ **knock-on effect** *noun* effect which an action will have on other situations **Schneeballeffekt, Anstoßwirkung;** *the strike by customs officers has had a knock-on effect on car production by slowing down exports of cars*

know *verb*
(a) to learn *or* to have information about something **wissen;** *I do not know how a computer works; does he know how long it takes to get to the airport? the managing director's secretary does not know where he is*
(b) to have met someone **kennen;** *do you know Mr Jones, our new sales director? he knows the African market very well*
NOTE: **knowing - known**
◇ **know-how** *noun* knowledge about how something works *or* how something is made **Know-how, Fachkenntnisse;** *electronic know-how; to acquire computer know-how*
NOTE: no plural
◇ **knowledge** *noun* what is known **Kenntnis, Wissen; he had no knowledge of the contract** = he did not know that the contract existed **er wußte nichts von dem Vertrag**
NOTE: no plural

Ll

l = LITRE

label
1 *noun*
(a) piece of paper *or* card attached to something to show its price *or* an address *or* instructions for use **Etikett, Anhängeschild; gummed label** = label which you wet to make it stick on the item **Aufkleber; self-sticking label** = sticky label, ready to stick on an item **Selbstklebeetikett; tie-on label** = label with a piece of string attached so that it can be tied on to an item **Anhänger**
(b) address label = label with an address on it **Adressenaufkleber; Adressenanhänger; price label** = label showing a price **Preisschild; quality label** = label which states the quality of something **Gütezeichen**
(c) own label goods = goods specially produced for a store with the store's name on them **Eigenmarkenwaren**
2 *verb* to attach a label to something **etikettieren; mit einem Anhänger od Aufkleber versehen; incorrectly labelled parcel** = parcel with the wrong information on the label **falsch beschriftetes Paket**

NOTE: **labelling - labelled** but US **labeling - labeled**

◇ **labelling** *noun* putting a label on something **Etikettierung; Anbringen eines Anhängers od Aufklebers; labelling department** = section of a factory where labels are attached to the product **Etikettierungsabteilung**
NOTE: no plural

laboratory *noun* place where scientific research is carried out **Labor;** *the product was developed in the company's laboratories; all products are tested in our own laboratories*

labour *or US* **labor** *noun*
(a) heavy work **(schwere) Arbeit; manual labour** = work done by hand **körperliche Arbeit; to charge for materials and labour** = to charge for both the materials used in a job and also the hours of work involved **Material und Arbeitslohn berechnen; labour costs** *or* **labour charges** = cost of the workers employed to make a product (not including materials or overheads) **Lohnkosten; indirect labour costs** = cost of wages of workers who are not directly involved in making the product (such as secretaries, cleaners) **Lohngemeinkosten; labour is charged at £5 an hour** = each hour of work costs £5 **der Arbeitslohn wird mit £5 pro Stunde in Rechnung gestellt**
(b) workers *or* the workforce **Arbeiter; Arbeitskräfte; Arbeiterschaft; Belegschaft; casual labour** = workers who are hired for a short period **Aushilfsarbeiter; cheap labour** = workers who do not earn much money **billige Arbeitskräfte; local labour** = workers recruited near a factory, not brought in from somewhere else **ortsansässige Arbeitskräfte; organized labour** = workers who are members of trade unions **gewerkschaftlich organisierte Arbeiter; skilled labour** = workers who have special knowledge or qualifications **Facharbeiter; labour force** = all workers **Belegschaft; Arbeitskräfte, Arbeiterschaft;** *the management has made an increased offer to the labour force; we are setting up a factory in the Far East because of the cheap labour force available;* **labour market** = number of workers who are available for work **Arbeitsmarkt; 25,000 young people have left school and have come on to the labour market** = 25,000 people have left school and become available for work **25.000 Personen haben die Schule verlassen und stehen dem Arbeitsmarkt zur Verfügung; labour shortage** *or* **shortage of labour** = situation where there are not enough workers to fill jobs **Arbeitskräftemangel; labour-intensive industry** = industry which needs large numbers of workers *or* where labour costs are high in relation to turnover **arbeitsintensiver Industriezweig**
(c) labour disputes = arguments between management and workers **Arbeitskämpfe; labour laws** *or* **labour legislation** = laws relating to the employment of workers **Arbeitsgesetze; Arbeitsgesetzgebung; labour relations** = relations between management and workers **Arbeitgeber-Arbeitnehmer-Beziehungen;** *US* **labor union** = organization which represents workers who are its members in discussions about wages and conditions of work with management **Arbeitergewerkschaft**
(d) International Labour Organization = section of the United Nations which tries to improve working conditions and workers' pay in member countries **Internationale Arbeitsorganisation**
NOTE: no plural

◇ **labourer** *noun* person who does heavy work **Arbeiter, Lohnarbeiter; agricultural labourer** = person who does heavy work on a farm **Landarbeiter; casual labourer** = worker who can be hired for a short period **Aushilfsarbeiter; manual labourer** = person who does heavy work with his hands **ungelernte Arbeitskraft**

◇ **labour-saving** *adjective* which saves you doing hard work **arbeitsparend;** *a labour-saving device*

> QUOTE the possibility that British goods will price themselves back into world markets is doubtful as long as sterling labour costs continue to rise faster than in competitor countries
> *Sunday Times*
>
> QUOTE 70 per cent of Australia's labour force is employed in service activity
> *Australian Financial Review*
>
> QUOTE European economies are being held back by rigid labor markets and wage structures
> *Duns Business Month*

lack
1 *noun* not having enough **Mangel; lack of data** *or* **lack of information** = not having enough information **fehlende Daten; fehlende Information;** *the decision has been put back for lack of up-to-date information;* **lack of funds** = not enough money **fehlende Geldmittel;** *the project was cancelled because of lack of funds*
NOTE: no plural
2 *verb* not to have enough of something **mangeln an, fehlen an;** *the company lacks capital;* **the sales staff lack motivation** = the sales staff are not motivated enough **dem Verkaufspersonal mangelt es an Motivation**

ladder *noun* series of steps made of wood or metal which can be moved about, and which you can climb **Leiter;** *you will need a ladder to look into the machine;* **promotion**

ladder = series of steps by which people can be promoted **Beförderungsleiter;** *by being appointed sales manager, he moved several steps up the promotion ladder*

laden *adjective* loaded **beladen; fully-laden ship** = ship with a full cargo **voll beladenes Schiff; ship laden in bulk** = ship which has a loose cargo (such as corn) which is not packed in containers **ein mit Massengut beladenes Schiff**

lading *noun* loading *or* putting goods on a ship **Verladen; bill of lading** = list of goods being shipped, which the transporter gives to the person sending the goods to show that they have been loaded **Konnossement**
NOTE: no plural

laissez-faire economy *noun* economy where the government does not interfere because it believes it is right to let the economy run itself **Laisser-faire-Wirtschaftspolitik**

lame *adjective* walking badly because of a bad leg **lahm**

◊ **lame duck** *noun* company which is in financial difficulties **unrentable Firma;** *the government has refused to help lame duck companies*

land

1 *noun* area of earth **Land; land agent** = person who runs a farm *or* a large area of land for someone **Gutsverwalter;** *GB* **land register** = register of land, showing who owns it and what buildings are on it **Grundbuch; land registration** = system of registering land and its owners **Grundbucheintragung; land registry** = government office where land is registered **Kataster-, Grundbuchamt; land taxes** = taxes on the amount of land someone owns **Grundsteuern**

2 *verb*

(a) to put goods *or* passengers on to land after a voyage by sea *or* by air **ab-, ausladen; von Bord gehen lassen; löschen;** *to land goods at a port; to land passengers at an airport;* **landed costs** = costs of goods which have been delivered to a port, unloaded and passed through customs **Fracht- und Löschungskosten**

(b) to come down to earth after a flight **landen;** *the plane landed ten minutes late*

◊ **landing** *noun* **landing card** = card given to passengers who have passed customs and can land from a ship *or* an aircraft **Einreisekarte; landing charges** = payment for putting goods on land and the customs duties **Löschungskosten und Löschungszölle; landing order** = permit which allows goods to be unloaded into a bonded warehouse without paying customs duty **Löscherlaubnis**

◊ **landlady** *noun* woman who owns a property which she lets **Vermieterin**

◊ **landlord** *noun* person *or* company which owns a property which is let **Vermieter; ground landlord** = person *or* company which owns the freehold of a property which is then let and sublet **Grundeigentümer;** *our ground landlord is an insurance company*

◊ **landowner** *noun* person who owns large areas of land **Grundbesitzer**

language *noun* words spoken or written by people in a certain country **Sprache;** *the managing director conducted the negotiations in three languages;* **programming language** = system of signs, letters and words used to instruct a computer **Programmiersprache;** *what language does the program run on?*

lapse

1 *noun* **a lapse of time** = a period of time which has passed **Zeitspanne**

2 *verb* to stop being valid *or* to stop being active **verfallen; ablaufen;** *the guarantee has lapsed;* **to let an offer lapse** = to allow time to pass so that an offer is no longer valid **ein Angebot verstreichen lassen**

large *adjective* very big *or* important **groß;** *our company is one of the largest suppliers of computers to the government; he is our largest customer; why has she got an office which is larger than mine?*

◊ **largely** *adverb* mainly *or* mostly **zum größten Teil;** *our sales are largely in the home market; they have largely pulled out of the American market*

◊ **large-scale** *adjective* working in a large way, with large numbers of people *or* large amounts of money involved **umfangreich, groß angelegt;** *large-scale investment in new technology; large-scale redundancies in the construction industry*

last

1 *adjective & adverb*

(a) coming at the end of a series **letzter;** *out of a queue of twenty people, I was served last; this is our last board meeting before we move to our new offices; we finished the last items in the order just two days before the promised delivery date;* **last quarter** = period of three months to the end of the financial year **letztes Quartal**

(b) most recent *or* most recently **letzter;** *where is the last batch of orders? the last ten orders were only for small quantities;* **last**

week *or* **last month** *or* **last year** = the week *or* month *or* year before this one **letzte Woche; letzten Monat; letztes Jahr;** *last week's sales were the best we have ever had; the sales managers have been asked to report on last month's drop in unit sales; last year's accounts have to be ready by the AGM*
(c) the week *or* **month** *or* **year before last** = the week *or* month *or* year before the one before this **vorletzte Woche; vorletzten Monat; vorletztes Jahr;** *last year's figures were bad, but they were an improvement on those of the year before last*
2 *verb* to go on *or* to continue **(an)dauern, halten;** *the boom started in the 1970s and lasted until the early 1980s; the discussions over redundancies lasted all day*

◇ **last in first out (LIFO)** *noun*
(a) redundancy policy, where the people who have been most recently appointed are the first to be made redundant **LIFO-Personalpolitik**
(b) accounting method where stock is valued at the price of the latest purchases **LIFO-Abschreibungsmethode**

late

1 *adjective*
(a) after the time stated or agreed **spät, verspätet;** *we apologize for the late arrival of the plane from Amsterdam;* **there is a penalty for late delivery** = if delivery is later than the agreed date, the supplier has to pay a fine **verspätete Lieferungen werden mit einer Strafe belegt**
(b) at the end of a period of time **letzter; latest date for signature of the contract** = the last acceptable date for signing the contract **der letzte Termin für die Vertragsunterzeichnung**
(c) latest = most recent **letzter, jüngster;** *he always drives the latest model of car; here are the latest sales figures*
2 *adverb* after the time stated or agreed **spät, verspätet;** *the shipment was landed late*

◇ **late-night** *adjective* happening late at night **Nacht-, spät am Abend;** *he had a late-night meeting at the airport; their late-night negotiations ended in an agreement which was signed at 3 a.m.*

launch

1 *verb* to put a new product on the market (usually spending money on advertising it) **herausbringen, auf den Markt bringen;** *they launched their new car model at the motor show; the company is spending thousands of pounds to launch a new brand of soap*
2 *noun* act of putting a new product on the market **Einführung;** *the launch of the new model has been put back three months; the company is geared up for the launch of the new brand of soap; the management has decided on a September launch date*

◇ **launching** *noun* act of putting a new product on the market **Einführung; launching costs** = costs of publicity for a new product **Anlaufkosten; launching date** = date when a new product is officially shown to the public for the first time **Einführungstermin; launching party** = party held to advertise the launching of a new product **Einführungsparty für ein neues Produkt**
NOTE: no plural

launder

verb to pass illegal profits *or* money which has not been taxed, etc. into the normal banking system **waschen;** *to launder money through an offshore bank*

law

noun
(a) laws = rules by which a country is governed and the activities of people and organizations controlled **Gesetze; labour laws** = laws concerning the employment of workers **Arbeitsgesetze; Arbeitsgesetzgebung**
(b) law = all the laws of a country taken together **Recht; civil law** = laws relating to arguments between individuals and the rights of individuals **Zivilrecht, bürgerliches Recht; commercial law** = laws regarding business **Handelsrecht (Teil des Wirtschaftsrechts); company law** = laws which refer to the way companies work **Unternehmensrecht; contract law** *or* **the law of contract** = laws relating to private agreements **Vertragsrecht; Schuldrecht; copyright law** = laws concerning the protection of copyright **Urheberrechtschutzgesetz; criminal law** = laws relating to crime **Strafrecht; international law** = laws referring to the way countries deal with each other **internationales Recht, Völkerrecht; maritime law** *or* **the law of the sea** = laws referring to ships, ports, etc. **Seerecht; law court** = place where a judge listens to cases and decides who is right legally **Gerichtshof, Gericht; to take someone to law** = to tell someone to appear in court to settle an argument **jdn vor Gericht bringen, jdn verklagen; inside the law** *or* **within the law** = obeying the laws of a country **im Rahmen des Gesetzes; against** *or* **outside the law** = not according to the laws of a country **außerhalb des Gesetzes;** *the company is operating outside the law;* **to break the law** = to do something which is not allowed by law **Gesetze übertreten, gegen das Gesetz verstoßen;** *he is breaking the law by selling goods on Sunday; you will be breaking the law if you try to take that computer out of the country without an export licence*

(c) general rule **Gesetz; law of supply and demand** = general rule that the amount of a product which is available is related to the needs of the possible customers **Gesetz von Angebot und Nachfrage; law of diminishing returns** = general rule that as more factors of production (land, labour and capital) are added to the existing factors, so the amount they produce is proportionately smaller **Gesetzmäßigkeit vom abnehmenden Ertragszuwachs**

NOTE: no plural for (b)

◇ **lawful** *adjective* acting within the law **rechtmäßig, gesetzlich; lawful practice** = action which is permitted by the law **rechtmäßiges Vorgehen; lawful trade** = trade which is allowed by law **rechtmäßiger Handel**

◇ **lawfully** *adverb* acting within the law **rechtmäßig, gesetzlich**

◇ **lawsuit** *noun* case brought to a court **Prozeß, Klage; to bring a lawsuit against someone** = to tell someone to appear in court to settle an argument **jdn verklagen; to defend a lawsuit** = to appear in court to state your case **einen Prozeß als Beklagter führen**

◇ **lawyer** *noun* person who has studied law and can act for people on legal business **Rechtsanwalt; commercial lawyer** *or* **company lawyer** = person who specializes in company law *or* who advises companies on legal problems **ein auf Handelsrecht spezialisierter Jurist; international lawyer** = person who specializes in international law **ein auf internationales Recht spezialisierter Jurist; maritime lawyer** = person who specializes in laws concerning ships **ein auf Seerecht spezialisierter Jurist**

lay *verb* to put **legen; to lay an embargo on trade with a country** = to forbid trade with a country **ein Handelsembargo über ein Land verhängen**

NOTE: **laying - laid**

◇ **lay off** *verb*

(a) to lay off workers = to dismiss workers for a time (until more work is available) **(vorübergehend) Arbeiter entlassen;** *the factory laid off half its workers because of lack of orders*

(b) to lay off risks = to protect oneself against risk in one investment by making other investments **sich gegen Risiken absichern**

◇ **lay-off** *noun* action of dismissing a worker for a time **vorübergehende Entlassung von Arbeitern;** *the recession has caused hundreds of lay-offs in the car industry*

◇ **lay out** *verb* to spend money **ausgeben;** *we had to lay out half our cash budget on equipping the new factory*

◇ **layout** *noun* arrangement of the inside of a building **Layout, Aufmachung;** *they have altered the layout of the offices*

◇ **lay up** *verb* to stop using a ship because there is no work **außer Dienst stellen;** *half the shipping fleet is laid up by the recession*

> QUOTE the company lost $52 million last year, and has laid off close to 2,000 employees
> *Toronto Star*
>
> QUOTE while trading conditions for the tanker are being considered, it is possible that the ship could be laid up
> *Lloyd's List*

lazy *adjective* (person) who does not want to work **faul;** *she is too lazy to do any overtime; he is so lazy he does not even send in his expense claims on time*

lb = pound

L/C = LETTER OF CREDIT

lead *verb*

(a) to be the first *or* to be in front **(an)führen, an der Spitze stehen;** *the company leads the market in cheap computers*

(b) to be the main person in a group **leiten, (an)führen;** *she will lead the trade mission to Nigeria; the tour of American factories will be led by the minister*

NOTE: **leading - led**

◇ **leader** *noun*

(a) person who manages *or* directs others **Leiter/-in, Vorsitzender/Vorsitzende;** *the leader of the construction workers' union or the construction workers' leader; she is the leader of the trade mission to Nigeria; the minister was the leader of the party of industrialists on a tour of American factories*

(b) product which sells best **Spitzenreiter, führender Artikel; a market leader** = product which sells most in a market *or* company which has the largest share of a market **ein Marktführer; loss-leader** = article which is sold very cheaply to attract customers **Lockartikel**

(c) important share *or* share which is often bought or sold on the Stock Exchange **Blue-chip**

◇ **leading** *adjective* most important **führend, Spitzen-, maßgebend, entscheidend;** *leading industrialists feel the end of the recession is near; leading shares rose on the Stock Exchange; leading shareholders in the company forced a change in management policy; they are the leading company in the field*

◇ **lead time** *noun* time between deciding to place an order and receiving the product

Lieferzeit; *the lead time on this item is more than six weeks*

◇ **lead (up) to** *verb* to be the cause of **führen zu;** *the discussions led to a big argument between the management and the union; we received a series of approaches leading up to the takeover bid*

leaflet *noun* sheet of paper giving information, used to advertise something **Hand-, Reklamezettel;** *to mail leaflets or to hand out leaflets describing services; they made a leaflet mailing to 20,000 addresses*

leak *verb* to pass on a secret **zuspielen;** *information on the contract was leaked to the press; they discovered the managing director was leaking information to a rival company*

◇ **leakage** *noun* amount of goods lost in storage (by going bad *or* by being stolen *or* by escaping from the container) **Schwund, Verlust**

leap-frogging *adjective* **leap-frogging pay demands** = pay demands where each section of workers asks for higher pay to do better than another section, which then asks for further increases in turn **sich sprunghaft entwickelnde Lohnforderungen**

lease
1 *noun*
(a) written contract for letting or renting of a building *or* a piece of land *or* a piece of equipment for a period against payment of a fee **Pachtvertrag; Mietvertrag; long lease** *or* **short lease** = lease which runs for fifty years or more *or* for up to two or three years **Pachtvertrag od Mietvertrag mit langer od kurzer Laufzeit;** *to take an office building on a long lease; we have a short lease on our current premises; to rent office space on a twenty-year lease;* **full repairing lease** = lease where the tenant has to pay for all repairs to the property **Pachtvertrag od Mietvertrag mit Reparaturklausel; headlease** = lease from the freeholder to a tenant **Hauptmietvertrag; Pachtvertrag; Vermietung; Verpachtung; sublease** *or* **underlease** = lease from a tenant to another tenant **Untermietvertrag; Unterpachtvertrag; Untervermietung; Unterverpachtung; the lease expires** *or* **runs out in 1989** = the lease comes to an end in 1989 **der Pacht- od Mietvertrag läuft 1989 aus; on expiration of the lease** = when the lease comes to an end **bei Ablauf des Pacht- od Mietvertrages**
(b) to hold an oil lease in the North Sea = to have a lease on a section of the North Sea to explore for oil **eine Ölkonzession in der Nordsee haben**
2 *verb*
(a) to let or rent offices *or* land *or* machinery for a period **verpachten; vermieten;** *to lease offices to small firms; to lease equipment*
(b) to use an office *or* land *or* machinery for a time and pay a fee **pachten; mieten;** *to lease an office from an insurance company; all our company cars are leased*

◇ **lease back** *verb* to sell a property *or* machinery to a company and then take it back on a lease **verkaufen mit Rückmietgarantie;** *they sold the office building to raise cash, and then leased it back for twenty-five years*

◇ **lease-back** *noun* arrangement where property is sold and then taken back on a lease **Verkauf mit Rückmietgarantie;** *they sold the office building and then took it back under a lease-back arrangement*

◇ **leasehold**
1 *noun* holding property on a lease **Mietvertrag; Pachtvertrag**
2 *adjective* held on a lease **gepachtet, Pacht-; gemietet, Miet-;** *leasehold property; the company has some valuable leaseholds; to buy a property leasehold*

◇ **leaseholder** *noun* person who holds a property on a lease **Pächter/-in; Mieter/-in**

◇ **leasing** *noun* which leases *or* working under a lease **Leasing;** *the company has branched out into car leasing; an equipment-leasing company; to run a copier under a leasing arrangement*
NOTE: no plural *see also* LESSEE

leave
1 *noun* permission to be away from work **Urlaub; six weeks' annual leave** = six weeks' holiday each year **sechs Wochen Jahresurlaub; leave of absence** = being allowed to be away from work **Beurlaubung; maternity leave** = permission given to a woman to be away from work to have a baby **Mutterschaftsurlaub; sick leave** = period when a worker is away from work because of illness **Genesungsurlaub; to go on leave** *or* **to be on leave** = to be away from work **Urlaub nehmen; Urlaub haben;** *she is away on sick leave or on maternity leave*
NOTE: no plural
2 *verb*
(a) to go away from **verlassen; gehen;** *he left his office early to go to the meeting; the next plane leaves at 10.20*
(b) to resign **aufgeben; kündigen;** *he left his job and bought a farm*
NOTE: **leaving - left**

◇ **leave out** *verb* not to include **aus-, weglassen;** *she left out the date on the letter; the contract leaves out all details of marketing arrangements*

ledger *noun* book in which accounts are written **Hauptbuch; bought ledger** *or* **purchase ledger** = book in which expenditure is noted **Einkaufsbuch; bought ledger clerk** *or* **sales ledger clerk** = office worker who deals with the bought ledger *or* the sales ledger **Einkaufsbuchhalter; nominal ledger** = book which records a company's income and expenditure in general **Hauptbuch; payroll ledger** = list of staff and their salaries **Lohn- und Gehaltsliste; sales ledger** = book in which sales are noted **Warenausgangsbuch**

left *adjective* on the side of the body which usually has the weaker hand *or* not right **links;** *the numbers run down the left side of the page; put the debits in the left column; see also* LEAVE

◊ **left-hand** *adjective* belonging to the left side **linker;** *the debits are in the left-hand column in the accounts; he keeps the personnel files in the left-hand drawer of his desk*

◊ **left luggage office** *noun* room where suitcases can be left while passengers are waiting for a plane or train **Gepäckaufbewahrung**

legacy *noun* property given by someone to someone else at his death **Vermächtnis**

legal *adjective*
(a) according to the law *or* allowed by the law **legal, rechtmäßig;** *the company's action was completely legal*
(b) referring to the law **juristisch, rechtlich, Rechts-; to take legal action** = to sue someone *or* to take someone to court **gerichtlich (gegen jdn) vorgehen; to take legal advice** = to ask a lawyer to advise about a legal problem **sich juristisch beraten lassen; legal adviser** = person who advises clients about the law **Rechtsberater;** *GB* **legal aid** = government scheme where someone who has little money can have his legal expenses paid for him **unentgeltliche Beratungs- und Prozeßkostenhilfe; legal claim** = statement that someone owns something legally **Rechtsanspruch;** *he has no legal claim to the property;* **legal costs** *or* **legal charges** *or* **legal expenses** = money spent on fees to lawyers **Anwaltskosten; legal currency** = money which is legally used in a country **gesetzliches Zahlungsmittel; legal department** *or* **legal section** = section of a company dealing with legal matters **Rechtsabteilung; legal expert** = person who knows a lot about the law **juristischer Sachverständiger; legal holiday** = day when banks and other businesses are closed **gesetzlicher Feiertag; legal tender** = coins or notes which can be legally used to pay a debt (small denominations cannot be used to pay large debts) **gesetzliches Zahlungsmittel**

◊ **legality** *noun* being allowed by law **Legalität, Gesetzmäßigkeit;** *there is doubt about the legality of the company's action in dismissing him*

◊ **legalize** *verb* to make something legal **legalisieren**

◊ **legalization** *noun* making something legal **Legalisierung**

◊ **legally** *adverb* according to the law **rechtlich; gesetzlich; juristisch; the contract is legally binding** = according to the law, the contract has to be obeyed **der Vertrag ist rechtsverbindlich; the directors are legally responsible** = the law says that the directors are responsible **die Direktoren sind vor dem Gesetz juristisch verantwortlich**

legatee *noun* person who receives property from someone who has died **Vermächtnisnehmer**

legislation *noun* laws **Gesetzgebung; labour legislation** = laws concerning the employment of workers **Arbeitsgesetzgebung; Arbeitsgesetze**
NOTE: no plural

lend *verb* to allow someone to use something for a period **ver-, ausleihen;** *to lend something to someone or to lend someone something; he lent the company money or he lent money to the company; to lend money against security; the bank lent him £50,000 to start his business*
NOTE: **lending - lent**

◊ **lender** *noun* person who lends money **Gläubiger; lender of the last resort** = central bank which lends money to commercial banks **Kreditgeber letzter Hand**

◊ **lending** *noun* act of letting someone use money for a time **Ver-, Ausleihen; lending limit** = limit on the amount of money a bank can lend **Kreditlimit**
NOTE: no plural

length *noun*
(a) measurement of how long something is **Länge;** *the boardroom table is twelve feet in length; inches and centimetres are measurements of length*
(b) to go to great lengths to get something = to do anything (even commit a crime) to get something **sich sehr viel Mühe geben, etwas zu bekommen;** *they went to considerable lengths to keep the turnover secret*

less
1 *adjective* smaller than *or* of a smaller size *or* of a smaller value **weniger;** *we do not grant credit for sums of less than £100; he sold it for less than he had paid for it*
2 *preposition* minus *or* with a sum removed **abzüglich;** *purchase price less 15% discount; interest less service charges*

lessee *noun* person who has a lease *or* who pays money for a property he leases **Pächter/-in; Mieter/-in**
◇ **lessor** *noun* person who grants a lease on a property **Verpächter; Vermieter**

let
1 *verb* to lend a house *or* an office *or* a farm to someone for a payment **vermieten; to let an office** = to allow someone to use an office for a time in return for payment of rent **ein Büro vermieten; offices to let** = offices which are available to be leased by companies **Büroräume zu vermieten**
NOTE: **letting - let**
2 *noun* **she has the house on a long let** period of the lease of a property **sie hat das Haus langfristig gemietet;** *they took the office on a short let*
◇ **let-out clause** *noun* clause which allows someone to avoid doing something in a contract **Rücktrittsklausel;** *he added a let-out clause to the effect that the payments would be revised if the exchange rate fell by more than 5%*

letter *noun*
(a) piece of writing sent from one person *or* company to another to give information **Brief; business letter** = letter which deals with business matters **Geschäftsbrief; circular letter** = letter sent to many people **Rundschreiben; Umlauf; covering letter** = letter sent with documents to say why they are being sent **Begleitschreiben; follow-up letter** = letter sent to someone after a previous letter *or* after a visit **Nachfaß-, Folgeschreiben; private letter** = letter which deals with personal matters **persönlicher Brief; standard letter** = letter which is sent without change to various correspondents **Standard-, Formbrief**
(b) letter of acknowledgement = letter which says that something has been received **Bestätigungsschreiben; letters of administration** = letter given by a court to allow someone to deal with the estate of someone who has died **Bestallungsurkunde zum Nachlaßverwalter; letter of allotment** *or* **allotment letter** = letter which tells someone how many shares in a new company he has been allotted **Zuteilungsanzeige; letter of application** = letter in which someone applies for a job **Bewerbungsschreiben; letter of appointment** = letter in which someone is appointed to a job **Einstellungsschreiben; Ernennungsschreiben; letter of comfort** = letter supporting someone who is trying to get a loan **Bonitätsbestätigung; letter of complaint** = letter in which someone complains **Beschwerdebrief; letter of credit** = letter from a bank allowing someone credit and promising to repay at a later date **Akkreditiv; letter of indemnity** = letter promising payment of compensation for a loss **(schriftliche) Schadloshaltungs-, Ausfallbürgschaftserklärung; letter of intent** = letter which states what a company intends to do if something happens **Absichtserklärung; letters patent** = official document which gives someone the exclusive right to make and sell something which he has invented **Patenturkunde; letter of reference** = letter in which an employer recommends someone for a new job **Zeugnis, Referenz**
(c) air letter = special thin blue paper which when folded can be sent by air without an envelope **Luftpostbrief(papier); airmail letter** = letter sent by air **Luftpostbrief; express letter** = letter sent very fast **Eilbrief; registered letter** = letter which is noted by the post office before it is sent, so that compensation can be claimed if it is lost **Einschreiben**
(d) to acknowledge receipt by letter = to write a letter to say that something has been received **den Empfang schriftlich bestätigen**
(e) written or printed sign (such as A, B, C, etc.) **Buchstabe;** *write your name and address in block letters or in capital letters*

◇ **letterhead** *noun* name and address of a company printed at the top of a piece of notepaper **Briefkopf**

letting *noun* **letting agency** = agency which deals in property to let **Wohnungsmakler; furnished lettings** = furnished property to let **möblierte Immobilien zu vermieten**

level
1 *noun* position where high is large and low is small **Stand, Niveau, Ebene;** *low level of productivity or low productivity levels; to raise the level of employee benefits; to lower the level of borrowings;* **high level of investment** = large amount of money invested **hohes Investitionsniveau; a decision taken at the highest level** = decision taken by the most important person or group **eine Entscheidung auf höchster Ebene; low-level** = not very important **untergeordnet, auf unterer Ebene;** *a low-level delegation;* **high-level** = very important **auf hoher Ebene;** *a high-level meeting or decision;* **decisions**

taken at managerial level = decisions taken by managers **Entscheidungen auf der Führungsebene; manning levels** *or* **staffing levels** = number of people required in each department of a company to do the work efficiently **Personalstärke, Personalbestand**
2 *verb* **to level off** *or* **to level out** = to stop rising or falling **sich ausgleichen/einpendeln;** *profits have levelled off over the last few years; prices are levelling out*
NOTE: **levelling - levelled** but US **leveling - leveled**

> QUOTE figures from the Fed on industrial production for April show a decline to levels last seen in June 1984
> *Sunday Times*
>
> QUOTE applications for mortgages are running at a high level
> *Times*
>
> QUOTE employers having got their staff back up to a reasonable level are waiting until the scope for overtime working is exhausted before hiring
> *Sydney Morning Herald*

leverage *noun*

(a) influence which you can use to achieve an aim **Einfluß;** *he has no leverage over the chairman*
(b) relation between a company's capital borrowed at a fixed interest and the value of its ordinary shares **Leverage (Verhältnis Eigen- zu Fremdkapital)**
(c) borrowing money at fixed interest which is then used to produce more money than the interest paid **Kreditaufnahme zu Anlagezwecken**
NOTE: no plural
◇ **leveraged buyout** *noun* buying all the shares in a company by borrowing money against the security of the shares to be bought **Leveraged Buyout, Aktienerwerb eines Unternehmens unter Ausnutzung des Leverage-Effektes (durch Leihkapital finanzierter Aufkauf)**

> QUOTE the offer came after management had offered to take the company private through a leveraged buyout for $825 million
> *Fortune*

levy

1 *noun* money which is demanded and collected by the government **Steuer; Abgabe; capital levy** = tax on the value of a person's property and possessions **Vermögenssteuer; import levy** = tax on imports, especially in the EC a tax on imports of farm produce from outside the EEC **Einfuhrzoll;** *EG* **Abschöpfung; levies on luxury items** = taxes on luxury items **Luxussteuer; training levy** = tax to be paid by companies to fund the government's training schemes **Ausbildungsabgabe**
2 *verb* to demand payment of a tax *or* an extra payment and to collect it **erheben; einziehen;** *the government has decided to levy a tax on imported cars; to levy a duty on the import of luxury items;* **to levy members for a new club house** = to ask members of the club to pay for the new building **von Mitgliedern Gelder für ein neues Clubhaus einziehen**

> QUOTE royalties have been levied at a rate of 12.5% of full production
> *Lloyd's List*

liability *noun*

(a) being legally responsible for damage *or* loss, etc. **Haftung; to accept liability for something** = to agree that you are responsible for something **für etwas Haftung übernehmen; to refuse liability for something** = to refuse to agree that you are responsible for something **es ablehnen, für etwas zu haften; contractual liability** = legal responsibility for something as stated in a contract **Vertragshaftung; employers' liability insurance** = insurance to cover accidents which may happen at work, and for which the company may be responsible **Unfallhaftpflichtversicherung der Arbeitgeber; limited liability** = situation where someone's liability for debt is limited by law **beschränkte Haftung; limited liability company** = company where a shareholder is responsible for repaying the company's debts only to the face value of the shares he owns **Gesellschaft mit beschränkter Haftung**
(b) liabilities = debts of a business **Verbindlichkeiten, Schulden;** *the balance sheet shows the company's assets and liabilities;* **current liabilities** = debts which a company should pay within the next accounting period **kurzfristige Verbindlichkeiten; long-term liabilities** = debts which are not due to be paid for some time **langfristige Verbindlichkeiten; he was not able to meet his liabilities** = he could not pay his debts **er konnte seinen Zahlungsverpflichtungen nicht nachkommen; to discharge one's liabilities in full** = to pay everything which you owe **seinen Verbindlichkeiten in voller Höhe nachkommen**
NOTE: no plural for (a)
◇ **liable** *adjective*
(a) liable for = legally responsible for **haftbar für;** *the customer is liable for breakages; the chairman was personally liable for the company's debts*
(b) liable to = which is officially due to be paid **unterliegen, unterworfen;** *goods which are liable to stamp duty*

libel

1 *noun* untrue written statement which damages someone's character **(schriftlich geäußerte) Verleumdung, Beleidigung; action for libel** *or* **libel action** = case in a law court

where someone says that another person has written a libel **Verleumdungsklage**
2 *verb* **to libel someone** = to damage someone's character in writing **jdn verleumden**
NOTE: **libelling - libelled** but US **libeling - libeled.** Compare SLANDER

licence *or US* **license** *noun*
(a) official document which allows someone to do something **Genehmigung; Konzession; Lizenz; driving licence** = document which allows someone to drive a car *or* a truck, etc. **Führerschein;** *applicants should hold a valid driving licence;* **import licence** *or* **export licence** = documents which allow goods to be exported or imported **Einfuhrlizenz; Ausfuhrlizenz; liquor licence** = government document allowing someone to sell alcohol **Schankkonzession; off licence** = licence to sell alcohol to be drunk away from the place where it is bought; shop which sells alcohol for drinking at home **Konzession zum Alkoholverkauf; Wein- und Spirituosenhandlung**
(b) goods manufactured under licence = goods made with the permission of the owner of the copyright or patent **in Lizenz hergestellte Waren**
◇ **license**
1 *noun US* = LICENCE
2 *verb* to give someone official permission to do something **eine Erlaubnis od Lizenz od Konzession erteilen, genehmigen;** *licensed to sell beers, wines and spirits; to license a company to manufacture spare parts; she is licensed to run an employment agency*
◇ **licensee** *noun* person who has a licence, especially a licence to sell alcohol *or* to manufacture something **Konzessionsinhaber;Lizenzinhaber**
◇ **licensing** *noun* which refers to licences **Schank-; Lizenz-; Konzessions-;** *a licensing agreement; licensing laws; GB* **licensing hours** = hours of the day when alcohol can be sold **Ausschankzeiten**

lien *noun* legal right to hold someone's goods and keep them until a debt has been paid **Sicherungspfandrecht**

lieu *noun* **in lieu of** = instead of **anstelle von; she was given two months' salary in lieu of notice** = she was given the salary and asked to leave immediately **sie bekam zwei Monatsgehälter an Stelle einer Kündigungsfrist**

life *noun*
(a) time when a person is alive **Leben; for life** = for as long as someone is alive **auf Lebenszeit, lebenslang;** *his pension gives him a comfortable income for life;* **life annuity** *or* **annuity for life** = annual payments made to someone as long as he is alive **Leibrente; life assurance** *or* **life insurance** = insurance which pays a sum of money when someone dies, or at a certain date if he is still alive **Lebensversicherung; the life assured** *or* **the life insured** = the person whose life has been covered by the life assurance **der Versicherte (in einer Lebensversicherung); life expectancy** = number of years a person is likely to live **Lebenserwartung; life interest** = interest in a property which stops when a person dies **lebenslanges Nutzungsrecht, lebenslange Nutznießung**
(b) period of time something exists **Laufzeit, Dauer;** *the life of a loan; during the life of the agreement;* **shelf life of a product** = length of time during which a product can stay in the shop and still be good to use **Haltbarkeit/Lagerfähigkeit eines Produktes**
◇ **lifeboat** *noun* boat used to rescue passengers from sinking ships **Rettungsboot; lifeboat operation** = rescue of a company (especially of a bank) which is in difficulties **Rettungsaktion**

LIFO = LAST IN FIRST OUT

lift
1 *noun* machine which takes people or goods from one floor to another in a building **Fahrstuhl, Aufzug;** *he took the lift to the 27th floor; the staff could not get into their office when the lift broke down*
2 *verb* to take away *or* to remove **aufheben;** *the government has lifted the ban on imports from Japan; to lift trade barriers; the minister has lifted the embargo on the export of computers to East European countries*

light *adjective* not heavy **leicht; shares fell back in light trading** = shares lost value on a day when there was little business done on the Stock Exchange **die Aktienwerte fielen bei schwachen Umsätzen; light industry** = industry which makes small products (such as clothes, books, calculators) **Leichtindustrie**

limit
1 *noun* point at which something ends *or* point where you can go no further **Grenze, Limit; to set limits to imports** *or* **to impose import limits** = to allow only a certain amount of imports **Importbeschränkungen einführen; age limit** = top age at which you are allowed to do a job **Altersgrenze;** *there is an age limit of thirty-five on the post of buyer;* **credit limit** = largest amount of money which a customer can borrow **Kreditlinie, Kreditlimit; he has exceeded his credit limit** = he has borrowed more money

than he is allowed **er hat seine Kreditlinie überzogen; lending limit** = restriction on the amount of money a bank can lend **Kreditlimit; time limit** = maximum time which can be taken to do something **Frist;** *to set a time limit for acceptance of the offer;* **weight limit** = maximum weight **Höchstgewicht**

2 *verb* to stop something from going beyond a certain point **begrenzen, be-, einschränken; the banks have limited their credit** = the banks have allowed their customers only a certain amount of credit **die Banken haben ihre Kreditvergabe begrenzt; each agent is limited to twenty-five units** = each agent is allowed only twenty-five units to sell **jeder Vertreter bekommt nur 25 Einheiten**

◇ **limitation** *noun*

(a) act of allowing only a certain quantity of something **Be-, Einschränkung, Begrenzung; limitation of liability** = making someone liable for only a part of the damage or loss **Haftungsbeschränkung; time limitation** = amount of time available **zeitliche Begrenzung;** *the contract imposes limitations on the number of cars which can be imported*

(b) statute of limitations = law which allows only a certain amount of time (a few years) for someone to claim damages or property **Verjährungsausschlußfrist**

◇ **limited** *adjective* restricted *or* not open **beschränkt, begrenzt; limited market** = market which can take only a certain quantity of goods **begrenzter Absatzmarkt; limited liability company** = company where a shareholder is responsible for the company's debts only to the face value of his shares **Gesellschaft mit beschränkter Haftung; private limited company** = company with a small number of shareholders, whose shares are not traded on the Stock Exchange; *entspricht* **Gesellschaft mit beschränkter Haftung;** *Smith and Sons, Ltd;* **Public Limited Company** = company whose shares can be bought on the Stock Exchange; *entspricht* **Aktiengesellschaft;** *Smith and Sons, plc*

◇ **limiting** *adjective* which limits **be-, einschränkend;** *a limiting clause in a contract; the short holiday season is a limiting factor on the hotel trade*

line *noun*

(a) long mark **Linie;** *paper with thin blue lines; I prefer notepaper without any lines; he drew a thick line across the bottom of the column to show which figure was the total*

(b) shipping line *or* **airline** = large shipping or aircraft company which carries passengers or cargo **Reederei; Fluggesellschaft;** *profits of major airlines have been affected by the rise in fuel prices*

(c) line of business *or* **line of work** = type of business or work **Branche, Sparte;** *what is his line?;* **line of product** *or* **product line** = series of different products which form a group, all made by the same company **Produktgruppe, Sortiment;** *we do not stock that line; computers are not one of our best-selling lines; they produce an interesting line in garden tools*

(d) row of letters *or* figures on a page **Zeile; bottom line** = last line in accounts, showing the net profit **Saldo;** *the boss is interested only in the bottom line;* **to open a line of credit** *or* **a credit line** = to make credit available to someone **eine Kreditlinie einräumen**

(e) assembly line *or* **production line** = production system where the product (such as a car) moves slowly through a factory with new sections added to it as it goes along **Montage-, Fließband, Fertigungsstraße;** *he works on the production line or he is a production line worker in the car factory*

(f) line chart *or* **line graph** = chart or graph using lines to indicate values **Linien-, Strichdiagramm; line printer** = machine which prints information from a computer one line at a time **Zeilendrucker**

(g) line of command *or* **line management** *or* **line organization** = organization of a business where each manager is responsible for doing what his superior tells him to do **Linienorganisation**

(h) telephone line = wire along which telephone messages travel **Telefonleitung; the line is bad** = it is difficult to hear clearly what someone is saying **die Verbindung ist schlecht; there is a crossed line** = when two telephone conversations get mixed **da ist jd in der Leitung; the line is engaged** = the person is already speaking on the phone **der Anschluß ist besetzt; the chairman is on the other line** = the chairman is speaking on his second telephone **der Vorsitzende telefoniert gerade; outside line** = line from an internal office telephone system to the main telephone exchange **Verbindung außer Haus**

◇ **lined** *adjective* with lines **liniert;** *he prefers lined paper for writing notes*

◇ **liner** *noun* large passenger ship **Passagier-, Linienschiff**

> QUOTE the best thing would be to have a few more plants close down and bring supply more in line with current demand
> *Fortune*
>
> QUOTE cash paid for overstocked lines, factory seconds, slow sellers, etc.
> *Australian Financial Review*

link *verb*

to join *or* to attach to something else **verbinden, koppeln;** *to link pensions to inflation; his salary is linked to the cost of* *living; to link bonus payments to productivity*

liquid *adjective* **liquid assets** = cash, or bills which can easily be changed into cash **flüssige Mittel; to go liquid** = to convert as many assets as possible into cash **Mittel flüssigmachen**

◇ **liquidate** *verb* **to liquidate a company** = to close a company and sell its assets **ein Unternehmen liquidieren/auflösen; to liquidate a debt** = to pay a debt in full **eine Schuld begleichen; to liquidate stock** = to sell stock to raise cash **Lagerbestände flüssig machen**

◇ **liquidation** *noun*
(a) liquidation of a debt = payment of a debt **Begleichung einer Schuld**
(b) closing of a company and selling of its assets **Liquidation, Auflösung; the company went into liquidation** = the company was closed and its assets sold **das Unternehmen ging in Liquidation; compulsory liquidation** = liquidation which is ordered by a court **Zwangsliquidation; voluntary liquidation** = situation where a company itself decides it must close **freiwillige Liquidation**

◇ **liquidator** *noun* person named to supervise the closing of a company which is in liquidation **Liquidator, Konkursverwalter**

◇ **liquidity** *noun* having cash or assets which can be changed into cash **Liquidität; liquidity crisis** = not having enough liquid assets **Liquiditätskrise**

lira *noun* money used in Italy **Lire;** *the book cost 2,700 lira or L2,700*
NOTE: **lira** is usually written **L** before figures: **L2,700**

list
1 *noun*
(a) several items written one after the other **Liste;** *list of products or product list; stock list; to add an item to a list; to cross an item off a list;* **address list** *or* **mailing list** = list of names and addresses of people and companies **Adressenliste; black list** = list of goods *or* companies *or* countries which are banned for trade **schwarze Liste; picking list** = list of items in an order, but listed according to where they can be found in the warehouse **Entnahmeliste**
(b) catalogue **Verzeichnis, Liste; list price** = price as given in a catalogue **Listenpreis; price list** = sheet giving prices of goods for sale **Preisliste**
2 *verb*
(a) to write a series of items one after the other **auflisten;** *to list products by category; to list representatives by area; to list products in a catalogue; the catalogue lists twenty-three models of washing machines*
(b) listed company = company whose shares can be bought or sold on the Stock Exchange **börsenfähiges/an der Börse notiertes Unternehmen; listed securities** = shares which can be bought or sold on the Stock Exchange *or* shares which appear on the official Stock Exchange list **an der Börse notierte Wertpapiere**

◇ **listing** *noun*
(a) Stock Exchange listing = being on the official list of shares which can be bought or sold on the Stock Exchange **amtliche Notierung an der Börse;** *the company is planning to obtain a Stock Exchange listing*
(b) computer listing = printout of a list of items taken from the data stored in a computer **Computerausdruck; listing paper** = paper made as a long sheet, used in computer printers **Tabellierpapier**

literature *noun* written information about something **Literatur; Prospekte;** *please send me literature about your new product range*
NOTE: no plural

litigation *noun* the bringing of a lawsuit against someone **Prozeß, Rechtsstreit**
NOTE: no plural

litre *or US* **liter** *noun* measure of liquids **Liter; the car does fifteen kilometres to the litre** *or* **fifteen kilometres per litre** = the car uses one litre of petrol to travel fifteen kilometres **der Wagen braucht einen Liter auf fünfzehn Kilometer**
NOTE: usually written **l** after figures: **25l**

lively *adjective* **lively market** = active stock market, with many shares being bought or sold **lebhafte Börse**

living *noun* **cost of living** = money which a person has to pay for rent, food, heating, etc. **Lebenshaltungskosten; cost-of-living index** = way of measuring the cost of living which is shown as a percentage increase on the figure for the previous year **Lebenshaltungskostenindex; he does not earn a living wage** = he does not earn enough to pay for essentials (food, heat, rent) **er verdient nicht genug zum leben; standard of living** *or* **living standards** = quality of personal home life (amount of food, clothes bought, size of the family car, etc.) **Lebensstandard;** *living standards fell as unemployment rose*
NOTE: no plural

Lloyd's *noun* central London insurance market **Lloyd's; Lloyd's Register** = classified list showing details of all the ships in the world **Lloyd's Register; ship which is A1 at Lloyd's** = ship in very good condition **ein Schiff, das bei Lloyd's als in erstklassigem Zustand beschrieben wird**

load

1 *noun*

(a) goods which are transported **Ladung; load of a lorry** *or* **of a container** = goods carried by a lorry or container **Lastwagenladung; Containerladung; lorry-load** *or* **container-load** = amount of goods carried on a lorry or container **Lastwagenladung; Containerladung;** *a container-load of spare parts is missing; they delivered six lorry-loads of coal;* **commercial load** = amount of goods *or* number of passengers which a bus *or* train *or* plane has to carry to make a profit **wirtschaftliche Auslastung; maximum load** = largest weight of goods which a lorry *or* plane can carry **Beladungsgrenze; load-carrying capacity** = amount of goods which a lorry is capable of carrying **Ladefähigkeit; load factor** = number of seats in a bus *or* train *or* plane which are occupied by passengers who have paid the full fare **Auslastungs-, Kapazitätsfaktor**

(b) workload = amount of work which a person has to do **Arbeitsbelastung;** *he has difficulty in coping with his heavy workload*

2 *verb*

(a) to load a lorry *or* **a ship** = to put goods into a lorry *or* a ship for transporting **einen Lastwagen beladen; ein Schiff beladen;** *to load cargo onto a ship; a truck loaded with boxes; a ship loaded with iron;* **fully loaded ship** = ship which is full of cargo **ein voll beladenes Schiff**

(b) *(Schiff)* to take on cargo **beladen;** *the ship is loading a cargo of wood*

(c) to put a program into a computer **laden;** *load the word-processing program before you start keyboarding*

◇ **loading** *noun* **loading bay** = section of road in a warehouse where lorries can drive in to be loaded **Ladeplatz; loading dock** = part of a harbour where ships can load or unload **Verladedock; loading ramp** = raised platform which makes it easier to load goods onto a lorry **Laderampe**

NOTE: no plural

◇ **load line** *noun* line painted on the side of a ship to show where the water should reach for maximum safety if the ship is fully loaded **Lademarke, Ladelinie**

NOTE: also called Plimsoll line

loan

1 *noun* money which has been lent **Kredit, Darlehen; loan capital** = part of a company's capital which is a loan to be repaid at a later date **Fremd-, Anleihekapital; loan stock** = money lent to a company at a fixed rate of interest **festverzinsliche Anleihen; convertible loan stock** = money which can be exchanged for shares at a later date **Wandelanleihe; bank loan** = money lent by a bank **Bankkredit, Bankdarlehen; bridging loan** = short-term loan to help someone buy a new house when he has not yet sold his old one **Überbrückungskredit; government loan** = money lent by the government **Staatsanleihe; home loan** = loan by a bank or building society to help someone buy a house **Kredit zum Hauskauf; short-term loan** *or* **long-term loan** = loans which have to be repaid within a few weeks or some years **kurzfristiges Darlehen; langfristiges Darlehen; soft loan** = loan (from a company to an employee *or* from one government to another) with no interest payable **zinsloses Darlehen; unsecured loan** = loan made with no security **ungesichertes Darlehen**

2 *verb* to lend **(aus)leihen, verleihen**

lobby

1 *noun* group of people who try to influence members of parliament, members of town councils, etc. **Lobby, Interessenverband; the energy-saving lobby** = people who try to persuade members of parliament to pass laws to save energy **die Lobby der Energiesparer**

2 *verb* to try to influence members of parliament, members of town councils, etc. **Einfluß nehmen (durch Lobbies);** *the group lobbied the chairmen of all the committees*

local

1 *adjective* referring to a particular area, especially one near where a factory *or* an office is based **örtlich, Orts-, lokal; local authority** = elected section of government which runs a small area of the country **örtliche Behörde; local call** = telephone call to a number in the same area as the person making the call **Ortsgespräch; local government** = elected administrative bodies which run areas of the country **Gemeinde-, Kommunalverwaltung; local labour** = workers who are recruited near a factory, and are not brought there from a distance **ortsansässige Arbeitskräfte**

2 *noun US* branch of a trade union **Ortsverein**

◇ **locally** *adverb* in the area near where an office or factory is based **am/vor Ort;** *we recruit all our staff locally*

QUOTE each cheque can be made out for the local equivalent of £100 rounded up to a convenient figure
Sunday Times

QUOTE the business agent for Local 414 of the Store Union said his committee will recommend that the membership ratify the agreement
Toronto Star

QUOTE EC regulations insist that customers can buy cars anywhere in the EC at the local pre-tax price
Financial Times

locate *verb* **to be located** = to be in a certain place **gelegen sein, seinen Sitz haben;** *the warehouse is located near to the motorway*
◇ **location** *noun* place where something is **Lage, Standort; the company has moved to a new location** = the company has moved to a new office or a different town **das Unternehmen hat seinen Standort verlegt**

lock
1 *noun* device for closing a door *or* box so that it can be opened only with a key **Schloß;** *the lock is broken on the petty cash box; I have forgotten the combination of the lock on my briefcase*
2 *verb* to close a door with a key, so that it cannot be opened **abschließen;** *the manager forgot to lock the door of the computer room; the petty cash box was not locked*
◇ **lock out** *verb* **to lock out workers** = to shut the factory door so that workers cannot get in and so force them not to work until the conditions imposed by the management are met **Arbeiter aussperren**
◇ **lockout** *noun* industrial dispute where the management will not let the workers into the factory until they have agreed to the management's conditions **Aussperrung**
◇ **lock up** *verb* **to lock up a shop** *or* **an office** = to close and lock the door at the end of the day's work **abschließen; to lock up capital** = to have capital invested in such a way that it cannot be used for other investments **Kapital anlegen**
◇ **locking up** *noun* **the locking up of money in stock** = investing money in stock so that it cannot be used for other, possibly more profitable, investments **die Festlegung von Geldern in Aktien**
◇ **lock-up** *adjective* **lock-up shop** = shop which has no living accommodation and which the proprietor locks at night when it is closed **Geschäft/Laden (ohne Nebenräume)**

lodge *verb* **to lodge a complaint against someone** = to make an official complaint about someone **gegen jdn Beschwerde einlegen; to lodge money with someone** = to deposit money with someone **Geld bei jdm hinterlegen/deponieren; to lodge securities as collateral** = to put securities into a bank to be used as collateral for a loan **Wertpapiere als Sicherheit hinterlegen**

log *verb* to write down all that happens **Buch führen über; to log phone calls** = to note all details of phone calls made **Telefonanrufe registrieren**
NOTE: **logging - logged**

logo *noun* symbol *or* design *or* group of letters used by a company as a mark on its products and in advertising **Firmenzeichen**

long
1 *adjective* for a large period of time **lang; long credit** = credit terms which allow the borrower a long time to pay **Kredit mit langer Laufzeit; in the long term** = over a long period of time **auf lange Sicht; to take the long view** = to plan for a long period before current investment becomes profitable **etwas langfristig betrachten; auf lange Sicht planen**
2 *noun* **longs** = government stocks which mature in over fifteen years' time **Longs, Langläufer**
◇ **long-dated** *adjective* **long-dated bills** = bills which are payable in more than three months' time **langfristige Wechsel**
◇ **long-distance** *adjective* **a long-distance call** = telephone call to a number which is not near **Ferngespräch; long-distance flight** = flight to a destination which is a long way away **Fern-, Langstreckenflug**
◇ **longhand** *noun* handwriting where the words are written out in full and not typed or in shorthand **Langschrift;** *applications should be written in longhand and sent to the personnel officer*
◇ **long-haul** *adjective* over a long distance **Fern-, Langstrecken-; long-haul flight** = long-distance flight especially between continents **Fern-, Langstreckenflug**
◇ **long-range** *adjective* for a long period of time in the future **langfristig; long-range economic forecast** = forecast which covers a period of several years **langfristige Konjunkturprognose**
◇ **long-standing** *adjective* which has been arranged for a long time **schon lange bestehend, alt;** *long-standing agreement;* **long-standing customer** *or* **customer of long standing** = person who has been a customer for many years **Stammkunde**
◇ **long-term** *adjective* **on a long-term basis** = for a long period of time **langfristig; long-term debts** = debts which will be repaid many years later **langfristige Verbindlichkeiten; long-term forecast** = forecast for a period of over three years **langfristige Prognose; long-term loan** = loan

to be repaid many years later **langfristiges Darlehen; long-term objectives** = aims which will take years to achieve **langfristige Ziele**

> QUOTE land held under long-term leases is not amortized
> *Hongkong Standard*
> QUOTE the company began to experience a demand for longer-term mortgages when the flow of money used to finance these loans diminished
> *Globe and Mail (Toronto)*

loophole *noun* **to find a loophole in the law** = to find a means of legally avoiding the law **eine Gesetzeslücke finden; to find a tax loophole** = to find a means of legally not paying tax **eine Lücke in der Steuergesetzgebung finden**

> QUOTE because capital gains are not taxed but money taken out in profits is taxed, owners of businesses will be using accountants and tax experts to find loopholes in the law
> *Toronto Star*

loose *adjective* not packed together **lose, unverpackt; loose change** = money in coins **Kleingeld; to sell loose sugar** *or* **to sell sugar loose** = to sell sugar in separately weighed quantities, not in packets **Zucker lose verkaufen**

◊ **loose-leaf book** *noun* book with loose pages which can be taken out and fixed back in again on rings **Ringbuch**

lorry *noun* large motor vehicle for carrying goods **Last(kraft)wagen;** *he drives a five-ton lorry;* **heavy lorry** = very large lorry which carries heavy loads **Schwergutlastwagen; lorry driver** = person who drives a lorry **Lastwagenfahrer**
NOTE: US English is **truck**

lose *verb*
(a) not to have something any more **verlieren; to lose an order** = not to get an order which you were hoping to get **einen Auftrag verlieren;** *during the strike, the company lost six orders to American competitors;* **to lose control of a company** = to find that you have less than 50% of the shares and so are no longer able to direct the company **die Aktienmehrheit an einem Unternehmen verlieren; to lose customers** = to have fewer customers **Kunden verlieren;** *their service is so slow that they have been losing customers;* **she lost her job when the factory closed** = she was made redundant **sie verlor ihre Stelle, als die Fabrik schloß**
(b) to have less money **verlieren;** *he lost £25,000 in his father's computer company;* **the pound has lost value** = the pound is worth less **das Pfund hat an Wert verloren**
(c) to drop to a lower price **einbüßen, verlieren;** *the dollar lost two cents against the yen; gold shares lost 5% on the market yesterday*
NOTE: **losing - lost**

◊ **lose out** *verb* to suffer as a result of something **Verluste hinnehmen müssen; den kürzeren ziehen;** *the company has lost out in the rush to make cheap computers*

loss *noun*
(a) loss of customers = not keeping customers because of bad service *or* high prices, etc. **Kundenabgänge; loss of an order** = not getting an order which was expected **Auftragsverlust; the company suffered a loss of market penetration** = the company found it had a smaller share of the market **das Unternehmen verlor Absatzgebiete; compensation for loss of earnings** = payment to someone who has stopped earning money *or* who is not able to earn money **Verdienstausfallentschädigung; compensation for loss of office** = payment to a director who is asked to leave a company before his contract ends **Entlassungsabfindung**
(b) having less money than before *or* not making a profit **Verlust, Einbuße; the company suffered a loss** = the company did not make a profit **die Firma mußte Verluste hinnehmen; to report a loss** = not to show a profit in the accounts at the end of the year **Verluste ausweisen;** *the company reported a loss of £1m on the first year's trading;* **capital loss** = loss made by selling assets **Kapitalverlust; the car was written off as a dead loss** *or* **a total loss** = the car was so badly damaged that the insurers said it had no value **das Auto wurde als Totalschaden abgeschrieben; paper loss** = loss made when an asset has fallen in value but has not been sold **nicht realisierter Verlust; trading loss** = situation where the company's receipts are less than its expenditure **Geschäftsverlust; at a loss** = making a loss *or* not making any profit **mit Verlust;** *the company is trading at a loss; he sold the shop at a loss;* **to cut one's losses** = to stop doing something which was losing money **seine Verluste verringern**
(c) being worth less *or* having a lower value **Verlust;** *shares showed losses of up to 5% on the Stock Exchange*
(d) loss in weight = goods which weigh less than when they were packed **Gewichtsverlust, Gewichtsschwund; loss in transport** = amount of weight which is lost while goods are being transported **Transportverlust, Transportschaden**

◊ **loss-leader** *noun* article which is sold at a loss to attract customers **Lockartikel;** *we use these cheap films as a loss-leader*

QUOTE against losses of FFr 7.7m in 1983, the company made a net profit of FFr 300,000 last year
Financial Times

lot *noun*
(a) large quantity **Menge, Masse;** *a lot of people or lots of people are out of work*
(b) group of items sold together at an auction **Los;** *to bid for lot 23; at the end of the auction half the lots were unsold*
(c) group of shares which are sold **Aktienpaket;** *to sell a lot of shares; to sell shares in small lots*
(d) *US* piece of land, especially one to be used for redevelopment **Bauplatz**

lottery *noun* game where numbered tickets are sold and prizes given for some of the numbers **Lotterie**

lounge *noun* comfortable room; *(Haus)* **Wohnzimmer;** *(Hotel)* **Gesellschaftsraum, Lounge; departure lounge** = room in an airport where passengers wait to board their planes **Abflughalle; transit lounge** = room in an airport where passengers wait for connecting flights **Transitraum**

low
1 *adjective* small *or* not high **niedrig, gering;** *low overhead costs keep the unit cost low; we try to keep our wages bill low; the company offered him a mortgage at a low rate of interest; the pound is at a very low rate of exchange against the dollar; our aim is to buy at the lowest price possible;;* **low sales** = small amount of money produced by sales **geringe Verkaufserträge; low volume of sales** = small number of items sold **geringer Absatz; the tender will go to the lowest bidder** = the contract will be awarded to the person who offers the best terms **der Auftrag wird an den preisgünstigsten Anbieter vergeben**
2 *noun* point where prices *or* sales are very small **Tiefstand;** *sales have reached a new low; the highs and lows on the stock market;* **shares have hit an all-time low** = shares have reached their lowest price ever **Aktien sind auf den niedrigsten Stand aller Zeiten gefallen**
◇ **lower**
1 *adjective* smaller *or* less high **niedriger, geringer;** *a lower rate of interest; sales were lower in December than in November*
2 *verb* to make smaller *or* less expensive **senken;** *to lower prices to secure a larger market share; to lower the interest rate*
◇ **lowering** *noun* making smaller *or* less expensive **Senkung, Verminderung;** *lowering of prices; we hope to achieve low prices with no lowering of quality*
NOTE: no plural
◇ **low-grade** *adjective* not very important *or* not of very good quality **untergeordnet; minderwertig; low-grade petrol Benzin mit niedriger Oktanzahl;** *a low-grade official from the Ministry of Commerce*
◇ **low-level** *adjective*
(a) not very important **untergeordnet, nieder, auf unterer Ebene;** *a low-level delegation visited the ministry; a low-level meeting decided to put off making a decision*
(b) low-level computer language = programming language similar to machine code **maschinenorientierte Programmiersprache**
◇ **low-pressure** *adjective* **low-pressure sales** = sales where the salesman does not force someone to buy, but only encourages him to do so **nicht-aggressive Verkaufsmethoden**
◇ **low-quality** *adjective* not of good quality **minderwertig;** *they tried to sell us some low-quality steel*

QUOTE after opening at 79.1 the index touched a peak of 79.2 and then drifted to a low of 78.8
Financial Times

QUOTE the pound which had been as low as $1.02 earlier this year, rose to $1.30
Fortune

QUOTE Canadian and European negotiators agreed to a deal under which Canada could keep its quotas but lower its import duties
Globe and Mail (Toronto)

loyalty *noun* **brand loyalty** = feeling of a customer who always buys the same brand of product **Markentreue; customer loyalty** = feeling of customers who always shop at the same shop **Kundentreue**

Ltd = LIMITED

luggage *noun* suitcases *or* bags for carrying clothes when travelling **Reisegepäck; hand luggage** *or* **cabin luggage** = small cases which passengers can take with them into the cabin of a plane *or* ship **Handgepäck; free luggage allowance** = amount of luggage which a passenger can take with him free of charge **Freigepäck**
NOTE: no plural; to show one suitcase, etc., say **a piece of luggage**

lull *noun* quiet period **Flaute;** *after last week's hectic trading this week's lull was welcome*

lump *noun* **lump sum** = money paid in one single amount, not in several small sums **Pauschalbetrag;** *when he retired he was given a lump-sum bonus; she sold her house and invested the money as a lump sum*

lunch *noun* meal eaten in the middle of the day **Mittagessen;** *the hours of work are from 9.30 to 5.30 with an hour off for lunch; the chairman is out at lunch;* **business lunch** = meeting between businessmen where they have lunch together to discuss business deals **Geschäftsessen**

◇ **lunch hour** *or* **lunchtime** *noun* time when people have lunch **Mittagspause;** *the office is closed during the lunch hour or at lunchtimes*

◇ **luncheon voucher** *noun* ticket given by an employer to a worker in addition to his wages, which can be exchanged for food in a restaurant **Essensmarke**

luxury *noun* expensive thing which is not necessary but which is good to have **Luxus;** *luxury items or luxury goods; a black market in luxury articles*

Mm

m = METRE, MILE, MILLION

M1 British measure of money supply, including all coins and notes plus personal money in current accounts **M1**

◇ **M2** British measure of money supply, including coins and notes and personal money in current and deposit accounts **M2**

◇ **M3** British measure of money supply, including coins and notes, personal money in current and deposit accounts, government deposits and deposits in currencies other than sterling; **£M3** = British measure of sterling money supply, including coins and notes, personal money in current and deposit accounts and government deposits **£M3**

NOTE: say "sterling M3"

machine *noun*

(a) device which works with power from a motor **Maschine, Apparat; adding machine** = machine which adds numbers **Addiermaschine; copying machine** *or* **duplicating machine** = machine which makes copies of documents **Kopiergerät, Kopierer; Vervielfältigungsgerät; dictating machine** = machine which records what someone dictates, which a typist can then play back and type out **Diktiergerät; automatic vending machine** = machine which provides food or drink when money is put in it **Automat; machine shop** = place where working machines are placed **Maschinensaal; machine tools** = tools worked by motors, used to work on wood or metal **Werkzeugmaschinen**

(b) machine-made *or* **machine-produced** = manufactured by a machine, not by people **maschinell hergestellt**

(c) machine code *or* **machine language** = instructions and information shown as a series of figures (0 and 1) which can be read by a computer **Maschinencode; Maschinensprache; machine-readable codes** = sets of signs or letters (such as bar codes, post codes) which a computer can read **maschinenlesbare Codes**

◇ **machinery** *noun*

(a) machines **Maschinen; idle machinery** *or* **machinery lying idle** = machines not being used **stilliegende Maschinen; machinery guards** = pieces of metal to prevent workers from getting hurt by the moving parts of a machine **Maschinen-Schutzvorrichtungen**

(b) organization *or* system **Apparat, Maschinerie;** *the government machinery; the machinery of local government; administrative machinery; the machinery for awarding government contracts*

NOTE: no plural

◇ **machinist** *noun* person who works a machine **Maschinist/-in**

macro- *prefix* very large, covering a wide area **makro-, Makro-; macro-economics** = study of the economics of a whole area *or* whole industry *or* whole group of the population *or* whole country, in order to help in economic planning **Makroökonomie**

Madam *noun* formal way of addressing a woman, especially one whom you do not know **Gnädige Frau; Dear Madam** = beginning of a letter to a woman whom you do not know **Sehr geehrte gnädige Frau; Madam Chairman** = way of addressing a woman who is in the chair at the meeting **Frau Vorsitzende**

made *adjective* produced *or* manufactured **gemacht, hergestellt;** *made in Japan or Japanese made; see also* MAKE

magazine *noun* paper, usually with pictures, which comes out regularly, every month or every week **Zeitschrift, Magazin; computer magazine** = magazine with articles on computers and programs **Computerzeitschrift; do-it-yourself magazine** = magazine with articles on work which the average person can do to repair or paint the house **Heimwerkermagazin; house magazine** = magazine produced for the workers in a company to give them news of the company's affairs **Werkszeitung; trade**

magazine = magazine produced for people or companies in certain trades **Fachzeitschrift; travel magazine** = magazine with articles on holidays and travel **Reisemagazin; women's magazine** = magazine aimed at the women's market **Frauenzeitschrift; magazine insert** = advertising sheet put into a magazine when it is mailed or sold **Werbebeilage; to insert a leaflet in a specialist magazine** = to put an advertising leaflet into a magazine before it is mailed or sold **einen Anzeigenteil in eine Fachzeitschrift einlegen; magazine mailing** = sending of copies of a magazine by post to subscribers **Zeitschriftenzustellung per Post**

magnate

noun important businessman **Magnat;** *a shipping magnate*

magnetic tape

or informal

mag tape

noun plastic tape for recording information on a large computer **Magnetband**

mail

1 *noun*

(a) system of sending letters and parcels from one place to another **Post;** *to put a letter in the mail; the cheque was lost in the mail; the invoice was put in the mail yesterday; mail to some of the islands in the Pacific can take six weeks;* **by mail** = using the postal services, not sending something by hand or by messenger **per Post; to send a package by surface mail** = to send a package by land or sea, not by air **ein Paket mit gewöhnlicher Post (auf dem Land- od Seeweg) schicken; by sea mail** = sent by post abroad, using a ship **auf dem Seeweg; to receive a sample by air mail** = by post using a plane **ein Muster per Luftpost erhalten; we sent the order by first-class mail** = by the most expensive mail service, designed to be faster **wir schicken die Bestellung per Post erster Klasse; electronic mail** = system of sending messages from one computer to another, using the telephone lines **elektronische Post, E-Mail**

(b) letters sent or received **Post;** *has the mail arrived yet? to open the mail; your cheque arrived in yesterday's mail; my secretary opens my mail as soon as it arrives; the receipt was in this morning's mail;* **incoming mail** = mail which arrives **Posteingang; outgoing mail** = mail which is sent out **Postausgang; mail room** = room in an office where incoming letters are sorted and sent to each department, and where outgoing mail is collected for sending **Poststelle**

(c) direct mail = selling a product by sending publicity material to possible buyers through the post **Direktversand; Direktwerbung;** *the company runs a successful direct-mail operation; these calculators are sold only by direct mail;* **direct-mail advertising** = advertising by sending leaflets to people by post **Briefwerbung; mail shot** = leaflets sent by mail to possible customers **Rundschreiben, Briefwerbeaktion**

NOTE: no plural

2 *verb* to send something by post **(mit der Post) schicken, aufgeben;** *to mail a letter; we mailed our order last Wednesday*

◊ **mail box** *noun* one of several boxes where incoming mail is put in a large building; box for putting letters, etc. which you want to post **Postfach; Briefkasten**

◊ **mailing** *noun* sending something in the post **Verschicken, Versenden;** *the mailing of publicity material;* **direct mailing** = sending of publicity material by post to possible buyers **Direktversand; Direktwerbung; mailing list** = list of names and addresses of people who might be interested in a product *or* list of names and addresses of members of a society **Adressenliste;** *his name is on our mailing list; to build up a mailing list;* **to buy a mailing list** = to pay a society, etc. money to buy the list of members so that you can use it to mail publicity material **eine Adressenliste kaufen; mailing piece** = leaflet suitable for sending by direct mail **Postwurfsendung; mailing shot** = leaflets sent by mail to possible customers **Rundschreiben, Briefwerbeaktion**

◊ **mail-order** *noun* system of buying and selling from a catalogue, placing orders and sending goods by mail **Postversand; mail-order business** *or* **mail-order firm** *or* **mail-order house** = company which sells a product by mail **Versandhaus; mail-order catalogue** = catalogue from which a customer can order items to be sent by mail **Versandhauskatalog**

main

adjective most important **Haupt-;** *main office; main building; one of our main customers;* US **Main Street** = most important street in a town, where the shops and banks are **Hauptstraße**

◊ **mainframe** *noun* large computer **Großrechner;** *the office micro interfaces with the mainframe in the head office*

◊ **mainly** *adverb* mostly *or* usually **hauptsächlich, in erster Linie;** *their sales are mainly in the home market; we are interested mainly in buying children's gift items*

maintain

verb

(a) to keep something going *or* working **aufrechterhalten, unter-, erhalten;** *to maintain good relations with one's customers; to maintain contact with an overseas market*

(b) to keep something working at the same level **(er)halten;** *the company has maintained the same volume of business in spite of the recession; to maintain an interest rate at 5%;* **to maintain a dividend** = to pay the same dividend as the previous year **eine Dividende in gleicher Höhe ausschütten**

◇ **maintenance** *noun*

(a) keeping things going *or* working **Aufrechterhaltung, Erhaltung;** *maintenance of contacts; maintenance of supplies*

(b) keeping a machine in good working order **Wartung; Instandhaltung; maintenance contract** = contract by which a company keeps a piece of equipment in good working order **Wartungsvertrag;** *we offer a full maintenance service*

> QUOTE responsibilities include the maintenance of large computerized databases
> *Times*
>
> QUOTE the federal administration launched a full-scale investigation into the airline's maintenance procedures
> *Fortune*

majeure *see* FORCE MAJEURE

major *adjective* important **Groß-, Haupt-, bedeutend; major shareholder** = shareholder with a large number of shares **Hauptaktionär**

◇ **majority** *noun* larger group than all others **Mehrheit, Majorität; majority of the shareholders** = more than 50% of the shareholders **die Mehrheit der Aktionäre; the board accepted the proposal by a majority of three to two** = three members of the board voted to accept and two voted against **der Vorstand nahm den Vorschlag mit einer Mehrheit von drei zu zwei Stimmen an; majority vote** *or* **majority decision** = decision made after a vote according to the wishes of the largest group **Mehrheitsbeschluß; majority shareholding** *or* **majority interest** = group of more than half of all the shares in a company **Mehrheitsbeteiligung; a majority shareholder** = person who owns more than half the shares in a company **ein Mehrheitsaktionär**

> QUOTE if the share price sinks much further the company is going to look tempting to any major takeover merchant
> *Australian Financial Review*
>
> QUOTE monetary officials have reasoned that coordinated greenback sales would be able to drive the dollar down against other major currencies
> *Duns Business Month*
>
> QUOTE a client base which includes many major commercial organizations and nationalized industries
> *Times*

make

1 *noun* type of product manufactured **Marke, Fabrikat;** *Japanese makes of cars; a standard make of equipment; what make is the new computer system or what is the make of the new computer system?*

2 *verb*

(a) to produce *or* to manufacture **herstellen, produzieren;** *to make a car or to make a computer; the workmen spent ten weeks making the table; the factory makes three hundred cars a day*

(b) to sign *or* to agree **(ab)schließen;** *to make a deal or to make an agreement;* **to make a bid for something** = to offer to buy something **ein Angebot machen; to make a payment** = to pay **eine Zahlung leisten; to make a deposit** = to pay money as a deposit **eine Anzahlung leisten**

(c) to earn *or* to increase in value **verdienen; erzielen;** *he makes £50,000 a year or £25 an hour; the shares made $2.92 in today's trading*

(d) to make a profit *or* **to make a loss** = to have more money *or* less money after a deal **einen Gewinn machen; einen Verlust machen; to make a killing** = to make a very large profit **einen (großen) Reibach machen**

NOTE: **making - made**

◇ **make good** *verb*

(a) to repair *or* to compensate **wiedergutmachen;** *the company will make good the damage; to make good a loss*

(b) to be a success **es schaffen, es zu etwas bringen; his son made good** = local person who becomes successful **sein Sohn hat es geschafft**

◇ **make out** *verb* to write **ausstellen;** *to make out an invoice; the bill is made out to Smith & Co.;* **to make out a cheque to someone** = to write someone's name on a cheque **jdm einen Scheck ausstellen**

◇ **make over** *verb* to transfer property legally **überschreiben;** *to make over the house to one's children*

◇ **make up** *verb*

(a) to compensate for something **wiedergutmachen; ausgleichen; to make up a loss** *or* **to make up the difference** = to pay extra so that the loss or difference is covered **einen Verlust ausgleichen; eine Differenz ausgleichen**

(b) to make up accounts = to complete the accounts **die Bücher abschließen**

◇ **make up for** *verb* to compensate for something **wiedergutmachen, ausgleichen;** *to make up for a short payment or to make up for a late payment*

◇ **maker** *noun* person who makes something **Hersteller;** *a major car maker; a furniture maker;* **decision maker** = person who decides *or* who takes decisions **Entscheidungsträger**

◊ **making** *noun* production of an item **Herstellung;** *ten tons of concrete were used in the making of the wall;* **decision making** = act of coming to a decision **Entscheidungsfindung**

maladministration *noun* incompetent administration **schlechte Verwaltung; Mißwirtschaft**

mall *noun US* **shopping mall** = enclosed covered area for shopping, with shops, restaurants, banks and other facilities **Einkaufspassage, Mall**

man
1 *noun* person *or* ordinary worker **Mann;** *all the men went back to work yesterday*
2 *verb* to provide the workforce for something **besetzen;** *to man a shift; to man an exhibition; the exhibition stand was manned by three salesgirls; see also* MANNED, MANNING

manage *verb*
(a) to direct *or* to be in charge of **leiten, führen;** *to manage a department; to manage a branch office*
(b) to manage property = to look after rented property for the owner **Immobilienbesitz verwalten**
(c) to manage to = to be able to do something **es schaffen, es fertigbringen;** *did you manage to see the head buyer? she managed to write six orders and take three phone calls all in two minutes*

◊ **manageable** *adjective* which can be dealt with easily **zu bewältigen;** *difficulties which are still manageable; the problems are too large to be manageable*

◊ **management** *noun*
(a) directing *or* running a business **Unternehmensführung, Management;** *to study management; good management or efficient management; bad management or inefficient management; a management graduate or a graduate in management;* **line management** = organization of a business where each manager is responsible for doing what his superior tells him to do **Linienmanagement; portfolio management** = buying and selling shares by a person or by a specialist on behalf of a client **Effekten-, Portfoliomanagement; product management** = directing the making and selling of a product as an independent item **Produkt-Management; management accountant** = accountant who prepares specialized information for managers so that they can make decisions **Finanzbuchhalter; management accounts** = financial information (on sales, costs, credit, profitability) prepared for a manager **Rechnungsbericht für die besonderen Zwecke der Unternehmensleitung; Geschäftsbilanz; management committee** = committee which manages a club, a pension fund, etc. **geschäftsführender Ausschuß; Vorstandsgremium; management consultant** = person who gives advice on how to manage a business **Unternehmensberater; management course** = training course for managers **Managerkurs; management by objectives** = way of managing a business by planning work for the managers and testing to see if it is completed correctly and on time **Unternehmensführung mit Zielvorgabe; management team** = a group of managers working together **Management-Team; management techniques** = ways of managing a business **Managementmethoden; management training** = training managers by making them study problems and work out ways of solving them **Management-Ausbildung; management trainee** = young person being trained to be a manager **Führungsnachwuchs**
(b) group of managers or directors **Unternehmensleitung, Management;** *the management has decided to give an overall pay increase;* **top management** = the main directors of a company **Unternehmensspitze, Top-Management; middle management** = the department managers of a company who carry out the policy set by the directors and organize the work of a group of workers **mittleres Management**
NOTE: no plural for (a)

◊ **manager** *noun*
(a) head of a department in a company **Abteilungsleiter;** *a department manager; personnel manager; production manager; sales manager;* **accounts manager** = head of the accounts department **Leiter/-in der Buchhaltung; area manager** = manager who is responsible for the company's work (usually sales) in an area **Bezirks-, Gebietsleiter; general manager** = manager in charge of the administration in a large company **geschäftsführender Direktor**
(b) person in charge of a branch or shop **Geschäftsleiter;** *Mr Smith is the manager of our local Lloyds Bank; the manager of our Lagos branch is in London for a series of meetings;* **bank manager** = person in charge of a branch of a bank **Bankdirektor; branch manager** = person in charge of a branch of a company **Filialleiter**

◊ **manageress** *noun* woman who runs a shop, or a department **Geschäftsleiterin; Abteilungsleiterin; Managerin**

◊ **managerial** *adjective* referring to managers **Management-, Führungs-;** *managerial staff;* **to be appointed to a managerial position** = to be appointed a manager **auf eine Manager-Position berufen werden; decisions taken at managerial level** = decisions taken by managers **auf der oberen Geschäftsebene getroffene Entscheidungen**

◇ **managership** *noun* job of being a manager **Managertätigkeit;** *after six years, he was offered the managership of a branch in Scotland*

◇ **managing** *adjective* **managing director** = director who is in charge of a whole company **geschäftsführender Direktor, Geschäftsführer; chairman and managing director** = managing director who is also chairman of the board of directors **Vorsitzender und Geschäftsführer**

> QUOTE the management says that the rate of loss-making has come down and it expects further improvement in the next few years
> *Financial Times*
>
> QUOTE the research director will manage and direct a team of graduate business analysts reporting on consumer behaviour throughout the UK
> *Times*
>
> QUOTE the No. 1 managerial productivity problem in America is managers who are out of touch with their people and out of touch with their customers
> *Fortune*

mandate *noun* **bank mandate** = written order allowing someone to sign cheques on behalf of a company **Bankvollmacht**

mandatory *adjective* **mandatory meeting** = meeting which all members have to attend **obligatorische Sitzung**

man-hour *noun* work done by one man in one hour **Mannstunde, Arbeitsstunde;** *one million man-hours were lost through industrial action*

manifest *noun* list of goods in a shipment **Ladeliste; passenger manifest** = list of passengers on a ship or plane **Passagierliste**

manilla *noun* thick brown paper **Hartpapier, braunes Papier;** *a manilla envelope*
NOTE: no plural

manipulate *verb* **to manipulate the accounts** = to make false accounts so that the company seems profitable **die Bücher schönen; to manipulate the market** = to work to influence share prices in your favour **die Börsenkurse manipulieren**

◇ **manipulation** *noun* **stock market manipulation** = trying to influence the price of shares **Kursmanipulation**

◇ **manipulator** *noun* **stock market manipulator** = person who tries to influence the price of shares in his own favour **Kursmanipulant**

manned *adjective* with someone working on it **besetzt; bemannt;** *the switchboard is manned twenty-four hours a day; the stand was manned by our sales staff*

◇ **manning** *noun* people who are needed to do a work process **Besetzung; Bemannung; manning levels** = number of people required in each department of a company to do the work efficiently **Personalstärke, Personalbestand; manning agreement** *or* **agreement on manning** = agreement between the company and the workers about how many workers are needed for a certain job; *entspricht* **Stellenbesetzungsplan**
NOTE: no plural

manpower *noun* number of workers **Personalbestand; manpower forecasting** = forecasting how many workers will be needed, and how many will be available **Personalbestandsprognose; manpower planning** = planning to obtain the right number of workers in each job **Personalplanung; manpower requirements** = number of workers needed **Bedarf an Arbeitskräften; manpower shortage** *or* **shortage of manpower** = lack of workers **Arbeitskräftemangel**
NOTE: no plural

manual
1 *adjective* done by hand *or* done using the hands **handgemacht, manuell; manual labour** *or* **manual work** = heavy work done by hand **körperliche Arbeit; manual labourer** = person who does heavy work with his hands **ungelernte Arbeitskraft; manual worker** = person who works with his hands **ungelernte Arbeitskraft**
2 *noun* book of instructions **Handbuch; operating manual** = book showing how to operate a machine **Bedienungsanleitung; service manual** = book showing how to service a machine **Wartungshandbuch**

◇ **manually** *adverb* done by hand, not by a machine **von Hand, manuell;** *invoices have had to be made manually because the computer has broken down*

manufacture
1 *verb* to make a product for sale, using machines **(maschinell) herstellen/fertigen;** *manufactured goods; the company manufactures spare parts for cars*
2 *noun* making a product for sale, using machines **Herstellung, Fertigung; products of**

foreign manufacture = products made in foreign countries **ausländische Fabrikate**
NOTE: no plural

◇ **manufacturer** *noun* person *or* company which produces machine-made products **Hersteller;** *foreign manufacturers; cotton manufacturer; sports car manufacturer;* **manufacturer's recommended price** = price at which the manufacturer suggests the product should be sold on the retail market, though often reduced by the retailer **empfohlener Herstellerpreis;** *all typewriters - 20% off the manufacturer's recommended price*

◇ **manufacturing** *noun* producing machine-made products for sale **Herstellung, Fertigung;** *manufacturing overheads; manufacturing processes;* **manufacturing capacity** = amount of a product which a factory is capable of making **Fertigungskapazität; manufacturing costs** = costs of making a product **Herstellungskosten; manufacturing industries** = industries which take raw materials and make them into finished products **verarbeitende Industrie**
NOTE: no plural

margin *noun*

(a) difference between the money received when selling a product and the money paid for it **Gewinnspanne, Marge; gross margin** = percentage difference between the unit manufacturing cost and the received price **Bruttomarge; net margin** = percentage difference between received price and all costs, including overheads **Nettomarge; we are cutting our margins very fine** = we are reducing our margins to the smallest possible to be competitive **wir haben unsere Gewinnspannen sehr eng bemessen; our margins have been squeezed** = profits have been reduced because our margins have to be smaller to stay competitive **unsere Gewinnspannen sind gedrückt worden**
(b) extra space *or* time allowed **Spielraum; margin of error** = number of mistakes which are accepted in a document *or* in a calculation **Fehlerspielraum; safety margin** = time *or* space allowed for something to be safe **Sicherheitsspielraum; margin of safety** = sales which are above the breakeven point **Sicherheitsmarge**

◇ **marginal** *adjective*
(a) marginal cost = cost of making a single extra unit above the number already planned **Grenzkosten; marginal pricing** = making the selling price the same as the marginal cost **Grenzkostenpreiskalkulation; marginal rate of tax** = percentage of tax which a taxpayer pays at the top rate **Grenzsteuersatz; marginal revenue** = income from selling a single extra unit above the number already sold **Grenzertrag**
(b) not very profitable *or* hardly worth the money paid **marginal, knapp, gering;** *marginal return on investment;* **marginal land** = land which is almost not worth farming **marginaler Boden; marginal purchase** = thing which a buyer feels is only just worth buying **Grenzkauf, gerade noch vertretbarer Kauf**

> QUOTE profit margins in the industries most exposed to foreign competition - machinery, transportation equipment and electrical goods - are significantly worse than usual
> QUOTE pensioner groups claim that pensioners have the highest marginal rates of tax. Income earned by pensioners above $30 a week is taxed at 62.5 per cent, more than the highest marginal rate
> *Australian Financial Review*

marine

1 *adjective* referring to the sea **Meeres-, See-; marine insurance** = insurance of ships and their cargoes **See(transport)versicherung; marine underwriter** = person who insures ships and their cargoes **Seeversicherer**
2 *noun* **the merchant marine** = all the commercial ships of a country **die Handelsmarine**

◇ **maritime** *adjective* referring to the sea **See-, Schiffahrts-; maritime law** = laws referring to ships, ports, etc. **Seerecht; maritime lawyer** = lawyer who specializes in legal matters concerning ships and cargoes **ein auf Seerecht spezialisierter Jurist; maritime trade** = transporting commercial goods by sea **Seehandel**

mark

1 *noun*
(a) sign put on an item to show something **Markierung, Zeichen; assay mark** = hallmark *or* mark put on gold or silver items to show that the metal is of the correct quality **Feingehaltsstempel;** *GB* **kite mark** = mark on goods to show that they meet official standards **(dreieckiges) Gütezeichen**
(b) money used in Germany **(D-)Mark;** *the price is twenty-five marks; the mark rose against the dollar*
NOTE: usually written **DM** after a figure: **25DM.** Also called **Deutschmark, D-Mark**
2 *verb* to put a sign on something **markieren, bezeichnen;** *to mark a product "for export only"; article marked at £1.50; to mark the price on something*

◇ **mark down** *verb* to make lower **heruntersetzen, senken; to mark down a price** = to lower the price of something **einen Preis heruntersetzen;** *this range has been marked down to $24.99; we have marked all prices down by 30% for the sale*

◇ **mark-down** *noun*

(a) reduction of the price of something to less than its usual price **Preissenkung**
(b) percentage amount by which a price has been lowered **Preisnachlaß, Rabatt;** *we have used a 30% mark-down to fix the sale price*

◇ **marker pen** *noun* felt pen which makes a wide coloured mark **Textmarker**

◇ **mark up** *verb* to increase **erhöhen, heraufsetzen; to mark prices up** = to increase prices **Preise erhöhen;** *these prices have been marked up by 10%*

◇ **mark-up** *noun*
(a) increase in price **Preiserhöhung, Preisaufschlag;** *we put into effect a 10% mark-up of all prices in June*
(b) amount added to the cost price to give the selling price **Handelsspanne; we work to a 3.5 times mark-up** *or* **to a 350% mark-up** = we take the unit cost and multiply by 3.5 to give the selling price **wir haben eine 350%ige Gewinnspanne**

market

1 *noun*
(a) place (often in the open air) where farm produce is sold **Markt;** *fish market; flower market; open-air market; here are this week's market prices for sheep;* **flea market** = market for secondhand goods **Flohmarkt; market day** = day when a market is regularly held **Markttag;** *Tuesday is market day, so the streets are closed to traffic;* **market dues** = rent for a stall in a market **Standmiete**
(b) the Common Market = the European Economic Community **der Gemeinsame Markt;** *the Common Market agricultural policy or the Common Market ministers;* **the Single Market** european trading market within the Common Market where no restrictions exist **der Binnenmarkt**
(c) place where a product might be sold *or* group of people who might buy a product **Markt, Absatzgebiet; home** *or* **domestic market** = market in the country where the selling company is based **Binnen-, Inlandsmarkt;** *sales in the home market rose by 22%*
(d) possible sales of a certain type of product *or* demand for a certain type of product **Markt, Absatzmarkt;** *the market for home computers has fallen sharply; we have 20% of the British car market; there is no market for electric typewriters;* **a growth market** = market where sales are likely to rise rapidly **ein Wachstumsmarkt; the labour market** = number of workers available for work **der Arbeitsmarkt; 25,000 graduates have come on to the labour market** = they have become available for work because they have left college **25.000 Hochschulabgänger stehen dem Arbeitsmarkt zur Verfügung; the property market** = sales of houses **Immobilien- und Grundstücksmarkt**
(e) the black market = buying and selling goods in a way which is not allowed by law **der Schwarzmarkt;** *there is a flourishing black market in spare parts for cars;* **to pay black market prices** = to pay high prices to get items which are not easily available **Schwarzmarktpreise bezahlen**
(f) a buyer's market = market where goods are sold cheaply because there is little demand **Käufermarkt; a seller's market** = market where the seller can ask high prices because there is a large demand for the product **Verkäufermarkt**
(g) closed market = market where a supplier deals with only one agent or distributor and does not supply any others direct **geschlossener Markt; free market economy** = system where the government does not interfere in business activity in any way **freie Marktwirtschaft; open market** = market where anyone can buy and sell **offener Markt**
(h) capital market = place where companies can look for investment capital **Kapitalmarkt; the foreign exchange markets** = places where currencies are bought or sold **die Devisenmärkte; forward markets** = places where foreign currency or commodities can be bought or sold for delivery at a later date **Terminmarkt; money market** *or* **finance market** = place where large sums of money are lent or borrowed **Finanzmarkt**
(i) commodity market = place where commodities are bought or sold **Warenbörse; stock market** = place where shares are bought and sold **Börse;** *the market in oil shares was very active or there was a brisk market in oil shares;* **to buy shares in the open market** = to buy shares on the Stock Exchange, not privately **Aktien im Freiverkehr kaufen; over-the-counter market** = secondary market in shares which are not listed on the main Stock Exchange **Freiverkehr(smarkt) (für nicht im offiziellen Börsenhandel zugelassene Aktien)**
(j) market analysis = detailed examination and report on a market **Marktanalyse; market capitalization** = value of a company calculated by multiplying the price of its shares on the Stock Exchange by the number of shares issued **Börsenkapitalisierung; market economist** = person who specializes in the study of financial structures and the return on investments in the stock market **Börsenanalytiker; market forces** = influences on the sales of a product **Marktkräfte; market forecast** = forecast of prices on the stock market **Marktprognose; market leader** = company with the largest market share **Marktführer;** *we are the market leader in*

home computers; **market opportunities** = possibility of finding new sales in a market **neue Absatzmöglichkeiten; market penetration** *or* **market share** = percentage of a total market which the sales of a company cover **Marktdurchdringung; Marktanteil;** *we hope our new product range will increase our market share;* **market price** = price at which a product can be sold **Marktpreis; market rate** = normal price in the market **Marktpreis, üblicher Tarif;** *we pay the market rate for secretaries or we pay secretaries the market rate;* **market research** = examining the possible sales of a product before it is put on the market **Marktforschung; market trends** = gradual changes taking place in a market **Marktentwicklung, Markttendenzen; market value** = value of a product *or* of a company if sold today **Marktwert**

(k) up market *or* **down market** = more expensive *or* less expensive **exklusiver/anspruchsvoller Markt; Massenmarkt; to go up market** *or* **to go down market** = to make products which appeal to a wealthy section of the market *or* to a wider, less wealthy, section of the market **sich an einen exklusiven Kundenkreis wenden; sich an Massenkundschaft wenden**

(l) to be in the market for secondhand cars = to look for secondhand cars to buy **in der Gebrauchtwagenbranche sein; to come on to the market** = to start to be sold **auf den Markt kommen;** *this soap has just come on to the market;* **to put something on the market** = to start to offer something for sale **etwas auf den Markt bringen;** *they put their house on the market; I hear the company has been put on the market;* **the company has priced itself out of the market** = the company has raised its prices so high that its products do not sell **das Unternehmen hat sich durch überhöhte Preise wettbewerbsunfähig gemacht**

2 *verb* to sell (products) **vertreiben, auf den Markt bringen;** *this product is being marketed in all European countries*

◇ **marketable** *adjective* which can be sold easily **absatz-, marktfähig**

◇ **marketing** *noun* techniques used in selling a product (such as packaging, advertising, etc.) **Marketing; marketing agreement** = contract by which one company will market another company's products **Vertriebsvereinbarung; marketing department** = department in a company which specializes in using marketing techniques to sell a product **Marketingabteilung; marketing manager** = person in charge of a marketing department **Marketingmanager; marketing policy** *or* **marketing plans** = ideas of how the company's products are going to be marketed **Absatzpolitik;** *to plan the marketing of a new product*

NOTE: no plural

◇ **market-maker** *noun* person who buys and sells shares for clients on the Stock Exchange **Market-maker**

◇ **marketplace** *noun*

(a) open space in the middle of a town where a market is held **Marktplatz**

(b) place where goods are sold **Markt;** *our salesmen find life difficult in the marketplace; what is the reaction to the new car in the marketplace? or what is the marketplace reaction to the new car?*

> QUOTE after the prime rate cut yesterday, there was a further fall in short-term market rates
> ***Financial Times***
>
> QUOTE market analysts described the falls in the second half of last week as a technical correction to a market which had been pushed by demand to over the 900 index level
> ***Australian Financial Review***
>
> QUOTE reporting to the marketing director, the successful applicant will be responsible for the development of a training programme for the new sales force
> ***Times***
>
> QUOTE most discounted fares are sold by bucket shops but in today's competitive marketplace any agent can supply them
> ***Business Traveller***

mart *noun* market *or* place where things are sold **Markt;** *car mart;* **auction mart** = auction rooms **Auktionsräume**

mass *noun*

(a) large group of people **Menge; mass marketing** = marketing which aims at reaching large numbers of people **Massenabsatzstrategie; mass media** = means of communication which reach large numbers of people (such as radio, television, newspapers) **Massenmedien; mass unemployment** = unemployment of large numbers of workers **Massenarbeitslosigkeit**

(b) large number **Masse, Menge;** *we have a mass of letters or masses of letters to write; they received a mass of orders or masses of orders after the TV commercials*

◇ **mass-produce** *verb* to manufacture in large quantities **in Massen produzieren;** *to mass-produce cars*

◇ **mass production** *noun* manufacturing large quantities of products **Massenproduktion, serienmäßige Herstellung**

master *noun* main *or* original **Original; master copy of a file** = main copy of a computer file, kept for security purposes **Stamm-, Bestandsdatei**

material *noun*

(a) substance which can be used to make a finished product **Material; building materials** = bricks, cement, etc., used in

building **Baustoffe; raw materials** = substances which have not been manufactured (such as wool, wood, sand) **Rohstoffe; synthetic materials** = substances made as products of a chemical process **Kunststoffe; materials control** = system to check that a company has enough materials in stock to do its work **Materialsteuerung; materials handling** = moving materials from one part of a factory to another in an efficient way **innerbetriebliches Transport- und Lagerwesen, Materialfluß**
(b) display material = posters, photographs, etc., which can be used to attract attention to goods which are for sale **Dekorationsmaterial**

maternity *noun* becoming a mother **Mutterschaft; maternity benefit** = money paid by the National Insurance to a mother when she has her child **Mutterschaftsgeld; maternity leave** = permission for a woman to be away from work to have a baby **Mutterschaftsurlaub**

matter
1 *noun*
(a) problem **Sache, Angelegenheit, Problem; it is a matter of concern to the members of the committee** = the members of the committee are worried about it **die Mitglieder des Komitees nehmen die Angelegenheit sehr ernst**
(b) printed matter = printed books, newspapers, publicity sheets, etc. **Drucksache; publicity matter** = sheets *or* posters *or* leaflets used for publicity **Werbematerial**
(c) question *or* problem to be discussed **Frage, Sache;** *the most important matter on the agenda; we shall consider first the matter of last month's fall in prices*
NOTE: no plural for (b)
2 *verb* to be important **von Bedeutung sein;** *does it matter if one month's sales are down?*

mature
1 *adjective* **mature economy** = fully developed economy **entwickelte Volkswirtschaft**
2 *verb* **bills which mature in three weeks' time** = bills which will be due for payment in three weeks **Wechsel, die in drei Wochen fällig werden**

◇ **maturity** *noun* **date of maturity** *or* **maturity date** = date when a government stock *or* an assurance policy *or* a debenture will become due for payment **Fälligkeitstermin; amount payable on maturity** = amount received by the insured person when the policy becomes mature **Betrag zahlbar bei Fälligkeit**

maximization *noun* making as large as possible **Maximierung;** *profit maximization or maximization of profit*

◇ **maximize** *verb* to make as large as possible **maximieren;** *to maximize profits*

maximum
1 *noun* largest possible number *or* price *or* quantity **Maximum; up to a maximum of £10** = no more than £10 **bis zu maximal £10; to increase exports to the maximum** = as much as possible **Exporte auf das Maximum erhöhen;** *it is the maximum the insurance company will pay*
NOTE: plural is **maxima**
2 *adjective* largest possible **maximal, Höchst-;** *maximum income tax rate or maximum rate of tax; maximum load; maximum production levels; maximum price;* **to increase production to the maximum level** = as much as possible **die Produktion auf das Maximum erhöhen**

MD = MANAGING DIRECTOR *the MD is in his office; she was appointed MD of a property company*

mean
1 *adjective* average **mittlerer, durchschnittlich, Mittel-;** *mean annual increase;* **mean price** = average price of a share in a day's trading **Mittelkurs**
2 *noun* average *or* number calculated by adding several figures together and dividing by the number of figures added **Mittelwert, Durchschnitt;** *unit sales are over the mean for the first quarter or above the first quarter mean*

◇ **means** *plural noun*
(a) way of doing something **Mittel;** *air freight is the fastest means of getting stock to South America; do we have any means of copying all these documents quickly?*
(b) money *or* resources **Mittel;** *the company has the means to launch the new product; such a level of investment is beyond the means of a small private company;* **means test** = inquiry into how much money someone earns to see if he is eligible for state benefits **Bedürftigkeitsüberprüfung; he has private means** = he has income from dividends *or* interest *or* rent which is not part of his salary **ihm stehen private Mittel zur Verfügung**

measure
1 *noun*
(a) way of calculating size *or* quantity **Maß(einheit); cubic measure** = volume in cubic feet or metres, calculated by multiplying height, width and length **Hohlmaß; dry measure** = way of calculating

the quantity of loose dry goods (such as corn) **Trockenmaß; square measure** = area in square feet or metres, calculated by multiplying width and length **Flächenmaß; inspector of weights and measures** = government inspector who inspects weighing machines and goods sold in shops to see if the quantities and weights are correct **Eichmeister; as a measure of the company's performance** = as a way of judging if the company's results are good or bad **als Maßstab der Leistung des Unternehmens**

(b) made to measure = made specially to fit **maßgefertigt;** *he has his clothes made to measure*

(c) tape measure = long tape with centimetres or inches marked on it, used to measure how long something is **Maßband, Bandmaß**

(d) type of action **Maßnahme; to take measures to prevent something happening** = to act to stop something happening **Maßnahmen ergreifen, um etwas zu verhindern; to take crisis** *or* **emergency measures** = to act rapidly to stop a crisis developing **Krisenmaßnahmen ergreifen; an economy measure** = an action to save money **eine Sparmaßnahme; fiscal measures** = tax changes made by the government to improve the working of the economy **finanzpolitische Maßnahmen; as a precautionary measure** = to prevent something taking place **als Vorsichtsmaßnahme; safety measures** = actions to make sure that something is safe **Sicherheitsvorkehrungen**

2 *verb*

(a) to find out the size *or* quantity of something; to be of a certain size *or* quantity **(ab)messen, aus-, vermessen;** *to measure the size of a package; a package which measures 10cm by 25cm or a package measuring 10cm by 25cm*

(b) to measure the government's performance = to judge how well the government is doing **die Leistung der Regierung bewerten**

◇ **measurement** *noun*

(a) measurements = size (in inches, centimetres, etc.) **Maße;** *to write down the measurements of a package*

(b) way of judging something **Beurteilung, Einschätzung;** *performance measurement or measurement of performance;* **measurement of profitability** = way of calculating how profitable something is **Rentabilitätsberechnung**

◇ **measuring tape** *noun* long tape with centimetres or inches marked on it, used to measure how long something is **Maßband, Bandmaß**

mechanic *noun* person who works with engines *or* machines **Mechaniker/-in;** *car mechanic*

◇ **mechanical** *adjective* worked by a machine **mechanisch;** *a mechanical pump*

◇ **mechanism** *noun* way in which something works **Mechanismus;** *a mechanism to slow down inflation; the company's discount mechanism*

◇ **mechanize** *verb* to use machines in place of workers **mechanisieren;** *the country is aiming to mechanize its farming industry*

◇ **mechanization** *noun* using machines in place of workers **Mechanisierung;** *farm mechanization or the mechanization of farms*

media *noun* **the media** *or* **the mass media** = means of communicating information to the public (such as television, radio, newspapers) **die Medien; die Massenmedien;** *the product attracted a lot of interest in the media or a lot of media interest;* **media analysis** *or* **media research** = examining different types of media (such as the readers of newspapers, television viewers) to see which is best for promoting a certain type of product **Medienforschung; media coverage** = reports about something in the media **Berichterstattung durch die Medien;** *we got good media coverage for the launch of the new model*

NOTE: **media** is followed by a singular or plural verb

median *noun* point in the middle of a list of numbers **Zentralwert, Median**

mediate *verb* to try to make the two sides in an argument come to to an agreement **vermitteln;** *to mediate between the manager and his staff; the government offered to mediate in the dispute*

◇ **mediation** *noun* attempt by a third party to make the two sides in an argument agree **Vermittlung;** *the employers refused an offer of government mediation; the dispute was ended through the mediation of union officials*

◇ **mediator** *noun* **official mediator** = government official who tries to make the two sides in an industrial dispute agree **Unterhändler, Schlichter**

medical *noun* referring to the study or treatment of illness **medizinisch, ärztlich; medical certificate** = certificate from a doctor to show that a worker has been ill **ärztliches Attest; medical inspection** = examining a place of work to see if the conditions will not make the workers ill **Gesundheitsüberprüfung; medical insurance** = insurance which pays the cost of medical treatment especially when travelling abroad **Krankenversicherung; medical officer of health** = person responsible for the health services in a town **Amtsarzt; he resigned for medical reasons** = he resigned because he was too ill to work **er schied aus gesundheitlichen Gründen aus**

medium

1 *adjective* middle *or* average **mittlerer;** *the company is of medium size*
2 *noun*
(a) way of doing something *or* means of doing something **Mittel; advertising medium** = type of advertisement (such as a TV commercial) **Werbeträger;** *the product was advertised through the medium of the trade press*
(b) mediums = government stocks which mature in five to fifteen years' time **mittelfristige Staatspapiere**
NOTE: plural for (a) is **media**

◇ **medium-sized** *adjective* **a medium-sized company** = company which is neither very large nor very small **eine Unternehmen mittlerer Größe**

◇ **medium-term** *adjective* referring to a point between short term and long terms **mittelfristig; medium-term forecast** = forecast for two or three years **mittelfristige Prognose**

meet *verb*

(a) to come together with someone **(sich) treffen;** *to meet a negotiating committee; to meet an agent at his hotel; the two sides met in the lawyer's office*
(b) to be satisfactory for **erfüllen, entsprechen;** *to meet a customer's requirements;* **to meet the demand for a new product** = to fill the demand for a product **die Nachfrage nach einem neuen Produkt befriedigen; we will try to meet your price** = we will try to offer a price which is acceptable to you **wir werden uns bemühen, Ihnen preislich entgegenzukommen; they failed to meet the deadline** = they were not able to complete in time **sie haben die Frist nicht einhalten können**
(c) to pay for **bezahlen, begleichen, decken;** *to meet someone's expenses; the company will meet your expenses; he was unable to meet his mortgage repayments*
NOTE: **meeting - met**

◇ **meet with** *verb*
(a) *US* to come together with someone **treffen, zusammenkommen mit; I hope to meet with him in New York** = I hope to meet him in New York **ich hoffe, ihn in New York zu treffen**
(b) his request met with a refusal = his request was refused **sein Ersuchen stieß auf Ablehnung**

◇ **meeting** *noun*
(a) coming together of a group of people **Besprechung, Sitzung;** *management meeting; staff meeting;* **board meeting** = meeting of the directors of a company; *entspricht* **Vorstands-, Aufsichtsratssitzung; general meeting** *or* **meeting of shareholders** *or* **shareholders' meeting** = meeting of all the shareholders of a company *or* meeting of all the members of a society **ordentliche Hauptversammlung; Annual General Meeting** = meeting of all the shareholders when a company's financial situation is discussed with the directors **ordentliche Jahreshauptversammlung; Extraordinary General Meeting** = special meeting of shareholders to discuss an important matter **außerordentliche Hauptversammlung**
(b) to hold a meeting = to organize a meeting of a group of people **eine Sitzung abhalten;** *the meeting will be held in the committee room;* **to open a meeting** = to start a meeting **eine Sitzung eröffnen; to conduct a meeting** = to be in the chair for a meeting **eine Sitzung leiten; to close a meeting** = to end a meeting **eine Sitzung schließen; to address a meeting** = to speak to a meeting **zu einer Versammlung sprechen; to put a resolution to a meeting** = to ask a meeting to vote on a proposal **einer Versammlung einen Resolutionsentwurf vorlegen**

QUOTE if corporate forecasts are met, sales will exceed $50 million in 1985
Citizen (Ottawa)
QUOTE in proportion to your holding you have a stake in every aspect of the company, including a vote in the general meetings
Investors Chronicle

megabyte

noun storage unit in computers, equal to 1,048,576 bytes **Megabyte**

member *noun*

(a) person who belongs to a group *or* a society **Mitglied;** *members of a committee or committee members; they were elected members of the board;* **ordinary member** = person who pays a subscription to belong to a group **ordentliches Mitglied; honorary member** = special person who does not have to pay a subscription **Ehrenmitglied**
(b) organization which belongs to a society **Mitglied;** *the member countries of the EC; the members of the United Nations; the member companies of a trade association*

◇ **membership** *noun*
(a) belonging to a group **Mitgliedschaft;** *membership qualifications; conditions of membership; membership card; to pay your membership or your membership fees; is Austria going to apply for membership of the Common Market?*

(b) all the members of a group **Mitglieder;** *the membership was asked to vote for the new president;* **the club's membership secretary** = committee member who deals with the ordinary members of a society **der Vereinsschriftführer/Clubsekretär; the club has a membership of five hundred** = the club has five hundred members **der Verein hat fünfhundert Mitglieder**

> QUOTE it will be the first opportunity for party members and trade union members to express their views on the tax package
> *Australian Financial Review*
>
> QUOTE the bargaining committee will recommend that its membership ratify the agreement at a meeting called for June
> *Toronto Star*
>
> QUOTE in 1984 exports to Canada from the member-states of the European Community jumped 38 per cent
> *Globe and Mail (Toronto)*
>
> QUOTE for EMS members, which means all EEC countries except Britain, the ecu has performed well
> *Economist*

memo *noun* short message sent from one person to another in the same organization **Mitteilung;** *to write a memo to the finance director; to send a memo to all the sales representatives; according to your memo about debtors; I sent the managing director a memo about your complaint*

◇ **memo pad** *noun* pad of paper for writing short notes **Notizblock**

◇ **memorandum** *noun* short message **Mitteilung; memorandum (and articles) of association** = legal document setting up a limited company and giving details of its aims, directors, and registered office **Gründungsurkunde**

memory *noun* facility for storing of data in a computer **Speicher**

mention *verb* to talk about something for a short time **erwähnen;** *the chairman mentioned the work of the retiring managing director; can you mention to the secretary that the date of the next meeting has been changed?*

mercantile *adjective* commercial **handeltreibend, Handels-; mercantile country** = country which earns income from trade **Handelsnation; mercantile law** = laws relating to business **Handelsrecht (Teil des Wirtschaftrechts); mercantile marine** = all the commercial ships of a country **Handelsmarine**

merchandise

1 *noun* goods which are for sale *or* which have been sold **Ware;** *the merchandise is shipped through two ports*
NOTE: no plural
2 *verb* to sell goods by a wide variety of means, including display, advertising, sending samples, etc. **Absatzplanung betreiben;** *to merchandise a product*

◇ **merchandiser** *noun* person *or* company which organizes the display and promotion of goods **Experte für Absatzpolitik**

◇ **merchandising** *noun* organizing the display and promotion of goods for sale **Merchandising, Absatzpolitik;** *merchandising of a product; merchandising department*

> QUOTE fill huge warehouses with large quantities but limited assortments of top-brand, first-quality merchandise and sell the goods at rock-bottom prices
> *Duns Business Month*

merchant *noun*
(a) businessman who buys and sells goods (especially imported goods) in bulk for retail sale **Händler;** *coal merchant; tobacco merchant; wine merchant*
(b) merchant bank = bank which lends money to companies and deals in international finance; *entspricht* **Investmentbank; merchant banker** = person who has a high position in a merchant bank; *entspricht* **Bankier in einer Investmentbank; merchant navy** *or* **merchant marine** = all the commercial ships of a country **Handelsmarine; merchant ship** *or* **merchant vessel** = commercial ship *or* ship which carries a cargo **Handelsschiff**

◇ **merchantman** *noun* commercial ship **Handelsschiff**

merge *verb* to join together **fusionieren, zusammenschließen;** *the two companies have merged; the firm merged with its main competitor*

◇ **merger** *noun* joining together of two or more companies **Fusion;** *as a result of the merger, the company is the largest in the field*

merit *noun* being good or efficient **Verdienst, Leistung; merit award** *or* **merit bonus** = extra money given to a worker because he has worked well **Leistungsprämie; merit increase** = increase in pay given to someone because his work is good **Leistungszulage; merit rating** = judging how well a worker does his work, so that he can be paid according to merit **Leistungsbeurteilung**

message *noun* piece of news which is sent to someone **Mitteilung, Nachricht;** *to send* *a message; I will leave a message with his secretary; can you give the director a message from his wife? he says he never received the message*

messenger *noun* person who brings a message **Bote;** *he sent the package by special messenger or by motorcycle messenger;* **office messenger** = person who carries messages from one person to another in a large office **Bürobote; messenger boy** = young man who carries messages **Botenjunge**

Messrs *noun* plural form of Mr, used only in names of firms **Firma, Herren;** *Messrs White and Smith*

method *noun* way of doing something **Methode, Verfahren;** *a new method of making something or of doing something; what is the best method of payment? his organizing methods are out of date; their manufacturing methods or production methods are among the most modern in the country;* **time and method study** = examining the way in which something is done to see if a cheaper or quicker way can be found **Verfahrens-Zeit-Studie**

metre *or US* **meter** *noun* measure of length (= 3.4 feet) **Meter**

NOTE: usually written **m** after figures: **the case is 2m wide by 3m long**

◇ **metric** *adjective* using the metre as a basic measurement **metrisch; metric ton** *or* **metric tonne** = 1000 kilograms **metrische Tonne; the metric system** = system of measuring, using metres, litres and grams **Dezimalsystem, metrisches System**

mg = MILLIGRAM

mi = MILE

micro *noun* microcomputer **Mikrocomputer;** *we put the sales statistics on to the office micro; our office micro interfaces with the mainframe computer in London*

◇ **micro-** *prefix* very small **mikro-, Mikro-; micro-economics** = study of the economics of persons or single companies **Mikroökonomie**

◇ **microcomputer** *noun* small computer for general use in the home or office **Mikrocomputer**

◇ **microfiche** *noun* index sheet, made of several microfilm photographs **Mikrofiche;** *we hold our records on microfiche*

◇ **microfilm**

1 *noun* roll of film on which a document is photographed in very small scale **Mikrofilm;** *we hold our records on microfilm*

2 *verb* to make a very small scale photograph **Mikrofilmaufnahmen machen;** *send the 1980 correspondence to be microfilmed or for microfilming*

◇ **microprocessor** *noun* small computer processing unit **Mikroprozessor**

mid- *prefix* middle **mittel-, Mittel-, mitten; from mid-1982** = from the middle of 1982 **von Mitte 1982;** *the factory is closed until mid-July*

◇ **mid-month** *adjective* taking place in the middle of the month **(in der) Mitte des Monats;** *mid-month accounts*

◇ **mid-week** *adjective* which happens in the middle of a week **(in der) Mitte der Woche;** *the mid-week lull in sales*

middle *adjective* in the centre *or* between two points **mittlerer, Mittel-; middle management** = department managers in a company, who carry out the policy set by the directors and organize the work of a group of workers **mittleres Management**

◇ **middle-income** *adjective* **people in the middle-income bracket** = people with average incomes, not very high or very low **Personen der mittleren Einkommensstufe**

◇ **middleman** *noun* businessman who buys from the manufacturer and sells to the public **Zwischenhändler;** *we sell direct from the factory to the customer and cut out the middleman*

NOTE: plural is **middlemen**

◇ **middle-sized** *adjective* neither small nor large **von mittlerer Größe, mittelgroß;** *a middle-sized company*

mile *noun* measure of length (= 1.625 kilometres) **Meile; the car does twenty-five miles to the gallon** *or* **twenty-five miles per gallon** = the car uses one gallon of petrol to travel twenty-five miles **der Wagen verbraucht eine Gallone auf 25 Meilen**

NOTE: miles per gallon is usually written **mpg** after figures: **the car does 25mpg**

◇ **mileage** *noun* distance travelled in miles **gefahrene Meilen; mileage allowance** = money allowed as expenses to someone who uses his own car for business travel; *entspricht* **Kilometerpauschale; the salesman's average annual mileage** = the number of miles which a salesman drives in a year **die im Jahresdurchschnitt gefahrene Meilenzahl eines Vertreters**

NOTE: no plural

mill *noun* building where a certain type of material is processed or made **Mühle; Fabrik,**

Werk; *after lunch the visitors were shown round the mill;* **cotton mill** = factory where raw cotton is processed **Spinnerei; paper mill** = factory where wood is made into paper **Papierfabrik**

milligram *noun* one thousandth of a gram **Milligramm**

NOTE: usually written **mg** after figures

◇ **millilitre** *noun* one thousandth of a litre **Milliliter**

NOTE: usually written **ml** after figures

◇ **millimetre** *noun* one thousandth of a metre **Millimeter**

NOTE: usually written **mm** after figures

million number 1,000,000 **Million;** *the company lost £10 million in the African market; our turnover has risen to $13.4 million*

NOTE: can be written **m** after figures: **$5m** (say "five million dollars")

◇ **millionaire** *noun* person who has more than one million pounds **Millionär/-in; dollar millionaire** = person who has more than one million dollars **Dollarmillionär; paper millionaire** = person who owns shares which, if sold, would be worth one million pounds or dollars **Aktienmillionär**

min = MINUTE, MINIMUM

mine

1 *noun* hole in the ground for digging out coal, gold, iron etc. **Bergwerk, Zeche, Mine;** *the mines have been closed by a strike*

2 *verb* to dig and bring out coal, gold, etc. **fördern, abbauen;** *the company is mining coal in the south of the country;* **mining concession** = right to use a piece of land for mining **Abbaurechte, Bergbaukonzession**

mini- *prefix* very small **Mini-**

◇ **minibudget** *noun* interim statement about financial plans from a finance minister; *entspricht* **Nachtragshaushalt**

◇ **minicomputer** *noun* computer which is larger than a micro but smaller than a mainframe **Minicomputer**

◇ **minicontainer** *noun* small container **Minicontainer**

◇ **minimarket** *noun* very small self-service store **Minimarkt, kleiner Selbstbedienungsladen**

minimal *adjective* the smallest possible **minimal;** *there was a minimal quantity of imperfections in the batch; the head office exercises minimal control over the branch offices*

◇ **minimize** *verb* to make something seem to be very small and not very important **bagatellisieren; herabsetzen;** *do not minimize the risks involved; he tends to minimize the difficulty of the project*

◇ **minimum**

1 *noun* smallest possible quantity *or* price *or* number **Minimum;** *to keep expenses to a minimum; to reduce the risk of a loss to a minimum*

NOTE: plural is **minima** or **minimums**

2 *adjective* smallest possible **Mindest-; minimum dividend** = smallest dividend which is legal and accepted by the shareholders **Mindestdividende; minimum payment** = smallest payment necessary **Mindestbetrag; minimum quantity** = smallest quantity which is acceptable **Mindestmenge; minimum wage** = lowest hourly wage which a company can legally pay its workers **garantierter Mindestlohn**

minister *noun* member of a government who is in charge of a ministry **Minister/-in;** *a government minister; the Minister of Trade or the Trade Minister; the Minister of Foreign Affairs or the Foreign Minister*

NOTE: in the USA, they are called **secretary: the Secretary for Commerce**

◇ **ministry** *noun* department in the government **Ministerium;** *he works in the Ministry of Finance or the Finance Ministry; he is in charge of the Ministry of Information or of the Information Ministry; a ministry official or an official from the ministry*

NOTE: in GB and the USA, important ministries are called **departments: the Department of Trade and Industry; the Commerce Department**

minor *adjective* less important **unbedeutend, unwichtig;** *minor expenditure; minor shareholders;* **a loss of minor importance** = not a very serious loss **ein Verlust von geringer Bedeutung**

◇ **minority** *noun* number *or* quantity which is less than half of the total **Minorität, Minderheit;** *a minority of board members opposed the chairman;* **minority shareholding** *or* **minority interest** = group of shares which are less than one half of the shares in a company **Minderheitsbeteiligung; minority shareholder** = person who owns a group of shares but less than half of the shares in a company **Minderheitsaktionär; in the minority** = being fewer than half **in der Minderheit;** *good salesmen are in the minority in our sales team*

mint

1 *noun* factory where coins are made **Prägeanstalt**

2 *verb* to make coins **prägen**

minus
1 *adverb* less *or* without **minus, abzüglich;** *net salary is gross salary minus tax and National Insurance deductions; gross profit is sales minus production costs*
2 *adjective* **the accounts show a minus figure** = show that more has been spent than has been received **die Bücher weisen ein Minus auf; minus factor** = unfavourable factor **Negativfaktor, Minus;** *to have lost sales in the best quarter of the year is a minus factor for the sales team*

minute
1 *noun*
(a) one sixtieth part of an hour **Minute;** *I can see you for ten minutes only; if you do not mind waiting, Mr Smith will be free in about twenty minutes' time*
(b) the minutes of the meeting = notes of what happened at a meeting, written by the secretary **das Protokoll einer Sitzung; to take the minutes** = to write notes of what happened at a meeting **Protokoll führen; the chairman signed the minutes of the last meeting** = he signed them to show that they are a correct record of what was said and what decisions were taken **der Vorsitzende zeichnete das Protokoll der letzten Sitzung ab; this will not appear in the minutes of the meeting** = this is unofficial and will not be noted as having been said **das wird nicht in das Protokoll der Sitzung aufgenommen**
2 *verb* to put something into the minutes of a meeting **protokollieren, zu Protokoll nehmen;** *the chairman's remarks about the auditors were minuted;* **I do not want that to be minuted** *or* **I want that not to be minuted** = do not put that remark into the minutes of the meeting **ich möchte nicht, daß das in das Protokoll aufgenommen wird**

◇ **minutebook** *noun* book in which the minutes of a meeting are kept **Protokollbuch**

misappropriate *verb* to use illegally money which is not yours, but with which you have been trusted **veruntreuen**

◇ **misappropriation** *noun* illegal use of money by someone who is not the owner but who has been trusted to look after it **Veruntreuung**

misc = MISCELLANEOUS

miscalculate *verb* to calculate wrongly **falsch berechnen/kalkulieren;** *the salesman miscalculated the discount, so we hardly broke even on the deal*

◇ **miscalculation** *noun* mistake in calculating **Fehlkalkulation**

miscellaneous *adjective* various *or* mixed *or* not all of the same sort **verschieden; gemischt;** *miscellaneous items; a box of miscellaneous pieces of equipment; miscellaneous expenditure*

miscount
1 *noun* mistake in counting **Rechenfehler**
2 *verb* to count wrongly **sich verzählen;** *the shopkeeper miscounted, so we got twenty-five bars of chocolate instead of two dozen*

misdirect *verb* to give wrong directions **irreleiten, irreführen**

mismanage *verb* to manage badly **schlecht verwalten**

◇ **mismanagement** *noun* bad management **Mißwirtschaft;** *the company failed because of the chairman's mismanagement*
NOTE: no plural

misrepresent *verb* to report facts wrongly **falsch darstellen**

◇ **misrepresentation** *noun* wrongly reporting facts **falsche Darstellung; fraudulent misrepresentation** = giving someone wrong information in order to cheat him **Vorspiegelung falscher Tatsachen, arglistige Täuschung**

Miss *noun* title given to a woman who is not married **Fräulein;** *Miss Smith is our sales manager*

miss *verb*
(a) not to hit **verfehlen; nicht erreichen;** *the company has missed its profit forecast again; the sales team has missed its sales targets*
(b) not to meet **verpassen;** *I arrived late, so missed most of the discussion;* **he missed the chairman by ten minutes** = he left ten minutes before the chairman arrived **er verpaßte den Vorsitzenden um zehn Minuten**

mission *noun* group of people going on a journey for a special purpose **Gesandtschaft, Delegation; trade mission** = visit by a group of businessmen to discuss trade **Handelsdelegation;** *he led a trade mission to China;* **inward mission** = visit to your home country by a group of foreign businessmen **Delegation aus dem Ausland; outward mission** = visit by a group of businessmen to a foreign country **Auslandsbesuch einer Delegation; a fact-finding mission** = visit to an area to search for information about a problem **Untersuchungsausschuß**

mistake *noun* wrong action *or* wrong decision **Fehler; to make a mistake** = to do something wrong **einen Fehler machen;** *the shop made a mistake and sent the wrong items; there was a mistake in the address; she made a mistake in addressing the letter;* **by mistake** = in error *or* wrongly **versehentlich;** *they sent the wrong items by mistake; she put my letter into an envelope for the chairman by mistake*

misunderstanding *noun* lack of agreement *or* mistake **Mißverständnis; Meinungsverschiedenheit;** *there was a misunderstanding over my tickets*

misuse *noun* wrong use **Zweckentfremdung; Mißbrauch;** *misuse of funds or of assets*

mix
1 *noun* things put together **Mischung; product mix** = range of different products which a company has for sale **Produktmix, Produktpalette; sales mix** = sales and profitability of a wide range of different products **Absatzmix**
2 *verb* to put different things together **(ver)mischen, verbinden;** *I like to mix business with pleasure - why don't we discuss the deal over lunch?*

◇ **mixed** *adjective*
(a) of different sorts *or* of different types together **gemischt; mixed economy** = system which contains both nationalized industries and private enterprise **Mischwirtschaft; mixed farm** = farm which has both animals and crops **gemischte Landwirtschaft**
(b) neither good nor bad **unterschiedlich, gemischt**

> QUOTE prices closed on a mixed note after a moderately active trading session
> *Financial Times*

ml = MILLILITRE

mm = MILLIMETRE

mobile *adjective* which can move about **beweglich, mobil; mobile shop** = van fitted out like a small shop which travels round selling groceries or vegetables **Verkaufswagen; mobile workforce** = workers who move from place to place to get work **mobile Arbeitskräfte**

◇ **mobility** *noun* being able to move from one place to another **Beweglichkeit, Mobilität; mobility of labour** = situation when workers agree to move from one place to another to get work **Freizügigkeit der Arbeitskräfte**

NOTE: no plural

◇ **mobilize** *verb* to bring together, especially to fight **mobilisieren, mobilmachen; to mobilize capital** = to collect capital to support something **Gelder flüssigmachen; to mobilize resources to defend a takeover bid** = to get the support of shareholders, etc., to stop a company being taken over **Mittel mobilisieren, um ein Übernahmeangebot abzuwehren**

mock-up *noun* model of a new product for testing or to show to possible buyers **Attrappe**

mode *noun* way of doing something **Art (und Weise), Form; mode of payment** = way in which payment is made (such as cash or cheque) **Zahlungsweise**

model
1 *noun*
(a) small copy of something to show what it will look like when finished **Modell;** *he showed us a model of the new office building*
(b) style *or* type of product **Modell;** *this is the latest model; the model on display is last year's; he drives a 1985 model Ford;* **demonstration model** = piece of equipment used in demonstrations and then sold cheaply **Vorführmodell**
(c) person whose job is to wear new clothes to show them to possible buyers **Mannequin, Model;** *männlich* **Dressman**
(d) economic model = computerized plan of a country's economic system, used for forecasting economic trends **(EDV-)Modell zur Wirtschaftsprognose**
2 *adjective* which is a perfect example to be copied **vorbildlich, mustergültig, Muster-, Modell-;** *a model agreement*
3 *verb* to wear new clothes to show them to possible buyers **als Mannequin arbeiten; als Dressman arbeiten**
NOTE: **modelling - modelled** but US **modeling - modeled**

modem *noun* device which links a computer to the telephone line, allowing data to be sent from one computer to another **Modem**

moderate
1 *adjective* not too large **gemäßigt, mäßig;** *the trade union made a moderate claim; the government proposed a moderate increase in the tax rate*
2 *verb* to make less strong *or* less large **mäßigen;** *the union was forced to moderate its claim*

modern *adjective* referring to the recent past or the present time **modern, neu;** *it is a fairly modern invention - it was patented only in the 1960s*
◊ **modernize** *verb* to make modern **modernisieren;** *he modernized the whole product range*
◊ **modernization** *noun* making modern **Modernisierung;** *the modernization of the workshop*

modest *adjective* small **mäßig, gering;** *oil shares showed modest gains over the week's trading*

modify *verb* to change *or* to make something fit a different use **modifizieren, ändern;** *the management modified its proposals; this is the new modified agreement; the car will have to be modified to pass the government tests; the refrigerator was considerably modified before it went into production*
◊ **modification** *noun* change **Modifizierung, Änderung;** *to make or to carry out modifications to the plan; the new model has had several important modifications; we asked for modifications to the contract*

modular *adjective* made of various sections **modular, aus Elementen zusammengesetzt**

momentum *noun* movement forwards **Schwung, Wucht; to gain** *or* **to lose momentum** = to move faster or more slowly **in Gang/Schwung kommen; den Schwung verlieren; the strike is gaining momentum** = more workers are joining the strike **der Streik weitet sich aus**
NOTE: no plural

monetary *adjective* referring to money or currency **monetär; währungspolitisch, Währungs-; the government's monetary policy** = the government's policy relating to finance (bank interest rates, taxes, government expenditure and borrowing) **die Geldmengenpolitik der Regierung; monetary standard** = fixing of a fixed exchange rate for a currency **Währungseinheit; the international monetary system** = methods of controlling and exchanging currencies between countries **das internationale Währungssystem; the European Monetary System** = system of controlled exchange rates between some member countries of the Common Market **das Europäisches Währungssystem; The International Monetary Fund** = (part of the United Nations) a type of bank which helps member states in financial difficulties, gives financial advice to members and encourages world trade **Internationaler Währungsfonds, der Weltwährungsfonds; monetary unit** = standard currency in a country (the pound, the dollar, the franc, etc.) **Währungseinheit**
◊ **monetarism** *noun* idea that inflation can be controlled by regulating the amount of money available in the economy **Monetarismus**
NOTE: no plural
◊ **monetarist**
1 *noun* person who believes in monetarism and acts accordingly **Monetarist**
2 *adjective* according to monetarism **monetaristisch;** *monetarist theories*

QUOTE the decision by the government to tighten monetary policy will push the annual inflation rate above the year's previous high
Financial Times

QUOTE it is not surprising that the Fed started to ease monetary policy some months ago
Sunday Times

QUOTE a draft report on changes in the international monetary system
Wall Street Journal

money *noun*
(a) coins and notes used for buying and selling **Geld; to earn money** = to have a salary **Geld verdienen; to earn good money** = to have a large salary **gut verdienen; to lose money** = to make a loss *or* not to make a profit **Geld verlieren/einbüßen; the company has been losing money for months** = the company has been working at a loss **das Unternehmen hat seit Monaten Geldeinbußen zu verzeichnen; to get your money back** = to earn enough to cover your original investment **sein Geld wieder herausbekommen; to make money** = to make a profit **Geld verdienen; to put money into the bank** = to deposit money into a bank account **Geld auf die Bank bringen; to put money into a business** = to invest money in a business **Geld in ein Geschäft investieren;** *he put all his redundancy money into a shop;* **to put money down** = to pay cash, especially as a deposit **eine Anzahlung leisten;** *he put £25 down and paid the rest in instalments;* **cheap money** = money which can be borrowed at a low rate of interest **billiges Geld; danger money** = extra salary paid to workers in dangerous jobs **Gefahrenzulage; dear money** = money which has to be borrowed at a high rate of interest **teures Geld; easy money** = money which can be earned with no difficulty **leicht verdientes Geld;** *selling insurance is easy money;* **hot money** = money which is moved from country to country to get the best returns **heißes Geld; paper money** = money in notes, not coins **Papiergeld; ready money** = cash *or* money which is immediately available

Bargeld, flüssige Mittel; money lying idle = money not being used to produce interest **totes Kapital; they are worth a lot of money** = they are valuable **sie sind viel Geld wert**
(b) money supply = amount of money which exists in a country **Geldreserve, Geldvolumen; money markets** = markets for buying and selling short-term loans **Geldmärkte;** *the international money markets are nervous;* **money rates** = rates of interest for borrowers or lenders **Geldmarktsätze**
(c) money order = document which can be bought for sending money through the post **Postanweisung; foreign money order** *or* **international money order** *or* **overseas money order** = money order in a foreign currency which is payable to someone living in a foreign country **Auslandszahlungsanweisung**
NOTE: no plural for (a), (b) and (c)
(d) monies = sums of money **Gelder;** *monies owing to the company; to collect monies due*
◇ **moneylender** *noun* person who lends money at interest **Geldverleiher**
◇ **money-making** *adjective* which makes money **einträglich, gewinnbringend;** *a money-making plan*
◇ **money-spinner** *noun* item which sells very well *or* which is very profitable **Kassenschlager**

monitor

1 *noun* screen (like a TV screen) on a computer **Monitor, Bildschirm**
2 *verb* to check *or* to examine how something is working **überwachen;** *he is monitoring the progress of sales; how do you monitor the performance of the sales reps?*

monopoly *noun* situation where one person or company controls all the market in the supply of a product **Monopol;** *to have the monopoly of alcohol sales or to have the alcohol monopoly; to be in a monopoly situation; the company has the absolute monopoly of imports of French wine; the factory has the absolute monopoly of jobs in the town;* **public monopoly** *or* **state monopoly** = situation where the state is the only suppliers of a product or service (such as the Post Office, the coal industry,etc.) **staatliches Monopol;** *GB* **the Monopolies Commission** = organization which examines takeovers and mergers to make sure that a monopoly is not being created **das Kartellamt**
NOTE: **trust** is used more often in US English
◇ **monopolize** *verb* to create a monopoly *or* to get control of all the supply of a product **monopolisieren, beherrschen**
◇ **monopolization** *noun* making a monopoly **Monopolisierung**

month *noun* one of twelve periods which make a year **Monat;** *the company pays him £100 a month; he earns £2,000 a month; bills due at the end of the current month;* **calendar month** = whole month as on a calendar **Kalendermonat; paid by the month** = paid once each month **monatlich bezahlt; to give a customer two months' credit** = to allow a customer to pay not immediately, but after two months **einem Kunden zwei Monate Kredit geben**
◇ **month end** *noun* the end of a calendar month, when accounts have to be drawn up **Monatsende;** *month-end accounts*
◇ **monthly**
1 *adjective* happening every month *or* which is received every month **monatlich;** *monthly statement; monthly payments; he is paying for his car by monthly instalments; my monthly salary cheque is late;* **monthly ticket** = ticket for travel which is good for one month **Monatskarte**
2 *adverb* every month **monatlich;** *to pay monthly; the account is credited monthly*

moonlight *verb informal* to do a second job for cash (often in the evening) as well as a regular job **schwarzarbeiten**
◇ **moonlighter** *noun* person who moonlights **Schwarzarbeiter**
◇ **moonlighting** *noun* doing a second job **Schwarzarbeit;** *he makes thousands a year from moonlighting*

mooring *noun* place where boats can be tied up in a harbour **Liegeplatz**

moratorium *noun* temporary stop to repayments of money owed **Moratorium; Zahlungsaufschub;** *the banks called for a moratorium on payments*
NOTE: plural is **moratoria**

mortality tables *plural noun* chart, used by insurers, which shows how long a person of a certain age can be expected to live on average **Sterbetafel**

mortgage

1 *noun* agreement where someone lends money to another person so that he can buy a property, the property being the security; money lent in this way **Hypothek;** *to take out a mortgage on a house; to buy a house with a £20,000 mortgage;* **mortgage payments** = money paid each month as interest on a mortgage, plus repayment of a small part of the capital borrowed **Hypothekentilgung; endowment mortgage** = mortgage backed by an endowment policy **mit einer Lebensversicherung gekoppelte Hypothek; first mortgage** = main mortgage on a property **Ersthypothek; second mortgage** = further mortgage on a property which is already mortgaged **Zweithypothek; to foreclose on a mortgaged property** = to sell a property because the owner cannot repay money which he has borrowed, using the property as security **aus eine Hypothek zwangsvollstrecken; to pay off a mortgage** = to pay back the principal and all the interest on a loan to buy a property **eine Hypothek abzahlen; mortgage bond** = certificate showing that a mortgage exists and that property is security for it **Hypothekenpfandbrief; mortgage debenture** = debenture where the lender can be repaid by selling the company's property **Hypothekenpfandbrief; mortgage famine** = situation where there is not enough money available to offer mortgages to house buyers **Hypothekenknappheit; mortgage queue** = list of people waiting for mortgages **Hypothekenwarteliste**

2 *verb* to accept a loan with a property as security **hypothekarisch belasten; eine Hypothek aufnehmen;** *the house is mortgaged; he mortgaged his house to set up in business*

◊ **mortgagee** *noun* person or company which lends money for someone to buy a property **Hypothekengläubiger**

◊ **mortgager** *or* **mortgagor** *noun* person who borrows money to buy a property **Hypothekenschuldner**

QUOTE mortgage money is becoming tighter. Applications for mortgages are running at a high level and some building societies are introducing quotas

Times

QUOTE for the first time since mortgage rates began falling a financial institution has raised charges on homeowner loans

Globe and Mail (Toronto)

most

1 *noun* very large amount *or* quantity **die meisten;** *most of the staff are graduates; most of our customers live near the factory; most of the orders come in the early part of the year*

2 *adjective* very large number of **die meisten;** *most orders are dealt with the same day; most salesmen have had a course of on-the-job training*

◊ **most favoured nation** *noun* country which has the best trade terms **meistbegünstigtes Land; most-favoured-nation clause** = agreement between two countries that each will offer the best possible terms in commercial contracts **Meistbegünstigungsklausel**

◊ **mostly** *adverb* mainly *or* generally **hauptsächlich, meistens;** *the staff are mostly girls of twenty to thirty years of age; he works mostly in the London office*

motion *noun*

(a) moving about **Bewegung; time and motion study** = study in an office *or* factory of the time taken to do certain jobs and the movements workers have to make to do them **Zeit- und Bewegungsstudie;** *entspricht* **REFA-Studie**

(b) proposal which will be put to a meeting to vote on **Antrag;** *to propose or to move a motion; the meeting voted on the motion; to speak against or for a motion; the motion was carried or was defeated by 220 votes to 196;* **to table a motion** = to put forward a proposal for discussion by putting details of it on the table at a meeting **einen Antrag einbringen**

NOTE: no plural

motivated *adjective*

highly motivated sales staff = sales staff who are very eager to sell **motiviert**

◊ **motivation** *noun* encouragement *or* being eager to sell **Motivation; the sales staff lack motivation** = the sales staff are not motivated enough **dem Verkaufspersonal mangelt es an Motivation**

NOTE: no plural

motor *noun*

car **Auto; motor insurance** = insuring a car, the driver and the passengers in case of accident **Kraftfahrzeugversicherung**

mountain *noun*

pile *or* large heap **Berg, Haufen;** *I have mountains of typing to do; there is a mountain of invoices on the sales manager's desk;* **butter mountain** = large amount of unsold butter kept in storage **Butterberg**

mounting *adjective*

increasing **steigend, zunehmend;** *he resigned in the face of mounting pressure from the shareholders; the company is faced with mounting debts*

◊ **mount up** *verb* to increase rapidly **steigen;** *costs are mounting up*

move *verb*

(a) to go from one place to another **umziehen; verlegen;** *the company is moving from London Road to the centre of town; we have decided to move our factory to a site near the airport*

(b) to be sold *or* to sell **absetzen;** *the stock is starting to move; the salesmen will have to work hard if they want to move all that stock by the end of the month*

(c) to propose formally that a motion be accepted by a meeting **beantragen;** *he moved that the accounts be agreed; I move that the meeting should adjourn for ten minutes*

◇ **moveable**
1 *adjective* which can be moved **beweglich;** *moveable property*
2 *plural noun* **moveables** = moveable property **bewegliches Vermögen**

◇ **movement** *noun*
(a) changing position *or* going up or down **Bewegung;** *movements in the money markets; cyclical movements of trade;* **movements of capital** = changes of investments from one country to another **Kapitalverkehr; stock movements** = passing of stock into *or* out of the warehouse **Warenbewegung;** *all stock movements are logged by the computer*
(b) group of people working towards the same aim **Bewegung;** *the labour movement; the free trade movement*

◇ **mover** *noun* person who proposes a motion **Antragsteller/-in**

mpg = MILES PER GALLON

Mr *noun* title given to a man **Herr;** *Mr Smith is the Managing Director*

MRP = MANUFACTURER'S RECOMMENDED PRICE

Mrs *noun* title given to a married woman **Frau;** *the chair was taken by Mrs Smith*

Ms *noun* title given to a woman where it is not known if she is married, or where she does not wish to indicate if she is married or not; *Ms Smith is the personnel officer*

multi- *prefix* referring to many things **multi-, Multi-**

◇ **multilateral** *adjective* between several parties **multilateral;** *a multilateral agreement;* **multilateral trade** = trade between several countries **multilateraler Handel**

◇ **multimillion** *adjective* referring to several million pounds or dollars **über mehrere Millionen, Millionen-;** *they signed a multimillion pound deal*

◇ **multimillionaire** *noun* person who owns several million pounds or dollars **Multimillionär**

◇ **multinational** *noun* company which has branches *or* subsidiary companies in several countries **multinational;** *the company has been bought by one of the big multinationals*

> QUOTE factory automation is a multi-billion-dollar business
> *Duns Business Month*

multiple
1 *adjective* many **mehr-, vielfach; multiple entry visa** = visa which allows a visitor to enter a country many times **Visum zur mehrmaligen Einreise; multiple store** = one store in a chain of stores **Filiale; multiple ownership** = situation where something is owned by several parties jointly **Gemeinschaftseigentum**
2 *noun* company with stores in several different towns **Einzelhandelskette**

multiply *verb*
(a) to calculate the sum of various numbers repeated a certain number of times **multiplizieren, malnehmen;** *to multiply twelve by three; square measurements are calculated by multiplying length by width*
(b) to grow *or* to increase **vermehren, vervielfachen;** *profits multiplied in the boom years*

◇ **multiplication** *noun* act of multiplying **Multiplikation; multiplication sign** = sign used to show that a number is being multiplied by another **Multiplikationszeichen**
NOTE: no plural

municipal *adjective* referring to a town **städtisch, Stadt-, kommunal, Kommunal-;** *municipal taxes; municipal offices*

Murphy's law *noun* law, based on wide experience, which says that in commercial life if something can go wrong it will go wrong

mutual *adjective* belonging to two or more people **gemeinsam; mutual (insurance) company** = company which belongs to insurance policy holders **Versicherungsverein auf Gegenseitigkeit;** *US* **mutual funds** = organizations which take money from small investors and invest it in stocks and shares for them, the investment being in the form of shares in the fund **offene Investmentfonds**
NOTE: the GB English for this is **unit trust**

Nn

nail *noun* small piece of metal, used to attach things together **Nagel; to pay on the nail** = to pay promptly *or* to pay rapidly **pünktlich bezahlen**

naira *noun* money used in Nigeria **Naira**
NOTE: no plural; naira is usually written **N** before figures: **N2,000** say "two thousand naira"

name *noun* word used to call a thing *or* a person **Name;** *I cannot remember the name of the managing director of Smith's Ltd; his first name is John, but I am not sure of his other names;* **brand name** = name of a particular make of product **Markenname; corporate name** = name of a large corporation **Firmenname; under the name of** = using a particular name **unter dem Namen; trading under the name of "Best Foods"** = using the name "Best Foods" as a commercial name, but not the name of the company **ein Produkt unter dem Namen "Best Foods" verkaufen**

◇ **named** *adjective* **person named in the policy** = person whose name is given on an insurance policy as the person insured **der (in der Police benannte) Versicherte**

nation *noun* country and the people living in it **Nation; Volk; most favoured nation** = country which has the best trade terms **meistbegünstigtes Land; most-favoured-nation clause** = agreement between two countries that each will give the other the best possible trade terms in commercial contracts **Meistbegünstigungsklausel; the United Nations** = organization linking almost all countries in the world **die Vereinten Nationen**

◇ **national** *adjective* referring to a particular country **national, National-; national advertising** = advertising in every part of a country, not just in the capital **landesweite/überregionale Werbung;** *we took national advertising to promote our new 24-hour delivery service;* **national campaign** = sales or publicity campaign in every part of a country **landesweite/überregionale Kampagne; the National Debt** = money borrowed by a government **die Staatsverschuldung;** *GB* **National Health Service** = scheme for free medical and hospital service for everyone, paid for by the National Insurance **Staatlicher Gesundheitsdienst; national income** = value of income from the sales of goods and services in a country **Volkseinkommen;** *GB* **National Insurance** = state insurance which pays for medical care, hospitals, unemployment benefits, etc. **Sozialversicherung; National Insurance contributions** = money paid into the National Insurance scheme by the employer and the worker **Sozialversicherungsbeiträge; national newspapers** *or* **the national press** = newspapers which sell in all parts of a country **überregionale Presse; gross national product** = annual value of goods and services in a country including income from other countries **Bruttosozialprodukt;** *GB* **National Savings** = savings scheme for small investors run by the Post Office (including a savings bank, savings certificates and premium bonds) **britisches Sparsystem**

◇ **nationality** *noun* **he is of British nationality** = he is a British citizen **er hat die britische Staatsangehörigkeit**

◇ **nationalize** *verb* to put a privately-owned industry under state ownership and control **verstaatlichen;** *the government are planning to nationalize the banking system*

◇ **nationalized** *adjective* **nationalized industry** = industry which was privately owned, but is now owned by the state **verstaatlichter Wirtschaftszweig**

◇ **nationalization** *noun* taking over of private industry by the state **Verstaatlichung**

◇ **nationwide** *adjective* all over a country **landesweit;** *the union called for a nationwide strike; we offer a nationwide delivery service; the new car is being launched with a nationwide sales campaign*

nature *noun* kind *or* type **Beschaffenheit, Natur;** *what is the nature of the contents of the parcel? the nature of his business is not known*

◇ **natural** *adjective*

(a) found in the earth **natürlich, Natur-; natural gas** gas found in the earth **Erdgas; natural resources** = raw materials (such as coal, gas, iron) which are found in the earth **Bodenschätze**

(b) not made by people **Natur-;** *natural fibres*

(c) normal **natürlich;** *it was natural for the shopkeeper to feel annoyed when the hypermarket was set up close to his shop;* **natural wastage** = losing workers because they resign or retire, not through redundancy or dismissals **natürlicher Abgang an Arbeitskräften;** *the company is hoping to avoid redundancies and reduce its staff by natural wastage*

navy *noun* **merchant navy** = all the commercial ships of a country **Handelsmarine**

NB = NOTE

necessary *adjective* which has to be done *or* which is needed **nötig, notwendig;** *it is necessary to fill in the form correctly if you are not to have difficulty at the customs; is it really necessary for the chairman to have six personal assistants? you must have all the necessary documentation before you apply for a subsidy*

◇ **necessity** *noun* thing which is absolutely important, without which nothing can be done **Notwendigkeit; das**

Notwendigste; *being unemployed makes it difficult to afford even the basic necessities*

negative *adjective* meaning "no" **negativ, verneinend; the answer was in the negative** = the answer was "no" **der Bescheid war negativ; negative cash flow** = situation where a company is spending more money than it receives **negativer Cashflow**

neglected *adjective* not well looked after **vernachlässigt; neglected shares** = shares which are not bought or sold often **wenig gefragte Aktien;** *bank shares have been a neglected sector of the market this week;* **neglected business** = company which has not been actively run by its owners and could therefore do better **vernachlässigtes Unternehmen**

negligence *noun* lack of proper care *or* not doing a duty **Nachlässigkeit; criminal negligence** = not doing a duty with the result that harm is done to the interests of people **grobe Fahrlässigkeit**
NOTE: no plural

◇ **negligible** *adjective* very small *or* not worth bothering about **unbedeutend, geringfügig; not negligible** = quite large **nicht unbedeutend**

negotiable *adjective* **not negotiable** = which cannot be exchanged for cash **unverkäuflich; "not negotiable"** = words written on a cheque to show that it can be paid only to a certain person **nicht übertragbar; negotiable cheque** = cheque made payable to bearer (i.e. to anyone who holds it) **Inhaberscheck; negotiable instrument** = document (such as a bill of exchange, or cheque) which can be exchanged for cash **begebbares Wertpapier**

◇ **negotiate** *verb* **to negotiate with someone** = to discuss a problem formally with someone, so as to reach an agreement **mit jdm verhandeln;** *the management refused to negotiate with the union;* **to negotiate terms and conditions** *or* **to negotiate a contract** = to discuss and agree terms of a contract **Bestimmungen und Bedingungen aushandeln; einen Vertrag aushandeln; he negotiated a £250,000 loan with the bank** = he came to an agreement with the bank for a loan of £250,000 **er handelte ein Darlehen in Höhe von £250.000 mit der Bank aus; negotiating committee** = group of representatives of management or unions who negotiate a wage settlement **Verhandlungsausschuß**

◇ **negotiation** *noun* discussion of terms and conditions to reach an agreement **Verhandlung; contract under negotiation** = contract which is being discussed **Vertrag wird verhandelt; a matter for negotiation** = something which must be discussed before a decision is reached **Verhandlungssache; to enter into negotiations** *or* **to start negotiations** = to start discussing a problem **Verhandlungen aufnehmen; to resume negotiations** = to start discussing a problem again, after talks have stopped for a time **Verhandlungen wiederaufnehmen; to break off negotiations** = to refuse to go on discussing a problem **Verhandlungen abbrechen; to conduct negotiations** = to negotiate **Verhandlungen führen; negotiations broke down after six hours** = discussions stopped because no agreement was possible **die Verhandlungen scheiterten nach sechs Stunden; pay negotiations** *or* **wage negotiations** = discussions between management and workers about pay **Lohnverhandlungen**

◇ **negotiator** *noun*
(a) person who discusses with the aim of reaching an agreement **Verhandlungsführer, Unterhändler; an experienced union negotiator** = member of a union who has a lot of experience of discussing terms of employment with management **ein erfahrener Gewerkschaftsunterhändler**
(b) *GB* person who works in an estate agency **Makler**

> QUOTE initial salary is negotiable around $45,000 per annum
> *Australian Financial Review*
>
> QUOTE after three days of tough negotiations, the company reached agreement with its 1,200 unionized workers
> *Toronto Star*
>
> QUOTE many of the large travel agency chains are able to negotiate even greater discounts
> *Duns Business Month*

net
1 *adjective*
(a) price *or* weight *or* pay, etc. after all deductions have been made **netto, Netto-; net assets** *or* **net worth** = value of all the property of a company after taking away what the company owes **Reinvermögen; net cash flow** = difference between money coming in and money going out of a firm **Netto-Cashflow; net earnings** *or* **net income** = total earnings of a business after tax and other deductions **Netto-, Reingewinn; net income** *or* **net salary** = person's income which is left after taking away tax and other deductions **Nettoverdienst, Nettogehalt; net loss** = actual loss, after deducting overheads **Nettoverlust; net margin** = net profit shown as a percentage of sales **Nettomarge; net price** = price which cannot be reduced by a discount **Nettopreis; net profit** = result where income from sales is more than all expenditure **Netto-, Reingewinn; net receipts** = receipts after

deducting commission *or* tax *or* discounts, etc. **Nettoeinnahmen; net sales** = sales less damaged or returned items **Nettoumsatz; net weight** = weight of goods after deducting the weight of packaging material and container **Nettogewicht; net yield** = profit from investments after deduction of tax **Nettoertrag**

(b) terms strictly net = payment has to be the full price, with no discount allowed **Bezahlung ohne jeden Abzug**

NOTE: the spelling **nett** is sometimes used on containers

2 *verb* to make a true profit **netto einnehmen/verdienen, Reingewinn erzielen;** *to net a profit of £10,000*

NOTE: **netting - netted**

> QUOTE out of its earnings a company will pay a dividend. When shareholders receive this it will be net, that is it will have had tax deducted at 30 per cent
>
> *Investors Chronicle*

network

1 *noun* system which links different points together **Netz(werk); a network of distributors** *or* **a distribution network** = series of points *or* warehouses from which goods are sent all over a country **Verteiler-, Vertriebsnetz; computer network** = computer system where several micros are linked so that they all draw on the same database **Computernetz(werk), Rechnerverbund; television network** = system of linked television stations covering the whole country **Sendenetz**

2 *verb* to link together in a network **vernetzen; to network a television programme** = to send out the same television programme through several TV stations **ein Fernsehprogramm im ganzen Netzbereich senden; networked system** = computer system where several micros are linked together so that they all draw on the same database **Mehrplatzsystem, Rechnerverbund**

new

adjective recent *or* not old **neu; under new management** = with a new owner **unter neuer Leitung; new issue** = issues of new shares **Neuemission; new issues department** = section of a bank which deals with issues of new shares **Abteilung für Neuemissionen; new technology** = electronic instruments which have recently been invented **neue Technologie**

◇ **news** *noun* information about things which have happened **Nachricht(en);** *business news; financial news; financial markets were shocked by the news of the devaluation;* **news agency** = office which distributes news to newspapers and television companies **Nachrichtenagentur, Nachrichtendienst; news release** = sheet giving information about a new event which is sent to newspapers and TV and radio stations so that they can use it **Pressenotiz;** *the company sent out a news release about the new managing director*

◇ **newsagent** *noun* person who runs a shop selling newspapers and magazines **Zeitungshändler**

◇ **newsletter** *noun* **company newsletter** = printed sheet or small newspaper giving news about a company **Firmenmitteilungsblatt**

niche

noun special place in a market, occupied by one company **Nische, Platz**

nickel

noun US five cent coin **Nickel, Fünfcentstück**

night

noun period of time from evening to morning **Nacht; night safe** = safe in the outside wall of a bank where money and documents can be deposited at night using a special door **Nachtsafe; night shift** = shift which works at night **Nachtschicht;** *there are thirty men on the night shift; he works nights or he works the night shift*

nil

noun zero *or* nothing **Null, Nichts;** *to make a nil return; the advertising budget has been cut to nil*

No

= NUMBER

no-claims bonus

noun reduction of premiums on an insurance policy because no claims have been made **Schadenfreiheitsrabatt**

nominal

adjective

(a) very small (payment) **gering, nominell;** *we make a nominal charge for our services; they are paying a nominal rent*

(b) nominal capital = the total of the face value of all the shares in a company **Nominalkapital; nominal ledger** = general accounts book showing income and expenditure **Hauptbuch; nominal value** = face value *or* value written on a share *or* a coin *or* a banknote **Nenn-, Nominalwert**

nominate

verb to suggest someone *or* to name someone for a job **nominieren; aufstellen; to nominate someone to a post** = to appoint someone to a post without an election **jdn auf eine Stelle berufen; to nominate someone as proxy** = to name someone as your proxy **jdn als Stellvertreter nominieren**

◊ **nomination** *noun* act of nominating **Nominierung; Aufstellung**

◊ **nominee** *noun* person who is nominated, especially someone who is appointed to deal with financial matters on your behalf **Nominierter/Nominierte, Kandidat/-in; nominee account** = account held on behalf of someone **Ander-, Mündelkonto**

non- *prefix* not **nicht-, Nicht-**

◊ **non-acceptance** *noun* situation where the person who is to pay a bill of exchange does not accept it **Akzeptverweigerung**

◊ **non-contributory** *adjective* **non-contributory pension scheme** = pension scheme where the employee does not make any contributions and the company pays everything **beitragsfreie Rentenversicherung;** *the company pension scheme is non-contributory*

◊ **non-delivery** *noun* situation where something is not delivered **Nichtlieferung**

◊ **non-durables** *plural noun* goods which are used up soon after they have been bought (such as food, newspapers) **kurzlebige Konsumgüter**

◊ **non-executive** *adjective* **non-executive director** = director who attends board meetings and gives advice, but does not work full-time for the company; *entspricht* **nichtgeschäftsführendes Aufsichtsratsmitglied**

◊ **non-feisance** *noun* not doing something which should be done by law **pflichtwidrige Unterlassung**

◊ **non-negotiable** *adjective* **non-negotiable instrument** = document (such as a crossed cheque) which cannot be exchanged for cash **Rektapapier**

◊ **non-payment** *noun* **non-payment of a debt** = not paying a debt due **Nichtzahlung einer Verpflichtung**

◊ **non profit-making organization** *or US* **non-profit corporation** *noun* organization (such as a club) which is not allowed by law to make a profit **gemeinnütziges Unternehmen;** *non-profit-making organizations are exempted from tax*

◊ **non-recurring** *adjective* **non-recurring items** = special items in a set of accounts which appear only once **einmalige Posten**

◊ **non-refundable** *adjective* which will not be refunded **nicht erstattungsfähig;** *non-refundable deposit*

◊ **non-resident** *noun* person who is not considered a resident of a country for tax purposes **Nichtansässiger, Ausländer/-in;** *he has a non-resident bank account*

◊ **non-returnable** *adjective* which cannot be returned **Einweg-; non-returnable packing** = packing which is to be thrown away when it has been used and not returned to the sender **Einweg(ver)packung**

◊ **non-stop** *adjective & adverb* without stopping **durchgehend, ununterbrochen;** *they worked non-stop to finish the audit on time*

◊ **non-taxable** *adjective* which is not subject to tax **steuerfrei, nicht steuerpflichtig;** *non-taxable income*

◊ **non-union** *adjective* **company using non-union labour** = company employing workers who do not belong to trade unions **Unternehmen, das nicht gewerkschaftlich organisierte Arbeiter beschäftigt**

◊ **non-voting** *adjective* **non-voting shares** = shares which do not allow the shareholder to vote at meetings **stimmrechtslose Aktien**

norm *noun* the usual quantity *or* the usual rate **Norm;** *the output from this factory is well above the norm for the industry or well above the industry norm*

◊ **normal** *adjective* usual *or* which happens regularly **normal, üblich;** *normal deliveries are made on Tuesdays and Fridays; now that the strike is over we hope to resume normal service as soon as possible;* **under normal conditions** = if things work in the usual way **unter normalen Bedingungen;** *under normal conditions a package takes two days to get to Copenhagen*

notary public *noun* lawyer who has the authority to witness documents and spoken statements, making them official **Notar**
NOTE: plural is **notaries public**

note

1 *noun*

(a) short document *or* short piece of information **Mitteilung; Bescheid; advice note** = written notice to a customer giving details of goods ordered and shipped but not yet delivered **Versandanzeige, Avis; contract note** = note showing that shares have been bought or sold but not yet paid for **Ausführungsanzeige; cover note** = letter from an insurance company giving details of an insurance policy and confirming that the policy exists **vorläufiger Versicherungsschein, Deckungszusage; covering note** = letter sent with documents to explain why you are sending them **Begleitschreiben; credit note** = note showing that money is owed to a customer **Gutschriftsanzeige; debit note** = note showing that a customer owes money **Lastschriftsanzeige;** *we undercharged Mr Smith and had to send him a debit note for the extra amount;* **delivery note** = list of goods being delivered, given to the customer with the goods **Lieferschein; dispatch note** = note saying that goods have

been sent **Versandschein; note of hand** *or* **promissory note** = document stating that someone promises to pay an amount of money on a certain date **Schuldschein**
(b) short letter *or* short piece of information **Notiz, Nachricht;** *to send someone a note; I left a note on his desk; she left a note for the managing director with his secretary*
(c) bank note *or* **currency note** = piece of printed paper money **Banknote;** *a £5 note; he pulled out a pile of used notes*
2 *verb* to write down details of something and remember them **zur Kenntnis nehmen; vermerken, notieren;** *we note that the goods were delivered in bad condition; your order has been noted and will be dispatched as soon as we have stock; your complaint has been noted*

◇ **notebook** *noun* book for writing notes in **Notizbuch**

◇ **notepad** *noun* pad of paper for writing short notes **Notizblock**

◇ **notepaper** *noun* good quality paper for letters **Briefpapier**

notice *noun*
(a) piece of written information **Mitteilung, Anschlag;** *the company secretary pinned up a notice about the pension scheme;* **copyright notice** = note in a book showing who owns the copyright and the date of ownership **Urheberrechtsvermerk**
(b) official warning that a contract is going to end *or* that terms are going to be changed **Bescheid; until further notice** = until different instructions are given **bis auf weiteres;** *you must pay £200 on the 30th of each month until further notice*
(c) written announcement that a worker is leaving his job on a certain date **Kündigung; period of notice** = time stated in the contract of employment which the worker or company has to allow between resigning or being fired and the worker actually leaving his job **Kündigungsfrist;** *we require three months' notice; he gave six months' notice; we gave him three months' wages in lieu of notice;* **she gave in** *or* **handed in her notice** = she resigned **sie hat ihre Kündigung eingereicht; he is working out his notice** = he is working during the time between resigning and actually leaving the company **er arbeitet bis zum Ende der Kündigungsfrist**
(d) time allowed before something takes place **Frist; at short notice** = with very little warning **kurzfristig;** *the bank manager will not see anyone at short notice;* **you must give seven days' notice of withdrawal** = you must ask to take money out of the account seven days before you want it **Sie haben sieben Tage Kündigungsfrist**
(e) legal document (such as telling a tenant to leave property which he is occupying) **Bescheid; Verfügung; Kündigungsschreiben; Vorladung;** *to give a tenant notice to quit:* **to serve notice on someone** = to give someone a legal notice **jdm eine rechtlich relevante Nachricht zustellen**
NOTE: no plural for (b), (c), (d) and (e)

◇ **noticeboard** *noun* board fixed to a wall where notices can be put up **Schwarzes Brett, Anschlagbrett;** *did you see the new list of prices on the noticeboard?*

notify *verb* **to notify someone of something** = to tell someone something formally **jdn von etwas in Kenntnis setzen/unterrichten;** *they were notified of the arrival of the shipment*

◇ **notification** *noun* informing someone **Benachrichtigung, Mitteilung**

notional *adjective* probable but not known exactly *or* not quantifiable **spekulativ, angenommen; notional income** = invisible benefit which is not money or goods and services **fiktives Einkommen; notional rent** = sum put into accounts as rent where the company owns the building it is occupying and so does not pay an actual rent **Mietwert einer eigengenutzten Eigentumswohnung**

nought number 0 **Null;** *a million pounds can be written as "£1m" or as one and six noughts*
NOTE: **nought** is commoner in GB English; in US English, **zero** is more usual

null *adjective* with no meaning *or* which cannot legally be enforced **nichtig, ungültig; contract was declared null and void** = the contract was said to be not valid **der Vertrag wurde für ungültig erklärt; to render a decision null** = to make a decision useless *or* to cancel a decision **eine Entscheidung für nichtig erklären/aufheben**

◇ **nullification** *noun* act of making something invalid **Annullierung, Aufhebung**

◇ **nullify** *verb* to make something invalid *or* to cancel something **annullieren, für nichtig erklären**

number
1 *noun*
(a) quantity of things *or* people **Zahl, Anzahl;** *the number of persons on the payroll has increased over the last year; the number of days lost through strikes has fallen; the number of shares sold;* **a number of** = some **eine Reihe von, einige;** *a number of the staff will be retiring this year*
(b) written figure **Zahl, Ziffer;** *account number; batch number; cheque number; invoice number; order number; page*

number; serial number; phone number or telephone number; **box number** = reference number used when asking for mail to be sent to a post office or when asking for replies to an advertisement to be sent to the newspaper's offices **Postfach; Chiffre;** *please reply to Box No. 209;* **index number** = (i) number of something in an index; (ii) number showing the percentage rise of something over a period **(i)(ii) Indexzahl**
NOTE: often written **No.** with figures
2 *verb* to put a figure on a document **numerieren;** *to number an order; I refer to your invoice numbered 1234;* **numbered account** = bank account (usually in Switzerland) which is referred to only by a number, the name of the person holding it being kept secret **Nummernkonto**

◇ **numeric** *or* **numerical** *adjective* referring to numbers **numerisch, zahlenmäßig; in numerical order** = in the order of figures (such as 1 before 2, 33 before 34) **in zahlenmäßiger Folge;** *file these invoices in numerical order;* **numeric data** = data in the form of figures **numerische Daten; numeric keypad** = part of a computer keyboard which is a programmable set of numbered keys **Zehnertastatur, numerische Tastatur**

Oo

O & M = ORGANIZATION AND METHODS

OAP = OLD AGE PENSIONER

oath *noun* legal promise stating that something is true **Eid; he was under oath** = he had promised in court to say what was true **er stand unter Eid**

object *verb* to refuse to do something *or* to say that you do not accept something **protestieren, Einwand erheben, gegen etwas sein;** *to object to a clause in a contract*
NOTE: you object **to** something

◇ **objection** *noun* **to raise an objection to something** = to object to something **gegen etwas Einwand/Einspruch erheben;** *the union delegates raised an objection to the wording of the agreement*

objective
1 *noun* something which you try to do **Ziel;** *the company has achieved its objectives; we set the sales forces certain objectives;* **long-term objective** *or* **short-term objective** = aim which you hope to achieve within a few years or a few months **langfristige Zielsetzung; kurzfristige Zielsetzung; management by objectives** = way of managing a business by planning work for the managers to do and testing if it is completed correctly and on time **Unternehmensführung mit Zielvorgabe**
2 *adjective* considered from a general point of view not from that of the person involved **objektiv, sachlich;** *you must be objective in assessing the performance of the staff; to carry out an objective survey of the market*

obligate *verb* **to be obligated to do something** = to have a legal duty to do something **verpflichtet sein, etwas zu tun**

◇ **obligation** *noun*
(a) duty to do something **Verpflichtung; to be under an obligation to do something** = to feel it is your duty to do something **sich verpflichtet fühlen, etwas zu tun;** *there is no obligation to buy; to be under no obligation to do something;* **he is under no contractual obligation to buy** = he has signed no contract which forces him to buy **er ist nicht vertraglich zum Kauf verpflichtet; to fulfill one's contractual obligations** = to do what is stated in a contract **seine Vertragspflicht erfüllen; two weeks' free trial without obligation** = the customer can try the item at home for two weeks without having to buy it at the end of the test **zwei Wochen Probezeit ohne Kaufzwang**
(b) debt **Verbindlichkeit; to meet one's obligations** = to pay one's debts **seinen Verbindlichkeiten nachkommen**

◇ **obligatory** *adjective* necessary according to the law or rules **obligatorisch, bindend;** *each person has to pass an obligatory medical examination*

◇ **oblige** *verb* **to oblige someone to do something** = to make someone feel he must do something **jdn zu etwas verpflichten;** *he felt obliged to cancel the contract*

obsolescence *noun* act of going out of date, and therefore becoming less useful and valuable **Veralten; built-in obsolescence** *or* **planned obsolescence** = situation where the manufacturer designs his products to become out of date so that the customers can be pressed to replace them with new models **eingeplantes Veralten**
NOTE: no plural

◇ **obsolescent** *adjective* becoming out of date **veraltend**

◇ **obsolete** *adjective* no longer used **überholt, veraltet;** *when the office was equipped with word-processors the typewriters became obsolete*

obtain *verb* to get **erhalten, beziehen, bekommen; erwirken;** *to obtain supplies from abroad; we find these items very difficult to obtain; to obtain an injunction against a company; he obtained control by buying the founder's shareholding*

◊ **obtainable** *adjective* which can be got **erhältlich, zu bekommen;** *prices fall when raw materials are easily obtainable; our products are obtainable in all computer shops*

occasional *adjective* which happens from time to time **gelegentlich**

occupancy *noun* act of occupying a property (such as a house, an office, a room in a hotel) **Besitz, Belegung; with immediate occupancy** = empty and available to be occupied immediately **sofort beziehbar; occupancy rate** = average number of rooms occupied in a hotel over a period of time shown as a percentage of the total number of rooms **Zimmerbelegung;** *during the winter months the occupancy rate was down to 50%*

NOTE: no plural

◊ **occupant** *noun* person or company which occupies a property **Bewohner/-in**

◊ **occupation** *noun*

(a) occupation of a building = act of occupying a building **Besitznahme/Beziehen eines Gebäudes**

(b) job *or* work **Beruf, Tätigkeit;** *what is her occupation? his main occupation is house building*

(c) occupations = types of work **Tätigkeiten;** *people in professional occupations*

◊ **occupational** *adjective* referring to a job **Berufs-, beruflich; occupational accident** = accident which takes place at work **Arbeitsunfall; occupational disease** = disease which affects people in certain jobs **Berufskrankheit; occupational hazards** = dangers which apply to certain jobs **Berufsrisiko;** *heart attacks are one of the occupational hazards of directors;* **occupational pension scheme** = pension scheme where the worker gets a pension from the company he has worked for **Betriebsaltersversorgung**

◊ **occupier** *noun* person who lives in a property **Bewohner/-in; beneficial occupier** = person who occupies a property but does not own it fully **Nießbrauchberechtigter; owner-occupier** = person who owns the property in which he lives **Bewohner des eigenen Grundbesitzes**

◊ **occupy** *verb*

(a) to live or work in a property (such as a house, an office, a hotel room) **bewohnen, belegen;** *all the rooms in the hotel are occupied; the company occupies three floors of an office block*

(b) to occupy a post = to be employed in a job **eine Stelle innehaben**

> QUOTE while occupancy rates matched those of 1984 in July, August has been a much poorer month than it was the year before
>
> *Economist*
>
> QUOTE employment in professional occupations increased by 40 per cent between 1974 and 1983, while the share of white-collar occupations in total employment rose from 44 per cent to 49 per cent
>
> *Sydney Morning Herald*

odd *adjective*

(a) odd numbers = numbers (like 17 or 33) which cannot be divided by two **ungerade Zahlen;** *odd-numbered buildings or buildings with odd numbers are on the south side of the street*

(b) a hundred odd = approximately one hundred **etwa hundert, um die hundert; keep the odd change** = keep the small change which is left over **behalte das Wechselgeld**

(c) one of a group **einzeln; an odd shoe** = one shoe of a pair **ein einzelner Schuh; we have a few odd boxes left** = we have a few boxes left out of the total shipment **wir haben einige wenige Kisten übrig; odd lot** = group of miscellaneous items for sale at an auction **Auktionsposten; to do odd jobs** = to do various pieces of work **Gelegenheitsarbeiten verrichten**

(d) odd sizes = strange sizes which are not usual **keine gängigen Größen; Übergrößen; Untergrößen**

◊ **odd-job-man** *noun* person who does various pieces of work **Gelegenheitsarbeiter**

◊ **oddments** *plural noun* items left over; pieces of large items sold separately **Restposten, Rest-, Einzelbestände**

off

1 *adverb*

(a) not working *or* not in operation **abgesagt, ausgefallen, nicht mehr geltend;** *the agreement is off; they called the strike off*

(b) taken away from a price **ermäßigt, mit Ermäßigung; £25 off the marked price; we give 5% off for quick settlement** £25 cheaper; 5% discount for quick settlement **£25 unter dem angegebenen Preis; wir geben 5% Ermäßigung für prompte Erledigung**

2 *preposition*

(a) away from a price **billiger, nachlassen, weniger;** *to take £25 off the price; we give 10% off our normal prices*

(b) away from work **frei;** *to take time off work; it is the secretary's day off tomorrow*

offer

1 *noun*

(a) statement that you are willing to pay a certain amount of money to buy something **Angebot;** *to make an offer for a company; he made an offer of £10 a share; we made a written offer for the house; £1,000 is the best offer I can make; to accept an offer of £1,000 for the car;* **the house is under offer** = someone has made an offer to buy the house and the offer has been accepted provisionally **für das Haus liegt ein Kaufangebot vor; we are open to offers** = we are ready to discuss the price which we are asking **Angebote werden entgegengenommen; cash offer** = being ready to pay in cash **Barangebot; or near offer** = or an offer of a price which is slightly less than the price asked **oder gegen Höchstgebot; Verhandlungsbasis, VB;** *the car is for sale at £2,000 or near offer* (NOTE: often shortened to **o.n.o.)**

(b) statement that you are willing to sell something **Verkaufsangebot; offer for sale** = situation where a company advertises new shares for sale **Zeichnungsangebot, Angebot; offer price** = price at which new shares are put on sale **Emissionskurs**

(c) he received six offers of jobs *or* **six job offers** = six companies told him he could have a job with them **ihm wurden sechs Stellen angeboten**

(d) bargain offer = sale of a particular type of goods at a cheap price **Sonderangebot;** *this week's bargain offer - 30% off all carpet prices;* **introductory offer** = special price offered on a new product to attract customers **Einführungspreis; special offer** = goods put on sale at a specially low price **Sonderangebot;** *we have a range of men's shirts on special offer*

2 *verb*

(a) to offer someone a job = to tell someone that he can have a job in your company **jdm eine Stelle anbieten;** *he was offered a directorship with Smith Ltd*

(b) to say that you are willing to pay a certain amount of money for something **bieten;** *to offer someone £100,000 for his house; he offered £10 a share*

(c) to say that you are willing to sell something **anbieten;** *we offered the house for sale*

office *noun*

(a) set of rooms where a company works *or* where business is done **Büro, Geschäftsstelle; Kanzlei; branch office** = less important office, usually in a different town or country from the main office **Filiale, Geschäftsstelle, Niederlassung; head office** *or* **main office** = office building where the board of directors works and meets **Hauptgeschäftsstelle, Zentrale, Direktion;** *GB* **registered office** = office address of a company which is officially registered with the Companies' Registrar **eingetragener Sitz**

(b) office block *or* **a block of offices** = building which contains only offices **Bürohaus; office boy** = young man who works in an office, usually taking messages from one department to another **Bürobote, Botenjunge; office equipment** = furniture and machines needed to make an office work **Büroeinrichtung; office hours** = time when an office is open **Dienststunden, Bürozeit;** *open during normal office hours; do not telephone during office hours; the manager can be reached at home out of office hours;* **office junior** = young man or woman who does all types of work in an office **Bürohilfe; office space** *or* **office accommodation** = space available for offices or occupied by offices **Büroräume;** *we are looking for extra office space;* **office staff** = people who work in offices **Büropersonal; office supplies** = stationery and furniture used in an office **Bürobedarf; an office supplies firm** = company which sells office supplies **Büroartikelfirma; for office use only** = something which must only be used in an office **nur für Bürozwecke; office worker** = person who works in an office **Büroangestellter**

(c) room where someone works and does business **Büro;** *come into my office; the manager's office is on the third floor*

(d) booking office = office where you can book seats at a theatre *or* tickets for the railway **Vorverkaufsstelle; Fahrkartenschalter; box office** = office at a theatre where tickets can be bought **Kasse, Theaterkasse; employment office** = office which finds jobs for people; *entspricht* **Arbeitsamt; Stellenvermittlung; general office** = main administrative office in a company **Zentrale; information office** = office which gives information to tourists *or* visitors **Fremdenverkehrsamt; Auskunft; inquiry office** = office where someone can answer questions from members of the public **Auskunft, Information; ticket office** = office where tickets can be bought **Kasse; Fahrkartenschalter**

(e) *GB* government department **Ministerium; the Foreign Office** = ministry dealing with foreign affairs **Außenministerium, Auswärtiges Amt; the Home Office** = ministry dealing with the internal affairs of the country **Innenministerium; Office of Fair Trading** = government department which protects consumers against unfair or illegal business **Amt für Verbraucherschutz**

(f) post *or* position **Amt, Posten;** *he holds or performs the office of treasurer;* **high office** = important position or job **hohe amtliche Stellung; compensation for loss of office** = payment to a director who is asked to leave a company before his contract ends **Entlassungsentschädigung**

officer *noun*
(a) person who has an official position **Beamter/Beamtin; Angestellter/Angestellte im öffentlichen Dienst; customs officer** = person working for the customs **Zollbeamter; fire safety officer** = person responsible for fire safety in a building **Betriebsfeuerwehrmann; information officer** = person who gives information about a company *or* about a government department to the public **Pressereferent; personnel officer** = person who deals with the staff, especially interviewing new workers **Personalchef, Personalreferent; training officer** = person who deals with the training of staff **Ausbildungsleiter; the company officers** *or* **the officers of a company** = the main executives *or* directors of a company **die Führungskräfte eines Unternehmens**
(b) official (usually unpaid) of a club *or* society, etc. **Vorstandsmitglied;** *the election of officers of an association*

official
1 *adjective*
(a) from a government department or organization **amtlich, Amts-; dienstlich, Dienst-;** *on official business; he left official documents in his car; she received an official letter of explanation;* **speaking in an official capacity** = speaking officially **in Ausübung seines Amtes sprechen; to go through official channels** = to deal with officials, especially when making a request **den Amtsweg/Dienstweg beschreiten; the official exchange rate** = exchange rate which is imposed by the government **der amtliche Wechselkurs;** *the official exchange rate is ten to the dollar, but you can get twice that on the black market*
(b) done or approved by a director *or* by a person in authority **offiziell, genehmigt;** *this must be an official order - it is written on the company's notepaper;* **the strike was made official** = the local strike was approved by the main trade union office **der Streik wurde genehmigt**
(c) the official receiver = government official who is appointed to close down a company which is in liquidation **Konkursverwalter**
2 *noun* person working in a government department **Beamter/Beamtin;** *airport officials inspected the shipment; government officials stopped the import licence;* **customs official** = person working for the customs **Zollbeamter; high official** = important person in a government department **höherer Beamter; minor official** = person in a low position in a government department **unterer Beamter;** *some minor official tried to stop my request for building permission;* **top official** = very important person in a government department **Spitzenbeamter; union officials** = paid organizers in a trade union **Gewerkschaftsfunktionäre**

◇ **officialese** *noun* language used in government documents which can be difficult to understand **Beamtendeutsch**

◇ **officially** *adverb* in an official way **offiziell;** *officially he knows nothing about the problem, but unofficially he has given us a lot of advice about it*

officio *see* EX OFFICIO

off-licence *noun GB*
(a) licence to sell alcohol for drinking away from the place where you buy it **Konzession zum Alkoholverkauf**
(b) shop which sells alcohol for drinking at home **Wein- und Spirituosenhandlung**

offload *verb* to pass something which is not wanted to someone else **abstoßen, abschieben; to offload excess stock** = to try to sell excess stock **Überbestand abstoßen; to offload costs onto a subsidiary company** = to try to get a subsidiary company to pay some charges so as to reduce tax **Kosten auf eine Tochtergesellschaft umlegen**
NOTE: you offload something **from** a thing or person **onto** another thing or person

off-peak *adjective* not during the most busy time **außerhalb der Stoßzeit/Hauptbelastungszeit/Hauptverkehrszeit; during the off-peak period** = at the time when business is less busy **außerhalb der Stoßzeit; off-peak tariff** *or* **rate** = lower charges used when the service is not busy **verbilligter Tarif (außerhalb der Stoßzeit)**

off-season
1 *adjective* **off-season tariff** *or* **rate** = cheap fares which are charged in a season when there is less business **Tarif außerhalb der Saison**
2 *noun* less busy season for travel (usually during the winter) **Nebensaison;** *to travel in the off-season; air fares are cheaper in the off-season*

offset *verb* to balance one thing against another so that they cancel each other out **ausgleichen, aufwiegen, anrechnen;** *to offset losses against tax; foreign exchange losses more than offset profits in the domestic market*
NOTE: **offsetting - offset**

off-shore *adjective & adverb*
(a) in the sea near to land **der Küste vorgelagert, Offshore;** *off-shore oil field; off-shore oil platform*
(b) on an island which is a tax haven **Offshore; off-shore fund** = fund which is based in the Bahamas, etc. **Offshore-Investmentfonds**

off-the-job *adjective* **off-the-job training** = training given to workers away from their place of work (such as at a college or school) **außerbetriebliche Ausbildung**

oil *noun* natural liquid found in the ground, used to burn to give power **Öl, Erdöl, Mineralöl; oil-exporting countries** = countries which produce oil and sell it to others **erdölexportierende Länder; oil field** = area of land or sea under which oil is found **Erdölvorkommen;** *the North Sea oil fields ;* **oil-importing countries** = countries which import oil **erdölimportierende Länder; oil-producing countries** = countries which produce oil **Ölförderländer; oil platform** *or* **oil rig** = large construction with equipment for making holes in the ground to find oil **Bohrinsel; oil well** = hole in the ground from which oil is pumped **Erdölquelle**

old *adjective* having existed for a long time **alt;** *the company is 125 years old next year; we have decided to get rid of our old computer system and install a new one*
◇ **old age** *noun* period when a person is old **Alter; old age pension** = state pension given to a man who is 65 or a woman who is 60 **Altersversorgung, Altersrente; old age pensioner** = person who receives the old age pension **Rentner/-in**
◇ **old-established** *adjective* (company *or* brand) which has been in existence for a long time **alteingesessen, seit langem bestehend**
◇ **old-fashioned** *adjective* out of date *or* not modern **altmodisch;** *he still uses an old-fashioned typewriter*

ombudsman *noun* official who investigates complaints by the public against government departments **Ombudsmann**
NOTE: plural is **ombudsmen**

omit *verb*
(a) to leave something out *or* not to put something in **aus-, weglassen;** *the secretary omitted the date when typing the contract*
(b) not to do something **unterlassen, versäumen;** *he omitted to tell the managing director that he had lost the documents*
NOTE: **omitting - omitted**

◇ **omission** *noun* thing which has been omitted **Aus-, Unterlassung, Versäumnis; errors and omissions excepted** = words written on an invoice to show that the company has no responsibility for mistakes in the invoice **Irrtümer und Auslassungen vorbehalten**

omnibus *noun* **omnibus agreement** = agreement which covers many different items **Globalabkommen**

on *preposition*
(a) to sit on a committee = to be a member of the committee **im Ausschuß sitzen; she is on the boards of two companies** = she is a member of the board **sie gehört dem Vorstand von zwei Unternehmen an; we have 250 people on the payroll** = we have 250 staff **wir haben 250 Beschäftigte auf unserer Lohnliste; she is on our full-time staff** = she works full-time for us **sie gehört zu unserem Ganztagspersonal**
(b) to buy something on approval = without commitment to buy **etwas auf Probe kaufen; on the average** = in general **im Durchschnitt; to buy a car on hire-purchase** = to pay for it in instalments **ein Auto auf Raten kaufen; to get a mortgage on easy terms** = to get favourable conditions for one's mortgage **eine Hypothek zu günstigen Bedingungen bekommen**
(c) on weekdays = not on weekends **an Wochentagen; on May 24th** = 24.5. **am 24. Mai**
(d) the director is on holiday = the director has time off **der Direktor ist in Urlaub; she is in the States on business** = she is in the States dealing with business matters **sie ist geschäftlich in den USA**

oncosts *plural noun* fixed costs *or* money paid in producing a product which does not rise with the quantity of the product made **Fixkosten**

on line *or* **online** *adverb* linked directly to a mainframe computer **online, angeschlossen, rechnerabhängig;** *the sales office is on line to the warehouse; we get our data on line from the stock control department*

on-the-job *adjective* **on-the-job training** = training given to workers at their place of work **betriebliche Ausbildung**

one-man *adjective* **one-man business** *or* **firm** *or* **company** *or* **operation** = business run by one person alone with no staff or partners **Einmannbetrieb**

◇ **one-off** *adjective* done or made only once **einmalig;** *one-off item; one-off deal*

◇ **one-sided** *adjective* which favours one side and not the other in a negotiation **einseitig, parteiisch;** *one-sided agreement*

◇ **one-way** *adjective* **one-way ticket** = ticket for a journey from one place to another **einfache Fahrkarte;** *US* **one-way fare** = fare for a journey from one place to another **einfacher Fahrpreis; einfacher Flugpreis; one-way trade** = situation where one country sells to another, but does not buy anything in return **einseitiger Handel**

◇ **one-way street** *noun* street where the traffic is allowed to go only in one direction **Einbahnstraße;** *the shop is in a one-way street, which makes it very difficult for parking*

onerous *adjective* heavy *or* needing a lot of effort or money **beschwerlich, lästig; the repayment terms are particularly onerous** = the loan is particularly difficult to pay back **die Rückzahlungsbedingungen sind extrem schwer**

o.n.o. = OR NEAR OFFER

OPEC = ORGANIZATION OF PETROLEUM EXPORTING COUNTRIES

open
1 *adjective*
(a) at work *or* not closed **geöffnet;** *the store is open on Sunday mornings; our offices are open from 9 to 6; they are open for business every day of the week*
(b) ready to accept something **offen, offenstehend; the job is open to all applicants** = anyone can apply for the job **die Stelle steht allen Bewerbern offen; we will keep the job open for you until you have passed your driving test** = we will not give the job to anyone else, and will wait until you have passed your test **wir werden die Stelle für Sie offen halten, bis Sie Ihren Führerschein gemacht haben; open to offers** = ready to accept a reasonable offer **Angebote werden entgegengenommen; the company is open to offers for the empty factory** = the company is ready to discuss an offer which is lower than the suggested price **die Firma zieht Angebote für die leerstehende Fabrik in Betracht**
(c) open account = account with unsecured credit **Kontokorrentkonto mit Kreditlinie; open cheque** = cheque which is not crossed and can be cashed anywhere **Barscheck; open credit** = bank credit given to good customers without security up to a certain maximum sum **Blankokredit; open market** = market where anyone can buy or sell **freier Markt; to buy shares on the open market** = to buy shares on the Stock Exchange, not privately **Wertpapiere auf dem freien Markt kaufen; open ticket** = ticket which can be used on any date **offenes Ticket**
2 *verb*
(a) to start a new business working **eröffnen, aufmachen;** *she has opened a shop in the High Street; we have opened an office in London*
(b) to start work *or* to be at work **aufmachen, öffnen, geöffnet sein;** *the office opens at 9 a.m.; we open for business on Sundays*
(c) to begin **eröffnen, beginnen; to open negotiations** = to begin negotiating **Verhandlungen beginnen/aufnehmen;** *he opened the discussions with a description of the product; the chairman opened the meeting at 10.30*
(d) to start *or* to allow something to start **eröffnen, einrichten;** *to open a bank account; to open a line of credit; to open a loan*
(e) the shares opened lower = share prices were lower at the beginning of the day's trading **bei Börsenbeginn standen die Aktien niedriger**

◇ **open-ended** *or US* **open-end** *adjective* with no fixed limit *or* with some items not specified **offen, unbeschränkt, unbefristet; Blanko-;** *open-ended agreement*

◇ **opening**
1 *noun*
(a) act of starting a new business **Eröffnung;** *the opening of a new branch; the opening of a new market or of a new distribution network*
(b) opening hours = hours when a shop *or* business is open **Öffnungs-, Geschäftszeit**
(c) job openings = jobs which are empty and need filling **freie Stellen;** *we have openings for office staff;* **a market opening** = possibility of starting to do business in a new market **Markterschließung**
2 *adjective* at the beginning *or* first **Eröffnungs-, einleitend; opening balance** = balance at the beginning of an accounting period **Eröffnungsbetrag; opening bid** = first bid at an auction **Eröffnungsgebot; opening entry** = first entry in an account **Eröffnungsbuchung; opening price** = price at the start of the day's trading **Eröffnungs-, Anfangskurs; opening stock** = stock at the beginning of the accounting period **Eröffnungsbestand**

◇ **open-plan** *adjective* **open-plan office** = large room divided into smaller working spaces with no fixed divisions between them **Großraumbüro**

◇ **open up** *verb* **to open up new markets** = to work to start business in markets where such business has not been done before **neue Märkte erschließen**

> QUOTE after opening at 79.1 the index touched a peak of 79.2 and then drifted to a low of 78.8
> *Financial Times*

operate *verb*
(a) to work **gelten, wirksam werden;** *the new terms of service will operate from January 1st; the rules operate on inland postal services*
(b) to operate a machine = to make a machine work **eine Maschine bedienen;** *he is learning to operate the new telephone switchboard*

◇ **operating** *noun* general running of a business *or* of a machine **Betrieb; operating budget** = forecast of income and expenditure over a period of time **Betriebswirtschaftsplan; operating costs** *or* **operating expenses** = costs of the day-to-day organization of a company **Betriebskosten, betriebliche Aufwendungen; operating manual** = book which shows how to work a machine **Benutzerhandbuch, Bedienungslanleitung; operating profit** *or* **operating loss** = profit or loss made by a company in its usual business **Betriebsgwinn; Betriebsverlust; operating system** = the main program which operates a computer **Betriebssystem**
NOTE: no plural

◇ **operation** *noun*
(a) business organization and work **Geschäft, Tätigkeit, Bereich;** *the company's operations in West Africa; he heads up the operations in Northern Europe;* **operations review** = examining the way in which a company or department works to see how it can be made more efficient and profitable **Betriebsanalyse; a franchising operation** = selling licences to trade as a franchise **Franchisevergabe**
(b) Stock Exchange operation = buying or selling of shares on the Stock Exchange **Börsengeschäft, Effektenhandel**
(c) in operation = working *or* being used **in Betrieb, in Kraft;** *the system will be in operation by June; the new system came into operation on June 1st*

◇ **operational** *adjective*
(a) referring to how something works **betrieblich, Betriebs-, Funktions-; operational budget** = forecast of expenditure on running a business **Betriebsbudget; operational costs** = costs of running a business **Betriebskosten; operational planning** = planning how a business is to be run **Betriebsplanung; operational research** = study of a company's way of working to see if it can be made more efficient and profitable **Unternehmensforschung, Operational-Research**
(b) the system became operational on June 1st = the system began working on June 1st **das System war ab 1. Juni einsatzbereit**

◇ **operative**
1 *adjective* **to become operative** = to start working **wirksam/gültig werden, in Kraft treten;** *the new system has been operative since June 1st*
2 *noun* person who operates a machine which makes a product **Fabrikarbeiter**

◇ **operator** *noun*
(a) person who works a machine **Operator; Maschinist;** *a keyboard operator; a telex operator*
(b) person who works a telephone switchboard **Telefonist/-in;** *switchboard operator; to call the operator or to dial the operator; to place a call through or via the operator*
(c) *(on the Stock Exchange)* person who buys and sells shares hoping to make a quick profit **Börsenspekulant**
(d) tour operator = person *or* company which organizes package tours **Reiseveranstalter**

> QUOTE the company blamed over-capacity and competitive market conditions in Europe for a £14m operating loss last year
> *Financial Times*
>
> QUOTE a leading manufacturer of business, industrial and commercial products requires a branch manager to head up its mid-western Canada operations based in Winnipeg
> *Globe and Mail (Toronto)*
>
> QUOTE the company gets valuable restaurant locations which will be converted to the family-style restaurant chain that it operates and franchises throughout most parts of the US
> *Fortune*
>
> QUOTE a number of block bookings by American tour operators have been cancelled
> *Economist*

opinion *noun*
(a) public opinion = what people think about something **öffentliche Meinung; opinion poll** *or* **opinion research** = asking a sample group of people what their opinion is, so as to guess the opinion of the whole population **Meinungsumfrage;** *opinion polls showed that the public preferred butter to margarine; before starting the new service, the company carried out nationwide opinion polls*
(b) piece of expert advice **Ansicht; Gutachten;** *the lawyers gave their opinion; to ask an adviser for his opinion on a case*

opportunity *noun* situation where you can do something successfully **Gelegenheit, Chance, Möglichkeit; investment opportunities** *or* **sales opportunities** = possibilities for making investments or sales which will be profitable **Investitionsmöglichkeiten;**

Verkaufsmöglichkeiten; a market opportunity = possibility of going into a market for the first time **neue Absätzmöglichkeiten; employment opportunities** *or* **job opportunities** = new jobs being available **Beschäftigungsmöglichkeiten;** *the increase in export orders has created hundreds of job opportunities*

> QUOTE the group is currently undergoing a period of rapid expansion and this has created an exciting opportunity for a qualified accountant
> *Financial Times*

oppose *verb* to try to stop something happening; to vote against something **ablehnen, Einspruch erheben, sich wiedersetzen, bekämpfen;** *a minority of board members opposed the motion; we are all opposed to the takeover*

opposite *noun* **opposite number** = person who has a similar job in another company **Pendant; John is my opposite number in Smith's** = John has the same job in Smith's as I have here **John hat bei Smith die gleiche Stelle wie ich**

optimal *adjective* best **optimal**

◇ **optimism** *noun* being sure that everything will work out well **Optimismus;** *he has considerable optimism about sales possibilities in the Far East;* **market optimism** = feeling that the stock market will rise **Börsenoptimismus**

NOTE: no plural

◇ **optimistic** *adjective* feeling sure that everything will work out well **optimistisch, zuversichtlich; he takes an optimistic view of the exchange rate** = he expects the exchange rate will go in his favour **er ist hinsichtlich des Wechselkurses zuversichtlich**

◇ **optimum** *adjective* best **optimal;** *the market offers optimum conditions for sales*

option *noun*

(a) option to purchase = giving someone the possibility to buy or sell something within a period of time **Option, Verkaufsoption, Vorkaufsrecht; first option** = allowing someone to be the first to have the possibility of deciding something **Vorhand; to grant someone a six-month option on a product** = to allow someone six months to decide if he wants to be the agent *or* if he wants to manufacture the product **jdm für ein Produkt ein sechsmonatiges Optionsrecht einräumen; to take up an option** *or* **to exercise an option** = to accept the option which has been offered and to put it into action **sein Optionsrecht ausüben;** *he exercised his option or he took up his option to acquire sole marketing rights to the product;* **I want to leave my options open** = I want to be able to decide what to do when the time is right **ich will mich nicht festlegen; ich will mir alle Möglichkeiten offenhalten; to take the soft option** = to decide to do something which involves the least risk, effort or problems **den Weg des geringsten Widerstandes wählen**

(b) *(Stock Exchange)* **call option** = option to buy shares at a certain price **Kaufoption; put option** = option to sell shares at a certain price **Verkaufsoption; share option** = right to buy or sell shares at a certain price at a time in the future **Aktienoption; stock option** = right to buy shares at a cheap price given by a company to its employees **Anrecht auf Belegschaftsaktien; option contract** = right to buy or sell shares at a fixed price **Optionsvertrag; option dealing** *or* **option trading** = buying and selling share options **Optionsgeschäft, Optionshandel**

◇ **optional** *adjective* which can be added if the customer wants **auf Wunsch erhältlich;** *the insurance cover is optional;* **optional extras** = items (such as a radio) which can be added (to a car) if wanted **Extras, Sonderzubehör**

order

1 *noun*

(a) arrangement of records (filing cards, invoices, etc.) **Anordnung, Reihenfolge; alphabetical order** = arrangement by the letters of the alphabet (A, B, C, etc.) **alphabetische Reihenfolge; chronological order** = arrangement by the order of the dates **zeitliche/chronologische Reihenfolge;** *the reports are filed in chronological order;* **numerical order** = arrangement by numbers **zahlenmäßige Reihenfolge;** *put these invoices in numerical order*

(b) to be out of order not working **nicht funktionieren/außer Betrieb sein; machine in full working order** = machine which is ready and able to work properly **Maschine, die voll betriebsfähig ist; the telephone is out of order** = the telephone is not working **das Telefon funktioniert nicht; is all the documentation in order?** = are all the documents valid and correct? **sind alle Dokumente in Ordnung?**

(c) pay to Mr Smith or order = pay money to Mr Smith or as he orders **zahlbar an Herrn Smith oder dessen Order; pay to the order of Mr Smith** = pay money directly into Mr Smith's account **zahlbar an Herrn Smith, auf Order Smith lautend**

(d) official request for goods to be supplied **Bestellung, Auftrag;** *to give someone an order or to place an order with someone for twenty filing cabinets;* **to fill** *or* **to fulfil an order** = to supply items which have been ordered **einer Bestellung nachkommen;** *we are so understaffed we cannot fulfil any more* *orders before Christmas; to supply an order for twenty filing cabinets;* **purchase order** = official paper which places an order for something **Auftrag, Bestellung; order fulfilment** = supplying items which have been ordered **Auftragsausführung, Ausführung der Bestellung; terms: cash with order** = the goods will be supplied only if payment in cash is made at the same time as the order is placed **Zahlungsbedingungen: Barzahlung bei Bestellung; items available to order only** = items which will be manufactured only if someone orders them **nur auf Bestellung erhältliche Ware; on order** = ordered but not delivered **bestellt;** *this item is out of stock, but is on order;* **unfulfilled orders** *or* **back orders** *or* **outstanding orders** = orders received in the past and not yet supplied **noch ausstehende Lieferungen, Auftragsrückstände, unerledigte Aufträge; order book** = record of orders **Bestellbuch; Auftragsbuch; the company has a full order book** = it has enough orders to work at full capacity **das Unternehmen hat volle Auftragsbücher; telephone orders** = orders received over the telephone **telefonische Bestellungen;** *since we mailed the catalogue we have had a large number of telephone orders;* **a pad of order forms** = a pad of blank forms for orders to be written on **ein Block Bestellformulare**

(e) item which has been ordered **Bestellung;** *the order is to be delivered to our warehouse;* **order picking** = collecting various items in a warehouse to make up an order to be sent to a customer **Zusammenstellung einer Bestellung**

(f) instruction **Anweisung, Anordnung; delivery order** = instructions given by the customer to the person holding his goods, telling him to deliver them **Lieferauftrag**

(g) document which allows money to be paid to someone **Zahlungsanweisung, Order;** *he sent us an order on the Chartered Bank;* **banker's order** *or* **standing order** = order written by a customer asking a bank to make a regular payment **Dauerauftrag;** *he pays his subscription by banker's order;* **money order** = document which can be bought for sending money through the post **Postanweisung**

2 *verb*

(a) to ask for goods to be supplied **bestellen;** *to order twenty filing cabinets to be delivered to the warehouse; they ordered a new Rolls Royce for the managing director*

(b) to put in a certain way **anordnen, ordnen;** *the address list is ordered by country; that filing cabinet contains invoices ordered by date*

ordinary *adjective* normal *or* not special **normal, gewöhnlich; ordinary member** = person who pays a subscription to belong to a group **ordentliches Mitglied; ordinary shares** = normal shares in a company, which have no special bonuses or restrictions **Stammaktien; ordinary shareholder** = person who owns ordinary shares in a company **Stammaktionär**

organization *noun*

(a) way of arranging something so that it works efficiently **Organisation, Planung, Aufbau, Einteilung;** *the chairman handles the organization of the AGM; the organization of the group is too centralized to be efficient; the organization of the head office into departments;* **organization and methods** = examining how an office works, and suggesting how it can be made more efficient **Organisation und Durchführung; organization chart** = list of people working in various departments, showing how a company *or* office is organized **Stellenbesetzungsplan; Diagramm der Unternehmensstruktur; line organization** = organization of a business where each manager is responsible for doing what his superior tells him to do **Linienorganisation**

(b) group or institution which is arranged for efficient work **Organisation; the Organization of Petroleum Exporting Countries** = group of major countries who are producers and exporters of oil **Organisation erdölexportierender Länder, OPEC; a government organization** = official body, run by the government **staatliche Organisation, Regierungsstelle; a travel organization** = body representing companies in the travel business **Verband der Reiseveranstalter; an employers' organization** = group of employers with similar interests **Arbeitgeberverband**

NOTE: no plural for (a)

◇ **organize** *verb* to arrange something so that it works efficiently **organisieren, planen, aufbauen, einteilen;** *the company is organized into six profit centres; the group is organized by areas of sales;* **organized labour** = workers who are members of trade unions **gewerkschaftlich organisierte Arbeiter**

◇ **organizational** *adjective* referring to the way in which something is organized **organisatorisch, Organisations-;** *the paper gives a diagram of the company's organizational structure*

◇ **organizer** *noun* person who arranges things efficiently **Organisator/-in**

◇ **organizing committee** *noun* group of people who arrange something **Organisationsausschuß, Gründungsausschuß;** *he is a member of the organizing committee for the conference*

> QUOTE working with a client base which includes many major commercial organizations and nationalized industries
>
> *Times*
>
> QUOTE we organize a rate with importers who have large orders and guarantee them space at a fixed rate so that they can plan their costs
>
> *Lloyd's List*
>
> QUOTE governments are coming under increasing pressure from politicians, organized labour and business to stimulate economic growth
>
> *Duns Business Month*

oriented *or* **orientated** *adjective* working in a certain direction **ausgerichtet, orientiert; a profit-oriented company** = company which does everything to make a profit **ein auf Profit ausgerichtetes Unternehmen; export-oriented company** = company which produces goods mainly for export **exportorientiertes Unternehmen**

origin *noun* where something comes from **Herkunft, Provenienz;** *spare parts of European origin;* **certificate of origin** = document showing where goods were made **Provenienz-, Herkunftszertifikat; country of origin** = country where a product is manufactured **Herkunftsland**

◇ **original**
1 *adjective* which was used or made first **original, Original-;** *they sent a copy of the original invoice; he kept the original receipt for reference*
2 *noun* first copy made **Original;** *send the original and file two copies*

◇ **originally** *adverb* first *or* at the beginning **ursprünglich**

ounce *noun* measure of weight (= 28 grams) **Unze**
NOTE: usually written **oz** after figures

out *adverb*
(a) on strike **im Ausstand, ausständig;** *the workers have been out on strike for four weeks; as soon as the management made the offer, the staff came out; the shop stewards called the workforce out*
(b) to be out = to be wrong in calculating something **sich verrechnen;** *the balance is £10 out;* **we are £20,000 out in our calculations** = we have £20,000 too much *or* too little **wir haben uns bei unseren Berechnungen um £20.000 verrechnet**

◇ **outbid** *verb* to offer a better price than someone else **überbieten;** *we offered £100,000 for the warehouse, but another company outbid us*
NOTE: **outbidding - outbid**

◇ **outfit** *noun* small, sometimes badly run, company **Laden, Unternehmen;** *umg* **Verein, Saftladen;** *they called in a public relations outfit; he works for some finance outfit*

◇ **outflow** *noun* **outflow of capital from a country** = capital which is sent out of a country for investment abroad **Kapitalabfluß/Kapitalabwanderung aus einem Land**

◇ **outgoing** *adjective*
(a) outgoing mail = mail which is being sent out **Postausgang**
(b) the outgoing chairman *or* **the outgoing president** = chairman *or* president who is about to retire **der ausscheidende Vorsitzende od Präsident**

◇ **outgoings** *plural noun* money which is paid out **Ausgaben, Ausgänge**

◇ **out-house** *adjective* working outside a company's buildings **außer Haus;** *the out-house staff; we do all our data processing out-house*

◇ **outlay** *noun* money spent *or* expenditure **Kosten, Auslagen, Ausgaben; capital outlay** = money spent on fixed assets (such as property, machinery, furniture) **Investitionsausgaben; for a modest outlay** = for a small sum **mit geringem Kostenaufwand**

◇ **outlet** *noun* place where something can be sold **Verkaufsstelle, Geschäft; retail outlets** = shops which sell to the general public **Einzelhandelsgeschäfte**

◇ **outline**
1 *noun* general description, without giving many details **Überblick, Abriß, Entwurf;** *they drew up the outline of a plan or an outline plan;* **outline planning permission** = general permission to build a property on a piece of land, but not final because there are no details **vorläufige Baugenehmigung**
2 *verb* to make a general description **skizzieren, entwerfen, einen Überblick geben;** *the chairman outlined the company's plans for the coming year*

◇ **outlook** *noun* view of what is going to happen in the future **Aussichten, Perspektive;** *the economic outlook is not good; the stock market outlook is worrying*

◇ **out of court** *adverb & adjective* **a settlement was reached out of court** = a dispute was settled between two parties privately without continuing a court case **es kam zu einem außergerichtlichen Vergleich;** *they are hoping to reach an out-of-court settlement*

◇ **out of date** *adjective & adverb* old-fashioned *or* no longer modern **veraltet, altmodisch, unzeitgemäß;** *their computer system is years out of date; they are still using out-of-date equipment*

◇ **out of pocket** *adjective & adverb* having paid out money personally **aus eigener Tasche;** *the deal has left me out of pocket;* **out-of-pocket expenses** = amount of money to pay a worker back for his own money which he has spent on company business **Spesen**

◇ **out of stock** *adjective & adverb* with no stock left **nicht vorrätig;** *those records are temporarily out of stock; several out-of-stock items have been on order for weeks*

◇ **out of work** *adjective & adverb* with no job **arbeitslos;** *the recession has put millions out of work; the company was set up by three out-of-work engineers*

◇ **output**
1 *noun*
(a) amount which a company or a person or a machine produces **Produktion, Ausstoß, Output;** *output has increased by 10%; 25% of our output is exported;* **output per hour** = amount produced in one hour **Produktionsleistung pro Stunde, Stundenleistung; output bonus** = extra payment for increased production **Produktionsprämie; output tax** = VAT charged by a company on goods or services sold **Bruttomehrwertsteuer**
(b) information which is produced by a computer **Ausgabe, Ausstoß, Ausgang, Output**
NOTE: no plural
2 *verb* to produce (by a computer) **ausgeben;** *the printer will output colour graphs; that is the information outputted from the computer*
NOTE: **outputting - outputted**

◇ **outright** *adverb & adjective* completely **total, ganz, vollständig; to purchase something outright** *or* **to make an outright purchase** = to buy something completely, including all rights in it **etwas komplett kaufen**

◇ **outsell** *verb* to sell more than someone **höhere Verkaufszahlen haben, mehr verkaufen;** *the company is easily outselling its competitors*
NOTE: **outselling - outsold**

◇ **outside** *adjective & adverb* not in a company's office or building **außer Haus, extern; to send work to be done outside** = to send work to be done in other offices **Arbeit außer Haus geben; outside office hours** = when the office is not open **außerhalb der Bürozeit; outside dealer** = person who is not a member of the Stock Exchange but is allowed to trade **Wertpapierhändler, der nicht der Börse angehört; outside director** = director who is not employed by the company **unternehmensfremder Direktor; outside line** = line from an internal office telephone system to the main telephone exchange **Verbindung außer Haus/nach außen;** *you dial 9 to get an outside line;* **outside worker** = worker who does not work in a company's offices **Angestellter außer Haus; Angestellter im Außendienst; Heimarbeiter**

◇ **outsize** *noun* size which is larger than usual; *von Kleidung* **Übergröße; an outsize order** = a very large order **eine Riesenbestellung**

◇ **outstanding** *adjective* not yet paid or completed **ausstehend, unbezahlt; outstanding debts** = debts which are waiting to be paid **Außenstände; outstanding orders** = orders received but not yet supplied **ausstehende Lieferungen, Auftragsrückstände, unerledigte Aufträge; what is the amount outstanding?** = how much money is still owed? **wie hoch ist der noch ausstehende Betrag?; matters outstanding from the previous meeting** = questions which were not settled at the previous meeting **von der vorhergehenden Besprechung noch offenstehende Punkte**

◇ **out tray** *noun* basket on a desk for letters or memos which have been dealt with and are ready to be dispatched **Ausgänge**

◇ **outturn** *noun* amount produced by a country *or* company **Produktionsleistung**

◇ **outvote** *verb* to defeat in a vote **überstimmen; the chairman was outvoted** = the majority voted against the chairman **der Vorsitzende wurde überstimmt**

◇ **outward** *adjective* going away from the home country **Hin-;** *the ship is outward bound; on the outward voyage the ship will call in at the West Indies;* **outward cargo** *or* **outward freight** = goods which are being exported **Hinfracht; outward mission** = visit by a group of businessmen to a foreign country **Delegation ins Ausland**

◇ **outwork** *noun* work which a company pays someone to do at home **Heimarbeit**

◇ **outworker** *noun* person who works at home for a company **Heimarbeiter**

> QUOTE crude oil output plunged during the last month and is likely to remain near its present level for the near future
> *Wall Street Journal*
>
> QUOTE American demand has transformed the profit outlook for many European manufacturers
> *Duns Business Month*
>
> QUOTE Nigeria recorded foreign exchange outflow of N972.9 million for the month of June 1985
> *Business Times (Lagos)*

over

1 *preposition*
(a) more than **über;** *the carpet costs over £100; packages not over 200 grams; the increase in turnover was over 25%*
(b) compared with **gegenüber;** *increase in output over last year; increase in debtors over the last quarter's figure*
(c) during **während;** *over the last half of the year profits doubled*
2 *adverb* **held over to the next meeting** = postponed *or* put back to the next meeting

bis zur nächsten Besprechung aufgeschoben; to carry over a balance = to take a balance from the end of one page or period to the beginning of the next **einen Saldo vortragen**
3 *plural noun* **overs** = extra items above the agreed total **Überschuß, Mehrbetrag;** *the price includes 10% overs to compensate for damage*

◊ **over-** *prefix* more than **über-; shop which caters to the over-60s** = shop which has goods which appeal to people who are more than sixty years old **Laden, der auf Kunden über sechzig ausgerichtet ist**

◊ **overall** *adjective* covering *or* including everything **gesamt, umfassend, Gesamt-; although some divisions traded profitably, the company reported an overall fall in profits** = the company reported a general fall in profits **obwohl einige Unternehmensbereiche einen Gewinn erzielten, meldete das Unternehmen insgesamt einen Gewinnverlust; overall plan** = plan which covers everything **Gesamtplan**

◊ **overbook** *verb* to book more people than there are seats or rooms available **überbuchen; überbelegen;** *the hotel or the flight was overbooked*

◊ **overbooking** *noun* booking of more people than there are seats or rooms available **Überbuchung; Überbelegung**

◊ **overbought** *adjective* **the market is overbought** = prices on the stock market are too high, because there have been too many buyers **der Markt ist ausgekauft worden**

◊ **overcapacity** *noun* unused capacity for producing something **Überkapazität**

◊ **overcapitalized** *adjective* with more capital in a company than it needs **überkapitalisiert**

◊ **overcharge**
1 *noun* charge which is higher than it should be **zuviel berechneter Betrag;** *to pay back an overcharge*
2 *verb* to ask too much money **zuviel berechnen;** *they overcharged us for meals; we asked for a refund because we had been overcharged*

◊ **overdraft** *noun* amount of money which a person withdraws from his account and which is more than he has in the account **Überziehung;** *the bank has allowed me an overdraft of £5,000;* **overdraft facilities** = arrangement with a bank to have an overdraft **Überziehungskredit; we have exceeded our overdraft facilities** = we have taken out more than the overdraft allowed by the bank **wir haben unseren Überziehungskredit überschritten**

◊ **overdraw** *verb* to take out more money from a bank account than there is in it **überziehen; your account is overdrawn** *or* **you are overdrawn** = you have paid out more money from your account than you have in it **Ihr Konto ist überzogen**
NOTE: **overdrawing - overdrew - overdrawn**

◊ **overdue** *adjective* which has not been paid on time **überfällig; interest payments are three weeks overdue** = interest payments which should have been made three weeks ago **die Zinszahlungen sind seit drei Wochen fällig**

◊ **overestimate** *verb* to think something is larger or worse than it really is **überschätzen, zu hoch ansetzen;** *he overestimated the amount of time needed to fit out the factory*

◊ **overextend** *verb* **the company overextended itself** = the company borrowed more money than its assets would allow **die Firma hat sich (finanziell) übernommen**

◊ **overhead**
1 *adjective* **overhead costs** *or* **expenses** = money spent on the day-to-day cost of a business **Betriebskosten, allgemeine Unkosten, Festkosten; overhead budget** = plan of probable overhead costs **Festkostenbudget**
2 *noun* **overheads** *or US* **overhead** = costs of the day-to-day running of a business **allgemeine Unkosten, Festkosten, Gemeinkosten;** *the sales revenue covers the manufacturing costs but not the overheads*

◊ **overlook** *verb*
(a) to look out over **überblicken;** *the Managing Director's office overlooks the factory*
(b) not to pay attention to **übersehen;** *in this instance we will overlook the delay*

◊ **overmanning** *noun* having more workers than are needed to do a company's work **zu große Belegschaft, Überbesetzung;** *to aim to reduce overmanning*

◊ **overpaid** *adjective* paid too much **überbezahlt;** *our staff are overpaid and underworked*

◊ **overpayment** *noun* paying too much **Überbezahlung**

◊ **overproduce** *verb* to produce too much **überproduzieren**

◊ **overproduction** *noun* manufacturing too much of a product **Überproduktion**

◊ **overrated** *adjective* valued more highly than it should be **überbewertet;** *the effect of the dollar on European business cannot be overrated; their "first-class service" is very overrated*

◊ **overrider** *or* **overriding commission** *noun* special extra commission which is above all other commissions **außerordentliche Provision, Superprovision**

◊ **overrun** *verb* to go beyond a limit **überschreiten, überziehen;** *the company*

overran the time limit set to complete the factory
NOTE: **overrunning - overran - overrun**

◇ **overseas**
1 *adjective* across the sea *or* to foreign countries **überseeisch, Übersee-; ausländisch, Auslands-; an overseas call** = phone call to another country **ein Auslandsgespräch; the overseas division** = section of a company dealing with trade with other countries **die Auslandsabteilung; overseas markets** = markets in foreign countries **Überseemärkte; Märkte im Ausland; overseas trade** = trade with foreign countries **Überseehandel; Handel mit dem Ausland**
2 *noun* foreign countries **Ausland;** *the profits from overseas are far higher than those of the home division*

◇ **overseer** *noun* person who supervises other workers **Aufseher/-in, Vorarbeiter**

◇ **oversell** *verb* to sell more than you can produce **zu große Mengen verkaufen; he is oversold** = he has agreed to sell more product than he can produce **er hat mehr verkauft, als er liefern kann; the market is oversold** = stock market prices are too low, because there have been too many sellers **die Kurse fallen aufgrund einer Überzahl an Verkäufern**
NOTE: **overselling - oversold**

◇ **overspend** *verb* to spend too much **zuviel ausgeben; to overspend one's budget** = to spend more money than is allowed in the budget **seine Budgetgrenze überschreiten**
NOTE: **overspending - overspent**

◇ **overspending** *noun* spending more than is allowed **mehr als vorgesehen ausgeben;** *the board decided to limit the overspending by the production departments*

◇ **overstaffed** *adjective* with more workers than are needed to do the work of the company **überbesetzt**

◇ **overstock**
1 *verb* to have more stock than is needed **sich übermäßig mit Waren eindecken, zu große Lagerbestände haben; to be overstocked with spare parts** = to have too many spare parts in stock **zu viele Ersatzteile auf Lager haben**
2 *plural noun US* **overstocks** = more stock than is needed to supply orders **Überbestand;** *we will have to sell off the overstocks to make room in the warehouse*

◇ **oversubscribe** *verb* **the share offer was oversubscribed six times** = people applied for six times as many new shares as were available **das Aktienangebot war sechsfach überzeichnet**

◇ **over-the-counter** *adjective* **over-the-counter sales** = legal selling of shares which are not listed in the official Stock Exchange list **Verkauf im Freiverkehr;** *this share is available on the over-the-counter market*

◇ **overtime**
1 *noun* hours worked more than the normal working time **Überstunden;** *to work six hours' overtime; the overtime rate is one and a half times normal pay;* **overtime ban** = order by a trade union which forbids overtime work by its members **Überstundenverbot; overtime pay** = pay for extra time worked **Überstundenlohn**
NOTE: no plural
2 *adverb* **to work overtime** = to work longer hours than in the contract of employment **Überstunden machen**

◇ **overvalue** *verb* to give a higher value than is right **überbewerten; these shares are overvalued at £1.25** = the shares are worth less than the £1.25 for which they are selling **mit £1.25 sind diese Aktien zu hoch angesetzt; the pound is overvalued against the dollar** = the exchange rate gives too many dollars to the pound, given the strength of the two countries' economies **gegenüber dem Dollar ist das Pfund überbewertet**

◇ **overweight** *adjective* **the package is sixty grams overweight** = the package weighs sixty grams too much **das Paket hat sechzig Gramm Übergewicht**

◇ **overworked** *adjective* having too much work to do **überarbeitet, überlastet;** *our staff complain of being underpaid and overworked*

> QUOTE they said the market was overbought when the index was between 860 and 870 points
> ***Australian Financial Review***
> QUOTE with the present over-capacity situation in the airline industry the discounting of tickets is widespread
> ***Business Traveller***
> QUOTE Cash paid for your stock: any quantity, any products, overstocked lines, factory seconds
> ***Australian Financial Review***
> QUOTE it ties up less capital in inventory and with its huge volume spreads out costs over bigger sales; add in low overhead (i.e. minimum staff, no deliveries, no credit cards) and a warehouse club can offer bargain prices
> ***Duns Business Month***

owe *verb* to have to pay money **schulden;** *he owes the bank £250,000;* **he owes the company for the stock he purchased** = he has not paid for the stock **er schuldet der Firma für die gekauften Waren**

◇ **owing** *adjective*
(a) which is owed **offenstehend;** *money owing to the directors; how much is still owing to the company by its debtors?*
(b) owing to = because of **wegen;** *the plane was late owing to fog; I am sorry that owing to pressure of work, we cannot supply your order on time*

own *verb* to have *or* to possess **besitzen;** *he owns 50% of the shares;* **a wholly-owned subsidiary** = a subsidiary which belongs completely to the parent company **eine hundertprozentige Tochtergesellschaft; a state-owned industry** = industry which is nationalized **ein staatseigener/verstaatlichter Industriebetrieb**

◇ **own brand goods** *noun* products specially packed for a store with the store's name on them **Eigenmarkenwaren, Hausmarke**

◇ **owner** *noun* person who owns something **Eigentümer/-in; sole owner** = person who owns something by himself **Alleineigentümer; owner-occupier** = person who owns and lives in a house **Bewohner des eigenen Grundbesitzes; goods sent at owner's risk** = situation where the owner has to insure the goods while they are being transported **Warensendung mit Gefahr beim Absender**

◇ **ownership** *noun* act of owning something **Eigentum; common** *or* **collective ownership** = situation where a business is owned by the workers who work in it **Miteigentum; Kollektivinhaberschaft; joint ownership** = situation where two people own the same property **Miteigentum; public ownership** *or* **state ownership** = situation where an industry is nationalized **Staatseigentum; private ownership** = situation where a company is owned by private shareholders **Privateigentum; the ownership of the company has passed to the banks** = the banks have become owners of the company **das Eigentumsrecht an dem Unternehmen ist auf die Banken übergegangen**

NOTE: no plural

◇ **own label goods** *noun* goods specially produced for a store with store's name on them **Eigenmarkenwaren, Hausmarkenwaren**

oz = OUNCE(S)

Pp

PA = PERSONAL ASSISTANT

p.a. = PER ANNUM

pack

1 *noun* **pack of items** = items put together in a container for selling **eine Packung Waren;** *pack of cigarettes; pack of biscuits; pack of envelopes;* **items sold in packs of 200** = sold in boxes containing 200 items **Waren in 200-Stück-Packungen; Waren, die in Packungen zu 200 Stück verkauft werden; blister pack** *or* **bubble pack** = type of packing where the item for sale is covered with a stiff plastic cover sealed to a card backing **Schrumpffolienverpackung; display pack** = specially attractive box for showing goods for sale **Schaupackung, Präsentationspackung; dummy pack** = empty pack for display in a shop **Attrappe, Schaupackung, Leerpackung; six-pack** = box containing six items (often bottles) **Sechserpack**

2 *verb* to put things into a container for selling *or* sending **ver-, einpacken;** *to pack goods into cartons; the biscuits are packed in plastic wrappers; the computer is packed in expanded polystyrene before being shipped*

◇ **package**

1 *noun*

(a) goods packed and wrapped for sending by mail **Paket;** *the Post Office does not accept bulky packages; the goods are to be sent in airtight packages*

(b) group of different items joined together in one deal **Paket; pay package** *or* **salary package** *or US* **compensation package** = salary and other benefits offered with a job **Gesamtvergütung;** *the job carries an attractive salary package;* **package deal** = agreement where several different items are agreed at the same time **Verhandlungspaket; Pauschalarrangement;** *we are offering a package deal which includes the whole office computer system, staff training and hardware maintenance;* **package holiday** *or* **package tour** = holiday *or* tour where the hotel, travel and meals are all included in the price **Pauschalreise;** *the travel company is arranging a package trip to the international computer exhibition*

2 *verb*

(a) to package goods = to wrap and pack goods in an attractive way **Waren (attraktiv) verpacken**

(b) to package holidays = to sell a holiday package including travel hotels and food **Pauschalreisen anbieten**

◇ **packaging** *noun*

(a) the action of putting things into packages **Packen, Verpacken**

(b) material used to protect goods which are being packed **Verpackungsmaterial;** *airtight packaging; packaging material*

(c) attractive material used to wrap goods for display **dekoratives Verpackungsmaterial**

NOTE: no plural

◇ **packager** *noun* company who creates a book for a publisher **Packager; Firma, die fertige Bücher an Verleger verkauft**

◇ **packer** *noun* person who packs goods **Packer/-in**

◇ **packet** *noun* small box of goods for selling **Päckchen;** *packet of cigarettes; packet of biscuits; packet of filing cards;* **item sold in packets of 20** = sold in boxes containing 20 items each **Ware, die in 20-Stück-Packungen verkauft wird; postal packet** = small container of goods sent by post **Postpaket**

◇ **packing** *noun*
(a) action of putting goods into boxes and wrapping them for shipping **Verpacken;** *what is the cost of the packing? packing is included in the price;* **packing case** = large wooden box for carrying easily broken items **Kiste; packing charges** = money charged for putting goods into boxes **Verpackungskosten; packing list** *or* **packing slip** = list of goods which have been packed, sent with the goods to show they have been checked **Packzettel**
(b) material used to protect goods **Verpackungsmaterial;** *packed in airtight packing;* **non-returnable packing** = packing which is to be thrown away when it has been used and not returned to the sender **Einwegpackung**
NOTE: no plural

QUOTE the remuneration package will include an attractive salary, profit sharing and a company car
Times
QUOTE airlines will book not only tickets but also hotels and car hire to provide a complete package
Business Traveller
QUOTE in today's fast-growing packaged goods area many companies are discovering that a well-recognized brand name can be a priceless asset
Duns Business Month

pad *noun*
(a) pile of sheets of paper attached together on one side **Block; desk pad** = pad of paper kept on a desk for writing notes **Schreibblock; memo pad** *or* **note pad** = pad of paper for writing memos or notes **Notizblock; phone pad** = pad of paper kept by a telephone for noting messages **Telefon-Notizblock**
(b) soft material like a cushion **Polster;** *the machine is protected by rubber pads;* **inking pad** = cushion with ink in it, used to put ink on a rubber stamp **Stempelkissen**

paid *adjective* with money given **bezahlt**
(a) paid holidays = holidays where the worker's wages are still paid even though he is not working **bezahlter Urlaub**
(b) paid assistant = assistant who receives a salary **fest engagierter Assistent**
(c) which has been settled **bezahlt, beglichen;** *carriage paid; tax paid;* **paid bills** = bills which have been settled **bezahlte Rechnungen;** *the invoice is marked "paid"*
(d) paid-up capital = all money paid for the issued capital shares **voll einbezahltes Kapital; paid-up shares** = shares which have been completely paid for by the shareholder **voll bezahlte Aktien**

pallet *noun* flat wooden base on which goods can be stacked for easy handling by a fork-lift truck **Palette**

◇ **palletize** *verb* to put goods on pallets **palettieren;** *palletized cartons*

pamphlet *noun* small booklet of advertising material or of information **Prospekt, Broschüre**

panel *noun*
(a) flat surface standing upright **Tafel, Brett; display panel** = flat area for displaying goods in a shop window **Auslage-, Anschlagfläche; advertisement panel** = specially designed large advertising space in a newspaper **Kasten**
(b) panel of experts = group of people who give advice on a problem **Sachverständigenausschuß, Expertengruppe; consumer panel** = group of consumers who report on goods they have used so that the manufacturer can improve the goods, or use the consumers' reports in his advertising **Verbraucherpanel, Verbrauchertestgruppe**

panic *adjective* frightened **Panik-; panic buying** = rush to buy something at any price because stocks may run out or because the price may rise **Angst-, Panikkäufe;** *panic buying of sugar or of dollars;* **panic selling of sterling** = rush to sell sterling at any price because of possible devaluation **panikartige Sterlingverkäufe**

paper *noun*
(a) thin material for writing on *or* for wrapping **Papier; brown paper** = thick paper for wrapping parcels **Packpapier; carbon paper** = sheet of paper with a black stuff on one side used in a typewriter to make a copy **Kohlepapier;** *she put the carbon paper in the wrong way round;* **duplicating paper** = special paper to be used in a duplicating machine **Saugpost-, Matrizenpapier; graph paper** = paper with small squares printed on it, used for drawing graphs **Millimeterpapier; headed paper** = notepaper with the name and address of the company printed on it **Papier mit Briefkopf; lined paper** = paper with thin lines printed on it **liniertes Papier; typing paper** = thin paper for use in a typewriter **Schreibmaschinenpapier; wrapping paper** = paper for wrapping **Packpapier;** (NOTE: no plural)

(b) paper bag = bag made of paper **Papiertüte; paper feed** = device which puts paper into a printer or photocopier **Papiervorschub, Papiereinzug**
(c) papers = documents **Papiere, Unterlagen;** *he sent me the relevant papers on the case; he has lost the customs papers; the office is asking for the VAT papers*
(d) on paper = in theory **auf dem Papier, theoretisch;** *on paper the system is ideal, but we have to see it working before we will sign the contract;* **paper loss** = loss made when an asset has fallen in value but has not been sold **nicht realisierter Verlust; paper profit** = profit made when an asset has increased in value but has not been sold **nicht realisierter Gewinn, Buchgewinn paper millionaire** = person who owns shares which, if he sold them, would make him a millionaire **Aktienmillionär**
(e) documents which can represent money (bills of exchange, promissory notes, etc.) **Geldmarktpapiere; bankable paper** = document which a bank will accept as security for a loan **bankfähiges Papier; negotiable paper** = document which can be transferred from one owner to another for money **begebbares Wertpapier**
(f) paper money *or* **paper currency** = banknotes **Papiergeld**
(g) newspaper **Zeitung; trade paper** = newspaper aimed at people working in a certain industry **Fachzeitschrift; free paper** *or* **giveaway paper** = newspaper which is given away free, and which relies for its income on its advertising **Werbe-, Anzeigenblatt**

◇ **paperclip** *noun* piece of bent wire, used to hold pieces of paper together **Büroklammer**

◇ **paperwork** *noun* office work, especially writing memos and filling in forms **Schreibarbeiten;** *exporting to Russia involves a large amount of paperwork*
NOTE: no plural

> QUOTE the profits were tax-free and the interest on the loans they incurred qualified for income tax relief; the paper gains were rarely changed into spending money
> *Investors Chronicle*

par *adjective* equal *or* at the same price **pari, gleich; par value** = face value *or* the value printed on a share certificate **Nennwert; shares at par** = shares whose market price is the same as their face value **Wertpapiere zum Nennwert/al pari; shares above par** *or* **below par** = shares with a market price higher or lower than their par value **Wertpapiere über od unter dem Nennwert/über od unter pari**

parachute *noun US* **golden parachute** = large, usually tax-free, sum of money given to an executive who retires from a company before the end of his service contract **großzügige Entlassungsabfindung**

paragraph *noun* group of several lines of writing which makes a separate section **Abschnitt, Absatz;** *the first paragraph of your letter or paragraph one of your letter; please refer to the paragraph in the contract on "shipping instructions"*

parameter *noun* fixed limit **Parameter;** *the budget parameters are fixed by the finance director; spending by each department has to fall within certain parameters*

parastatal *noun (in Africa)* large state-controlled organization **staatliches Unternehmen**

parcel
1 *noun*
(a) goods wrapped up in paper *or* plastic, etc., to be sent by post **Paket;** *to do up goods into parcels;* **to tie up a parcel** = to fasten a parcel with string **ein Paket verschnüren; parcel delivery service** = private company which delivers parcels within a certain area **Kurierdienst; parcels office** = office where parcels can be handed in for sending by mail **Paketannahme; parcel post** = mail service for sending parcels **Paketpost;** *to send a box by parcel post;* **parcel rates** = charges for sending parcels by post **Paketgebühren, Pakettarife**
(b) parcel of shares = group of shares (such as 50 or 100) which are sold as a group **Aktienpaket;** *the shares are on offer in parcels of 50*
2 *verb* to wrap and tie to make a parcel **(als Paket) verpacken;** *to parcel up a consignment of books*
NOTE: **parcelling - parcelled** but US **parceling - parceled**

parent *noun* **parents** = father and mother **Eltern; parent company** = company which owns more than 50% of the shares of another company **Muttergesellschaft**

pari passu *phrase* equally **gleichwertig;** *the new shares will rank pari passu with the existing ones*

parity *noun* being equal **Gleichheit; Parität; the female staff want parity with the men** = they want to have the same rates of pay and perks as the men **die weibliche Belegschaft will mit der männlichen gleichgestellt werden; the pound fell to parity with the dollar** = the pound fell to a point where one pound

equalled one dollar **das Pfund fiel, bis es den Kurs von 1:1 gegenüber dem Dollar erreichte**
NOTE: no plural

> QUOTE the draft report on changes in the international monetary system casts doubt about any return to fixed exchange-rate parities
> *Wall Street Journal*

park

1 *noun* open space with grass and trees **Park; business park** = group of small factories or warehouses, especially near a town **Gewerbegebiet; car park** = place where you can leave your car **Parkplatz;** *he left his car in the hotel car park; if the car park is full, you can park in the street for thirty minutes;* **industrial park** = area of land near a town specially set aside for factories and warehouses **Industriegebiet; science park** = area near a town or university set aside for technological industries **Technologiezentrum**
2 *verb* to leave your car in a place while you are not using it **parken;** *the rep parked his car outside the shop; you cannot park here during the rush hour; parking is difficult in the centre of the city*

Parkinson's law

noun law, based on wide experience, that in business as in government the amount of work increases to fill the time available for it **Parkinsonsches Gesetz**

part

noun
(a) piece *or* section **Teil;** *part of the shipment was damaged; part of the workforce is on overtime;* **part of the expenses will be refunded** = some of the expenses, but not all **ein Teil der Ausgaben wird zurückerstattet**
(b) in part = not completely **teilweise, zum Teil;** *to contribute in part to the costs or to pay the costs in part*
(c) spare part = small piece of machinery to replace a part of a machine which is broken **Ersatzteil;** *the photocopier will not work - we need to replace a part or a part needs replacing*
(d) part-owner = person who owns something jointly with one or more other persons **Miteigentümer;** *he is part-owner of the restaurant;* **part-ownership** = situation where two or more persons own the same property **Miteigentum**
(e) to offer *or* **take something in part exchange** = giving an old product as part of the payment for a new one **etwas in Zahlung geben od nehmen;** *they refused to take my old car as part exchange for the new one;* **part payment** = paying of part of a whole payment **Teilzahlung, Abschlagzahlung;** *I gave him £250 as part payment for the car;* **part delivery** *or* **part order** *or* **part shipment** = delivering *or* shipping only some of the items in an order **Teillieferung, Teilsendung**

◊ **part-time** *adjective & adverb* not working for the whole working day **Teilzeit-;** *she works part-time; he is trying to find part-time work when the children are in school; a part-time worker; we are looking for part-time staff to work our computers;* **part-time work** *or* **part-time employment** = work for part of a working day *or* part of the week **Halbtagsbeschäftigung, Teilzeitbeschäftigung, Teilzeitarbeit**

◊ **part-timer** *noun* person who works part-time **Teilzeitkraft**

partial

adjective not complete **Teil-, partiell, teilweise; partial loss** = situation where only part of the insured property has been damaged or lost **Teilverlust, Teilschaden; he got partial compensation for the damage to his house** = he was compensated for part of the damage **der Schaden an seinem Haus wurde zum Teil ersetzt**

participation

noun taking part **Teilnahme, Beteiligung, Mitwirkung; worker participation** = situation where the workers take part in making management decisions **Mitbestimmung**
NOTE: no plural

◊ **participative** *adjective* where both sides take part **partizipativ;** *we do not treat management-worker relations as a participative process*

particular

1 *adjective* special *or* different from others **besonderer, speziell;** *the photocopier only works with a particular type of paper;* **particular average** = situation where part of a shipment is lost or damaged and the insurance costs are borne by the owner of the lost goods and not shared among all the owners of the shipment **besondere Havarie**
2 *noun*
(a) particulars = details **Einzelheiten, nähere Angaben;** *sheet which gives particulars of the items for sale; the inspector asked for particulars of the missing car;* **to give full particulars of something** = to list all the known details about something **genaue/detaillierte Angaben zu etwas machen**
(b) in particular = specially *or* as a special point **besonders, insbesondere, vor allem;** *fragile goods, in particular glasses, need special packing*

partly

adverb not completely **teilweise, zum Teil; partly-paid capital** = capital which represents partly-paid shares **teilweise eingezahltes Aktienkapital; partly-paid up shares** = shares where the shareholders have not paid the full face value **teilweise eingezahlte Aktien; partly-secured creditors** = creditors whose debts are not fully covered by the value of the security **nur zum Teil gesicherter Gläubiger**

partner *noun* person who works in a business and has an equal share in it with other partners **Partner/-in;** *he became a partner in a firm of solicitors;* **active partner** *or* **working partner** = partner who works in a partnership **tätiger Teilhaber, Geschäftspartner; junior partner** *or* **senior partner** = person who has a small or large part of the shares in a partnership **Juniorpartner; Seniorpartner; sleeping partner** = partner who has a share in a business but does not work in it **stiller Teilhaber**

◇ **partnership** *noun*
(a) unregistered business where two or more people share the risks and profits equally **Partnerschaft, Teilhaberschaft, Personengesellschaft;** *to go into partnership with someone; to join with someone to form a partnership;* **to offer someone a partnership** *or* **to take someone into partnership with you** = to have a working business and bring someone in to share it with you **jdn zum Teilhaber machen; to dissolve a partnership** = to bring a partnership to an end **eine Gesellschaft/Partnerschaft auflösen**
(b) limited partnership = registered business where the liability of the partners is limited to the amount of capital they have each provided to the business and where the partners may not take part in the running of the business **Kommanditgesellschaft**

party *noun*
(a) company *or* person involved in a legal dispute *or* legal agreement **Partei;** *one of the parties to the suit has died; the company is not a party to the agreement*
(b) third party = any third person, in addition to the two main people involved in a contract **Dritter, dritte Person; third party insurance** *or* **third party policy** = insurance to cover damage to any person who is not one of the people named in the insurance contract (that is, not the insured person nor the insurance company) **Haftpflichtversicherung**
(c) working party = group of experts who study a problem **Arbeitsausschuß;** *the government has set up a working party to study the problems of industrial waste; Professor Smith is the chairman of the working party on computers in society*

pass
1 *noun* permit to allow someone to go into a building **Ausweis, Passierschein;** *you need a pass to enter the ministry offices; all members of staff must show a pass*
2 *verb*
(a) to pass a dividend = to pay no dividend in a certain year **keine Dividende ausschütten, eine Dividende ausfallen lassen**
(b) to approve **genehmigen, annehmen;** *the finance director has to pass an invoice before it is sent out; the loan has been passed by the board;* **to pass a resolution** = to vote to agree to a resolution **eine Resolution annehmen;** *the meeting passed a proposal that salaries should be frozen*
(c) to be successful **bestehen;** *he passed his typing test; she has passed all her exams and now is a qualified accountant*

◇ **passbook** *noun* book given by a bank *or* building society which shows money which you deposit *or* withdraw from your savings account *or* building society account **Sparbuch**

> QUOTE instead of customers having transactions recorded in their passbooks, they will present plastic cards and have the transactions printed out on a receipt
> *Australian Financial Review*

◇ **pass off** *verb* **to pass something off as something else** = to pretend that it is another thing in order to cheat a customer **etwas für/als etwas anderes ausgeben;** *he tried to pass off the wine as French, when in fact it came from outside the Common Market*

passage *noun* voyage by ship **Überfahrt**

passenger *noun* person who travels in a plane, bus, taxi, plane, etc., but is not the driver or member of the crew **Passagier/-in; passenger terminal** = air terminal for people going on planes, not for cargo **Abfertigungsgebäude für Passagiere; passenger train** = train which carries passengers but not freight **Personenzug**

passport *noun* official document proving that you are a citizen of a country, which you have to show when you travel from one country to another **Paß;** *we had to show our passports at the customs post; his passport is out of date; the passport officer stamped my passport*

patent
1 *noun*
(a) official document showing that a person has the exclusive right to make and sell an invention **Patenturkunde, Patent;** *to take out a patent for a new type of light bulb; to apply for a patent for a new invention;* **letters**

patent = official term for a patent **Patenturkunde; patent applied for** *or* **patent pending** = words on a product showing that the inventor has applied for a patent for it **Patent angemeldet, angemeldetes Patent; to forfeit a patent** = to lose a patent because payments have not been made **ein Patent verfallen lassen/verwirken; to infringe a patent** = to make and sell a product which works in the same way as a patented product and not pay a royalty for it **ein Patent verletzen; infringement of patent** *or* **patent infringement** = act of illegally making or selling a product which is patented **Patentverletzung**
(b) patent agent = person who advises on patents and applies for patents on behalf of clients **Patentanwalt; to file a patent application** = to apply for a patent **ein Patent anmelden, eine Patentanmeldung einreichen; patent medicine** = medicine which is registered as a patent **patentrechtlich geschütztes Arzneimittel; patent office** = government office which grants patents and supervises them **Patentamt; patent rights** = rights which an inventor holds under a patent **Patentschutz**
2 *verb* **to patent an invention** = to register an invention with the patent office to prevent other people from copying it **eine Erfindung patentieren lassen**

◊ **patented** *adjective* which is protected by a patent **gesetzlich/patentrechtlich geschützt**

paternity

paternity *noun* **paternity leave** = permission for a man to be away from work when his wife is having a baby **Arbeitsfreistellung zur Geburt**

pattern

pattern *noun*
(a) pattern book = book showing examples of design **Musterbuch**
(b) general way in which something usually happens **Struktur, übliches Schema;** *pattern of prices or price pattern; pattern of sales or sales pattern;* **pattern of trade** *or* **trading pattern** = general way in which trade is carried on **Handelsstruktur;** *the company's trading pattern shows high export sales in the first quarter and high home sales in the third quarter*

pawn

pawn
1 *noun* **to put something in pawn** = to leave a valuable object with someone in exchange for a loan which has to be repaid if you want to take back the object **etwas verpfänden;** *umg* **etwas versetzen/ins Leihhaus bringen; to take something out of pawn** = to repay the loan and so get back the object **ein Pfand auslösen; pawn ticket** = receipt given by the pawnbroker for the object left in pawn **Pfandschein**
NOTE: no plural
2 *verb* **to pawn a watch** = to leave a watch with a pawnbroker who gives a loan against it **eine Uhr verpfänden**

◊ **pawnbroker** *noun* person who lends money against the security of valuable objects **Pfandleiher/-in**

◊ **pawnshop** *noun* pawnbroker's shop **Leihhaus, Pfandleihanstalt**

pay

pay
1 *noun*
(a) salary *or* wage *or* money given to someone for regular work **Gehalt, Lohn; back pay** = salary which has not been paid **Lohnrückstand; basic pay** = normal salary without extra payments **Ecklohn, Grundgehalt; take-home pay** = pay left after tax and insurance have been deducted **Nettoverdienst; holidays with pay** = holiday which a worker can take by contract and for which he is paid **bezahlter Urlaub; unemployment pay** = dole *or* money given by the government to someone who is unemployed **Arbeitslosengeld; Arbeitslosenhilfe**
(b) pay cheque = monthly cheque which pays a salary to a worker **Gehalts-, Lohnscheck; pay day** = day on which wages are paid to workers (usually Friday for workers paid once a week, and during the last week of the month for workers who are paid once a month) **Zahltag; pay negotiations** *or* **pay talks** = discussions between management and workers about pay increases **Lohnverhandlungen; pay packet** = envelope containing the pay slip and the cash pay **Lohntüte; pay rise** = increase in pay **Gehalts-, Lohnerhöhung; pay slip** = piece of paper showing the full amount of a worker's pay, and the money deducted as tax, pension and insurance contributions **Gehalts-, Lohnstreifen, Gehalts-, Lohnabrechnung**
(c) pay desk = place in a store where you pay for goods bought **Kasse; pay phone** = telephone which works if you put coins into it **Münzfernsprecher**
2 *verb*
(a) to give money to buy an item or a service **(be)zahlen;** *to pay £1,000 for a car; how much did you pay to have the office cleaned?;* **to pay in advance** = to give money before you receive the item bought *or* before the service has been completed **im voraus bezahlen;** *we had to pay in advance to have the new telephone system installed;* **to pay in instalments** = to give money for an item by giving small amounts regularly **in Raten zahlen;** *we are paying for the computer by paying instalments of £50 a month;* **to pay cash** = to pay the complete sum in cash **bar bezahlen; "pay cash"** = words written on

a crossed cheque to show that it can be paid in cash if necessary; *GB* **Barauszahlung; to pay by cheque** = to pay by giving a cheque, not by using cash or credit card **mit (einem) Scheck bezahlen; to pay by credit card** = to pay, using a credit card and not a cheque or cash **mit Kreditkarte bezahlen**
(b) to give money **(be)zahlen; to pay on demand** = to pay money when it is asked for, not after a period of credit **auf Anforderung bezahlen; please pay the sum of £10** = please give £10 in cash or by cheque **bitte bezahlen Sie den Betrag von £10; to pay a dividend** = to give shareholders a part of the profits of a company **eine Dividende ausschütten;** *these shares pay a dividend of 1.5p;* **to pay interest** = to give money as interest on money borrowed *or* invested **Zinsen zahlen;** *building societies pay an interest of 10%;* **pay as you earn** *or* *US* **pay-as-you-go** = tax system, where income tax is deducted from the salary before it is paid to the worker **Lohnsteuerabzug vor Auszahlung des Lohns**
(c) to give a worker money for work done **zahlen;** *the workforce has not been paid for three weeks; we pay good wages for skilled workers; how much do they pay you per hour?;* **to be paid by the hour** = to get money for each hour worked **stundenweise bezahlt werden, einen Stundenlohn erhalten; to be paid at piece-work rates** = to get money for each piece of work finished **einen Akkordlohn erhalten, im Akkord bezahlt werden**
(d) to give money which is owed *or* which has to be paid **(be)zahlen, begleichen;** *to pay a bill; to pay an invoice; to pay duty on imports; to pay tax*
(e) to pay a cheque into an account = to deposit money in the form of a cheque **einen Scheck auf ein Konto einzahlen**
NOTE: **paying - paid**

◊ **payable** *adjective* which is due to be paid **zahlbar, fällig; payable in advance** = which has to be paid before the goods are delivered **im voraus zahlbar; payable on delivery** = which has to be paid when the goods are delivered **zahlbar bei Lieferung; payable on demand** = which must be paid when payment is asked for **zahlbar bei Sicht/auf Verlangen; payable at sixty days** = which has to be paid by sixty days after the date of invoice **zahlbar innerhalb von sechzig Tagen; payable to bearer** = cheque which will be paid to the person who has it, not to any particular name written on it **zahlbar an Überbringer; shares payable on application** = shares which must be paid for when you apply to buy them **bei Antragstellung zahlbare Wertpapiere; accounts payable** = money owed by a company **Verbindlichkeiten; bills payable** = bills which a debtor will have to pay **Wechselverbindlichkeiten; electricity charges are payable by the tenant** = the tenant (and not the landlord) must pay for the electricity **Elektrizitätskosten sind vom Mieter zu tragen**

◊ **pay back** *verb* to give money back to someone **zurückzahlen;** *to pay back a loan; I lent him £50 and he promised to pay me back in a month; he has never paid me back the money he borrowed*

◊ **payback** *noun* paying back money which has been borrowed **Rückzahlung; payback clause** = clause in a contract which states the terms for repaying a loan **Rückzahlungsklausel; payback period** = period of time over which a loan is to be repaid *or* an investment is to pay for itself **Tilgungszeitraum; Amortisationszeit**
NOTE: no plural

◊ **paycheck** *noun* salary cheque given to an employee **Lohn-, Gehaltsscheck**

◊ **pay down** *verb* **to pay money down** = to make a deposit **Geld anzahlen;** *he paid £50 down and the rest in monthly instalments*

◊ **PAYE** = PAY AS YOU EARN

◊ **payee** *noun* person who receives money from someone *or* person whose name is on a cheque **Zahlungsempfänger**

◊ **payer** *noun* person who gives money to someone **Zahler; slow payer** = person *or* company which does not pay debts on time **säumiger Schuldner;** *he is well known as a slow payer*

◊ **paying**
1 *adjective* which makes a profit **rentabel, gewinnbringend, lukrativ, einträglich;** *it is a paying business;* **it is not a paying proposition** = it is not a business which is going to make a profit **das ist kein lukratives/lohnendes Geschäft**
2 *noun* giving money **Zahlen;** *paying of a debt;* **paying-in book** = book of forms for paying money into a bank account *or* building society; *GB* **Einzahlungsbuch; paying-in slip** = form which is filled in when money is being deposited in a bank account *or* building society **Einzahlungsbeleg**
NOTE: no plural

◊ **payload** *noun* cargo *or* passengers carried by a ship *or* train *or* plane for which payment is made **Nutzlast**

◊ **payment** *noun*
(a) giving money **Zahlung, Bezahlung, Begleichung;** *payment in cash or cash payment; payment by cheque; payment of interest or interest payment;* **payment on account** = paying part of the money owed **Abschlagszahlung, Akontozahlung; full payment** *or* **payment in full** = paying all money owed **Zahlung in voller Höhe; payment on invoice** = paying money as soon as an invoice is received **Zahlung bei Erhalt der**

Rechnung; payment in kind = paying by giving goods or food, but not money **Sachleistung, Bezahlung in Naturalien; payment by results** = money given which increases with the amount of work done or goods produced **Leistungslohn**

(b) money paid **Zahlung; back payment** = paying money which is owed **Nach-, Rückzahlung; deferred payments** = money paid later than the agreed date **aufgeschobene Zahlung;** *the company agreed to defer payments for three months;* **down payment** = part of a total payment made in advance **Anzahlung; repayable in easy payments** = repayable with small sums regularly **zahlbar in bequemen Raten; incentive payments** = extra pay offered to a worker to make him work better **Leistungszulage, Prämie; balance of payments** = the international financial position of a country including visible and invisible trade **Zahlungsbilanz**

◊ **pay off** *verb*

(a) to finish paying money which is owed **vollständig abbezahlen, tilgen;** *to pay off a mortgage; to pay off a loan*

(b) to pay all the money owed to someone and terminate his employment **auszahlen;** *when the company was taken over the factory was closed and all the workers were paid off*

◊ **payoff** *noun* money paid to finish paying something which is owed **Tilgungssumme, Rückzahlungsbetrag**

◊ **pay out** *verb* to give money **ausbezahlen, ausgeben;** *the company pays out thousands of pounds in legal fees; we have paid out half our profits in dividends*

◊ **payout** *noun* money paid to help a company in difficulty *or* subsidy **Subventionszahlungen;** *the company only exists on payouts from the government*

◊ **payroll** *noun* list of people employed and paid by a company *or* money paid by a company in salaries **Lohn-, Gehaltsliste; Lohn-, Gehaltssumme;** *the company has 250 on the payroll;* **payroll ledger** = list of staff and their salaries **Lohn- und Gehaltsliste; payroll tax** = tax on the people employed by a company **Arbeitgeberanteil an der Sozialversicherung**

◊ **pay up** *verb* to give money which is owed **zahlen, voll/ganz bezahlen;** *the company only paid up when we sent them a letter from our solicitor; he finally paid up six months late*

> QUOTE the yield figure means that if you buy the shares at their current price you will be getting 5% before tax on your money if the company pays the same dividend as in its last financial year
> ***Investors Chronicle***
>
> QUOTE after a period of recession followed by a rapid boost in incomes, many tax payers embarked upon some tax planning to minimize their payouts
> ***Australian Financial Review***
>
> QUOTE recession encourages communication not because it makes redundancies easier, but because it makes low or zero pay increases easier to accept
> ***Economist***

P/E *abbreviation* = PRICE/EARNINGS; **P/E ratio** = ratio between the market price of a share and the current dividend it produces **Kurs-Gewinn-Verhältnis;** *the shares sell at a P/E ratio of 7*

peak
1 *noun* highest point **Höhepunkt, Höchststand; peak period** = time of the day when most commuters are travelling *or* when most electricity is being used **Hauptverkehrszeit, Stoßzeit; Hauptbelastungszeit; time of peak demand** = time when something is being used most **Spitzenbedarfszeit; peak output** = highest output **Höchstproduktion; peak year** = best year *or* year when the largest quantity of products was produced *or* when sales were highest **Spitzenjahr;** *the shares reached their peak in January; the share index has fallen 10% since the peak in January*
2 *verb* to reach the highest point **den Höchststand erreichen;** *productivity peaked in January; shares have peaked and are beginning to slip back*

pecuniary *adjective* referring to money **finanziell, pekuniär; he gained no pecuniary advantage** = he made no profit **er erzielte keinen finanziellen Vorteil**

peddle *verb* to sell goods from door to door *or* in the street **hausieren; Wandergewerbe betreiben**

peg *verb* to hold something at a certain point **festsetzen, halten; to peg prices** = to fix prices to stop them rising **Preise stützen/stabilisieren; to peg wage increases to the cost-of-living index** = to limit increases in wages to the increases in the cost-of-living index **Lohnerhöhungen auf dem Niveau des Lebenshaltungsindexes halten**
NOTE: **pegging - pegged**

pen *noun* thing for writing with, using ink **Füllhalter, Kugelschreiber; felt pen** = pen with a point made of hard cloth **Filzstift; light pen**

= type of pen which when passed over a bar code can read it and send information back to a computer **Lichtstift, Lesepistole; marker pen** = pen which makes a wide coloured mark **Textmarker**

penalty *noun* punishment (such as a fine) which is imposed if something is not done **Strafe; Geldstrafe, Buße; penalty clause** = clause which lists the penalties which will be imposed if the contract is not obeyed **Strafklausel, Bestimmung der Vertragsstrafe;** *the contract contains a penalty clause which fines theB company 1% for every week the completion date is late*

◇ **penalize** *verb* to punish *or* to fine **bestrafen; mit einer Geldstrafe belegen;** *to penalize a supplier for late deliveries; they were penalized for bad service*

pence *see* PENNY

pending
1 *adjective* waiting **schwebend, anstehend; pending tray** = basket on a desk for papers which cannot be dealt with immediately **Wiedervorlage; patent pending** = situation where an invention is put on the market before a patent is granted **angemeldetes Patent**
2 *adverb* **pending advice from our lawyers** = while waiting for advice from our lawyers **bis zur Benachrichtigung durch unsere Anwälte**

penetrate *verb* **to penetrate a market** = to get into a market and capture a share of it **in einen Markt vordringen, sich auf einem Markt durchsetzen**

◇ **penetration** *noun* **market penetration** = percentage of a total market which the sales of a company cover **Marktdurchdringung**
NOTE: no plural

penny *noun*
(a) *GB* small coin, of which one hundred make a pound **Penny;** (NOTE: usually written **p** after a figure: **26p;** the plural is **pence)**
(b) *US informal* small coin, one cent **Centstück**

◇ **penny share** *or US* **penny stock** *noun* very cheap share, costing about 10p or less than $1 **Kleinaktie**

pension
1 *noun*
(a) money paid regularly to someone who no longer works **Rente, Pension, Ruhegehalt; retirement pension** *or* **old age pension** = state pension given to a man who is over 65 or and woman who is over 60 **Altersrente, Altersversorgung; government pension** *or* **state pension** = pension paid by the state **staatliche Altersversorgung; occupational pension** = pension which is paid by the company by which a worker has been employed **betriebliche Altersversorgung, Betriebsrente; portable pension** = pension entitlement which can be moved from one company to another without loss (as a worker changes jobs); *GB* **(auf eine andere Firma) übertragbarer Rentenanspruch; pension contributions** = money paid by a company or worker into a pension fund **Rentenversicherungsbeiträge**
(b) pension plan *or* **pension scheme** = plan worked out by an insurance company which arranges for a worker to pay part of his salary over many years and receive a regular payment when he retires **Alterssicherungssystem, Ruhegeldordnung, Rentenversicherungs- system; company pension scheme** = pension which is organized by a company for its staff **Betriebsrentenplan, betriebliche Altersversorgung;** *he decided to join the company's pension scheme;* **contributory pension scheme** = scheme where the worker has to pay a proportion of his salary **beitragspflichtige Rentenversicherung; graduated pension scheme** = pension scheme where the benefit is calculated as a percentage of the salary of each person in the scheme; *GB* **gestaffeltes Rentensystem; non-contributory pension scheme** = scheme where the employer pays in all the money on behalf of the worker **beitragsfreie Rentenversicherung; personal pension plan** = pension plan which applies to one worker only, usually a self-employed person, not to a group **private Rentenversicherung; portable pension plan** = pension plan which a worker can carry from one company to another as he changes jobs (auf eine andere Firma) übertragbares Altersversorgungssystem
(c) pension entitlement = amount of pension which someone has the right to receive when he retires **Rentenanspruch; pension fund** = money which provides pensions for retired members of staff **Rentenfonds**
2 *verb* **to pension someone off** = to ask someone to retire and take a pension **jdn vorzeitig pensionieren, jdn in den Ruhestand versetzen**

◇ **pensionable** *adjective* able to receive a pension **pensionsberechtigt; rentenberechtigt; pensionable age** = age after which someone can take a pension **Pensionsalter, Rentenalter**

◇ **pensioner** *noun* person who receives a pension **Rentner/-in; old age pensioner** = person who receives the retirement pension **Rentner/-in, Rentenempfänger**

peppercorn rent *noun* very small *or* nominal rent **nominelle Miete; nominelle Pacht;** *to pay a peppercorn rent; to lease a property for or at a peppercorn rent*

per *preposition*
(a) as per = according to **gemäß, laut; as per invoice** = as stated in the invoice **laut Rechnung; as per sample** = as shown in the sample **gemäß dem Muster; as per previous order** = according to the details given in our previous order **gemäß der vorausgegangenen Bestellung**
(b) at a rate of **pro; per hour** *or* **per day** *or* **per week** *or* **per year** = for each hour *or* day *or* week *or* year **pro Stunde; pro Tag; pro Woche; pro Jahr;** *the rate is £5 per hour; he makes about £250 per month;* **we pay £10 per hour** = we pay £10 for each hour worked **wir bezahlen £10 pro/die Stunde; the car was travelling at twenty-five miles per hour** = at a speed which covered 25 miles in one hour **das Auto fuhr 25 Meilen pro Stunde; the earnings per share** = dividend received by each share **der Gewinn pro Aktie; the average sales per representative** = the average sales achieved by one representative **der durchschnittliche Absatz pro Vertreter; per head** = for each person **pro Kopf/Person;** *allow £15 per head for expenses; representatives cost on average £25,000 per head per annum*
(c) out of **pro;** *the rate of imperfect items is about twenty-five per thousand; the birth rate has fallen to twelve per hundred*
◇ **per annum** *adverb* in a year **im/pro Jahr;** *what is their turnover per annum?*
◇ **per capita** *adjective & adverb* for each person **pro Person/Kopf; average income per capita** *or* **per capita income** = average income of one person **Durchschnittseinkommen pro Person, Pro-Kopf-Einkommen; per capita expenditure** = total money spent divided by the number of people involved **Pro-Kopf- Ausgaben**
◇ **per cent** *adjective & adverb* out of each hundred *or* for each hundred **prozentig** *noun* per hundred **Prozent; 10 per cent** = ten in every hundred **10 Prozent;** *what is the increase per cent? fifty per cent of nothing is still nothing*
◇ **percentage** *noun* amount shown as part of one hundred **Prozentsatz, Prozent; percentage discount** = discount calculated at an amount per hundred **Rabatt in Prozenten ausgedrückt; percentage increase** = increase calculated on the basis of a rate for one hundred **prozentualer Anstieg; percentage point** = one per cent **Prozentpunkt**
◇ **percentile** *noun* one of a series of ninety-nine figures below which a certain percentage of the total falls **Hundertstel**

QUOTE a 100,000 square-foot warehouse generates $600 in sales per square foot of space
Duns Business Month

QUOTE this would represent an 18 per cent growth rate - a slight slackening of the 25 per cent turnover rise in the first half
Financial Times

QUOTE buildings are depreciated at two per cent -per annum on the estimated cost of construction
Hongkong Standard

QUOTE state-owned banks cut their prime rates a percentage point to 11%
Wall Street Journal

QUOTE a good percentage of the excess stock was taken up during the last quarter
Australian Financial Review

perfect
1 *adjective* completely correct *or* with no mistakes **perfekt, fehlerlos, vollkommen;** *we check each batch to make sure it is perfect; she did a perfect typing test*
2 *verb* to make something which is completely correct **vervollkommnen, perfektionieren;** *he perfected the process for making high grade steel*
◇ **perfectly** *adverb* with no mistakes *or* correctly **perfekt, fehlerlos;** *she typed the letter perfectly*

perform *verb* to do well or badly **abschneiden; how did the shares perform?** = did the shares go up or down? **wie haben die Aktien abgeschnitten?; the company** *or* **the shares performed badly** = the company's share price fell **das Unternehmen hat/die Aktien haben schlecht abgeschnitten**
◇ **performance** *noun* way in which someone *or* something acts **Leistung; the poor performance of the shares on the stock market** = the fall in the share price on the stock market **das schlechte Abschneiden der Aktien an der Börse;** *last year saw a dip in the company's performance;* **as a measure of the company's performance** = as a way of judging if the company's results are good or bad **als Maßstab für die Leistung/den Erfolg des Unternehmens; performance of personnel against objectives** = how personnel have worked, measured against the objectives set **Leistung des Personals gemessen an den Zielen; performance review** = yearly interview between a manager and each worker to discuss how the worker has worked during the year **Leistungsbeurteilung; earnings performance** = way in which shares earn dividends **Gewinnentwicklung; job performance** = doing a job well or badly **Arbeitsleistung**

QUOTE inflation-adjusted GNP edged up at a 1.3% annual rate, its worst performance since the economic expansion began
Fortune

period *noun*
(a) length of time **Zeit, Zeitspanne, Zeitraum, Periode;** *for a period of time or for a period of months or for a six-year period; sales over a period of three months; sales over the holiday period; to deposit money for a fixed period*
(b) accounting period = period of time at the end of which the firm's accounts are made up **Abrechnungszeitraum**
◇ **periodic** *or* **periodical**
1 *adjective* from time to time **periodisch, periodisch erscheinend;** *a periodic review of the company's performance*
2 *noun* **periodical** = magazine which comes out regularly **Zeitschrift, Magazin**

peripherals *plural noun* items of hardware (such as terminals, printers, monitors, etc.) which are attached to a main computer system **Peripheriegeräte, periphäre Geräte**

perishable
1 *adjective* which can go bad *or* become rotten easily **leicht verderblich;** *perishable goods or items or cargo*
2 *plural noun* **perishables** = goods which can go bad easily **(leicht) verderbliche Ware**

perjury *noun* telling lies when you have made an oath in court to say what is true **Meineid;** *he was sent to prison for perjury; she appeared in court on a perjury charge*
◇ **perjure** *verb* **to perjure yourself** = to tell lies when you have made an oath to say what is true **einen Meineid leisten**

perks *plural noun* extra items given by a company to workers in addition to their salaries (such as company cars, private health insurance) **Leistungsanreize für Arbeitnehmer**

permanent *adjective* which will last for a very long time *or* for ever **dauerhaft, fest, unbefristet;** *he has found a permanent job; she is in permanent employment; the permanent staff and part-timers*
◇ **permanency** *noun* being permanent **Dauerhaftigkeit, Beständigkeit**
NOTE: no plural
◇ **permanently** *adverb* for ever **fest, ständig**

permission *noun* being allowed to do something **Erlaubnis, Genehmigung, Bewilligung; written permission** = document which allows someone to do something **schriftliche Genehmigung; verbal permission** = telling someone that he is allowed to do something **mündliche Genehmigung; to give someone permission to do something** = to allow someone to do something **jdm gestatten, etwas zu tun; jdm die Erlaubnis erteilen;** *he asked the manager's permission to take a day off*

permit
1 *noun* official document which allows someone to do something **Genehmigung, Erlaubnis; building permit** = official document which allows someone to build on a piece of land **Baugenehmigung; export permit** *or* **import permit** = official document which allows goods to be exported *or* imported **Exportgenehmigung; Importgenehmigung; work permit** = official document which allows someone who is not a citizen to work in a country **Arbeitserlaubnis**
2 *verb* to allow someone to do something **genehmigen, erlauben, gestatten;** *this document permits you to export twenty-five computer systems; the ticket permits three people to go into the exhibition*

per pro = PER PROCURATIONEM with the authority of **per Prokura, im Auftrag;** *the secretary signed per pro the manager*

perquisites *plural noun* = PERKS

person *noun*
(a) someone *or* man *or* woman **Person;** *insurance policy which covers a named person;* **the persons named in the contract** = people whose names are given in the contract **die im Vertrag genannten Personen; the document should be witnessed by a third person** = someone who is not named in the document should witness it **das Dokument sollte von einem Dritten/einer dritten Person als Zeuge unterschrieben werden**
(b) in person = someone himself *or* herself **persönlich; this important package is to be delivered to the chairman in person** = the package has to be given to the chairman himself (and not to his secretary, assistant, etc.) **dieses wichtige Paket muß dem Vorsitzenden persönlich übergeben werden; he came to see me in person** = he himself came to see me **er kam persönlich zu mir**
◇ **person-to-person call** *noun* telephone call where you ask the operator to connect you with a named person **Gespräch mit namentlicher Voranmeldung**
◇ **personal** *adjective*
(a) referring to one person **persönlich; personal allowances** = part of a person's income which is not taxed **persönlicher Steuerfreibetrag; personal assets** = moveable assets which belong to a person **bewegliches Privatvermögen; personal call** = (i) telephone

call where you ask the operator to connect you with a particular person; (ii) telephone call not related to business **(i) Gespräch mit Voranmeldung, (ii) Privatgespräch; personal computer** = small computer which can be used at home **Personal-Computer, PC; personal effects** *or* **personal property** = things which belong to someone **Gegenstände des persönlichen Gebrauchs; Privateigentum; personal income** = income received by an individual person before tax is paid **persönliches Einkommen; apart from the family shares, he has a personal shareholding in the company** = he has shares which he owns himself **neben dem der Familie gehörenden Aktien besitzt er persönliche Aktien des Unternehmens/hat er persönlich Aktienbesitz an dem Unternehmen; the car is for his personal use** = the car is for him to use himself **das Auto ist für seinen Privatgebrauch bestimmt**

(b) private **privat, Privat-;** *I want to see the director on a personal matter;* **personal assistant** = secretary who also helps the boss in various ways **Privatsekretär**

◊ **personalized** *adjective* with the name or initials of a person printed on it **mit dem Namen oder den Initialien versehen;** *personalized cheques; personalized briefcase*

◊ **personally** *adverb* in person **persönlich, eigenhändig;** *he personally opened the envelope; she wrote to me personally*

personnel *noun* people who work in a certain place *or* for a certain company **Personal, Belegschaft;** *the personnel of the warehouse or the warehouse personnel;* **the personnel department** = section of the company which deals with the staff **Personalabteilung; personnel management** = organizing and training of staff so that they work well and profitably **Personalführung; personnel manager** = head of the personnel department **Personalchef**

persuade *verb* to talk to someone and get him to do what you want **überreden, dazubringen;** *after ten hours of discussion, they persuaded the MD to resign; we could not persuade the French company to sign the contract*

peseta *noun* money used in Spain **Peseta**
NOTE: usually written **ptas** after a figure: **2,000ptas**

peso *noun* money used in Mexico and many other countries **Peso**

pessimism *noun* expecting that everything will turn out badly **Pessimismus; market pessimism** *or* **pessimism on the market** = feeling that the stock market prices will fall **Pessimismus am Aktienmarkt;** *there is considerable pessimism about job opportunities*
NOTE: no plural

◊ **pessimistic** *adjective* feeling sure that things will work out badly **pessimistisch; he takes a pessimistic view of the exchange rate** = he expects the exchange rate to fall **er sieht die Entwicklung des Wechselkurses pessimistisch**

peter out *verb* to come to an end gradually **auslaufen, sich legen, allmählich zu Ende gehen**

> QUOTE economists believe the economy is picking up this quarter and will do better in the second half of the year, but most expect growth to peter out in 1986
> *Sunday Times*

Peter principle *noun* law, based on wide experience, that people are promoted until they occupy positions for which they are incompetent **das Peter-Prinzip**

petition
1 *noun* official request **Antrag, Gesuch, Petition, Eingabe; to file a petition in bankruptcy** = to ask officially to be made bankrupt *or* to ask officially for someone else to be made bankrupt **einen Antrag auf Konkurseröffnung stellen, einen Konkursantrag stellen**
2 *verb* to make an official request **beantragen, ersuchen, eine Petition einreichen, eine Eingabe machen;** *he petitioned the government for a special pension*

petrodollar *noun* dollar earned by a country from exporting oil, then invested outside that country **Petro-Dollar**

petrol *noun* liquid, made from petroleum, used to drive a car engine **Benzin;** *the car is very economic on petrol; we are looking for a car with a low petrol consumption*
NOTE: no plural

◊ **petroleum** *noun* raw natural oil, found in the ground **Erdöl, Mineralöl; crude petroleum** = raw petroleum which has not been processed **Rohöl; petroleum exporting countries** = countries which produce petroleum and sell it to others **erdölexportierende Länder; petroleum industry** = industry which uses petroleum to make other products (petrol, soap, etc.) **erdölverarbeitende Industrie; petroleum products** = products (such as petrol, soap, paint) which are made from crude petroleum **Rohölprodukte; petroleum**

revenues = income from selling oil **Erdöleinnahmen**

petty *adjective* not important **unwichtig, belanglos, unbedeutend; petty cash** = small amount of money kept in an office to pay small debts **Portokasse; petty cash book** = book in which petty cash payments are noted **Portokassenbuch; petty cash box** = locked metal box in an office where the petty cash is kept **Portokasse; petty expenses** = small sums of money spent **geringfügige Ausgaben**

phase *noun* period *or* part of something which takes place **Phase, Abschnitt, Stadium, Stufe;** *the first phase of the expansion programme*

◇ **phase in** *verb* to bring something in gradually **schrittweise einführen;** *the new invoicing system will be phased in over the next two months*

◇ **phase out** *verb* to remove something gradually **auslaufen lassen, allmählich einstellen;** *Smith Ltd will be phased out as a supplier of spare parts*

> QUOTE the budget grants a tax exemption for $500,000 in capital gains, phased in over the next six years
>
> *Toronto Star*

phoenix syndrome *noun* situation where a company goes into liquidation leaving debts, and the directors form an identical company with a slightly different name to carry on the business; *entspricht* **Phönix-Syndrom**

phone

1 *noun* telephone *or* machine used for speaking to someone over a long distance **Telefon;** *we had a new phone system installed last week;* **house phone** *or* **internal phone** = telephone for calling from one office to another **Haustelefon; by phone** = using the telephone **telefonisch;** *to place an order by phone;* **to be on the phone** = to be speaking to someone on the telephone **telefonieren;** *she has been on the phone all morning; he spoke to the manager on the phone;* **phone book** = book which lists names of people and companies with their addresses and phone numbers **Telefonbuch;** *look up his address in the phone book;* **phone call** = speaking to someone on the phone **Telefongespräch, Anruf; to make a phone call** = to speak to someone on the telephone **jdn anrufen, telefonieren; to answer the phone** *or* **to take a phone call** = to reply to a call on the phone **das Telefon abnehmen, ans Telefon gehen; phone number** = set of figures for a particular telephone **Telefonnummer;** *he keeps a list of phone numbers in a little black book; the phone number is on the company notepaper; can you give me your phone number?*

2 *verb* **to phone someone** = to call someone by telephone **jdn anrufen;** *don't phone me, I'll phone you; his secretary phoned to say he would be late; he phoned the order through to the warehouse;* **to phone for something** = to make a phone call to ask for something **etwas telefonisch bestellen;** *he phoned for a taxi;* **to phone about something** = to make a phone call to speak about something **wegen etwas anrufen;** *he phoned about the January invoice*

◇ **phone back** *verb* to reply by phone **zurückrufen;** *the chairman is in a meeting, can you phone back in about half an hour? Mr Smith called while you were out and asked if you would phone him back*

photocopier *noun* machine which makes a copy of a document by photographing and printing it **Fotokopiergerät, Kopierer**

◇ **photocopy**

1 *noun* copy of a document made by photographing and printing it **Fotokopie;** *make six photocopies of the contract*

2 *verb* to make a copy of a document by photographing and printing it **fotokopieren;** *she photocopied the contract*

◇ **photocopying** *noun* making photocopies **Fotokopieren;** *photocopying costs are rising each year;* **photocopying bureau** = office which photocopies documents for companies which do not possess their own photocopiers **Copy-Shop, Kopierzentrum; there is a mass of photocopying to be done** = there are many documents waiting to be photocopied **es gibt Unmengen zum Fotokopieren**

NOTE: no plural

◇ **photostat**

1 *noun* trademark for a type of photocopy; *entspricht* **Fotokopie**

2 *verb* to make a photostat of a document; *entspricht* **fotokopieren**

pick

1 *noun* thing chosen **Wahl; take your pick** = choose what you want **suchen Sie sich etwas aus; the pick of the group** = the best item in the group **das Allerbeste, das Beste von allem**

2 *verb* to choose **auswählen, aussuchen;** *the board picked the finance director to succeed the retiring MD; the Association has picked Paris for its next meeting*

◇ **picking** *noun* **order picking** = collecting various items in a warehouse to make up an order to be sent to a customer **Zusammenstellung einer Bestellung; picking list** = list of items in an order, listed according to where they can be found in the warehouse **Entnahmeliste**

◇ **pick out** *verb* to choose (something *or* someone) out of a lot **auswählen, aussuchen;** *he was picked out for promotion by the chairman*

◇ **pick up** *verb* to get better *or* to improve **sich erholen;** *business or trade is picking up*

◇ **pickup** *noun* **pickup (truck)** = type of small van for transporting goods **offener Kleintransporter; pickup and delivery service** = service which takes goods from the warehouse and delivers them to the customer **Abhol- und Zustelldienst**

picket

1 *noun* striking worker who stands at the gate of a factory to try to persuade other workers not to go to work **Streikposten; flying pickets** = pickets who travel round the country to try to stop workers going to work **mobile Streikposten; picket line** = line of pickets at the gate of a factory **Streikpostenkette;** *to man a picket line or to be on the picket line;* **to cross a picket line** = to go into a factory to work, even though pickets are trying to prevent workers from going in **eine Streikpostenkette durchbrechen**
2 *verb* **to picket a factory** = to put pickets at the gate of a factory to try to prevent other workers from going to work **vor einer Fabrik Streikposten aufstellen**

◇ **picketing** *noun* act of standing at the gates of a factory to prevent workers going to work **Streikpostenstehen; lawful picketing** = picketing which is allowed by law **rechtmäßiges/erlaubtes Aufstellen von Streikposten; mass picketing** = picketing by large numbers of pickets who try to frighten workers who want to work **massives Aufgebot an Streikposten; peaceful picketing** = picketing which does not involve fighting **friedlich durchgeführtes Streikpostenstehen; secondary picketing** = picketing of another factory, not directly connected with the strike, to prevent it supplying the striking factory *or* receiving supplies from it **Bestreikung eines nur indirekt beteiligten Betriebes**
NOTE: no plural

piece

piece *noun* small part of something **Stück, Teil;** *to sell something by the piece; the price is 25p the piece;* **mailing piece** = leaflet suitable for sending by direct mail **Postwurfsendung**

◇ **piece rate** *noun* rate of pay for a product produced *or* for a piece of work done and not paid for at an hourly rate **Akkord-, Stücklohnsatz;** *to earn piece rates*

◇ **piecework** *noun* work for which workers are paid for the products produced *or* the piece of work done and not at an hourly rate **Akkordarbeit**
NOTE: no plural

pie chart

pie chart *noun* diagram where information is shown as a circle cut up into sections of different sizes **Kreisdiagramm**

pigeonhole

1 *noun* one of a series of small spaces for filing documents *or* for putting letters for delivery to separate offices **Fach; Brieffach**
2 *verb* to file a plan or document as the best way of forgetting about it **auf Eis legen;** *the whole expansion plan was pigeonholed*

pile

1 *noun* lot of things put one on top of the other **Stapel;** *the Managing Director's desk is covered with piles of paper; she put the letter on the pile of letters waiting to be signed*
2 *verb* to put things on top of one another **stapeln;** *he piled the papers on his desk*

◇ **pile up** *verb* to put *or* get into a pile **aufstapeln; sich anhäufen;** *the invoices were piled up on the table; complaints are piling up about the after-sales service*

pilferage

pilferage *or* **pilfering** *noun* stealing small amounts of money *or* small items from an office *or* shop **geringfügiger Diebstahl;** *umg* **Mitgehenlassen von unbedeutenden Beträgen/Gegenständen**
NOTE: no plural

pilot

pilot *noun*
(a) person who flies a plane *or* guides a ship into port **Pilot; Lotse**
(b) used as a test, which if successful will then be expanded into a full operation **Pilot-, Probe-, Modellversuch;** *the company set up a pilot project to see if the proposed manufacturing system was efficient; the pilot factory has been built to test the new production processes; he is directing a pilot scheme for training unemployed young people*

pin

1 *noun* sharp piece of metal for attaching papers together, etc. **Nadel; drawing pin** = pin with a flat head for attaching a sheet of paper to something hard **Reißzwecke, Heftzwecke;** *she used drawing pins to pin the poster to the door*
2 *verb* to attach with a pin **heften, festmachen;** *she pinned the papers together; pin your cheque to the application form*

◇ **pin up** *verb* to attach something with pins to a wall **(an)heften;** *they pinned the* *posters up at the back of the exhibition stand*

pint *noun* measure of liquids (= 0.568 of a litre) **Pint**

pioneer
1 *noun* first to do a type of work **Pionier, Wegbereiter, Vorreiter; pioneer project** *or* **pioneer development** = project or development which is new and has never been tried before **Pionierprojekt; bahnbrechende Entwicklung**
2 *verb* to be the first to do something **Pionierarbeit leisten, initiieren, den Weg bahnen;** *the company pioneered developments in the field of electronics*

pirate
1 *noun* person who copies a patented invention or a copyright work and sells it **Plagiator, Markenpirat; Hersteller von Raubdrucken;** *a pirate copy of a book*
2 *verb* to copy a copyright work **unerlaubt nachahmen/nachbauen, plagiieren; einen Raubdruck herstellen;** *a pirated book or a pirated design; the designs for the new dress collection were pirated in the Far East*
◇ **piracy** *noun* copying of patented inventions or copyright works **Patentverletzung, unerlaubte Nachahmung; Raubdruck; Markenpiraterie**
NOTE: no plural

pit *noun* coal mine **Kohlebergwerk, Zeche**

pitch *noun* **sales pitch** = talk by a salesman to persuade someone to buy **Verkaufsgespräch**

pix *plural noun informal* pictures (used in advertising or design) **Bildchen**

place
1 *noun*
(a) where something is *or* where something happens **Platz, Ort, Stelle; to take place** = to happen **stattfinden;** *the meeting will take place in our offices;* **meeting place** = room *or* area where people can meet **Treffpunkt; place of work** = office *or* factory, etc. where people work **Arbeitsplatz**
(b) position (in a competition) **Platz;** *three companies are fighting for first place in the home computer market*
(c) job **Stelle, Anstellung;** *he was offered a place with an insurance company; she turned down three places before accepting the one we offered*
(d) position in a text **Stelle;** *she marked her place in the text with a red pen; I have lost my place and cannot remember where I have reached in my filing*
2 *verb*
(a) to put **legen, setzen, stellen; to place money in an account** = to deposit money **Geld auf ein Konto einzahlen; to place a block of shares** = to find a buyer for a block of shares **ein Aktienpaket plazieren; to place a contract** = to decide that a certain company shall have the contract to do work **einen Auftrag vergeben; to place something on file** = to file something **etwas abheften**
(b) to place an order = to order something **eine Bestellung aufgeben;** *he placed an order for 250 cartons of paper*
(c) to place staff = to find jobs for staff **Personal unterbringen; how are you placed for work?** = have you enough work to do? **sind Sie mit Arbeit eingedeckt?**
◇ **placement** *noun* finding work for someone **Stellenvermittlung, Unterbringung**
◇ **placing** *noun* **the placing of a line of shares** = finding a buyer for a large number of shares in a new company or a company which is going public **die Plazierung eines Aktienpaketes**
NOTE: no plural

plain *adjective*
(a) easy to understand **klar, deutlich;** *we made it plain to the union that 5% was the management's final offer;* **the manager is a very plain-spoken man** = the manager says exactly what he thinks **der Manager drückt sich sehr direkt /offen aus**
(b) simple **einfach, schlicht;** *the design of the package is in plain blue and white squares; we want the cheaper models to have a plain design*
◇ **plain cover** *noun* **to send something under plain cover** = to send something in an ordinary envelope with no company name printed on it **etwas in einem neutralen Umschlag schicken**

plaintiff *noun* person who starts a legal action against someone **Kläger/-in**

plan
1 *noun*
(a) organized way of doing something **Plan; contingency plan** = plan which will be put into action if something happens which no one expects to happen **Krisenplan; the government's economic plans** = the government's proposals for running the country's economy **das Wirtschaftsprogramm der Regierung; a Five-Year Plan** = proposals for running a country's economy over a five-year period **ein Fünfjahresplan**
(b) way of saving or investing money **Plan, Programm;** *investment plan; pension plan; savings plan*

(c) drawing which shows how something is arranged *or* how something will be built **Plan, Entwurf;** *the designers showed us the first plans for the new offices;* **floor plan** = drawing of a floor in a building, showing where different departments are **Raumverteilungsplan; street plan** *or* **town plan** = map of a town showing streets and buildings **Stadtplan**

2 *verb* to organize carefully how something should be done **planen; to plan for an increase in bank interest charges** = to change a way of doing things because you think there will be an increase in bank interest charges **sich einstellen auf eine Erhöhung der Bankzinsen; to plan investments** = to propose how investments should be made **Investitionen planen**
NOTE: **planning - planned**

◇ **planned** *adjective* **planned economy** = system where the government plans all business activity **Planwirtschaft**

◇ **planner** *noun*

(a) person who plans **Planer/-in; the government's economic planners** = people who plan the future economy of the country for the government **die Wirtschaftsplaner der Regierung**

(b) desk planner *or* **wall planner** = book *or* chart which shows days *or* weeks *or* months so that the work of an office can be shown by diagrams **Tischkalender od Wandkalender zur Arbeitsplanung**

◇ **planning** *noun*

(a) organizing how something should be done, especially how a company should be run to make increased profits **Planung;** *long-term planning or short-term planning;* **economic planning** = planning the future financial state of the country for the government **Wirtschaftsplanung; corporate planning** = planning the future financial state of a group of companies **langfristige Unternehmensplanung; manpower planning** = planning to get the right number of workers in each job **Personalplanung**

(b) *GB* **planning permission** = official document allowing a person *or* company to plan new buildings on empty land **Baugenehmigung;** *to be refused planning permission; we are waiting for planning permission before we can start building; the land is to be sold with planning permission;* **the planning department** = section of a local government office which deals with requests for planning permission **Bauordnungsamt**
NOTE: no plural

> QUOTE the benefits package is attractive and the compensation plan includes base, incentive and car allowance totalling $50,000+
> *Globe and Mail (Toronto)*
>
> QUOTE buildings are closely regulated by planning restrictions
> *Investors Chronicle*

plane *noun* aircraft *or* machine which flies in the air, carrying passengers or cargo **Flugzeug;** *I plan to take the 5 o'clock plane to New York; he could not get a seat on Tuesday's plane, so he had to wait until Wednesday; there are ten planes a day from London to Paris*

plant *noun*
(a) machinery **Maschinenanlage, Anlagen; plant-hire firm** = company which lends large machines (such as cranes and tractors) to building companies **Baumaschinenvermietung;** (NOTE: no plural)
(b) large factory **Werk, Fabrikanlage;** *they are planning to build a car plant near the river; to set up a new plant; they closed down six plants in the north of the country; he was appointed plant manager*

platform *noun* high pavement in a station, so that passengers can get on or off trains **Bahnsteig;** *the train for Birmingham leaves from Platform 12; the ticket office is on Platform 2*

PLC *or* **plc** = PUBLIC LIMITED COMPANY

plead *verb* to speak on behalf of a client in court **jdn (bei Gericht) vertreten**

pledge
1 *noun* object given to a pawnbroker as security for money borrowed **Pfand(sache); to redeem a pledge** = to pay back a loan and interest and so get back the security **ein Pfand einlösen; unredeemed pledge** = pledge which the borrower has not claimed back by paying back his loan **nicht eingelöstes Pfand**
2 *verb* **to pledge share certificates** = to deposit share certificates with the lender as security for money borrowed **Aktienzertifikate verpfänden**

plenary *noun* **plenary meeting** *or* **plenary session** = meeting at a conference when all the delegates meet together **Vollversammlung, Plenarsitzung**

plough back *verb* **to plough back profits into the company** = to invest the profits in the business (and not pay them out as dividends to the shareholders) by using them to buy new equipment *or* create new products **Gewinne in das Unternehmen reinvestieren**

plug

1 *noun*

(a) device at the end of a wire for connecting a machine to the electricity supply **Stecker;** *the printer is supplied with a plug*

(b) to give a plug to a new product = to publicize a new product **für ein neues Produkt Reklame machen**

2 *verb*

(a) to plug in = to attach a machine to the electricity supply **in die Steckdose stecken, anschließen;** *the computer was not plugged in*

(b) to publicize *or* to advertise **anpreisen, Reklame machen für;** *they ran six commercials plugging holidays in Spain*

(c) to block *or* to stop **stoppen, zum Halt bringen;** *the company is trying to plug the drain on cash reserves*

NOTE: **plugging - plugged**

plummet *or* plunge

verb to fall sharply **stark fallen, stürzen, absacken;** *share prices plummeted or plunged on the news of the devaluation*

> QUOTE in the first six months of this year secondhand values of tankers have plummeted by 40%
>
> *Lloyd's List*
>
> QUOTE crude oil output plunged during the past month
>
> *Wall Street Journal*

plus

1 *preposition*

(a) added to **plus, und, zuzüglich;** *his salary plus commission comes to more than £25,000; production costs plus overheads are higher than revenue*

(b) more than **über, mehr als; houses valued at £100,000 plus** = houses valued at over £100,000 **Häuser, die auf über £100.000 geschätzt werden**

2 *adjective* favourable *or* good and profitable **positiv, Plus-;** *a plus factor for the company is that the market is much larger than they had originally thought;* **the plus side of the account** = the credit side of the account **die Habenseite des Kontos; on the plus side** = this is a favourable point **als Pluspunkt;** *on the plus side, we must take into account the new product line*

3 *noun* a good *or* favourable point **Plus, Pluspunkt;** *to have achieved £1m in new sales in less than six months is certainly a plus for the sales team*

p.m.

adverb in the afternoon *or* in the evening *or* after 12 o'clock midday **nachmittags;** *the train leaves at 6.50 p.m.; if you phone New York after 6 p.m. the calls are at a cheaper rate*

PO

= POST OFFICE

pocket

noun **pocket calculator** *or* **pocket diary** = calculator *or* diary which can be carried in the pocket **Taschenrechner, Taschenkalender; to be £25 in pocket** = to have made a profit of £25 **£25 besser bei Kasse sein; to be £25 out of pocket** = to have lost £25 **um £25 ärmer sein; out-of-pocket expenses** = amount of money to pay back a worker for his own money which he has spent on company business **Spesen**

point

1 *noun*

(a) place *or* position **Stelle, Ort; point of sale** = place where a product is sold (such as a shop) **Verkaufsstelle, Verkaufsort; point of sale material** = display material (such as posters, dump bins) to advertise a product where it is being sold **Werbematerial für den Verkaufsort, POS-Werbematerial; breakeven point** = position at which sales cover costs but do not show a profit **Kostendeckungspunkt, Break-even-Point; customs entry point** = place at a border between two countries where goods are declared to customs **Zollanmeldungsstelle, Grenzübergangsstelle; starting point** = place where something starts **Ausgangspunkt**

(b) decimal point = dot which indicates the division between a whole unit and its smaller parts (such as 4.25) **Dezimalstelle; percentage point** = 1 per cent **Prozentpunkt; half a percentage point** = 0.5 per cent **ein halbes Prozent; the dollar gained two points** = the dollar increased in value against another currency by two hundredths of a cent **der Dollar stieg um zwei Punkte; the exchange fell ten points** = the stock market index fell by ten units **der Börsenindex fiel um zehn Punkte**

2 *verb* **to point out** = to show **hinweisen auf, aufzeigen, verdeutlichen;** *the report points out the mistakes made by the company over the last year; he pointed out that the results were better than in previous years*

> QUOTE sterling M3, the most closely watched measure, rose by 13% in the year to August - seven percentage points faster than the rate of inflation
>
> *Economist*
>
> QUOTE banks refrained from quoting forward US/Hongkong dollar exchange rates as premiums of 100 points replaced discounts of up to 50 points
>
> *South China Morning Post*

policy *noun*
(a) decisions on the general way of doing something **Kurs, Politik, Linie, Taktik, Verfahrensweise;** *government policy on wages or government wages policy; the government's prices policy or incomes policy; the country's economic policy; a company's trading policy;* **the government made a policy statement** *or* **made a statement of policy** = the government declared in public what its plans were **die Regierung gab eine Grundsatzerklärung ab; budgetary policy** = policy of expected income and expenditure **Budgetpolitik**
(b) company policy = the company's agreed plan of action *or* the company's way of doing things **Unternehmenspolitik;** *what is the company policy on credit? it is against company policy to give more than thirty days' credit; our policy is to submit all contracts to the legal department*
(c) insurance policy = document which shows the conditions of an insurance contract **Versicherungspolice; an accident policy** = an insurance contract against accidents **Unfallversicherung(spolice); all-risks policy** = insurance policy which covers risks of any kind, with no exclusions **Universalversicherung(spolice), Allgefahrendeckung; a comprehensive** *or* **an all-in policy** = an insurance which covers all risks **Kombination mehrerer Versicherungsdeckungen, Pauschaldeckung; contingent policy** = policy which pays out only if something happens (as if the person named in the policy dies before the person due to benefit) **Eventualversicherung; Risikoversicherung; endowment policy** = policy where a sum of money is paid to the insured person on a certain date, or to his estate if he dies earlier **Versicherung auf den Erlebens- und Todesfall; policy holder** = person who is insured by an insurance company **Versicherungsnehmer; to take out a policy** = to sign the contract for an insurance and start paying the premiums **eine Versicherung abschließen;** *she took out a life insurance policy or a house insurance policy;* **the insurance company made out a policy** *or* **drew up a policy** = the company wrote the details of the contract on the policy **die Versicherungsgesellschaft stellte eine Police aus**

polite *adjective* behaving in a pleasant way **höflich;** *we stipulate that our salesgirls must be polite to customers; we had a polite letter from the MD*

◇ **politely** *adverb* in a pleasant way **höflich;** *she politely answered the customers' questions*

political *adjective* referring to a certain idea of how a country should be run **politisch; political levy** = part of the subscription of a member of a trade union which the union pays to support a political party; *GB* **politische Abgaben; political party** = group of people who believe a country should be run in a certain way **politische Partei**

poll
1 *noun* **opinion poll** = asking a sample group of people, taken at random, what they feel about something, so as to guess the opinion of the whole population **Meinungsumfrage;** *opinion polls showed the public preferred butter to margarine; before starting the service the company carried out a nationwide opinion poll*
2 *verb* **to poll a sample of the population** = to ask a sample group of people what they feel about something **eine repräsentative Bevölkerungsgruppe befragen; to poll the members of the club on an issue** = to ask the members for their opinion on an issue **die Klubmitglieder zu einem Punkt befragen**

◇ **pollster** *noun* expert in understanding what polls mean **Meinungsforscher**

polystyrene *noun* **expanded polystyrene** = light solid plastic used for packing **Styropor;** *the computer is delivered packed in expanded polystyrene*
NOTE: no plural

pool
1 *noun*
(a) typing pool = group of typists, working together in a company, offering a secretarial service to several departments **zentraler Schreibdienst**
(b) unused supply **Bestand, Reserve, Vorrat, Ressourcen;** *a pool of unemployed labour or of expertise*
2 *verb* **to pool resources** = to put all resources together so as to be more powerful or profitable **seine Ressourcen zusammenlegen**

poor *adjective*
(a) without much money **arm, bedürftig, mittellos;** *the company tries to help the poorest members of staff with soft loans; it is one of the poorest countries in the world*
(b) not very good **schlecht ,schwach, dürftig;** *poor quality; poor service; poor turnround time of orders or poor order turnround time*

◇ **poorly** *adverb* badly **schlecht, dürftig;** *the offices are poorly laid out; the plan was poorly presented;* **poorly-paid staff** = staff with low wages **schlecht bezahltes Personal**

popular *adjective* liked by many people **beliebt, populär;** *this is our most popular model; the South Coast is the most popular area for holidays;* **popular prices** = prices which are low and therefore liked **populäre Preise**

population *noun* number of people who live in a country *or* in a town **Bevölkerung;** *Paris has a population of over one million; the working population; population statistics; population trends;* **floating population** = people who move from place to place **nicht seßhafte Bevölkerung**

port *noun*
(a) harbour *or* place where ships come to load *or* unload **Hafen;** *the port of Rotterdam;* **inland port** = port on a river *or* canal **Binnenhafen; to call at a port** = to stop at a port to load or unload cargo **einen Hafen anlaufen; port authority** = organization which runs a port **Hafenbehörde; port of call** = port at which a ship often stops **Anlaufhafen; port charges** *or* **port dues** = payment which a ship makes to the port authority for the right to use the port **Hafengebühren; port of embarkation** = port at which you get on a ship **Einschiffungshafen; port installations** = buildings and equipment of a port **Hafenanlagen; commercial port** = port which has only goods traffic **Handelshafen; fishing port** = port which is used mainly by fishing boats **Fischereihafen; free port** = port where there are no customs duties to be paid **Freihafen**
(b) part of a computer where a lead can be attached **Anschluß, Port, Schnittstelle**

portable
1 *adjective* which can be carried **tragbar; a portable typewriter** a small typewriter **eine Reiseschreibmaschine;** *a portable computer;* **portable pension** = pension rights which a worker can take with him from one company to another as he changes jobs **(auf eine andere Firma) übertragbarer Rentenanspruch**
2 *noun* **a portable** = a computer *or* television set which can be carried **Portable, tragbares Gerät**

portfolio *noun* **a portfolio of shares** = all the shares owned by someone **Aktienportefeuille; portfolio management** = buying and selling shares to make profits for a person **Effekten-, Portfoliomanagement**

portion *noun* small quantity, especially enough food for one person **Portion;** *we serve ice cream in individual portions*

p.o.s. = POINT OF SALE

position *noun*
(a) situation *or* state of affairs **Lage, Situation; what is the cash position?** = what is the state of the company's current account? **wieviel Geld haben wir flüssig?; bargaining position** = statement of position by one group during negotiations **Verhandlungsposition; to cover a position** = to have enough money to pay for a forward purchase **eine Position abdecken**
(b) job *or* paid work in a company **Stellung, Stelle, Position;** *to apply for a position as manager; we have several positions vacant; all the vacant positions have been filled; she retired from her position in the accounts department;* **he is in a key position** = he has an important job **er hat eine leitende Stelle**

positive *adjective* meaning "yes" **bejahend, positiv, zustimmend;** *the board gave a positive reply ;* **positive cash flow** = situation where more money is coming in than is being spent **positiver Cashflow**

possess *verb* to own **besitzen;** *the company possesses property in the centre of the town; he lost all he possessed in the collapse of his company*
◇ **possession** *noun*
(a) owning something **Besitz; the documents are in his possession** = he is holding the documents **die Unterlagen befinden sich in seinem Besitz; vacant possession** = being able to occupy a property immediately after buying it because it is empty **sofort beziehbar;** *the property is to be sold with vacant possession* (NOTE: no plural)
(b) possessions = property *or* things owned **Besitz(tümer);** *they lost all their possessions in the fire*

possible *adjective* which might happen **möglich;** *the 25th and 26th are possible dates for our next meeting; it is possible that production will be held up by industrial action;* **there are two possible candidates for the job** = two candidates are good enough to be appointed **für die Stelle kommen zwei Kandidaten in Frage**
◇ **possibility** *noun* being likely to happen **Möglichkeit;** *there is a possibility that the plane will be early*

post
1 *noun*
(a) system of sending letters and parcels from one place to another **Post;** *to send an invoice by post; he put the letter in the post; the cheque was lost in the post;* **to send a reply by return of post** = to reply to a letter

immediately **postwendend antworten; letter post** *or* **parcel post** = service for sending letters or parcels **Briefpost; Paketpost; post room** = room in an office where the post is sorted and sent to each department or collected from each department for sending **Poststelle**
(b) letters sent or received **Post;** *has the post arrived yet? my secretary opens the post as soon as it arrives; the receipt was in this morning's post; the letter did not arrive by first post this morning*
(c) job *or* paid work in a company **Stelle, Stellung, Posten;** *to apply for a post as cashier; we have three posts vacant; all our posts have been filled; we advertised three posts in the "Times"*
NOTE: no plural for (a) or (b)
2 *verb*
(a) to send something by post **abschicken, mit der Post schicken;** *to post a letter or to post a parcel*
(b) to post an entry = to transfer an entry to an account **einen Posten buchen; to post up a ledger** = to keep a ledger up to date **ein Hauptbuch nachbuchen/auf den neuesten Stand bringen**
(c) to post up a notice = to put a notice on a wall *or* on a noticeboard **einen Anschlag machen**
(d) to post an increase = to let people know that an increase has taken place **eine Erhöhung bekanntgeben**

> QUOTE Toronto stocks closed at an all-time high, posting their fifth day of advances in heavy trading
> *Financial Times*

post- *prefix* later **nach-, Nach-, post-, Post-**

postage *noun* payment for sending a letter or parcel by post **Porto, Postgebühren;** *what is the postage to Nigeria?;* **postage paid** = words printed on an envelope to show that the sender has paid the postage even though there is no stamp on it **Gebühr/Porto bezahlt, gebührenfrei; postage stamp** = small piece of paper attached to a letter or parcel to show that you have paid for it to be sent through the post **Briefmarke**
NOTE: no plural

postal *adjective* referring to the post **Post-; postal charges** *or* **postal rates** = money to be paid for sending letters or parcels by post **Postgebühren, Posttarife;** *postal charges are going up by 10% in September;* **postal order** = document bought at a post office, as a method of paying small amounts of money by post **Postanweisung**

postcard *noun* piece of cardboard for sending a message by post (often with a picture on one side) **Postkarte; Ansichtskarte**

postcode *noun* letters and numbers used to indicate a town in an address on an envelope **Postleitzahl**
NOTE: US English is **zip code**

postdate *verb* to put a later date on a document **vordatieren;** *he sent us a postdated cheque; his cheque was postdated to June*

poster *noun* large notice *or* advertisement to be stuck up on a wall **Plakat, Poster**

poste restante *adjective* system where letters can be addressed to someone at a post office, where they can be collected **postlagernd;** *send any messages poste restante to Athens*

post free *adverb* without having to pay any postage **portofrei;** *the game is obtainable post free from the manufacturer*

postmark
1 *noun* mark stamped by the Post Office on a letter, covering the postage stamp, to show that the Post Office has accepted it **Poststempel;** *letter with a London postmark*
2 *verb* to stamp a letter with a postmark **(ab)stempeln;** *the letter was postmarked New York*

post office *noun*
(a) (i) building where the postal services are based; (ii) shop where you can buy stamps, send parcels, etc. **(i) Post(amt); (ii);** *GB* **Zweigstelle der Post;** *main post office;* **sub-post office** = small post office, usually part of a general store; *GB* **Zweigstelle der Post**
(b) the Post Office = national organization which deals with sending letters and parcels; *entspricht* **Deutsche Bundespost;** *Post Office officials or officials of the Post Office; Post Office van;* **Post Office box number** = reference number given for delivering mail to a post office, so as not to give the actual address of the person who will receive it **Postfach**

> QUOTE travellers cheques cost 1% of their face value and can be purchased from any bank, main post offices, travel agents and several building societies
> *Sunday Times*

postpaid *adjective* with the postage already paid **Gebühr bezahlt;** *the price is £5.95 postpaid*

postpone *verb* to arrange for something to take place later than planned **auf-, verschieben, vertagen;** *he postponed the meeting to tomorrow; they asked if they could postpone payment until the cash situation was better*

◇ **postponement** *noun* arranging for something to take place later than planned **Aufschub, Vertagung;** *I had to change my appointments because of the postponement of the board meeting*

potential
1 *adjective* possible **potentiell; potential customers** = people who could be customers **potentielle Kunden, Interessenten; potential market** = market which could be exploited **potentieller Markt; the product has potential sales of 100,000 units** = the product will possibly sell 100,000 units **das Produkt hat ein Umsatzpotential von 100.000 Einheiten; he is a potential managing director** = he is the sort of man who could become managing director **er kommt als Generaldirektor in Frage**
2 *noun* possibility of becoming something **Potential; share with a growth potential** *or* **with a potential for growth** = share which is likely to increase in value **Aktie mit Wachstumspotential; product with considerable sales potential** = product which is likely to have very large sales **Produkt mit beträchtlichen Absatzchancen; to analyze the market potential** = to examine the market to see how large it possibly is **die Absatzmöglichkeiten analysieren; earning potential** = amount of money which someone should be able to earn *or* amount of dividend which a share is capable of earning **Erwerbsfähigkeit; Ertragsfähigkeit**

> QUOTE career prospects are excellent for someone with growth potential
> *Australian Financial Review*
> QUOTE for sale: established general cleaning business; has potential to be increased to over 1 million dollar turnover
> *Australian Financial Review*

pound *noun*
(a) measure of weight (= 0.45 kilos); *entspricht* **Pfund;** *to sell oranges by the pound; a pound of oranges; oranges cost 50p a pound*
NOTE: usually written **lb** after a figure: **25lb**
(b) money used in the UK and many other countries **Pfund; pound sterling** = official term for the British currency **Pfund Sterling;** *a pound coin; a five pound note; it costs six pounds; the pound/dollar exchange rate*
NOTE: usually written **£** before a figure: **£25**

◇ **poundage** *noun* (i) rate charged per pound in weight; (ii) tax charged per pound in value **(i) pro Pfund berechnete Gebühr; (ii) nach dem Wert in Pfunden berechnete Abgaben**
NOTE: no plural

power *noun*
(a) strength *or* ability **Macht, Stärke, Kraft, Vermögen, Fähigkeit; purchasing power** = quantity of goods which can be bought by a group of people *or* with a sum of money **Kaufkraft;** *the purchasing power of the school market; the purchasing power of the pound has fallen over the last five years;* **the power of a consumer group** = ability of a group to influence the government *or* manufacturers **das Einflußvermögen einer Verbrauchergruppe; bargaining power** = strength of one person *or* group when discussing prices *or* wages **Verhandlungsstärke; earning power** = amount of money someone should be able to earn **Verdienstmöglichkeit;** *he is such a fine designer that his earning power is very large;* **borrowing power** = amount of money which a company can borrow **Kreditfähigkeit**
(b) force *or* legal right **Vollmacht, Ermächtigung, Befugnis; executive power** = right to put decisions into action **Exekutivgewalt, ausübende Gewalt; power of attorney** = legal document which gives someone the right to act on someone's behalf in legal matters **Vollmacht; the full power of the law** = the full force of the law when applied **die volle Gesetzeskraft;** *we will apply the full power of the law to get possession of our property again*

p.p. *verb* = PER PROCURATIONEM; **to p.p. a letter** = to sign a letter on behalf of someone **einen Brief im Auftrag unterschreiben;** *the secretary p.p.'d the letter while the manager was at lunch*

PR = PUBLIC RELATIONS *a PR firm is handling all our publicity; he is working in PR; the PR people gave away 100,000 balloons*

practice *noun*
(a) way of doing things **Gewohnheit, Verfahrensweise;** *his practice was to arrive at work at 7.30 and start counting the cash;* **business practices** *or* **industrial practices** *or* **trade practices** = ways of managing *or* working in business, industry or trade **Geschäftspraktiken, Geschäftsgepflogenheiten; Industriepraktiken; Handelspraktiken; restrictive practices** = ways of working which make people less free (such as stopping, by trade unions, of workers from doing certain jobs *or* not allowing customers a free choice of product) **restriktive Praktiken; sharp practice** = way of doing business which is not honest, but is not illegal

unsauberes/unlauteres Geschäftsgebaren; code of practice = rules drawn up by an association which the members must follow when doing business **Richtlinien**
(b) in practice = when actually done **in der Praxis;** *the marketing plan seems very interesting, but what will it cost in practice?*

> QUOTE the EC demanded international arbitration over the pricing practices of the provincial boards
> *Globe and Mail (Toronto)*

pre- *prefix* before **Vor-, vor- Prä-, prä-;** *a pre-stocktaking sale; there will be a pre-AGM board meeting or there will be a board meeting pre the AGM; the pre-Christmas period is always very busy*

precautionary *adjective* **as a precautionary measure** = in case something takes place **als Vorsichtsmaßnahme**
◊ **precautions** *plural noun* care taken to avoid something unpleasant **Vorkehrungen, Vorsichtsmaßnahmen;** *to take precautions to prevent thefts in the office; the company did not take proper fire precautions;* **safety precautions** = actions to try to make sure that something is safe **Sicherheitsvorkehrungen**

precinct *noun*
(a) pedestrian precinct *or* **shopping precinct** = part of a town which is closed to traffic so that people can walk about and shop **Fußgängerzone**
(b) *US* administrative district in a town **Verwaltungsbezirk**

predecessor *noun* person who had a job *or* position before someone else **Vorgänger/-in;** *he took over from his predecessor last May; she is using the same office as her predecessor*

predict *verb* to say that something will certainly happen **voraussagen, prophezeien**

> QUOTE lower interest rates are a bull factor for the stock market and analysts predict that the Dow Jones average will soon challenge the 1,300 barrier
> *Financial Times*

pre-empt *verb* to get an advantage by doing something quickly before anyone else **zuvorkommen;** *they staged a management buyout to pre-empt a takeover bid*
◊ **pre-emptive** *adjective* which has an advantage by acting early **Präventiv-; Vorkaufs-; Bezugs-; pre-emptive strike against a takeover bid** = rapid action taken to prevent a takeover bid **Präventivstreik gegen ein Übernahmeangebot; a pre-emptive right** = (i) right of a government *or* of a local authority to buy a property before anyone else; (ii); *US* right of a shareholder to be first to buy a new stock issue **(i) Vorkaufsrecht; (ii) Bezugsrecht**

prefer *verb* to like something better than another thing **vorziehen, bevorzugen;** *we prefer the small corner shop to the large supermarket; most customers prefer to choose clothes themselves, rather than take the advice of the sales assistant*
◊ **preference** *noun* thing which is preferred **Vorliebe;** *the customers' preference for small corner shops;* **preference shares** = shares (often with no voting rights) which receive their dividend before all other shares and which are repaid first (at face value) if the company is liquidated **Vorzugsaktien; preference shareholders** = owners of preference shares **Vorzugsaktienbesitzer; cumulative preference share** = preference share where the dividend will be paid at a later date even if the company cannot pay a dividend in the current year **nachzugsberechtigte/kumulative Vorzugsaktien**
◊ **preferential** *adjective* showing that something is preferred more than another **bevorzugt, Vorzugs-; preferential creditor** = creditor who must be paid first if a company is in liquidation **bevorrechtigter Gläubiger; preferential duty** *or* **preferential tariff** = special low rate of tax **Vorzugszoll, Vorzugstarif; preferential terms** *or* **preferential treatment** = terms *or* way of dealing which is better than usual **Vorzugskonditionen; bevorzugte Behandlung;** *subsidiary companies get preferential treatment when it comes to subcontracting work*
◊ **preferred** *adjective* **preferred creditor** = creditor who must be paid first if a company is in liquidation **bevorrechtigter Gläubiger; preferred shares** *or US* **preferred stock** = shares which receive their dividend before all other shares, and which are repaid first (at face value) if the company is in liquidation **Vorzugsaktien;** *US* **cumulative preferred stock** = preference share where the dividend will be paid at a later date even if the company cannot pay a dividend in the current year **kumulative Vorzugsaktie**

pre-financing *noun* financing in advance **Vorfinanzierung**

prejudice
1 *noun* harm done to someone **Schaden; without prejudice** = without harming any interests (words written on a letter to indicate that the writer is not legally bound

to do what he offers to do in the letter) **ohne Verbindlichkeit/Obligo; to act to the prejudice of a claim** = to do something which may harm a claim **auf eine einer Forderung abträgliche Weise handeln**
2 *verb* to harm **beeinträchtigen, schädigen;** *to prejudice someone's claim*

preliminary *adjective* early *or* happening before anything else **vorbereitend, vorausgehend, Vor-; preliminary discussion** *or* **a preliminary meeting** = discussion *or* meeting which takes place before the main discussion *or* meeting starts **Vorbesprechung**

> QUOTE preliminary indications of the level of business investment and activity during the March quarter will be available this week
> *Australian Financial Review*

premises *plural noun* building and the land it stands on **Gelände, Besitz, Haus mit Grund; business premises** *or* **commercial premises** = building used for commercial use **Geschäftsräume; office premises** *or* **shop premises** = building which houses an office or shop **Bürogebäude; Ladenräume; lock-up premises** = shop which is locked up at night when the owner goes home **Geschäft/Laden (ohne Nebenräume); licensed premises** = shop *or* restaurant *or* public house which is licensed to sell alcohol **Laden od Gaststätte mit Schankkonzession; on the premises** = in the building **am Ort, im Gebäude;** *there is a doctor on the premises at all times*

premium *noun*
(a) premium offer = free gift offered to attract more customers **Werbegeschenk**
(b) insurance premium = annual payment made by the insured person *or* a company to an insurance company **Versicherungsbeitrag, Versicherungsprämie; additional premium** = payment made to cover extra items in an existing insurance **Beitrags-, Prämienzuschlag;** *you pay either an annual premium of £360 or twelve monthly premiums of £32*
(c) amount to be paid to a landlord or a tenant for the right to take over a lease **Abstandssumme;** *flat to let with a premium of £10,000; annual rent: £8,500, premium: £25,000*
(d) extra charge **Zuschlag, Aufgeld; exchange premium** = extra cost above the normal rate for buying foreign currency **Agio, Aufgeld;** *the dollar is at a premium;* **shares sold at a premium** = shares whose price is higher than their face value; new shares whose market price is higher than their issue price **mit Aufgeld verkaufte Aktien**
(e) *GB* **premium bonds** = government bonds, part of the national savings scheme, which pay no interest, but give the owner the chance to win a weekly *or* monthly prize **Sparprämienanleihe**
(f) premium quality = top quality **erstklassige Qualität**

> QUOTE greenmail, the practice of buying back stock at a premium from an acquirer who threatens a takeover
> *Duns Business Month*
>
> QUOTE responsibilities include the production of premium quality business reports
> *Times*

prepacked *or* **prepackaged** *adjective* to pack something before putting it on sale **abgepackt, vorverpackt;** *the fruit are prepacked or prepackaged in plastic trays; the watches are prepacked in attractive display boxes*

prepaid *adjective* paid in advance **vorausbezahlt; carriage prepaid** = note showing that the transport costs have been paid in advance **frachtfrei; prepaid reply card** = stamped addressed card which is sent to someone so that he can reply without paying the postage **frankierte/freigemachte Antwortkarte**
◇ **prepay** *verb* to pay in advance **im voraus bezahlen**
NOTE: **prepaying - prepaid**
◇ **prepayment** *noun* payment in advance **Vorauszahlung; to ask for prepayment of a fee** = to ask for the fee to be paid before the work is done **Vorauszahlung des Honorars verlangen**

present
1 *noun* thing which is given **Geschenk;** *these calculators make good presents; the office gave her a present when she got married*
2 *adjective*
(a) happening now **gegenwärtig, augenblicklich, derzeitig, jetzig;** *the shares are too expensive at their present price; what is the present address of the company?*
(b) being there when something happens **anwesend;** *only six directors were present at the board meeting*
3 *verb*
(a) to give someone something **überreichen, übergeben; schenken;** *he was presented with a watch on completing twenty-five years' service with the company*
(b) to bring *or* send and show a document **vorlegen; to present a bill for acceptance** = to send a bill for payment by the person who has accepted it **einen Wechsel zur Annahme vorlegen; to present a bill for payment** = to send a bill to be paid **eine Rechnung zur Zahlung vorlegen**
◇ **presentation** *noun*
(a) showing a document **Vorlage; cheque payable on presentation** = cheque which

will be paid when it is presented **Scheck bei Vorlage zahlbar; free admission on presentation of the card** = you do not pay to go in if you show this card **Eintritt kostenlos bei Vorlage der Karte**
(b) demonstration *or* exhibition of a proposed plan **Präsentation, Vorführung;** *the manufacturer made a presentation of his new product line to possible customers; the distribution company made a presentation of the services they could offer; we have asked two PR firms to make presentations of proposed publicity campaigns*

◇ **present value** *noun*
(a) the value something has now **gegenwärtiger Wert;** *in 1974 the pound was worth five times its present value*
(b) sum of money which if invested now at a given rate of interest would produce a certain amount in the future **Barwert**

preside *verb* to be chairman **den Vorsitz führen/haben;** *to preside over a meeting; the meeting was held in the committee room, Mr Smith presiding*

◇ **president** *noun* head of a company *or* a club **Präsident/-in;** *he was elected president of the sports club; A.B.Smith has been appointed president of the company*
NOTE: in GB, president is sometimes a title given to a non-executive former chairman of a company; in the USA, the president is the main executive director of a company

press *noun* newspapers and magazines **Presse; the local press** = newspapers which are sold in a small area of the country **Lokalblätter; the national press** = newspapers which sell in all parts of the country **die überregionale Presse;** *the new car has been advertised in the national press; we plan to give the product a lot of press publicity; there was no mention of the new product in the press;* **press conference** = meeting where reporters from newspapers are invited to hear news of a new product *or* of a court case *or* of a takeover bid, etc. **Pressekonferenz; press coverage** = reports about something in the press **Presseberichte, Berichterstattung durch die Presse;** *we were very disappointed by the press coverage of the new car;* **press cutting** = piece cut out of a newspaper *or* magazine, which refers to an item which you find interesting **Zeitungsausschnitt;** *we have kept a file of press cuttings about the new car;* **press release** = sheet giving news about something which is sent to newspapers and TV and radio stations so that they can use the information **Pressemitteilung;** *the company sent out a press release about the launch of the new car*
NOTE: no plural

◇ **pressing** *adjective* urgent **dringend; pressing engagements** = meetings which have to be attended **dringende Termine; pressing bills** = bills which have to be paid **dringende Rechnungen**

pressure *noun* something which forces you to do something **Druck; he was under considerable financial pressure** = he was forced to act because he owed money **er stand unter erheblichen finanziellem Druck; to put pressure on someone to do something** = to try to force someone to do something **jdn unter Druck setzen, etwas zu tun;** *the group tried to put pressure on the government to act; the banks put pressure on the company to reduce its borrowings;* **working under high pressure** = working with customers asking for supplies urgently *or* with a manager telling you to work faster **unter Druck/Streß arbeiten; high-pressure salesman** = salesman who forces a customer to buy something he does not really need **aggressiver Verkäufer; pressure group** = group of people who try to influence the government *or* the local town council, etc. **Interessengruppe**

prestige *noun* importance because of high quality *or* high value, etc. **Prestige; prestige advertising** = advertising in high quality magazines to increase a company's reputation **Prestigewerbung, Repräsentationswerbung; prestige product** = expensive luxury product **Luxus-, Prestigeartikel; prestige offices** = expensive offices in a good area of the town **Repräsentationsbüro**

presume *verb* to suppose something is correct **annehmen;** *I presume the account has been paid; the company is presumed to be still solvent; we presume the shipment has been stolen*

◇ **presumption** *noun* thing which is assumed to be correct **Annahme**

pre-tax *or* **pretax** *adjective* before tax has been deducted *or* paid **vor Steuern, vor Abzug der Steuern; pretax profit** = profit before tax has been paid **Gewinn vor (Abzug der) Steuern;** *the dividend paid is equivalent to one quarter of the pretax profit*

QUOTE the company's goals are a growth in sales of up to 40 per cent, a rise in pre-tax earnings of nearly 35 per cent and a rise in after-tax earnings of more than 25 per cent
Citizen (Ottawa)

QUOTE EEC regulations which came into effect in July insist that customers can buy cars anywhere in the EEC at the local pre-tax price
Financial Times

pretences *plural noun* **false pretences** = doing or saying something to cheat someone **Vorspiegelung falscher Tatsachen;** *he was sent to prison for obtaining money by false pretences*

pretend *verb* to act like someone else in order to trick *or* to act as if something is true when it really is not **vorgeben, vortäuschen;** *he got in by pretending to be a telephone engineer; the chairman pretended he knew the final profit; she pretended she had 'flu and asked to have the day off*

prevent *verb* to stop something happening **verhindern, verhüten;** *we must try to prevent the takeover bid; the police prevented anyone from leaving the building; we have changed the locks on the doors to prevent the former MD from getting into the building*

◇ **preventive** *adjective* which tries to stop something happening **vorbeugend, präventiv; to take preventive measures against theft** = to try to stop things from being stolen **vorbeugende Maßnahmen gegen Diebstahl ergreifen**

previous *adjective* which happens earlier **vorig, vorhergehend, Vor-; he could not accept the invitation because he had a previous engagement** = because he had earlier accepted another invitation to go somewhere **er konnte die Einladung nicht annehmen, weil er anderweitig verabredet war**

◇ **previously** *adverb* happening earlier **vorher**

price

1 *noun*

(a) money which has to be paid to buy something **Preis; agreed price** = price which has been accepted by both the buyer and seller **vereinbarter Preis; all-in price** = price which covers all items in a purchase (goods, insurance, delivery, etc.) **Pauschalpreis, Gesamtpreis; asking price** = price which the seller is hoping to be paid for the item when it is sold **geforderter Preis; Verhandlungsbasis; bargain price** = very cheap price **Sonder-, Spottpreis; catalogue price** *or* **list price** = price as marked in a catalogue or list **Katalog-, Listenpreis; competitive price** = low price aimed to compete with a rival product **wettbewerbsfähiger Preis; cost price** = selling price which is the same as the price which the seller paid for the item (either the manufacturing price or the wholesale price) **Selbstkostenpreis; cut price** = very cheap price **Niedrigpreis; discount price** = full price less a discount **Diskontpreis, Preis nach Abzug des Rabatts; factory price** *or* **price ex factory** = price not including transport from the maker's factory **Preis ab Werk; fair price** = good price for both buyer and seller **fairer/angemessener Preis; firm price** = price which will not change **Festpreis;** *they are quoting a firm price of $1.23 a unit;* **going price** *or* **current price** *or* **usual price** = the price which is being charged now **gängiger/jetziger/üblicher Preis; to sell goods off at half price** = to sell goods at half the price at which they were being sold before **Waren zum halben Preis losschlagen; market price** = price at which a product can be sold **Marktpreis; net price** = price which cannot be reduced by a discount **Nettopreis; retail price** = price at which the retailer sells to the final customer **Einzelhandels-, Laden-, Endpreis; retail price index** = index which shows how prices of consumer goods have increased or decreased over a period of time **Index der Einzelhandelspreise; spot price** = price for immediate delivery of a commodity **Lokopreis;** *the spot price of oil on the commodity markets;* **price ceiling** = highest price which can be reached **oberste Preisgrenze; price controls** = legal measures to stop prices rising too fast **Preiskontrollen; Preisüberwachung; price cutting** = sudden lowering of prices **plötzliche Preissenkung; price war** *or* **price-cutting war** = competition between companies to get a larger market share by cutting prices **Preiskrieg; price differential** = difference in price between products in a range **Preisgefälle, Preisunterschied; price fixing** = illegal agreement between companies to charge the same price for competing products **Preisabsprache; price label** *or* **price tag** = label which shows a price **Preisschild;** *the takeover bid put a $2m price tag on the company;* **price list** = sheet giving prices of goods for sale **Preisliste; price range** = series of prices for similar products from different suppliers **Preisklasse; cars in the £6-7,000 price range** = cars of different makes, selling for between £6,000 and £7,000 **Wagen in der Preisklase von £6000 bis £7000; price-sensitive product** = product which will not sell if the price is increased **preisempfindliches Produkt**

(b) to increase in price = to become more expensive **teurer werden;** *petrol has increased in price or the price of petrol has increased;* **to increase prices** *or* **to raise prices** = to make items more expensive **Preise erhöhen; we will try to meet your price** = we will try to offer a price which is acceptable to you **wir werden versuchen, ihrer Preisvorstellung zu entsprechen; to cut prices** = to reduce prices suddenly **Preise plötzlich senken; to lower prices** *or* **to reduce prices** = to make items cheaper **Preise**

senken/herabsetzen/reduzieren, mit dem Preis heruntergehen
(c) *(on the Stock Exchange)* **asking price** = price which sellers are asking for shares **Briefkurs; closing price** = price at the end of a day's trading **Schlußkurs, Schlußnotierung; opening price** = price at the start of a day's trading **Eröffnungskurs; price/earnings ratio** = ratio between the market price of a share and the current earnings it produces **Kurs-Gewinn-Verhältnis**
2 *verb* to give a price to a product **einen Preis festsetzen;** *car priced at £5,000;* **competitively priced** = sold at a low price which competes with that of similar goods from other companies **zu einem wettbewerbsfähigen Preis; the company has priced itself out of the market** = the company has raised its prices so high that its products do not sell **das Unternehmen ist durch seine überhöhten Preise wettbewerbsunfähig geworden**

◇ **pricing** *noun* giving a price to a product **Preisfestsetzung, Preiskalkulation, Preisbildung; pricing policy** = a company's policy in giving prices to its products **Preispolitik;** *our pricing policy aims at producing a 35% gross margin;* **common pricing** = illegal fixing of prices by several businesses so that they all charge the same price **Preisabsprache; competitive pricing** = putting a low price on a product so that it competes with similar products from other companies **wettbewerbsfähige Auspreisung; marginal pricing** = making the selling price the same as the cost of a single extra unit above the number already planned **Grenzkostenpreiskalkulation**
NOTE: no plural

QUOTE that British goods will price themselves back into world markets is doubtful as long as sterling labour costs continue to rise
Sunday Times

QUOTE the average price per kilogram for this season has been 300c
Australian Financial Review

QUOTE European manufacturers rely heavily on imported raw materials which are mostly priced in dollars
Duns Business Month

primary *adjective* basic **grundlegend; primary commodities** = raw materials or food **Grundstoffe; primary industry** = industry dealing with basic raw materials (such as coal, wood, farm produce) **Rohstoffindustrie; primary products** = products (such as wood, milk, fish) which are basic raw materials **Primärprodukte**

◇ **primarily** *adverb* mainly **hauptsächlich**

QUOTE farmers are convinced that primary industry no longer has the capacity to meet new capital taxes or charges on farm inputs
Australian Financial Review

prime *adjective*
(a) most important **Haupt-, wesentlich; prime time** = most expensive advertising time for TV commercials **Hauptsendezeit;** *we are putting out a series of prime-time commercials*
(b) basic **ursprünglich; prime bills** = bills of exchange which do not involve any risk **erstklassige Wechsel; prime cost** = cost involved in producing a product, excluding overheads **Gestehungs-, Herstellungs-, Selbstkostenpreis; prime rate** *or* **prime** = best rate of interest at which a bank lends to its customers **Prime Rate, Leitzins (für erste Adressen)**

◇ **Prime Minister** *noun* head of a government **Premierminister, Ministerpräsident;** *the Australian Prime Minister or the Prime Minister of Australia*

◇ **priming** *noun see* PUMP PRIMING

QUOTE the base lending rate, or prime rate, is the rate at which banks lend to their top corporate borrowers
Wall Street Journal

principal
1 *noun*
(a) person *or* company which is represented by an agent **Auftraggeber/-in;** *the agent has come to London to see his principals*
(b) money invested *or* borrowed on which interest is paid **Kapital(summe), Kapitaleinlage, Hauptsumme, Darlehensbetrag;** *to repay principal and interest*
2 *adjective* most important **Haupt-, wichtigster;** *the principal shareholders asked for a meeting; the country's principal products are paper and wood*

QUOTE the company was set up with funds totalling NorKr 145m with the principal aim of making capital gains on the secondhand market
Lloyd's List

principle *noun* basic point *or* general rule **Prinzip; in principle** = in agreement with a general rule **prinzipiell, im Prinzip; agreement in principle** = agreement with the basic conditions of a proposal **grundsätzliche Übereinstimmung**

print
1 *noun* words made (on paper) with a machine **Gedrucktes; to read the small print** *or* **the fine print on a contract** = to read the conditions of a contract which are often printed very small so that people will not be able to read them easily **das Kleingedruckte in einem Vertrag lesen**
2 *verb*
(a) to make letters on paper with a machine **drucken;** *printed agreement; printed regulations*

(b) to write in capital letters **in Druckbuchstaben/Druckschrift schreiben;** *please print your name and address on the top of the form*

◇ **printer** *noun* machine which prints **Druckmaschine; computer printer** *or* **line printer** = machine which prints information from a computer, printing one line at a time **Drucker; Zeilendrucker; dot-matrix printer** = machine which prints by forming letters from many tiny dots **Matrixdrucker**

◇ **print out** *verb* to print information from a computer through a printer **ausdrucken**

◇ **printout** *noun* **computer printout** = printed copy of information from a computer **Computer-Ausdruck;** *the sales director asked for a printout of the agents' commissions*

prior *adjective* earlier **früher, vorausgehend; prior agreement** = agreement which was reached earlier **frühere Vereinbarung; without prior knowledge** = without knowing before **ohne vorheriges Wissen; prior charge** = security (such as a preference share) which is repaid before other securities when a company goes into liquidation **bevorrechtigte Forderung**

◇ **priority** *noun* **to have priority** = to have the right to be first **Vorrang haben; to have priority over** *or* **to take priority over something** = to be more important than something **vor etwas Vorrang haben;** *reducing overheads takes priority over increasing turnover; debenture holders have priority over ordinary shareholders;* **to give something top priority** = to make something the most important item **etwas vorrangig behandeln**

private *adjective*
(a) belonging to a single person, not a company *or* the state **privat, Privat-; letter marked "private and confidential"** = letter which must not be opened by anyone other than the person it is addressed to **ein Brief mit der Aufschrift "streng vertraulich"; private client** *or* **private customer** = client dealt with by a salesman as a person, not as a company **Privatkunde; private income** = income from dividends *or* interest *or* rents which is not part of a salary **Privateinkommen; private investor** = ordinary person with money to invest **Privatanleger; private property** = property which belongs to a private person, not to the public **Privatbesitz; Privatgrundstück**
(b) in private = away from other people **unter vier Augen;** *he asked to see the managing director in private; in public he said the company would break even soon, but in private he was less optimistic*
(c) private limited company = company with a small number of shareholders whose shares are not traded on the Stock Exchange; *entspricht* **Gesellschaft mit beschränkter Haftung**
(d) private enterprise = businesses which are owned by private shareholders, not by the state **Privatunternehmen;** *the project is funded by private enterprise;* **the private sector** = all companies which are owned by private shareholders, not by the state **Privatsektor**

◇ **privately** *adverb* away from other people **unter vier Augen;** *the deal was negotiated privately*

◇ **privatization** *noun* selling a nationalized industry to private owners **Privatisierung, Zurückführung in Privateigentum**

◇ **privatize** *verb* to sell a nationalized industry to private owners **privatisieren**

> QUOTE in the private sector the total number of new house starts was 3 per cent higher than in the corresponding period last year, while public sector starts were 23 per cent lower
> *Financial Times*
>
> QUOTE management had offered to take the company private through a leveraged buyout for $825 million
> *Fortune*

pro *preposition* for **für; pro tem** = for the time being *or* temporarily **zur Zeit, z.Zt.; per pro** = with the authority of **per Prokura, im Auftrag;** *the secretary signed per pro the manager;* **pro forma invoice** = invoice sent to a buyer before the goods are sent, so that payment can be made in advance *or* that business documents can be produced **Proforma-Rechnung; pro rata** = at a rate which varies according to the size or importance of something **anteilig, anteilsmäßig; dividends are paid pro rata** = dividends are paid according to the number of shares held **Dividenden werden anteilsmäßig bezahlt**

probable *adjective* likely to happen **wahrscheinlich, zu erwarten;** *he is trying to prevent the probable collapse of the company*

◇ **probably** *adverb* likely **wahrscheinlich, vermutlich;** *the MD is probably going to retire next year; this shop is probably the best in town for service*

probate *noun* proving legally that a document, especially a will, is valid **gerichtliche Testamentsbestätigung; the executor was granted probate** = the executor was told officially that the will was valid **dem Testamentsvollstrecker wurde das Testament bestätigt und ein Erbschein erteilt;**

probate court = court which examines wills to see if they are valid **Nachlaßgericht**
NOTE: no plural

◊ **probation** *noun* period when a new worker is being tested before getting a permanent job **Probezeit;** *he is on three months' probation; to take someone on probation*
NOTE: no plural

◊ **probationary** *adjective* while someone is being tested **Probe-;** *a probationary period of three months; after the probationary period the company decided to offer him a full-time contract*

problem *noun* thing to which it is difficult to find an answer **Problem;** *the company suffers from cash flow problems or staff problems;* **to solve a problem** = to find an answer to a problem **ein Problem lösen;** *problem solving is a test of a good manager;* **problem area** = area of a company's work which is difficult to run **Problembereich;** *overseas sales is one of our biggest problem areas*

> QUOTE everyone blames the strong dollar for US trade problems, but they differ on what should be done
> *Duns Business Month*

procedure *noun* way in which something is done **Verfahren, Vorgehen, Vorgehensweise;** *to follow the proper procedure;* **this procedure is very irregular** = this is not the set way to do something **diese Vorgehensweise ist unvorschriftsmäßig; accounting procedures** = set ways of doing the accounts of a company **Buchungsverfahren; disciplinary procedure** = way of warning a worker that he is breaking the rules of a company **Disziplinarverfahren; complaints procedure** *or* **grievance procedure** = way of presenting complaints formally from a trade union to a management **Beschwerdeweg;** *the trade union has followed the correct complaints procedure;* **dismissal procedures** = correct way to dismiss someone, following the rules in the contract of employment **Entlassungsverfahren**

proceed *verb* to go on *or* to continue **fortfahren, fortsetzen;** *the negotiations are proceeding slowly;* **to proceed against someone** = to start a legal action against someone **gegen jdn prozessieren/gerichtlich vorgehen; to proceed with something** = to go on doing something **mit etwas weitermachen;** *shall we proceed with the committee meeting?*

◊ **proceedings** *plural noun*
(a) conference proceedings = written report of what has taken place at a conference **Konferenzprotokoll**
(b) legal proceedings = legal action *or* lawsuit **Gerichtsverfahren, Prozeß, Klage;** *to take proceedings against someone; the court proceedings were adjourned;* **to institute proceedings against someone** = to start a legal action against someone **gegen jdn gerichtlich vorgehen**

◊ **proceeds** *plural noun* **the proceeds of a sale** = money received from a sale after deducting expenses **Verkaufserlös;** *he sold his shop and invested the proceeds in a computer repair business*

process
1 *noun*
(a) industrial process = process involved in manufacturing products in factories **Herstellungsprozeß; decision-making processes** = ways in which decisions are reached **Entscheidungsprozeß**
(b) the due processes of the law = the formal work of a legal action **ordentliches Gerichtsverfahren**
2 *verb*
(a) to process figures = to sort out information to make it easily understood **Zahlen aufbereiten;** *the sales figures are being processed by our accounts department; data is being processed by our computer*
(b) to deal with something in the usual routine way **bearbeiten;** *to process an insurance claim; orders are processed in our warehouse*

◊ **processing** *noun*
(a) sorting of information **Aufarbeitung;** *processing of information or of statistics;* **batch processing** = computer system, where information is collected into batches before being loaded into the computer **Stapelverarbeitung, Batch-Betrieb; data processing** *or* **information processing** = selecting and examining data in a computer to produce information in a special form **Datenverarbeitung; word processing** *or* **text processing** = working with words, using a computer to produce, check and change texts, reports, letters, etc. **Textverarbeitung**
(b) the processing of a claim for insurance = putting a claim for insurance through the usual office routine in the insurance company **Schadensbearbeitung der Versicherung; order processing** = dealing with orders **Auftragsabwicklung**
NOTE: no plural

◊ **processor** *noun* **word processor** = small computer which is used for working with words, to produce texts, reports, letters, etc. **Textverarbeitungsanlage**

produce
1 *noun* foodstuffs grown on the land

Agrarerzeugnisse, landwirtschaftliche Produkte; *home produce; agricultural produce or farm produce*
NOTE: no plural
2 *verb*
(a) to bring out **vorzeigen, vorlegen;** *he produced documents to prove his claim; the negotiators produced a new set of figures; the customs officer asked him to produce the relevant documents*
(b) to make *or* to manufacture **herstellen, produzieren, erzeugen, fertigen;** *to produce cars or engines or books;* **to mass produce** = to make large quantities of a product **in Massenanfertigung/serienweise herstellen**
(c) to give an interest **bringen, erzielen, abwerfen;** *investments which produce about 10% per annum*

◇ **producer** *noun* person *or* company *or* country which manufactures **Hersteller, Erzeuger, Produzent;** *country which is a producer of high quality watches; the company is a major car producer*

◇ **producing** *adjective* which produces **Herstellungs-, Produktions-, erzeugend; producing capacity** = capacity to produce **Produktionskapazität; oil-producing country** = country which produces oil **erdölförderndes Land**

product *noun*
(a) thing which is made *or* manufactured **Produkt, Erzeugnis; basic product** = main product made from a raw material **Grundprodukt; by-product** = secondary product made as a raw material is being processed **Nebenprodukt; end product** *or* **final product** *or* **finished product** = product made at the end of a production process **Endprodukt**
(b) manufactured item for sale **Produkt, Artikel, Ware; product advertising** = advertising a particular named product, not the company which makes it **Produktwerbung; product analysis** = examining each separate product in a company's range to see why it sells *or* who buys it, etc. **Produktanalyse; product design** = design of consumer products **Produktgestaltung; product development** = improving an existing product line to meet the needs of the market **Produktentwicklung; product engineer** = engineer in charge of the equipment for making a product **Fertigungsingenieur; product line** *or* **product range** = series of different products made by the same company which form a group (such as cars in different models, pens in different colours, etc.) **Sortiment; product management** = directing the making and selling of a product as an independent item **Produkt-Management; product mix** = group of quite different products made by the same company **Produktmix, Produktpalette**
(c) gross domestic product = annual value of goods sold and services paid for inside a country **Bruttoinlandsprodukt; gross national product** = annual value of goods and services in a country, including income from other countries **Bruttosozialprodukt**

◇ **production** *noun*
(a) showing something **Vorlage, Vorzeigen; on production of** = when something is shown **bei Vorlage von;** *the case will be released by the customs on production of the relevant documents; goods can be exchanged only on production of the sales slip*
(b) making *or* manufacturing of goods for sale **Herstellung, Produktion, Erzeugung, Fertigung;** *production will probably be held up by industrial action; we are hoping to speed up production by installing new machinery;* **batch production** = production in batches **Serienfertigung; domestic production** = production of goods in the home market **Inlandsproduktion; mass production** = manufacturing of large quantities of goods **Massenproduktion, serienmäßige Herstellung;** *mass production of cars or of calculators;* **rate of production** *or* **production rate** = speed at which items are made **Produktionsleistung; production cost** = cost of making a product **Produktionskosten; production department** = section of a company which deals with the making of the company's products **Fertigungsabteilung; production line** = system of making a product, where each item (such as a car) moves slowly through the factory with new sections added to it as it goes along **Fertigungsstraße, Fließband;** *he works on the production line; she is a production line worker;* **production manager** = person in charge of the production department **Produktionsleiter, Leiter der Fertigung; production unit** = separate small group of workers producing a certain product **Produktionseinheit**
NOTE: no plural

◇ **productive** *adjective* which produces **produktiv; productive capital** = capital which is invested to give interest **arbeitendes/gewinnbringendes Kapital; productive discussions** = useful discussions which lead to an agreement *or* decision **produktive Gespräche**

◇ **productively** *adverb* in a productive way **produktiv**

◇ **productivity** *noun* rate of output per worker *or* per machine in a factory **Produktivität;** *bonus payments are linked to productivity; the company is aiming to increase productivity; productivity has fallen or risen since the company was taken*

over; **productivity agreement** = agreement to pay a productivity bonus **Produktivitätsabkommen; productivity bonus** = extra payments made to workers because of increased production **Produktivitätsprämie, Leistungszulage; productivity drive** = extra effort to increase productivity **Produktivitätskampagne**
NOTE: no plural

> QUOTE though there has been productivity growth, the absolute productivity gap between many British firms and their foreign rivals remains
> *Sunday Times*

profession *noun*
(a) work which needs special skills learnt over a period of time **Beruf;** *the managing director is an accountant by profession*
(b) group of specialized workers **Berufsstand; the legal profession** = all lawyers **der Anwaltsstand, die Anwälte; the medical profession** = all doctors **die Ärzteschaft**

◇ **professional**
1 *adjective*
(a) referring to one of the professions **beruflich, Berufs-; fachlich, fachmännisch;** *the accountant sent in his bill for professional services; we had to ask our lawyer for professional advice on the contract;* **a professional man** = man who works in one of the professions (such as a lawyer, doctor, accountant) **Angehöriger der gehobenen Berufe; professional qualifications** = documents showing that someone has successfully finished a course of study which allows him to work in one of the professions **berufliche Qualifikationen**
(b) expert *or* skilled **professionell;** *his work is very professional; they did a very professional job in designing the new office*
(c) doing work for money **Berufs-;** *a professional tennis player;* **he is a professional troubleshooter** = he makes his living by helping companies to sort out their problems **er ist ein professioneller Krisenmanager**
2 *noun* skilled person *or* person who does skilled work for money **Fachmann, Profi**

proficiency *noun* skill *or* being capable of doing something **Fertigkeit, Leistung;** *she has a certificate of proficiency in English; to get the job he had to pass a proficiency test*
NOTE: no plural

◇ **proficient** *adjective* capable of doing something well **tüchtig;** *she is quite proficient in English*

profile *noun* brief description **Kurzübersicht, Profil;** *he asked for a company profile of the possible partners in the joint venture; the customer profile shows our average buyer to be male, aged 25-30, and employed in the service industries*

profit *noun* money gained from a sale which is more than the money spent **Gewinn, Profit, Erlös; clear profit** = profit after all expenses have been paid **Rein-, Nettogewinn;** *we made $6,000 clear profit on the deal;* **gross profit** = profit calculated as sales income less the cost of the goods sold **Bruttogewinn; net profit** = result where income from sales is larger than all expenditure **Nettogewinn; operating profit** = result where sales from normal business activities are higher than the costs **Betriebsgewinn; trading profit** = result where the company' receipts are higher than its expenditure **Geschäftsgewinn; profit and loss account** = accounts for a company which show expenditure and income balanced to show a final profit *or* loss **Gewinn- und Verlustrechnung; profit margin** = percentage difference between sales income and the cost of sales **Gewinnspanne; profits tax** *or* **tax on profits** = tax to be paid on profits **Gewinnsteuer; profit before tax** *or* **pretax profit** = profit before any tax has been paid **Gewinn vor (Abzug der) Steuern; profit after tax** = profit after tax has been paid **Gewinn nach Steuern; to take one's profit** = to sell shares at a higher price than was paid for them, rather than to keep them as an investment **seinen Gewinn mitnehmen; to show a profit** = to make a profit and state it in the company accounts **einen Gewinn aufweisen;** *we are showing a small profit for the first quarter;* **to make a profit** = to have more money as a result of a deal **einen Gewinn machen; to move into profit** = to start to make a profit **in die schwarzen Zahlen kommen;** *the company is breaking even now, and expects to move into profit within the next two months;* **to sell at a profit** = to sell at a price which gives you a profit **mit Gewinn verkaufen; excess profit** = profit which is higher than what is thought to be normal **Mehrgewinn; excess profits tax** = tax on excess profits **Steuer zur Abschöpfung von Höchstgewinnen; healthy profit** = quite a large profit **stattlicher Gewinn; paper profit** = profit on an asset which has increased in price but has not been sold **Buchgewinn;** *he is showing a paper profit of £25,000 on his investment*

◇ **profit centre** *noun* person *or* department which is considered separately for the purposes of calculating a profit **Kostenstelle, Profit-Center**

◇ **profit-making** *adjective* which makes a profit **gewinnbringend, rentabel;** *the whole project was expected to be profit-making by 1985;* **non profit-making** = (organization, such as a club) which is not allowed by law to make a profit **gemeinnützig, nicht auf Erwerbszwecke ausgerichtet;** *non profit-making organizations are exempt from tax*

◇ **profit-sharing** *noun* arrangement where workers get a share of the profits of the company they work for **Gewinnbeteiligung;** *the company runs a profit-sharing scheme*
NOTE: no plural

◇ **profit-taking** *noun* selling investments to realize the profit, rather than keeping them **Gewinnmitnahme, Gewinnrealisierung;** *share prices fell under continued profit-taking*
NOTE: no plural

◇ **profitability** *noun*
(a) ability to make a profit **Rentabilität**
(b) amount of profit made as a percentage of costs **Profitabilität; measurement of profitability** = way of calculating how profitable something is **Rentabilitätsberechnung**
NOTE: no plural

◇ **profitable** *adjective* which makes a profit **rentabel, gewinnbringend, ertragreich, einträglich**

◇ **profitably** *adverb* making a profit **rentabel, gewinnbringend, ertragreich**

◇ **profiteer** *noun* person who makes too much profit, especially when goods are rationed *or* in short supply **Geschäftemacher**

◇ **profiteering** *noun* making too much profit **Geschäftemacherei, Preistreiberei**

> QUOTE because capital gains are not taxed and money taken out in profits and dividends is taxed, owners of businesses will be using accountants and tax experts to find loopholes in the law
> *Toronto Star*
>
> QUOTE the bank transferred $5 million to general reserve compared with $10 million in 1983 which made the consolidated profit and loss account look healthier
> *Hongkong Standard*
>
> QUOTE some profit-taking was seen yesterday as investors continued to lack fresh incentives to renew buying activity
> *Financial Times*

pro forma

noun **pro forma invoice** = invoice sent to a buyer before the goods are sent, so that payment can be made or that business documents can be produced **Proforma-Rechnung;** *they sent us a pro forma*

program

1 *noun* **computer program** = instructions to a computer telling it to do a particular piece of work **Computer-, Rechnerprogramm;** *to buy a word-processing program; the accounts department is running a new payroll program*
2 *verb* to write a program for a computer **programmieren; to program a computer** = to install a program in a computer **einen Computer programmieren;** *the computer is programmed to print labels*
NOTE: **programming - programmed**

◇ **programme** *or US* **program** *noun* plan of things which will be done **Programm, Plan;** *development programme; research programme; training programme; to draw up a programme of investment or an investment programme*

◇ **programmable** *adjective* which can be programmed **programmierbar**

◇ **programmer** *noun* **computer programmer** = person who writes computer programs **Programmierer/-in**

◇ **programming** *noun* **computer programming** = writing programs for computers **Programmierung; programming engineer** = engineer in charge of programming a computer system **Systemanalytiker, Systemprogrammierer; programming language** = system of signs, letters and words used to instruct a computer **Programmiersprache**

progress

1 *noun* movement of work forward **Fortschreiten, Verlauf;** *to report on the progress of the work or of the negotiations;* **to make a progress report** = to report how work is going **einen Fortschrittsbericht anfertigen; in progress** = which is being done but is not finished **laufend;** *negotiations in progress; work in progress;* **progress payments** = payments made as each stage of a contract is completed **Abschlagszahlungen;** *the fifth progress payment is due in March*
NOTE: no plural
2 *verb* to move forward *or* to go ahead **Fortschritte machen, vordringen;** *the contract is progressing through various departments*

◇ **progress chaser** *noun* person whose job is to check that work is being carried out on schedule *or* that orders are being fulfilled on time, etc. **Terminprüfer**

◇ **progressive** *adjective* which moves forward in stages **progressiv, gestaffelt;** *progressive taxation*

prohibitive

adjective with a price so high that you cannot afford to pay it **untragbar, unerschwinglich;** *the cost of redeveloping the product is prohibitive*

project

noun
(a) plan **Plan;** *he has drawn up a project for developing new markets in Europe*
(b) particular job of work which follows a plan **Projekt, Vorhaben;** *we are just completing an engineering project in North Africa; the company will start work on the*

project next month; **project analysis** = examining all costs *or* problems of a project before work on it is started **Projektanalyse; project engineer** = engineer in charge of a project **Projektingenieur; project manager** = manager in charge of a project **Projektleiter**

◊ **projected** *adjective* planned *or* expected **geplant, erwartet; projected sales** = forecast of sales **erwarteter Absatz, Verkaufsprognose;** *projected sales in Europe next year should be over £1m*

◊ **projection** *noun* forecast of something which will happen in the future **Vorhersage, Prognose;** *projection of profits for the next three years; the sales manager was asked to draw up sales projections for the next three years*

promise

1 *noun* saying that you will do something **Versprechen, Zusage; to keep a promise** = to do what you said you would do **ein Versprechen halten;** *he says he will pay next week, but he never keeps his promises;* **to go back on a promise** = not to do what you said you would do **ein Versprechen brechen;** *the management went back on its promise to increase salaries across the board;* **a promise to pay** = a promissory note **Zahlungsversprechen**

2 *verb* to say that you will do something **versprechen, zusagen;** *they promised to pay the last instalment next week; the personnel manager promised he would look into the grievances of the office staff*

◊ **promissory note** *noun* document stating that someone promises to pay an amount of money on a certain date **Schuldschein**

promote *verb*

(a) to give someone a more important job **befördern;** *he was promoted from salesman to sales manager*

(b) to advertise **werben, Reklame machen; to promote a new product** = to increase the sales of a new product by a sales campaign *or* TV commercials *or* free gifts **durch Werbung den Verkauf eines neuen Produktes fördern**

(c) to promote a new company = to organize the setting up of a new company **eine neue Firma gründen**

◊ **promoter** *noun* **company promoter** = person who organizes the setting up of a new company **Firmengründer**

◊ **promotion** *noun*

(a) moving up to a more important job **Beförderung;** *promotion chances or promotion prospects; he ruined his chances of promotion when he argued with the managing director;* **to earn promotion** = to work hard and efficiently and so be promoted **sich seine Beförderung verdienen**

(b) promotion of a company = setting up a new company **Firmengründung**

(c) promotion of a product = selling a new product by publicity *or* sales campaign *or* TV commercials *or* free gifts **Werbekampagne für ein Produkt;** *promotion budget; promotion team; sales promotion; special promotion*

◊ **promotional** *adjective* used in an advertising campaign **Werbe-;** *the admen are using balloons as promotional material;* **promotional budget** = forecast cost of promoting a new product **Werbeetat**

prompt

adjective rapid *or* done immediately **prompt, sofortig;** *prompt service; prompt reply to a letter;* **prompt payment** = payment made rapidly **pünktliche Zahlung; prompt supplier** = supplier who delivers orders rapidly **Lieferant, der sofort liefert**

◊ **promptly** *adverb* rapidly **prompt, pünktlich;** *he replied to my letter very promptly*

> QUOTE they keep shipping costs low and can take advantage of quantity discounts and other allowances for prompt payment
> *Duns Business Month*

proof

noun thing which shows that something is true **Nachweis, Beweis; documentary proof** = proof in the form of a document **Urkundenbeweis**

◊ **-proof** *suffix* which prevents something getting in *or* getting out *or* harming **-dicht, -sicher;** *dustproof cover; inflation-proof pension; soundproof studio*

property *noun*

(a) personal property = things which belong to a person **Privateigentum;** *the storm caused considerable damage to personal property; the management is not responsible for property left in the hotel rooms*

(b) land and buildings **Grundbesitz, Immobilien, Liegenschaften;** *property tax; damage to property or property damage; the commercial property market is booming;* **the office has been bought by a property company** = by a company which buys buildings to lease them **das Büro ist von einer Immobiliengesellschaft gekauft worden; property developer** = person who buys old buildings *or* empty land and builds new buildings for sale or rent **Bauunternehmer, der zum Wiederverkauf baut od renoviert; private property** = property which belongs to a private person and not to the public **Privatgrundstück**

(c) a building **Gebäude;** *we have several properties for sale in the centre of the town*

NOTE: no plural for (a) or (b)

proportion *noun* part (of a total) **Teil, Anteil;** *a proportion of the pre-tax profit is set aside for contingencies; only a small proportion of our sales comes from retail shops;* **in proportion to** = showing how something is related to something else **im Verhältnis zu;** *profits went up in proportion to the fall in overhead costs; sales in Europe are small in proportion to those in the USA*

◇ **proportional** *adjective* directly related **proportional;** *the increase in profit is proportional to reduction in overheads*

◇ **proportionately** *adverb* in proportion **verhältnismäßig**

proposal *noun*
(a) suggestion *or* thing suggested **Vorschlag, Antrag;** *to make a proposal or to put forward a proposal to the board;* **the committee turned down the proposal** = the committee refused to accept what was suggested **der Ausschuß hat den Antrag abgewiesen**
(b) official document with details of a property *or* person to be insured which is sent to the insurance company when asking for an insurance **Versicherungsantrag**

◇ **propose** *verb*
(a) to suggest that something should be done **vorschlagen; to propose a motion** = to ask a meeting to vote for a motion and explain the reasons for this **einen Antrag stellen; to propose someone as president** = to ask a group to vote for someone to become president **jdn als Vorsitzenden vorschlagen**
(b) to propose to = to say that you intend to do something **vorhaben;** *I propose to repay the loan at £20 a month*

◇ **proposer** *noun* person who proposes a motion at a meeting **Antragsteller/-in**

◇ **proposition** *noun* commercial deal which is suggested **Angebot; it will never be a commercial proposition** = it is not likely to make a profit **es wird nie ein rentables Angebot sein**

proprietary *adjective*
(a) product (such as a medicine) which is made and owned by a company **gesetzlich geschützt, Marken-; proprietary drug** = drug which is made by a particular company and marketed under a brand name **patentrechtlich geschütztes Arzneimittel**
(b) *(in South Africa and Australia)* **proprietary company** = private limited company **Gesellschaft mit beschränkter Haftung**

◇ **proprietor** *noun* owner **Eigentümer, Inhaber;** *the proprietor of a hotel or a hotel proprietor*

◇ **proprietress** *noun* woman owner **Eigentümerin, Inhaberin;** *the proprietress of an advertising consultancy*

pro rata *adjective & adverb* at an amount which varies according to the rate applied **anteilmäßig, anteilig;** *a pro rata payment; to pay someone pro rata*

prosecute *verb* to bring (someone) to court to answer a criminal charge **anklagen, strafrechtlich verfolgen;** *he was prosecuted for embezzlement*

◇ **prosecution** *noun*
(a) act of bringing someone to court to answer a charge **Anklage, strafrechtliche Verfolgung;** *his prosecution for embezzlement*
(b) people who have prosecuted someone **Staatsanwaltschaft, Anklagevertretung;** *the costs of the case will be borne by the prosecution;* **prosecution counsel** *or* **counsel for the prosecution** = lawyer acting for the prosecution **Vertreter der Anklage**
NOTE: no plural for (b)

prospect *noun*
(a) prospects = possibilities for the future **Aussichten; his job prospects are good** = he is very likely to find a job **er hat gute Berufsaussichten; prospects for the market** *or* **market prospects are worse than those of last year** = sales in the market are likely to be lower than they were last year **die Markterwartungen sind schlechter als letztes Jahr**
(b) possibility that something will happen **Chance, Möglichkeit;** *there is no prospect of negotiations coming to an end soon*
(c) person who may become a customer **Interessent/-in;** *the salesmen were looking out for possible prospects*

◇ **prospective** *adjective* which may happen in the future **voraussichtlich; a prospective buyer** = someone who may buy in the future **ein potentieller Käufer;** *there is no shortage of prospective buyers for the computer*

◇ **prospectus** *noun*
(a) document which gives information to attract buyers *or* customers **Prospekt;** *the restaurant has girls handing out prospectuses in the street*
(b) document which gives information about a company whose shares are being sold to the public for the first time **Subskriptions-, Emissionsprospekt**
NOTE: plural is **prospectuses**

prosperous *adjective* rich **wohlhabend; gutgehend, blühend;** *a prosperous shopkeeper; a prosperous town*

◇ **prosperity** *noun* being rich **Wohlstand, Prosperität; in times of prosperity** = when people are rich **in Zeiten allgemeinen Wohlstandes**

NOTE: no plural

protect *verb* to defend something against harm **schützen, absichern;** *the workers are protected from unfair dismissal by government legislation; the computer is protected by a plastic cover; the cover is supposed to protect the machine from dust;* **to protect an industry by imposing tariff barriers** = to stop a local industry from being hit by foreign competition by stopping foreign products from being imported **die Industrie durch die Einführung von Zollschranken schützen**

◇ **protection** *noun* thing which protects **Schutz;** *the legislation offers no protection to part-time workers;* **consumer protection** = protecting consumers against unfair *or* illegal traders **Verbraucherschutz**
NOTE: no plural

◇ **protective** *adjective* which protects **Schutz-; protective tariff** = tariff which tries to ban imports to stop them competing with local products **Schutzzoll; protective cover** = cover which protects a machine **Schutzhülle**

pro tem *adverb* temporarily *or* for a time **zur Zeit, z.Zt.**

protest
1 *noun*
(a) statement *or* action to show that you do not approve of something **Protest;** *to make a protest against high prices;* **sit-down protest** = action by members of the staff who occupy their place of work and refuse to leave **Sit-in; in protest at** = showing that you do not approve of something **aus Protest gegen;** *the staff occupied the offices in protest at the low pay offer;* **to do something under protest** = to do something, but say that you do not approve of it **etwas unter Protest tun**
(b) official document which proves that a bill of exchange has not been paid **Wechselprotest**
2 *verb*
(a) to protest against something = to say that you do not approve of something **gegen etwas protestieren/Einspruch erheben;** *the importers are protesting against the ban on luxury goods* (NOTE: GB English is **to protest against something,** but US English is **to protest something)**
(b) to protest a bill = to draw up a document to prove that a bill of exchange has not been paid **Wechselprotest einlegen**

prototype *noun* first model of a new machine before it goes into production **Prototyp;** *prototype car or prototype plane; the company is showing the prototype of the new model at the exhibition*

provide *verb*
(a) to provide for = to allow for something which may happen in the future **vorsehen, Vorsorge treffen für etwas;** *the contract provides for an annual increase in charges; £10,000 of expenses have been provided for in the budget*
(b) to put money aside in accounts to cover expenditure *or* loss in the future **bereitstellen;** *£25,000 is provided against bad debts*
(c) to provide someone with something = to supply something to someone **jdm etwas zur Verfügung stellen, jdn mit etwas versorgen;** *each rep is provided with a company car; staff uniforms are provided by the hotel*

◇ **provided that** *or* **providing** *conjunction* on condition that **vorausgesetzt, daß;** *the goods will be delivered next week provided or providing the drivers are not on strike*

◇ **provident** *adjective* which provides benefits in case of illness *or* old age, etc. **Unterstützungs-, Fürsorge-;** *a provident fund; a provident society*

province *noun*
(a) large division of a country **Gebiet, Provinz, Region;** *the provinces of Canada*
(b) the provinces = parts of any country away from the main capital town **Provinz;** *there are fewer retail outlets in the provinces than in the capital*

◇ **provincial** *adjective* referring to a province *or* to the provinces **Provinz-, regional; provinziell, kleinstädtisch;** *a provincial government; a provincial branch of a national bank*

provision *noun*
(a) to make provision for = to see that something is allowed for in the future **Vorkehrungen/Vorsorge treffen für; there is no provision for** *or* **no provision has been made for car parking in the plans for the office block** = the plans do not include space for cars to park **in den Plänen für das Bürogebäude sind keine Parkplätze vorgesehen**
(b) money put aside in accounts in case it is needed in the future **Rücklage, Rückstellung;** *the bank has made a £2m provision for bad debts*
(c) legal condition **Klausel, Bestimmung; we have made provision to this effect** = we have put into the contract terms which will make this work **wir haben für diesen Fall Klauseln eingebaut**
(d) provisions = food **Lebensmittel, Proviant**

◇ **provisional** *adjective* temporary *or* not final or permanent **vorläufig, provisorisch, Interims-;** *provisional forecast of sales; provisional budget; they telexed their provisional acceptance of the contract*

◇ **provisionally** *adverb* not finally **vorläufig, provisorisch;** *the contract has been accepted provisionally*

> QUOTE landlords can create short lets of dwellings which will be free from the normal security of tenure provisions
>
> *Times*

proviso *noun* condition in a contract **Vorbehalt, Vorbehaltsklausel;** *we are signing the contract with the proviso that the terms can be discussed again after six months*

proxy *noun*
(a) document which gives someone the power to act on behalf of someone else **Vollmacht, Handlungsvollmacht;** *to sign by proxy;* **proxy vote** = votes made by proxy **durch einen Stimmrechtsbevollmächtigten/Stellvertreter abgegebene Stimme;** *the proxy votes were all in favour of the board's recommendation*
(b) person who acts on behalf of someone else **Bevollmächtigter, Stellvertreter;** *to act as proxy for someone*

P.S. *noun* = POST SCRIPTUM additional note at the end of a letter **P.S.;** *did you read the P.S. at the end of the letter?*

PSBR = PUBLIC SECTOR BORROWING REQUIREMENT

pt = PINT

ptas = PESETAS

Pty = PROPRIETARY COMPANY

public
1 *adjective*
(a) referring to all the people in general **öffentlich; public holiday** = day when all workers rest and enjoy themselves instead of working **Feiertag; public image** = idea which the people have of a company *or* a person **Image;** *the minister is trying to improve his public image;* **public transport** = transport (such as buses, trains) which is used by any member of the public **öffentliche Verkehrsmittel**
(b) referring to the government or the state **staatlich; public expenditure** = spending of money by the local *or* central government **öffentliche Ausgaben; public finance** = the raising of money by governments (by taxes or borrowing) and the spending of it **Staatsfinanzen; public funds** = government money available for expenditure **öffentliche Mittel/Gelder; public ownership** = situation where an industry is nationalized **Staatsbesitz**
(c) Public Limited Company = company whose shares can be bought on the Stock Exchange **Aktiengesellschaft; the company is going public** = the company is going to place some of its shares for sale on the stock market so that anyone can buy them **das Unternehmen wird in eine Aktiengesellschaft umgewandelt**
2 *noun* **the public** *or* **the general public** = the people **Öffentlichkeit; in public** = in front of everyone **in der Öffentlichkeit, öffentlich;** *in public he said that the company would soon be in profit, but in private he was less optimistic*
NOTE: no plural

◇ **public relations** *plural noun* keeping good relations between a company *or* a group and the public so that people know what the company is doing and can approve of it **PR-Arbeit, Public Relations, Öffentlichkeitsarbeit;** *a public relations man; he works in public relations; a public relations firm handles all our publicity;* **a public relations exercise** = a campaign to improve public relations **eine PR-Kampagne, eine Kampagne zur Verbesserung der Public Relations**

◇ **public sector** *noun* nationalized industries and services **öffentlicher Bereich, staatlicher Sektor;** *a report on wage rises in the public sector or on public sector wage settlements;* **public sector borrowing requirement** = amount of money which a government has to borrow to pay for its own spending **Kreditbedarf der öffentlichen Hand**

publication *noun*
(a) making something public **Veröffentlichung, Bekanntgabe, Bekanntmachung;** *the publication of the latest trade figures*
(b) printed document which is to be sold *or* given to the public **Publikation, Veröffentlichung;** *he asked the library for a list of government publications;* **the company has six business publications** = the company publishes six magazines or newspapers referring to business **das Unternehmen gibt sechs Wirtschaftspublikationen heraus**
NOTE: no plural for (a)

publicity *noun* attracting the attention of the public to products or services by mentioning them in the media **Werbung, Reklame; publicity agency** *or* **publicity**

bureau = office which organizes publicity for companies who do not have publicity departments **Werbeagentur; publicity budget** = money allowed for expenditure on publicity **Werbeetat; publicity campaign** = period when planned publicity takes place **Werbeaktion, Werbekampagne; publicity copy** = text of an advertisement before it is printed **Werbetextentwurf; publicity department** = section of a company which organizes the company's publicity **Werbeabteilung; publicity expenditure** = money spent on publicity **Werbekosten; publicity manager** = person in charge of a publicity department **Werbeleiter; publicity matter** = sheets *or* posters *or* leaflets used for publicity **Werbematerial**

NOTE: no plural

◊ **publicize** *verb* to attract people's attention to a product for sale *or* a service *or* an entertainment **werben, Werbung/Reklame machen;** *the campaign is intended to publicize the services of the tourist board; we are trying to publicize our products by advertisements on buses*

publish

publish *verb* to have a document (such as a catalogue *or* book *or* magazine *or* newspaper) written and printed and then sell *or* give it to the public **veröffentlichen, herausgeben, verlegen;** *the society publishes its list of members annually; the government has not published the figures on which its proposals are based; the company publishes six magazines for the business market*

◊ **publisher** *noun* person *or* company which publishes **Verleger, Verlag**

pull off

pull off *verb informal* to succeed in negotiating a deal **mit Erfolg abwickeln, an Land ziehen**

◊ **pull out** *verb* to stop being part of a deal *or* agreement **zurücktreten, aussteigen;** *our Australian partners pulled out of the contract*

pump priming

pump priming *noun* government investment in new projects which it hopes will benefit the economy **Ankurbelung durch staatliche Investitionen**

punched card

punched card *noun* card with holes in it which a computer can read and store as information **Lochkarte**

punt

1 *noun* money used in the Republic of Ireland **irisches Pfund**

2 *verb* to gamble *or* to bet (on something) **spielen, wetten**

◊ **punter** *noun* person who gambles *or* who hopes to make money on the Stock Exchange **Spieler, Wetter; Börsenspekulant**

purchase

1 *noun* thing which has been bought **Kauf; to make a purchase** = to buy something **einen Kauf tätigen, eine Anschaffung machen; purchase book** = records of purchases **Wareneingangsbuch; purchase ledger** = book in which expenditure is noted **Einkaufsbuch; purchase order** = official order made out by a purchasing department for goods which a company wants to buy **Auftrag, Bestellung;** *we cannot supply you without a purchase order number;* **purchase price** = price paid for something **Kaufpreis; purchase tax** = tax paid on things which are bought **Kaufsteuer;** *entspricht* **Verbrauchsteuer; bulk purchase** *or* **quantity purchase** = buying of large quantities of goods at low prices **Mengen-, Posteneinkauf; cash purchase** = purchase made in cash **Barkauf; hire purchase** = system of buying something by paying a sum regularly each month **Raten-, Teilzahlungskauf;** *he is buying a refrigerator on hire purchase;* **hire purchase agreement** = contract to pay for something by instalments **Teilzahlungskaufvertrag**

2 *verb* to buy **kaufen, erwerben, erstehen, einkaufen, ankaufen; to purchase something for cash** = to pay cash for something **etwas bar kaufen**

◊ **purchaser** *noun* person *or* company which purchases **Käufer/-in, Erwerber/-in; the company is looking for a purchaser** = the company is trying to find someone who will buy it **für das Unternehmen wird ein Käufer gesucht;** *the company has found a purchaser for its warehouse*

◊ **purchasing** *noun* buying **Einkauf, Warenbeschaffung; purchasing department** = section of a company which deals with buying of stock, raw materials, equipment, etc. **Abteilung Einkauf; purchasing manager** = head of a purchasing department **Einkaufsleiter; purchasing officer** = person in a company *or* organization who is responsible for buying stock, raw materials, equipment, etc. **Einkäufer; purchasing power** = quantity of goods which can be bought by a group of people *or* with an amount of money **Kaufkraft;** *the decline in the purchasing power of the pound;* **central purchasing** = purchasing organized by the main office for all departments or branches **zentraler Einkauf**

NOTE: no plural

purpose

purpose *noun* aim *or* plan **Zweck; we need the invoice for tax purposes** *or* **for the purpose of declaration to the tax authorities** = in order for it to be declared to the tax authorities **wir benötigen die Rechnung zu Steuerzwecken**

put

1 *noun* **put option** = right to sell shares at a certain price at a certain date **Verkaufsoption**

2 *verb* to place *or* to fix **festsetzen, festlegen, setzen, legen; the accounts put the stock value at £10,000** = the accounts state that the value of the stock is £10,000 **in den Büchern wird der Warenwert auf £10.000 festgesetzt; to put a proposal to the vote** = to ask a meeting to vote for *or* against the proposal **über einen Antrag abstimmen lassen; to put a proposal to the board** = to ask the board to consider a suggestion **dem Vorstand einen Antrag unterbreiten**

NOTE: **putting - put**

◇ **put down** *verb*

(a) to make a deposit **anzahlen;** *to put down money on a house*

(b) to write an item in a ledger *or* an account book **eintragen, aufschreiben;** *to put down a figure for expenses*

◇ **put in** *verb* **to put an ad in a paper** = to have an ad printed in a newspaper **ein Inserat aufgeben; to put in a bid for something** = to offer (usually in writing) to buy something **für etwas ein Angebot machen; to put in an estimate for something** = to give someone a written calculation of the probable costs of carrying out a job **für etwas einen Kostenvoranschlag machen; to put in a claim for damage** = to ask an insurance company to pay for damage **einen Schadensersatzanspruch stellen; the union put in a 6% wage claim** = the union asked for a 6% increase in wages **die Gewerkschaft stellte eine Lohnforderung von 6%**

◇ **put into** *verb* **to put money into a business** = to invest money in a business **Geld in ein Geschäft stecken**

◇ **put off** *verb* to arrange for something to take place later than planned **ver-, aufschieben;** *the meeting was put off for two weeks; he asked if we could put the visit off until tomorrow*

◇ **put on** *verb* **to put an item on the agenda** = to list an item for discussion at a meeting **einen Punkt auf die Tagesordnung setzen; to put an embargo on trade** = to forbid trade **ein Handelsembargo verhängen; property shares put on gains of 10%-15%** = shares in property companies increased in value by 10%-15% **Immobilienaktien verzeichnen einen Wertzuwachs von 10-15%**

◇ **put out** *verb* to send out **vergeben, außer Haus geben;** *to put work out to freelancers; we put all our typing out to a bureau;* **to put work out to contract** = to decide that work should be done by a company on a contract, rather than employ members of staff to do it **Unteraufträge vergeben**

◇ **put up** *verb*

(a) who put up the money for the shop? = who provided the investment money for the shop to start? **wer hat das Geld für den Laden zur Verfügung gestellt?; to put something up for sale** = to advertise that something is for sale **etwas zum Verkauf anbieten;** *when he retired he decided to put his town flat up for sale*

(b) to increase *or* to make higher **erhöhen, heraufsetzen;** *the shop has put up all its prices by 5%*

Qq

quadruplicate *noun* **in quadruplicate** = with the original and three copies **in vierfacher Ausfertigung;** *the invoices are printed in quadruplicate*

NOTE: no plural

qualification *noun*

(a) proof that you have completed a specialized course of study **Qualifikation;** *to have the right qualifications for the job;* **professional qualifications** = documents which show that someone has successfully finished a course of study which allows him to work in one of the professions **fachliche Qualifikation; Zeugnis**

(b) period of qualification = time which has to pass before someone qualifies for something **Zulassungsfrist**

◇ **qualify** *verb*

(a) to qualify for = to be in the right position for *or* to be entitled to **berechtigt sein zu;** *the company does not qualify for a government grant; she qualifies for unemployment pay*

(b) to qualify as = to follow a specialized course and pass examinations so that you can do a certain job **seine Ausbildung zum ... abschließen;** *she has qualified as an accountant; he will qualify as a solicitor next year*

(c) the auditors have qualified the accounts = the auditors have found something in the accounts of the company which they do not agree with, and have noted it **die Wirtschaftsprüfer haben den Jahresabschluß mit einschränkenden Bemerkungen verabschiedet**

◇ **qualified** *adjective*

(a) having passed special examinations in a subject **ausgebildet, qualifiziert;** *she is a qualified accountant; we have appointed a qualified designer to supervise the new*

factory project; **highly qualified** = with very good results in examinations **hochqualifiziert;** *all our staff are highly qualified; they employ twenty-six highly qualified engineers*
(b) with some reservations *or* conditions **bedingt, mit Einschränkungen;** *qualified acceptance of a contract; the plan received qualified approval from the board*
(c) qualified accounts = accounts which have been noted by the auditors because they contain something with which the auditors do not agree **berichtigter Jahresabschluß**

◇ **qualifying** *adjective*
(a) qualifying period = time which has to pass before something qualifies for a grant *or* subsidy, etc. **Wartezeit;** *there is a six-month qualifying period before you can get a grant from the local authority*
(b) qualifying shares = number of shares which you need to earn to get a bonus issue *or* to be a director of the company, etc. **Pflichtaktien**

> QUOTE federal examiners will also determine which of the privately insured savings and loans qualify for federal insurance
> *Wall Street Journal*
>
> QUOTE applicants will be professionally qualified and ideally have a degree in Commerce and post graduate management qualifications
> *Australian Financial Review*

quality *noun*
(a) what something is like *or* how good or bad something is **Qualität;** *good quality or bad quality;* **we sell only quality farm produce** = we sell only farm produce of the best quality **wir verkaufen nur Agrarprodukte bester Qualität;** *there is a market for good quality secondhand computers;* **high quality** *or* **top quality** = very best quality **Spitzenqualität, erstklassige Qualität;** *the store specializes in high quality imported items*
(b) quality control = checking that the quality of a product is good **Qualitätskontrolle; quality controller** = person who checks the quality of a product **Qualitätskontrolleur**
NOTE: no plural

quango *noun* official body, set up by a government to investigate or deal with a special problem; *entspricht* **halbstaatliche Organisation**

quantify *verb* **to quantify the effect of something** = to show the effect of something in figures **die Wirkung von etwas in Zahlen/quantitativ ausdrücken;** *it is impossible to quantify the effect of the new legislation on our turnover*

◇ **quantifiable** *adjective* which can be quantified **meßbar, in Zahlen ausdrückbar;** *the effect of the change in the discount structure is not quantifiable*

quantity *noun*
(a) amount *or* number of items **Menge, Quantität, Anzahl;** *a small quantity of illegal drugs; he bought a large quantity of spare parts*
(b) large amount **große Stückzahl;** *the company offers a discount for quantity purchase;* **quantity discount** = discount given to a customer who buys large quantities of goods **Mengenrabatt**
(c) to carry out a quantity survey = to estimate the amount of materials and the cost of the labour required for a construction project **eine Baukostenschätzung erstellen; quantity surveyor** = person who carries out a quantity survey **Baukostenschätzer**

quart *noun* old measure of liquids *or* of loose goods, such as seeds (= 1.136 litres) **Quart**

quarter *noun*
(a) one of four equal parts **Viertel; a quarter of a litre** *or* **a quarter litre** = 250 millilitres **ein Viertelliter; a quarter of an hour** = 15 minutes **eine Viertelstunde; three quarters** = 75% **drei Viertel;** *three quarters of the staff are less than thirty years old; he paid only a quarter of the list price*
(b) period of three months **Quartal, Vierteljahr; first quarter** *or* **second quarter** *or* **third quarter** *or* **fourth quarter** *or* **last quarter** = periods of three months from January to the end of March *or* from April to the end of June *or* from July to the end of September *or* from October to the end of the year **das erste od zweite od dritte od vierte/letzte Quartal;** *the instalments are payable at the end of each quarter; the first quarter's rent is payable in advance;* **quarter day** = day at the end of a quarter, when rents *or* fees, etc. should be paid **Quartalsende, Quartalstag**
(c) *US informal* 25 cent coin **25 Centstück**

◇ **quarterly** *adjective & adverb* happening every three months *or* happening four times a year **vierteljährlich, quartalsweise;** *there is a quarterly charge for electricity; the bank sends us a quarterly statement; we agreed to pay the rent quarterly or on a quarterly basis*

> QUOTE corporate profits for the first quarter showed a 4 per cent drop from last year's final three months
> *Financial Times*
>
> QUOTE economists believe the economy is picking up this quarter and will do better still in the second half of the year
> *Sunday Times*

quartile *noun* one of three figures below which 25%, 50% *or* 75% of a total falls **Quartil**

quasi- *prefix* almost *or* which seems like **Quasi, quasi-;** *a quasi-official body*

quay *noun* place in a harbour where ships tie up **Kai; price ex quay** = price of goods after they have been unloaded, not including transport from the harbour **Preis ab Kai**

QC = QUEEN'S COUNSEL

query
1 *noun* question **Frage, Rückfrage;** *the chief accountant had to answer a mass of queries from the auditors*
2 *verb* to ask a question about something *or* to suggest that something may be wrong **erkundigen; in Frage stellen, bezweifeln, beanstanden;** *the shareholders queried the payments to the chairman's son*

question
1 *noun*
(a) words which need an answer **Frage;** *the managing director refused to answer questions about redundancies; the market research team prepared a series of questions to test the public's reactions to colour and price*
(b) problem **Problem;** *he raised the question of moving to less expensive offices; the main question is that of cost; the board discussed the question of redundancy payments*
2 *verb*
(a) to ask questions **befragen, Fragen stellen, verhören;** *the police questioned the accounts staff for four hours; she questioned the chairman on the company's investment policy*
(b) to query *or* to suggest that something may be wrong **in Frage stellen, bezweifeln;** *we all question how accurate the computer printout is*

◊ **questionnaire** *noun* printed list of questions, especially used in market research **Fragebogen;** *to send out a questionnaire to test the opinions of users of the system; to answer or to fill in a questionnaire about holidays abroad*

queue
1 *noun*
(a) line of people waiting one behind the other **(Warte)schlange;** *to form a queue or to join a queue; queues formed at the doors of the bank when the news spread about its possible collapse;* **dole queue** = line of people waiting to collect their unemployment money **Arbeitslosenschlange**
(b) series of documents (such as orders, application forms) which are dealt with in order **Unterlagenstapel his order went to the end of the queue** = his order was dealt with last **seine Bestellung landete zuunterst, seine Bestellung wanderte an das Ende des Stapels; mortgage queue** = list of people waiting for mortgages **Hypotheken-Warteliste**
2 *verb* to form a line one after the other for something **Schlange stehen, anstehen, sich anstellen;** *when food was rationed, people had to queue for bread; we queued for hours to get tickets; a list of companies queueing to be launched on the Stock Exchange*

quick *adjective* fast *or* not taking any time **schnell;** *the company made a quick recovery; he is looking for a quick return on his investments; we are hoping for a quick sale*

◊ **quickly** *adverb* without taking much time **schnell;** *the sale of the company went through quickly; the accountant quickly looked through the pile of invoices*

quiet *adjective* calm *or* not excited **ruhig, lustlos, flau;** *the market is very quiet; currency exchanges were quieter after the government's statement on exchange rates;* **on the quiet** = in secret **heimlich;** *he transferred his bank account to Switzerland on the quiet*

quit *verb* to resign *or* to leave (a job) **kündigen, seine Stelle aufgeben;** *he quit after an argument with the managing director; several of the managers are quitting to set up their own company*
NOTE: **quitting - quit**

quite *adverb*
(a) more or less **ziemlich, recht;** *he is quite a good salesman; she can type quite fast; sales are quite satisfactory in the first quarter*
(b) very *or* completely **durchaus, sehr wohl;** *he is quite capable of running the department alone; the company is quite possibly going to be sold*
(c) quite a few *or* **quite a lot** = many **recht viele;** *quite a few of our sales staff are women; quite a lot of orders come in the pre-Christmas period*

quorum *noun* number of people who have to be present at a meeting to make it valid **beschlußfähige Anzahl; to have a quorum** = to have enough people present for a meeting to go ahead **beschlußfähig sein;** *do we have a quorum?*

quota *noun* fixed amount of something which is allowed **Kontingent, Quote; import quota** = fixed quantity of a particular type of goods which the government allows to be imported **Einfuhrkontingent, Importquote;** *the government has imposed a quota on the importation of cars; the quota on imported cars has been lifted;* **quota system** = system where imports *or* supplies are regulated by fixing maximum amounts **Kontingentierungssystem, Quotensystem; to arrange distribution through a quota system** = to arrange distribution by allowing each distributor only a certain number of items **den Vertrieb durch ein Quotensystem regeln**

> QUOTE Canada agreed to a new duty-free quota of 600,000 tonnes a year
> *Globe and Mail (Toronto)*

quote
1 *verb*
(a) to repeat words used by someone else; to repeat a reference number **zitieren, anführen; angeben;** *he quoted figures from the annual report; in reply please quote this number; when making a complaint please quote the batch number printed on the box; he replied, quoting the number of the account*
(b) to estimate *or* to say what costs may be **(einen Preis) angeben/nennen;** *to quote a price for supplying stationery; their prices are always quoted in dollars; he quoted me a price of £1,026; can you quote for supplying 20,000 envelopes?*
2 *noun informal* estimate of how much something will cost **Angebot;** *to give someone a quote for supplying computers; we have asked for quotes for refitting the shop; his quote was the lowest of three; we accepted the lowest quote*

◇ **quotation** *noun*
(a) estimate of how much something will cost **Kostenvoranschlag;** *they sent in their quotation for the job; to ask for quotations for refitting the shop; his quotation was much lower than all the others; we accepted the lowest quotation*
(b) quotation on the Stock Exchange *or* **Stock Exchange quotation** = listing of the price of a share on the Stock Exchange **Notierung, Kursnotierung; the company is going for a quotation on the Stock Exchange** = the company has applied to the Stock Exchange to have its shares listed **das Unternehmen hat die Börsennotierung beantragt;** *we are seeking a stock market quotation*

◇ **quoted** *adjective* **quoted company** = company whose shares can be bought *or* sold on the Stock Exchange **Unternehmen, dessen Aktien an der Börse zugelassen sind; quoted shares** = shares which can be bought *or* sold on the Stock Exchange **(an der Börse) notierte Aktien**

> QUOTE a Bermudan-registered company quoted on the Luxembourg stock exchange
> *Lloyd's List*
>
> QUOTE banks operating on the foreign exchange market refrained from quoting forward US/Hongkong dollar exchange rates
> *South China Morning Post*

qty = QUANTITY

qwerty *or* **QWERTY** *noun* **qwerty keyboard** = English language keyboard for a typewriter *or* computer, where the first letters are Q-W-E-R-T-Y **englische Tastatur;** *the computer has a normal qwerty keyboard*

Rr

R&D = RESEARCH AND DEVELOPMENT *the R&D department; the company spends millions on R&D*

rack *noun*
(a) frame to hold items for display **Ständer, Gestell, Regal;** *card rack; display rack; magazine rack;* **rack jobber** = wholesaler who sells goods by putting them on racks in retail shops **Regalgroßhändler**
(b) rack rent = (i) very high rent; (ii) full yearly rent of a property let on a normal lease **(i) Wuchermiete; (ii) Jahresmiete**

racket *noun* illegal deal which makes a lot of money **betrügerisches Geschäft, Betrügerei, Gaunerei;** *he runs a cut-price ticket racket*

◇ **racketeer** *noun* person who runs a racket **Betrüger/-in, Gauner/-in**

raid *noun* **dawn raid** = buying large numbers of shares in a company at the beginning of a day's trading **überraschende Aktienaufkaufaktion bei Börseneröffnung; bear raid** = selling large numbers of shares to try to bring down prices **Baissemanöver, Baissierangriff**

◇ **raider** *noun* company which buys shares in another company before making a takeover bid **Raider, agressiver Aktienaufkäufer (mit Übernahmeabsicht)**

rail *noun* railway *or* system of travel using trains **Bahn;** *six million commuters travel to work by rail each day; we ship all our goods by rail; rail travellers are complaining about* *rising fares; rail travel is cheaper than air travel;* **free on rail** = price including all the seller's costs until the goods are delivered to the railway for shipment **frei Waggon**

◊ **railhead** *noun* end of a railway line **Endbahnhof;** *the goods will be sent to the railhead by lorry*

◊ **railroad** *noun US* system using trains to carry passengers and goods **Bahn**

◊ **railway** *noun* system using trains to carry passengers and goods **Bahn;** *a railway station; a railway line; the British railway network*

raise

1 *noun US* increase in salary **Gehalts-, Lohnerhöhung;** *he asked the boss for a raise; she is pleased - she has had her raise*

NOTE: GB English is **rise**

2 *verb*

(a) to ask a meeting to discuss a question **vorbringen;** *to raise a question or a point at a meeting; in answer to the questions raised by Mr Smith; the chairman tried to prevent the question of redundancies being raised*

(b) to raise an invoice = to write out an invoice **eine Rechnung ausstellen**

(c) to increase *or* to make higher **erhöhen, anheben, heraufsetzen;** *the government has raised the tax levels; air fares will be raised on June 1st; the company raised its dividend by 10%; when the company raised its prices, it lost half of its share of the market*

(d) to obtain (money) *or* to organize (a loan) **beschaffen, aufbringen;** *the company is trying to raise the capital to fund its expansion programme; the government raises more money by indirect taxation than by direct; where will he raise the money from to start up his business?*

> QUOTE the company said yesterday that its recent share issue has been oversubscribed, raising A$225.5m
>
> *Financial Times*
>
> QUOTE investment trusts can raise capital, but this has to be done as a company does, by a rights issue of equity
>
> *Investors Chronicle*

rake in

verb to gather together **zusammenbringen, einstreichen; to rake in cash** *or* **to rake it in** = to make a lot of money **Geld scheffeln**

◊ **rake-off** *noun* commission **Provision;** *the group gets a rake-off on all the company's sales; he got a £100,000 rake-off for introducing the new business*

NOTE: plural is **rake-offs**

rally

1 *noun* rise in price when the trend has been downwards **Aufschwung, Erholung;** *shares staged a rally on the Stock Exchange; after a brief rally shares fell back to a new low*

2 *verb* to rise in price, when the trend has been downwards **sich erholen, anziehen;** *shares rallied on the news of the latest government figures*

ramp

noun **loading ramp** = raised platform which makes it easier to load goods onto a lorry **Laderampe**

random

adjective done without making any special choice **Zufalls-, zufällig, willkürlich; random check** = check on items taken from a group without any special choice **Stichprobe; random error** = computer error which has no special reason **Zufallsfehler; random sample** = sample for testing taken without any choice **zufällige Stichprobe; random sampling** = choosing samples for testing without any special selection **Stichprobenauswahl; at random** = without special choice **wahllos, aufs Geratewohl;** *the chairman picked out two salesmen's reports at random*

range

1 *noun*

(a) series of items from which the customer can choose **Sortiment, Angebot, Auswahl;** *we offer a wide range of sizes or range of styles; their range of products or product range is too narrow; we have the most modern range of models or model range on the market*

(b) price range variation in price from small to large **Preislage, Preisklasse;** *I am looking for something in the £2 - £3 price range; we make shoes in a wide range of prices*

(c) type of variety **Bereich;** *this falls within the company's range of activities*

2 *verb* to vary *or* to be different **reichen/gehen von ... bis, variieren;** *the company sells products ranging from the cheap down-market pens to imported luxury items; the company's salary scale ranges from £5,000 for a trainee to £50,000 for the managing director; our activities range from mining in the USA to computer servicing in Scotland*

rank

1 *noun* position in a company *or* an organization **Stellung, Rang;** *all managers are of equal rank;* **in rank order** = in order according to position of importance **nach Rangordnung**

2 *verb*

(a) to classify in order of importance **einordnen;** *candidates are ranked in order of appearance*

(b) to be in a certain position **Rang einnehmen;** *the non-voting shares rank equally with the voting shares;* **all managers**

rank equally = all managers have the same status in the company **alle Manager haben den gleichen Status**

◇ **rank and file** *noun* ordinary members of a trade union **Basis einer Gewerkschaft;** *the rank and file of the trade union membership; the decision was not liked by the rank and file;* **rank-and-file members** = ordinary members **einfache Mitglieder**

◇ **ranking** *adjective* in a certain position **rangmäßig;** *high-ranking official;* **he is the top-ranking** *or* **the senior-ranking official in the delegation** = the member of the delegation who occupies the highest official post **er ist der ranghöchste Beamte der Delegation**

rapid *adjective* fast *or* quick **schnell, rasch, prompt; we offer 5% discount for rapid settlement** = we take 5% off the price if the customer pays quickly **wir geben 5% Skonto für prompte Bezahlung**

◇ **rapidly** *adverb* quickly *or* fast **schnell, rasch;** *the company rapidly ran up debts of over £1m; the new clothes shop rapidly increased sales*

rare *adjective* not common **selten, rar;** *experienced salesmen are rare these days; it is rare to find a small business with good cash flow*

◇ **rarely** *adverb* not often **selten;** *the company's shares are rarely sold on the Stock Exchange; the chairman is rarely in his office on Friday afternoons*

rata *see* PRO RATA

rate

1 *noun*

(a) money charged for time worked *or* work completed **Satz, Gebühr, Preis; all-in rate** = price which covers all items in a purchase (such as delivery, tax and insurance, as well as the goods themselves) **Inklusivpreis; fixed rate** = charge which cannot be changed **fester Satz/Preis; flat rate** = charge which always stays the same **Pauschale; Grundgebühr; Einheitstarif;** *a flat-rate increase of 10%; we pay a flat rate for electricity each quarter; he is paid a flat rate of £2 per thousand;* **full rate** = full charge, with no reductions **voller Satz/Preis; the going rate** = the usual *or* the current rate of payment **der übliche Satz; the market rate** = normal price in the market **Marktpreis, üblicher Preis;** *we pay the going rate or the market rate for typists; the going rate for offices is £10 per square foot;* **reduced rate** = specially cheap charge **ermäßigter Tarif**

(b) discount rate = percentage taken by a bank when it buys bills **Diskontsatz; insurance rates** = amount of premium which has to be paid per £1000 of insurance **Versicherungsprämiensatz; interest rate** *or* **rate of interest** = percentage charge for borrowing money **Zinssatz; rate of return** = amount of interest *or* dividend which comes from an investment, shown as a percentage of the money invested **Rendite**

(c) bank base rates = basic rate of interest which a bank uses to calculate the actual rate of interest on loans to customers **Eckzins, Bankleitzinssatz; cross rate** = exchange rate between two currencies expressed in a third currency **Kreuzkurs; exchange rate** *or* **rate of exchange** = rate at which one currency is exchanged for another **Wechselkurs;** *what is today's rate or the current rate for the dollar?;* **to calculate costs on a fixed exchange rate** = to calculate costs on an exchange rate which does not change **die Kosten berechnen anhand eines festen Wechselkurses; forward rate** = rate for purchase of foreign currency at a fixed price for delivery at a later date **Devisenterminkurs; freight rates** = charges for transporting goods **Frachtgebühren; letter rate** *or* **parcel rate** = postage (calculated by weight) for sending a letter *or* a parcel **Briefgebühr; Paketgebühr;** *it is more expensive to send a packet letter rate but it will get there quicker;* **night rate** = cheap telephone calls at night **Nachttarif**

(d) amount *or* number *or* speed compared with something else **Rate;** *the rate of increase in redundancies; the rate of absenteeism or the absenteeism rate always increases in fine weather;* **birth rate** = number of children born per 1,000 of the population **Geburtenrate; call rate** = number of calls (per day *or* per week) which a salesman makes on customers **Besuchshäufigkeit; depreciation rate** = rate at which an asset is depreciated each year in the company accounts **Abschreibungssatz; error rate** = number of mistakes per thousand entries *or* per page **Fehlerquote; rate of sales** = speed at which units are sold **Absatzgeschwindigkeit**

(e) *GB* local taxes on property; *entspricht* **Gemeindeabgaben, Grundsteuer;** *the local authority has fixed or has set the rate for next year; our rates have gone up by 25% this year*

2 *verb*

(a) to rate someone highly = to value someone *or* to think someone is very good **jdn hoch einschätzen**

(b) highly-rated part of London = part of London with high local taxes **ein Londoner Stadtteil mit hohen Gemeindeabgaben**

◇ **rateable** *adjective* **rateable value** = value of a property as a basis for calculating local taxes **Einheitswert**

◇ **ratepayer** *noun* **domestic ratepayer** = person who pays local taxes on a house *or* flat **privater Gemeindeabgabenzahler; business ratepayer** = business which pays local taxes on a shop *or* factory, etc. **kommerzieller Gemeindeabgabenzahler**

> QUOTE state-owned banks cut their prime rate a percentage point to 11%
> *Wall Street Journal*
>
> QUOTE the unions had argued that public sector pay rates had slipped behind rates applying in private sector employment
> *Australian Financial Review*
>
> QUOTE royalties have been levied at a rate of 12.5% of full production
> *Lloyd's List*

ratify *verb* to approve officially **ratifizieren, genehmigen;** *the agreement has to be ratified by the board*

◇ **ratification** *noun* official approval **Ratifizierung, Genehmigung;** *the agreement has to go to the board for ratification*

rating *noun*
(a) valuing of property **Veranlagung, Schätzung; rating officer** = official in a local authority who decides the rateable value of a house **Beamter, der den Einheitswert festlegt**
(b) credit rating = amount which a credit agency feels a customer will be able to repay **Bonitätsbeurteilung; merit rating** = judging how well a worker does his work, so that he can be paid according to merit **Leistungsbeurteilung; performance rating** = judging how well a share *or* a company has performed **Leistungsbeurteilung**
(c) ratings = estimated number of people who watch TV programmes **Einschaltquote;** *the show is high in the ratings, which means it will attract good publicity*

ratio *noun* proportion *or* quantity of something compared to something else **Verhältnis;** *the ratio of successes to failures; our product outsells theirs by a ratio of two to one;* **price/earnings ratio (P/E ratio)** = comparison between the market price of a share and the current dividend it produces **Kurs-Gewinn-Verhältnis;** *the shares sell at a P/E ratio of 7*

ration *verb* to allow someone only a certain amount (of food *or* money) **rationieren, zuteilen;** *to ration investment capital or to ration funds for investment;* **to ration mortgages** = to make only a certain amount of money available for house mortgages, and so restrict the number of mortgages which can be given **die Hypothekenvergabe einschränken;** *mortgages are rationed for first-time buyers*

◇ **rationing** *noun* allowing only a certain amount of something to be sold **Rationierung;** *there may be a period of food rationing this winter; building societies are warning of mortgage rationing*
NOTE: no plural

rationale *noun* set of reasons for doing something **Gründe;** *I do not understand the rationale behind the decision to sell the warehouse*

rationalization *noun* streamlining *or* making more efficient **Rationalisierung**

◇ **rationalize** *verb* to streamline *or* to make more efficient **rationalisieren;** *the rail company is trying to rationalize its freight services*

rat race *noun* competition for success in business *or* in a career **beruflicher Existenzkampf;** *he decided to get out of the rat race and buy a small farm*
NOTE: no plural

raw *adjective* in the original state *or* not processed **roh, unverarbeitet; raw data** = data as it is put into a computer, without being analyzed **Ausgangsdaten, Urdaten; raw materials** = substances which have not been manufactured (such as wool, wood, sand) **Rohstoffe**

> QUOTE it makes sense for them to produce goods for sale back home in the US from plants in Britain where raw materials are relatively cheap
> *Duns Business Month*

re *preposition* about *or* concerning *or* referring to **betreffs, bezüglich, in Bezugnahme auf;** *re your inquiry of May 29th; re: Smith's memo of yesterday; re: the agenda for the AGM*

re- *prefix* again **wieder-**

reach *verb*
(a) to arrive at a place *or* at a point **erreichen, ankommen;** *the plane reaches Hong Kong at midday; sales reached £1m in the first four months of the year; I did not reply because your letter never reached me*
(b) to come to **erzielen, kommen zu; to reach an agreement** = to agree **eine Vereinbarung treffen; to reach an accommodation with creditors** = to agree terms for a settlement with creditors **eine Einigung mit den Gläubigern erzielen; to reach a decision** = to decide **zu einer Entscheidung kommen;** *the two parties reached an agreement over the terms for the contract; the board reached a decision about closing the factory*

react *verb* **to react to** = to do *or* to say something in reply to what someone has done *or* said **reagieren auf;** *shares reacted sharply to the fall in the exchange rate; how will the chairman react when we tell him the news?*

◇ **reaction** *noun* change *or* action in reply to something said or done **Reaktion;** *the reaction of the shares to the news of the takeover bid*

read *verb* to look at printed words and understand them **lesen;** *the terms and conditions are printed in very small letters so that they are difficult to read; has the managing director read your report on sales in India?;* **can the computer read this information?** = can the computer take in this information and understand it or analyze it? **kann der Computer diese Information lesen?**

◇ **readable** *adjective* which can be read **lesbar; machine-readable codes** = sets of signs or letters (such as bar codes, post codes) which can be read and understood by a computer **computerlesbare Codes; the data has to be presented in computer-readable form** = in a form which a computer can read **die Daten müssen in computerlesbarer Form gegeben werden**

readjust *verb* to adjust again **anpassen;** *to readjust prices to take account of the rise in the costs of raw materials; shares prices readjusted quickly to the news of the devaluation*

◇ **readjustment** *noun* act of readjusting **Anpassung, Neuregelung;** *a readjustment in pricing; after the devaluation there was a period of readjustment in the exchange rates*

readvertise *verb* to advertise again **nochmals inserieren; to readvertise a post** = to put in a second advertisement for a vacant post **eine Stelle nochmals inserieren;** *all the candidates failed the test, so we will just have to readvertise*

◇ **readvertisement** *noun* second advertisement for a vacant post **Zweitinserat**

ready *adjective*
(a) fit to be used *or* to be sold **fertig, bereit;** *the order will be ready for delivery next week; the driver had to wait because the shipment was not ready;* **make-ready time** = time to get a machine ready to start production **Rüstzeit**
(b) ready cash = money which is immediately available for payment **Bargeld; these items find a ready sale in the Middle East** = these items sell rapidly *or* easily in the Middle East **diese Waren finden im Nahen Osten schnellen/reißenden Absatz**

◇ **ready-made** *or* **ready-to-wear** *adjective* (clothes) which are mass-produced, not made for each customer personally **Fertig-, fertig, gebrauchsfertig; Konfektions-, von der Stange;** *the ready-to-wear trade has suffered from foreign competition*

real *adjective*
(a) true *or* not an imitation **echt;** *his case is made of real leather or he has a real leather case; that car is a real bargain at £300;* **real income** *or* **real wages** = income which is available for spending after tax, etc. has been deducted **Realeinkommen; Reallohn; in real terms** = actually *or* really **Real-, in reeller Kaufkraft;** *prices have gone up by 3% but with inflation running at 5% that is a fall in real terms*
(b) real time = time when a computer is working on the processing of data while the problem to which the data refers is actually taking place **Echtzeit, Real-time; real-time system** = computer system where data is inputted directly into the computer which automatically processes it to produce information which can be used immediately **Echtzeitsystem**
(c) real estate = property (land or buildings) **Grundbesitz, Immobilien;** *he made his money from real estate deals in the 1970s; US* **real estate agent** = person who sells property for customers **Immobilienmakler**

◇ **really** *adverb* in fact **in Wirklichkeit, tatsächlich;** *the company is really making an acceptable profit; the office building really belongs to the chairman's father; the shop is really a general store, though it does carry some books*

◇ **realtor** *noun US* estate agent *or* person who sells real estate for customers **Immobilienhändler**

◇ **realty** *noun* property *or* real estate **Immobilien, Grundbesitz**

QUOTE real wages have been held down dramatically: they have risen as an annual rate of only 1% in the last two years
Sunday Times

QUOTE sterling M3 rose by 13.5% in the year to August - seven percentage points faster than the rate of inflation and the biggest increase in real terms since 1972-3
Economist

QUOTE on top of the cost of real estate, the investment in inventory and equipment to open a typical warehouse comes to around $5 million
Duns Business Month

realize *verb*
(a) to understand clearly **begreifen, sich klarmachen, sich über etwas im klaren sein;** *he soon realized the meeting was going to vote*

against his proposal; the small shopkeepers realized that the hypermarket would take away some of their trade; when she went into the manager's office she did not realize she was going to be promoted
(b) to make something become real **verwirklichen, realisieren, durchführen; to realize a project** *or* **a plan** = to put a project *or* a plan into action **einen Plan ausführen**
(c) to sell for money **veräußern, realisieren, zu Geld machen; erzielen;** *to realize property or assets; the sale realized £100,000*

◇ **realizable** *adjective* **realizable assets** = assets which can be sold for money **Effektivbestand, flüssige Mittel, leicht realisierbare Aktivposten**

◇ **realization** *noun*
(a) gradual understanding **Erkenntnis;** *the chairman's realization that he was going to be outvoted*
(b) making real **Verwirklichung, Realisierung, Durchführung; the realization of a project** = putting a project into action **die Ausführung eines Planes;** *the plan moved a stage nearer realization when the contracts were signed*
(c) realization of assets = selling of assets for money **Veräußerung von Vermögenswerten**

reapply *verb* to apply again **erneut bewerben;** *when he saw that the job had still not been filled, he reapplied for it*

◇ **reapplication** *noun* second application **erneute Bewerbung**

reappoint *verb* to appoint someone again **wiederernennen, wiedereinstellen;** *he was reappointed chairman for a further three-year period*

◇ **reappointment** *noun* being reappointed **Wiederernennung, Wiedereinstellung**

reason *noun* thing which explains why something has happened **Grund, Motiv, Begründung;** *the airline gave no reason for the plane's late arrival; the personnel officer asked him for the reason why he was late again; the chairman was asked for his reasons for closing the factory*

◇ **reasonable** *adjective*
(a) sensible *or* not annoyed **vernünftig, verständnisvoll;** *the manager of the shop was very reasonable when she tried to explain that she had left her credit cards at home;* **no reasonable offer refused** = we will accept any offer which is not extremely low **jedes reelle Angebot wird angenommen**
(b) moderate *or* not expensive **annehmbar, angemessen, vernünftig;** *the restaurant offers good food at reasonable prices*

reassess *verb* to assess again **neu bewerten; neu veranlagen; neu schätzen**

◇ **reassessment** *noun* new assessment **Neubewertung; Neuveranlagung; Neuschätzung**

reassign *verb* to assign again **wiederernennen; zurückübertragen, wiederabtreten**

◇ **reassignment** *noun* new assignment **Wiederernennung; Rückübertragung, Wiederabtretung**

reassure *verb*
(a) to make someone calm *or* less worried **beruhigen;** *the markets were reassured by the government statement on import controls; the manager tried to reassure her that she would not lose her job*
(b) to reinsure *or* to spread the risk of an insurance by asking another insurance company to cover part of it and receive part of the premium **rückversichern**

◇ **reassurance** *noun* making someone calm **Beruhigen**
NOTE: no plural

rebate *noun*
(a) reduction in the amount of money to be paid **Rabatt, Preisnachlaß;** *to offer a 10% rebate on selected goods*
(b) money returned to someone because he has paid too much **Rückzahlung, Rückvergütung, Rückerstattung;** *he got a tax rebate at the end of the year*

rebound *verb* to go back up again quickly **wieder ansteigen;** *the market rebounded on the news of the government's decision*

recd = RECEIVED

receipt
1 *noun*
(a) paper showing that money has been paid *or* that something has been received **Quittung, Beleg, Empfangsbestätigung;** *customs receipt; rent receipt; receipt for items purchased; please produce your receipt if you want to exchange items;* **receipt book** *or* **book of receipts** = book of blank receipts to be filled in when purchases are made **Quittungsblock**
(b) act of receiving something **Empfang, Eingang, Erhalt; to acknowledge receipt of a letter** = to write to say that you have received a letter **den Empfang eines Schreibens bestätigen;** *we acknowledge receipt of your letter of the 15th; goods will be supplied within thirty days of receipt of order; invoices are payable within thirty*

days of receipt; on receipt of the notification, the company lodged an appeal
(c) receipts = money taken in sales **Einnahmen, Einkünfte;** *to itemize receipts and expenditure; receipts are down against the same period of last year*
NOTE: no plural for (b)
2 *verb* to stamp *or* to sign a document to show that it has been received *or* to stamp an invoice to show that it has been paid **Empfang bestätigen, quittieren**

> QUOTE the public sector borrowing requirement is kept low by treating the receipts from selling public assets as a reduction in borrowing
> *Economist*
>
> QUOTE gross wool receipts for the selling season to end June appear likely to top $2 billion
> *Australian Financial Review*

receive *verb* to get something which has been delivered **erhalten, empfangen, entgegennehmen;** *we received the payment ten days ago; the workers have not received any salary for six months; the goods were received in good condition;* **"received with thanks"** = words put on an invoice to show that a sum has been paid **"dankend erhalten"**

◇ **receivable** *adjective* which can be received **offen, ausstehend; accounts receivable** = money owed to a company **Außenstände; bills receivable** = bills which a creditor will receive **Wechselforderungen**

◇ **receivables** *plural noun* money which is owed to a company **Außenstände, Forderungen**

◇ **receiver** *noun*
(a) person who receives something **Empfänger/-in;** *the receiver of the shipment*
(b) official receiver = government official who is appointed to run a company which is in financial difficulties, to pay off its debts as far as possible, and to close it down **Konkursverwalter;** *the court appointed a receiver for the company; the company is in the hands of the receiver*

◇ **receivership** *noun* **the company went into receivership** = the company was put into the hands of a receiver **das Unternehmen hat Konkurs gemacht**

◇ **receiving** *noun*
(a) act of getting something which has been delivered **Empfang, Annahme; receiving clerk** = official who works in a receiving office **Angestellter in der Warenannahme; receiving department** = section of a company which deals with incoming goods *or* payments **Warenannahme; receiving office** = office where goods *or* payments are received **Warenannahme, Einzahlungsschalter**
(b) receiving order = order from a court appointing a receiver to a company **Konkurseröffnungsbeschluß**
NOTE: no plural

recent *adjective* which happened not very long ago **kürzlich/vor kurzem stattfindend; neuester;** *the company's recent acquisition of a chain of shoe shops; his recent appointment to the board; we will mail you our most recent catalogue*

◇ **recently** *adverb* not very long ago **vor kurzem;** *the company recently started on an expansion programme; they recently decided to close the branch office in Australia*

reception *noun* place (in a hotel *or* office) where visitors register *or* say who they have come to see **Empfang, Rezeption; reception clerk** = person who works at the reception desk **Herr am Empfang, Empfangsdame; reception desk** = desk where customers *or* visitors check in **Rezeption, Empfang**

◇ **receptionist** *noun* person in a hotel *or* office who meets guests *or* clients, answers the phone, etc. **Empfangsdame, Herr am Empfang**

recession *noun* fall in trade *or* in the economy **Rezession, Konjunkturrückgang;** *the recession has reduced profits in many companies; several firms have closed factories because of the recession*

recipient *noun* person who receives **Empfänger/-in;** *the recipient of an allowance from the company*

reciprocal *adjective* applying from one country *or* person *or* company to another and vice versa **wechsel-, gegenseitig;** *reciprocal agreement; reciprocal contract;* **reciprocal holdings** = situation where two companies own shares in each other to prevent takeover bids **gegenseitige Beteiligung; reciprocal trade** = trade between two countries **zweiseitiger Handel**

◇ **reciprocate** *verb* to do the same thing to someone as he has just done to you **etwas im Gegenzug/als Gegenleistung tun; mitziehen, sich revanchieren;** *they offered us an exclusive agency for their cars and we reciprocated with an offer of the agency for our buses*

> QUOTE in 1934 Congress authorized President Roosevelt to seek lower tariffs with any country willing to reciprocate
> *Duns Business Month*

reckon *verb*
(a) to calculate **berechnen, ansetzen, kalkulieren;** *to reckon the costs at £25,000; we reckon the loss to be over £1m*

(b) to reckon on = to depend on *or* to expect something to happen **mit (etwas) rechnen;** *they reckon on being awarded the contract; he can reckon on the support of the managing director*

recognize *verb*

(a) to know someone *or* something because you have seen *or* heard them before **erkennen, wiedererkennen;** *I recognized his voice before he said who he was; do you recognize the handwriting on the letter?*
(b) to recognize a union = to accept that a union can act on behalf of staff **eine Gewerkschaft anerkennen;** *although all the staff had joined the union, the management refused to recognize it;* **recognized agent** = agent who is approved by the company for which he acts **zugelassener Vertreter**

◇ **recognition** *noun* act of recognizing **Anerkennung, Zulassung; to grant a trade union recognition** = to recognize a trade union **eine Gewerkschaft anerkennen**

recommend *verb*

(a) to suggest that something should be done **empfehlen, raten zu;** *the investment adviser recommended buying shares in aircraft companies; we do not recommend bank shares as a safe investment;* **manufacturer's recommended price (MRP)** *or* **recommended retail price (RRP)** = price which a manufacturer suggests the product should be sold at on the retail market, though often reduced by the retailer **empfohlener Herstellerpreis, empfohlener Einzelhandelspreis, unverbindliche Preisempfehlung;** *"all typewriters - 20% off MRP"*
(b) to say that someone *or* something is good **empfehlen;** *he recommended a shop in the High Street for shoes; I certainly would not recommend Miss Smith for the job; the board meeting recommended a dividend of 10p a share; can you recommend a good hotel in Amsterdam?*

◇ **recommendation** *noun* saying that someone *or* something is good **Empfehlung;** *we appointed him on the recommendation of his former employer*

reconcile *verb* to make two accounts *or* statements agree **abstimmen;** *to reconcile one account with another; to reconcile the accounts*

◇ **reconciliation** *noun* making two accounts *or* statements agree **Abstimmung; reconciliation statement** = statement which explains why two accounts do not agree **Erklärung von Kontenabstimmungsdifferenzen**

reconstruction *noun* building again **Wiederaufbau;** *the economic reconstruction of an area after a disaster*

record

1 *noun*
(a) report of something which has happened **Protokoll, Aufzeichnung;** *the chairman signed the minutes as a true record of the last meeting;* **for the record** *or* **to keep the record straight** = to note something which has been done **der Ordnung halber;** *for the record, I would like these sales figures to be noted in the minutes;* **it is on record** = correctly reported **es ist schriftlich/im Protokoll festgehalten/belegt;** *the chairman is on record as saying that profits are set to rise;* **off the record** = unofficially *or* in private **inoffiziell;** *he made some remarks off the record about the disastrous home sales figures*
(b) records = documents which give information **Unterlagen, Aufzeichnungen, Akten;** *the names of customers are kept in the company's records; we find from our records that our invoice number 1234 has not been paid*
(c) description of what has happened in the past **Vergangenheit;** *the company's record in industrial relations*
(d) personal file **Personalakte;** *the salesman's record of service or service record;* **track record** = success or failure of a company *or* salesman in the past **Erfolgs- und Leistungsnachweis;** *he has a good track record as a salesman; the company has no track record in the computer market*
(e) success which is better than anything before **Rekord; record sales** *or* **record losses** *or* **record profits** = sales *or* losses *or* profits which are higher than ever before **Spitzenumsätze; Rekordverluste; Höchstgewinne;** *1985 was a record year for the company; sales for 1983 equalled the record of 1980; our top salesman has set a new record for sales per call;* **we broke our record for June** = we sold more than we have ever sold before in June **wir haben unseren Rekord für Juni gebrochen**
2 *verb* to note *or* to report **aufzeichnen, protokollieren; registrieren, verzeichnen;** *the company has recorded another year of increased sales; your complaint has been recorded and will be investigated;* **recorded delivery** = mail service where the letters are signed for by the person receiving them **Einschreiben**

◇ **record-breaking** *adjective* which is better than anything which has happened before **Rekord-;** *we are proud of our record-breaking profits in 1984*

◇ **recording** *noun* making of a note **Aufzeichnung, Eintragung; Registrierung;** *the recording of an order or of a complaint*

recoup *verb* **to recoup one's losses** = to get back money which you thought you had lost **seine Verluste wieder hereinholen/hereinbekommen**

recourse *noun* **to decide to have recourse to the courts** = to decide in the end to sue someone **beschließen, den Rechtsweg zu beschreiten**

recover *verb*
(a) to get back something which has been lost **zurückbekommen, (wieder) hereinholen;** *he never recovered his money; the initial investment was never recovered; to recover damages from the driver of the car; to start a court action to recover property*
(b) to get better or to rise **sich erholen, einen Aufschwung nehmen;** *the market has not recovered from the rise in oil prices; the stock market fell in the morning, but recovered during the afternoon*

◇ **recoverable** *adjective* which can be got back **eintreibbar, erstattungsfähig**

◇ **recovery** *noun*
(a) getting back something which has been lost **Wiederbeschaffung, Wiedererlangung, Wiedergewinnung;** *we are aiming for the complete recovery of the money invested; to start an action for recovery of property*
(b) movement upwards of shares or of the economy **Aufschwung, Wiederbelebung;** *the economy staged a recovery; the recovery of the economy after a slump;* **recovery shares** = shares which are likely to go up in value because the company's performance is improving **im Aufschwung begriffene Aktien**

recruit *verb* **to recruit new staff** = to get new staff to join a company **weiteres Personal einstellen;** *we are recruiting staff for our new store*

◇ **recruitment** or **recruiting** *noun* **the recruitment of new staff** = looking for new staff to join a company **Personalbeschaffung**

rectify *verb* to correct something or to make something right **berichtigen, korrigieren, bereinigen;** *to rectify an entry*

◇ **rectification** *noun* correction **Berichtigung, Korrektur, Bereinigung**

recurrent *adjective* which happens again and again **sich wiederholend, ständig wiederkehrend;** *a recurrent item of expenditure*

recycle *verb* to take waste material and process it so that it can be used again **(wieder)aufbereiten, recycle; recycled paper** = paper made from waste paper **Umweltschutzpapier, Recycling-Papier**

red *noun* **in the red** = showing a debit or loss **in den roten Zahlen;** *my bank account is in the red; the company went into the red in 1984; the company is out of the red for the first time since 1950*
NOTE: no plural

◇ **red tape** *noun* official paperwork which takes a long time to complete **Bürokratie, Papierkrieg, Amtsschimmel;** *the Australian joint venture has been held up by government red tape*
NOTE: no plural

redeem *verb*
(a) to pay off a loan or a debt **abzahlen, tilgen, ablösen;** *to redeem a mortgage; to redeem a debt*
(b) to redeem a bond = to sell a bond for cash **eine Obligation verkaufen**

◇ **redeemable** *adjective* which can be sold for cash **einlösbar**

redemption *noun*
(a) repayment of a loan **Abzahlung, Tilgung; redemption date** = date on which a loan, etc., is due to be repaid **Tilgungstermin; redemption before due date** = paying back a loan before the date when repayment is due **Rückzahlung vor Fälligkeit; redemption value** = value of a security when redeemed **Rückzahlungswert; redemption yield** = yield on a security including interest and its redemption value **Tilgungserlös, Aktienrendite**
(b) repayment of a debt **Rückzahlung, Tilgung;** *redemption of a mortgage*
NOTE: no plural

redeploy *verb* to move workers from one place to another or to give workers totally different jobs to do **versetzen; anderweitig einsetzen;** *we closed the design department and redeployed the workforce in the publicity and sales departments*

◇ **redeployment** *noun* moving workers from one place to another **Versetzung**

redevelop *verb* to knock down the buildings on a site, and build new ones **sanieren**

◇ **redevelopment** *noun* knocking down of existing buildings to replace them with new ones **Sanierung;** *the redevelopment plan was rejected by the planning committee*

redistribute *verb* to move items *or* work *or* money to different areas *or* people **umverteilen, umschichten, neu verteilen;** *the government aims to redistribute wealth by taxing the rich and giving grants to the poor; the orders have been redistributed among the company's factories*

◇ **redistribution** *noun* **redistribution of wealth** = sharing wealth among the whole population **Vermögensumverteilung**

redraft *verb* to draft again **umformulieren, neu abfassen;** *the whole contract had to be redrafted to take in the objections from the chairman*

reduce *verb* to make smaller *or* lower **reduzieren, verringern, herabsetzen, ermäßigen, senken;** *to reduce expenditure; to reduce a price; to reduce taxes; we have made some staff redundant to reduce overmanning; prices have been reduced by 15%; carpets are reduced from £100 to £50; the company reduced output because of a fall in demand; the gove;* **to reduce staff** = to sack employees in order to have a smaller number of staff **den Personalbestand abbauen**

◇ **reduced** *adjective* lower **reduziert, ermäßigt, herabgesetzt, geringer;** *reduced prices have increased unit sales; prices have fallen due to a reduced demand for the goods*

reduction *noun* lowering (of prices, etc.) **Reduzierung, Ermäßigung, Herabsetzung, Verringerung, Senkung;** *price reductions; tax reductions; staff reductions; reduction of expenditure; reduction in demand; the company was forced to make job reductions*

redundancy *noun*
(a) being no longer employed, because the job is no longer necessary **Arbeitslosigkeit nach Rationalisierung; redundancy payment** = payment made to a worker to compensate for losing his job **Entlassungsabfindung; voluntary redundancy** = situation where the worker asks to be made redundant, usually in return for a large payment **freiwillige Arbeitsplatzaufgabe**
(b) person who has lost a job because he is not needed any more **Arbeitsloser;** *the takeover caused 250 redundancies*

◇ **redundant** *adjective*
(a) more than is needed *or* useless **überflüssig, überzählig;** *redundant capital; redundant clause in a contract; the new legislation has made clause 6 redundant*
(b) to make someone redundant = to decide that a worker is not needed any more **jdn entlassen; redundant staff** = staff who have lost their jobs because they are not needed any more **entlassene Arbeitskräfte**

re-elect *verb* to elect again **wiederwählen;** *he was re-elected chairman*

◇ **re-election** *noun* being elected again **Wiederwahl; she is eligible to stand for re-election** = it is possible for her to be re-elected if she wants **sie ist wiederwählbar**

re-employ *verb* to employ someone again **wiedereinstellen, wiederbeschäftigen**

◇ **re-employment** *noun* employing someone again **Wiedereinstellung, Wiederbeschäftigung**

re-engage *verb* **to re-engage staff** = to employ staff again **Personal wiedereinstellen**

re-entry *noun* coming back in again **Wiedereinreise; re-entry visa** *or* **permit** = visa which allows someone to leave a country and go back in again **Visum mit Rückkehrberechtigung**

re-examine *verb* to examine something again **erneut prüfen, nachprüfen**

◇ **re-examination** *noun* examining something which has already been examined before **erneute Prüfung, Nachprüfung**

re-export
1 *noun* exporting of goods which have been imported **Wiederausfuhr;** *re-export trade; we import wool for re-export; the value of re-exports has increased*
2 *verb* to export something which has been imported **wiederausführen**

◇ **re-exportation** *noun* exporting goods which have been imported **Wiederausfuhr**

ref = REFERENCE

refer *verb*
(a) to mention *or* to deal with *or* to write about something **erwähnen, sich beziehen auf;** *we refer to your estimate of May 26th; he referred to an article which he had seen in the "Times"; referring to your letter of June 4th*
(b) to pass a problem on to someone else to decide **weiterleiten;** *to refer a question to a committee; we have referred your complaint to our supplier*
(c) the bank referred the cheque to drawer = the bank returned the cheque to the person who wrote it because there was not enough money in the account to pay it **die Bank schickte den Scheck an den Aussteller zurück; "refer to drawer"** = words written on a

cheque which a bank refuses to pay **"vorgelegt und nicht eingelöst"**
NOTE: **referring - referred**

◇ **referee** *noun* person who can give a report on someone's character *or* ability *or* speed of work, etc. **Referenz;** *to give someone's name as referee; she gave the name of her boss as a referee; when applying please give the names of three referees*

◇ **reference** *noun*
(a) terms of reference = areas which a committee *or* an inspector can deal with **Aufgabenbereich;** *under the terms of reference of the committee, it cannot investigate complaints from the public; the committee's terms of reference do not cover exports*
(b) mentioning *or* dealing with **Bezug;** *with reference to your letter of May 25th*
(c) numbers *or* letters which make it possible to find a document which has been filed **Zeichen;** *our reference: PC/MS 1234; thank you for your letter (reference 1234); please quote this reference in all correspondence; when replying please quote reference 1234*
(d) written report on someone's character *or* ability, etc. **Referenz;** *to write someone a reference or to give someone a reference; to ask applicants to supply references;* **to ask a company for trade references** *or* **for bank references** = to ask a company to give names of traders or banks who can report on the company's financial status and reputation **ein Unternehmen um Handelsauskünfte/Bankreferenzen ersuchen; letter of reference** = letter in which an employer *or* former employer recommends someone for a job **Zeugnis, Referenz;** *he enclosed letters of reference from his two previous employers*
(e) person who reports on someone's character *or* ability, etc. **Referenz;** *to give someone's name as reference; please use me as a reference if you wish*

refinancing *noun* **refinancing of a loan** = floating a new loan to pay back a previous loan **Refinanzierung eines Kredites**

refit *verb* to fit out (a shop *or* factory *or* office) again **neu ausstatten**
NOTE: **refitting - refitted**

◇ **refitting** *noun* fitting out (of a shop *or* factory *or* office) again **Neuausstattung**

reflate *verb* **to reflate the economy** = to stimulate the economy by increasing the money supply *or* by reducing taxes, leading to increased inflation **die Wirtschaft ankurbeln (durch Geldvermehrung);** *the government's attempts to reflate the economy were not successful*

◇ **reflation** *noun* act of stimulating the economy by increasing the money supply *or* by reducing taxes **Reflation, Ankurbelung der Wirtschaft durch Geldvermehrung**
NOTE: no plural

◇ **reflationary** *adjective* **reflationary measures** = acts which are likely to stimulate the economy **Reflationsmaßnahmen**

refresher course *noun* course of study to make you practise your skills again in order to improve them **Auffrischungskurs;** *he went on a refresher course in bookkeeping*

refund
1 *noun* money paid back **Rückerstattung;** *to ask for a refund; she got a refund after she had complained to the manager;* **full refund** *or* **refund in full** = refund of all the money paid **Rückerstattung in voller Höhe;** *he got a full refund when he complained about the service*
2 *verb* to pay back money **erstatten, rückerstatten, zurückzahlen;** *to refund the cost of postage; all money will be refunded if the goods are not satisfactory*

◇ **refundable** *adjective* which can be paid back **zurückerstattbar;** *refundable deposit; the entrance fee is refundable if you purchase £5 worth of goods*

refuse *verb* to say that you will not do something *or* will not accept something **ablehnen, nicht gewähren, verweigern, sich weigern;** *they refused to pay; the bank refused to lend the company any more money; he asked for a rise but it was refused; the loan was refused by the bank; the customer refused the goods or refused to accept the goods*
NOTE: you refuse **to do something** or refuse **something**

◇ **refusal** *noun* saying no **Ablehnung, Weigerung, Verweigerung, Absage; his request met with a refusal** = his request was refused **auf sein Gesuch bekam er einen abschlägigen Bescheid; to give someone first refusal of something** = to allow someone to be the first to decide if they want something or not **jdm das Vorkaufsrecht einräumen; blanket refusal** = refusal to accept many different items **allgemeine Ablehnung**

regard *noun* **with regard to** = concerning *or* dealing with **in bezug auf, bezüglich, betreffend;** *with regard to your request for unpaid leave*

◇ **regarding** *preposition* concerning *or* dealing with **bezüglich, betreffend;**

instructions regarding the shipment of goods to Africa

◇ **regardless** *adjective* **regardless of** = in spite of **ungeachtet; the chairman furnished his office regardless of expense** = without thinking of how much it would cost **der Vorsitzende richtete sein Büro ein, ohne auf die Kosten zu achten**

region *noun* large area of a country **Gebiet, Gegend, Region; in the region of** = about *or* approximately **um die;** *he was earning a salary in the region of £25,000; the house was sold for a price in the region of £100,000*

◇ **regional** *adjective* referring to a region **regional, Regional-; gebietsweise; regional planning** = planning the industrial development of a region **Regionalplanung**

register
1 *noun*
(a) official list **Verzeichnis, Liste;** *to enter something in a register; to keep a register up to date;* **companies' register** *or* **register of companies** = list of companies, showing their directors and registered addresses **Handelsregister; register of debentures** *or* **debenture register** = list of debenture holders of a company **Verzeichnis der Obligationäre; register of directors** = official list of the directors of a company which has to be sent to the registrar of companies **Vorstandsverzeichnis; land register** = list of pieces of land, showing who owns it and what buildings are on it **Grundbuch; Lloyd's register** = classified list showing details of all the ships in the world **Lloyd's Register; register of shareholders** *or* **share register** = list of shareholders in a company with their addresses **Aktienbuch**
(b) large book for recording details (as in a hotel, where guests sign in, or in a registry where deaths are recorded) **Eintragungsbuch, Register**
(c) cash register = machine which shows and adds the prices of items bought in a shop, with a drawer for keeping the cash received **Registrierkasse**
2 *verb*
(a) to write something in an official list **eintragen, registrieren, eintragen lassen, erfassen;** *to register a company; to register a sale; to register a property; to register a trademark*
(b) to arrive at a hotel *or* at a conference, sign your name and write your address on a list **sich eintragen/anmelden;** *they registered at the hotel under the name of Macdonald*
(c) to send (a letter) by registered post **als/per Einschreiben schicken;** *I registered the letter, because it contained some money*

◇ **registered** *adjective*
(a) which has been noted on an official list **eingetragen, registriert, angemeldet;** *registered share transaction; registered trademark;* **the company's registered office** = the head office of the company as noted in the register of companies **der eingetragene Sitz der Gesellschaft**
(b) registered letter *or* **registered parcel** = letter *or* parcel which is noted by the post office before it is sent, so that compensation can be claimed if it is lost **Einschreibebrief; eingeschriebenes Päckchen;** *to send documents by registered mail or registered post*

◇ **registrar** *noun* person who keeps official records **Registrator, Registerführer, Archivar; Standesbeamter;** *registrar of companies or the company registrar*

◇ **registration** *noun*
(a) act of having something noted on an official list **Eintragung, Registrierung, Anmeldung, Erfassung;** *registration of a trademark or of a share transaction;* **certificate of registration** *or* **registration certificate** = document showing that an item has been registered **Eintragungsbescheinigung, Meldeschein;** *für Kraftfahrzeuge* **Zulassungspapiere; registration fee** = money paid to have something registered *or* money paid to attend a conference **Anmeldegebühr; registration number** = official number; the number of a car **Eintragungsnummer; Kraftfahrzeugkennzeichen**
(b) land registration = system of registering land and its owners **Grundbucheintragung**

◇ **registry** *noun*
(a) place where official records are kept **Registratur; Amt, in dem die Eintragung vorgenommen wird;** *GB* **land registry** = government office where details of land are kept **Grundbuch-, Katasteramt; registry office** = office where records of births, marriages and deaths are kept **Standesamt**
(b) port of registry = port where a ship is registered **Heimathafen**

regret *verb* to be sorry **bedauern;** *I regret having to make so many staff redundant; we regret the delay in answering your letter; we regret to inform you of the death of the chairman*
NOTE: you **regret doing something** or **regret to do something** or **regret something.** Note also: **regretting - regretted**

regular *adjective*
(a) which happens *or* comes at the same time each day *or* each week *or* each month *or* each year **regelmäßig, regulär;** *his regular train is the 12.45; the regular flight to Athens leaves at 06.00;* **regular customer** = customer who always buys from the same

shop **Stammkunde; regular income** = income which comes in every week or month **geregeltes/festes Einkommen;** *she works freelance so she does not have a regular income;* **regular staff** = full-time staff **ständiges/festangestelltes Personal**
(b) ordinary *or* standard **normal, regulär;** *the regular price is $1.25, but we are offering them at 99c;* **regular size** = ordinary size (smaller than economy size, family size, etc.) **Normalformat, Standardgröße**

◊ **regularly** *adverb* happening often each day *or* week *or* /month *or* year **regelmäßig, ständig;** *the first train in the morning is regularly late*

◊ **regulate** *verb*
(a) to adjust something so that it works well *or* is correct **regulieren, einstellen, ordnen**
(b) to change *or* maintain something by law **regeln; prices are regulated by supply and demand** = prices are increased or lowered according to supply and demand **Preise werden durch Angebot und Nachfrage bestimmt; government-regulated price** = price which is imposed by the government **staatlich vorgeschriebener Preis**

◊ **regulation** *noun*
(a) act of making sure that something will work well **Regelung, Regulierung;** *the regulation of trading practices*
(b) regulations = laws *or* rules **Vorschriften, Satzung, Statuten;** *the new government regulations on housing standards; fire regulations or safety regulations; regulations concerning imports and exports*
NOTE: no plural for (a)

> QUOTE EEC regulations which came into effect in July insist that customers can buy cars anywhere in the EEC at the local pre-tax price
> *Financial Times*
>
> QUOTE a unit trust is established under the regulations of the Department of Trade, with a trustee, a management company and a stock of units
> *Investors Chronicle*

reimburse

reimburse *verb* **to reimburse someone his expenses** = to pay someone back for money which he has spent **jdm seine Auslagen erstatten;** *you will be reimbursed for your expenses or your expenses will be reimbursed*

◊ **reimbursement** *noun* paying back money **Erstattung;** *reimbursement of expenses*

reimport

1 *noun* importing of goods which have been exported from the same country **Wiedereinfuhr**
2 *verb* to import goods which have been exported **wieder einführen**

◊ **reimportation** *noun* importing goods which have been exported **Wiedereinfuhr**

reinstate

reinstate *verb* to put someone back into a job from which he was dismissed **wiedereinstellen;** *the union demanded that the sacked workers should be reinstated*

◊ **reinstatement** *noun* putting someone back into a job from which he was dismissed **Wiedereinstellung**

reinsure

reinsure *verb* to spread the risk of an insurance, by asking another insurance company to cover part of it and receive part of the premium **rückversichern**

◊ **reinsurance** *noun* act of reinsuring **Rückversicherung**

◊ **reinsurer** *noun* insurance company which accepts to insure part of the risk for another insurer **Rückversicherer**

reinvest

reinvest *verb* to invest again **neu anlegen, reinvestieren;** *he reinvested the money in government stocks*

◊ **reinvestment** *noun* investing again in the same securities; investing a company's earnings in its own business by using them to create new products for sale **Wiederanlage, Reinvestition**

reissue

1 *noun* issue of something again **Neuausgabe; Neuauflage**
2 *verb* to issue something again **neu herausgeben; neu auflegen;** *the company reissued its catalogue with a new price list*

reject

1 *noun* thing which has been thrown out because it is not of the usual standard **Ausschußware; zweite Wahl, B-Sortiment;** *sale of rejects or of reject items; to sell off reject stock;* **reject shop** = shop which specializes in the sale of rejects **Laden für Partiewaren/Waren zweiter Wahl**
2 *verb* to refuse to accept *or* to say that something is not satisfactory **ablehnen, zurückweisen;** *the union rejected the management's proposals;* **the company rejected the takeover bid** = the directors recommended that the shareholders should not accept the bid **das Unternehmen wies das Übernahmeangebot zurück**

◊ **rejection** *noun* refusal to accept **Ablehnung, Zurück-, Abweisung**

related

related *adjective* connected *or* linked **zusammenhängend;** *related items on the agenda;* **related company** = company which is partly owned by another company **Konzerngesellschaft; earnings-related**

pension = pension which is linked to the size of the salary **dynamische Rente**

◇ **relating to** *adverb* referring to *or* connected with **in Zusammenhang mit;** *documents relating to the agreement*

◇ **relation** *noun*
(a) in relation to = referring to *or* connected with **in Zusammenhang mit, in bezug auf;** *documents in relation to the agreement*
(b) relations = links (with other people *or* other companies) **Beziehungen;** *we try to maintain good relations with our customers;* **to enter into relations with a company** = to start discussing a business deal with a company **zu einem Unternehmen Beziehungen aufnehmen; to break off relations with someone** = to stop dealing with someone **die Beziehungen zu jdm abbrechen; industrial relations** *or* **labour relations** = relations between management and workers **Arbeitgeber-Arbeitnehmer-Beziehungen;** *the company has a history of bad labour relations*
(c) public relations (PR) = keeping good links between a company *or* a group and the public so that people know what the company is doing and approve of it **PR-Arbeit, Public Relations, Öffentlichkeitsarbeit; public relations department** = section of a company which deals with relations with the public **PR-Abteilung, Abteilung für Öffentlichkeitsarbeit; public relations officer** = official who deals with relations with the public **Leiter der PR-Abteilung**

◇ **relatively** *adverb* more or less **verhältnismäßig, relativ;** *we have appointed a relatively new PR firm to handle our publicity*

release

1 *noun*
(a) setting free **Freistellung, Freigabe, Entbindung; Entlassung;** *release from a contract; release of goods from customs*
(b) day release = arrangement where a company allows a worker to go to college to study for one day each week **Freistellung zur beruflichen Fortbildung;** *the junior sales manager is attending a day release course*
(c) press release = sheet giving news about something which is sent to newspapers and TV and radio stations so that they can use the information in it **Pressemitteilung;** *the company sent out or issued a press release about the launch of the new car*
(d) new releases = new records put on the market **Neuerscheinungen auf dem Plattenmarkt**
NOTE: no plural for (a)
2 *verb*
(a) to free **freigeben, freistellen, entbinden, befreien; entlassen;** *to release goods from customs; the customs released the goods against payment of a fine; to release someone from a debt*
(b) to make something public **veröffentlichen;** *the company released information about the new mine in Australia; the government has refused to release figures for the number of unemployed women*
(c) to put on the market **herausbringen, veröffentlichen;** *to release a new record;* **to release dues** = to send off orders which had been piling up while a product was out of stock **überfällige Bestellungen abwickeln**

> QUOTE pressure to ease monetary policy mounted yesterday with the release of a set of pessimistic economic statistics
> *Financial Times*
>
> QUOTE the national accounts for the March quarter released by the Australian Bureau of Statistics showed a real increase in GDP
> *Australian Financial Review*

relevant *adjective* which has to do with what is being discussed **entsprechend, relevant, zuständig;** *which is the relevant government department? can you give me the relevant papers?*

reliable *adjective* which can be trusted **zuverlässig, seriös, verläßlich; sicher;** *reliable company; the sales manager is completely reliable; we have reliable information about our rival's sales; the company makes a very reliable product*

◇ **reliability** *noun* being reliable **Zuverlässigkeit, Verläßlichkeit; Sicherheit;** *the product has passed its reliability tests*
NOTE: no plural

◇ **rely on** *verb* to depend on *or* to trust **angewiesen sein auf, sich verlassen auf;** *the chairman relies on the finance department for information on sales; we rely on part-time staff for most of our mail-order business; do not rely on the agents for accurate market reports*

relief *noun* help **Hilfe, Unterstützung, Erleichterung; tax relief** = allowing someone to pay less tax **Steuerermäßigung; there is full tax relief on mortgage interest payments** = no tax is payable on income used to pay interest on a mortgage **für Hypothekenzahlungen werden Steuervergünstigungen in voller Höhe gewährt; mortgage relief** = allowing someone to pay no tax on mortgage interest payments **Vergünstigungen bei Hypothekenzahlungen; relief shift** = shift which comes to take the place of another shift, usually the shift between the day shift and the night shift **Ablösungsschicht**
NOTE: no plural

remain *verb*
(a) to be left **(übrig)bleiben;** *half the stock remained unsold; we will sell off the old stock at half price and anything remaining will be thrown away*
(b) to stay **bleiben;** *she remained behind at the office after 6.30 to finish her work*

◊ **remainder**
1 *noun*
(a) things left behind **Rest(bestand);** *the remainder of the stock will be sold off at half price*
(b) remainders = new books sold cheaply **Restauflage; remainder merchant** = book dealer who buys unsold new books from publishers at a very low price **auf Restauflagen spezialisierter Buchhändler**
NOTE: in (a) **remainder** is usually singular and is written with **the**
2 *verb* **to remainder books** = to sell new books off cheaply **Restauflagen billig verkaufen;** *the shop was full of piles of remaindered books*

remember *verb* to bring back into your mind something which you have seen *or* heard *or* read before **sich erinnern, sich entsinnen; denken an;** *do you remember the name of the Managing Director of Smith Ltd? I cannot remember the make of photocopier which he said was so good; did you remember to ask the switchboard to put my calls through to the boardroom? she remembered seeing the item in a*
NOTE: you **remember doing something** which you did in the past; you **remember to do something** in the future

remind *verb* to make someone remember **erinnern;** *I must remind my secretary to book the flight for New York; he reminded the chairman that the meeting had to finish at 6.30*

◊ **reminder** *noun* letter to remind a customer that he has not paid an invoice **Mahnung;** *to send someone a reminder*

remission *noun* **remission of taxes** = refund of taxes which have been overpaid **Steuerrückzahlung**

remit *verb* to send (money) **überweisen;** *to remit by cheque*
NOTE: **remitting - remitted**

◊ **remittance** *noun* money which is sent **Überweisung;** *please send remittances to the treasurer; the family lives on a weekly remittance from their father in the USA*

remnant *noun* odd piece of a large item sold separately **Rest;** *remnant sale or sale of remnants*

remove *verb* to take something away **entfernen, streichen, aufheben;** *we can remove his name from the mailing list; the government has removed the ban on imports from Japan; the minister has removed the embargo on the sale of computer equipment;* **two directors were removed from the board at the AGM** = two directors were dismissed from the board **bei der Jahreshauptversammlung wurden zwei Direktoren aus dem Vorstand ausgeschlossen**

◊ **removal** *noun*
(a) moving to a new house *or* office **Umzug; removal** *or* **removals company** = company which specializes in moving the contents of a house *or* an office to a new building **Spedition(sfirma), Spediteur**
(b) sacking someone (usually a director) from a job **Entlassung, Absetzung;** *the removal of the managing director is going to be very difficult*

remunerate *verb* to pay someone for doing something **bezahlen, entlohnen;** *to remunerate someone for their services*

◊ **remuneration** *noun* payment for services **Bezahlung, Lohn, Honorar;** *she has a monthly remuneration of £400*
NOTE: no plural

◊ **remunerative** *adjective* (job) which pays well **einträglich, lukrativ;** *he is in a very remunerative job*

render *verb* **to render an account** = to send in an account **eine Rechnung vorlegen;** *payment for account rendered; please find enclosed payment per account rendered*

renew *verb* to continue something for a further period of time **verlängern, erneuern;** *von Wechsel* **prolongieren;** *to renew a bill of exchange or to renew a lease ;* **to renew a subscription** = to pay a subscription for another year **ein Abonnement erneuern; to renew an insurance policy** = to pay the premium for another year's insurance **eine Versicherung erneuern**

◊ **renewal** *noun* act of renewing **Verlängerung, Erneuerung;** *von Wechsel* **Prolongation;** *renewal of a lease or of a subscription or of a bill; the lease is up for renewal next month; when is the renewal date of the bill?;* **renewal notice** = note sent by an insurance company asking the insured person to renew the insurance **Prämienrechnung; renewal premium** = premium to be paid to renew an insurance **Folgeprämie**
NOTE: no plural

rent

1 *noun* money paid to use an office *or* house *or* factory for a period of time **Miete, Pacht; high rent** *or* **low rent** = expensive *or* cheap rent **hohe Miete; niedrige Miete;** *rents are high in the centre of the town; we cannot afford to pay High Street rents; to pay three months' rent in advance;* **back rent** = rent owed **Mietrückstand; the flat is let at an economic rent** = at a rent which covers all costs to the landlord **die Wohnung ist zur Kostenmiete vermietet; ground rent** = rent paid by the main tenant to the ground landlord; *entspricht* **Grundzins; nominal rent** = very small rent **geringe/symbolische Miete; rent control** = government regulation of rents **Mietpreisbindung, Mietpreisregelung; income from rents** *or* **rent income** = income from letting offices *or* houses, etc. **Mieteinkünfte**

2 *verb*

(a) to pay money to hire an office *or* house *or* factory *or* piece of equipment for a period of time **mieten, pachten; leihen;** *to rent an office or a car; he rents an office in the centre of town; they were driving a rented car when they were stopped by the police*

(b) to rent (out) = to own a car *or* office, etc. and let it to someone for money **vermieten, verpachten; verleihen;** *we rented part of the building to an American company*

◇ **rental** *noun* money paid to use an office *or* house *or* factory *or* car *or* piece of equipment, etc., for a period of time **Miete, Pacht; Leihgebühr;** *the telephone rental bill comes to over £500 a quarter;* **rental income** *or* **income from rentals** = income from letting offices *or* houses, etc. **Mieteinkünfte; car rental firm** = company which specializes in offering cars for rent **Autovermietung; fleet rental** = renting all a company's cars from the same company at a special price **Anmietung des gesamten Fuhrparks**

> QUOTE top quality office furniture: short or long-term rental 50% cheaper than any other rental company
>
> *Australian Financial Review*
>
> QUOTE office rental growth has been faster in Britain in the first six months of 1985 than in 1984
>
> *Lloyd's List*

renunciation *noun* act of giving up ownership of shares **Verzicht; letter of renunciation** = form sent with new shares, which allows the person who has been allotted the shares to refuse to accept them and so sell them to someone else **Abtretungsformular für Bezugsrechte**

NOTE: no plural

reopen *verb* to open again **wiedereröffnen;** *the office will reopen soon after its refit*

◇ **reopening** *noun* opening again **Wiedereröffnung;** *the reopening of the store after refitting*

reorder

1 *noun* further order for something which has been ordered before **Nachbestellung;** *the product has only been on the market ten days and we are already getting reorders;* **reorder level** = minimum amount of stock of an item which must be reordered when stock falls to this amount **Mindestnachbestellung**

2 *verb* to place a new order for something **nachbestellen;** *we must reorder these items because stock is getting low*

reorganize *verb* to organize in a new way **neu organisieren, umstrukturieren, reorganisieren**

◇ **reorganization** *noun* new way of organizing **Umstrukturierung, Reorganisation, Neuordnung;** *his job was downgraded in the office reorganization or in the reorganization of the office;* **the reorganization of a company** *or* **a company reorganization** = restructuring the finances of a company **Unternehmenssanierung**

rep

1 *noun* = REPRESENTATIVE *to hold a reps' meeting; our reps make on average six calls a day;* **commission rep** = representative who is not paid a salary but receives a commission on sales **Provisionsvertreter**

2 *verb informal* = REPRESENT *he reps for two firms on commission*

NOTE: **repping - repped**

repack *verb* to pack again **umpacken, wieder verpacken**

◇ **repacking** *noun* packing again **Umpacken**

repair

1 *noun* mending *or* making good something which was broken **Reparatur, Instandsetzung;** *to carry out repairs to the machinery; his car is in the garage for repair*

2 *verb* to mend *or* to make good something which is broken **reparieren, instandsetzen;** *the photocopier is being repaired;* **repairing lease** = lease where the tenant is responsible for repairs to the building which he is renting **Miet-, Pachtvertrag mit Reparaturklausel**

◇ **repairer** *or* **repair man** *noun* person who carries out repairs **Handwerker, Techniker;** *the repair man has come to mend the photocopier*

repay *verb* to pay back **zurückzahlen; erstatten;** *to repay money owed; the company had to cut back on expenditure in order to repay its debts;* **he repaid me in full** = he paid me back all the money he owed me **er hat mir alles zurückbezahlt**
NOTE: **repaying - repaid**

◇ **repayable** *adjective* which can be paid back **rückzahlbar;** *loan which is repayable over ten years*

◇ **repayment** *noun* paying back; money which is paid back **Rückzahlung; Rückerstattung;** *the loan is due for repayment next year;* **he fell behind with his mortgage repayments** = he was late in paying back the instalments on his mortgage **er kam mit seinen Hypothekenzahlungen in Verzug**

repeat *verb*
(a) to say something again **wiederholen;** *he repeated his address slowly so that the salesgirl could write it down; when asked what the company planned to do, the chairman repeated "Nothing"*
(b) to repeat an order = to order something again **eine Nachbestellung aufgeben, etwas nachbestellen**

◇ **repeat order** *noun* new order for something which has been ordered before **Nachbestellung;** *the product has been on the market only ten days and we are already flooded with repeat orders*

replace *verb* to put someone *or* something in the place of something else **ersetzen;** *the cost of replacing damaged stock is very high; the photocopier needs replacing; the company will replace any defective item free of charge; we are replacing all our salaried staff with freelancers*

◇ **replacement** *noun*
(a) replacement cost *or* **cost of replacement** = cost of an item to replace an existing asset **Wiederbeschaffungskosten; replacement value** = value of something for insurance purposes if it were to be replaced **Wiederbeschaffungswert;** *the computer is insured at its replacement value*
(b) item which replaces something **Ersatz;** *we are out of stock and are waiting for replacements*
(c) person who replaces someone **Nachfolger/-in, Vertretung;** *my secretary leaves us next week, so we are advertising for a replacement*
NOTE: no plural for (a)

reply
1 *noun* answer **Antwort, Erwiderung;** *there was no reply to my letter or to my phone call; I am writing in reply to your letter of the 24th; the company's reply to the takeover bid;* **reply coupon** = form attached to a coupon ad which has to be filled in and returned to the advertiser **Antwortkarte, Coupon; international postal reply coupon** = coupon which can be used in another country to pay the postage of replying to a letter **internationaler Antwortschein;** *he enclosed an international reply coupon with his letter;* **reply paid card** = card to be sent back to the sender with a reply, the sender having already paid for the return postage **freigemachte/frankierte Antwortkarte**
2 *verb* to answer **antworten, erwidern;** *to reply to a letter; the company has replied to the takeover bid by offering the shareholders higher dividends*

report
1 *noun*
(a) statement describing what has happened *or* describing a state of affairs **Bericht;** *to draft a report; to make a report or to present a report or to send in a report; the sales manager reads all the reports from the sales team; the chairman has received a report from the insurance company;* **the company's annual report** *or* **the chairman's report** *or* **the directors' report** = document sent each year by the chairman of a company or the directors to the shareholders, explaining what the company has done during the year **Geschäftsbericht; Jahresbericht des Aufsichtsratsvorsitzenden; confidential report** = secret document which must not be shown to other people **vertraulicher Bericht; feasibility report** = document which says if something can be done **Durchführbarkeitsstudie; financial report** = document which gives the financial position of a company *or* of a club, etc. **Finanzbericht; progress report** = document which describes what progress has been made **Fortschrittsbericht; the treasurer's report** = document from the honorary treasurer of a society to explain the financial state of the society to its members **Kassenwartbericht**
(b) a report in a newspaper *or* **a newspaper report** = article *or* news item **Zeitungsbericht, Meldung in der Zeitung;** *can you confirm the report that the company is planning to close the factory?*
(c) official document from a government committee **Untersuchungsbericht;** *the government has issued a report on the credit problems of exporters*
2 *verb*
(a) to make a statement describing something **berichten, melden;** *the salesmen reported an increased demand for the product; he reported the damage to the insurance company; we asked the bank to*

report on his financial status; he reported seeing the absentee in a shop
(b) to report to someone = to be responsible to *or* to be under someone **jdm unterstehen;** *he reports direct to the managing director; the salesmen report to the sales director*
(c) to go to a place *or* to attend **sich melden;** *to report for an interview; please report to our London office for training*
NOTE: for (a), you **report something** or **report on something** or **report doing something**

> QUOTE a draft report on changes in the international monetary system
> *Wall Street Journal*
> QUOTE responsibilities include the production of premium quality business reports
> *Times*
> QUOTE the research director will manage a team of business analysts monitoring and reporting on the latest development in retail distribution
> *Times*
> QUOTE the successful candidate will report to the area director for profit responsibility for sales of leading brands
> *Times*

repossess *verb* to take back an item which someone is buying under a hire-purchase agreement, because the purchaser cannot continue the payments **wieder in Besitz nehmen**

represent *verb*
(a) to work for a company, showing goods or services to possible buyers **vertreten;** *he represents an American car firm in Europe; our French distributor represents several other competing firms*
(b) to act for someone **vertreten, repräsentieren;** *he sent his solicitor and accountant to represent him at the meeting; three managers represent the workforce in discussions with the directors*

◇ **re-present** *verb* to present something again **nochmals vorlegen;** *he re-presented the cheque two weeks later to try to get payment from the bank*

◇ **representation** *noun*
(a) act of selling goods for a company **Vertretung;** *we offered them exclusive representation in Europe; they have no representation in the USA*
(b) having someone to act on your behalf **Stellvertretung, Repräsentation;** *the minority shareholders want representation on the board*
(c) complaint made on behalf of someone **Vorhaltungen, Vorstellungen;** *the managers made representations to the board on behalf of the hourly-paid members of staff*

◇ **representative**
1 *adjective* which is an example of what all others are like **repräsentativ, typisch;** *we displayed a representative selection of our product range; the sample chosen was not representative of the whole batch*
2 *noun*
(a) sales representative = person who works for a company, showing goods or services for sale **Verkaufsvertreter, Vertreter/-in;** *we have six representatives in Europe; they have vacancies for representatives to call on accounts in the north of the country*
(b) company which works for another company, selling their goods **Agent, Repräsentant, Vertretung;** *we have appointed Smith & Co our exclusive representatives in Europe*
(c) person who acts on someone's behalf **Stellvertreter, Repräsentant/-in;** *he sent his solicitor and accountant to act as his representatives at the meeting; the board refused to meet the representatives of the workforce*

repudiate *verb* to refuse to accept **nicht anerkennen; to repudiate an agreement** = to refuse to continue with an agreement **eine Vereinbarung nicht anerkennen**

◇ **repudiation** *noun* refusal to accept **Nichtanerkennung**

reputable *adjective* with a good reputation **angesehen, seriös;** *we only use reputable carriers; a reputable firm of accountants*

◇ **reputation** *noun* opinion of someone *or* something held by other people **Ruf;** *company with a reputation for quality; he has a reputation for being difficult to negotiate with*

request
1 *noun* asking for something **Bitte, Gesuch, Antrag;** *they put in a request for a government subsidy; his request for a loan was turned down by the bank;* **on request** = if asked for **auf Wunsch/Anforderung;** *we will send samples on request or "samples available on request"*
2 *verb* to ask for **bitten, ersuchen, beantragen, anfordern;** *to request assistance from the government; I am sending a catalogue as requested*

require *verb*
(a) to ask for *or* to demand something **verlangen;** *to require a full explanation of expenditure; the law requires you to submit all income to the tax authorities*
(b) to need **brauchen, benötigen, erfordern;** *the document requires careful study; to write the program requires a computer specialist*

◇ **requirement** *noun* what is needed **Erfordernis, Bedarf; public sector borrowing**

requirement = amount of money which a government has to borrow to pay for its own spending **Kreditbedarf der öffentlichen Hand**

◇ **requirements** *plural noun* things which are needed **Bedarf;** *to meet a customer's requirements; if you will supply us with a list of your requirements, we shall see if we can meet them;* **the requirements of a market** *or* **market requirements** = things which are needed by the market **Marktbedarf; budgetary requirements** = spending or income needed to meet the budget forecasts **Budgeterfordernisse; manpower requirements** = number of workers needed **Bedarf an Arbeitskräften**

requisition

1 *noun* official order for something **Anforderung;** *what is the number of your latest requisition?;* **cheque requisition** = official note from a department to the company accounts staff asking for a cheque to be written **Scheckanforderung**

2 *verb* to put in an official order for something; to ask for supplies to be sent **anfordern**

resale *noun* selling goods which have been bought **Wieder-, Weiterverkauf;** *to purchase something for resale; the contract forbids resale of the goods to the USA*

NOTE: no plural

◇ **resale price maintenance** *noun* system where the price for an item is fixed by the manufacturer and the retailer is not allowed to sell it for a lower price **Preisbindung zweiter Hand, vertikale Preisbindung**

rescind *verb* to annul *or* to cancel **annullieren, aufheben, rückgängig machen, für nichtig erklären;** *to rescind a contract or an agreement*

rescue

1 *noun* saving someone *or* something from danger **Rettung, Hilfe; rescue operation** = arrangement by a group of people to save a company from collapse **Rettungsaktion, Sanierung;** *the banks planned a rescue operation for the company*

2 *verb* to save someone *or* something from danger **retten;** *the company nearly collapsed, but was rescued by the banks*

research

1 *noun* trying to find out facts *or* information **Forschung; consumer research** = research into why consumers buy goods and what goods they may want to buy **Konsumforschung; market research** = examining the possible sales of a product and the possible customers for it before it is put on the market **Marktforschung; research and development** = scientific investigation which leads to making new products or improving existing products **Forschung und Entwicklung;** *the company spends millions on research and development;* **scientific research** = study to try to find out information **wissenschaftliche Forschung;** *he is engaged in research into the packaging of the new product line; the company is carrying out research into finding a medicine to cure colds;* **research department** = section of a company which does research **Forschungsabteilung; a research institute** *or* **organization** = place which exists only to carry out research **Forschungsinstitut, Forschungsanstalt; research unit** = separate small group of research workers **Forschungsgruppe; research worker** = person who works in a research department **Angestellter in einer Forschungsanstalt**

2 *verb* to study *or* to try to find out information about something **forschen, Forschung betreiben;** *to research the market for a product*

◇ **researcher** *noun* person who carries out research **Forscher/-in**

reservation *noun* booking a seat *or* table *or* room **Reservierung;** *I want to make a reservation on the train to Plymouth tomorrow evening;* **room reservations** = department in a hotel which deals with bookings for rooms **Zimmerreservierung;** *can you put me through to reservations?*

reserve

1 *noun*

(a) money from profits not paid as dividend, but kept back by a company in case it is needed for a special purpose **Rücklage; bank reserves** = cash and securities held by a bank to cover deposits **Mindest-, Bankreserve; capital reserves** = money from profits, which forms part of the capital of a company and can be used for distribution to shareholders only when a company is wound up **Kapitalrücklagen; capitalization of reserves** = issuing free bonus shares to shareholders **Kapitalisierung von Rücklagen; cash reserves** = a company's reserves in cash deposits or bills kept in case of urgent need **Bar-, Liquiditätsreserven;** *the company was forced to fall back on its cash reserves; to have to draw on reserves to pay the dividend;* **contingency reserve** *or* **emergency reserves** = money set aside in case it is needed urgently **Fonds für außerordentliche Rückstellungen; reserve for bad debts** = money kept by a company to cover debts which may not be paid **Rücklagen für uneinbringliche Forderungen; hidden reserves** = illegal reserves which are not declared in the company's balance sheet **stille Reserven; sums chargeable to the reserve** = sums which can be debited to a company's reserves **auf die Rücklage zurechenbare Beträge; reserve fund** = profits in a business which have not been paid out as dividend but have been ploughed back into the business **Rücklagefonds**

(b) reserve currency = strong currency held by other countries to support their own weaker currencies **Reservewährung; currency reserves** = foreign money held by a government to support its own currency and to pay its debts **Währungsreserven; a country's foreign currency reserves** = a country's reserves in currencies of other countries **die Devisenreserven eines Landes;** *the UK's gold and dollar reserves fell by $200 million during the quarter*

(c) in reserve = kept to be used at a later date **in Reserve;** *to keep something in reserve; we are keeping our new product in reserve until the launch date*

(d) reserves = supplies kept in case of need **Reserven, Rücklagen;** *our reserves of fuel fell during the winter; the country's reserves of gas or gas reserves are very large*

(e) reserve price = lowest price which a seller will accept at an auction **Vorbehaltspreis;** *the painting was withdrawn when it did not reach its reserve*

2 *verb* **to reserve a room** *or* **a table** *or* **a seat** = to book a room *or* table *or* seat *or* to ask for a room *or* table *or* seat to be kept free for you **ein Zimmer od einen Tisch od einen Platz reservieren;** *I want to reserve a table for four people; can your secretary reserve a seat for me on the train to Glasgow?*

residence *noun*

(a) house *or* flat where someone lives **Wohnsitz, Wohnung;** *he has a country residence where he spends his weekends*

(b) act of living *or* operating officially in a country **Aufenthalt; residence permit** = official document allowing a foreigner to live in a country **Aufenthaltsgenehmigung;** *he has applied for a residence permit; she was granted a residence permit for one year*

NOTE: no plural for (b)

◊ **resident** *adjective* living or operating in a country **wohnhaft, ansässig;** *the company is resident in France;* **non-resident** = not officially resident in a country **auswärtig, im Ausland ansässig;** *he has a non-resident account with a French bank; she was granted a non-resident visa*

residue *noun* money left over **Restbetrag;** *after paying various bequests the residue of his estate was split between his children*

◊ **residual** *adjective* remaining after everything else has gone **übrig, restlich**

resign *verb* to give up a job **zurücktreten, kündigen, sein Amt niederlegen;** *he resigned from his post as treasurer; he has resigned with effect from July 1st; she resigned as finance director*

◊ **resignation** *noun* act of giving up a job **Rücktritt, Kündigung, Amtsniederlegung;** *he wrote his letter of resignation to the chairman;* **to hand in** *or* **to give in** *or* **to send in one's resignation** = to resign from a job **seine Kündigung einreichen**

resist *verb* to fight against something *or* not to give in to something **Widerstand leisten, sich wehren, sich widersetzen;** *the chairman resisted all attempts to make him resign; the company is resisting the takeover bid*

◊ **resistance** *noun* showing that people are opposed to something **Widerstand;** *there was a lot of resistance from the shareholders to the new plan; the chairman's proposal met with strong resistance from the banks;* **consumer resistance** = lack of interest by consumers in buying a new product **Kaufunlust;** *the new product met no consumer resistance even though the price was high*

NOTE: no plural

resolution *noun* decision to be reached at a meeting **Beschluß, Resolution; to put a resolution to a meeting** = to ask a meeting to vote on a proposal **einen Beschluß einbringen;** *the meeting passed or carried or adopted a resolution to go on strike; the meeting rejected the resolution or the resolution was defeated by ten votes to twenty*

resolve *verb* to decide to do something **beschließen, einen Beschluß fassen;** *the meeting resolved that a dividend should not be paid*

resources *plural noun*

(a) source of supply of something **Mittel, Ressourcen; natural resources** = supplies of gas, oil, coal, etc. which are available in the ground **Bodenschätze;** *the country is rich in natural resources;* **we are looking for a site with good water resources** = a site with plenty of water available **wir suchen ein Gelände mit guter Wasserversorgung**

(b) financial resources = supply of money for something **finanzielle Mittel;** *the costs of* *the London office are a drain on the company's financial resources; the company's financial resources are not strong enough to support the cost of the research programme;* **the cost of the new project is easily within our resources** = we have enough money to pay for the new project **die Kosten für das neue Projekt liegen durchaus im Rahmen unserer finanziellen Möglichkeiten**

respect
1 *noun* **with respect to** = concerning **in bezug auf, hinsichtlich, was ... betrifft**
2 *verb* to pay attention to **anerkennen, berücksichtigen;** *to respect a clause in an agreement; the company has not respected the terms of the contract*

◊ **respectively** *adverb* referring to each one separately **beziehungsweise;** *Mr Smith and Mr Jones are respectively MD and Sales Director of Smith Ltd*

response *noun* reply *or* reaction **Antwort, Reaktion;** *there was no response to our mailing shot; we got very little response to our complaints*

responsibility *noun*
(a) being responsible **Verantwortung, Verantwortlichkeit;** *there is no responsibility on the company's part for loss of customers' property; the management accepts no responsibility for loss of goods in storage*
(b) responsibilities = duties **Pflichten;** *he finds the responsibilities of being managing director too heavy*
NOTE: no plural for (a)

◊ **responsible** *adjective*
(a) responsible for = directing *or* being in charge of **verantwortlich/zuständig für;** *he is responsible for all sales*
(b) responsible to someone = being under someone's authority **jdm unterstellt sein;** *he is directly responsible to the managing director*
(c) a responsible job = job where important decisions have to be taken *or* where the employee has many responsibilities **eine verantwortungsvolle Stelle;** *he is looking for a responsible job in marketing*

rest *noun* what is left **Rest;** *the chairman went home, but the rest of the directors stayed in the boardroom; we sold most of the stock before Christmas and hope to clear the rest in a sale; the rest of the money is invested in gilts*
NOTE: usually singular, written with **the**

restaurant *noun* place where you can buy a meal **Restaurant, Gaststätte;** *he runs a French restaurant in New York*

◊ **restaurateur** *noun* person who runs a restaurant **Restaurantbesitzer; Gastwirt**

restitution *noun*
(a) giving back (property) **Rückerstattung, Rückgabe;** *the court ordered the restitution of assets to the company*
(b) compensation *or* payment for damage or loss **Entschädigung, Schadensersatz**
(c) *(in the EC)* **export restitution** = subsidies to European food exporters **Exporterstattung**
NOTE: no plural

restock *verb* to order more stock **Lager auffüllen;** *to restock after the Christmas sales*

◊ **restocking** *noun* ordering more stock **Lagerauffüllung**
NOTE: no plural

restraint *noun* control **Be-, Einschränkung; pay restraint** *or* **wage restraint** = keeping increases in wages under control **Politik der Lohnkontrolle; restraint of trade** = (i) situation where a worker is not allowed to use his knowledge in another company if he changes jobs; (ii) attempt by companies to fix prices *or* create monopolies *or* reduce competition, which could affect free trade **(i) Geheimhaltungspflicht; (ii) Wettbewerbs-, Handelsbeschr- änkung**

restrict *verb* to limit *or* to impose controls on **be-, einschränken;** *to restrict credit; we are restricted to twenty staff by the size of our offices; to restrict the flow of trade or to restrict imports;* **to sell into a restricted market** = to sell goods into a market where the supplier has agreed to limit sales to avoid competition **Waren auf einem beschränkten Markt absetzen**

◊ **restriction** *noun* limit *or* controlling **Be-, Einschränkung;** *import restrictions or restrictions on imports;* **to impose restrictions on imports** *or* **on credit** = to start limiting imports *or* credit **Importbeschränkungen od Kreditrestriktionen einführen; to lift credit restrictions** = to allow credit to be given freely **Kreditrestriktionen aufheben**

◊ **restrictive** *adjective* which limits **einschränkend, restriktiv; restrictive trade practices** = arrangement between companies to fix prices *or* to share the market, etc. **wettbewerbsbeschränkende Geschäftspraktiken**

restructure *verb* to reorganize the (financial) basis of a company **(finanziell) umstrukturieren, reorganisieren**

◊ **restructuring** *noun* **the restructuring of the company** = reorganizing the (financial) basis of a company **die (finanzielle) Neuorganisation des Unternehmens**
NOTE: no plural

result
1 *noun*
(a) profit or loss account for a company at the end of a trading period **Jahresergebnis;** *the company's results for 1984*
(b) something which happens because of something else **Resultat, Folge;** *what was the result of the price investigation? the company doubled its sales force with the result that the sales rose by 26%;* **the expansion programme has produced results** = the expansion programme has produced increased sales **das Expansionsprogramm hat gut Resultate erzielt; payment by results** = being paid for profits *or* increased sales **Leistungsgehalt**
2 *verb*
(a) **to result in** = to produce as a result **führen zu, zur Folge haben**
(b) **to result from** = to happen because of something **sich ergeben aus; zur Folge haben, hinauslaufen auf;** *the increase in debt resulted from the expansion programme; the doubling of the sales force resulted in increased sales; the extra orders resulted in overtime work for all the factory staff*

> QUOTE the company has received the backing of a number of oil companies who are willing to pay for the results of the survey
> *Lloyd's List*
>
> QUOTE some profit-taking was noted, but underlying sentiment remained firm in a steady stream of strong corporate results
> *Financial Times*

resume *verb* to start again **wiederaufnehmen;** *the discussions resumed after a two hour break*

resumé *noun US* summary of a person's life story with details of education and work experience **Lebenslauf**
NOTE: GB English is **curriculum vitae**

resumption *noun* starting again **Wiederaufnahme; we expect an early resumption of negotiations** = we expect negotiations will start again soon **wir rechnen mit einer baldigen Wiederaufnahme der Verhandlungen**
NOTE: no plural

retail
1 *noun* sale of small quantities of goods to ordinary customers **Einzelhandel; retail dealer** = person who sells to the general public **Einzelhändler; retail price** = full price paid by a customer in a shop **Einzelhandels-, Laden-, Endpreis; retail price index** = index showing how prices of retail goods have risen over a period of time **Index der Einzelhandelspreise; retail shop** *or* **retail outlet** = shop which sells goods to the general public **Einzelhandelsgeschäft; the retail trade** = all people *or* businesses selling goods retail **der Einzelhandel; the goods in stock have a retail value of £1m** = the value of the goods if sold to the public is £1m, before discounts etc. are taken into account **der Wiederverkaufswert der Waren auf Lager beträgt £1 Mio**
2 *adverb* **he sells retail and buys wholesale** = he buys goods in bulk at a wholesale discount and sells in small quantities to the public **er verkauft im Einzelhandel und kauft im Großhandel**
3 *verb*
(a) **to retail goods** = to sell goods direct to the public **Waren im Einzelhandel verkaufen**
(b) to sell for a price **wiederverkauft werden für; these items retail at** *or* **for 25p** = the retail price of these items is 25p **diese Waren kosten im Einzelhandel 25 Pence**

◊ **retailer** *noun* person who runs a retail business, selling goods direct to the public **Einzelhändler**

◊ **retailing** *noun* selling of full price goods to the public **Einzelhandel;** *from car retailing the company branched out into car leasing*
NOTE: no plural

retain *verb*
(a) to keep **(ein)behalten, zurückbehalten;** *out of the profits, the company has retained £50,000 as provision against bad debts;* **retained income** = profit not distributed to the shareholders as dividend **nicht ausgeschüttete Gewinne;** *the balance sheet has £50,000 in retained income*
(b) **to retain a lawyer to act for a company** = to agree with a lawyer that he will act for you (and pay him a fee in advance) **einen Anwalt beauftragen, für ein Unternehmen tätig zu werden**

◊ **retainer** *noun* money paid in advance to someone so that he will work for you, and not for someone else **Honorarvorschuß;** *we pay him a retainer of £1,000*

retire *verb*
(a) to stop work and take a pension **sich pensionieren lassen, in Pension gehen, in den Ruhestand treten, sich zur Ruhe setzen;** *she retired with a £6,000 pension; the founder of the company retired at the age of 85; the shop is owned by a retired policeman*

(b) to make a worker stop work and take a pension **in den Ruhestand versetzen;** *they decided to retire all staff over 50*
(c) to come to the end of an elected term of office **ausscheiden, zurücktreten;** *the treasurer retires from the council after six years; two retiring directors offer themselves for re-election*

◇ **retiral** *noun US* = RETIREMENT

◇ **retirement** *noun* act of retiring from work **Pensionierung; to take early retirement** = to leave work before the usual age **vorzeitig in den Ruhestand treten, sich vorzeitig pensionieren lassen; retirement age** = age at which people retire (in the UK usually 65 for men and 60 for women) **Rentenalter; retirement pension** = pension which someone receives when he retires **Altersruhegeld, Altersversorgung, Altersrente**
NOTE: no plural

retrain *verb* to train someone for a new job, or to do the same job in a more modern way **umschulen**

◇ **retraining** *noun* act of training again **Umschulung;** *the shop is closed for staff retraining; he had to attend a retraining session*
NOTE: no plural

retrenchment *noun* reduction of expenditure *or* of new plans **Kürzung, Senkung, Abbau, Einschränkung;** *the company is in for a period of retrenchment*

retrieve *verb* to get back (something) which has been lost; to get back (information) which is stored in a computer **zurückbekommen, wiedererlangen, zurückgewinnen; wiedergewinnen, wiederauffinden;** *the company is fighting to retrieve its market share; all of the information was accidentally wiped off the computer so we cannot retrieve our sales figures for the last month*

◇ **retrieval** *noun* getting back **Wiedererlangung, Zurückgewinnung; data retrieval** *or* **information retrieval** = getting information from the data stored in a computer **Datenwiedergewinnung; retrieval system** = system which allows information to be retrieved **System zur Datenrückgewinnung**
NOTE: no plural

retroactive *adjective* which takes effect from a time in the past **rückwirkend;** *retroactive pay rise; they got a pay rise retroactive to last January*

◇ **retroactively** *adverb* going back to a time in the past **rückwirkend**

return
1 *noun*
(a) going back *or* coming back **Rückkehr; return journey** = journey back to where you came from **Rückfahrt; a return ticket** *or* **a return** = a ticket for a journey to a place and back again **eine Rückfahrkarte;** *I want two returns to Edinburgh;* **return fare** = fare for a journey from one place to another and back again **Preis für eine Rückfahrkarte**
(b) sending back **Rückgabe, Rücksendung; he replied by return of post** = he replied by the next post service back **er antwortete postwendend; return address** = address to send back something **Absender; these goods are all on sale or return** = if the retailer does not sell them, he sends them back to the supplier, and pays only for the items sold **alle diese Waren haben wir auf Kommission**
(c) profit *or* income from money invested **Gewinn, Ertrag, Rendite;** *to bring in a quick return; what is the gross return on this line?;* **return on investment (ROI)** *or* **on capital** = profit shown as a percentage of money invested **Ertrag aus investiertem Kapital, Kapitalrendite, Investitionsrentabiliät; rate of return** = amount of interest *or* dividend produced by an investment, shown as a percentage **Rendite**
(d) official return = official report **amtliche Meldung, öffentliche Erklärung; to make a return to the tax office** *or* **to make an income tax return** = to send a statement of income to the tax office **eine Einkommenssteuererklärung abgeben; to fill in a VAT return** = to complete the form showing VAT receipts and expenditure **eine Mehrwertsteuererklärung ausfüllen; nil return** = report showing no sales *or* income *or* tax etc. **keinerlei Erträge; daily** *or* **weekly** *or* **quarterly sales return** = report of sales made each day *or* week *or* quarter **täglicher od wöchentlicher od vierteljährlicher Absatzbericht**
2 *verb*
(a) to send back **zurückgeben, zurückschicken, zurücksenden;** *to return unsold stock to the wholesaler; to return a letter to sender;* **returned empties** = empty bottles *or* containers which are sent back to a supplier **Leergut**
(b) to make a statement **erklären, angeben, melden;** *to return income of £15,000 to the tax authorities*

◇ **returnable** *adjective* **returnable bottles** which can be returned **Mehrwegflaschen;** *these bottles are not returnable*

◇ **returns** *plural noun*
(a) profits *or* income from investment **Gewinn, Einkünfte;** *the company is looking for quick returns on its investment;* **law of diminishing returns** = general rule that as more factors of production (land, labour

and capital) are added to the existing factors, so the amount they produce is proportionately smaller **Gesetzmäßigkeit vom abnehmenden Ertragszuwachs**
(b) unsold goods, especially books *or* newspapers *or* magazines sent back to the supplier **Retourwaren, Rücksendungen**

revalue *verb* to value something again (at a higher value than before) **aufwerten;** *the company's properties have been revalued; the dollar has been revalued against all world currencies*

◇ **revaluation** *noun* act of revaluing **Aufwertung;** *the balance sheet takes into account the revaluation of the company's properties; the revaluation of the dollar against the franc*

revenue *noun*
(a) money received **Einnahmen, Einkünfte, Einkommen;** *revenue from advertising or advertising revenue; oil revenues have risen with the rise in the dollar;* **revenue accounts** = accounts of a business which record money received as sales, commission etc. **Ertragskonto**
(b) money received by a government in tax **Steueraufkommen; Inland Revenue** *or US* **Internal Revenue Service** = government department which deals with tax **Finanzamt, Finanzverwaltung; revenue officer** = person working in the government tax offices **Finanzbeamter**

reversal *noun* change from being profitable to unprofitable **Umschwung, Rückschlag;** *the company suffered a reversal in the Far East*

reverse
1 *adjective* opposite *or* in the opposite direction **umgekehrt, entgegengesetzt; reverse takeover** = takeover of a large company by a small company **gegenläufige Fusion; reverse charge call** = telephone call where the person receiving the call agrees to pay for it **R-Gespräch**
2 *verb*
(a) to change a decision to the opposite **(ins Gegenteil) umkehren;** *the committee reversed its decision on import quotas*
(b) to reverse the charges = to make a phone call, asking the person receiving it to pay for it **ein R-Gespräch führen**

> QUOTE the trade balance sank $17 billion, reversing last fall's brief improvement
> *Fortune*

reversion *noun* return of property to an original owner **Rückfall, Zurückfallen; he has the reversion of the estate** = he will receive the estate when the present lease ends **der Grundbesitz wird an ihn zurückfallen**

◇ **reversionary** *adjective* (property) which passes to another owner on the death of the present one **Anwartschafts-; reversionary annuity** = annuity paid to someone on the death of another person **Rente auf den Überlebensfall**

review
1 *noun*
(a) general examination **Überblick, Überprüfung;** *to conduct a review of distributors;* **financial review** = examination of an organization's finances **Finanzprüfung; wage review** *or* **salary review** = examination of salaries *or* wages in a company to see if the workers should earn more **Gehaltsrevision; she had a salary review last April** = her salary was examined (and increased) in April **ihr Gehalt wurde letzten April revidiert**
(b) magazine *or* monthly or weekly journal **Zeitschrift**
2 *verb* to examine something generally **überprüfen; to review salaries** = to look at all salaries in a company to decide on increases **die Gehälter revidieren;** *his salary will be reviewed at the end of the year; the company has decided to review freelance payments in the light of the rising cost of living;* **to review discounts** = to look at discounts offered to decide whether to change them **Preisnachlässe neu überdenken**

revise *verb* to change something which has been calculated *or* planned **überarbeiten, neu bearbeiten;** *sales forecasts are revised annually; the chairman is revising his speech to the AGM*

revive *verb* to make more lively; to increase (after a recession) **beleben; wieder aufblühen;** *the government is introducing measures to revive trade; industry is reviving after the recession*

◇ **revival** *noun* **revival of trade** = increase in trade after a recession **Konjunkturaufschwung, Konjunkturbelebung**

revoke *verb* to cancel **aufheben, rückgängig machen, annullieren;** *to revoke a clause in an agreement; the quota on luxury items has been revoked*

revolving *adjective* **revolving credit** = system where someone can borrow money at any time up to an agreed amount, and continue to borrow while still paying off the original loan **Revolving-Kredit, revolvierender Kredit**

rich *adjective*
(a) having a lot of money **reich, wohlhabend;** *a rich stockbroker; a rich oil company*
(b) having a lot of natural resources **reich;** *the country is rich in minerals; oil-rich territory*

rid *verb* **to get rid of something** = to throw something away because it is useless **etwas abstoßen/loswerden;** *the company is trying to get rid of all its old stock; our department has been told to get rid of twenty staff*
NOTE: **getting rid - got rid**

rider *noun* additional clause **Zusatzklausel, Anhang;** *to add a rider to a contract*

rig
1 *noun* **oil rig** = platform which holds the equipment for taking oil out of the earth **Bohrinsel**
2 *verb* to arrange for a result to be changed **manipulieren;** *they tried to rig the election of officers;* **to rig the market** = to make share prices go up or down so as to make a profit **die Kurse manipulieren; rigging of ballots** *or* **ballot-rigging** = trying to change the result of an election by altering or destroying voting papers **Wahlmanipulation**
NOTE: **rigging - rigged**

right
1 *adjective*
(a) good *or* correct **richtig;** *the chairman was right when he said the figures did not add up; this is not the right plane for Paris*
(b) not left **rechts;** *the credits are on the right side of the page*
2 *noun*
(a) legal title to something **Recht, Berechtigung, Anrecht, Anspruch;** *right of renewal of a contract; she has a right to the property; he has no right to the patent; the staff have a right to know how the company is doing;* **foreign rights** = legal title to sell something (especially a book) in a foreign country **Auslandsrechte; right to strike** = legal title for workers to stop working if they have a good reason for it **Streikrecht; right of way** = legal title to go across someone's property **Wegerecht**
(b) rights issue = giving shareholders the right to buy more shares at a lower price **Bezugsrechtsausgabe**

◇ **rightful** *adjective* legally correct **rechtmäßig; rightful claimant** = person who has a legal claim to something **Anspruchsberechtigter; rightful owner** = legal owner **rechtmäßiger Besitzer**

◇ **right-hand** *adjective* belonging to the right side **rechts;** *the credit side is the right-hand column in the accounts; he keeps the address list in the right-hand drawer of his desk;* **right-hand man** = main assistant **rechte Hand**

ring
1 *noun* group of people who try to fix prices so as not to compete with each other and still make a large profit **Ring, Kartell, Syndikat**
2 *verb* to call using the telephone **anrufen;** *he rang (up) his stockbroker*
NOTE: **ringing - rang - has rung**

◇ **ring back** *verb* to telephone in reply to a phone call **zurückrufen;** *the managing director rang - can you ring him back?*

rise
1 *noun*
(a) increase *or* growing high **Anstieg, Erhöhung, Zunahme, Steigerung;** *rise in the price of raw materials; oil price rises brought about a recession in world trade; there is a rise in sales of 10%* *or* *sales show a rise of 10%; salaries are increasing to keep up with the rises in the cost of living; the recent rise in inter*
(b) increase in salary **Lohn-, Gehaltserhöhung;** *she asked her boss for a rise; he had a 6% rise in January*
NOTE: US English for (b) is **raise**
2 *verb* to move upwards *or* to become higher **ansteigen, sich erhöhen, zunehmen, steigen, in die Höhe gehen;** *prices are rising faster than inflation; interest rates have risen to 15%*
NOTE: **rising - rose - has risen**

> QUOTE the index of industrial production sank 0.2 per cent for the latest month after rising 0.3 per cent in March
> *Financial Times*
>
> QUOTE the stock rose to over $20 a share, higher than the $18 bid
> *Fortune*
>
> QUOTE customers' deposit and current accounts also rose to $655.31 million at the end of December
> *Hongkong Standard*

risk *noun*
(a) possible harm *or* chance of danger **Risiko; to run a risk** = to be likely to suffer harm **Gefahr laufen; to take a risk** = to do something which may make you lose money or suffer harm **ein Risiko eingehen; financial risk** = possibility of losing money **finanzielles Risiko;** *there is no financial risk in selling to East European countries on credit; he is running the risk of overspending his promotion budget; the company is taking a considerable risk in manufacturing 25m units without doing any market research*
(b) risk capital = capital for investment which may easily be lost in risky projects,

but which can also provide high returns **Risiko-, Wagniskapital**
(c) at owner's risk = situation where goods shipped *or* stored are insured by the owner, not by the transport company or the storage company **auf Gefahr des Eigentümers;** *goods left here are at owner's risk; the shipment was sent at owner's risk*
(d) loss *or* damage against which you are insured **Risiko, Gefahr, Gefährdung; fire risk** = situation *or* goods which could start a fire **Feuergefahr;** *that warehouse full of paper is a fire risk*
(e) he is a good *or* **bad risk** = it is not likely *or* it is very likely that the insurance company will have to pay out against claims where he is concerned **bei ihm besteht ein geringes od hohes Schadensrisiko**

◇ **risk-free** *adjective* with no risk involved **risikolos, wenig riskant;** *a risk-free investment*

◇ **risky** *adjective* dangerous *or* which may cause harm **gewagt, riskant;** *he lost all his money in some risky ventures in South America*

> QUOTE there is no risk-free way of taking regular income from your money higher than the rate of inflation and still preserving its value
> *Guardian*

rival *noun* person *or* company which competes in the same market **Konkurrent/-in; Konkurrenz;** *a rival company; to undercut a rival; we are analyzing the rival brands on the market*

road *noun*
(a) way used by cars *or* lorries, etc. to move from one place to another **Straße;** *road transport costs have risen; the main office is in London Road; use the Park Road entrance to get to the buying department*
(b) on the road = travelling **unterwegs;** *the salesmen are on the road thirty weeks a year; we have twenty salesmen on the road*

robot *noun* machine which can be programmed to work like a person **Roboter;** *the car is made by robots*

◇ **robotics** *noun* study of robots *or* making of robots **Roboter-Technologie; Roboter-Herstellung**
NOTE: takes a singular verb

rock *noun* large stone **Fels(en); the company is on the rocks** = the company is in great financial difficulties **das Unternehmen ist vom Pleitegeier bedroht**

◇ **rock bottom** *noun* **rock-bottom prices** = the lowest prices possible **Tiefst-, Niedrigst-, Schleuderpreise; sales have reached rock bottom** = sales have reached the lowest point possible **der Absatz hat einen Tiefpunkt erreicht**

> QUOTE investment companies took the view that secondhand prices had reached rock bottom and that levels could only go up
> *Lloyd's List*

rocket *verb* to rise fast **emporschnellen, sprunghaft ansteigen;** *rocketing prices; prices have rocketed*

ROI = RETURN ON INVESTMENT

roll
1 *noun* something which has been turned over and over to wrap round itself **Rolle;** *the desk calculator uses a roll of paper*
2 *verb* to make something go forward by turning it over **rollen;** *they rolled the computer into position*

◇ **roll on/roll off** *adjective* (ferry) where lorries and cars can drive straight into or off the boat **Ro Ro-**

◇ **roll over** *verb* **to roll over credit** *or* **a debt** = to make credit available over a continuing period *or* to allow a debt to stand after the repayment date **bei Fälligkeit einen Kredit erneuern/umschulden**

◇ **rolling plan** *noun* plan which runs for a period of time and is updated regularly for the same period **revolvierende Planung**

◇ **rolling stock** *noun* wagons, etc., used on the railway **rollendes Material**

room *noun*
(a) part of a building, divided off from other parts by walls **Zimmer, Raum;** *the chairman's room is at the end of the corridor;* **conference room** = room where a small meeting can take place **Besprechungszimmer; mail room** = section of a building where incoming letters are sorted and distributed to departments **Poststelle**
(b) bedroom in a hotel **Zimmer;** *I want a room with bath for two nights;* **double room** = room with two beds, for two people **Doppelzimmer; room service** = arrangement in a hotel where food or drink can be served in a guest's bedroom **Zimmerservice**
(c) space **Platz;** *the filing cabinets take up a lot of room; there is no more room in the computer file*
NOTE: no plural for (c)

rotation *noun* taking turns **Wechsel, Turnus, Rotation; to fill the post of chairman by rotation** = each member of the group is chairman for a period then gives the post to another member **die Positon des Vorsitzenden im Turnus vergeben; two directors retire by rotation** = two directors

retire because they have been directors longer than any others, but can offer themselves for re-election **zwei Direktoren treten turnusmäßig zurück**
NOTE: no plural

rouble *noun* money used in Russia **Rubel**

rough *adjective*
(a) approximate *or* not very accurate **ungefähr, grob; rough calculation** *or* **rough estimate** = approximate answer **grobe Berechnung/Schätzung;** *I made some rough calculations on the back of an envelope*
(b) not finished **Roh-; rough copy** = draft of a document which will have changes made to it before it is complete **Konzept, Entwurf;** *he made a rough draft of the new design*
◇ **roughly** *adverb* more or less **ungefähr;** *the turnover is roughly twice last year's; the development cost of the project will be roughly £25,000*
◇ **rough out** *verb* to make a draft *or* a general design **grob entwerfen;** *the finance director roughed out a plan of investment*

round
1 *adjective*
(a) in round figures = not totally accurate, but correct to the nearest 10 or 100 **aufgerundet; abgerundet**
(b) round trip = journey from one place to another and back again **Hin- und Rückfahrt;** *round-trip ticket; round-trip fare*
◇ **round down** *verb* to decrease to the nearest full figure **abrunden**
◇ **round up** *verb* to increase to the nearest full figure **aufrunden;** *to round up the figures to the nearest pound*

> QUOTE each cheque can be made out for the local equivalent of £100 rounded up to a convenient figure
> *Sunday Times*

route *noun*
(a) way which is regularly taken **Route, Strecke; bus route** = normal way taken by a bus from one place to another **Busstrecke;** *companies were warned that normal shipping routes were dangerous because of the war*
(b) en route = on the way **unterwegs, auf dem Weg;** *the tanker sank when she was en route to the Gulf*

routine
1 *noun* normal *or* regular way of doing something **Routine;** *he follows a daily routine - he takes the 8.15 train to London, then the bus to his office, and returns by the same route in the evening; refitting the conference room has disturbed the office routine*
2 *adjective* normal *or* which happens regularly **Routine-, routinemäßig;** *routine work; routine call; a routine check of the fire equipment*

royalty *noun*
(a) money paid to an inventor **Lizenz-, Patentgebühren**
(b) money paid to a writer **Tantiemen, Autorenhonorar**
(c) money paid to the owner of land for right to use his property (usually a certain percentage of sales, or a certain amount per sale) **Nutzungsgebühr;** *he is receiving royalties from his invention; book royalties are linked to book sales; oil royalties make up a large proportion of the country's revenue*

RPM = RESALE PRICE MAINTENANCE

RRP = RECOMMENDED RETAIL PRICE

RSVP = REPONDEZ S'IL VOUS PLAIT letters on an invitation showing the person to whom replies should be sent **u.A.w.g.**

rubber *noun* elastic material from the juice of a tree **Gummi, Kautschuk;** *US* **rubber check** = cheque which cannot be cashed because the person writing it does not have enough money in the account to pay it **ungedeckter Scheck**
◇ **rubber stamp**
1 *noun* stamp with rubber letters or figures on it to put the date *or* a note on a document **(Gummi)stempel;** *he stamped the invoice with the rubber stamp "Paid"*
2 *verb* to agree to something without discussing it **bedenkenlos zustimmen/genehmigen;** *the board simply rubber stamped the agreement*

rule
1 *noun*
(a) general way of conduct **Regel; as a rule** = usually **in der Regel, normalerweise;** *as a rule, we do not give discounts over 20%;* **company rules** = general way of working in a company **Betriebsvorschriften;** *it is a company rule that smoking is not allowed in the offices*
(b) to work to rule = to work strictly according to the rules agreed by the company and union, and therefore to work very slowly **Dienst nach Vorschrift tun**
2 *verb*
(a) to give an official decision **entscheiden, anordnen, bestimmen;** *the commission of inquiry ruled that the company was in*

breach of contract; the judge ruled that the documents had to be deposited with the court
(b) to be in force *or* to be current **gelten;** *prices which are ruling at the moment*

◊ **ruling**
1 *adjective* in operation at the moment *or* current **geltend, laufend;** *we will invoice at ruling prices*
2 *noun* decision **Entscheidung;** *the inquiry gave a ruling on the case; according to the ruling of the court, the contract was illegal*

run

1 *noun*
(a) making a machine work **Durchlauf, Maschinenlauf; a cheque run** = series of cheques processed through a computer **Ausstellung von Schecks durch Computer; a computer run** = period of work of a computer **Arbeitsgang/Durchlauf eines Computers; test run** = trial made on a machine **Probelauf**
(b) rush to buy something **Ansturm, Andrang, Run;** *the Post Office reported a run on the new stamps;* **a run on the bank** = rush by customers to take deposits out of a bank which they think may close down **Bankrun, Ansturm auf die Bank; a run on the pound** = rush to sell pounds and buy other currencies **Panikverkäufe des Pfundes**
(c) regular route (of a plane *or* bus) **Strecke**
2 *verb*
(a) to be in force **gelten, gültig sein;** *the lease runs for twenty years; the lease has only six months to run*
(b) to amount to **sich belaufen auf, gehen;** *the costs ran into thousands of pounds*
(c) to manage *or* to organize **betreiben, leiten, führen;** *she runs a mail-order business from home; they run a staff sports club; he is running a multimillion-pound company*
(d) to work on a machine **bedienen, betreiben;** *do not run the photocopier for more than four hours at a time*
(e) *(of buses, trains etc.)* to be working **verkehren, fahren;** *there is an evening plane running between Manchester and Paris; this train runs on weekdays*
NOTE: **running - ran - has run**

◊ **runaway** *adjective* **runaway inflation** = very rapid inflation, which is almost impossible to reduce **galoppierende Inflation**

◊ **run down** *verb*
(a) to reduce a quantity gradually **abbauen;** *to run down stocks or to let stocks run down*
(b) to slow down the business activities of a company before it is going to be closed **nach und nach auflösen;** *the company is being run down*

◊ **run into** *verb*
(a) to run into debt = to start to have debts **in Schulden geraten**
(b) to amount to **gehen, sich belaufen auf;** *costs have run into thousands of pounds;* **he has an income running into five figures** = he earns more than £10,000 **er hat ein Einkommen, das sich auf fünfstellige Zahlen beläuft**

◊ **running** *noun*
(a) running total = total carried from one column of figures to the next **laufende Summe**
(b) running costs *or* **running expenses** *or* **costs of running a business** = money spent on the day-to-day cost of keeping a business going **Betriebskosten, allgemeine Unkosten, Festkosten**
(c) the company has made a profit for six years running = the company has made a profit for six years one after the other **der Betrieb hat sechs Jahre hintereinander Profit gemacht**

◊ **run out of** *verb* **she ran out of coins** she used them all up **ihr gingen die Münzen aus;** *we have run out of headed notepaper; the printer has run out of paper*

◊ **run up** *verb* to make debts go up quickly **(Schulden) anwachsen lassen;** *he quickly ran up a bill for £250*

> QUOTE applications for mortgages are running at a high level
> *Times*
>
> QUOTE business is booming for airlines on the London to Manchester run
> *Business Traveller*

rupee *noun* money used in India and some other countries **Rupie**

rush

1 *noun* doing something fast **Eile, Hast; rush hour** = time when traffic is worst *or* when everyone is trying to travel to work or from work back home **Hauptverkehrszeit, Rush-hour;** *the taxi was delayed in the rush hour traffic;* **rush job** = job which has to be done fast **Eilauftrag; rush order** = order which has to be supplied fast **Eilbestellung**
2 *verb* to make something go fast **treiben, hetzen; schnell transportieren;** *to rush an order through the factory; to rush a shipment to Africa*

Ss

sack

1 *noun*
(a) large bag made of strong cloth or plastic **Sack;** *a sack of potatoes; we sell onions by the sack*

(b) to get the sack = to be dismissed from a job **rausgeschmissen werden**
NOTE: no plural for (b)
2 *verb* **to sack someone** = to dismiss someone from a job **jdn rausschmeißen;** *he was sacked after being late for work*

◇ **sacking** *noun* dismissal from a job **Rausschmiß, Entlassung;** *the union protested against the sackings*

SAE *or* **s.a.e.** = STAMPED ADDRESSED ENVELOPE

safe
1 *noun* heavy metal box which cannot be opened easily, in which valuable documents, money, etc. can be kept **Safe, Tresor;** *put the documents in the safe; we keep the petty cash in the safe;* **fire-proof safe** = safe which cannot be harmed by fire **feuersicherer Tresor; night safe** = safe in the outside wall of a bank, where money and documents can be deposited at night, using a special door **Nachttresor; wall safe** = safe installed in a wall **Wandtresor**
2 *adjective*
(a) out of danger **sicher; keep the documents in a safe place** = in a place where they cannot be stolen or destroyed **bewahre die Unterlagen an einem sicheren Ort auf; safe keeping** = being looked after carefully **Verwahrung;** *we put the documents into the bank for safe keeping*
(b) safe investments = shares, etc., which are not likely to fall in value **risikofreie Investitionen, sichere Kapitalanlagen**

◇ **safe deposit** *noun* bank safe where you can leave jewellery or documents **Tresor**

◇ **safe deposit box** *noun* small box which you can rent to keep jewellery or documents in a bank's safe **Bankschließfach**

◇ **safely** *adverb* without being harmed **sicher, wohlbehalten;** *the cargo was unloaded safely from the sinking ship*

◇ **safeguard** *verb* to protect **schützen, sichern;** *to safeguard the interests of the shareholders*

◇ **safety** *noun*
(a) being free from danger or risk **Sicherheit; safety margin** = time *or* space allowed for something to be safe **Sicherheitsspielraum; margin of safety** = sales which are above the breakeven point **Sicherheitsmarge; to take safety precautions** *or* **safety measures** = to act to make sure something is safe **Vorsichtsmaßnahmen ergreifen; safety regulations** = rules to make a place of work safe for the workers **Sicherheitsvorschriften**
(b) fire safety = making a place of work safe for the workers in case of fire **Brandschutz; fire safety officer** = person in a company responsible for seeing that the workers are safe if a fire breaks out **Betriebsfeuerwehrmann**
(c) for safety = to make something safe *or* to be safe **sicherheitshalber;** *put the documents in the cupboard for safety; to take a copy of the disk for safety*
NOTE: no plural

sail *verb* to travel on water *or* to leave harbour **fahren; ablegen, auslaufen, in See stechen;** *the ship sails at 12.00*

◇ **sailing** *noun* departure (of a ship) **Abfahrt;** *there are no sailings to France because of the strike*

salary *noun* payment for work, made to an employee usually as a cheque at the end of each month **Gehalt;** *she got a salary increase in June; the company froze all salaries for a six-month period;* **basic salary** = normal salary without extra payments **Ecklohn; Grundgehalt; gross salary** = salary before tax is deducted **Bruttogehalt; net salary** = salary which is left after deducting tax and national insurance contributions **Nettogehalt; starting salary** = amount of payment for an employee when starting work **Anfangsgehalt;** *he was appointed at a starting salary of £10,000;* **salary cut** = sudden reduction in salary **Gehaltskürzung; salary cheque** = monthly cheque by which an employee is paid **Gehaltsscheck; salary deductions** = money which a company removes from salaries to give to the government as tax, national insurance contributions, etc. **Lohnabzüge; salary review** = examination of salaries in a company to see if workers should earn more **Gehaltsrevision;** *she had a salary review last April or her salary was reviewed last April;* **scale of salaries** *or* **salary scale** = list of salaries showing different levels of pay in different jobs in the same company **Gehaltstabelle; the company's salary structure** = organization of salaries in a company, with different rates for different types of job **die Gehaltsstrukur des Unternehmens**

◇ **salaried** *adjective* earning a salary **fest angestellt;** *the company has 250 salaried staff*

> QUOTE the union of hotel and personal service workers has demanded a new salary structure and uniform conditions of service for workers in the hotel and catering industry
> *Business Times (Lagos)*

sale *noun*
(a) act of selling *or* of giving an item in exchange for money **Verkauf; cash sale** = selling something for cash **Barverkauf; credit card sale** = selling something for credit, using a credit card **Verkauf auf Kreditkarte;**

forced sale = selling something because a court orders it *or* because it is the only thing to do to avoid a financial crisis **Zwangsverkauf; sale and lease-back** = situation where a company sells a property to raise cash and then leases it back from the purchaser **Verkauf bei gleichzeitiger Vermietung an den Verkäufer; sale or return** = system where the retailer sends goods back if they are not sold, and pays the supplier only for goods sold **Verkauf auf Kommission, Kauf mit Rückgaberecht;** *we have taken 4,000 items on sale or return;* **bill of sale** = document which the seller gives to the buyer to show that a sale has taken place **Kaufvertrag; conditions of sale** = agreed ways in which a sale takes place (such as discounts and credit terms) **Verkaufsbedingungen**

(b) for sale = ready to be sold **zu verkaufen; to offer something for sale** *or* **to put something up for sale** = to announce that something is ready to be sold **etwas zum Verkauf anbieten;** *they put the factory up for sale; his shop is for sale; these items are not for sale to the general public*

(c) to be on sale = ready to be sold in a shop **zum Verkauf stehen;** *these items are on sale in most chemists*

(d) sales = money received for selling something *or* number of items sold **Umsatz, Absatz;** *sales have risen over the first quarter;* **sales analysis** = examining the reports of sales to see why items have or have not sold well **Umsatz-, Absatzanalyse; sales appeal** = quality which makes customers want to buy **Kaufanreiz; sales book** = record of sales **Verkaufsbuch, Warenausgangsjournal; book sales** = sales as recorded in the sales book **Absatz laut Verkaufsbuch; sales budget** = plan of probable sales **Absatzplanung; sales campaign** = planned work to achieve higher sales **Verkaufsaktion; sales conference** *or* **sales meeting** = meeting of sales managers, representatives, publicity staff, etc., to discuss results and future sales plans **Konferenz zur Absatzplanung; cost of sales** = all the costs of a product sold, including manufacturing costs and the staff costs of the production department **Absatz-, Vertriebskosten; sales department** = section of a company which deals in selling the company's products or services **Verkaufsabteilung, Abteilung Verkauf; domestic sales** *or* **home sales** = sales in the home market **Inlandsabsatz; sales drive** = vigorous work to increase sales **Verkaufskampagne; sales executive** = person in a company in charge of sales **Verkaufsleiter; sales figures** = total sales, or sales broken down by category **Verkaufs-, Absatzzahlen; sales force** = group of salesmen **Verkäuferstab, Verkaufspersonal; sales forecast** = calculation of future sales **Absatzprognose; forward sales** = sales (of shares, commodities, foreign exchange) for delivery at a later date **Terminverkäufe; sales ledger** = book in which income from sales is recorded **Warenausgangsbuch; sales ledger clerk** = office worker who deals with the sales ledger **für das Warenausgangsbuch zuständiger Angestellter; sales literature** = printed information (such as leaflets, prospectuses) which help sales **Werbematerial, Verkaufsprospekte; sales manager** = person in charge of a sales department **Verkaufsleiter; monthly sales report** = report made showing the number of items *or* amount of money received for selling stock **monatlicher Absatzbericht;** *in the sales reports all the European countries are bracketed together;* **sales revenue** = money received from sales **Verkaufserlös; sales tax** = tax to be paid on each item sold **Warenumsatzsteuer; sales volume** *or* **volume of sales** = number of units sold **Absatz-, Umsatzvolumen, Absatz**

(e) selling of goods at specially low prices **Ausverkauf;** *the shop is having a sale to clear old stock; the sale price is 50% of the normal price;* **bargain sale** = sale of all goods in a store at cheap prices **Ausverkauf; clearance sale** = sale of items at low prices to get rid of the stock **Räumungsverkauf; half-price sale** = sale of items at half the usual price **Verkauf zum halben Preis; jumble sale** = sale of old used household goods; *entspricht* **Wohltätigkeitsbasar; the sales** = period when major stores sell many items at specially low prices **Schlußverkauf;** *I bought this in the sales or at the sales or in the January sales*

◇ **saleability** *noun* quality of an item which makes it easy to sell **Absatzfähigkeit**
NOTE: no plural

◇ **saleable** *adjective* which can easily be sold **gut verkäuflich, absatzfähig**

◇ **saleroom** *noun* room where an auction takes place **Auktionsraum**

◇ **salesclerk** *noun US* person who sells goods to customers in a store **Verkäufer/-in**

◇ **salesgirl** *noun* girl who sells goods to customers in a store **Verkäuferin**

◇ **saleslady** *noun* woman who sells goods to customers in a store **Verkäuferin**

◇ **salesman** *noun*

(a) man who sells goods or services to members of the public **Verkäufer;** *he is the head salesman in the carpet department; a used car salesman;* **door-to-door salesman** = man who goes from one house to the next, asking people to buy something **Vertreter; insurance salesman** = man who encourages clients to take out insurance policies **Versicherungsvertreter**

(b) person who represents a company, selling its products or services to retail shops **Vertreter, Handelsvertreter;** *we have six salesmen calling on accounts in central London*

NOTE: plural is **salesmen**

◇ **salesmanship** *noun* art of selling *or* of persuading customers to buy **Gewandheit beim Verkaufen, Verkaufstechnik**

NOTE: no plural

◇ **saleswoman** *noun* woman in a shop who sells goods to customers **Verkäuferin**

NOTE: plural is **saleswomen**

> QUOTE the latest car sales for April show a 1.8 per cent dip from last year's total
> *Investors Chronicle*
>
> QUOTE the wage agreement includes sales clerks and commission sales people in stores in Toronto
> *Toronto Star*

salvage

1 *noun*

(a) saving a ship *or* a cargo from being destroyed **Bergung; salvage money** = payment made by the owner of a ship *or* a cargo to the person who has saved it **Bergelohn; salvage vessel** = ship which specializes in saving other ships and their cargoes **Bergungsschiff**

(b) goods saved from a wrecked ship *or* from a fire, etc. **Bergungsgut;** *a sale of flood salvage items*

NOTE: no plural

2 *verb*

(a) to save goods *or* a ship from being wrecked **bergen;** *we are selling off a warehouse full of salvaged goods*

(b) to save something from loss **retten;** *the company is trying to salvage its reputation after the managing director was sent to prison for fraud; the receiver managed to salvage something from the collapse of the company*

sample

1 *noun*

(a) specimen *or* a small part of an item which is used to show what the whole item is like **Muster, Probe, Warenprobe;** *a sample of the cloth or a cloth sample;* **check sample** = sample to be used to see if a whole consignment is acceptable **Prüfmuster; free sample** = sample given free to advertise a product **Gratisprobe; sample book** *or* **book of samples** = book showing samples of different types of cloth *or* paper, etc. **Musterbuch**

(b) small group taken to show what a larger group is like **Auswahl;** *we interviewed a sample of potential customers;* **a random sample** = a sample taken without any selection **Stichprobe**

2 *verb*

(a) to test *or* to try something by taking a small amount **probieren, testen, kosten;** *to sample a product before buying it*

(b) to ask a representative group of people questions to find out what the reactions of a much larger group would be **eine Repräsentativerhebung durchführen;** *they sampled 2,000 people at random to test the new drink*

◇ **sampling** *noun*

(a) testing a product by taking a small amount **Probeentnahme;** *sampling of Common Market produce;* **acceptance sampling** = testing a small sample of a batch to see if the whole batch is good enough to be accepted **Qualitätskontrolle mittels Stichproben**

(b) testing the reactions of a small group of people to find out the reactions of a larger group of consumers **Stichprobenverfahren, Befragung eines repräsentativen Querschnitts;** *random sampling*

sanction

1 *noun*

(a) permission **Zustimmung, Genehmigung;** *you will need the sanction of the local authorities before you can knock down the office block*

(b) economic sanctions = restrictions on trade with a country in order to influence its political situation *or* in order to make its government change its policy **Wirtschaftssanktionen;** *to impose sanctions on a country or to lift sanctions*

2 *verb* to approve **sanktionieren, genehmigen,;** *the board sanctioned the expenditure of £1.2m on the development project*

sandwich *noun* two pieces of bread with meat *or* cheese, etc. between them **Sandwich**

◇ **sandwich boards** *noun* boards carried in front of and behind a person to carry advertisements **Sandwich-Plakat, von Plakatträger getragene Werbetafel**

◇ **sandwich course** *noun* course of study where students spend a period of time working in a factory *or* office as part of a college course **Studium mit integriertem Praktikum**

◇ **sandwich man** *noun* man who carries sandwich boards **Sandwichmann, Plakatträger**

satisfaction *noun* feeling of being happy *or* good feeling **Zufriedenheit, Befriedigung, Zufriedenstellung; customer satisfaction** = making a customer pleased with what he has bought **Zufriedenstellung des Kunden; job satisfaction** = a worker's feeling that he is happy in his place of work and pleased with

the work he does **Zufriedenheit am Arbeitsplatz**
NOTE: no plural

◇ **satisfy** *verb*
(a) to satisfy a client = to make a client pleased with what he has purchased **einen Kunden zufriedenstellen; a satisfied customer** = a customer who has got what he wanted **ein zufriedener Kunde**
(b) to satisfy a demand = to fill a demand **Nachfrage stillen/befriedigen;** *we cannot produce enough to satisfy the demand for the product*

saturation *noun* filling completely **Sättigung; saturation of the market** *or* **market saturation** = situation where the market has taken as much of the product as it can buy **Marktsättigung; the market has reached saturation point** = the market is at a point where it cannot buy any more of the product **der Markt hat den Sättigungsgrad erreicht**
NOTE: no plural

◇ **saturate** *verb* to fill something completely **sättigen;** *to saturate the market; the market for home computers is saturated*

save *verb*
(a) to keep (money) *or* not to spend (money) **sparen;** *he is trying to save money by walking to work; she is saving to buy a house*
(b) not to waste *or* to use less **(ein)sparen;** *to save time, let us continue the discussion in the taxi to the airport; the government is encouraging companies to save energy*
(c) to store data on a computer disk **sichern;** *do not forget to save your files when you have finished keyboarding them*

◇ **save-as-you-earn** *noun GB* **save-as-you-earn scheme** = scheme where workers can save money regularly by having it deducted automatically from their wages and invested in National Savings **steuerfreies Sparprogramm, bei dem der Sparbetrag automatisch vom Lohn abgezogen wird**

◇ **save on** *verb* not to waste *or* to use less **(ein)sparen;** *by introducing shift work we find we can save on fuel*

◇ **saver** *noun* person who saves money **Sparer/-in**

◇ **save up** *verb* to put money aside for a special purpose **sparen;** *they are saving up for a holiday in the USA*

◇ **saving**
1 *noun* using less **Einsparung;** *we are aiming for a 10% saving in fuel*
2 *suffix* which uses less **-sparend; an energy-saving** *or* **labour-saving device** = machine which saves energy *or* labour **ein energiesparendes od arbeitsparendes Gerät; time-saving** = which takes less time **zeitsparend**

◇ **savings** *plural noun* money saved **Ersparnisse;** *he put all his savings into a deposit account; GB* **National Savings** = scheme run by the Post Office, where small investors can invest in government savings certificates, premium bonds, etc. **britisches Sparsystem; savings certificate** *or US* **savings bond** = document showing that you have invested money in a government savings scheme **Sparschuldverschreibung, Sparbrief; savings account** = bank account where you can put money in regularly and which pays interest, often at a higher rate than a deposit account **Sparkonto**

◇ **savings bank** *noun* bank where you can deposit money and receive interest on it **Sparkasse**

◇ **savings and loan (association)** *noun US* financial association which accepts and pays interest on deposits from investors and lends money to people who are buying property; *entspricht* **Bausparkasse**
NOTE: the GB English for this is **building society**

SAYE = SAVE-AS-YOU-EARN

scab *noun informal* worker who goes on working when there is a strike **Streikbrecher/-in**

scale
1 *noun*
(a) system which is graded into various levels **Skala, Tabelle; scale of charges** *or* **scale of prices** = list showing various prices **Preisliste, Gebührenordnung, Tarife; fixed scale of charges** = rate of charging which does not change **verbindliche Gebührenordnung; scale of salaries** *or* **salary scale** = list of salaries showing different levels of pay in different jobs in the same company **Gehaltstabelle;** *he was appointed at the top end of the salary scale;* **incremental scale** = salary scale with regular annual salary increases **Gehaltssteigerungstabelle**
(b) large scale *or* **small scale** = working with large or small amounts of investment *or* staff, etc. **in großem Umfang; in begrenztem Umfang; to start in business on a small scale** = to start in business with a small staff *or* few products *or* little investments **er fing sein Geschäft klein an; economies of scale** = making a product more economical by manufacturing it or buying it in larger quantities **Größendegression**
(c) scales = machine for weighing **Waage**
2 *verb* **to scale down** *or* **to scale up** = to lower *or* to increase in proportion **verringern, herabsetzen; erhöhen, heraufsetzen**

scam *noun US informal* case of fraud **Betrug**

scarce *adjective* not easily found *or* not common **rar, selten, knapp;** *scarce raw materials; reliable trained staff are scarce*
◇ **scarceness** *or* **scarcity** *noun* lack *or* being scarce **Knappheit, Seltenheit, Mangel;** *the scarceness of trained staff; there is a scarcity of trained staff;* **scarcity value** = value of something because it is rare and there is a large demand for it **Seltenheitswert**
NOTE: no plural

schedule
1 *noun*
(a) timetable *or* plan of time drawn up in advance **Zeitplan; Arbeitsplan; Terminplan; to be ahead of schedule** = to be early **vorzeitig, dem Zeitplan voraus sein; to be on schedule** = to be on time **pünktlich/rechtzeitig fertig sein; plangemäß vorankommen; to be behind schedule** = to be late **in Verzug sein;** *the project is on schedule; the building was completed ahead of schedule; I am sorry to say that we are three months behind schedule; the managing director has a busy schedule of appointments; his secretary tried to fit me into his schedule*
(b) list (especially additional documents attached to a contract) **Verzeichnis, Liste, Aufstellung; Anhang;** *please find enclosed our schedule of charges; schedule of territories to which a contract applies; see the attached schedule or as per the attached schedule*
(c) *GB* **tax schedules** = six types of income as classified for tax **Steuerklassen**
2 *verb*
(a) to list officially **festlegen, aufführen;** *scheduled prices or scheduled charges*
(b) to plan the time when something will happen **ansetzen, anberaumen;** *the building is scheduled for completion in May;* **scheduled flight** = regular flight which is in the airline timetable **Linienflug;** *he left for Helsinki on a scheduled flight*
◇ **scheduling** *noun* drawing up a plan *or* a timetable **Ablauf-, Terminplanung**
NOTE: no plural

scheme *noun* plan *or* arrangement *or* way of working **Plan, Programm, Vorhaben, Projekt;** *bonus scheme; pension scheme; profit-sharing scheme*

science *noun* study *or* knowledge based on observing and testing **Wissenschaft; business science** *or* **management science** = the study of business *or* management techniques **Wirtschaftswissenschaft; Managementlehre;** *he has a master's degree in business science;* **science park** = area near a town or university set aside for technological industries **Technologiezentrum**

scope *noun* opportunity *or* possibility **Möglichkeiten; there is scope for improvement in our sales performance** = the sales performance could be improved **unsere Verkaufsleistung könnte verbessert werden;** *there is considerable scope for expansion into the export market*

scrap
1 *noun* waste material *or* pieces of metal to be melted down to make new metal ingots **Altmaterial, Schrott;** *to sell a ship for scrap; its scrap value is £2,500;* **scrap dealer** *or* **scrap merchant** = person who deals in scrap **Schrotthändler**
2 *verb*
(a) to give up *or* to stop working on **aufgeben, fallenlassen;** *to scrap plans for expansion*
(b) to throw (something) away as useless **verschrotten;** *they had to scrap 10,000 spare parts*
NOTE: **scrapping - scrapped**

screen
1 *noun* glass surface on which computer information *or* TV pictures, etc., can be shown **Bildschirm;** *a TV screen; he brought up the information on the screen*
2 *verb* **to screen candidates** = to examine candidates to see if they are completely suitable **Bewerber sieben/aussondern**
◇ **screening** *noun* **the screening of candidates** = examining candidates to see if they are suitable **das Aussondern geeigneter Bewerber**

scrip *noun* **scrip issue** = new shares given free to shareholders **Ausgabe von Gratisaktien**

sea *noun* area of salt water **Meer, See;** *to send a shipment by sea;* **by sea mail** = sent by post abroad, using a ship, not by air **Postsendung auf dem Seeweg**
◇ **seaport** *noun* port by the sea **Seehafen**

seal
1 *noun*
(a) common seal *or* **company's seal** = metal stamp for stamping documents with the name of the company to show they have been approved officially **Firmensiegel;** *to attach the company's seal to a document;* **contract under seal** = contract which has been legally approved with the seal of the company **beurkundeter/besiegelter Vertrag**
(b) piece of paper *or* metal *or* wax attached to close something, so that it can be opened

only if the paper *or* metal *or* wax is removed or broken **Versiegelung; customs seal** = seal attached by customs office to a box, to show that the contents have not passed through the customs **Plombe, Zollverschluß**
2 *verb*
(a) to close something tightly **fest verschließen, zukleben;** *the computer disks were sent in a sealed container;* **sealed envelope** = envelope where the back has been stuck down to close it **verschlossener Briefumschlag;** *the information was sent in a sealed envelope;* **sealed tenders** = tenders sent in sealed envelopes, which will all be opened at a certain time **versiegelte Submissionsofferten;** *the company has asked for sealed bids for the warehouse*
(b) to attach a seal *or* to stamp something with a seal **versiegeln; plombieren;** *the customs sealed the shipment*

search *noun* examination of records by the lawyer acting for someone who wants to buy a property, to make sure that the vendor has the right to sell it **Einsichtnahme in das Grundbuch, um festzustellen, ob etwaige Rechte Dritter an dem zu kaufenden Grundbesitz bestehen**

season *noun*
(a) one of four parts which a year is divided into (spring, summer, autumn, winter) **Jahreszeit**
(b) a period of time when something usually takes place **Saison; low season** *or* **high season** = period when there are few travellers *or* lots of travellers **Nachsaison; Haupt-, Hochsaison;** *air fares are cheaper in the low season;* **tourist season** *or* **holiday season** = period when there are many people on holiday **Urlaubszeit; busy season** *or* **slack season** = period when a company is busy *or* not very busy **umsatzstarke/belebte Jahreszeit; umsatzschwache Jahreszeit, Zeit der Flaute; dead season** = time of year when there are few tourists about **Nebensaison; end of season sale** = selling goods cheaply when the season in which they would be used is over (such as summer clothes sold cheaply in the autumn) **Saisonschlußverkauf**

◇ **seasonal** *adjective* which lasts for a season *or* which only happens during a particular season **Saison-, saisonbedingt, jahreszeitlich bedingt;** *the demand for this item is very seasonal; seasonal variations in sales patterns;* **seasonal adjustments** = changes made to figures to take account of seasonal variations **Saisonbereinigungen; seasonal demand** = demand which exists only during the high season **saisonbedingte Nachfrage; seasonal unemployment** = unemployment which rises and falls according to the season **saisonbedingte Arbeitslosigkeit**

◇ **seasonally** *adverb* **seasonally adjusted figures** = statistics which are adjusted to take account of seasonal variations **saisonbereinigte Beträge**

◇ **season ticket** *noun* rail *or* bus ticket which can be used for any number of journeys over a period (normally 1, 3, 6 or 12 months) **Zeitkarte**

sec = SECRETARY; **hon sec** = honorary secretary **ehrenamtlicher Sekretär**

second
1 *adjective* (thing) which comes after the first **zweiter; second half-year** = six month period from July to the end of December **zweites Halbjahr; second mortgage** = further mortgage on a property which is already mortgaged **Zweithypothek; second quarter** = three month period from April to the end of June **zweites Quartal**
2 *verb*
(a) to second a motion = to be the first person to support a proposal put forward by someone else **einen Antrag unterstützen;** *Mrs Smith seconded the motion or the motion was seconded by Mrs Smith*
(b) to lend a member of staff to another company *or* to a government department, etc., for a fixed period of time **abstellen;** *he was seconded to the Department of Trade for two years*

◇ **secondary** *adjective* second in importance **sekundär, Sekundär-, Neben-, zweitrangig; secondary banks** = companies which provide money for hire-purchase deals **Teilzahlungsinstitute; secondary industry** = industry which uses basic raw materials to make manufactured goods **verarbeitende Industrie; secondary picketing** = picketing of a second factory, which is not directly connected with a strike, to prevent it supplying a striking factory or receiving supplies from it **Bestreikung eines indirekt beteiligten Betriebes**

◇ **second-class** *adjective & adverb* less expensive *or* less comfortable way of travelling **zweite Klasse;** *to travel second-class; the price of a second-class ticket is half that of a first class; I find second-class hotels are just as comfortable as the best ones;* **second-class mail** = (i); *GB* less expensive, slower, mail service; (ii); *US* mail service for sending newspapers and magazines **(i) Postsendungen zweiter Klasse; (ii);** *entspricht* **Drucksache;** *a second-class letter is slower than a first-class; send it second-class if it is not urgent*

◇ **seconder** *noun* person who seconds a proposal **Befürworter/-in;** *there was no* *seconder for the motion so it was not put to the vote*

◇ **second half** *noun* period of six months from 1st July to end of December **zweites Halbjahr;** *the figures for the second half are up on those for the first part of the year*

◇ **secondhand** *adjective & adverb* used *or* not new *or* which has been owned by someone before **gebraucht, Gebraucht-;** *a secondhand car salesman; the secondhand computer market or the market in secondhand computers; to buy something secondhand; look at the prices of secondhand cars or look at secondhand car prices;* **secondhand dealer** = dealer who buys and sells secondhand items **Gebrauchtwarenhändler**

◇ **secondment** *noun* being seconded to another job for a period **(vorübergehende) Versetzung;** *he is on three years' secondment to an Australian college*

◇ **second-rate** *adjective* not of good quality **zweitklassig, minderwertig;** *never buy anything second-rate*

◇ **seconds** *plural noun* items which have been turned down by the quality controller as not being top quality **zweite Wahl, B-Sortiment;** *the shop has a sale of seconds*

secret

1 *adjective* (something) hidden *or* not known by many people **geheim, Geheim-;** *the MD kept the contract secret from the rest of the board; they signed a secret deal with their main rivals*
2 *noun* something hidden **Geheimnis; to keep a secret** = not to tell someone a secret which you know **etwas geheim halten**

◇ **secretary** *noun*
(a) person who helps to organize work *or* types letters *or* files documents *or* arranges meetings, etc. for someone **Sekretär/-in;** *secretary and personal assistant; my secretary deals with incoming orders; his secretary phoned to say he would be late*
(b) official of a company *or* society **Geschäftsführer; Schriftführer;** *GB* **company secretary** = person who is responsible for a company's legal and financial affairs **Manager mit Aufgabenbereich Finanzen und Verwaltung; honorary secretary** = person who keeps the minutes and official documents of a committee *or* club, but is not paid a salary **ehrenamtlicher Sekretär;** *he was elected secretary of the committee or committee secretary;* **membership secretary** = committee member who deals with the ordinary members of a society **Schriftführer**
(c) *GB* member of the government in charge of a department **Minister/-in;** *Education Secretary; Foreign Secretary; US* **Secretary of the Treasury** = senior member of the government in charge of financial affairs **Finanzminister**

◇ **Secretary of State** *noun*
(a) *GB* member of the government in charge of a department **Minister/-in**
(b) *US* senior member of the government in charge of foreign affairs **Außenminister**

◇ **secretarial** *adjective* referring to the work of a secretary **als Sekretär, Sekretärinnen-;** *she is taking a secretarial course; he is looking for secretarial work; we need extra secretarial help to deal with the mailings;* **secretarial college** = college which teaches typing, shorthand and word-processing **Sekretärinnenschule**

◇ **secretariat** *noun* important office and the officials who work in it **Sekretariat;** *the United Nations secretariat*

section

noun part of something **Abteilung; Abschnitt, Absatz; legal section** = department in a company dealing with legal matters **Rechtsabteilung**

sector

noun part of the economy *or* the business organization of a country **Sektor, Bereich;** *all sectors of the economy suffered from the fall in the exchange rate; technology is a booming sector of the economy;* **public sector** = nationalized industries and public services **öffentlicher Bereich, staatlicher Sektor; public sector borrowing requirement** = amount of money which a government has to borrow to pay for its own spending **Kreditbedarf der öffentlichen Hand; private sector** = all companies which are owned by private shareholders, not by the state **Privatsektor;** *the expansion is funded completely by the private sector; salaries in the private sector have increased faster than in the public*

QUOTE government services form a large part of the tertiary or service sector
Sydney Morning Herald

QUOTE in the dry cargo sector, a total of 956 dry cargo vessels are laid up - 3% of world dry cargo tonnage
Lloyd's List

secure

1 *adjective* safe *or* which cannot change **sicher, gesichert; secure job** = job from which you are not likely to be made redundant **sicherer Arbeitsplatz; secure investment** = investment where you are not likely to lose money **sichere/risikofreie Investition**
2 *verb*
(a) to secure a loan = to pledge a property as a security for a loan **ein Darlehen sichern**
(b) to get (something) safely into your control **sich sichern;** *to secure funds; he secured the backing of an Australian group*

◇ **secured** *adjective* **secured loan** = loan which is guaranteed by the borrower giving valuable property as security **(dinglich) gesichertes Darlehen; secured creditor** = person who is owed money by someone, and can legally claim the same amount of the borrower's property if he fails to pay back the money owed **Vorzugsgläubiger; secured debts** = debts which are guaranteed by assets **gesicherte Verbindlichkeiten**

◇ **securities** *plural noun* investments in stocks and shares; certificates to show that someone owns stock **Wertpapiere, Effekten; gilt-edged securities** *or* **government securities** = investments in British government stock **Staatspapiere; listed securities** = shares which can be bought or sold on the Stock Exchange *or* shares which appear on the official Stock Exchange list **an der Börse notierte Wertpapiere; the securities market** = Stock Exchange *or* place where stocks and shares can be bought or sold **Effektenmarkt; securities trader** = person whose business is buying and selling stocks and shares **Effektenhändler**

◇ **security** *noun*

(a) job security = feeling which a worker has that he has a right to keep his job *or* that his job will never end **Sicherheit des Arbeitsplatzes; security of employment** = feeling by a worker that he has the right to keep his job until he retires **Arbeitsplatzsicherheit; security of tenure** = right to keep a job *or* rented accommodation, provided that certain conditions are met **gesetzliche Kündigungsschutz**

(b) being protected **Schutz, Sicherheit; airport security** = actions taken to protect aircraft and passengers against attack **Flugsicherheit; security guard** = person who protects an office *or* factory against burglars **Wachmann; office security** = protecting an office against theft **Sicherheitsvorkehrungen (gegen Diebstahl) im Büro**

(c) being secret **Diskretion, Geheimhaltung; security in this office is nil** = nothing can be kept secret in this office **in diesem Büro wird alles ausgeplaudert; security printer** = printer who prints paper money, secret government documents, etc. **Notenpresse**

(d) social security = money *or* help provided by the government to people who need it **Sozialunterstützung;** *he lives on social security payments*

(e) guarantee that someone will repay money borrowed **Bürgschaft, Garantie; to stand security for someone** = to guarantee that if the person does not repay a loan, you will repay it for him **für jdn Bürgschaft leisten, für jdn bürgen;** *to give something as security for a debt; to use a house as security for a loan; the bank lent him £20,000 without security*

NOTE: no plural

see-safe *noun* agreement where a supplier will give credit for unsold goods at the end of a period **Kauf mit Rückgaberecht/auf Kommission;** *we bought the stock see-safe*

seek *verb* to ask for **anstreben, beantragen;** *they are seeking damages for loss of revenue;* **to seek an interview** = to ask if you can see someone **um ein Gespräch bitten;** *she sought an interview with the minister*
NOTE: **seeking - sought**

seize *verb* to take hold of something *or* to take possession of something **einziehen, beschlagnahmen, pfänden;** *the customs seized the shipment of books; the court ordered the company's funds to be seized*

◇ **seizure** *noun* taking possession of something **Einziehung, Beschlagnahme, Pfändung;** *the court ordered the seizure of the shipment or of the company's funds*

select

1 *adjective* of top quality *or* specially chosen **exklusiv, auserwählt, auserlesen;** *our customers are very select; a select range of merchandise*

2 *verb* to choose **auswählen, aussuchen; selected items are reduced by 25%** = some items have been reduced by 25% **einige ausgewählte Artikel sind um 25% herabgesetzt**

◇ **selection** *noun* choice; thing which has been chosen **Auswahl;** *a selection of our product line;* **selection board** *or* **selection committee** = committee which chooses a candidate for a job **Auswahlkomitee, Bewerbungsausschuß; selection procedure** = general method of choosing a candidate for a job **Auswahlverfahren**

◇ **selective** *adjective* which chooses **selektiv, gezielt; selective strikes** = strikes in certain areas *or* at certain factories, but not everywhere **Schwerpunktstreiks**

self *pronoun* your own person **selbst;** *(on cheques)* **"pay self"** = pay the person who has signed the cheque **"Zahlung an Aussteller"**

◇ **self-** *prefix* referring to oneself **Selbst-**

◇ **self-contained office** *noun* office which has all facilities inside it, and its own entrance, so that it is separate from other offices in the same building **abgeschlossenes Büro**

◇ **self-employed**

1 *adjective* working for yourself *or* not on the payroll of a company **selbständig, freiberuflich;** *a self-employed engineer; he*

worked for a bank for ten years but now is self-employed
2 *noun* **the self-employed** = people who work for themselves **die Selbständigen**
NOTE: can be followed by a verb in the plural

◇ **self-financed** *adjective* **the project is completely self-financed** = the project pays its development costs out of its own revenue, with no subsidies **das Projekt finanziert sich selbst**

◇ **self-financing**
1 *noun* the financing of development costs, purchase of capital assets etc., of a company from its own resources **Eigen-, Selbstfinanzierung;** NOTE: no plural
2 *adjective* **the company is completely self-financing** = the company finances its development costs *or* capital assets, etc. from its own resources **das Unternehmen finanziert sich selbst**

◇ **self-made man** *noun* man who is rich and successful because of his work, not because he inherited money or position **Selfmademan**

◇ **self-regulation** *noun* regulating by a body (such as the Stock Exchange) of its own members **Selbstverwaltung**

◇ **self-regulatory** *adjective* (group) which regulates itself **selbstverwaltend**

◇ **self-service** *adjective* **a self-service store** = shop where customers take goods from the shelves and pay for them at the checkout **ein Selbstbedienungsgeschäft; self-service petrol station** = petrol station where the customers put the petrol in their cars themselves **Tankstelle mit Selbstbedienung**

◇ **self-sufficiency** *noun* being self-sufficient **Autarkie, Selbstversorgung**
NOTE: no plural

◇ **self-sufficient** *adjective* producing enough food *or* raw materials for its own needs **autark;** *the country is self-sufficient in oil*

◇ **self-supporting** *adjective* which finances itself from its own resources, with no subsidies **finanziell unabhängig**

sell

1 *noun* act of selling **Verkauf, Verkaufstaktik, Verkaufsstrategie; to give a product the hard sell** = to make great efforts to persuade customers to buy it **ein Produkt aggressiv verkaufen; he tried to give me the hard sell** = he put a lot of effort into trying to persuade me to buy his product **er versuchte auf aggressive Art, mich zum Kauf zu bewegen; soft sell** = persuading people to buy, by encouraging and not forcing them to do so **diskreter/zurückhaltender Verkauf**
NOTE: no plural
2 *verb*
(a) to give goods in exchange for money **verkaufen;** *to sell cars* or *to sell refrigerators; they have decided to sell their house; they tried to sell their house for £100,000; to sell something on credit; her house is difficult to sell; their products are easy to sell;* **to sell forward** = to sell foreign currency, commodities, etc., for delivery at a later date **auf Termin verkaufen**
(b) to be bought **sich verkaufen, Absatz finden, verkauft werden;** *these items sell well in the pre-Christmas period; those packs sell for £25 a dozen*
NOTE: **selling - sold**

◇ **sell-by date** *noun* date on a food packet which is the last date on which the food is guaranteed to be good **Mindesthaltbarkeitsdatum**

◇ **seller** *noun*
(a) person who sells **Verkäufer;** *there were few sellers in the market, so prices remained high;* **seller's market** = market where the seller can ask high prices because there is a large demand for the product **Verkäufermarkt**
(b) thing which sells **gängiger Artikel;** *this book is a steady seller;* **best-seller** = item (especially a book) which sells very well **Bestseller**

◇ **selling**
1 *noun* **direct selling** = selling a product direct to the customer without going through a shop **Direktverkauf; mail-order selling** = selling by taking orders and supplying a product by post **Versandhandel; selling costs** = amount of money to be paid for advertising, reps' commissions, etc., involved in selling something **Vertriebskosten; selling price** = price at which someone is willing to sell **Verkaufspreis**
2 *suffix* **fast-selling items** = items which sell quickly **leichtverkäuflicher Artikel, Artikel mit reißendem Absatz; best-selling car** = car which sells better than other models **der Wagen, der am besten geht, der Verkaufsschlager unter den Autos**

◇ **sell off** *verb* to sell goods quickly to get rid of them **abstoßen**

◇ **sell out** *verb*
(a) to sell all stock **ausverkaufen;** *to sell out of a product line; we have sold out of electronic typewriters; this item has sold out*
(b) to sell out = to sell one's business **seine Firma verkaufen;** *he sold out and retired to the seaside*

◇ **sellout** *noun* **this item has been a sellout** = all the stock of the item has been sold **dieser Artikel ist ausverkauft**

◇ **sell up** *verb* to sell a business and all the stock **eine Firma komplett verkaufen**

semi-

prefix half **halb, Halb-**

◊ **semi-finished** *adjective* **semi-finished products** = products which are partly finished **Halbfabrikate**

◊ **semi-skilled** *adjective* **semi-skilled workers** = workers who have had some training **angelernte Arbeitskräfte**

send *verb* to make someone *or* something go from one place to another **(zu)schicken, (ver)senden;** *to send a letter or an order or a shipment; the company is sending him to Australia to be general manager of the Sydney office; send the letter airmail if you want it to arrive next week; the shipment was sent by rail*
NOTE: **sending - sent**

◊ **send away for** *verb* to write asking for something to be sent to you **etwas bestellen/anfordern;** *we sent away for the new catalogue*

◊ **sender** *noun* person who sends **Absender; "return to sender"** = words on an envelope *or* parcel to show that it is to be sent back to the person who sent it **zurück an Absender**

◊ **send in** *verb* to send (a letter) **einsenden;** *he sent in his resignation; to send in an application*

◊ **send off** *verb* to put (a letter) in the post **abschicken**

◊ **send off for** *verb* to write asking for something to be sent to you **etwas bestellen/anfordern;** *we sent off for the new catalogue*

◊ **send on** *verb* to post a letter which you have received, and address it to someone else **nachsenden;** *he sent the letter on to his brother*

senior *adjective* older; more important; (worker) who has been employed longer than another **älter; leitend, übergeordnet, höher; dienstälter; senior manager** *or* **senior executive** = manager *or* director who has a higher rank than others **obere Führungskraft, leitender Angestellter; senior partner** = most important partner in a firm of solicitors *or* accountants **Seniorpartner; John Smith, Senior** = the older John Smith (i.e. the father of John Smith, Junior) **John Smith, senior**

◊ **seniority** *noun* being older; being an employee of the company longer **höheres Alter; höheres Dienstalter; the managers were listed in order of seniority** = the manager who had been an employee the longest was put at the top of the list **die Manager wurden entsprechend der Betriebszugehörigkeitsdauer aufgeführt**
NOTE: no plural

sensitive *adjective* able to feel something sharply **empfindlich, sensibel;** *the market is very sensitive to the result of the elections;* **price-sensitive product** = product which will sell less if the price is increased **preisempfindliches Produkt**

separate
1 *adjective* not together **getrennt, gesondert, einzeln, separat; to send something under separate cover** = to send something in a different envelope **etwas mit getrennter Post schicken**
2 *verb* to divide **trennen, aufteilen;** *the personnel are separated into part-timers and full-time staff*

◊ **separately** *adverb* not together **getrennt, gesondert, einzeln, separat;** *each job was invoiced separately*

◊ **separation** *noun US* leaving a job (resigning, retiring, or being fired or made redundant) **Aufgabe einer Stellung**

sequester *or* **sequestrate** *verb* to take and keep (property) because a court has ordered it **konfiszieren, sequestrieren**

◊ **sequestration** *noun* taking and keeping of property on the order of a court **Konfiszierung, Sequestration, Zwangsverwaltung**

◊ **sequestrator** *noun* person who takes and keeps property on the order of a court **Sequester, Zwangsverwalter**

serial number *noun* number in a series **Fabrikationsnummer; Seriennummer;** *this batch of shoes has the serial number 25-02*

series *noun* group of items following one after the other **Serie;** *a series of successful takeovers made the company one of the largest in the trade*
NOTE: plural is **series**

serious *adjective* bad *or* important **schwer, schlimm; ernsthaft;** *the storm caused serious damage; the management is making serious attempts to improve working conditions; the damage to the computer was not very serious*

◊ **seriously** *adverb* badly **schwer, schlimm;** *the cargo was seriously damaged by water*

servant *noun* person who is paid to work in someone's house **Diener/-in; civil servant** = person who works for the government **Beamter im öffentlichen Dienst**

serve *verb* to deal with (a customer) **bedienen; to serve a customer** = to take a customer's order and provide what he wants **einen Kunden bedienen; to serve in a shop** *or* **in a restaurant** = to deal with customers' orders **in einem Laden od Restaurant bedienen; to serve someone with a writ** *or* **to serve a writ on someone** = to give someone a writ officially, so that he has to obey it **jdm eine Ladung od Verfügung zustellen**

service

1 *noun*

(a) working for a company *or* in a shop, etc. **Dienst; length of service** = number of years someone has worked **Beschäftigungsdauer; service agreement** *or* **service contract** = contract between a company and a director showing all conditions of work **Dienst-, Arbeitsvertrag**

(b) the work of dealing with customers *or* payment for help for the customer **Bedienung;** *the service in that restaurant is extremely slow; to add on 10% for service;* **the bill includes service** = includes a charge added for the work involved **die Rechnung ist einschließlich Bedienung;** *is the service included?;* **service charge** = charge added to the bill in a restaurant to pay for service *or* amount paid by tenants in a block of flats for general cleaning **Bedienung(szuschlag); Reinigungskosten**

(c) keeping a machine in good working order **Wartung;** *the machine has been sent in for service; the routine service of equipment;* **service contract** = contract by which a company keeps a piece of equipment in good working order **Wartungsvertrag; after-sales service** = service of a machine carried out by the seller for the buyer **Kundendienst; service centre** = office *or* workshop which specializes in keeping machines in good working order **Kundendienstvertragswerkstatt; service department** = section of a company which keeps customers' machines in good working order **technischer Kundendienst; service engineer** = engineer who specializes in keeping machines in good working order **Kundendienstmechaniker; service handbook** *or* **service manual** = book which shows how to service a machine **Wartungshandbuch; service station** = garage where you can buy petrol and have small repairs done to a car **Tankstelle mit Reparaturwerkstatt**

(d) business *or* office which gives help when it is needed **Dienst, Service; answering service** = office which answers the telephone and takes messages for a company **Fernsprechauftragsdienst; 24-hour service** = help which is available for the whole day **Tag- und Nachtdienst; service bureau** = office which specializes in helping other offices **Büro-Service; service department** = department of a company which does not deal with production or sales (accounts, personnel, etc.) **allgemeine Kostenstelle; service industry** = industry which does not make products, but offers a service (such as banking, insurance, transport) **Dienstleistungsbranche**

(e) to put a machine into service = to start using a machine **eine Maschine in Betrieb nehmen**

(f) regular working of a public organization **Versorgung, Service;** *the postal service is efficient; the bus service is very irregular; we have a good train service to London;* **the civil service** = the administration of a country **öffentlicher Dienst, Staatsdienst;** *he has a job in the civil service; civil service pensions are index-linked*

2 *verb*

(a) to keep a machine in good working order **warten;** *the car needs to be serviced every six months; the computer has gone back to the manufacturer for servicing*

(b) to service a debt = to pay interest on a debt **Schuldzinsen bezahlen;** *the company is having problems in servicing its debts*

session *noun* meeting *or* period when a group of people meets **Sitzung;** *the morning session or the afternoon session will be held in the conference room;* **opening session** *or* **closing session** = first part *or* last part of a conference **Eröffnungsitzung; Schlußsitzung**

set

1 *noun* group of items which go together *or* which are used together *or* which are sold together **Set, Satz, Sortiment;** *set of tools or set of equipment;* **boxed set** = set of items sold together in a box **in einer Schachtel verpacktes Set**

2 *adjective* fixed *or* which cannot be changed **fest, festgelegt, Fix-;** *set price;* **set menu** = cheaper menu in a restaurant where there are only a few choices **Tagesmenü**

3 *verb* to fix *or* to arrange **festlegen, festsetzen;** *we have to set a price for the new computer; the price of the calculator has been set low, so as to achieve maximum unit sales;* **the auction set a record for high prices** = the prices at the auction were the highest ever reached **bei der Auktion wurden Rekordpreise erzielt**

NOTE: **setting - set**

◇ **set against** *verb* to balance one group of figures against another group to try to make them cancel each other out **gegenüberstellen, absetzen;** *to set the costs against the invoice; can you set the expenses against tax?*

◇ **set aside** *verb* to decide not to apply a decision **aufheben, annullieren;** *the arbitrator's award was set aside on appeal*

◇ **set back** *verb* to make something late **verzögern, zurückwerfen;** *the project was set back six weeks by bad weather*

◇ **setback** *noun* stopping progress **Rückschlag;** *the company suffered a series of setbacks in 1984; the shares had a setback on the Stock Exchange*

◇ **set out** *verb* to put clearly in writing **darlegen;** *to set out the details in a report*

◇ **set up** *verb*
(a) to begin (something) *or* to organize (something) new **eröffnen, gründen; veranlassen, einsetzen;** *to set up an inquiry or a working party;* **to set up a company** = to start a company legally **eine Firma gründen**
(b) to set up in business = to start a new business **sich niederlassen;** *he set up in business as an insurance broker; he set himself up as a freelance engineer*

◇ **setting up costs** *or* **setup costs** *plural noun* costs of getting a machine *or* a factory ready to make a new product after finishing work on another one **Rüstkosten**

◇ **setup** *noun*
(a) arrangement *or* organization **Organisation, Anlage, Anordnung; the setup in the office** = the way the office is organized **der Aufbau des Büros**
(b) commercial firm **Firma;** *he works for a PR setup*

> QUOTE the concern announced that it had acquired a third large tanker since being set up in 1983
> *Lloyd's List*
>
> QUOTE a sharp setback in foreign trade accounted for most of the winter slowdown
> *Fortune*
>
> QUOTE for sale: top quality office furniture, which includes executive desks, filing cabinets, typewriters and complete office setup
> *Australian Financial Review*

settle *verb*
(a) to settle an account = to pay what is owed **ein Konto be-, ausgleichen**
(b) to settle a claim = to agree to pay what is asked for **eine Forderung regulieren;** *the insurance company refused to settle his claim for storm damage;* **the two parties settled out of court** = the two parties reached an agreement privately without continuing the court case **die beiden Parteien haben einen außergerichtlichen Vergleich getroffen**

◇ **settlement** *noun*
(a) payment of an account **Abrechnung, Bezahlung; settlement day** = day when accounts have to be settled **Abrechnungstag, Stichtag; our basic discount is 20% but we offer an extra 5% for rapid settlement** = we take a further 5% off the price if the customer pays quickly **wir geben normalerweise 20% Rabatt, aber wir bieten weitere 5% für prompte Bezahlung; settlement in cash** *or* **cash settlement** = payment of an invoice in cash, not by cheque **Barzahlung**
(b) agreement after an argument **Beilegung, Schlichtung, Vergleich; to effect a settlement between two parties** = to bring two parties together to make them agree **einen Vergleich zustande bringen**

◇ **settle on** *verb* to leave property to someone when you die **vermachen;** *he settled his property on his children*

> QUOTE he emphasised that prompt settlement of all forms of industrial disputes would guarantee industrial peace in the country and ensure increased productivity
> *Business Times (Lagos)*

several *adjective* more than a few *or* some **einige, mehrere;** *several managers are retiring this year; several of our products sell well in Japan*

◇ **severally** *adverb* separately *or* not jointly **einzeln; they are jointly and severally liable** = they are liable both as a group and as individuals **sie haften gesamtschuldnerisch**

severance pay *noun* money paid as compensation to someone who is losing his job **Entlassungsabfindung**

severe *adjective* bad *or* serious **schwer, hart, streng;** *the company suffered severe losses in the European market; the government imposed severe financial restrictions*

◇ **severely** *adverb* badly *or* in a serious way **schwer, hart, streng;** *train services have been severely affected by snow*

shady *adjective* not honest **zweifelhaft, fragwürdig;** *shady deal*

shake *verb*
(a) to move something quickly from side to side **schütteln**
(b) to surprise *or* to shock **erschüttern;** *the markets were shaken by the company's results*
NOTE: **shaking - shook - has shaken**

◇ **shakeout** *noun* reorganization, where some people are left, but others go **Personalabbau, Gesundschrumpfen;** *a shakeout in the top management; only three companies were left after the shakeout in the computer market*

◇ **shakeup** *noun* total reorganization **Umstrukturierung;** *the managing director ordered a shakeup of the sales departments*

◇ **shaky** *adjective* not very sure *or* not very reliable **unsicher;** *the year got off to a shaky start*

share

1 *noun*

(a) to have a share in = to take part in *or* to contribute to **an etwas beteiligt sein;** *to have a share in management decisions;* **market share** *or* **share of the market** = percentage of a total market which the sales of a company cover **Marktanteil;** *the company hopes to boost its market share; their share of the market has gone up by 10%*

(b) one of many parts into which a company's capital is divided **Aktie;** *he bought a block of shares in Marks and Spencer; shares fell on the London market; the company offered 1.8m shares on the market;* **"A" shares** = ordinary shares with limited voting rights **dividendenberechtigte Aktien mit beschränktem Stimmrecht; "B" shares** = ordinary shares with special voting rights (often owned by the founder of the company and his family) **Aktien mit besonderem Stimmrecht; bonus share** = extra share given to an existing shareholder **Gratisaktie; deferred shares** = shares which receive a dividend only after all other dividends have been paid **Nachzugsaktien; founder's shares** = special shares issued to the person who starts a company **Gründeraktien; ordinary shares** = normal shares in a company, which have no special benefits or restrictions **Stammaktien; preference shares** = shares (often with no voting rights) which receive their dividend before all other shares and are repaid first (at face value) if the company goes into liquidation **Vorzugsaktien; share allocation** *or* **share allotment** = sharing of a small number of shares among a large number of people who have applied to buy them **Aktienzuteilung; to allot shares** = to give a certain number of shares to people who have applied to buy them **Aktien zuteilen; share capital** = value of the assets of a company held as shares **Aktienkapital; share certificate** = document proving that someone owns shares **Aktienzertifikat; share issue** = selling new shares in a company to the public **Aktienemission**

2 *verb*

(a) to own *or* use something together with someone else **sich teilen, gemeinsam haben;** *to share a telephone; to share an office*

(b) to divide something up among several people **sich teilen, auf-, verteilen;** *three companies share the market; to share computer time; to share the profits among the senior executives;* **to share information** *or* **to share data** = to give someone information which you have **Information/Daten zugänglich machen**

◇ **shareholder** *noun* person who owns shares in a company **Aktionär/-in;** *to call a shareholders' meeting;* **shareholders' equity** = ordinary shares owned by shareholders in a company **Eigenkapital; majority** *or* **minority shareholder** = person who owns more *or* less than half the shares in a company **Mehrheitsaktionär; Minderheitsaktionär;** *the solicitor acting on behalf of the minority shareholders*

◇ **shareholding** *noun* group of shares in a company owned by one person **Aktienbestand; a majority shareholding** *or* **a minority shareholding** = group of shares which are more *or* less than half the total **Mehrheitsbeteiligung; Minderheitsbeteiligung;** *he acquired a minority shareholding in the company; she has sold all her shareholdings;* **dilution of shareholding** = situation where the ordinary share capital of a company has been increased, but without an increase in the assets so that each share is worth less than before **Wertminderung von Aktien**

◇ **shareout** *noun* dividing something among many people **Verteilung;** *a shareout of the profits*

◇ **sharing** *noun* dividing up **Ver-, Aufteilung; profit sharing** = dividing profits among workers **Gewinnbeteiligung;** *the company operates a profit-sharing scheme;* **time-sharing** = (i) owning a property in part, with the right to use it for a period each year; (ii) sharing a computer system with different users using different terminals **(i) Timesharing; (ii) Time-sharing**

NOTE: no plural

> QUOTE falling profitability means falling share prices
>
> *Investors Chronicle*
>
> QUOTE the share of blue-collar occupations declined from 48 per cent to 43 per cent
>
> *Sydney Morning Herald*
>
> QUOTE as of last night the bank's shareholders no longer hold any rights to the bank's shares
>
> *South China Morning Post*
>
> QUOTE the company said that its recent issue of 10.5% convertible preference shares at A$8.50 has been oversubscribed, boosting shareholders' funds to A$700 million plus
>
> *Financial Times*

shark

noun **loan shark** = person who lends money at a very high interest rate **Kredithai**

sharp

adjective

(a) sudden **plötzlich, steil;** *sharp rally on the stock market; sharp drop in prices*

(b) sharp practice = way of doing business which is not honest, but not illegal **unlauteres/unsauberes Geschäftsgebaren**

◇ **sharply** *adverb* suddenly **plötzlich, steil;** *shares dipped sharply in yesterday's trading*

sheet

noun

(a) sheet of paper = piece of paper **Blatt Papier; sheet feed** = device which puts one

sheet at a time into a computer printer or photocopier **Einzelblatteinzug; sales sheet** = paper which gives details of a product and explains why it is good **Werbeschreiben; time sheet** = paper showing when a worker starts work and when he leaves work in the evening **Arbeitsnachweisbogen, Stundenzettel**
(b) balance sheet = statement of the financial position of a company at the end of a financial year or at the end of a period **Bilanz;** *the company's balance sheet for 1984; the accountants prepared a balance sheet for the first half-year*

shelf *noun* flat surface attached to a wall *or* in a cupboard on which items for sale are displayed **Regal;** *the shelves in the supermarket were full of items before the Christmas rush;* **shelf filler** = person whose job it is to make sure that the shelves in a shop are kept full of items for sale **Regalauffüller; shelf life of a product** = number of days or weeks when the product will stay on the shelf in the shop and still be good to use **Haltbarkeit/Lagerfähigkeit eines Produktes; shelf space** = amount of space on shelves in a shop **Regalfläche**
NOTE: plural is **shelves**

shell company *noun* company which does not trade, but exists only as a name to be used to hold shares in other companies **Firmenmantel**

shelter *noun* protected place **Schutz, Unterstand; tax shelter** = financial arrangement (such as a pension scheme) where investments can be made without tax **Steuerbegünstigung**

shelve *verb* to postpone *or* to put back to another date **aufschieben, zurückstellen, auf Eis/ad acta legen;** *the project was shelved; discussion of the problem has been shelved*

◊ **shelving** *noun*
(a) rows of shelves *or* space on shelves **Regale;** *we installed metal shelving in the household goods department*
(b) postponing **Aufschub, Zurückstellung;** *the shelving of the project has resulted in six redundancies*

shift
1 *noun*
(a) group of workers who work for a period, and then are replaced by another group; period of time worked by a group of workers **Schicht; day shift** = shift worked during the daylight hours (from early morning to late afternoon) **Tagesschicht; night shift** = shift worked during the night **Nachtschicht;** *there are 150 men on the day shift; he works the day shift or night shift; we work an 8-hour shift; the management is introducing a shift system or shift working;* **they work double shifts** = two groups of workers are working shifts together **sie arbeiten Doppelschichten**
(b) movement *or* change **Änderung, Wandel, Trend, Verlagerung;** *a shift in the company's marketing strategy; the company is taking advantage of a shift in the market towards higher priced goods*
2 *verb* to move *or* to sell **verkaufen;** *umg* **loswerden;** *we shifted 20,000 items in one week*

◊ **shift key** *noun* key on a typewriter *or* computer which makes capital letters **Umschalt-, Shifttaste**

◊ **shift work** *noun* system of work in a factory with shifts **Schichtarbeit**

shilling *noun* money used in Kenya **Shilling**

ship
1 *noun* large boat for carrying passengers and cargo on the sea **Schiff; cargo ship** = ship which carries cargo, not passengers **Frachter, Fracht-, Transportschiff; container ship** = ship made specially to carry containers **Containerschiff; ship chandler** = person who supplies goods (such as food) to ships **Schiffsausrüster; to jump ship** = to leave the ship on which you are working and not come back **ohne Erlaubnis abheuern**
2 *verb* to send (goods), but not always on a ship **versenden, befördern, transportieren; verschiffen;** *to ship goods to the USA; we ship all our goods by rail; the consignment of cars was shipped abroad last week;* **to drop ship** = to deliver a large order direct to a customer's shop or warehouse, without going through an agent **direkt liefern**
NOTE: **shipping - shipped**

◊ **ship broker** *noun* person who arranges shipping *or* transport of goods for customers on behalf of ship owners **Schiffsmakler**

◊ **shipment** *noun* goods sent **Sendung, Ladung;** *two shipments were lost in the fire; a shipment of computers was damaged; we make two shipments a week to France;* **bulk shipment** = shipments of large quantities of goods **Massengütertransport; consolidated shipment** = goods from different companies grouped together into a single shipment **Sammelladung; drop shipment** = delivery of a large order from a manufacturer direct to a customer's shop or warehouse, without going through an agent **Direktlieferung**

◊ **shipper** *noun* person who sends goods *or* who organizes the sending of goods for other customers **Spediteur;** *(Überseefrachtverkehr)* **Ablader**

◇ **shipping** *noun* sending of goods **Versand, Transport; Versschiffung;** *shipping charges or shipping costs;* **shipping agent** = company which specializes in the sending of goods **Spediteur, Speditionsfirma; shipping clerk** = clerk who deals with shipping documents **Reedereiangestellter; shipping company** *or* **shipping line** = company which owns ships **Reederei; shipping instructions** = details of how goods are to be shipped and delivered **Versandanweisungen; shipping note** = note which gives details of goods being shipped **Frachtbrief, Versandanzeige**

NOTE: no plural. Note also that **shipping** does not always mean using a ship

◇ **shipyard** *noun* factory where ships are built **Werft**

shoot up

verb to go up fast **in die Höhe schießen, sprunghaft ansteigen;** *prices have shot up during the strike*

NOTE: **shooting - shot**

shop

1 *noun*

(a) place where goods are stored and sold **Laden, Geschäft;** *bookshop; computer shop; electrical goods shop; he has bought a shoe shop in the centre of town; she opened a women's wear shop; all the shops in the centre of town close on Sundays;* **retail shop** = shop where goods are sold only to the public **Einzelhandelsgeschäft; a corner shop** = small privately owned general store **ein Tante-Emma-Laden; shop assistant** = person who serves customers in a shop **Verkäufer/-in; shop front** = part of a shop which faces the street, including the entrance and windows **Ladenfront; shop window** = window in a shop where goods are displayed so that customers can see them *or* place where goods or services can be exhibited **Schaufenster;** (NOTE: US English usually uses **store)**

(b) place where goods are made *or* workshop **Werkstatt; machine shop** = place where working machines are kept **Maschinensaal; repair shop** = small factory where machines are repaired **Reparaturwerkstatt; on the shop floor** = in the factory *or* in the works *or* among the ordinary workers **im Betrieb;** *the feeling on the shop floor is that the manager does not know his job*

(c) closed shop = system where a company agrees to employ only union members in certain jobs **gewerkschaftspflichtiger Betrieb;** *the union is asking the management to agree to a closed shop*

2 *verb* **to shop (for)** = to look for things in shops **einkaufen**

NOTE: **shopping - shopped**

◇ **shop around** *verb* to go to various shops or offices and compare prices before making a purchase *or* before placing an order **sich umsehen;** *you should shop around before getting your car serviced; he is shopping around for a new computer; it pays to shop around when you are planning to ask for a mortgage*

◇ **shopkeeper** *noun* person who owns or runs a shop **Laden-, Geschäftsinhaber**

◇ **shoplifter** *noun* person who steals goods from shops **Ladendieb**

◇ **shoplifting** *noun* stealing goods from shops **Ladendiebstahl**

NOTE: no plural

◇ **shopper** *noun* person who buys goods in a shop **Käufer/-in;** *the store stays open to midnight to cater for late-night shoppers;* **shoppers' charter** = law which protects the rights of shoppers against shopkeepers who are not honest **Verbraucherschutzgesetz**

◇ **shopping** *noun*

(a) buying goods in a shop; goods bought in a shop **Einkaufen; Einkäufe;** *to go shopping; to buy one's shopping or to do one's shopping in the local supermarket*

(b) shopping basket = basket for carrying shopping **Einkaufskorb; shopping centre** = group of shops linked together with car parks and restaurants **Einkaufszentrum;** *US* **shopping mall** = enclosed covered area for shopping, with shops, restaurants, banks and other facilities **Einkaufspassage; shopping precinct** = part of town which is closed to traffic so that people can walk about and shop **Fußgängerzone; window shopping** = looking at goods in shop windows, without buying anything **Schaufensterbummel; shopping around** = looking at prices in various shops before buying what you want **preisbewußter Einkauf**

NOTE: no plural

◇ **shop-soiled** *adjective* dirty because of having been on display in a shop **angeschmutzt**

◇ **shop steward** *noun* elected trade union representative of workers who reports their complaints to the management **betrieblicher Vertrauensmann**

◇ **shopwalker** *noun* employee of a department store who advises the customers and supervises the shop assistants in a department **Abteilungsleiter**

short

1 *adjective*

(a) for a small period of time **kurz, Kurz-; short credit** = terms which allow the customer only a little time to pay **kurzfristiger Kredit; in the short term** = in the

near future *or* quite soon **in kurzer Zeit, in Kürze, kurzfristig**
(b) not as much as should be **zu wenig;** *the shipment was three items short;* **when we cashed up we were £10 short** = we had £10 less than we should have had **als wir Kasse machten, fehlten £10; to give short weight** = to sell something which is lighter than it should be **etwas zu knapp abwiegen**
(c) short of = with less than needed *or* with not enough of **knapp an;** *we are short of staff or short of money; the company is short of new ideas*
(d) to sell short = to agree to sell something (such as shares) which you do not possess, but which you think you will be able to buy for less **leerverkaufen; short selling** *or* **selling short** = arranging to sell something in the future which you think you can buy for less than the agreed selling price **Fixgeschäft, Leerverkauf; to borrow short** = to borrow for a short period **kurzfristig aufnehmen**
2 *noun* **shorts** = government stocks which mature in less than five years' time **Papiere mit kurzer/bis zu fünfjähriger Laufzeit**

◇ **shortage** *noun* lack *or* not having enough **Mangel, Verknappung, Engpaß;** *a chronic shortage of skilled staff; we employ part-timers to make up for staff shortages; the import controls have resulted in the shortage of spare parts;* **manpower shortage** *or* **shortage of manpower** = lack of workers **Arbeitskräftemangel; there is no shortage of investment advice** = there are plenty of people who want to give advice on investments **es herrscht kein Mangel an Tips zur Kapitalanlage/Kapitalanlageberatern**

◇ **short change** *verb* to give a customer less change than is right, hoping that he will not notice **zu wenig herausgeben**

◇ **short-dated** *adjective* **short-dated bills** = bills which are payable within a few days **kurzfristige Wechsel; short-dated securities** = government stocks which mature in less than five years time **Papiere mit kurzer/bis zu fünfjähriger Laufzeit**

◇ **shorten** *verb* to make shorter **verkürzen;** *to shorten credit terms*

◇ **shortfall** *noun* amount which is missing which would make the total expected sum **Fehlbetrag, Defizit;** *we had to borrow money to cover the shortfall between expenditure and revenue*

◇ **shorthand** *noun* rapid way of writing using a system of signs **Stenographie, Kurzschrift; shorthand secretary** = secretary who takes dictation in shorthand **Stenograph/-in; shorthand typist** = typist who can take dictation in shorthand and then type it **Stenotypist/-in; to take shorthand** = to write using shorthand **stenographieren;** *he took down the minutes in shorthand*

◇ **shorthanded** *adjective* without enough staff **knapp an Personal;** *we are rather shorthanded at the moment*

◇ **short-haul** *adjective* **short-haul flight** = flight over a short distance (up to 1,000 km) **Kurzstreckenflug**

◇ **shortlist**
1 *noun* list of some of the better people who have applied for a job, who can be asked to come for a test or an interview **Auswahlliste;** *to draw up a shortlist; he is on the shortlist for the job*
2 *verb* to make a shortlist **eine Auswahlliste aufstellen;** *four candidates have been shortlisted; shortlisted candidates will be asked for an interview*

◇ **short-range** *adjective* **short-range forecast** = forecast which covers a period of a few months **kurzfristige Prognose**

◇ **short-staffed** *adjective* with not enough staff **unterbesetzt;** *we are rather short-staffed at the moment*

◇ **short-term** *adjective* for a short period **kurzfristig;** *to place money on short-term deposit; short-term contract;* **on a short-term basis** = for a short period **kurzfristig, auf kurze Sicht; short-term debts** = debts which have to be repaid within a few weeks **kurzfristige Schulden; short-term forecast** = forecast which covers a period of a few months **kurzfristige Prognose; short-term gains** = gains made over a short period (less than 12 months) **rasch zu erzielende Gewinne; short-term loan** = loan which has to be repaid within a few weeks **kurzfristiger Kredit**

◇ **short time** *noun* shorter working hours than usual **Kurzarbeit;** *to be on short time; the company has had to introduce short-time working because of lack of orders*

shot *noun* **mail shot** *or* **mailing shot** = leaflets sent by post to possible customers **Briefwerbeaktion, Rundschreiben**

show
1 *noun*
(a) exhibition *or* display of goods or services for sale **Ausstellung, Messe;** *motor show; computer show;* **show house** *or* **show flat** = house *or* flat built and furnished so that possible buyers can see what similar houses could be like **Musterhaus; Musterwohnung**
(b) show of hands = vote where people show how they vote by raising their hands **Abstimmung durch Handheben;** *the motion was carried on a show of hands*
2 *verb* to make something be seen **zeigen, aufweisen;** *to show a gain or a fall; to show a profit or a loss*
NOTE: **showing - showed - has shown**

◇ **showcard** *noun* piece of cardboard with advertising material, put near an item for sale **Schaufensterschild, Schaufensterplakat**

◇ **showcase** *noun* cupboard with a glass front or top to display items **Schaukasten, Vitrine**

◇ **showroom** *noun* room where goods are displayed for sale **Ausstellungsraum;** *car showroom*

shrink *verb* to get smaller **schrumpfen, zurückgehen;** *the market has shrunk by 20%; the company is having difficulty selling into a shrinking market*
NOTE: **shrinking - shrank - has shrunk**

◇ **shrinkage** *noun*
(a) amount by which something gets smaller **Schwund, Einbußen, Minderung;** *to allow for shrinkage*
(b) *informal* losses of stock through theft (especially by members of the staff of the shop) **Ladendiebstahl**

◇ **shrink-wrapped** *adjective* covered in tight plastic protective cover **eingeschweißt**

◇ **shrink-wrapping** *noun* book, fruit, record etc. in a tight plastic cover **Schrumpfpackung**

shut
1 *adjective* closed *or* not open **geschlossen;** *the office is shut on Saturdays*
2 *verb* to close **schließen;** *to shut a shop or a warehouse*
NOTE: **shutting - shut**

◇ **shut down** *verb* **to shut down a factory** = to make a factory stop working for a time **eine Fabrik schließen;** *the offices will shut down for Christmas; six factories have shut down this month*

◇ **shutdown** *noun* shutting of a factory **(vorübergehende) Stillegung**

◇ **shutout** *noun* locking of the door of a factory *or* office to stop the staff getting in **Aussperrung**

sick *adjective* ill *or* not well **krank; to be on sick leave** = to be away from work because of illness **krank geschrieben sein; sick pay** = pay paid to a worker who is sick, even if he cannot work **Krankengeld**

◇ **sickness** *noun* being ill **Krankheit; sickness benefit** = payment paid by the government or private insurance to someone who is ill and cannot work **Krankengeld;** *the sickness benefit is paid monthly*

side *noun*
(a) part of something near the edge **Rand, Spalte; credit side** = right-hand side of accounts showing money received **Habenseite; debit side** = left-hand side of accounts showing money owed or paid **Debetseite, Debet**
(b) one of the surfaces of a flat object **Seite;** *please write on one side of the paper only*
(c) on the side = separate from your normal work, and hidden from your employer **nebenbei;** *he works in an accountant's office, but he runs a construction company on the side; her salary is too small to live on, so the family lives on what she can make on the side*

◇ **sideline** *noun* business which is extra to your normal work **Nebenbeschäftigung;** *he runs a profitable sideline selling postcards to tourists*

sight *noun* seeing **Sicht, Anblick; bill payable at sight** = bill which must be paid when it is presented **Wechsel zahlbar bei Sicht; sight bill** *or* **sight draft** = bill of exchange which is payable at sight **Sichtwechsel, Sichttratte; to buy something sight unseen** = to buy something without having inspected it **etwas ungesehen kaufen**
NOTE: no plural

sign
1 *noun* advertising board *or* notice which advertises something **Schild, Ladenschild;** *they have asked for planning permission to put up a large red shop sign; advertising signs cover most of the buildings in the centre of the town*
2 *verb* to write your name in a special way on a document to show that you have written it or approved it **unterschreiben;** *to sign a letter or a contract or a document or a cheque; the letter is signed by the managing director; the cheque is not valid if it has not been signed by the finance director;* **the warehouse manager signed for the goods** = the manager signed a receipt to show that the goods had been received **der Lagerleiter bestätigte den Empfang der Waren; he signed the goods in** *or* **he signed the goods out** = he signed the stock report to show that the goods had arrived *or* had been dispatched **er bestätigte den Wareneingang; er bestätigte den Warenabgang**

◇ **signatory** *noun* person who signs a contract, etc. **Unterzeichner;** *you have to get the permission of all the signatories to the agreement if you want to change the terms*

◇ **signature** *noun* name written in a special way by someone **Unterschrift;** *a pile of letters waiting for the managing director's signature; he found a pile of cheques on his desk waiting for signature; all cheques need two signatures*

◇ **sign on** *verb* to start work, by signing your name in the personnel office **die Arbeit aufnehmen; to sign on for the dole** = to register as unemployed **sich arbeitslos melden**

silent *adjective* not speaking **still; silent partner** = partner who has a share of the business but does not work in it **stiller Teilhaber/Gesellschafter**

simple interest *noun* interest calculated on the capital only, and not added to it **einfache Zinsen**

sincerely *adverb* **Yours sincerely** *or US* **Sincerely yours** = words used as an ending to a business letter addressed to a named person; *entspricht* **Mit freundlichen Grüßen**

sine die *phrase* **to adjourn a case sine die** = to postpone the hearing of a case without fixing a new date for it **einen Fall auf unbestimmte Zeit vertagen**

single *adjective* one alone **einzeln, Einzel-; einzige**
(a) single fare *or* **single ticket** *or* **a single** = fare *or* ticket for one journey from one place to another **einfacher Fahrpreis; einfache Fahrkarte;** *I want two singles to London*
(b) single premium policy = insurance policy where only one premium is paid rather than regular annual premiums **Einmalprämienpolice; single-entry bookkeeping** = method of bookkeeping where payments or sales are noted with only one entry **einfache Buchführung; in single figures** = less than ten **in einstelligen Zahlen;** *sales are down to single figures; inflation is now in single figures;* **single-figure inflation** = inflation rising at less than 10% per annum **einstellige Inflationsrate; single market** European trading market within the Common Market where no restrictions exist **Binnenmarkt**

sink *verb*
(a) to go to the bottom of the water **sinken, untergehen;** *the ship sank in the storm and all the cargo was lost*
(b) to go down suddenly **sinken, fallen;** *prices sank at the news of the closure of the factory*
(c) to invest money (into something) **anlegen, investieren;** *he sank all his savings into a car-hire business*
NOTE: **sinking - sank - sunk**
◇ **sinking fund** *noun* fund built up out of amounts of money put aside regularly to meet a future need **Tilgungsfonds**

sir *noun* **Dear Sir** = way of addressing a letter to a man whom you do not know or to a limited company **Sehr geehrte Herren; Dear Sirs** = way of addressing a letter to a firm **Sehr geehrte Damen und Herren**

sister *adjective* **sister company** = one of several companies which are part of the same group **Schwestergesellschaft; sister ship** = ship which is of the same design and belongs to the same company as another ship **Schwesterschiff**

sit-down *adjective* **sit-down protest** *or* **sit-down strike** = strike where the workers stay in their place of work and refuse to work or to leave **Sitzstreik, Sit-in**
◇ **sit-in** *noun* strike where the workers stay in their place of work and refuse to work or leave **Sit-in, Sitzstreik**
NOTE: plural is **sit-ins**

site
1 *noun* place where something is built **Bauplatz;** *we have chosen a site for the new factory; the supermarket is to be built on a site near the station;* **building site** *or* **construction site** = place where a building is being constructed **Baustelle;** *all visitors to the site must wear safety helmets;* **green field site** = site for a factory which is in the country, and not surrounded by other buildings **Industrieansiedlungsplatz in unbewohntem Gebiet; site engineer** = engineer in charge of a building being constructed **Bauleiter**
2 *verb* **to be sited** = to be placed **liegen;** *the factory will be sited near the motorway*

situated *adjective* placed **gelegen;** *the factory is situated on the edge of the town; the office is situated near the railway station*
◇ **situation** *noun*
(a) state of affairs **Lage, Situation;** *financial situation of a company; the general situation of the economy*
(b) job **Stelle; situations vacant** *or* **situations wanted** = list in a newspaper of vacancies for workers *or* of people wanting work **Stellenangebote; Stellengesuche**
(c) place where something is **Lage;** *the factory is in a very pleasant situation by the sea*

size *noun* measurements of something *or* how big something is *or* how many there are of something **Größe, Maße, Umfang, Format;** *what is the size of the container? the size of the staff has doubled in the last two years; this packet is the maximum size allowed by the post office*

skeleton *noun* **skeleton staff** = few staff left to carry on essential work while most of the workforce is away **Rumpfbelegschaft**

skill *noun* ability to do something because you have been trained **Kenntnisse, Fertigkeit, Qualifikation;** *she has acquired some very useful office management skills; he will have to learn some new skills if he is going to direct the factory*

◇ **skilled** *adjective* having learnt certain skills **ausgebildet, qualifiziert, Fach-; skilled workers** *or* **skilled labour** = workers who have special skills *or* who have had long training **Facharbeiter**

slack *adjective* not busy **flau, ruhig;** *business is slack at the end of the week; January is always a slack period*

◇ **slacken off** *verb* to become less busy **abnehmen, nachlassen;** *trade has slackened off*

slander

1 *noun* untrue spoken statement which damages someone's character **Verleumdung, üble Nachrede; action for slander** *or* **slander action** = case in a law court where someone says that another person had slandered him **Verleumdungsklage**

2 *verb* **to slander someone** = to damage someone's character by saying untrue things about him **jdn verleumden**

NOTE: compare **LIBEL**

slash *verb* to cut *or* to reduce sharply **radikal herabsetzen, stark reduzieren;** *to slash prices or credit terms; prices have been slashed in all departments; the bank has been forced to slash interest rates*

sleeper *noun* share which has not risen in value for some time, but which may suddenly do so in the future **im Wert unterschätzte Aktie**

◇ **sleeping** *adjective* **sleeping partner** = partner who has a share in the business but does not work in it **stiller Teilhaber**

slide *verb* to move down steadily **absinken, abrutschen;** *prices slid after the company reported a loss*

NOTE: **sliding - slid**

◇ **sliding** *adjective* which rises in steps **gleitend; a sliding scale of charges** = list of charges which rises gradually according to value *or* quantity *or* time, etc. **eine gleitende Gebührentabelle**

slight *adjective* not very large *or* not very important **leicht, unwesentlich, geringfügig;** *there was a slight improvement in the balance of trade; we saw a slight increase in sales in February*

◇ **slightly** *adverb* not very much **etwas, leicht;** *sales fell slightly in the second quarter; the Swiss bank is offering slightly better terms*

slip

1 *noun*

(a) small piece of paper **Zettel, Beleg; compliments slip** = piece of paper with the name of the company printed on it, sent with documents, gifts, etc., instead of a letter **Kurzmitteilung; deposit slip** = piece of paper stamped by the cashier to prove that you have paid money into your account **Einzahlungsbeleg; distribution slip** = paper attached to a document *or* to a magazine, showing all the people in an office who should read it; *entspricht* **Verteilerzettel; pay slip** = piece of paper showing the full amount of a worker's pay, and the money deducted as tax, pension and insurance contributions **Gehalts-, Lohnstreifen; Gehalts-, Lohnabrechnung; paying-in slip** = printed form which is filled in when money is being deposited in a bank **Einzahlungsbeleg; sales slip** = paper showing that an article was bought at a certain shop **Kassenbeleg, Kassenzettel, Bon;** *goods can be exchanged only on production of a sales slip*

(b) mistake **Versehen, Schnitzer;** *he made a couple of slips in calculating the discount*

2 *verb* to go down and back **abrutschen, fallen;** *profits slipped to £1.5m; shares slipped back at the close*

NOTE: **slipping - slipped**

◇ **slip up** *verb* to make a mistake **sich versehen, einen Schnitzer machen;** *we slipped up badly in not signing the agreement with the Chinese company*

◇ **slip-up** *noun* mistake **Versehen, Schnitzer**

NOTE: plural is **slip-ups**

slogan *noun* **publicity slogan** = group of words which can be easily remembered, and which is used in publicity for a product **Werbespruch;** *we are using the slogan "Smiths can make it" on all our publicity*

slot machine *noun* machine which provides drinks *or* cigarettes, plays music, etc., when a coin is put in it **Automat**

slow

1 *adjective* not going fast **langsam, allmählich;** *a slow start to the day's trading; the sales got off to a slow start, but picked up later; business is always slow after Christmas; they were slow to reply or slow at replying to the customer's complaints; the board is slow to come to a decision; there*

was a slow improvement in sales in the first half of the year
2 *adverb* **to go slow** = to protest against management by working slowly **einen Bummelstreik machen**

◇ **slow down** *verb* to stop rising *or* moving *or* falling **verlangsamen; verringern; abflauen;** *inflation is slowing down; the fall in the exchange rate is slowing down; the management decided to slow down production*

◇ **slowdown** *noun* becoming less busy **Verlangsamung; Verringerung;** *a slowdown in the company's expansion*

◇ **slowly** *adverb* not fast **langsam, allmählich;** *the company's sales slowly improved; we are slowly increasing our market share*

> QUOTE a general price freeze succeeded in slowing the growth in consumer prices
> *Financial Times*
>
> QUOTE cash paid for stock: overstocked lines, factory seconds, slow sellers
> *Australian Financial Review*
>
> QUOTE the fall in short-term rates suggests a slowing economy
> *Financial Times*

slump
1 *noun*
(a) rapid fall **Sturz, Fall, plötzlicher Rückgang; Baisse;** *slump in sales; slump in profits; slump in the value of the pound; the pound's slump on the foreign exchange markets*
(b) period of economic collapse with high unemployment and loss of trade **Depression, starker Konjunkturrückgang;** *we are experiencing slump conditions;* **the Slump** = the world economic crisis of 1929 - 1933 **die Weltwirtschaftskrise**
2 *verb* to fall fast **stürzen, plötzlich fallen;** *profits have slumped; the pound slumped on the foreign exchange markets*

slush fund *noun* money kept to one side to give to people to persuade them to do what you want **Schmiergelder**

small *adjective* not large **klein; small ads** = short private advertisements in a newspaper (selling small items, asking for jobs, etc.) **Kleinanzeigen; small businesses** = little companies with low turnover and few employees **Kleinbetriebe; small businessman** = man who runs a small business **Kleinunternehmer; small change** = loose coins **Kleingeld;** *GB* **small claims court** = court which deals with disputes over small amounts of money **Gericht, das für Geldansprüche bis zu einer gewissen Höhe zuständig ist;** *entspricht* **Amtsgericht the small investor** = person who has a small amount of money to invest **Kleinanleger; small shopkeepers** = owners of small shops **kleine Ladenbesitzer**

◇ **small-scale** *adjective* working in a small way, with few staff and not much money **in begrenztem Umfang/Rahmen; a small-scale enterprise** = a small business **ein Kleinbetrieb**

smash *verb* to break (a record) *or* to do better than (a record) **brechen;** *to smash all production records; sales have smashed all records for the first half of the year*

smuggle *verb* to take goods into a country without declaring them to the customs **schmuggeln;** *they had to smuggle the spare parts into the country*

◇ **smuggler** *noun* person who smuggles **Schmuggler/-in**

◇ **smuggling** *noun* taking goods illegally into a country **Schmuggel;** *he made his money in arms smuggling*
NOTE: no plural

snap *adjective* rapid *or* sudden **plötzlich, spontan;** *the board came to a snap decision; they carried out a snap check or a snap inspection of the expense accounts*

◇ **snap up** *verb* to buy something quickly **aufkaufen, wegschnappen;** *to snap up a bargain; he snapped up 15% of the company's shares*
NOTE: **snapping - snapped**

snip *noun informal* bargain **Schnäppchen;** *these typewriters are a snip at £50*

soar *verb* to go up rapidly **sprunghaft ansteigen, in die Höhe schnellen;** *food prices soared during the cold weather; share prices soared on the news of the takeover bid or the news of the takeover bid sent share prices soaring*

social *adjective* referring to society in general **Sozial-, gesellschaftlich; social costs** = ways in which something will affect people **gesellschaftliche Kosten;** *the report examines the social costs of building the factory in the middle of the town;* **social security** = money from contributions paid to the National Insurance provided by the government to people who need it **Sozialunterstützung;** *he gets weekly social security payments;* **the social system** = the way society is organized **Gesellschaftsordnung**

◇ **society** *noun*
(a) way in which people in a country are organized **Gesellschaft; consumer society** = type of society where consumers are encouraged to buy goods **Konsumgesellschaft; the affluent society** =

type of society where most people are rich **Wohlstandsgesellschaft**
(b) club *or* group of people with the same interests **Verein, Gesellschaft;** *he has joined a computer society;* **building society** = financial institution which accepts and pays interest on deposits, and lends money to people who are buying property **Bausparkasse**
NOTE: the US English for this is **savings and loans association** **cooperative society** = organization where customers and workers are partners and share the profits **Genossenschaft; friendly society** = group of people who pay regular subscriptions to a fund which is used to help members who are ill or in financial trouble **Versicherungsverein auf Gegenseitigkeit**
◇ **socio-economic** *adjective* referring to social and economic conditions **sozio-ökonomisch, sozialökonomisch;** *the socio-economic system in capitalist countries;* **socio-economic groups** = groups in society divided according to income and position **sozialökonomische Gruppierungen**

soft *adjective* not hard **weich; soft currency** = currency of a country with a weak economy, which is cheap to buy and difficult to exchange for other currencies **weiche Währung; soft loan** = loan (from a company to an employee or from a government to another government) at very low or nil interest **zinsgünstiger od zinsloser Kredit; to take the soft option** = to decide to do something which involves least risk, effort or problems **den Weg des geringsten Widerstandes gehen; soft sell** = persuading people to buy by encouraging them, but not forcing them to do so **diskreter/zurückhaltender Verkauf**
◇ **software** *noun* computer programs (as opposed to machines) **Software**
NOTE: no plural

sole *adjective* only **Allein-, alleinig; sole agency** = agreement to be the only person to represent a company *or* to sell a product in a certain area **Alleinvertretung; Alleinvertrieb;** *he has the sole agency for Ford cars;* **sole agent** = person who has the sole agency for a product in an area **Alleinvertreter; sole distributor** = retailer who is the only one in an area who is allowed to sell a certain product **Alleinvertrieb; sole owner** = person who owns a business on his own, with no partners **Alleineigentümer; sole trader** = person who runs a business by himself but has not registered it as a company **Einzelkaufmann**

solemn *adjective* **solemn and binding agreement** = agreement which is not legally binding, but which all parties are supposed to obey **förmliches und bindendes Abkommen**

solicit *verb* **to solicit orders** = to ask for orders *or* to try to get people to order goods **sich um Aufträge bemühen**
◇ **solicitor** *noun GB* lawyer who gives advice to members of the public and acts for them legally **Anwalt/Anwältin; to instruct a solicitor** = to give orders to a solicitor to start legal proceedings on your behalf **einen Anwalt beauftragen; einen Fall einem Anwalt übergeben**

solus (advertisement) *noun* advertisement which does not appear near other advertisements for similar products **alleinstehende Anzeige, Inselanzeige**

solution *noun* answer to a problem **Lösung;** *to look for a solution to the financial problems; the programmer came up with a solution to the systems problem; we think we have found a solution to the problem of getting skilled staff*

solve *verb* **to solve a problem** = to find an answer to a problem **ein Problem lösen;** *the loan will solve some of our short-term problems*

solvent *adjective* having enough money to pay debts **zahlungsfähig, solvent;** *when he bought the company it was barely solvent*
◇ **solvency** *noun* being able to pay all debts **Zahlungsfähigkeit, Solvenz**
NOTE: no plural

sort *verb* to put (a lot of things) in order **sortieren, (ein)ordnen;** *she is sorting index cards into alphabetical order*
◇ **sort out** *verb* to put into order; to settle (a problem) **(aus)sortieren, ordnen; klären, lösen;** *did you sort out the accounts problem with the auditors?*

sound *adjective* reasonable *or* which can be trusted **solide, stabil; gesund; vernünftig;** *the company's financial situation is very sound; he gave us some very sound advice*
◇ **soundness** *noun* being reasonable **Solidität, Stabilität; Vernünftigkeit**
NOTE: no plural

source *noun* place where something comes from **Quelle, Ursprung;** *source of income; you must declare income from all sources to the tax office;* **income which is taxed at source** = where the tax is removed before the income is paid **Einkommen mit Quellenbesteuerung**

space *noun* empty place *or* empty area **Platz, Raum; advertising space** = space in a newspaper set aside for advertisements **Anzeigenraum; to take advertising space in a newspaper** = to place a large advertisement in a newspaper **Anzeigenraum belegen; floor space** = area of the floor in an office **Bodenfläche; office space** = area available for offices or used by offices **Büroraum;** *we are looking for extra office space for our new accounts department*

◊ **space bar** *noun* key on a typewriter *or* computer which makes a single space between letters **Leertaste**

◊ **space out** *verb* to place things with spaces between them **(mit Abstand) verteilen;** *the company name is written in spaced-out letters; payments can be spaced out over a period of ten years*

spare *adjective* extra *or* not being used **übrig, überschüssig;** *he has invested his spare capital in a computer shop;* **to use up spare capacity** = to make use of time or space which has not been fully used **ungenutzte Kapazität aufbrauchen; spare part** = small piece of machinery used to replace part of a machine which is broken **Ersatzteil;** *the photocopier will not work - it needs a spare part;* **spare time** = time when you are not at work **Freizeit;** *he built himself a car in his spare time*

spec *noun* **to buy something on spec** = to buy something as a speculation, without being sure of its value **etwas auf gut Glück kaufen**

◊ **specs** *plural noun* = SPECIFICATIONS

special *adjective* different *or* not normal *or* referring to one particular thing **Sonder-, besonderer, speziell;** *he offered us special terms; the car is being offered at a special price;* **special deposits** = large sums of money which banks have to deposit with the Bank of England **Mindestreserven**

◊ **specialist** *noun* person *or* company which deals with one particular type of product or one subject **Fachmann, Experte/Expertin, Spezialist/- in; Fachhandel;** *you should go to a specialist in computers or to a computer specialist for advice*

◊ **speciality** *or* **specialty** *noun* particular interest *or* special type of product which a company deals in **Spezialität, Spezialgebiet, Fachgebiet;** *their speciality is computer programs;* *US* **specialty store** = shop selling a limited range of items of good quality **Spezialgeschäft**

◊ **specialization** *noun* study of one particular thing *or* dealing with one particular type of product **Spezialisierung;** *the company's area of specialization is accounts packages for small businesses*

◊ **specialize** *verb* to trade in one particular type of product or service **(sich) spezialisieren;** *the company specializes in electronic components; they have a specialized product line; he sells very specialized equipment for the electronics industry*

> QUOTE the group specializes in the sale, lease and rental of new and second-user hardware
> *Financial Times*
>
> QUOTE airlines offer special stopover rates and hotel packages to attract customers to certain routes
> *Business Traveller*

specie *plural noun* coins **Münz-, Hartgeld**

specify *verb* to state clearly what is needed **angeben, einzeln aufführen, spezifizieren;** *to specify full details of the goods ordered; do not include VAT on the invoice unless specified*

◊ **specification** *noun* detailed information about what is needed *or* about a product to be supplied **Beschreibung, Spezifikation;** *to detail the specifications of a computer system;* **job specification** = very detailed description of what is involved in a job **Stellen-, Arbeitsplatzbeschreibung; to work to standard specifications** = to work to specifications which are acceptable anywhere in the industry **nach Norm arbeiten; the work is not up to specification** *or* **does not meet our specifications** = the product is not made in the way which was detailed **die Arbeit wurde nicht den Spezifikationen nach ausgeführt**

specimen *noun* thing which is given as a sample **Muster, Probe, Probeexemplar; to give specimen signatures on a bank mandate** = to write the signatures of all people who can sign cheques for an account so that the bank can recognize them **auf einer Kontovollmacht Unterschriftproben geben**

speculate *verb* to take a risk in business which you hope will bring you profits **spekulieren; to speculate on the Stock Exchange** = to buy shares which you hope will rise in value **an der Börse spekulieren**

◊ **speculation** *noun* risky deal which may produce a short-term profit **Spekulation;** *he bought the company as a speculation; she lost all her money in Stock Exchange speculations*

◊ **speculative** *adjective* **speculative builder** = builder who builds houses in the hope that someone will want to buy them **Bauspekulant; speculative share** = share which may go up or down in value **Spekulationsaktie**

◇ **speculator** *noun* person who buys goods *or* shares *or* foreign currency in the hope that they will rise in value **Spekulant/-in;** *a property speculator; a currency speculator; a speculator on the Stock Exchange or a Stock Exchange speculator*

speed *noun* rate at which something moves **Geschwindigkeit, Schnelligkeit; dictation speed** = number of words per minute which a secretary can write down in shorthand **Silben pro Minute; typing speed** = number of words per minute which a typist can type **Anschläge pro Minute**

◇ **speed up** *verb* to make something go faster **beschleunigen;** *we are aiming to speed up our delivery times*

spend *verb*

(a) to pay money **ausgeben;** *they spent all their savings on buying the shop; the company spends thousands of pounds on research*

(b) to use time **verbringen;** *the company spends hundreds of man-hours on meetings; the chairman spent yesterday afternoon with the auditors*

NOTE: **spending - spent**

◇ **spending** *noun* paying money **Ausgaben;** *cash spending or credit card spending;* **consumer spending** = spending by consumers **Ausgaben der Privathaushalte; spending money** = money for ordinary personal expenses **Taschengeld; spending power** = having money to spend on goods; amount of goods which can be bought for a certain sum of money **Kaufkraft;** *the spending power of the pound has fallen over the last ten years; the spending power of the student market*

NOTE: no plural

sphere *noun* area **Bereich, Gebiet;** *sphere of activity; sphere of influence*

spin off *verb* **to spin off a subsidiary company** = to take a part of a large company and make a smaller subsidiary from it **eine Tochtergesellschaft ausgliedern**

NOTE: **spinning - span - spun**

◇ **spinoff** *noun* useful product developed as a secondary product from a main item **Nebenprodukt;** *one of the spinoffs of the research programme has been the development of the electric car*

spiral

1 *noun* thing which twists round and round getting higher all the time **Spirale; the economy is in an inflationary spiral** *or* **wage-price spiral** = the economy is in a situation where price rises encourage higher wage demands which in turn make prices rise **die Wirtschaft befindet sich in einer Inflationsspirale od Lohn-Preis-Spirale**

2 *verb* to twist round and round, getting higher all the time **klettern, hochschnellen;** *a period of spiralling prices;* **spiralling inflation** = inflation where price rises make workers ask for higher wages which then increase prices again **eine sich spiralartig entwickelnde Inflation**

NOTE: **spiralling - spiralled** but US English **spiraling - spiraled**

split

1 *noun*

(a) dividing up **Aufteilung; share split** = dividing of shares into smaller denominations **Aktiensplit; the company is proposing a five for one split** = the company is proposing that each existing share should be divided into five smaller shares **das Unternehmen plant einen Aktiensplit im Verhältnis eins zu fünf**

(b) lack of agreement **Entzweiung, Spaltung;** *a split in the family shareholders*

2 *verb*

(a) to split shares = to divide shares into smaller denominations **Aktien splitten; the shares were split five for one** = five new shares were given for each existing share held **die Aktien wurden im Verhältnis eins zu fünf gesplittet**

(b) to split the difference = to come to an agreement over a price by dividing the difference between the amount the seller is asking and amount the buyer wants to pay and agreeing on a price between the two **sich die Differenz teilen**

NOTE: **splitting - split**

spoil *verb* to ruin *or* to make something bad **verderben;** *half the shipment was spoiled by water; the company's results were spoiled by a disastrous last quarter*

sponsor

1 *noun*

(a) person who pays money to help research *or* to pay for a business venture; company which pays to help a sport, in return for advertising rights **Sponsor**

(b) company which advertises on TV **Fernsehwerbungstreibender, Sponsor**

2 *verb* to pay money to help research *or* business development **als Sponsor finanzieren, sponsoren;** *to sponsor a television programme; the company has sponsored the football match; government-sponsored trade exhibition*

◇ **sponsorship** *noun* act of sponsoring **finanzielle Förderung, Sponsoring;**

government sponsorship of overseas selling missions

spot *noun*
(a) buying something for immediate delivery **Lokoware; spot cash** = cash paid for something bought immediately **sofortige Bezahlung, Sofortliquidität; the spot market in oil** = the market for buying oil for immediate delivery **der Kassamarkt für Öl; spot price** *or* **spot rate** = price *or* rate for something which is delivered immediately **Lokopreis**
(b) place **Ort, Platz, Stelle; to be on the spot** = to be at a certain place **an Ort und Stelle sein;** *we have a man on the spot to deal with any problems which happen on the building site*
(c) TV spot = period on TV which is used for commercials **Werbesendezeit;** *we are running a series of TV spots over the next three weeks*

> QUOTE with most of the world's oil now traded on spot markets, Opec's official prices are much less significant than they once were
> *Economist*
> QUOTE the averager spot price of Nigerian light crude oil for the month of July was 27.21 dollars per barrel
> *Business Times (Lagos)*

spread
1 *noun*
(a) range **Reihe; Streuung; he has a wide spread of investments** *or* **of interests** = he has shares in many different types of companies **er hat in seinen Investitionen eine breite Streuung**
(b) *(on the Stock Exchange)* difference between buying and selling prices **Marge, Spanne**
2 *verb* to space out over a period of time **verteilen;** *to spread payments over several months;* **to spread a risk** = to make the risk of insurance less great by asking other companies to help cover it **das Risiko verteilen**
NOTE: **spreading - spread**

◊ **spreadsheet** *noun* computer printout showing a series of columns of figures **Tabellenkalkulation**

> QUOTE dealers said markets were thin, with gaps between trades and wide spreads between bid and ask prices on the currencies
> *Wall Street Journal*
> QUOTE to ensure an average return you should hold a spread of different shares covering a wide cross-section of the market
> *Investors Chronicle*

square *noun*
(a) shape with four equal sides and four right angles **Quadrat;** *graph paper is drawn with a series of small squares*
(b) way of measuring area, by multiplying the length by the width **Quadrat(zahl);** *the office is ten metres by twelve - its area is one hundred and twenty square metres;* **square measure** = area in square feet or metres **Flächenmaß**
NOTE: written with figures as
ten square feet;
six square metres

◊ **squared paper** *noun* graph paper *or* paper printed with a series of small squares **Millimeterpapier**

squeeze
1 *noun* government control carried out by reducing amounts available **Verknappung; credit squeeze** = period when lending by the banks is restricted by the government **Kreditrestriktionen; profit squeeze** = control of the amount of profits which companies can pay out as dividend **Verminderung der Gewinnspanne**
2 *verb* to crush *or* to press; to make smaller **drücken, verkleinern;** *to squeeze margins or profits or credit;* **our margins have been squeezed by the competition** = profits have been reduced because our margins have to be smaller for us to stay competitive **unsere Gewinnspannen sind von der Konkurrenz heruntergedrückt worden**

stability *noun* being steady *or* not moving up or down **Stabilität, Beständigkeit;** *price stability; a period of economic stability; the stability of the currency markets*
NOTE: no plural

◊ **stabilization** *noun* making stable *or* preventing sudden changes in prices, etc. **Stabilisierung, Festigung; stabilization of the economy** = keeping the economy stable by preventing inflation from rising, cutting high interest rates and excess money supply **Stabilisierung der Wirtschaft**

◊ **stabilize** *verb* to make steady **(sich) stabilisieren, festigen; prices have stabilized** = prices have stopped moving up or down **die Preise haben sich stabilisiert; to have a stabilizing effect on the economy** = to make the economy more stable **eine stabilisierende Wirkung auf die Wirtschaft haben**

◊ **stable** *adjective* steady *or* not moving up or down **stabil, beständig, gleichbleibend;** *stable prices; stable exchange rate; stable currency; stable economy*

stack
1 *noun* pile *or* heap of things on top of each other **Stapel, Stoß;** *there is a stack of replies to our advertisement*

2 *verb* to pile things on top of each other **stapeln;** *the boxes are stacked in the warehouse*

staff

1 *noun* people who work for a company *or* for an organization **Personal, Mitarbeiter, Belegschaft, Angestellte; to be on the staff** *or* **a member of staff** *or* **a staff member** = to be employed permanently by a company **zum Personal gehören; staff agency** = agency which looks for office staff for companies **Büropersonalvermittlung; staff appointment** = a job on the staff **feste Anstellung; staff association** = society formed by members of staff of a company to represent them to the management and to organize entertainments **Personalvertretung; accounts staff** = people who work in the accounts department **Buchhalter/-in; clerical staff** *or* **office staff** = people who work in offices **Büropersonal; counter staff** = sales staff who work behind counters **Verkaufspersonal hinter dem Ladentisch; senior staff** *or* **junior staff** = older *or* younger members of staff; people in more important *or* less important positions in a company **ältere od jüngere Angestellte; Personal in führender od untergeordneter Position**

NOTE: **staff** refers to a group of people and so is often followed by a verb in the plural

2 *verb* to employ workers **mit Personal besetzen;** *to be staffed with skilled part-timers; to have difficulty in staffing the factory*

◇ **staffer** *noun US* member of the permanent staff **ständiger Mitarbeiter**

◇ **staffing** *noun* providing workers for a company **Einstellung von Personal; staffing levels** = numbers of members of staff required in a department of a company for it to work efficiently **Personalstärke; the company's staffing policy** = the company's views on staff - how many are needed for each department *or* if they should be full-time or part-time *or* what the salaries should be, etc. **die Personalplanung des Unternehmens**

NOTE: no plural

stag

1 *noun* person who buys new issues of shares and sells them immediately to make a profit **Neuemissionsspekulant**

2 *verb* **to stag an issue** = to buy a new issue of shares not as an investment, but to sell immediately at a profit **mit Neuemissionen spekulieren**

NOTE: **stagging - stagged**

stage

1 *noun* period *or* one of several points of development **Stadium, Phase, Etappe, Stufe, Abschnitt;** *the different stages of the production process;* **the contract is still in the drafting stage** = the contract is still being drafted **der Vertrag befindet sich noch im Entwurfsstadium; in stages** = in different steps **in Etappen, etappenweise;** *the company has agreed to repay the loan in stages*

2 *verb*

(a) to put on *or* to organize (a show) **veranstalten;** *the exhibition is being staged in the conference centre;* **to stage a recovery** = to recover **sich erholen;** *the company has staged a strong recovery from a point of near bankruptcy*

(b) staged payments = payments made in stages **Zahlungen in Etappen**

stagflation

noun inflation and stagnation of an economy **Stagflation, realer Stillstand bei steigenden Preisen**

stagger

verb to arrange (holidays, working hours) so that they do not all begin and end at the same time **staffeln;** *staggered holidays help the tourist industry; we have to stagger the lunch hour so that there is always someone on the switchboard*

stagnant

adjective not active *or* not increasing **stagnierend, stockend;** *turnover was stagnant for the first half of the year; a stagnant economy*

◇ **stagnate** *verb* not to increase *or* not to make progress **stagnieren, stocken;** *the economy is stagnating; after six hours the talks were stagnating*

◇ **stagnation** *noun* not increasing *or* not making any progress **Stagnation, Stillstand;** *the country entered a period of stagnation;* **economic stagnation** = lack of expansion in the economy **Wirtschaftsstagnation**

NOTE: no plural

stake

1 *noun* money invested **Beteiligung, Einlage; to have a stake in a business** = to have money invested in a business **einen Anteil an einem Unternehmen haben; to acquire a stake in a business** = to buy shares in a business **einen Anteil an einem Unternehmen erwerben;** *he acquired a 25% stake in the business*

2 *verb* **to stake money on something** = to risk money on something **Geld setzen auf**

> QUOTE other investments include a large stake in a Chicago-based insurance company, as well as interests in tobacco products and hotels
> *Lloyd's List*

stamp

1 *noun*

(a) device for making marks on documents; mark made in this way **Stempel;** *the invoice*

has the stamp "Received with thanks" on it; the customs officer looked at the stamps in his passport; **date stamp** = stamp with rubber figures which can be moved, used for marking the date on documents **Datumsstempel; rubber stamp** = stamp made of hard rubber cut to form words **(Gummi)stempel; stamp pad** = soft pad of cloth with ink on which a stamp is pressed, before marking the paper **Stempelkissen**
(b) small piece of gummed paper which you buy from a post office and stick on a letter *or* parcel to pay for the postage **Briefmarke;** *a postage stamp; a £1 stamp*
(c) stamp duty = tax on legal documents (such as the conveyance of a property to a new owner) **Stempelgebühr**
2 *verb*
(a) to mark a document with a stamp **(ab)stempeln;** *to stamp an invoice "Paid"; the documents were stamped by the customs officials*
(b) to put a postage stamp on (an envelope, etc.) **frankieren; stamped addressed envelope** = envelope with your own address written on it and a stamp stuck on it to pay for the return postage **frankierter/freigemachter Rückumschlag;** *send a stamped addressed envelope for further details and catalogue*

stand

1 *noun* arrangement of shelves *or* tables, etc. at an exhibition for showing a company's products **Stand; display stand** = special stand for displaying goods for sale **Auslagenstand, Vollsichtregal; exhibition stand** = separate section of an exhibition where a company exhibits its products or services **Messestand; news stand** = small wooden shop on a pavement, for selling newspapers **Zeitungsstand**
2 *verb* to be *or* to stay **sein, stehen; to stand liable for damages** = to be liable to pay damages **schadensersatzpflichtig sein; the company's balance stands at £24,000** = the balance is £24,000 **das Firmenguthaben liegt bei £24.000**
NOTE: **standing - stood**

◇ **stand down** *verb* to withdraw your name from an election **seine Kandidatur zurückziehen**

◇ **stand in for** *verb* to take someone's place **jdn vertreten, für jdn einspringen;** *Mr Smith is standing in for the chairman, who is ill*

standard

1 *noun* normal quality *or* normal conditions which other things are judged against **Norm, Standard, Niveau; standard of living** *or* **living standards** = quality of personal home life (such as amount of food or clothes bought, size of family car, etc.) **Lebensstandard; production standards** = quality of production **Produktionsstandard; up to standard** = of acceptable quality **den Anforderungen genügend;** *this batch is not up to standard or does not meet our standards;* **gold standard** = linking of the value of a currency to value of a quantity of gold **Goldwährung**
2 *adjective* normal *or* usual **Standard-, üblich, handelsüblich, normal;** *a standard model car; we have a standard charge of £25 for a thirty-minute session;* **standard agreement** *or* **standard contract** = normal printed contract form **Mustervertrag; standard letter** = letter which is sent without any change to various correspondents **Standard-, Formbrief; standard rate** = basic rate of income tax which is paid by most taxpayers **Standardsteuersatz**

◇ **standardization** *noun* making sure that everything fits a standard *or* is produced in the same way **Normung, Standardisierung, Typung;** *standardization of design; standardization of measurements;* **standardization of products** = reducing a large number of different products to a series which have the same measurements *or* design *or* packaging, etc. **Produkttypung**
NOTE: no plural

◇ **standardize** *verb* to make sure that everything fits a standard *or* is produced in the same way **normen, standardisieren, vereinheitlichen**

standby *noun*

(a) standby ticket = cheap air ticket which allows the passenger to wait until the last moment to see if there is an empty seat on the plane **Standby-Ticket; standby fare** = cheap fare for a standby ticket **Standby-Flugpreis**
(b) standby arrangements = plans for what should be done if an emergency happens, especially money held in reserve in the International Monetary Fund for use by a country in financial difficulties **Beistandsabkommen; standby credit** = credit which is available from the International Monetary Fund **Beistandskredit, Standby-Kredit**

standing

1 *adjective* **standing order** = order written by a customer asking a bank to pay money regularly to an account **Dauerauftrag;** *I pay my subscription by standing order*
2 *noun*
(a) long-standing customer *or* **customer of long standing** = person who has been a customer for many years **ein treuer/langjähriger Kunde**
(b) good reputation **Ansehen, Ruf; Bonität;** *the financial standing of a company;*

company of good standing = very reputable company **eine angesehene Firma**
NOTE: no plural

standstill
noun situation where work has stopped **Stillstand;** *production is at a standstill; the strike brought the factory to a standstill*

staple
1 *adjective*
(a) staple commodity = basic food or raw material **Haupterzeugnis; staple industry** = main industry in a country **Hauptindustriezweig; staple product** = main product **Hauptprodukt**
(b) small piece of bent metal for attaching papers together **Heftklammer;** *he used a pair of scissors to take the staples out of the documents*
2 *verb* **to staple papers together** = to attach papers with staples **Blätter zusammenheften;** *he could not take away separate pages, because the documents were stapled together*

◊ **stapler** *noun* small device used to attach papers together with staples **Hefter**

start
1 *noun* beginning **Beginn, Anfang, Start; cold start** = beginning a new business *or* opening a new shop with no previous turnover to base it on **ein völliger Neubeginn; house starts** *or US* **housing starts** = number of new private houses or flats of which construction has been started during a year **Neubauten**
2 *verb* **to start a business from cold** *or* **from scratch** = to begin a new business, with no previous turnover to base it on **ein Unternehmen von Grund auf aufbauen**

◊ **starting** *noun* beginning **Start-, Anfangs-; starting date** = date on which something starts **Anfangsdatum; starting salary** = salary for an employee when he starts work with a company **Anfangsgehalt**

◊ **start-up** *noun* beginning of a new company *or* new product **Neugründung; Anlauf;** *start-up costs*
NOTE: plural is **start-ups**

state
1 *noun*
(a) independent country; semi-independent section of a federal country (such as the USA or FRG) **Staat; Bundesstaat**
(b) government of a country **Regierung; state enterprise** = company run by the state **Staatsbetrieb, staatliches Unternehmen;** *the bosses of state industries are appointed by the government;* **state ownership** = situation where an industry is nationalized **Staatseigentum**
2 *verb* to say clearly **angeben, festlegen, feststellen;** *the document states that all revenue has to be declared to the tax office*

◊ **state-controlled** *adjective* run by the state **unter staatlicher Aufsicht;** *state-controlled television*

◊ **state-of-the-art** *adjective* technically as advanced as possible **technisch auf dem neuesten Stand**

◊ **state-owned** *adjective* owned by the state or by a state **staatseigen**

> QUOTE the unions had argued that public sector pay rates had slipped behind rates applying in state and local government areas
> ***Australian Financial Review***
>
> QUOTE state-owned banks cut their prime rates a percentage point to 11%
> ***Wall Street Journal***
>
> QUOTE each year American manufacturers increase their budget for state-of-the-art computer-based hardware and software
> ***Duns Business Month***

statement
noun saying something clearly **Angabe, Feststellung, Stellungnahme; to make a false statement** = to give wrong details **falsche Angaben machen; statement of expenses** = detailed list of money spent **Spesenaufstellung; bank statement** = written document from a bank showing the balance of an account **Kontoauszug; monthly** *or* **quarterly statement** = statement which is sent every month *or* every quarter by the bank **monatlicher od vierteljährlicher Kontoauszug**
(b) financial statement = document which shows the financial situation of a company **Finanzbericht, Abschluß;** *the accounts department have prepared a financial statement for the shareholders*
(c) statement of account = list of invoices and credits and debits sent by a supplier to a customer at the end of each month **Abrechnung**

station
noun
(a) place where trains stop for passengers **Bahnhof;** *the train leaves the Central Station at 14.15*
(b) TV station *or* **radio station** = building where TV or radio programmes are produced **Sendestation**

stationery
noun office supplies for writing, such as paper, carbons, pens, etc. **Schreibwaren;** *stationery supplier; office stationery;* **continuous stationery** = paper made as a long sheet used in computer printers **Endlospapier**
NOTE: no plural

statistics *plural noun* study of facts in the form of figures *or* statistical figures **Statistik; Statistiken, statistische Unterlagen;** *to examine the sales statistics for the previous six months; government trade statistics show an increase in imports*

◇ **statistical** *adjective* based on figures **statistisch;** *statistical analysis; statistical information;* **statistical discrepancy** = amount by which sets of figures differ **statistische Abweichung**

◇ **statistician** *noun* person who analyzes statistics **Statistiker/-in**

status *noun*
(a) importance *or* position in society **Stellung, Rang, Status; the chairman's car is a status symbol** = the size of the car shows how important the company is **der Wagen des Direktors ist ein Statussymbol; loss of status** = becoming less important in a group **Prestigeverlust; status inquiry** = checking on a customer's credit rating **Kreditauskunft**
(b) legal status = legal position **Personenstand; Rechtslage**
NOTE: no plural

◇ **status quo** *noun* state of things as they are now **Status quo;** *the contract does not alter the status quo*

statute *noun* law made by parliament **Gesetz; statute book** = list of laws passed by parliament **Gesetzbuch; statute of limitations** = law which allows only a certain amount of time (a few years) for someone to claim damages or property **Verjährungsausschlußfrist**

◇ **statutory** *adjective* fixed by law **gesetzlich;** *there is a statutory period of probation of thirteen weeks;* **statutory holiday** = holiday which is fixed by law **gesetzlicher Feiertag**

stay
1 *noun*
(a) length of time spent in one place **Aufenthalt;** *the tourists were in town only for a short stay;* **long-stay guests** = customers who spend a long time at a hotel **Dauergäste**
(b) stay of execution = temporary stopping of a legal order **Vollstreckungsaufschub;** *the court granted the company a two-week stay of execution*
2 *verb* to stop at a place **bleiben; übernachten;** *the chairman is staying at the Hotel London; profits have stayed below 10% for two years; inflation has stayed high in spite of the government's efforts to bring it down*

STD = SUBSCRIBER TRUNK DIALLING

steady
1 *adjective* continuing in a regular way **beständig, stabil;** *steady increase in profits; the market stayed steady; there is a steady demand for computers*
2 *verb* to become firm *or* to stop fluctuating **sich beruhigen, sich festigen;** *the markets steadied after last week's fluctuations; prices steadied on the commodity markets; the government's figures had a steadying influence on the exchange rate*

◇ **steadily** *adverb* in a regular *or* continuous way **ständig, fortwährend;** *output increased steadily over the last two quarters; the company has steadily increased its market share*

◇ **steadiness** *noun* being firm *or* not fluctuating **Beständigkeit, Stabilität, Festigkeit;** *the steadiness of the markets is due to the government's intervention*
NOTE: no plural

steal *verb* to take something which does not belong to you **stehlen;** *the rival company stole our best clients; one of our biggest problems is stealing in the wine department*
NOTE: **stealing - stole - has stolen**

steep *adjective* very sharp *or* very high (price) **steil, jäh;** *a steep increase in interest charges; a steep decline in overseas sales*

stencil *noun* sheet of special paper which can be written or typed on, and used in a duplicating machine **Matrize**

stenographer *noun* official person who can write in shorthand **Stenograph/-in**

step *noun*
(a) type of action **Maßnahme;** *the first step taken by the new MD was to analyse all the expenses;* **to take steps to prevent something happening** = to act to stop something happening **Maßnahmen zur Verhinderung von etwas ergreifen**
(b) movement **Schritt;** *becoming assistant to the MD is a step up the promotion ladder;* **in step with** = moving at the same rate as **in Einklang mit;** *the pound rose in step with the dollar;* **out of step with** = not moving at the same rate as **nicht in Einklang mit;** *the pound was out of step with other European currencies; wages are out of step with the cost of living*

◇ **step up** *verb* to increase **steigern, erhöhen; verstärken;** *to step up industrial action; the company has stepped up production of the latest models*
NOTE: **stepping - stepped**

sterling *noun* standard currency used in the United Kingdom **Sterling;** *to quote prices in sterling or to quote sterling prices;* **pound sterling** = official term for the British currency **Pfund Sterling; sterling area** = area of the world where the pound sterling is the main trading currency **Sterlingzone; sterling balances** = a country's trade balances expressed in pounds sterling **Außenhandelsbilanz in Pfund Sterling; sterling crisis** = fall in the exchange rate of the pound sterling **Sterlingkrise**
NOTE: no plural

> QUOTE it is doubtful that British goods will price themselves back into world markets as long as sterling labour costs continue to rise faster than in competitor countries
> *Sunday Times*

stevedore *noun* person who works in a port, loading or unloading ships **Schauermann, Stauer**

steward *noun*
(a) man who serves drinks *or* food on a ship *or* plane **Steward**
(b) shop steward = elected union representative of workers, who represents their complaints to the management **betrieblicher Vertrauensmann**
◇ **stewardess** *noun* woman who serves drinks *or* food on a ship *or* plane **Stewardeß**

stick *verb*
(a) to attach with glue **kleben;** *to stick a stamp on a letter; they stuck a poster on the door*
(b) to stay still *or* not to move **steckenbleiben;** *sales have stuck at £2m for the last two years*
NOTE: **sticking - stuck**
◇ **sticker**
1 *noun* small piece of gummed paper or plastic to be stuck on something as an advertisement *or* to indicate a price **Aufkleber, Etikett; airmail sticker** = blue sticker with the words "By air mail" which can be stuck on an envelope or parcel to show that it is being sent by air **Luftpostaufkleber**
2 *verb* to put a price sticker on an article for sale **auszeichnen, mit Preisschildern versehen;** *we had to sticker all the stock*

stiff *adjective* strong *or* difficult **hart, schwierig;** *stiff competition; he had to take a stiff test before he qualified*

stimulate *verb* to encourage *or* to make (something) become more active **anregen, ankurbeln, beleben;** *to stimulate the economy; to stimulate trade with the Middle East*

◇ **stimulus** *noun* thing which encourages activity **Anreiz, Ansporn**
NOTE: plural is **stimuli**

stipulate *verb* to demand that a condition be put into a contract **(vertraglich) vereinbaren;** *to stipulate that the contract should run for five years; to pay the stipulated charges; the company failed to pay on the date stipulated in the contract; the contract stipulates that the seller pays the buyer's legal costs*
◇ **stipulation** *noun* condition in a contract **Vereinbarung, Bedingung, Klausel**

stock
1 *noun*
(a) quantity of raw materials **Vorrat;** *we have large stocks of oil or coal; the country's stocks of butter or sugar*
(b) quantity of goods for sale **Lager-, Warenbestand; opening stock** = details of stock at the beginning of an accounting period **Eröffnungsbestand; closing stock** = details of stock at the end of an accounting period **Schlußbestand; stock code** = number and letters which indicate an item of stock **Warencode; stock control** = making sure that enough stock is kept and that quantities and movements of stock are noted **Lagersteuerung; stock depreciation** = reduction in value of stock which is held in a warehouse for some time **Lagerbestandsabschreibung; stock figures** = details of how many goods are in the warehouse *or* store etc. **Lagerbestandsverzeichnis; stock level** = quantity of goods kept in stock **Lagerbestandshöhe;** *we try to keep stock levels low during the summer;* **stock turn** *or* **stock turnround** *or* **stock turnover** = total value of stock sold in a year divided by the average value of goods in stock **Lagerumschlag; stock valuation** = estimating the value of stock at the end of an accounting period **Bewertung des Lagerbestandes; to buy a shop with stock at valuation** = to pay for the stock the same amount as its value as estimated by the valuer **ein Geschäft inklusive des Warenbestandes zum Schätzpreis kaufen; stock in hand** = stock held in a shop *or* warehouse **Waren auf Lager; to purchase stock at valuation** = to pay for stock the price it is valued at **den Warenbestand zum Schätzpreis kaufen**
(c) in stock *or* **out of stock** = available *or* not available in the warehouse *or* store **vorrätig sein; nicht vorrätig/ausverkauft sein;** *to hold 2,000 lines in stock; the item went out of stock just before Christmas but came back into stock in the first week of January; we are out of stock of this item;* **to take stock** =

to count the items in a warehouse **Inventur machen**
(d) stocks and shares = shares in ordinary companies **Effekten, Aktien, Wertpapiere; stock certificate** = document proving that someone owns stock in a company **Aktienzertifikat, Anteilsschein; debenture stock** = capital borrowed by a company, using its fixed assets as security **Anleihekapital; dollar stocks** = shares in American companies **US-Aktien; government stock** = government securities **Staatsanleihen; loan stock** = money lent to a company at a fixed rate of interest **festverzinsliche Anleihen; convertible loan stock** = money lent to a company which can be converted into shares at a later date **Wandelanleihen;** *US* **common stock** = ordinary shares in a company giving the shareholders the right to vote at meetings and receive a dividend **Stammaktien**
(e) the stock market = place where shares are bought and sold **Börse;** *stock market price or price on the stock market;* **stock market valuation** = value of shares based on the current market price **Aktienbewertung an der Börse**
(f) normal *or* usually kept in stock **Grundbestand;** *butter is a stock item for any good grocer;* **stock size** = normal size **gängige Größe;** *we only carry stock sizes of shoes*
2 *verb* to hold goods for sale in a warehouse *or* store **führen, auf Lager halten;** *to stock 200 lines*

◊ **stockbroker** *noun* person who buys or sells shares for clients **Börsenmakler; stockbroker's commission** = payment to a broker for a deal carried out on behalf of a client **Courtage**

◊ **stockbroking** *noun* trade of dealing in shares for clients **Effektenhandel, Aktiengeschäft;** *a stockbroking firm*
NOTE: no plural

◊ **stock controller** *noun* person who notes movements of stock **Lagerverwalter**

◊ **Stock Exchange** *noun* place where stocks and shares are bought and sold **Börse, Effekten-, Wertpapierbörse;** *he works on the Stock Exchange; shares in the company are traded on the Stock Exchange;* **Stock Exchange listing** = official list of shares which can be bought or sold on the Stock Exchange **Börsennotierung**

◊ **stockholder** *noun* person who holds shares in a company **Aktionär/-in**

◊ **stockholding** *noun* shares in a company held by someone **Aktienbestand, Aktienbeteiligung**

◊ **stock-in-trade** *noun* goods held by a business for sale **Bestände, Sortiment**
NOTE: no plural

◊ **stockist** *noun* person *or* shop which stocks a certain item **Fachhändler, Fachgeschäft**

◊ **stock jobber** *noun* person who buys and sells shares from other traders on the Stock Exchange **Börsenhändler**

◊ **stock jobbing** *noun* buying and selling shares from other traders on the Stock Exchange **Handel an der Börse**
NOTE: no plural

◊ **stocklist** *noun* list of items carried in stock **Warenverzeichnis, Lagerbestandsverzeichnis**

◊ **stockpile**
1 *noun* supplies kept by a country *or* a company in case of need **Vorrat, Reserve;** *a stockpile of raw materials*
2 *verb* to buy items and keep them in case of need **Vorräte anlegen, horten;** *to stockpile raw materials*

◊ **stockroom** *noun* room where stores are kept **Lager**

◊ **stocktaking** *noun* counting of goods in stock at the end of an accounting period **Inventur, Bestandsaufnahme;** *the warehouse is closed for the annual stocktaking;* **stocktaking sale** = sale of goods cheaply to clear a warehouse before stocktaking **Ausverkauf wegen Inventur**
NOTE: no plural

◊ **stock up** *verb* to buy supplies of something which you will need in the future **einen Vorrat anlegen, Lager auffüllen;** *they stocked up with computer paper*

> QUOTE US crude oil stocks fell last week by nearly 2.5m barrels
> *Financial Times*
>
> QUOTE to stock rose to over $20 a share, higher than the $18 bid
> *Fortune*
>
> QUOTE the news was favourably received on the Sydney Stock Exchange, where the shares gained 40 cents to A$9.80
> *Financial Times*

stop

1 *noun*
(a) end of an action **Halt, Stillstand;** *work came to a stop when the company could not pay the workers' wages; the new finance director put a stop to the reps' expense claims*
(b) not supplying **Sperrung; account on stop** = account which is not supplied because it has not paid its latest invoices **gesperrtes Konto;** *to put an account on stop;* **to put a stop on a cheque** = to tell the bank not to pay a cheque which you have written **einen Scheck sperren**
2 *verb*
(a) to make (something) not to move any more **anhalten, zum Stillstand bringen,**

stoppen; *the shipment was stopped by the customs*
(b) not to do anything any more **aufhören, einstellen;** *the work force stopped work when the company could not pay their wages; the office staff stop work at 5.30; we have stopped supplying Smith & Co.*
(c) to stop an account = not to supply an account any more on credit because bills have not been paid **ein Konto sperren; to stop a cheque** = to ask a bank not to pay a cheque you have written **einen Scheck sperren lassen; to stop payments** = not to make any further payments **Zahlungen einstellen**
(d) to stop someone's wages = to take money out of someone's wages **einen Lohnanteil von jdm einbehalten;** *we stopped £25 from his pay because he was late*
NOTE: **stopping - stopped**

◇ **stop over** *verb* to stay for a short time in a place on a long journey **Zwischenstation machen;** *we stopped over in Hong Kong on the way to Australia*

◇ **stopover** *noun* staying for a short time in a place on a long journey **Zwischenstation; Zwischenlandung;** *the ticket allows you two stopovers between London and Tokyo*

◇ **stoppage** *noun*
(a) act of stopping **Unterbrechung, Stillstand;** *stoppage of deliveries; stoppage of payments; deliveries will be late because of stoppages on the production line*
(b) money taken from a worker's wage packet for insurance, tax, etc. **Gehalts-, Lohnabzug**

storage *noun*
(a) keeping in store *or* in a warehouse **Lagerung, Aufbewahrung;** *we put our furniture into storage;* **storage capacity** = space available for storage **Lagerkapazität; storage company** = company which keeps items for customers **Lagerungsfirma, Lagerhaus; storage facilities** = equipment and buildings suitable for storage **Lagereinrichtungen; storage unit** = device attached to a computer for storing information on disk or tape **Speichergerät; cold storage** = keeping food, etc., in a cold store to prevent it going bad **Kaltlagerung, Kühlhauslagerung; to put a plan into cold storage** = to postpone work on a plan, usually for a very long time **einen Plan auf Eis legen**
(b) cost of keeping goods in store **Lagerkosten, Lagergeld;** *storage was 10% of value, so we scrapped the stock*
(c) facility for storing data in a computer **Speicher, Speicherung;** *disk with a storage capacity of 10Mb*
NOTE: no plural

◇ **store**
1 *noun*
(a) place where goods are kept **Lager(halle), Lagerhaus, Magazin; cold store** = warehouse *or* room where food can be kept cold **Kühlhaus**
(b) quantity of items *or* materials kept because they will be needed **Vorrat, Bestände;** *I always keep a store of envelopes ready in my desk*
(c) large shop **Geschäft;** *a furniture store; a big clothing store;* **chain store** = one store in a number of stores **Filiale, Kettenladen; department store** = large store with sections for different types of goods **Kaufhaus, Warenhaus; discount store** = shop which specializes in cheap goods sold at a high discount **Diskont-, Billigladen; general store(s)** = small country shop which sells a wide range of products **Gemischtwarenhandlung**
2 *verb*
(a) to keep in a warehouse **(ein)lagern;** *to store goods for six months*
(b) to keep for future use **aufbewahren, speichern;** *we store our pay records on computer*

◇ **storekeeper** *or* **storeman** *noun* person in charge of a storeroom **Lagerverwalter, Lagerist**

◇ **storeroom** *noun* room where stock can be kept *or* small warehouse attached to a factory **Lager, Lagerraum**

straight line *noun* **straight line depreciation** = depreciation calculated by dividing the cost of an asset by the number of years it is likely to be used **lineare Abschreibung**

strategy *noun* plan of future action **Strategie;** *business strategy; company strategy; marketing strategy; financial strategy*

◇ **strategic** *adjective* based on a plan of action **strategisch; strategic planning** = planning the future work of a company **strategische Planung**

stream *noun* mass of people *or* traffic, all going in the same direction **Strom;** *we had a stream of customers on the first day of the sale;* **to come on stream** = to start production **in Betrieb nehmen**

◇ **streamer** *noun* device for attaching a tape storage unit to a computer **Magnetbandstation**

◇ **streamline** *verb* to make (something) more efficient *or* more simple **rationalisieren;** *to streamline the accounting system; to streamline distribution services*

◇ **streamlined** *adjective* efficient *or* rapid **rationalisiert;** *streamlined production; the* *company introduced a streamlined system of distribution*

◇ **streamlining** *noun* making efficient **Rationalisierung, Straffung**
NOTE: no plural

street *noun* road in a town **Straße; High Street** = main shopping street in a British town **Hauptgeschäftsstraße; the High Street banks** = main British banks which accept deposits from individual customers **die größten öffentlichen Banken; street directory** = (i) list of people living in a street; (ii) map of a town with all the streets listed in alphabetical order in an index **(i) Adreßbuch; (ii) Stadtplan**

strength *noun* being strong *or* at a high level **Stärke;** *the company took advantage of the strength of the demand for home computers; the strength of the pound increases the possibility of high interest rates*

stretch *verb* to pull out *or* make longer **strecken, dehnen;** *the investment programme has stretched the company's resources;* **he is not fully stretched** = his job does not make him work as hard as he could **er ist nicht voll ausgelastet**

strict *adjective* exact **genau, strikt, präzise;** *in strict order of seniority*

◇ **strictly** *adverb* exactly **genau, strikt, präzise;** *the company asks all staff to follow strictly the buying procedures*

strike
1 *noun*
(a) stopping of work by the workers (because of lack of agreement with management *or* because of orders from a union) **Streik, Ausstand; all-out strike** = complete strike by all workers **Totalstreik; general strike** = strike of all the workers in a country **Generalstreik; official strike** = strike which has been approved by the main office of a union **offizieller Streik, gewerkschaftlich organisierter Streik; protest strike** = strike in protest at a particular grievance **Proteststreik; sit-down strike** = strike where workers stay in their place of work and refuse to work or leave **Sitzstreik; sympathy strike** = strike to show that workers agree with another group of workers who are on strike **Solidaritätsstreik, Sympathiestreik; token strike** = short strike to show that workers have a grievance **Warnstreik; unofficial strike** = strike by local workers, which has not been approved by the main union **wilder Streik; wildcat strike** = strike organized by workers without the main union office knowing about it **wilder Streik**
(b) to take strike action = to go on strike **in den Ausstand treten; strike call** = demand by a union for a strike **Streikaufruf; no-strike agreement** *or* **no-strike clause** = (clause in an) agreement where the workers say that they will never strike **Streikverbotsklausel; strike fund** = money collected by a trade union from its members, used to pay strike pay **Streikkasse; strike pay** = wages paid to striking workers by their trade union **Streikgeld; strike ballot** *or* **strike vote** = vote by workers to decide if a strike should be held **Streik-, Urabstimmung**
(c) to come out on strike *or* **to go on strike** = to stop work **in den Ausstand treten;** *the office workers are on strike for higher pay;* **to call the workforce out on strike** = to tell the workers to stop work **zum Streik in einem Unternehmen aufrufen;** *the union called its members out on strike*
2 *verb*
(a) to stop working because there is no agreement with management **streiken;** *to strike for higher wages or for shorter working hours; to strike in protest against bad working conditions;* **to strike in sympathy with the postal workers** = to strike to show that you agree with the postal workers who are on strike **aus Solidarität mit den Postbeamten streiken**
(b) to strike a bargain with someone = to come to an agreement **ein Geschäft abschließen; a deal was struck at £25 a unit** = we agreed the price of £25 a unit **der Vertrag wurde für £25 pro Einheit abgeschlossen**
NOTE: **striking - struck**

◇ **strikebound** *adjective* not able to work *or* to move because of a strike **bestreikt, vom Streik betroffen;** *six ships are strikebound in the docks*

◇ **strikebreaker** *noun* worker who goes on working while everyone else is on strike **Streikbrecher**

◇ **striker** *noun* worker who is on strike **Streikender**

stripper *noun* **asset stripper** = person who buys a company to sell its assets **Aufkäufer (un)rentabler Unternehmen, der anschließend deren Vermögenswerte verkauft**

◇ **stripping** *noun* **asset stripping** = buying a company in order to sell its assets **Aufkauf (un)rentabler Unternehmen, deren Vermögenswerte anschließend verkauft werden**

strong *adjective* with a lot of force *or* strength **stark;** *a strong demand for home computers; the company needs a strong chairman;* **strong pound** = pound which is high against other currencies **starkes Pfund**

◇ **strongbox** *noun* safe *or* heavy metal box which cannot be opened easily, in which valuable documents, money, etc., can be kept **Stahlkassette**

◇ **strongroom** *noun* special room (in a bank) where valuable documents, money, golds, etc., can be kept **Stahlkammer, Tresorraum**

> QUOTE everybody blames the strong dollar for US trade problems
> *Duns Business Month*
> QUOTE in a world of floating exchange rates the dollar is strong because of capital inflows rather than weak because of the nation's trade deficit
> *Duns Business Month*

structure
1 *noun* way in which something is organized **Struktur, Aufbau, Gefüge;** *the paper gives a diagram of the company's organizational structure; the price structure in the small car market; the career structure within a corporation; the company is reorganizing its discount structure;* **capital structure of a company** = way in which a company's capital is set up **die Kapitalstruktur einer Firma; the company's salary structure** = organization of salaries in a company with different rates of pay for different types of job **die Gehaltsstruktur eines Unternehmens**
2 *verb* to arrange in a certain way **aufbauen, gestalten, strukturieren;** *to structure a meeting*

◇ **structural** *adjective* referring to a structure **strukturell;** *to make structural changes in a company;* **structural unemployment** = unemployment caused by the changing structure of an industry *or* society **strukturelle Arbeitslosigkeit**

stub *noun* **cheque stub** = piece of paper left in a cheque book after a cheque has been written and taken out **Scheckabschnitt**

studio *noun* place where designers, film producers, artists, etc., work **Atelier, Studio; design studio** = independent firm which specializes in creating designs for companies **Design-Studio**

study
1 *noun* examining something carefully **Studie;** *the company has asked the consultants to prepare a study of new production techniques; he has read the government study on sales opportunities;* **to carry out a feasibility study on a project** = to examine the costs and possible profits to see if the project should be started **eine Vorstudie zu einem Projekt/eine Projektstudie ausführen**
2 *verb* to examine (something) carefully **sorgfältig untersuchen/prüfen;** *we are studying the possibility of setting up an office in New York; the government studied the committee's proposals for two months; you will need to study the market carefully before deciding on the design of the product*

stuff *verb* to put papers, etc., into envelopes **stecken;** *we pay casual workers £2 an hour for stuffing envelopes or for envelope stuffing*

◇ **stuffer** *noun US* advertising paper to be put in an envelope for mailing **Anzeigen-, Werbebeilage**

style *noun* way of doing *or* making something **Stil, Art;** *a new style of product; old-style management techniques*

sub *noun*
(a) wages paid in advance **Vorschuß, Lohnvorauszahlung**
(b) = SUBSCRIPTION

sub- *prefix* under *or* less important **Unter-, unter-, Sub-, sub-**

◇ **sub-agency** *noun* small agency which is part of a large agency **Untervertretung**

◇ **sub-agent** *noun* person who is in charge of a sub-agency **Untervertreter**

◇ **subcommittee** *noun* small committee which is part of *or* set up by a main committee **Unterausschuß;** *the next item on the agenda is the report of the finance subcommittee*

◇ **subcontract**
1 *noun* contract between the main contractor for a whole project and another firm who will do part of the work **Unterauftrag, Untervertrag;** *they have been awarded the subcontract for all the electrical work in the new building; we will put the electrical work out to subcontract*
2 *verb* to agree with a company that they will do part of the work for a project **Unteraufträge vergeben/weitervergeben;** *the electrical work has been subcontracted to Smith Ltd*

◇ **subcontractor** *noun* company which has a contract to do work for a main contractor **Subunternehmer**

◇ **subdivision** *noun US* piece of empty land to be used for building new houses **Bauplatz**

subject to *adjective*
(a) depending on **abhängig von; the contract is subject to government approval** = the contract will be valid only if it is approved by the government **der Vertrag hängt von der Genehmigung der Regierung ab; agreement** *or*

sale subject to contract = agreement *or* sale which is not legal until a proper contract has been signed **Vereinbarung od Verkauf im Fall eines Vertragsabschlusses; offer subject to availability** = the offer is valid only if the goods are available **Angebot solange Vorrat reicht**
(b) these articles are subject to import tax = import tax has to be paid on these articles **auf diese Artikel wird Einfuhrzoll erhoben**

sub judice
adverb being considered by a court (and so not to be mentioned in the media) **noch nicht entschieden (vor Gericht), rechtshängig;** *the papers cannot report the case because it is still sub judice*

sublease
1 *noun* lease from a tenant to another tenant **Untermietvertrag; Unterpachtvertrag; Untervermietung; Unterverpachtung**
2 *verb* to lease a leased property from another tenant **untervermieten; unterverpachten;** *they subleased a small office in the centre of town*

◇ **sublessee** *noun* person *or* company which takes a property on a sublease **Untermieter; Unterpächter**

◇ **sublessor** *noun* tenant who lets a leased property to another tenant **Untervermieter; Unterverpächter**

◇ **sublet** *verb* to let a leased property to another tenant **untervermieten; unterverpachten;** *we have sublet part of our office to a financial consultancy*
NOTE: **subletting - sublet**

submit
verb to put (something) forward to be examined **einreichen, vorlegen;** *to submit a proposal to the committee; he submitted a claim to the insurers; the reps are asked to submit their expenses claims once a month*
NOTE: **submitting - submitted**

subordinate
1 *adjective* less important **untergeordnet; subordinate to** = governed by *or* which depends on **bestimmt durch, abhängig von**
2 *noun* member of staff who is directed by someone **Untergebener;** *his subordinates find him difficult to work with*

subpoena
1 *noun* order telling someone to appear in court as a witness **Vorladung (vor Gericht)**
2 *verb* to order someone to appear in court **(vor Gericht) vorladen;** *the finance director was subpoenaed by the prosecution*

subscribe
verb
(a) to subscribe to a magazine = to pay for a series of issues of a magazine **eine Zeitschrift abonnieren**
(b) to subscribe for shares = to apply for shares in a new company **neue Aktien zeichnen**

◇ **subscriber** *noun*
(a) subscriber to a magazine *or* **magazine subscriber** = person who has paid in advance for a series of issues of a magazine **Zeitschriftenabonnent;** *the extra issue is sent free to subscribers*
(b) subscriber to a share issue = person who has applied for shares in a new company **Zeichner von neuen Aktien**
(c) telephone subscriber = person who has a telephone **Fernsprechteilnehmer; subscriber trunk dialling** = telephone system where you can dial international numbers direct from your own telephone without going through the operator **Selbstwählferndienst**

◇ **subscription** *noun*
(a) money paid in advance for a series of issues of a magazine *or* for membership of a society **Abonnement; Mitgliedsbeitrag;** *did you remember to pay the subscription to the computer magazine? he forgot to renew his club subscription;* **to take out a subscription to a magazine** = to start paying for a series of issues of a magazine **eine Zeitschrift abonnieren; to cancel a subscription to a magazine** = to stop paying for a magazine **eine Zeitschrift abbestellen, ein Zeitschriftenabonnement kündigen; subscription rates** = amount of money to be paid for a series of issues of a magazine **Abonnementspreis**
(b) subscription to a new share issue = offering shares in a new company for sale **Zeichnungsangebot, Auslegung zur öffentlichen Zeichnung; subscription list** = list of subscribers to a new share issue **Zeichnungsbogen; the subscription lists close at 10.00 on September 24th** = no new applicants will be allowed to subscribe for the share issue after that date **die Zeichnung wird am 24. September um 10 Uhr geschlossen**

> QUOTE the rights issue is to be a one-for-four, at FFr 1,000 a share; it will grant shareholders free warrants to subscribe to further new shares
> *Financial Times*

subsidiary
1 *adjective* (thing) which is less important **nebensächlich, Neben-;** *they agreed to most of the conditions in the contract but queried one or two subsidiary items;* **subsidiary company** = company which is owned by a parent company **Tochtergesellschaft**
2 *noun* company which is owned by a parent company **Tochtergesellschaft;** *most of the group profit was contributed by the subsidiaries in the Far East*

subsidize *verb* to help by giving money **subventionieren;** *the government has refused to subsidize the car industry;* **subsidized accommodation** = cheap accommodation which is partly paid for by an employer or a local authority, etc. **subventionierte Wohnung**

◇ **subsidy** *noun*
(a) money given to help something which is not profitable **Subvention;** *the industry exists on government subsidies; the government has increased its subsidy to the car industry*
(b) money given by a government to make something cheaper **Subvention;** *the subsidy on butter or the butter subsidy*

> QUOTE a serious threat lies in the estimated 400,000 tonnes of subsidized beef in EEC cold stores
> *Australian Financial Review*

subsistence *noun* minimum amount of food, money, housing, etc., which a person needs **Lebensunterhalt; subsistence allowance** = money paid by a company to cover the cost of hotels, meals, etc., for a member of staff who is travelling on business **Tagegeld; at subsistence level** = to have only just enough money to live on **Existenzminimum**
NOTE: no plural

substantial *adjective* large *or* important **beträchtlich, erheblich, stattlich; she was awarded substantial damages** = she received a large sum of money as damages **ihr wurde eine stattliche Schadensersatzsumme zugesprochen; to acquire a substantial interest in a company** = to buy a large number of shares in a company **einen stattlichen Anteil an einem Unternehmen erwerben**

substitute
1 *noun* person *or* thing which takes the place of someone *or* something else **Vertreter/-in, Vertretung, Stellvertreter; Ersatz**
2 *verb* to take the place of something else **ersetzen, austauschen**

subtenancy *noun* agreement to sublet a property **Untermiete; Unterpacht**

◇ **subtenant** *noun* person *or* company to which a property has been sublet **Untermieter; Unterpächter**

subtotal *noun* total of one section of a complete set of figures **Zwischensumme**

subtract *verb* to take away (something) from a total **subtrahieren, abziehen;** *if the profits from the Far Eastern operations are subtracted, you will see that the group has not been profitable in the European market*

subvention *noun* subsidy **Subvention**

succeed *verb*
(a) to do well *or* to be profitable **Erfolg haben, erfolgreich sein;** *the company has succeeded best in the overseas markets; his business has succeeded more than he had expected*
(b) to do what was planned **gelingen;** *she succeeded in passing her shorthand test; they succeeded in putting their rivals out of business*
(c) to follow (someone) **folgen;** *Mr Smith was succeeded as chairman by Mr Jones*

◇ **success** *noun*
(a) doing something well **Erfolg;** *the launch of the new model was a great success; the company has had great success in the Japanese market*
(b) doing what was intended **Erfolg;** *we had no success in trying to sell the lease; he has been looking for a job for six months, but with no success*

◇ **successful** *adjective* which does well **erfolgreich;** *a successful businessman; a successful selling trip to Germany*

◇ **successfully** *adverb* done well **erfolgreich, mit Erfolg;** *he successfully negotiated a new contract with the unions; the new model was successfully launched last month*

◇ **successor** *noun* person who takes over from someone **Nachfolger/-in;** *Mr Smith's successor as chairman will be Mr Jones*

sue *verb* to take someone to court *or* to start legal proceedings against someone to get money as compensation **klagen, Klage erheben, einen Prozeß anstrengen, prozessieren, verklagen, gerichtlich belangen;** *to sue someone for damages; he is suing the company for $50,000 compensation*

suffer *verb* to be in a bad situation *or* to do badly **leiden, erleiden;** *exports have suffered during the last six months;* **to suffer from something** = to do badly because of something **unter etwas leiden;** *the company's products suffer from bad design; the group suffers from bad management*

> QUOTE the bank suffered losses to the extent that its capital has been wiped out
> *South China Morning Post*
> QUOTE the holding company has seen its earnings suffer from big writedowns in conjunction with its agricultural loan portfolio
> *Duns Business Month*

sufficient *adjective* enough **ausreichend, genügend, genug;** *the company has sufficient funds to pay for its expansion programme*

suggest *verb* to put forward a proposal **vorschlagen, empfehlen, anregen;** *the chairman suggested (that) the next meeting should be held in October; we suggested Mr Smith for the post of treasurer*

◇ **suggestion** *noun* proposal *or* idea which is put forward **Vorschlag, Empfehlung, Anregung; suggestion box** = place in a company where members of staff can put forward their ideas for making the company more efficient and profitable **Kasten für Verbesserungsvorschläge**

suitable *adjective* convenient *or* which fits **passend, geeignet;** *Wednesday is the most suitable day for board meetings; we had to readvertise the job because there were no suitable candidates*

suitcase *noun* box with a handle for carrying clothes and personal belongings when travelling **Koffer;** *the customs officer made him open his three suitcases*

sum *noun*
(a) quantity of money **Betrag;** *a sum of money was stolen from the personnel office; he lost large sums on the Stock Exchange; she received the sum of £500 in compensation;* **the sum insured** = the largest amount which an insurer will pay under the terms of an insurance **Versicherungssumme; lump sum** = money paid in one payment, not in several small payments **Pauschalbetrag, Pauschale**
(b) total of a series of figures added together **Summe**

summary *noun* short account of what has happened *or* of what has been written **Zusammenfassung, Übersicht;** *the chairman gave a summary of his discussions with the German trade delegation; the sales department has given a summary of sales in Europe for the first six months*

summons *noun* official order to appear in court to be tried **Vorladung, Ladung;** *he threw away the summons and went on holiday to Spain*

sundry
1 *adjective* various **verschiedene**
2 *noun* various items **Verschiedenes; sundry items** *or* **sundries** = small items which are not listed in detail **Verschiedenes**

superannuation *noun* pension paid to someone who is too old *or* ill to work any more **Rente, Pension; superannuation plan** *or* **scheme** = pension plan *or* scheme **Alterssicherungssystem**
NOTE: no plural

superintend *verb* to be in charge of **beaufsichtigen, verantwortlich sein für;** *he superintends the company's overseas sales*

◇ **superintendent** *noun* person in charge **Leiter/-in, Aufsicht**

superior
1 *adjective* better *or* of better quality **besser, überlegen;** *our product is superior to all competing products; their sales are higher because of their superior distribution service*
2 *noun* more important person **Vorgesetzter;** *each manager is responsible to his superior for accurate reporting of sales*

supermarket *noun* large store, usually selling food, where customers serve themselves and pay at a checkout **Supermarkt;** *sales in supermarkets or supermarket sales account for half the company's turnover*

superstore *noun* very large self-service store which sells a wide range of goods **Einkaufs-, Verbrauchermarkt**

supertanker *noun* very large oil tanker **Supertanker**

supervise *verb* to watch work carefully to see if it is well done **überwachen, beaufsichtigen, die Aufsicht haben;** *the move to the new offices was supervised by the administrative manager; she supervises six girls in the accounts department*

◇ **supervision** *noun* being supervised **Aufsicht;** *new staff work under supervision for the first three months; she is very experienced and can be left to work without any supervision; the cash was counted under the supervision of the finance manager*
NOTE: no plural

◇ **supervisor** *noun* person who supervises **Aufsicht, Aufsichtsbeamter, Aufseher, Kontrolleur**

◇ **supervisory** *adjective* as a supervisor **Aufsichts-, Überwachungs-;** *supervisory staff; he works in a supervisory capacity*

supplement
1 *noun* thing which is added **Zusatz, Ergänzung; Zulage, Aufbesserung;** *the company gives him a supplement to his pension*

2 *verb* to add **ergänzen; aufbessern;** *we will supplement the warehouse staff with six part-timers during the Christmas rush*

◇ **supplementary** *adjective* in addition to **Zusatz-, zusätzlich, ergänzend; supplementary benefit** = payments from the government to people with very low incomes **Sozialhilfe**

supply

1 *noun*

(a) providing something which is needed **Versorgung, Angebot, Lieferung; money supply** = amount of money which exists in a country **Geldreserve, Geldvolumen; supply price** = price at which something is provided **Angebotspreis; supply and demand** = amount of a product which is available and the amount which is wanted by customers **Angebot und Nachfrage; the law of supply and demand** = general rule that the amount of a product which is available is related to the needs of the possible customer **das Gesetz von Angebot und Nachfrage**

(b) in short supply = not available in large enough quantities to meet the demand **knapp sein;** *spare parts are in short supply because of the strike*

(c) stock of something which is needed **Vorrat, Bestand;** *the factory is running short of supplies of coal; supplies of coal have been reduced;* **office supplies** = goods needed to run an office (such as paper, pens, typewriters) **Bürobedarf**

2 *verb* to provide something which is needed **liefern, beliefern, versorgen;** *to supply a factory with spare parts; the finance department supplied the committee with the figures; details of staff addresses and phone numbers can be supplied by the personnel staff*

◇ **supply side economics** *noun* economic theory, that governments should encourage producers and suppliers of goods by cutting taxes, rather than encourage demand by making more money available in the economy **angebotsorientierte Wirtschaftspolitik**

◇ **supplier** *noun* person *or* company which supplies *or* sells goods or services **Lieferant, Zulieferer;** *office equipment supplier; they are major suppliers of spare parts to the car industry*

support

1 *noun*

(a) giving money to help **Unterstützung, Hilfe;** *the government has provided support to the electronics industry; we have no financial support from the banks*

(b) agreement *or* encouragement **Unterstützung, Beistand;** *the chairman has the support of the committee;* **support price** = price (in the EC) at which a government will buy agricultural produce to stop the price falling **Stützungspreis**

NOTE: no plural

2 *verb*

(a) to give money to help **finanziell unterstützen, stützen;** *the government is supporting the electronics industry to the tune of $2m per annum; we hope the banks will support us during the expansion period*

(b) to encourage *or* to agree with **unterstützen, beistehen, befürworten;** *she hopes the other members of the committee will support her; the market will not support another price increase*

surcharge *noun* extra charge **Zuschlag, Aufschlag, Aufpreis; import surcharge** = extra duty charged on imported goods, to try to stop them from being imported and to encourage local manufacture **Importabgabe**

surety *noun*

(a) person who guarantees that someone will do something **Bürge;** *to stand surety for someone*

(b) deeds *or* share certificates, etc., deposited as security for a loan **Sicherheit, Garantie**

surface *noun* top part of the earth **Erdoberfläche; to send a package by surface mail** = to send it by land or sea, but not by air **ein Paket mit gewöhnlicher Post (auf dem Landweg od Seeweg) schicken; surface transport** = transport on land or sea **Transport auf dem Land- und Seeweg, Bodentransport**

NOTE: no plural

surplus *noun* extra stock *or* something which is more than is needed **Überschuß;** *surplus government equipment; surplus butter is on sale in the shops; we are holding a sale of surplus stock; governments are trying to find ways of reducing the agricultural surpluses in the Common Market; we are trying to let surplus capacity in the warehouse;* **a budget surplus** = more revenue than was planned for in the budget **Etatüberschuß; these items are surplus to our requirements** = we do not need these items **diese Waren sind überschüssig; to absorb a surplus** = to take a surplus into a larger amount **einen Mehrbetrag verrechnen**

surrender

1 *noun* giving up of an insurance policy before the contracted date for maturity **Rückkauf; surrender value** = money which

an insurer will pay if an insurance policy is given up **Rückkaufwert**
2 *verb* **to surrender a policy** = to give up an insurance **eine Versicherungspolice zum Rückkauf bringen**

surtax *noun* extra tax on high income **Zusatzsteuer**

survey
1 *noun*
(a) general report on a problem **Studie, Untersuchungsbericht;** *the government has published a survey of population trends; we have asked the sales department to produce a survey of competing products*
(b) examining something to see if it is in good condition **Gutachten, Expertise;** *we have asked for a survey of the house before buying it; the insurance company is carrying out a survey of the damage;* **damage survey** = survey of damage done **Schadensprüfung**
(c) measuring exactly **Vermessung; quantity survey** = calculating the amount of materials and cost of labour needed for a construction project **Baukostenschätzung**
2 *verb* to examine (something) to see if it is in good condition **begutachten, inspizieren**

◇ **surveyor** *noun* person who examines buildings to see if they are in good condition **Gutachter/-in (für Gebäude); quantity surveyor** = person who calculates the amount of materials and cost of labour needed for a construction project **Ersteller/-in von Kostenschätzungen**

suspend *verb*
(a) to stop (something) for a time **zeitweilig einstellen, aussetzen, unterbrechen;** *we have suspended payments while we are waiting for news from our agent; sailings have been suspended until the weather gets better; work on the construction project has been suspended; the management decided to suspend negotiations*
(b) to stop (someone) working for a time **suspendieren;** *he was suspended on full pay while the police investigations were going on*

◇ **suspension** *noun* stopping something for a time **zeitweilige Einstellung, Aussetzung, Aufschub;** *suspension of payments; suspension of deliveries*

swap
1 *noun* exchange of one thing for another **Tausch**
2 *verb* to exchange one thing for another **tauschen;** *he swapped his old car for a new motorcycle;* **he swapped jobs with her** = each of them took the other's job **er hat seine Stelle mit ihr getauscht**
NOTE: **swapping - swapped**

swatch *noun* small sample **Muster; colour swatch** = small sample of colour which the finished product must look like **Farbmuster**

sweat *noun* drops of liquid which come through your skin when you are hot **Schweiß**

◇ **sweated labour** *noun*
(a) people who work hard for very little money **billige Arbeitskräfte;** *of course the firm makes a profit - it employs sweated labour*
(b) hard work which is very badly paid **Arbeit für einen Hungerlohn**

◇ **sweatshop** *noun* factory using sweated labour **Fabrik mit ausbeuterischen Bedingungen**

switch *verb* to change from one thing to another **wechseln, übertragen;** *to switch funds from one investment to another; the job was switched from our British factory to the States*

◇ **switchboard** *noun* central point in a telephone system, where all lines meet **Telefonzentrale; switchboard operator** = person who works the central telephone system **Telefonist/-in**

◇ **switch over to** *verb* to change to something quite different **überwechseln, umstellen;** *we have switched over to a French supplier; the factory has switched over to gas for heating*

swop = SWAP

symbol *noun* sign *or* picture *or* object which represents something **Symbol;** *they use a bear as their advertising symbol*

sympathy *noun* feeling sorry because someone else has problems **Mitleid, Verständnis;** *the manager had no sympathy for his secretary who complained of being overworked;* **sympathy strike** = strike to show that workers agree with another group of workers who are on strike **Solidaritätsstreik, Sympathiestreik; to strike in sympathy** = to stop work to show that you agree with another group of workers who are on strike **aus Solidarität streiken;** *the postal workers went on strike and the telephone engineers came out in sympathy*

◇ **sympathetic** *adjective* showing sympathy **mitfühlend, verständnisvoll; sympathetic strike** = sympathy strike **Sympathiestreik**

syndicate
1 *noun* group of people *or* companies working together to make money **Syndikat,**

Konsortium, Verband; *a German finance syndicate;* **arbitrage syndicate** = group of people who together raise the capital to invest in arbitrage deals **Arbitrage-Konsortium; underwriting syndicate** = group of underwriters who insure a large risk **Übernahme-, Emissionskonsortium**
2 *verb* to produce an article, drawing, etc., which is published in several newspapers or magazines **in mehreren Zeitungen zugleich veröffentlichen**
◇ **syndicated** *adjective* published in several newspapers or magazines **in mehreren Zeitungen zugleich veröffentlicht;** *he writes a syndicated column on personal finance*

synergy *noun* producing greater effects by joining forces than by acting separately **Synergismus**

synthetic *adjective* artificial *or* made by man **synthetisch; synthetic fibres** *or* **synthetic materials** = materials made as products of a chemical process **Kunstfasern; Kunststoff**

system *noun*
(a) arrangement *or* organization of things which work together **System;** *our accounting system has worked well in spite of the large increase in orders;* **decimal system** = system of mathematics based on the number 10 **Dezimalsystem; filing system** = way of putting documents in order for easy reference **Ablagesystem; to operate a quota system** = to regulate supplies by fixing quantities which are allowed **ein Quotensystem anwenden;** *we arrange our distribution using a quota system - each agent is allowed only a certain number of units*
(b) computer system = set of programs, commands, etc., which run a computer **Computersystem**
(c) systems analysis = using a computer to suggest how a company should work by analyzing the way in which it works at present **Systemanalyse; systems analyst** = person who specializes in systems analysis **Systemanalytiker, Systemberater**
◇ **systematic** *adjective* in order *or* using method **systematisch;** *he ordered a systematic report on the distribution service*

Tt

tab *noun* = TABULATOR

table
1 *noun*
(a) piece of furniture with a flat top and legs **Tisch; typing table** = table for a typewriter **Schreibmaschinentisch**
(b) list of figures *or* facts set out in columns **Tabelle, Übersicht; table of contents** = list of contents in a book **Inhaltsverzeichnis; actuarial tables** = lists showing how long people of certain ages are likely to live **Sterbetabellen**
2 *verb* to put items of information on the table before a meeting **einbringen; vorlegen;** *the report of the finance committee was tabled;* **to table a motion** = to put forward a proposal for discussion by putting details of it on the table at a meeting **einen Antrag einbringen**

◇ **tabular** *adjective* **in tabular form** = arranged in a table **tabellarisch**

◇ **tabulate** *verb* to set out in a table **tabellarisieren, tabellarisch darstellen**

◇ **tabulation** *noun* arrangement of figures in a table **Tabellarisierung, tabellarische Aufstellung**

◇ **tabulator** *noun* part of a typewriter *or* computer which sets words or figures automatically in columns **Tabulator**

tachograph *noun* device in a lorry, which shows details of distance travelled and time of journeys **Fahrtenschreiber, Tachograph**

tacit *adjective* agreed but not stated **stillschweigend;** *tacit approval; tacit agreement to a proposal*

tactic *noun* way of doing things so as to be at an advantage **Taktik;** *his usual tactic is to buy shares in a company, then mount a takeover bid, and sell out at a profit; the directors planned their tactics before going into the meeting with the union representatives*

tag *noun* label **Schild, Etikett;** *price tag; name tag*

take
1 *noun* money received in a shop **Einnahme**
2 *verb*
(a) to receive *or* to get **nehmen; einnehmen; bekommen; the shop takes £2,000 a week** = the shop receives £2,000 a week in cash sales **das Geschäft nimmt £2.000 pro Woche ein; he takes home £250 a week** = his salary, after deductions for tax, etc., is £250 a week **er verdient pro Woche £250 netto**

(b) to do a certain action **unternehmen, durchführen; to take action** = to do something **Schritte unternehmen;** *you must take immediate action if you want to stop thefts;* **to take a call** = to answer the telephone **einen Anruf entgegennehmen; to take the chair** = to be chairman of a meeting **den Vorsitz führen/übernehmen;** *in the absence of the chairman his deputy took the chair;* **to take dictation** = to write down what someone is saying **ein Diktat aufnehmen;** *the secretary was taking dictation from the managing director;* **to take stock** = to count the items in a warehouse **Inventur machen, inventarisieren; to take stock of a situation** = to examine the state of things before deciding what to do **sich von einer Situation ein Bild machen**
(c) to need (a time *or* a quantity) **brauchen, benötigen;** *it took the factory six weeks or the factory took six weeks to clear the backlog of orders; it will take her all morning to do my letters; it took six men and a crane to get the computer into the office*
NOTE: **taking - took - has taken**

◇ **take away** *verb*
(a) to remove one figure from a total **abziehen;** *if you take away the home sales, the total turnover is down*
(b) to remove **wegnehmen, abziehen;** *we had to take the work away from the supplier because the quality was so bad; the police took away piles of documents from the office;* **sales of food to take away** = cooked food sold by a shop to be eaten at some other place **Straßenverkauf**

◇ **takeaway** *noun* shop which sells food to be eaten at some other place **Imbißstube, Restaurant für Außer-Haus-Verkauf;** *a takeaway meal; a Chinese takeaway*

◇ **take back** *verb*
(a) to return with something **zurückbringen;** *when the watch went wrong, he took it back to the shop; if you do not like the colour, you can take it back to change it*
(b) to take back dismissed workers = to allow former workers to join the company again **entlassene Arbeiter wieder einstellen**

◇ **take-home pay** *noun* amount of money received in wages, after tax, etc., has been deducted **Nettoverdienst**
NOTE: no plural

◇ **take into** *verb* to take inside **auf-, hineinnehmen;** *to take items into stock or into the warehouse*

◇ **take off** *verb*
(a) to remove *or* to deduct **wegnehmen; abziehen, nachlassen;** *he took £25 off the price*
(b) to start to rise fast **anlaufen, schnell steigen;** *sales took off after the TV commercials*

(c) she took the day off = she decided not to work for the day **sie nahm sich einen Tag frei**

◇ **take on** *verb* to agree to employ someone **einstellen** to agree to do something **über-, annehmen;** *she took on the job of preparing the VAT returns; to take on more staff; he has taken on a lot of extra work*

◇ **take out** *verb* to remove **hinausbringen; to take out a patent for an invention** = to apply for and receive a patent **ein Patent für eine Erfindung anmelden; to take out insurance against theft** = to pay a premium to an insurance company, so that if a theft takes place the company will pay compensation **eine Diebstahlversicherung abschließen**

◇ **take over** *verb*
(a) to start to do something in place of someone else **übernehmen, ablösen;** *Miss Black took over from Mr Jones on May 1st; the new chairman takes over on July 1st;* **the take-over period is always difficult** = the period when one person is taking over work from another **die Übernahmezeit ist immer problematisch**
(b) to take over a company = to buy (a business) by offering to buy most of its shares **ein Unternehmen übernehmen;** *the buyer takes over the company's liabilities; the company was taken over by a large multinational*

◇ **takeover** *noun* buying a business **Übernahme; takeover bid** = offer to buy all or most of the shares in a company so as to control it **Übernahmeangebot; to make a takeover bid for a company** = to offer to buy most of the shares in a company **ein Übernahmeangebot für ein Unternehmen machen; to withdraw a takeover bid** = to say that you no longer offer to buy the shares in a company **ein Übernahmeangebot zurückziehen; the company rejected the takeover bid** = the directors recommended that the shareholders should not accept the offer **das Unternehmen wies das Übernahmeangebot zurück;** *the disclosure of the takeover bid raised share prices;* **contested takeover** = takeover where the board of the company being bought do not recommend it, and try to fight it **angefochtene Übernahme**

◇ **taker** *noun* buyer *or* person who wants to buy **Abnehmer/-in;** *there were no takers for the new shares*

◇ **take up** *verb* **to take up an option** = to accept an option which has been offered and put into action **ein Optionsrecht ausüben;** *half the rights issue was not taken up by the shareholders;* **take up rate** = percentage of acceptances for a rights issue **Annahmequote (von Bezugsrechtemissionen)**

◇ **takings** *plural noun* money received in a shop *or* a business **Einnahmen;** *the week's takings were stolen from the cash desk*

> QUOTE many takeovers result in the new managers/owners rationalizing the capital of the company through better asset management
> *Duns Business Month*
>
> QUOTE capital gains are not taxed, but money taken out in profits and dividends is taxed
> *Toronto Star*

tally
1 *noun* note of things counted *or* recorded **Kontrolliste;** *to keep a tally of stock movements or of expenses;* **tally clerk** = person whose job is to note quantities of cargo **Ladungskontrolleur; tally sheet** = sheet on which quantities are noted **Kontrolliste**
2 *verb* to agree *or* to be the same **übereinstimmen;** *the invoices do not tally; the accounts department tried to make the figures tally*

tangible *adjective* **tangible assets** = assets which are solid (such as furniture, jewellery, etc.) **materielle Vermögenswerte; bilanzirbare Sachwerte**

tanker *noun* special ship for carrying liquids (especially oil) **Tanker**

tap *noun GB* government stocks issued through the Bank of England **Staatsanleihen (durch die Bank von England begeben)**
◊ **tap stock** *noun* issue of government securities **Staatsanleihe**

tape *noun* long, flat, narrow piece of plastic **Klebestreifen; magnetic tape** = sensitive tape for recording information **Magnetband; computer tape** = magnetic tape used in computers **Magnetband; measuring tape** *or* **tape measure** = long tape with centimetres *or* inches marked on it for measuring how long something is **Maßband, Bandmaß**

tare *noun* (allowance made for the) weight of a container and packing which is deducted from the total weight; (allowance made for the) weight of a vehicle in calculating transport costs **Tara, Verpackungsgewicht;** *to allow for tare*
NOTE: no plural

target
1 *noun* thing to aim for **Ziel; production targets** = amount of units a factory is expected to produce **Produktionsziel; sales targets** = amount of sales a representative is expected to achieve **Verkaufsziel; target market** = market in which a company is planning to sell its goods **Zielmarkt, Zielgruppe; to set targets** = to fix amounts *or* quantities which workers have to produce *or* reach **Ziele setzen; to meet a target** = to produce the quantity of goods *or* sales which are expected **ein (gestecktes) Ziel erreichen; to miss a target** = not to produce the amount of goods *or* sales which are expected **ein (gestecktes) Ziel nicht erreichen;** *they missed the target figure of £2m turnover*
2 *verb* to aim to sell **anstreben, abzielen auf; to target a market** = to plan to sell goods in a certain market **auf einen Markt abzielen**

> QUOTE in a normal leveraged buyout the acquirer raises money by borrowing against the assets of the target company
> *Fortune*
>
> QUOTE the minister is persuading the oil, gas, electricity and coal industries to target their advertising towards energy efficiency
> *Times*

tariff *noun*
(a) customs tariffs = tax to be paid for importing *or* exporting goods **Zolltarife; tariff barriers** = customs duty intended to make imports more difficult **Zollschranken;** *to impose tariff barriers on or to lift tariff barriers from a product;* **differential tariffs** = different duties for different types of goods **Staffeltarif, Differentialzoll; General Agreement on Tariffs and Trade** = international agreement to try to reduce restrictions in trade between countries **Allgemeines Zoll- und Handelsabkommen**
(b) rate of charging for electricity, hotel rooms, train tickets, etc. **Tarif, Preis**

task *noun*
(a) work which has to be done **Aufgabe; to list task processes** = to make a list of various parts of a job which have to be done **Arbeitsabläufe auflisten**
(b) task force = special group of workers *or* managers who are chosen to carry out a special job *or* to deal with a special problem **Arbeitsgruppe, Arbeitsstab**

tax
1 *noun*
(a) money taken by the government *or* by an official body to pay for government services **Steuer; airport tax** = tax added to the price of an air ticket to cover the cost of running an airport **Flughafengebühr; capital gains tax** = tax on capital gains **Veräußerungsgewinnsteuer; capital transfer tax** = tax on gifts or bequests of money or property **Kapitaltransfersteuer; corporation tax** = tax on profits made by companies **Körperschaftssteuer; excess profits tax** = tax on profits which are higher than what is thought to be normal **Steuer zur Abschöpfung von Höchstgewinnen; income tax** = tax on salaries and wages **Lohnsteuer,**

Einkommenssteuer; land tax = tax on the amount of land owned **Grundsteuer; sales tax** = tax on the price of goods sold **Warenumsatzsteuer; turnover tax** = tax on company turnover **Umsatzsteuer; value added tax** = tax on goods and services, added as a percentage to the invoiced sales price **Mehrwertsteuer**

(b) ad valorem tax = tax calculated according to the value of the goods taxed **Wertsteuer; back tax** = tax which is owed **Steuerschulden; basic tax** = tax paid at the normal rate **Basis-, Eingangssteuer; direct tax** = tax paid directly to the government (such as income tax) **direkte Steuer; indirect tax** = tax paid to someone who then pays it to the government (such as VAT) **indirekte Steuer; to levy a tax** *or* **to impose a tax** = to make a tax payable **eine Steuer erheben;** *the government has imposed a 15% tax on petrol;* **to lift a tax** = to remove a tax **eine Steuer aufheben;** *the tax on company profits has been lifted;* **exclusive of tax** = not including tax **ohne Steuer; tax abatement** = reduction of tax **Steuernachlaß; tax adjustments** = changes made to tax **Steueranpassungen; tax adviser** *or* **tax consultant** = person who gives advice on tax problems **Steuerberater; tax allowance** *or* **allowances against tax** = part of the income which a person is allowed to earn and not pay tax on **Steuerfreibetrag; tax avoidance** = trying (legally) to minimize the amount of tax to be paid **Steuerverkürzung; in the top tax bracket** = paying the highest level of tax **in der höchsten Steuerklasse; tax code** = number given to indicate the amount of tax allowances a person has **Abgabenordnung; tax concession** = allowing less tax to be paid **Steuervergünstigung; tax credit** = part of a dividend on which the company has already paid tax, so that the shareholder is not taxed on it again **Steuergutschrift; tax deductions** = (i) money removed from a salary to pay tax; (ii); *US* business expenses which can be claimed against tax **(i) Steuerabzüge; (ii) (von der Steuer) absetzbare Ausgaben; tax deducted at source** = tax which is removed from a salary or interest before the money is paid out **Quellensteuer; tax evasion** = trying illegally not to pay tax **Steuerhinterziehung; tax exemption** = (i) being free from payment of tax; (ii); *US* part of income which a person is allowed to earn and not pay tax on **(i) Steuerbefreiung; (ii) Steuerfreibetrag; tax form** = blank form to be filled in with details of income and allowances and sent to the tax office each year **Vordruck für die Steuererklärung; tax haven** = country where taxes are low, encouraging companies to set up their main offices there **Steueroase; tax holiday** = period when a new company pays no tax **Steuerbefreiung; tax inspector** *or* **inspector of taxes** = official of the Inland Revenue who examines tax returns and decides how much tax someone should pay **Steuerprüfer; Leiter des Finanzamtes; tax loophole** = legal means of not paying tax **Lücke in der Steuergesetzgebung; tax relief** = allowing someone not to pay tax on certain parts of his income **Steuerermäßigung; tax return** *or* **tax declaration** = completed tax form, with details of income and allowances **Steuererklärung; tax shelter** = financial arrangement (such as a pension scheme) where investments can be made without tax **Steuerbegünstigung; tax year** = twelve month period on which taxes are calculated (in the UK, 6th April to 5th April of the following year) **Steuerjahr**

2 *verb* to make someone pay a tax *or* to impose a tax on something **jdn mit einer Steuer belegen; besteuern;** *to tax businesses at 50%; income is taxed at 35%; luxury items are heavily taxed*

◇ **taxable** *adjective* which can be taxed **besteuerbar; steuerpflichtig; taxable items** = items on which a tax has to be paid **steuerpflichtige Posten; taxable income** = income on which a person has to pay tax **steuerpflichtiges Einkommen**

◇ **taxation** *noun* act of taxing **Besteuerung; Veranlagung; direct taxation** = taxes (such as income tax) which are paid direct to the government **Direktbesteuerung; indirect taxation** = taxes (such as sales tax) which are not paid direct to the government **indirekte Besteuerung;** *the government raises more money by indirect taxation than by direct;* **double taxation** = taxing the same income twice **Doppelbesteuerung; double taxation agreement** = agreement between two countries that a person living in one country will not be taxed in both countries on the income earned in the other country **Abkommen zur Doppelbesteuerung**

NOTE: no plural

◇ **tax-deductible** *adjective* which can be deducted from an income before tax is calculated **steuerlich absetzbar/abzugsfähig; these expenses are not tax-deductible** = tax has to be paid on these expenses **diese Ausgaben sind nicht steuerlich abzugsfähig**

◇ **tax-exempt** *adjective* not required to pay tax; (income *or* goods) which are not subject to tax **steuerbefreit**

◇ **tax-free** *adjective* on which tax does not have to be paid **steuerfrei**

◇ **taxpayer** *noun* person *or* company which has to pay tax **Steuerzahler;** *basic taxpayer or taxpayer at the basic rate; corporate taxpayers*

taxi *noun* car which takes people from one place to another for money **Taxi, Taxe;** *he* *took a taxi to the airport; taxi fares are very high in New York*

team *noun* group of people who work together **Team, Mannschaft; management team** = group of all the managers working in the same company **Management-Team; sales team** = all representatives, salesmen and sales managers working in a company **Verkaufsteam**

◇ **teamster** *noun US* truck driver **Lastwagenfahrer**

◇ **teamwork** *noun* being able to work together as a group **Team-, Gruppenarbeit**
NOTE: no plural

technical *adjective*
(a) referring to a particular machine *or* process **technisch;** *the document gives all the technical details on the new computer*
(b) technical correction = situation where a share price *or* a currency moves up or down because it was previously too low or too high **technische Kurskorrektur**

◇ **technician** *noun* person who is specialized in industrial work **Facharbeiter; Techniker;** *computer technician;* **laboratory technician** = person who deals with practical work in a laboratory **Labortechniker**

◇ **technique** *noun* skilled way of doing a job **Technik, Verfahren;** *the company has developed a new technique for processing steel; he has a special technique for answering complaints from customers;* **management techniques** = skill in managing a business **Managementmethoden; marketing techniques** = skill in marketing a product **Marketing-Methoden**

◇ **technology** *noun* applying scientific knowledge to industrial processes **Technik, Technologie; information technology** = working with data stored on computers **Informationstechnologie; the introduction of new technology** = putting new electronic equipment into a business or industry **die Einführung neuer Technologien**

◇ **technological** *adjective* referring to technology **technologisch, technisch; the technological revolution** = changing of industry by introducing new technology **die technologische Revolution**

> QUOTE market analysts described the falls in the second half of last week as a technical correction
> *Australian Financial Review*

tel = TELEPHONE

telecommunications *plural noun* systems of passing messages over long distances (by cable, radio, etc.) **Fernmeldewesen**

telegram *noun* message sent to another country by telegraph **Telegramm;** *to send an international telegram*

◇ **telegraph**
1 *noun* system of sending messages along wires **Telegraf;** *to send a message by telegraph;* **telegraph office** = office from which telegrams can be sent **Telegrafenamt**
2 *verb* to send a message by telegram **telegrafieren;** *to telegraph an order*

◇ **telegraphic** *adjective* referring to a telegraph system **telegrafisch; telegraphic address** = short address used for sending telegrams **Telegrammadresse**

◇ **telemessage** *noun GB* message sent by telephone, and delivered as a card **Telebrief**

telephone
1 *noun* machine used for speaking to someone over a long distance **Telefon;** *we had a new telephone system installed last week;* **he is on the telephone** = to be speaking to someone using the telephone **er telefoniert;** *the managing director is on the telephone to Hong Kong; she has been on the telephone all day;* **by telephone** = using the telephone **per Telefon;** *to place an order by telephone; to reserve a room by telephone;* **house telephone** *or* **internal telephone** = telephone for calling from one room to another in an office or hotel **Haustelefon; telephone book** *or* **telephone directory** = book which lists all people and businesses in alphabetical order with their telephone numbers **Telefonbuch;** *he looked up the number of the company in the telephone book;* **telephone call** = speaking to someone on the telephone **Telefongespräch; to make a telephone call** = to speak to someone on the telephone **telefonieren, ein Telefongespräch führen; to answer the telephone** *or* **to take a telephone call** = to speak in reply to a call on the telephone **ein Telefongespräch annehmen; telephone exchange** = central office where the telephones of a whole district are linked **Telefonzentrale, Vermittlung; telephone number** = set of figures for a particular telephone subscriber **Telefon-, Fernsprech-, Rufnummer;** *can you give me your telephone number?;* **telephone operator** = person who operates a telephone switchboard **Telefonist/-in; telephone orders** = orders received by telephone **telefonische Bestellung;** *since we mailed the catalogue we have received a large number of telephone orders;* **telephone subscriber** = person who has a telephone **Fernsprechteilnehmer; telephone switchboard** = central point in a telephone system where all internal and external lines meet **Telefonzentrale**
2 *verb* **to telephone a person** = to call a place *or* someone by telephone **jdn anrufen;** *his*

secretary telephoned to say he would be late; **he telephoned the order through to the warehouse** = he telephoned the warehouse to place an order **er gab den Auftrag per Telefon an das Lager; to telephone about something** = to make a telephone call to speak about something **wegen etwas anrufen;** *he telephoned about the January invoice;* **to telephone for something** = to make a telephone call to ask for something **etwas telefonisch bestellen;** *he telephoned for a taxi*

◇ **telephonist** *noun* person who works a telephone switchboard **Telefonist/-in**

◇ **teleprinter** *noun* machine like a typewriter, which can send messages by telegraph and print incoming messages **Fernschreiber;** *teleprinter operator*

◇ **telesales** *plural noun* sales made by telephone **Telefonverkauf**

◇ **teletypewriter** *noun US* = TELEPRINTER

telex
1 *noun*
(a) system of sending messages by teleprinter **Fernschreiber, Telex;** *to send information by telex; the order came by telex;* **telex line** = wire linking a telex machine to the telex system **Fernschreibleitung;** *we cannot communicate with our Nigerian office because of the breakdown of the telex lines;* **telex operator** = person who operates a telex machine **Fernschreibkraft; telex subscriber** = company which has a telex **Fernschreibteilnehmer**
(b) a telex = (i) a machine for sending and receiving telex messages; (ii) a message sent by telex **(i) Fernschreiber; (ii) Telex, Fernschreiben;** *he sent a telex to his head office; we received his telex this morning*
2 *verb* to send a message using a teleprinter **(per) Telex schicken;** *can you telex the Canadian office before they open? he telexed the details of the contract to New York*

teller *noun* person who takes cash or pays cash to customers at a bank **Kassierer/-in**

tem *see* PRO TEM

temp
1 *noun* temporary secretary **Zeitarbeiterin, Büroaushilfskraft;** *we have had two temps working in the office this week to clear the backlog of letters;* **temp agency** = office which deals with finding temporary secretaries for offices **Vermittlung für Zeitarbeiter/Aushilfskräfte**
2 *verb* to work as a temporary secretary **als Büroaushilfskraft arbeiten**

◇ **temping** *noun* working as a temporary secretary **Zeitarbeit;** *she can earn more money temping than from a full-time job*
NOTE: no plural

temporary *adjective* which only lasts a short time **befristet, vorübergehend;** *he was granted a temporary export licence; to take temporary measures; he has a temporary post with a construction company; he has a temporary job as a filing clerk or he has a job as a temporary filing clerk;* **temporary employment** = full-time work which does not last for more than a few days or months **Zeitarbeit; temporary staff** = staff who are appointed for a short time **Zeitarbeitskräfte**

◇ **temporarily** *adverb* lasting only for a short time **befristet, vorübergehend**

tenancy *noun* (i) agreement by which a tenant can occupy a property; (ii) period during which a tenant has an agreement to occupy a property **(i) Mietverhältnis; Pachtverhältnis (ii) Mietdauer; Pachtdauer**

◇ **tenant** *noun* person *or* company which rents a house *or* flat *or* office to live or work in **Mieter/-in; Pächter/-in;** *the tenant is liable for repairs;* **sitting tenant** = tenant who is living in a house when the freehold or lease is sold **durch Mietschutz geschützter Mieter**

tend *verb* to be likely to do something **tendieren, neigen;** *he tends to appoint young girls to his staff*

◇ **tendency** *noun* being likely to do something **Tendenz;** *the market showed an upward tendency; there has been a downward tendency in the market for several days;* **the market showed a tendency to stagnate** = the market seemed to stagnate rather than advance **die Börse wies Tendenzen der Stagnation auf**

tender
1 *noun*
(a) offer to work for a certain price **Submission, Angebot;** *a successful tender or an unsuccessful tender;* **to put a project out to tender** *or* **to ask for** *or* **to invite tenders for a project** = to ask contractors to give written estimates for a job **Angebote für ein Projekt einholen; ein Projekt ausschreiben; to put in a tender** *or* **to submit a tender** = to make an estimate for a job **ein Angebot machen; to sell shares by tender** = to ask people to offer in writing a price for shares **Aktien auf dem Angebotsweg verkaufen; sealed tenders** = tenders sent in sealed envelopes which will all be opened together at a certain time **versiegelte Submissionsofferten**

(b) legal tender = coins or notes which can be legally used to pay a debt (small denominations cannot be used to pay large debts) **gesetzliches Zahlungsmittel**
2 *verb*
(a) to tender for a contract = to put forward an estimate of cost for work to be carried out under contract **sich (im Ausschreibungsweg) um einen Auftrag bewerben;** *to tender for the construction of a hospital*
(b) to tender one's resignation = to give in one's resignation **seine Kündigung einreichen**

◇ **tenderer** *noun* person *or* company which tenders for work **Submittent;** *the company was the successful tenderer for the project*

◇ **tendering** *noun* act of putting forward an estimate of cost **Angebot(sabgabe);** *to be successful, you must follow the tendering procedure as laid out in the documents*

tentative *adjective* not certain **vorläufig; unverbindlich; vorsichtig;** *they reached a tentative agreement over the proposal; we suggested Wednesday May 10th as a tentative date for the next meeting*

◇ **tentatively** *adverb* not sure **vorläufig; unverbindlich;** *we tentatively suggested Wednesday as the date for our next meeting*

tenure *noun*
(a) right to hold property *or* position **Innehaben einer Position; Pachtverhältnis, Landbesitzrecht; security of tenure** = right to keep a job *or* rented accommodation provided certain conditions are met **gesetzliche Kündigungsschutz**
(b) time when a position is held **Dienst-, Amtszeit;** *during his tenure of the office of chairman*

term *noun*
(a) period of time when something is legally valid **Dauer, Zeitraum;** *the term of a lease; the term of the loan is fifteen years; to have a loan for a term of fifteen years; during his term of office as chairman;* **term deposit** = money invested for a fixed period at a higher rate of interest **Termineinlagen; term insurance** = life assurance which covers a person's life for a period of time **zeitlich begrenzte Lebensversicherung;** *he took out a ten-year term insurance;* **term loan** = loan for a fixed period of time **befristeter Kredit; term shares** = type of building society deposit for a fixed period of time at a higher rate of interest **Fristeinlagen (bei einer Bausparkasse); short-term** = for a period of months **kurzfristig; long-term** = for a long period of time **langfristig; medium-term** = for a period of one or two years **mittelfristig**
(b) terms = conditions *or* duties which have to be carried out as part of a contract *or* arrangements which have to be agreed before a contract is valid **Bedingungen;** *he refused to agree to some of the terms of the contract; by or under the terms of the contract, the company is responsible for all damage to the property; to negotiate for better terms;* **terms of payment** *or* **payment terms** = conditions for paying something **Zahlungsbedingungen; terms of sale** = conditions attached to a sale **Verkaufsbedingungen; cash terms** = lower terms which apply if the customer pays cash **Barzahlungsbedingungen; "terms: cash with order"** = terms of sale showing that payment has to be made in cash when the order is placed **"Bedingungen: Barzahlung bei Bestellung"; easy terms** = terms which are not difficult to accept *or* price which is easy to pay **günstige Bedingungen; Zahlungserleichterungen;** *the shop is let on very easy terms; to pay for something on easy terms;* **on favourable terms** = on especially good terms **sehr günstige Bedingungen;** *the shop is let on very favourable terms;* **trade terms** = special discount for people in the same trade **Händlerrabatt**
(c) part of a legal *or* university year; *entspricht* **Semester**
(d) terms of employment = conditions set out in a contract of employment **Einstellungsbedingungen**

> QUOTE companies have been improving communications, often as part of deals to cut down demarcation and to give everybody the same terms of employment
>
> *Economist*
>
> QUOTE the Federal Reserve Board has eased interest rates in the past year, but they are still at historically high levels in real terms
>
> *Sunday Times*

terminal
1 *noun*
(a) computer terminal = keyboard and screen, by which information can be put into a computer or can be called up from a database **Computerterminal;** *computer system consisting of a microprocessor and six terminals*
(b) air terminal = building in a town where passengers meet to be taken by bus to an airport outside the town **Terminal/Abfertigungsgebäude in der Innenstadt; airport terminal** *or* **terminal building** = main building at an airport where passengers arrive and leave **Terminal, Abfertigungshalle; container terminal** = area of a harbour where container ships are loaded or unloaded **Containerterminal; ocean terminal** = building at a port where

passengers arrive and depart **Überseeterminal**
2 *adjective* at the end **End-, Abschluß-; terminal bonus** = bonus received when an insurance comes to an end **Schlußdividende**

terminate *verb* to end (something) *or* to bring (something) to an end **(be)enden; lösen; kündigen; ablaufen;** *to terminate an agreement; his employment was terminated; the offer terminates on July 31st; the flight from Paris terminates in New York*

◊ **terminable** *adjective* which can be terminated **künd-, auflösbar**

◊ **termination** *noun*
(a) bringing to an end **Beendigung; Lösung; Kündigung; termination clause** = clause which explains how and when a contract can be terminated **Kündigungsklausel**
(b) *US* leaving a job (resigning, retiring, or being fired or made redundant) **Kündigung**

territory *noun* area visited by a salesman **Bezirk, Gebiet;** *a rep's territory; his territory covers all the north of the country*

tertiary *adjective* **tertiary industry** = service industry *or* industry which does not produce or manufacture but offers a service (such as banking, retailing or accountancy) **Dienstleistungsbranche; tertiary sector** = section of the economy containing the service industries **Dienstleistungssektor**

test
1 *noun*
(a) examination to see if something works well *or* is possible **Test, Prüfung; test certificate** = certificate to show that something has passed a test **Abnahme-, Zulassungsbescheinigung; driving test** = examination to see if someone is able to drive a car **Führerscheinprüfung; feasibility test** = test to see if something is possible **Durchführbarkeitstest; market test** = examination to see if a sample of a product will sell in a market **Markttest**
(b) test case = legal action where the decision will fix a principle which other cases can follow **Musterprozeß**
2 *verb* to examine something to see if it is working well **testen, prüfen;** *to test a computer system;* **to test the market for a product** *or* **to test market a product** = to show samples of a product in a market to see if it will sell well **den Markt für ein Produkt testen;** *we are test marketing the toothpaste in Scotland*

◊ **test-drive** *verb* **to test-drive a car** = to drive a car (before buying it) to see if it works well **ein Auto probefahren**

◊ **testing** *noun* examining something to see if it works well **Erprobung, Prüfung;** *during the testing of the system several defects were corrected*

testimonial *noun* written report about someone's character *or* ability **Zeugnis, Referenz;** *to write someone a testimonial;* **unsolicited testimonial** = letter praising someone *or* a product, without the writer having been asked to write it **ohne Aufforderung gegebene Empfehlung**

text *noun* written part of something **Text;** *he wrote notes at the side of the text of the agreement;* **text processing** = working with words, using a computer to produce, check and change documents, reports, letters, etc. **Textverarbeitung**

thank *verb* to show someone that you are grateful for what has been done **danken, sich bedanken bei;** *the committee thanked the retiring chairman for his work; "Thank you for your letter of June 25th"*

◊ **thanks** *plural noun* word showing that someone is grateful **Danke;** *"many thanks for your letter of June 25th";* **vote of thanks** = official vote at a meeting to show that the meeting is grateful for what someone has done **Danksagungsadresse;** *the meeting passed a vote of thanks to the organizing committee for their work in setting up the international conference*

◊ **thanks to** *adverb* because of **dank;** *the company was able to continue trading thanks to a loan from the bank;* **it was no thanks to the bank that we avoided making a loss** = we avoided making a loss in spite of the bank's actions **daß wir es vermeiden konnten, Verluste zu machen, haben wir nicht der Bank zu verdanken**

theft *noun* stealing **Diebstahl;** *we have brought in security guards to protect the store against theft; they are trying to cut their losses by theft; to take out insurance against theft*

theory *noun* statement of the general principle of how something should work **Theorie; in theory the plan should work** = the plan may work, but it has not been tried in practice **theoretisch sollte der Plan gelingen**

think tank *noun* group of experts who advise *or* put forward plans **Denkfabrik, Think-tank**

third *noun* part of something which is divided into three **Drittel; to sell everything at one third off** = to sell everything at a discount of 33% **alles mit einem Drittel Rabatt verkaufen; the company has two thirds of the total market** = the company has 66% of the total market **das Unternehmen kontrolliert zwei Drittel des Gesamtmarktes**

◇ **third party** *noun* any person other than the two main parties involved in a contract **dritte Person, Dritte; third-party insurance** = insurance to cover damage to any person who is not one of the people named in the insurance contract **Haftpflichtversicherung; the case is in the hands of a third party** = the case is being dealt with by someone who is not one of the main interested parties **der Fall befindet sich in der Hand Dritter /S/ third quarter** *noun* three months' period from July to September **drittes Quartal**

◇ **Third World** *noun* countries of Africa, Asia and South America which do not have highly developed industries **Dritte Welt;** *we sell tractors into the Third World or to Third World countries*

threshold *noun* limit *or* point at which something changes **Schwelle; threshold agreement** = contract which says that if the cost of living goes up by more than a certain amount, pay will go up to match it **Lohnindexierung; threshold price** = in the EC, the lowest price at which farm produce imported into the EC can be sold **Schwellenpreis; pay threshold** = point at which pay increases because of a threshold agreement **Lohnschwelle, Lohnindexstufe; tax threshold** = point at which another percentage of tax is payable **Schwelle zu einer anderen Steuerstufe;** *the government has raised the minimum tax threshold from £6,000 to £6,500*

thrift *noun*
(a) saving money by spending carefully **Sparsamkeit**
(b) *US* private local bank *or* savings and loan association *or* credit union, which accepts and pays interest on deposits from small investors **Sparkasse, Bausparkasse**
NOTE: no plural for (a)

◇ **thrifty** *adjective* careful not to spend too much money **sparsam**

> QUOTE the thrift, which had grown from $4.7 million in assets in 1980 to 1.5 billion this year, has ended in liquidation
> *Barrons*

thrive *verb* to grow well *or* to be profitable **blühen, florieren;** *a thriving economy; thriving black market in car radios; the company is thriving in spite of the recession*

throughput *noun* amount of work done *or* of goods produced in a certain time **Kapazität;** *we hope to increase our throughput by putting in two new machines; the invoice department has a throughput of 6,000 invoices a day*

throw out *verb*
(a) to reject *or* to refuse to accept **verwerfen;** *the proposal was thrown out by the planning committee; the board threw out the draft contract submitted by the union*
(b) to get rid of (something which is not wanted) **weg-, herauswerfen;** *we threw out the old telephones and installed a computerized system; the AGM threw out the old board of directors*
NOTE: **throwing - threw - has thrown**

tick
1 *noun*
(a) *informal* credit **Pump;** *all the furniture in the house is bought on tick*
(b) mark on paper to show that something is correct *or* that something is approved **Haken;** *put a tick in the box marked "R"*
NOTE: no plural for (a). Note also US English for (b) is **check**
2 *verb* to mark with a sign to show that something is correct **abhaken;** *tick the box marked "R" if you require a receipt*

◇ **ticker** *noun US* machine (operated by telegraph) which prints details of share prices and transactions rapidly on paper tape **Börsenticker**

ticket *noun*
(a) piece of paper *or* card which allows you to do something **Karte; entrance ticket** *or* **admission ticket** = ticket which allows you to go in **Eintrittskarte; theatre ticket** = ticket which allows you a seat in a theatre **Theaterkarte**
(b) piece of paper *or* card which allows you to travel **Fahrkarte, Ticket;** *train ticket or bus ticket or plane ticket;* **season ticket** = train *or* bus ticket which can be used for any number of journeys over a period (usually one, three, six or twelve months) **Zeit-, Dauerkarte; single ticket** *or US* **one-way ticket** = ticket for one journey from one place to another **einfache Fahrkarte; return ticket** *or US* **round-trip ticket** = ticket for a journey from one place to another and back again **Rückfahrkarte**
(c) ticket agency = shop which sells tickets to theatres **Kartenvorverkaufsstelle; ticket counter** = counter where tickets are sold **Fahrkartenschalter**
(d) paper which shows something **Etikett, Schild; baggage ticket** = paper showing that you have left a piece of baggage with

someone **Gepäckschein; price ticket** = piece of paper showing a price **Preisschild**

tie *verb* to attach *or* to fasten (with string, wire, etc.) **binden, befestigen;** *he tied the parcel with thick string; she tied two labels on to the parcel*
NOTE: **tying - tied**

◇ **tie-on label** *noun* label with a piece of string attached so that it can be tied to an item **Anhänger**

◇ **tie up** *verb*
(a) to attach *or* to fasten tightly **verschnüren; festmachen;** *the parcel is tied up with string; the ship was tied up to the quay;* **he is rather tied up at the moment** = he is very busy **er ist sehr beschäftigt im Moment**
(b) to invest money in one way, so that it cannot be used for other investments **fest anlegen, festlegen;** *he has £100,000 tied up in long-dated gilts; the company has £250,000 tied up in stock which no one wants to buy*

◇ **tie-up** *noun* link *or* connection **Verbindung;** *the company has a tie-up with a German distributor*
NOTE: plural is **tie-ups**

> QUOTE a lot of speculator money is said to be tied up in sterling because of the interest-rate differential between US and British rates
> *Australian Financial Review*

tight *adjective* which is controlled *or* which does not allow any movement **eng, streng;** *the manager has a very tight schedule today - he cannot fit in any more appointments; expenses are kept under tight control;* **tight money** = money which is borrowed at a high interest rate **knappes Geld; tight money policy** = government policy to restrict money supply **restriktive Geldmengenpolitik**

◇ **-tight** *suffix* which prevents something getting in **-dicht;** *the computer is packed in a watertight case; send the films in an airtight container*

◇ **tighten** *verb* to make (something) tight *or* to control (something) **anziehen, verschärfen;** *the accounts department is tightening its control over departmental budgets*

◇ **tighten up on** *verb* to control (something) more **härter durchgreifen bei;** *the government is tightening up on tax evasion; we must tighten up on the reps' expenses*

> QUOTE mortgage money is becoming tighter
> *Times*
> QUOTE the decision by the government to tighten monetary policy will push the annual inflation rate above the previous high
> *Financial Times*

till *noun* drawer for keeping cash in a shop **Ladenkasse; cash till** = cash register *or* machine which shows and adds prices of items bought, with a drawer for keeping the cash received **Kasse;** *there was not much money in the till at the end of the day*

time *noun*
(a) period when something takes place (such as one hour, two days, fifty minutes, etc.) **Zeit; computer time** = time when a computer is being used (paid for at an hourly rate) **Betriebszeit; real time** = time when a computer is working on the processing of data while the problem to which the data refers is actually taking place **Echtzeit, Real-time; time and motion study** = study in an office *or* factory of how long it takes to do certain jobs and the movements workers have to make to do them **Zeit- und Bewegungsstudie;** *entspricht* **REFA-Studie; time and motion expert** = person who analyzes time and motion studies and suggests changes in the way work is done; *entspricht* **REFA-Fachmann**
(b) hour of the day (such as 9.00, 12.15, ten o'clock at night, etc.) **Zeit;** *the time of arrival or the arrival time is indicated on the screen; departure times are delayed by up to fifteen minutes because of the volume of traffic;* **on time** = at the right time **pünktlich;** *the plane was on time; you will have to hurry if you want to get to the meeting on time or if you want to be on time for the meeting;* **opening time** *or* **closing time** = time when a shop or office starts or stops work **Öffnungszeit; Geschäftsschluß**
(c) system of hours on the clock **Zeit, Uhrzeit; Summer Time** *or* **Daylight Saving Time** = system where clocks are set back one hour in the summer to take advantage of the longer hours of daylight **Sommerzeit; Standard Time** = normal time as in the winter months **Normalzeit**
(d) hours worked **Arbeitszeit; he is paid time and a half on Sundays** = he is paid the normal rate plus 50% extra when he works on Sundays **sonntags bekommt er 50% Zuschlag; full-time** = working for the whole normal working day **Ganztags-, ganztägig; overtime** = hours worked more than the normal working time **Überstunden; part-time** = not working for a whole working day **Halbtags-, Teilzeit-**
(e) period before something happens **Zeitspanne; Frist; time deposit** = deposit of money for a fixed period, during which it cannot be touched **Termineinlagen, Festgelder; delivery time** = number of days before something will be delivered **Lieferzeit; lead time** = time between placing an order and receiving the goods **Lieferzeit; time limit** = period during which something

should be done **Frist; to keep within the time limits** *or* **within the time schedule** = to complete work by the time stated **die Fristen einhalten**
NOTE: no plural for (a), (c) and (d)

◇ **time-card** *or US* **time-clock card** *noun* card which is put into a timing machine when a worker clocks in *or* clocks out, and records the time when he starts and stops work **Stechkarte**

◇ **time-keeping** *noun* being on time for work **Pünktlichkeit;** *bad time-keeping* not being on time **Unpünktlichkeit;** *he was warned for bad time-keeping*
NOTE: no plural

◇ **time rate** *noun* rate for work which is calculated as money per hour *or* per week, and not money for work completed **Zeitlohn**

◇ **time saving**
1 *adjective* which saves time **zeitsparend;** *a time-saving device*
2 *noun* trying to save time **Zeiteinsparung;** *the management is keen on time saving*

◇ **time scale** *noun* time which will be taken to complete work **zeitlicher Rahmen;** *our time scale is that all work should be completed by the end of August; he is working to a strict time scale*

◇ **time share** *noun* system where several people each own part of a property (such as a holiday flat), each being able to use it for a certain period each year **Timeshare**

◇ **time-sharing** *noun*
(a) = TIME SHARE
(b) sharing a computer system, with different users using different terminals **Time-sharing, Mehrbenutzersystem**
NOTE: no plural

◇ **time sheet** *noun* paper showing when a worker starts work in the morning and leaves work in the evening **Arbeitsnachweisbogen, Stundenzettel**

◇ **timetable**
1 *noun*
(a) list showing times of arrivals *or* departures of buses *or* trains *or* planes, etc. **Fahrplan;** *according to the timetable, there should be a train to London at 10.22; the bus company has brought out its winter timetable*
(b) list of appointments *or* events **Terminkalender, Programm;** *the manager has a very full timetable, so I doubt if he will be able to see you today;* **conference timetable** = list of speakers *or* events at a conference **Konferenzprogramm**
2 *verb* to make a list of times **einen Zeitplan aufstellen**

◇ **time work** *noun* work which is paid for at a rate per hour *or* per day, not per piece of work completed **Zeitarbeit**

◇ **timing** *noun* way in which something happens at a particular time **Terminierung, Timing;** *the timing of the conference is very convenient, as it comes just before my annual holiday; his arrival ten minutes after the meeting finished was very bad timing*
NOTE: no plural

tip

1 *noun*
(a) money given to someone who has helped you **Trinkgeld;** *I gave the taxi driver a 10 cent tip; the staff are not allowed to accept tips*
(b) advice on something to buy *or* to do which could be profitable **Tip;** *a stock market tip; he gave me a tip about a share which was likely to rise because of a takeover bid;* **tip sheet** = newspaper which gives information about shares which should be bought or sold **Börsenratgeber**
2 *verb*
(a) to give money to someone who has helped you **Trinkgeld geben;** *he tipped the receptionist £5*
(b) to say that something is likely to happen *or* that something might be profitable **einen Tip geben;** *two shares were tipped in the business section of the paper; he is tipped to become the next chairman*
NOTE: **tipping - tipped**

TIR = TRANSPORT INTERNATIONAL ROUTIER

title *noun*
(a) right to own a property **Anspruch, Anrecht; Rechtstitel;** *she has no title to the property; he has a good title to the property;* **title deeds** = document showing who is the owner of a property **Grundeigentumsurkunde;** *entspricht* **Grundbucheintrag**
(b) name given to a person in a certain job **Amtsbezeichnung, Titel;** *he has the title "Chief Executive"*
(c) name of a book *or* film, etc. **Titel**

token *noun*
(a) thing which acts as a sign *or* symbol **Zeichen; Symbol; token charge** = small charge which does not cover the real costs **symbolische Gebühr;** *a token charge is made for heating;* **token payment** = small payment to show that a payment is being made **symbolische Zahlung; token rent** = very low rent payment to show that a rent is being asked **geringe/symbolische Miete; token strike** = short strike to show that workers have a grievance **Warnstreik**
(b) book token *or* **flower token** *or* **gift token** = card bought in a store which is given as a present and which must be exchanged in

that store for goods **Büchergutschein; Blumengutschein; Geschenkgutschein;** *we gave her a gift token for her birthday*

toll *noun* payment for using a service (usually a bridge or a ferry) **Benutzungsgebühr;** *we had to cross a toll bridge to get to the island; you have to pay a toll to cross the bridge*

◇ **toll call** *noun US* long-distance telephone call **Ferngespräch**

◇ **toll free** *adverb US* without having to pay a charge for a long-distance telephone call **gebührenfrei;** *to call someone toll free; toll free number*

tombstone *noun informal* official announcement in a newspaper showing that a loan has been subscribed **Emissionsanzeige (der Emissionshäuser)**

ton *noun* measure of weight **Tonne;** *GB* **long ton** = measure of weight (= 1016 kilos) **(britische) Tonne;** *US* **short ton** = measure of weight (= 907 kilos) **(amerikanische) Tonne; metric ton** = 1,000 kilos **metrische Tonne**

◇ **tonne** *noun* metric ton *or* 1,000 kilos **Tonne**

◇ **tonnage** *noun* space for cargo in a ship, measured in tons **Tonnage; gross tonnage** = amount of total space in a ship **Bruttotonnage; deadweight tonnage** = largest amount of cargo which a ship can carry safely **Gesamttonnage**

NOTE: no plural

> QUOTE Canada agreed to the new duty-free quota of 600,000 tonnes a year
>
> *Globe and Mail (Toronto)*
>
> QUOTE in the dry cargo sector a total of 956 cargo vessels of 11.6m tonnes are laid up - 3% of world dry cargo tonnage
>
> *Lloyd's List*

tone *noun* **dialling tone** = noise made by a telephone to show that it is ready for you to dial a number **Freizeichen**

tool *noun* instrument used for doing manual work (such as a hammer, screwdriver) **Werkzeug; machine tools** = tools worked by motors, used to work on wood or metal **Werkzeugmaschinen**

◇ **tool up** *verb* to put machinery into a factory **(mit Maschinen) ausrüsten**

top

1 *noun* upper surface *or* upper part; highest point *or* most important place **oberer Teil; Spitze;** *the top of the computer is not the place to put coffee cups; the company is in the top six exporters;* **top copy** = first sheet of a document which is typed with several carbon copies or photocopies **Original; top management** = the main directors of a company **Unternehmensspitze, Top-Management; top-hat pension** = special extra pension for senior managers **Sonderpension für leitende Angestellte; to give something top priority** = to make something the most important item, so that it is done very fast **etwas auf höchste Dringlichkeitsstufe setzen; top quality** = very best quality **Spitzenqualität**

2 *adjective* upper; high; highest **oberer; oberster; hoher; höchster;** *the top floor is unfurnished; the car's top speed is 140 m.p.h.;* **top-flight** *or* **top-ranking** = in the most important position **von hohem Rang, hoher, Spitzen-;** *top-flight managers can earn very high salaries; he is the top-ranking official in the delegation;* **top-grade** = most important *or* of the best quality **Spitzen-, hoher; erstklassig;** *the car only runs on top-grade petrol;* **top-selling** = selling better than anything else **meistverkauft;** *Utopia is the top-selling holiday destination; top-selling brands of toothpaste*

3 *verb* to go higher than **übersteigen;** *sales topped £ 1m in the first quarter*

NOTE: **topping - topped top up** = to fill up something which is not full **auffüllen;** *to top up stocks before the Christmas rush*

> QUOTE gross wool receipts for the selling season appear likely to top $2 billion
>
> *Australian Financial Review*
>
> QUOTE the base lending rate, or prime rate, is the rate at which banks lend to their top corporate borrowers
>
> *Wall Street Journal*
>
> QUOTE fill huge warehouses with large quantities of top-brand, first-quality merchandise, sell the goods at rock-bottom prices
>
> *Duns Business Month*

tort *noun* harm done to someone *or* property which can be the basis of a lawsuit **Delikt**

total

1 *adjective* complete *or* with everything added together **gesamt, ganz; völlig, absolut;** *total amount; total assets; total cost; total expenditure; total income; total output; total revenue;* **the cargo was written off as a total loss** = the cargo was so badly damaged that the insurers said it had no value **die Fracht wurde als Totalverlust abgeschrieben**

2 *noun* amount which is complete *or* with everything added up **Summe, Endbetrag;** *the total of the charges comes to more than £1,000;* **grand total** = final total made by adding several subtotals **Gesamtsumme, Endbetrag**

3 *verb* to add up to **ergeben, sich belaufen auf;** *costs totalling more than £25,000*

NOTE: **totalling - totalled** but US English **totaling - totaled**

◇ **totally** *adverb* completely **völlig, total;** *the factory was totally destroyed in the fire; the cargo was totally ruined by water*

tour *noun* (holiday) journey to various places, coming back in the end to the place the journey started from **Rundreise, Tour;** *the group went on a tour of Italy; the minister went on a fact-finding tour of the region;* **conducted tour** = tour with a guide who shows places to the tourists **Rundfahrt mit Führer; package tour** = tour where the hotel, travel, and meals are all arranged in advance and paid for in one payment **Pauschalreise; tour operator** = person *or* company which organizes tours **Reiseveranstalter; to carry out a tour of inspection** = to visit various places *or* offices *or* factories to inspect them **eine Inspektionstour machen**

◇ **tourism** *noun* business of providing travel, hotel rooms, food, entertainment, etc., for tourists **Tourismus**
NOTE: no plural

◇ **tourist** *noun* person who goes on holiday to visit places away from his home **Tourist/-in; tourist bureau** *or* **tourist information office** = office which gives information to tourists about the place where it is situated **Fremdenverkehrsbüro; tourist class** = lower quality or less expensive way of travelling **Touristenklasse;** *he always travels first class, because he says tourist class is too uncomfortable;* **tourist visa** = visa which allows a person to visit a country for a short time on holiday **Touristenvisum**

tout
1 *noun* person who sells tickets (to games *or* shows) for more than the price printed on them **Kartenschwarzhändler**
2 *verb* **to tout for custom** = to try to attract customers **auf Kundenfang sein**

track record *noun* success or failure of a company *or* salesman in the past **Erfolgs- und Leistungsnachweis;** *he has a good track record as a secondhand car salesman; the company has no track record in the computer market*

trade
1 *noun*
(a) business of buying and selling **Handel; Gewerbe; export trade** *or* **import trade** = the business of selling to other countries *or* buying from other countries **Exporthandel; Importhandel; foreign trade** *or* **overseas trade** *or* **external trade** = trade with other countries **Außenhandel; Überseehandel; home trade** = trade in the country where a company is based **Binnenhandel; trade cycle** = period during which trade expands, then slows down, then expands again **Konjunkturzyklus; balance of trade** *or* **trade balance** = international trading position of a country, excluding invisible trade **Handelsbilanz;** *the country had an adverse balance of trade for the second month running;* **favourable balance of trade** = situation where a country's exports are larger than its imports **aktive Handelsbilanz**
(b) to do a good trade in a range of products = to sell a large number of the range of products **mit einer Produktenserie guten Absatz erzielen; fair trade** = international business system where countries agree not to charge import duties on certain items imported from their trading partners **Nichtdiskriminierung im Außenhandel; free trade** = system where goods can go from one country to another without any restrictions **Freihandel; free trade area** = group of countries practising free trade **Freihandelszone; trade agreement** = international agreement between countries over general terms of trade **Handelsabkommen; trade bureau** = office which specializes in commercial enquiries **Handels-, Wirtschaftsbüro; to impose trade barriers on** = to restrict the import of certain goods by charging high duty **mit Importrestriktionen belegen; trade deficit** *or* **trade gap** = difference in value between a country's high imports and low exports **Außenhandelsdefizit; trade description** = description of a product to attract customers **Warenkennzeichnung;** *GB* **Trade Descriptions Act** = act which limits the way in which products can be described so as to protect customers from wrong descriptions made by manufacturers **Warenkennzeichnungsgesetz; trade directory** = book which lists all the businesses and business people in a town **Branchenadreßbuch; trade mission** = visit to a country by a group of foreign businessmen to discuss trade **Handelsmission; to ask a company to supply trade references** = to ask a company to give names of traders who can report on the company's financial situation and reputation **ein Unternehmen um Handelsauskünfte ersuchen**
(c) people *or* companies dealing in the same type of product **Branche, Gewerbe;** *he is in the secondhand car trade; she is very well known in the clothing trade;* **trade association** = group which links together companies in the same trade **Wirtschafts-, Handelsverband; trade counter** = shop in a factory *or* warehouse where goods are sold to retailers **Warenausgabe für den Einzelhandel, Großhandelsverkauf; trade**

discount *or* **trade terms** = reduction in price given to a customer in the same trade **Händlerrabatt; trade fair** = large exhibition and meeting for advertising and selling a certain type of product **Handelsmesse;** *there were two trade fairs running in London at the same time; to organize or to run a trade fair* ; **trade journal** *or* **trade magazine** *or* **trade paper** *or* **trade publication** = magazine or newspaper produced for people and companies in a certain trade **Fachzeitschrift; trade press** = all magazines produced for people working in a certain trade **Fachpresse; trade price** = special wholesale price paid by a retailer to the manufacturer or wholesaler **Großhandelspreis**
NOTE: no plural for (a) or (b)
2 *verb* to buy and sell *or* to carry on a business **handeln, Handel treiben;** *to trade with another country; to trade on the Stock Exchange; the company has stopped trading; the company trades under the name "Eeziphitt"*

◇ **trade in** *verb*
(a) to buy and sell certain items **handeln mit, Handel treiben mit;** *the company trades in imported goods; he trades in French wine*
(b) to give in an old item as part of the payment for a new one **in Zahlung geben;** *the chairman traded in his old Rolls Royce for a new model*

◇ **trade-in** *noun* old item (such as a car *or* washing machine) given as part of the payment for a new one **in Zahlung gegebener Gegenstand;** *to give the old car as a trade-in;* **trade-in price** = amount allowed by the seller for an old item being traded in for a new one **Preis bei Inzahlungnahme**

◇ **trademark** *or* **trade name** *noun* particular name, design, etc., which has been registered by the manufacturer and which cannot be used by other manufacturers **Warenzeichen, Handelsmarke;** *you cannot call your beds "Softn'kumfi" - it is a registered trademark*

◇ **trade-off** *noun* exchanging one thing for another as part of a business deal **Austausch**

◇ **trader** *noun* person who does business **Händler/-in, Kaufmann/Kauffrau; commodity trader** = person whose business is buying and selling commodities **Warenterminhändler; free trader** = person who is in favour of free trade **Befürworter des Freihandels; sole trader** = person who runs a business, usually by himself, but has not registered it as a company **Einzelkaufmann**

◇ **tradesman** *noun* shopkeeper *or* person who runs a shop **Einzelhändler, Kaufmann/Kauffrau**
NOTE: plural is **tradesmen**

◇ **tradespeople** *plural noun* shopkeepers **Geschäftsleute**

◇ **trade union** *or* **trades union** *noun* organization which represents workers who are its members in discussions with employers about wages and conditions of employment **Gewerkschaft;** *they are members of a trades union or they are trade union members; he has applied for trade union membership or he has applied to join a trades union;* **Trades Union Congress (TUC)** = organization linking all British trade unions; *entspricht* **Gewerkschaftsbund**
NOTE: although **Trades Union Congress** is the official name for the organization, **trade union** is commoner than **trades union** in GB English. US English is **labor union**

◇ **trade unionist** *noun* member of a trade union **Gewerkschaft(l)er/-in**

◇ **trading** *noun* business of buying and selling **Handel; trading account** = account of a company's gross profit **Erfolgskonto; trading area** = group of countries which trade with each other **Handelszone, Absatzgebiet; trading company** = company which specializes in buying and selling goods **Handelsgesellschaft; adverse trading conditions** = bad conditions for trade **erschwerte Handelsbedingungen; trading estate** = area of land near a town specially for factories and warehouses **Industrie-, Gewerbegebiet; trading loss** = situation where a company's receipts are less than its expenditure **Geschäftsverlust; trading partner** = company *or* country which trades with another **Handelspartner; trading profit** = situation where a company's gross receipts are more than its gross expenditure **Geschäftsgewinn; trading stamp** = special stamp given away by a shop, which the customer can collect and exchange later for free goods **Rabattmarke; fair trading** = way of doing business which is reasonable and does not harm the customer **lauterer Wettbewerb;** *GB* **Office of Fair Trading** = government department which protects consumers against unfair or illegal business **Amt für Verbraucherschutz; insider trading** = illegal buying or selling of shares by staff of a company who have secret information about the company's plans **Insiderhandel**
NOTE: no plural

QUOTE a sharp setback in foreign trade accounted for most of the winter slowdown. The trade balance sank $17 billion

Fortune

QUOTE at its last traded price, the bank was capitalized around $1.05 billion

South China Morning Post

QUOTE with most of the world's oil now traded on spot markets, Opec's official prices are much less significant than they once were

Economist

traffic *noun*
(a) movement of cars *or* lorries *or* trains *or* planes; movement of people *or* goods in vehicles **Verkehr;** *there is an increase in commuter traffic or goods traffic on the motorway; passenger traffic on the commuter lines has decreased during the summer;* **air traffic controller** = person who controls the landing and taking off of planes at an airport **Fluglotse**
(b) illegal trade **Dealen, Handel;** *drugs traffic or traffic in drugs*
NOTE: no plural

train
1 *noun* set of coaches *or* wagons pulled by an engine along railway lines **Zug;** *a passenger train or a goods train; to take the 09.30 train to London; he caught his train or he missed his train; to ship goods by train;* **freight train** *or* **goods train** = train used for carrying goods **Güterzug**
2 *verb* to teach (someone) to do something; to learn how to do something **ausbilden;** *he trained as an accountant; the company has appointed a trained lawyer as its managing director*

◇ **trainee** *noun* person who is learning how to do something **Auszubildender, Lehrling;** *we employ a trainee accountant to help in the office at peak periods; graduate trainees come to work in the laboratory when they have finished their courses at university;* **management trainee** = young member of staff being trained to be a manager **Führungsnachwuchs**

◇ **traineeship** *noun* post of trainee **Ausbildungsplatz**

◇ **training** *noun* being taught how to do something **Ausbildung, Schulung;** *there is a ten-week training period for new staff; the shop is closed for staff training;* **industrial training** = training of new workers to work in an industry **Fachausbildung; betriebliche Ausbildung; management training** = training staff to be managers, by making them study problems and work out solutions to them **Management-Ausbildung; on-the-job training** = training given to workers at their place of work **innerbetriebliche Ausbildung; off-the-job training** = training given to workers away from their place of work (such as at a college or school) **außerbetriebliche Ausbildung; training levy** = tax to be paid by companies to fund the government's training schemes **Ausbildungsabgabe; training officer** = person who deals with the training of staff **Ausbildungsleiter; training unit** = special group of teachers who organize training for companies **Aus- und Weiterbildungsabteilung**
NOTE: no plural

transact *verb* **to transact business** = to carry out a piece of business **Geschäfte abschließen/abwickeln**

◇ **transaction** *noun* **business transaction** = piece of business *or* buying or selling **geschäftliche Transaktion; cash transaction** = transaction paid for in cash **Bar-, Kassegeschäft; a transaction on the Stock Exchange** = purchase *or* sale of shares on the Stock Exchange **Börsentransaktion;** *the paper publishes a daily list of Stock Exchange transactions;* **exchange transaction** = purchase *or* sale of foreign currency **Devisengeschäft; fraudulent transaction** = transaction which aims to cheat someone **Schwindelgeschäft**

transfer
1 *noun* moving someone *or* something to a new place **Transfer; Versetzung; Verlegung; Übertragung;** *he applied for a transfer to our branch in Scotland;* **transfer of property** *or* **transfer of shares** = moving the ownership of property *or* shares from one person to another **Eigentumsüberschreibung; Aktientransfer; airmail transfer** = sending money from one bank to another by airmail **Luftpostüberweisung; bank transfer** = moving money from a bank account to an account in another country **Banküberweisung; credit transfer** *or* **transfer of funds** = moving money from one account to another **Kredittransfer; Geldtransfer; stock transfer form** = form to be signed by the person transferring shares **Aktienübertragungsformular**
2 *verb*
(a) to move someone *or* something to a new place **transferieren; versetzen; verlegen; übertragen;** *the accountant was transferred to our Scottish branch; he transferred his shares to a family trust; she transferred her money to a deposit account;* **transferred charge call** = phone call where the person receiving the call agrees to pay for it **R-Gespräch**
(b) to change from one type of travel to another **umsteigen;** *when you get to London airport, you have to transfer onto an internal flight*
NOTE: **transferring - transferred**

◇ **transferable** *adjective* which can be passed to someone else **übertragbar; the season ticket is not transferable** = the ticket cannot be given or lent to someone else to use **die Zeitkarte ist nicht übertragbar**

tranship *verb* to move cargo from one ship to another **umladen**
NOTE: **transhipping - transhipped**

transit *noun*
(a) movement of passengers *or* goods on the way to a destination **Transit; Transport;** *to pay compensation for damage suffered in transit or for loss in transit; some of the goods were damaged in transit;* **goods in transit** = goods being transported from warehouse to customer **Transitgüter**
(b) transit lounge = room in an airport where passengers wait for connecting flights **Transitraum; transit visa** *or* **transit permit** = document which allows someone to spend a short time in one country while travelling to another country **Transit-, Durchreisevisum**
NOTE: no plural

translate *verb* to put something which is said *or* written in one language into another language **übersetzen;** *he asked his secretary to translate the letter from the German agent; we have had the contract translated from French into Japanese*

◇ **translation** *noun* something which has been translated **Übersetzung;** *she passed the translation of the letter to the accounts department;* **translation bureau** = office which translates documents for companies **Übersetzungsbüro**

◇ **translator** *noun* person who translates **Übersetzer/-in**

transmission *noun* sending **Übermittlung;** *transmission of a message*

◇ **transmit** *verb* to send (a message) **übermitteln**
NOTE: **transmitting - transmitted**

transport
1 *noun* moving of goods or people **Transport, Beförderung;** *air transport or transport by air; rail transport or transport by rail; road transport or transport by road; passenger transport or the transport of passengers; the passenger transport services of British Rail; what means of transport will you use to get to the factory?;* **the visitors will be using public transport** *or* **private transport** = the visitors will be coming by bus *or* train, etc., or in their own cars **die Besucher werden öffentliche od private Verkehrsmittel benutzen; public transport system** = system of trains, buses, etc., used by the general public **öffentliches Verkehrsnetz**
NOTE: no plural
2 *verb* to move goods *or* people from one place to another in a vehicle **transportieren, befördern;** *the company transports millions of tons of goods by rail each year; the visitors will be transported to the factory by air or by helicopter or by taxi*

◇ **transportable** *adjective* which can be moved **transportfähig, transportabel**

◇ **transportation** *noun*
(a) moving goods *or* people from one place to another **Transport, Beförderung**
(b) vehicles used to move goods *or* people from one place to another **Beförderungs-, Verkehrsmittel;** *the company will provide transportation to the airport;* **ground transportation** = buses, taxis, etc., available to take passengers from an airport to the town **Bodentransport**
NOTE: no plural

◇ **transporter** *noun* company which transports goods **Transportunternehmen**

◇ **Transport International Routier, TIR** *noun* system with international documents which allows dutiable goods to cross several European countries by road without paying duty until they reach their final destination **TIR**

travel
1 *noun* moving of people from one place to another *or* from one country to another **Reisen;** *business travel is a very important part of our overhead expenditure;* **travel agent** = person in charge of a travel agency **Reisebürokaufmann; travel agency** = office which arranges travel for customers **Reisebüro; travel allowance** = money which an employee is allowed to spend on travelling **Reisekostenzuschuß; travel magazine** = magazine with articles on holidays and travel **Reisemagazin; the travel trade** = all businesses which organize travel for people **die Reisebranche**
NOTE: no plural
2 *verb*
(a) to move from one place to another *or* from one country to another **reisen;** *he travels to the States on business twice a year; in her new job, she has to travel abroad at least ten times a year*
(b) to go from one place to another, showing a company's goods to buyers and taking orders from them **Vertreter sein; bereisen;** *he travels in the north of the country for an insurance company*
NOTE: **travelling - travelled** but US **traveling - traveled**

◇ **traveller** *or US* **traveler** *noun*
(a) person who travels **Reisender; business traveller** = person who is travelling on business **Geschäftsreisender; traveller's cheques** *or US* **traveler's checks** = cheques taken by a traveller which can be cashed in a foreign country **Reiseschecks**
(b) commercial traveller = salesman who travels round an area visiting customers on behalf of his company **Handelsvertreter**

◊ **travelling** *noun* **travelling expenses** = money spent on travelling and hotels for business purposes **Reisespesen**

tray *noun* **filing tray** = container kept on a desk for documents which have to be filed **Ablage; in tray** = basket on a desk for letters *or* memos which have been received and are waiting to be dealt with **Eingänge; out tray** = basket on a desk for letters *or* memos which have been dealt with and are ready to be sent out **Ausgänge; pending tray** = basket on a desk for papers which cannot be dealt with immediately **Wiedervorlage**

treasurer *noun*
(a) person who looks after the money *or* finances of a club or society, etc. **Finanzverwalter(chef); honorary treasurer** = treasurer who does not receive any fee **ehrenamtlicher Finanzverwalter**
(b) *US* main financial officer of a company **Finanzmanager**

◊ **treasury** *noun* **the Treasury** = government department which deals with the country's finance **das Finanzministerium; treasury bill** = bill of exchange which does not give any interest and is sold by the government at a discount **Schatzwechsel; treasury bonds** = bonds issued by the Treasury of the USA **Schatzobligation**

treaty *noun*
(a) agreement between countries **Staatsvertrag; Abkommen;** *commercial treaty*
(b) agreement between individual persons **Vertrag; to sell a house by private treaty** = to sell a home to another person not by auction **ein Haus privat verkaufen**

treble *verb* to increase three times **verdreifachen;** *the company's borrowings have trebled*

trend *noun* general way things are going **Trend, Tendenz;** *there is a trend away from old-established food stores; a downward trend in investment; we notice a general trend to sell to the student market; the report points to inflationary trends in the economy; an upward trend in sales;* **economic trends** = way in which a country's economy is moving **ökonomische Entwicklungen; market trends** = gradual changes taking place in a market **Marktentwicklungen, Markttendenzen**

> QUOTE the quality of building design and ease of accessibility will become increasingly important, adding to the trend towards out-of-town office development
>
> *Lloyd's List*

trial *noun*
(a) court case to judge a person accused of a crime **Gerichtsverhandlung; Prozeß;** *he is on trial or is standing trial for embezzlement*
(b) test to see if something is good **Probe; Erprobung; Prüfung; on trial** = being tested **getestet werden; zur Prüfung/Probe;** *the product is on trial in our laboratories;* **trial period** = time when a customer can test a product before buying it **Probezeit; trial sample** = small piece of a product used for testing **Muster, Probestück; free trial** = testing of a machine *or* product with no payment involved **kostenlos zur Probe**
(c) trial balance = draft adding of debits and credits to see if they balance **vorläufige Bilanz**

tribunal *noun* official court which examines special problems and makes judgements **Gericht; Schiedsgericht; Tribunal; adjudication tribunal** = group which adjudicates in industrial disputes **Schlichtungskommission; industrial tribunal** = court which can decide in disputes about employment **Arbeitsgericht; rent tribunal** = court which can decide if a rent is too high or low **Schiedsgericht für Mietstreitigkeiten**

trick *noun* clever act to make someone believe something which is not true **Trick; confidence trick** = business where someone gains another person's confidence and then tricks him **Schwindel**

◊ **trickster** *noun* **confidence trickster** = person who carries out a confidence trick on someone **Schwindler/-in**

trip *noun* journey **Trip, Reise; business trip** = journey to discuss business matters with people who live a long way away or overseas **Geschäftsreise**

triple
1 *verb* to multiply three times **(sich) verdreifachen;** *the company's debts tripled in twelve months; the acquisition of the chain of stores has tripled the group's turnover*
2 *adjective* three times as much **dreifach;** *the cost of airfreighting the goods is triple their manufacturing cost*

triplicate *noun* **in triplicate** = with an original and two copies **in dreifacher Ausfertigung;** *to print an invoice in triplicate;* **invoicing in triplicate** = preparing three copies of invoices **Rechnungen in dreifacher Ausfertigung ausstellen**

trouble *noun* problem *or* difficult situation **Schwierigkeiten; Probleme;** *we are having some computer trouble or some* *trouble with the computer; there was some trouble in the warehouse after the manager was fired*

◊ **troubleshooter** *noun* person whose job is to solve problems in a company **Trouble Shooter; Krisenmanager**

trough *noun* low point in the economic cycle **Konjunkturtief, Talsohle**

truck *noun*

(a) large motor vehicle for carrying goods **Last(kraft)wagen; fork-lift truck** = type of small tractor with two metal arms in front, used for lifting and moving pallets **Gabelstapler**

(b) open railway wagon for carrying goods **Güterwagen**

◊ **trucker** *noun* person who drives a truck **Lastwagenfahrer**

◊ **trucking** *noun* carrying goods in trucks **Güter(kraft)verkehr, Spedition;** *trucking firm*

NOTE: no plural

true *adjective* correct *or* accurate **wahr; true copy** = exact copy **getreue Kopie;** *I certify that this is a true copy; certified as a true copy*

truly *adverb* **Yours truly** *or US* **Truly yours** = ending to a formal business letter where you do not know the person you are writing to **Hochachtungsvoll**

trunk call *noun* telephone call to a number which is in a different area **Ferngespräch**

trust

1 *noun*

(a) being confident that something is correct, will work, etc. **Vertrauen; we took his statement on trust** = we accepted his statement without examining it to see if it was correct **wir akzeptierten seine Aussage auf Treu und Glauben**

(b) passing goods *or* money *or* secrets to someone who will look after them well **Treuhand(schaft);** *he left his property in trust for his grandchildren;* **he was guilty of a breach of trust** = he did not act correctly *or* honestly when people expected him to **er verletzte die Treuhandpflicht; he has a position of trust** = his job shows that people believe he will act correctly and honestly **er hat eine Vertrauensstellung**

(c) management of money *or* property for someone **Vermögensverwaltung;** *they set up a family trust for their grandchildren; US* **trust company** = organization which supervises the financial affairs of private trusts, executes wills, and acts as a bank to a limited number of customers **Treuhandgesellschaft; trust deed** = document which sets out the details of a private trust **Treuhandvertrag; trust fund** = assets (money, securities, property) held in trust for someone **Treuhandfonds; investment trust** = company whose shares can be bought on the Stock Exchange and whose business is to make money by buying and selling stocks and shares **Investmenttrust, Kapitalanlagegesellschaft; unit trust** = organization which takes money from investors and invests it in stocks and shares for them under a trust deed **offener Investmentfonds, Unit Trust**

NOTE: the US English for this is **mutual funds**

(d) *US* small group of companies which (illegally) control the supply of a product **Syndikat**

NOTE: no plural for (a) and (b)

2 *verb* **to trust someone with something** = to give something to someone to look after **jdm etwas anvertrauen;** *can he be trusted with all that cash?*

◊ **trustbusting** *noun US* breaking up monopolies to encourage competition **Monopol-, Trustzerschlagung**

◊ **trustee** *noun* person who has charge of money in trust *or* person who is responsible for a family trust **Vermögensverwalter, Treuhänder;** *the trustees of the pension fund;* **Trustee Savings Bank** = bank which takes savings from small savers, and is guaranteed by the government **öffentlich-rechtliches Bankinstitut**

◊ **trustworthy** *adjective* (person) who can be trusted **vertrauenswürdig;** *our cashiers are completely trustworthy*

TUC = TRADES UNION CONGRESS

tune *noun* piece of music **Lied, Melodie; the bank is backing him to the tune of £10,000** = the bank is helping him with a loan of £10,000 **die Bank unterstützt ihn mit einem Betrag in Höhe von £10.000**

turn

1 *noun*

(a) movement in a circle *or* change of direction **Drehung**

(b) profit *or* commission **Gewinn(spanne); Courtage; jobber's turn** = profit made by a stock jobber **Courtage**

(c) stock turn = total value of stocks sold in a year divided by the average value of goods in stock **Lagerumschlag;** *the company has a stock turn of 6.7*

2 *verb* to change direction *or* to go round in a circle **abbiegen; (sich) drehen**

◊ **turn down** *verb* to refuse **ablehnen;** *the board turned down their takeover bid; the* *bank turned down their request for a loan; the application for a licence was turned down*

◊ **turnkey** *noun* **turnkey operation** = deal where a company takes all responsibility for constructing, fitting and staffing a building (such as a school *or* hospital *or* factory) so that it is completely ready for the purchaser to take over **Erfüllung einer geschäftlichen Operation**

◊ **turn out** *verb* to produce **produzieren, herstellen;** *the factory turns out fifty units per day*

◊ **turn over** *verb* to have a certain amount of sales **umsetzen;** *we turn over £2,000 a week*

◊ **turnover** *noun*
(a) *GB* amount of sales **Umsatz;** *the company's turnover has increased by 235%; we based our calculations on the forecast turnover;* **stock turnover** = total value of stock sold in a year divided by the average value of goods held in stock **Lagerumschlag**
(b) changes in staff, when some leave and others join **Fluktuation;** *staff turnover or turnover of staff*
(c) *US* number of times something is used *or* sold in a period (usually one year), expressed as a percentage of a total **Umschlaggeschwindigkeit**

◊ **turn round** *verb* to make (a company) change from making a loss to become profitable **sanieren; he turned the company round in less than a year** = he made the company profitable in less than a year **in weniger als einem Jahr sanierte er das Unternehmen**

◊ **turnround** *noun*
(a) value of goods sold during a year divided by the average value of goods held in stock **mittlerer Lagerumschlag**
(b) action of emptying a ship, plane, etc., and getting it ready for another commercial journey **Entladung und Wiederfahrbereitmachung**
(c) making a company profitable again **Sanierung**

QUOTE a 100,000 square foot warehouse can turn its inventory over 18 times a year, more than triple a discounter's turnover
Duns Business Month

QUOTE he is turning over his CEO title to one of his teammates, but will remain chairman for a year
Duns Business Month

QUOTE the US now accounts for more than half our world-wide sales; it has made a huge contribution to our earnings turnround
Duns Business Month

two-part paper *noun* paper (for computers *or* typewriters) with a top sheet for the original and a second sheet for a copy **zweilagiges Papier;** *two-part invoices; two-part stationery*

tycoon *noun* important businessman **Magnat**

type *verb* to write with a typewriter **tippen, (mit der) Schreibmaschine schreiben;** *he can type quite fast; all his reports are typed on his portable typewriter*

◊ **typewriter** *noun* machine which prints letters *or* figures on a piece of paper when a key is pressed **Schreibmaschine;** *portable typewriter; electronic typewriter*

◊ **typewritten** *adjective* written on a typewriter **maschinengeschrieben;** *he sent in a typewritten job application*

◊ **typing** *noun* writing letters with a typewriter **Tippen, Schreibmaschineschreiben; typing error** = mistake made when using a typewriter **Tippfehler;** *the secretary must have made a typing error;* **typing pool** = group of typists, working together in a company, offering a secretarial service to several departments **zentraler Schreibdienst; copy typing** = typing documents from originals, not from dictation **Abtippen von Dokumenten**
NOTE: no plural

◊ **typist** *noun* person whose job is to write letters using a typewriter **Schreibkraft; copy typist** = person who types documents from originals not from dictation **Schreibkraft (ohne Diktat); shorthand typist** = typist who takes dictation in shorthand and then types it **Stenotypist/-in**

Uu

ultimate *adjective* last *or* final **letzter, End-; ultimate consumer** = the person who actually uses the product **Endverbraucher**

◊ **ultimately** *adverb* in the end **schließlich, letzten Endes;** *ultimately, the management had to agree to the demands of the union*

◊ **ultimatum** *noun* statement to a someone that unless he does something within a period of time, action will be taken against him **Ultimatum;** *the union officials argued among themselves over the best way to deal with the ultimatum from the management*
NOTE: plural is **ultimatums** or **ultimata**

umbrella *noun* **umbrella organization** = large organization which includes several smaller ones **Dachorganisation**

UN = THE UNITED NATIONS

unable *adjective* not able **außerstande sein;** *the chairman was unable to come to the meeting*

unacceptable *adjective* which cannot be accepted **unannehmbar, nicht akzeptabel;** *the terms of the contract are quite unacceptable*

unaccounted for *adjective* lost, without any explanation **nicht ausgewiesen;** *several thousand units are unaccounted for in the stocktaking*

unanimous *adjective* where everyone votes in the same way **einstimmig, einmütig;** *there was a unanimous vote against the proposal; they reached unanimous agreement*

◇ **unanimously** *adverb* with everyone agreeing **einstimmig, einmütig;** *the proposals were adopted unanimously*

unaudited *adjective* which has not been audited **ungeprüft;** *unaudited accounts*

unauthorized *adjective* not permitted **unbefugt, unzulässig;** *unauthorized access to the company's records; unauthorized expenditure; no unauthorized persons are allowed into the laboratory*

unavailable *adjective* not available **nicht erhältlich, nicht verfügbar;** *the following items on your order are temporarily unavailable*

◇ **unavailability** *noun* not being available **Nichtverfügbarkeit**

NOTE: no plural

unavoidable *adjective* which cannot be avoided **unvermeidlich, unumgänglich;** *planes are subject to unavoidable delays*

unbalanced *adjective* (budget) which does not balance *or* which is in deficit **nicht ausgeglichen**

uncalled *adjective* (capital) which a company is authorized to raise and has been issued but is not fully paid **nicht eingefordert; nachschußpflichtig**

uncashed *adjective* which has not been cashed **nicht eingelöst;** *uncashed cheques*

unchanged *adjective* which has not changed **unverändert**

> QUOTE the dividend is unchanged at L90 per ordinary share
> *Financial Times*

unchecked *adjective* which has not been checked **ungeprüft;** *unchecked figures*

unclaimed *adjective* which has not been claimed **nicht geltend gemacht; unclaimed baggage** = cases which have been left with someone and have not been claimed by their owners **nicht abgeholtes Gepäck;** *unclaimed property or unclaimed baggage will be sold by auction after six months*

uncollected *adjective* which has not been collected **nicht eingezogen; nicht abgeholt;** *uncollected subscriptions; uncollected taxes*

unconditional *adjective* with no conditions **vorbehaltlos;** *unconditional acceptance of the offer by the board;* **the offer went unconditional last Thursday** = the takeover bid was accepted by the majority of the shareholders and therefore the conditions attached to it no longer apply **das Angebot wurde am letzten Donnerstag vorbehaltlos angenommen**

◇ **unconditionally** *adverb* without imposing any conditions **vorbehaltlos;** *the offer was accepted unconditionally by the trade union*

unconfirmed *adjective* which has not been confirmed **unbestätigt;** *there are unconfirmed reports that our agent has been arrested*

unconstitutional *adjective* not allowed by the rules *or* laws of a country *or* organization **verfassungswidrig, nicht verfassungsmäßig;** *the chairman ruled that the meeting was unconstitutional*

uncontrollable *adjective* which cannot be controlled **nicht unter Kontrolle zu bringen, unkontrollierbar;** *uncontrollable inflation*

uncrossed cheque *noun* cheque which can be cashed anywhere **Barscheck**

undated *adjective* with no date written **undatiert;** *he tried to cash an undated cheque;* **undated bond** = bond with no maturity date **Schuldverschreibung ohne Fälligkeitstermin**

under *preposition*
(a) lower than *or* less than **unter;** *the interest rate*

is under 10%; under half of the shareholders accepted the offer
(b) controlled by *or* according to **nach, gemäß, laut;** *under the terms of the agreement, the goods should be delivered in October; he is acting under rule 23 of the union constitution*

◇ **under-** *prefix* less important than *or* lower than **Unter-**

◇ **underbid** *verb* to bid less than someone **unterbieten**
NOTE: **underbidding - underbid**

◇ **underbidder** *noun* person who bids less than the person who buys at an auction **Mitbieter**

◇ **undercapitalized** *adjective* without enough capital **unterkapitalisiert;** *the company is severely undercapitalized*

◇ **undercharge** *verb* to ask for too little money **zu wenig berechnen;** *he undercharged us by £25*

◇ **undercut** *verb* to offer something at a lower price than someone else **unterbieten**

◇ **underdeveloped** *adjective* which has not been developed **unterentwickelt;** *Japan is an underdeveloped market for our products;* **underdeveloped countries** = countries which are not fully industrialized **Entwicklungsländer**

◇ **underemployed** *adjective* with not enough work **unterbeschäftigt, nicht ausgelastet;** *the staff is underemployed because of the cutback in production;* **underemployed capital** = capital which is not producing enough interest **nicht voll genutztes Kapital**

◇ **underemployment** *noun*
(a) situation where workers in a company do not have enough work to do **Unterbeschäftigung**
(b) situation where there is not enough work for all the workers in a country **Unterbeschäftigung, Arbeitslosigkeit**
NOTE: no plural

◇ **underequipped** *adjective* with not enough equipment **unzulänglich ausgerüstet**

◇ **underestimate**
1 *noun* estimate which is less than the actual figure **Unterschätzung; Unterbewertung;** *the figure of £50,000 in turnover was a considerable underestimate*
2 *verb* to think that something is smaller *or* not as bad as it really is **unterschätzen; unterbewerten;** *they underestimated the effects of the strike on their sales; he underestimated the amount of time needed to finish the work*

◇ **underlease** *noun* lease from a tenant to another tenant **Untermietvertrag; Unterpachtvertrag; Untervermietung; Unterverpachtung**

◇ **undermanned** *adjective* with not enough staff to do the work **unterbesetzt**

◇ **undermanning** *noun* having too few workers than are needed to do the company's work **Unterbesetzung;** *the company's production is affected by undermanning on the assembly line*
NOTE: no plural

◇ **undermentioned** *adjective* mentioned lower down in a document **untengenannt**

◇ **underpaid** *adjective* not paid enough **unterbezahlt;** *our staff say that they are underpaid and overworked*

◇ **underrate** *verb* to value less highly than should be **unterbewerten, unterschätzen;** *do not underrate the strength of the competition in the European market; the power of the yen is underrated*

◇ **undersell** *verb* to sell more cheaply than **unterbieten; unter Preis verkaufen;** *to undersell a competitor;* **the company is never undersold** = no other company sells goods as cheaply as this one **diese Firma wird nie unterboten/ist der billigste Anbieter**
NOTE: **underselling - undersold**

◇ **undersigned** *noun* person who has signed a letter **Unterzeichneter; we, the undersigned** = we, the people who have signed below **wir, die Unterzeichnenden**
NOTE: can be followed by a plural verb

◇ **underspend** *verb* to spend less **zu wenig ausgeben; he has underspent his budget** = he has spent less than was allowed in the budget **er hat sein Budget nicht voll ausgeschöpft**
NOTE: **underspending - underspent**

◇ **understaffed** *adjective* with not enough staff to do the company's work **unterbesetzt**

◇ **understand** *verb* to know *or* to see what something means **verstehen**
NOTE: **understanding - understood**

◇ **understanding** *noun* private agreement **Vereinbarung, Übereinkunft;** *to come to an understanding about the divisions of the market;* **on the understanding that** = on condition that *or* provided that **unter der Voraussetzung, daß;** *we accept the terms of the contract, on the understanding that it has to be ratified by our main board*

◇ **understate** *verb* to make something seem less than it really is **zu niedrig angeben, untertreiben;** *the company accounts understate the real profit*

◇ **undertake** *verb* to agree to do something **übernehmen, sich verpflichten;** *to undertake an investigation of the market; they have undertaken not to sell into our territory*
NOTE: **undertaking - undertook - has undertaken**

◇ **undertaking** *noun*
(a) business **Unternehmen, Projekt;** *commercial undertaking*

(b) (legally binding) promise **Zusicherung;** *they have given us a written undertaking not to sell their products in competition with ours*

◇ **underutilized** *adjective* not used enough **nicht voll ausgelastet**

◇ **undervalued** *adjective* not valued highly enough **unterbewertet, zu niedrig geschätzt;** *the properties are undervalued on the balance sheet; the dollar is undervalued on the foreign exchanges*

◇ **undervaluation** *noun* being valued at a lower worth than should be **Unterbewertung, zu niedrige Schätzung**

◇ **underweight** *adjective* **the pack is twenty grams underweight** = the pack weighs twenty grams less than it should **das Gewicht der Packung liegt zwanzig Gramm unter dem Normalgewicht**

◇ **underworked** *adjective* not given enough work to do **nicht ausgelastet;** *the directors think our staff are overpaid and underworked*

◇ **underwrite** *verb*
(a) to accept responsibility for **bürgen für; haften; to underwrite a share issue** = to guarantee that a share issue will be sold by agreeing to buy all shares which are not subscribed **eine Aktienemission zeichnen/fest übernehmen;** *the issue was underwritten by three underwriting companies*
(b) to insure *or* to cover (a risk) **versichern;** *to underwrite an insurance policy*
(c) to agree to pay for costs **Haftung übernehmen für;** *the government has underwritten the development costs of the project*
NOTE: **underwriting - underwrote - has underwritten**

◇ **underwriter** *noun* person *or* bank underwriting a share issue **Anleihegarant** company which underwrites an insurance **Versicherungsträger, Versicherer; Lloyd's underwriter** = member of an insurance group at Lloyd's who accepts to underwrite insurances **Versicherungsträger bei Lloyd's; marine underwriter** = person who insures ships and their cargoes **Seetransportversicherer**

undischarged bankrupt *noun* person who has been declared bankrupt and has not been released from that state **nicht entlasteter Konkursschuldner**

undistributed profit *noun* profit which has not been distributed as dividends to shareholders **einbehaltene Gewinne**

unearned income *noun* money received from interest or dividends, not from salary or profits of one's business **Kapitalertrag**

uneconomic *adjective* which does not make a commercial profit **unwirtschaftlich, unökonomisch; it is an uneconomic proposition** = it will not be commercially profitable **das ist ein unrentables Geschäft; uneconomic rent** = rent which is not enough to cover costs **nicht kostendeckende Miete**

unemployed *adjective* not employed *or* without any work **arbeitslos; unemployed office workers** = office workers with no jobs **arbeitslose Büroangestellte; the unemployed** = the people without any jobs **die Arbeitslosen**

◇ **unemployment** *noun* lack of work **Arbeitslosigkeit; mass unemployment** = unemployment of large numbers of workers **Massenarbeitslosigkeit; unemployment benefit** *or US* **unemployment compensation** = payment made to someone who is unemployed **Arbeitslosengeld; Arbeitslosenhilfe**
NOTE: no plural

> QUOTE tax advantages directed toward small businesses will help create jobs and reduce the unemployment rate
> *Toronto Star*

unfair *adjective* **unfair competition** = trying to do better than another company by using techniques such as importing foreign goods at very low prices or by wrongly criticizing a competitor's products **unlauterer Wettbewerb; unfair dismissal** = removing someone from a job for reasons which are not fair **ungerechtfertigte Entlassung**

unfavourable *adjective* not favourable **ungünstig, negativ; unfavourable balance of trade** = situation where a country imports more than it exports **passive Handelsbilanz; unfavourable exchange rate** = exchange rate which gives an amount of foreign currency for the home currency which is not good for trade **ungünstiger Wechselkurs;** *the unfavourable exchange rate hit the country's exports*

unfulfilled *adjective* (order) which has not yet been supplied **unerfüllt, nicht ausgeführt**

ungeared *adjective* with no borrowings **ohne Fremdkapitalaufnahme**

unilateral *adjective* on one side only *or* done by one party only **unilateral, einseitig;**

they took the unilateral decision to cancel the contract

◇ **unilaterally** *adverb* by one party only **unilateral, einseitig;** *they cancelled the contract unilaterally*

uninsured *adjective* not insured **nicht versichert**

union *noun*
(a) trade union *or* **trades union** *or US* **labor union** = organization which represents workers who are its members in discussions with management about wages and conditions of work **Gewerkschaft; union agreement** = agreement between a management and a trade union over wages and conditions of work **Tarifvertrag; union dues** *or* **union subscription** = payment made by workers to belong to a union **Gewerkschaftsbeiträge; union officials** = paid organizers of a union **Gewerkschaftsfunktionäre; union recognition** = act of agreeing that a union can act on behalf of staff in a company **Anerkennung der Gewerkschaft**
(b) customs union = agreement between several countries that goods can go between them without paying duty, while goods from other countries have special duties charged on them **Zollunion**

◇ **unionist** *noun* member of a trade union **Gewerkschaftsmitglied**

◇ **unionized** *adjective* (company) where the members of staff belong to a trade union **gewerkschaftlich organisiert**

> QUOTE the blue-collar unions are the people who stand to lose most in terms of employment growth
> *Sydney Morning Herald*
>
> QUOTE after three days of tough negotiations, the company reached agreement with its 1,200 unionized workers
> *Toronto Star*

unique *adjective* special *or* with nothing like it **einmalig, einzigartig; unique selling proposition** = special quality of a product which makes it different from other goods and therefore attractive to customers **einmaliges Verkaufsangebot**

unissued capital *noun* capital which a company is authorized to issue but has not issued as shares **genehmigte Kapital, aber noch nicht als Aktien emittiert**

unit *noun*
(a) single product for sale **Einheit, Stück; unit cost** = the cost of one item (i.e total product costs divided by the number of units produced) **Einheits-, Stückkosten; unit price** = the price of one item **Einheits-, Stückpreis**
(b) separate piece of equipment or furniture **Element; display unit** = special stand for showing goods for sale **Auslagenstand; visual display unit** = screen attached to a computer which shows the information stored in the computer **Bildschirm**
(c) factory unit = single building on an industrial estate **Fabrikgebäude**
(d) production unit = separate small group of workers which produces a certain product **Produktionseinheit; research unit** = separate small group of research workers **Forschungsgruppe**
(e) monetary unit *or* **unit of currency** = main item of currency of a country (a dollar, pound, yen etc.) **Währungseinheit; unit of account** = currency used for calculating the EC budget and farm prices **Rechnungseinheit**
(f) single share in a unit trust **Anlageeinheit**

◇ **unit trust** *noun* organization which takes money from small investors and invests it in stocks and shares for them under a trust deed, the investment being in the form of shares (or units) in the trust **offener Investmentfonds, Unit Trust**
NOTE: the US English for this is **mutual funds**

unite *verb* to join together **(sich) zusammenschließen/vereinigen;** *the directors united with the managers to reject the takeover bid;* **United Nations** = organization which links the countries of the world to promote good relations between them **die Vereinten Nationen**

unladen *adjective* empty *or* without a cargo **unbeladen**

unlawful *adjective* against the law *or* not legal **ungesetzlich; gesetzwidrig**

unlimited *adjective* with no limits **unbegrenzt;** *the bank offered him unlimited credit;* **unlimited liability** = situation where a sole trader or each partner is responsible for all the firm's debts with no limit at the amount each may have to pay **unbeschränkte Haftung**

unlined *adjective* **unlined paper** = paper with no lines printed on it **unliniertes Papier**

unlisted *adjective* **unlisted securities** = shares which are not listed on the Stock Exchange **Freiverkehrswerte; unlisted securities market** = market for buying and selling shares which are not listed on the Stock Exchange **Freiverkehr**

unload *verb*
(a) to take goods off (a ship, etc.) **ent-, ausladen; löschen;** *the ship is unloading at Hamburg; we need a fork-lift truck to unload the lorry; we unloaded the spare parts at Lagos; there are no unloading facilities for container ships*
(b) to sell (shares which do not seem attractive) **abstoßen;** *we tried to unload our shareholding as soon as the company published its accounts*

unobtainable *adjective* which cannot be obtained **nicht erhältlich**

unofficial *adjective* not official **inoffiziell; unofficial strike** = strike by local workers which has not been approved by the main union **wilder Streik**
◊ **unofficially** *adverb* not officially **inoffiziell;** *the tax office told the company unofficially that it would be prosecuted*

unpaid *adjective* not paid **unbezahlt; unpaid holiday** = holiday where the worker does not receive any pay **unbezahlter Urlaub; unpaid invoices** = invoices which have not been paid **unbezahlte Rechnungen**

unprofitable *adjective* which is not profitable **unrentabel**

> QUOTE the airline has already eliminated a number of unprofitable flights
> *Duns Business Month*

unquoted shares *plural noun* shares which have no Stock Exchange quotation **unnotierte Aktien**

unredeemed pledge *noun* pledge which the borrower has not claimed back by paying back his loan **uneingelöstes Pfand**

unregistered *adjective* (company) which has not been registered **nicht eingetragen**

unreliable *adjective* which cannot be relied on **unzuverlässig;** *the postal service is very unreliable*

unsealed envelope *noun* envelope where the flap has been pushed into the back of the envelope, not stuck down **offener Briefumschlag**

unsecured *adjective* **unsecured creditor** = creditor who is owed money, but has no security from the debtor for it **Gläubiger ohne Sicherheiten; unsecured debt** = debt which is not guaranteed by assets **ungesicherte Verbindlichkeit; unsecured loan** = loan made with no security **ungesichertes Darlehen**

unseen *adverb* not seen **unsichtbar; unbesehen; to buy something sight unseen** = to buy something without having inspected it **etwas unbesehen kaufen**

unsettled *adjective* which changes often *or* which is upset **unbeständig, veränderlich;** *the market was unsettled by the news of the failure of the takeover bid*

unskilled *adjective* without any particular skill **ungelernt;** *unskilled labour or unskilled workforce or unskilled workers*

unsocial *adjective* **to work unsocial hours** = to work at times (i.e. in the evening *or* at night *or* during public holidays) when most people are not at work **außerhalb der normalen Arbeitszeiten arbeiten**

unsold *adjective* not sold **unverkauft;** *unsold items will be scrapped*

unsolicited *adjective* which has not been asked for **unverlangt;** *an unsolicited gift* ; **unsolicited testimonial** = letter praising someone *or* a product without the writer having been asked to write it **ohne Aufforderung gegebene Empfehlung**

unstable *adjective* not stable *or* changing frequently **schwankend, unsicher;** *unstable exchange rates*

unsubsidized *adjective* with no subsidy **nicht subventioniert**

unsuccessful *adjective* not successful **erfolglos;** *an unsuccessful businessman; the project was expensive and unsuccessful*
◊ **unsuccessfully** *adverb* with no success **erfolglos, vergeblich;** *the company unsuccessfully tried to break into the South American market*

untrue *adjective* not true **unwahr, falsch**

unused *adjective* which has not been used **ungebraucht, unbenutzt;** *we are trying to sell off six unused typewriters*

unwaged *adjective* **the unwaged** = people with no jobs **die Erwerbslosen**
NOTE: is followed by a plural verb

unwritten *adjective* **unwritten agreement** = agreement which has been reached in speaking (such as in a telephone conversation) but has not been written down **mündliche Vereinbarung**

up *adverb & preposition* in a higher position *or* to a higher position **hinauf; höher; gestiegen;** *the inflation rate is going up steadily; shares were up slightly at the end of the day*

◇ **up to** *adverb* as far as *or* as high as **bis zu;** *we will buy at prices up to £25*

◇ **up to date** *adjective & adverb* current *or* recent *or* modern **aktuell, auf dem neuesten Stand;** *an up-to-date computer system;* **to bring something up to date** = to add the latest information or equipment to something **etwas auf den neuesten Stand bringen; to keep something up to date** = to keep adding information to something so that it always has the latest information in it **etwas auf dem laufenden halten, etwas aktualisieren;** *we spend a lot of time keeping our mailing list up to date*

update
1 *noun* information added to something to make it up to date **Aktualisierung**
2 *verb* to revise something so that it is always up to date **aktualisieren, auf den neuesten Stand bringen;** *the figures are updated annually*

up front *adverb* in advance **im voraus; money up front** = payment in advance **Vorauszahlung;** *they are asking for £100,000 up front before they will consider the deal; he had to put money up front before he could clinch the deal*

upgrade *verb* to increase the importance of someone *or* of a job **befördern; anheben;** *his job has been upgraded to senior manager level*

upkeep *noun* cost of keeping a building *or* machine in good order **Instandhaltungskosten**
NOTE: no plural

uplift *noun* increase **Anhebung;** *the contract provides for an annual uplift of charges*

up market *adjective & adverb* more expensive *or* appealing to a wealthy section of the population **anspruchsvoll, exklusiv; the company has decided to move up market** = the company has decided to start to produce more luxury items **die Firma entschied sich, anspruchsvollere Produkte anzubieten**

upset price *noun* lowest price which the seller will accept at an auction **Vorbehaltspreis**

upturn *noun* movement towards higher sales or profits **Aufschwung;** *an upturn in the economy; an upturn in the market*

upward *adjective* towards a higher position **Aufwärts-, nach oben;** *an upward movement*

◇ **upwards** *adverb* towards a higher position **aufwärts, nach oben;** *the market moved upwards after the news of the budget*
NOTE: US English uses **upward** as both adjective and adverb

urgent *adjective* which has to be done quickly **dringend, Eil-, eilig**

◇ **urgently** *adverb* immediately **dringend, dringlich**

usage *noun* how something is used **Gebrauch, Anwendung**
NOTE: no plural

use
1 *noun* way in which something can be used **Verwendung, Benutzung, Gebrauch; directions for use** = instructions on how to run a machine **Gebrauchsanweisung; to make use of something** = to use something **von etwas Gebrauch machen; in use** = being worked **in Gebrauch/Betrieb;** *the computer is in use twenty-four hours a day;* **items for personal use** = items which a person will use for himself, not on behalf of the company **Gegenstände des persönlichen Gebrauchs; he has the use of a company car** = he has a company car which he uses privately **er hat einen Firmenwagen; land zoned for industrial use** = land where planning permission has been given to build factories **für Leichtindustrie vorgesehenes Land**
2 *verb* to take a machine, a company, a process, etc., and work with it **benutzen, verwenden, einsetzen;** *we use airmail for all our overseas correspondence; the photocopier is being used all the time; they use freelancers for most of their work*

◇ **useful** *adjective* which can help **nützlich, brauchbar**

◇ **user** *noun* person who uses something **Benutzer/-in, Anwender/-in; end user** = person who actually uses a product **Endverbraucher; user's guide** *or* **handbook** = book showing someone how to use something **Benutzerhandbuch**

◇ **user-friendly** *adjective* which a user finds easy to work **benutzerfreundlich;** *these programs are really user-friendly*

USM = UNLISTED SECURITIES MARKET

USP = UNIQUE SELLING PROPOSITION

usual *adjective* normal *or* ordinary **gewöhnlich, normal, üblich;** *our usual terms or usual conditions are thirty days' credit; the usual practice is to have the contract signed by the MD; the usual hours of work are from 9.30 to 5.30*

usury *noun* lending money at high interest **Wucher, Kreditwucher**
NOTE: no plural

utilize *verb* to use **verwenden, (be)nutzen**
◇ **utilization** *noun* making use of something **Verwendung, Benutzung, Nutzung; capacity utilization** = using something as much as possible **Kapazitätsausnutzung**
NOTE: no plural

> QUOTE control permits the manufacturer to react to changing conditions on the plant floor and to keep people and machines at a high level of utilization
> *Duns Business Month*

Vv

vacancy *noun* empty place *or* room; job which is not filled **freier Platz; freies Zimmer; freie Stelle;** *we advertised a vacancy in the local press; we have been unable to fill the vacancy for a skilled machinist; they have a vacancy for a secretary;* **job vacancies** = jobs which are empty and need people to do them **offene Stellen, Stellenangebote; vacancy rate** = average number of rooms empty in a hotel over a period of time, shown as a percentage of the total number of rooms **Zimmerbelegung**
◇ **vacant** *adjective* empty *or* not occupied **frei, unbesetzt; unbewohnt; vacant possession** = being able to occupy a property immediately after buying it because it is empty **sofort beziehbar;** *the house is for sale with vacant possession;* **situations vacant** *or* **appointments vacant** = list (in a newspaper) of jobs which are available **Stellenangebote**

vacate *verb* **to vacate the premises** = to leave premises, so that they become empty **das Gebäude räumen**

◇ **vacation** *noun*
(a) *GB* period when the law courts are closed **Gerichtsferien**
(b) *US* holiday *or* period when people are not working **Urlaub;** *the CEO is on vacation in Florida*

valid *adjective*
(a) which is acceptable because it is true **begründet, stichhaltig, triftig;** *that is not a valid argument or excuse*
(b) which can be used lawfully **gültig, rechtsgültig;** *the contract is not valid if it has not been witnessed; ticket which is valid for three months; he was carrying a valid passport*
◇ **validate** *verb*
(a) to check to see if something is correct **für gültig erklären, bestätigen;** *the document was validated by the bank*
(b) to make (something) valid **rechtsgültig machen, legalisieren**
◇ **validation** *noun* act of making something valid **Gültigkeitserklärung, Bestätigung**
NOTE: no plural
◇ **validity** *noun* being valid **Gültigkeit, Rechtsgültigkeit; period of validity** = length of time for which a document is valid **Gültigkeitsdauer, Laufzeit**
NOTE: no plural

valorem *see* AD VALOREM

valuable *adjective* which is worth a lot of money **wertvoll, kostbar; valuable property** *or* **valuables** = personal items which are worth a lot of money **Wertgegenstände**
◇ **valuation** *noun* estimate of how much something is worth **Schätzung, Bewertung;** *to ask for a valuation of a property before making an offer for it;* **stock valuation** = estimating the value of stock at the end of an accounting period **Bewertung des Lagerbestandes; to buy a shop with stock at valuation** = to pay for the stock the same amount as its value as estimated by a valuer **ein Geschäft inklusive des Warenbestandes zum Schätzpreis kaufen**
◇ **value**
1 *noun* amount of money which something is worth **Wert;** *he imported goods to the value of £250; the fall in the value of sterling; the valuer put the value of the stock at £25,000;* **good value (for money)** = a bargain *or* something which is worth the price paid for it **preiswert, preisgünstig;** *that restaurant gives value for money; buy that computer now - it is very good value; holidays in Italy are good value because of the exchange rate;* **to rise in value** *or* **to fall in value** = to be worth more *or* less **im Wert**

steigen; im Wert fallen; asset value = value of a company calculated by adding together all its assets **Vermögenswert; book value** = value as recorded in the company's accounts **Buch-, Bilanzwert; "sample only - of no commercial value"** = not worth anything if sold **"unentgeltliche Werbeprobe"; declared value** = value of goods entered on a customs declaration form **angemeldeter/angegebener Wert; discounted value** = difference between the face value of a share and its lower market price **Diskontwert; face value** = value written on a coin *or* banknote *or* share **Nominal-, Nennwert; market value** = value of an asset *or* of a product *or* of a company, if sold today **Marktwert; par value** = value written on a share certificate **Nennwert; scarcity value** = value of something which is worth a lot because it is rare and there is a large demand for it **Seltenheitswert; surrender value** = money which an insurer will pay if an insurance policy is given up before maturity date **Rückkaufwert**

2 *verb* to estimate how much money something is worth **schätzen;** *he valued the stock at £25,000; we are having the jewellery valued for insurance*

◇ **Value Added Tax** *noun* tax imposed as a percentage of the invoice value of goods and services **Mehrwertsteuer**

◇ **valuer** *noun* person who estimates how much money something is worth **Schätzer**

van *noun* small goods vehicle **Lieferwagen; delivery van** = van for delivering goods to customers **Lieferwagen**

variable *adjective* which changes **variabel, veränderlich, schwankend; variable costs** = money paid to produce a product which increases with the quantity made (such as wages, raw materials) **variable Kosten**

◇ **variability** *noun* being variable **Variabilität, Veränderlichkeit**

NOTE: no plural

◇ **variance** *noun* difference **Diskrepanz, Abweichung, Unterschied; budget variance** = difference between the cost as estimated for the budget, and the actual cost **Budgetabweichung; to be at variance with** = not to agree with **unvereinbar sein mit;** *the actual sales are at variance with the sales reported by the reps*

◇ **variation** *noun* amount by which something changes **Abweichung; seasonal variations** = changes which take place because of the seasons **saisonbedingte Abweichungen;** *seasonal variations in buying patterns*

variety *noun* different types of things **Auswahl, Vielfalt, Anzahl;** *the shop stocks a variety of goods; we had a variety of visitors at the office today;* US **variety store** = shop selling a wide range of usually cheap items **Gemischtwarenladen**

◇ **vary** *verb* to change *or* to differ **sich (ver)ändern, schwanken, variieren;** *the gross margin varies from quarter to quarter; we try to prevent the flow of production from varying in the factory*

VAT = VALUE ADDED TAX *the invoice includes VAT at 15%; the government is proposing to increase VAT to 17.5%; some items (such as books) are zero-rated for VAT; he does not charge VAT because he asks for payment in cash;* **VAT declaration** = statement declaring VAT income to the VAT office **Mehrwertsteuererklärung; VAT invoicing** = sending of an invoice including VAT **Mehrwertsteuerabrechnung; VAT invoice** = invoice which shows VAT separately **Mehrwertsteuerrechnung; VAT inspector** = government official who examines VAT returns and checks that VAT is being paid **Finanzbeamter (zuständig für Mehrwertsteuer); VAT office** = government office dealing with the collection of VAT in an area; *entspricht* **Umsatzsteuerstelle**

NOTE: no plural

◇ **VATman** *or* **vatman** *noun* VAT inspector **Finanzbeamter (zuständig für Mehrwertsteuer)**

VDU *or* **VDT** = VISUAL DISPLAY UNIT *or* VISUAL DISPLAY TERMINAL

vehicle *noun* machine with wheels, used to carry goods *or* passengers on a road **Fahrzeug; commercial vehicle** *or* **goods vehicle** = van *or* truck used for business purposes **Nutzfahrzeug; heavy goods vehicle** = very large lorry **Schwerfahrzeug;** *goods vehicles can park in the loading bay*

vending *noun* selling **Verkauf; (automatic) vending machine** = machine which provides drinks, cigarettes, etc., when a coin is put in **Automat**

◇ **vendor** *noun*

(a) person who sells (a property) **Grundstücksverkäufer;** *the solicitor acting on behalf of the vendor*

(b) street vendor = person who sells food or small items in the street **Straßenhändler**

venture

1 *noun* business *or* commercial deal which involves a risk **gewagtes Unternehmen;** *he lost money on several import ventures; she has started a new venture - a computer shop;* **joint venture** = very large business project where two or more companies, often from

different countries, join together **Joint venture, Gemeinschaftsunternehmen; venture capital** = capital for investment which may easily be lost in risky projects, but can also provide high returns **Risiko-, Wagniskapital**
2 *verb* to risk (money) **riskieren, aufs Spiel setzen**

venue *noun* place where a meeting is to be held **Tagungsort, Ort;** *we have changed the venue for the conference; what is the venue for the exhibition?*

verbal *adjective* using spoken words, not writing **mündlich; verbal agreement** = agreement which is spoken (such as over the telephone) **mündliche Vereinbarung**
◊ **verbally** *adverb* using spoken words, not writing **mündlich;** *they agreed to the terms verbally, and then started to draft the contract*

verify *verb* to check to see if something is correct **(über)prüfen**
◊ **verification** *noun* checking if something is correct **Überprüfung;** *the shipment was allowed into the country after verification of the documents by the customs*

vertical *adjective* upright *or* straight up or down **senkrecht, vertikal; vertical communication** = communication between senior managers via the middle management to the workers **vertikale Kommunikation; vertical integration** = joining two businesses together which deal with different stages in the production or sale of a product **vertikale Integration**

vessel *noun* ship **Schiff; merchant vessel** = commercial ship which carries a cargo **Handelsschiff**

vested *adjective* **vested interest** = special interest in keeping an existing state of affairs **festbegründetes/persönliches Interesse; she has a vested interest in keeping the business working** = she wants to keep the business working because she will make more money if it does **sie hat ein persönliches Interesse am Weiterbestehen des Unternehmens**

vet *verb* to examine something carefully **überprüfen;** *all candidates have to be vetted by the managing director; the contract has been sent to the legal department for vetting*
NOTE: **vetting - vetted**

via *preposition* using (a means *or* a route) **via, über;** *the shipment is going via the Suez Canal; we are sending the cheque via our office in New York; they sent the message via the telex line*

viable *adjective* which can work in practice **durchführbar, realisierbar, brauchbar; not commercially viable** = not likely to make a profit **nicht rentabel**
◊ **viability** *noun* being viable *or* being able to make a profit **Durchführbarkeit; Rentabilität**
NOTE: no plural

vice- *prefix* deputy *or* second in command **stellvertretend, Vize-;** *he is the vice-chairman of an industrial group; she was appointed to the vice-chairmanship of the committee*
◊ **vice-president** *noun US* one of the executive directors of a company **Vice President;** *entspricht* **Hauptabteilungsleiter; senior vice-president** = one of a few main executive directors of a company **Senior Vice President**

view *noun* way of thinking about something **Ansicht, Meinung;** *we asked the sales manager for his views on the reorganization of the reps' territories; the chairman takes the view that credit should never be longer than thirty days;* **to take the long view** = to plan for a long period before your current investment will become profitable **auf lange Sicht planen; etwas langfristig betrachten; in view of** = because of **angesichts, in Anbetracht;** *in view of the falling exchange rate, we have redrafted our sales forecasts*

vigorous *adjective* energetic *or* very active **aktiv, dynamisch, schwungvoll;** *we are planning a vigorous publicity campaign*

VIP = VERY IMPORTANT PERSON; **VIP lounge** = special room at an airport for important travellers **VIP-Lounge; we laid on VIP treatment for our visitors** *or* **we gave our visitors a VIP reception** = we arranged for our visitors to be looked after and entertained well **unsere Besucher wurden als VIPs behandelt**

visa *noun* special document *or* special stamp in a passport which allows someone to enter a country **Visum, Sichtvermerk;** *you will need a visa before you go to the USA; he filled in his visa application form;* **entry visa** = visa allowing someone to enter a country **Einreisevisum; multiple entry visa** = visa allowing someone to enter a country many times **Visum zur mehrmaligen Einreise; tourist visa** = visa which allows a person to visit a country for a short time on holiday **Touristenvisum; transit visa** = visa which allows someone to spend a short time in one country while travelling to another country **Transitvisum**

visible *adjective* which can be seen **sichtbar; visible imports** *or* **exports** = real products which are imported *or* exported **sichtbare Importe; sichtbare Exporte**

visit

1 *noun* short stay in a place **Besuch;** *we are expecting a visit from our German agents; he is on a business visit to London; we had a visit from the VAT inspector*

2 *verb* to go to a place *or* to see someone for a short time **besuchen, aufsuchen;** *he spent a week in Scotland, visiting clients in Edinburgh and Glasgow; the trade delegation visited the Ministry of Commerce*

◇ **visitor** *noun* person who visits **Besucher/-in;** *the chairman showed the Japanese visitors round the factory;* **visitors' bureau** = office which deals with visitors' questions **Besucherinformation**

visual *adjective* which can be seen **sichtbar, visuell, Anschauungs-; visual display terminal** *or* **visual display unit** = screen attached to a computer which shows the information stored in the computer **Monitor, Bildschirm**

vivos *noun* **gift inter vivos** = present given to another living person **Schenkung zu Lebzeiten**

vocation *noun* type of job which you feel you want to do; wanting to be in a certain type of job **Berufung, Berufsideal;** *he followed his vocation and became an accountant*

◇ **vocational** *adjective* referring to a choice of job **Berufs-; vocational guidance** = helping young people to choose a suitable job **Berufsberatung; vocational training** = training for a particular job **Berufsausbildung**

void

1 *adjective* not legally valid **ungültig,; the contract was declared null and void** = the contract was said to be no longer valid **der Vertrag wurde für ungültig erklärt**

2 *verb* **to void a contract** = to make a contract invalid **einen Vertrag für ungültig erklären/aufheben**

volume *noun* quantity of items **Menge, Umfang, Volumen; volume discount** = discount given to customer who buys a large quantity of goods **Mengenrabatt; volume of output** = number of items produced **Produktionsvolumen; volume of sales** *or* **sales volume** = number of items sold **Absatz(volumen); low** *or* **high volume of sales** = small *or* large number of items sold **geringer Absatz; hoher Absatz; volume of trade** *or* **volume of business** = number of items sold *or* number of shares sold on the Stock Exchange during a day's trading **Umsatzvolumen;** *the company has maintained the same volume of business in spite of the recession*

voluntary *adjective*

(a) done without being forced **freiwillig; voluntary liquidation** = situation where a company itself decides it must close and sell its assets **freiwillige Liquidation; voluntary redundancy** = situation where a worker asks to be made redundant **freiwillige Arbeitsplatzaufgabe**

(b) done without being paid **freiwillig; voluntary organization** = organization which has no paid staff **Wohltätigkeitsorganisation**

◇ **voluntarily** *adverb* without being forced or paid **freiwillig**

vote

1 *noun* marking a paper, holding up your hand, etc., to show your opinion *or* to show who you want to be elected **Abstimmung, Wahl; to take a vote on a proposal** *or* **to put a proposal to the vote** = to ask people present at a meeting to say if they do or do not agree with the proposal **über einen Vorschlag abstimmen lassen; block vote** = casting of a large number of votes (such as of a trade union delegation) all together in the same way **Blockabstimmung, geschlossene Stimmabgabe; casting vote** = vote used by the chairman in the case where the votes for and against a proposal are equal **ausschlaggebende Stimme;** *the chairman has the casting vote; he used his casting vote to block the motion;* **postal vote** = election where the voters send in their voting papers by post **Briefwahl**

2 *verb* to show an opinion by marking a paper *or* by holding up your hand at a meeting **abstimmen, wählen;** *the meeting voted to close the factory; 52% of the members voted for Mr Smith as chairman;* **to vote for a proposal** *or* **to vote against a proposal** = to say that you agree *or* do not agree with a proposal **für od gegen einen Vorschlag stimmen; two directors were voted off the board at the AGM** = the AGM voted to dismiss two directors **bei der Jahresversammlung wurden zwei Direktoren des Board of Directors abgewählt; she was voted on to the committee** = she was elected a member of the committee **sie wurde in den Ausschuß gewählt**

◊ **voter** *noun* person who votes **Wähler/-in**

◊ **voting** *noun* act of making a vote **Wahl, Stimmabgabe; voting paper** = paper on which the voter puts a cross to show for whom he wants to vote **Stimmzettel; voting rights** = rights of shareholders to voting at company meetings **Stimmrecht; non-voting shares** = shares which do not allow the shareholder to vote at company meetings **stimmrechtslose Aktien**

NOTE: no plural

voucher *noun*

(a) paper which is given instead of money **Gutschein; cash voucher** = paper which can be exchanged for cash **Bargeldgutschein;** *with every £20 of purchases, the customer gets a cash voucher to the value of £2;* **gift voucher** = card, bought in a store, which is given as a present and which must be exchanged in that store for goods **Geschenkgutschein; luncheon voucher** = ticket, given by an employer to a worker, which can be exchanged in a restaurant for food **Essensmarke**

(b) written document from an auditor to show that the accounts are correct *or* that money has really been paid **Buchungsbeleg; Beleg, Quittung**

voyage *noun* long journey by ship **Seereise**

Ww

wage *noun* money paid (usually in cash each week) to a worker for work done **Arbeitslohn;** *she is earning a good wage or good wages in the supermarket;* **basic wage** = normal pay without any extra payments **Ecklohn, Grundlohn;** *the basic wage is £110 a week, but you can expect to earn more than that with overtime;* **hourly wage** *or* **wage per hour** = amount of money paid for an hour's work **Stundenlohn; minimum wage** = lowest hourly wage which a company can legally pay its workers **Mindestlohn; wage adjustments** = changes made to wages **Lohnregulierung; wage claim** = asking for an increase in wages **Lohnforderung; wages clerk** = office worker who deals with the pay of other workers **Lohnbuchhalter; wage differentials** = differences in salary between workers in similar types of jobs **Lohngefälle; wage freeze** *or* **freeze on wages** = period when wages are not allowed to increase **Lohnstopp; wage levels** = rates of pay for different types of work **Lohnniveau; wage negotiations** = discussions between management and workers or their representatives about pay **Lohnverhandlungen; Tarifverhandlungen; wage packet** = envelope containing money and pay slip **Lohntüte; wages policy** = government policy on what percentage increases should be paid to workers **Lohnpolitik; wage-price spiral** = situation where price rises encourage higher wage demands which in turn make prices rise **Lohn-Preis-Spirale; wage scale** = list of wages, showing different rates of pay for different jobs in the same company **Lohnskala**

NOTE: **wages** is more usual when referring to money earned, but **wage** is used before other nouns

◊ **wage-earner** *noun* person who earns money paid weekly in a job **Lohnempfänger**

◊ **wage-earning** *adjective* **the wage-earning population** = people who have jobs and earn money **die erwerbstätige Bevölkerung**

> QUOTE European economies are being held back by rigid labor markets and wage structures
> *Duns Business Month*
>
> QUOTE real wages have been held down dramatically: they have risen at an annual rate of only 1% in the last two years
> *Sunday Times*

wagon *noun* goods truck used on the railway **Güterwagen, Waggon**

waive *verb* to give up (a right) **verzichten auf;** *he waived his claim to the estate;* **to waive a payment** = to say that payment is not necessary **die Bezahlung erlassen**

◊ **waiver** *noun* giving up (a right) *or* removing the conditions (of a rule) **Verzicht, Aufgabe;** *if you want to work without a permit, you will have to apply for a waiver;* **waiver clause** = clause in a contract giving the conditions under which the rights in the contract can be given up **Verzichtklausel**

walk *verb* to go on foot **gehen, laufen;** *he walks to the office every morning; the visitors walked round the factory*

◊ **walk off** *verb* to go on strike *or* to stop working and leave an office *or* factory **die Arbeit niederlegen;** *the builders walked off the site because they said it was too dangerous*

◊ **walk out** *verb* to go on strike *or* to stop working and leave an office *or* factory **die Arbeit niederlegen;** *the whole workforce walked out in protest*

◊ **walk-out** *noun* strike *or* stopping work **Arbeitsniederlegung;** *production has been held up by the walk-out of the workers*

NOTE: plural is **walk-outs**

Wall Street *noun* street in New York where the Stock Exchange is situated; the American financial centre **Wall Street;** *a Wall Street analyst; she writes the Wall Street column in the newspaper*

want *noun* thing which is needed **Bedarf, Bedürfnis; want ads** = advertisements listed in a newspaper under special headings (such as "property for sale", or "jobs wanted") **Kleinanzeigen; to draw up a wants list** = to make a list of things which you need **eine Bedarfsliste aufstellen**

war *noun* fighting *or* argument between countries *or* companies **Krieg;** *price war; tariff war*

warehouse
1 *noun* large building where goods are stored **Lager(haus); bonded warehouse** = warehouse where goods are stored until excise duty has been paid **Zollager; warehouse capacity** = space available in a warehouse **Lagerhauskapazität; price ex warehouse** = price for a product which is to be collected from the manufacturer's or agent's warehouse and so does not include delivery **Preis ab Lager**
2 *verb* to store (goods) in a warehouse **lagern**

◊ **warehousing** *noun* act of storing goods **Lagerung;** *warehousing costs are rising rapidly*
NOTE: no plural

◊ **warehouseman** *noun* person who works in a warehouse **Lagerarbeiter**

warn *verb* to say that there is a possible danger **warnen;** *he warned the shareholders that the dividend might be cut; the government warned of possible import duties*
NOTE: you warn someone **of** something, or **that** something may happen

◊ **warning** *noun* notice of possible danger **Warnung;** *to issue a warning; warning notices were put up around the construction site*

warrant
1 *noun* official document which allows someone to do something **Vollmacht; dividend warrant** = cheque which makes payment of a dividend **Dividendenscheck, Kupon; share warrant** = document which says that someone has the right to a number of shares in a company **Aktienbezugsrechtschein**
2 *verb*
(a) to guarantee **garantieren;** *all the spare parts are warranted*
(b) to show that something is reasonable **rechtfertigen;** *the company's volume of trade with the USA does not warrant six trips a year to New York by the sales director*

◊ **warrantee** *noun* person who is given a warranty **Garantieempfänger**

◊ **warrantor** *noun* person who gives a warranty **Garant**

◊ **warranty** *noun*
(a) guarantee *or* legal document which promises that a machine will work properly *or* that an item is of good quality **Garantie;** *the car is sold with a twelve-month warranty; the warranty covers spare parts but not labour costs*
(b) promise in a contract **Gewähr; breach of warranty** = failing to do something which is a part of a contract **Verletzung der Gewährleistungspflicht; Garantieverletzung**
(c) statement made by an insured person which declares that the facts stated by him are true **Gewähr(leistung); wahrheitsgemäße Angabe**

> QUOTE the rights issue will grant shareholders free warrants to subscribe for further new shares
> *Financial Times*

wastage *noun* amount lost by being wasted **Verlust, Schwund;** *allow 10% extra material for wastage;* **natural wastage** = losing workers because they resign *or* retire, not because they are made redundant or are sacked **natürlicher Arbeitskräfteabgang**
NOTE: no plural

◊ **waste**
1 *noun* rubbish *or* things which are not used **Abfall;** *the company was fined for putting industrial waste into the river; it is a waste of time asking the chairman for a rise; that computer is a waste of money - there are plenty of cheaper models which would do the work just as well*
NOTE: no plural
2 *adjective* not used **überschüssig; Abfall-;** *waste materials; cardboard is made from recycled waste paper;* **waste paper basket** = container near an office desk into which pieces of rubbish can be put **Papierkorb**
3 *verb* to use more than is needed **verschwenden, vergeuden;** *to waste money or paper or electricity or time; the MD does not like people wasting his time with minor details; we turned off all the heating so as not to waste energy*

◊ **wasteful** *adjective* which wastes a lot of something **verschwenderisch; unwirtschaftlich;** *this photocopier is very wasteful of paper*

waterproof *adjective* which will not let water through **wasserdicht, wasserfest;** *the parts are sent in waterproof packing*

waybill *noun* list of goods carried, made out by the carrier **Frachtbrief**

weak *adjective* not strong *or* not active **schwach; weak market** = share market where prices tend to fall because there are no buyers **flaue Börse (mit fallenden Aktienkursen); share prices remained weak** = share prices did not rise **die Aktienkurse reagierten schwach**
◇ **weaken** *verb* to become weak **schwächer werden, nachlassen; the market weakened** = share prices fell **die Aktienkurse fielen**
◇ **weakness** *noun* being weak **Schwäche**

> QUOTE the Fed started to ease monetary policy months ago as the first stories appeared about weakening demand in manufacturing industry
> *Sunday Times*
> QUOTE indications of weakness in the US economy were contained in figures from the Fed on industrial production
> *Financial Times*

wealth *noun* large quantity of money owned by someone **Vermögen, Wohlstand; wealth tax** = tax on money *or* property *or* investments owned by someone **Vermögenssteuer**
NOTE: no plural
◇ **wealthy** *adjective* very rich **wohlhabend**

wear and tear *noun* **fair wear and tear** = acceptable damage caused by normal use **normale Abnutzungs- und Verschleißerscheinungen;** *the insurance policy covers most damage but not fair wear and tear to the machine*
NOTE: no plural

week *noun* period of seven days (from Monday to Sunday) **Woche; to be paid by the week** = to be paid a certain amount of money each week **wöchentlich bezahlt werden;** *he earns £500 a week or per week; she works thirty-five hours per week or she works a thirty-five-hour week*
◇ **weekday** *noun* normal working day (not Saturday or Sunday) **Wochentag**
◇ **weekly** *adjective* done every week **wöchentlich;** *the weekly rate for the job is £250;* **a weekly magazine** *or* **a weekly** = magazine which is published each week **eine Wochenzeitschrift**

weigh *verb*
(a) to measure how heavy something is **(ab)wiegen;** *he weighed the packet at the post office*
(b) to have a certain weight **wiegen;** *the packet weighs twenty-five grams*
◇ **weighbridge** *noun* platform for weighing a lorry and its load **Brückenwaage**
◇ **weighing machine** *noun* machine which measures how heavy a thing *or* a person is **Waage**
◇ **weight** *noun* measurement of how heavy something is **Gewicht; to sell fruit by weight** = the price is per pound *or* per kilo of the fruit **Obst nach Gewicht verkaufen; false weight** = weight on a shop scales which is wrong and so cheats customers **falsches Gewicht; gross weight** = weight of both the container and its contents **Bruttogewicht; net weight** = weight of goods after deducting the packing material and container **Nettogewicht; to give short weight** = to give less than you should **zu knapp abwiegen; inspector of weights and measures** = government official who inspects goods sold in shops to see if the quantities and weights are correct **Eichmeister**
◇ **weighted** *adjective* **weighted average** = average which is calculated taking several factors into account, giving some more value than others **Bewertungsdurchschnitt; weighted index** = index where some important items are given more value than less important ones **Bewertungsindex**
◇ **weighting** *noun* additional salary *or* wages paid to compensate for living in an expensive part of the country **Zulage;** *salary plus a London weighting*

welfare *noun*
(a) looking after people **Fürsorge;** *the chairman is interested in the welfare of the workers' families;* **welfare state** = country which looks after the health, education, etc., of the people **Sozial-, Wohlfahrtsstaat**
(b) money paid by the government to people who need it **Sozialhilfe**
NOTE: no plural

> QUOTE California become the latest state for enact a program forcing welfare recipients to work for their benefits
> *Fortune*

well-known *adjective* known by many people **(wohl)bekannt**
◇ **well-paid** *adjective* earning a high salary **gut bezahlt**

wharf *noun* place in a dock where a ship can tie up to load or unload **Kai, Dock**
NOTE: plural is **wharfs** or **wharves**
◇ **wharfage** *noun* charge for tying up at a wharf **Kaigebühren**
NOTE: no plural
◇ **wharfinger** *noun* person who works on a wharf **Kaimeister**

wheeler-dealer *noun* person who lives on money from a series of profitable business deals **(gerissener) Geschäftemacher**

whereof *adverb (formal)* **in witness whereof I sign my hand** = I sign as a witness that this is correct **ich bestätige hiermit die Richtigkeit durch meine Unterschrift**

white *adjective* the colour of snow **weiß; white sale** = sale of sheets *or* towels, etc. **Ausverkauf von Bett- und Tischwäsche**
◊ **white-collar union** *noun* trade union formed of white-collar workers **Angestelltengewerkschaft**
◊ **white-collar worker** *noun* worker in an office, not in a factory **Angestellter**
◊ **white goods** *plural noun*
(a) machines (such as refrigerators, washing machines) which are used in the kitchen **elektrische Haushaltsgeräte**
(b) sheets *or* towels, etc. **Bett- und Tischwäsche**
◊ **white knight** *noun* person *or* company which rescues a firm in financial difficulties, especially which saves a firm from being taken over by an unacceptable purchaser **"Retter in der Not" (bei Übernahmespekulation)**
◊ **White Paper** *noun GB* report from the government on a particular problem **Weißbuch**

> QUOTE the share of white-collar occupations in total employment rose from 44 per cent to 49 per cent
> *Sydney Morning Herald*

whole-life insurance *noun* insurance where the insured person pays a fixed premium each year and the insurance company pays a sum when he dies **Lebensversicherung auf den Todesfall; Risikoversicherung**

wholesale *noun & adverb* buying goods from manufacturers and selling in large quantities to traders who then sell in smaller quantities to the general public **(im) Großhandel;** *wholesale discount; wholesale shop;* **wholesale dealer** = person who buys in bulk from manufacturers and sells to retailers **Großhändler; wholesale price index** = index showing the rises and falls of prices of manufactured goods as they leave the factory **Großhandelspreisindex; he buys wholesale and sells retail** = he buys goods in bulk at a wholesale discount and then sells in small quantities to the public **er kauft im Großhandel und verkauft im Einzelhandel**
NOTE: no plural
◊ **wholesaler** *noun* person who buys goods in bulk from manufacturers and sells them to retailers **Großhändler**

wholly-owned subsidiary *noun* company which is owned completely by another company **100%ige Tochtergesellschaft**

wildcat strike *noun* strike organized suddenly by workers without the main union office knowing about it **wilder Streik**

will *noun* legal document where someone says what should happen to his property when he dies **Testament;** *he wrote his will in 1964; according to her will, all her property is left to her children*

win *verb* to be successful **gewinnen; to win a contract** = to be successful in tendering for a contract **einen Vertrag bekommen;** *the company announced that it had won a contract worth £25m to supply buses and trucks*
NOTE: **winning - won**

windfall *noun* sudden winning of money *or* sudden profit which is not expected **unerwartete Einkünfte, unerwarteter Gewinn; windfall tax** = tax on sudden profits **Sondergewinnsteuer**

wind up *verb*
(a) to end (a meeting) **(be)schließen;** *he wound up the meeting with a vote of thanks to the committee*
(b) to wind up a company = to put a company into liquidation **eine Firma liquidieren;** *the court ordered the company to be wound up*
NOTE: **winding - wound**
◊ **winding up** *noun* liquidation *or* closing of a company and selling its assets **Liquidation; a compulsory winding up order** = order from a court saying that a company must be wound up **gerichtlicher Liquidationsbeschluß**

window *noun* opening in a wall, with glass in it **Fenster; shop window** = large window in a shop front, where customers can see goods displayed **Schaufenster; window display** = display of goods in a shop window **Auslage, Schaufensterdekoration; window envelope** = envelope with a hole in it covered with plastic like a window, so that the address on the letter inside can be seen **Fenster(brief)umschlag; window shopping** = looking at goods in shop windows, without buying anything **Schaufensterbummel**
◊ **window dressing** *noun*
(a) putting goods on display in a shop window, so that they attract customers **Dekoration**

(b) putting on a display to make a business seem better *or* more profitable *or* more efficient than it really is **Bilanzschönung**

wire

1 *noun* telegram **Telegramm;** *to send someone a wire*

2 *verb* to send a telegram to (someone) **telegraphieren, ein Telegramm schicken;** *he wired the head office to say that the deal had been signed*

withdraw *verb*

(a) to take (money) out of an account **abheben;** *to withdraw money from the bank or from your account; you can withdraw up to £50 from any bank on presentation of a banker's card*

(b) to take back (an offer) **zurückziehen; widerrufen; one of the company's backers has withdrawn** = he stopped supporting the company financially **einer der Kapitalgeber der Firma ist ausgeschieden;** *to withdraw a takeover bid; the chairman asked him to withdraw the remarks he has made about the finance director*

NOTE: **withdrawing - withdrew - has withdrawn**

◇ **withdrawal** *noun* removing money from an account **Abhebung; withdrawal without penalty at seven days' notice** = money can be taken out of a deposit account, without losing any interest, provided that seven days' notice has been given **bei Einhaltung der 7-tägigen Kündigungsfrist entstehen keine Gebühren;** *to give seven days' notice of withdrawal*

withholding tax

withholding tax *noun* (i) tax which takes money away from interest *or* dividend before it is paid to the investor; (ii); *US* income tax deducted from the paycheck of a worker before he is paid **(i) (ii) Quellensteuer**

within

within *preposition* inside **innerhalb, in**

witness

1 *noun* person who sees something happen **Zeuge/Zeugin; to act as a witness to a document** *or* **a signature** = to sign a document to show that you have watched the main signatory sign it **ein Dokument od eine Unterschrift bestätigen;** *the MD signed as a witness; the contract has to be signed in front of two witnesses*

2 *verb* to sign (a document) to show that you guarantee that the other signatures on it are genuine **bestätigen, bezeugen;** *to witness an agreement or a signature*

wording

wording *noun* series of words **Formulierung; Wortlaut;** *did you read the wording on the contract?*

NOTE: no plural

word-processing

word-processing *noun* working with words, using a computer to produce, check and change texts, reports, letters, etc. **Textverarbeitung;** *load the word-processing program before you start keyboarding;* **word-processing bureau** = office which specializes in word-processing for other companies **(Computer-)Schreibbüro**

NOTE: no plural

◇ **word-processor** *noun* small computer *or* typewriter with a computer in it, used for working with words to produce texts, reports, letters, etc. **Textverarbeitungsanlage**

work

1 *noun*

(a) things done using the hands *or* brain **Arbeit; casual work** = work where the workers are hired for a short period **Aushilfsarbeit; clerical work** = work done in an office **Schreib-, Büroarbeit; manual work** = heavy work done by hand **körperliche Arbeit; work in progress** = value of goods being manufactured which are not complete at the end of an accounting period **unfertige Erzeugnisse**

(b) job *or* something done to earn money **Arbeit;** *he goes to work by bus; she never gets home from work before 8 p.m.; his work involves a lot of travelling; he is still looking for work; she has been out of work for six months ;* **work permit** = official document which allows someone who is not a citizen to work in a country **Arbeitserlaubnis**

NOTE: no plural

2 *verb*

(a) to do things with your hands *or* brain, for money **arbeiten;** *the factory is working hard to complete the order; she works better now that she has been promoted;* **to work a machine** = to make a machine function **eine Maschine bedienen; to work to rule** = to work strictly according to rules agreed between the company and the trade union, and therefore work very slowly **Dienst nach Vorschrift tun**

(b) to have a paid job **arbeiten;** *she works in an office; he works at Smith's; he is working as a cashier in a supermarket*

◇ **worker** *noun*

(a) person who is employed **Berufstätiger, Arbeiter/-in; blue-collar worker** = manual worker in a factory **Fabrikarbeiter; casual worker** = worker who can be hired for a short period **Aushilfsarbeiter; clerical worker** = person who works in an office **Büroangestellter; factory worker** = person who works in a factory **Fabrikarbeiter;**

manual worker = worker who works with his hands **ungelernte Arbeitskraft; white-collar worker** = office worker **Büroangestellter; worker director** = director of a company who is a representative of the workforce **Arbeitsdirektor; worker representation on the board** = having a representative of the workers as a director of the company **Betriebsrat; Belegschaftsvertretung**
(b) person who works hard **Arbeiter/-in;** *she's a real worker*

◇ **working** *adjective*
(a) (person) who works **arbeitend, berufstätig;** *the working population of a country;* **working partner** = partner who works in a partnership **tätiger Teilhaber; working party** = group of experts who study a problem **Arbeitsausschuß;** *the government set up a working party to examine the problem of computers in schools*
(b) referring to work **arbeitend, Arbeits-; working capital** = capital in cash and stocks needed for a company to be able to work **Working Capital; working conditions** = general state of the place where people work (if it is hot, noisy, dark, dangerous, etc.) **Arbeitsbedingungen; the normal working week** = the usual number of hours worked per week **die normale Arbeitswoche;** *even though he is a freelance, he works a normal working week*

◇ **workforce** *noun* all the workers (in an office *or* factory) **Belegschaft; Arbeitskräfte, Arbeiterschaft**

◇ **workload** *noun* amount of work which a person has to do **Arbeitsbelastung;** *he has difficulty in coping with his heavy workload*

◇ **workman** *noun* man who works with his hands **Arbeiter**
NOTE: plural is **workmen**

◇ **work out** *verb*
(a) to calculate **aus-, be-, errechnen;** *he worked out the costs on the back of an envelope; he worked out the discount at 15%; she worked out the discount on her calculator*
(b) he is working out his notice = he is working during the time between resigning and actually leaving the company **er arbeitet bis zum Ablauf seiner Kündigungsfrist**

◇ **workplace** *noun* place where you work **Arbeitsplatz**

◇ **works** *noun* factory **Werk, Fabrik;** *an industrial works; an engineering works; the steel works is expanding;* **works committee** *or* **works council** = committee of workers and management which discusses the organization of work in a factory **Belegschaftsvertretung; price ex works** = price not including transport from the manufacturer's factory **Preis ab Werk; the works manager** = person in charge of a works **Betriebsleiter**
NOTE: not plural, and takes a singular verb

◇ **work-sharing** *noun* system where two part-timers share one job **Arbeitsteilung**

◇ **workshop** *noun* small factory **Werkstatt**

◇ **workspace** *noun* memory *or* space available on a computer for temporary work **Arbeitsspeicher**

◇ **workstation** *noun* desk with a computer terminal, printer, telephone, etc., where a word-processing operator works **Workstation, Arbeitsplatz**

◇ **work-to-rule** *noun* working strictly according to the rules agreed between the union and management and therefore very slowly, as a protest **Dienst nach Vorschrift**

> QUOTE the control of materials from purchased parts through work in progress to finished goods provides manufacturers with an opportunity to reduce the amount of money tied up in materials
> *Duns Business Month*
>
> QUOTE the quality of the work environment demanded by employers and employees alike
> *Lloyd's List*
>
> QUOTE every house and workplace in Britain is to be directly involved in an energy efficiency campaign
> *Times*

world *noun*
(a) the earth **Welt; the world market for steel** = the possible sales of steel in the whole world **der Weltmarkt für Stahl; he has world rights to a product** = he has the right to sell the product anywhere in the world **die Rechte für ein Produkt weltweit haben**
(b) people in a particular business *or* people with a special interest **Welt, Berufssphäre;** *the world of big business; the world of publishing or the publishing world; the world of lawyers or the legal world*

◇ **World Bank** *noun* central bank, controlled by the United Nations, whose funds come from the member states of the UN and which lends money to member states **Weltbank**

◇ **worldwide** *adjective & adverb* everywhere in the world **weltweit;** *the company has a worldwide network of distributors; worldwide sales or sales worldwide have topped two million units; this make of computer is available worldwide*

> QUOTE the EC pays farmers 27 cents a pound for sugar and sells it on the world market for 5 cents
> *Duns Business Month*
>
> QUOTE manufactures and services were the fastest growing sectors of world trade
> *Australian Financial Review*

worth
1 *adjective* having a value *or* a price **wert;** *do not get it repaired - it is worth only £25; the car is worth £6,000 on the secondhand market;* **he is worth £10m** = his property *or* investments, etc. would sell for £10m **er besitzt £10 Mio; what are ten pounds worth in dollars?** = what is the equivalent of £10 in dollars? **wieviel sind zehn Pfund in Dollar?**
NOTE: always follows the verb **to be**
2 *noun* value **Wert; give me ten pounds' worth of petrol** = give me as much petrol as £10 will buy **geben Sie mir für zehn Pfund Benzin**

◇ **worthless** *adjective* having no value **wertlos;** *the cheque is worthless if it is not signed*

wrap (up) *verb* to cover something all over (in paper) **einwickeln, einpacken;** *he wrapped (up) the parcel in green paper;* **to gift-wrap a present** = to wrap a present in special coloured paper **ein Geschenk verpacken**
NOTE: **wrapping - wrapped**

◇ **wrapper** *noun* material which wraps something **Verpackung;** *the biscuits are packed in plastic wrappers*

◇ **wrapping** *noun* **wrapping paper** = special coloured paper for wrapping presents **Geschenkpapier; gift-wrapping** = (i) service in a store for wrapping presents for customers; (ii) coloured paper for wrapping presents **(i) Geschenkverpackungsdienst ; (ii) Geschenkpapier**

wreck
1 *noun*
(a) ship which has sunk *or* which has been badly damaged and cannot float **Wrack;** *they saved the cargo from the wreck; oil poured out of the wreck of the tanker*
(b) company which has collapsed **Ruin;** *he managed to save some of his investment from the wreck of the company; investors lost thousands of pounds in the wreck of the investment company*
2 *verb* to damage badly *or* to ruin **zerstören: zum Scheitern bringen;** *they are trying to salvage the wrecked tanker; the negotiations were wrecked by the unions*

writ *noun* legal document ordering someone to do something *or* not to do something **gerichtliche Verfügung;** *the court issued a writ to prevent the trade union from going on strike;* **to serve someone with a writ** *or* **to serve a writ on someone** = to give someone a writ officially, so that he has to obey it **jdm eine gerichtliche Verfügung zustellen**

write *verb* to put words *or* figures on to paper **schreiben;** *she wrote a letter of complaint to the manager; the telephone number is written at the bottom of the notepaper*
NOTE: **writing - wrote - has written**

◇ **write down** *verb* to note an asset at a lower value than previously **(teil)abschreiben;** *written down value; the car is written down in the company's books*

◇ **writedown** *noun* noting of an asset at a lower value **Teilabschreibung**

◇ **write off** *verb* to cancel (a debt) *or* to remove an asset from the accounts as having no value **vollständig abschreiben;** *to write off bad debts;* **two cars were written off after the accident** = the insurance company considered that both cars were a total loss **zwei Autos wurden nach dem Unfall als Totalschaden abgeschrieben; the cargo was written off as a total loss** = the cargo was so badly damaged that the insurers said it had no value **die Fracht wurde als Totalverlust abgeschrieben**

◇ **write-off** *noun* total loss *or* cancellation of a bad debt *or* removal of an asset's value in a company's accounts **Vollabschreibung;** *the car was a write-off; to allow for write-offs in the yearly accounts*

◇ **write out** *verb* to write in full **ausschreiben;** *she wrote out the minutes of the meeting from her notes;* **to write out a cheque** = to write the words and figures on a cheque and then sign it **einen Scheck ausstellen**

◇ **writing** *noun* something which has been written **Schriftstück; Schrift;** *to put the agreement in writing; he has difficulty in reading my writing*
NOTE: no plural

> QUOTE $30 million from usual company borrowings will either be amortized or written off in one sum
> ***Australian Financial Review***
>
> QUOTE the holding company has seen its earnings suffer from big writedowns in conjunction with its $1 billion loan portfolio
> ***Duns Business Month***

wrong *adjective* not right *or* not correct **falsch;** *the total in the last column is wrong; the sales director reported the wrong figures to the meeting; I tried to phone, but I got the wrong number*

◇ **wrongful** *adjective* unlawful **unrechtmäßig, widerrechtlich; wrongful dismissal** = removing someone from a job for reasons which are wrong **unrechtmäßige Entlassung**

◇ **wrongly** *adverb* not correctly *or* badly **zu Unrecht; fälschlicherweise;** *he wrongly invoiced Smith Ltd for £250, when he* *should have credited them with the same amount*

Xx

X = EXTENSION

Xerox
1 *noun*
(a) trade mark for a type of photocopier **Xerox;** *to make a xerox copy of a letter; we must order some more xerox paper for the copier; we are having a new xerox machine installed tomorrow*
(b) photocopy made with a xerox machine **Fotokopie;** *to send the other party a xerox of the contract; we have sent xeroxes to each of the agents*
2 *verb* to make a photocopy with a xerox machine **fotokopieren;** *to xerox a document; she xeroxed all the file*

Yy

yard *noun*
(a) measure of length (= 0.91 metres) **Yard;** (NOTE: can be written **yd** after figures: **10yd)**
(b) factory which builds ships **Werft**

yd = YARD

year *noun* period of twelve months **Jahr; calendar year** = year from January 1st to December 31st **Kalenderjahr; financial year** = the twelve month period for a firm's accounts **Geschäfts-, Rechnungsjahr; fiscal year** = twelve month period on which taxes are calculated (in the UK it is April 6th to April 5th of the following year) **Steuerjahr; year end** = the end of the financial year, when a company's accounts are prepared **Jahresabschluß;** *the accounts department has started work on the year-end accounts*
◊ **yearbook** *noun* reference book which is published each year with updated or new information **Jahrbuch**
◊ **yearly** *adjective* happening once a year **jährlich;** *yearly payment; yearly premium of £250*

yellow pages *plural noun* section of a telephone directory (printed on yellow paper) which lists businesses under various headings (such as computer shops or newsagents, etc.) **Gelbe Seiten, Branchenverzeichnis**

yen *noun* money used in Japan **Yen**
NOTE: usually written as **Y** before a figure: **Y2,700** (say "two thousand seven hundred yen")

yield
1 *noun* money produced as a return on an investment **Ertrag; Rendite; current yield** = dividend calculated as a percentage of the price paid per share **laufende Ertrag;** *share with a current yield of 5%;* **dividend yield** = dividend expressed as a percentage of the price of a share **Dividendenertrag; earnings yield** = money earned in dividends per share as a percentage of the market price of the share **Gewinnrendite; effective yield** = actual yield shown as a percentage of the price paid **Effektivertrag; fixed yield** = fixed percentage return which does not change **Festertrag; gross yield** = profit from investments before tax is deducted **Bruttoertrag**
2 *verb* to produce (as interest *or* dividend, etc.) **ein-, erbringen; rentieren;** *government stocks which yield a small interest; shares which yield 10%*

> QUOTE if you wish to cut your risks you should go for shares with yields higher than average
> *Investors Chronicle*

Zz

zero *noun* nought *or* number 0 **Null;** *the code for international calls is zero one zero (010);* **zero inflation** = inflation at 0% **Nullinflation**
NOTE: **nought** is more common in GB English
◊ **zero-rated** *adjective* (item) which has a VAT rate of 0% **mehrwertsteuerfrei**
◊ **zero-coupon bonds** *noun* bonds which do not carry any interest *or* where the interest is contained in the capital gain **Zero-Bonds**
◊ **zero-rating** *noun* rating of an item at 0% VAT **Mehrwertsteuerbefreiung**

zip code *noun US* letters and numbers used to indicate a town or street in an address on an envelope **Postleitzahl**
NOTE: the GB English for this is **postcode**

zone
1 *noun* area of a town *or* country (for administrative purposes) **Zone, Gebiet;**

development zone *or* **enterprise zone** = area which has been given special help from the government to encourage businesses and factories to set up there **Förderungsgebiet; free trade zone** = area where there are no customs duties **Freihandelszone**
2 *verb* to divide (a town) into different areas for planning purposes **in Zonen aufteilen; land zoned for light industrial use** = land where planning permission has been given to build small factories for light industry **für Leichtindustrie vorgesehenes Land**

Deutsch-Englisches Register

Aa

abändern: *alter; amend*
Abänderung: *alteration; amendment*
Abandon: *abandonment of a ship*
Abbau einschränkender Bestimmungen: *deregulation (US)*
abbauen: *axe; cut; mine; run down*
Abbaurecht: *mining concession*
abbiegen: *turn*
abbrechen: *break off; call off*
abbrennen: *burn down*
abdecken: *cover*
Abend: spät am ~ *late-night*
abfahren: *depart*
Abfahrt: *departure; sailing*
Abfall: *waste*
Abfallprodukt: *by-product*
Abfertigung: *check-in counter; forwarding*
Abfertigungshalle: *airport terminal, terminal building*
Abfertigungsschalter: *check-in counter*
Abflauen: *downturn*
abflauen: *slow down*
abfliegen: *depart*
Abflug: *departure*
Abflughalle: *departure lounge*
Abfluß: *efflux*
Abflußrohr: *drain*
Abgaben: politische ~ *political levy*
Abgabenordnung: *tax code*
abgeben: *hand in*
abgeholt: nicht ~ *uncollected*
abgemacht: *agreed*
abgepackt: *prepacked* or *prepackaged*
abgerundet: *in round figures*
abgesagt: *called off*
abgeworben: er wurde ~ *he was headhunted*
abhaken: *check (US); tick*
abhalten: *hold*
abhängig von: *depending on; subject to; subordinate to*
abheben: *draw; withdraw*
Abhebung: *withdrawal*
abheften: etwas ~ *to place something on file*
abholen: *collect; fetch*
Abholgebühren: *collection charges* or *collection rates*
Abholmarkt: *cash and carry*
Abhol- und Zustelldienst: *pickup and delivery service*
Abholung: *collection*
Abkommen: *agreement; covenant; deal; treaty*
Abkommen zur Doppelbesteuerung: *double taxation agreement*
abladen: *land*
Ablader: *shipper*
Ablage: *filing basket; filing tray*
Ablagesystem: *filing system*
Ablauf: *expiration; expiry*
Ablaufdatum: *expiry date*
ablaufen: *expire; lapse; terminate*
Ablaufplanung: *scheduling*
Ableben: *demise*
ablegen: *sail*
ablehnen: *refuse; reject; turn down*
Ablehnung: *refusal; rejection* **allgemeine ~** *blanket refusal*
ablösen: *take over*
Ablösungsschicht: *relief shift*
Abmachung: *agreement* **faire ~** *fair deal*
Abmachungen: zwischenbetriebliche ~ *inter-company dealings*
abmessen: *measure*
Abnahme: *decline; decrease*
Abnahmebescheinigung: *test certificate*
abnehmen: *decline; decrease; diminish; fall away; fall off; slacken off*
abnehmend: *falling*
Abnehmer: *taker*
Abonnement: *subscription* **ein ~ erneuern** *to renew a subscription*
Abonnementspreis: *subscription rates*
Abordnung: *delegation*
abraten: *advise against*
Abrechnung: *account; invoicing; settlement; statement of account* **spezifizierte ~** *itemized account*
Abrechnungsbank: *clearing bank*
Abrechnungstag: *account day; settlement day*
Abrechnungszeitraum: *accounting period*
Abreise: *departure*
abreisen: *check out; depart*
Abriß: *outline*
abrunden: *round down*
abrutschen: *slide; slip*
absacken: *plummet* or *plunge*
Absage: *cancellation; refusal*
absagen: *call off; cancel*
Absatz: *clause; paragraph; sales volume* or *volume of sales* **erwarteter ~** *projected sales* **geringer ~** *low volume of sales* **hoher ~** *high volume (of sales)*
Absatzanalyse: *sales analysis*
Absatzbericht: monatlicher ~ *monthly sales report*
Absatzdiagramm: *sales chart*
absatzfähig: *marketable; saleable*
Absatzfähigkeit: *saleability*
Absatzgebiet: *market; trading area*
Absatzgeschwindigkeit: *rate of sales*
Absatzkosten: *cost of sales*
Absatzkurve: *sales curve*
Absatz laut Verkaufsbuch: *book sales*
Absatzmarkt: *market* **begrenzter ~** *limited market* **monopolistischer ~** *captive market* **wachsender ~** *growth area* or *growth market*
Absatzmix: *sales mix*

Absatzmöglichkeiten: **die ~ analysieren** *to analyze the market potential* **neue ~** *market opportunities*

Absatzplanung: *sales budget*

Absatzpolitik: *marketing policy or marketing plans; merchandising*

Absatzprognose: *sales forecast*

absatzstark: *best-selling*

Absatzvolumen: *sales volume or volume of sales*

Absatzzahlen: *sales figures*

abschätzen: *appraise; evaluate*

Abschätzung: *appraisal; evaluation*

abschicken: *post; send off*

abschieben: *offload*

Abschlagsdividende: *interim dividend*

Abschlagszahlung: *interim payment; payment on account*

Abschlagszahlungen: *progress payments*

abschließen: *clinch; close; conclude; finalize; finish; firm up; lock*

abschließend: *closing*

Abschluß: *completion; deal* **zum ~ bringen** *finalize*

Abschluß-: *closing; final; terminal*

Abschluß auf Termin: *forward contract*

Abschlußtermin: *completion date*

abschneiden: *perform*

Abschnitt: *paragraph; phase; section; stage*

Abschöpfung: *import or levy*

abschreiben: *depreciate; write down*

Abschreibung: **jährliche ~** *annual depreciation* **lineare ~** *straight line depreciation* **vorzeitige ~** *accelerated depreciation*

Abschreibungssatz: *depreciation rate*

abschwächen: *damp down*

Abschwächung: *decline*

Absender: *dispatcher; return address* **zurück an ~** *"return to sender"*

absetzen: *move; set against*

Absetzung: *removal*

absichern: *protect* **sich ~** *to hedge one's bets*

Absicht: *intent*

Absichtserklärung: *letter of intent*

absinken: *slide*

absolut: *absolute; absolutely; total*

absorbieren: *absorb*

abspalten: *hive off*

Abstand: *key money*

Abstandssumme: *premium*

abstempeln: *postmark; stamp*

abstimmen: *ballot; reconcile; vote*

Abstimmung: *reconciliation; vote*

Abstimmung durch Handheben: *show of hands*

abstoßen: *offload; sell off; unload* **etwas ~** *to get rid of something*

abstufen: *grade*

Absturz: *crash* **abstürzen** *to crash*

Abteilung: *department; division; section* **technische ~** *the engineering department*

Abteilung Einkauf: *purchasing department*

Abteilung für Neuemissionen: *new issues department*

Abteilung für Öffentlichkeitsarbeit: *public relations department*

Abteilungs-: *departmental; divisional*

Abteilungsleiter: *head of department or department head or department manager; departmental manager; floor manager (US); shopwalker*

Abteilungsleiterin: *manageress*

Abteilung Verkauf: *sales department*

Abtippen von Dokumenten: *copy typing*

abtreten: *assign*

Abtretender: *assignor*

Abtretung: *assignation; assignment; cession*

Abtretungsempfänger: *assignee*

Abtretungsformular für Bezugsrechte: *letter of renunciation*

abwarten: *hold on*

abwärts: *downward; downwards*

Abwehr: *defence or defense (US)*

Abweichung: *variance; variation* **statistische ~** *statistical discrepancy* **saisonbedingte ~** *seasonal variations*

Abweisung: *rejection*

abwerten: *devalue*

Abwertung: *devaluation*

abwesend: *absent; away*

Abwesender: *absentee*

Abwesenheit: *absence; absenteeism* **in ~ von** *in the absence of*

abwiegen: *weigh*

abzahlen: *redeem*

Abzahlung: *redemption*

Abzahlungskredit: *consumer credit*

abzeichnen: *initial*

abziehbar: *deductible*

Abziehen: *deduction*

abziehen: *deduct; subtract; take away; take off*

abzielen auf: *target*

Abzug: *hard copy; deduction*

abzüglich: *less; minus*

Acker: *field*

adäquat: *adequate*

addieren: *add; add up*

Addiermaschine: *adding machine*

Addition: *addition*

administrativ: *administrative*

Adressat: *addressee*

Adreßbuch: *directory; street directory*

Adresse: *address*

Adressenanhänger: *address label*

Adressenaufkleber: *address label*

Adressenliste: *address list or mailing list*

adressieren: *address*

Adressiermaschine: *addressing machine*

affirmativ: *affirmative*

Agent: *agent; representative*
Agentur: *agency*
agieren: *act*
Agio: *agio; exchange premium*
Agrar-: *agricultural*
Agrarerzeugnisse: *agricultural produce*
Agrarindustrie: *agribusiness*
Agrarökonom: *agricultural economist*
Airline: *airline*
Akademiker: *graduate*
Akkordarbeit: *piecework*
Akkordlohn: **einen ~ erhalten** *to be paid at piece-work rates*
Akkordsatz: *piece rate*
akkreditiert: *accredited*
Akkreditiv: *letter of credit* **unwiderrufliches ~** *irrevocable letter of credit*
akkumulieren: *accumulate*
Akontozahlung: *payment on account*
Akte: *document; file*
Akten: *records*
Aktenkoffer: *attaché case; briefcase*
Aktenkopie: *file copy*
Aktenmappe: *folder*
Aktenordner: *file* **kastenförmiger ~** *box file*
Aktenschrank: *filing cabinet*
Aktie: *share* **schnell steigende ~** *high flier or boom share* **stimmrechtslose ~** *non-voting share*
Aktie mit Wachstumspotential: *share with growth potential or with a potential for growth*
Aktien: *stocks and shares* **neue ~ zeichnen** *to subscribe for shares* **notierte ~** *quoted shares* **teilweise eingezahlte ~** *partly-paid up shares* **unnotierte ~** *unquoted shares* **voll bezahlte ~** *fully-paid shares* **wenig gefragte ~** *neglected shares*
Aktienaufkäufer: **agressiver ~** *raider*
Aktienausgabe: *issue of new shares or share issue*
Aktienbank: *joint-stock bank*
Aktienbesitz: *holding* **wechselseitiger ~** *cross holding; cross holdings*
Aktienbestand: *shareholding; stockholding*
Aktienbeteiligung: *stockholding*
Aktienbezugsrechtschein: *share warrant*
Aktienbuch: *register of shareholders or share register*
Aktienemission: *share issue*
Aktiengeschäft: *stockbroking*
Aktiengesellschaft: *joint-stock company; public limited company (plc); corporation (US)*
Aktienkapital: *share capital*
Aktienkurse: **die ~ fielen** *the market weakened*
Aktienmillionär: *paper millionaire*
Aktienoption: *share option*
Aktienpaket: *lot; parcel of shares* **ein ~ plazieren** *to place a block of shares*
Aktienportefeuille: *a portfolio of shares*
Aktienrendite: *redemption yield*
Aktiensplit: *share split*
Aktien splitten: *to split shares*
Aktientransfer: *transfer of shares*
Aktienübertragungsformular: *stock transfer form*
Aktienzertifikat: *share certificate; stock certificate*
Aktienzertifikate verpfänden: *to pledge share certificates*
Aktien zuteilen: *to allot shares*
Aktienzuteilung: *share allocation or share allotment*
Aktion: *campaign*
Aktionär: *shareholder; stockholder*
aktiv: *active; actively; energetic; keen; vigorous*
Aktiva: *asset*
Aktivität: *activity*
Aktivposten: **leicht realisierbare ~** *realizable assets*
Aktivsaldo: *credit balance*
Aktualisierung: *update* **aktualisieren** *to update*
aktuell: *up to date*
Akzept: *acceptance*
akzeptabel: *acceptable* **nicht ~** *unacceptable*
Akzepthaus: *accepting house*
akzeptieren: *accept*
Akzeptverweigerung: *non-acceptance*
Akzidenzdrucker: *jobbing printer*
Allein-: *sole* **Alleineigentümer** *sole owner*
alleinig: *sole*
Alleinvertreter: *sole agent*
Alleinvertretung: *sole agency*
Alleinvertretungsvereinbarung: *exclusive agreement*
Alleinvertrieb: *sole agency; sole distributor*
allem: **vor ~** *in particular*
Allerbeste: **das ~** *the pick of the group*
Allgefahrendeckung: *all-risks policy*
allgemein: *across-the-board; common; general*
allmählich: *gradual; gradually; slow; slowly*
allmählich einstellen: *phase out*
Alphabet: *alphabet*
alt: *long-standing; old*
alteingesessen: *old-established*
Alter: *old age* **höheres ~** *seniority*
älter: *senior*
Alternative: *alternative*
Altersgrenze: *age limit*
Altersrente: *retirement pension or old age pension*
Altersruhegeld: *retirement pension*
Alterssicherungssystem: *pension plan or pension scheme; superannuation plan or scheme*
Altersversorgung: **betriebliche ~** *occupational pension; company pension scheme* **staatliche ~** *government pension or state pension*
Altmaterial: *scrap*
altmodisch: *out of date; old-fashioned; out of date*
Amortisation: *amortization*
Amortisationszeit: *payback period*
amortisierbar: *amortizable*
amortisieren: *amortize*

Amt: *appointment; office; registry* **sein ~ niederlegen** *resign*
amtlich: *official*
amtlich eintragen: *incorporate*
Amts: von ~ wegen *ex officio*
Amtsarzt: *medical officer of health*
Amtsbezeichnung: *title*
Amtsniederlegung: *resignation*
Amtsschimmel: *red tape*
Amtsweg: den ~ beschreiten *to go through the official channels*
Amtszeit: *tenure*
Analogrechner: *analog computer*
Analyse: *analysis*
analysieren: *analyse* or *analyze*
Analytiker: *analyst*
anberaumen: *schedule*
Anbetracht: in ~ *in view of*
anbieten: *offer*
Anblick: *sight*
andauern: *continue; last*
Anderkonto: *nominee account*
ändern: *amend; modify* **sich ~** *vary*
Änderung: *alteration; amendment; modification; shift*
anderweitig einsetzen: *redeploy*
Andrang: *run*
anerkennen: *allow; respect* **nicht ~** *disallow; repudiate*
Anerkennung: *appreciation; recognition*
Anerkennung der Gewerkschaft: *union recognition*
Anfang: *beginning; start*
anfangen: *begin*
anfänglich: *initial*
Anfangs-: *initial; starting*
Anfangsbuchstaben: *initials*
Anfangsdatum: *starting date*
Anfangsgehalt: *starting salary*
Anfangskurs: *opening price*
Anfangsverkauf: *initial sales*
anfordern: *request; requisition* **etwas ~** *send away for; send off for*
Anforderung: *requisition* **auf ~** *on request* **auf ~ bezahlen** *to pay on demand*
Anforderungen: den ~ genügend *up to standard*
Anfrage: *inquiry*
anfügen: *join*
anführen: *head; lead; quote*
Angabe: *statement* **wahrheitsgemäße ~** *warranty*
Angaben: falsche ~ machen *to make a false statement* **nähere ~** *particulars*
angeben: *quote; return; specify; state*
Angeber: *kite flier*
Angebot: *bid; offer; proposition; quote (informal); range; supply; tender* **ein ~ abgeben** *to put in a bid for something* or *to enter a bid for something* **ein ~ machen** *to make a bid for something; to put in a tender* or *to submit a tender* **günstiges ~** *bargain offer*
Angebote werden entgegengenommen: *open to offers*
Angebotsabgabe: *tendering*
Angebotspreis: *supply price*
Angebot und Nachfrage: *supply and demand*
angehen: *affect; concern*
Angelegenheit: *affair; business; matter*
angemeldet: *registered*
angemessen: *adequate; reasonable*
angenommen: *notional*
angesammelt: *aggregate*
angeschlossen: *affiliated; on line* or *online*
angeschmutzt: *shop-soiled*
angesehen: *reputable*
angesichts: *in view of*
angestellt: *employed*
Angestellte: *staff* **zwanzig ~ haben** *to employ twenty staff*
Angestellten: einen ~ entlassen *to dismiss an employee*
Angestelltengewerkschaft: *white-collar union*
Angestelltenstelle: *office job* or *white-collar job*
Angestellte(r): *employee; white-collar worker* **leitende(r) ~** *executive; senior manager* or *senior executive* **untere(r) ~** *junior clerk*
Angestellter außer Haus: *outside worker*
Angestellter im Außendienst: *outside worker*
angewiesen sein auf: *to depend on; rely on*
angleichen: *adjust; equalize*
Angleichung: *adjustment; equalization*
Angstkäufe: *panic buying*
anhalten: *stop*
Anhang: *rider; schedule*
anhängen: *attach*
Anhänger: *tie-on label*
Anhängeschild: *label*
anhäufen: *accumulate* **sich ~** *pile up*
anhäufend: *cumulative*
anheben: *raise; upgrade*
Anhebung: *uplift*
anheften: *pin up*
anheizen: *fuel*
ankaufen: *purchase*
Ankäufer: *acquirer*
Anklage: *charge; prosecution*
anklagen: *accuse; charge; prosecute*
Anklagevertretung: *prosecution*
ankommen: *arrive; get; reach*
ankündigen: *announce*
Ankündigung: *announcement*
Ankunft: *arrival; arrivals*
ankurbeln: *boost; stimulate*
Anlage: *enc* or *encl; enclosure; facility (US); installation; setup* **in der ~** *herewith* **kurzfristige ~** *short-term investment* **langfristige ~** *long-term investment*

Anlageberater: *investment adviser*
Anlagegüter: *capital goods*
Anlagekapital: *fixed capital*
Anlagen: *plant*
Anlagevermögen: *capital assets or fixed assets*
Anlauf: *start-up*
anlaufen: *take off*
Anlaufhafen: *port of call*
Anlaufkosten: *launching costs*
anlegen: *berth; invest*
Anlegen von Karteikarten: *card-indexing*
Anleihe: **eine ~ auflegen** *to float a loan* **unkündbare ~** *irredeemable bond* **untilgbare ~** *irredeemable bond*
Anleihegarant: *underwriter*
Anleihekapital: *debenture capital or debenture stock; loan capital*
Anleihen: **festverzinsliche ~** *loan stock*
Anmeldegebühr: *registration fee*
anmelden: **sich ~** *check in; register*
Anmeldung: *registration*
annähernd: *approximate; approximately*
Annahme: *acceptance; presumption; receiving* **unwiderrufliche ~** *irrevocable acceptance*
Annahme eines Angebotes: *acceptance of an offer*
Annahmequote: *take up rate*
annehmbar: *acceptable; reasonable*
annehmen: *accept; adopt; carry; pass; presume; take on*
Annonce: *advertisement*
annoncieren: *advertise*
annullierbar: *annullable*
Annullieren: *cancellation*
annullieren: *annul; cancel; nullify; rescind; revoke; set aside*
Annullierung: *annulling; annulment; invalidation; nullification*
anordnen: *arrange; order*
Anordnung: *order; setup*
anpassen: *adjust; readjust*
anpassen an: *gear*
Anpassung: *adjustment; readjustment*
anpreisen: *plug*
anrechenbar: *chargeable*
anrechnen: *offset*
Anrecht: *right; title*
Anrecht auf Belegschaftsaktien: *stock option*
anregen: *encourage; stimulate; suggest*
Anregung: *encouragement; suggestion*
Anreiz: *incentive; inducement; stimulus*
Anreizsystem: *incentive scheme*
Anruf: *call; phone call* **einen ~ entgegennehmen** *to take a call*
Anrufbeantworter: *answering machine*
anrufen: *to make a call; call; ring* **jdn ~** *to phone someone*
Anrufer: *caller*
ansammeln: *hoard*
ansässig: *resident*
Anschaffung: *acquisition; purchase*
Anschaffungskosten: **ursprüngliche ~** *historic(al) cost*
Anschauungs-: *visual*
Anschlag: *notice* **einen ~ machen** *to post up a notice*
Anschlagbrett: *noticeboard*
Anschlagfläche: *display panel*
anschließen: *interface; to plug in*
Anschluß: *extension; port*
Anschlußflug: *connecting flight*
Anschlußstelle: *interface*
Ansehen: *standing*
ansetzen: *reckon; schedule*
Ansicht: *opinion; view*
Ansichtskarte: *card; postcard*
ansonsten: *failing*
Ansporn: *inducement; stimulus*
ansprechen: *appeal*
Anspruch: *claim; entitlement; right; title* **rechtmäßiger ~** *legal claim*
Anspruch erheben auf: *claim*
Anspruchsberechtigter: *rightful claimant*
Anspruchsteller: *claimant*
Anspruchstellung: *claiming*
anstehen: *queue*
anstehend: *pending*
ansteigen: *escalate; increase; rise*
anstellen: *employ* **sich ~** *queue*
anstelle von: *in lieu of*
Anstellung: *employment; place* **feste ~** *staff appointment*
Anstieg: *hike (US); rise* **prozentualer ~** *percentage increase* **sprunghafter ~** *jump*
anstoßen: *hit*
Anstoßwirkung: *knock-on effect*
anstreben: *seek; target*
Anstrengung: *effort*
Ansturm: *run*
Anteil: *concern; cut; holding; interest; proportion*
anteilig or **anteilmäßig:** *pro rata*
Anteilschein: *stock certificate*
ante meridiem: *a.m.*
Anti-Dumping-: *anti-dumping*
antiinflationär: *anti-inflationary*
Antitrust-: *anti-trust*
Antrag: *application; motion; petition; proposal; request* **einen ~ einbringen** *to table a motion* **einen ~ stellen** *to propose a motion* **einen ~ unterstützen** *to second a motion*
Antragsformular: *application form*
Antragsformular auf Schadensersatz: *claim form*
Antragsteller: *applicant; claimant; mover; proposer*
antreiben: *chase; hurry*
Antrieb: *drive*
Antwort: *answer; reply; response*

Antwortcoupon: *reply coupon*

Antwortkarte: frankierte *or* **freigemachte** ~ *reply paid card; prepaid reply card*

Antwortschein: internationaler ~ *international postal reply coupon*

anwachsen: *accrue*

anwachsen lassen: *run up*

Anwalt: *counsel; solicitor (GB)* **einen ~ beauftragen** *to instruct a solicitor; to retain a lawyer to act for a company*

Anwälte: die ~ *the legal profession*

Anwältin: *counsel; solicitor (GB)*

Anwaltskosten: *legal costs or legal charges or legal expenses*

Anwaltsreferendar: *articled clerk*

Anwaltsstand: der ~ *the legal profession*

Anwartschafts-: *reversionary*

anweisen: *instruct*

Anweisung: *instruction; order*

anwenden: *exercise*

Anwender: *user*

Anwendung: *exercise; usage*

anwesend: *present*

anwesend sein: *attend*

Anzahl: *number; quantity; variety* **beschlußfähige** ~ *quorum*

Anzahl der Abschlüsse: *bargains done*

Anzahl der Börsengeschäfte: *bargains done*

anzahlen: *put down*

Anzahlung: *advance; deposit; down payment* **eine ~ leisten** *to pay money on account; to make a deposit; to put money down* **eine ~ verlieren** *or* **verwirken** *to forfeit a deposit*

Anzeige: *advertisement* **alleinstehende** ~ *solus (advertisement)*

anzeigen: *indicate*

Anzeigenbeilage: *stuffer (US)*

Anzeigenblatt: *free paper or giveaway paper*

Anzeigenkosten: *advertising rates*

Anzeigenkunde: *advertiser*

Anzeigenleiter: *advertisement manager*

Anzeigenraum: *advertising space*

Anzeigenraum belegen: *to take advertising space in a newspaper*

anziehen: *advance; attract; rally; tighten*

Anziehungskraft: *appeal*

Apparat: *extension; instrument; machine*

Äquivalenz: *equivalence*

Arbeit: *employment; job; labour or labor (US); work* **die ~ aufnehmen** *sign on* **die ~ niederlegen** *to down tools; walk off; walk out* **doppelte** ~ *duplication of work* **eine ~ erledigen** *to do a job of work* **körperliche** ~ *manual labour or manual work*

arbeiten: *work*

arbeitend: *employed; working*

Arbeiter: *blue-collar worker; hand; labourer; worker; workman* **gewerkschaftlich organisierte** ~ *organized labour* **stundenweise bezahlter** ~ *hourly-paid worker*

Arbeiter aussperren: *to lock out workers*

Arbeiter entlassen: *to lay off workers*

Arbeitergewerkschaft: *blue-collar union; labor union (US)*

Arbeiterschaft: *labour force or workforce*

Arbeitgeber: *employer*

Arbeitgeberanteil: *employer's contribution*

Arbeitgeber-Arbeitnehmer-Beziehungen: *industrial relations; labour relations*

Arbeitgeberverband: *employers' organization or association*

Arbeitnehmer: *employed; employee*

Arbeitsablaufdiagramm: *flow chart; flow diagram*

Arbeitsabläufe auflisten: *to list task processes*

Arbeitsamt: *job centre (GB); employment office*

Arbeitsausschuß: *working party*

Arbeitsbedingungen: *working conditions*

Arbeitsbeginn registrieren: *clock in or clock on*

Arbeitsbelastung: *workload*

Arbeitsbeschaffungsprogramm: *job creation scheme*

Arbeitsdirektor: *worker director*

Arbeitseinkommen: *earned income*

Arbeitserlaubnis: *green card; work permit*

Arbeitsfreistellung zur Geburt: *paternity leave*

Arbeitsgang eines Computers: *a computer run*

Arbeitsgerät: *implement*

Arbeitsgesetze: *labour laws*

Arbeitsgesetzgebung: *labour legislation*

Arbeitsgruppe: *task force*

Arbeitskampf: *industrial dispute or labour dispute*

Arbeitskampfmaßnahmen ergreifen: *to take industrial action*

Arbeitskraft: ungelernte ~ *manual labourer; manual worker*

Arbeitskräfte: *labour or labor (US); labour force; workforce* **angelernte** ~ *semi-skilled workers* **billige** ~ *cheap labour; sweated labour* **entlassene** ~ *redundant staff* **mobile** ~ *mobile workforce* **ortsansässige** ~ *local labour*

Arbeitskräfteabgang: natürlicher ~ *natural wastage*

Arbeitskräftemangel: *labour or manpower shortage*

Arbeitsleistung: *job performance*

Arbeitslohn: *wage*

arbeitslos: *out of work; unemployed* **sich ~ melden** *to sign on for the dole*

Arbeitslosen: die ~ *the jobless; the unemployed*

Arbeitslosengeld *or* **Arbeitslosenhilfe:** *dole; unemployment pay; unemployment benefit or unemployment compensation (US)*

Arbeitslosenschlange: *dole queue*

Arbeitslosigkeit: saisonbedingte ~ *seasonal unemployment* **strukturelle** ~ *structural unemployment*

Arbeitslosigkeit nach Rationalisierung: *redundancy*

arbeitslos sein: *to be out of a job*

Arbeitsmarkt: *labour market*

Arbeitsnachweisbogen: *time sheet*
Arbeitsniederlegung: *walk-out*
arbeitsparend: *labour-saving*
Arbeitsplan: *schedule*
Arbeitsplatz: *job; place of work; workplace; workstation* **sicherer ~** *secure job*
Arbeitsplatzanalyse: *job analysis*
Arbeitsplatzaufgabe: freiwillige ~ *voluntary redundancy*
Arbeitsplatzbeschaffungsprogramm: *job creation scheme*
Arbeitsplatzbeschreibung: *job specification*
Arbeitsplatzbewertung: *job evaluation*
Arbeitsplätze streichen: *to cut jobs*
Arbeitsplatzkürzungen: *job cuts*
Arbeitsplatzsicherheit: *security of employment*
Arbeitsschluß registrieren: *clock out or clock off*
Arbeitsstab: *task force*
Arbeitsstunde: *man-hour*
Arbeitsteilung: *work-sharing*
Arbeitsunfall: *industrial accident; occupational accident*
Arbeitsvermittlung: *job centre*
Arbeitsvertrag: *contract of employment; service agreement or service contract*
Arbeitsvertragsbedingungen: *conditions of employment or conditions of service*
Arbeitswoche: die normale ~ *the normal working week*
Arbeitszeit: flexible ~ *flexible working hours*
Arbeit weitervergeben: *to farm out work*
Arbitrage: *arbitrage*
Arbitragehändler: *arbitrager or arbitrageur*
Arbitrage-Konsortium: *arbitrage syndicate*
Arbitrageur: *arbitrager or arbitrageur*
Archivar: *registrar*
arm: *poor*
Arrangement: *arrangement*
arrangieren: *arrange*
Arrest: dinglicher ~ *attachment*
Art: *kind; mode; style*
Artikel: *article; item; product* **führender ~** *leader* **gängiger ~** *seller* **leichtverkäuflicher** *or* **schnellverkäufliche ~** *fast-selling items*
Arzneimittel: *drug* **patentrechtlich geschütztes ~** *patent medicine; proprietary drug*
Arzt: *doctor*
Ärzteschaft: die ~ *the medical profession*
Ärztin: *doctor*
ärztlich: *medical*
Assistent: *assistant* **persönlicher ~** *personal assistant*
assoziiert: *associate; associated*
Atelier: *studio*
Attaché: *attaché*
Attest: ärztliches ~ *medical certificate*
attraktiv: *attractive*
Attrappe: *dummy pack; mock-up*
Aufarbeitung: *processing*
Aufbau: *organization; structure*
aufbauen: *build; build up; organize; structure*
aufbessern: *supplement*
Aufbesserung: *supplement*
aufbewahren: *store*
Aufbewahrung: *storage*
aufblühen: wieder ~ *revive*
aufbrauchen: *drain*
aufbringen: *afford; raise*
aufdecken: *disclose*
Aufdeckung: *disclosure*
Aufenthalt: *residence; stay*
Aufenthaltsgenehmigung: *residence permit*
auffordern: *invite*
Aufforderung: *demand; invitation*
Auffrischungskurs: *refresher course*
aufführen: *schedule* **einzeln ~** *itemize; specify*
auffüllen: *top up*
Aufgabe: *abandonment; assignment; function; job; task; waiver* **eine ~ erledigen** *to do a job of work*
Aufgabe einer Stellung: *separation (US)*
Aufgabe eines Schiffes: *abandonment of a ship*
Aufgabenbereich: *terms of reference*
Aufgaben der Betriebsleitung: *management function*
aufgeben: *abandon; get out of; leave; mail; scrap*
Aufgeld: *agio; exchange premium*
aufgerundet: *in round figures*
aufgeschoben: *deferred*
aufgrund: *due*
aufhalten: *delay; hold up*
aufhängen: *hang; hang up*
aufhebbar: *annullable*
aufheben: *cancel; cancel out; dissolve; lift; remove; rescind; revoke; set aside*
Aufhebung: *annulment; cancellation; dissolution; invalidation; nullification*
aufhören: *stop*
aufkaufen: *snap up*
Aufkleber: *gummed label; sticker*
aufkommen für: *defray*
Auflage: *batch; circulation; condition*
Auflagen: mit ~ *conditional*
Auflagenhöhe: *circulation*
Auflagennummer: *batch number*
Auflaufen: *accrual* **auflaufen** *to accrue*
auflegen: *hang up*
auflisten: *list*
auflösbar: *terminable*
auflösen: *break up; dissolve*
Auflösung: *dissolution; liquidation*
aufmachen: *open*
Aufmachung: *layout*
Aufmerksamkeit: *attention*
aufnehmen: *absorb; to enter into; take into*
Aufpreis: *surcharge*
aufrechterhalten: *keep up; maintain*

Aufrechterhaltung: *maintenance*
Aufruf: *call*
aufrufen: *access; call; call up*
aufrunden: *round up*
aufschieben: *defer; postpone; put off; shelve*
Aufschlag: *surcharge*
Aufschlüsselung: *breakdown*
aufschlüsseln: *to break down*
aufschreiben: *put down*
Aufschub: *deferment; grace; postponement; shelving; suspension*
Aufschwung: *boom; boost; rally; recovery; upturn*
Aufseher: *overseer; supervisor*
aufsetzen: *draw up*
Aufsicht: *control; superintendent; supervision; supervisor* **unter staatlicher ~** *government-controlled; state-controlled*
Aufsichts-: *supervisory*
Aufsichtsbeamter: *supervisor*
Aufsichtsbehörde: *the factory inspectorate*
Aufsichtsrat: *board; directorate*
Aufsichtsratsmitglied: *director* **nichtgeschäftsführendes ~** *non-executive director*
Aufsichtsratssitzung: *board meeting*
aufstapeln: *pile up*
Aufstellen: *installation*
aufstellen: *draw up; install; nominate*
Aufstellung: *nomination; schedule* **tabellarische ~** *tabulation*
aufsuchen: *visit*
aufteilen: *break up; divide; separate; share*
Aufteilung: *sharing; split*
Auftrag: *assignment; instruction; job; order; purchase order* **einen ~ stornieren** *to countermand an order* **einen ~ vergeben** *to place a contract* **einen ~ verlieren** *to lose an order* **im ~ von** *on behalf of; per pro*
Auftrag an Vertreter: *journey order*
Aufträge: unerledigte ~ *back orders; unfulfilled orders; outstanding orders*
Aufträge weitervergeben: *to farm out work*
Auftraggeber: *client; principal*
Auftragnehmer: *contractor*
Auftragsabwicklung: *order processing*
Auftragsarbeit: *contract work*
Auftragsausführung: *order fulfilment*
Auftragsbuch: *order book*
Auftragserfüllung: *order fulfilment*
auftragsgemäß: *in accordance with* or *according to instructions*
Auftragsrückstände: *unfulfilled orders* or *back orders* or *outstanding orders*
Auftragsverlust: *loss of an order*
Auftrieb: *boost*
Aufwandsentschädigung: *entertainment allowance*
Aufwands- und Ertragsrechnung: *income statement (US)*
aufwärts: *upwards*
aufweisen: *bear; show*
Aufwendungen: außerordentliche ~ *below-the-line expenditure* **betriebliche ~** *operating costs* or *operating expenses*
Aufwertung: *revaluation* **aufwerten** *to revalue*
aufwiegen: *offset*
aufzehren: *drain*
aufzeichnen: *record*
Aufzeichnung: *record; recording*
aufzeigen: *to point out*
Aufzug: *elevator (US); lift*
Augen: unter vier ~ *in private; privately*
augenblicklich: *present*
Auktion: *auction*
Auktionator: *auctioneer*
Auktionshammer: *auctioneer's hammer*
Auktionsposten: *odd lot*
Auktionsraum: *saleroom*
Auktionsräume: *auction mart*
Ausbau: *expansion* **ausbauen** *to expand*
ausbeuten: *exploit*
ausbezahlen: *disburse; pay out*
ausbilden: *train*
Ausbilder: *instructor*
Ausbildung: *apprenticeship; background; training* **außerbetriebliche ~** *off-the-job training* **betriebliche ~** *industrial training; on-the-job training* **innerbetriebliche ~** *in-house training; on-the-job training*
Ausbildungsabgabe: *training levy*
Ausbildungsleiter: *training officer*
Ausbildungsplatz: *traineeship*
Ausbildungsprogramm für Hochschulabgänger: *graduate training scheme*
Ausbildungsvertrag: *indentures* or *articles of indenture*
Ausbruch: *escape*
Ausdruck: *hard copy*
ausdrucken: *print out*
ausdrücken: *express*
ausdrücklich: *express; expressly*
auseinandersetzen: sich ~ *argue*
Auseinandersetzung: *argument*
auserlesen: *select*
auserwählt: *select*
Ausfall: *breakdown* **ausfallen** *to break down*
Ausfallbürgschaftserklärung: *letter of indemnity*
Ausfallzeit: *down time*
Ausfertigung: *copy* **in doppelter** or **zweifacher ~** *in duplicate* **in dreifacher ~** *in triplicate* **in vierfacher ~** *in quadruplicate*
ausfindig machen: *discover*
Ausfuhr: *export; exportation*
Ausfuhren: unsichtbare ~ *invisible exports*
ausführen: *describe; effect; execute; export; fulfil* or *fulfill (US); implement*
ausführlich: *detailed*
Ausfuhrlizenz: *export licence*

Ausführung: *execution; fulfilment; implementation*
Ausführung der Bestellung: *order fulfilment*
Ausführungsanzeige: *contract note*
Ausfuhrzoll: *export duty*
ausfüllen: *fill in; fill out; fill up*
Ausgabe: *copy; disbursement; expense; issue; issuing; output*
Ausgabekurs: *issue price*
Ausgaben: *expenditure; outgoings; outlay; spending* **abzugsfähige ~** *allowable expenses* **geringfügige ~** *petty expenses* **hohe ~** *heavy costs or heavy expenditure* **öffentliche ~** *public expenditure*
Ausgaben der Privathaushalte: *consumer spending*
Ausgabeposten: *item of expenditure*
Ausgabe von Gratisaktien: *bonus issue; scrip issue*
Ausgabe von Schuldverschreibungen: *debenture issue*
Ausgang: *exit; output*
Ausgänge: *outgoings; out tray*
Ausgangsdaten: *raw data*
Ausgangspunkt: *base; starting point*
ausgeben: *disburse; issue; lay out; output; pay out; spend*
ausgebildet: *qualified; skilled*
ausgedehnt: *extensive*
ausgeführt: nicht ~ *unfulfilled*
ausgeglichen: nicht ~ *unbalanced*
ausgelastet: nicht ~ *underemployed; underworked*
ausgenommen: *excepted; excluding; exempt*
ausgerichtet: *oriented or orientated*
ausgerichtet auf: *catering for*
ausgewiesen: nicht ~ *unaccounted for*
ausgezeichnet: *excellent*
Ausgleich: *equalization*
ausgleichen: *balance; equalize; make up for; offset* **sich ~** *to level off or to level out*
ausgliedern: *hive off*
Aushandeln: *bargaining* **aushandeln** *to bargain*
Aushilfsarbeit: *casual work*
Aushilfsarbeiter: *casual labourer; casual worker*
aushöhlen: *erode*
Ausklarierungsschein: *clearance certificate*
auskommen mit: *get on with*
Auskunft: *information bureau or office; inquiry office*
ausladen: *unload*
Auslage: *disbursement; display; window display*
Auslagefläche: *display panel*
Auslagen: *outlay*
Auslagenstand: *display stand; display unit*
Ausland: *overseas* **im ~ ansässig** *resident abroad*
Ausländer: *foreigner*
ausländisch: *foreign; overseas*
Auslandsabteilung: die ~ *the overseas division*
Auslandsauftrag: *indent* **einen ~ erteilen** *to indent for something*
Auslandsbesuch einer Delegation: *outward mission*
Auslandsgespräch: *overseas call; international call*
Auslandsinvestitionen: *foreign investments*
Auslandskonto: *external account*
Auslandsrechte: *foreign rights*
Auslandsvorwahl: *international dialling code*
Auslandswaren: *foreign goods*
Auslandszahlungsanweisung: *foreign money order or international money order or overseas money order*
auslassen: *leave out; omit*
Auslassung: *omission*
Auslastung: wirtschaftliche ~ *commercial load*
Auslastungsfaktor: *load factor*
auslaufen: *to come to an end; finish; peter out; sail*
auslaufen lassen: *discontinue; phase out*
Ausleihen: *lending* **ausleihen** *to lend or to loan*
ausmessen: *measure*
ausnutzen: *exploit*
Auspreisung: konkurrenzfähige *or* **wettbewerbsfähige ~** *competitive pricing*
ausräumen: *empty*
ausrechnen: *compute; work out*
Ausrede: *excuse*
ausreichend: *sufficient*
ausrichten auf: *gear*
ausrüsten: *equip; fit out; tool up*
Ausrüstung: *equipment*
Aussage: *evidence*
ausschalten: *eliminate*
Ausschankzeiten: *licensing hours (GB)*
ausscheiden: *retire*
ausschließen: *eliminate; exclude*
ausschließlich: *exclusive of*
Ausschluß: *exclusion*
Ausschluß der Gewährleistung: *caveat emptor*
Ausschlußklausel: *exclusion clause*
ausschreiben: *write out*
Ausschreibungsschluß: *closing date*
Ausschuß: *board; commission; committee* **einem ~ vorsitzen** *to chair a committee* **gemeinsamer ~** *joint commission of inquiry or joint committee* **geschäftsführender ~** *management committee* **im ~ sitzen** *to sit on a committee*
Ausschußware: *reject*
ausschütten: *distribute*
Außendienst: im ~ *in the field*
Außendienstleiter: *field sales manager*
Außenhandel: *external trade; foreign trade*
Außenhandelsdefizit: *trade gap; trade deficit*
Außenminister: *Foreign Minister; Foreign Secretary (GB); Secretary of State (US)*
Außenministerium: *the Foreign Office; the State Department (US)*

Außenstände: *accounts receivable; outstanding debts; receivables* **nicht einziehbare ~** *bad debts*
außer: *except; excluding*
außerbetrieblich: *external*
außergewöhnlich: *exceptional; extraordinary*
Außerkurssetzung: *demonetization*
außerordentlich: *extraordinary*
äußerst: *extremely*
außerstande sein: *unable*
Aussetzung: *suspension* **aussetzen** *to suspend*
Aussichten: *outlook; prospects*
aussortieren: *sort out*
Aussperrung: *lockout; shutout*
Ausstand: *strike* **im ~** *out (on strike)*
ausständig: *out*
ausstatten: *equip; fit out; furnish*
Ausstattung: *equipment*
ausstehend: *outstanding; receivable*
aussteigen: *back out; get out; pull out*
ausstellen: *display; draw; issue; make out*
Ausstellen von Rechnungen: *billing (US)*
Aussteller: *drawer; exhibitor* **"Zahlung an ~"** *"pay self"*
Ausstellung: *exhibition; show*
Ausstellungsraum: *exhibition room or hall; showroom*
Ausstellungsstück: *exhibit*
Ausstoß: *output*
aussuchen: *pick; pick out; select*
Austausch: *exchange; trade-off*
austauschbar: *exchangeable*
austauschen: *substitute*
Ausübung einer Option: *exercise of an option*
Aus- und Weiterbildungsabteilung: *training unit*
Ausverkauf: *bargain sale; close-out sale (US)*
ausverkaufen: *clear; sell out*
Ausverkauf wegen Inventur: *stocktaking sale*
Auswahl: *choice; range; sample; selection; variety*
auswählen: *choose; pick; pick out; select*
Auswahlkomitee: *selection board or committee*
Auswahlliste: *shortlist* **eine ~ aufstellen** *shortlist*
Auswahlverfahren: *selection procedure*
auswärtig: *non-resident*
Auswärtiges Amt: *the Foreign Office*
auswaschen: *erode*
Ausweichen: *evasion* **ausweichen** *to evade*
Ausweis: *pass*
Ausweitung: *expansion* **ausweiten** *to expand*
Auswertung: *analysis* **auswerten** *to analyse or analyze*
auswirken: sich ~ auf *affect*
Auswirkung: *effect; impact; influence*
Auswirkungen: langanhaltende ~ *durable effects*
auszahlen: *disburse; pay off*
Auszahlung: *disbursement*
Auszubildender: *apprentice; trainee*
Auszug: *extract*
autark: *self-sufficient*
Autarkie: *self-sufficiency*
Auto: ein ~ probefahren *to test-drive a car*
Autofähre: *car ferry*
Automat: *automatic vending machine; dispenser; slot machine*
automatisiert: *automated*
Automatisierung: *automation*
Auto-Montagewerk: *car assembly plant*
Autorenhonorar: *royalty*
autorisieren: *authorize*
autorisiert: *accredited; authorized*
Autoverleihfirma: *car hire firm*
Autovermietung: *car rental firm*
Avis: *advice note* **laut ~** *as per advice*

Bb

Baby Bonds: *baby bonds (US)*
bagatellisieren: *minimize*
Bahn: *rail; railroad (US); railway* **frei ~** *free on rail*
Bahnhof: *station*
Bahnsteig: *platform*
Baisse: *slump*
Baissemanöver: *bear raid*
Baissemarkt: *bear market; a falling market*
Baissier: *bear*
Baissierangriff: *bear raid*
bald: *at an early date*
baldmöglichst: *at your earliest convenience*
Balkendiagramm: *bar chart*
Ballen: *bale* **in ~ packen** *bale*
Bandmaß: *tape measure; measuring tape*
Bank: *bank*
Bankakzept: *bank bill*
Bank-an-Bank-Kredit: *inter-bank loan*
Bankangestellter: *bank clerk*
Bankdarlehen: *bank loan or bank advance; bank borrowing*
Bankdirektor: *bank manager*
Bankeinlagen: *bank deposits*
Bankenkrise: *a banking crisis*
Banker: *banker*
bankfähig: *bankable*
Bankgebühren: *bank charges*
Bankgeschäft: *banking*
Bankgewerbe: *banking*
Bankgiro: *bank giro (GB)*
Bankier: *banker*
Bankinstitut: öffentlich-rechtliches ~ *Trustee Savings Bank*
Bankkonto: *bank account; banking account (US)*
Bankkonzession: *bank charter*
Bankkredit: *bank loan or bank advance; bank credit*

Bankleitzinssatz: *bank base rates*
Banknote: *bank bill (US); bank note or banknote; currency note*
Banköffnungszeiten: *banking hours*
Bankreserve: *bank reserves*
Bankrott: *bankruptcy* **bankrott** *bankrupt*
bankrott gehen: *crash; fail*
Bankrun: *a run on the bank*
Bankschließfach: *safe deposit box*
Banktratte: *bank draft*
Banküberweisung: *bank transfer*
Bankvollmacht: *bank mandate*
Bankwechsel: *bank bill (GB); bank draft; banker's bill*
bar: **etwas ~ kaufen** *to purchase something for cash*
Bär: *bear*
Barangebot: *cash offer*
Barauszahlung: *"pay cash"*
Barbestand: *cash in hand; cash balance*
bar bezahlen: *to pay cash*
Bar-Code: *bar code*
Bargebot: **ein ~ machen** *to make a cash bid*
Bargeld: *cash; cash in hand; hard cash; ready cash*
Bargeldgutschein: *cash voucher*
Bargeschäft: *cash sale; cash transaction*
Barkasse: *petty cash*
Barkauf: *cash purchase*
Barposten: *cash items*
Barpreis: *cash price or cash terms*
Barrel: *barrel*
Barren: *bullion; ingot*
Barrengold: *gold bullion*
Barreserven: *cash reserves*
Barrister: *barrister (GB)*
Barscheck: *open or uncrossed cheque*
Barverkauf: *cash deal; cash sale*
Barvorschuß: *cash advance*
Barwert: *present value*
bar zahlen: *to pay cash down*
Barzahlung: *cash payment; cash; settlement in cash or cash settlement*
Barzahlungsangebot: *cash offer*
Barzahlungsbedingungen: *cash terms*
Barzahlungspreis: *cash price*
Barzahlungsrabatt: *cash discount or discount for cash*
basieren: *base*
Basis: *base; basis*
Basis einer Gewerkschaft: *rank and file*
Basisjahr: *base year*
Basissteuer: *basic tax*
Batch-Betrieb: *batch processing*
Batterie: *battery*
Bau: *construction* **im ~** *under construction*
bauen: *build; construct*
Bauernfänger: *confidence trickster*
Bauernfängerei: *confidence trick*
Bauernhof: *farm*
Baugenehmigung: *building permit; planning permission (GB)* **vorläufige ~** *outline planning permission*
Bauingenieur: *civil engineer*
Bauingenieurwesen: *civil engineering*
Baukostenschätzer: *quantity surveyor*
Baukostenschätzung: *quantity survey* **eine ~ erstellen** *to carry out a quantity survey*
Bauleiter: *site engineer*
Baumaschinenvermietung: *plant-hire firm*
Bauordnungsamt: *the planning department*
Bauplatz: *lot (US); site*
Bausparkasse: *building society (GB); savings and loan (association) (US); thrift (US)*
Bauspekulant: *speculative builder*
Baustelle: *building site or construction site*
Baustoffe: *building materials*
Bauunternehmen: *construction company*
Bauunternehmer: *property developer*
beabsichtigen: *to be going to do something; intend*
Beachtung: *attention*
Beamtendeutsch: *officialese*
Beamtenschaft: *civil service*
Beamter: *officer; official* **höherer ~** *high official* **unterer ~** *minor official*
Beamtin: *officer; official*
beanstanden: *query*
beantragen: *apply; move; petition; request; seek*
beantworten: *answer*
bearbeiten: *handle; process*
Bearbeitung: *handling*
Bearbeitungsgebühr: *handling charge*
beaufsichtigen: *superintend; supervise*
beauftragen: *assign; instruct*
bedanken: **sich ~ bei** *thank*
Bedarf: *demand; requirement(s); want* **den ~ decken** *to meet a demand or to fill a demand*
Bedarf an Arbeitskräften: *manpower requirements*
Bedarfsliste: **eine ~ aufstellen** *to draw up a wants list*
bedauern: *regret*
bedenken: *consider*
bedenkenlos genehmigen *or* **zustimmen:** *rubber stamp*
bedeutend: *grand; important; major*
Bedeutung: *importance* **von ~ sein** *matter*
bedienen: *run; serve*
Bedienung: *service*
Bedienungsanleitung: *handbook; operating manual*
Bedienungszuschlag: *service charge*
bedingt: *conditional; qualified*
Bedingung: *condition; stipulation* **unter der ~** *on condition that*

Bedingungen: günstige ~ *easy or favourable terms* **harte ~ stellen** *to drive a hard bargain* **unter normalen ~** *under normal conditions*
Bedürfnis: *want*
bedürftig: *poor*
Bedürftigkeitsüberprüfung: *means test*
beeilen: sich ~ *hurry*
beeinflussen: *influence*
beeinträchtigen: *prejudice*
beenden: *close; complete; end; finish; terminate*
Beendigung: *completion; end; termination*
Befähigung: *capacity*
befassen: sich ~ mit *to deal with; to be engaged in; handle*
befestigen: *attach; tie*
befinden: *find*
Befolgung: *compliance* **befolgen** *to keep to; to comply*
befördern: *carry; promote; ship; transport; upgrade*
Beförderung: *carrying; handling; promotion; transport; transportation*
Beförderungskosten: *haulage*
Beförderungsleiter: *promotion ladder*
Beförderungsmittel: *transportation*
Befrachter: *freighter*
befragen: *canvass; question*
Befragter: *interviewee*
Befragung: *interview*
befreien: *exempt; release* **befreit** *exempt*
Befreiung: *exemption*
Befreiungsklausel: *escape clause*
Befriedigung: *satisfaction*
befristet: *temporary; temporarily*
Befugnis: *authority; power*
befugt: *authorized*
befürworten: *support*
Befürworter: *seconder*
Befürworter des Freihandels: *free trader*
begehen: *commit*
Beginn: *beginning; start*
beginnen: *begin; open* **mit etwas ~** *to embark on*
beglaubigen: *authenticate; certify*
Beglaubigung: *certificate*
begleichen: *honour; meet; pay*
Begleichung: *discharge; payment*
Begleichung einer Schuld: *liquidation of a debt*
begleiten: *accompany*
Begleitschreiben: *covering letter; covering note*
beglückwünschen: *congratulate*
begreifen: *realize*
begrenzen: *limit*
Begrenzung: *limitation* **zeitliche ~** *time limitation*
begründet: *valid*
Begründung: *reason*
begünstigen: *encourage; favour or favor (US)*
Begünstigter: *beneficiary*
begutachten: *survey*
behalten: *hold; retain*
Behälter: *bin; container*
Behandlung: bevorzugte ~ *preferential treatment*
behaupten: *claim*
beherrschen: *monopolize; dominate*
Behörde: örtliche ~ *local authority*
Behörden: die ~ *the authorities*
bei: *care of*
beibehalten: *keep up*
beifügen: *enclose*
beiheften: *attach*
Beihilfe: *allowance; benefit; grant*
Beilage: *enclosure; insert*
beilegen: *enclose; insert*
Beilegung: *settlement*
beiliegend: *herewith*
beimessen: *attach*
Beirat: *advisory board*
beiseite: *aside*
Beispiel: zum ~ *for example*
Beistand: *support*
Beistandsabkommen: *standby arrangements*
Beistandskredit: *standby credit*
beistehen: *support*
beisteuern: *contribute*
Beitrag: *contribution* **einen ~ leisten** *contribute*
beitragend: *contributory*
Beitragszuschlag: *additional premium*
beiwohnen: *attend*
bejahend: *affirmative; positive*
bekämpfen: *oppose*
bekannt: *well-known*
Bekanntgabe: *publication*
bekanntgeben: *announce; declare*
Bekanntmachung: *announcement; publication*
beklagen: sich ~ *complain*
Beklagter: *defendant*
bekommen: *get; obtain* **zu ~** *obtainable*
Bekräftigung: *confirmation* **bekräftigen** *to confirm*
beladen: *laden; load*
Beladungsgrenze: *maximum load*
belanglos: *petty*
belastbar: *debitable*
Belastung: *charge; strain*
belaufen: sich ~ auf *add up to; to amount to; run; run into; total*
beleben: *revive; stimulate*
Beleg: *receipt; slip; voucher*
belegen: *occupy*
belegen mit: *impose*
Belegschaft: *labour force; personnel; staff; workforce* **zu große ~** *overmanning*
Belegschaftsvertretung: *worker representation on the board*
Belegung: *occupancy*

beliebig: *discretionary*
beliebt: *popular*
beliefern: *furnish; supply*
bemannt: *manned*
Bemannung: *manning*
bemühen: **sich** ~ *attempt*
Bemühung: *attempt*
benachrichtigen: *inform*
Benachrichtigung: *notification* **laut** ~ *as per advice*
benötigen: *require*
benutzen: *use; utilize*
Benutzer: *user*
benutzerfreundlich: *user-friendly*
Benutzerhandbuch: *operating manual; user's guide or handbook*
Benutzung: *use; utilization*
Benutzungsgebühr: *toll*
Benzin: *petrol*
beratend: *advisory; consulting*
Berater: *adviser or advisor; consultant*
Beratung: *consultancy*
Beratungsgremium: *advisory board*
berechenbar: *computable*
berechnen: *bill; calculate; charge; compute; evaluate; reckon; work out* **zu** ~ *chargeable*
Berechnung: *calculation; computation* **annähernde** ~ *approximation* **grobe** ~ *rough estimate; rough calculation*
Berechnungsfehler: *computational error*
berechtigen: *entitle*
berechtigt sein zu: *to qualify for*
Berechtigung: *entitlement; right*
Bereich: *area; operation; range; sector; sphere* **öffentlicher** ~ *public sector*
Bereinigung: *rectification* **bereinigen** *to rectify*
bereisen: *travel*
bereit: *ready* **sich** ~ **machen** *gear up*
bereitstellen: *appropriate; provide*
Bereitstellung: *appropriation*
Bergbaukonzession: *mining concession*
Bergelohn: *salvage money*
Bergung: *salvage* **bergen** *to salvage*
Bergungsgut: *salvage*
Bergungsschiff: *salvage vessel*
Bergwerk: *mine*
Bericht: *report* **vertraulicher** ~ *confidential report*
berichten: *report*
berichtigen: *amend; rectify*
Berichtigung: *rectification*
berücksichtigen: *respect*
Berücksichtigung: *account*
Beruf: *career; occupation; profession* **gefährlicher** ~ *dangerous job*
berufen: *appoint*
beruflich: *occupational; professional*
Berufsausbildung: *vocational training*
Berufsberatung: *vocational guidance*
Berufsbezeichnung: *job title*
Berufsideal: *vocation*
Berufsklassifikation: *job classification*
Berufskrankheit: *occupational disease*
Berufsrisiko: *occupational hazards*
Berufsschäden: *industrial injuries*
Berufsstand: *profession*
berufstätig: *working*
Berufstätiger: *worker*
Berufung: *appeal; appointment; vocation*
Berufung einlegen: *appeal*
Berufungsantrag: *appeal*
Beruhigen: *reassurance* **beruhigen** *to reassure*
berühmt: *famous*
Besatzung: *crew*
Beschädigung: *damage* **beschädigen** *to damage*
beschaffen: *fix up with*
Beschaffenheit: *nature*
beschäftigen: *employ*
beschäftigt: *busy; employed*
Beschäftigter: **ganztätig** ~ *full-timer*
Beschäftigung: *employment* **einträgliche** ~ *gainful employment*
Beschäftigungsdauer: *length of service*
Beschäftigungsmöglichkeiten: *employment or job opportunities*
Beschäftigungsprogramm: *job creation scheme*
Bescheid: *answer; note; notice*
bescheinigen: *certify*
Bescheinigung: **ärztliche** ~ *doctor's certificate*
Beschlagnahme: *seizure*
beschlagnahmen: *impound; seize*
beschleunigen: *hurry; speed up*
beschleunigt: *accelerated*
beschließen: *decide; fix; resolve; wind up*
Beschluß: *decision; resolution* **einen** ~ **fassen** *resolve*
beschlußfähig sein: *to have a quorum*
Beschlußfassung: *decision making*
beschränken: *limit; restrict*
beschränkt: *limited*
Beschränkung: *limitation; restraint; restriction*
beschreiben: *describe*
Beschreibung: *description; specification*
beschuldigen: *accuse; blame*
Beschwerde: *complaint; grievance* **eine** ~ **vorbringen** *to air a grievance*
Beschwerdeabteilung: *complaints department*
Beschwerdebrief: *letter of complaint*
Beschwerdeweg: *complaints procedure; grievance procedure*
beschweren: **sich** ~ *complain*
beschwerlich: *onerous*
beseitigen: *eliminate*
besetzen: *man*
besetzt: *engaged; manned*
Besetztzeichen: *engaged tone*
Besetzung: *manning*

Besitz: *fortune; occupancy; possession(s); property* **beweglicher ~** *goods and chattels*
besitzen: *hold; own; possess*
Besitzer: *holder* **den ~ wechseln** *to change hands*
Besitznahme eines Gebäudes: *occupation of a building*
Besitztümer: *possessions*
besonderer: *particular; special*
besonders: *in particular*
besorgen: *fix up with*
Besorgnis: *concern*
besprechen: *discuss*
Besprechung: *briefing; conference; discussion; meeting*
Besprechungszimmer: *conference room*
besser: *better; superior*
Besserung: *improvement*
Bestallungsurkunde zum Nachlaßverwalter: *letters of administration*
Bestand: *pool; supply*
Bestände: *stock-in-trade; store*
Bestände aufnehmen: *inventory*
beständig: *firm; stable; steady*
Beständigkeit: *firmness; permanency; stability; steadiness*
Bestandsaufnahme: *stocktaking*
Bestandsdatei: *master copy of a file*
Bestandskontrolle: *inventory control*
Bestandteil: *component*
bestätigen: *acknowledge; certify; confirm; validate; witness*
Bestätigung: *acknowledgement; certificate; confirmation; validation*
Bestätigungsschreiben: *confirmation; letter of acknowledgement*
Bestechungsgeld: *bribe* **bestechen** *to bribe*
bestehen: *pass* **auf etwas ~** *hold out for*
bestehen aus: *consist of*
Bestellbuch: *order book*
bestellen: *book; order* **etwas ~** *send away for; send off for*
bestellt: *on order*
Bestellung: *order; purchase order* **auf ~ anfertigen** *customize* **eine ~ aufgeben** *to place an order* **eine ~ ausführen** *to deal with an order; to fulfil an order* **einer ~ nachkommen** *to fill* or *to fulfil an order*
bestens verkaufen: *sell at best*
besteuern: *tax* **besteuerbar** *taxable*
Besteuerung: *taxation*
bestimmen: *determine; rule*
bestimmt durch: *subordinate to*
bestimmter: ein ~ *a certain*
Bestimmung: *provision*
Bestimmung der Vertragsstrafe: *penalty clause*
Bestimmungsort: *destination*
bestrafen: *penalize*
Bestrebung: *aim*
bestreikt: *strikebound*
Besuch: *call; visit* **unangemeldeter ~** *cold call*
besuchen: *visit* **jdn ~** *to call on someone*
Besucher: *caller; visitor*
Besucherinformation: *visitors' bureau*
Besuchshäufigkeit: *call rate*
Beteiligter: *interested party*
Beteiligung: *holding; interest; participation; stake* **gegenseitige ~** *cross holdings; reciprocal holdings*
Beteiligungen: seine ~ offenlegen *to declare an interest*
Beteiligungsgesellschaft: *associate company*
Betracht: in ~ ziehen *entertain*
beträchtlich: *considerable; considerably; substantial*
Betrag: *amount; sum*
Beträge: historische ~ *historical figures* **saisonbereinigte ~** *seasonally adjusted figures*
betragen: *to amount to*
betrauen: *assign*
betreffen: *affect; concern; hit*
betreffend: *with regard to; regarding*
betreffs: *re*
betreiben: *run*
Betreuung: gastronomische ~ *catering*
Betrieb: *business; establishment; operating* **gewerkschaftspflichtiger ~** *closed shop* **im ~** *on the shop floor* **in ~** *going; in operation; in use* **in ~ nehmen** *to come on stream*
betrieblich: *operational*
Betrieb mit Staatsaufträgen: *government contractor*
Betriebsaltersversorgung: *occupational pension scheme*
Betriebsamkeit: *activity*
Betriebsanalyse: *operations review*
Betriebsanlage: *facility (US)*
Betriebsarzt: *company doctor*
Betriebsbudget: *operational budget*
Betriebsfeuerwehrmann: *fire safety officer*
Betriebsgewinn: *operating profit*
betriebsintern: *in-house*
Betriebskosten: *business expenses; operating costs* or *running costs; overhead costs*
Betriebsleiter: *works manager*
Betriebsplanung: *operational planning*
Betriebsrat: *worker representation on the board*
Betriebsratsgespräch: *joint discussions*
Betriebsrente: *occupational pension*
Betriebsrentenplan: *company pension scheme*
Betriebsstörung: *breakdown*
Betriebssystem: *operating system*
Betriebsunfall: *industrial accident*
Betriebsverein: *staff club*
Betriebsverlust: *operating loss*
Betriebsvorschriften: *company rules*
Betriebswirtschaftsplan: *operating budget*
Betriebszeit: *computer time*
Betriebszeitung: *house journal* or *house magazine* or *house organ (US)*

betrifft: was ... ~ *with respect to*
Betrug: *confidence trick; deceit or deception; fraud; scam (informal)*
betrügen: *cheat*
Betrüger: *confidence trickster; racketeer*
Betrügerei: *deceit or deception; racket*
betrügerisch: *fraudulent*
Betrugsdezernat: *fraud squad*
Bett- und Tischwäsche: *white goods*
beurkunden: *authenticate*
Beurlaubung: *leave of absence*
beurteilen: *judge*
Beutel: *bag*
Bevölkerung: die erwerbstätige ~ *the wage-earning population* **nicht seßhafte ~** *floating population*
bevollmächtigen: *authorize; delegate*
bevollmächtigt: *accredited; authorized*
Bevollmächtigter: *attorney; delegate; proxy*
Bevollmächtigung: *authorization; delegation*
bevorzugen: *favour or favor (US); prefer*
bevorzugt: *favourite; preferential*
bewältigen: zu ~ *manageable*
beweglich: *mobile; moveable*
Beweglichkeit: *mobility*
Bewegung: *motion; movement*
Beweis: *proof*
bewerben: sich ~ *apply*
Bewerber: *applicant; candidate*
Bewerber aussondern *or* **sieben:** *to screen candidates*
Bewerbung: *application* **erneute ~** *reapplication*
Bewerbungsausschuß: *selection board or selection committee*
Bewerbungsformular: *application form*
Bewerbungsschreiben: *letter of application*
bewerten: *appraise*
Bewertung: *appraisal; valuation*
Bewertung des Lagerbestandes: *stock valuation*
Bewertungsdurchschnitt: *weighted average*
Bewertungsindex: *weighted index*
bewilligen: *allow; authorize; grant*
Bewilligung: *permission*
bewirtschaften: *farm*
Bewirtung: *entertainment* **bewirten** *to entertain*
Bewirtungsentschädigung: *entertainment allowance*
Bewirtungsspesen: *entertainment expenses*
bewohnen: *occupy*
Bewohner: *occupant; occupier*
bezahlen: *pay; remunerate* **ganz ~** *pay up* **nicht ~** *default*
Bezahlung: *payment; remuneration; settlement* **die ~ erlassen** *to waive a payment* **sofortige ~** *spot cash*
Bezahlung in Naturalien: *payment in kind*
bezeichnen: *mark*
bezeugen: *witness*
beziehen: *obtain* **sich ~ auf** *refer*
Beziehen eines Gebäudes: *occupation of a building*
Beziehungen: *connections; relations*
beziehungsweise: *respectively*
Bezirk: *territory*
Bezirksleiter: *area manager*
Bezogener: *drawee*
Bezug: *reference*
bezug: in ~ auf *with regard to; in relation to; with respect to*
Bezüge: *emoluments*
bezüglich: *re; with regard to; regarding*
Bezugnahme: in ~ auf *re*
Bezugsrecht: *a pre-emptive right (US)*
Bezugsrechtsausgabe: *rights issue*
Bezugsrechtsemission: *rights issue*
bezweifeln: *query; question*
Bieten: *bidding*
bieten: *offer* **auf** *or* **für etwas ~** *to bid for something*
Bieter: *bidder*
Bilanz: *balance sheet* **eine gesunde ~** *a healthy balance sheet* **eine ~ saldieren** *bring down* **konsolidierte ~** *consolidated accounts* **vorläufige ~** *trial balance*
Bilanzschönung: *window dressing*
Bilanzwert: *book value*
bilateral: *bilateral*
Bildchen: *pix (informal)*
bilden: *establish*
Bildschirm: *monitor; screen*
Billig-: *budget; down market*
billig: *cheap; cheaply; down market*
billigen: *to approve of*
Billigladen: *cut-price store; discount store*
Billion: *billion (Brit)*
binden: *bind; tie*
bindend: *binding; obligatory*
Binnenhafen: *inland port*
Binnenhandel: *internal trade; home trade*
Binnenmarkt: *home or domestic market* **der ~** *the Single Market*
bis jetzt: *to date*
Bitte: *request*
bitten: *ask; ask for; request*
bitte nachsenden: *please forward or to be forwarded*
bitte warten: *hold the line please*
Blanko-: *open-ended or open-end (US)*
Blankokredit: *open credit*
Blankoscheck: *blank cheque*
Blätter zusammenheften: *to staple papers together*
Blatt Papier: *sheet of paper*
bleiben: *remain; stay*
Blindband: *dummy (book)*
Block: *pad*
Blockabstimmung: *block vote*

blockieren: *block; jam*
blockiert: *frozen*
Blockschrift: *block capitals or block letters*
Blue-chips: *blue-chip investments or blue-chip shares*
blühen: *flourish; thrive*
blühend: *booming; flourishing; prosperous*
Blumengutschein: *flower token*
Blüte: *dud (informal)*
Blütezeit: *bonanza*
Boden: *floor; ground* **marginaler ~** *marginal land*
Bodenfläche: *floor space*
Bodenpersonal: weibliches ~ *ground hostess*
Bodenschätze: *natural resources*
Bodentransport: *surface transport*
Bohrinsel: *oil platform; oil rig*
Bon: *chit; sales slip*
Bona-Fide-Angebot: *bona fide offer*
Bonität: *creditworthiness; standing*
Bonitätsbestätigung: *comfort letter; letter of comfort*
Bonitätsbeurteilung: *credit rating*
Bonus aus Kapitalerträgen: *capital bonus*
Boom: *boom*
Boot: *boat*
Bord: an ~ *on board* **an ~ gehen** *board* **frei an ~** *free on board (f.o.b.)* **über ~ werfen** *jettison*
Bordkarte: *boarding card or boarding pass; embarkation card*
borgen: *borrow*
Börse: *Stock Exchange; stock market* **flaue ~** *weak market* **lebhafte ~** *lively market*
Börsenanalytiker: *market economist*
Börsengeschäft: *bargain; Stock Exchange operation*
Börsenhändler: *(stock) jobber*
Börsenkapitalisierung: *market capitalization*
Börsenkrach: *crash*
Börsenkurse: die ~ manipulieren *to manipulate the market*
Börsenmakler: *(stock)broker*
Börsennotierung: *Stock Exchange listing*
Börsenoptimismus: *market optimism*
Börsenratgeber: *tip sheet*
Börsenspekulant: *operator; punter; speculator*
Börsenticker: *ticker (US)*
Börsentransaktion: *a transaction on the Stock Exchange*
Boss: *boss (informal)*
Bote: *messenger*
Botenjunge: *messenger boy; office boy*
Boutique: *boutique*
Boykott: *boycott*
boykottieren: *black; boycott*
Branche: *industry; line of business or line of work; trade*
Branchenadreßbuch: *commercial directory; trade directory*
Branchenblatt: *trade journal*
Branchenverzeichnis: *classified directory; yellow pages*
Brand: in ~ geraten *to catch fire*
Brandschaden: *fire damage*
Brandschutz: *fire safety*
brauchbar: *useful; viable*
brauchen: *require; take*
Break-even-Point: *breakeven point*
brechen: *smash*
breit: *extensive*
bremsen: *check*
Brennstoff: *fuel*
Brett: *panel*
Brief: *letter*
Briefeschreiber: *correspondent*
Brieffach: *pigeonhole*
Briefgebühr: *letter rate or parcel rate*
Briefkasten: *letter box; mail box*
Briefkastenadresse: *accommodation address*
Briefkopf: *letter heading or heading on notepaper; letterhead*
Briefkurs: *asking price*
Briefmarke: *(postage) stamp*
Briefpapier: *notepaper*
Briefpost: *letter post or parcel post*
Briefpost erster Klasse: *first-class mail*
Briefumschlag: *envelope* **offener ~** *unsealed envelope* **verschlossener ~** *sealed envelope*
Briefwahl: *postal ballot; postal vote*
Briefwerbeaktion: *mail shot; mailing shot*
Briefwerbung: *direct-mail advertising*
bringen: *bear; bring; bring in; carry; earn; produce*
Broschüre: *booklet; brochure; pamphlet*
Bruchschaden: *breakages*
Bruchteil: *fraction*
Bruchteilsaktie: *fractional certificate*
Brückenwaage: *weighbridge*
brutto: *gross*
Bruttoeinkommen: *gross earnings; gross income*
Bruttoeinnahmen: *gross earnings; gross receipts*
brutto einnehmen: *gross*
Bruttoertrag: *gross yield*
Bruttogehalt: *gross salary*
Bruttogewicht: *gross weight*
Bruttogewinn: *gross profit*
Bruttoinlandsprodukt: *gross domestic product*
Bruttomarge: *gross margin*
Bruttomehrwertsteuer: *output tax*
Bruttosozialprodukt: *gross national product*
Bruttotonnage: *gross tonnage*
brutto verdienen: *gross*
Bruttoverdienst: *gross income or gross salary*
B-Sortiment: *reject; seconds*
Buch: *book* **buchen** *to book*
Bücher: *a company's accounts* **die ~ abschließen** *to close the accounts* **die ~ führen** *to keep the accounts* **die ~ schönen** *to manipulate the accounts*

Büchergutschein: *book token*
Bücherstand: *bookstall*
Buch führen über: *log*
Buchführung: *bookkeeping* **doppelte ~** *double-entry bookkeeping* **einfache ~** *single-entry bookkeeping*
Buchführungsarbeit: *bookwork*
Buchgewinn: *paper profit*
Buchhalter: *accountant; bookkeeper*
Buchhaltung: *accounts department; accountancy; accounting*
Buchhaltungsabteilung: *counting house*
Buchhändler: *bookseller*
Buchhandlung: *bookshop; bookstore (US)*
Buchprüfung: *audit* **ordentliche ~** *general audit*
Buchstabe: *letter*
Buchung: *booking* **eine ~ bestätigen** *to confirm a booking*
Buchungsbeleg: *voucher*
Buchungsbestätigung: *confirmation of a booking*
Buchungsverfahren: *accounting procedures*
Buchwert: *book value*
Budget: *budget* **das ~ planen** *budget*
Budgetabweichung: *budget variance*
Budgetbedarf: *budgetary requirements*
Budgeterfordernisse: *budgetary requirements*
Budgetgrenze: **seine ~ überschreiten** *to overspend one's budget*
budgetieren: *budget*
Budget-Konto: *budget account*
Budgetkontrolle: *budgetary control*
Budgetpolitik: *budgetary policy*
Bummelstreik: *go-slow*
Bund: *association*
bündeln: *bale*
Bundes-: *federal*
Bundesstaat: *state*
Bundestagswahl: *general election*
Bürge: *guarantor; surety*
bürgen: **für jdn ~** *to go guarantee for someone; to stand security for someone*
bürgen für: *underwrite*
bürgerlich: *civil*
Bürgschaft: *guarantee; security*
Büro: *bureau; office* **abgeschlossenes ~** *self-contained office*
Büroangestellte: *clerkess* **arbeitslose ~** *unemployed office workers*
Büroangestellter: *clerical worker; clerk; white-collar worker; office worker*
Büroarbeit: *clerical work*
Büroartikelfirma: *office supplies firm*
Büroaushilfskraft: *temp* **als ~ arbeiten** *temp*
Büroausstattung: *business equipment*
Bürobedarf: *office supplies*
Bürobote: *office messenger; office boy*
Bürochef: *chief clerk or head clerk*
Büroeinrichtung: *business equipment; office equipment*
Bürogebäude: *office premises or shop premises*
Bürohaus: *a block of offices or an office block*
Bürohilfe: *office junior*
Büroklammer: *paperclip*
Bürokratie: *red tape*
Büromöbel: *office furniture*
Büropersonal: *clerical staff; office staff*
Büropersonalvermittlung: *staff agency*
Büroraum: *office space*
Büro-Service: *service bureau*
Bürovorsteher: *administrator*
Bürozeit: *office hours*
Bürozwecke: **nur für ~** *for office use only*
Bus: *bus*
Business Class: *business class*
Buße: *penalty*
Busstrecke: *bus route*
Busunternehmer: *bus company*
Butterberg: *butter mountain*
Byte: *byte*

Cc

Carnet: *carnet*
Cashflow: *cash flow* **diskontierter ~** *discounted cash flow*
Cashflow-Bericht: *cash flow statement*
Cashflow-Prognose: *cash flow forecast*
Cent: *cent*
Centstück: *penny (informal)* **25 ~** *quarter (informal)*
Chance: *chance; opportunity; prospect*
Chancengleichheitsplan: *equal opportunities programme*
Charterer: *charterer*
Charterflug: *charter flight*
Charterflugzeug: *charter plane*
chartern: *charter*
Chartist: *chartist*
Chef: *boss (informal); head*
Chiffre: *box number; code*
Chiffrierung: *coding*
chronisch: *chronic*
cif: *cost, insurance and freight*
circa: *approximately; around*
City: **die ~** *the City*
Clearingbank: *clearing bank*
Clearingkasse: *clearing house*
Code: *code*
Codes: **computerlesbare** *or* **maschinenlesbare ~** *machine-readable codes*
Computer: *computer* **auf ~ umstellen** *computerize*
Computerausdruck: *computer listing*
Computer-Ausdruck: *computer printout*
Computerchip: *computer chip*
Computerdatei: *computer file*

Computerfehler: *computer error*
computerisieren: *computerize*
Computernetz: *computer network*
Computerprogramm: *computer program*
Computerprogrammierer: *computer programmer*
Computer-Schreibbüro: *word-processing bureau*
Computersprache: *computer language*
Computersystem: *computer system*
Computerterminal: *computer terminal*
Computerzeitschrift: *computer magazine*
Container: *container* **auf ~ umstellen** *containerize*
Containerladung: *lorry-load or container-load*
Containerschiff: *container ship*
Containerterminal: *container terminal*
Containerzug: *freightliner*
Copy-Shop: *photocopying bureau*
Coupon: *coupon; reply coupon* **cum** *or* **mit ~** *cum coupon*
Couponanzeige: *coupon ad (informal)*
Courtage: *brokerage or broker's commission; jobber's turn*
Couvert: *cover charge*
Crash: *crash*

Dd

Dachgesellschaft: *holding company*
Dachorganisation: *umbrella organization*
dämpfen: *damp down*
dank: *thanks to*
Danke: *thanks*
danken: *thank*
"dankend erhalten": *"received with thanks"*
Danksagungsadresse: *vote of thanks*
darlegen: *set out*
Darlehen: *advance; credit; loan* **ein ~ sichern** *to secure a loan* **gesichertes ~** *secured loan* **kurzfristiges ~** *short-term loan* **langfristiges ~** *long-term loan* **ungesichertes ~** *unsecured loan* **zinsfreies** *or* **zinsloses ~** *interest-free credit; soft loan*
Darlehensbetrag: *principal*
Darlehensnehmer: *borrower*
Darstellung: falsche ~ *misrepresentation* **grafische ~** *diagram*
Datei: *file*
Daten: *data* **fehlende ~** *lack of data* **numerische ~** *numeric data*
Datenabruf: *information retrieval*
Datenbank: *data bank; database*
Dateneingabe: *input of information; keyboarding*
Daten eingeben: *to input information*
Datenerfassung: *data acquisition*
Datenkasse: *electronic point of sale*
Datentypist: *keyboarder*
Datenverarbeitung: elektronische ~ *electronic data processing*
Datenverarbeitung/EDV: auf ~ umstellen *computerize*
Datenwiedergewinnung: *data retrieval*
Daten zugänglich machen: *to share data*
datieren: *date* **datiert** *dated*
Datum: *date*
Datumsstempel: *date stamp*
Dauer: *life; term*
Dauerarbeitslosigkeit: *chronic unemployment*
Dauerauftrag: *banker's order; standing order*
Dauergäste: *long-stay guests*
dauerhaft: *permanent*
Dauerhaftigkeit: *permanency*
Dauerkarte: *season ticket*
dauern: *last*
dazu: *in addition to*
dazubringen: *persuade*
Dealen: *traffic*
Debatte: *discussion*
Debet: *debit*
Debetseite: *debit side*
Debetspalte: *debit column*
Decke: *blanket; ceiling*
decken: *cover; meet*
Deckenleuchte: *ceiling light*
Deckladung: *deck cargo*
Deckung: *collateral; cover*
Deckungszusage: *binder (US); cover note*
Defekt: *defect; fault*
defekt: *defective; faulty*
Defizit: *deficiency; deficit; shortfall* **ein ~ ausgleichen** *to make good a deficit*
defizitär: *adverse*
Defizitwirtschaft: *deficit financing*
Deflation: *deflation*
deflationär: *deflationary*
dehnen: *stretch*
Deklaration: *declaration*
Dekoration: *window dressing*
Dekorationsmaterial: *display material*
Delegation: *delegation; mission*
Delegation ins Ausland: *outward mission*
delegieren: *delegate*
Delegierter: *delegate*
Delikt: *crime; tort*
Delkredereagent: *del credere agent*
dementsprechend: *accordingly*
denken an: *remember*
Denkfabrik: *think tank*
deponieren: *deposit*
Deport: *backwardation*
Depot: *depositary (US); depository; depot*
Depression: *depression; slump*
Deregulation: *deregulation (US)*
derzeitig: *current; present*

Design-Abteilung: *design department*
designiert: *designate; -elect*
desinvestieren: *disinvest*
Desinvestition: *disinvestment*
Detail: *detail*
detailliert: *in detail; detailed*
deutlich: *clear; plain*
Deutsche Bundespost: *the Post Office*
Devisen: *foreign currency; foreign exchange*
Devisenhandel: *foreign exchange dealing*
Devisenhändler: *foreign exchange broker or dealer*
Devisenkonto: *foreign currency account*
Devisenkontrolle: *exchange controls*
Devisenmakler: *foreign exchange broker or dealer*
Devisenmarkt: *foreign exchange market*
Devisenreserven: *foreign currency reserves; foreign exchange reserves*
Devisenterminkurs: *forward (exchange) rate*
Devisentransfer: *foreign exchange transfer*
dezentralisieren: *decentralize*
Dezentralisierung: *decentralization*
Dezimalisierung: *decimalization*
Dezimalstelle: *decimal point*
Dezimalsystem: *decimal or metric system*
d.h.: *i.e.*
Diagramm: *chart; diagram; graph* **in einem ~** *diagrammatically*
Diagramm der Unternehmensstruktur: *organization chart*
-dicht: *-proof; -tight*
Diebstahl: *theft* **geringfügiger ~** *pilferage or pilfering*
Diebstahlversicherung: eine ~ abschließen *to take out insurance against theft*
Diener: *servant*
Dienst: *service* **außer ~ stellen** *lay up* **öffentlicher ~** *civil service*
Dienstalter: höheres ~ *seniority*
dienstälter: *senior*
Dienstleistungsbranche: *service industry; tertiary industry*
Dienstleistungssektor: *tertiary sector*
dienstlich: *on business; official*
Dienst nach Vorschrift: *work-to-rule*
Dienstreise: *business trip*
Dienststunden: *office hours*
Dienstvertrag: *service contract; service agreement*
Dienstweg: den ~ beschreiten *to go through the official channels*
Dienstzeit: *tenure*
Differentialtarif: *differential tariffs*
Differenz: eine ~ ausgleichen *to make up a loss or to make up the difference*
Digitalcomputer: *digital computer*
Digitaluhr: *digital clock*
Diktaphon: *Dictaphone*
Diktat: *dictation*
diktieren: *dictate*
Diktiergerät: *dictating machine*
Dime: *dime (informal)*
Diplomat: *diplomat or diplomatist*
diplomatisch: *diplomatic*
direkt: *direct; directly*
Direktabbuchung: *direct debit*
Direktaktion: *direct action*
Direktbesteuerung: *direct taxation*
Direktion: *directorate; head office; headquarters*
direkt liefern: *to drop ship*
Direktlieferung: *drop shipment*
Direktor: *director* **geschäftsführender ~** *chief executive or chief executive officer (US); company director; managing director; executive director* **unternehmensfremder ~** *outside director*
Direktorenstelle: *directorship*
Direktorium: *directorate*
Direktverkauf: *direct selling; house-to-house selling*
Direktversand: *direct mail; direct mailing*
Direktwerbung: *direct mail; direct mailing*
Diskette: *disk; diskette*
Diskettenlaufwerk: *disk drive*
Diskont: *cash discount or discount for cash*
Diskontbank: *discount house*
Diskonter: *discount house; discounter*
diskontfähig: *discountable*
Diskonthaus: *discounter*
Diskontladen: *discount house; discount store; discounter*
Diskontpreis: *discount price*
Diskontsatz: *discount rate*
Diskontwert: *discount value*
Diskrepanz: *discrepancy; variance*
Diskriminierung: *discrimination*
Diskussion: *discussion*
diskutieren: *discuss*
Dispache: *average adjustment*
Disponibilität: *availability*
Disput: einen ~ schlichten *to adjudicate or to mediate in a dispute*
Disziplinarverfahren: *disciplinary procedure*
Diversifikation: *diversification*
diversifizieren: *diversify*
Dividende: *dividend* **cum ~** *cum dividend* **eine ~ ausschütten** *to pay a dividend* **ex ~** *ex dividend* **keine ~ ausschütten** *to pass the dividend* **mit ~** *cum dividend* **ohne ~** *ex dividend*
Dividende erhöhen: *to raise or to increase the dividend*
Dividenden: aufgelaufene ~ *accrued dividend*
Dividendendeckung: *dividend cover*
Dividendenertrag: *dividend yield*
Dividendenscheck: *dividend warrant*
Dividendenzahlungsanweisung: *dividend warrant*
D-Mark: *mark*
Dock: *wharf* **ins ~ gehen** *dock*
Dockgebühren: *dock dues*

Do-it-yourself: *do-it-yourself*
Dokument: *deed; document*
dokumentarisch: *documentary*
Dokumentation: *documentation*
Dollar: *buck (informal); dollar* **halber ~** *half-dollar (US)* **tausend ~** *grand (informal)*
Dollarkrise: *dollar crisis*
Dollarlücke: *dollar gap*
Dollarmillionär: *dollar millionaire*
Dollarschein: *greenback (informal)*
Dollarzone: *dollar area*
Dolmetscher: *interpreter* **dolmetschen** *to interpret*
Doppelbelegung: *double-booking*
Doppelbesteuerung: *double taxation*
Doppelbesteuerungsabkommen: *double taxation agreement*
Doppelbuchung: *double-booking*
Doppelschichten: *double shifts*
doppelt: *double*
doppelt belegen *or* **doppelt buchen:** *double-book*
Doppelte: das ~ verdienen *to be on double time*
Doppelzimmer: *double room*
Dow-Jones Aktienindex: *Dow Jones Average*
dranbleiben: *hang on*
Draufgeld: *earnest*
Drehung: *turn* **drehen** *to turn*
dreifach: *triple*
Dressman: als ~ arbeiten *to model*
dringend: *pressing; urgent; urgently*
dringlich: *urgently*
Drittel: *third*
Dritte(r): *third party*
Dritte Welt: *Third World*
Druck: *impact; pressure* **großer ~** *high pressure*
Druckbuchstaben: in ~ schreiben *print*
drucken: *print*
drücken: *beat; depress; force down; squeeze*
Drucker: *computer printer or line printer*
Druckmaschine: *printer*
Drucksache: *printed matter*
Druckschrift: *block capitals or block letters* **in ~ schreiben** *print*
Drucktaste: *key*
Dumping: *dumping*
dünn: *fine*
Duplikat: *duplicate*
durchaus: *quite*
durchführbar: *viable*
Durchführbarkeit: *feasibility; viability*
Durchführbarkeitsstudie: *feasibility report*
Durchführbarkeitstest: *feasibility test*
durchführen: *effect; implement; realize*
Durchführung: *execution; implementation; realization*
durchgehend: *non-stop*
durchkommen: *get through*
Durchlauf: *run*
durchmachen: *experience*
Durchreisevisum: *transit visa*
Durchschlag: *carbon copy*
Durchschlagpapier: *carbon paper*
Durchschnitt: *average; mean*
durchschnittlich betragen: *average; average out*
Durchschnittseinkommen pro Person: *average income per capita or per capita income*
durchsetzen: *enforce*
Durchsetzung: *enforcement*
durchstreichen: *cross out*
durchwählen: *to dial direct*
dürftig: *poor; poorly*
Duty-free-Shop: *duty-free shop*
Dutzend: *dozen* **ein halbes ~** *half a dozen or a half-dozen* **im ~ billiger** *cheaper by the dozen*
dynamisch: *go-ahead; vigorous*

Ee

Ebene: *echelon; level* **auf hoher ~** *high-level* **auf unterer ~** *low-level*
echt: *genuine; real*
Echtheit: *genuineness*
Echtzeit: *real time*
Echtzeitsystem: *real-time system*
Ecke: *corner*
Eckladen: *corner shop*
Ecklohn: *basic pay; basic wage*
Eckwert: *benchmark*
Eckzins: *bank base rate*
EDV-Abteilung: *computer department*
EDV-Modell zur Wirtschaftsprognose: *economic model*
EDV-Servicebüro: *computer bureau*
Effekt: *effect*
Effekten: *securities; stocks and shares* **erstklassige ~** *blue-chip investments*
Effektenbörse: *Stock Exchange*
Effektenhandel: *dealing; stockbroking* **geordneter ~** *fair dealing*
Effektenhändler: *securities trader*
Effektenmanagement: *portfolio management*
Effektenmarkt: *the securities market*
effektiv: *actual; effective*
Effektivbestand: *realizable assets*
Effektivertrag *or* **Effektivrendite:** *effective yield*
effizient: *efficient; efficiently*
Effizienz: *efficiency*
ehemalig: *ex-; former*
ehrenamtlich: *honorary*
Ehrenmitglied: *honorary member*
ehrlich: *honest; honestly*
Eichmeister: *inspector of weights and measures*
Eid: *oath*
eifrig: *keen*

Eigenfinanzierung: *self-financing*
eigenhändig: *personally*
Eigenkapital: *equity capital; shareholders' equity*
Eigenmarkenwaren: *own label goods; own brand goods*
Eigenschaft: in einer ~ *in a capacity*
eigentlich: *basic; basically; in fact*
Eigentum: *ownership*
Eigentümer: *owner; proprietor*
Eigentümerin: *proprietress*
Eigentumsnachweis: *search*
Eigentumsüberschreibung: *transfer of property or transfer of shares*
Eigentumsübertragung: *conveyancing*
Eigentumsurkunde: *title deeds*
Eigentumswohnung: *condominium (US)*
Eignung: *capacity*
Eil-: *express; urgent*
Eilauftrag: *rush job*
Eilbestellung: *rush order*
Eilbote: *courier*
Eilbrief: *express letter*
Eile: *hurry; rush*
eilen: *hurry*
eilig: *urgent*
Eilzustellung: *express delivery*
Einbahnstraße: *one-way street*
Einbau: *installation*
Einbauten: *fittings*
einbehalten: *dock; keep back; retain*
einberufen: *convene*
einbeziehen: *build into; include*
einbringen: *bring in; earn; fetch; table; yield*
Einbuße: *loss*
einbüßen: *lose*
Einbußen: *shrinkage*
einchecken: *check in*
Eincheckzeit: *check-in time*
einfach: *easy; easily; plain*
Einfluß: *influence; leverage*
Einfluß nehmen: *lobby*
einfordern: *claim*
einfrieren: *freeze*
Einfrieren von Krediten: *credit freeze*
einfügen: *insert*
Einfuhr: *importation; importing*
Einfuhren: unsichtbare ~ *invisible imports*
einführen: *import; introduce* **wieder ~** *reimport*
Einfuhrkontingent: *import quota*
Einfuhrlizenz: *import licence*
Einfuhrstopp: *import ban*
Einführung: *induction; introduction; launch; launching*
Einführungsbrief: *introduction*
Einführungskurse: *induction courses or induction training*
Einführungspreis: *introductory offer*
Einführungstermin: *launching date*
Einfuhrverbot: *import ban*
Einfuhrzoll: *customs duty; import duty; import levy*
Eingabe: *petition* **eine ~ machen** *petition*
Eingang: *arrival; entrance; entry; receipt*
Eingänge: *in tray*
Eingangsdatum: *date of receipt*
Eingangssteuer: *basic tax*
eingebaut: *built-in*
eingeben: *feed; keyboard*
eingefordert: nicht ~ *uncalled*
eingefroren: *frozen*
eingehen: *arrive; to enter into; to fold (up) (informal); incur*
eingelöst: nicht ~ *uncashed*
eingeschweißt: *shrink-wrapped*
Eingeständnis: *admission*
eingestehen: *admit*
eingetragen: nicht ~ *unregistered*
eingezogen: nicht ~ *uncollected*
eingliedern: *incorporate*
Eingreifen: *interference*
Eingriff: *intervention*
Einhalt: *check*
einhalten: *hold to; keep* **nicht ~** *break*
Einhaltung: *compliance*
einheimisch: *domestic; homegrown*
Einheitskosten: *unit cost*
Einheitspreis: *unit price*
Einheitssatz: *flat rate*
Einheitstarif: *flat rate*
Einheitswert: *rateable value*
einige: *a few; a number of; several*
Einkauf: *purchasing* **preisbewußter ~** *shopping around*
einkaufen: *buy; purchase; to shop (for)*
Einkäufer: *buyer; purchasing officer*
Einkaufsabteilung: *buying department*
Einkaufsbuch: *bought ledger; purchase ledger*
Einkaufsbuchhalter: *bought ledger clerk or sales ledger clerk*
Einkaufskorb: *shopping basket*
Einkaufsleiter: *head buyer; purchasing manager*
Einkaufsmarkt: *superstore*
Einkaufspassage: *shopping mall (US)*
Einkaufstasche: *shopping bag*
Einkaufszentrum: *shopping centre*
Einklang: in ~ mit *in step with*
Einkommen: *earnings; emoluments; income; revenue* **festes ~** *fixed income; regular income* **fiktives ~** *notional income* **geregeltes ~** *regular income* **persönliches ~** *personal income* **steuerpflichtiges ~** *taxable income* **verfügbares ~** *disposable income*
Einkommen mit Quellenbesteuerung: *income which is taxed at source*
Einkommenssteuer: *income tax*

Einkommenssteuererklärung: *declaration of income; income tax return* **eine ~ abgeben** *to make a return to the tax office* or *to make an income tax return*
Einkommenssteuerformular: *income tax form*
Einkommensstufe: hohe ~ *upper income bracket* **niedrige ~** *lower income bracket*
Einkünfte: *earnings; income; receipts; returns; revenue* **feste ~** *fixed income* **unerwartete ~** *windfall* **unsichtbare ~** *invisible earnings*
Einlage: *deposit; stake*
einlagern: *store*
Einleger: *depositor*
einleiten: *initiate; institute*
einleitend: *opening*
einlösbar: *cashable; encashable; redeemable* **nicht ~** *inconvertible; irredeemable*
einlösen: *encash*
Einlösen eines Schecks: *clearance of a cheque*
Einlösung: *encashment*
einmalig: *one-off; unique*
Einmalprämienpolice: *single premium policy*
Einmannbetrieb: *one-man business* or *firm* or *company* or *operation*
einmischen: sich ~ *interfere; intervene*
Einmischung: *interference; intervention*
einmütig: *unanimous; unanimously*
Einnahmen: *receipts; revenue; takings*
Einnahmen- und Ausgabenplanung: *cash budget*
einnehmen: *capture; take*
einordnen: *rank; sort*
einpacken: *pack; wrap (up)*
einpendeln: sich ~ *to level off* or *to level out*
einrechnen: *allow for*
einreichen: *file; submit*
Einreisekarte: *landing card*
Einreisevisum: *entry visa*
einrichten: *to open an account; arrange; establish; furnish; institute; open*
Einrichtung: *equipment*
Einrichtungen: *facilities*
Einrückung: *indent* **einrücken** *to indent*
Einschaltquote: *ratings*
einschätzen: *appraise; evaluate*
Einschätzung: *appraisal; evaluation*
einschiffen: *embark*
Einschiffungshafen: *port of embarkation*
einschließen: *include*
einschließlich: *inclusive*
einschränken: *limit; restrict*
einschränkend: *limiting; restrictive*
Einschränkung: *limitation; restraint; restriction; retrenchment*
Einschränkungen: mit ~ *qualified*
Einschreibebrief: *registered letter*
Einschreiben: *recorded delivery; registered letter*
einseitig: *one-sided; unilateral; unilaterally*
einsenden: *send in*
einsetzen: *set up; use*
Einsetzung: *appointment*
einsparen: *save*
Einsparung: *saving*
einspringen: für jdn ~ *stand in for*
Einspruch einlegen: *to enter a caveat*
Einspruch erheben: *oppose*
einsteigen: *board; enter*
einstellen: *employ; regulate; stop; take on* **jdn ~** *engage*
einstellen und entlassen: *to hire and fire*
Einstellung: *hiring* **zeitweilige ~** *suspension*
Einstellungsbedingungen: *terms of employment*
Einstellungsschreiben: *letter of appointment*
Einstellung von Hochschulabgängern: *graduate entry*
Einstellung von Personal: *staffing*
einstimmig: *unanimous; unanimously*
einstreichen: *rake in*
einstufen: *classify; grade*
Einstufung: *classification* **niedrigere ~** *demotion*
einstweilig: *in the interim*
eintausend: *K*
Einteilung: *organization* **einteilen** *to organize*
Eintrag: einen ~ zurückbuchen *to contra an entry*
eintragen: *enter; fill in; put down; register* **sich ~** *register*
einträglich: *money-making; paying; profitable; remunerative*
Eintragung: *entering; recording; registration* **amtliche ~** *incorporation*
Eintragungsbescheinigung: *registration certificate*
Eintragungsbuch: *register*
Eintragungsnummer: *registration number*
Eintreffen: *arrival* **eintreffen** *to arrive*
eintreibbar: *recoverable*
eintreiben: *to collect* **Eintreibung** *collection*
Eintritt: *admission; entrance (charge); entry (charge)*
Eintrittsgebühr: *admission charge* or *entry charge*
Eintrittskarte: *entrance ticket* or *admission ticket*
einverstanden: sich ~ erklären *agree*
Einwand erheben: *object*
Einweg-: *disposable; non-returnable*
Einweg(ver)packung: *non-returnable packing*
Einweisung: *induction*
einwickeln: *wrap (up)*
einzahlen: *deposit* **Einzahler** *depositor*
Einzahlungsbeleg: *deposit slip; paying-in slip*
Einzahlungsbuch: *paying-in book*
Einzahlungsschalter: *receiving office*
Einzahlungsschein: *certificate of deposit*
Einzel-: *single*
Einzelbestände: *oddments*
Einzelblatteinzug: *sheet feed*
Einzelhandel: *retail; retailing* **der ~** *the retail trade*
Einzelhandelsgeschäft: *retail outlet; retail shop*

Einzelhandelskette: *multiple*
Einzelhandelspreis: *retail price* **empfohlener ~** *manufacturer's recommended price (MRP) or recommended retail price (RRP)*
Einzelhändler: *retail dealer; retailer*
Einzelheit: *detail*
Einzelheiten: *particulars*
Einzelkaufmann: *sole trader*
einzeln: *individual; odd; separate; separately; severally; single*
Einzelperson: *individual*
einziehbar: nicht ~ *irrecoverable*
einziehen: *collect; demonetize; indent; levy; seize*
Einziehung: *collection; seizure*
Einziehungsbeamter: *collector*
einzigartig: *unique*
einzige: *single*
Einzug: *feed; indent*
Eis: auf ~ legen *pigeonhole*
Eisenwaren: *hardware*
Elan: *drive*
elastisch: *elastic*
Elastizität: *elasticity*
elektrisch: *electric; electrical*
Elektrizität: *electricity*
Elektronik: *electronics*
Elektroniker: *electronic engineer*
elementar: *basic*
Elementen: aus ~ zusammengesetzt *modular*
eliminieren: *eliminate*
Eltern: *parents*
E-Mail: *electronic mail*
Embargo: ein ~ aufheben *to lift an embargo* **ein ~ verhängen** *embargo* **einem ~ unterliegen** *to be under an embargo*
Emission neuer Aktien: *issue of new shares or share issue*
Emissionsabteilung: *new issues department*
Emissionsanzeige: *tombstone (informal)*
Emissionsbank: *issuing bank or issuing house*
Emissionskonsortium: *underwriting syndicate*
Emissionskurs: *issue price; offer price*
Emissionsprospekt: *prospectus*
emittieren: *issue*
Empfang: *receipt; receiving; reception (desk)*
empfangen: *receive*
Empfänger: *addressee; consignee; receiver; recipient*
Empfangsbestätigung: *receipt*
Empfangsdame: *reception clerk; receptionist*
Empfangsdatum: *date of receipt*
empfehlen: *advise; recommend; suggest*
Empfehlung: *advice; recommendation; suggestion*
empfindlich: *sensitive*
emporschnellen: *jump; rocket*
End-: *final; terminal; ultimate*
Endbahnhof: *railhead*
Endbetrag: *grand total*
Ende des Buchungszeitraumes: *account end*
enden: *end up; finish; terminate*
enden mit: *end in*
Endes: letzten ~ *ultimately*
endgültig festlegen: *finalize*
Endlospapier: *continuous stationery*
Endlospapiereinzug: *continuous feed*
Endpreis: *retail price*
Endprodukt: *end product; final product; finished product*
Endverbraucher: *end user; ultimate consumer*
Energie: *energy*
energiesparend: *energy-saving*
eng: *tight*
engagieren: *engage*
Engpaß: *bottleneck; shortage*
en gros: *in bulk*
Enquettekommissionsbericht: *Green Paper*
entbinden: *to release* **Entbindung** *release*
entdecken: *discover*
entfernen: *remove*
entgegengesetzt: *reverse*
entgegennehmen: *receive*
enthalten: *contain; hold; include*
enthüllen: *to disclose* **Enthüllung** *disclosure*
Entkommen: *escape*
entladen: *unload*
Entladung und Wiederfahrbereitmachung: *turnround*
entlassen: *discharge; release* **jdn ~** *to fire someone; to make someone redundant*
entlassen werden: *to get one's cards*
Entlassung: *dismissal; release; removal; sacking* **ungerechtfertigte ~** *unfair dismissal* **unrechtmäßige ~** *wrongful dismissal*
Entlassungsabfindung: *compensation for loss of office; redundancy payment; severance pay* **großzügige ~** *golden handshake or golden parachute (US)*
Entlassungsentschädigung: *compensation for loss of office*
Entlassungsverfahren: *dismissal procedures*
Entlastung eines Konkursschuldners: *discharge in bankruptcy*
Entleiher: *borrower*
entlohnen: *remunerate*
Entnahmeliste: *picking list*
entnehmen: *gather*
entschädigen: *compensate; indemnify*
Entschädigung: *damages; indemnification; indemnity; restitution*
entscheiden: *adjudicate; decide; find; judge; rule*
entscheidend: *leading*
Entscheidung: *adjudication; decision; ruling*
Entscheidungsfindung: *decision making*
Entscheidungsfreiheit: *discretion*
Entscheidungsprozeß: *decision-making process*
Entscheidungsträger: *decision maker*
entschieden: noch nicht ~ *sub judice*

entschließen: **sich ~** *decide*
Entschluß: *decision*
entschuldigen: *excuse* **sich ~** *apologize*
Entschuldigung: *apology; excuse*
entsinnen: **sich ~** *remember*
entsprechen: *to correspond with something*
entsprechend: *accordingly; relevant*
entwerfen: *design; draft; outline*
entwerten: *demonetize*
Entwertung: *demonetization*
entwickeln: *develop*
Entwicklung: *development* **bahnbrechende ~** *pioneer project or pioneer development*
Entwicklungen: **ökonomische ~** *economic trends*
Entwicklungsland: *developing country or developing nation*
Entwicklungsländer: *underdeveloped countries*
Entwurf: *rough copy; design; draft; outline; plan*
entziehen: **sich ~** *evade*
Entzweiung: *split*
Enwicklung: **wirtschaftliche ~** *economic development*
Erbauer: *constructor*
Erbe: *heir; inheritance*
erben: *inherit*
Erbin: *heir*
erbringen: *yield*
Erbschaft: *inheritance*
Erbschaftssteuer: *death duty or death tax (US); estate duty*
Erdboden: *ground*
Erdgas: *natural gas*
Erdgeschoß: *ground floor*
Erdoberfläche: *surface*
Erdöl: *oil; petroleum*
Erdöleinnahmen: *petroleum revenues*
Erdölquelle: *oil well*
Erdölvorkommen: *oil field*
ereignen: **sich ~** *happen*
Ereignis: **unvorhergesehenes ~** *contingency*
erfahren: *experience; experienced*
Erfahrung: *experience*
erfassen: *to register* **Erfassung** *registration*
erfinden: *to invent* **Erfinder** *inventor*
Erfindung: *invention*
Erfolg: *success* **keinen ~ haben** *fail* **mit ~** *successfully* **mit ~ abwickeln** *pull off (informal)*
Erfolg haben: *succeed*
erfolglos: *unsuccessful; unsuccessfully*
erfolgreich: *successful; successfully*
erfolgreich sein: *succeed*
Erfolgs- und Leistungsnachweis: *track record*
erforderlich machen: *entail*
erfordern: *require*
Erfordernis: *requirement*
erfreut: *happy*
erfüllen: *fulfil or fulfill (US); meet* **nicht ~** *default*
Erfüllung: *fulfilment*
ergänzen: *supplement*
ergänzend: *supplementary*
Ergänzung: *addition; supplement*
ergeben: *add up to; total* **sich ~ aus** *to result from*
Ergebnisse einer Untersuchungskommission: *the findings of a commission of enquiry*
Ergonomie *or* **Ergonomik:** *ergonomics*
Ergonomiker: *ergonomist*
Erhalt: *receipt*
erhalten: *get; maintain; obtain; receive*
erhältlich: **nicht ~** *unavailable; unobtainable*
Erhaltung: *maintenance*
erheben: *charge; file; impose; levy*
erheblich: *considerable; considerably; substantial*
erhöhen: *hike (US); increase; mark up; put up; raise; to scale up; step up* **sich ~** *rise*
Erhöhung: *advance; hike (US); increase; rise* **eine ~ bekanntgeben** *to post an increase*
Erhöhung eines Angebotes: *improvement on an offer*
erholen: **sich ~** *pick up; rally; recover; to stage a recovery*
Erholung: *rally*
Erholungspause: *allowed time*
erinnern: *remind* **sich ~** *remember*
erkennen: *recognize*
Erkenntnis: *realization*
erklären: *declare; explain; return*
Erklärung: *declaration; explanation* **öffentliche ~** *official return*
Erklärung abgeben: *declare*
Erklärung von Kontenabstimmungsdifferenzen: *reconciliation statement*
erkundigen: *query* **sich ~** *inquire*
Erkundungs-: *fact-finding*
erlangen: *achieve; gain*
Erlaß: *act*
erlauben: *permit* **nicht ~** *forbid*
Erlaubnis: *permission; permit* **ohne ~ abheuern** *to jump ship*
erlaubt: *allowable*
erleben: *experience*
erledigen: *finish; handle*
Erledigung: *handling*
Erleichterung: *facility; relief*
erleiden: *suffer*
Erlös: *profit*
erlöschen: *expire*
Erlöschen: *expiration; expiry*
ermächtigen: *authorize; empower*
Ermächtigung: *authority; authorization; power*
ermäßigen: *reduce*
ermäßigt: *off; reduced*
Ermäßigung: *reduction*
Ermessen: *discretion* **nach jds ~** *at the discretion of someone*
ermitteln: *calculate; investigate*
Ermittlung: *calculation*

Ermittlungsbeamter: *investigator*
ermutigen: *encourage*
Ermutigung: *encouragement*
Ernannter: *appointee*
ernennen: *appoint*
Ernennungsschreiben: *letter of appointment*
erneuern: *to renew* **Erneuerung** *renewal*
erneut bewerben: *reapply*
erneut prüfen: *re-examine*
erneut sinken: *fall back*
ernsthaft: *serious*
erobern: *capture*
eröffnen: *open; set up*
Eröffnung: *opening*
Eröffnungsbestand: *opening stock*
Eröffnungsbetrag: *opening balance*
Eröffnungsbuchung: *opening entry*
Eröffnungsgebot: *opening bid*
Eröffnungsitzung: *opening session*
Eröffnungskurs: *opening price*
erörtern: *to discuss* **Erörterung** *discussion*
erpicht: *eager*
Erprobung: *testing; trial*
errechenbar: *computable*
errechnen: *compute; work out*
Errechnung: *computation*
erreichen: *achieve; reach* **nicht ~** *miss*
Ersatz: *replacement; substitute*
Ersatzteil: *spare part*
erschließen: *develop*
Erschließung: industrielle ~ *industrial development*
erschüttern: *shake*
ersetzen: *replace; substitute*
Ersparnisse: *savings*
erstatten: *refund; repay*
Erstattung: *reimbursement*
erstattungsfähig: *recoverable* **nicht ~** *non-refundable*
erstehen: *purchase*
Ersteller von Kostenschätzungen: *quantity surveyor*
Erster Klasse: *first-class*
Ersthypothek: *first mortgage*
erstklassig: *A1; first-class; excellent; high-grade; top-grade*
Ersuchen: *application*
ersuchen: *petition; request*
Ertrag: *earnings; return; yield* **laufende ~** *current yield*
Erträge: keinerlei ~ *nil return*
ertragreich: *profitable; profitably*
Ertragsfähigkeit: *earning potential*
Ertragskonto: *revenue accounts*
erwägen: *entertain*
Erwägung: *consideration* **in ~ ziehen** *entertain*
erwähnen: *mention; refer*
erwarten: *await; expect* **zu ~** *probable*
erwartet: *projected*
erweitern: *diversify; expand*
Erweiterung: *expansion*
Erweiterung des Produktangebots: *product diversification*
Erwerb: *acquisition*
erwerben: *acquire; gain; purchase*
Erwerber: *acquirer; purchaser*
Erwerbseinkünfte: *earned income*
Erwerbsfähigkeit: *earning potential*
Erwerbslosen: die ~ *the unwaged*
Erwerbstätigkeit: *gainful employment*
erwidern: *to reply* **Erwiderung** *reply*
erwirken: *obtain*
erzeugen: *to produce* **Erzeuger** *producer*
Erzeugnis: *product*
Erzeugnisse: einheimische ~ *home-produced products* **unfertige ~** *work in progress*
Erzeugung: *production*
erzielen: *fetch; make; produce; reach; realize*
erzwingen: *to enforce* **Erzwingung** *enforcement*
eskalieren: *escalate*
Essen: *food*
Essensmarke: *luncheon voucher*
Etage: *floor*
Etappe: *stage*
etappenweise: *in stages*
Etat: *budget* **den ~ ausgleichen** *to balance the budget*
Etatüberschuß: *budget surplus*
Etikett: *label; sticker; tag; ticket*
etikettieren: *label*
Etikettierung: *labelling*
Etikettierungsabteilung: *labelling department*
etwa: *approximately*
etwas: *slightly*
Eurobond: *Eurobond*
Eurodollar: *Eurodollar*
Euromarkt: *Euromarket*
Europa: *Europe*
europäisch: *European*
Europäische: das ~ Währungssystem *the European Monetary System* **die ~ Gemeinschaft** *the European Community*
Euroscheck: *Eurocheque*
Eurowährung: *Eurocurrency*
exakt: *accurate; accurately; exact*
Examen: *examination*
exekutiv: *executive*
Exekutivgewalt: *executive power*
Exemplar: *copy*
Existenzkampf: beruflicher ~ *rat race*
Existenzminimum: *at subsistence level*
existieren: *exist*
exklusiv: *select; up market*
exklusive: *exclusive of*
expandieren: *expand*
Expansion: industrielle ~ *industrial expansion*

Expedient: *dispatcher*
Experte: *expert; specialist*
Experte für Absatzpolitik: *merchandiser*
Expertengruppe: *panel of experts*
Expertin: *expert; specialist*
Expertise: *expert's report; survey*
Export: *export; exportation*
Exportabteilung: *export department*
Exporte: **sichtbare ~** *visible exports*
Exporterstattung: *export restitution*
Exporteur: *exporter*
Exportfirma: *export house; exporter*
Exportgenehmigung: *export permit*
Exporthandel: *export trade*
exportieren: *export*
Exportkreditversicherung: **staatliche ~** *Export Credit Guarantee Department*
Exportleiter: *export manager*
Exportlizenz: *export licence*
Exportzoll: *export duty*
Expreß: **per ~** *express*
extern: *external; outside*
extra: *in addition to; extra*
Ezil: *decile*

Ff

Fabrik: *factory; mill; works*
Fabrikanlage: *plant*
Fabrikarbeiter: *blue-collar worker; factory hand; operative; factory worker*
Fabrikat: *make*
Fabrikationsnummer: *serial number*
Fabrikgebäude: *factory unit*
Fabrikhalle: *the factory floor*
Fabrikpreis: *factory price or price ex factory*
Fach: *pigeonhole*
-fach: *-fold*
Facharbeiter: *skilled worker(s) or skilled labour; technician*
Fachausbildung: *industrial training*
Fachblatt: *trade journal*
Fachgebiet: *speciality or specialty*
Fachgeschäft: *stockist*
Fachhandel: *specialist*
Fachhändler: *stockist*
Fachkenntnisse: *know-how*
fachlich: *professional*
Fachmann: *expert; professional; specialist*
fachmännisch: *professional*
Fachmesse: *trade fair*
Fachpresse: *trade press*
Fachwissen: *expertise*
Fachzeitschrift: *trade magazine; trade paper; trade journal or trade magazine or trade paper or trade*

Factor: *factor*
Factoring-Gebühren: *factoring charges*
fähig: *capable; competent; efficient*
Fähigkeit: *efficiency; power*
Fahne: *flag*
Fähre: *ferry*
fahren: *drive; run; sail*
Fahrkarte: *ticket* **einfache ~** *one-way ticket; single fare or single ticket or a single*
Fahrkartenschalter: *booking office; ticket office; ticket counter*
Fahrlässigkeit: **grobe ~** *criminal negligence*
Fahrplan: *timetable*
Fahrpreis: *fare* **einfacher ~** *single fare or one-way fare (US)* **halber ~** *half fare* **voller ~** *full fare*
Fahrstuhl: *elevator (US); lift*
Fahrtenschreiber: *tachograph*
Fahrzeug: *vehicle*
fair: *fair*
Faktor: *factor* **ausschlaggebender** *or* **entscheidender ~** *deciding factor*
Faktoren: **zyklische ~** *cyclical factors*
Faktum: *fact*
fakturieren: *invoice*
Fakturist: *invoice clerk*
Fall: *decrease; depreciation; instance; slump*
Fallen: *fall*
fallen: *decrease; depreciate; dip; drop; fall; fall off; sink; slip*
fallenlassen: *scrap*
fällig: *due; payable*
Fälligkeitstag: *expiry date*
Fälligkeitstermin: *maturity date; date of maturity*
Fälligwerden: *expiration*
falsch: *dud; false; fictitious; incorrectly; untrue; wrong*
falsch berechnen: *miscalculate*
falsch darstellen: *misrepresent*
fälschen: *counterfeit; fake; falsify; forge*
Fälschen: *forgery*
falsch kalkulieren: *miscalculate*
fälschlicherweise: *wrongly*
Fälschung: *fake; falsification; forgery*
Falsifikat: *fake*
falten: *fold*
Familienunternehmen: *family company*
Farbmuster: *colour swatch*
Faß: *barrel*
Fassade: *front*
fassen: *hold*
Fassung: *draft*
Fassungsvermögen: *capacity*
faul: *lazy*
Fax: *fax or FAX* **faxen** *to fax*
Fazilität: *facility*
Feedback: *feedback*
Fehlbetrag: *deficiency; shortfall*
fehlen an: *lack*

Fehler: *defect; error; failing; fault; imperfection; mistake*
fehlerfrei: *accurate; accurately*
fehlerhaft: *defective; faulty; imperfect; incorrect*
fehlerlos: *perfect; perfectly*
Fehlerquote: *error rate*
Fehlerspielraum: *margin of error*
Fehlkalkulation: *miscalculation*
fehlschlagen: *fall through*
Feierabend machen: *knock off*
Feiertag: *bank holiday; public holiday* **gesetzlicher ~** *statutory holiday; legal holiday* **öffentlicher ~** *bank holiday*
feilschen: *haggle*
Feingehaltsstempel: *assay mark; hallmark; assay mark*
Feld: *field*
Felduntersuchung: *field work*
Fenster: *window*
Fensterumschlag: *aperture* or *window envelope*
Fernbleiben: *absence*
Fernflug: *long-haul* or *long-distance flight*
Ferngespräch: *long-distance call; toll call (US); trunk call*
Fernmeldewesen: *telecommunications*
Fernschreiben: *telex*
Fernschreiber: *teleprinter; telex*
Fernschreibkraft: *telex operator*
Fernschreibleitung: *telex line*
Fernschreibteilnehmer: *telex subscriber*
Fernsehwerbungstreibender: *sponsor*
Fernspediteur: *road haulier*
Fernsprechauftragsdienst: *answering service*
Fernsprechnummer: *telephone number*
Fernsprechteilnehmer: *telephone subscriber*
fertig: *ready; ready-made* or *ready-to-wear*
fertigbringen: **es ~** *to manage to*
fertigen: *manufacture; produce*
Fertiggerichte: *convenience foods*
Fertigkeit: *proficiency; skill*
fertig machen: *finish*
fertigstellen: *complete*
Fertigstellung: *completion*
Fertigung: *manufacture; manufacturing; production*
Fertigungsabteilung: *production department*
Fertigungsingenieur: *product engineer*
Fertigungskapazität: *industrial capacity; manufacturing capacity*
Fertigungsstraße: *assembly line; production line*
Fertigwaren: *finished goods*
fertigwerden: *cope*
fest: *firm; fixed; permanent; permanently; set*
fest angestellt: *salaried*
fest anlegen: *tie up*
Festertrag: *fixed yield*
Festgeld: *fixed deposit*
Festgelder: *time deposit*
festgelegt: *set*
festhalten an: *hold on; hold to*
festigen: *stabilize*
Festigkeit: *firmness; steadiness*
Festigung: *stabilization*
Festkosten: *overhead expenses* or *general expenses* or *running expenses; overhead costs* or *running costs; overheads* or *overhead (US)*
Festkostenbudget: *overhead budget*
festlegen: *determine; fix; put; schedule; set; state; tie up*
Festlegung: *fixing*
festmachen: *pin; tie up*
Festplatte: *hard disk*
Festpreis: *firm price*
Festpreisvereinbarung: *fixed-price agreement*
festsetzen: *determine; evaluate; fix; peg; put; set*
Festsetzung: *evaluation; fixing*
feststellen: *to state* **Feststellung** *statement*
fest verschließen: *seal*
Feuer: *fire* **Feuer fangen** *to catch fire*
feuerfest: *fireproof*
Feuergefahr: *fire risk* **eine ~ darstellen** *to be a fire hazard* or *fire risk*
Feuerleiter: *fire escape*
feuern: **jdn ~** *to fire someone*
Feuerrisiko: *fire hazard*
Feuerschaden: *fire damage*
feuersicher: *fireproof*
Feuertreppe: *fire escape*
Feuertür: *fire door*
Feuerversicherung: *fire insurance*
Fideikommiß: *entail*
FIFO-Abschreibungsmethode: *first in first out (FIFO)*
fifty-fifty machen: *to go fifty-fifty*
fiktiv: *fictitious*
Filiale: *branch; chain store; multiple store; branch office; chain store*
Filialleiter: *branch manager*
Filzstift: *felt pen*
Financier: *financier*
Finanz-: *budgetary; financial; fiscal*
Finanzamt: *Inland Revenue* or *Internal Revenue Service (US)*
Finanzbeamter: *revenue officer; VAT inspector; VATman* or *vatman*
Finanzberater: *financial adviser*
Finanzbericht: *financial statement; financial report*
Finanzbuchhalter: *management accountant*
Finanzenmittel: *finances*
Finanzhilfe: *financial assistance*
finanziell: *financial; financially; pecuniary*
finanziell unabhängig: *self-supporting*
finanziell unterstützen: *support*
finanzieren: *bankroll (informal); finance; fund*
Finanzierung: *financing; funding*

Finanzierungsgesellschaft: *finance company; finance corporation; finance house*
Finanzinstitut: *financial institution*
Finanzlage: *financial position*
Finanzmanager: *treasurer (US)*
Finanzmarkt: *finance market; money market*
Finanzminister: *Chancellor of the Exchequer (GB); Secretary of the Treasury (US)*
Finanzministerium: *the Exchequer (GB)*
Finanzplanung: *budgeting*
Finanzprüfung: *financial review*
Finanz- und Wirtschaftsredakteur: *City editor*
Finanz- und Wirtschaftsredaktion: *City desk*
Finanzverwalter: *treasurer*
Finanzverwaltung: *Inland Revenue* or *Internal Revenue Service (US)*
fingieren: *fake*
Finish: *finish*
Firma: *company; establishment; firm; house* **eine angesehene ~** *company of good standing* **eine ~ gründen** *to set up a company* **eine ~ liquidieren** *to wind up a company* **unrentable ~** *lame duck*
Firmenansehen: *goodwill*
Firmengründer: *company promoter*
Firmengründung: *promotion of a company*
Firmengruppe: *group*
Firmenimage: *corporate image* **das ~ pflegen** *to promote a corporate image*
Firmenmantel: *shell company*
Firmenmitteilungsblatt: *company newsletter*
Firmenname: *corporate name*
Firmensiegel: *common seal* or *company's seal*
Firmenvorstand: *board*
Firmenwagen: *company car*
Firmenwohnung: *company flat*
Firmenzeichen: *logo*
Fischereihafen: *fishing port*
Fischzucht: *fish farm*
Fixer: *fixer (informal)*
Fixgeschäft: *short selling* or *selling short*
Fixkosten: *fixed costs; fixed expenses*
Fläche: *area*
Flächenmaß: *square measure*
Flagge: *flag*
flau: *inactive; quiet; slack*
Flaute: *depression; downturn; dullness; lull*
flexibel: *flexible*
Flexibilität: *flexibility*
fliegen: *fly*
Fließband: *assembly line; production line*
Flip-Chart: *flip chart*
floaten: *float*
Flohmarkt: *flea market*
Flop: *flop*
Floppy Disk: *floppy disk*
florieren: *flourish; thrive*
florierend: *booming; flourishing*
Flucht: *flight*
flüchtig: *casual*
Flug: *flight*
Flugabfertigung: *check-in*
Flugblatt: *publicity handout*
Fluggesellschaft: *air carrier; airline*
Flughafen: *airport*
Flughafenbus: *airport bus*
Flughafengebühr: *airport tax*
Fluginformation: *flight information*
Fluglotse: *air traffic controller*
Flugpreis: *fare*
Flugsicherheit: *airport security*
Flugsteig: *gate*
Flugtauglichkeit: *airworthiness*
Flugzeug: *aircraft; plane*
Fluktuation: *fluctuation; turnover*
fluktuieren: *fluctuate*
Flußdiagramm: *flow chart; flow diagram*
flüssigmachen: *free*
Flut: *flood*
f.o.b: *free on board (f.o.b.)*
Folge: *result* **in zahlenmäßiger ~** *in numerical order* **zur ~ haben** *entail; to result in*
folgen: *follow; gather; succeed*
folgenden: **im ~** *hereafter*
Folgeprämie: *renewal premium*
Folgeschreiben: *follow-up letter*
Folio: *folio*
Fonds: *fund*
fordern: *ask for; claim; demand*
fördern: *boost; encourage; further; mine*
Forderung: *claim; claiming; demand* **bevorrechtigte ~** *prior charge* **uneinbringliche ~** *bad debt; irrecoverable debt*
Förderung: *boost* **finanzielle ~** *sponsorship*
Forderungen: *receivables*
Forderungen ankaufen: *factor*
Forderungseinziehung: *debt collection*
Förderungsgebiet: *development area* or *development zone; enterprise zone*
Form: *form of words; mode*
Formalität: *formality*
Format: *size*
Formbrief: *standard letter*
formell: *formal; formally*
förmlich: *formal*
Formular: *form*
Formulieren: *drafting*
Formulierung: *form of words; wording*
forschen: *to research* **Forscher** *researcher*
Forschung: *research* **wissenschaftliche ~** *scientific research*
Forschung betreiben: *research*
Forschungsabteilung: *research department*
Forschungsanstalt: *research institute* or *organization*
Forschungsgruppe: *research unit*
Forschungsinstitut: *research institute*

Forschung und Entwicklung: *research and development*
fortfahren: *proceed; continue*
Fortführung: *continuation*
Fortschreiten: *progress*
Fortschritt: *advance*
Fortschritte machen: *get on; progress*
Fortschrittsbericht: *progress report*
fortsetzen: *continue; proceed*
Fortsetzung: *continuation*
fortwährend: *steadily*
Fotokopie: *photocopy; photostat; Xerox*
fotokopieren: *photocopy; photostat; Xerox*
Fotokopiergerät: *photocopier*
Fracht: *cargo* **f.o.b. einschließlich ~** *free on board (US)*
Fracht auflade *or* **aufnehmen:** *to take on freight*
Frachtbrief: *shipping note; waybill*
Frachter: *cargo ship; freighter*
frachtfrei: *carriage free; carriage paid*
Frachtgebühren: *freight charges; freight rates*
Frachtkosten: *freight costs; freightage*
Frachtnachnahme: *carriage forward; freight forward*
Frachtschiff: *cargo ship*
Fracht- und Löschungskosten: *landed costs*
Frage: *matter; query; question* **in ~ stellen** *query; question*
Fragebogen: *questionnaire*
fragen: *ask*
Fragen stellen: *question*
fragwürdig: *shady*
Franc: *franc*
Franchise: *franchise*
Franchise-Basis: auf ~ vergeben *franchise*
Franchisegeber: *franchiser*
Franchisenehmer: *franchisee*
Franchisevergabe: *franchising operation*
Franchising: *franchising*
Franc-Konto: *franc account*
frankieren: *frank; stamp*
Frankiermaschine: *franking machine*
Frau: *Mrs*
Frauenzeitschrift: *women's magazine*
Fräulein: *Miss*
Frau Vorsitzende: *Madam Chairman*
frei: *clear; floating; franco; free; freely; off; vacant*
"frei": *"for hire"*
freiberuflich: *freelance; self-employed*
freiberuflich tätig sein: *freelance*
Freibetrag für Erwerbseinkünfte: *earned income allowance*
Freigabe: *release*
freigeben: *decontrol; float; release*
Freigepäck: *baggage allowance; free baggage allowance*
Freihafen: *free port*
Freihandel: *free trade*
Freihandelszone: *free trade area; free trade zone*
Freikarte: *complimentary ticket*
freimachen: *frank*
frei schwankend: *floating*
freistellen: *to release* **Freistellung** *release*
Freiverkehr: *unlisted securities market*
Freiverkehrswerte: *unlisted securities*
freiwillig: *voluntary; voluntarily*
Freizeichen: *dialling tone*
Freizeichnungsklausel: *exclusion clause*
Freizeit: *spare time*
Freizügigkeit der Arbeitskräfte: *mobility of labour*
Fremdenverkehrsamt: *information bureau; information office*
Fremdenverkehrsbüro: *tourist bureau or tourist information office*
Fremdkapital: *borrowings; loan capital*
Fremdkapitalaufnahme: festverzinsliche ~ *gearing* **ohne ~** *ungeared*
Fremdwährung: *foreign currency*
Fremdwährungskonto: *foreign currency account*
Friedenspflicht: *cooling off period*
frisieren: *fiddle (informal)*
Frist: *time limit; notice; time* **eine ~ einhalten** *to meet a deadline*
Fristeinlagen: *term shares*
führen: *carry; conduct; direct; handle; head up; keep; lead; manage; run; stock*
führend: *leading*
führend sein: *to be first in the field*
Führerschein: *driving licence*
Führerscheinprüfung: *driving test*
Fuhrpark: *fleet*
Führung: *administration; direction*
Führungsfunktion: *management function*
Führungskraft: *executive* **obere ~** *senior manager or senior executive*
Führungskräften: nach ~ suchen *headhunt*
Führungsnachwuchs: *management trainee*
Fuhrunternehmer: *carter; haulage contractor*
füllen: *fill*
Füller: *filler*
Füllhalter: *pen*
Fundieren: *funding*
fundiert: *funded*
Fünfcentstück: *nickel (US)*
Fünfdollarschein: *five dollar bill*
Fünfjahresplan: *Five-Year Plan*
fungieren: *act*
Funktion: *function* **in einer ~** *in a capacity*
funktionieren: *function*
Funktions-: *operational*
für: *in favour of; pro*
Fürsorge: *welfare*
Fusion: *merger* **gegenläufige ~** *reverse takeover*
fusionieren: *merge*
Fuß: *foot* **zu ~** *on foot*

Fußboden: *floor*
Fußgängerzone: *pedestrian precinct; shopping precinct*
Futures: *futures*

Gg

Gabelstapler: *fork-lift truck*
Gag: *gimmick*
Gallone: *gallon*
Gang: **in ~ kommen** *to gain momentum* **in ~ setzen** *initiate*
ganz: *clear; in full; fully; outright; total*
ganztägig: *full-time*
Ganztagsbeschäftigung: *full-time employment*
Garant: *warrantor*
Garantie: *guarantee; security; surety; warranty*
Garantieempfänger: *warrantee*
garantieren: *guarantee; warrant*
Garantieverletzung: *breach of warranty*
Garderobe: *checkroom (US)*
Gaststätte: *restaurant*
Gaststättengewerbe: *catering trade*
Gastwirt: *restaurateur*
Gate: *gate*
Gattung: *kind*
Gauner: *racketeer*
Gaunerei: *racket*
Gebäude: *building; property* **das ~ räumen** *to vacate the premises* **im ~** *on the premises*
Gebiet: *area; district; province; region; sphere; territory; zone*
Gebietsleiter: *area manager*
gebietsweise: *regional*
Gebot: *bid; bidding*
Gebrauch: *usage; use*
Gebrauchsanweisung: *directions for use*
gebrauchsfertig: *ready-made or ready-to-wear*
Gebrauchsgüter: **langlebige ~** *consumer durables*
gebraucht: *secondhand*
Gebrauchtwarenhändler: *secondhand dealer*
Gebühr: *charge; fee; rate* **symbolische ~** *token charge*
Gebühr bezahlt: *postage paid; postpaid*
Gebühr bezahlt Empfänger: *charges forward; freepost (GB)*
gebührenfrei: *free of charge; postage paid; toll free (US)*
Gebührenordnung: **verbindliche ~** *fixed scale of charges*
Gebührentabelle: **eine gleitende ~** *a sliding scale of charges*
gebunden: *fixed*
Geburtenrate: *birth rate*
Gedanke: *idea*
Gedeck: *cover charge*
Gedrucktes: *print*
geeignet: *suitable*
Gefahr: *danger; risk*
Gefährdung: *risk*
Gefahrenzulage: *danger money*
Gefahr laufen: *to be in danger of; to run a risk*
gefährlich: *dangerous*
Gefälligkeit: **aus ~** *as a favour*
Gefälligkeitswechsel: *accommodation bill*
gefälscht: *counterfeit; dud*
Gefüge: *structure*
Gegen-: *counter-*
gegen: *against*
Gegenbuchung: *contra entry* **als ~** *per contra or as per contra*
Gegend: *region*
gegen etwas sein: *object*
Gegenforderung: *counter-claim* **eine ~ stellen** *counter-claim*
Gegengebot: *counterbid; counter-offer*
gegeninflationär: *anti-inflationary*
Gegenkonto: *contra account*
Gegenleistung: *consideration*
gegenseitig: *reciprocal*
Gegenstand: *item*
Gegenstück: *counterpart*
Gegenteil: *contrary* **im ~** *on the contrary*
gegenüberstellen: *set against*
gegenwärtig: *current; currently; present*
gegenzeichnen: *countersign*
Gehalt: *compensation (US); pay; salary* **ansprechendes ~** *attractive salary* **ein ~ beziehen** *to draw a salary* **verlockendes ~** *attractive salary*
Gehälter: **die ~ revidieren** *to review salaries*
Gehaltsabrechnung: *pay slip*
Gehaltsabzug: *stoppage*
Gehaltsaufbesserung: *increase*
Gehaltserhöhung: *increase; increment; pay rise; raise (US)*
Gehaltskürzung: *salary cut*
Gehaltsliste: *payroll*
Gehaltsrevision: *salary review*
Gehaltsscheck: *pay cheque; paycheck; salary cheque*
Gehaltssteigerungstabelle: *incremental scale*
Gehaltsstreifen: *pay slip*
Gehaltssumme: *payroll*
Gehaltstabelle: *scale of salaries or salary scale*
Gehaltszulage: **jährliche ~** *incremental increase*
"Gehalt über £15.000": *"salary: £15K+ "*
geheim: *secret* **etwas ~ halten** *to keep a secret*
Geheimhaltung: *security*
Geheimhaltungspflicht: *restraint of trade*
Geheimnis: *secret*
Gehilfe: *assistant*
gehören zu: *to belong to*
Gelände: *premises*
gelangen zu: *to arrive at*

Gelbe Seiten: *yellow pages*

Geld: *money* **billiges ~** *cheap money; easy money* **heißes ~** *hot money* **knappes ~** *tight money* **leicht verdientes ~** *easy money* **stilliegendes ~** *money lying idle or idle money* **teures ~** *dear money* **ungedecktes ~** *fiat money* **zu ~ machen** *realize*

Geld anzahlen: *to pay money on account; to pay money down*

Geldautomat: *automatic telling machine or; cash dispenser*

Geldautomatenkarte: *cash card*

Geld einbüßen: *to lose money*

Gelder: *monies* **flüssige ~** *available capital* **öffentliche ~** *public funds*

Gelder flüssigmachen: *to mobilize capital*

Gelder umleiten: *to convert funds to one's own use*

Gelder veruntreuen: *to convert funds to one's own use; to convert funds to another purpose*

Geldgeber: *backer; financier*

Geldgeschenk: *gratuity*

Geldhändler: *authorized dealer*

Geldkassette: *cash box*

Geldmärkte: *money markets*

Geldmarktsätze: *money rates*

Geldmengenpolitik: **restriktive ~** *tight money policy*

Geldmittel: **fehlende ~** *lack of funds*

Geldreserve: *money supply*

Geld scheffeln: *to rake in cash or to rake it in*

Geldschwemme: *glut of money*

Geld setzen auf: *to stake money on something*

Geldstrafe: *fine; penalty*

Geldstück: *coin*

Geldtransfer: *credit transfer or transfer of funds*

Geld verdienen: *to earn money; to make money*

Geldverleiher: *moneylender*

Geld verlieren: *to lose money*

Geldvolumen: *money supply*

Geldwechsler: *change machine; changer*

gelegen: *situated*

Gelegenheit: *opportunity*

Gelegenheitsarbeiten verrichten: *to do odd jobs*

Gelegenheitsarbeiter: *odd-job-man*

Gelegenheitskauf: *bargain*

gelegen sein: *to be located*

gelegentlich: *occasional*

gelingen: *succeed*

gelten: *apply; operate; rule; run*

Geltung verschaffen: *enforce*

gemäß: *according to; as per; under*

gemäßigt: *moderate*

Gemein-: *common*

Gemeinde: *community*

Gemeindeabgaben: *rate (GB)*

Gemeindeabgabenzahler: **kommerzieller ~** *business ratepayer* **privater ~** *domestic ratepayer*

Gemeindeverwaltung: *local government*

Gemeinkosten: *fixed costs; overheads or overhead (US)*

gemeinnützig: *non profit-making*

gemeinsam: *collective; common; joint; jointly; mutual*

Gemeinsame: **der ~ Markt** *the Common Market*

Gemeinschaft: *community*

gemeinschaftlich-: *joint*

Gemeinschafts-: *collective; common; joint*

Gemeinschaftseigentum: *multiple ownership*

Gemeinschaftskonto: *joint account*

Gemeinschaftsunternehmen: *joint venture*

gemischt: *miscellaneous; mixed*

Gemischtwarenhandlung: *general store(s)*

Gemischtwarenladen: *variety store (US)*

genau: *accurate; accurately; exact; exactly; strict; strictly*

genehmigen: *agree; approve; authorize; license; pass; permit; ratify; sanction*

Genehmigung: *approval; authorization; licence or license (US); permission; permit; ratification; sanction* **mündliche ~** *verbal permission* **schriftliche ~** *written permission*

Genehmigungszertifikat: *certificate of approval*

Generalstreik: *general strike*

generell: *general*

Genesungsurlaub: *sick leave*

Genossenschaft: *co-operative society* **landwirtschaftliche ~** *agricultural co-operative*

Gentleman's Agreement: *gentleman's agreement or gentlemen's agreement (US)*

genug or genügend: *sufficient*

geöffnet: *open*

gepachtet: *leasehold*

Gepäck: *baggage* **nicht abgeholtes ~** *unclaimed baggage*

Gepäckaufbewahrung: *baggage room (US); checkroom (US); left luggage office*

Gepäck aufgeben: *to check baggage in*

Gepäckkontrolle: *baggage check*

Gepäckschein: *baggage ticket*

geplant: *projected*

Gerät: *device; implement; instrument*

Geräte: **periphäre ~** *peripherals*

Geräteverleih: *equipment hire firm*

Geräte vermieten: *to hire out equipment*

Geratewohl: **aufs ~** *at random*

gerecht: *fair*

Gericht: *court; law court; tribunal*

Gericht für Bagatellsachen: *small claims court*

gerichtlich belangen: *sue*

gerichtlich vorgehen: *to take legal action*

Gerichtsentscheidung: *adjudication*

Gerichtsferien: *vacation (GB)*

Gerichtshof: *law court*

Gerichtskosten: *costs*

Gerichtssaal: *court*

Gerichtsurteil: *judgement or judgment*

Gerichtsverfahren: *court case; legal proceedings* **ordentliches ~** *the due processes of the law*

Gerichtsverhandlung: *trial*

gering: *low; marginal; modest; nominal*
geringer: *lower; reduced*
geringer werden: *decline*
geringfügig: *fractional; negligible; slight*
gesamt: *aggregate; overall; total*
Gesamtgebühr: *inclusive charge; inclusive sum*
Gesamtnutzlast: *deadweight capacity or deadweight tonnage*
Gesamtplan: *overall plan*
Gesamtpreis: *all-in price*
Gesamtsumme: *grand total*
Gesamttonnage: *deadweight tonnage*
Gesamtvereinbarung: *blanket agreement*
Gesamtvergütung: *pay package or salary package or compensation package (US)*
Gesandtschaft: *mission*
Geschädigte: *injured party*
Geschäft: *affair; bargain; business; deal; establishment; operation; outlet; shop; store* **betrügerisches ~** *racket* **das ~ aufgeben** *to go out of business* **ein ~ abschließen** *to strike a bargain with someone* **ein ~ ausstatten** *fitting out of a shop* **ein ~ betreiben** *to carry on a business* **ein ~ einrichten** *fitting out of a shop* **ein ~ gründen** *to go into business* **im ~ sein** *to be in business* **kein gewinnbringendes ~** *not a commercial proposition* **schlechtes ~** *bad bargain* **unabhängiges ~** *independent trader or independent shop* **"Näheres im ~"** *"inquire within"*
Geschäfte abschließen *or* **abwickeln:** *to transact business*
Geschäftemacher: *profiteer; wheeler-dealer*
Geschäftemacherei: *profiteering*
geschäftlich: *on business; commercially* **sich ~ durchsetzen** *or* **etablieren** *to establish oneself in business*
Geschäftsadresse: *business address*
Geschäftsbericht: *annual report*
Geschäftsbesuch: *business call*
Geschäftsbilanz: *management accounts*
Geschäftsbrief: *business letter*
Geschäftsbriefe: *business correspondence*
Geschäftsbücher: *the accounts of a business or a company's accounts; a company's books*
Geschäftsessen: *business lunch*
Geschäftsfrau: *businesswoman*
Geschäftsführer: *managing director*
Geschäftsführung: **gemeinsame ~** *joint management*
Geschäftsgebaren: **unlauteres** *or* **unsauberes ~** *sharp practice*
Geschäftsgepflogenheiten: *business practices or industrial practices or trade practices*
Geschäftsgewinn: *trading profit*
Geschäftsinhaber: *shopkeeper*
Geschäftsjahr: *financial year*
Geschäftskorrespondenz: *business correspondence*
Geschäftsleiter: *manager*
Geschäftsleiterin: *manageress*
Geschäftsleitung: *directorate*
Geschäftsleute: *tradespeople*
Geschäftsmann: *businessman*
Geschäftspartner: *active partner; associate; working partner*
Geschäftspraktiken: *business practices or industrial practices or trade practices* **wettbewerbsbeschränkende ~** *restrictive trade practices*
Geschäftsräume: *business premises or commercial premises*
Geschäftsreise: *business trip*
Geschäftsreisender: *business traveller*
Geschäftsschluß: *closing time*
Geschäftsstelle: *branch office*
Geschäftsstunden: *business hours*
Geschäftsverlust: *trading loss*
Geschäftsviertel: *the commercial district or the business district; downtown*
Geschäftswelt: **die örtliche ~** *the local business community*
Geschäftszeit: *business hours; opening hours*
geschätzt: *estimated*
Geschenk: *gift; present* **als ~ einpacken** *gift-wrap*
Geschenkboutique: *gift shop*
Geschenkgutschein: *gift coupon or gift token or gift voucher*
Geschenkpapier: *gift-wrapping; wrapping paper*
geschickt: *clever*
geschlossen: *closed; shut*
Geschwindigkeit: *speed*
Geselle: *journeyman (US)*
Gesellschaft: *association; company; institution; society* **eine ~ auflösen** *to dissolve a partnership*
Gesellschafter: **stiller ~** *silent partner*
gesellschaftlich: *social*
Gesellschaftsgründung: *incorporation*
Gesellschaftsgründung durch Aktienemission: *floating of a company*
Gesellschaftsordnung: *the social system*
Gesellschaftsraum: *lounge*
Gesellschaftsvertrag: *articles of association or articles of incorporation (US); deed of partnership*
Gesetz: *act; law; statute*
Gesetzbuch: *statute book*
Gesetzentwurf: *bill*
Gesetzes: **außerhalb des ~** *against or outside the law*
Gesetzeskraft: **die volle ~** *the full power of the law*
Gesetzeslücke: **eine ~ finden** *to find a loophole in the law*
Gesetzesvorlage: *bill*
Gesetze übertreten: *to break the law*
Gesetzgebung: *legislation*
gesetzlich: *lawful; lawfully; legally; statutory*
gesetzlich geschützt: *patented; proprietary*
Gesetzmäßigkeit: *legality*
gesetzwidrig: *unlawful*

gesichert: *secure*
gesondert: *separate; separately*
gesperrt: *frozen*
Gespräch: *call* **ein ~ annehmen** *to take a call*
Gespräche: produktive ~ *productive discussions*
Gespräche registrieren: *to log calls*
Gespräch mit Voranmeldung: *personal call*
Gesprächsleiter: *interviewer*
gestaffelt: *graduated; progressive*
gestalten: *structure*
Geständnis: *admission*
gestatten: *allow; permit*
Gestehungspreis: *prime cost*
Gestell: *rack*
gesteuert: *controlled*
gestreut anlegen: *diversify*
Gesuch: *application; petition; request*
gesund: *sound*
Gesundheit: *health*
Gesundheitsüberprüfung: *medical inspection*
Gesundschrumpfen: *shakeout*
getrennt: *separate; separately*
getrennt bezahlen: *to go Dutch*
gewagt: *risky*
Gewähr: *warranty*
gewähren: *allow; extend; grant* **nicht ~** *refuse*
Gewährleistung: *warranty*
Gewalt: ausübende ~ *executive power* **höhere ~** *act of God; force majeure*
Gewandheit beim Verkaufen: *salesmanship*
Gewerbe: *business; trade*
Gewerbeaufsichtsamt: *the factory inspectorate*
Gewerbeaufsichtsbeamter: *factory inspector or inspector of factories*
Gewerbegebiet: *commercial district; industrial estate or trading estate; business park*
gewerblich: *commercially*
Gewerkschaft: *trade union or trades union or labor union (US)* **eine ~ anerkennen** *to recognize a union; to grant a trade union recognition*
Gewerkschaft(l)er: *convenor; trade unionist*
gewerkschaftlich organisiert: *unionized*
Gewerkschaftsbeiträge: *union dues or union subscription*
Gewerkschaftsbund: *Trades Union Congress (TUC)*
Gewerkschaftsfunktionäre: *union officials*
Gewerkschaftsmitglied: *unionist*
Gewerkschaftsunterhändler: ein erfahrener ~ *an experienced union negotiator*
Gewerkschaftsvertreter: *business agent (US)*
Gewicht: *weight*
Gewichtsschwund *or* **Gewichtsverlust:** *loss in weight*
Gewinn: *earnings; gain; profit; return; turn* **mit ~ verkaufen** *to sell at a profit* **nicht realisierter ~** *paper profit* **seinen ~ mitnehmen** *to take one's profit* **stattlicher ~** *healthy profit* **unerwarteter ~** *windfall*
Gewinn an Erfahrung: *gain in experience*
Gewinnbeteiligung: *profit-sharing*
gewinnbringend: *money-making; paying; profit-making; profitable*
Gewinne: einbehaltene ~ *retained earnings; undistributed profit* **kurfristige ~** *short-term gains* **zurechenbare ~** *attributable profits*
gewinnen: *attract; win*
Gewinnentwicklung: *earnings performance*
Gewinnmitnahme: *profit-taking*
Gewinn nach Steuern: *profit after tax*
Gewinnrealisierung: *profit-taking*
Gewinnrendite: *earnings per share; earnings yield*
Gewinnspanne: *margin; profit margin; turn*
Gewinnsteuer: *profits tax or tax on profits*
Gewinn- und Verlustrechnung: *profit and loss account; income statement (US)*
Gewinnverteilungsrechnung: *appropriation account*
Gewinn vor Steuern: *pretax profit; profit before tax*
Gewinnvortrag: *accumulated profit*
Gewohnheit: *practice*
gezielt: *selective*
Gilde: *guild*
Gipfel: *height*
Girobank: *clearing bank; Girobank*
Girokasse: *clearing house*
Girokonto: *current account or cheque account or checking account (US); drawing account*
Gitterstruktur: *grid structure*
Glaskasten: *display case*
Glauben: in gutem ~ *bona fide*
Gläubiger: *chargee; creditor; lender* **bevorrechtigter ~** *preferential creditor; preferred creditor* **nachrangiger ~** *deferred creditor*
Gläubiger ohne Sicherheiten: *unsecured creditor*
Gläubigerversammlung: *creditors' meeting*
gleich: *directly; equal; immediately; par*
gleichbleibend: *stable*
gleichermaßen: *equally*
Gleichheit: *parity*
gleichkommen: *equal; to be equivalent to*
gleichmäßig: *continuous; equally*
gleichwertig: *pari passu*
Gleichwertigkeit: *equivalence*
gleichwertig sein: *to be equivalent to*
gleitend: *sliding*
Gleitzeit: *flexible working hours; flexitime*
global: *across-the-board*
Globalabkommen: *omnibus agreement*
Glückwünsche: *congratulations*
Gnädige Frau: *Madam*
Gold: *gold*
Goldgrube: *bonanza*
Goldmine: *goldmine*
Goldminenaktien: *gold shares or golds*
Goldpunkt: *gold point*

Goldstandard: *gold standard*
Goodwill: *goodwill*
Graduierte(r): *graduate*
grafisch dargestellt: *in diagrammatic form*
Gramm: *gram or gramme*
Gratifikation: *gratuity*
gratis: *free; gratis*
Gratisaktie: *bonus share*
Gratisprobe: *free sample*
Gratulationen: *congratulations*
gratulieren: *congratulate*
greifbar: nicht ~ *intangible*
Gremium: *committee* **einem ~ vorsitzen** *to chair a committee*
Grenze: *limit*
Grenzertrag: *marginal revenue*
Grenzkauf: *marginal purchase*
Grenzkosten: *incremental cost; marginal cost*
Grenzkostenpreiskalkulation: *marginal pricing*
Grenzsteuersatz: *marginal rate of tax*
Grenzübergangsstelle: *customs entry point*
grob: *rough*
grob entwerfen: *rough out*
Gros: *gross*
Großanzeige: *display ad (informal); display advertisement*
großartig: *grand*
Großbuchstaben: *capital letters or block capitals*
Größe: *size* **gängige ~** *stock size* **von mittlerer ~** *middle-sized*
Größendegression: *economies of scale*
Großhandel: *wholesale*
Großhandelspreis: *trade price*
Großhandelspreisindex: *wholesale price index*
Großhandelsverkauf: *trade counter*
Großhändler: *wholesale dealer; jobber (US); wholesaler*
Großindustrie: *big business*
Großraumbüro: *open-plan office*
Großrechner: *mainframe*
Großstadt: *city*
Großunternehmertum: *big business*
großzügig: *generous*
Grund: *cause; grounds; reason*
Grundbau: *engineering*
Grundbesitz: *hereditament; property; real estate; realty* **unbeschränkter ~** *freehold property*
Grundbesitzer: *landowner*
Grundbestand: *stock*
Grundbestandteil: *element*
Grundbuch: *land register*
Grundbuchamt: *land registry*
Grundbucheintragung: *land registration*
Grunddienstbarkeit: *easement*
Grunde: im ~ *basically*
Gründe: *rationale*
Grundeigentümer: *ground landlord* **freier ~** *freeholder*
gründen: *base; establish; form; institute; set up*
Gründer: *founder*
Gründeraktien: *founder's shares*
Grundfläche: *floor space*
Grundgebühr: *flat rate*
Grundgehalt: *basic pay; basic salary*
Grundkapital: genehmigtes ~ *authorized capital*
Grundlage: *base; basis; element*
Grundlagen: *basics*
grundlegend: *primary*
Grundlohn: *basic wage*
Grundnahrungsmittel: *essential foodstuffs*
Grundprodukt: *basic product*
Grundrabatt: *basic discount*
Grundsachverhalt: *basics*
Grundsteuer: *rate (GB); land tax*
Grundstoffe: *primary or basic commodities*
Grundstoffindustrie: *basic industry*
Grundstruktur: *infrastructure*
Grundstückspacht: *ground lease*
Grundstücks- und Immobilienfirma: *estate agency*
Grundstücks- und Immobilienmakler: *estate agent*
Grundstücks- und Immobilienmaklerbüro: *estate agency*
Grundstücksverkäufer: *vendor*
Gründung: *formation or forming*
Gründungsausschuß: *organizing committee*
Gründungskapital: *initial capital*
Gründungsurkunde: *memorandum (and articles) of association*
Grundzins: *ground rent*
Grüne Karte: *green card*
Gruppe: *bracket; group*
Gruppenarbeit: *teamwork*
Gruppenbuchung: *block booking*
gruppieren: *arrange*
Gruppierungen: sozialökonomische ~ *socio-economic groups*
gültig: *valid* **für ~ erklären** *validate*
gültig bleiben: *to remain in effect*
Gültigkeit: *validity*
Gültigkeitsdauer: *period of validity*
Gültigkeitserklärung: *validation*
gültig werden: *to become operative*
Gummiband: *rubber band*
gummiert: *gummed*
Gummistempel: *rubber stamp*
günstig: *favourable*
Gutachten: *opinion; survey*
Gutachter: *consultant; surveyor*
gut bezahlt: *well-paid*
Güteklasse: *class*
Güteklassen: in ~ einteilen *grade*
Güter: langlebige ~ *durable goods* **zu verzollende ~** *goods which are liable to duty*
Güterdepot: *freight depot; goods depot*

Güterkraftverkehr: *road haulage; trucking*
Güterkraftverkehrdepot: *road haulage depot*
Güterverkehr: *trucking*
Güterwagen: *freight car (US); truck; wagon*
Güter zollamtlich abfertigen: *to clear goods through the customs*
Güterzug: *freight train; goods train*
Gütezeichen: *kite mark (GB); quality label*
gutgehend: *flourishing; going; prosperous*
gutheißen: *to approve of*
Gutschein: *chit; coupon; voucher*
gutschreiben: *credit*
Gutschrift: *credit entry*
Gutschriftsanzeige: *credit note*
Gutsverwalter: *land agent*
gut verdienen: *to earn good money*
gut verkäuflich: *saleable*

Hh

Haben: *credit*
Habenbuchung: *credit entry*
Habenseite: *credit side*
Habenspalte: *credit column*
Hab und Gut: *goods and chattels*
Hafen: *docks; harbour; port* **einen ~ anlaufen** *to call at a port*
Hafenanlagen: *harbour installations or harbour facilities; port installations*
Hafenarbeiter: *docker*
Hafenbehörde: *port authority*
Hafengebühren: *dock dues or port dues or harbour dues; harbour dues; port charges or port dues*
haftbar für: *liable for*
haften: *underwrite* **für jdn ~** *to go guarantee for someone* **sie ~ gesamtschuldnerisch** *they are jointly and severally liable*
Haftpflichtversicherung: *third-party insurance*
Haftung: **beschränkte ~** *limited liability* **unbeschränkte ~** *unlimited liability*
Haftungsablehnungserklärung: *disclaimer*
Haftungsbeschränkung: *limitation of liability*
Haftung übernehmen für: *underwrite*
Haken: *check (US); tick*
halb: *half; semi-*
halbe-halbe machen: *to go fifty-fifty*
Halbfabrikate: *semi-finished products*
Halbjahr: *half-year* **erstes ~** *first half or first half-year* **zweites ~** *second half-year or second half*
Halbjahresbericht: *interim report*
halbjährlich: *bi-annually; half-yearly*
Halbtagsbeschäftigung: *part-time employment; part-time work*
Hälfte: *half*
Halt: *stop*
Haltbarkeit eines Produktes: *shelf life of a product*
halten: *hold; keep; last; maintain; peg*
Halter: *holder*
hämmern: *hammer*
Hamsterer: *hoarder* **hamstern** *to hoard*
Hand: **rechte ~** *right-hand man or woman* **von ~** *by hand; manually* **von ~ bedient** *hand-operated* **von ~ geschrieben** *handwritten* **zur ~** *to hand*
handbetrieben: *hand-operated*
Handbuch: *handbook; manual*
Handel: *affair; bargain; commerce; deal; dealing; trade; trading; traffic* **allgemeiner ~** *general trading* **einseitiger ~** *one-way trade* **florierender ~** *flourishing trade* **legaler ~** *fair dealing* **multilateraler ~** *multilateral trade* **rechtmäßiger ~** *lawful trade* **reger ~** *flourishing trade* **zweiseitiger ~** *reciprocal trade*
Handeln: *bargaining*
handeln: *act; bargain; deal; haggle; trade*
Handelsabkommen: *trade agreement*
Handelsattaché: *commercial attaché*
Handelsbedingungen: **erschwerte** *or* **ungünstige** *or* **widrige ~** *adverse trading conditions*
Handelsbeschränkung: *restraint of trade*
Handelsbilanz: *balance of trade or trade balance* **aktive ~** *favourable trade balance* **passive ~** *adverse balance of trade*
Handelsbilanz in Dollar: *dollar balance*
Handelsbrauch: *the customs of the trade*
Handelsbüro: *trade bureau*
Handelsdelegation: *trade mission* **eine hochgestellte** *or* **hochrangige ~** *a high-grade trade delegation*
Handelsembargo: **ein ~ verhängen** *to put an embargo on trade*
Handelsgesellschaft: *trading company*
Handelsgewicht: **britisches ~** *avoirdupois*
Handelshafen: *commercial port*
Handelsinstitut: *commercial college*
Handelskammer: *Chamber of Commerce*
Handelsmarine: *mercantile marine; merchant navy or merchant marine*
Handelsmarke: *trademark or trade name*
Handelsmesse: *trade fair*
Handelsmission: *trade mission*
Handelsnation: *mercantile country*
Handelspartner: *trading partner*
Handelspraktiken: *business practices or industrial practices or trade practices*
Handelsrecht: *commercial law; mercantile law*
Handelsregister: *companies' register*
Handelsschiff: *merchant ship or merchant vessel; merchantman*
Handelsspanne: *mark-up*
Handelsstruktur: *pattern of trade or trading pattern*
handelsüblich: *standard*
Handelsverband: *trade association*
Handelsverbot: *embargo*
Handelsverkehr: *commerce*
Handelsvertreter: *commercial traveller; salesman*

Handelszone: *trading area* **freie ~** *free trade area*
Handel treiben: *deal; trade*
handeltreibend: *mercantile*
handgearbeitet: *handmade*
Handgeld: *earnest*
handgemacht: *handmade*
Handgepäck: *hand luggage; cabin luggage*
handgeschrieben: *handwritten*
Handhabung: *handling*
Händler: *broker; dealer; distributor; merchant; trader* **selbständiger ~** *independent trader or independent shop*
Händlerrabatt: *trade discount; trade terms*
handlich: *handy*
Handlung: *action*
Handlungsvollmacht: *power of attorney; proxy*
Handschrift: *handwriting*
Handwerker: *repairer or repair man*
Handzettel: *flier or flyer; handbill; leaflet*
hängen: *hang*
hart: *hard; severe; severely; stiff*
Hartgeld: *specie*
Hartgeldwährung: *coinage*
Hartpapier: *manilla*
hart verhandeln: *to drive a hard bargain*
Hast: *rush*
häufig: *common; frequent; frequently*
Haupt-: *basic; chief; head; main; major; prime; principal*
Hauptaktionär: *major shareholder*
Hauptaspekte eines Abkommens: *heads of agreement*
Hauptbelastungszeit: *peak period*
Hauptbelastungszeit/Hauptverkehrszeit: außerhalb der ~ *off-peak*
hauptberuflich: *full-time*
Hauptbuch: *ledger*
Hauptbüro: *central office*
Haupterzeugnis: *staple commodity*
Hauptgeschäftsstelle: *head office; headquarters*
Hauptgeschäftsstraße: *High Street*
Hauptindustriezweig: *staple industry*
Hauptmietvertrag *or* **Hauptpachtvertrag:** *headlease*
Hauptprodukt: *staple product*
Hauptsaison: *high season*
Hauptsendezeit: *prime time*
Hauptsitz: *headquarters*
Hauptstadt: *capital city*
Hauptstraße: *Main Street (US)*
Hauptsumme: *principal*
Hauptverkehrszeit: *peak period; rush hour*
Hauptversammlung: außerordentliche ~ *Extraordinary General Meeting* **ordentliche ~** *general meeting or meeting of shareholders or shareholders' meeting*
Haus: *home; house* **außer ~** *out-house; outside* **außer ~ geben** *put out*
Hausbesitz: *house property*
Hausbesitzer: *homeowner; householder*
Hause: nach ~ *homewards*
Häusermakler: *house agent*
hausgemacht: *homemade*
Haushalt: *budget; household*
Haushaltsgeräte: elektrische ~ *white goods*
Haushaltswaren: *household goods; hardware*
Haushaltungskosten: *household expenses*
Hausieren: *door-to-door canvassing*
hausieren: *hawk; peddle*
Hausierer: *hawker*
Hausmarke: *own brand*
Hausmarkenwaren: *own label goods*
Haus mit Grund: *premises*
Hausnachrichten: *house journal or house magazine or house organ (US)*
Hausse: *boom*
Haussemarkt: *bull market*
Haussier: *bull*
Haustelefon: *house (tele)phone; internal (tele)phone*
Haus- und Hausratsversicherung: *house insurance*
Havarie: besondere ~ *particular average* **große ~** *general average*
Headhunter: *headhunter*
Hedging: *hedging*
heften: *pin; pin up*
Hefter: *binder; stapler*
Heftklammer: *staple*
Heftzwecke: *drawing pin*
Heimarbeit: *outwork*
Heimarbeiter: *outside worker; outworker*
Heimathafen: *port of registry*
Heimatland: *home country*
heimlich: *on the quiet*
Heimwerkermagazin: *do-it-yourself magazine*
Heizkostenpauschale: nominelle ~ *a token heating charge*
Hektar: *hectare*
hektisch: *hectic*
helfen: *assist; help*
hemmen: *check*
Hemmnis: *bar; check*
herabgesetzt: *reduced*
herabsetzen: *depress; minimize; reduce; to scale down*
Herabsetzung: *reduction*
Herangehen *or* **Herantreten:** *approach*
heraufsetzen: *mark up; put up; raise; to scale up*
herausbringen: *bring out; get out; launch; release*
herausfinden: *discover*
herausgeben: *issue; publish*
herausgehen: *get out of*
herausschneiden: *excise*
herauswerfen: *throw out*
hereinholen: *recover*
hereinkommen: *enter*

hergestellt: *made*
Herkunft: *origin*
Herkunftsland: *country of origin*
Herkunftszertifikat: *certificate of origin*
Hermes Kreditversicherung: *Export Credit Guarantee Department*
Herr: *gentleman; Mr*
Herr am Empfang: *reception clerk; receptionist*
Herren: *Messrs* **"meine ~"** *"gentlemen"*
Herr Vorsitzender: *Mr Chairman*
herstellen: *make; manufacture; produce; turn out*
Hersteller: *maker; manufacturer; producer*
Herstellerpreis: empfohlener ~ *manufacturer's recommended price (MRP) or recommended retail price (RRP)*
Hersteller von Raubdrucken: *pirate*
Herstellung: *making; manufacture; manufacturing; production* **serienmäßige ~** *mass production*
Herstellungskosten: *manufacturing costs or production costs* **ursprüngliche ~** *historic(al) cost*
Herstellungspreis: *prime cost*
Herstellungsprozeß: *industrial process*
heruntersetzen: *mark down*
herunterstufen: *downgrade*
hervorragend: *excellent*
hetzen: *rush*
heute: bis ~ *to date*
hiermit: *hereby*
Hilfe: *assistance; help; relief; rescue; support*
Hilfe aus Schwierigkeiten: *bail-out*
hinaus: über ... ~ *further to*
hinausbringen: *take out*
hinausgehen über: *exceed*
hinauslaufen auf: *to result from*
Hindernis: *bar; check*
hineingehen: *enter*
hineinnehmen: *take into*
hineinpassen: *fit in*
hineinstecken: *insert*
Hinfracht: *outward cargo or outward freight*
hinlänglich: *adequate*
hinsichtlich: *with respect to*
hinter: *behind*
Hintergründe: *background*
Hinterlegungsstelle: *depositary (US); depository*
Hintermann: *backer*
Hin- und Rückfahrpreis: *return fare or round-trip fare (US)*
Hin- und Rückfahrt: *round trip*
hinweisen auf: *indicate; to point out*
hinzufügen *or* **hinzurechnen:** *add*
historisch: *historic(al)*
hoch: jdn ~ einschätzen *to rate someone highly* **zu ~ ansetzen** *overestimate*
Hochachtungsvoll: *yours faithfully; Yours truly or Truly yours (US)*
hochbezahlt: *highly-paid*
hochbleiben: *hold up*
Hochfinanz: *high finance*
hochgestellt: *highly-placed*
Hochkonjunktur: *boom*
hochqualifiziert: *highly qualified*
Hochsaison: *high season*
hochschnellen: *spiral*
höchst: *extremely; highly*
höchster: *chief; top*
Höchstgebot: *closing bid* **oder gegen ~** *or near offer*
Höchstgewicht: *weight limit*
Höchstgewinne: *record sales or record profits*
Höchstgrenze: *ceiling*
Höchstproduktion: *peak output*
Höchststand: *high; peak* **absoluter ~** *all-time high* **den ~ erreichen** *peak*
Hochtouren: auf ~ *flat out*
hochtreiben: *force up*
hochwertig: *high-grade; high-quality*
hoffen: *hope*
höflich: *polite; politely*
Höhe: *height*
Höhepunkt: *height; peak*
hoher: *high; top; top-flight or top-ranking; top-grade*
höher: *improved; senior*
Hohlmaß: *cubic measure*
Holdinggesellschaft: *holding company*
Honorar: *emoluments; fee; honorarium; remuneration*
Honorarvorschuß: *retainer*
horizontal: *horizontal*
horten: *hoard; stockpile*
Horten von Vorräten: *hoarding of supplies*
Hosteß: *hostess*
Hotel: *hotel*
Hotelgewerbe: *the hotel trade*
Hotelier: *hotelier*
Hotelkette: *hotel chain or chain of hotels*
Hotelunterbringung: *hotel accommodation*
Hubschrauber: *helicopter*
Hülle: *cover; holder*
hundert: etwa ~ *a hundred odd* **um die ~** *a hundred odd*
Hundertstel: *percentile*
Hyperinflation: *hyperinflation*
Hypothek: *mortgage* **eine ~ abzahlen** *to pay off a mortgage* **eine ~ aufnehmen** *mortgage*
hypothekarisch belasten: *mortgage*
Hypothekengläubiger: *mortgagee*
Hypothekenknappheit: *mortgage famine*
Hypothekenpfandbrief: *mortgage bond; mortgage debenture*
Hypothekenschuldner: *mortgager or mortgagor*
Hypothekentilgung: *mortgage payments*
Hypothekenvergabe: die ~ einschränken *to ration mortgages*

Hypothekenwarteliste: *mortgage queue*

Ii

ideal: *ideal*
Idee: *idea*
illegal: *hot; illegal; illegally*
Illegalität: *illegality*
Image: *image*
Imbißstube: *snack bar; takeaway*
Imitation: *fake; imitation*
imitieren: *fake; imitate*
immateriell: *intangible*
immer mehr: *increasingly*
Immobilien: *real estate; property; realty*
Immobilienbesitz verwalten: *to manage property*
Immobilienhändler: *realtor (US)*
Immobilienmakler: *house agent; real estate agent (US)*
Immobilien- und Grundstücksmarkt: *the property market*
Immunität: diplomatische ~ *diplomatic immunity*
Import: *importation; importing*
Importabgabe: *import surcharge*
Importbeschränkungen einführen: *to set limits to imports or to impose import limits*
Importe: sichtbare ~ *visible imports* **unsichtbare ~** *invisible imports*
Importe beschränken: *to put a check on imports*
Importeur *or* **Importfirma:** *importer*
Importgenehmigung: *import licence or import permit*
Importhandel: *import trade*
importieren: *import*
Importkonnossement: *inward bill*
Importlizenz: *import licence or import permit*
Importquote: *import quota*
Importrestriktionen: mit ~ belegen *to impose trade barriers on*
Impuls: *impulse*
impulsiv: etwas ~ tun *to do something on impulse*
Impulskauf: *impulse purchase*
inbegriffen: alles ~ *all-in*
Incentive: *incentive*
Inch: *inch*
Indentgeschäft: *indent*
Index: *index*
Indexbindung: *indexation*
Index der Einzelhandelspreise: *retail price index*
indexgebunden: *index-linked*
Indexierung: *indexation*
Indexierung von Gehaltserhöhungen: *indexation of wage increases*
Indexzahl *or* **Indexziffer:** *index number*
Indikator: *indicator*
indirekt: *indirect*
individuell: *individual*
individuell anpassen: *customize*
Individuum: *individual*
Indossament: *endorsement*
Indossant: *endorser*
Indossat: *endorsee*
industrialisieren: *industrialize*
Industrialisierung: *industrialization*
Industrie: erdölverarbeitende ~ *petroleum industry* **verarbeitende ~** *secondary industry; manufacturing industries*
Industriebetrieb: ein staatseigener *or* **ein verstaatlichter ~** *a state-owned industry*
Industriedesign: *industrial design*
Industriegebiet: *industrial estate or trading estate; industrial park*
Industriegelände: *industrial estate or industrial park*
Industriegüter: *heavy equipment; manufactured goods*
industriell: *industrial*
Industrieller: *industrialist*
Industriepraktiken: *business practices or industrial practices or trade practices*
Industriewerte: *industrials*
Industriezentrum: *industrial centre*
Industriezweig: arbeitsintensiver ~ *labour-intensive industry* **expandierender ~** *a growth industry*
ineffizient: *inefficient* **Ineffizienz** *inefficiency*
Inflation: galoppierende ~ *galloping inflation; runaway inflation* **kostentreibende ~** *cost-push inflation*
inflationsbedingt: *inflationary*
Inflationsbekämpfung: *disinflation*
Inflationsrate: *rate of inflation or inflation rate* **der ~ angeglichen** *index-linked* **einstellige ~** *single-figure inflation*
Inflationssicherung: *a hedge against inflation*
Inflationswährung: *inflated currency*
inflatorisch: *inflationary*
Information: *information (bureau); inquiry office* **fehlende ~** *lack of data or lack of information*
Informationsmaterial: *information*
Informationstechnologie: *information technology*
Information zugänglich machen: *to share information or to share data*
informieren: *advise; brief; inform*
Infrastruktur: *infrastructure*
Ingenieur: beratender ~ *consulting engineer*
Inhaber: *bearer; holder; proprietor*
Inhaberin: *proprietress*
Inhaberscheck: *cheque to bearer; negotiable cheque*
Inhaberschuldverschreibung: *bearer bond*
Inhalt: *contents*
Inhaltsbeschreibung: unkorrekte ~ *false description of contents*
Inhaltsverzeichnis: *docket; table of contents*

Initialien: *initials*
Initiative: **die ~ ergreifen** *to take the initiative* **eine ~ aufgreifen** *to follow up an initiative*
initiieren: *pioneer*
Inkasso: *encashment*
Inkassobeauftragter: *(debt) collector*
Inkassobüro *or* **Inkassofirma:** *debt collection agency; collecting agency*
Inkassowechsel: fälliger ~ *bills for collection*
inklusive: *inclusive*
Inklusivpreis: *all-in price or rate; all-in rate*
inkompetent: *incompetent; inefficient*
Inkompetenz: *inefficiency*
Inlandmarkt: *domestic market*
Inlandsabsatz: *home sales or sales in the home market; domestic sales*
Inlandsflug: *internal flight*
Inlandsfrachtkosten: *inland freight charges*
Inlandsmarkt: *home or domestic market*
Inlandsporto: *inland postage*
Inlandsproduktion: *domestic production*
Inlandsverbrauch: *home consumption or domestic consumption*
Innehaben einer Position: *tenure*
Innenministerium: *the Home Office*
Innenstadt: *downtown*
innerbetrieblich: *in-house; internal; internally*
innovatorisch: *innovative*
Innung: *guild*
inoffiziell: *off the record; unofficial; unofficially*
insbesondere: *in particular*
Inselanzeige: *solus (advertisement)*
Inserat: ein ~ aufgeben *to put an ad in a paper*
Inserent: *advertiser*
insgesamt: *altogether*
Insider: *insider*
Insiderhandel: *insider dealing; insider trading*
insolvent: *bankrupt; insolvent*
Insolvenz: *insolvency*
Insolvenzfeststellung: *hammering*
Inspektionstour: eine ~ machen *to carry out a tour of inspection*
inspizieren: *survey*
Instabilität: *instability*
Installation: *installation*
Installationen und Einbauten: *fixtures and fittings*
installieren: *install*
Instandhaltung: *maintenance*
Instandhaltungskosten: *upkeep*
instandsetzen: *repair*
Instandsetzung: *repair*
Institut: *college; institute; institution*
institutionell: *institutional*
instruieren: *brief*
Instrument: *instrument*
Integration: horizontale ~ *horizontal integration* **vertikale ~** *vertical integration*
integrieren: *incorporate; integrate*
Intercity-: *inter-city*
Interesse: *concern; interest* **im ~ von** *on behalf of* **persönliches ~** *vested interest*
Interesse hervorrufen: *interest*
Interessengruppe: *pressure group*
Interessenkonflikt: *conflict of interest*
Interessent: *prospect*
Interessenten: *potential customers*
Interessenverband: *lobby*
interessieren: *interest* **sich ~ für** *interested in*
Interface: *interface*
Interimszahlung: *interim payment*
intern: *internal; internally*
international: *international*
Internationale Arbeitsorganisation: *International Labour Organization*
intervenieren: *interfere; intervene*
Intervention: *interference; intervention*
Interventionspreis: *intervention price*
Interview: *interview*
Interviewer: *interviewer*
Interviewter: *interviewee*
Inventar aufnehmen: *inventory*
inventarisieren: *inventory; to take stock*
Inventarliste: *inventory*
Inventarverzeichnis: *inventory*
Inventur: *stocktaking*
Inventur machen: *to take stock*
investieren: *invest; sink*
Investition: *contribution of capital; investment* **risikofreie** *or* **sichere ~** *secure investment*
Investitionsausgaben: *capital outlay*
Investitionsbeihilfe: *investment grant*
Investitionsgüter: *capital equipment*
Investitionsmöglichkeiten: *investment opportunities*
Investitionsniveau: hohes ~ *high level of investment*
Investitionsrentabiliät: *return on investment (ROI) or on capital*
Investitionszuschuß: *investment grant*
Investmentbank: *merchant bank*
Investmentfonds: offene ~ *mutual funds (US)* **offener ~** *unit trust*
Investmenttrust: *investment company or investment trust*
Investor: *contributor of capital; investor*
irreführen *or* **irreleiten:** *misdirect*
irrtümlich: *in error or by error*

Jj

jagen: *chase*
jäh: *steep*

Jahr: *year* **einmal pro ~** *on an annual basis* **im ~** *per annum* **pro ~** *per year; per annum* **vorletztes ~** *the year before last*
Jahrbuch: *yearbook*
Jahre des Aufschwungs: *the boom years*
Jahresabschluß: *annual accounts; year end* **berichtigter ~** *qualified accounts*
Jahresbericht: *directors' report*
Jahresbericht des Aufsichtsratsvorsitzenden: *the chairman's report*
Jahresbilanz: *annual accounts*
Jahreseinkommen: *annual income*
Jahreshälfte: die erste ~ *the first half of the year*
Jahreshauptversammlung: ordentliche ~ *annual general meeting; Annual General Meeting*
Jahresmiete: *rack rent*
Jahrespension *or* **Jahresrente:** *annuity*
Jahreszeit: umsatzschwache ~ *slack season* **umsatzstarke ~** *busy season*
jahreszeitlich bedingt: *seasonal*
Jahreszinssatz: *annualized percentage rate*
jährlich: *annual; annualized; annually; yearly*
je nach: *depending on*
jetzig: *present*
Jingle: *advertising jingle or publicity jingle*
Jobben: *jobbing*
Joint-venture: *joint venture*
Journal: *daybook; journal*
Journalist: *journalist*
junior: *junior*
Juniorpartner: *junior partner*
Junk Bonds: *junk bonds*
juristisch: *legal; legally*
Justiz-: *judicial*

Kk

Kabine: *booth*
Kaffeepause: *coffee break*
Kai: *dock; quay; wharf* **am ~ festmachen** *dock*
Kaigebühren: *wharfage*
Kaimeister: *wharfinger*
Kalender: *calendar*
Kalenderjahr: *calendar year*
Kalendermonat: *calendar month*
Kalfaktor: *dogsbody (informal); gofer (US)*
Kalkulation: *budgeting; computation* **grobe ~** *rough calculation*
Kalkulationen vornehmen: *to work out the figures*
kalkulierbar: *computable*
kalkulieren: *calculate; compute; reckon*
Kaltlagerung: *cold storage*
Kampagne: *campaign* **landesweite** *or* **überregionale ~** *national campaign*
Kampf: *battle*
Kanal: *channel*
Kandidat: *appointee; candidate; interviewee; nominee*
Kandidatur: seine ~ zurückziehen *stand down*
Kante: *edge*
Kanzlei: *office*
Kapazität: *capacity; throughput* **ungenutzte ~ aufbrauchen** *to use up spare capacity*
Kapazitätsausnutzung: *capacity utilization*
Kapazitätsfaktor: *load factor*
Kapital: *capital; finance; principal* **arbeitendes ~** *productive capital* **ausgegebenes ~** *issued capital* **einbezahltes ~** *paid-up capital* **eingezahltes ~** *called up capital* **genehmigte ~** *unissued capital* **gewinnbringendes ~** *productive capital* **nicht arbeitendes ~** *money lying idle or idle money* **totes ~** *dead money; idle capital* **verfügbares ~** *available capital; fund* **voll einbezahltes ~** *fully paid-up capital*
Kapitalanlage: sichere ~ *safe investment*
Kapitalanlagegesellschaft: *investment company or investment trust*
Kapitalanlagen: festverzinsliche ~ *fixed-interest investments*
Kapitalanleger: *investor*
Kapitaleinkommen: *unearned income*
Kapitaleinkünfte: *investment income*
Kapitaleinlage: *principal*
Kapitalertrag: *interest; unearned income*
Kapitalerträge: *investment income*
Kapitalflucht: *flight of capital*
Kapitalgesellschaft: *corporation* **eine ~ gründen** *incorporate*
kapitalisieren: *capitalize*
Kapitalisierung von Rücklagen: *capitalization of reserves*
Kapitalismus: *capitalism*
Kapitalist: *capitalist*
kapitalistisch: *capitalist*
Kapitalkonto: *capital account*
Kapitalmarkt: *capital market*
Kapitalrendite: *return on investment (ROI) or on capital*
Kapitalreserven *or* **Kapitalrücklagen:** *capital reserves*
Kapital schlagen aus: *capitalize on*
Kapitalstruktur eines Unternehmens: *capital structure of a company*
Kapitalsumme: *principal*
Kapitaltransfersteuer: *capital transfer tax*
Kapitalverkehr: *movements of capital; circulation of capital*
Kapitalverlust: *capital loss*
Karat: *carat*
Kargo: *cargo*
Karriere: *career*
Karrierefrau: *career woman*
Karte: *card; ticket*
Kartei: *card index*
Karteibuchstabe: *index letter*
Karteikarte: *filing card; index card*

Karteikarten anlegen: *card-index*
Karteinummer: *index number*
Kartell: *cartel; combine; ring*
Kartellamt: das ~ *the Monopolies Commission (GB)*
Kartenhülle: *card holder*
Kartenschalter: *ticket counter*
Kartenschwarzhändler: *tout*
Kartenverkäufer: *booking clerk*
Kartenverkaufsstand: *ticket booth*
Kartenvorverkaufsstelle: *ticket agency*
Karton: *card; cardboard; carton*
Kassakonto: *cash account*
Kasse: *cash desk; checkout; box office; ticket office; pay desk; cash till* **gemeinsame ~** *kitty* **getrennte ~ machen** *to go Dutch*
Kassegeschäft: *cash sale; cash transaction*
Kasse machen: *cash up*
Kassenbeleg: *sales slip*
Kassenbestand: *balance in hand; cash balance*
Kassenbuch: *cash book*
Kassenkonto: *cash account*
Kassenschlager: *money-spinner*
Kassenterminal: *electronic point of sale*
Kassenwartbericht: *treasurer's report*
Kassenzettel: *sales slip*
Kassette: *cassette*
Kassierer: *cashier; teller*
Kasten: *box; advertisement panel*
Kasten für Verbesserungsvorschläge: *suggestion box*
Katalog: *catalogue or catalog (US)*
katalogisieren: *catalogue or catalog (US)*
Katalogpreis: *catalogue price; list price*
Katasteramt: *land registry*
katastrophal: *disastrous*
Katastrophe: *disaster*
Kategorie: *category; class*
Kauf: *purchase* **ein guter ~** *a good buy*
Kaufanreiz: *sales appeal*
Kauf eines Aktienpakets: *greenmail*
kaufen: *buy; purchase*
Käufer: *buyer; purchaser; shopper* **ein potentieller ~** *a prospective buyer* **ernsthafter ~** *genuine purchaser*
Käufermarkt: *a buyers' market*
Kauffrau: *dealer; trader*
Kaufhaus: *department store*
Kaufkraft: *buying power; purchasing power; spending power*
Kaufmann: *dealer; trader; tradesman*
Kauf mit Rückgaberecht: *sale or return*
Kaufoption: *call option*
Kaufpreis: *purchase price*
Kaufsteuer: *purchase tax*
Kaufunlust: *consumer resistance*
Kaufvertrag: *bill of sale*
Kaution: *bail*
Kautschuk: *rubber*
Kenntnis: *knowledge* **in ~ setzen** *advise; inform* **zur ~ nehmen** *note*
Kennzahl: internationale ~ *international dialling code*
Kennzeichen: *flag*
Kettenladen: *chain store*
Kilobyte: *kilobyte*
Kilo(gramm): *kilo(gram)*
Kilometer: *kilometre or kilometer (US)*
Kilometerpauschale: *mileage allowance*
Kiosk: *kiosk*
Kiste: *bin; case; crate; packing case*
Kisten: in ~ verpacken *case; crate* **sechs ~ Wein** *six cases of wine*
Klage: *action; lawsuit; legal proceedings* **eine ~ zurückziehen** *to abandon an action* **zivilrechtliche ~** *civil action*
Klage erheben or **klagen:** *to take legal action; to sue*
Kläger: *claimant; plaintiff*
klären: *sort out*
klarmachen: sich ~ *realize*
Klasse: *bracket; category; class* **zweite ~** *second-class*
klassifizieren: *classify; grade*
Klassifizierung: *classification*
Klausel: *article; clause; provision; stipulation*
Klebeetikett: *gummed label*
Klebestreifen: *tape*
Klebstoff: *glue; gum*
Kleinaktie: *penny share or penny stock (US)*
Kleinanleger: *the small investor or the private investor*
Kleinanzeigen: *classified ads or small ads or want ads (informal)*
Kleinbetrieb: ein ~ *a small-scale enterprise*
Kleinbetriebe: *small businesses*
Kleingeld: *small change; float; loose change; small change*
kleinstädtisch: *provincial*
Kleintastatur: *keypad*
Kleintransporter: offener ~ *pickup (truck)*
Kleinunternehmer: *small businessman*
klettern: *climb; spiral*
Klientel: *clientele; custom*
Klienten: einen ~ einführen *to introduce a client*
Klubbeitrag: *club subscription*
Klubmitgliedschaft: *club membership*
knapp: *marginal; scarce* **zu ~ abwiegen** *to give short weight*
knapp an: *short of*
Knappheit: *scarceness or scarcity*
knapp sein: *in short supply*
Know-how: *know-how*
Kodex: *code*
Kodierung: *coding*
Koffer: *case; suitcase*
Kohlebergwerk: *pit*

Kohlepapier: *carbon paper*
Kollege: *counterpart*
Kollektivinhaberschaft: *collective ownership*
kollidieren: *crash*
Kollision: *crash*
Kolonne: *column*
Kolumne: *column*
Kombination: *combination*
Kombination mehrerer Versicherungsarten: *blanket insurance*
Kombination mehrerer Versicherungsdeckungen: *a comprehensive or an all-in policy*
Kombination verschiedener Versicherungsarten: *all-risks policy*
Komitee: *committee*
Kommanditgesellschaft: *limited partnership*
kommerzialisieren: *commercialize*
Kommerzialisierung: *commercialization*
kommerziell: *commercial; commercially*
Kommission: *commission*
Kommissionsgebühr: *commission*
Kommissionsware: *goods on consignment*
kommunal: *municipal*
Kommunalobligation: *municipal bond or local authority bond*
Kommunalverwaltung: *local government*
Kommunikation: **horizontale ~** *horizontal communication*
Kommunikationswege: **neue ~ erschließen** *to open up new channels of communication*
kommunizieren: *communicate*
kompetent: *competent*
Kompetenzstreit: *demarcation dispute*
komplett: *complete* **etwas ~ kaufen** *to purchase something outright or to make an outright purchase*
Komplex/komplex: *complex*
Kompromiß: *compromise* **einen ~ schließen** *compromise*
Kondition: *condition*
Konferenzprogramm: *conference timetable*
Konferenzprotokoll: *conference proceedings*
Konferenz zur Absatzförderung *or* **Absatzplanung:** *sales conference or sales meeting*
Konfiskation: *forfeiture*
konfiszieren: *forfeit; sequester or sequestrate*
Konfiszierung: *sequestration*
Konjunkturaufschwung *or* **Konjunkturbelebung:** *revival of trade*
Konjunkturindikatoren: **staatliche ~** *government economic indicators*
Konjunkturindustrie: *boom industry*
Konjunkturprognose: **langfristige ~** *long-range economic forecast*
Konjunkturrückgang: *recession* **starker ~** *slump*
Konjunkturtief: *trough*
Konjunkturzyklus: *economic cycle or trade cycle or business cycle*
Konkurrent: *competitor; rival*
Konkurrenz: *competition*
Konkurrenzartikel: *competitive product(s)*
konkurrenzfähig: *competitive*
Konkurrenzfähigkeit: *competitiveness*
Konkurrenzprodukte: *competing products; competitive products*
Konkurrenz verdrängen: *to freeze out competition*
konkurrierend: *competing*
Konkurs: *bankruptcy* **den ~ anmelden** *or* **einen ~ stellen** *to file a petition in bankruptcy*
Konkursaufhebung: *discharge in bankruptcy*
Konkurseröffnungsbeschluß: *adjudication of bankruptcy or declaration of bankruptcy*
Konkursgläubiger: **nachrangiger ~** *deferred creditor*
Konkursschuldner: *bankrupt* **entlasteter ~** *discharged bankrupt* **nicht entlasteter ~** *undischarged bankrupt* **rehabilitierter ~** *certificated bankrupt*
Konkursverwalter: *liquidator; official receiver*
Konnossement: *bill of lading* **unreines ~** *foul bill of lading*
Konsolidieren: *funding*
konsolidieren: *consolidate*
Konsols: *consols (GB)*
Konsortium: *consortium; syndicate*
konstruieren: *construct*
Konstrukteur: *constructor*
Konstruktion: *construction*
konstruktiv: *constructive*
konsultieren: *consult*
Konsum: *consumption*
Konsument: *consumer*
Konsumforschung: *consumer research*
Konsumgesellschaft: *consumer society*
Konsumgüter: *consumable goods; consumer goods* **kurzlebige ~** *non-durables* **langlebige ~** *consumer durables*
Kontakt aufnehmen mit: *contact*
Kontaktperson: *contact*
Kontingent: *quota*
Kontingentierungssystem: *quota system*
kontinuierlich: *continuous*
Konto: *account* **ein ~ auflösen** *to close an account* **ein ~ ausgleichen** *or* **begleichen** *to settle an account* **ein ~ belasten** *to debit an account* **ein ~ einrichten** *or* **eröffnen** *to open an account* **ein ~ sperren** *to stop an account* **gemeinsames ~** *joint account* **gesperrtes ~** *frozen account; account on stop* **laufendes ~** *checking account (US); cheque account; current account; drawing account* **umsatzloses ~** *dead account* **überzogenes ~** *overdrawn account*
Kontoauszug: *bank statement*
Kontokorrentkonto: *demand deposit (US); drawing account*
Kontokorrentkonto mit Kreditlinie: *open account*
Konto mit Habensaldo: *account in credit*

Kontostand: *bank balance*
Kontrollabschnitt: *counterfoil*
Kontrolle: *check; control; inspection* **außer ~** *out of control* **eine ~ anordnen** *to issue an inspection order* **unter ~** *under control*
Kontrolleur: *inspector; supervisor*
Kontrollgruppe: *control group*
kontrollieren: *check; control; inspect*
Kontrolliste: *tally; tally sheet*
Kontrollsiegel: *inspection stamp*
Kontrolltaste: *control key*
konvertierbar: nicht ~ *inconvertible*
Konvertierbarkeit: *convertibility*
Konvertierung: *conversion*
Konzept: *rough copy; draft*
Konzern: *concern; group*
Konzernergebnisse: *group results*
Konzerngesellschaft: *related company*
Konzession: *concession; licence or license (US)*
Konzessionär: *concessionnaire*
Konzessionsinhaber: *licensee*
Konzession zum Alkoholverkauf: *off licence*
konzipieren: *draft; draw up*
Kooperation: *co-operation*
kooperativ: *co-operative*
Kooperative: *co-operative*
kooperieren: *co-operate*
Kopf: pro ~ *per head; per capita*
Kopie: *copy; duplicate; hard copy; imitation* **beglaubigte ~** *certified copy* **getreue ~** *true copy*
kopieren: *copy; imitate*
Kopierer: *copier or copying machine*
Kopiergerät: *duplicating machine; duplicator; copying machine*
Kopierzentrum: *photocopying bureau*
koppeln: *link*
Korb: *basket*
Körperschaftssteuer: *corporation tax*
Korrektur: *correction; rectification*
Korrespondent: *correspondence clerk; correspondent*
Korrespondenz: *correspondence*
korrigieren: *correct; rectify*
kostbar: *valuable*
Kosten: *charge; cost; expense; outlay* **die ~ decken** *to cover costs* **gesellschaftliche ~** *social costs* **mit hohen ~** *at great expense*
kosten: *cost; sample*
Kostenanalyse: *cost analysis*
Kostenanschlag: *bid*
Kostenaufwand: mit geringem ~ *for a modest outlay*
Kostenberechnung: *costing*
kostendeckend arbeiten: *break even*
Kostendeckungspunkt: *breakeven point*
Kostenfaktor: *cost factor*
kostenintensiv: *at great expense*
kostenlos: *free (of charge)*
Kosten-Nutzen-Analyse: *cost-benefit analysis*
Kostenrechner: *cost accountant*
Kostenrechnung: *cost accounting*
Kostenrentabilität: *cost-effectiveness*
Kostensenkung: *cost-cutting*
Kostenstelle: *cost centre*
Kostenvoranschlag: *bid; estimate; quotation* **einen ~ machen** *to put in an estimate*
kostenwirksam: *cost-effective*
kostspielig: *costly; dear; expensive*
Kosumgesellschaft: *consumer society*
Kraft: *energy; force; power* **in ~** *in operation* **in ~ sein** *to be in force* **in ~ treten** *to come into force; to become operative*
Kraftfahrzeugkennzeichen: *registration number*
Kraftfahrzeugversicherung: *motor insurance*
Kraftstoff: *fuel*
Kragen: *collar*
Kran: *crane*
krank: *sick*
Krankengeld: *sick pay; sickness benefit*
Krankenversicherung: *health insurance; medical insurance* **private ~** *a private health scheme*
krank geschrieben sein: *to be on sick leave*
Krankheit: *sickness*
Kredit: *credit; loan* **auf ~** *on credit* **befristeter ~** *term loan* **kurzfristiger ~** *short credit; short-term loan* **langfristiger ~** *extended credit* **offener ~** *open credit* **prolongierter ~** *extended credit* **revolvierender ~** *revolving credit* **verlängerter ~** *extended credit*
Kreditaufnahme: *borrowing*
Kreditaufnahme zu Anlagezwecken: *leverage*
Kreditauskunft: *status inquiry*
Kreditauskunftei: *credit agency or credit bureau (US)*
Kreditbank: *credit bank*
Kredite: eingefrorene ~ *frozen credits*
Kreditfähigkeit: *borrowing power*
Kreditgeber letzter Hand: *lender of the last resort*
Kreditgenossenschaft: *credit union (US)*
Kredithai: *loan shark*
Kreditinstitut: *financial institution*
Kreditkarte: *credit card*
Kreditkartenhülle or Kreditkarteninhaber: *credit card holder*
Kreditkontrolle: *credit control*
Kreditlimit: *credit limit; lending limit*
Kreditlinie: eine ~ einräumen *to open a line of credit*
Kreditmodalitäten: *credit facilities*
Kreditnehmer: *borrower*
Kreditrestriktionen: *credit squeeze* **Kreditrestriktionen aufheben** *to lift credit restrictions*
Kreditsaldo: *credit balance*
Kreditspalte: *credit column*
Kredittransfer: *credit transfer or transfer of funds*
Kreditvergaben: *bank borrowings*

Kreditwucher: *usury*
kreditwürdig: *creditworthy*
Kreditwürdigkeit: *creditworthiness*
Kredit zum Hauskauf: *home loan*
Kreisdiagramm: *pie chart*
Kreislauf: *cycle*
Kreuzkurs: *cross rate*
kriminell: *criminal*
Krise: *crisis*
Krisenmanager: *company doctor; troubleshooter*
Krisenmaßnahmen ergreifen: *to take crisis* or *emergency measures*
Krisenplan: *contingency plan*
kritisieren: *criticize*
Kronanwalt: *Queen's Counsel (GB)*
Kubikmaß: *cubic measure*
Kugelschreiber: *pen*
Kuhhandel: *horse trading*
Kühlhaus: *cold store*
Kühlhauslagerung: *cold storage*
kümmern: sich ~ um *attend to*
kumulativ: *cumulative*
kündbar: *terminable*
Kunde: *client; customer* **ein langjähriger** or **ein treuer ~** *long-standing customer* or *customer of long standing*
Kundenabgänge: *loss of customers*
Kundenattraktivität: *customer appeal*
Kundenbetreuer: *account executive*
Kundendienst: *after-sales service; customer service department* **technischer ~** *service department*
Kundendienstmechaniker: *service engineer*
Kundendienstvertragswerkstatt: *service centre*
Kundenfang: auf ~ sein *to tout for custom*
Kundenkonto: *account* **ein ~ einrichten** or **eröffnen** *to open an account* **ein ~ sperren** *to close an account*
Kundenkredit: *consumer credit*
Kundenkreditkarte: *charge card*
Kundenkreditkonto: *charge account; credit account*
Kundenkreis: *clientele*
Kundentreue: *customer loyalty*
kündigen: *leave; quit; resign; terminate*
Kündigung: *notice; resignation; termination* **erzwungene ~** *constructive dismissal* **seine ~ einreichen** *to tender one's resignation*
Kündigungsfrist: *period of notice*
Kündigungsklausel: *termination clause*
Kündigungsschreiben: *notice*
Kündigungsschutz: gesetzliche ~ *security of tenure*
Kundin: *customer*
Kundschaft: *clientele; custom*
künftig: *hereafter*
Kunstfasern: *synthetic fibres*
Kunststoff: *synthetic materials*
Kupon: *dividend warrant* **cum** or **mit ~** *cum coupon* **ex** or **ohne ~** *ex coupon*
Kurier: *courier*
Kurierdienst: *parcel delivery service*
Kurs: *course; policy*
Kurse: die ~ manipulieren *to rig the market*
Kurs-Gewinn-Verhältnis: *price/earnings ratio (P/E ratio)*
Kurskorrektur: technische ~ *technical correction*
Kursmanipulant: *stock market manipulator*
Kursmanipulation: *stock market manipulation*
Kursnotierung: *quotation on the Stock Exchange* or *Stock Exchange quotation*
Kurssicherungsgeschäft: *hedging*
Kursus: *course*
Kurve: *curve*
Kurzarbeit: *short time*
Kürze: in ~ *in the short term*
kurzem: vor ~ *recently*
kürzen: *cut; cut down (on); dock*
kürzeren: den ~ ziehen *lose out*
kurzfristig: *at short notice; short-term; on a short-term basis*
kurzfristig aufnehmen: *to borrow short*
Kurzmitteilung: *compliments slip*
Kurzschrift: *shorthand*
Kurzstreckenflug: *short-haul flight*
Kurzübersicht: *profile*
Kürzung: *abatement; cut; cutback; retrenchment*
Küste: der ~ vorgelagert *off-shore*

Ll

Labor: *laboratory*
Labortechniker: *laboratory technician*
Ladefähigkeit: *load-carrying capacity*
Ladelinie or **Lademarke:** *load line*
Ladeliste: *manifest*
Laden: *outfit; shop*
laden: *load*
Ladenaufsicht: *floorwalker*
Ladenbesitzer: kleine ~ *small shopkeepers*
Ladendieb: *shoplifter*
Ladendiebstahl: *shoplifting; shrinkage (informal)*
Ladenfront: *shop front*
Ladenhüter: *a drug on the market*
Ladeninhaber: *shopkeeper*
Ladenkasse: *till*
Ladenpreis: *retail price*
Ladenräume: *shop premises*
Ladenschluß: *closing time*
Ladentisch: *counter*
Ladeplatz: *loading bay*
Laderampe: *loading ramp*
Ladung: *cargo; load; shipment; summons*
Ladungskontrolleur: *tally clerk*

Lage: *location; position; situation*
Lager: *stockroom; store; storeroom; warehouse* **auf ~ haben** *carry* **auf ~ halten** *keep; stock*
Lagerarbeiter: *warehouseman*
Lager auffüllen: *restock; stock up*
Lagerauffüllung: *restocking*
Lagerbestand: *stock*
Lagerbestände: *inventory*
Lagerbestände flüssig machen: *to liquidate stock*
Lagerbestandsabschreibung: *stock depreciation*
Lagerbestandshöhe: *stock level*
Lagerbestandsverzeichnis: *stock figures; stocklist*
Lagereinrichtungen: *storage facilities*
Lagerfähigkeit eines Produktes: *shelf life of a product*
Lagergeld: *storage*
Lagerhalle: *store*
Lagerhaus: *depot; godown; storage company; store; warehouse*
Lagerhauskapazität: *warehouse capacity*
Lagerist: *storekeeper or storeman*
Lagerkapazität: *storage capacity*
Lagerkosten: *storage*
lagern: *store; warehouse*
Lagerraum: *storeroom*
Lagersteuerung: *stock control*
Lagerumschlag: *stock turn or stock turnround or stock turnover*
Lagerung: *storage; warehousing*
Lagerungsfirma: *storage company*
Lagerverwalter: *stock controller; storekeeper or storeman*
lahm: *dull; lame*
lahmlegen: *check*
Laisser-faire-Wirtschaftspolitik: *laissez-faire economy*
Land: *country; land* **an ~ ziehen** *pull off (informal)* **erdölförderndes ~** *oil-producing country* **meistbegünstigtes ~** *most favoured nation*
Landarbeiter: *agricultural labourer*
Landbesitzrecht: *tenure*
landen: *land*
Länder: erdölexportierende ~ *oil-exporting countries* **erdölimportierende ~** *oil-importing countries*
Landesregierung: *provincial government or state government*
landesweit: *nationwide*
Landwirtschaft: *agriculture; farming* **gemischte ~** *mixed farming*
Landwirtschaft betreiben: *farm*
landwirtschaftlich: *agricultural*
lange: schon ~ bestehend *long-standing*
Länge: *length*
langfristig: *on a long-term basis; long-term* **etwas ~ betrachten** *to take the long view*
Langläufer: *longs*
langsam: *slow; slowly* **sich ~ bewegen** *drift; edge*
Langschrift: *longhand*
Langstreckenflug: *long-haul or long-distance flight*
lästig: *onerous*
Lastkraftwagen: *lorry; truck*
Lastschrift: *debit entry*
Lastschriftanzeige: *debit note*
Lastwagen: *lorry; truck*
Lastwagenfahrer: *lorry driver; teamster (US); trucker*
Lastwagenladung: *lorry-load*
Lauf: im ~ *in the course of*
Laufbahn: *career*
laufend: *in progress; ruling*
Laufzeit: *life; period of validity*
laut: *according to; as per; under*
Layout: *layout*
Leasing: *leasing*
Lebenserwartung: *life expectancy*
Lebenshaltungskosten: *cost of living*
Lebenshaltungskostenindex: *cost-of-living index*
lebenslang: *for life*
Lebenslauf: *curriculum vitae; résumé (US)*
Lebensmittel: *food; provisions*
Lebensmittellieferant: *caterer*
Lebensstandard: *standard of living or living standards*
Lebensunterhalt: *subsistence*
Lebensversicherung: *life assurance; life insurance* **zeitlich begrenzte ~** *term insurance*
Lebenszeit: auf ~ *for life*
lebhaft: *brisk*
leer: *blank; empty*
leeren: *empty*
Leergut: *empties*
Leerpackung: *dummy pack*
Leertaste: *space bar*
Leerung: *collection*
Leerverkauf: *short selling or selling short*
leerverkaufen: *to sell short*
legal: *over the counter; legal*
legalisieren: *legalize; validate*
Legalisierung: *legalization*
Legalität: *legality*
legen: *lay; place; put* **sich ~** *peter out*
Lehre: *apprenticeship*
Lehrer: *instructor*
Lehrgang: kaufmännischer ~ *commercial course*
Lehrling: *apprentice; trainee*
Lehrvertrag: *indentures or articles of indenture*
Leibrente: *annuity for life or life annuity*
leicht: *easy; easily; light; slight; slightly*
Leichtindustrie: *light industry*
leicht verderblich: *perishable*
leiden: *suffer*
Leihen: *hire*

leihen: *advance; borrow; loan; rent*
Leihgebühr: *rental*
Leihhaus: *pawnshop*
Leihwagen: *hire car*
Leim: *glue* **leimen** *to glue*
leisten: sich ~ *afford*
Leistung: *benefit; merit; performance; proficiency*
Leistungsanreize für Arbeitnehmer: *fringe benefits; perks*
Leistungsbeurteilung: *merit rating; performance review*
leistungsfähig: *capable; efficient*
Leistungsfähigkeit: *efficiency*
Leistungsgehalt *or* **Leistungslohn:** *payment by results*
Leistungsprämie: *incentive bonus; merit award or merit bonus*
Leistungszulage: *incentive bonus or incentive payment; merit increase; productivity bonus*
Leitartikel: *editorial*
leiten: *conduct; direct; head; head up; lead; manage; run*
leitend: *senior*
Leiter: *director; head; ladder; leader; superintendent*
Leiter der Buchhaltung: *accounts manager; controller (US)*
Leiter der EDV-Abteilung: *computer manager*
Leiter der Fertigung: *production manager*
Leiter der PR-Abteilung: *public relations officer*
Leiter der Schadenabteilung: *claims manager*
Leiter des Finanzamtes: *inspector of taxes or tax inspector*
Leitung: *chairmanship; control; direction* **unter neuer ~** *under new management*
Leitungsebene: unterste ~ *first-line management; front-line management*
Leitzins: *prime rate*
lesbar: *readable*
Lesepistole: *light pen*
letzter: *final; last; late; latest; ultimate*
Leverage: *leverage*
Leveraged Buyout: *leveraged buyout*
liberalisieren: *decontrol*
Lichtstift: *light pen*
Liebe(r): *dear*
Lieblings-: *favourite*
Lieferant: *supplier*
Lieferauftrag: *delivery order*
liefern: *deliver; supply*
Lieferpreis: *delivered price*
Lieferschein: *delivery note*
Lieferung: *delivery; supply* **zahlbar bei ~** *payable on delivery*
Lieferungen: ausstehende ~ *outstanding orders; back orders*
Liefervertrag: *contract*
Lieferwagen: *delivery van*
Lieferzeit: *delivery time; lead time*
Liegegeld: *demurrage*
Liegenschaften: *property*
Liegeplatz: *berth; mooring*
LIFO-Abschreibungsmethode: *last in first out (LIFO)*
LIFO-Personalpolitik: *last in first out (LIFO)*
Lift: *elevator (US)*
Limit: *limit*
Linie: *line; policy* **in erster ~** *mainly* **punktierte ~** *dotted line*
Linien: feine ~ *feint*
Liniendiagramm: *line chart or line graph*
Linienflug: *scheduled flight*
Linienmanagement: *line management*
Linienorganisation: *line organization*
Linienschiff: *liner*
liniert: *lined*
linker: *left-hand*
Liquidation: *liquidation; winding up* **freiwillige ~** *voluntary liquidation*
Liquidationsbeschluß: gerichtlicher ~ *compulsory winding up order*
Liquidator: *liquidator*
Liquiditätskrise: *liquidity crisis*
Liquiditätsreserven: *cash reserves*
Lire: *lira*
Liste: *catalogue or catalog (US); list; register; schedule*
Listenpreis: *catalogue price; list price*
Liter: *litre or liter (US)*
Literatur: *literature*
Lizenz: *licence or license (US)*
Lizenzgebühren: *royalty*
Lobby: *lobby*
Lochkarte: *punched card*
Lockartikel: *loss-leader*
Lohn: *compensation (US); pay; remuneration*
Lohnabrechnung: *pay slip*
Lohnabzug: *stoppage*
Lohnabzüge: *deductions from salary or salary deductions or deductions at source*
Lohnarbeiter: *labourer*
Lohnbuchhalter: *wages clerk*
Lohnempfänger: *wage-earner*
Lohnerhöhung: *pay hike; pay rise; raise (US)*
Lohnforderung: *wage claim*
Lohngärtner: *jobbing gardener*
Lohngefälle abbauen: *to erode wage differentials*
Lohngemeinkosten: *indirect labour costs*
Lohnindexierung: *threshold agreement*
Lohnindexstufe: *pay threshold*
Lohnkontrollen aufheben: *to decontrol wages*
Lohnkosten: *labour costs; labour charges*
Lohnliste: *payroll*
Lohnniveau: *wage levels*
Lohnpolitik: *wages policy*
Lohn-Preis-Spirale: *wage-price spiral*
Lohnregulierung: *wage adjustments*

Lohnrückstand: *back pay*
Lohnscheck: *pay cheque; paycheck*
Lohnschwelle: *pay threshold*
Lohnskala: *wage scale*
Lohnsteuer: *income tax*
Lohnstopp: *wage freeze*
Lohnstreifen: *pay slip*
Lohnsumme: *payroll*
Lohntüte: *pay packet; wage packet*
Lohn- und Gehaltsliste: *payroll ledger*
Lohn- und Preisstopp: *wages and prices freeze*
Lohnunterschiede abbauen: *to erode wage differentials*
Lohnverhandlungen: *pay negotiations or wage negotiations; pay talks*
Lohnvorauszahlung: *sub*
Lohnzulage: *increase*
Lokal: *bar*
lokal: *local*
Lokalblätter: *the local press*
Lokopreis: *spot price; spot rate*
Lokoware: *spot*
Longs: *longs*
Los: *lot*
löschen: *land; unload*
Löscherlaubnis: *landing order*
Löschungskosten und Löschungszölle: *landing charges*
lose: *loose*
lösen: *break; sort out; terminate*
losschlagen: *to dispose of*
Lösung: *solution; termination*
Losverfahren: *ballot*
loswerden: *shift* **etwas ~** *to get rid of something*
Lotse: *pilot*
Lotterie: *lottery*
Lounge: *lounge*
Lücke: *blank; gap*
Lückenfüller: *filler*
luftdicht: *airtight*
Luftfahrtsgesellschaft: *air carrier*
Luftfracht: *air cargo; air freight* **per ~ senden** *to airfreight*
Luftfrachtgebühren: *air freight charges or rates*
Luftfrachtspedition: *air forwarding*
Luftpost: *airmail* **per ~** *by air* **per ~ schicken** *airmail*
Luftpostaufkleber: *airmail sticker*
Luftpostbrief: *air letter; airmail letter*
Luftpostüberweisung: *airmail transfer*
Luftpostumschlag: *airmail envelope*
Lufttüchtigkeitszeugnis: *certificate of airworthiness*
Luftwege: auf dem ~ *by air*
lukrativ: *paying; remunerative*
lustlos: *flat; quiet*
Luxus: *luxury*
Luxusartikel: *luxury goods; prestige product*
Luxussteuer: *levies on luxury items*

Mm

Macht: *control; power*
Mädchen für alles: *dogsbody (informal); gofer (US)*
Magazin: *magazine; periodical; store*
Magnat: *magnate; tycoon*
Magnetband: *magnetic tape or mag tape (informal)*
Magnetbandstation: *streamer*
Mahnung: *chaser; reminder* **letzte ~** *final demand*
Majorität: *majority*
Makler: *agent; broker; negotiator (GB)*
Maklergebühr: *brokerage or broker's commission*
Maklergeschäft: *broking*
Makroökonomie: *macro-economics*
Mall: *shopping mall (US)*
malnehmen: *multiply*
Management: *management* **mittleres ~** *middle management*
Management-Ausbildung: *management training*
Managementlehre: *business science or management science*
Managementmethoden: *management techniques*
Management-Team: *management team*
Manager: **geschäftsführender ~** *company director* **stellvertretender ~** *assistant manager*
Managerin: *manageress*
Managerkurs: *management course*
Managertätigkeit: *managership*
Mangel: *defect; deficiency; imperfection; lack; scarceness or scarcity; shortage*
mangeln an: *lack*
mangels: *failing*
Manipulation: *fiddle (informal)*
Manipulation der Wahlresultate: *ballot-rigging*
manipulieren: *rig*
Mannequin: *model* **als ~ arbeiten** *model*
Mannschaft: *crew; team*
Mannstunde: *man-hour*
manuell: *manual; manually*
Marge: *margin; spread*
marginal: *marginal*
Mark: *Deutschmark; mark*
Marke: *brand; make*
Marken-: *proprietary*
Markenartikel: *branded goods; the genuine article*
Markenname: *brand name*
Markenpirat: *pirate* **Markenpiraterie** *piracy*
Markenprofil: *brand image*
Markentreue: *brand loyalty*
Marketingabteilung: *marketing department*
Marketingmanager: *marketing manager*
Marketing-Methoden: *marketing techniques*

Market-maker: *market-maker*
markieren: *mark*
Markierung: *flag; mark*
Markt: *market; marketplace; mart* **den ~ beherrschen** *to corner the market* **flauer ~** *depressed market; dull market* **freier ~** *open market* **geschlossener ~** *closed market* **lustloser ~** *inactive market* **offener ~** *open market* **potentieller ~** *potential market* **ruhiger ~** *easy market* **umsatzschwacher ~** *inactive market*
Marktanalyse: *market analysis*
Marktanteil: *market share*
Marktbedarf: *market requirements*
Marktdurchdringung: *market penetration*
Märkte: neue ~ erschließen *to open up new markets*
Märkte im Ausland: *overseas markets*
Marktentwicklungen: *market trends*
marktfähig: *marketable*
Marktforschung: *market research*
Marktführer: *market leader*
Marktkräfte: *market forces*
Marktlücke: *gap in the market*
Marktplatz: *marketplace*
Marktpreis: *market price; market rate*
Marktprognose: *market forecast*
Marktsättigung: *market saturation*
Markttag: *market day*
Markttendenzen: *market trends*
Markttest: *market test*
Marktwert: *market value*
Marktwirtschaft: freie ~ *free market economy*
Marmelade: *jam*
Maschine: *machine* **eine ~ bedienen** *to operate a machine; to work a machine*
maschinell hergestellt: *machine-made or machine-produced*
maschinell lesbar: *computer-readable*
Maschinen: *machinery* **stilliegende** *or* **stillstehende ~** *idle machinery or machines lying idle*
Maschinenanlage: *plant*
Maschinencode: *machine code*
maschinengeschrieben: *typewritten*
Maschinenlauf: *run*
Maschinensaal: *machine shop*
Maschinen-Schutzvorrichtungen: *machinery guards*
Maschinensprache: *machine language*
Maschinerie: *machinery*
Maschinist: *machinist; operator*
Maß: *measure*
Maßband: *tape measure; measuring tape*
Masse: *bulk; lot; mass*
Maße: *measurements; size*
Maßeinheit: *measure*
Massen: in ~ *in bulk* **in ~ produzieren** *mass-produce*
Massenabsatzstrategie: *mass marketing*
Massenanfertigung: in ~ herstellen *to mass produce*
Massenarbeitslosigkeit: *mass unemployment*
Massengütertransport: *bulk shipment*
Massengutfrachter: *bulk carrier*
Massenmedien: *mass media*
Massenproduktion: *mass production*
maßgebend: *leading*
maßgefertigt: *made to measure*
mäßig: *moderate; modest*
mäßigen: *moderate*
massiv: *all-out*
Maßnahmen: finanzpolitische *or* **steuerpolitische ~** *fiscal measures*
Maßnahmen zur Inflationsbekämpfung: *anti-inflationary measures*
Material: *material* **rollendes ~** *rolling stock*
Materialfluß: *materials handling*
Materialsteuerung: *materials control*
Matrixdrucker: *dot-matrix printer*
Matrize: *stencil*
Matrizenpapier: *duplicating paper*
maximal: *maximum*
maximieren: *maximize*
Maximierung: *maximization*
Maximum: *maximum*
Mechaniker: *mechanic*
mechanisch: *mechanical*
mechanisieren: *mechanize*
Mechanisierung: *mechanization*
Mechanismus: *mechanism*
Median: *median*
Medien: die ~ *the media*
Medienforschung: *media research*
medizinisch: *medical*
Meer: *sea*
Meeres-: *marine*
Megabyte: *megabyte*
Mehrbenutzersystem: *time-sharing*
Mehrbetrag: *excess; overs* **einen ~ verrechnen** *to absorb a surplus*
mehrfach: *multiple*
Mehrgewinn: *excess profit*
Mehrheit: *majority*
Mehrheitsaktionär: *majority shareholder*
Mehrheitsbeschluß: *majority vote or majority decision*
Mehrheitsbeteiligung: *majority interest; majority shareholding*
Mehrplatzsystem: *networked system*
Mehrwegflaschen: *returnable bottles*
Mehrwertsteuer: *value added tax; Value Added Tax*
Mehrwertsteuerabrechnung: *VAT invoicing*
Mehrwertsteuerbefreiung: *zero-rating*
Mehrwertsteuererklärung: *VAT declaration*
mehrwertsteuerfrei: *zero-rated*
Mehrwertsteuerrechnung: *VAT invoice*

Meile: *mile*
Meilen: gefahrene ~ *mileage*
Meineid: *perjury* **einen ~ leisten** *to perjure yourself*
Meinung: *view* **öffentliche ~** *public opinion*
Meinungsforscher: *canvasser; pollster*
Meinungsumfrage: *canvassing; opinion poll*
Meinungsverschiedenheit: *misunderstanding*
Meistbegünstigungsklausel: *most-favoured-nation clause*
Meistbietender: *highest bidder*
meisten: am ~ verkauft *best-selling*
meistverkauft: *top-selling*
melden: *report; return*
Meldeschein: *certificate of registration*
Meldung: amtliche ~ *official return*
Menge: *bulk; lot; mass; quantity; volume* **eine ~** *a great deal; a good deal of*
Mengen: in ~ *in bulk*
Mengeneinkauf: *bulk buying or bulk purchase*
Mengenrabatt: *quantity discount; volume discount*
Merchandising: *merchandising*
meßbar: *quantifiable*
Messe: *show*
Messehalle: *exhibition room or hall*
messen: *measure*
Messestand: *booth (US); exhibition stand*
Meter: *metre or meter (US)*
Methode: *method*
metrisch: *metric*
Miete: *rent; rental* **geringe ~** *nominal rent; token rent* **nicht kostendeckende ~** *uneconomic rent* **nominelle ~** *peppercorn rent* **symbolische ~** *nominal rent; token rent*
Mieteinkünfte: *income from rents; rental income*
mieten: *charter; lease; rent*
Mieter: *charterer; leaseholder; lessee; tenant*
Mietpreisbindung or preisregelung: *rent control*
Mietrückstand: *back rent*
Mietverhältnis: *tenancy*
Mietvertrag: *lease*
Mietvertrag mit Reparaturklausel: *repairing lease*
Mietvorauszahlung: *key money*
Mietwagen: *hire car*
Mikrocomputer: *micro(computer)*
Mikrofiche: *microfiche*
Mikrofilm: *microfilm*
Mikroökonomie: *micro-economics*
Mikroprozessor: *microprocessor*
Milliarde: *billion (US)*
Milligramm: *milligram*
Milliliter: *millilitre*
Millimeter: *millimetre*
Millimeterpapier: *graph paper; squared paper*
Million: *million*
Millionär: *millionaire*
Millionen-: *multimillion*
Minderheit: *minority*
Minderheitsaktionär: *minority shareholder*
Minderheitsbeteiligung: *minority shareholding or minority interest*
Minderung: *shrinkage*
minderwertig: *low-grade; inferior; low-quality; second-rate*
Mindestbetrag: *minimum payment*
Mindestdividende: *minimum dividend*
Mindesthaltbarkeitsdatum: *sell-by date*
Mindestlohn: *minimum wage*
Mindestmenge: *minimum quantity*
Mindestnachbestellung: *reorder level*
Mindestpreis: garantierter ~ *intervention price*
Mindestreserve: *bank reserves*
Mine: *mine*
Mineralöl: *oil; petroleum*
Minicomputer: *minicomputer*
Minicontainer: *minicontainer*
minimal: *minimal*
Minimarkt: *minimarket*
Minimum: *minimum*
Minister: *minister; secretary (GB)*
Ministerium: *department; ministry; office (GB)*
Ministerpräsident: *Prime Minister*
Minorität: *minority*
minus: *minus*
Minusbetrag: *deficit*
Minute: *minute*
mischen: *mix*
Mischkonzern: *conglomerate*
Mischung: *mix*
Mischwirtschaft: *mixed economy*
Mißbrauch: *misuse*
Mißerfolg: kommerzieller ~ *commercial failure*
mißlingen: *fall through*
Mißverständnis: *misunderstanding*
Mißwirtschaft: *maladministration; mismanagement*
Mit-: *co-; joint*
Mitarbeit: *co-operation*
Mitarbeiter: *assistant; staff* **freier ~** *freelance; freelancer* **ständiger ~** *staffer (US)*
Mitbestimmung: *worker participation*
Mitbieter: *underbidder*
Mitdirektor: *co-director*
Miteigentum: *co-ownership; coproperty; joint ownership*
Miteigentümer: *co-owner; coproprietor*
Mit freundlichen Grüßen: *yours faithfully; Yours sincerely or Sincerely yours (US)*
mitfühlend: *sympathetic*
Mitglied: ordentliches ~ *ordinary member*
Mitglieder: einfache ~ *rank-and-file members*
Mitgliedsbeitrag: *subscription*
Mitgliedschaft: *membership*
Mitinhaber: *co-owner*

Mitleid: *sympathy*
mitrechnen: *count*
Mittagessen: *lunch*
Mittagspause: *lunch hour or lunchtime*
Mitte der Woche: *mid-week*
Mitte des Monats: *mid-month*
mitteilen: *inform*
Mitteilung: *communication; memo(randum); message; note; notice; notification*
Mittel: *means; medium; resources* **finanzielle ~** *finance; financial resources* **flüssige ~** *liquid assets; ready money; realizable assets* **öffentliche ~** *public funds*
Mittel-: *mean; mid-; middle*
mittelbar: *indirect*
Mittel flüssigmachen: *to go liquid*
mittelfristig: *medium-term*
mittelgroß: *average-sized; middle-sized*
Mittelkurs: *mean price*
mittellos: *poor*
Mittelwert: *average; mean*
Mitversicherung: *co-insurance*
mitverursachend: *contributory*
Mitwirkung: *participation*
mitzählen: *count*
mitziehen: *reciprocate*
Möbellager: *furniture depository*
mobil: *mobile*
Mobiliar: *furniture*
mobilisieren: *mobilize*
Mobilität: *mobility*
mobilmachen: *mobilize*
möblieren: *furnish*
Modeartikel: *fancy goods*
Model: *model*
Modell: *example; model*
Modellversuch: *pilot*
Modell zur Wirtschaftsprognose: *economic model*
Modem: *modem*
modern: *modern*
modernisieren: *modernize*
Modernisierung: *modernization*
modifizieren: *modify*
Modifizierung: *modification*
modular: *modular*
möglich: *possible*
Möglichkeit: *chance; opportunity; possibility; prospect*
Monat: **vorletzten ~** *the month before last*
monatlich: *monthly*
Monatsende: *month end*
Monatskarte: *monthly ticket*
monetär: *monetary*
Monetarismus: *monetarism*
Monetarist: *monetarist*
monetaristisch: *monetarist*
Monitor: *monitor; visual display terminal*
Monopol: **staatliches ~** *public monopoly or state monopoly* **unumschränktes ~** *absolute monopoly*
monopolisieren: *monopolize*
Monopolisierung: *monopolization*
Monopolzerschlagung: *trustbusting (US)*
Montage: *assembly*
Montageband: *assembly line; production line*
montieren: *assemble*
Moratorium: *moratorium*
Morgen: *acre*
Motiv: *reason*
Motivation: *motivation*
Motor: *engine*
Motorrad-Bote: *dispatch rider*
Mühe: *effort*
Mühle: *mill*
multilateral: *multilateral*
Multimillionär: *multimillionaire*
multinational: *multinational*
Multiplikation: *multiplication*
Multiplikationszeichen: *multiplication sign*
multiplizieren: *multiply*
Mündelkonto: *nominee account*
mündlich: *verbal; verbally*
Münze: *coin*
Münzfernsprecher: *pay phone*
Münzgeld: *specie*
Muster: *example; sample; specimen; swatch* **gemäß dem ~** *as per sample*
Musterbuch: *pattern book; sample book or book of samples*
mustergültig: *model*
Musterhaus: *show house*
Musterprozeß: *test case*
Mustervertrag: *standard agreement or standard contract*
Musterwohnung: *show flat*
Muttergesellschaft: *parent company*
Mutterschaftsgeld: *maternity benefit*
Mutterschaftsurlaub: *maternity leave*

Nn

Nachahmung: *imitation* **unerlaubte ~** *piracy*
nachbestellen: *reorder*
Nachbestellung: *reorder; repeat order*
Nachbörse: *after-hours dealing*
nachfassen: *follow up*
Nachfaßschreiben: *follow-up letter*
nachfolgend: *incoming*
Nachfolger: *replacement; successor*
Nachforschungen anstellen: *inquire into*
Nachfrage: *demand; inquiry* **effektive ~** *effective demand* **große ~** *keen demand* **saisonbedingte ~** *seasonal demand*

Nachfrage befriedigen *or* **stillen:** *to satisfy a demand*
Nachfrageinflation: *demand-led inflation*
Nachfragepreis: *demand price*
Nachfrist: *grace*
nachgeben: *ease*
nachgehen: *follow up*
Nachlaß: *allowance; estate*
nachlassen: *decrease; ease; knock off; slacken off; take off; weaken*
Nachlaßgericht: *probate court*
Nachlässigkeit: *negligence*
Nachlaßverwalter: *administrator*
Nachlösegebühr: *excess fare*
nachmachen: *forge; imitate*
nachmittags: *p.m.*
Nachnahme: *charges forward* **gegen** *or* **per** ~ *cash on delivery*
nachprüfen: *re-examine*
Nachprüfung: *re-examination*
Nachrede: üble ~ *slander*
Nachrichtenagentur: *news agency*
Nachsaison: *low season*
nachschußpflichtig: *uncalled*
Nachsendeadresse: *forwarding address*
nachsenden: *send on* **nicht** ~ *"to await arrival"*
nachstehend: *hereafter*
nachsuchen: *apply*
Nachteil: *drawback*
nachteilig: *adverse*
Nachtrag: im ~ *further to*
Nachtragshaushalt: *minibudget*
Nachtschicht: *night shift*
Nachttarif: *night rate*
Nachttresor: *night safe*
Nachweis: *proof*
Nachwuchsmanager: *junior executive* *or* *junior manager*
Nachzahlung: *back payment*
Nachzugsaktien: *deferred stock; deferred shares*
Nadel: *pin*
Nagel: *nail*
Näherungswert: *approximation*
Nahrung: *food*
Nahverkehrszug: *commuter train*
Naira: *naira*
Namen: im ~ **von** *on behalf of*
Nation: *nation*
national: *national*
Natur: *nature*
Neben-: *collateral; incidental; secondary; subsidiary*
Nebenausgaben: *extras; incidental expenses*
nebenbei: *on the side*
Nebenbeschäftigung: *sideline*
Nebenkosten: *incidental expenses; extras; incidentals*
Nebenprodukt: *by-product; spinoff*
nebensächlich: *incidental; subsidiary*
Nebensaison: *dead season; off-season*
Nebenstelle: *extension*
negativ: *negative; unfavourable*
Negativfaktor: *minus factor*
nehmen: auf sich ~ *incur*
neigen: *tend*
nennen: *quote*
Nennwert: *denomination; face value; par value*
nervös: *jumpy*
Netto-Cashflow: *net cash flow*
Nettoeinkommen: *disposable income; net income*
Nettoeinnahmen: *net receipts*
netto einnehmen: *net*
Nettoertrag: *net yield*
Nettogehalt: *net salary*
Nettogewicht: *net weight*
Nettogewinn: *net earnings; net profit; clear profit*
Nettomarge: *net margin*
Nettopreis: *net price*
Nettoumsatz: *net sales*
netto verdienen: *net*
Nettoverdienst: *net income* *or* *net salary; take-home pay*
Nettoverlust: *net loss*
Netz(werk): *network*
neu abfassen: *redraft*
neu anlegen: *reinvest*
Neuauflage: *reissue*
neu auflegen: *reissue*
Neuausgabe: *reissue*
neu ausstatten: *refit*
Neuausstattung: *refitting*
Neubauten: *house starts* *or* *housing starts (US)*
neu bearbeiten: *revise*
Neubeginn: *departure* **ein völliger** ~ *cold start*
neu bewerten: *reassess*
Neubewertung: *reassessment*
Neueinführung: *innovation*
Neuemission: *new issue*
Neuemissionsspekulant: *stag*
Neuerer: *innovator*
Neuerung: *departure*
Neuerungen einführen: *innovate*
Neugründung: *start-up*
Neuheit: *innovation*
neu herausgeben: *reissue*
Neuordnung: *reorganization*
neu organisieren: *reorganize*
Neuregelung: *readjustment*
neu schätzen *or* **veranlagen:** *reassess*
Neuschätzung *or* **Neuveranlagung:** *reassessment*
neu verteilen: *redistribute*
Nichtanerkennung: *repudiation*
Nichtansässiger: *non-resident*
Nichtdiskriminierung im Außenhandel: *fair trade*
Nichterfüllung: *default*

Nichterscheinen: *absence; absenteeism*
Nichterschienener: *absentee*
nichtig: *invalid; null* **für ~ erklären** *nullify; rescind*
Nichtigkeit: *invalidity*
Nichtlieferung: *non-delivery*
Nichtverfügbarkeit: *unavailability*
Nichtzahlung: bei ~ *in default of payment*
Nichtzahlung einer Verpflichtung: *non-payment of a debt*
Nickel: *nickel (US)*
Niederlage: *defeat*
niederlassen: sich ~ *to set up in business*
Niederlassung: *branch; domicile*
niedriger einstufen: *demote; downgrade*
niedrig halten: *hold down*
Niedrigpreisgeschäft: *cut-price store*
Niedrigstpreise: *rock-bottom prices*
Nießbrauch: *beneficial interest*
Nießbrauchberechtigter: *beneficial occupier*
Nische: *niche*
Niveau: *level; standard*
nochmals inserieren: *readvertise*
nochmals vorlegen: *re-present*
Nominalkapital: *nominal capital*
Nominalwert: *face value; nominal value*
nominell: *nominal*
nominieren: *nominate*
Nominierte(r): *nominee*
Nominierung: *nomination*
Norm: *norm; standard* **nach ~ arbeiten** *to work to standard specifications*
normal: *common; normal; ordinary; regular; standard; usual*
normalerweise: *as a rule*
Normalformat: *regular size*
Normalrabatt: *basic discount*
Normalzeit: *Standard Time*
normen: *standardize*
Normung: *standardization*
Notar: *conveyancer; notary public*
Notausgang: *fire exit*
Notenbank: *central bank*
Notenpresse: *security printer*
Notfall: *emergency*
Notfonds: *emergency reserves*
notieren: *note*
Notierung: *Stock Exchange quotation*
Notiz: *note*
Notizblock: *memo pad; notepad*
Notizbuch: *notebook*
Notlage *or* **Notstand:** *emergency*
Notverkauf: *forced sale*
Notwendigkeit: *necessity*
Null: *nil; nought; zero*
Nullinflation: *zero inflation*
numerieren: *number*
numerisch: *numeric or numerical*
Nummernkonto: *numbered account*
nutzen: *exploit; utilize*
nützen: *benefit*
Nutzfahrzeug: *commercial vehicle; goods vehicle*
Nutzlast: *payload*
nützlich: *useful*
Nutznießer: *beneficiary*
Nutznießung: lebenslange ~ *life interest*
Nutzung: *utilization*
Nutzungsgebühr: *royalty*
Nutzungsrecht auf Lebensdauer: *life interest*

Oo

Oberflächenfinish: *finish*
objektiv: *objective*
Obligation: *(debenture) bond* **eine ~ verkaufen** *to redeem a bond*
Obligationär: *debenture holder*
Obligationsinhaber: *bondholder*
obligatorisch: *compulsory; obligatory*
Obligo: ohne ~ *without prejudice*
offen: *open; open-ended or open-end (US); receivable*
Offenlegung vertraulicher Informationen: *disclosure of confidential information*
offenstehend: *open; owing*
öffentlich: *public*
Öffentlichkeit: *the general public* **in der ~** *in public*
Öffentlichkeitsarbeit: *public relations (PR)*
offiziell: *formal; formally; official; officially*
Öffnung: *aperture*
Öffnungszeit: *opening hours; opening time*
Offshore: *off-shore*
Offshore-Investmentfonds: *off-shore fund*
Ökonometrie: *econometrics*
Ökonomie: *economics*
Ölförderländer: *oil-producing countries*
Ombudsmann: *ombudsman*
online: *on line or online*
OPEC: *the Organization of Petroleum Exporting Countries*
Operator: *operator*
optimal: *optimal; optimum*
Optimismus: *optimism*
optimistisch: *optimistic*
Option: *option to purchase* **negative ~** *inertia selling*
Optionsgeschäft *or* **Optionshandel:** *option dealing or option trading*
Optionsrecht: ein ~ ausüben *to take up an option or to exercise an option*
Optionsvertrag: *option contract*
Order: *order*
ordnen: *arrange; order; regulate; sort; sort out*

Ordnung: der ~ halber *for the record* or *to keep the record straight*
ordnungsgemäß: nicht ~ *irregular*
Organisation: *organization; setup*
Organisation erdölexportierender Länder: *the Organization of Petroleum Exporting Countries*
Organisationsausschuß: *organizing committee*
Organisation und Durchführung: *organization and methods*
Organisator: *organizer*
organisatorisch: *organizational*
organisieren: *organize*
orientiert: *oriented* or *orientated*
Original: *top copy; master; original*
original: *original*
Ort: *place; point; spot; venue* **am ~** *locally; on the premises* **vor ~** *locally*
örtlich: *local*
Ortsgespräch: *local call*
Ortsnetzkennzahl: *area code*
Ortsverein: *local (US)*
Output: *output*

Pp

Pacht: *rent; rental* **nominelle ~** *peppercorn rent*
Pacht-: *leasehold*
Pachtdauer: *tenancy*
pachten: *lease; rent*
Pächter: *leaseholder; lessee; tenant*
Pachtverhältnis: *tenure*
Pachtvertrag: *lease; headlease; leasehold*
Pachtvertrag mit Reparaturklausel: *repairing lease*
Packager: *packager*
Päckchen: *packet* **eingeschriebenes ~** *registered parcel*
Packen: *packaging*
Packer: *packer*
Packpapier: *brown paper; wrapping paper*
Packzettel: *packing list* or *packing slip*
paginieren: *folio*
Paket: *block; package; parcel* **falsch beschriftetes ~** *incorrectly labelled parcel*
Paketannahme: *parcels office*
Paketgebühr: *parcel rate*
Paketpost: *parcel post*
Pakettarife: *parcel rates*
Palette: *pallet*
palettieren: *palletize*
Panikkäufe: *panic buying*
Panikverkäufe des Pfundes: *a run on the pound*
Papier: bankfähiges ~ *bankable paper* **braunes ~** *manilla* **zweilagiges ~** *two-part paper*
Papiere: *papers*
Papiereinzug: *paper feed*
Papierfabrik: *paper mill*
Papiergeld: *paper money*
Papierkorb: *waste paper basket*
Papierkrieg: *red tape*
Papier mit Briefkopf: *headed paper*
Papierschneider: *guillotine*
Papiertüte: *paper bag*
Papiervorschub: *paper feed*
Pappe: *card; cardboard*
Pappkarton: *cardboard box; carton*
Pappschachtel: *cardboard box*
Paragraph: *article; clause*
Parameter: *parameter*
paraphieren: *initial*
pari: *par*
Parität: *parity*
parken: *park*
Parkinsonsches Gesetz: *Parkinson's law*
Parkplatz: *car park*
Parlamentswahl: *general election*
Partei: geschädigte ~ *injured party* **politische ~** *political party*
parteiisch: *one-sided*
Partie: *block*
partiell: *partial*
partizipativ: *participative*
Partner: *partner*
Partnerschaft: *partnership* **eine ~ auflösen** *to dissolve a partnership*
Paß: *passport*
Passagierfähre: *passenger ferry*
Passagierliste: *passenger manifest*
Passagierschiff: *liner*
passen: *fit; fit in*
passend: *convenient; suitable*
passieren: *happen*
Passierschein: *pass*
Patent: *patent* **angemeldetes ~** *patent applied for* or *patent pending* **ein ~ anmelden** *to file a patent application* **ein ~ verletzen** *to infringe a patent*
Patentamt: *patent office*
Patent angemeldet: *patent applied for* or *patent pending*
Patentanmeldung: eine ~ einreichen *to file a patent application*
Patentanwalt: *patent agent*
Patentgebühren: *royalty*
Patentrecht: das ~ verletzen *to infringe a patent*
patentrechtlich geschützt: *patented*
Patentschutz: *patent rights*
Patenturkunde: *letters patent*
Patentverletzung: *patent infringement; piracy*
Pauschalarrangement: *package deal*
Pauschalbetrag: *lump sum*
Pauschaldeckung: *comprehensive* or *all-in policy*
Pauschale: *inclusive sum* or *inclusive charge; flat rate; lump sum*
Pauschalpreis: *all-in price*
Pauschalreise: *package holiday* or *package tour*

Pause: *break*
PC: *personal computer or home computer*
peinlich: *awkward*
pekuniär: *pecuniary*
Pendant: *counterpart; opposite number*
pendeln: *commute*
Pendler: *commuter*
Pendlerzug: *commuter train*
Penny: *penny (GB)*
Pension: *pension; superannuation* **in ~ gehen** *retire*
pensionieren: sich ~ lassen *retire*
Pensionierung: *retirement*
Pensionsalter: *pensionable age*
Pensionsbegünstigter: *annuitant*
pensionsberechtigt: *pensionable*
perfekt: *perfect; perfectly*
perfektionieren: *perfect*
Periode: *period*
periodisch: *periodic or periodical*
Peripheriegeräte: *peripherals*
Person: dritte ~ *third party* **pro ~** *per head; per capita*
Personal: *personnel; staff* **festangestelltes ~** *regular staff* **knapp an ~** *shorthanded* **mit ~ besetzen** *staff* **schlecht bezahltes ~** *poorly-paid staff* **ständiges ~** *regular staff* **weiteres ~ einstellen** *to recruit new staff* **zum ~ gehören** *to be on the staff or a member of staff or a staff member*
Personalabbau: *shakeout*
Personalabteilung: *personnel department*
Personalakte: *record*
Personalbeschaffung: *recruitment of new staff*
Personalbesetzungsplan: *manpower forecasting*
Personalbestand: *manning levels or staffing levels* **den ~ abbauen** *to reduce staff*
Personalbestandsprognose: *manpower forecasting*
Personalbeurteilung: *staff appraisal; staff assessment*
Personalchef: *personnel officer; personnel manager*
Personal-Computer: *personal computer*
Personalführung: *personnel management*
Personalplanung: *manpower planning*
Personalreferent: *personnel officer*
Personalstärke: *manning levels or staffing levels*
Personal unterbringen: *to place staff*
Personalvertretung: *staff association*
Personengesellschaft: *close company or close(d) corporation (US)*
Personenstand: *legal status*
Personenzug: *passenger train*
persönlich: *in person; personal; personally*
Perspektive: *outlook*
Peseta: *peseta*
Peso: *peso*
Pessimismus: *pessimism*
Pessimismus am Aktienmarkt: *market pessimism*
pessimistisch: *pessimistic*
Peter-Prinzip: *Peter principle*
Petition: *petition* **eine ~ einreichen** *petition*
Petro-Dollar: *petrodollar*
Pfand: *pledge* **ein ~ auslösen** *to take something out of pawn* **ein ~ einlösen** *to redeem a pledge* **nicht eingelöstes ~** *unredeemed pledge*
Pfandbriefinhaber: *bondholder*
pfänden: *seize*
Pfandleihanstalt: *pawnshop*
Pfandleiher: *pawnbroker*
Pfandsache: *pledge*
Pfandschein: *pawn ticket*
Pfändung: *seizure*
Pflicht-: *compulsory*
Pflichtaktien: *qualifying shares*
Pflichten: *responsibilities*
Pfund: *pound* **grünes ~** *green pound* **irisches ~** *punt* **tausend ~** *grand (informal)*
Pfund Sterling: *pound sterling*
Phase: *phase; stage*
Phönix-Syndrom: *phoenix syndrome*
Phonotypist: *audio-typist*
Pilotversuch: *pilot*
Pint: *pint*
Pionier: *pioneer*
Pionierarbeit leisten: *pioneer*
Pionierprojekt: *pioneer project or pioneer development*
Plagiator: *pirate*
plagiieren: *pirate*
Plakat: *poster*
Plakatträger: *sandwich man*
Plakatwand: *advertisement hoarding*
Plan: *arrangement; plan; programme or program (US); project; scheme* **einen ~ ausführen** *to realize a project or a plan*
planen: *organize; plan*
Planer: *planner*
plangemäß vorankommen: *to be on schedule*
Planquadrat: *grid*
Planung: *organization; planning* **strategische ~** *strategic planning*
Planwirtschaft: *planned economy*
Platz: *niche; place; room; space; spot* **freier ~** *vacancy*
platzen: *bounce*
Pleite: *flop* **kommerzielle ~** *commercial failure*
pleite: *broke (informal)*
Plenarsitzung: *plenary meeting or plenary session*
Plombe: *customs seal*
plombieren: *seal*
plötzlich fallen: *slump*
plötzlich steigen: *jump*
Plunder: *junk*
Pluspunkt: als ~ *on the plus side*

Politik: *policy*
Politik der Lohnkontrolle: *pay restraint or wage restraint*
politisch: *political*
Polster: *cushion; pad*
populär: *popular*
Port: *port*
Portable: *a portable*
Portfoliomanagement: *portfolio management*
Portion: *portion*
Porto: *postage* **Porto bezahlt** *postage paid*
portofrei: *post free*
Portokasse: *petty cash*
Portokassenbuch: *petty cash book*
Position: eine ~ abdecken *to cover a position*
positiv: *plus; positive*
Post: *mail; post* **elektronische ~** *electronic mail* **per ~** *by mail*
Postanweisung: *money order; postal order*
Postausgang: *outgoing mail*
Posteingang: *incoming mail*
Posten: *item; office; post* **einen ~ buchen** *to post an entry* **einmalige ~** *non-recurring items* **steuerpflichtige ~** *taxable items*
Posteneinkauf: *bulk buying or bulk purchase*
Poster: *poster*
Postfach: *box; mail box*
Postgebühren: *postage; postal charges or postal rates*
Postgirodienst: *National Giro (GB)*
Postkarte: *card; postcard*
postlagernd: *poste restante*
Postleitzahl: *post code or zip code (US)*
Postpaket: *postal packet*
Postsendungen zweiter Klasse: *second-class mail*
Poststelle: *mail room; post room*
Poststempel: *postmark*
Posttarife: *postal charges or postal rates*
Postversand: *mail-order*
postwendend antworten: *to send a reply by return of post*
Postwurfsendung: *mailing piece*
Post(amt): *post office*
POS-Werbematerial: *point of sale material*
Potential: *potential* **potentiell** *potential*
PR-Abteilung: *public relations department*
Prägeanstalt: *mint*
prägen: *mint*
Praktiken: restriktive ~ *restrictive practices*
praktisch: *convenient; handy*
Prämie: *bonus*
Prämienrechnung: *renewal notice*
Prämienzuschlag: *additional premium*
PR-Arbeit: *public relations (PR)*
Präsentation: *presentation*
Präsentationspackung: *display pack*
Präsident: *president*
präventiv: *preventive*
Präventiv-: *pre-emptive*
Praxis: in der ~ *in practice*
präzise: *strict; strictly*
Preis: *cost; price; rate; tariff* **angemessener** or **fairer ~** *fair price* **fester ~** *fixed rate* **gängiger/jetziger/üblicher ~** *going price or current price or usual price* **geforderter ~** *asking price* **konkurrenzfähiger ~** *competitive price* **niedrigster ~** *bottom price* **staatlich vorgeschriebener ~** *government-regulated price* **unter ~ verkaufen** *undersell* **vereinbarter ~** *agreed price* **voller ~** *full price; full rate* **wettbewerbsfähiger ~** *competitive price*
Preis ab Kai: *price ex quay*
Preis ab Lager: *price ex warehouse*
Preisabsprache: *common pricing; price fixing*
Preis ab Werk: *price ex works or ex factory*
Preisanstieg: *escalation of prices*
Preisaufschlag: *mark-up*
Preis bei Inzahlungnahme: *trade-in price*
Preisbildung: *pricing*
Preisbindung zweiter Hand: *resale price maintenance*
Preise: die ~ drücken *to force prices down* **die ~ hochtreiben** *to force prices up* **günstige ~** *keen prices* **überhöhte ~** *inflated prices* **verlockende ~** *attractive prices*
Preise drastisch senken: *to hammer prices*
Preise erhöhen: *to mark prices up; to increase prices or to raise prices*
Preise herabsetzen/reduzieren: *to lower prices or to reduce prices*
Preisempfehlung: unverbindliche ~ *manufacturer's recommended price (MRP) or recommended retail price (RRP)*
Preisen: mit wettbewerbsfähigen ~ *competitively priced* **zu herabgesetzten ~** *cut-price*
Preiserhöhung: *mark-up*
Preise senken: *to lower prices or to reduce prices*
Preiseskalation: *escalation of prices*
Preise stabilisieren: *to peg prices*
Preisfestsetzung: *pricing*
Preisgabe: *disclosure*
preisgeben: *disclose*
Preisgefälle: *price differential*
Preisgleitklausel: *escalator clause*
Preisgrenze: oberste ~ *ceiling price or price ceiling*
preisgünstig: *inexpensive; good value (for money)*
Preiskalkulation: *pricing*
Preisklasse: *price range*
Preiskontrolle: *price control*
Preiskrieg: *price war or price-cutting war*
Preislage: *price range*
Preisliste: *price list; scale of charges or scale of prices*
Preisnachlaß: *discount; mark-down; rebate*
Preispolitik: *pricing policy*
Preisschild: *price label; price tag; price ticket*

Preissenkung: *price cutting; mark-down*
Preistreiberei: *profiteering*
Preisüberwachung: *price controls*
Preisunterschied: *price differential*
preiswert: *cheap; inexpensive; good value (for money)*
Premierminister: *Prime Minister*
Presse: *press* **überregionale ~** *national newspapers or the national press*
Presseausschnittdienst: *clipping service; press cutting agency*
Presseberichte: *press coverage*
Pressekonferenz: *press conference*
Pressemitteilung: *press release*
Pressenotiz: *news release*
Pressereferent: *information officer*
Prestigeartikel: *prestige product*
Prestigeverlust: *loss of status*
Prestigewerbung: *prestige advertising*
Primärprodukte: *primary products*
Prime Rate: *prime rate or prime*
Prinzip: *principle* **im ~** *in principle*
prinzipiell: *in principle*
privat: *personal; private*
Privatabkommen: durch ~ *by private contract*
Privatadresse: *home address*
Privataltersversorgung: *Individual Retirement Account (US)*
Privatanleger: *private investor*
Privatbesitz: *private property*
Privateigentum: *private ownership; personal effects or personal property*
Privateinkommen: *private income*
Privatgespräch: *personal call*
Privatgrundstück: *private property*
privatisieren: *denationalize; privatize*
Privatisierung: *denationalization; privatization*
Privatkunde: *private client or private customer*
Privatsekretär: *personal assistant*
Privatsektor: *private sector*
Privatunternehmen: *private enterprise*
Privatvermögen: bewegliches ~ *personal assets*
Privatwirtschaft: *private enterprise*
pro: *per*
Probe: *example; sample; specimen; trial* **kostenlos zur ~** *free trial* **zur ~** *on approval; on trial*
Probeentnahme: *sampling*
Probeexemplar: *specimen*
Probelauf: *dummy run; test run*
Probestück: *trial sample*
Probeversuch: *pilot*
Probezeit: *probation; trial period*
probieren: *sample*
Problem: *difficulty; matter; problem; question*
Problembereich: *problem area*
Produkt: preisempfindliches ~ *price-sensitive product*
Produktanalyse: *product analysis*
Produktentwicklung: *product development*
Produktgestaltung: *product design*
Produktgruppe: *product line*
Produkt-Image: *brand image*
Produktion: *output; production* **die ~ einstellen** *discontinue* **die ~ zurückschrauben** *to cut (back) production*
Produktionseinheit: *production unit*
Produktionsfaktoren: *factors of production*
Produktionsgenossenschaft: landwirtschaftliche ~ *collective farm*
Produktionskapazität: *producing capacity*
Produktionskosten: *manufacturing costs or production costs*
Produktionsleistung: *outturn; rate of production or production rate*
Produktionsleiter: *production manager*
Produktionsmittel: *capital equipment*
Produktionsprämie: *output bonus*
Produktionsstandard: *production standards*
Produktionsvolumen: *volume of output*
Produktionsziel: *production targets*
produktiv: *productive; productively*
Produktivität: *productivity*
Produktivitätsabkommen: *productivity agreement*
Produktivitätskampagne: *productivity drive*
Produktivitätsprämie: *productivity bonus*
Produkt-Management: *product management*
Produktmix or **Produktpalette:** *product mix*
Produkttypung: *standardization of products*
Produktüberangebot: *a glut of produce*
Produktwerbung: *product advertising*
Produzent: *producer*
produzieren: *make; produce; turn out*
professionell: *professional*
Profi: *professional*
Profil: *profile*
Profit: *earnings; profit*
Profitabilität: *profitability*
Profit-Center: *profit centre*
profitieren von: *to benefit from or by*
Proforma-Rechnung: *pro forma invoice*
Prognose: *forecast; forecasting; projection* **kurzfristige ~** *short-range forecast; short-term forecast* **langfristige ~** *long-term forecast* **mittelfristige ~** *medium-term forecast*
prognostizieren: *forecast*
Programm: *plan; programme or program (US); scheme; timetable* **subventioniertes ~** *grant-aided scheme*
programmierbar: *programmable*
programmieren: *program*
Programmierer: *computer programmer*
Programmiersprache: *programming language* **höhere ~** *high-level computer language* **maschinenorientierte ~** *low-level computer language*
Programmierung: *computer programming*

Progression: **der ~ unterliegend** *graduated*
progressiv: *go-ahead; innovative; progressive*
Projekt: *project; scheme; undertaking* **ein ~ ausschreiben** *to put a project out to tender or to ask for or to invite tenders for a project*
Projektanalyse: *project analysis*
Projektingenieur: *project engineer*
Projektleiter: *project manager*
Pro-Kopf-Ausgaben: *per capita expenditure*
Pro-Kopf-Einkommen: *average income per capita or per capita income*
Prokura: **per ~** *per pro*
Prolongation: *extension; renewal*
prolongieren: *extend; renew*
prompt: *immediate; prompt; rapid*
prophezeien: *predict*
proportional: *proportional*
Prospekt: *broadside (US); brochure; catalogue or catalog (US); pamphlet; prospectus*
Prosperität: *prosperity*
Protest: **aus ~ gegen** *in protest at*
protestieren: *object*
Proteststreik: *protest strike*
Protokoll: *record* **zu ~ nehmen** *minute*
Protokollbuch: *minutebook*
Protokoll führen: *to take the minutes*
protokollieren: *minute; record*
Prototyp: *prototype*
Provenienz: *origin*
Provenienzzertifikat: *certificate of origin*
Proviant: *provisions*
Provinz: *province; the provinces*
Provinzialregierung: *provincial government or state government*
provinziell: *provincial*
Provision: *commission; rake-off* **außerordentliche ~** *overrider or overriding commission*
Provisionsagent: *commission agent*
Provisionsvertreter: *commission rep*
provisorisch: *provisional; provisionally*
Prozent: *per cent; percentage* **ein halbes ~** *half a per cent or a half per cent; half a percentage point*
prozentig: *per cent*
Prozentpunkt: *percentage point*
Prozentsatz: *percentage*
Prozeß: *action; court case; lawsuit; litigation; legal proceedings; trial* **einen ~ anstrengen** *sue*
prozessieren: *sue*
prüfen: *examine; inspect; test; verify*
Prüfer: *inspector*
Prüfmuster: *check sample*
Prüfung: *examination; inspection; test; testing; trial* **erneute ~** *re-examination* **zur ~** *on trial*
Publikation: *publication*
Puffer: *cushion*
Pump: *tick (informal)*
Punkt: *dot; item*
Pünktchen: *dot*
pünktlich: *promptly; on time*
pünktlich bezahlen: *to pay on the nail*
pünktlich fertig sein: *to be on schedule*

Qq

Quadrat: *square*
Quadratzahl: *square*
Qualifikation: *qualification; skill* **fachliche or berufliche ~** *professional qualification*
qualifiziert: *qualified; skilled*
Qualität: *quality* **erstklassige ~** *premium quality; high quality or top quality*
Qualitätskontrolle: *quality control*
Qualitätskontrolle mittels Stichproben: *acceptance sampling*
Qualitätskontrolleur: *quality controller*
Quantität: *quantity*
Quart: *quart*
Quartal: *quarter*
Quartalstag: *quarter day*
quartalsweise: *quarterly*
Quartil: *quartile*
Quelle: *source*
Quellensteuer: *tax deducted at source; withholding tax (US)*
quittieren: *receipt*
Quittung: *receipt; voucher* **ordnungsgemäße ~** *receipt in due form*
Quittungsblock: *receipt book or book of receipts*
Quittungsduplikat: *duplicate receipt*
Quote: *quota*
Quotensystem: *quota system*

Rr

Rabatt: *allowance; discount; mark-down; rebate*
Rabatt gewähren: *discount*
radikal herabsetzen: *slash*
radikal kürzen: *axe*
Rahmen: **in begrenztem ~** *small-scale* **zeitlicher ~** *time scale*
Raider: *raider*
Rand: *edge; side*
Rang: *grade; rank; status* **von hohem ~** *top-flight or top-ranking*
Rang einnehmen: *rank*
rangmäßig: *ranking*
Rangordnung: **nach ~** *in rank order*
rar: *rare; scarce*
rasch: *rapid; rapidly*
Rat: *advice; council*
Rate: *instalment or installment (US); rate* **zu ~ ziehen** *consult*
Raten: **in ~ zahlen** *to pay in instalments*

raten: *advise* **etwas ~** *to guess (at) something*
Ratenkauf: *hire purchase*
Ratenzahlung: *deferred payment; installment plan (US)*
raten zu: *recommend*
Ratgeber: *adviser or advisor*
ratifizieren: *approve; ratify*
Ratifizierung: *ratification*
rationalisieren: *rationalize; streamline*
rationalisiert: *streamlined*
Rationalisierung: *rationalization; streamlining*
rationell: *economical*
rationieren: *ration*
Rationierung: *rationing*
Raubdruck: *piracy* **einen ~ herstellen** *pirate*
Rauchverbot: das ~ aufheben *to lift the ban on smoking* **Rauchverbot erlassen** *to impose a ban on smoking*
Raum: *area; room; space*
räumen: *clear*
Raummaß: *cubic measure*
Räumungsverkauf: *clearance sale; close-out sale (US); closing-down sale*
Raumverteilungsplan: *floor plan*
rausgeschmissen werden: *to get the sack*
rausschmeißen: jdn ~ *to sack someone*
Rausschmiß: *sacking*
reagieren auf: *to react to*
Reaktion: *feedback; reaction; response*
Realeinkommen: *real income*
realisierbar: *viable*
Realisierbarkeit: *feasibility*
realisieren: *realize*
Realisierung: *realization*
Reallohn: *real income or real wages*
Real-time: *real time*
Rechenfehler: *computational error; miscount*
Rechengeschwindigkeit: *computing speed*
Rechenmaschine: *calculating machine*
Rechenschaft ablegen: *to account for*
Rechenzentrum: *computer bureau*
Rechercheur: *investigator*
rechnen: *calculate; count*
rechnen mit: *count on*
Rechner: *computer* **kommerzieller ~** *business computer*
rechnerabhängig: *on line or online*
Rechnerprogramm: *computer program*
Rechnerverbund: *computer network; networked system*
Rechnung: *bill; check (US); invoice* **aufgegliederte ~** *itemized invoice* **detaillierte ~** *detailed account* **die ~ begleichen** *or* **bezahlen** *to foot the bill* **eine ~ ausstellen** *to raise an invoice* **eine ~ vorlegen** *to render an account* **in ~ stellen** *bill; charge* **laut ~** *as per invoice*
Rechnung ausstellen: *invoice*
Rechnungen: bezahlte ~ *paid bills* **dringende ~** *pressing bills* **fällige ~** *bills for collection* **unbezahlte ~** *unpaid invoices*
Rechnungsabteilung: *invoicing department*
Rechnungsausstellung: *invoicing*
Rechnungsausstellung inklusive Mehrwertsteuer: *VAT invoicing*
Rechnungsbetrag: fälliger ~ *balance due* **voller ~** *total invoice value*
Rechnungsbuch: *account book*
Rechnungseinheit: *unit of account*
Rechnungsjahr: *financial year*
Rechnungslegung zum Wiederbeschaffungswert: *current cost accounting*
Rechnungspreis: *invoice price*
Rechnungsprüfer: *accountant; auditor; comptroller* **betriebsinterner ~** *internal auditor* **unabhängiger ~** *external auditor*
Rechnungsprüfungen vornehmen: *audit*
Rechnungsprüfung/Revision: außerbetriebliche *or* **unabhängige ~** *external audit or independent audit* **innerbetriebliche ~** *internal audit*
Rechnungswesen: *accountancy; accounting*
Recht: *law; right* **bürgerliches ~** *civil law*
rechtfertigen: *warrant*
rechtlich: *legal; legally*
rechtmäßig: *lawful; lawfully; legal; rightful*
rechts: *right; right-hand*
Rechtsabteilung: *legal department or legal section*
Rechtsanspruch: *legal claim*
Rechtsanwalt/Rechtsanwältin: *attorney (US); barrister (GB); lawyer*
Rechtsberater: *legal adviser*
rechtsgültig: *in due form; valid*
Rechtsgültigkeit: *validity*
rechtsgültig machen: *validate*
rechtshängig: *sub judice*
Rechtslage: *legal status*
Rechtsstreit: *action; court case; litigation*
Rechtstitel: *title*
Rechtsungültigkeit: *invalidity*
rechtsunwirksam: *invalid*
Rechtsweg: *judicial processes*
rechtswidrig: *illegal*
Rechtswidrigkeit: *illegality*
recht viele: *quite a few or quite a lot*
rechtzeitig fertig sein: *to be on schedule*
Recycling-Papier: *recycled paper*
Redakteur: *editor*
Redaktion: *editorial board*
redaktionell: *editorial*
Redaktionskomitee: *editorial board*
redlich: *honest*
reduzieren: *cut; reduce* **sich ~** *decrease*
Reduzierung: *decrease; reduction*
Reederei: *shipping company or shipping line*
Reedereiangestellter: *shipping clerk*
REFA-Fachmann: *time and motion expert*

Referenz: *referee; reference; testimonial*
Refinanzierung eines Kredites: *refinancing of a loan*
Reflation: *reflation*
Reflationsmaßnahmen: *reflationary measures*
Regal: *rack; shelf*
Regalauffüller: *shelf filler*
Regale: *shelving*
Regalfläche: *shelf space*
Regalgroßhändler: *rack jobber*
rege: *brisk*
regelmäßig: *regular; regularly*
regeln: *regulate*
Regelung: *regulation*
regieren: *govern*
Regierung: *government*
Region: *province; region*
regional: *provincial; regional*
Regionalplanung: *regional planning*
Register: *index; register*
Registerführer *or* **Registrator:** *registrar*
Registratur: *registry*
registrieren: *record; register*
Registrieren des Arbeitsbeginns: *clocking in or clocking on*
Registrieren des Arbeitsschlusses: *clocking out or clocking off*
Registrierkasse: *cash register or cash till*
registriert: *registered*
Registrierung: *recording; registration*
regulär: *regular*
regulieren: *regulate*
Regulierung: *regulation*
Reibach: einen ~ machen *to make a killing (informal)*
reich: *affluent; rich*
Reihe: *spread* **eine ~ von** *a number of*
Reihenfolge: alphabetische ~ *alphabetical order* **chronologische** *or* **zeitliche ~** *chronological order* **zahlenmäßige ~** *numerical order*
Reinfall: *flop*
Reingewinn: *clear profit; net profit*
Reinigungskosten: *service charge*
Reinschrift: *fair copy or final copy*
Reinvermögen: *net assets or net worth*
reinvestieren: *reinvest*
Reinvestition: *reinvestment*
Reise: *journey; trip*
Reisebranche: die ~ *the travel trade*
Reisebüro: *travel agency* **unseriöses ~** *bucket shop (informal)*
Reisebürokaufmann: *travel agent*
Reisegepäck: *luggage*
Reisekostenzuschuß: *travel allowance*
Reiseleiter: *courier*
Reisemagazin: *travel magazine*
reisen: *travel*
Reisender: *traveller or traveler (US)*
Reiseroute: *itinerary*
Reiseschecks: *traveller's cheques or traveler's checks (US)*
Reiseschreibmaschine: *portable typewriter*
Reisespesen: *travelling expenses*
Reiseveranstalter: *tour operator*
Reißzwecke: *drawing pin*
Reiz: *appeal*
reizen: *appeal*
Reklamationsabteilung: *complaints department*
Reklame: *advertisement; advertising; publicity*
Reklame machen: *promote; publicize; advertise; plug*
Reklamesendungen: *junk mail*
Reklamewand: *advertisement hoarding*
Reklamezettel: *handbill; publicity handout; leaflet*
Rekord: *record*
Rekordernte: *bumper crop*
Rekordverluste: *record losses*
Rektapapier: *non-negotiable instrument*
relativ: *relatively*
Rendite: *(rate of) return; yield*
rentabel: *economic; paying; profit-making; profitable* **nicht ~** *not commercially viable*
Rentabilität: *profitability; viability*
Rentabilitätsberechnung: *measurement of profitability*
Rentabilitätssteigerung: *gain in profitability*
Rente: *pension; superannuation* **dynamische ~** *earnings-related pension* **staatliche ~** *government annuity*
Rentenalter: *pensionable or retirement age*
Rentenanspruch: *pension entitlement* **übertragbarer ~** *portable pension*
Rentenbegünstigter: *annuitant*
rentenberechtigt: *pensionable*
Rentenempfänger: *old age pensioner*
Rentenfonds: *pension fund*
Rentensystem: gestaffeltes ~ *graduated pension scheme*
Rentenversicherung: beitragsfreie ~ *non-contributory pension scheme* **beitragspflichtige ~** *contributory pension plan or scheme* **private ~** *personal pension plan*
Rentenversicherungsbeiträge: *pension contributions*
rentieren: *yield*
Rentner: *old age pensioner*
reorganisieren: *reorganize; restructure*
Reparatur: *repair*
Reparaturwerkstatt: *repair shop*
reparieren: *fix; repair*
Reportgeschäft: *contango*
Reporttag: *contango day*
Repräsentant: *representative*
Repräsentation: *representation*
Repräsentationsbüro: *prestige office*
Repräsentationswerbung: *prestige advertising*

repräsentativ: *representative*
repräsentieren: *represent*
Reprivatisierung: *denationalization*
Reserve: *pool; stockpile* **in ~** *in reserve*
Reserven: stille ~ *hidden assets; hidden reserves*
Reservewährung: *reserve currency*
reservieren: *book*
Reservierung: *reservation*
Resolution: eine ~ annehmen *to pass a resolution*
Resonanz: *feedback*
Ressort: *desk; department*
Ressourcen: ~ zusammenlegen *to pool resources*
Rest: *remainder; remnant; rest*
Restauflage: *remainders*
Restaurant: *restaurant*
Restaurantbesitzer: *restaurateur*
Restaurant für Außer-Haus-Verkauf: *takeaway*
Restbestand: *remainder*
Restbestände: *oddments*
Restbetrag: *balance; residue*
Restdividende: *final dividend*
restlich: *residual*
Restposten: *oddments*
restriktiv: *restrictive*
Resultat: *result*
Retourwaren: *returns*
retten: *rescue; salvage*
Rettung: *rescue*
Rettungsaktion: *rescue operation*
Rettungsboot: *lifeboat*
revanchieren: sich ~ *reciprocate*
Revision: *appeal; audit; auditing* **betriebsinterne** *or* **innerbetriebliche** *or* **interne ~** *internal audit*
Revision einlegen: *appeal*
Revisionsantrag: *appeal*
Revisor: betriebsinterner ~ *internal auditor* **unabhängiger ~** *external auditor*
Revolving-Kredit: *revolving credit*
Rezeption: *reception; reception desk*
Rezession: *recession*
R-Gespräch: *collect call (US); reverse charge call; transferred charge call*
richten an: *address*
Richter: *judge*
Richterzimmer: *chambers*
richtig: *correct; right*
Richtlinien: *code of practice; guidelines*
Richtpreis: *administered price (US)*
Riesenbestellung: eine ~ *an outsize order*
Ringbuch: *ring binder; loose-leaf book*
Risiko: *danger; exposure; risk* **das ~ verteilen** *to spread the risk* **ein ~ decken** *to cover a risk* **ein ~ eingehen** *to take a risk*
Risikoanleihen: *junk bonds*
Risikokapital: *risk capital; venture capital*
risikolos: *risk-free*
Risikoversicherung: *contingent policy; whole-life insurance*
riskant: *dangerous; risky*
riskieren: *venture*
Roboter: *robot*
Roboter-Herstellung *or* **Roboter-Technologie:** *robotics*
Rohentwurf: *rough draft*
Rohgewicht: *gross weight*
Rohöl: *crude (oil); crude petroleum*
Rohölprodukte: *petroleum products*
Rohstoffe: *raw materials*
Rohstoffindustrie: *primary industry*
Rolle: *roll*
rollen: *roll*
Ro Ro-: *roll on/roll off*
Rotation: *rotation*
Route: *route*
Routine: *routine*
routinemäßig: *routine*
Rubel: *rouble*
rückerstatten: *refund*
Rückerstattung: *rebate; refund; repayment; restitution*
Rückfahrkarte: *return ticket* *or* *round-trip ticket (US)*
Rückfahrt: *return journey*
Rückfall: *reversion*
Rückforderung: *clawback*
Rückfrage: *query*
Rückgabe: *restitution; return*
Rückgang: *decline; decrease; downturn; drop* **kurzfristiger ~** *dip* **plötzlicher ~** *slump*
rückgängig machen: *annul; call off; rescind; revoke*
rückkaufen: *buy in*
Rückkaufwert: *surrender value*
Rückkehr: *return*
Rücklage: *provision; reserve*
Rücklagefonds: *reserve fund*
Rücklagen: *reserves*
rückläufig: *downward*
Rückschlag: *reversal; setback*
Rückseite: *back*
Rücksendung: *return*
Rückstand: *backlog* **im ~** *in arrears* **in ~ geraten** *fall behind*
Rückstände: *arrears; back payments*
Rückstellung: *provision*
Rücktritt: *resignation*
Rücktrittsklausel: *cancellation clause; escape clause; let-out clause*
Rückübertragung: *reassignment*
Rückumschlag: frankierter *or* **freigemachter ~** *stamped addressed envelope*
Rückvergütung: *rebate*
Rückversicherer: *reinsurer*
rückversichern: *reassure; reinsure*
Rückversicherung: *reinsurance*
rückwirkend: *retroactive*

rückzahlbar: *repayable*
Rückzahlung: *back payment; payback; rebate; redemption; repayment*
Rückzahlungsbetrag: *payoff*
Rückzahlungsklausel: *payback clause*
Rückzahlungswert: *redemption value*
Rückzahlung vor Fälligkeit: *redemption before due date*
Rückzoll: *drawback*
Ruf: *reputation; standing*
Rufnummer: *telephone number*
Ruhegehalt: *pension*
Ruhegeldordnung: *pension plan or pension scheme*
ruhig: *calm; quiet; slack*
Ruin: *wreck*
ruinieren: *bankrupt*
Rumpfbelegschaft: *skeleton staff*
Run: *run*
Rundfahrt mit Führer: *conducted tour*
Rundreise: *tour*
Rundschreiben: *circular (letter); mail shot; mailing shot*
Rundschreiben verschicken: *circularize*
Rupie: *rupee*
Rüstkosten: *setting up costs or setup costs*
Rüstzeit: *make-ready time*

Ss

Sachbearbeiter: *clerk*
Sachbearbeiterin: *clerkess*
Sache: *affair; business; matter* **einer ~ nachgehen** *investigate*
Sachkenntnis: *expertise*
sachkundig: *experienced*
Sachleistung: *payment in kind*
sachlich: *objective*
Sachverständigenausschuß: *panel of experts*
Sachverständigengutachten: *expert's report*
Sachverständiger: *expert* **juristischer ~** *legal expert*
Sachwerte: bilanzirbare ~ *tangible assets*
Safe: *safe*
Saftladen: *sloppy outfit*
Saison: *season*
saisonbedingt: *seasonal*
Saisonbereinigungen: *seasonal adjustments*
Saisonschlußverkauf: *end of season sale*
saldieren: *balance*
Saldo: *balance; balance brought down; bottom line*
Saldovortrag: *balance brought forward or carried forward*
Sammelladung: *consolidated shipment*
sammeln: *gather*
Sammlung: *collection*
Sandwich Bar: *sandwich bar*
Sandwich-Plakat: *sandwich board*
sanieren: *redevelop; turn round*
Sanierung: *redevelopment; rescue operation; turnround*
sanktionieren: *sanction*
Sattelkraftfahrzeug *or* **Sattelschlepper:** *articulated lorry or articulated vehicle*
sättigen: *saturate* **Sättigung** *saturation*
Satz: *rate; set* **der übliche ~** *the going rate* **fester ~** *fixed rate* **voller ~** *full rate*
Satzung: *articles of association or articles of incorporation (US); constitution; regulations*
satzungsgemäß: *constitutional*
Saugpostpapier: *duplicating paper*
Säulendiagramm: *bar chart*
Schachtel: *box*
Schaden: *damage; harm; prejudice*
schaden: *harm; hurt*
Schadenabteilung: *claims department*
Schaden anrichten: *to cause damage*
Schaden erleiden: *to suffer damage*
Schadenfreiheitsrabatt: *no-claims bonus*
Schadenregulierer: *average adjuster*
Schadensanspruch: *insurance claim*
Schadensbearbeitung der Versicherung: *the processing of a claim for insurance*
Schadensersatz: *compensation for damage; damages; indemnification; restitution*
Schadensersatz leisten: *indemnify*
schadensersatzpflichtig sein: *to stand liable for damages*
Schadensformular: *claim form*
Schadensprüfung: *damage survey*
Schadenssachverständiger: *adjuster*
Schaden verursachen: *to cause damage*
schadhaft: *damaged; defective*
schädigen: *prejudice*
Schadloshaltungserklärung: *letter of indemnity*
schaffen: *achieve; create; establish*
Schaffung: *creation*
Schalterbeamter: *booking clerk*
Schalterstunden: *banking hours*
Schankkonzession: *liquor licence*
Schattenwirtschaft: *black economy*
Schatzamt: *the Exchequer (GB)*
Schatzanweisung: *government bonds*
schätzen: *appreciate; assess; calculate; estimate; value*
Schätzer: *estimator; valuer*
Schatzkanzler: *Chancellor of the Exchequer (GB)*
Schatzobligation: *treasury bonds*
Schätzung: *assessment; estimate; estimation; guess; rating; valuation* **bei vorsichtiger ~** *at a conservative estimate* **grobe ~** *rough estimate; guesstimate (informal); rough calculation* **zu niedrige ~** *undervaluation*
Schatzwechsel: *treasury bill*

Schaubild: *diagram; graph* **in einem ~** *diagrammatically*
Schauermann: *stevedore*
Schaufenster: *shop window*
Schaufensterbummel: *window shopping*
Schaufensterdekoration: *window display*
Schaufensterplakat *or* **Schaufensterschild:** *showcard*
Schaukasten: *display case; display cabinet; showcase*
Schaupackung: *display pack; dummy pack*
Scheck: bestätigter ~ *certified cheque or certified check (US)* **einen ~ ausstellen** *to write out a cheque* **einen ~ einlösen** *to cash a cheque; to clear a cheque* **einen ~ girieren** *to endorse a cheque* **einen ~ sperren** *to put a stop on a cheque* **einen ~ stornieren** *to cancel a cheque* **einen ~ unterschreiben** *to sign a cheque* **einen ~ vordatieren** *to date a cheque forward* **mit ~ bezahlen** *to pay by cheque* **nichteingelöster ~** *dishonoured cheque* **ungedeckter ~** *dud cheque or bouncing cheque or cheque which bounces or rubber check (US)*
Scheckabschnitt: *cheque stub*
Scheckanforderung: *cheque requisition*
Scheckheft: *cheque book*
Scheckkarte: *cheque (guarantee) card*
Scheffel: *bushel*
Schein: *bank bill (US); bank note or banknote*
Scheinaktiva: *fictitious assets*
Scheitern: *breakdown; failure*
scheitern: *break down; fail; fall through*
Schema: übliches ~ *pattern*
schenken: *give; present*
Schenkung zu Lebzeiten: *gift inter vivos*
Schicht: *echelon; shift*
Schichtarbeit: *shift work*
schicken: *dispatch; mail; send*
Schiebung: *fiddle (informal)*
Schiedsgericht: *industrial court (GB); tribunal*
Schiedsgericht für Mietstreitigkeiten: *rent tribunal*
Schiedsrichter: *arbitrator*
Schiedsspruch: *award*
Schiff: *boat; ship; vessel* **voll beladenes ~** *fully-laden ship*
Schiffahrts-: *maritime*
Schiffsausrüster: *ship chandler*
Schiffshypothek: *bottomry*
Schiffslieferant: *chandler*
Schiffsmakler: *ship broker*
Schild: *sign; tag; ticket*
schildern: *describe*
Schilderung: *description*
schlagen: *beat; defeat; hit*
Schlange: *queue*
Schlange stehen: *queue*
Schlappe: *hammering*
schlau: *clever*
schlecht verwalten: *mismanage*
schleppend: *dull*
Schleuderpreis: *rock-bottom price*
schlicht: *plain*
schlichten: *arbitrate*
Schlichter: *adjudicator; arbitrator; official mediator*
Schlichtung: *arbitration; conciliation; settlement*
Schlichtungskommission: *adjudication tribunal; arbitration board or arbitration tribunal*
Schlichtungsverfahren: *arbitration*
schließen: *close; close down; gather; shut; wind up*
schließlich: *in the end; finally; ultimately*
Schließung: *closing; closure*
Schließungstag: *closing date*
schlimm: *serious; seriously*
Schloß: *lock*
Schluß: *close* **zum ~** *finally*
Schlußbestand: *closing stock*
Schlußdividende: *final dividend*
Schlüssel: *key*
Schlüsselindustrie: *basic industry*
schlußfolgern: *conclude*
Schlußkurs: *closing price*
Schlußnotierung: *closing price*
Schlußsitzung: *closing session*
Schlußverkauf: *the sales*
schmieren: *bribe*
Schmiergeld: *backhander (informal); bribe; kickback*
Schmiergelder: *slush fund*
Schmuggel: *smuggling*
schmuggeln: *smuggle*
Schmuggelware: *contraband (goods)*
Schmuggler: *smuggler*
Schnäppchen: *bargain; snip (informal)*
Schneeballeffekt: *knock-on effect*
Schnelligkeit: *speed*
schnell steigen: *take off*
Schnittstelle: *interface; port*
Schnitzer: *slip; slip-up* **einen ~ machen** *slip up*
Schrank: *cabinet*
Schranke: *barrier*
schreckhaft: *jumpy*
Schreibarbeit: *clerical work or paperwork*
Schreibblock: *desk pad*
Schreibbüro: *word-processing bureau*
Schreibdienst: zentraler ~ *typing pool*
Schreibfehler: *clerical error*
Schreibkraft: *(copy) typist*
Schreibkräfte: *clerical staff*
Schreibmaschine: *typewriter*
Schreibmaschinenpapier: *typing paper*
Schreibmaschinentisch: *typing table*
Schreibmaschineschreiben: *typing*
Schreibtisch: *desk*
Schreibtischjob: *office job or white-collar job*
Schreibwaren: *stationery*

Schrift: *writing*
Schriftführer: *secretary*
Schriftstück: *writing*
Schriftwechsel: *correspondence*
Schritt: *step*
Schritte unternehmen: *to take action*
schrittweise einführen: *phase in*
Schrott: *scrap*
Schrotthändler: *scrap dealer or scrap merchant*
schrumpfen: *shrink*
Schrumpffolienverpackung: *blister pack or bubble pack*
Schrumpfpackung: *shrink-wrapping*
Schuld: *blame; fault* **eine ~ begleichen** *to discharge or to liquidate a debt* **fundierte ~** *funded debt*
Schulden: *debts; liabilities* **aufgenommene ~** *borrowings* **fällige ~** *debts due* **in ~ geraten** *to run into debt* **kurzfristige ~** *short-term debts*
schulden: *owe*
Schulden begleichen: *to clear off or to pay off a debt*
Schuldenbegleichung: *clearing of a debt*
Schulden eintreiben: *to collect a debt*
Schuldeneintreiber: *debt collector*
Schuldeneintreibung: *debt collection*
Schulden haben: *to be in debt*
Schulden machen: *to get into debt; to incur debts*
Schulden tilgen: *to clear off or to pay off a debt*
Schuldentilgung: *clearing of a debt*
Schulden zurückzahlen: *to pay back a debt*
schuldig: *guilty*
Schuldner: *debtor* **flüchtiger ~** *fly-by-night* **säumiger ~** *defaulter; slow payer*
Schuldnerland: *debtor nation*
Schuldposten: *debit*
Schuldrecht: *contract law or law of contract*
Schuldschein: *bond; note of hand; IOU; promissory note*
Schuldverschreibung: *bond; debenture bond* **gesicherte ~** *debenture* **kündbare ~** *callable bond*
Schuldverschreibung ohne Fälligkeitstermin: *undated bond*
Schuldzinsen bezahlen: *to service a debt*
Schulung: *training*
schütteln: *shake*
Schutz: *cover; hedge; protection; security; shelter*
schützen: *protect; safeguard*
Schutzhülle: *protective cover*
Schutzzoll: *protective tariff*
Schwäche: *failing; weakness*
schwanken: *fluctuate; vary*
schwankend: *fluctuating; unstable; variable*
Schwankung: *fluctuation*
Schwarzarbeit: *moonlighting (informal)*
schwarzarbeiten: *moonlight (informal)*
Schwarzarbeiter: *moonlighter (informal)*
Schwarzes Brett: *noticeboard*
Schwarzmarkt: *black market*
schwebend: *pending*
Schweiß: *sweat*
Schwelle: *threshold*
Schwellenpreis: *threshold price*
Schwerfahrzeug: *heavy goods vehicle*
Schwergut: *deadweight cargo*
Schwergutlastwagen: *heavy lorry*
Schwerindustrie: *heavy industry*
Schwermaschinen: *heavy equipment; heavy machinery*
Schwerpunktstreiks: *selective strikes*
Schwestergesellschaft: *sister company*
Schwesterschiff: *sister ship*
Schwierigkeit: *difficulty*
Schwierigkeiten: aus ~ helfen *bail out*
Schwindel: *con (informal); confidence trick*
Schwindelgeschäft: *fraudulent transaction*
Schwindler: *confidence trickster*
Schwund: *leakage; shrinkage; wastage*
Schwung: *drive; momentum* **in ~ kommen** *to gain momentum*
schwungvoll: *vigorous*
Sechserpack: *six-pack*
Seehafen: *seaport*
Seehandel: *maritime trade*
Seemann: unausgebildeter ~ *deck hand*
Seerecht: *maritime law or the law of the sea*
Seereise: *voyage*
See(transport)versicherer: *marine underwriter*
See(transport)versicherung: *marine insurance*
Seeweg: auf dem ~ *by sea mail*
Sehr geehrte(r): *dear*
Seite: *side* **zur ~** *aside*
Seitenende: *foot*
Seitenzahlen: mit ~ versehen *folio*
seit langem bestehend: *old-established*
Sekretär: *secretary* **ehrenamtlicher ~** *hon sec; honorary secretary*
Sekretariat: *secretariat*
Sekretärinnenschule: *secretarial college*
Sektor: staatlicher ~ *public sector*
sekundär: *secondary*
selbständig: *self-employed*
Selbständigen: die ~ *the self-employed*
Selbstbedienungsgeschäft: *self-service store*
Selbstbedienungsladen: kleiner ~ *minimarket*
selbstdurchschreibend: *carbonless*
Selbstfinanzierung: *self-financing*
Selbstklebeetikett: *self-sticking label*
Selbstkosten: *direct cost*
Selbstkostenpreis: *cost price; prime cost* **zum ~ verkaufen** *to sell at cost*
Selbstläufer: *fast-selling items*
Selbstversorgung: *self-sufficiency*
selbstverständlich: *of course*
selbstverwaltend: *self-regulatory*
Selbstverwaltung: *self-regulation*

Selbstwählferndienst: *subscriber trunk dialling* **internationaler ~** *international direct dialling*
selektiv: *selective*
selten: *rare; rarely; scarce*
Seltenheit: *scarceness or scarcity*
Seltenheitswert: *scarcity value*
Semester: *term*
senden: *dispatch; send*
Sendenetz: *television network*
Sendestation: *TV station or radio station*
Sendung: *dispatch; shipment*
senken: *bring down; cut; depress; lower; mark down; reduce*
senkrecht: *vertical*
Senkrechtstarter: *high flier*
Senkung: *abatement; cut; lowering; reduction*
sensibel: *sensitive*
separat: *separate; separately*
Sequester: *sequestrator*
Sequestration: *sequestration*
sequestrieren: *sequester or sequestrate*
Serie: *batch; series*
Serienfertigung: *batch production*
Seriennummer: *batch number; serial number*
serienweise: in ~ herstellen *to mass produce*
seriös: *reliable; reputable*
Service: *service*
SERVICE 130: *freephone (GB)*
Set: *set*
Shifttaste: *shift key*
Shilling: *shilling*
sicher: *certain; reliable; safe; secure*
-sicher: *-proof*
Sicherheit: *collateral; cover; guarantee; reliability; safety; security; surety*
Sicherheit des Arbeitsplatzes: *job security*
sicherheitshalber: *for safety*
Sicherheitsmarge: *margin of safety*
Sicherheitsspielraum: *safety margin*
Sicherheitsvorkehrungen: *safety measures; safety precautions* **~ im Büro** *office security*
Sicherheitsvorschriften: *safety regulations*
sichern: *safeguard; save*
Sicherstellung: *impounding*
Sicherungskopie: *backup copy*
Sicherungspfandrecht: *lien*
Sicht: *sight* **auf kurze ~** *on a short-term basis* **auf lange ~** *in the long term*
sichtbar: *visible; visual*
Sichteinlage: *demand deposit (US)*
Sichttratte: *sight draft; sight bill*
Sichtvermerk: *visa*
Sichtwechsel: *demand bill; sight draft; sight bill*
Silben(zahl) pro Minute: *dictation speed*
sinken: *decline; depreciate; dip; fall; fall away; sink*
Sinn: *effect*
Situation: *position; situation*
Sitz: *base; domicile* **eingetragener ~** *registered office (GB)* **seinen ~ haben** *to be located*
Sitzstreik: *sit-down protest or sit-down strike*
Sitzung: *meeting; session* **eine ~ abhalten** *to hold a meeting* **eine ~ eröffnen** *to open a meeting* **eine ~ leiten** *to conduct a meeting* **eine ~ schließen** *to close a meeting* **obligatorische ~** *mandatory meeting*
Sitzungssaal: *boardroom*
Skala: *scale*
skizzieren: *outline*
sofort beziehbar: *with immediate occupancy; vacant possession*
sofortig: *prompt*
Sofortliquidität: *spot cash*
Software: *software*
Solidargläubiger: *co-creditor*
Solidaritätsstreik: *sympathy strike*
solide: *sound*
Solidität: *soundness*
Soll: *debit*
Sollbuchung: *debit entry*
Sollsaldo: *debit balance*
Sollspalte: *debtor side*
Soll und Haben: *debit and credit*
Sollzinsen: *interest charges*
solvent: *solvent*
Solvenz: *solvency*
Sommerferien: *the summer holidays*
Sommerzeit: *Summer Time or Daylight Saving Time*
Sonderabschreibung: *accelerated depreciation*
Sonderangebot: *bargain offer; special offer*
Sonderangebotsabteilung: *budget department*
Sonderangebotsstand: *bargain counter*
Sonderausgaben: *extras* **unvorhergesehene ~** *contingent expenses*
Sondergewinnsteuer: *windfall tax*
Sonderposten: *exceptional or extraordinary items*
Sonderpreis: *bargain price*
Sondertisch: *bargain counter*
Sonderzubehör: *optional extras*
sondieren: *explore*
Sonntag: geschäftsfreier ~ *Sunday closing*
sonst: *failing that*
Sorge: *concern*
sorgfältig prüfen or untersuchen: *study*
Sorte: *kind*
sortieren: *sort; sort out*
Sortiment: *choice; product line or product range*
Sortimentserweiterung: *product diversification or diversification into new products*
Sozialhilfe: *supplementary benefit; welfare*
Sozialstaat: *welfare state*
Sozialunterstützung: *social security*
Sozialversicherung: *National Insurance (GB)*
Sozialversicherungsbeiträge: *National Insurance contributions*
sozio-ökonomisch: *socio-economic*

Spalte: *column; side*
Spaltung: *split*
Spanne: *spread*
Sparbrief: *savings certificate or savings bond (US)*
Sparbuch: *bank book; passbook*
Spareinlagen: **zinstragende ~** *interest-bearing deposits*
sparen: *save; save up*
Sparer: *saver*
Sparkampagne: *economy drive*
Sparkasse: *savings bank; thrift (US)*
Sparkonto: *deposit account; savings account* **steuerfreies ~** *Individual Retirement Account (US)*
Sparmaßnahmen einführen: *to introduce economies or economy measures*
Sparpackung: *economy size*
Sparprämienanleihe: *premium bond (GB)*
Sparpreise: *budget prices*
Sparprogramm: **steuerfreies ~** *save-as-you-earn scheme (GB)*
sparsam: *economical; thrifty*
Sparsamkeit: *economy; thrift*
Sparschuldverschreibung: *savings certificate or savings bond (US)*
Sparsystem: **britisches ~** *National Savings (GB)*
Sparte: *line of business or line of work*
Spediteur: *forwarding agent; clerk (US); haulage contractor; (freight) forwarder; road haulier; removal(s) company; shipper; shipping agent*
Spedition(sfirma): *(common) carrier; (freight) forwarder; haulage firm or company; removal(s) company*
Speicher: *memory; storage*
Speichergerät: *storage unit*
speichern: *store*
Speicherung: *storage*
speisen: *feed*
Spekulant: *speculator*
Spekulation: *speculation*
Spekulationsaktie: *speculative share*
spekulativ: *notional*
spekulieren: *speculate*
Sperre: *check*
sperren: *block*
sperrig: *bulky*
Sperrung: *stop*
Sperrung eines Kundenkreditkontos: *closing of an account*
Spesen: *allowance; expenses*
Spesenaufstellung: *statement of expenses*
Spesenkonto: *expense account*
spezialangefertigt: *custom-built or custom-made*
Spezialgebiet: *speciality or specialty*
Spezialgeschäft: *specialty store (US)*
spezialisieren: *specialize*
Spezialisierung: *specialization*
Spezialist in: *specialist*
Spezialität: *speciality or specialty*
speziell: *particular; special*
Spezifikation: *specification*
spezifizieren: *break down; itemize; specify*
Spezifizierung: *breakdown*
Spiel: **aufs ~ setzen** *venture*
spielen: *punt*
Spieler: *punter*
Spielraum: *margin*
Spinnerei: *cotton mill*
Spirale: *spiral*
Spitze: *head; top*
Spitzen-: *favourite; first-class; top-flight; high-level; leading; top-ranking; top-grade*
Spitzenanlagen: *blue-chip investments*
Spitzenbeamter: *top official*
Spitzenbedarfszeit: *time of peak demand*
Spitzendelegation: *high-level delegation*
Spitzenjahr: *peak year*
Spitzenqualität: *high quality or top quality*
Spitzenreiter: *leader*
Spitzenumsätze: *record sales*
Sponsor: *backer; sponsor* **als ~ finanzieren** *sponsor*
sponsoren: *sponsor*
Sponsoring: *sponsorship*
spontan: *snap* **etwas ~ tun** *to do something on impulse*
Spontankäufer: *impulse buyer*
Spottpreis: *bargain or knockdown price*
Sprache: *language* **zur ~ bringen** *bring up*
sprechen zu: *address*
springen: *jump*
Sprung: *jump*
sprunghaft ansteigen: *rocket; shoot up; soar*
Staat: *state*
Staatlicher Gesundheitsdienst: *National Health Service (GB)*
staatlich gefördert: *government-sponsored*
staatlich gelenkt or vorgeschrieben: *government-regulated*
Staatsanleihen: *government bonds; government stock; tap (stock) (GB)* **konsolidierte ~** *consols (GB)*
Staatsanwaltschaft: *prosecution*
Staatsbesitz: *public ownership*
Staatsbetrieb: *state enterprise*
Staatsdienst: *the civil service*
staatseigen: *state-owned*
Staatseigentum: *public ownership or state ownership*
Staatsfinanzen: *public finance*
Staatshaushalt: **der ~** *the Budget*
Staatspapiere: *gilts (GB); gilt-edged securities or government securities* **mittelfristige ~** *mediums*
Staatsverschuldung: **die ~** *the National Debt*
Staatsvertrag: *treaty*
Stabdiagramm: *bar chart*
stabil: *firm; sound; stable; steady*

stabilisieren: *stabilize*
Stabilisierung: *stabilization*
Stabilität: *firmness; soundness; stability; steadiness*
Stadium: *phase; stage*
Stadt: *city*
städtisch: *municipal*
Stadtplan: *directory; street plan* or *town plan; street directory*
Stadtrat: *town council*
Stadtteil: *district*
staffeln: *grade; stagger*
Staffeltarife: *differential tariffs*
Stagflation: *stagflation*
Stagnation: *dullness; stagnation*
stagnieren: *stagnate*
stagnierend: *stagnant*
Stahlkammer: *strongroom*
Stahlkassette: *strongbox*
Stammaktien: *equities; ordinary shares; common stock (US)*
Stammaktionär: *ordinary shareholder*
Stammdatei: *master copy of a file*
Stammkunde: *long-standing* or *regular customer*
Stand: *booth (US); level; stand*
Standardbrief: *standard letter*
Standardgröße: *regular size*
standardisieren: *standardize*
Standardisierung: *standardization*
Standardsteuersatz: *standard rate*
Standby-Flugpreis: *standby fare*
Standby-Kredit: *standby credit*
Ständer: *rack*
Standesamt: *registry office*
Standesbeamter: *registrar*
ständig wiederkehrend: *recurrent*
Standmiete: *market dues*
Standort: *base; location*
Stange: *carton* **von der ~** *ready-made* or *ready-to-wear*
Stapel: *batch; pile; stack* **stapeln** *batch; pile; stack*
Stapelverarbeitung: *batch processing*
Stärke: *power; strength*
stark fallen: *plummet* or *plunge*
stark reduzieren: *slash*
Start: *departure; start*
Startkapital: *initial capital*
stationieren: *base*
Statistik(en): *statistics*
Statistiker: *statistician*
statistisch: *statistical*
stattfinden: *hold; take place*
stattgeben: *allow*
stattlich: *substantial*
Status: *status*
Status quo: *status quo*
Statuten: *regulations*
Stau: *jam*
Stauer: *stevedore*
Stechkarte: *clock card; time-card* or *time-clock card (US)*
steckenbleiben: *stick*
Stecker: *plug*
stehlen: *steal*
steigen: *advance; appreciate; climb; gain; increase; mount up; rise*
steigern: *increase; step up*
Steigerung: *buildup; increase; rise* **~ der Lebenshaltungskosten** *increase in the cost of living*
steil: *sharp(ly); steep(ly)*
Stelle: *appointment; employment; place; point; position; post; situation; spot* **eine verantwortungsvolle ~** *a responsible job* **eine ~ besetzen** *to fill a post* or *a vacancy* **eine ~ innehaben** *to occupy a post* **freie ~** *vacancy* **leere ~** *blank* **seine ~ aufgeben** *to give up one's job; quit*
Stellen: freie or **offene ~** *job openings* or *vacancies*
stellen: *place*
Stellenangebote: *situations vacant; job vacancies*
Stellenbeschreibung: *job description; job specification*
Stellenbesetzungsplan: *organization chart*
Stellengesuch: *job application*
Stellengesuche: *situations wanted*
Stellenvermittlung: *job centre (GB); employment office* or *bureau* or *agency; placement*
Stellung: *job; position; post; rank; status* **hohe amtliche ~** *high office*
Stellungnahme: *statement*
stellvertretend: *acting; vice-*
Stellvertreter: *deputy; proxy; representative; substitute*
Stellvertretung: *representation*
Stempel: *rubber stamp*
Stempelgebühr: *stamp duty*
Stempelkissen: *inking pad; stamp pad*
Stempeln: *clocking in* or *clocking on; clocking out* or *clocking off*
stempeln: *clock in* or *clock on; clock out* or *clock off; postmark; stamp* **stempeln gehen** *to go on the dole*
Stenograph: *shorthand secretary; stenographer*
Stenographie: *shorthand*
stenographieren: *to take shorthand*
Stenotypist: *shorthand typist*
Sterbegeld: *death benefit*
Sterbetafel: *actuarial* or *mortality tables*
Sterlingkrise: *sterling crisis*
Sterlingverkäufe: panikartige ~ *panic selling of sterling*
Sterlingzone: *sterling area*
stetig: *continuous*
Steuer: *duty; levy; tax* **eine ~ erheben** *to levy a tax* or *to impose a tax* **ohne ~** *exclusive of tax*
Steuerabzüge: *tax deductions*
Steueranpassungen: *tax adjustments*
Steueraufkommen: *revenue*

steuerbefreit: *tax-exempt*
Steuerbefreiung: *exemption from tax or tax exemption; tax holiday*
Steuerbegünstigung: *tax shelter*
Steuerberater: *accountant; tax adviser or tax consultant*
Steuereinnehmer: *exciseman*
Steuererklärung: *tax return or tax declaration*
Steuerermäßigung: *tax relief*
steuerfrei: *exempt from tax or tax-exempt; free of tax or tax-free; non-taxable*
Steuerfreibetrag: *allowance; tax allowance or allowances against tax; tax exemption (US)* **persönlicher ~** *personal allowance*
Steuergesetz: *Finance Act; Finance Act (GB)*
Steuergutschrift: *tax credit*
Steuer hinterziehen: *to evade tax*
Steuerhinterziehung: *tax evasion*
Steuerjahr: *fiscal year; tax year*
Steuerklasse: höchste ~ *highest tax bracket*
Steuerklassen: *tax schedules (GB)*
steuerlich: *fiscal*
steuerlich absetzbar *or* **abzugsfähig:** *tax-deductible*
Steuern: vor ~ *pre-tax or pretax*
steuern: *control*
Steuernachlaß: *tax abatement*
Steueroase: *tax haven*
steuerpflichtig: *taxable* **nicht ~** *non-taxable*
Steuerprüfer: *inspector of taxes or tax inspector*
Steuerrückzahlung: *remission of taxes*
Steuerschulden: *back tax*
Steuersystem mit Progression: *graduated taxation*
Steuerungssysteme: *control systems*
Steuervergünstigung: *tax concession*
Steuerverkürzung: *tax avoidance*
Steuerzahler: *taxpayer*
Steward: *steward*
Stewardeß: *air hostess or stewardess*
stichhaltig: *valid*
Stichprobe: *check sample* **zufällige ~** *random sample*
Stichprobenauswahl: *random sampling*
Stichprobenverfahren: *sampling*
Stichtag: *deadline; effective date; settlement day*
Stiftung: *endowment*
Stil: *style*
stillegen: *close down*
Stillegung: *closure; shutdown*
stillschweigend: *tacit*
Stillstand: *deadlock; stagnation; standstill; stop; stoppage*
Stillstandzeit: *down time*
Stimmabgabe: *voting* **geschlossene ~** *block vote*
Stimme: ausschlaggebende ~ *casting vote*
Stimmrecht: *voting rights*
Stimmzettel: *ballot paper; voting paper*
Stipendium: *grant*
stocken: *stagnate*
stockend: *stagnant*
Stockung: *jam*
Stockwerk: *floor*
stoppen: *block; plug; stop*
stornieren: *cancel*
Stornierung: *cancellation*
Stoß: *batch; stack*
Stoßzeit: *peak period* **außerhalb der ~** *off-peak; during the off-peak period*
strafbar: *criminal*
Strafe: *penalty*
Straffung: *streamlining*
Strafklausel: *penalty clause*
Strafprozeß: *criminal action*
Strafrecht: *criminal law*
strafrechtlich verfolgen: *prosecute*
Straftat: *crime*
Strandgut: *flotsam and jetsam*
Straße: *road; street*
Straßenecke: *corner*
Straßenhändler: *street vendor*
Strategie: *strategy*
strategisch: *strategic*
Strecke: *route; run*
streichen: *axe; cross off; cut; delete; remove*
Streik: *strike* **gewerkschaftlich organisierter** *or* **offizieller ~** *official strike* **vom ~ betroffen** *strikebound* **wilder ~** *unofficial or wildcat strike*
Streikabstimmung: *strike ballot or strike vote*
Streikaufruf: *strike call*
Streikbrecher: *blackleg; fink (informal) (US); scab (informal); strikebreaker*
streiken: *strike*
Streikender: *striker*
Streikgeld: *strike pay*
Streikkasse: *strike fund*
Streikposten: *picket* **mobile ~** *flying pickets*
Streikpostenkette: *picket line* **eine ~ durchbrechen** *to cross a picket line*
Streikpostenstehen: *picketing* **friedlich durchgeführtes ~** *peaceful picketing*
Streikrecht: *right to strike*
Streikverbotsklausel: *no-strike agreement or no-strike clause*
Streit: *argument* **streiten** *to argue*
Streß: unter ~ arbeiten *work under high pressure*
Streuung: *spread*
Strichdiagramm: *line chart or line graph*
Strichkodierung: *bar code*
Strohmann: *front; front man*
Strom: *electricity; flood; stream*
Stromzufuhrkabel: *input lead*
Struktur: *pattern; structure*
strukturell: *structural*
strukturieren: *structure*
Stück: *piece; unit*

Stückelung: *denomination*
Stückkosten: *unit cost*
Stücklohnsatz: *piece rate*
Stückpreis: *unit price*
Stückzahl: große ~ *quantity*
Studie: *study; survey*
Studio: *studio*
Stufe: *bracket; grade; phase; stage*
Stunde: pro ~ *per hour*
Stunden: eine 35-~-Woche arbeiten *to work a thirty-five hour week*
Stundenleistung: *output per hour*
Stundenlohn: *hourly rate; hourly wage*
stundenweise: *hourly* ~ **bezahlt werden** *to be paid by the hour*
Stundenzettel: *time sheet*
stündlich: *hourly*
Sturmschaden: *storm damage*
Sturz: *collapse; drop; slump*
stürzen: *drop; plummet or plunge; slump*
stützen: *support*
Stützungspreis: *support price*
Styropor: *expanded polystyrene*
Submission: *tender*
Submissionsofferten: versiegelte ~ *sealed tenders*
Submittent: *tenderer*
Subskriptionsprospekt: *prospectus*
subtrahieren: *subtract*
Subunternehmer: *subcontractor*
Subvention: *bounty; grant; subsidy; subvention*
subventionieren: *subsidize*
Summe: *amount; figure; sum; total* **laufende** ~ *running total*
Supermarkt: *supermarket*
Superprovision: *overrider or overriding commission*
Supertanker: *supertanker*
suspendieren: *suspend*
Symbol: *symbol; token*
Sympathiestreik: *sympathy strike*
Syndikat: *federation; ring; syndicate; trust (US)*
Synergismus: *synergy*
synthetisch: *synthetic*
System: leistungsabhängiges ~ *incentive scheme* **metrisches** ~ *the metric system*
Systemanalyse: *systems analysis*
Systemanalytiker: *systems analyst*
systematisch: *systematic*
Systemberater: *systems analyst*
Systemprogrammierer: *programming engineer*
System zur Datenrückgewinnung: *retrieval system*

Tt

tabellarisch: *in tabular form*
tabellarisch darstellen *or* **tabellarisieren:** *tabulate*
Tabellarisierung: *tabulation*
Tabelle: *scale; table*
Tabellenkalkulation: *spreadsheet*
Tabellierpapier: *listing paper*
Tabulator: *tabulator*
Tachograph: *tachograph*
Tafel: *panel*
Tag: pro ~ *per day*
Tagarbeiter: *day worker*
Tag des Inkrafttretens: *effective date*
Tage: drei ganze *or* **drei volle** ~ *three clear days*
Tagebuch: *diary*
Tagegeld: *subsistence allowance*
Tagesgeld: *money at call or money on call or call money*
Tageskurs: *current rate of exchange*
Tagesmenü: *set menu*
Tagesordnung: *agenda*
Tagespreis: *current price*
Tagesproduktion an Autos: *daily production of cars*
Tagesumsatz: *daily sales returns*
Tagesverbrauch: *daily consumption*
Tageszeitung: *a daily newspaper or a daily*
täglich: *daily; day-to-day*
Tagschicht: *day shift*
Tag- und Nachtdienst: *24-hour service*
Tagung: *conference*
Tagungsort: *venue*
Taktik: *policy; tactic*
Talentsucher: *headhunter*
Talsohle: *trough*
Tanker: *tanker*
Tankstelle: *filling or petrol station*
Tankstelle mit Reparaturwerkstatt: *service station*
Tankstelle mit Selbstbedienung: *self-service petrol station*
Tante-Emma-Laden: *corner shop*
Tantiemen: *royalty*
Tara: *tare*
Tarif: *tariff* **ermäßigter** ~ *reduced rate* **niedriger** ~ *cheap rate* **üblicher** ~ *market rate* **verbilligter** ~ *off-peak tariff or rate*
Tarife: *scale of charges or scale of prices*
Tarifverhandlungen: *wage negotiations* **autonome** ~ *free collective bargaining*
Tarifvertrag: *union agreement*
Tarnung: *front*
Tasche: *bag*
Taschengeld: *spending money*
Taschenkalender: *pocket diary*
Taschenrechner: *pocket calculator*
Tastatur: *keyboard* **englische** ~ *qwerty keyboard* **numerische** ~ *numeric keypad*

tätig: *active; actively*
Tätigkeit: *occupation; operation*
Tätigkeitsbericht: **monatlicher ~** *monthly activity report*
Tätigkeitsbeschreibung: *job description*
tätig sein: *to be engaged in*
Tatsache: *fact*
Tatsache ist: *the fact of the matter is*
tatsächlich: *actual; in fact; really*
Tausch: *exchange; swap*
Tauschabkommen: *barter agreement or barter arrangement or barter deal*
tauschen: *change; convert; exchange; swap*
Tauschhandel: *barter; bartering*
Tauschhandel treiben: *barter*
Täuschung: *deceit or deception* **arglistige ~** *fraudulent misrepresentation*
Taxe *or* **Taxi:** *taxi*
Teamarbeit: *teamwork*
Technik: *technique*
Techniker: *engineer; repairer or repair man; technician*
technisch: *technical*
Technologie: *technology*
Technologiezentrum: *science park*
technologisch: *technological*
Teepause: *tea break*
Teil: **zum größten ~** *largely* **zum ~** *in part; partly*
teilabschreiben: *write down*
Teilabschreibung: *writedown*
teilen: *divide* **sich ~** *share*
Teilhaber: *copartner* **stiller ~** *sleeping or silent partner* **tätiger ~** *active or working partner*
Teilhaberschaft: *(co)partnership*
Teillieferung *or* **Teilsendung:** *part delivery or part order or part shipment*
Teilnahme: *participation*
Teilschaden *or* **Teilverlust:** *partial loss*
Teilzahlung: *part payment* **als ~** *on account* **eine ~ leisten** *advance on account*
Teilzahlungsfinanzierungsgesellschaft: *hire-purchase company*
Teilzahlungsinstitute: *secondary banks*
Teilzahlungskauf: *hire purchase*
Teilzahlungskaufvertrag: *hire purchase agreement*
Teilzahlungssystem: *installment plan (US)*
Teilzeitarbeit: *part-time work*
Teilzeitbeschäftigung: *part-time employment*
Teilzeitkraft: *part-timer*
Telebrief: *telemessage (GB)*
Telefax: *fax or FAX*
telefaxen: *fax or FAX*
Telefon: *(tele)phone* **ans ~ gehen** *to answer the phone or to take a phone call* **das ~ abnehmen** *to answer the (tele)phone; to take a phone call*
Telefonanrufe registrieren: *to log phone calls*
Telefonbuch: *(tele)phone book; telephone directory*
Telefongespräch: *(tele)phone call* **ein ~ führen** *to make a telephone call* **eingehendes ~** *incoming call*
telefonieren: *to be on the phone; to make a (tele)phone call*
telefonisch: *by phone*
Telefonist: *(switchboard) operator; telephone operator; telephonist*
Telefonleitung: *telephone line*
Telefon-Notizblock: *phone pad*
Telefonnummer: *(tele)phone number*
Telefonverkauf: *telesales*
Telefonzelle: *telephone booth; call box; telephone kiosk*
Telefonzentrale: *switchboard; telephone exchange*
Telegrafenamt: *telegraph office*
telegrafieren: *cable; telegraph*
Telegramm: *cable; cablegram; telegram; wire*
Telegrammadresse: *telegraphic address*
Telegrammanschrift: *cable address*
Telex: *telex* **Telex schicken** *to telex*
Tendenz: *tendency; trend*
tendieren: *tend*
Termin: *appointment; deadline* **auf ~ kaufen** *to buy forward* **auf ~ verkaufen** *to sell forward*
Terminal: *terminal building*
Termine: **dringende ~** *pressing engagements*
Termineinlagen: *term deposit; time deposit*
Termingeschäfte: *forward dealings*
Terminierung: *timing*
Terminkalender: *appointments book; diary; timetable*
Terminkauf: *forward buying or buying forward*
Terminlieferung: *future delivery*
Terminmarkt: *forward market*
Terminplan: *activity chart; schedule*
Terminplanung: *scheduling*
Terminprüfer: *progress chaser*
Terminverkäufe: *forward sales*
Testament: *will*
Testamentsbestätigung: **gerichtliche ~** *probate*
Testamentsvollstrecker: *executor*
testen: *sample; test*
teuer: *costly; dear; expensive; highly-priced*
Teuerungszulage: *cost-of-living allowance*
Teuerungszuschlag: *cost-of-living bonus*
Text: *text*
Textmarker: *marker pen*
Textverarbeitung: *text processing; word-processing*
Textverarbeitungsanlage: *word-processor*
Theaterkarte: *theatre ticket*
Theaterkasse: *box office*
theoretisch: *on paper*
Theorie: *theory*
Think-tank: *think tank*
Tiefbau: *engineering*

Tiefpunkt: *bottom; low (point)*
Tiefstand: *depression; low* **absoluter ~** *all-time low*
Tiefstpreis: *rock-bottom price*
Tiefststand: *bottom*
tilgen: *pay off; redeem*
Tilgung: *discharge; redemption*
Tilgungserlös: *redemption yield*
Tilgungsfonds: *sinking fund*
Tilgungsrate: letzte ~ *final discharge*
Tilgungssumme: *payoff*
Tilgungstermin: *redemption date*
Tilgungszeitraum: *payback period*
Timeshare: *time share*
Timing: *timing*
Tip: *tip* **einen ~ geben** *tip*
Tippen: *typing*
tippen: *type*
Tippen nach Phonodiktat: *audio-typing*
Tippfehler: *typing error*
TIR: *Transport International Routier, TIR*
Titel: *title*
Tochter-: *affiliated*
Tochtergesellschaft: *subsidiary (company)* **eine hundertprozentige ~** *a wholly-owned subsidiary* **eine ~ ausgliedern** *to spin off a subsidiary company*
Tod: *death; demise*
Tonnage: *tonnage*
Tonne: *ton* **metrische ~** *metric ton or metric tonne*
Tor: *gate*
Totalausverkauf: *closing-down sale*
Totalstreik: *all-out strike*
Totalverlust: *dead loss*
Tourismus: *tourism*
Touristenklasse: *economy class; tourist class*
Touristenvisum: *tourist visa*
tragbar: *portable*
tragen: *bear; carry; defray*
Trägheit: *inertia*
Trägheitsverkauf: *inertia selling*
Transaktion: geschäftliche ~ *business transaction*
Transfer: *transfer* **transferieren** *to transfer*
Transitgüter: *goods in transit*
Transitraum: *transit lounge*
Transitvisum: *transit visa*
Transport: *carriage; carrying; cartage; shipping; transport; transportation*
transportabel *or* **transportfähig:** *transportable*
Transporter: *carrier*
Transportflugzeug: *cargo or freight plane*
transportieren: *ship; transport*
Transportkosten: *carriage; freight costs; haulage costs or haulage rates; haulage*
Transportschaden: *loss in transport*
Transportschiff: *cargo ship*
Transportunternehmen: *(common) carrier; transporter*
Transportunternehmer: *haulage contractor*
Transportverlust: *loss in transport*
Transportweg: *haul*
Transportwesen: innerbetriebliches ~ *materials handling*
Trassant: *drawer*
Trassat: *drawee*
Tratte: *bill; bill of exchange*
Treffpunkt: *meeting place*
treiben: *drift; rush*
Treibgut: *flotsam and jetsam*
Trend: *shift; trend*
trennen: *separate*
Tresen: *counter*
Tresor: *safe (deposit)* **feuersicherer ~** *fire-proof safe*
Tresorraum: *strongroom*
Treuhand: *trust*
Treuhänder: *fiduciary; trustee*
treuhänderisch: *fiduciary*
treuhänderisch hinterlegt: *in escrow*
Treuhandfonds: *trust fund*
Treuhandgesellschaft: *trust company (US)*
Treuhandkonto: *escrow account (US)*
Treuhandschaft: *trust*
Treuhandvertrag: *trust deed*
Tribunal: *tribunal*
Trick: *con (informal); trick*
tricksen: *fiddle (informal)*
Trickserei: *fiddle (informal)*
triftig: *valid*
Trinkgeld: *tip*
Trinkgeld geben: *tip*
Trockenmaß: *dry measure*
Trödel: *junk*
Trouble Shooter: *troubleshooter*
Trustzerschlagung: *trustbusting (US)*
tüchtig: *efficient; proficient*
tun: etwas weiter ~ *go on; keep on*
Tupfen: *dot*
Turnus: *rotation*
Tüte: *bag*
typisch: *representative*
Typung: *standardization*

Uu

u.A.w.g.: *RSVP*
überarbeiten: *revise; overwork*
überbelegen: *overbook* **Überbelegung** *overbooking*
überbesetzt: *overstaffed* **Überbesetzung** *overmanning*
Überbestand: ~ abstoßen *to offload excess stock or overstocks (US)*
überbewerten: *overvalue* **überbewertet** *overrated*

überbezahlt: *overpaid* **Überbezahlung** *overpayment*
überbieten: *improve on; outbid*
Überblick: *outline; review* **einen ~ geben** *outline*
überblicken: *overlook*
Überbringer: zahlbar an ~ *payable to bearer*
Überbringerscheck: *cheque to bearer*
Überbrückungskredit: *accommodation; bridging loan*
überbuchen: *overbook* **Überbuchung** *overbooking*
Übereignungsurkunde: *deed of assignment*
Übereinkunft: *arrangement; understanding*
übereinstimmen: *agree; to correspond with something; tally*
Übereinstimmung: grundsätzliche ~ *agreement in principle* **in ~ mit** *in accordance with*
Überfahrt: *passage*
überfällig: *overdue*
überflüssig: *redundant*
Übergabe: *handover*
übergeben: *hand over; present*
übergeordnet: *senior*
Übergewicht: *excess baggage*
Übergröße: *outsize*
überholt: *obsolete*
Überkapazität: *excess capacity; overcapacity*
überkapitalisiert: *overcapitalized*
überlastet: *overworked*
Überlebensrente: einseitige ~ *reversionary annuity*
überlegen: *consider; superior*
Überlegung: *consideration* **nach reiflicher ~** *after due consideration*
Überlegungsfrist: *cooling off period*
übermäßig: *excessive*
übermitteln: *transmit*
Übermittlung: *transmission*
übernachten: *stay*
Übernahme: *absorption; assumption; takeover* **angefochtene ~** *contested takeover*
Übernahmeangebot: *takeover bid*
Übernahmekonsortium: *underwriting syndicate*
übernehmen: *assume; take on; take over; undertake*
Überproduktion: *overproduction*
überproduzieren: *overproduce*
überprüfen: *check; examine; go into; investigate; review; verify; vet*
Überprüfung: *check; examination; inspection; investigation; review; verification*
überqueren: *cross*
überreden: *persuade*
überreichen: *give; hand over; present*
überschätzen: *overestimate*
Überschlag: *computation*
überschlagbar: *computable*
überschlagen: *compute*
überschreiben: *make over*
überschreiten: *exceed; overrun*
Überschrift: *heading*
Überschuß: *excess; overs; surplus*
überschüssig: *spare; waste*
überschwemmen: *flood; glut*
Überseehandel: *foreign trade or overseas trade or external trade*
überseeisch: *overseas*
Überseemärkte: *overseas markets*
Überseeterminal: *ocean terminal*
übersehen: *overlook*
übersetzen: *translate*
Übersetzer: *translator*
Übersetzung: *translation*
Übersetzungsbüro: *translation bureau*
Übersicht: *abstract; summary*
übersteigen: *exceed; top*
überstimmen: *outvote*
Überstunden: *overtime*
Überstundenlohn: *call-back pay; overtime pay*
Überstunden machen: *to work overtime*
Überstundenverbot: *overtime ban*
übertragbar: *transferable* **nicht ~** *"not negotiable"*
übertragen: *assign; bring forward; switch; transfer*
Übertragung: *assignation; assignment; delegation; delivery; transfer*
Übertragungsurkunde: *conveyance*
übertreffen: *improve on*
übertreten: *infringe*
Übertretung: *infringement*
übervorteilen: *cheat*
überwachen: *monitor; supervise*
Überwachung: *control*
Überwachungs-: *supervisory*
überwechseln: *switch over to*
überweisen: *remit*
Überweisung: *remittance*
überzählig: *redundant*
überziehen: *overdraw*
Überziehung: *overdraft*
Überziehungskredit: *overdraft facility*
üblich: *normal; standard; usual*
übrig: *residual; spare*
übrigbleiben: *remain*
Ultimatum: *ultimatum*
Umfang: *size; volume* **in begrenztem ~** *small scale* **in großem ~** *large scale*
umfangreich: *extensive; heavy; large-scale*
umfassend: *comprehensive; extensive; full-scale; overall*
umformulieren: *redraft*
umgehen: *avoid; evade; get round*
umgehend: *immediate; immediately*
Umgehung: *avoidance; evasion*
umgekehrt: *reverse*
umkehren: *reverse*
umladen: *tranship*

Umlauf: *circular letter* **im ~ befindlich** *circulating* **in ~ bringen** *circulate*
umlaufend: *circulating*
Umlaufvermögen: *current assets; circulating capital*
umlegen: *apportion*
Umlegung: *apportionment*
umpacken: *repack*
Umrechnungskurs: *conversion price or conversion rate*
Umsatz: *sales; turnover*
Umsatzanalyse: *sales analysis*
Umsatzdiagramm: *sales chart*
Umsatzsteuer: *turnover tax*
Umsatzsteuerstelle: *VAT office*
Umsatzvolumen: *sales volume; volume of trade or volume of business*
Umschalttaste: *shift key*
umschichten: *redistribute*
Umschlag: *handling*
Umschlaggeschwindigkeit: *turnover (US)*
Umschlagspesen: *handling charges*
umschulen: *retrain* **Umschulung** *retraining*
Umschwung: *reversal*
umsehen: sich ~ *shop around*
umsetzen: *turn over*
umsonst: *gratis*
umsteigen: *transfer*
umstellen: *switch over to*
Umstellung auf Containertransport: *containerization*
umstrukturieren: *reorganize; restructure*
Umstrukturierung: *reorganization; shakeup*
umtauschbar: *exchangeable*
umtauschen: *convert*
umverteilen: *redistribute*
umwandeln: *commute*
Umwandlung: *conversion*
Umweltschutzpapier: *recycled paper*
umziehen: *move*
Umzug: *removal*
unabhängig: *free; independent*
unannehmbar: *unacceptable*
unausgefüllt: *blank*
unbedeutend: *minor; negligible; petty*
unbedingt notwendig: *essential*
unbefristet: *open-ended or open-end (US)*
unbefugt: *unauthorized*
unbegrenzt: *unlimited*
unbeladen: *unladen*
unbelebt: *inactive*
unbenutzt: *unused*
unbeschäftigt: *idle*
unbeschränkt: *absolute; unlimited*
unbesehen: *unseen* **etwas ~ kaufen** *to buy something sight unseen*
unbesetzt: *free; vacant*
unbeständig: *unsettled*
Unbeständigkeit: *instability*
unbestätigt: *unconfirmed*
unbeweglich: *immovable*
unbewohnt: *vacant*
unbezahlt: *outstanding; unpaid*
undatiert: *undated*
unerfüllt: *unfulfilled*
unerläßlich: *essential*
unerlaubt: *illicit*
unerschwinglich: *prohibitive*
unfähig: *incompetent; inefficient*
Unfähigkeit: *inefficiency*
Unfall: *accident*
Unfallgeld: *injury benefit*
Unfallhaftpflichtversicherung der Arbeitgeber: *employers' liability insurance*
Unfallversicherung: *accident insurance*
Unfallversicherungspolice: *accident policy*
ungeachtet: *regardless of*
ungebraucht: *unused*
ungebunden: *independent*
ungefähr: *approximate; rough; roughly*
ungelernt: *unskilled*
ungenau: *incorrect; incorrectly*
ungeprüft: *unaudited; unchecked*
ungesetzlich: *illegal; unlawful*
Ungesetzlichkeit: *illegality*
Unglück: *accident; disaster*
Unglücksfall: *disaster*
ungültig: *defective; invalid; null; void* **für ~ erklären** *annul; invalidate*
Ungültigkeit: *invalidity*
Ungültigkeitserklärung: *invalidation*
ungünstig: *adverse; unfavourable*
Unit Trust: *unit trust*
Universalversicherungspolice: *all-risks policy*
unkontrollierbar: *uncontrollable*
Unkosten: allgemeine ~ *overhead expenses or general expenses; overhead costs; overheads or overhead (US)*
unmittelbar: *direct; directly*
unmöglich: *impossible*
unökonomisch: *uneconomic*
unpersönlich: *impersonal*
Unpünktlichkeit: *bad time-keeping*
Unrecht: zu ~ *wrongly*
unrechtmäßig: *illegal; wrongful*
Unrechtmäßigkeit: *illegality*
Unregelmäßigkeit: *irregularity*
unrentabel: *not commercially viable; unprofitable*
unrichtig: *false*
unschlüssig sein: *hesitate*
unsichtbar: *unseen*
unstatthaft: *irregular*
untätig: *inactive*
untengenannt: *undermentioned*
Unterauftrag: *subcontract*

Unterausschuß: *subcommittee*
unterbeschäftigt: *underemployed*
Unterbeschäftigung: *underemployment*
unterbesetzt: *short-staffed; undermanned; understaffed*
Unterbesetzung: *undermanning*
unterbewerten: *underestimate; underrate*
unterbewertet: *undervalued*
Unterbewertung: *underestimate; undervaluation*
unterbezahlt: *underpaid*
unterbieten: *underbid; undercut; undersell*
unterbrechen: *suspend*
Unterbrechung: *stoppage*
Unterbringung: *placement*
unterentwickelt: *underdeveloped*
Untergebener: *subordinate*
untergeordnet: *junior; low-grade; low-level; subordinate*
Untergeschoß: *basement*
unterhalten: *entertain; maintain*
Unterhändler: *official mediator; negotiator*
Unterhaus: *House of Commons*
unterkapitalisiert: *undercapitalized*
Unterkunft: **möblierte** ~ *furnished accommodation*
Unterlagen: *information; papers; records* **statistische** ~ *statistics*
unterlassen: *default; fail; omit*
Unterlassung: *default; omission* **pflichtwidrige** ~ *non-feisance*
Unterlassungsfall: **im** ~ *by default*
unterliegen: *liable to*
Untermiete: *subtenancy*
Untermieter: *sublessee; subtenant*
Untermietvertrag: *sublease; underlease*
Unternehmen: *business; company; corporation; enterprise; establishment; firm; outfit; undertaking* **exportorientiertes** ~ *export-oriented company* **gemeinnütziges** ~ *non profit-making organization or non-profit corporation (US)* **gewagtes** ~ *venture* **staatliches** ~ *state enterprise; parastatal ((in Africa))* **unseriöses** ~ *fly-by-night outfit*
Unternehmen mit Staatsaufträgen: *government contractor*
Unternehmensberater: *management consultant*
Unternehmensbereich: *division*
Unternehmens-Fixkosten: *establishment charges*
Unternehmensforschung: *operational research*
Unternehmensführung mit Zielvorgabe: *management by objectives*
Unternehmensgewinne: *corporate profits*
Unternehmensleitung: *management*
Unternehmensplan: **langfristiger** ~ *corporate plan*
Unternehmenspolitik: *company policy*
Unternehmensrecht: *Companies Act (GB); company law*
Unternehmenssanierung: *the reorganization of a company or a company reorganization*
Unternehmensspitze: *top management*
Unternehmer: *entrepreneur*
unternehmerisch: *entrepreneurial*
Unternehmertum: **freies** ~ *free enterprise*
Unterpacht: *subtenancy*
Unterpächter: *sublessee; subtenant*
Unterpachtvertrag: *sublease; underlease*
unterrichten: *advise; inform*
unterschätzen: *underestimate; underrate* **Unterschätzung** *underestimate*
unterscheiden: **sich** ~ *differ*
Unterschied: *difference; variance*
unterschiedlich: *different; differential; mixed*
unterschlagen: *embezzle*
Unterschlagung: *concealment; defalcation; embezzlement*
unterschreiben: *sign*
Unterschrift: *signature* **seine** ~ **einlösen** *to honour a signature*
Unterstand: *shelter*
unterstützen: *assist; back up; further; help; support*
Unterstützung: *assistance; help; relief; support* **finanzielle** ~ *backing* **mit staatlicher** ~ *government-backed*
untersuchen: *examine; explore; go into; inspect; investigate*
Untersuchung: *examination; inspection; investigation*
Untersuchungsausschuß: **gemeinsamer** ~ *joint commission of inquiry or joint committee*
Untersuchungsbeamter: *investigator*
Untersuchungsbericht: *report; survey*
untertreiben: *understate*
untervermieten: *sublease; sublet*
Untervermieter: *sublessor*
Untervermietung: *sublease; underlease*
unterverpachten: *sublease; sublet*
Unterverpächter: *sublessor*
Unterverpachtung: *sublease; underlease*
Untervertrag: *subcontract*
Untervertreter: *sub-agent* **Untervertretung** *sub-agency*
unterworfen: *liable to*
Unterzeichnenden: **die** ~ *the undersigned*
Unterzeichner: *signatory*
Unterzeichneter: *undersigned*
untragbar: *prohibitive*
unumgänglich: *unavoidable*
ununterbrochen: *continual; on end; non-stop*
unverändert: *unchanged*
unverarbeitet: *raw*
unverbindlich: *tentative*
unvereinbar sein mit: *to be at variance with*
unverkäuflich: *not negotiable*
unverkauft: *unsold*
unverlangt: *unsolicited*
unvermeidlich: *unavoidable*
unverpackt: *loose*
unverzüglich: *instant*

unvorbereitet: *cold*
unwahr: *untrue*
unwesentlich: *slight*
unwichtig: *minor; petty*
unwiderruflich: *irrevocable*
unwirtschaftlich: *uneconomic; wasteful*
Unze: *ounce*
unzeitgemäß: *out of date*
unzulänglich: *defective; incompetent*
unzulänglich ausgerüstet: *underequipped*
unzulässig: *unauthorized*
unzuverlässig: *unreliable*
Urabstimmung: *strike ballot or strike vote*
Urdaten: *raw data*
Urheberrecht: *copyright* **das ~ verletzen** *to infringe a copyright*
urheberrechtlich schützen: *copyright*
Urheberrechtschutzgesetz: *copyright law*
Urheberrechtsvermerk: *copyright notice*
Urkunde: *deed; document; instrument*
Urkundenbeweis: *documentary evidence or proof*
urkundlich: *documentary*
Urlaub: *holiday; leave; vacation (US)*
Urlaubsanspruch: *holiday entitlement*
Urlaubsgeld: *holiday pay*
Urlaubszeit: *tourist season or holiday season*
Ursache: *cause*
Ursprung: *source*
ursprünglich: *originally; prime*
Urteil: *judgement or judgment* **ein ~ verkünden** *to pronounce judgement*
urteilen: *find*
Urteil fällen: *adjudicate*
Urteilsschuldner: *judgment debtor*
US-Aktien: *dollar stocks*
usw.: *etc.*

Vv

variabel: *floating; variable*
Variabilität: *variability*
variieren: *range; vary*
VB: *or near offer*
Verabredung: **eine ~ einhalten** *to keep an appointment*
Veralten: **eingeplantes ~** *built-in obsolescence or planned obsolescence*
veraltend: *obsolescent*
veraltet: *out of date; obsolete*
veränderlich: *unsettled; variable*
Veränderlichkeit: *instability; variability*
verändern: *alter* **sich ~** *vary*
Veranlagung: *rating; taxation*
veranlassen: *set up*
veranschlagt: *estimated*
veranstalten: *give; stage*
verantworten: **sich ~** *to account for*
verantwortlich für: *responsible for*
Verantwortlichkeit: *responsibility*
Verantwortung: *responsibility*
Verarbeitung: *finish*
veräußern: *to dispose of; realize*
Veräußerung: *disposal*
Veräußerungsgewinne: *capital gains*
Veräußerungsgewinnsteuer: *capital gains tax*
Veräußerung von Vermögenswerten: *realization of assets*
Verband: *association; combine; federation; syndicate*
verbessern: *correct; improve*
Verbesserung: *advance; correction; improvement*
verbieten: *ban; forbid*
verbinden: *connect; incorporate; interface; join; link; mix*
verbindlich: *binding; compulsory; firm*
Verbindlichkeit: *obligation* **eine ~ erfüllen** *to discharge a debt or to discharge one's liabilities* **ohne ~** *without prejudice*
Verbindlichkeiten: *accounts payable; liabilities* **gesicherte ~** *secured debts* **kurzfristige ~** *current liabilities* **langfristige ~** *long-term liabilities* **seinen ~ nachkommen** *to meet one's obligations* **ungesicherte ~** *unsecured debts*
Verbindung: *combination; connection; contact; tie-up*
Verbindung außer Haus: *outside line*
verborgen: *hidden*
Verbot: **ein ~ umgehen** *to beat a ban*
verboten: *illicit*
Verbrauch: **täglicher ~** *daily consumption*
Verbraucher: *consumer*
Verbraucher-Abholmarkt: *cash and carry*
Verbraucherberatung: *consumer council*
Verbrauchergroßmarkt: *hypermarket*
Verbrauchermarkt: *superstore*
Verbraucherpanel: *consumer panel*
Verbraucherpreisindex: *retail price index or consumer price index (US)*
Verbraucherschutz: *consumer protection*
Verbraucherschutzgesetz: *shoppers' charter*
Verbrauchertestgruppe: *consumer panel*
Verbrauchsgüter: *consumer goods; consumables*
Verbrauchssteuer: *excise duty*
Verbrechen: *crime* **verbrecherisch** *criminal*
verbreiten: *circulate* **Verbreitung** *circulation*
verbrennen: *burn*
verbringen: *spend*
verbürgen: **sich ~** *guarantee*
verdeckt: *hidden*
verderben: *spoil*
verdeutlichen: *point out*
verdienen: *earn; make*
Verdienst: *merit*
Verdienstausfallentschädigung: *compensation for loss of earnings*

Verdienstmöglichkeit: *earning capacity; earning power*
verdoppeln: *double*
verdreifachen: *treble; triple*
Verein: *club; outfit; society*
vereinbaren: *agree; stipulate*
Vereinbarung: *agreement; contract; engagement; stipulation; understanding* **eine ~ ausarbeiten** *or* **aushandeln** *to hammer out an agreement* **eine ~ treffen** *to reach an agreement* **frühere ~** *prior agreement* **mündliche ~** *unwritten or verbal agreement*
vereinheitlichen: *standardize*
vereinigen: *unite*
Vereinsbeitrag: *club subscription*
Vereinsmitgliedschaft: *club membership*
Vereinsschriftführer: *a club's membership secretary*
Vereinten: die ~ Nationen *the United Nations*
Verfahren: *method; procedure; technique*
Verfahrensformen: *judicial processes*
Verfahrensweise: *policy; practice*
Verfahrens-Zeit-Studie: *time and method study*
Verfall: *expiry; forfeit*
verfallen: *lapse*
Verfallsdatum: *expiry date*
Verfallsklausel: *forfeit clause*
Verfälschung: *falsification*
Verfassen: *drafting* **Verfasser** *drafter*
Verfassung: *constitution*
verfassungsmäßig: *constitutional*
verfassungswidrig: *unconstitutional*
verfehlen: *miss*
verfolgen: *chase*
Verfolgung: strafrechtliche ~ *criminal action; prosecution*
verfrachten: *to freight goods*
verfügbar: *available* **nicht ~** *unavailable*
Verfügbarkeit: *availability*
Verfügung: *notice* **einstweilige ~** *injunction* **gerichtliche ~** *writ* **zur ~** *in hand*
vergeben: *give away; put out*
vergeblich: *unsuccessfully*
Vergehen: *irregularities*
vergessen: *forget*
vergeuden: *waste*
Vergleich: *arrangement; comparison; composition; settlement*
vergleichbar: *comparable* **Vergleichbarkeit** *comparability*
vergleichen: *compare*
Vergleichsjahr: *base year*
Vergleichslohn: *pay comparability*
vergrößern: *expand* **Vergrößerung** *expansion*
Vergünstigung: *concession*
Vergünstigungen bei Hypothekenzahlungen: *mortgage relief*
vergüten: *allow for*
Vergütung: *compensation (US); indemnity*

Verhältnis: *ratio* **im ~ zu** *in proportion to*
Verhältnis Gewinn-Dividende: *dividend cover*
verhältnismäßig: *proportionately; relatively*
Verhandlung: *negotiation*
Verhandlungsausschuß: *negotiating committee*
Verhandlungsbasis: *asking price; or near offer*
Verhandlungsführer: *negotiator*
Verhandlungspaket: *package deal*
Verhandlungsposition: *bargaining position*
Verhandlungssache: *a matter for negotiation*
Verhandlungsstärke: *bargaining power*
verhängen: *impose* **Verhängung** *imposition*
verheerend: *disastrous*
verhindern: *prevent*
verhören: *question*
verhüten: *prevent*
Verjährungsausschlußfrist: *statute of limitations*
Verkauf: *disposal; sale; sell; vending* **diskreter** *or* **zurückhaltender ~** *soft sell*
Verkauf auf Kommissionsbasis: *commission sale or sale on commission*
Verkauf auf Kreditkarte: *credit card sale*
Verkäufe: ungesetzliche ~ *under-the-counter sales*
verkaufen: *sell; shift* **mehr ~** *outsell* **zu ~** *for sale*
Verkäufer: *shop assistant; sales clerk (US); salesman; seller* **aggressiver ~** *high-pressure salesman*
Verkäuferin: *salesgirl; saleslady; saleswoman; shop assistant*
Verkäufermarkt: *seller's market*
Verkäuferstab: *sales force*
Verkauf im Freiverkehr: *over-the-counter sales*
Verkauf mit Rückmietgarantie: *lease-back sale*
Verkaufsabteilung: *sales department*
Verkaufsaktion: *sales campaign*
Verkaufsangebot: *offer* **einmaliges ~** *unique selling proposition*
Verkaufsbedingungen: *conditions or terms of sale*
Verkaufsbuch: *sales book*
Verkaufserlös: *proceeds of a sale; sales revenue*
Verkaufserträge: geringe ~ *low sales*
Verkaufsgespräch: *sales pitch*
Verkaufskampagne: *sales drive*
Verkaufsleiter: *sales executive; sales manager*
Verkaufsmethoden: aggressive ~ *high-pressure sales techniques or high-pressure selling* **nicht-aggressive ~** *low-pressure sales*
Verkaufsmöglichkeiten: *sales opportunities*
Verkaufsoption: *option to purchase; put option*
Verkaufsort: *point of sale*
Verkaufspersonal: *sales force*
Verkaufspolitik: aggressive ~ *hard selling*
Verkaufspreis: *selling price*
Verkaufsprognose: *projected sales*
Verkaufsprospekte: *sales literature*
Verkaufsschlager: *best-seller*
Verkaufsstelle: *outlet; point of sale*

Verkaufstechnik: *salesmanship*
Verkaufsvertreter: *sales representative*
Verkaufswagen: *mobile shop*
Verkaufszahlen: *sales figures* **höhere ~ haben** *outsell*
Verkaufsziel: *sales targets*
Verkehr: *traffic*
verkehren: *run*
Verkehrsflugzeug: *commercial aircraft*
Verkehrsmittel: öffentliche ~ *public transport*
Verkehrsnetz: öffentliches ~ *public transport system*
Verkehrsstau: *traffic jam*
Verkehrsunternehmen: *common carrier*
Verkehrsverbindung: *communications*
verklagen: *to take legal action; sue* **jdn ~** *to bring a lawsuit against someone; to take someone to law*
verklemmen: *jam*
Verknappung: *shortage; squeeze*
verkürzen: *shorten*
Verladedock: *loading dock*
Verladen: *lading*
Verlag: *publisher*
Verlagerung: *shift*
verlagsrechtlich geschützt: *copyrighted*
verlangen: *ask for; demand; require*
verlängern: *extend; renew*
Verlängerung: *extension; renewal*
verlangsamen: *slow down*
Verlangsamung: *slowdown*
Verlassen: *abandonment*
verlassen: *abandon; leave* **sich ~ auf** *bank on; count on; rely on*
verläßlich: *reliable* **Verläßlichkeit** *reliability*
Verlauf: *progress* **im ~** *in the course of*
verlegen: *move; publish; transfer*
Verleger: *publisher*
Verlegung: *transfer*
verleihen: *lend; loan; to rent (out)*
verletzen: *break; infringe; injure*
Verletzung: *breach; infringement; injury*
Verletzung der Gewährleistungspflicht: *breach of warranty*
Verletzung des Urheberrechts: *infringement of copyright or copyright infringement*
verleumden: jdn ~ *to libel or to slander someone*
Verleumdung: *libel; slander*
Verleumdungsklage: *action for libel or libel action; action for slander or slander action*
verlieren: *lose*
Verlust: *deficit; leakage; loss; wastage* **einen ~ ausgleichen** *to make up a loss or to make up the difference* **mit ~** *at a loss* **nicht realisierter ~** *paper loss*
Verluste: seine ~ verringern *to cut one's losses*
Verlustfaktor: *downside factor*
Verlustzeit: *down time*
vermachen: *settle on*
Vermächtnis: *bequest; legacy*
Vermächtnisnehmer: *legatee*
vermehren: *multiply*
vermeiden: *avoid*
vermerken: *note*
vermessen: *measure*
Vermessung: *survey*
vermieten: *lease; let; to rent (out)*
Vermieter: *landlord; lessor*
Vermieterin: *landlady*
Vermietung: *headlease*
vermindern: *depress* **sich ~** *decrease; diminish*
Verminderung: *decrease; lowering*
Verminderung der Gewinnspanne: *profit squeeze*
vermischen: *mix*
vermitteln: *mediate*
Vermittler: *intermediary*
Vermittlung: *mediation; telephone exchange*
Vermittlung für Aushilfskräfte *or* **Zeitarbeiter:** *temp agency*
Vermögen: *fortune; power; wealth* **bewegliches ~** *chattels; moveables* **unbewegliches ~** *immovable property*
Vermögensanlage: *investment*
Vermögenseinkünfte: *unearned income*
Vermögenssteuer: *capital levy; wealth tax*
Vermögensumverteilung: *redistribution of wealth*
Vermögensverschleierung: *concealment of assets*
Vermögensverwalter: *trustee*
Vermögenswert: *asset (value)*
Vermögenswerte: blockierte *or* **eingefrorene ~** *frozen assets* **immaterielle ~** *intangible assets* **materielle ~** *tangible assets* **unsichtbare ~** *invisible assets*
vernachlässigt: *neglected*
verneinend: *negative*
vernetzen: *network*
vernünftig: *reasonable; sound*
veröffentlichen: *issue; publish; release*
Veröffentlichung: *publication*
verpachten: *lease; to rent (out)*
Verpächter: *lessor*
Verpachtung: *demise; headlease*
Verpacken: *packaging; packing*
verpacken: *pack; parcel*
Verpackung: *wrapper*
Verpackungsgewicht: *tare*
Verpackungskosten: *packing charges*
Verpackungsmaterial: *packaging; packing*
verpassen: *miss*
verpfänden: etwas ~ *to put something in pawn*
verpflichten: sich ~ *undertake*
verpflichtet sein: *to be obligated to do something*
Verpflichtung: *engagement; obligation*
verramschen: *dispose*
verrechnen: sich ~ *to be out; miscalculate*
Verrechnungsscheck: *crossed cheque*

verringern: *depress; reduce; to scale down; slow down* **sich ~** *diminish*
Verringerung: *reduction; slowdown*
Versagen: *failure*
Versalien: *capital letters or block capitals*
Versammlung: *assembly*
Versand: *consignation; consignment; dispatch; shipping*
Versandabteilung: *dispatch department*
Versandanweisungen: *forwarding or shipping instructions*
Versandanzeige: *advice note; consignment note; shipping note*
Versandhandel: *mail-order selling*
Versandhaus: *mail-order business or firm or house*
Versandhauskatalog: *mail-order catalogue*
Versandschein: *dispatch note*
Versandvorschriften: *forwarding or shipping instructions*
versäumen: *omit*
Versäumnis: *default; omission*
verschärfen: *tighten*
verschenken: *give away*
Verschicken: *mailing*
verschieben: *defer; hold over; postpone; put off*
verschieden: *different; differential; miscellaneous*
Verschiedenes: *AOB; any other business; sundry items or sundries*
verschiffen: *ship*
Verschleierung: *concealment*
Verschlüsselung: *coding*
verschnüren: *tie up*
verschrotten: *scrap*
Verschulden: *fault*
verschulden: **sich ~** *to get into debt*
verschuldet: *indebted*
Verschuldung: *state of indebtedness*
Verschuldungsgrad: *gearing*
verschwenden: *waste*
verschwenderisch: *wasteful*
Versehen: *slip; slip-up*
versehentlich: *in error or by error; by mistake*
Versehrtenrente: *injury benefit*
Versenden: *mailing*
versenden: *dispatch; send; ship*
Versender: *consignor*
Versendung: *consignation; consignment*
versetzen: *redeploy; transfer*
Versetzung: *redeployment; secondment; transfer*
versicherbar: *insurable*
Versicherer: *insurer; underwriter*
versichern: *assure; insure; underwrite*
Versicherte: **der ~** *the life assured; the life insured*
Versicherung: *assurance; insurance*
Versicherungsagent: *insurance agent or broker*
Versicherungsanspruch regulieren: *to settle a claim*
Versicherungsantrag: *proposal*
Versicherungsbeitrag: *insurance premium*
versicherungsfähig: *insurable*
Versicherungsgesellschaft: *insurance company*
Versicherungskarte: **grüne ~** *green card*
Versicherungsmathematiker: *actuary*
Versicherungsnehmer: *policy holder*
Versicherungspolice: *insurance policy*
Versicherungsprämie: *insurance premium*
Versicherungsprämiensatz: *insurance rates*
Versicherungsschein: **vorläufiger ~** *binder (US); cover note*
Versicherungsschutz: *insurance cover; coverage (US)*
Versicherungssumme: *the sum insured*
Versicherungsträger: *assurer or assuror; insurer; underwriter*
Versicherungsverein auf Gegenseitigkeit: *mutual (insurance) company*
Versicherungsvertrag: *insurance contract*
Versicherungsvertreter: *insurance agent; insurance broker; insurance salesman*
versiegeln: *to seal* **Versiegelung** *seal*
versorgen: *furnish; supply*
Versorgung: *service; supply*
verspäten: **sich ~** *to delay* **Verspätung** *delay*
Versprechen: *promise*
Versschiffung: *shipping*
verstaatlichen: *nationalize*
Verstaatlichung: *nationalization*
verständigen: **sich ~** *communicate*
Verständigung: *communication*
verständlich: *clear*
verständlich machen: *get across*
Verständnis: *sympathy*
verständnisvoll: *reasonable; sympathetic*
verstärken: *step up*
versteckt: *hidden*
verstehen: *understand* **sich ~ mit** *get on with*
versteigern: *auction*
versteigert werden: *to go under the hammer*
Versteigerung: **holländische ~** *Dutch auction*
Verstopfung: *jam*
verstorben: *dead*
Verstoß: *breach*
Verstöße: *irregularities*
Versuch: *attempt* **versuchen** *to attempt*
versuchsweise: *on approval*
vertagen: *adjourn; defer; hold over; postpone* **Vertagung** *adjournment; deferment; postponement*
verteidigen: *defend*
Verteidiger: *defence counsel*
Verteidigung: *defence or defense (US)*
verteilen: *apportion; share; space out; spread*
Verteiler: *distributor*
Verteilernetz: *distribution network; network of distributors*
Verteilerzettel: *distribution slip*
verteilt anlegen: *diversify*

Verteilung: *apportionment; shareout; sharing*
Vertrag: *contract; covenant; treaty* **besiegelter ~** *contract under seal* **unter ~ stehen** *to be under contract*
vertraglich: *contractual; contractually* **sich ~ verpflichten** *contract*
vertraglich vereinbaren: *covenant*
Vertragsabschluß: *completion of a contract*
Vertragsbedingungen: *terms of a contract*
Vertragsbruch: *breach of contract*
Vertragshaftung: *contractual liability*
vertragsmäßig: *contractual*
Vertragspartner: *contracting party*
Vertragspflicht: seine ~ erfüllen *to fulfill one's contractual obligations*
Vertragsrecht: *contract law or law of contract*
Vertragsunterzeichnung: *exchange of contracts*
Vertragsurkunde: *deed of covenant*
Vertragsverlängerung: *extension of a contract*
Vertragsverletzung: *default*
Vertrag wird verhandelt: *contract under negotiation*
Vertrauen: *confidence; trust*
Vertrauensmann: betrieblicher ~ *shop steward*
vertrauenswürdig: *trustworthy*
vertraulich: *in confidence; confidential*
Vertraulichkeit: *confidentiality*
vertreiben: *distribute; market*
vertreten: *represent* **jdn ~** *to deputize for someone; plead for; stand in for*
Vertreter: *agent; canvasser; (door-to-door) salesman; sales representative; substitute* **rechtlicher ~** *attorney* **zugelassener ~** *recognized agent*
Vertreterbesuch: unangemeldeter ~ *cold call*
Vertreterbesuche: *canvassing*
Vertreter der Anklage: *prosecution counsel or counsel for the prosecution*
Vertreterprovision: *agent's commission*
Vertretung: *agency; replacement; representation; representative; substitute*
Vertrieb: *distribution; distributorship*
Vertriebskosten: *cost of sales; selling costs*
Vertriebsnetz: *distribution network; network of distributors*
Vertriebsvereinbarung: *marketing agreement*
Vertriebswege: *distribution channels*
veruntreuen: *embezzle; misappropriate*
Veruntreuung: *defalcation; embezzlement; misappropriation*
Veruntreuung von Geldmitteln: *conversion of funds*
verursachen: *cause*
vervielfachen: *multiply*
Vervielfältigung: *duplication*
Vervielfältigungsgerät: *duplicator; copying or duplicating machine*
vervollkommnen: *perfect*
Verwahrer: *depositary (US); depository*
Verwahrung: *safe keeping* **gerichtliche ~** *impounding* **in ~ geben** *deposit*
verwalten: *administer* **Verwalter** *administrator*
Verwaltung: *admin (informal); administration* **schlechte ~** *maladministration*
Verwaltungsbezirk: *precinct (US)*
Verwaltungskosten: *administration expenses*
Verwaltungsratsmitglied: außerordentliches ~ *associate director*
verwaltungstechnisch: *administrative*
Verwarnung: gebührenpflichtige ~ *fine*
verwechseln: *confuse*
verweigern: *refuse* **Verweigerung** *refusal*
verwenden: *use; utilize* **Verwendung** *use; utilization*
verwerfen: *throw out*
verwirken: *forfeit*
verwirklichen: *realize* **Verwirklichung** *realization*
Verwirkung: *forfeit; forfeiture*
verwirren: *confuse*
verzählen: sich ~ *miscount*
verzeichnen: *record*
Verzeichnis: *list; register; schedule*
Verzeichnis der Obligationäre: *debenture register*
Verzicht: *renunciation; waiver*
verzichten auf: *waive*
Verzichtklausel: *waiver clause*
verzögern: *hold up; set back; delay*
Verzögerung: *delay; hold-up*
Verzollung von Waren: *clearing of goods through the customs*
Verzug: *delay* **in ~ geraten** *default; fall behind* **in ~ sein** *to be behind schedule*
vielfach: *multiple*
Vielfalt: *variety*
Vierfache: um das ~ *four-fold*
Viertel: *area; district; quarter*
Vierteljahr: *quarter* **vierteljährlich** *quarterly*
Viertelliter: ein ~ *a quarter of a litre or a quarter litre*
Visitenkarte: *business card*
Visum mit Rückkehrberechtigung: *re-entry visa*
Vitrine: *display cabinet or case; showcase*
Völkerrecht: *international law*
Volkseinkommen: *national income*
Volkswirt: *economist*
Volkswirtschaft: *economics* **entwickelte ~** *mature economy*
voll: nicht ~ ausgelastet *underutilized*
Vollabschreibung: *write-off*
voll ausgelastet sein: *to work at full capacity*
Vollbeschäftigung: *full employment*
völlig neu: *brand new*
vollkommen: *completely; perfect*
Vollkosten: *full costs*
Vollmacht: *power of attorney; proxy; warrant*
Vollmacht erteilen: *delegate; empower*

Vollsichtregal: *display stand or display unit*
vollständig: *complete; (in) full; fully; outright*
vollständig abbezahlen: *pay off*
vollständig abschreiben: *write off*
Vollstreckungsaufschub: *stay of execution*
voll und ganz: *absolutely*
Vollversammlung: *plenary meeting or plenary session*
vollziehen: *implement* **Vollzug** *implementation*
vorab: *(in) advance*
vorankommen: *get on with*
vorantreiben: *chase; hurry up*
Vorarbeiter: *chargehand; foreman or forewoman; overseer*
voraus: *ahead* **im ~** *in advance; advance; forward; up front* **im ~ bezahlen** *to pay in advance; prepay* **im ~ zahlbar** *payable in advance*
Vorausberechnung: *forecast*
vorausbezahlt: *prepaid*
vorausgehend: *preliminary; prior*
vorausgesetzt: *provided that or providing*
Voraussage: *forecast; forecasting*
voraussagen: *forecast; predict*
Voraussetzung: **unter der ~** *on the understanding that*
voraussichtlich: *prospective*
Vorauszahlung: *money up front; prepayment*
Vorbehalt: *proviso* **unter ~** *conditional* **unter ~ annehmen** *to give a conditional acceptance*
vorbehaltlos: *unconditional*
Vorbehaltsklausel: *proviso*
Vorbehaltspreis: *reserve or upset price*
vorbeikommen: *call in*
vorbereitend: *preliminary*
Vorbesprechung: *preliminary discussion or meeting*
Vorbestellungen: *dues*
vorbeugend: *preventive*
vorbildlich: *model*
Vorbildung: *background*
vorbringen: *raise*
vordatieren: *postdate*
Vorderseite: *front*
vordrängeln: **sich ~** *to jump the queue*
vordringen: *progress*
Vordruck: *form*
voreilig handeln *or* **sein:** *to jump the gun*
Vorfinanzierung: *pre-financing*
vorführen: *demonstrate* **Vorführer** *demonstrator*
Vorführmodell: *demonstration model*
Vorführung: *demonstration; presentation*
Vorgänger: *predecessor*
vorgeben: *pretend*
Vorgehen: *action; procedure* **rechtmäßiges ~** *lawful practice*
Vorgehensweise: *procedure*
Vorgesetzter: *superior*
Vorhaben: *project; scheme*
vorhaben: *intend; to propose to*
Vorhaltungen: *representation*
Vorhand: *first option*
Vorhersage: *projection*
Vorkaufsrecht: *option to purchase; a pre-emptive right (US)*
Vorkehrungen treffen für: *to make provision for*
vorladen: *subpoena*
Vorladung: *notice; subpoena; summons*
Vorlage: *presentation; production*
vorläufig: *provisional; tentative*
vorlegen: *file; get out; present; produce; submit; table*
Vorliebe: *preference*
vormittags: *a.m.*
Vorrang haben: *to have priority*
vorrangig: **etwas ~ behandeln** *to give something top priority*
Vorrat: *pool; stock; stockpile; store; supply* **einen ~ anlegen** *stock up* **solange ~ reicht** *subject to availability*
Vorräte anlegen: *stockpile*
vorrätig: *in stock* **nicht ~** *out of stock*
Vorreiter: *pioneer*
Vorrichtung: *device*
vorschießen: *advance*
Vorschlag: *proposal; suggestion* **vorschlagen** *to propose or suggest*
Vorschriften: *regulations*
vorschriftsmäßig: *in due form; duly; in accordance with or according to instructions*
Vorschriftswidrigkeiten: *irregularities*
Vorschub: *feed*
Vorschuß: *advance; sub*
vorsehen: *earmark; to provide for* **sich ~** *beware*
Vorsichtsmaßnahme: **als ~** *as a precautionary measure*
Vorsichtsmaßnahmen ergreifen: *to take safety precautions or safety measures*
Vorsitz: *chair; chairmanship* **den ~ führen** *preside; to take the chair*
Vorsitzende: *chairwoman; leader*
Vorsitzender: *chairman; chairperson; leader*
Vorsitzender des Aufsichtsrates: *chairman*
Vorsitzender und Geschäftsführer: *chairman and managing director*
Vorsorge treffen für: *to make provision for*
Vorspiegelung falscher Tatsachen: *fraudulent misrepresentation; false pretences*
Vorstand: *board; director; executive committee; head*
Vorstandsgremium: *management committee*
Vorstandsmitglied: *board member*
Vorstandssitzung: *board meeting*
Vorstandsverzeichnis: *register of directors*
vorstehen: *head*
vorstellen: *introduce*
Vorstellungen: *representation*
Vorstellungsgespräch: *interview*

Vorsteuer: *input tax*
vortäuschen: *pretend*
Vorteil: *advantage; edge*
vorteilhaft: *favourable*
vortragen: *bring or carry forward*
vorübergehend: *temporary*
Vorverkaufskasse *or* **Vorverkaufsstelle:** *booking office*
vorverlegen: *advance; bring forward*
vorverpackt: *prepacked or prepackaged*
Vorwahl: *area code; dialling code*
Vorwürfe machen: *blame*
Vorzeigen: *production* **vorzeigen** *to produce*
vorziehen: *prefer*
Vorzugsaktien: *preference shares; preferred shares or preferred stock (US)* **kumulative ~** *cumulative preference shares or cumulative preferred stock (US)* **nachzugsberechtigte ~** *cumulative preference shares*
Vorzugsaktienbesitzer: *preference shareholders*
Vorzugsfahrpreis: *concessionary fare*
Vorzugsgläubiger: *secured creditor*
Vorzugskonditionen: *preferential terms*
Vorzugstarif: *preferential tariff*
Vorzugszoll: *preferential duty*

Ww

Waage: *scales; weighing machine*
waagerecht: *horizontal*
Wachmann: *security guard*
wachsen: *grow; increase*
Wachstum: *growth*
Wachstumsaktie: *growth share or growth stock*
Wachstumsbranche: *boom industry or growth industry*
Wachstumsindex: *growth index*
Wachstumsmarkt: *growth market*
Wachstumsrate: *growth rate*
Wagen: **einen ~ mieten** *to hire a car*
Wagenpark: *fleet*
Wagen vermieten: *to hire out cars*
Waggon: *freight car (US); wagon* **frei ~** *free on rail*
Wagniskapital: *risk capital; venture capital*
Wahl: *ballot; choice; election; pick; vote; voting* **eine ~ abhalten** *ballot* **geheime ~** *secret ballot* **zweite ~** *reject; seconds*
wählbar: *eligible* **Wählbarkeit** *eligibility*
wählen: *choose; dial; elect; vote*
Wählen: *dialling*
Wähler: *voter*
Wahlhelfer: *canvasser*
wahllos: *at random*
Wahlmanipulation: *ballot-rigging*
Wahlrecht: **das ~ entziehen** *disenfranchise*
Wahlurne: *ballot box*
Wahlwerbung: *canvassing*
Wahlwerbung betreiben: *canvass*
Wahlzettel: *ballot paper*
Währung: **frei konvertierbare ~** *convertible currency; free currency* **harte ~** *hard currency* **weiche ~** *soft currency*
Währungsausgleichsfonds: *Exchange Equalization Account (GB)*
Währungseinheit: *monetary unit or unit of currency*
Währungsfonds: **internationaler ~** *the International Monetary Fund*
Währungsgarantie: *currency backing*
Währungskorb: *basket of currencies*
währungspolitisch: *monetary*
Währungsreserven: *currency reserves*
Währungssystem: **das internationale ~** *the international monetary system*
Wandel: *shift*
Wandelanleihe: *convertible loan stock*
Wandergewerbe betreiben: *peddle*
Wandtresor: *wall safe*
Ware: *commodity; merchandise; product* **schwer verkäufliche ~** *a drug on the market* **stark herabgesetzte ~** *distress merchandise (US)* **unverkaufte ~** *goods left on hand*
Waren: **brandgeschädigte ~** *fire-damaged goods* **verderbliche ~** *perishables* **verzollte ~** *duty-paid goods*
Warenannahme: *receiving department or office*
Waren auf Lager: *stock in hand*
Warenaufzug: *freight elevator*
Warenausgangsbuch: *sales ledger*
Warenausgangsjournal: *sales book*
Warenbegleitschein: *docket*
Warenbeschaffung: *purchasing*
Warenbestand: *stock*
Warenbestände: *inventory*
Warenbestellung: *indent*
Warenbewegung: *stock movements*
Warenbörse: *commodity exchange; commodity market*
Warencode: *stock code*
Wareneingangsbuch: *purchase book*
Warenhaus: *emporium; department store*
Warenkennzeichnungsgesetz: *Trade Descriptions Act (GB)*
Warenlieferung: *delivery of goods*
Warenposten: *job lot*
Warenprobe: *sample* **unverkäufliche ~** *sample only - not for resale*
Warensendung: *consignment*
Warentermingeschäft: *commodity futures*
Warenterminhändler: *commodity trader*
Waren übertragen: *to carry over stock*
Warenumsatzsteuer: *sales tax*
Waren unter Zollverschluß: *goods (held) in bond*
Warenverkaufsbuch: *sales book*
Warenverzeichnis: *stocklist*

Warenzeichen: *trademark or trade name*
Warenzustellung: *delivery of goods*
Warnstreik: *token strike*
Warnung: *caveat; warning*
warten: *hang on; hold on; service*
warten auf: *await*
Warteschlange: *queue*
Wartezeit: *qualifying period*
Wartung: *maintenance; service*
Wartungshandbuch: *service handbook or manual*
Wartungsvertrag: *maintenance or service contract*
waschen: *launder*
wasserdicht *or* **wasserfest:** *waterproof*
Wechsel: *bill (of exchange); rotation* **einen ~ diskontieren** *to discount a bill* **einen ~ indossieren** *to endorse a bill* **einen ~ unterzeichnen** *to back a bill* **erstklassige ~** *prime bills* **kurzfristige ~** *short-dated bills* **langfristige ~** *long-dated bills*
Wechselautomat: *change machine*
Wechselbürgschaft: eine ~ leisten *to guarantee a bill of exchange*
Wechselforderungen: *bills receivable*
Wechselgarant: *backer of a bill*
Wechselgeld: *cash float; change* **behalte das ~** *keep the (odd) change*
Wechselkurs: *rate of exchange or exchange rate* **der amtliche ~** *the official exchange rate* **ungünstiger ~** *unfavourable exchange rate*
wechseln: *change; exchange; switch*
Wechselprotest: *protest*
wechselseitig: *reciprocal*
Wechselstube: *bureau de change*
Wechselverbindlichkeiten: *bills payable*
Weg: *channel* **auf dem ~** *en route* **den ~ bahnen** *pioneer*
Wegbereiter: *pioneer*
Wegerecht: *right of way*
weglassen: *leave out; omit*
wegnehmen: *take away; take off*
wegschnappen: *snap up*
Wegwerf-: *disposable*
wegwerfen: *throw out*
wehren: sich ~ *resist*
Wehrmaterial: *military hardware*
Weide: *field*
weigern: sich ~ *refuse*
Weigerung: *refusal*
Weihnachtsgeld: *Christmas bonus*
Wein- und Spirituosenhandlung: *off-licence*
Weise: auf betrügerische ~ *fraudulently*
weiß: *white* **das ~ keiner** *it is anyone's guess*
Weißbuch: *White Paper (GB)*
weiteres: bis auf ~ *until further notice*
weiterleiten: *refer*
Weiterverkauf: *resale*
weitverbreitet: *common*
Weltbank: *World Bank*
Welthandel: *international trade*
Weltwährungsfonds: *International Monetary Fund*
weltweit: *worldwide*
Weltwirtschaftskrise: die ~ *the Great Depression; the Slump*
wenden: sich ~ an *approach*
Werbeabteilung: *publicity department*
Werbeagentur: *advertising agency; publicity agency or bureau*
Werbeaktion: *publicity or advertising campaign*
Werbebeilage: *magazine insert; stuffer (US)*
Werbeblatt: *free paper or giveaway paper*
Werbeetat: *advertising or publicity budget*
Werbefachmann: *adman (informal)*
Werbegeschenk: *free gift; giveaway; premium offer*
Werbegrafiker: *commercial artist*
Werbekampagne: *publicity or advertising campaign*
Werbekosten: *publicity expenditure*
Werbeleiter: *advertising or publicity manager*
Werbematerial: *publicity matter; sales literature*
werben: *canvass; promote; publicize*
Werbeprobe: "unentgeltliche ~" *"sample only - of no commercial value"*
Werbeprospekt: *publicity handout*
Werbesätze: degressive ~ *graded advertising rates*
Werbeschreiben: *sales sheet*
Werbesendezeit: *TV spot*
Werbespot: *commercial*
Werbespruch: *publicity slogan*
Werbetarif: *advertising rates*
Werbetext: herabsetzender ~ *knocking copy*
Werbetextentwurf: *publicity copy*
Werbetexter: *copywriter*
Werbeträger: *advertising medium*
Werbung: *advertisement; advertising; blurb; commercial; publicity* **reißerische** *or* **übertriebene ~** *hype* **~ machen** *publicize*
Werbungsbranche: *advertising*
Werdegang: *background*
Werft: *dockyard; shipyard*
Werk: *factory; mill; plant; works* **urheberrechtlich geschütztes ~** *work still in copyright*
Werksspionage: *industrial espionage*
Werkstatt: *workshop*
Werkszeitung: *house journal or magazine*
Werkzeug: *implement; tool*
Werkzeugmaschinen: *machine tools*
Wert: *value; worth* **an ~ gewinnen** *appreciate* **an ~ verlieren** *depreciate* **angegebener ~** *declared value* **gegenwärtiger ~** *present value*
Wertgegenstände: *valuable property or valuables*
wertlos: *dud; worthless*
Wertminderung: *depreciation*
Wertminderung von Aktien: *dilution of equity or of shareholding*
Wertpapier: begebbares ~ *negotiable paper*

Wertpapieranlage: **sichere** ~ *blue-chip investments or blue-chip shares or blue chips*
Wertpapierbörse: *Stock Exchange*
Wertpapiere: *securities; stocks and shares*
Wertschätzung: *appreciation*
Wertsteigerung: *appreciation*
Wertsteuer: *ad valorem duty or tax*
Wertverlust: *depreciation*
wertvoll: *valuable*
Wertzuwachs: *appreciation*
wesentlich: *basic; essential; prime*
Wettbewerb: **freier** ~ *free competition* **mörderischer** ~ *cut-throat competition* **scharfer** ~ *keen competition* **unlauterer** ~ *unfair competition*
Wettbewerbsbeschränkung: *restraint of trade*
wettbewerbsfähig: *competitive*
Wettbewerbsfähigkeit: *competitiveness*
Wettbewerbsfreiheit: *free competition*
Wette or **Wetteinsatz:** *bet*
wetten: *bet; punt*
Wetter: *punter*
Wettsteuer: *betting tax*
wichtigster: *principal*
Widerklage: *counter-claim*
widerrechtlich: *wrongful*
widerrufen: *withdraw*
widersetzen: **sich** ~ *resist*
Widerstand: *resistance*
widrigenfalls: *failing that*
wiederabtreten: *reassign* **Wiederabtretung** *reassignment*
Wiederanlage: *reinvestment*
Wiederaufbau: *reconstruction*
wiederaufbereiten: *recycle*
Wiederauffinden von Information: *information retrieval*
Wiederaufnahme: *resumption*
wiederaufnehmen: *resume*
Wiederausfuhr: *re-export; re-exportation*
wiederausführen: *re-export*
Wiederausfuhrhafen: *entrepot port*
Wiederbelebung: *recovery*
Wiederbeschaffungskosten: *replacement cost*
Wiederbeschaffungswert: *replacement value*
wiederbeschäftigen: *re-employ*
Wiedereinfuhr: *reimport; reimportation*
Wiedereinreise: *re-entry*
wiedereinstellen: *reappoint; re-employ; reinstate*
wiedererkennen: *recognize*
wiedererlangen: *retrieve*
Wiedererlangung: *recovery; retrieval*
wiederernennen: *reappoint; reassign*
wiedereröffnen: *reopen*
wiedergewinnen: *retrieve*
Wiedergewinnung: *recovery*
wiedergutmachen: *make good; make up (for)*
wiederholen: *repeat*
wiederholend: **sich** ~ *recurrent*
wiedersetzen: **sich** ~ *oppose*
Wiederverkauf: *resale*
Wiederverkäufer: *distributor*
Wiederverkäuferrabatt: *trade discount*
Wiedervorlage: *pending tray*
Wiederwahl: *re-election*
wiederwählbar: *eligible for re-election*
wiederwählen: *re-elect*
wiegen: *weigh*
willkürlich: *random*
wirksam: *effective; effectual*
wirksam bleiben: *to remain in effect*
Wirksamkeit: *effectiveness*
Wirkung: *impact*
Wirtschaft: **die** ~ **anheizen** *to inflate the economy* **die** ~ **ankurbeln** *to reflate the economy* **staatlich gelenkte** ~ *controlled economy*
wirtschaftlich: *commercial*
Wirtschaftsbüro: *trade bureau*
Wirtschaftsgeld: *household expenses*
Wirtschaftsinstitut: *business college or school*
Wirtschaftskorrespondent: *business or financial correspondent*
Wirtschaftskrise: *economic crisis*
Wirtschaftsplanung: *economic planning*
Wirtschaftspolitik: **angebotsorientierte** ~ *supply side economics*
Wirtschaftsprüfer: *accountant* **beeidigter** ~ *chartered accountant*
Wirtschaftsredakteur: *the City editor*
Wirtschaftsredaktion: *the city desk*
Wirtschaftssanktionen: *economic sanctions*
Wirtschaftsspionage: *industrial espionage*
Wirtschaftsstagnation: *economic stagnation*
Wirtschaftsverband: *trade association*
Wirtschaftswachstum: *economic growth*
Wirtschaftswissenschaft: *economics; business science*
Wirtschaftswissenschaftler: *economist*
Wirtschaftszweig: **verstaatlichter** ~ *nationalized industry*
Wissen: **ohne vorheriges** ~ *without prior knowledge*
Wissenschaft: *science*
Woche: **pro** ~ *per week* **vorletzte** ~ *the week before last*
Wochen: **sechs** ~ **Jahresurlaub** *six weeks' annual leave* **zwei** ~ *fortnight*
Wochentagen: **an** ~ *on weekdays*
wöchentlich: *weekly*
Wochenzeitschrift: *weekly magazine or weekly*
wohlbehalten: *safely*
wohlbekannt: *well-known*
Wohlfahrtsstaat: *welfare state*
wohlhabend: *affluent; prosperous; rich; wealthy*
Wohlstand: *prosperity; wealth*
Wohlstandsgesellschaft: *the affluent society*
Wohltätigkeitsbasar: *jumble sale*

Wohltätigkeitsorganisation: *voluntary organization*
wohnhaft: *resident*
Wohnsitz: *domicile; residence*
Wohnung: *flat; home; residence* **subventionierte ~** *subsidized accommodation*
Wohnungsmakler: *letting agency*
Wohnzimmer: *lounge*
Workstation: *workstation*
Wortlaut: *wording*
Wrack: *wreck*
Wucher: *usury*
Wuchermiete: *rack rent*
Wucht: *momentum*
Wühltisch: *dump bin*
Wunsch: auf ~ *on request* **auf ~ erhältlich** *optional*
Würdigung: *appreciation*

Xx

Xerox: *Xerox*

Yy

Yen: *yen*

Zz

zahlbar: *payable*
Zahlen: in einstelligen ~ *in single figures* **in ~ ausdrückbar** *quantifiable* **ungerade ~** *odd numbers*
zahlen: *pay (up)*
zählen: *count*
Zahlen aufbereiten: *to process figures*
zahlenmäßig: *numeric or numerical*
Zahler: *payer*
Zählmaschine: *comptometer*
Zahltag: *pay day*
Zahlung: *payment* **aufgeschobene ~** *deferred payment* **eine ~ leisten** *to effect or to make a payment* **in ~ geben** *trade in* **pünktliche ~** *prompt payment* **symbolische ~** *token payment*
Zahlungen in Etappen: *staged payments*
Zahlungsanweisung: *order*
Zahlungsaufforderung: letzte ~ *final demand*
Zahlungsaufschub: *moratorium*
Zahlungsbedingungen: *terms of payment*
Zahlungsbilanz: *balance of payments*
Zahlungsbilanzdefizit: *balance of payments deficit*
Zahlungsempfänger: *payee*
Zahlungserleichterungen: *easy terms*
zahlungsfähig: *solvent* **Zahlungsfähigkeit** *solvency*
Zahlungsmittel: gesetzliches ~ *legal currency or tender*
Zahlungstermin: letzter ~ *final date for payment* **mittlerer ~** *average due date*
zahlungsunfähig: *bankrupt; insolvent*
Zahlungsunfähigkeit: *insolvency*
Zahlungsweise: *mode of payment*
z.B.: *e.g.*
Zeche: *mine; pit*
Zehncentstück: *dime (informal)*
Zehnertastatur: *numeric keypad*
Zehntelstelle: *decile*
Zeichen: *mark; reference; token*
zeichnen: *apply*
Zeichner: *applicant*
Zeichnung: *application*
Zeichnungsangebot: *offer for sale; subscription to a new share issue*
Zeichnungsbogen: *subscription list*
zeigen: *display; indicate; show*
Zeile: *line* **Zeilendrucker** *line printer*
Zeit: *period; time* **in kurzer ~** *in the short term* **zur ~** *currently; pro tem*
Zeitarbeit: *temporary employment; temping; time work*
Zeitarbeiterin: *temp*
Zeitarbeitskräfte: *temporary staff*
Zeit der Flaute: *slack season*
Zeiteinsparung: *time saving*
Zeitkarte: *season ticket*
Zeitlohn: *time rate*
Zeitplan: *schedule* **einen ~ aufstellen** *timetable*
Zeitraum: *period; term*
Zeitschrift: *journal; magazine; periodical; review* **eine ~ abonnieren** *to subscribe to a magazine; to take out a subscription to a magazine*
Zeitschriftenabonnement: ein ~ kündigen *to cancel a subscription to a magazine*
Zeitschriftenabonnent: *subscriber to a magazine or magazine subscriber*
Zeitschriftenzustellung per Post: *magazine mailing*
Zeitspanne: *a lapse of time; period; time*
zeitsparend: *time-saving*
Zeit- und Bewegungsstudie: *time and motion study*
Zeitung: *paper*
Zeitungsausschnitt: *press cutting*
Zeitungsbericht: *newspaper report*
Zeitungshändler: *newsagent*
Zeitungsstand: *news stand*
zeitweilig einstellen: *suspend*
Zentimeter: *centimetre*
Zentner: *hundredweight*
Zentralbank: *central bank; Federal Reserve Bank (US)*

Zentrale: *central* or *general* or *head office; headquarters; main office*
Zentraleinkauf: *central purchasing*
Zentralisierung: *centralization*
Zentralregierung: *central government*
Zentralwert: *median*
Zentrum: *centre* or *center (US)*
zerbrechlich: *fragile*
Zero-Bonds: *zero-coupon bonds*
Zession: *cession*
Zessionsurkunde: *deed of transfer*
Zettel: *slip*
Zeuge or **Zeugin:** *witness*
Zeugnis: *letter of reference; testimonial*
Ziel: *aim; goal; objective; target*
Zielmarkt: *target market*
Zielort: *final* or *ultimate destination*
Ziffer: *digit; figure; number*
Zimmer: *room* **freies** ~ *vacancy*
Zimmerbelegung: *occupancy rate*
Zimmerreservierung: *room reservations*
Zimmerservice: *room service*
Zinsbelastung: *interest charges*
Zinsen: **aufgelaufene** ~ *accrued interest* **einfache** ~ *simple interest* **feste** ~ *fixed interest*
Zinseszins: *compound interest*
Zinsrückstand: *back interest*
Zinssatz: *interest rate* or *rate of interest*
Zinsschein: *interest coupon*
Zinsthesaurierung: *accrual of interest*
zirkulierend: *circulating*
zitieren: *quote*
Zivilprozeß: *civil action*
Zivilrecht: *civil law*
zögern: *hesitate; hold back*
Zoll: *customs (duty); inch*
Zollabfertigung: *customs clearance*
Zollabfertigungsschein: *clearance certificate*
Zollabgabe: *customs duty*
Zollagent: *customs broker*
Zollager: *bonded warehouse*
zollamtlich abfertigen lassen: *to effect customs clearance*
Zollanmeldungsstelle: *customs entry point*
Zollbeamter: *customs officer; customs official*
Zollbehörden: *customs*
Zolldeklaration: *customs declaration*
Zollformalitäten: *customs formalities*
zollfrei: *duty-free; free of duty*
Zollgebühren: *customs tariffs*
Zollkontrolle: *customs examination*
zollpflichtig: *dutiable goods* or *items*
Zollrückvergütung: *drawback*
Zollschranken: *customs* or *tariff barriers*
Zolltarife: *customs tariffs*
Zollunion: *customs union*
Zollverschluß: *customs seal* **unter** ~ *bonded*
Zone: *area; zone*
zudecken: *cover*
zuerkennen: *award*
zufällig: *random*
Zufallsfehler: *random error*
Zufluchtsort: *haven*
Zufluß: *influx*
Zufriedenheit am Arbeitsplatz: *job satisfaction*
zufriedenstellend: *adequate*
Zufriedenstellung des Kunden: *customer satisfaction*
Zufuhr: *influx*
Zugang: *addition*
zugeben: *admit*
zugehen auf: *head for*
zugkräftig: *attractive*
Zugriffszeit: *access time*
zugunsten: *in favour of*
zugute kommen: *benefit*
zukleben: *seal*
Zukunft: **in** ~ *hereafter*
zukünftig: *future*
Zulage: *bonus; supplement; weighting*
zulässig: *allowable*
Zulassung: *recognition*
Zulassungsbescheinigung: *test certificate*
Zulassungsfrist: *period of qualification*
Zulassungspapiere: *registration*
Zulieferer: *supplier*
zumachen: *close*
Zunahme: *gain; growth; increase; rise*
zunehmend: *increasing; incremental; mounting*
Zunft: *guild*
zurechtkommen: *cope; get along* or *on*
zurückbehalten: *keep back; retain*
zurückbekommen: *get back; recover; retrieve*
zurückdatieren: *antedate; backdate*
zurückerstattbar: *refundable*
Zurückfallen: *reversion*
zurückfordern: *call in; claim back*
Zurückführung in Privateigentum: *privatization*
zurückgeben: *return*
zurückgehen: *decline; decrease; drop; fall away; fall off; shrink*
zurückgewinnen: *retrieve*
Zurückgewinnung: *retrieval*
zurückgreifen auf: *fall back on*
zurückholen: **sich** ~ *claw back*
zurückkaufen: *buy back*
zurücknehmen: *go back on*
zurückrufen: *phone* or *ring back*
zurückschicken or **zurücksenden:** *return*
zurückstellen: *defer; shelve*
zurückstufen: *demote*
zurücktreten: *pull out; resign; retire*
zurückübertragen: *reassign*
zurückweisen: *reject*

zurückwerfen: *set back*
zurückzahlen: *pay back; refund; repay*
zurückziehen: *withdraw*
zusagen: *promise*
zusammenarbeiten: *collaborate; co-operate*
zusammenbauen: *assemble*
zusammenbrechen: *collapse; crash*
Zusammenbruch: *collapse* **finanzieller ~** *crash*
zusammenfassen: *to bracket or group together; to integrate*
Zusammenfassung: *abstract; integration; summary*
Zusammenhang: in ~ mit *in connection with; relating to; in relation to*
Zusammenhänge: *background*
zusammenlegen: *consolidate; fold*
zusammenpacken: *gather*
zusammenrufen: *convene*
zusammenschließen: *integrate; merge; unite* **sich ~** *combine*
zusammensetzen: sich ~ aus *consist of*
Zusammenstellung einer Bestellung: *order picking*
zusammenzählen: *add up; count*
Zusatz: *supplement*
Zusatzklausel: *endorsement; rider*
zusätzlich: *in addition to; additional; backup; extra; further; supplementary*
Zusatzsteuer: *surtax*
Zuschauerzahl: *gate*
zuschicken: *send*
Zuschlag: *premium; surcharge*
Zuschuß: *allowance; benefit; grant*
Zusicherung: *undertaking*
zuspielen: *leak*
zusprechen: *award*
Zustand: *condition*
zuständig für: *responsible for*
zustellen: *deliver*
zusteuern auf: *head for*
zustimmen: *agree*
zustimmend: *affirmative; positive*
Zustimmung: *sanction*
Zustrom: *inflow; influx*
zuteilen: *allocate; allot; apportion; ration*
Zuteilungsanzeige: *allotment letter*
Zutritt: *admission; admittance*
zuverlässig: *reliable*
zuversichtlich: *confident; optimistic*
zuviel ausgeben: *overspend*
zuviel berechnen: *overcharge*
zuvorkommen: *pre-empt*
Zuwachs: *accrual; gain; increase*
zuweisen: *allocate; allot; appropriate*
Zuwendung: *handout*
zuzüglich: *additional; plus*
Zwangsliquidation: *compulsory liquidation*
Zwangsverkauf: *forced sale*
Zwangsverwalter: *sequestrator*
Zwangsverwaltung: *sequestration*
zwangsvollstrecken lassen: *foreclose*
Zwangsvollstreckung: *foreclosure*
Zweck: *purpose*
Zweckentfremdung: *misuse*
zweifelhaft: *shady*
Zweigstelle: *branch*
Zweigstelle der Post: *(sub-)post office*
zweimal jährlich: *bi-annually*
zweimal monatlich: *bi-monthly*
zweiseitig: *bilateral*
zweistellig: *in double figures*
Zweithypothek: *second mortgage*
Zweitinserat: *readvertisement*
zweitklassig: *inferior; second-rate*
zweitrangig: *secondary*
Zweitschrift: *duplicate*
zwingen: *force*
Zwischenbericht: *interim report*
Zwischendividende: *interim dividend*
Zwischenhändler: *middleman*
Zwischenlandung *or* **Zwischenstation:** *stopover*
Zwischensumme: *subtotal*
Zwischenzeit: in der ~ *in the interim*
zyklisch: *cyclical*
Zyklus: *cycle*
z.Zt.: *pro tem*

Anhang

Numbers

you write	*you say*
0	zero *or* nought *or* oh
0.4[1]	point four *or* nought point four
0.5126[2]	nought point five one two six
¼	one quarter *or* (informal) a quarter
½	one half *or* (informal) a half
¾	three quarters
5/16	five sixteenths
1	one
2	two
3	three
4	four
5	five
6	six
7	seven
8	eight
9	nine
10	ten
12	twelve *or* (informal) one dozen[3] *or* a dozen
15	fifteen *or* one-five[4]
50	fifty *or* five-oh
67	sixty-seven
100	one hundred *or* (informal) a hundred
106	one hundred and six[5] *or* (US) one hundred six
556	five hundred and fifty-six
1000	one thousand *or* (informal) a thousand *or* one K
5001	five thousand and one[6]
10,000	ten thousand
1,000,000 *or* 1m	one million *or* (informal) a million
1000,000,000 *or* 1bn	one billion *or* (informal) a billion
	Telephone
01-608-9940[7]	oh one, six oh eight, double nine four oh
	Year
1987	nineteen eighty-seven
1621	sixteen twenty-one
2000	the year two thousand
1905	nineteen five *or* nineteen hundred and five *or* nineteen oh five
	Date
2.1.70[8]	the second of January nineteen seventy *or*
2/1/70	(US) the first of February nineteen seventy
2 Jan 70	
2 January 1970	the second of January, nineteen seventy
2nd January, 1970	
	Code number
1600	sixteen hundred *or* one six oh oh *or* one six zero zero
45038	four five oh three eight

Note

1. The point (.) is used to show decimals. The comma (,) to show thousands or millions or billions
2. After the decimal point you read number by number
3. The plural is 'two dozen', 'three dozen', etc
4. The difference between numbers like 13 (thirteen) and 30 (thirty) is sometimes difficult to hear so it may be necessary to say 'one-three', 'three-oh' when repeating
5. 'and' is normally said after hundreds; Americans often leave the word out
6. A comma (,) or a space is used to show thousands or millions or billions. There is usually no comma or space in 1000.
7. see also section on *telephone*
8. American dates use the order: month/date/year
   European and British dates use the order: day/month/year

Movement of Numbers

A Graph

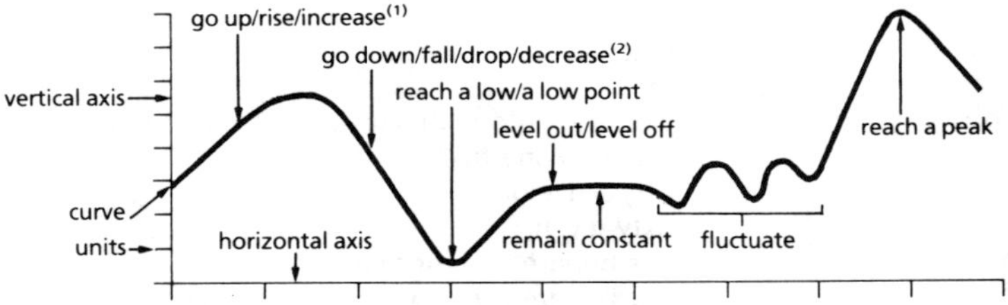

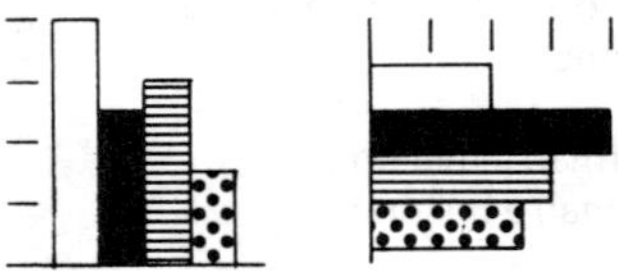

A column chart/bar chart

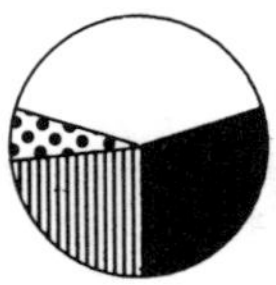

A pie chart

Note:

1. when describing increase or decrease you can say:

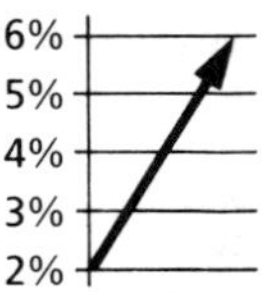

"inflation	rose/fell went up/went down increased/decreased	*to*	6%"
"inflation	went up/went down increased/decreased rose/fell	*by*	4%"
"inflation	now stands	*at*	6%"

2. when describing increase or decrease you can say:

"inflation fell/rose sharply"

"inflation fell/rose gradually"

Measurement

When you describe measurements you say:
"The pipe is five metres (5m) long" *or* "the pipe is five metres in length" *but* "It is a five-metre (5m) pipe".

You can say: "The cable is two hundred feet (200ft) long" *but* "It is a two-hundred-foot (200ft) cable"

The most common measurements are given on the table below:

British and American				*Metric*	
we say	*we write*			*we say*	*we write*
		Length			
inch	in *or* "	0.039	25.40	millimetre	mm
		0.394	2.540	centimetre	cm
foot	ft *or* '	3.218	0.305	metre[(1)]	m
yard	yd	1.094	0.914		
mile	m *or* mi	0.621	1.609	kilometre	km
		Weight			
ounce	oz	0.035	28.350	gram	gm
pound	lb	2.205	0.454	kilogram[(2)]	kg
hundredweight	cwt	0.196	50.18		
ton		0.984	1.016	metric tonne	tonne
		Capacity			
pint	pt	1.70	0.568	litre[(1)]	l
gallon	gal	0.220	4.546		
		Area			
square inch	sq in *or* in^2	0.155	6.452	square centimetre	cm^2
square foot	sq ft *or* ft^2	10.764	0.093	square metre	m^2
square yard	sq yd *or* yd^2	1.196	0.836		
acre		2.471	0.4047	hectare	ha
square mile	sq m *or* mi^2	0.387	2.59	square kilometre	km^2
		Volume			
cubic inch	cu in *or* in^3	0.061	16.4	cubic centimetre	cm^3 *or* cc
cubic foot	cu ft *or* ft^3	35.315	0.0283	cubic metre	m^3
cubic yard	cu yd *or* yd^3	1.308	0.765		

Note

1. metre, litre, etc=US: "meter, liter", etc.
2. informal: 'kilo'

Abbreviations

You can find abbreviations of business terms in the body of the dictionary and abbreviations of measurements in the measurement section.
These are commonly used abbreviations[1]. If the abbreviation is marked (*), you can *say* it as well as *write* it[2].

a/c *or* acc *or* acct	account
a.m.* *or* am	in the morning, before midday
approx	approximately
arr	arrival or arrived
cc	copies (on a letter, to show that copies of the letter have been sent
c/o*	care of (on an address to show that the person lives at the address but only as a visitor)
COD* *or* c.o.d.	cash on delivery
cont *or* cont'd	continued
dep *or* dept	department
ditto *or* do	the same (to show that an item, for example in a list, is the same as the previous one)
e.g.* *or* eg	for example
encl *or* enc	enclosure (on a letter, to show that another written paper has been sent in the same envelope)
esp	especially
et al	and others
etc	etcetera, and so on
fig	figure
HQ*[3]	headquarters
i.e.*	that is, in other words
K*	thousand
max	maximum
misc	miscellaneous, mixed and various
NB	note, take special note that...
no	number
ono *or* o.n.o	or near offer (after a price)
p.m.* *or* pm	in the afternoon, in the evening, after 12 midday
ps *or* PS	post script (in a letter, to introduce an added message after the signature)
qty	quantity
recd	received
re* *or* ref	reference, with reference to
RSVP	please reply (on an invitation)
SAE *or* sae	stamped addressed envelope
tel	telephone
v *or* vs	versus, against
wk	week
x *or* ext	extension (after a telephone number)

Note:

1. abbreviations can be written in different ways and sometimes the same letters can have more than one meaning:

m	million *or* mile *or* metre
min	minimum *or* minute
MD	managing director* *or* doctor of medicine
p.a. *or* P.A.	per annum (every year) *or* personal assistant*
pp*	on behalf of (used on letters below a signature when one person signs on behalf of another) or pages

2. in modern English writing, many abbreviations can be written with or without punctuation, in capital letters or small letters:
   fmcg *or* FMCG *or* F.M.C.G. fast-moving customer goods
   plc *or* p.l.c. *or* PLC *or* P.L.C. public limited company
3. you say *a* headquarters, but *an* HQ
   a managing director, but *an* MD

PUNCTUATION

.	full stop *or* point, US: period
,	comma
:	colon
;	semi-colon
-	dash *or* hyphen
/	stroke *or* oblique *or* solidus
( )	brackets
[ ]	square brackets

SYMBOLS

%	per cent
°	degrees
=	equals
≈	is approximately equal to
≠	is not equal to
<	is less than
>	is more than
+	plus
−	minus
÷	divided by
×	multiplied by
∴	therefore
&	and
∝	infinity
√	root

ROMAN NUMERALS

I *or* i	1
II *or* ii	2
III *or* iii	3
IV *or* iv	4
V *or* v	5
VI *or* vi	6
VII *or* vii	7
VIII *or* viii	8
IX *or* ix	9
X *or* x	10
XI *or* xi	11
XX *or* xx	20
L	50
C	100
D	500
M	1000

Business Letters

A letter to a company

- printed letterhead (company name, address, postcode, telephone and telex numbers
- company name & address
- reference codes
- "salutation" or opening phrase[1]
- opening sentence
- text
- closing sentence
- "complimentary close"[2]
- writer's signature
- name and position of writer

Colville International plc
65 Holt Street, London W5 2LJ
tel: 01-221 6010
telex: 359126 Colin

Export Components
245 Ocean Road
SYDNEY
N.S.W.
AUSTRALIA

11 July 1987

Your ref: AK/341

Our ref: OS/6

Dear Sirs

With reference to your advertisement in the 5th July edition of "Export Magazine", we would want to draw your attention to the services we can offer, and therefore the possibility of co-operating on the project, as it is in an area which we understand and have experience

We look forward to your reply.

Yours faithfully

H. Roberts

H. Roberts
Purchasing Manager

A letter to an individual[3]

Bennet R. Lee
Production Director
Micro Aerospace
175 Golden Crescent
Aberdeen, SCOTLAND

11 July 1987

Dear Mr Lee

Thank you for your letter of 3rd July which I found very encouraging.

I look forward to hearing from you with few weeks.

Yours Sincerely

Harold Roberts

H. Roberts
Purchasing Manager

A letter to a colleague or friend

11.7.87

Dear John

Further to our short telephone conversation yesterday, I'd like to say how glad we are

Best wishes

Yours

Harry

H. Roberts

Note:

1. In modern business letters punctuation is kept to a minimum. Commas (,) are possible after "Dear Sir", "Yours faithfully", etc, but are not necessary.
2. If you begin a letter "Dear Sir", you must end with "Yours faithfully". If you begin "Dear Mr X", you must end with "Yours sincerely" or "Sincerely yours".
3. If you are writing to a woman, begin the letter "Dear Madam" if you don't know her name. If you know her name, you can begin "Dear Miss X" or "Dear Mrs X", but many women now prefer "Dear Ms X". (Ms is pronounce "Miz")
4. For business and personal letters in English many styles and layouts are acceptable. The examples shown here are probably the most common and widely accepted forms.

The Telephone

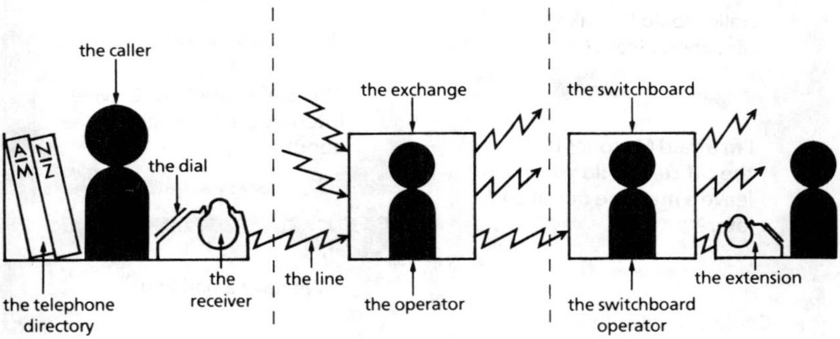

country code | code | private number | extension

we write: (44) 01-221 6010 x142

we say: "four four, oh one, two two one, six oh one oh, extension one four two"

Certain key phrases are used in most telephone conversations. Opposite are three model telephone calls and five phrases used when there are problems on the line.

Note:
1. American: 'speak *with*'
2. = it is difficult to hear
3. 'You are speaking too quietly'
4. 'You are speaking too quickly'

Financial Documents

British cheque-American check

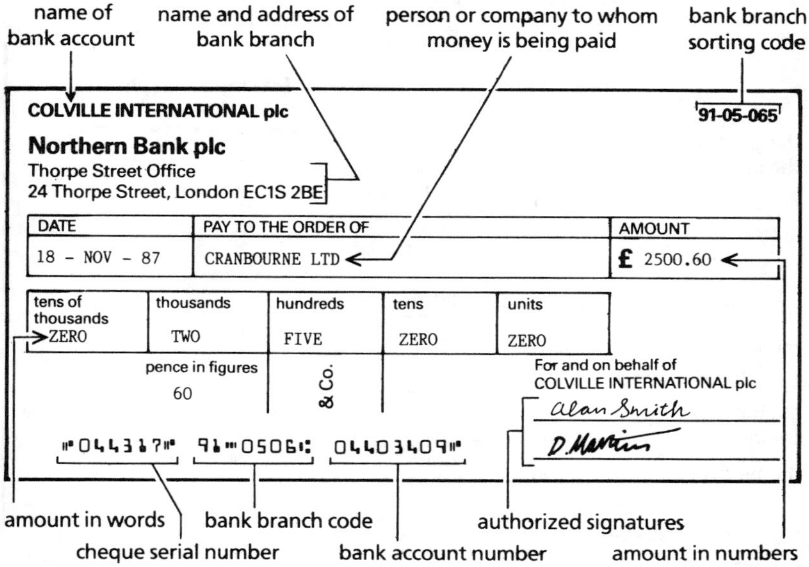

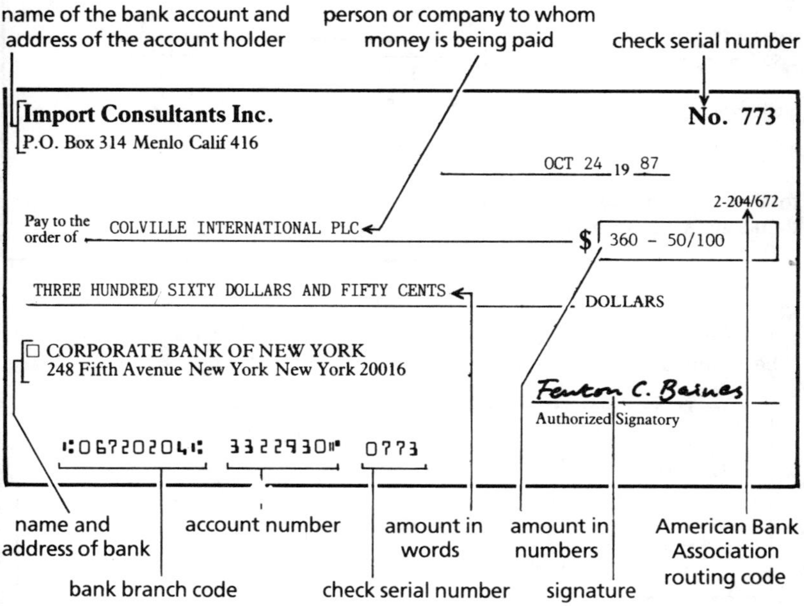

The balance sheet

A balance sheet shows the financial position of a company at a particular time, such as the end of a financial year or the end of a quarter:

Colville International plc

Balance sheet[1] as at 31 December 1987

		£000	
things of value owned by the company →	**ASSETS**	**£000**	
	Fixed Assets		
	Land	210	
	Buildings	160	
	Plant and machinery	90	
	Total fixed assets		460
	Current Assets		
US: inventory → Stocks	Raw materials, Work in progress, Finished goods } Stocks	110	
money owed to the company US: 'accounts receivable' →	Debtors	45	
	Cash in hand at bank	35	
	Total current assets		190
amounts owed by the company →	**Current Liabilities**		
money owed by the company US: 'accounts payable' →	Creditors	40	
money owed to a bank account →	Bank overdraft	25	
	Taxation	35	
	Total current liabilities		100
current assets less current liabilities →	*Net current assets (working capital)*		90
fixed assets plus net current assets →	*Net assets*		550
	CAPITAL		
	Share capital		
give a variable dividend →	Ordinary shares	400	
give a fixed dividend →	Preference shares	100	
	Reserves	50	
total capital employed should equal net assets →	*Total*		550

Note:

1. This is the normal layout of a modern balance sheet. The balance sheet can also be arranged:

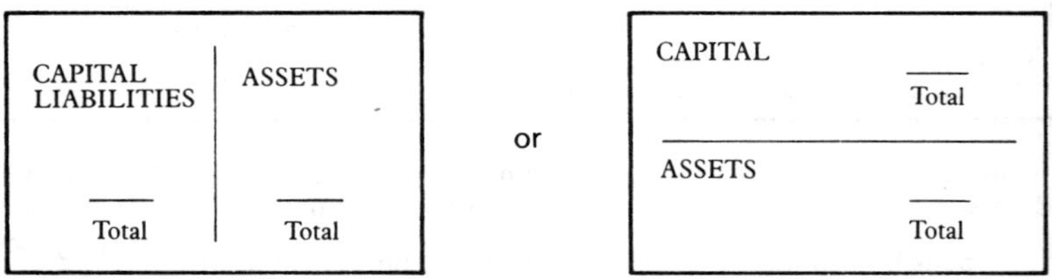

The bank statement

name of bank where account is held
name of bank branch
number of statement
name and address of account holder
period covered by statement
serial number of account
details of deposits and withdrawals
money out of the account (debit)
money paid into the account (credit)
* (or 'C' or 'CR') means the account is in credit; 'DR' or ('OD') means the account is overdrawn

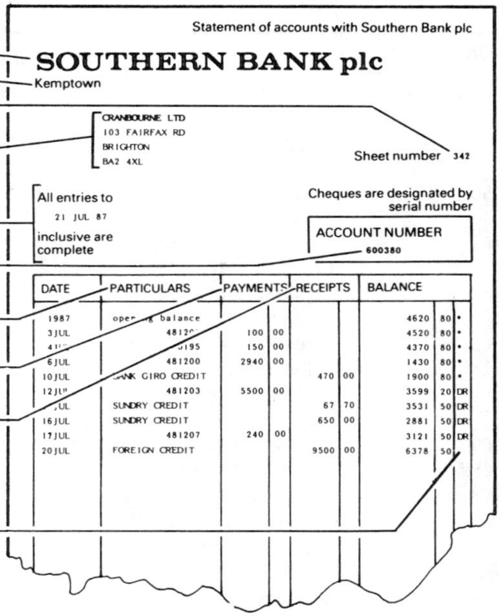
Statement of accounts with Southern Bank plc

SOUTHERN BANK plc
Kemptown

CRANBOURNE LTD
103 FAIRFAX RD
BRIGHTON
BA2 4XL

Sheet number 342

All entries to
21 JUL 87
inclusive are complete

Cheques are designated by serial number

ACCOUNT NUMBER
600380

DATE	PARTICULARS	PAYMENTS	RECEIPTS	BALANCE
1987	opening balance			4620 80 •
3 JUL	4812[illegible]	100 00		4520 80 •
4 [illegible]	[illegible]195	150 00		4370 80 •
6 JUL	481200	2940 00		1430 80 •
10 JUL	[illegible]ANK GIRO CREDIT		470 00	1900 80 •
12 JU[illegible]	481203	5500 00		3599 20 DR
[illegible] JUL	SUNDRY CREDIT		67 70	3531 50 DR
16 JUL	SUNDRY CREDIT		650 00	2881 50 DR
17 JUL	481207	240 00		3121 50 DR
20 JUL	FOREIGN CREDIT		9500 00	6378 50

The profit and loss account

A profit and loss account shows the income and expenditure of a company over a particular period balanced to show the pre-tax profit (or loss) made by the company:

Cranbourne Limited

PROFIT AND LOSS ACCOUNT
Year ending 31 December 1987

		£000	£000	£000
Sales income			853	
Cost of sales				
Materials		340		
Labour		300		
			640	
Gross margin (profit)				213
Expenses				
Salaries		30		
Distribution		30		
Advertising		18		
Administration		25		
Financial charges		15		
Rent and rates				
Heat	Overheads	35		
Light				
Depreciation		10		
			163	
Profit before tax				50

Money

British		*American*	
you write	*you say*	*you write*	*you say*
1p	one penny *or* one pence *or* one p	1¢ $0.01	one cent
56p £0.56	fifty six pence *or* fifty six p	56¢	fifty six cents
£1	a pound *or* one pound	$1	a dollar *or* one dollar
£1.20	one pound twenty *or* one pound and twenty pence	$1.20	one dollar twenty *or* one dollar and twenty cents
£3.75	three pounds seventy five *or* three pounds (and) seventy five pence	$3.75	three dollars seventy five *or* three dollars and seventy five cents
£5m	five million pounds	$3bn	three billion dollars
£5.5m	five point five million pounds *or* five and a half million pounds *or* five million, five hundred thousand pounds		

Note:
1. The letters 'p' and ¢ are written when no pounds or dollars are shown
2. A decimal point is used to divide pounds from pence and dollars from cents. A comma is used after millions and thousands: $15,621,202.75
3. You say: 'The bonus is worth two thousand pounds' but 'it is a two thousand pound bonus'
4. When we write, the symbol or abbreviation ($, DM, F, etc) comes first, when we say the figure, the number comes first

In the list of world currencies that follows, words marked (*) usually have no plural e.g. 1 kyat, 'one kyat', 200 kyat, 'two hundred kyat'

Country	*Currency*	*Divided into*	*Abbreviation*
Afghanistan	Afghani*	puli	Af *or* Afs
Albania	Lek*	qindars	Lk
Algeria	Algerian dinar	centimes	AD *or* DA
Andorra	French Franc	centimes	
Angola	Kwanza*	cents	KW
Antigua	East Caribbean Dollar	cents	ECar$ *or* EC$
Argentina	Austral	centavos	
Australia	Australian Dollar	cents	A$
Austria	Schilling	groschen	Sch *or* ASch
Bahamas	Bahamian Dollar	cents	Ba$
Bahrein	Bahreini Dinar	fils	BD

Country	*Currency*	*Divided into*	*Abbreviation*
Bangladesh	Taka*	poisha	Tk
Barbados	Barbados Dollar	cents	Bds$ BD$
Belgium	Belgian Franc	centimes	BFr *or* Bf *or* FB
Belize	Belize Dollar	cents	B$ *or* $B
Benin	CFA Franc	centimes	CFA Fr
Bermuda	Bermuda Dollar	cents	Bda$
Bhutan	Ngultrum*	tikchung	N
Bolivia	Bolivian peso	centavos	B$ *or* $b
Botswana	Pula	cents	Pu *or* P
Brazil	Cruzeiro	centavos	Cr *or* Cr$
Brunei	Brunei Dollar	cents	Br$ *or* B$
Bulgaria	Lev*	stotinki	Lv
Burkina Faso	CFA Franc	centimes	CFA Fr
Burma	Kyat*	pyas	Kt
Burundi	Burundi Franc	centimes	Bur Fr *or* FrBr
Cambodia (see Kampuchea)			
Cameroon	CFA Franc	centimes	CFA Fr
Canada	Canadian Dollar	cents	Can$ *or* C$
Cape Verde Islands	Escudo Caboverdianos	centavos	CV esc
Cayman Islands	Cayman Island Dollar	cents	Cayl$
Central African Republic	CFA Franc	centimes	CFA Fr
Chad	Cfa Franc	centimes	CFA Fr
Chile	Chilean Peso	centavos	Ch$
China	Yuan* *or* renminbi*	fen	Y
Colombia	Colombian Peso	centavos	Col$
Comoros	CFA Franc	centimes	CFA Fr
Congo	CFA Franc	centimes	CFA Fr
Costa Rica	Colón*	centimos	CR¢ *or* ¢
Cuba	Cuban Peso	centavos	Cub$
Cyprus	Cyprus Pound	Mils	£C *or* C£
Czechoslovakia	Crown *or* Koruna	hellers, halern	Kčs
Dahomey (see Benin)			
Denmark	Krone	örer	DKr *or* DKK
Djibouti	Djibouti Franc	centimes	Dj Fr
Dominica	East Caribbean Dollar	cents	ECar$ *or* EC$
Dominican Republic	Dominican Peso	centavos	DR$
Ecuador	Sucre*	centavos	Su
Egypt	Egyptian Pound	piastres	£E *or* E£
Eire (see Irish Republic)			
El Salvador	Colón*	centavos	ES¢ *or* ¢
Equatorial Guinea	Ekuele* *or* ekpwele *or* peseta Guineana	centimos	E
Ethiopia	Birr* *or* Ethiopian Dollar	cents	Br
Fiji	Fijian Dollar	cents	$F *or* F$
Finland	Marakka* *or* Finnmark	pennia	Fmk
France	French Franc	centimes	Fr *or* F *or* FF
French Guiana	French Franc	centimes	Fr *or* F *or* FF

Country	*Currency*	*Divided into*	*Abbreviation*
Gabon	CFA Franc	centimes	CFA Fr
Gambia, The	Dalasi*	butut	Di
Germany			
East – Democratic Republic	Ostmark *or* DDR-Mark	pfennig	M
West – Federal Republic	Deutsche Mark	pfennig	DM
Ghana	Cedi*	pesewas	₵
Great Britain (see note above)			
Greece	Drachma	lepta	Dr
Grenada	East Caribbean Dollar	cents	ECar$ *or* EC$
Guatemala	Quetzal	centavos	Q
Guinea	Syli*	cauris	Sy
Guinea – Bissau	Guinea – Bissau Peso	centavos	GB P
Guyana	Guyana Dollar	cents	G$ *or* Guy$
Haiti	Gourde*	centimes	Gde
Holland (see Netherlands)			
Honduras	Lempira*	centavos	La
Hong Kong	Hong Kong Dollar	cents	HK$
Hungary	Forint	filler	Ft
Iceland	Króna	aurar	IKr
India	Rupee	paise	R *or* Re *or* Rs
Indonesia	Rupiah*	sen	Rp
Iran	Rial*	dinars	RI
Iraq	Iraqui Dinar	fils	ID
Irish Republic	Irish Pound *or* Punt	pence	IR£ *or* £
Israel	Shekel	agorot	IS
Italy	Lira	centesimi	L
Ivory Coast	CFA Franc	centimes	CFA Fr
Jamaica	Jamaican Dollar	cents	J$ *or* Jam$
Japan	Yen*	sen	Y *or* ¥
Jordan	Jordanian Dinar	fils	JD
Kampuchea	Riel*	sen	RI
Kenya	Kenyan Shilling	cents	KSh *or* Sh
Korea:			
North Korea	North Korean Won*	jon	NK W
South Korea	South Korean Won*	chon	SK W
Kuwait	Kuwaiti Dinar	fils	KD
Laos	Kip*	at	K *or* Kp
Lebanon	Lebanese Pound	piastres	£Leb *or* L£
Lesotho	Loti*	lisente	L
Liberia	Liberian Dollar	cents	L$
Libya	Libyan dinar	dirhams	LD
Liechtenstein	Swiss Franc	centimes	SFr *or* FS
Luxembourg	Luxembourg Franc	centimes	LFr
Macau	Pataca*	avos	P *or* $
Madeira	Portuguese Escudo	centavos	Esc
Malagasy Republic	Malagasy Franc	centimes	FMG *or* Mal Fr

Country	*Currency*	*Divided into*	*Abbreviation*
Malawi	Kwacha*	tambala	K *or* MK
Malaysia	Ringgit* *or* Malaysian Dollar	cents	M$
Maldives	Maldivian Rupee	paise	MvRe
Mali	Mali Franc	centimes	MFr *or* MF
Malta	Maltese Pound	cents	£M *or* M£
Mauritania	Ouguiya*	khoums	U
Mauritius	Mauritian Rupee	cents	Mau Rs *or* R
Mexico	Peso	centavos	Mex$
Monaco	French Franc	centimes	Fr *or* F *or* FF
Mongolian Republic	Tugrik*	möngös	Tug
Montserrat	E. Caribbean Dollar	cents	ECar$ *or* EC$
Morocco	Dirham	centimes	Dh *or* DH
Mozambique	Metical*	centavos	M
Namibia	South African Rand	cents	R
Nauru	Australian Dollar	cents	A$
Nepal	Nepalese Rupee	Paise	NR *or* NRe
Netherlands, The	Guilder *or* Gulden *or* Florin	cents	HFl *or* DFl *or* Gld *or* Fl
New Hebrides (see Vanuatu)			
New Zealand	New Zealand Dollar	cents	NZ$
Nicaragua	Córdoba	centavos	C$ *or* C
Niger	CFA Franc	centimes	CFA Fr
Nigeria	Naira*	kobo	N *or* ₦
Norway	Krone	örer	NKr
Oman	Omani Ryal *or* Rial	baizas	RO
Pakistan	Pakistan rupee	paise	R *or* Pak Re
Panama	Balboa	centesimos	Ba
Papua New Guinea	Kina*	toea	Ka *or* K
Paraguay	Guaraní*	centimos	G
Peru	Sol*	centavos	S
Philippines	Philippine Peso	centavos	P *or* PP
Poland	Zloty*	groszy	Zl
Portugal	Escudo	centavos	Esc
Puerto Rico	US Dollar	cents	$ *or* US$
Qatar	Qatar Riyal	dirhams	QR
Reunion	CFA Franc	centimes	CFA Fr
Romania	Leu*	bani	L *or* l
Rwanda	Rwanda Franc	centimes	Rw Fr
St Lucia	E. Caribbean Dollar	cents	ECar$ *or* EC$
St Vincent	E. Caribbean Dollar	cents	ECar$ *or* EC$
Saudi Arabia	Saudi Riyal *or* Rial	halalah	SA R
Senegal	CFA Franc	centimes	CFA Fr
Seychelles	Seychelles Rupee	cents	SRe *or* R
Sierra Leone	Leone	cents	Le
Singapore	Singapore Dollar	cents	S$ *or* Sing$
Solomon Islands	Solomon Island Dollar	cents	SI$
Somalia	Somali Shilling	cents	Som Sh *or* So Sh

Country	*Currency*	*Divided into*	*Abbreviation*
South Africa	Rand*	cents	R
Spain	Peseta	centimos	Pta
Sri Lanka	Sri Lanka Rupee	cents	SC Re
Sudan	Sudanese Pound	piastres	Sud£ *or* £S
Surinam	Surinam Guilder	cents	S Gld
Swaziland	Lilangeni*	cents	Li *or* E
Sweden	Krona	örer	SKr
Switzerland	Swiss Franc	centimes	SFr *or* FS *or* SWFr
Syria	Syrian Pound	piastres	£Syr *or* S£
Taiwan	New Taiwan Dollar	cents	T$ *or* NT$
Tanzania	Tanzanian Shilling	cents	TSh
Thailand	Baht*	satang	Bt
Tonga	Pa'anga*	senik	
Togo	CFA Franc	centimes	CFA Fr
Trinidad & Tobago	Trinidad & Tobago Dollar	cents	TT$
Tunisia	Tunisian Dinar	millimes	TD
Turkey	Turkish Lira	kurus	TL
Tuvalu	Australian Dollar	cents	$A
Uganda	Uganda Shilling	cents	USh
Union of Soviet Socialist Republics	Rouble	kopecks	Rub
United Arab Emirates	UAE Dirham	fils	UAE Dh *or* UD
United Kingdom	Pound (Sterling)	pence	£ *or* £Stg
United States of America	Dollar	cents	$ *or* US$
Upper Volta (see Burkina Faso)			
Uruguay	Uruguayan New Peso	centesimos	N$
Vanuatu			
Venezuela		vatu	
Vietnam	Bolívar	centimos	B
Virgin Islands	Dong*	xu	D
Western Samoa	US Dollar	cents	$ *or* US$
	Tala *or* Dollar *or* Western Samoan Dollar	cents *or* sene	WS$ *or* $WS
Yemen:			
South Yemen	South Yemen Dinar	fils	YD
Northern Yemen	Yemeni Riyal	fils	YR
Yugoslavia	Dinar	paras	Din *or* DN
Zaire	Zaire	makata	Z
Zambia	Kwacha*	ngwee	K
Zimbabwe	Zimbabwe Dollar	cents	Z$